World Economic For...
Geneva, Switzerland ...

Professor Klaus Schwab
World Economic Forum

Professor Michael E. Po...
Harvard University

Co-Directors, The Global Competitiveness Report

The Global Competitiveness Report 2005–2006

Dr Augusto Lopez-Claros
Director, Global Competitiveness Programme, World Economic Forum
Editor

palgrave
macmillan

The Global Competitiveness Report 2005 2006
is published by the World Economic Forum
within the framework of the Global
Competitiveness Programme.

Professor Klaus Schwab
Executive Chairman

Augusto Lopez-Claros
Director

Jennifer Blanke
Simone Droz
Margareta Drzeniek
Kerry Jaggi
Emma Loades
Irene Mia
Saadia Zahidi

Special thanks to Professor Xavier Sala-i-Martin
for his valuable advice during the past two
years and to Mario Blejer, Peter Heller, and
Daniel Kaufmann for their long-standing support
and collaboration.

We thank AmadeaEditing and Hope Steele for
their superb editing work and Ha Nguyen for
her excellent graphic design and layout. We are
very grateful to Ibrahim Cotran, Justina Roberts,
and Shubhra Saxena for their invaluable
research assistance.

The terms *country* and *nation* as used in this
report do not in all cases refer to a territorial
entity that is a state as understood by international law and practice. The term covers well-
defined, geographically self-contained economic
areas that may not be states but for which statistical data are maintained on a separate and
independent basis.

First published 2005 by
PALGRAVE MACMILLAN
Houndmills, Basingstoke, Hampshire RG21 6XS and
175 Fifth Avenue, New York, N. Y. 10010
Companies and representatives throughout the world.

PALGRAVE MACMILLAN is the global academic imprint of the
Palgrave Macmillan division of St. Martin's Press, LLC and of
Palgrave Macmillan Ltd. Macmillan® is a registered trademark
in the United States, United Kingdom and other countries.
Palgrave is a registered trademark in the European Union and
other countries.

ISBN-13: 978-1-4039-9844-6
ISBN-10: 1-4039-9844-2

This book is printed on paper suitable for recycling and made
from fully managed and sustained forest sources.

A catalogue record for this book is available from the British Library.
A catalogue record for this book is available from the Library of
Congress.

10   9   8   7   6   5   4   3   2
14 13 12 11 10 09 08 07 06 05

Printed and bound in Great Britain by
Ashford Colour Press Ltd, Gosport.

Contents

Partner Institutes

Albania
Institute for Contemporary Studies (ISB)
Artan Hoxha, Research Director
Selami Xhepa, Research Manager, ACIT Program
Juli Dhimitri, Researcher

Algeria
Centre de Recherche en Economie Appliquée pour le
    Développement (CREAD)
Professor Yassine Ferfera, Director

Argentina
IAE—Universidad Austral
Marcelo Paladino, Vice Dean
Ariel A. Casarin, Assistant Professor

Armenia
Economy and Values Research Center
Manuk Hergnyan, Chairman
Sevak Hovhannisyan, Senior Fellow
Anna Makaryan, Research Analyst

Australia
Australian Industry Group
Heather Ridout, Chief Executive, Australian Industry Group
Tony Pensabene, Associate Director—Economics & Research

Austria
Austrian Institute of Economic Research (WIFO)
Professor Karl Aiginger, Deputy Director
Gerhard Schwarz, Coordinator, Survey Department

Azerbaijan
Azerbaijan Marketing Society
Sanar Mammadov, Executive Director
Ashraf Hajiyev, Project Coordinator
Saida Mammadova, Consultant

Bahrain
Economic Development Board
Sulaf Zakharia, Manager, Research Services Unit

Bangladesh
Centre for Policy Dialogue (CPD)
Dr Debapriya Bhattacharya, Executive Director
Professor Mustafizur Rahman, Research Director
Dr Khondaker Golam Moazzem, Research Fellow

Belgium
Vlerick Leuven Gent Management School
Professor Dr Lutgart Van den Berghe, Executive Director; Chairman,
    Competence Centre Entrepreneurship, Governance and Strategy
Professor Dr Harry P. Bowen, Economics and International Business

Benin
Micro Impacts of Macroeconomic Adjustment Policies (MIMAP)
    Benin
Epiphane Adjovi, Business Coodinator
Marie-Odile Attanasso, Deputy Coordinator

Bosnia and Herzegovina
MIT Center—The Faculty of Economics, Sarajevo University
Professor Zlatko Lagumdzija
Professor Bozidar Matic
Dr Zeljko Sain

Botswana
Botswana Institute for Development Policy Analysis (BIDPA)
Dr N.H. Fidzani, Executive Director
Kedikilwe P. Maroba, Programme Coordinator

Brazil
Fundação Dom Cabral
Professor Carlos Arruda, Associate Dean for Research and
    Development
Rafael Tello, Researcher
Diogo Lara, Research Assistant

Movimento Brasil Competitivo (MBC)
José Fernando Mattos, President
Claudio Leite Gastal, Director
Jorge H. S. Lima, Project Coordinator

Bulgaria
Center for Economic Development
Anelia Damianova, PhD, Senior Expert

Cambodia
Economic Institute of Cambodia
Sok Hach, Director
Chan Vuthy, Researcher
Tuy Chak Riya, Research Associate

Cameroon
Comité de Compétitivité (Competitiveness Committee)
Lucien Sanzouango, Permanent Secretary

Canada
Institute for Competitiveness and Prosperity
Roger Martin, Dean of the Rotman School of Management,
    University of Toronto and Chairman of the Institute for
    Competitiveness and Prosperity
James Milway, Executive Director of the Institute for
    Competitiveness and Prosperity

Chad
Groupe de Recherches Alternatives et de Monitoring du Projet
    Pétrole-Tchad-Cameroun (GRAMP-TC)
Professor Gilbert Maoundonodji, Director
Lydie Beassemda, Program Officer
Yode Miangotar, Researcher

Chile
Universidad Adolfo Ibáñez—School of Government
Andres Allamand, Dean
Victoria Hurtado, Academic Director
Sergio Selman, Project Coordinator

v

Israel
Manufacturers' Association of Israel (MAI)
Shraga Brosh, President
Yoram Blizovsky, Managing Director
Dan Catarivas, Director, Foreign Trade and International Relations
  Division

Investment Promotion Center
Rachel Roei-Rothler, Director

Italy
SDA Bocconi
Carlo Secchi, Full Professor of Economic Policy, Bocconi University
Paola Dubini, Associate Professor, Strategic and Entrepreneurial
  Management Department
Olga E. Annushkina, Assistant Professor, Strategic and
  Entrepreneurial Management Department

Jamaica
Private Sector Organisation of Jamaica (PSOJ)
Lola Fong Wright, Chief Executive Officer

Mona School of Business at the University of the West Indies (MSB)
Neville Ying, Acting Executive Director
Maxine Garvey

Japan
Hitotsubashi University Graduate School of International Corporate
  Strategy (ICS)
Professor Yoko Ishikura

Jordan
Ministry of Planning, Competitiveness Unit
Naseem Al-Rahahleh, Director

Kazakhstan
Ministry of Economy & Budget Planning
Centre for Market and Analytical Research
Prasad Bhamre, Advisor

Kenya
Institute for Development Studies, University of Nairobi
Professor Dorothy McCormick, Director
Dr Walter Odhiambo, Research Fellow

Korea
Korea Development Institute
Dr Cho Byung-Koo, Director, Economic Information and Education
  Center (EIEC)

Kuwait
Kuwait Economic Society (KES) Kuwait University
Dr Rola Dashti, Chairman, Kuwait Economic Society
Kuwait University
Dr Reyadh Faras, Assistant Professor, Economics Department
Dr Mohammad Ali Alomar, Assistant Professor, Economics
  Department
Dr Abdullah AlSalman, Assistant Professor, Economics Department
Dr Mohammed El-Sakka, Professor, Economics Department

Kyrgyz Republic
Economic Policy Institute "Bishkek Consensus"
Chorobek Imashev, Deputy Director
Genoura Alybaeva, Programme Coordinator

Latvia
Institute of Economics, Latvian Academy of Sciences, Riga
Dr Raita Karnite, Director

Lithuania
Statistikos Tyrimai—Statistical Surveys, Vilnius
Benonas Miksas, Director

Luxembourg
Chamber of Commerce of the Grand Duchy of Luxembourg
Carlo Thelen, Member of the Managing Board
Jean-Christophe Burkel, Attaché, Economic Department

Macedonia, FYR
National Entrepreneurship and Competitiveness Council (NECC)
Svetozar Janevski, Co-chair of the NECC, Managing Director of
  Skopsko Brewery
Stevce Jakimovski, Co-chair of the NECC, Minister of Economy
Ana Nikovska, Advisor to the NECC, Macedonia Competitiveness
  Activity

Madagascar
Centre of Economic Studies, University of Antananarivo
Pépé Andrianomanana, Director

Malawi
Malawi Investment Promotion Agency
Alick C. E. Sukasuka, Acting Deputy General Manager

Malaysia
Institute of Strategic and International Studies (ISIS)
Tan Sri Dato' Dr Mohamed Noordin Sopiee, Chairman and Chief
  Executive Officer

Mali
Groupe de Recherche en Economie Appliquée et Théorique (GREAT)
Massa Coulibaly, Coordinator

Malta
Competitive Malta—Foundation for National Competitiveness
Dr John C. Grech
Margrith Lutschg-Emmenegger, Vice President
Adrian Said, Chief Coordinator

Mauritius
Joint Economic Council of Mauritius
Raj Makoond, Director

Mexico
Ministry of the Economy
Dr Eduardo J. Solis Sanchez, Chief of the Office for the Co-ordination
  of International Trade and Investment Promotion
Lic. Veronica Orendain De Los Santos, Assistant in the Office for the
  Co-ordination of International Trade and Investment Promotion

Center for Intellectual Capital and Competitiveness
Dr Rene Villarreal, President
Dra Rocio Ramos de Villarreal, Vice-President

Moldova
Center for Strategic Territorial Development
Serghei Ostaf, President of the Board
Ruslan Codreanu, Programme Coordinator
Roman Smolnitchi, Consultant, Regional Economic Planning

Mongolia
Economic Policy Reform and Competitiveness Project (EPRC)
Janusz Szyrmer, Senior Economic Policy Advisor

Morocco
Université Hassan II
Fouzi Mourji, Professor of Economics

Mozambique
EconPolicy Research Group, Lda
Dr Peter Coughlin, Partner
Professor Dr Paulo N. Mole, Partner

Namibia
Namibian Economic Policy Research Unit (NEPRU)
Dr Christoph Stork, Senior Researcher

Netherlands
Erasmus Strategic Renewal Center, Erasmus University Rotterdam
Professor Frans A. J. van den Bosch
Professor Henk W. Volberda

New Zealand
Business New Zealand
Phil O'Reilly, Chief Executive
Marcia Dunnett, Manager—Business Services

Nigeria
Nigerian Economic Summit Group (NESG)
Chris E. Onyemenam, Director, Operations & Administration
Dr Felix Ogbera, Associate Director, Research

Norway
BI Norwegian School of Management
Professor Torger Reve
Eskil Goldeng, Researcher

Pakistan
Pakistan Institute of Development Economics
Dr A. R. Kemal
Dr Zafar Mueen Nasir, Chief of Research

Paraguay
Centro de Analisis y Difusion de Economia Paraguaya (CADEP)
Fernando Masi, Director
Dionisio Borda, Research Member
Nelson Aguilera Alfred, Research Member

Peru
Centro de Desarrollo Industrial (CDI)—Sociedad Nacional de Industrias
Luis Tenorio, Executive Director
Néstor Asto, Project Director

Philippines
Makati Business Club
Guillermo M. Luz, Executive Director
Marc P. Opulencia, Deputy Director
Michael B. Mundo, Chief Economist

Poland
Warsaw School of Economics
Professor Bogdan Radomski, Associate Professor

Portugal
PROFORUM, Associação para o Desenvolvimento da Engenharia
Ilídio António de Ayala Serôdio, Vice President of the Board of Directors

Qatar
Qatari Businessmen Association (QBA)
Issa Abdul Salam Abu Issa, Secretary-General
Bassam Ramzi Massouh, General Manager
Ahmad Elshaffee, Economist

Romania
Romanian Economic Society (SOREC)
Prof. Daniel Daianu, President

Group of Applied Economics (GEA)
Dragos Pislaru, Executive Director
Dr Liviu Voinea, Research Director
Diana Spiridon, Programme Coordinator

Russian Federation
Academy of National Economy under the Government of Russian Federation, Bauman Innovation
Dr Alexei Prazdnitchnykh, Associate Professor

Institute for Private Sector Development and Socio-Economic Analysis (IPSSA)
Irina Evseyeva

Stockholm School of Economics, Russia
Professor Carl F. Fey, Associate Dean of Research
Dr Igor Dukeov, Research Fellow

Serbia and Montenegro
USAID Serbia Enterprise Development Project
Booz Allen Hamilton
Andrew Vonnegut, Chief of Party
Jelena Sevo, Deputy Chief of Party

Singapore
Economic Development Board
Shirley Chen, Assistant Managing Director, Corporate Services
Chua Kia Chee, Head, Research and Statistics Unit

Slovak Republic
Business Alliance of Slovakia (PAS)
Robert Kicina, Executive Director
Gabriel Machlica, Project Manager
Institute for Economic and Social Reforms (INEKO)
Eugen Jurzyca, Director

Slovenia
Institute for Economic Research
Professor Peter Stanovnik
Dr Art Kovačič
Dr Mateja Drnovšek, Faculty of Economics

South Africa
Business Unity South Africa (BUSA)
Bheki Sibiya, Chief Executive Officer
Friede Dowie, Chief Officer, Strategic Services

Spain
IESE Business School-Anselmo Rubiralta Center for Globalization and Strategy
Professor Eduardo Ballarín
María Luisa Blázquez, Research Associate

Sri Lanka
Institute of Policy Studies
Indika Siriwardena, Database Manager

Sweden
Center for Strategy and Competitiveness
Stockholm School of Economics
Professor Örjan Sölvell
Dr Christian Ketels

Switzerland
University of St. Gallen
Professor Dr Franz Jaeger, Director, Research Institute for Empirical Economics and Economic Policy

Taiwan
Council for Economic Planning and Development
Dr Sheng Cheng Hu, Chairman
J. B. Hung, Director, Economic Research Department
Chung Chung Shieh, Researcher, Economic Research Department

Tajikistan
The Center for Sociological Researches "Zerkalo"
Qahramon Baqoev, Director
Isoev Alikul Ismankulovich, Sociologist/Economist
Es'kina Ol'ga Konstsntinovna, Researcher

Preface

KLAUS SCHWAB

Executive Chairman, World Economic Forum

The publication of this year's *Global Competitiveness Report* provides an opportunity to examine some of the key economic issues confronting the international community. The global economy is expected to grow by some 4 ¼ percent in 2005, nearly one percentage point less than in 2004, when the rapid expansion of global trade delivered the best growth performance for world output of the past decade. Notwithstanding a slowdown in industrial production and global trade, and the adverse impact of higher oil prices, the short-term outlook suggests solid growth, at least through the end of 2006.

However, while developments in the oil markets will continue to pose a risk to this relatively benign scenario, there are other worries on the horizon. Some of these, such as the persistence of large global imbalances, pose risks of a systemic nature; their likely impact is difficult to assess, but there appears to be broad consensus that, if unchecked, they are a potential threat to future global prosperity. Other risks are more narrowly defined, but, in an increasingly integrated world, the dividing line between "local" and "global" is becoming increasingly blurred. We can ill afford to dismiss some of these as "too small" to challenge the positive global economic outlook. Widespread poverty and its consequences may be a good example of the latter.

With the emergence of a record United States current account deficit in 2004, equivalent to close to 6 percent of GDP, there has been increasing discussion about its sustainability and the implications for exchange rates, for trade, and for the distribution of the future burden of adjustment. Some have argued that a combination of tighter fiscal policies in the United States, greater exchange rate flexibility in Asia supported by ambitious reform of China's banking system, and the elimination of well-known and long-standing rigidities and structural inefficiencies in Europe and Japan will be part of the solution.

We are particularly concerned about the potential consequences of global imbalances for the world's trading system. Rising protectionist sentiment in the rich industrial countries has already raised its ugly head. Over the past half century the growth of international trade has been one of the primary engines of economic growth; increasing protectionism would entail large welfare losses for the global economy.

One early casualty has been the Doha round of trade liberalization talks, which have been slow in coming to a successful conclusion. This has coincided with increased efforts on the part of the industrial countries to broaden the scope of aid to Africa. It is widely acknowledged, however, that the most effective way to tackle poverty in the developing world is to open the markets of the rich countries, particularly for agricultural exports from the low-income countries. Agricultural subsidies in the OECD, amounting to close to US$300 billion per year are neither "a policy for the future," as has been suggested, nor a source of strength for the economies of the countries where these massive transfers take place. They distort markets and competition in international trade; only 25 cents of every dollar of support provided to farmers actually ends up in farmers' pockets; the overproduction they imply has harsh consequences for the quality of farmland and wildlife; what is worse, the excess output they generate depresses prices of farm products for developing country exports. The United States, Japan, the EU and some non-EU members, such as Norway and Switzerland, bear a special responsibility to ensure that Doha does not fail.

The move to a more rational system of financing agriculture—less destructive of global welfare—is only one among many challenges currently facing governments in Europe. The EU finds itself at a critical crossroads. There is little doubt that the impressive strides in economic integration, made over the last several decades, have been tremendously successful: 12 of the 20 countries with the highest per capita income in the world are members of the EU. Furthermore, the incorporation last year of ten new members was a signal achievement, an imaginative new way to create a cooperative and institutionalized framework for economic convergence between nations at different stages of development. However, a proper reading of the history of the EU shows that it has been characterized by achievements followed by crises, progress tempered by setbacks. The recent rejection of the European Constitution in referenda in France and the Netherlands is one such setback. Initially, it raised questions—at least in these two founding members of the EU—about public commitment to the European project of strengthening the mechanisms of integration. But it is gradually giving way to a lively debate on the future direction of change, on what should be the priorities of economic reform in Europe, on how its members will rise to the competitive challenges posed by the rapid ascendancy of China, India, and other emerging markets. We feel this debate is long overdue, fundamentally salutary in nature, and a powerful catalyst for constructive change.

Policymakers are presently struggling with ways of intelligently managing these global risks, while preparing their economies to perform well in an economic landscape characterized by growing complexity. The World Economic Forum has for many years played a facilitating role in this process, by providing detailed assessments of the economic conditions of nations worldwide. *The Global Competitiveness Report* is a contribution to enhancing our understanding of the key ingredients of economic growth and prosperity. By highlighting the strengths and weaknesses of an economy, policymakers and business leaders are offered an important tool to assist them in the formulation of improved economic policies and institutional reforms.

Earlier this year, as part of its series of associated regional competitiveness reports, the Forum's Global Competitiveness Programme published its second *Arab World Competitiveness Report,* identifying the key economic problems and challenges facing the region. Triggered by the *Report* and a number of workshops held in connection with its release, and in collaboration with governments and organizations of civil society, members of the Arab Business Council have since established National Competitiveness Councils in a number of countries in the region, to act as catalysts for accelerating the process of economic reforms. In time, these councils might well inspire the creation of similar organizations elsewhere in the world.

Given the importance of capacity-building in developing countries, we have expanded our worldwide country coverage from 104 countries last year, to 117 countries in this year's *Global Competitiveness Report.* Particular attention has been paid to including more countries from Africa, as well as several from Central Asia, given the increasing importance of this region on the global stage. We will continue to increase our geographic coverage in coming years, to ensure that we provide the most accurate snapshot possible of the overall global economic landscape.

The Global Competitiveness Report could not have been put together without the support of a number of colleagues. We thank Professor Michael E. Porter, Director of the Institute for Strategy and Competitiveness at the Harvard Business School, and would also like to express our gratitude to the distinguished authors and scholars who have shared with us their knowledge and experience, and contributed to this year's *Report.* Appreciation also goes to Augusto Lopez-Claros, the Forum's Chief Economist and Director of the Global Competitiveness

Programme, and to his team, Jennifer Blanke, Simone Droz, Margareta Drzeniek, Kerry Jaggi, Emma Loades, Irene Mia, and Saadia Zahidi. We also thank FedEx, Gallup International, and USAID, our partners in this *Report,* for their invaluable support in this important venture. We would also like to convey our sincere gratitude to all the business executives around the world, who took the time to participate in our Executive Opinion Survey, and without whose valuable input the preparation of this *Report* would not have been possible.

Executive Summary

AUGUSTO LOPEZ-CLAROS, World Economic Forum

The World Economic Forum's definition of competitiveness goes beyond notions of exchange rate competitiveness, and links the concept to productivity. Thus, competitiveness is defined as that collection of factors, policies and institutions which determine the level of productivity of a country and that, therefore, determine the level of prosperity that can be attained by an economy. However, productivity is also the key driver of the rates of return on investment, which, in turn, determine the aggregate growth rates of the economy. Thus, a more competitive economy is one that is likely to grow faster over the medium to long term.

Much of the work at the World Economic Forum in the area of competitiveness is aimed at highlighting the factors, policies, and institutions that determine the sharply different growth experiences of over 100 economies. What explains the differences in the evolution of per capita income in, say, Argentina, Ghana, and Taiwan over the last five decades?

Perhaps few questions are more pertinent in the area of comparative development. There are at least three key insights that emerge from the Forum's work in this field: first, that the significant factors are many, and wide-ranging. The quality of the macroeconomic environment is certainly crucial: how many countries can we point to which have shown sustained growth while *mismanaging* the public finances or pursuing misguided or inconsistent exchange rate policies?

But cautious management of the macroeconomy is not the only concern of the public sector. One must also ask: Does the government maintain an arm's-length relationship with respect to the private sector, or does it play favorites? Does the judicial system allow for the reasonable, expeditious, transparent, and low-cost settlement of disputes, or is justice for sale? Is tax revenue channeled back into the economy through productivity-enhancing investments in human capital and infrastructure, or is the money wasted on inefficient projects, or, what is worse, mostly stolen? Is the regulatory environment hampered by unnecessary layers of bureaucracy and red tape, reducing competitiveness and raising the costs of transactions and operations? How efficiently are new technological innovations absorbed, and is attention being paid to constantly upgrading the country's educational system? Does the country engage with the outside world with openness and self confidence, or with fear and ambivalence? What is the role of property rights and institutions?

The answers to the above questions will vary greatly across countries and, not surprisingly, will have an important bearing on whether the economy grows in a predictable and sustained way (e.g., Taiwan), fails to fulfill its potential (e.g., Argentina), or whether it stagnates, and actually suffers a reduction in per capita income (e.g., Ghana).

Second, these factors matter differently for different countries, depending on their stage of development. Management of the public finances in Finland is less of a concern than in India or Turkey, both of which have a long history of fiscal indiscipline. On the one hand, putting many large European countries to shame, Finland is facing the aging of its population by running surpluses now to pay for future pension liabilities. India and Turkey, on the other hand, are running budget deficits, although the latter, it must be said, has made remarkable progress recently in abandoning irresponsible fiscal policies, which resulted in the accumulation of large levels of public debt. In Finland, the pace of technological innovation is absolutely central to the country's future growth prospects. Whether Nokia is able to maintain its technological edge over its Asian rivals is a far more important determinant of the future evolution of per capita income in Finland, than whether there is a slight rise in inflation.

Third, the importance of these factors changes over time, a trend enhanced by the forces of globalization. Inflation—on a downward trend worldwide, and fallen to some of the lowest levels in the post-war period—is not as much of a worry as it used to be in the 1970s and 1980s, when even the United States suffered from double-digit inflation. But, with increasing capital mobility and skittish financial markets, countries that do not manage their public finances well do so at increasing risk, as Argentina found out in late 2001. Education, the acquisition of relevant skills, and the level of training of the labor force have acquired growing importance in recent years, as swift reductions in the costs of transport and communications have made it easier for global corporations to shift production to places in the world which are capable of bringing together the right combination of skills and low labor costs with political and social stability. This has become evident during the past decade in Central and Eastern Europe, whose economies have been growing at twice the average of the rest of Europe.

The Growth Competitiveness Index

The World Economic Forum has been measuring national competitiveness and producing Competitiveness *Reports* for well over two decades. Over the years, the specific methodology used to measure competitiveness has necessarily evolved, as we have taken into account the latest thinking about what drives the underlying productivity, critical to a country's ability to ensure sufficient and rising prosperity for its citizens. Since 2001, our methodology has been based on a model developed for the World Economic Forum by Jeffrey Sachs and John McArthur, called the Growth Competitiveness Index (GCI).

The GCI brings together a number of complementary concepts aimed at providing a quantified framework for measuring competitiveness. In formulating the range of factors that go into explaining the evolution of growth in a country, it identifies "three pillars": the *quality of the macroeconomic environment,* the *state of the country's public institutions,* and, given the importance of technology and innovation, the *level of its technological readiness.* The GCI uses a combination of hard data—e.g., university enrollment rates, inflation performance, the state of the public finances, the level of penetration of new technologies, such as mobile telephones and the Internet—and data drawn from the World Economic Forum's Executive Opinion Survey (Survey). The latter helps to capture concepts for which hard data are typically unavailable, but which are, nevertheless, central to an appropriate understanding of the factors fuelling economic growth. Examples of the latter might include such concepts as judicial independence, the prevalence of institutionalized corruption, or the extent of inefficient government intervention in an economy.

These various pieces are brought together under different subindexes, each capturing a different aspect of the growth process (e.g., the importance of contracts and law, the stability of the macroeconomic environment) and are aggregated to give an overall competitiveness "score." A second concept introduced by Sachs and McArthur is the notion that, while technology matters a great deal, it matters in different ways for different countries, depending on their stage of development. Innovation will be key in Switzerland, but the adoption of foreign technologies and technology transfer may be relatively more important in Chile, a distinction that led them to separate countries into two sets, called *core innovators* and *non-core innovators,* based on the number of US utility patents (patents for invention) per capita registered in the most recent year. Table 1 lists the core innovators, all with at least 15 patents per million population in 2004. A third concept was the idea that the factors which explain a nation's competitiveness will vary in importance across these two sets of countries. So, macroeconomic stability is likely to be a more important factor in Turkey than in Sweden. The exact methodology underlying the construction of this index is described in Chapter 1.1.

The Competitiveness Rankings for 2005

The rankings from this year's GCI are presented in Table 1. Finland maintains its position at the top of the ranking. The country owes its strong showing to one of the most innovative business environments in the world, particularly critical to driving productivity in the country, given its advanced stage of development. This is coupled with a very healthy macroeconomic environment, at a time when many other industrial countries are struggling in this area. The willingness of Finnish governments to run budget surpluses, so as to be able to meet future social commitments linked to the aging of the population is particularly impressive. This approach to macroeconomic policy highlights a degree of political maturity in Finnish society worthy of emulation. Furthermore, Finland has an institutional environment that is among the world's finest: the business community operates in a climate of respect for the law, unusually low levels of corruption, and an openness and transparency which other countries would do well to study.

The United States is ranked second, its strong performance attributable to its continuing technological supremacy, and a pipeline of innovation second to none in the world. The US has companies that are aggressive in adopting new technologies, and spend heavily on research and development. However, the country's technological prowess is offset by its significantly weaker performance in other areas measured by the index, in particular aspects of the macroeconomic environment. This is not surprising in the context of intensifying international concern regarding macroeconomic imbalances in the country, especially in the area of the public finances.

As has been the case in recent years, the other Nordic countries continue to do very well in the competitiveness rankings. After Finland and the United States, Sweden and Denmark take the next two places in the ranking at 3rd and 4th places, respectively. Iceland and Norway follow closely behind, still among the top ten, at 7th and 9th places, respectively. These countries share a number of characteristics that make them extremely competitive, including very healthy macroeconomic environments and public institutions that are highly transparent and efficient. There is no evidence that relatively high tax rates are preventing these countries from competing effectively in world markets, or from delivering to their respective populations some of the highest standards of living in the world.

The United Kingdom (13th) and Germany (15th) continue to occupy relatively privileged positions in the overall rankings. Both countries have world-class public institutions, although the German business community views the property rights environment in their country and the functioning of their judicial system as being second to none in the world. Both countries have particularly strong scores on such variables as spending on R&D, collaboration between academia and the business community, and a broad range of variables which capture the use of various new technologies. Germany's overall GCI rank would be higher, were it not for the pessimism of its business community about the short-term economic growth outlook, and the presence of a large public sector deficit. Italy's performance (47th) is analyzed in detail in a special box in Chapter 1.1.

Among the ten countries recently acceding to the EU, Estonia leads the pack, at 20th place, ahead of several of the wealthier original EU15 members. Estonia's ranking is impressive, having bridged the gap between the inefficiencies of central planning and competent economic performance in less than 15 years. The worst performer among the accession countries continues to be Poland. However, on a positive note, some progress in Poland's performance is visible, with the country moving up 9 places to 51st since 2004. This is in line with a trend we see among many of the new accession countries, where there is a measured improvement in levels of competitiveness over recent years, likely due in large part to the general benefits of EU membership, and the incentives it provides for a proactive stance on the part of the government in the area of economic reform.

Unlike some other regions, where countries often cluster behind one or two top performers, Asian economies are spread throughout the full range of the index, pointing to their very different levels of development and growth potential. Leading within the region are Asian tigers, notably Taiwan and Singapore, ranked 5th and 6th respectively, several places ahead of the next Asian country covered by the GCI, Japan, ranked 12th. Japan's rank has been adversely affected by the deterioration of its public finances. However, what Japan lacks in fiscal discipline is more than compensated for by the country's impressive technology performance, with extremely high rankings in R&D, firm-level technology absorption, and patent registration, where the scores are second only to the United States, by a small margin.

China and India, 49th and 50th, respectively, ranked much more closely than in previous years. While China dropped three ranks, India moved up five places. The Chinese authorities have been trying to rein in the growth of credit, and the strength of demand has resulted in an acceleration of inflation in 2004. India's improved rank mirrors the country's somewhat higher position in the technology index. The increasing inflows of FDI to skill and technology-intensive sectors observed over the past few years have certainly succeeded in boosting the mood of the business community. Remaining worries in India, however, stem from the slight progress made in fiscal adjustment, the low penetration rates of new technologies and low enrollment rates for higher education. The latter two are also a problem in China. Both countries continue to suffer from institutional weaknesses, which, unless addressed, are likely to slow down their ascension to the top tier of the most competitive economies in the world. Chapter 1.1 features a box providing a detailed analysis of India's situation.

As in previous years, Chile, ranked 23rd, leads the way in Latin America by a wide margin. Indeed, the gap with respect to the next best performer in the region has widened from 26 places in 2004 to 31 places in 2005, a characteristic not seen in any other region of the world. The country continues to benefit from a combination of remarkably competent macroeconomic management, and public institutions which have achieved EU levels of transparency and efficiency. Indeed, only eight of the 25 EU members have higher ranks on the public institutions subindex.

Mexico has fallen seven places since last year to 55th, ceding its second spot in the regional ranking to Uruguay, while Brazil fell by eight places to 65th place. Both Mexico and Brazil suffered drops in those indicators which capture the quality of their public institutions. In Mexico, the political uncertainties in the run-up to the 2006 presidential election, and the resulting paralysis in policymaking, considerably soured the mood of the business community. In Brazil business confidence may have been adversely affected by a weakening of the ruling party's coalition in the wake of bribery scandals and other events, which have cast the underlying strength of the country's public institutions in an unfavorable light.

Venezuela, which had a ranking of 62 in 2001, continues its precipitous decline to the bottom of the rankings, falling another four places to 89th position overall this year. Venezuela's performance is quite extraordinary from a number of perspectives: notwithstanding huge terms of trade gains from high oil prices, the government has managed to run budget deficits for a number of years, suggesting massive waste. It has one of the worst inflation performances in the world (115th) and has the distinction of having *the* worst property rights climate in the world (117th).

Within the Middle East and North Africa region, the small Gulf States perform quite well in the overall GCI rankings, including two new entrants to the index from the region this year: Qatar and Kuwait. The United Arab Emirates (UAE) and Qatar are ranked 18th and 19th, respectively. These countries are going through a particularly good phase. Terms-of-trade gains have boosted growth rates and reinforced already high levels of confidence in the business community, resulting from ongoing institutional modernization and improvements in macroeconomic management. The authorities have proven reasonably adept at not squandering the gains from higher oil prices, but, rather, are using these resources to reduce debt, to invest, and to save.

While most of the countries of the sub-Saharan African region are not very competitive, the region does have a number of relative success stories, including South Africa (42nd), Botswana (48th), and Mauritius (52nd). Zimbabwe, however, is a particularly sad case, whose quick descent to the bottom of the world's competitiveness rankings reflects the continued deterioration of the institutional climate, including the disappearance of property

rights, the corruption of the rule of law, and the implications these and other factors have had for macroeconomic management. The country has the world's worst ranking (117th) for the quality of its macroeconomic environment. Table 2 contains the rankings for the three component indexes of the GCI for the 117 countries covered in this year's *Report*.

The Business Competitiveness Index

The Business Competitiveness Index (BCI) focuses on the underlying *microeconomic* factors which determine economies' current sustainable levels of productivity and competitiveness, thus providing a complementary approach to the forward-looking macroeconomic approach of the GCI described in the section above. The BCI rests on the idea that microeconomic factors are critical for national competitiveness, since wealth is actually created at the level of firms operating in an economy. The BCI specifically measures two areas that are critical to the microeconomic business environment in an economy: the sophistication of company operations and strategy, as well as the quality of the overarching national business environment in which they are operating.

This year's BCI rankings are shown in Table 3. The first column shows the overall rankings, while the second two columns show the rankings in each of the two subindexes: company operations and strategy and the quality of the national business environment.

The United States remains the leader in fundamental competitiveness ahead of Finland, the two countries occupying the number one and two spots since 1998. The United States benefited in 2005 from improvements relative to its peers in telecommunication infrastructure, the quality of electricity supply, and, notably, the quality of the education system.

High-income nations improving their rankings the most include Cyprus (up 8 ranks, with all rank changes referring to a constant sample of countries), based especially on improvements in foreign ownership related to EU accession, the Czech Republic (up 7 ranks), owing to more effective corporate boards, less corruption and bureaucratic red tape, and better availability of scientists and engineers, Austria (up 6 ranks), for improvements in the extent of bureaucratic red tape and several indicators of financial market strengths, and Singapore (up 5 ranks), for improvements in the intensity of local competition and the availability of scientists and engineers.

Advanced countries falling in the rankings include Hong Kong, Sweden, and Italy. Hong Kong (down 9 ranks) lost the ground it gained last year, due to increasing concerns over favoritism by government officials and growing bureaucracy. Sweden (down 8 ranks) dropped, due to concerns over judicial independence, and erosion

Table 1: Growth Competitiveness Index rankings and 2004 comparisons

Country	GCI 2005 Rank	GCI 2005 Score	GCI 2004 Rank	Country	GCI 2005 Rank	GCI 2005 Score	GCI 2004 Rank
Finland	1	5.94	1	Namibia	63	3.72	52
United States	2	5.81	2	Costa Rica	64	3.72	50
Sweden	3	5.65	3	Brazil	65	3.69	57
Denmark	4	5.65	5	Turkey	66	3.68	66
Taiwan	5	5.58	4	Romania	67	3.67	63
Singapore	6	5.48	7	Peru	68	3.66	67
Iceland	7	5.48	10	Azerbaijan	69	3.64	—
Switzerland	8	5.46	8	Jamaica	70	3.64	65
Norway	9	5.40	6	Tanzania	71	3.57	82
Australia	10	5.21	14	Argentina	72	3.56	74
Netherlands	11	5.21	12	Panama	73	3.55	58
Japan	12	5.18	9	Indonesia	74	3.53	69
United Kingdom	13	5.11	11	Russian Federation	75	3.53	70
Canada	14	5.10	15	Morocco	76	3.49	56
Germany	15	5.10	13	Philippines	77	3.47	76
New Zealand	16	5.09	18	Algeria	78	3.46	71
Korea, Rep.	17	5.07	29	Armenia	79	3.44	—
United Arab Emirates	18	4.99	16	Serbia and Montenegro	80	3.38	89
Qatar	19	4.97	—	Vietnam	81	3.37	77
Estonia	20	4.95	20	Moldova	82	3.37	—
Austria	21	4.95	17	Pakistan	83	3.33	91
Portugal	22	4.91	24	Ukraine	84	3.30	86
Chile	23	4.91	22	Macedonia, FYR	85	3.26	84
Malaysia	24	4.90	31	Georgia	86	3.25	94
Luxembourg	25	4.90	26	Uganda	87	3.24	79
Ireland	26	4.86	30	Nigeria	88	3.23	93
Israel	27	4.84	19	Venezuela	89	3.22	85
Hong Kong SAR	28	4.83	21	Mali	90	3.22	88
Spain	29	4.80	23	Mozambique	91	3.19	92
France	30	4.78	27	Kenya	92	3.19	78
Belgium	31	4.63	25	Honduras	93	3.18	97
Slovenia	32	4.59	33	Gambia	94	3.18	75
Kuwait	33	4.58	—	Bosnia and Herzegovina	95	3.17	81
Cyprus	34	4.54	38	Mongolia	96	3.16	—
Malta	35	4.54	32	Guatemala	97	3.12	80
Thailand	36	4.50	34	Sri Lanka	98	3.10	73
Bahrain	37	4.48	28	Nicaragua	99	3.08	95
Czech Republic	38	4.42	40	Albania	100	3.07	—
Hungary	39	4.38	39	Bolivia	101	3.06	98
Tunisia	40	4.32	42	Dominican Republic	102	3.05	72
Slovak Republic	41	4.31	43	Ecuador	103	3.01	90
South Africa	42	4.31	41	Tajikistan	104	3.01	—
Lithuania	43	4.30	36	Malawi	105	3.00	87
Latvia	44	4.29	44	Ethiopia	106	3.00	101
Jordan	45	4.28	35	Madagascar	107	2.95	96
Greece	46	4.26	37	East Timor	108	2.93	—
Italy	47	4.21	47	Zimbabwe	109	2.89	99
Botswana	48	4.21	45	Bangladesh	110	2.86	102
China	49	4.07	46	Cameroon	111	2.84	—
India	50	4.04	55	Cambodia	112	2.82	—
Poland	51	4.00	60	Paraguay	113	2.80	100
Mauritius	52	4.00	49	Benin	114	2.74	—
Egypt	53	3.96	62	Guyana	115	2.73	—
Uruguay	54	3.93	54	Kyrgyz Republic	116	2.62	—
Mexico	55	3.92	48	Chad	117	2.37	104
El Salvador	56	3.86	53				
Colombia	57	3.84	64				
Bulgaria	58	3.83	59				
Ghana	59	3.82	68				
Trinidad and Tobago	60	3.81	51				
Kazakhstan	61	3.77	—				
Croatia	62	3.74	61				

(cont'd.)

Table 2: Growth Competitiveness Index components

Growth Competitiveness Index (GCI)

Country	GCI 2005 Rank	GCI 2005 Score	Country	GCI 2005 Rank	GCI 2005 Score
Finland	1	5.94	Kazakhstan	61	3.77
United States	2	5.81	Croatia	62	3.74
Sweden	3	5.65	Namibia	63	3.72
Denmark	4	5.65	Costa Rica	64	3.72
Taiwan	5	5.58	Brazil	65	3.69
Singapore	6	5.48	Turkey	66	3.68
Iceland	7	5.48	Romania	67	3.67
Switzerland	8	5.46	Peru	68	3.66
Norway	9	5.40	Azerbaijan	69	3.64
Australia	10	5.21	Jamaica	70	3.64
Netherlands	11	5.21	Tanzania	71	3.57
Japan	12	5.18	Argentina	72	3.56
United Kingdom	13	5.11	Panama	73	3.55
Canada	14	5.10	Indonesia	74	3.53
Germany	15	5.10	Russian Federation	75	3.53
New Zealand	16	5.09	Morocco	76	3.49
Korea, Rep.	17	5.07	Philippines	77	3.47
United Arab Emirates	18	4.99	Algeria	78	3.46
Qatar	19	4.97	Armenia	79	3.44
Estonia	20	4.95	Serbia and Montenegro	80	3.38
Austria	21	4.95	Vietnam	81	3.37
Portugal	22	4.91	Moldova	82	3.37
Chile	23	4.91	Pakistan	83	3.33
Malaysia	24	4.90	Ukraine	84	3.30
Luxembourg	25	4.90	Macedonia, FYR	85	3.26
Ireland	26	4.86	Georgia	86	3.25
Israel	27	4.84	Uganda	87	3.24
Hong Kong SAR	28	4.83	Nigeria	88	3.23
Spain	29	4.80	Venezuela	89	3.22
France	30	4.78	Mali	90	3.22
Belgium	31	4.63	Mozambique	91	3.19
Slovenia	32	4.59	Kenya	92	3.19
Kuwait	33	4.58	Honduras	93	3.18
Cyprus	34	4.54	Gambia	94	3.18
Malta	35	4.54	Bosnia and Herzegovina	95	3.17
Thailand	36	4.50	Mongolia	96	3.16
Bahrain	37	4.48	Guatemala	97	3.12
Czech Republic	38	4.42	Sri Lanka	98	3.10
Hungary	39	4.38	Nicaragua	99	3.08
Tunisia	40	4.32	Albania	100	3.07
Slovak Republic	41	4.31	Bolivia	101	3.06
South Africa	42	4.31	Dominican Republic	102	3.05
Lithuania	43	4.30	Ecuador	103	3.01
Latvia	44	4.29	Tajikistan	104	3.01
Jordan	45	4.28	Malawi	105	3.00
Greece	46	4.26	Ethiopia	106	3.00
Italy	47	4.21	Madagascar	107	2.95
Botswana	48	4.21	East Timor	108	2.93
China	49	4.07	Zimbabwe	109	2.89
India	50	4.04	Bangladesh	110	2.86
Poland	51	4.00	Cameroon	111	2.84
Mauritius	52	4.00	Cambodia	112	2.82
Egypt	53	3.96	Paraguay	113	2.80
Uruguay	54	3.93	Benin	114	2.74
Mexico	55	3.92	Guyana	115	2.73
El Salvador	56	3.86	Kyrgyz Republic	116	2.62
Colombia	57	3.84	Chad	117	2.37
Bulgaria	58	3.83			
Ghana	59	3.82			
Trinidad and Tobago	60	3.81			

(cont'd.)

Technology Index

Country	Rank	Score	Country	Rank	Score
United States	1	6.19	Bulgaria	61	3.31
Finland	2	6.02	Trinidad and Tobago	62	3.25
Taiwan	3	5.85	Uruguay	63	3.19
Sweden	4	5.78	China	64	3.18
Denmark	5	5.30	Panama	65	3.17
Switzerland	6	5.29	Indonesia	66	3.13
Korea, Rep.	7	5.26	Dominican Republic	67	3.13
Japan	8	5.24	Serbia and Montenegro	68	3.12
Iceland	9	5.16	Ghana	69	3.11
Singapore	10	4.93	El Salvador	70	3.09
Netherlands	11	4.88	Kenya	71	3.04
Israel	12	4.87	Venezuela	72	3.03
Norway	13	4.87	Russian Federation	73	3.01
Australia	14	4.82	Colombia	74	3.01
Canada	15	4.79	Peru	75	3.01
Germany	16	4.78	Botswana	76	2.99
United Kingdom	17	4.66	Kazakhstan	77	2.99
Estonia	18	4.62	Morocco	78	2.96
New Zealand	19	4.47	Namibia	79	2.95
Portugal	20	4.39	Pakistan	80	2.94
Austria	21	4.35	Mongolia	81	2.93
Czech Republic	22	4.31	Uganda	82	2.93
Malta	23	4.29	Mozambique	83	2.91
France	24	4.26	Georgia	84	2.84
Malaysia	25	4.22	Ukraine	85	2.82
Hong Kong SAR	26	4.21	Tanzania	86	2.81
Spain	27	4.21	Azerbaijan	87	2.79
Belgium	28	4.18	Sri Lanka	88	2.79
Luxembourg	29	4.11	Moldova	89	2.76
Hungary	30	4.08	Nigeria	90	2.74
Ireland	31	4.07	Macedonia, FYR	91	2.73
Slovenia	32	4.07	Vietnam	92	2.72
United Arab Emirates	33	4.04	Albania	93	2.69
Slovak Republic	34	3.99	Armenia	94	2.69
Chile	35	3.93	Honduras	95	2.68
Cyprus	36	3.87	Guatemala	96	2.67
Greece	37	3.85	Gambia	97	2.65
Latvia	38	3.83	Zimbabwe	98	2.62
Poland	39	3.77	Bosnia and Herzegovina	99	2.61
Qatar	40	3.76	Ecuador	100	2.61
Bahrain	41	3.73	Bangladesh	101	2.60
Lithuania	42	3.70	Nicaragua	102	2.52
Thailand	43	3.69	Mali	103	2.52
Italy	44	3.68	Tajikistan	104	2.52
Jamaica	45	3.64	Cambodia	105	2.51
South Africa	46	3.62	Madagascar	106	2.48
Mauritius	47	3.57	Malawi	107	2.46
Kuwait	48	3.56	Bolivia	108	2.42
Romania	49	3.53	East Timor	109	2.42
Brazil	50	3.51	Cameroon	110	2.36
Croatia	51	3.48	Paraguay	111	2.35
Jordan	52	3.46	Guyana	112	2.34
Turkey	53	3.45	Kyrgyz Republic	113	2.34
Philippines	54	3.43	Algeria	114	2.29
India	55	3.42	Ethiopia	115	2.22
Costa Rica	56	3.39	Benin	116	2.09
Mexico	57	3.39	Chad	117	1.80
Egypt	58	3.36			
Argentina	59	3.35			
Tunisia	60	3.35			

(cont'd.)

Table 2: Growth Competitiveness Index components *(cont'd.)*

Public Institutions Index

Country	Rank	Score	Country	Rank	Score
New Zealand	1	6.35	Turkey	61	4.25
Denmark	2	6.35	Bulgaria	62	4.23
Iceland	3	6.33	Moldova	63	4.20
Singapore	4	6.25	Poland	64	4.14
Finland	5	6.19	Jamaica	65	4.14
Norway	6	6.13	Armenia	66	4.11
Luxembourg	7	6.08	Azerbaijan	67	4.09
Germany	8	6.04	Malawi	68	4.08
Switzerland	9	6.02	Serbia and Montenegro	69	4.07
Australia	10	6.01	Brazil	70	4.06
Austria	11	6.00	Mexico	71	4.03
United Kingdom	12	5.98	Mali	72	4.00
Ireland	13	5.93	Croatia	73	3.99
Japan	14	5.84	Argentina	74	3.96
Portugal	15	5.83	Panama	75	3.90
Netherlands	16	5.83	Kazakhstan	76	3.89
Sweden	17	5.82	Gambia	77	3.88
United States	18	5.77	Romania	78	3.84
Qatar	19	5.75	Ethiopia	79	3.79
France	20	5.72	Zimbabwe	80	3.79
Canada	21	5.67	Algeria	81	3.77
Chile	22	5.58	Nicaragua	82	3.74
Hong Kong SAR	23	5.58	Trinidad and Tobago	83	3.73
United Arab Emirates	24	5.52	Bolivia	84	3.71
Estonia	25	5.51	Morocco	85	3.69
Taiwan	26	5.47	Bosnia and Herzegovina	86	3.67
Cyprus	27	5.44	Georgia	87	3.65
Belgium	28	5.38	Honduras	88	3.61
Malaysia	29	5.36	Indonesia	89	3.58
Israel	30	5.35	Ukraine	90	3.56
Jordan	31	5.28	Russian Federation	91	3.55
Malta	32	5.23	Mozambique	92	3.54
Uruguay	33	5.19	Mongolia	93	3.53
Hungary	34	5.15	Kenya	94	3.50
Slovenia	35	5.14	Uganda	95	3.49
Spain	36	5.13	Macedonia, FYR	96	3.47
Kuwait	37	5.11	Vietnam	97	3.43
Bahrain	38	5.10	Nigeria	98	3.43
Botswana	39	5.08	Madagascar	99	3.39
Tunisia	40	5.02	Sri Lanka	100	3.34
Thailand	41	4.88	Tajikistan	101	3.33
Korea, Rep.	42	4.78	Albania	102	3.32
Greece	43	4.77	Pakistan	103	3.31
Lithuania	44	4.73	Philippines	104	3.30
Slovak Republic	45	4.73	Dominican Republic	105	3.24
Italy	46	4.70	Venezuela	106	3.23
South Africa	47	4.63	Guatemala	107	3.22
Czech Republic	48	4.63	East Timor	108	3.20
Colombia	49	4.55	Guyana	109	3.10
Latvia	50	4.55	Benin	110	3.06
Ghana	51	4.54	Cameroon	111	3.05
India	52	4.52	Paraguay	112	2.97
Egypt	53	4.46	Ecuador	113	2.93
El Salvador	54	4.45	Cambodia	114	2.90
Mauritius	55	4.41	Kyrgyz Republic	115	2.89
China	56	4.41	Chad	116	2.64
Namibia	57	4.38	Bangladesh	117	2.55
Costa Rica	58	4.32			
Peru	59	4.27			
Tanzania	60	4.25			

(cont'd.)

Macroeconomic Environment Index

Country	Rank	Score	Country	Rank	Score
Singapore	1	5.82	Colombia	61	3.95
Norway	2	5.76	Bulgaria	62	3.95
Denmark	3	5.64	Hungary	63	3.91
Finland	4	5.52	Indonesia	64	3.89
United Arab Emirates	5	5.43	Namibia	65	3.84
Qatar	6	5.40	Ghana	66	3.82
Ireland	7	5.38	Morocco	67	3.82
Hong Kong SAR	8	5.34	Croatia	68	3.76
Luxembourg	9	5.30	Pakistan	69	3.74
Netherlands	10	5.26	Peru	70	3.71
Iceland	11	5.24	Philippines	71	3.69
Sweden	12	5.24	Tanzania	72	3.65
Switzerland	13	5.23	Romania	73	3.65
Australia	14	5.21	Panama	74	3.60
Chile	15	5.20	Macedonia, FYR	75	3.58
Canada	16	5.16	Nigeria	76	3.54
Taiwan	17	5.15	Armenia	77	3.53
United Kingdom	18	5.13	Ukraine	78	3.52
Malaysia	19	5.12	Brazil	79	3.50
New Zealand	20	5.10	Ecuador	80	3.50
Kuwait	21	5.09	Guatemala	81	3.47
Austria	22	5.07	Costa Rica	82	3.44
United States	23	5.07	Bangladesh	83	3.43
Spain	24	5.07	Uruguay	84	3.40
Korea, Rep.	25	4.98	Venezuela	85	3.39
Thailand	26	4.94	Argentina	86	3.37
France	27	4.90	Turkey	87	3.34
Germany	28	4.81	Uganda	88	3.30
Belgium	29	4.76	Honduras	89	3.25
Estonia	30	4.73	Georgia	90	3.25
South Africa	31	4.68	Bosnia and Herzegovina	91	3.23
Bahrain	32	4.62	Albania	92	3.20
China	33	4.61	East Timor	93	3.18
Tunisia	34	4.59	Sri Lanka	94	3.17
Slovenia	35	4.57	Tajikistan	95	3.17
Botswana	36	4.55	Moldova	96	3.14
Portugal	37	4.51	Mali	97	3.13
Latvia	38	4.48	Mozambique	98	3.13
Lithuania	39	4.47	Jamaica	99	3.13
Trinidad and Tobago	40	4.44	Cameroon	100	3.12
Kazakhstan	41	4.42	Benin	101	3.08
Japan	42	4.40	Paraguay	102	3.07
Mexico	43	4.35	Bolivia	103	3.05
Algeria	44	4.33	Cambodia	104	3.04
Cyprus	45	4.33	Mongolia	105	3.03
Czech Republic	46	4.31	Kenya	106	3.01
Italy	47	4.26	Gambia	107	3.01
Israel	48	4.25	Ethiopia	108	2.99
Slovak Republic	49	4.23	Madagascar	109	2.98
India	50	4.17	Nicaragua	110	2.96
Greece	51	4.16	Serbia and Montenegro	111	2.95
Jordan	52	4.10	Dominican Republic	112	2.78
Poland	53	4.09	Guyana	113	2.77
Malta	54	4.09	Chad	114	2.67
Egypt	55	4.07	Kyrgyz Republic	115	2.62
Azerbaijan	56	4.05	Malawi	116	2.47
El Salvador	57	4.03	Zimbabwe	117	2.25
Russian Federation	58	4.02			
Mauritius	59	4.01			
Vietnam	60	3.96			

(cont'd.)

along a number of different measures of educational quality. Italy fell despite improvements in its absolute BCI score, overtaken by the Czech Republic, Cyprus, Hungary, and Thailand, all of which recorded a faster rate of improvement.

Middle-income nations improving their competitiveness ranking include Poland, Argentina, Croatia, Botswana, El Salvador, Hungary, and Bosnia and Herzegovina. Poland jumped by 5 ranks, driven by strong improvements in many areas of business environment quality; most pronounced in the effectiveness of antitrust policy and improving financial market sophistication. The country is now back at its 2001 level when it suffered a decline. Argentina, benefiting especially from improving measures of innovative capacity, and its neighbor Uruguay, with reductions in bureaucracy and improvements in the reliability of police services, jump by 13 and 10 ranks respectively. Both are still below their 2001/02 levels, however. Finally, Croatia improved by 12 ranks, regaining the ground lost last year based on a stronger assessment of the business environment, especially in the areas of fewer foreign ownership restrictions, better reliability of police services, and improving overall infrastructure quality.

Middle-income countries falling in competitiveness rank include Morocco, Namibia, the Dominican Republic, Russia, Brazil, Romania, and China. Morocco registered a large drop (down 29 ranks), dragged down by lower assessments especially in bureaucracy, foreign ownership restrictions, and corruption. Namibia dropped by 19 ranks after having registered a stable ranking since entering the GCR in 2002, driven especially by lower assessments of bureaucracy, favoritism of government officials, and corruption. The Dominican Republic (down 11 places) continues its downward trend.

Among low-income countries, Ghana, Tanzania, and Pakistan made the largest improvements. Ghana benefited especially from improved public schools and less corruption, with Tanzania and Pakistan both reporting better labor-employer relations.

Gambia and Indonesia experienced the largest drops among low-income countries. Indonesia lost almost all the ground gained last year when a change in government had created high expectations about imminent improvements. A sharply lower assessment of physical infrastructure and financial markets were key reasons for the drop.

Since both macroeconomic and microeconomic factors are critical for driving productivity, the BCI and the GCI provide complementary perspectives on national competitiveness. Not surprisingly, the results of the two indexes are highly correlated, as shown in Figure 1.

The latest in competitiveness research: The Global Competitiveness Index

The GCI described in the foregoing was a major step forward in the Forum's efforts to present a quantified framework for the analysis of the key determinants of growth. When it was created, it represented an intelligent compromise between the need for complexity, reflecting the multiplicity of factors affecting the evolution of growth, and the need for a structure that was transparent and simple enough that it could be estimated for a large number of countries. Thus, the GCI has served its purpose well, providing important insights into a number of the key areas central to the growth process. In particular, it provides a useful linkage with the past, especially relevant for countries wanting to see the evolution of a key competitiveness indicator in an inter-temporal perspective.

However, it has become increasingly apparent to us that we need a more comprehensive vehicle, one that better reflects changes in the nature of the global economy and the relative importance of key factors in explaining the evolution of growth in a large number of countries, with a considerable degree of institutional and structural diversity.

A few examples will suffice. It is difficult to make a meaningful analysis of the sluggish growth performance of the EU15 without entering into a discussion of structural weaknesses and the slow pace of reform in a number of areas, be it the prevalence of labor market rigidities, or delays in the completion of key elements of the single market, which have prevented the European economies from benefiting from the economies of scale associated with a large, single, truly unified market. The GCI does not address the issue of labor market rigidities, nor does it look more broadly at the issue of efficiencies in the operation of various markets.

The poor growth performance seen in most of the African continent during the past quarter century cannot be divorced from public health considerations; as important as good management of the public finances is for assessing the macroeconomic environment in African countries, it is not appropriate to analyze competitiveness trends in the region, without taking into consideration the impact on business of HIV/AIDS, or of other major epidemics. The GCI is silent on these issues, not because its original authors did not see these as being central to an understanding of development in Africa or other parts of the world, but rather because coverage of Africa in the Forum's competitiveness work in 2001 was still limited, and there was no compelling reason to include factors that were not essential to explaining growth in places other than Africa.

Education and the extent to which countries are able to upgrade the skills and training of the labor force have acquired growing importance as indicators of a country's

Table 3: The Business Competitiveness Index

Country	BCI ranking	Company operations and strategy ranking	Quality of the national business environment ranking
United States	1	1	2
Finland	2	9	1
Germany	3	2	4
Denmark	4	4	3
Singapore	5	14	5
United Kingdom	6	6	6
Switzerland	7	5	7
Japan	8	3	10
Netherlands	9	8	8
Austria	10	11	9
France	11	10	11
Sweden	12	7	14
Canada	13	18	13
Taiwan	14	13	15
Australia	15	23	12
Belgium	16	12	17
Iceland	17	15	18
New Zealand	18	21	16
Ireland	19	16	20
Hong Kong SAR	20	20	19
Norway	21	22	21
Israel	22	19	22
Malaysia	23	24	23
Korea, Rep.	24	17	24
Spain	25	25	26
Estonia	26	33	25
Czech Republic	27	29	27
South Africa	28	26	30
Chile	29	31	29
Portugal	30	39	28
India	31	30	31
Slovenia	32	27	35
United Arab Emirates	33	36	33
Hungary	34	40	32
Tunisia	35	46	34
Cyprus	36	48	36
Thailand	37	35	37
Italy	38	28	39
Slovak Republic	39	47	38
Greece	40	42	40
Lithuania	41	41	41
Poland	42	43	46
Jordan	43	59	42
Qatar	44	64	43
Ghana	45	56	47
Malta	46	61	44
Kuwait	47	63	45
Latvia	48	51	48
Brazil	49	32	52
Costa Rica	50	34	53
Turkey	51	38	51
Mauritius	52	45	49
Jamaica	53	54	54
Bahrain	54	67	55
Botswana	55	76	50
Colombia	56	49	57
China	57	53	58
El Salvador	58	57	56
Indonesia	59	50	59
Mexico	60	55	62
Panama	61	37	68
Kazakhstan	62	72	60
Croatia	63	70	61
Argentina	64	52	64
Trinidad and Tobago	65	62	63
Pakistan	66	68	65
Romania	67	69	67
Kenya	68	60	69
Philippines	69	44	78
Uruguay	70	79	66

Country	BCI ranking	Company operations and strategy ranking	Quality of the national business environment ranking
Egypt	71	58	74
Sri Lanka	72	73	73
Namibia	73	75	72
Russian Federation	74	77	70
Ukraine	75	71	76
Nigeria	76	65	79
Azerbaijan	77	74	80
Bulgaria	78	82	71
Morocco	79	80	75
Vietnam	80	81	77
Peru	81	66	82
Tanzania	82	93	81
Macedonia, FYR	83	89	83
Zimbabwe	84	78	84
Uganda*	85	91	87
Serbia and Montenegro	86	108	86
Mali*	87	109	85
Armenia	88	87	90
Cameroon*	89	84	92
Gambia	90	100	89
Malawi	91	86	93
Venezuela	92	85	97
Moldova	93	90	94
Bosnia and Herzegovina	94	101	91
Algeria	95	111	88
Georgia	96	94	95
Madagascar	97	102	96
Mozambique	98	97	99
Benin*	99	106	98
Bangladesh	100	99	101
Dominican Republic	101	88	103
Tajikistan	102	107	100
Guatemala	103	83	104
Mongolia	104	98	102
Honduras	105	95	105
Nicaragua	106	110	106
Ecuador	107	96	108
Kyrgyz Republic	108	92	111
Cambodia	109	103	107
Guyana	110	105	109
Ethiopia	111	113	110
Albania	112	104	113
Bolivia	113	115	112
Paraguay	114	112	114
East Timor*	115	114	115
Chad*	116	116	116

* Survey data for these countries have high within-country variance; until the reliability of survey responses improves with future educational efforts and improved sampling in these countries, their rankings should be interpreted with caution.

(cont'd.)

Figure 1: Growth and Business Competitiveness rankings

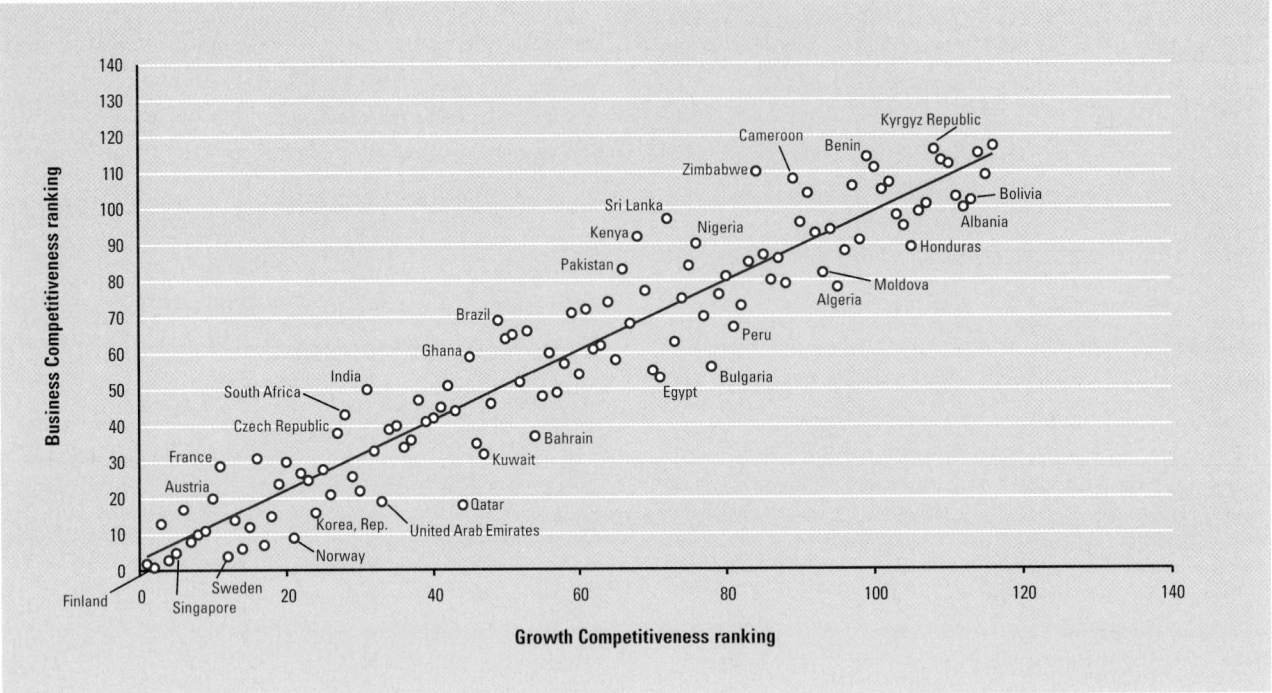

future growth potential. A country's ability to absorb new technologies, to produce goods and services that can reach standards of quality and performance acceptable in international markets, to engage with the rest of the world in ways that are value-creating, is intimately linked to the quality of its schools, to the priority given to training in mathematics and science, and to the existence and accessibility of specialized research and training centres. The GCI brought in some concepts in this area, but we feel there is an obvious need to do more.

In the interest of taking the Forum's competitiveness work further, and in order to capture a broader set of factors crucial to a clear understanding of the determinants of economic growth, we have worked closely for the past two years with Professor Xavier Sala-i-Martin, a leading expert on the process of economic growth at Columbia University. In last year's *Report*, we provided a preliminary version of a new and more comprehensive competitiveness index, which we called the *Global Competitiveness Index*. This new index allows us to measure and benchmark many critical factors, absent from the Growth Competitiveness Index described in the previous section.

The new Global Competitiveness Index is built around nine different pillars, each of which is critical to driving productivity and competitiveness in national economies. The pillars include all of the elements that were previously included in the GCI, as well as many other factors discussed earlier.

Beyond these pillars, which capture a more comprehensive set of growth factors, the Global Competitiveness Index has a number of other important distinguishing features. One is the formal incorporation, from its conception, of the notion that countries around the world are functioning at different stages of economic development. The relative importance of particular factors for improving the competitiveness of a country will be a function of its particular stage of development. What presently drives productivity in the United States is necessarily different from what drives it in Brazil. Thus, the Global Competitiveness Index separates countries into three specific stages, adding degrees of complexity at each stage, called *factor driven, efficiency-driven,* and *innovation-driven*. A fuller description of the index is provided in Chapter 1.1

The Global Competitiveness Index is a logical extension of the Forum's competitiveness work. It builds on the strengths of the GCI, by widening the scope of analysis through the introduction of concepts not previously considered. Our strategy—already announced last year upon publication of *The Global Competitiveness Report 2004–2005*—is to make the Global Competitiveness Index the centerpiece of our analytical work. The conceptual framework upon which this index has been built and its methodological underpinnings are strong, and its

Table 4: Top performers in the nine pillars of the Global Index

Country	Institutions	Infrastructure	Macroeconomy	Health and primary education	Higher education and training	Market efficiency	Technological readiness	Business sophistication	Innovation
Singapore	**1**	5	9	69	8	4	**1**	20	9
Denmark	2	**1**	16	23	3	5	2	4	10
Chile	27	34	**1**	25	42	24	36	31	41
Japan	26	9	93	**1**	16	16	17	**1**	2
Finland	3	10	10	10	**1**	12	12	12	4
United States	16	8	62	47	2	**1**	5	3	**1**

broader coverage of factors central to a proper study of the growth process is yet another attractive feature. Both the Growth and the Global indexes will co-exist for a while longer. The former, because it provides a useful link to the past; the latter, because it represents a deepening of the Forum's competitiveness work. However, the Global Competitiveness Index is expected to become the main analytical tool in our competitiveness work, and in 2006, it will be the results of this index that will be featured. Table 4 presents the top performers among the 117 countries covered in each of the nine pillars of the Global Competitiveness Index.

The *Report* also includes specific country profiles for all 117 countries covered, outlining the index scores for each country, as well as their relative competitive advantages and disadvantages. In addition to the country profiles, detailed data tables give an account of countries' rankings on the variables utilized to compute the indexes, as well as others. Guidelines on how to read the country profiles and data tables are included in an Appendix at the end of the *Report,* together with technical notes on data sources, and the full definition of certain variables.

Selected issues of competitiveness and special topics

As in previous *Reports,* this year's edition features several outstanding contributions from eminent scholars and experts, dealing with specific competitiveness issues or broader development themes. While some of them build on the findings of the Survey for their analysis, and others explore the facets of competitiveness highlighted by the Forum indexes, all are concerned with the conditions for sustained growth and development and represent a very insightful reading for policymakers, business, and the general public. Each addresses a different aspect of competitiveness, and provides in-depth analysis of one or another of the central questions at the heart of the work we do at the World Economic Forum. These special studies are highly business relevant, and complement the competitiveness indexes, country profiles and data tables elsewhere in the *Report.*

On governance and corruption

Daniel Kaufmann's challenging chapter "Myths and Realities of Governance and Corruption," counters some of the prevailing misconceptions about concepts which scholars, aid agencies, the NGO community, and governments themselves have begun to take more and more seriously in recent years. Many questions remain unresolved, and the author helps us sift through the issues, by highlighting eight "myths" about governance and corruption, and offering insightful explanations of why each is mistaken.

For example, answering myth #1, that *governance and anti-corruption are synonymous,* he points out the broader scope of governance, and the fact that corruption is not limited to those who govern, but implicates the private sector as well. To those who say that *governance and corruption cannot be measured,* myth #2, he describes the variety and scale of impressive and comprehensive measures, which have become available, and are in wide use for monitoring performance. Kaufmann answers those who *dismiss the importance of governance and anti-corruption as "overrated,"* by sharing the results of exhaustive research on the impact of governance on development, and explaining the "development dividend" that results from better governance. He points out the crucial importance of governance practices on the success or failure of aid projects, and debunks the notion that donors can somehow "ringfence" development projects, insulating them from a surrounding corrupt environment.

The chapter concludes with a call for a bolder approach to improving governance and reducing corruption. Basing his suggestions on the innovative work at the World Bank on transparency reforms, Kaufmann lists some highly practical and specific reforms which countries can implement to enhance freedom of the press and further gender equality.

Managing exchange rates

"Rethinking Exchange Rate Competitiveness" by Kenneth Rogoff is a welcome contribution to the debate on the role of exchange rate policy for a country's overall competitiveness. Rogoff argues that the importance of maintaining competitive exchange rates is enshrined in the "Washington consensus," which firmly warns against maintaining grossly overvalued exchange rates. Nevertheless, the days are gone when one could simply look at black (or "parallel") market premia, and instantly have a sense of whether a country's exchange rate was grossly overvalued. Today, with fewer countries imposing heavy-handed currency conversion restrictions, exchange rates are increasingly driven by market forces. Monetary policy still reacts to exchange rates—at a minimum through their influence on inflation—but today intervention is more likely to involve market-based instruments. As a result, identifying cases of large exchange rate misalignments has become more subtle, and must typically involve assessing a country's overall macroeconomic stance. The mercantilist view that countries should maintain low (competitive) real exchange rates in order to run trade balance surpluses is as misguided as ever. Despite these caveats, Rogoff insists that it is still important to try to assess the real purchasing value of a country's currency, and discuss in detail the practical challenges involved in constructing real exchange rate indices to make international comparisons.

Safeguarding property rights in Africa

In her thoughtful, carefully researched paper "Securing Land and Property Rights in Africa: Improving the Investment Climate," Camilla Toulmin makes the case for secure property rights as the key to promoting investment in Africa, and examines options for securing land rights, particularly for the more vulnerable poor. In many areas, land, which once seemed a virtually inexhaustible asset in Africa, has succumbed to market development and population growth, resulting in mounting competition, especially in urban and peri-urban areas. Toulmin highlights the obstacles and costs involved not only in acquiring and registering property itself, but for safeguarding land use rights, for both small and large investors, and especially for farmers, herders, and women, and the importance of preserving and protecting common resources, such as grazing, wetlands, and woodlands, which are best managed at the community level.

Governments across the continent, traditionally the sole "owners" of African land, are revising land law and administration, and experimenting with new ways to register land rights, with both positive and negative results, which Toulmin describes. Historical experience shows that in the transition from oral to written culture, those who stand to lose most are those with secondary rights, who rely on common resources, such as women, pastoral herders, urban squatters, and migrants. Past experience with titling in Africa shows that many hoped-for benefits were not achieved, with land registers becoming rapidly

out of date, the most vulnerable dispossessed, and rights made less, rather than more, secure. On the basis of her exhaustive experience on the African continent, and her close familiarity with its many cultures, Toulmin concludes with a proposal for the phased design of institutions for managing rights, answerable and relevant to the needs and capacities of local populations, and giving priority to areas of greatest contest.

Can we protect the environment competitively?

In his intriguing paper "The Environment as a Source of Competitive Advantage," Allen Hammond offers interesting counter arguments to the prevailing idea that environmental regulations place a potential constraint on, or worse, pose risks for business. Increasingly, he explains, environmental and social development issues are also coming to be understood as a source of opportunity for new products and services, new technology, and new markets. It is only when both risk and opportunity are taken into account, that the full implications for business can be evaluated. Hammond reports on the broader perspective of the environment and sustainable development as sources of competitive advantage, and draws on a number of analyses, surveys, and reports, including the results of the Executive Opinion Survey for 2005. The Survey results show that, in the opinion of business leaders, economic development and performance in environmental and social responsibility are reasonably well correlated. Although the responses also show that major improvements are needed, there is significant consensus, even among low-income respondents, that complying with environmental standards improves long-term competitiveness, that lack of clean water hinders business expansion, and that clean production and waste reduction are important to company success. In addition to the Survey results, the paper looks at some of the business opportunities offered by global environmental problems—principally climate change and ecosystem degradation—and by critical global social and sustainable development challenges—principally poverty. The author examines in considerable detail the competitiveness implications of climate policies, and how they are playing out in the auto sector. He also considers the competitive implications of disturbing new data on the degradation of ecosystem services, and the impact on economic sectors dependent on fresh water, timber, fisheries, or other severely stressed natural resources. Finally, he offers some thought-provoking ideas about how the private sector can approach low-income markets in ways which will help to alleviate poverty.

The case for Europe

In a timely contribution entitled "Can Europe Compete? The International and Technological Competitiveness of Europe," Beatrice Weder di Mauro argues, contrary to much current perception, that Europe is actually outperforming its main competitors in terms of international competitiveness. However, although European exporters have by far the largest share in world trade and have been gaining market shares, she concedes that Europe is, indeed, underperforming in terms of "technological" competitiveness, as shown by most conventional indicators of technological performance, and also by the evidence from the 2005 Survey. However, Weder di Mauro argues that the technological gap may be overstated, since it can be explained, in part, by differences in industrial composition. For instance, she finds no significant differences between the EU and the United States, when restricting the sample to the manufacturing sector. Relative specialization patterns may explain why industrial composition matters more than country characteristics: Europe specializes in chemical products, machinery and cars. These are conventionally classified as medium-tech products, even if they are highly differentiated and research intensive. Moreover, world demand for these particular products has been robust, and in some cases stronger, than for so-called high-tech products. Finally, a role can also be found for country characteristics: high labor market rigidities, and, in particular, the ease of hiring and firing contribute to explaining why Europe lags behind US performance. The author recommends, by way of policy implication, that improving the flexibility of labor markets should be high on Europe's reform agenda.

What does Russia's future look like?

In "Russia: Competitiveness, Growth, and the Next Stage of Development," Augusto Lopez-Claros examines the factors that are likely to play a key role in enhancing the productivity of the Russian economy, and improving its levels of competitiveness. He argues that there is no intrinsic reason why the Russian economy could not enter a period of high, sustained growth in coming years, and points to a number of structural features which create the conditions for rapid growth: gains in efficiency from the continued elimination of distortions, the country's impressive natural resource endowment (likely to spur the continued interest of foreign investors), and its human capital stock, which—weaknesses in the public sector notwithstanding—can be considered a competitive advantage. While the brain drain has dealt a severe blow to Russia's ability to return to the outer limits of the technology frontier, her impressive tradition of world-class research in the basic sciences, especially mathematics and physics, provide the foundation for a comeback.

Tight conditions in the global oil markets suggest that the external environment is likely to remain favorable to Russia, creating an ideal opportunity to push ahead with structural and institutional reforms. Particular attention will have to be paid to reforms to improve Russia's woefully inadequate public institutions, to improve the judicial and legal climate, to safeguard property rights, and reduce the prevalence of corruption and crime. He notes that Russian policymakers will have their hands full in the period ahead, dealing with large inflows from record high energy prices, which, indeed, create opportunities, but which also pose important challenges. Liquidity management has now moved to the centre of macroeconomic policy. A loosening of fiscal policy, particularly one aimed at boosting public sector wages and pensions, not investments in education, public health, and infrastructure, all of which would boost productivity, will need to be avoided. But beyond these issues, it is incumbent on the authorities to broaden their focus, and deal with a broad range of emerging stresses. Foremost among these are how to arrest the disturbing demographic trends, how to better utilize surplus public resources to enhance the economy's capacity for innovation, and how to put the country back on a path of world-class scientific and technological achievement, so that Russia may join the ranks of the most competitive economies in the world.

The Washington Consensus

In a thoughtful contribution John Williamson poses the question "Should There Be a Development Consensus?" He traces the history of the "Washington consensus," speculates about the possibility of a global development consensus, and outlines in detail—under the three main themes of macroeconomic discipline, microeconomic liberalization, and globalization—the ten policy pillars, which in 1989 were widely regarded as necessary to achieve economic modernization in most Latin American countries. The paper also identifies two alternative meanings given to the term, namely (a) the set of policies urged on developing countries by "official" Washington (especially the international financial institutions) and (b) "neoliberalism" or "market fundamentalism." When first applied, the first alternative meaning came close to Williamson's original meaning, but diverged in the 1990s as a result of the enthusiasm—questionable, he feels—of the IFIs for capital account liberalization, and the bipolar solution to the exchange rate issue, as well as their increasing focus—highly desirable, he argues—on institutional issues and financial sector stability.

While most of the policies summarized in the author's original version of the Washington consensus remain relevant, time has moved on, and several additional issues should be taken into consideration in any policy agenda designed to address the needs of Latin America today. The author concludes that the current agenda should emphasize the importance of macroeconomic policies which will minimize the dangers of crises (and their costs), continue rather than reverse, the efforts to liberalize the economy, build and strengthen institutions and frame policies appropriately, and pay closer attention to improving income distribution, and accelerating the rate of economic growth.

Impending aging in the developing world

Readers may be shocked by the findings in Nicholas Eberstadt's exhaustively researched essay "Aging in Low-Income Countries: Looking to 2025," in which the author convincingly demonstrates that over the coming decades a dramatic graying of much of the "third world" lies in store. Although the phenomenon of population aging has become a topic of sustained policy analysis and concern in the already-affluent OECD societies, the subject has attracted relatively little attention in low-income regions of the world. This neglect is not only surprising, but dangerous, for, as the author shows, the burdens of pronounced population aging are unlikely to be borne as easily by poor countries as by rich ones, since they have vastly fewer, and much less attractive, options for dealing with the resulting problems.

In considerable, insightful detail, Eberstadt describes the economic and cultural situations of three countries, China, Russia and India, and compares their growth, income-per-capita, and fertility replacement patterns with those of Japan, the United States, and various European countries, and projects the likelihood that by 2025, a large proportion of their populations will have to cope with aged populations on income levels far lower than those yet witnessed in any society with comparable degrees of graying. Referring to the "slow motion humanitarian tragedy," Eberstadt describes what he calls China's "triple bind": sub-replacement fertility rates, the "son deficit," and ill health, Russia's unnaturally high mortality rates and disastrous health problems, and India's non-existent retirement/pension provisions and inadequate educational base. For such countries, although differing in the details, the social and economic consequences of aging could be harsh, and the options for mitigating the adverse effects of population aging limited. In all of them, aging may emerge as an important constraint on long-term growth and development. As Eberstadt's compelling analysis demonstrates, rapid and pronounced population aging represents a highly uneven, largely unappreciated, and, as yet, almost entirely undiscounted long-term risk for the world's emerging markets.

Lessons from market crises

In "Emerging Market Crises and Crisis Resolution: A Decade of Experience," Nouriel Roubini and Brad Setser provide a thorough examination of the recurring severe crises in emerging market economies in the last ten years. Major emerging economies have proved vulnerable to sudden swings in capital flows, which have led to severe crises and steep falls in output. Sustained and stable growth in emerging market economies depends, above all, on the ability of emerging economies themselves to maintain sound macroeconomic policies and debt structures that protect them against sudden shifts in capital flows. Countries that get into trouble usually have important policy weaknesses, weaknesses that are exposed when market conditions change, and, as the authors remind us, the current, rather favorable, conditions for emerging markets are unlikely to be permanent. The IMF, the G7, and others who have a stake in the health of the global financial system should expect that emerging economies will continue to experience occasional crises, and must be ready to ensure that the right policies and institutions are in place to handle future ones. In the authors' judgment, although the basic tools needed to respond to a wide range of crises generally exist, the main challenge is to use those available tools better, and map them more adequately to different types of crises. Thus, what is needed is better "software," rather than new "hardware."

The authors argue that it is unrealistic to expect that sovereign governments or, for that matter, the banking system of a major emerging-market economy, can go under without drawing the IMF into either the country's decision to default or into the often messy restructuring process that follows. Thus, they argue, IMF financial support, combined with appropriate policy adjustment, remains an essential element of crisis resolution. Because the nature of financial crises differs from one country to another, simply giving all countries access to large amounts of emergency financing to avoid a debt restructuring, or, on the other hand, denying all countries access to it, is unwise. Although large IMF-led rescue packages can work in the right circumstances, the odds of success, they say, are far greater when the crisis country's problems stem primarily from having too few reserves relative to their short-term debts, not too much debt. For countries with higher levels of debt, the right approach may not be to use IMF funds to try to avoid any form of debt restructuring, but rather to use IMF borrowing to soften the blow.

Unemployment and happiness

In his thoughtful paper on "Full Employment for Europe," Richard Layard maintains that unemployment, not productivity or general economic weakness, is the problem in Europe. Many European countries have reduced their unemployment rates to US levels or below, including some, such as Denmark, which have very high tax rates. It is precisely the variation of experience among the different countries, in terms of policy and the treatment of the unemployed, which helps us to understand what must be done by those large continental countries where unemployment remains so shockingly high. By the early 1990s there was clear evidence that the keys to reducing unemployment were welfare-to-work policies and more flexible wages. Countries such as Denmark, the Netherlands, and Britain, which acted on this evidence, have halved their unemployment since then. Those which did not, such as France and Germany, have continued to have high unemployment, even at the peak of the European boom in 2000. In that year, both had record levels of vacancies, despite massive unemployment, demonstrating that the main reason for unemployment was a failure to mobilize the unemployed.

On the basis of his intriguing research on happiness, Layard reminds us that almost any job is better than being unemployed, and that being out of work has as devastating an effect on a person's happiness as divorce, and is three times worse than losing a third of one's income. So he maintains that unemployed people, after a while, should be expected to fill most types of vacancy. They should also automatically receive offers of activity, which they are required to accept, rather than staying at home on benefits. This *activation* principle has been a major factor in lowering unemployment in many countries, but must be accompanied by an active and energetic service, which combines job search assistance and benefit monitoring. Wage flexibility is also vital in regions where productivity is low, and should be adequately reflected in lower wages. This applies to East Germany, southern Italy, and southern Spain. The lessons learned from elsewhere in Europe and the United States apply equally to the transition countries, where high unemployment will only be reduced through more flexible relative wages across regions, and better policies toward the unemployed themselves.

What's good about globalization?

In "Globalization as an Agent of Prosperity" Jagdish Bhagwati makes an engaging and insightful contribution to our understanding of how globalization makes nations more prosperous. Drawing on his recently-published book *In Defense of Globalization,* Bhagwati gives examples of how globalization has advanced gender equality, helped to alleviate poverty and child labor, promoted better governance, and enabled economies to reap the benefits of freer trade and growth. He introduces his subject by describing the nature of the anti-globalization arguments and their origin, and exposing the misconceptions underlying the anti-capitalist, anti-corporation mindset driving most anti-

globalization protest. Focusing on economic—as differentiated from cultural—globalization, he carefully illustrates his conviction that, despite the contentions of its critics, globalization has a human face, that its effects are benign, not malign, and that social agendas creating such concern are, in fact, advanced by it.

He cites compelling evidence to support his views, such as a study showing how peasant Vietnamese parents responded to increased income from liberalized rice exports by sending their children to school. On the topic of gender equality, he cites the work of Harvard researchers, who found that increased competition through trade contributed to the improvement in female wages in traded industries. In discussing the economic benefits of freer trade, Bhagwati warns of the dangers of advising poor countries to seek protectionism for themselves, while demanding that rich countries lower *their* trade barriers, citing the disastrous history of non-reciprocity. Finally, on the topic of growth—which he defines as an active, *pull-up,* as opposed to a *trickle-down* strategy—he looks at the experience of India and China, both of which have moved from insular policies to outward-oriented trade regimes over the past two decades, and dramatically reduced poverty. Bhagwati speaks eloquently of the importance of coupling economic globalization with social policies, that will ensure the wise allocation of increased economic resources, and argues forcefully for the implementation of policy interventions which "preserve, celebrate and enhance the good effects" of globalization, while addressing its occasional downsides.

Part 1

The Competitiveness Indexes

CHAPTER 1.1

Policies and Institutions Underpinning Economic Growth: Results from the Competitiveness Indexes

AUGUSTO LOPEZ-CLAROS

JENNIFER BLANKE

MARGARETA DRZENIEK

IRENE MIA

SAADIA ZAHIDI

at the World Economic Forum

What is *competitiveness* and why does it matter?

The word *competitiveness* means different things to different people. For many it is a reference to the real exchange rate, defined as the nominal exchange rate adjusted for differences in the price level between the country in question and the rest of the world. From this vantage point, a low value for the real exchange rate is good for exporters, whose goods gain in competitiveness in global markets, while a high value makes imports inexpensive relative to domestically produced goods. The importance of the real exchange rate is not in doubt—indeed, we wholeheartedly agree with Kenneth Rogoff who, in a paper elsewhere in this volume,[1] examines the role of the exchange rate in assessing competitiveness and states: "Ask any good international macroeconomist what key variables they most want to know in assessing a country's overall macroeconomic stance, and the real exchange rate will often be near the top of the list."[2]

At the World Economic Forum we use a broader definition of competitiveness, one that goes beyond notions of exchange rate competitiveness, and that links the concept to that of productivity. We think of competitiveness as that collection of factors, policies, and institutions which determine the level of productivity of a country and that, therefore, determine the level of prosperity that can be attained by an economy. As put by Xavier Sala-i-Martin: "more competitive economies tend to be able to produce higher levels of income for their citizens."[3] However, productivity is also the key driver of the rates of return associated with investment in an economy which, in turn, unambiguously determine the aggregate growth rates of the economy. Thus, a more competitive economy is one that is likely to grow faster over the medium to long term.

Much of the work at the World Economic Forum in the area of competitiveness is aimed at shedding some light on the factors, policies, and institutions that determine the sharply different growth experiences of over 100 economies. What explains the differences in the evolution of per capita income in Argentina, Ghana, and Taiwan over the last five decades? (Figure 1). Perhaps few questions are more pertinent in the area of comparative development. There are at least three key insights that emerge from the Forum's work in this field: first, the factors that matter are many, and are spread over a wide range of areas. The quality of the macroeconomic environment is certainly key— we do not have many examples of countries able to show sustained growth while mismanaging the public finances or, as noted above, pursuing misguided or inconsistent exchange rate policies.

But so are other aspects of the role of the public sector, which go beyond cautious management of the macroeconomy. Does the government maintain an arm's-length relationship with respect to the private sector, or does it play favorites? Does the judicial system operate in a way

Figure 1: GDP per capita, PPP in international dollars

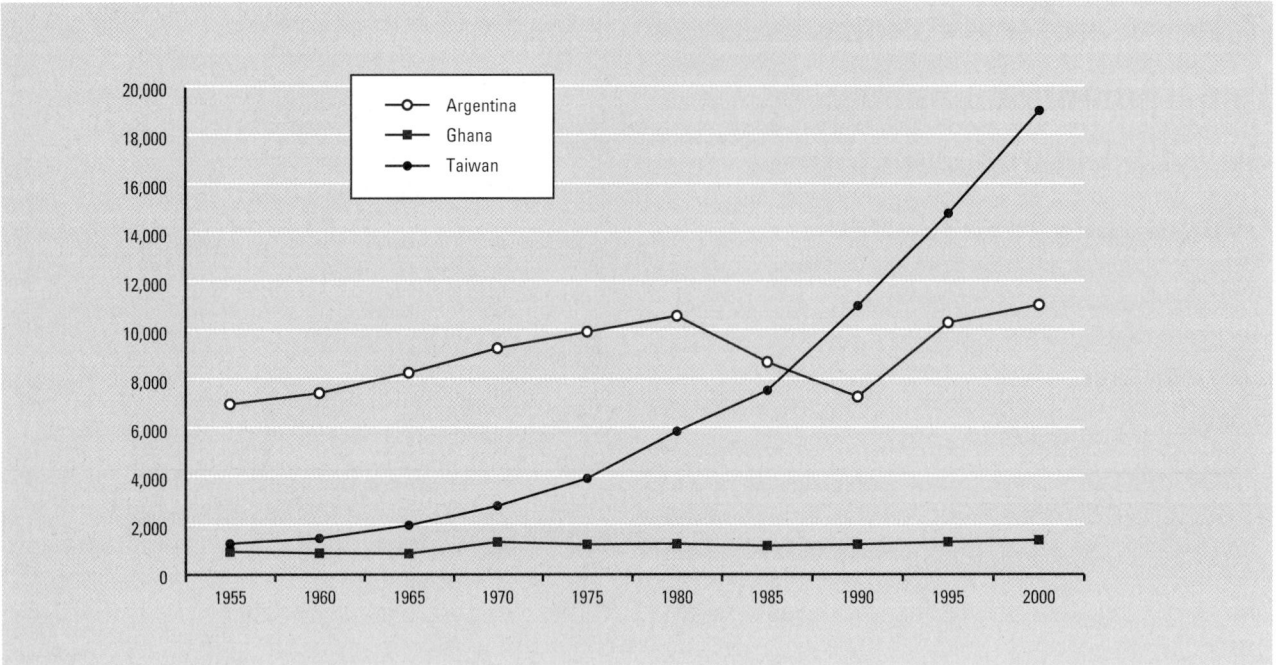

Sources: Heston et al., 2002; International Monetary Fund, 2005.

4

that allows for the settlement of disputes in a reasonably expeditious, transparent, low-cost manner, or is "justice" for sale? Is tax revenue channeled back into the economy through productivity-enhancing investments in human capital and infrastructure, or is the money wasted on inefficient projects, or, even worse, mostly stolen? Is the regulatory environment laden with bureaucracy and red tape, thereby reducing competitiveness by raising the costs of transactions and operations? How efficiently are new technological innovations being absorbed and is enough attention being given to the quality of the country's educational system? Does the country engage with the outside world with openness and self-confidence, or with fear and ambivalence?

More generally, what is the role of property rights and institutions? Acemoglu (2001) makes a compelling case for their central importance to the development process: "Countries with better 'institutions,' more secure property rights, and less distortionary policies will invest more in physical and human capital, and will use these factors more efficiently to achieve a greater level of income."[4] The answers to the above questions will vary greatly across countries and, not surprisingly, will have an important bearing on whether the economy grows in a predictable and sustained way (e.g., Taiwan), fails to fulfil its potential (e.g., Argentina), or whether it stagnates, or,

worse, actually suffers a reduction in per capita income (e.g., Ghana). The growth experiences of these three countries are shown in Figure 1.

Second, these factors matter differently for different countries, depending on their stage of development. Management of the public finances in Finland is less of a concern than it is in India or Turkey, both of which have a long history of fiscal indiscipline. Finland, facing an aging population problem, is running surpluses now to pay for future pension liabilities—and in so doing puts to shame many larger countries in Europe. India and Turkey run budget deficits, although the latter has made remarkable progress in the last couple of years in leaving behind irresponsible fiscal policies, which have resulted in the accumulation of large levels of public debt. In Finland, however, the pace of technological innovation is absolutely central to the country's future growth prospects. Whether Nokia is able to maintain its technological edge over its Asian rivals is a far more important determinant of the future evolution of per capita income in Finland than whether there is a slight rise in inflation.

Third, the importance of these factors changes over time, a trend enhanced by the forces of globalization. Inflation, which has been on a downward trend worldwide, and has fallen to some of the lowest levels in the post-war period, is not as much of a worry as it used to be in the 1970s and 1980s, when even the United States suffered from double digit inflation. But, with increasing capital mobility and skittish financial markets, countries that do not manage their public finances well do so at increasing risk, as Argentina found out in late 2001. Education, the acquisition of relevant skills, and the level of training of the labor force have acquired growing importance in recent years, as swift reductions in the costs of transport and communications have made it much easier for global corporations to shift production to places in the world which can bring together the right combination of skills, low labor costs, and political and social stability. This has become evident during the past decade in Central and Eastern Europe, whose economies have been growing at twice the average of the rest of Europe.

The Growth Competitiveness Index

The World Economic Forum has been measuring national competitiveness and producing *Competitiveness Reports* since 1979. Over the years, the specific methodology used to measure competitiveness has necessarily evolved, as we have taken into account the latest thinking about what drives the underlying productivity so critical to a country's ability to ensure sufficient and rising prosperity for its citizens. Since 2001, our methodology has been based on a model developed for the World Economic Forum by Jeffrey Sachs and John McArthur, called the Growth Competitiveness Index (GCI).[5]

The GCI brings together a number of complementary concepts aimed at providing a quantified framework for measuring competitiveness. In formulating the range of factors that go into explaining the evolution of growth in a country, it identifies "three pillars": the quality of the macroeconomic environment, the state of the country's public institutions, and, given the importance of technology and innovation, the level of its technological readiness. The GCI uses a combination of hard data—e.g., university enrollment rates, inflation performance, the state of the public finances, the level of penetration of new technologies, such as mobile telephones and the Internet—and data drawn from the World Economic Forum's Executive Opinion Survey (Survey). The latter helps to capture concepts for which hard data are typically unavailable, but which are, nevertheless, central to an appropriate understanding of the factors fueling economic growth. Examples of the latter might include such concepts as judicial independence, the prevalence of institutionalized corruption, or the extent of inefficient government intervention in an economy.

These various pieces are brought together under different subindexes, each capturing a different aspect of the growth process (e.g., the importance of contracts and law, the stability of the macroeconomic environment) and are aggregated to give an overall competitiveness "score." A second concept introduced by Sachs and McArthur is the notion that, while technology matters a great deal, it matters in different ways for different countries, depending on the stage of development. Innovation will be key in Switzerland, but the adoption of foreign technologies and technology transfer may be relatively more important in Chile, a distinction that led them to separate countries in two sets, so-called *core innovators* and *non-core innovators,* based on the number of US utility patents (patents for invention) per capita registered in the most recent year. Table 1 lists the core innovators, all with at least 15 patents per million population in 2004. A third concept was the idea that the factors which explain a nation's competitiveness will vary in importance across these two sets of countries. So, macroeconomic stability is likely to be a more important factor in Turkey than in Sweden. The exact methodology underlying the construction of this index is described in Appendix A, at the end of this chapter.

Table 1: Core technology-innovating economies, 2004

Country	Average annual US utility patents granted per million population	Rank
United States	283.7	1
Japan	276.6	2
Taiwan	263.9	3
Switzerland	177.4	4
Finland	176.5	5
Israel	155.8	6
Sweden	144.9	7
Germany	130.7	8
Canada	106.4	9
Singapore	104.4	10
Korea, Rep.	92.3	11
Luxembourg	88.0	12
Netherlands	78.6	13
Denmark	76.7	14
Austria	66.7	15
Iceland	66.7	15
Belgium	59.4	17
United Kingdom	58.1	18
France	56.0	19
Norway	52.8	20
Australia	47.9	21
Ireland	46.5	22
Hong Kong SAR	43.8	23
New Zealand	36.4	24
Italy	27.6	25

Source: United States Patent and Trademark Office

Growth Competitiveness Index rankings 2005–2006

Europe and the United States

Finland maintains its position at the top of the ranking. The country owes its strong showing to one of the most innovative business environments in the world, particularly critical to driving productivity in the country, given its advanced stage of development. This is coupled with a very healthy macroeconomic environment, at a time when many other industrial countries are struggling in this area. The willingness of Finnish governments to run budget surpluses, so as to be able to meet future social commitments linked to the aging of the population is particularly impressive. This approach to macroeconomic policy highlights a degree of political maturity in Finnish society worthy of emulation. Furthermore, Finland has an institutional environment that is among the world's finest: the business community operates in a climate of respect for the law, unusually low levels of corruption, and an openness and transparency which, again, other countries would do well to study.[6]

The **United States** is ranked second, with its strong performance attributable to its continuing technological supremacy, with a pipeline of innovation second to none in the world. The US has companies that are aggressive in adopting new technologies, and spend heavily on research and development. This environment, coupled with one of the highest tertiary enrollment rates in the world, provides the basis for an economy in which there is a powerful culture of innovation. However, the country's undeniable technological prowess, which explains its very high overall rank, is offset by its significantly weaker performance in other areas measured by the index. The GCI shows that the country's institutional environment is not a competitive strength. The US has a relatively low rank of 20 for the contracts and law indicator used in the GCI, with particular concerns on the part of the business community about the government's ability to maintain arm's-length relationships with the private sector, and in the formulation of policies more generally. But the country's greatest weakness concerns the stability of its macroeconomic environment, where it ranks a low 47th overall. This is not surprising in the context of intensifying international concern regarding macroeconomic imbalances in the country, especially as regards the public finances. According to the latest data made available by the International Monetary Fund, the United States is running a fiscal deficit in 2005 in excess of 4 percent of GDP for the fourth year in a row, and is projected to run a similar deficit in 2006. Little additional fiscal adjustment is envisaged through 2010. As would be expected, particular weaknesses are the very low national savings rate, and a growing level of public indebtedness. Our analysis indicates that weaknesses in key macroeconomic indicators pose a non-negligible risk to the United States' overall competitiveness rankings in future years, as well as to the overall world economy, requiring serious attention by the authorities.

As has been the case in recent years, the other Nordic countries continue to do very well in the competitiveness rankings. After Finland and the United States, **Sweden** and **Denmark** take the next two places in the ranking at 3rd and 4th places, respectively. **Iceland** and **Norway** follow closely behind, still among the top-ten, at 7th and 9th places, respectively. These countries share a number of characteristics that make them extremely competitive, such as very healthy macroeconomic environments and public institutions that are highly transparent and efficient, with general agreement within society on the spending priorities to be met in the government budget. While the business communities in the Nordic countries, when asked, point to high tax rates as a potential problem area, there is no evidence that these are adversely affecting the ability of these countries to compete effectively in world markets, or to deliver to their respective populations some of the highest standards of living in the world. Indeed, the high levels of government tax revenue have delivered world-class educational establishments, an extensive safety net, and a highly motivated and skilled labor force.

The **United Kingdom** (13th) and **Germany** (15th) continue to occupy relatively privileged positions in the overall rankings. Both countries have world-class public institutions, although the German business community views the property rights environment in their country and the functioning of their judicial system as being second to none in the world, a slightly more upbeat assessment than that made by their United Kingdom counterparts. Both countries also have broadly similar rankings on the technology subindex (17th and 16th, respectively) with particularly strong scores on such variables as spending on R&D, collaboration between academia and the business community, the legal framework underpinning the ICT sector and, of course, a broad range of variables which capture the use of various new technologies. Both countries have a well-developed capacity for innovation, although, as measured by US patents registration, Germany is more of a powerhouse. Germany's overall GCI rank would be higher, were it not for the pessimism of its business community about the short-term economic growth outlook and the presence of a large public sector deficit—a rank of 86th among the 117 countries covered —for which the macroeconomic environment subindex penalizes the country's score. **France** does not quite come up to the levels of performance seen in the United Kingdom and Germany. France, like Germany, is running large budget deficits (at least since 2002), and has also suffered from a relatively sluggish growth performance, which may have colored the mood of its business community. Its macroeconomic environment rank is 27th, falling

Table 2: Growth Competitiveness Index rankings and 2004 comparisons

Country	GCI 2005 rank	GCI 2005 score	GCI 2004 rank	Country	GCI 2005 rank	GCI 2005 score	GCI 2004 rank
Finland	1	5.94	1	Tanzania	71	3.57	82
United States	2	5.81	2	Argentina	72	3.56	74
Sweden	3	5.65	3	Panama	73	3.55	58
Denmark	4	5.65	5	Indonesia	74	3.53	69
Taiwan	5	5.58	4	Russian Federation	75	3.53	70
Singapore	6	5.48	7	Morocco	76	3.49	56
Iceland	7	5.48	10	Philippines	77	3.47	76
Switzerland	8	5.46	8	Algeria	78	3.46	71
Norway	9	5.40	6	Armenia	79	3.44	—
Australia	10	5.21	14	Serbia and Montenegro	80	3.38	89
Netherlands	11	5.21	12	Vietnam	81	3.37	77
Japan	12	5.18	9	Moldova	82	3.37	—
United Kingdom	13	5.11	11	Pakistan	83	3.33	91
Canada	14	5.10	15	Ukraine	84	3.30	86
Germany	15	5.10	13	Macedonia, FYR	85	3.26	84
New Zealand	16	5.09	18	Georgia	86	3.25	94
Korea, Rep.	17	5.07	29	Uganda	87	3.24	79
United Arab Emirates	18	4.99	16	Nigeria	88	3.23	93
Qatar	19	4.97	—	Venezuela	89	3.22	85
Estonia	20	4.95	20	Mali	90	3.22	88
Austria	21	4.95	17	Mozambique	91	3.19	92
Portugal	22	4.91	24	Kenya	92	3.19	78
Chile	23	4.91	22	Honduras	93	3.18	97
Malaysia	24	4.90	31	Gambia	94	3.18	75
Luxembourg	25	4.90	26	Bosnia and Herzegovina	95	3.17	81
Ireland	26	4.86	30	Mongolia	96	3.16	—
Israel	27	4.84	19	Guatemala	97	3.12	80
Hong Kong SAR	28	4.83	21	Sri Lanka	98	3.10	73
Spain	29	4.80	23	Nicaragua	99	3.08	95
France	30	4.78	27	Albania	100	3.07	—
Belgium	31	4.63	25	Bolivia	101	3.06	98
Slovenia	32	4.59	33	Dominican Republic	102	3.05	72
Kuwait	33	4.58	—	Ecuador	103	3.01	90
Cyprus	34	4.54	38	Tajikistan	104	3.01	—
Malta	35	4.54	32	Malawi	105	3.00	87
Thailand	36	4.50	34	Ethiopia	106	3.00	101
Bahrain	37	4.48	28	Madagascar	107	2.95	96
Czech Republic	38	4.42	40	East Timor	108	2.93	—
Hungary	39	4.38	39	Zimbabwe	109	2.89	99
Tunisia	40	4.32	42	Bangladesh	110	2.86	102
Slovak Republic	41	4.31	43	Cameroon	111	2.84	—
South Africa	42	4.31	41	Cambodia	112	2.82	—
Lithuania	43	4.30	36	Paraguay	113	2.80	100
Latvia	44	4.29	44	Benin	114	2.74	—
Jordan	45	4.28	35	Guyana	115	2.73	—
Greece	46	4.26	37	Kyrgyz Republic	116	2.62	—
Italy	47	4.21	47	Chad	117	2.37	104
Botswana	48	4.21	45				
China	49	4.07	46				
India	50	4.04	55				
Poland	51	4.00	60				
Mauritius	52	4.00	49				
Egypt	53	3.96	62				
Uruguay	54	3.93	54				
Mexico	55	3.92	48				
El Salvador	56	3.86	53				
Colombia	57	3.84	64				
Bulgaria	58	3.83	59				
Ghana	59	3.82	68				
Trinidad and Tobago	60	3.81	51				
Kazakhstan	61	3.77	—				
Croatia	62	3.74	61				
Namibia	63	3.72	52				
Costa Rica	64	3.72	50				
Brazil	65	3.69	57				
Turkey	66	3.68	66				
Romania	67	3.67	63				
Peru	68	3.66	67				
Azerbaijan	69	3.64	—				
Jamaica	70	3.64	65				

(cont'd.)

Table 3: Growth Competitiveness Index components

Growth Competitiveness Index (GCI)			Technology index			Public institutions index			Macroeconomic environment index		
Country	GCI 2005 Rank	GCI 2005 Score	Country	Rank	Score	Country	Rank	Score	Country	Rank	Score
Finland	1	5.94	United States	1	6.19	New Zealand	1	6.35	Singapore	1	5.82
United States	2	5.81	Finland	2	6.02	Denmark	2	6.35	Norway	2	5.76
Sweden	3	5.65	Taiwan	3	5.85	Iceland	3	6.33	Denmark	3	5.64
Denmark	4	5.65	Sweden	4	5.78	Singapore	4	6.25	Finland	4	5.52
Taiwan	5	5.58	Denmark	5	5.30	Finland	5	6.19	United Arab Emirates	5	5.43
Singapore	6	5.48	Switzerland	6	5.29	Norway	6	6.13	Qatar	6	5.40
Iceland	7	5.48	Korea, Rep.	7	5.26	Luxembourg	7	6.08	Ireland	7	5.38
Switzerland	8	5.46	Japan	8	5.24	Germany	8	6.04	Hong Kong SAR	8	5.34
Norway	9	5.40	Iceland	9	5.16	Switzerland	9	6.02	Luxembourg	9	5.30
Australia	10	5.21	Singapore	10	4.93	Australia	10	6.01	Netherlands	10	5.26
Netherlands	11	5.21	Netherlands	11	4.88	Austria	11	6.00	Iceland	11	5.24
Japan	12	5.18	Israel	12	4.87	United Kingdom	12	5.98	Sweden	12	5.24
United Kingdom	13	5.11	Norway	13	4.87	Ireland	13	5.93	Switzerland	13	5.23
Canada	14	5.10	Australia	14	4.82	Japan	14	5.84	Australia	14	5.21
Germany	15	5.10	Canada	15	4.79	Portugal	15	5.83	Chile	15	5.20
New Zealand	16	5.09	Germany	16	4.78	Netherlands	16	5.83	Canada	16	5.16
Korea, Rep.	17	5.07	United Kingdom	17	4.66	Sweden	17	5.82	Taiwan	17	5.15
United Arab Emirates	18	4.99	Estonia	18	4.62	United States	18	5.77	United Kingdom	18	5.13
Qatar	19	4.97	New Zealand	19	4.47	Qatar	19	5.75	Malaysia	19	5.12
Estonia	20	4.95	Portugal	20	4.39	France	20	5.72	New Zealand	20	5.10
Austria	21	4.95	Austria	21	4.35	Canada	21	5.67	Kuwait	21	5.09
Portugal	22	4.91	Czech Republic	22	4.31	Chile	22	5.58	Austria	22	5.07
Chile	23	4.91	Malta	23	4.29	Hong Kong SAR	23	5.58	United States	23	5.07
Malaysia	24	4.90	France	24	4.26	United Arab Emirates	24	5.52	Spain	24	5.07
Luxembourg	25	4.90	Malaysia	25	4.22	Estonia	25	5.51	Korea, Rep.	25	4.98
Ireland	26	4.86	Hong Kong SAR	26	4.21	Taiwan	26	5.47	Thailand	26	4.94
Israel	27	4.84	Spain	27	4.21	Cyprus	27	5.44	France	27	4.90
Hong Kong SAR	28	4.83	Belgium	28	4.18	Belgium	28	5.38	Germany	28	4.81
Spain	29	4.80	Luxembourg	29	4.11	Malaysia	29	5.36	Belgium	29	4.76
France	30	4.78	Hungary	30	4.08	Israel	30	5.35	Estonia	30	4.73
Belgium	31	4.63	Ireland	31	4.07	Jordan	31	5.28	South Africa	31	4.68
Slovenia	32	4.59	Slovenia	32	4.07	Malta	32	5.23	Bahrain	32	4.62
Kuwait	33	4.58	United Arab Emirates	33	4.04	Uruguay	33	5.19	China	33	4.61
Cyprus	34	4.54	Slovak Republic	34	3.99	Hungary	34	5.15	Tunisia	34	4.59
Malta	35	4.54	Chile	35	3.93	Slovenia	35	5.14	Slovenia	35	4.57
Thailand	36	4.50	Cyprus	36	3.87	Spain	36	5.13	Botswana	36	4.55
Bahrain	37	4.48	Greece	37	3.85	Kuwait	37	5.11	Portugal	37	4.51
Czech Republic	38	4.42	Latvia	38	3.83	Bahrain	38	5.10	Latvia	38	4.48
Hungary	39	4.38	Poland	39	3.77	Botswana	39	5.08	Lithuania	39	4.47
Tunisia	40	4.32	Qatar	40	3.76	Tunisia	40	5.02	Trinidad and Tobago	40	4.44
Slovak Republic	41	4.31	Bahrain	41	3.73	Thailand	41	4.88	Kazakhstan	41	4.42
South Africa	42	4.31	Lithuania	42	3.70	Korea, Rep.	42	4.78	Japan	42	4.40
Lithuania	43	4.30	Thailand	43	3.69	Greece	43	4.77	Mexico	43	4.35
Latvia	44	4.29	Italy	44	3.68	Lithuania	44	4.73	Algeria	44	4.33
Jordan	45	4.28	Jamaica	45	3.64	Slovak Republic	45	4.73	Cyprus	45	4.33
Greece	46	4.26	South Africa	46	3.62	Italy	46	4.70	Czech Republic	46	4.31
Italy	47	4.21	Mauritius	47	3.57	South Africa	47	4.63	Italy	47	4.26
Botswana	48	4.21	Kuwait	48	3.56	Czech Republic	48	4.63	Israel	48	4.25
China	49	4.07	Romania	49	3.53	Colombia	49	4.55	Slovak Republic	49	4.23
India	50	4.04	Brazil	50	3.51	Latvia	50	4.55	India	50	4.17
Poland	51	4.00	Croatia	51	3.48	Ghana	51	4.54	Greece	51	4.16
Mauritius	52	4.00	Jordan	52	3.46	India	52	4.52	Jordan	52	4.10
Egypt	53	3.96	Turkey	53	3.45	Egypt	53	4.46	Poland	53	4.09
Uruguay	54	3.93	Philippines	54	3.43	El Salvador	54	4.45	Malta	54	4.09
Mexico	55	3.92	India	55	3.42	Mauritius	55	4.41	Egypt	55	4.07
El Salvador	56	3.86	Costa Rica	56	3.39	China	56	4.41	Azerbaijan	56	4.05
Colombia	57	3.84	Mexico	57	3.39	Namibia	57	4.38	El Salvador	57	4.03
Bulgaria	58	3.83	Egypt	58	3.36	Costa Rica	58	4.32	Russian Federation	58	4.02
Ghana	59	3.82	Argentina	59	3.35	Peru	59	4.27	Mauritius	59	4.01
Trinidad and Tobago	60	3.81	Tunisia	60	3.35	Tanzania	60	4.25	Vietnam	60	3.96
Kazakhstan	61	3.77	Bulgaria	61	3.31	Turkey	61	4.25	Colombia	61	3.95
Croatia	62	3.74	Trinidad and Tobago	62	3.25	Bulgaria	62	4.23	Bulgaria	62	3.95
Namibia	63	3.72	Uruguay	63	3.19	Moldova	63	4.20	Hungary	63	3.91
Costa Rica	64	3.72	China	64	3.18	Poland	64	4.14	Indonesia	64	3.89
Brazil	65	3.69	Panama	65	3.17	Jamaica	65	4.14	Namibia	65	3.84
Turkey	66	3.68	Indonesia	66	3.13	Armenia	66	4.11	Ghana	66	3.82
Romania	67	3.67	Dominican Republic	67	3.13	Azerbaijan	67	4.09	Morocco	67	3.82
Peru	68	3.66	Serbia and Montenegro	68	3.12	Malawi	68	4.08	Croatia	68	3.76
Azerbaijan	69	3.64	Ghana	69	3.11	Serbia and Montenegro	69	4.07	Pakistan	69	3.74
Jamaica	70	3.64	El Salvador	70	3.09	Brazil	70	4.06	Peru	70	3.71
(cont'd.)			(cont'd.)			(cont'd.)			(cont'd.)		

Table 3: Growth Competitiveness Index components *(cont'd.)*

Growth Competitiveness Index (GCI)	GCI 2005 Rank	GCI 2005 Score	Technology index	Rank	Score	Public institutions index	Rank	Score	Macroeconomic environment index	Rank	Score
Tanzania	71	3.57	Kenya	71	3.04	Mexico	71	4.03	Philippines	71	3.69
Argentina	72	3.56	Venezuela	72	3.03	Mali	72	4.00	Tanzania	72	3.65
Panama	73	3.55	Russian Federation	73	3.01	Croatia	73	3.99	Romania	73	3.65
Indonesia	74	3.53	Colombia	74	3.01	Argentina	74	3.96	Panama	74	3.60
Russian Federation	75	3.53	Peru	75	3.01	Panama	75	3.90	Macedonia, FYR	75	3.58
Morocco	76	3.49	Botswana	76	2.99	Kazakhstan	76	3.89	Nigeria	76	3.54
Philippines	77	3.47	Kazakhstan	77	2.99	Gambia	77	3.88	Armenia	77	3.53
Algeria	78	3.46	Morocco	78	2.96	Romania	78	3.84	Ukraine	78	3.52
Armenia	79	3.44	Namibia	79	2.95	Ethiopia	79	3.79	Brazil	79	3.50
Serbia and Montenegro	80	3.38	Pakistan	80	2.94	Zimbabwe	80	3.79	Ecuador	80	3.50
Vietnam	81	3.37	Mongolia	81	2.93	Algeria	81	3.77	Guatemala	81	3.47
Moldova	82	3.37	Uganda	82	2.93	Nicaragua	82	3.74	Costa Rica	82	3.44
Pakistan	83	3.33	Mozambique	83	2.91	Trinidad and Tobago	83	3.73	Bangladesh	83	3.43
Ukraine	84	3.30	Georgia	84	2.84	Bolivia	84	3.71	Uruguay	84	3.40
Macedonia, FYR	85	3.26	Ukraine	85	2.82	Morocco	85	3.69	Venezuela	85	3.39
Georgia	86	3.25	Tanzania	86	2.81	Bosnia and Herzegovina	86	3.67	Argentina	86	3.37
Uganda	87	3.24	Azerbaijan	87	2.79	Georgia	87	3.65	Turkey	87	3.34
Nigeria	88	3.23	Sri Lanka	88	2.79	Honduras	88	3.61	Uganda	88	3.30
Venezuela	89	3.22	Moldova	89	2.76	Indonesia	89	3.58	Honduras	89	3.25
Mali	90	3.22	Nigeria	90	2.74	Ukraine	90	3.56	Georgia	90	3.25
Mozambique	91	3.19	Macedonia, FYR	91	2.73	Russian Federation	91	3.55	Bosnia and Herzegovina	91	3.23
Kenya	92	3.19	Vietnam	92	2.72	Mozambique	92	3.54	Albania	92	3.20
Honduras	93	3.18	Albania	93	2.69	Mongolia	93	3.53	East Timor	93	3.18
Gambia	94	3.18	Armenia	94	2.69	Kenya	94	3.50	Sri Lanka	94	3.17
Bosnia and Herzegovina	95	3.17	Honduras	95	2.68	Uganda	95	3.49	Tajikistan	95	3.17
Mongolia	96	3.16	Guatemala	96	2.67	Macedonia, FYR	96	3.47	Moldova	96	3.14
Guatemala	97	3.12	Gambia	97	2.65	Vietnam	97	3.43	Mali	97	3.13
Sri Lanka	98	3.10	Zimbabwe	98	2.62	Nigeria	98	3.43	Mozambique	98	3.13
Nicaragua	99	3.08	Bosnia and Herzegovina	99	2.61	Madagascar	99	3.39	Jamaica	99	3.13
Albania	100	3.07	Ecuador	100	2.61	Sri Lanka	100	3.34	Cameroon	100	3.12
Bolivia	101	3.06	Bangladesh	101	2.60	Tajikistan	101	3.33	Benin	101	3.08
Dominican Republic	102	3.05	Nicaragua	102	2.52	Albania	102	3.32	Paraguay	102	3.07
Ecuador	103	3.01	Mali	103	2.52	Pakistan	103	3.31	Bolivia	103	3.05
Tajikistan	104	3.01	Tajikistan	104	2.52	Philippines	104	3.30	Cambodia	104	3.04
Malawi	105	3.00	Cambodia	105	2.51	Dominican Republic	105	3.24	Mongolia	105	3.03
Ethiopia	106	3.00	Madagascar	106	2.48	Venezuela	106	3.23	Kenya	106	3.01
Madagascar	107	2.95	Malawi	107	2.46	Guatemala	107	3.22	Gambia	107	3.01
East Timor	108	2.93	Bolivia	108	2.42	East Timor	108	3.20	Ethiopia	108	2.99
Zimbabwe	109	2.89	East Timor	109	2.42	Guyana	109	3.10	Madagascar	109	2.98
Bangladesh	110	2.86	Cameroon	110	2.36	Benin	110	3.06	Nicaragua	110	2.96
Cameroon	111	2.84	Paraguay	111	2.35	Cameroon	111	3.05	Serbia and Montenegro	111	2.95
Cambodia	112	2.82	Guyana	112	2.34	Paraguay	112	2.97	Dominican Republic	112	2.78
Paraguay	113	2.80	Kyrgyz Republic	113	2.34	Ecuador	113	2.93	Guyana	113	2.77
Benin	114	2.74	Algeria	114	2.29	Cambodia	114	2.90	Chad	114	2.67
Guyana	115	2.73	Ethiopia	115	2.22	Kyrgyz Republic	115	2.89	Kyrgyz Republic	115	2.62
Kyrgyz Republic	116	2.62	Benin	116	2.09	Chad	116	2.64	Malawi	116	2.47
Chad	117	2.37	Chad	117	1.80	Bangladesh	117	2.55	Zimbabwe	117	2.25

Table 4: Technology index components

Country	Technology index Rank	Score	Innovation subindex Rank	Score	ICT subindex Rank	Score	Tech transfer subindex Rank	Score
Albania	93	2.69	94	1.75	91	1.91	66	4.05
Algeria	114	2.29	84	2.01	110	1.80	89	3.03
Argentina	59	3.35	34	3.18	59	2.51	39	4.54
Armenia	94	2.69	71	2.21	97	1.88	70	3.92
Australia	14	4.82	15	4.36	9	5.27	—	—
Austria	21	4.35	21	3.97	18	4.74	—	—
Azerbaijan	87	2.79	81	2.05	78	2.21	72	3.81
Bahrain	41	3.73	52	2.45	42	3.08	19	5.01
Bangladesh	101	2.60	105	1.61	112	1.73	59	4.10
Belgium	28	4.18	19	4.20	26	4.17	—	—
Benin	116	2.09	113	1.44	104	1.82	91	2.66
Bolivia	108	2.42	59	2.38	106	1.81	86	3.25
Bosnia and Herzegovina	99	2.61	82	2.02	76	2.22	84	3.33
Botswana	76	2.99	98	1.69	75	2.23	46	4.44
Brazil	50	3.51	68	2.25	52	2.70	18	5.02
Bulgaria	61	3.31	50	2.47	48	2.91	58	4.12
Cambodia	105	2.51	110	1.49	113	1.67	68	3.97
Cameroon	110	2.36	106	1.61	107	1.81	85	3.33
Canada	15	4.79	11	4.69	16	4.89	—	—
Chad	117	1.80	117	1.30	117	1.39	92	2.52
Chile	35	3.93	38	2.86	37	3.37	17	5.04
China	64	3.18	75	2.15	60	2.48	43	4.47
Colombia	74	3.01	67	2.26	71	2.28	53	4.24
Costa Rica	56	3.39	72	2.20	58	2.52	22	4.95
Croatia	51	3.48	48	2.54	40	3.19	56	4.18
Cyprus	36	3.87	51	2.46	29	3.88	50	4.32
Czech Republic	22	4.31	39	2.80	31	3.75	2	5.57
Denmark	5	5.30	10	4.70	1	5.90	—	—
Dominican Republic	67	3.13	55	2.42	65	2.35	47	4.40
East Timor	109	2.42	103	1.62	115	1.58	74	3.80
Ecuador	100	2.61	87	1.88	95	1.89	73	3.81
Egypt	58	3.36	64	2.36	68	2.33	14	5.07
El Salvador	70	3.09	85	2.00	66	2.34	45	4.46
Estonia	18	4.62	27	3.51	21	4.56	15	5.07
Ethiopia	115	2.22	116	1.36	116	1.50	83	3.47
Finland	2	6.02	2	6.43	5	5.61	—	—
France	24	4.26	20	4.05	22	4.46	—	—
Gambia	97	2.65	112	1.45	93	1.90	65	4.05
Georgia	84	2.84	60	2.38	87	2.03	62	4.08
Germany	16	4.78	9	4.92	20	4.63	—	—
Ghana	69	3.11	96	1.71	82	2.08	21	4.95
Greece	37	3.85	24	3.54	38	3.36	35	4.62
Guatemala	96	2.67	95	1.72	100	1.84	61	4.09
Guyana	112	2.34	111	1.48	94	1.90	88	3.22
Honduras	95	2.68	90	1.80	101	1.84	60	4.09
Hong Kong SAR	26	4.21	32	3.19	10	5.23	—	—
Hungary	30	4.08	36	3.10	35	3.46	8	5.24
Iceland	9	5.16	14	4.45	2	5.88	—	—
India	55	3.42	76	2.13	67	2.33	6	5.32
Indonesia	66	3.13	80	2.05	85	2.04	23	4.95
Ireland	31	4.07	22	3.82	24	4.33	—	—
Israel	12	4.87	6	5.38	23	4.37	—	—
Italy	44	3.68	30	3.38	28	3.98	—	—
Jamaica	45	3.64	78	2.11	46	2.97	16	5.05
Japan	8	5.24	5	5.74	17	4.75	—	—
Jordan	52	3.46	47	2.57	53	2.66	31	4.82
Kazakhstan	77	2.99	41	2.79	74	2.24	64	4.05
Kenya	71	3.04	97	1.70	108	1.81	12	5.14
Korea, Rep.	7	5.26	8	5.29	11	5.23	—	—
Kuwait	48	3.56	69	2.23	45	3.01	33	4.73
Kyrgyz Republic	113	2.34	63	2.36	90	1.91	90	2.91
Latvia	38	3.83	25	3.52	39	3.36	36	4.57
Lithuania	42	3.70	26	3.51	41	3.15	41	4.48
Luxembourg	29	4.11	37	3.03	13	5.19	—	—
Macedonia, FYR	91	2.73	77	2.11	70	2.29	82	3.51
Madagascar	106	2.48	108	1.54	102	1.83	77	3.66
Malawi	107	2.46	115	1.42	114	1.66	71	3.88
Malaysia	25	4.22	40	2.80	33	3.56	1	5.57
Mali	103	2.52	109	1.53	88	1.98	80	3.57
Malta	23	4.29	58	2.40	25	4.32	26	4.89

(cont'd.)

Country	Technology index		Innovation subindex		ICT subindex		Tech transfer subindex	
	Rank	Score	Rank	Score	Rank	Score	Rank	Score
Mauritius	47	3.57	79	2.07	47	2.93	25	4.93
Mexico	57	3.39	73	2.20	57	2.57	27	4.88
Moldova	89	2.76	74	2.19	72	2.27	78	3.59
Mongolia	81	2.93	53	2.44	81	2.08	55	4.23
Morocco	78	2.96	93	1.77	83	2.07	38	4.54
Mozambique	83	2.91	114	1.43	105	1.81	28	4.87
Namibia	79	2.95	91	1.79	80	2.11	42	4.47
Netherlands	11	4.88	17	4.33	7	5.43	—	—
New Zealand	19	4.47	18	4.22	19	4.71	—	—
Nicaragua	102	2.52	86	1.89	109	1.80	75	3.69
Nigeria	90	2.74	99	1.69	103	1.83	51	4.30
Norway	13	4.87	12	4.62	14	5.12	—	—
Pakistan	80	2.94	100	1.65	77	2.21	49	4.35
Panama	65	3.17	42	2.75	73	2.24	37	4.54
Paraguay	111	2.35	83	2.01	111	1.77	87	3.24
Peru	75	3.01	62	2.36	84	2.07	40	4.49
Philippines	54	3.43	65	2.34	63	2.42	11	5.15
Poland	39	3.77	31	3.22	43	3.03	24	4.94
Portugal	20	4.39	35	3.15	30	3.84	3	5.55
Qatar	40	3.76	70	2.22	44	3.02	7	5.25
Romania	49	3.53	54	2.44	50	2.71	20	4.97
Russian Federation	73	3.01	29	3.41	62	2.43	76	3.66
Serbia and Montenegro	68	3.12	61	2.37	64	2.36	48	4.37
Singapore	10	4.93	13	4.47	8	5.40	—	—
Slovak Republic	34	3.99	46	2.62	36	3.41	9	5.21
Slovenia	32	4.07	23	3.60	27	4.06	54	4.23
South Africa	46	3.62	66	2.27	55	2.63	4	5.39
Spain	27	4.21	28	3.44	32	3.74	13	5.09
Sri Lanka	88	2.79	101	1.65	89	1.94	52	4.30
Sweden	4	5.78	4	5.89	4	5.66	—	—
Switzerland	6	5.29	7	5.37	12	5.21	—	—
Taiwan	3	5.85	3	6.19	6	5.51	—	—
Tajikistan	104	2.52	89	1.85	92	1.91	81	3.56
Tanzania	86	2.81	107	1.54	96	1.89	44	4.46
Thailand	43	3.69	43	2.72	51	2.70	5	5.33
Trinidad and Tobago	62	3.25	92	1.77	61	2.43	30	4.84
Tunisia	60	3.35	57	2.41	56	2.61	34	4.64
Turkey	53	3.45	56	2.42	54	2.66	29	4.85
Uganda	82	2.93	104	1.62	98	1.84	32	4.82
Ukraine	85	2.82	33	3.19	79	2.17	79	3.57
United Arab Emirates	33	4.04	44	2.67	34	3.53	10	5.16
United Kingdom	17	4.66	16	4.35	15	4.98	—	—
United States	1	6.19	1	6.66	3	5.72	—	—
Uruguay	63	3.19	49	2.50	49	2.71	63	4.07
Venezuela	72	3.03	45	2.67	69	2.30	57	4.13
Vietnam	92	2.72	88	1.87	86	2.04	69	3.92
Zimbabwe	98	2.62	102	1.64	99	1.84	67	3.98

Table 5: Public institutions index components

Country	Public institutions index		Contracts and law subindex		Corruption subindex	
	Rank	Score	Rank	Score	Rank	Score
Albania	102	3.32	108	2.80	93	3.84
Algeria	81	3.77	67	3.66	91	3.87
Argentina	74	3.96	100	2.98	57	4.94
Armenia	66	4.11	72	3.51	61	4.70
Australia	10	6.01	10	5.67	10	6.35
Austria	11	6.00	13	5.61	9	6.39
Azerbaijan	67	4.09	61	3.75	72	4.44
Bahrain	38	5.10	39	4.54	34	5.65
Bangladesh	117	2.55	104	2.88	117	2.22
Belgium	28	5.38	23	5.11	35	5.65
Benin	110	3.06	95	3.12	113	3.00
Bolivia	84	3.71	97	3.05	75	4.36
Bosnia and Herzegovina	86	3.67	101	2.97	74	4.36
Botswana	39	5.08	30	4.93	48	5.23
Brazil	70	4.06	77	3.42	62	4.70
Bulgaria	62	4.23	103	2.90	38	5.57
Cambodia	114	2.90	102	2.91	115	2.89
Cameroon	111	3.05	91	3.15	114	2.95
Canada	21	5.67	24	5.09	17	6.24
Chad	116	2.64	113	2.54	116	2.73
Chile	22	5.58	34	4.88	13	6.29
China	56	4.41	62	3.74	50	5.08
Colombia	49	4.55	83	3.32	30	5.79
Costa Rica	58	4.32	49	4.16	68	4.48
Croatia	73	3.99	80	3.33	65	4.66
Cyprus	27	5.44	25	5.09	31	5.78
Czech Republic	48	4.63	50	4.11	49	5.15
Denmark	2	6.35	1	6.17	4	6.54
Dominican Republic	105	3.24	106	2.85	99	3.63
East Timor	108	3.20	96	3.06	107	3.34
Ecuador	113	2.93	115	2.30	101	3.56
Egypt	53	4.46	45	4.37	67	4.55
El Salvador	54	4.45	70	3.56	44	5.33
Estonia	25	5.51	35	4.87	21	6.16
Ethiopia	79	3.79	75	3.47	84	4.12
Finland	5	6.19	3	5.90	5	6.49
France	20	5.72	18	5.30	22	6.15
Gambia	77	3.88	55	4.05	97	3.71
Georgia	87	3.65	84	3.25	87	4.04
Germany	8	6.04	6	5.88	20	6.19
Ghana	51	4.54	36	4.79	77	4.29
Greece	43	4.77	40	4.53	54	5.00
Guatemala	107	3.22	114	2.47	89	3.97
Guyana	109	3.10	110	2.74	105	3.45
Honduras	88	3.61	107	2.82	73	4.40
Hong Kong SAR	23	5.58	22	5.16	26	5.99
Hungary	34	5.15	43	4.43	29	5.86
Iceland	3	6.33	4	5.89	1	6.78
India	52	4.52	37	4.78	78	4.26
Indonesia	89	3.58	66	3.66	103	3.49
Ireland	13	5.93	11	5.63	18	6.24
Israel	30	5.35	27	5.03	33	5.66
Italy	46	4.70	68	3.66	32	5.74
Jamaica	65	4.14	74	3.47	58	4.81
Japan	14	5.84	21	5.24	8	6.44
Jordan	31	5.28	26	5.05	40	5.51
Kazakhstan	76	3.89	71	3.56	81	4.23
Kenya	94	3.50	90	3.19	94	3.81
Korea, Rep.	42	4.78	41	4.53	52	5.04
Kuwait	37	5.11	31	4.91	45	5.31
Kyrgyz Republic	115	2.89	112	2.71	112	3.07
Latvia	50	4.55	52	4.09	53	5.00
Lithuania	44	4.73	58	3.83	36	5.63
Luxembourg	7	6.08	9	5.71	7	6.45
Macedonia, FYR	96	3.47	111	2.73	82	4.21
Madagascar	99	3.39	88	3.23	100	3.58
Malawi	68	4.08	56	3.95	83	4.21
Malaysia	29	5.36	17	5.30	43	5.42
Mali	72	4.00	51	4.09	90	3.90
Malta	32	5.23	29	4.95	41	5.51

(cont'd.)

Country	Public institutions index Rank	Score	Contracts and law subindex Rank	Score	Corruption subindex Rank	Score
Mauritius	55	4.41	53	4.07	59	4.76
Mexico	71	4.03	79	3.35	60	4.71
Moldova	63	4.20	93	3.12	47	5.28
Mongolia	93	3.53	81	3.32	96	3.73
Morocco	85	3.69	60	3.76	98	3.63
Mozambique	92	3.54	86	3.23	92	3.85
Namibia	57	4.38	54	4.06	63	4.69
Netherlands	16	5.83	14	5.53	23	6.12
New Zealand	1	6.35	2	5.97	2	6.74
Nicaragua	82	3.74	98	3.03	70	4.45
Nigeria	98	3.43	69	3.59	109	3.27
Norway	6	6.13	7	5.80	6	6.45
Pakistan	103	3.31	87	3.23	106	3.39
Panama	75	3.90	63	3.72	86	4.08
Paraguay	112	2.97	117	2.17	95	3.77
Peru	59	4.27	99	2.98	39	5.55
Philippines	104	3.30	82	3.32	108	3.28
Poland	64	4.14	65	3.68	66	4.61
Portugal	15	5.83	16	5.46	19	6.20
Qatar	19	5.75	15	5.52	27	5.98
Romania	78	3.84	85	3.25	71	4.44
Russian Federation	91	3.55	109	2.78	76	4.33
Serbia and Montenegro	69	4.07	92	3.14	55	5.00
Singapore	4	6.25	5	5.88	3	6.62
Slovak Republic	45	4.73	57	3.85	37	5.61
Slovenia	35	5.14	48	4.28	25	6.01
South Africa	47	4.63	46	4.31	56	4.96
Spain	36	5.13	47	4.30	28	5.95
Sri Lanka	100	3.34	89	3.21	104	3.48
Sweden	17	5.82	19	5.30	11	6.34
Switzerland	9	6.02	8	5.79	15	6.26
Taiwan	26	5.47	33	4.88	24	6.07
Tajikistan	101	3.33	76	3.46	110	3.20
Tanzania	60	4.25	44	4.40	85	4.09
Thailand	41	4.88	42	4.48	46	5.28
Trinidad and Tobago	83	3.73	78	3.41	88	4.04
Tunisia	40	5.02	28	4.99	51	5.04
Turkey	61	4.25	59	3.82	64	4.68
Uganda	95	3.49	73	3.48	102	3.51
Ukraine	90	3.56	105	2.87	79	4.26
United Arab Emirates	24	5.52	38	4.78	16	6.25
United Kingdom	12	5.98	12	5.62	12	6.33
United States	18	5.77	20	5.27	14	6.27
Uruguay	33	5.19	32	4.91	42	5.48
Venezuela	106	3.23	116	2.22	80	4.25
Vietnam	97	3.43	64	3.71	111	3.16
Zimbabwe	80	3.79	94	3.12	69	4.46

Table 6: Macroeconomic environment index components

Country	Macroeconomic environment index		Macroeconomic stability subindex		Government waste		Country credit rating	
	Rank	Score	Rank	Score	Rank	Score	Rank	Score
Albania	92	3.20	85	4.10	95	2.57	96	2.02
Algeria	44	4.33	12	5.30	51	3.30	68	3.44
Argentina	86	3.37	50	4.59	91	2.61	107	1.68
Armenia	77	3.53	55	4.52	63	3.12	98	1.97
Australia	14	5.21	25	5.05	16	4.34	18	6.39
Austria	22	5.07	38	4.73	22	4.07	12	6.76
Azerbaijan	56	4.05	18	5.13	57	3.19	78	2.74
Bahrain	32	4.62	20	5.11	36	3.68	47	4.58
Bangladesh	83	3.43	67	4.36	85	2.68	86	2.30
Belgium	29	4.76	52	4.56	50	3.33	16	6.61
Benin	101	3.08	92	4.03	104	2.33	101	1.92
Bolivia	103	3.05	105	3.69	97	2.51	87	2.29
Bosnia and Herzegovina	91	3.23	70	4.30	110	2.14	89	2.17
Botswana	36	4.55	53	4.56	15	4.37	43	4.70
Brazil	79	3.50	81	4.14	111	2.13	62	3.58
Bulgaria	62	3.95	51	4.59	89	2.65	56	3.96
Cambodia	104	3.04	100	3.78	70	2.94	107	1.68
Cameroon	100	3.12	87	4.09	102	2.36	100	1.94
Canada	16	5.16	23	5.07	33	3.76	13	6.74
Chad	114	2.67	110	3.56	114	1.80	104	1.73
Chile	15	5.20	3	5.66	19	4.23	32	5.25
China	33	4.61	27	5.02	44	3.45	37	4.96
Colombia	61	3.95	48	4.61	66	3.02	65	3.55
Costa Rica	82	3.44	109	3.62	83	2.69	60	3.85
Croatia	68	3.76	90	4.05	74	2.84	55	4.10
Cyprus	45	4.33	76	4.21	30	3.83	36	5.05
Czech Republic	46	4.31	44	4.64	78	2.80	34	5.15
Denmark	3	5.64	11	5.31	4	5.12	8	6.83
Dominican Republic	112	2.78	108	3.63	115	1.72	92	2.14
East Timor	93	3.18	93	4.03	61	3.15	113	1.51
Ecuador	80	3.50	33	4.84	113	1.95	84	2.35
Egypt	55	4.07	59	4.47	34	3.75	64	3.57
El Salvador	57	4.03	63	4.42	35	3.71	62	3.58
Estonia	30	4.73	14	5.27	43	3.45	38	4.93
Ethiopia	108	2.99	106	3.66	59	3.16	114	1.50
Finland	4	5.52	13	5.30	10	4.61	4	6.87
France	27	4.90	61	4.43	29	3.88	7	6.84
Gambia	107	3.01	113	3.45	45	3.43	106	1.69
Georgia	90	3.25	74	4.23	69	2.96	111	1.58
Germany	28	4.81	65	4.38	37	3.67	10	6.81
Ghana	66	3.82	66	4.37	21	4.18	83	2.37
Greece	51	4.16	96	3.91	60	3.15	25	5.68
Guatemala	81	3.47	73	4.24	106	2.30	72	3.11
Guyana	113	2.77	115	3.13	86	2.67	92	2.14
Honduras	89	3.25	84	4.11	94	2.59	88	2.22
Hong Kong SAR	8	5.34	6	5.55	11	4.60	26	5.66
Hungary	63	3.91	95	3.93	73	2.88	40	4.90
Iceland	11	5.24	21	5.10	6	4.97	23	5.80
India	50	4.17	41	4.68	63	3.12	53	4.20
Indonesia	64	3.89	56	4.51	40	3.58	75	2.94
Ireland	7	5.38	7	5.47	28	3.89	14	6.68
Israel	48	4.25	62	4.42	41	3.50	44	4.68
Italy	47	4.26	89	4.08	87	2.66	20	6.22
Jamaica	99	3.13	107	3.63	88	2.66	80	2.59
Japan	42	4.40	78	4.19	68	2.96	19	6.28
Jordan	52	4.10	57	4.50	23	4.03	70	3.39
Kazakhstan	41	4.42	24	5.06	39	3.60	57	3.95
Kenya	106	3.01	99	3.81	105	2.32	94	2.10
Korea, Rep.	25	4.98	8	5.38	32	3.77	28	5.39
Kuwait	21	5.09	1	5.72	38	3.63	31	5.26
Kyrgyz Republic	115	2.62	114	3.25	107	2.30	109	1.67
Latvia	38	4.48	28	5.00	49	3.34	48	4.57
Lithuania	39	4.47	29	4.91	46	3.41	46	4.63
Luxembourg	9	5.30	26	5.04	18	4.25	3	6.88
Macedonia, FYR	75	3.58	46	4.62	84	2.69	81	2.40
Madagascar	109	2.98	112	3.50	47	3.37	112	1.56
Malawi	116	2.47	117	2.83	92	2.60	110	1.62
Malaysia	19	5.12	19	5.12	2	5.13	35	5.12
Mali	97	3.13	104	3.73	56	3.21	102	1.87
Malta	54	4.09	80	4.15	79	2.77	30	5.28

(cont'd.)

Table 6: Macroeconomic environment index components *(cont'd.)*

Country	Macroeconomic environment index		Macroeconomic stability subindex		Government waste		Country credit rating	
	Rank	Score	Rank	Score	Rank	Score	Rank	Score
Mauritius	59	4.01	86	4.09	41	3.50	51	4.35
Mexico	43	4.35	36	4.76	55	3.22	45	4.65
Moldova	96	3.14	75	4.22	80	2.75	115	1.39
Mongolia	105	3.03	94	3.96	109	2.22	97	1.98
Morocco	67	3.82	88	4.09	54	3.23	58	3.87
Mozambique	98	3.13	102	3.76	72	2.91	95	2.08
Namibia	65	3.84	71	4.30	52	3.24	66	3.51
Netherlands	10	5.26	39	4.69	9	4.81	9	6.82
New Zealand	20	5.10	22	5.09	25	4.02	21	6.18
Nicaragua	110	2.96	97	3.88	101	2.38	105	1.72
Nigeria	76	3.54	45	4.64	81	2.74	91	2.14
Norway	2	5.76	5	5.61	8	4.86	2	6.94
Pakistan	69	3.74	49	4.61	48	3.35	82	2.39
Panama	74	3.60	91	4.03	99	2.45	59	3.86
Paraguay	102	3.07	79	4.16	117	1.62	85	2.34
Peru	70	3.71	54	4.53	103	2.34	67	3.45
Philippines	71	3.69	58	4.49	100	2.44	71	3.35
Poland	53	4.09	68	4.33	77	2.80	39	4.92
Portugal	37	4.51	64	4.40	58	3.17	22	6.08
Qatar	6	5.40	4	5.66	3	5.13	33	5.17
Romania	73	3.65	83	4.13	90	2.64	61	3.70
Russian Federation	58	4.02	42	4.65	93	2.59	54	4.19
Serbia and Montenegro	111	2.95	101	3.77	108	2.28	98	1.97
Singapore	1	5.82	10	5.36	1	5.90	15	6.64
Slovak Republic	49	4.23	40	4.69	82	2.70	41	4.82
Slovenia	35	4.57	35	4.78	62	3.15	27	5.55
South Africa	31	4.68	30	4.90	14	4.41	49	4.53
Spain	24	5.07	31	4.87	24	4.02	17	6.51
Sri Lanka	94	3.17	103	3.75	98	2.47	79	2.70
Sweden	12	5.24	16	5.20	31	3.77	11	6.79
Switzerland	13	5.23	37	4.76	13	4.43	1	7.00
Taiwan	17	5.15	17	5.15	12	4.53	24	5.76
Tajikistan	95	3.17	72	4.28	71	2.91	116	1.19
Tanzania	72	3.65	77	4.21	26	4.02	89	2.17
Thailand	26	4.94	9	5.37	17	4.32	42	4.70
Trinidad and Tobago	40	4.44	15	5.23	75	2.83	50	4.48
Tunisia	34	4.59	43	4.65	7	4.86	52	4.20
Turkey	87	3.34	111	3.56	76	2.82	69	3.41
Uganda	88	3.30	82	4.13	65	3.08	102	1.87
Ukraine	78	3.52	69	4.31	96	2.54	76	2.92
United Arab Emirates	5	5.43	2	5.70	5	5.00	29	5.32
United Kingdom	18	5.13	32	4.86	27	3.94	4	6.87
United States	23	5.07	47	4.61	20	4.21	6	6.85
Uruguay	84	3.40	98	3.85	67	2.99	77	2.92
Venezuela	85	3.39	60	4.46	116	1.71	74	2.95
Vietnam	60	3.96	34	4.80	52	3.24	73	3.01
Zimbabwe	117	2.25	116	3.00	112	2.00	117	1.00

Box 1: Is Italy's ranking too low?

Italy's ranking in the Growth Competitiveness Index has been on a downward trend, falling from 26 in 2001 to 47 in both 2004 and 2005. Only Poland in the EU25 has a lower ranking at 51. It is useful to examine the factors that explain this precipitous decline in Italy's competitive position.

First, on the macroeconomic side, Italy has seen a fairly steady deterioration of the public sector accounts. In the 1990s, the country made remarkable progress in bringing the budget under control, as part of its efforts to qualify for membership in the euro area. Indeed, by 2000 the budget deficit had fallen under 1 percent of GDP for the first time in several decades. However, according to the latest data released by the IMF, the country has been running large—and growing—deficits since then, and there appear to be no prospects for improvement, with the deficit in 2006 (4.3 percent of GDP) projected to be even larger than in 2005. The levels of public indebtedness, already well in excess of 100 percent of GDP in the early part of the decade, have remained stubbornly high. Italy's growth performance has been extremely sluggish and on a sharply decelerating trend. After growing by an average of 2.3 percent during the period 1980–90, GDP growth slowed down to 1.3 percent during the period 1991–2000 and to a further 1.1 percent during 2001–2005. Not surprisingly, this has considerably dampened the mood in the business community. Our "recession expectations" indicator—a Survey measure of how the private sector views the short-term outlook—is particularly low for Italy, 110th in the world in this year's rankings.

Second, on the technology side, Italy ranks 44th in the world, well below the corresponding ranks for its G7 partners in the EU where Germany is 16th, the United Kingdom 17th and France 24th. The GCI's technology index has a large number of hard data variables (personal computer use, Internet access, availability of fixed telephone line, patents registration as a measure of innovation, and university enrollment rates, as leading indicators of a country's future innovation potential), and, across the board, Italy's rankings are mediocre for its level of per capita income and stage of development. For example, personal computer use in Italy is lower than in Korea, Taiwan, Estonia, Ireland, Slovenia, Cyprus, Malta, and the Slovak Republic, among others. Internet use is lower than in Singapore, Taiwan, Estonia, and Korea. Patents registration rates are lower in Italy than in Israel, Korea, Ireland, Hong Kong, and New Zealand; indeed of the 25 "core innovator" countries identified in the GCI, Italy is at the bottom.

While the above assessment is based overwhelmingly on hard data variables—and thus beyond the criticism that it simply reflects the subjective opinions of the business community—Italy is weakest in terms of the public institutions indicators used in the GCI, as reflected in a low ranking of 68th with regard to the general state of Italy's *contracts and law* environment. Of particular concern is the lack of independence of the judiciary (59th), the perception that the government favors well-connected firms and individuals in deciding upon contracts and policies (72nd), and the high costs imposed by organized crime on Italian businesses

(103rd). While there is no doubt that these perceptions involve a degree of subjectivity, they are not necessarily off target. In the course of 2005, there have been a number of unfavorable analyses of the Italian economy in the leading international press. An article in *The Economist*[1] refers, in rather unkind language, to glaring weaknesses in Italy's system of corporate governance, as well as to widespread evidence of "political graft and favors." Indeed, a number of scandals in the course of the past year are thought to have adversely affected confidence. *The Financial Times* has focused on what *The Economist* calls "the extraordinary saga" of the attempted takeover of some Italian banks by banks elsewhere in the EU, strenuously resisted, allegedly, by the Bank of Italy.[2]

Beyond these particular factors, Italian competitiveness is hindered by its heavy reliance on low-growth mature industries (textiles, clothing, shoes, and white goods), which need a low-cost base to be able to prosper, and which are more and more exposed to international competition. With the adoption of the euro, the option to devalue as a way of maintaining a lower-cost base has been permanently foreclosed. Moreover, companies have to cope with high labor costs, Italian workers being among the best paid and most protected in the world.[3]

Italy's ranking in the Global Competitiveness Index (see below) is 38, somewhat better than with the GCI, because it gets credit for good scores on health and primary education, and, to a lesser extent, on business sophistication. In light of the above, we do not think that Italy's ranking is too low. On the contrary, the World Economic Forum's indexes seem to capture quite well Italy's competitiveness deficiencies. Regardless of the measure of competitiveness used, it is clear that there are onerous challenges ahead, especially in the area of fiscal policy and strengthening of the institutional environment, if Italy's competitiveness rankings are to improve.

Notes

1 See article "The Real Sick Man of Europe," *The Economist*, 2005.

2 *The London Financial Times*, various issues, February–June, 2005.

3 This is not to suggest, for a moment, that Italy should consider abandoning the euro and returning to the days of 10 percent of GDP budget deficits, sky-high interest rates and a weak and unstable lira. Far better for the government to focus attention on structural and microeconomic reforms aimed at enhancing productivity and boosting the innovative potential of the manufacturing sector. In terms of policy formulation and implementation, Italy should aim to be more like Finland than Argentina.

two places since last year, although this is explained by the incorporation of two other countries, Kuwait and Qatar, both of which have a higher rank on this component of the GCI. However, French businesses take a considerably tougher line in assessing those aspects of the competitiveness climate which involve the quality of public institutions. Whether one looks at the operations and independence of the courts, at the property rights environment, or at issues of evenhandedness of government officials in their dealings with the private sector, France does not meet the standards seen not only in Germany, but in other countries such as Finland, Denmark, New Zealand, Switzerland, and Singapore, among others. On a more positive note, France's rankings are likely to rise in coming years, as our focus shifts to the Global Competitiveness Index (see below), where the country will get credit for a number of concepts not presently being captured in the GCI—e.g., the sophistication of its companies, its strong human capital endowment, including excellent levels of public health, and so on.[7]

Among the ten countries recently acceding to the EU, **Estonia** leads the pack, coming in at 20th place, ahead of several of the wealthier original EU15 members. Estonia's ranking is impressive for a number of reasons, perhaps the most important among them being that it has bridged the gap between the inefficiencies of central planning and competent economic performance in less than 15 years. The country ranks 14th overall in terms of the stability of its macroeconomic environment, and 18th in the area of technology, slightly ahead of New Zealand and Portugal. The worst performer among the accession countries continues to be **Poland,** with serious weaknesses in the country's institutional and macroeconomic environments. Noteworthy areas of concern are the poor outlook for the public finances, as well as mediocre scores in a number of areas which capture essential elements of the role of the public sector in the economy. However, on a positive note, we do note some progress in Poland's performance, with the country moving up 9 places to 51st, up from 60th last year. This is in line with a trend we see among many of the new accession countries, where there is a measured improvement in levels of competitiveness over recent years, likely due in large part to the general benefits of EU membership, and the incentives it provides for a proactive stance on the part of the government in the area of economic reform.

Asia
Unlike some other regions, where countries often cluster behind one or two top performers, Asian economies are spread throughout the full range of the index, pointing to their very different levels of development and growth potential. Leading within the region are Asian tigers, notably **Taiwan** and **Singapore,** ranked 5th and 6th

respectively, some places ahead of the next Asian country covered by the GCI, **Japan,** ranked 12th. We note that the distance between these top-ranked economies and Japan has increased since last year, reflecting Japan's relatively poor macroeconomic performance. Indeed, Japan has some of the worst rankings in the world for the budget deficit (113th) and the levels of public indebtedness (114th). However, what Japan lacks in fiscal discipline is more than compensated for by the country's impressive technology performance, with extremely high rankings in R&D, firm-level technology absorption, and patent registration, where the scores are second only to the United States, by a small margin.

Compared with the other tigers, **Hong Kong** ranked lower at 28th place, having dropped seven places since last year. A perceived worsening of the quality of the country's public institutions was primarily to blame for this weakening, with Hong Kong dropping 14 places on this subindex, from 9th to 23rd place. This in turn, is the result of significant shifts on both the contracts and law subindex and the corruption subindex. Hong Kong deteriorated on practically all components of the public institutions part of the GCI: judicial independence (from 14th place to 25th), property rights (from 3rd to 15th), favoritism (from 10th to 32nd). Hong Kong's ranks on irregular payments (corruption) have fallen well below its previously excellent performance. These results suggest a tangible deterioration in Hong Kong's institutional environment during the past year.

China and **India,** 49th and 50th, respectively, ranked much more closely to one another than in previous years. While China dropped three ranks, India moved up five places. In China, the change in rank reflects the inclusion in this year's index of two new countries entering at a higher rank. In addition, China had a slightly deteriorating score with regard to the country's macroeconomic environment. The authorities have been trying to rein in the growth of credit—China's ranking on the access to credit variable dropped considerably—and the strength of demand has resulted in an acceleration of inflation in 2004. India's improved rank mirrors the country's somewhat higher position in the technology index. The increasing inflows of FDI to skill and technology-intensive sectors observed over the past few years have certainly succeeded in boosting the mood of the business community. Remaining worries in India, however, stem from the slight progress made in fiscal adjustment—the country has one of the world's largest budget deficits, ranked 116th among 117 countries—the low penetration rates of new technologies (mobile telephones, personal computers, Internet use), and low enrollment rates for higher education. (For a fuller description of competitiveness issues in India, see Box 2.) The latter two are also a problem in China. Both China and India have had an excellent growth

Box 2: What will it take to boost India's competitiveness rankings?

India ranks 50th in this year's Growth Competitiveness Index, moving up five ranks as compared to last year. The country's recent economic success is beyond doubt and reflected in the GDP growth rates of over 7 percent over the past few years, an important achievement, which has brought with it a substantial reduction in the incidence of poverty.[1]

The key question at the moment is whether India will be able to sustain and, indeed, accelerate its growth performance over the next decade. To be sure, just as China has benefited from a massive process of urbanization, India has a similar "structural" feature which is likely to fuel growth: its favorable demographics. For the next 20 years, the share of the working-age population will rise rapidly. However, to benefit from this, India will have to find ways to bring its masses of young people into the workforce, by spending on education, and improving the quality of its educational institutions, in order to boost the productivity of its young, particularly the poor.

There has also been a significant improvement in recent years in the quality of India's business environment, and in the degree of sophistication of its private sector. Whether we look at such things as the sophistication of production processes, levels of company spending on R&D, the prevalence of foreign technology licensing, the sophistication of financial markets, the greater openness in the economy associated with a much more sensible approach to trade, India has made tangible progress over the past decade. No doubt, the better growth performance seen during this period reflects these improvements in the policy framework and the institutional environment.

However, to quicken the pace of growth to, let us say, 8 percent per year, a number of weaknesses will have to be addressed. Key among them are:

- *High illiteracy rates* and relatively *low enrollment rates* across all segments of the educational ladder. The needs are particularly urgent at the primary and secondary level, but even tertiary enrollment rates are low by international standards—India ranks 91st among the 117 countries covered in the *Global Competitiveness Report*. The scope for improvement in girls' education is especially wide. India will have to educate and train its young poor, to enable them to join the labor force with usable skills, particularly in those sectors of potential comparative advantage. There is every expectation that world demand for outsourcing will rise in coming years, reflecting the continued shift of backoffice operations to the developing world associated with the drop in the cost of communications. For India to be able to take full advantage of these opportunities—particularly at the high end of the outsourcing market—it will have to improve the level of skills and training of its workforce.

- The extent of *bureaucratic red tape* and *excessive regulation* remains a serious problem in India. There is a pervasive culture of government intervention and control, best characterized as "self-inflicted injuries," which add to business costs, and discourage the development of small and medium-sized enterprises. That is, things that developing countries do to themselves which have little or no discernible value, other than to make life difficult for business. India has made progress in this area over the past decade, but not nearly enough.

- The government has identified glaring needs in the area of *infrastructure:* India's roads, ports, airports, and power generation are in a sorry state of repair. Some progress has been made to improve the telecom infrastructure, but major investments are necessary, across the board, to sustain private sector development, and boost inflows of FDI to much higher levels. The government would like to attract US$150 billion of FDI during the next decade, but there is little chance that this will materialize purely on the strength of India's large and growing market. The infrastructure will have to be upgraded to create a friendlier environment for investment. Whether these plans are fully realized will, in turn, be closely linked to a major improvement in the public finances.

- India has a serious *fiscal deficit* problem. Essentially, it has been running deficits of some 10 percent of GDP for the last several years, among the highest in the world—among the 117 countries covered in the *Global Competitiveness Report* only Turkey scores lower. There are several aspects to this problem: first, India's consolidated public debt level, at 83 percent of GDP, is already very high, by both emerging market standards, and those of developed economies; second, the revenue-to-debt ratio is among the highest in the world, due to India's very narrow revenue base; India collects only about 19 percent of GDP in revenues, compared to some 26 percent of GDP on average for the developing countries and much higher levels still for industrial countries with widespread safety nets.

  In an attempt to bring about some measure of medium-term fiscal adjustment, the government brought into force in 2003 a Fiscal Responsibility Budget Management law (FRBMA) which sets out a plan for deficit reduction through 2009. But the law has some flaws: first, it applies only to the central government, whereas, in fact, about half of the deficit problem is with the states; second, the law does not establish any penalties and/or sanctions for departures with respect to the path of fiscal adjustment laid down in the FRBMA.

  Why is all of this important? For a number of reasons. First, the bulk of the public debt is denominated in rupees. This is seen by the markets as a positive, since it isolates the country from exchange rate risk. However, since the debt is large, it means that the banking system is essentially playing the role of cashier to the government. It taps household savings and then finances the government and sits on several hundred billion dollars of government paper. This is profitable, safe business for the banks, which then do not have to worry excessively about intermediating

(cont'd.)

Box 2: What will it take to boost India's competitiveness rankings? *(cont'd.)*

savings to the private productive sectors, the small and medium-sized companies, which need finance to grow. They also do not have to worry much about further developing the internal capacity to price risk—why should they, if they have, in the form of the government, a large, reliable client? India is unlikely to see 8 percent growth on a sustained basis without a thriving financial sector channeling household savings into private sector productive investments. But this will not happen as long as the government does not curtail its own appetite for savings. Furthermore, with a huge stock of government securities sitting in the balance sheets of the banks, these are vulnerable to interest rate risk and, thus, potential capital losses.

Finally, India's good growth performance would seem to provide an ideal context for fiscal adjustment, whether in the form of higher taxes or lower expenditures, or some combination thereof. A growing economy provides the cushion, in political economy terms, for belt-tightening. The alternative is to do it in the middle of an economic downturn or a crisis, and this is traditionally more difficult. Fiscal discipline is always difficult in the context of a multiparty democracy, particularly one with the (still) large levels of poverty seen in India. Without doubt the deficit is a drag on the economy; a much lower deficit would have been associated with higher growth rates and higher levels of revenue, boosting the ability of the government to respond to pressing social needs. So, perversely, lack of fiscal discipline is having the opposite of the intended effect: by reducing growth, it has turned into an anti-poor measure.

The Indian economy has the potential to become an engine of growth for the world. To realize its full potential, the authorities and the business community will have to join forces to address a number of important challenges: special priority will have to be given to boosting the country's human capital endowment, improving the quality of physical infrastructure, reducing the burden on business of needless over-regulation and moving the public finances onto a more sustainable path. Real GDP growth of 8 percent per year over the longer term would allow further gains in poverty reduction, always a central concern of good economic policy. Along the way, provided these challenges are met, there is no reason why India could not join the ranks of the most competitive economies in the world.

Note

1 India's average annual real GDP growth during the period 1990–2004 has been about 5.7 percent, compared to close to 9 percent in China. So, during this period Indian GDP doubled but Chinese GDP tripled. Not surprisingly, China has much lower infant mortality, higher life expectancy, and lower illiteracy rates than India.

performance in recent years. In both cases, it has reflected efficiency gains stemming from the elimination of gross distortions in resource allocation (particularly in China); the move to more open and better policies has contributed to major improvements in productivity. Furthermore, in China, the economy has also benefited from several structural transformations, including a massive process of urbanization, which continues to account for a not insignificant share of GDP growth.[8] However, both countries continue to suffer from institutional weaknesses, which, unless addressed, are likely to slow down their ascension to the top tier of the most competitive economies in the world.

Korea moved up by an impressive 12 places in this year's ranking, certainly the most significant and one of the largest improvements of all 117 countries ranked this year. This is due in part to Korea's recovery from the credit card crisis of 2003. The effects of the crisis on the country's macroeconomic environment brought about an 11 place drop in last year's ranking, while the subsequent improvement over the last year allowed Korea to regain its previous position.

This year's ranking has for the first time included three central Asian economies. While **Kazakhstan,** with a relatively strong performance in the macroeconomic subindex comes in 61st, its neighbors **Tajikistan** and the **Kyrgyz Republic** occupy ranks in the lowest part of the list: 104 and 116, respectively. Several other Asian countries have been added to the ranking this year including **Mongolia** (ranked 96th), **East Timor** (ranked 108th), **Cambodia** (ranked 112th), and **Azerbaijan** (ranked 69th). The agenda for reform in these countries is quite heavy, across a broad range of areas. In the central Asian economies, in particular, there are important issues of concern as regards the role of the government—often heavy-handed—in its relations with the private sector. An additional area of concern is evidence of widespread corruption.

Latin America

As in previous years, **Chile,** ranked 23rd, leads the way in Latin America by a wide margin. Indeed, the gap with respect to the next best performer in the region has widened from 26 places in 2004 to 31 places in 2005, a characteristic not seen in any other region of the world. The country continues to benefit from a combination of remarkably competent macroeconomic management (see the discussion below on the Global Competitiveness Index, where Chile ranks number 1 in the world in the macroeconomy pillar of that index), and public institutions, which have achieved EU levels of transparency and efficiency. Indeed, only eight of the 25 EU members have higher ranks on the public institutions subindex. Chile looks set to grow by 6.1 percent in 2005—the highest growth in Latin America according to the latest projections by the IMF—and the upcoming presidential election is unlikely to dent this impressive performance. Indeed, a distinguishing feature of Chile's performance over the past decade and a half is the extent to which commitment to sound policies is not a function of political cycles.

Mexico has fallen seven places since last year to 55th, ceding its second spot in the regional ranking to **Uruguay,** while **Brazil** fell by eight places to 65th place. Both Mexico and Brazil suffered major plunges in those indicators which capture the quality of their public institutions. In Mexico, the political uncertainties in the run-up to the 2006 presidential election, and the resulting paralysis in policymaking, considerably soured the mood of the business community, contributing to the country's 71st position in the public institutions index. Mexico continues to suffer from high levels of crime and has also seen a gradual erosion of relative rankings in the ICT area reflecting both the incorporation into the index calculations of countries with a more sophisticated technology infrastructure and faster progress made in these areas in other parts of the world (particularly in Asia). In Brazil business confidence may have been adversely affected by a weakening of the ruling party's coalition in the wake of bribery scandals and other events, which have cast the underlying strength of the country's public institutions in an unfavorable light. This is illustrated by Brazil's weak performance with regards to judicial independence (72nd), the wastefulness of government spending (ranked 111th on this indicator), and favoritism in the decisions of government officials (69th).

Argentina has seen an overall improvement over the past year, moving up from a rank of 74 to 72, despite the inclusion of a number of new countries, several of which have entered ahead of Argentina. It is particularly notable that the country's macroeconomic performance rose from a rank of 94 to 86th place, in part reflecting reduced inflation levels, a smaller interest rate spread, and the nation's successful debt restructuring. However, public debt levels remain high, and the country's private sector continues to have deep scepticism about the strength of the institutional environment, with Argentina scoring poorly on property rights, independence of the judiciary, and several measures of corruption. On the other hand, **Venezuela,** which had a ranking of 62 in 2001, continues its precipitous decline to the bottom of the rankings, falling another four places to 89th position overall this year. Venezuela's performance is quite extraordinary from a number of perspectives: notwithstanding huge terms of trade gains because of high oil prices, the government has managed to run budget deficits for a number of years, suggesting massive waste; indeed, its score for waste in government spending, at 116th, is next to last. It has one of the worst inflation performances in the world (115th) and has the

distinction of having the worst property rights climate in the world (117th). Venezuela performs feebly across all the other dimensions of the contracts and law subindex, including judicial independence (ranked 114th), favoritism in the decisions of government officials (ranked 116th), and organized crime (ranked 104th). Not surprisingly, in this calamitous environment, Venezuela has also suffered an erosion of a broad range of technology indicators: penetration ranks for Internet use, personal computers, and fixed line telephones are all down, as are other indicators, important to the country's future growth potential, such as spending on R&D, FDI, and technology transfer, and the priority given by government to ICT promotion. Finally, **Guyana,** a new addition to this year's rankings, comes in last in the Latin American and Caribbean region, and third to last overall, at 115th out of the 117 countries.

Middle East-North Africa

Within the Middle East and North Africa (MENA) region, the small Gulf States perform quite well in the overall GCI rankings, including two new entrants to the index from the region this year: Qatar and Kuwait. The **United Arab Emirates** (UAE) and **Qatar** are ranked 18th and 19th, respectively. These countries are going through a particularly good phase. Terms-of-trade gains have boosted growth rates and reinforced already high levels of confidence in the business community, resulting from ongoing institutional modernization and improvements in macroeconomic management. The authorities have proven reasonably adept at not squandering the gains from higher oil prices, but, rather, are using these resources to reduce debt, to invest, and to save. Their competitiveness rankings are thus quite high. **Kuwait** and **Bahrain** follow relatively closely at positions ranked 33rd and 37th, respectively, while **Tunisia** and **Jordan** are ranked somewhat lower, at 40th and 45th respectively. The lowest ranked countries from the region are **Morocco,** ranked 76th, and **Algeria,** ranked 78th.

The range of ranks is in keeping with the high degree of heterogeneity of the region. These countries have very different income levels and productive structures, ranging from almost complete reliance on the oil sector (in most of the Gulf States), to much more diversified economies.[9]

Compared to 2004, the competitiveness performance of the region has been rather disappointing. With the exception of Tunisia, all countries covered last year dropped in the rankings. The most extreme case was Morocco, which fell by 20 places. This can be traced to a very significant weakening of the country's macroeconomic environment, and its public institutions. The ranking in the macroeconomic environment subindex went down 21 places (from 46th to 67th) and the contract and law subindex registered an equally precipitous drop of 20 places (from 40th to 60th). In this context, macroeconomic reforms, involving a substantial trimming of the large and growing budget deficit and public debt, as well as a better targeting of public spending, should be at the top of policymakers' agenda. Improvements in the country's rule of law framework also require immediate attention.

The problems and the challenges faced by policymakers in the MENA region are serious indeed: notwithstanding the encouraging steps and structural reforms undertaken by most countries, the region displays the highest unemployment rate in the world, at 15 percent, with a working population projected to grow from 104 million in 2000 to 185 million by 2020,[10] a heavy dependence on the energy sector, and growing competition from other regions of the world. For this reason, much needs to be done in terms of microeconomic and macroeconomic reforms in order to diversify and increase trade and to attract FDI. Egypt deserves much praise for its initiative to create a National Competitiveness Council to work together with the government to identify obstacles to growth.[11]

Sub-Saharan Africa

While most of the countries of the sub-Saharan African region are not very competitive, the region does have a number of relative success stories. This includes **South Africa** (42nd), **Botswana** (48th), **Mauritius** (52nd), and **Ghana** (59th), the latter's competitiveness performance being even more notable, having improved by 9 places since 2004. **Tanzania** has also seen a significant improvement over the past year, moving up 11 places in the overall rankings. On the other hand, **Namibia,** a relatively good performer overall, lost 11 places over the past year, as, predictably, did **Madagascar** and **Zimbabwe,** losing 11 and 10, respectively. Zimbabwe is a particularly sad case, whose quick descent to the bottom of the world's competitiveness rankings reflects the continued deterioration of the institutional climate, including the disappearance of property rights, the corruption of the rule of law, and the implications these and other factors have had for macroeconomic management. The country has the world's worst ranking (117th) for the quality of its macroeconomic environment.

Most sub-Saharan African countries continue to lag behind the rest of the world in competitiveness terms, including two countries just added to the index from the region: Cameroon and Benin. Seven of the 13 lowest-ranked countries in the overall index are from this region. These include **Malawi** (105th), **Ethiopia** (106th), **Madagascar** (107th), **Zimbabwe** (109th), **Cameroon** (111th), **Benin** (114th), and **Chad** (117th). The GCI rankings thus confirm sub-Saharan Africa's status as the world's least developed region, with stagnating foreign trade, investment, and per capita income. In fact, the Millennium Development Goals (MDG) progress report of 2004 predicted that sub-Saharan Africa would not achieve most of the MDG goals—in particular the elimination of extreme poverty and hunger—by 2015, unless it could benefit from a freer and fairer international trading system, and a significantly higher volume of overseas development assistance. The recent decision of the G8 countries to write off US$40 billion debt owed by 18 mainly African countries is surely a step in the right direction, but African countries must also make a considerable effort *internally* to improve macroeconomic fundamentals, and those governance practices aimed at enhancing the rule of law and boosting the legitimacy of government, through adoption of the practices and institutions of democracy.

The latest in competitiveness research: The new "Global Competitiveness Index"

The Growth Competitiveness Index described above (and in Appendix A) was a major step forward in the Forum's efforts to present a quantified framework for the analysis of the key determinants of growth. When it was put together, it represented an intelligent compromise between the need for complexity, reflecting the multiplicity of factors affecting the evolution of growth, on the one hand, and the need for a structure that was transparent and simple enough that it could be estimated for a large number of countries. The GCI has thus served its purpose well, providing important insights into a number of the key areas central to the growth process. In particular, it provides a useful linkage with the past, especially relevant for countries wanting to see the evolution of a key competitiveness indicator in an inter-temporal perspective. However, it has become increasingly apparent to us that we need a more comprehensive vehicle, one that better reflects changes in the nature of the global economy and the relative importance of key factors in explaining the evolution of growth in a large number of countries, with a considerable degree of institutional and structural diversity.

A few examples will suffice. It is difficult to make a meaningful analysis of the sluggish growth performance of the EU15 without entering into a discussion of structural weaknesses and the slow pace of reform in a number of areas, be it the prevalence of labor market rigidities, or delays in the completion of key elements of the single market, which have prevented the European economies from benefiting from the economies of scale associated with a large, single, truly unified market, such as exists in the United States. The GCI does not address the issue of labor market rigidities, nor does it look more broadly at the issue of efficiencies in the operation of various markets; the GCI framework simply does not encompass the sophistication of financial institutions and their ability to intermediate resources, or the presence of unnecessary regulatory red tape, or the existence of adequate levels of competition in the domestic economy.

The poor growth performance seen in most of the African continent during the past quarter century cannot be divorced from public health considerations; as important as good management of the public finances is for assessing the macroeconomic environment in African countries, it is not appropriate to analyze competitiveness trends in the region, without taking into consideration the impact on business of HIV/AIDS, or of other major epidemics. The GCI is silent on these issues, not because its original authors did not see these as being central to an understanding of development in Africa,[12] but rather because coverage of Africa in the Forum's competitiveness work in 2001 was still limited, and there was no compelling reason to include factors that were not essential to explaining growth in Europe or Latin America.

Education and the extent to which countries are able to upgrade the skills and training of the labor force have acquired growing importance as indicators of a country's future growth potential. A country's ability to absorb new technologies, to produce goods and services that can reach standards of quality and performance acceptable in international markets, to engage with the rest of the world in ways that are value-creating, is intimately linked to the quality of its schools, to the priority given to training in mathematics and science, and to the existence and accessibility of specialized research and training centers. The GCI brought in some concepts in this area, but we feel there is an obvious need to do more.

In the interest of taking the Forum's competitiveness work further, in order to capture a broader set of factors crucial to understanding more clearly the determinants of economic growth, we have worked closely for the past two years with Professor Xavier Sala-i-Martin, a leading expert on the process of economic growth at Columbia University. In last year's *Report,* we provided a preliminary version of a new, and more comprehensive competitiveness index, which we called the *Global Competitiveness Index* (Global CI). This new index allows us to measure and benchmark many critical factors, which were absent from the Growth Competitiveness Index described in the previous section. The Global CI aims to measure "the set of institutions, policies, and factors that set the sustainable current and medium-term levels of economic prosperity."[13]

The new Global CI is built around nine different pillars, each of which is critical to driving productivity and competitiveness in national economies. The pillars include all of the elements that were previously included in the GCI, as well as many other factors as discussed above. A brief description of these pillars will be useful here; the full details on the construction of the index are provided in Appendix B at the end of this chapter, and in the Technical Notes section (Appendix C).

Pillar 1: Institutions

The institutional environment in an economy is fundamental for establishing the context in which the development process takes place. The quality of a country's public and private institutions constitutes the framework within which the economy's main players interact. Regarding the public sector in particular, factors such as the strength of the property rights environment, the efficiency with which the government uses scarce financial resources, the extent to which public sector officials clearly distinguish between the public good and private gain, the prevalence of crime and its impact on business costs are all of critical importance. It is clear that business cannot be carried out efficiently in an economy where property rights are poorly defined; when property owners (material or intellectual) are not guaranteed owners' rights, they will be unwilling to invest further, while new entrants to the market will have little incentive to join the formal economy, preferring instead to disguise their activities outside the reach of tax authorities, in the outer margins of the "informal sector."[14] Lack of transparency in government operations and evidence of corruption undermine business confidence, lead to misallocation of resources, and may entail large welfare losses to society at large. Favoritism in the decisions of government officials and meddling in the judicial system lead to inefficiency, erode property rights, and hinder dispute settlement, increasing business costs. In addition to these more hidden factors, there are also the more visible inefficiencies created by governments, such as red tape and needless bureaucracy, which create waste. Finally, business is disrupted in an insecure environment, when additional costs are imposed by terrorism, organized crime and violence, especially when combined with a lack of reliable police services.

But "good governance" is not a concept that applies to the public sector only. Quality and transparency of private institutions are also crucial for economic efficiency. An economy is well served by businesses that are run honestly, where managers abide by strong ethical practices in their dealings with the government, other firms, and the public. Private sector transparency is indispensable to business, notably the financial sector, using standards, auditing, and accounting practices that ensure access to information in a timely manner.[15]

Pillar 2: Infrastructure

The existence of high-quality infrastructure is critical for ensuring the efficient functioning of the economy, as it is an important factor determining the location of economic activity, and the kinds of projects or sectors that can develop over time. High-quality infrastructure facilitates closer interaction between regions, encouraging the internal integration of the national market, and the development of linkages with other countries and regions.

Effective modes of transport for goods, people, and services, such as quality railroads, ports, and air transport are vitally important, enabling entrepreneurs to get their goods to market in a secure, cost-effective, and timely manner, and facilitating the movement of workers around the country to the most suitable jobs. Economies must also be able to depend on electricity supplies that are free of interruptions and shortages, to ensure that businesses and factories can work unimpeded. Finally, a solid and extensive telecommunications network, allowing for a rapid and free flow of information, is vital for increasing overall economic efficiency, and by helping to ensure that decisions by economic actors take into account all available, relevant information.

Pillar 3: Macroeconomy

Macroeconomic stability has come to be accepted as an essential ingredient of sustainable growth.[16] It is a challenging task to come up with examples of countries that have grown on a sustained basis without due regard for budget constraints or the importance of price stability. Management of the public finances is particularly important, as far too many countries have suffered the debilitating effects of fiscal indiscipline which, over time, leads to rising levels of public indebtedness, and severely constrains the ability of governments to respond to pressing needs, such as public health, infrastructure, or education. Conversely, governments that have managed the public sector accounts with caution, transparency, and efficiency have been able to allocate resources to these areas, all critical to enhance the country's competitiveness. The macroeconomic indicators captured in this pillar broadly correspond to those included in the Growth Competitiveness Index, although in a more streamlined fashion.

Pillar 4: Health and primary education

A healthy workforce is vital to a country's competitiveness and productivity. Workers who are ill cannot function to their potential, and will be less productive. Poor health leads to significant costs to business, as sick workers are often absent or operate at lower levels of efficiency. In the extreme case of death of an employee, selection of new staff and training is also costly. In acute cases, such as the HIV/AIDS epidemic in Africa, which primarily affects the working-age population, we see a shortage of qualified workers in the short term; and in the long term as well, because orphaned children will inevitably have to work to support their families, and will almost certainly receive less education. The health of the workforce is measured by basic health indicators, such as life expectancy and infant mortality, as well as the prevalence and cost to business of three major world illnesses: malaria, tuberculosis, and HIV/AIDS.

In addition to health, this pillar takes into account the years of basic education received by the population, which, as noted above, is increasingly important in today's economy. Basic education increases the efficiency of each individual worker, making the economy more productive. In addition, a workforce that has received little formal education can only carry out basic manual work and finds it much more difficult to adapt to more advanced production processes and techniques. A shortage of qualified administrative staff might also have a negative impact on overall business performance. Lack of basic education can therefore become a constraint on business development, with firms finding it difficult to move up the value chain, by producing more sophisticated or value-intensive products.

Pillar 5: Higher education and training

The quality and quantity of higher education provided within an economy are critical for competitiveness, for preparing qualified staff for more complex roles in areas, such as production, marketing, management, and R&D.[17] More generally, the technological adaptation required in a fast changing globalizing world economy demands a large pool of well-educated talent.

Aside from formal education, on-the-job training has become an increasingly important method of upgrading an economy's human resources. Companies that continuously update and improve the skill level of their employees are more likely to adapt to a changing environment, and to maintain their competitive edge, contributing more to overall economic productivity. Keeping up with constantly improving production processes, introducing new marketing techniques, or entering new markets requires specific professional skills, which firms can provide through staff training, assisted in this task by appropriate professional training institutions in the country.

Pillar 6: Market efficiency

The efficiency with which the various factor markets in the economy function is critical for its underlying productivity and competitiveness, as it ensures the proper allocation of economic factors to their best use. Three vital types of market efficiency are measured in the Global Competitiveness Index: *goods markets, labor markets,* and *financial markets.*

Countries with efficient goods markets are positioned to produce the right mix of products and services, given supply and demand conditions, and also ensure that these goods can be most effectively traded in the economy. Healthy market competition, both domestic and foreign, is important in driving market efficiency, and thus business productivity, by ensuring that the most efficient firms, producing goods demanded by the market, are those that survive. And to ensure the best possible environment for the exchange of goods, there must be a minimum of impediments to business activity from government intervention. For example, competitiveness is hindered by distortionary or burdensome taxes, or an inefficient legal framework which does not provide for businesses to settle disputes in an impartial and timely manner.

Productivity and competitiveness are also boosted by labor market efficiency. In a productive economy, workers are allocated properly to their best use, and provided with incentives to give their best effort in their jobs. Labor markets must have the flexibility to shift workers from one economic activity to another quickly, and to allow for wage fluctuations without social disruption. Efficient labor markets must also ensure a clear relationship between worker incentives and their efforts, as well as equity in the business environment between women and men.

Finally, economies with efficient financial markets see financial resources allocated most effectively in the economy to their best investment use. Most critical to productivity is business investment, so economies require sophisticated financial markets that can make capital available for private sector investment from such sources as loans from a sound banking sector, well-regulated securities exchanges, and venture capital.

Pillar 7: Technological readiness

Technology has become an increasingly central element in today's knowledge-based global economy, affecting the range, quality, and price of goods produced in, and ultimately exported by, a country. In this sense, the degree to which a country can sustain rates of growth and productivity depends more and more on its technological readiness, and on whether, and to what extent, it can benefit from new technologies, whether developed internally or imported.[18]

Technological readiness specifically relates to those factors which facilitate and enable the technological capacity of a country. This includes the general availability of technologies, and the penetration rate of information and communication technologies (ICT), as these tools are seen as critical indicators of the overall technological readiness of a country. Access to ICT is critical, not only for the establishment of an effective and rapid communication system but also for providing an efficient infrastructure for commercial transactions.

Pillar 7 complements, and is, in turn, complemented by, Pillar 9 (Innovation). While both highlight the importance of technology for overall national competitiveness, Pillar 7 deals with the stock of technology available in a given economy, regardless of its original source, while Pillar 9 addresses the innovation potential of a country, i.e., its capacity to generate new technologies internally.

Pillar 8: Business sophistication

Business sophistication is conducive to higher efficiency in the production of goods and services, which leads, in turn, to increased productivity, thus enhancing a nation's competitiveness. Business sophistication concerns the quality of a country's overall business networks, as well as the quality of individual firms' operations and strategies.[19] This pillar is particularly important for economies in the innovation-driven stage of development (see below).

The quality of a country's business networks and supporting industries, which we capture by using Survey variables on the quantity and quality of local suppliers, is important for a variety of reasons. When companies and suppliers are interconnected in geographically proximate groups ("clusters") efficiency is heightened, leading to greater opportunities for innovation, and to the reduction of barriers to entry for new firms. Individual firms' operations and strategies (branding, marketing, the presence of a value chain, and the production of unique and sophisticated products) all lead to sophisticated and modern business processes.

Pillar 9: Innovation

It is widely accepted that one of the principal conditions for a rising living standard is the development of dynamic, national competitive advantages, based on technology and skills-intensive industries, as opposed to static ones, based on lower production costs. Thus, as countries develop, national competitiveness depends to an increasing extent on their innovative potential. Whereas the dimensions captured in the previous eight pillars run into diminishing returns, common sense suggests that there is no limit to the possible number of new ideas.

Innovative capability is particularly crucial for countries already functioning at, or close to, the frontiers of knowledge, and for which the adoption or use of exogenous technology no longer ensures sustained and continuous rates of productivity growth. These countries must focus on research and development, and on the endogenous generation of knowledge and new products.[20]

The innovative capability of a nation depends on whether it exists in an appropriate and conducive environment, supported by the joint and coherent efforts of both the public and private sectors. It cannot exist without high quality scientific research institutions, a highly skilled workforce, including scientists and engineers, sufficient R&D spending by private companies, and intellectual property protection to make R&D worthwhile. Also vital to innovation is the private-public synergy provided by the active collaboration of universities and R&D companies.

Using these 9 pillars, covering a wide variety of institutional, macroeconomic, and microeconomic factors critical to boosting an economy's productive potential, we are confident that the Global CI will deliver a state-of-the-art competitiveness index, sufficiently comprehensive in scope to replace the Growth Competitiveness Index, and allow for an enhanced dialogue between the World Economic Forum and the users of our work.

Stages of development and transitions

Beyond the above pillars, which capture a more comprehensive set of growth factors, the Global CI has a number of other important distinguishing features. One of them is the formal incorporation—from its conception—of the notion that countries around the world find themselves at different stages of economic development. The relative importance of particular factors for improving the competitiveness of a country will be a function of its particular stage of development. What presently drives productivity in the United States is necessarily different from what drives it in the Ukraine. Thus, the Global CI separates countries into three specific stages, adding degrees of complexity at each stage, called *factor-driven, efficiency-driven, and innovation-driven.*

In the first factor-driven stage, countries generally compete based on low prices. They sell commodities or simple products, taking advantage of low-cost labor and readily available natural resources. At this stage of development, the basic ingredients of competitiveness include strong public and private institutions (pillar 1), adequate infrastructure (pillar 2), a healthy macroeconomic environment (pillar 3), and a healthy workforce, with at least a basic level of education (pillar 4).

As countries move into stage 2, the efficiency-driven stage, it becomes important for them to develop more efficient production practices. Product quality, rather than low price, drives competitiveness at this stage, and is dependent on higher education and training programs to prepare the workforce for more advanced production processes (pillar 5), goods, labor, and financial markets that operate at increasing levels of efficiency (pillar 6), as well as access to the latest technologies invented around the world (pillar 7).

In the third innovation-driven stage, countries can no longer compete simply by being efficient. In countries at this advanced stage of development, companies must compete through innovation (pillar 9), producing new and different goods, and using the most sophisticated production processes (pillar 8).

So while, to varying degrees, all nine pillars matter for all countries, the importance of each for national competitiveness depends on a country's particular stage of development. To take this into account, the pillars are organized into three subindexes, each critical to one particular stage of development. The basic requirements subindex groups those pillars most critical for countries in the factor-driven stage. The efficiency enhancers subindex includes those

pillars critical for countries in the efficiency-driven stage. The innovation and sophistication factor subindex includes all pillars critical to countries in the innovation-driven stage. The three subindexes are composed as follows:

Basic requirements subindex (Stage 1: factor-driven)
- Institutions (pillar 1)
- Infrastructure (pillar 2)
- Macroeconomy (pillar 3)
- Health and basic education (pillar 4)

Efficiency enhancers subindex (Stage 2: efficiency-driven)
- Higher education and training (pillar 5)
- Market efficiency (pillar 6)
- Technological readiness (pillar 7)

Innovation and sophistication factor subindex (Stage 3: innovation-driven)
- Business sophistication (pillar 8)
- Innovation (pillar 9)

The Global CI implements the concept of developmental stages by weighting each of the subindexes differently, depending on the stage of a given country. More specifically, the index places more weight on those pillars that are most important at a given stage of a country's development.

The specific weights given to each of the subindexes for countries in the different stages of development are shown in Table 7. The table shows that for countries at the factor-driven stage, most weight is placed on basic requirements (50 percent), considerable weight is placed on efficiency enhancers (40 percent), and only 10 percent weight is placed on innovation and sophistication factors. For countries at the efficiency-driven stage, the weights between basic requirements and efficiency enhancers are reversed, with little weight still placed on innovation factors. Finally, for the countries at the innovation-driven stage, considerable weight is still placed on the two first subindexes, but the weight placed on the innovation and sophistication factors subindex is higher, reflecting the fact that at this most advanced stage of development, these are the factors that matter the most for improving productivity and competitiveness.

Table 7: Weights of the three main groups of pillars at each stage of development

Weights	Basic requirements	Efficiency enhancers	Innovation and sophistication factors
Factor-driven stage	50%	40%	10%
Efficiency-driven stage	40%	50%	10%
Innovation-driven stage	30%	40%	30%

Table 8: List of countries in each stage of development

Stage 1	Transition from 1 to 2	Stage 2	Transition from 2 to 3	Stage 3
Income of less than US$2,000	Income US$2,000–US$3,000	Income US$3,000–US$9,000	Income US$9,000–US$17,000	Income more than US$17,000
Armenia	Albania	Argentina	Bahrain	Australia
Azerbaijan	Algeria	Botswana	Czech Republic	Austria
Bangladesh	Colombia	Brazil	Hungary	Belgium
Benin	Dominican Republic	Bulgaria	Korea	Canada
Bolivia	Ecuador	Chile	Malta	Cyprus
Bosnia and Herzegovina	El Salvador	Costa Rica	Portugal	Denmark
Cambodia	Guatemala	Croatia	Slovenia	Finland
Cameroon	Kazakhstan	Estonia	Taiwan	France
Chad	Macedonia, FYR	Jamaica	Trinidad and Tobago	Germany
China	Namibia	Latvia		Greece
East Timor	Peru	Lithuania		Hong Kong SAR
Egypt	Serbia and Montenegro	Malaysia		Iceland
Ethiopia	Thailand	Mauritius		Ireland
Gambia	Tunisia	Mexico		Israel
Georgia		Panama		Italy
Ghana		Poland		Japan
Guyana		Romania		Kuwait
Honduras		Russia		Luxembourg
India		Slovak Republic		Netherlands
Indonesia		South Africa		New Zealand
Jordan		Turkey		Norway
Kenya		Uruguay		Qatar
Kyrgyz Republic		Venezuela		Singapore
Madagascar				Spain
Malawi				Sweden
Mali				Switzerland
Moldova				United Arab Emirates
Mongolia				United Kingdom
Morocco				United States
Mozambique				
Nicaragua				
Nigeria				
Pakistan				
Paraguay				
Philippines				
Sri Lanka				
Tajikistan				
Tanzania				
Uganda				
Ukraine				
Vietnam				
Zimbabwe				

Of course, countries do not suddenly jump from one stage of development to another, but rather, move along a continuum. We therefore take into account the fact that many countries are in transition between stages. For these countries, the weights change smoothly as a country develops, reflecting the gradual transition from one stage of development to the next. This is an important characteristic of the index, as, by introducing this type of transition between stages into the model—i.e., by placing increasing weight on those areas that are becoming more important for the country's competitiveness at its particular stage of development—the Global CI can begin to "penalize" those countries that are not yet preparing for the next stage of development.

Countries are separated into stages as follows. The factor-driven stage includes countries that have GDP per

capita below US$2,000. The efficiency-driven stage includes countries with per capita income between US$3,000 and US$9,000. The innovation-driven stage includes countries with GDP per capita higher than US$17,000. The countries in transition are those between the categories. Table 8 shows how the 117 countries covered in this *Report* are allocated into the different stages of development.

The reason that we use income levels as the separating criterion for the stages is, as the authors explain, because "factor-driven economies are those that compete in low prices. We proxy low wages with low income levels, which is why we assign countries with … income per capita below US$2,000 to this group."[21] The same reasoning applies to countries in stages 2 and 3: rising GDP per capita proxies for wages that are rising, pulling countries into higher stages of development, where they must improve their productivity based on more complex factors. Tables 9–12 present the results of the Global Competitiveness Index rankings for 2005.

The top performers in the nine pillars of the Global Competitiveness Index

Table 13 displays the countries with the number one ranking in each of the nine pillars of the Global Competitiveness Index. Singapore, Japan, and the United States are notable for being the three countries that are first in two pillars. Denmark, Chile, and Finland hold the first places in the other three pillars.

Singapore holds first place on the institutions and technological readiness pillars. Singapore performs well on both subindexes of the Institutions pillar, but particularly so on the public institutions subindex where it holds the first place out of the 117 countries. This subindex is made up of five components and Singapore performs remarkably well on all five of them: property rights (6), ethics and corruption (1), undue influence (9), government inefficiency: red tape, bureaucracy and waste (1), and security (6). It is clear that the public has a high level of trust in the financial honesty of politicians; compliance with administrative regulations does not put an unnecessary burden on business; government spending provides the necessary goods and services that are not provided by the market; government decisions are neutral and police services are reliable; all these characteristics serve to make Singapore the country with the best institutions at a global level. Singapore's number one ranking on the technological readiness pillar can be attributed to the existing technological infrastructure (the large penetration rates for the Internet and personal computers), to the high levels of technological absorption by firms, to proficiency at adopting new technologies through FDI, and to a highly developed regulatory environment for ICT. This ranking is fully consistent with Singapore's number one ranking in the Forum's *Global Information Technology Report 2004–2005* and the Networked Readiness Index contained therein.

Japan holds first place on the health and primary education, and business sophistication pillars. Japan has very low levels of HIV/AIDS, high life expectancy, and very low levels of infant mortality. In addition, in Japan the impact on business of worker illness is very low. This makes Japan the top country in the world in terms of the quality of basic human capital. Japan also holds the number one ranking on the business sophistication pillar. Japan has the best business networks (large numbers of high-quality local suppliers) as well as among the best individual company operations and strategies. This includes factors such as local control over international distribution and marketing (2), the production of sophisticated and

high-value added products (1), and high-quality production processes (1).

The United States holds first place on the market efficiency and innovation pillars. Market efficiency is composed of three subindexes (goods markets, labor markets, and financial markets) and the United States holds the number one spot on both goods markets and financial markets, and the second spot on labor markets. In terms of goods markets, the United States has fairly low levels of distortions (9), and a very strong domestic and foreign competition environment. The availability of venture capital, the ease of obtaining bank loans, the highly sophisticated stock markets, and the ease of raising money by issuing shares on local stock markets, all explain the United States' top spot on the financial markets subindex. Finally, the wage-setting process, the flexibility of hiring and firing workers, the relative absence of nepotism, and the fact that salaries are strongly related to worker productivity all boost the efficiency and flexibility of the US labor markets. The United States also occupies first place on the innovation pillar. This can be attributed to the fact that the United States holds the highest ranks on practically all of the variables that enter this index: quality of scientific research institutions (1), company spending on R&D (1), business collaboration with universities on R&D (1), intellectual property protection (1), government procurement of advanced technology products (8), availability of scientists and engineers (13), capacity for innovation (4), and the number of registered patents (1). The United States is clearly ahead of its closest competitor, Japan.

Denmark holds the top spot on the infrastructure pillar. High-quality railroads, ports, telephones, air transport, and electricity supply all contribute to Denmark's having the highest-quality overall infrastructure in the world. Chile ranks in first place on the macroeconomy pillar: the authorities have managed the public finances with admirable caution and consistency and, given the country's strong growth performance, public debt levels have been on a rapidly declining trend (12 percent of GDP in 2004), enabling the government to invest in productivity-enhancing areas, as well as making impressive progress in reducing the incidence of poverty. With an excellent inflation performance, the monetary authorities have focused considerable attention in efficiently regulating an otherwise sophisticated financial sector. Finally, Finland, the number two country overall on the Global Competitiveness Index, holds the top spot on the higher education and training pillar, with the highest tertiary education enrollment ratio in the world (87.5 percent), high-quality math and science education, excellent management schools, and a very high level of employee training and development.

Table 9: The Global Competitiveness Index 2005

| | OVERALL INDEX | | THREE SUBINDEXES | | | | | |
| | | | Basic requirements | | Efficiency enhancers | | Innovation factors | |
Country	Rank	Score	Rank	Score	Rank	Score	Rank	Score
United States	1	5.85	18	5.61	1	5.85	1	6.07
Finland	2	5.73	2	6.05	5	5.54	5	5.68
Denmark	3	5.73	1	6.15	3	5.60	7	5.47
Switzerland	4	5.67	6	5.91	7	5.44	4	5.73
Singapore	5	5.67	3	6.05	2	5.70	14	5.24
Germany	6	5.56	8	5.79	19	5.16	3	5.86
Sweden	7	5.55	7	5.80	9	5.40	6	5.50
Taiwan	8	5.52	19	5.60	6	5.50	8	5.44
United Kingdom	9	5.51	17	5.63	4	5.56	11	5.33
Japan	10	5.50	25	5.43	17	5.19	2	5.98
Netherlands	11	5.39	9	5.77	16	5.21	12	5.26
France	12	5.39	16	5.65	18	5.18	9	5.41
Canada	13	5.39	11	5.73	11	5.32	16	5.14
Hong Kong SAR	14	5.35	4	5.98	12	5.29	21	4.80
Austria	15	5.34	14	5.67	21	5.15	13	5.25
Iceland	16	5.34	13	5.68	10	5.34	18	4.99
Norway	17	5.31	5	5.94	15	5.22	20	4.81
Australia	18	5.31	12	5.71	8	5.43	23	4.75
Korea, Rep.	19	5.28	20	5.58	20	5.16	17	5.06
Belgium	20	5.23	21	5.53	23	5.04	15	5.19
Ireland	21	5.22	22	5.52	14	5.23	19	4.91
New Zealand	22	5.22	15	5.66	13	5.24	22	4.75
Israel	23	5.22	31	5.18	22	5.11	10	5.40
Luxembourg	24	5.04	10	5.77	26	4.76	24	4.69
Malaysia	25	5.03	26	5.42	25	4.79	25	4.67
Estonia	26	5.03	29	5.30	24	5.00	34	4.05
Chile	27	4.84	24	5.46	31	4.49	32	4.09
Spain	28	4.80	28	5.33	27	4.68	28	4.41
Czech Republic	29	4.76	37	5.03	28	4.64	27	4.44
Slovenia	30	4.62	32	5.14	29	4.52	31	4.20
Portugal	31	4.60	30	5.29	32	4.47	35	4.04
United Arab Emirates	32	4.59	23	5.51	33	4.42	42	3.90
Thailand	33	4.59	34	5.10	41	4.22	38	4.01
Lithuania	34	4.51	43	4.84	35	4.36	40	3.94
Hungary	35	4.50	49	4.68	30	4.50	39	3.98
Slovak Republic	36	4.48	47	4.74	34	4.40	43	3.88
Tunisia	37	4.48	33	5.13	48	4.02	33	4.08
Italy	38	4.47	44	4.79	36	4.35	30	4.32
Latvia	39	4.46	41	4.84	37	4.33	62	3.57
South Africa	40	4.43	46	4.77	43	4.17	29	4.32
Cyprus	41	4.40	36	5.05	40	4.26	41	3.93
Jordan	42	4.38	40	4.89	49	3.92	50	3.73
Poland	43	4.38	57	4.60	38	4.30	45	3.87
Malta	44	4.34	39	4.94	39	4.29	70	3.47
India	45	4.32	65	4.47	46	4.09	26	4.48
Qatar	46	4.31	27	5.34	45	4.13	67	3.52
Greece	47	4.28	42	4.84	42	4.19	47	3.84
China	48	4.26	45	4.79	62	3.70	48	3.83
Kuwait	49	4.24	35	5.05	44	4.13	61	3.58
Bahrain	50	4.19	38	5.00	47	4.08	83	3.30
Kazakhstan	51	4.17	51	4.66	56	3.83	58	3.59
Egypt	52	4.10	53	4.64	68	3.59	71	3.47
Russian Federation	53	4.10	60	4.53	53	3.87	66	3.53
Argentina	54	4.09	62	4.52	57	3.81	52	3.72
Mauritius	55	4.08	64	4.51	58	3.78	46	3.85
Costa Rica	56	4.08	73	4.32	50	3.90	37	4.01
Brazil	57	4.08	77	4.32	51	3.89	36	4.03
Colombia	58	4.07	63	4.52	67	3.63	49	3.74
Mexico	59	4.07	55	4.61	61	3.73	57	3.60
El Salvador	60	4.05	50	4.67	73	3.53	73	3.45
Bulgaria	61	4.04	58	4.54	59	3.78	74	3.39
Azerbaijan	62	4.04	48	4.71	79	3.33	64	3.55
Jamaica	63	4.03	72	4.33	52	3.87	59	3.59
Croatia	64	4.01	67	4.46	60	3.75	65	3.54
Panama	65	4.00	59	4.54	65	3.64	54	3.68
Trinidad and Tobago	66	3.99	56	4.60	66	3.63	69	3.49
Romania	67	3.98	76	4.32	55	3.84	76	3.37
Ukraine	68	3.97	74	4.32	64	3.64	60	3.59
Indonesia	69	3.96	71	4.38	74	3.52	55	3.63
Uruguay	70	3.95	54	4.61	71	3.53	75	3.39

(cont'd.)

Table 9: The Global Competitiveness Index 2005 *(cont'd.)*

| | OVERALL INDEX | | THREE SUBINDEXES | | | | | |
| | | | Basic requirements | | Efficiency enhancers | | Innovation factors | |
Country	Rank	Score	Rank	Score	Rank	Score	Rank	Score
Turkey	71	3.94	89	4.05	54	3.86	44	3.88
Botswana	72	3.94	61	4.53	69	3.58	77	3.37
Philippines	73	3.93	81	4.20	63	3.67	56	3.61
Vietnam	74	3.91	68	4.43	77	3.39	79	3.36
Macedonia, FYR	75	3.84	69	4.42	81	3.32	81	3.31
Morocco	76	3.83	70	4.38	84	3.27	78	3.37
Peru	77	3.83	82	4.20	70	3.57	82	3.31
Ghana	78	3.82	86	4.07	72	3.53	53	3.70
Namibia	79	3.80	66	4.46	86	3.25	89	3.15
Sri Lanka	80	3.77	84	4.13	78	3.37	68	3.52
Armenia	81	3.75	80	4.20	82	3.29	80	3.35
Algeria	82	3.75	52	4.66	94	3.02	97	3.01
Nigeria	83	3.74	78	4.26	90	3.17	72	3.46
Venezuela	84	3.71	79	4.23	76	3.42	92	3.11
Serbia and Montenegro	85	3.67	92	3.98	75	3.43	85	3.19
Georgia	86	3.61	88	4.05	88	3.23	103	2.94
Ecuador	87	3.59	75	4.32	104	2.93	101	2.94
Bosnia and Herzegovina	88	3.58	87	4.06	91	3.14	98	2.97
Moldova	89	3.58	93	3.98	89	3.22	96	3.05
Mongolia	90	3.57	98	3.89	80	3.33	105	2.89
Dominican Republic	91	3.56	97	3.91	85	3.26	93	3.10
Tajikistan	92	3.53	85	4.11	99	2.96	102	2.94
Kenya	93	3.52	108	3.67	83	3.29	51	3.72
Pakistan	94	3.51	105	3.70	87	3.25	63	3.57
Guatemala	95	3.50	90	4.05	103	2.93	94	3.08
Nicaragua	96	3.48	91	4.02	97	2.99	107	2.79
Honduras	97	3.47	83	4.14	110	2.77	104	2.93
Bangladesh	98	3.45	95	3.92	100	2.95	90	3.13
Cameroon	99	3.42	101	3.84	101	2.94	84	3.29
Albania	100	3.40	96	3.91	95	3.02	112	2.64
Bolivia	101	3.39	99	3.89	98	2.97	114	2.57
Paraguay	102	3.36	94	3.96	107	2.80	115	2.56
Uganda	103	3.36	107	3.67	96	3.00	86	3.18
Kyrgyz Republic	104	3.35	106	3.69	92	3.08	109	2.75
Tanzania	105	3.35	103	3.75	105	2.90	88	3.16
Benin	106	3.33	100	3.88	111	2.73	100	2.94
Madagascar	107	3.30	102	3.75	109	2.79	95	3.07
Guyana	108	3.27	111	3.64	102	2.93	110	2.75
Gambia	109	3.26	110	3.64	106	2.90	108	2.78
Zimbabwe	110	3.25	113	3.43	93	3.05	87	3.17
Cambodia	111	3.20	104	3.71	114	2.71	113	2.61
Mozambique	112	3.17	112	3.61	113	2.71	106	2.86
East Timor	113	3.09	109	3.66	115	2.55	117	2.39
Malawi	114	3.08	114	3.31	108	2.80	99	2.97
Mali	115	2.94	116	3.08	112	2.72	91	3.13
Ethiopia	116	2.85	115	3.19	116	2.48	111	2.67
Chad	117	2.65	117	3.03	117	2.22	116	2.50

Table 10: Global Competitiveness Index: Basic Requirements

Country	Basic requirements		1. Institutions		2. Infrastructure		3. Macroeconomy		4. Health and primary education	
	Rank	Score	Rank	Score	Rank	Score	Rank	Score	Rank	Score
Albania	96	3.91	107	2.94	116	1.77	85	4.10	36	6.83
Algeria	52	4.66	74	3.42	80	2.88	3	5.69	66	6.63
Argentina	62	4.52	98	3.08	63	3.53	46	4.67	41	6.81
Armenia	80	4.20	77	3.40	95	2.57	70	4.31	75	6.52
Australia	12	5.71	8	5.38	19	5.42	27	5.08	3	6.97
Austria	14	5.67	9	5.38	18	5.47	33	4.89	13	6.95
Azerbaijan	48	4.71	67	3.61	51	3.73	12	5.44	92	6.05
Bahrain	38	5.00	45	4.18	42	4.10	28	5.06	63	6.64
Bangladesh	95	3.92	108	2.90	101	2.38	68	4.35	94	6.03
Belgium	21	5.53	29	4.70	13	5.74	40	4.74	20	6.93
Benin	100	3.88	101	3.04	110	2.09	60	4.41	95	6.00
Bolivia	99	3.89	112	2.81	98	2.49	94	3.89	82	6.37
Bosnia and Herzegovina	87	4.06	106	2.94	100	2.40	52	4.54	84	6.36
Botswana	61	4.53	31	4.59	60	3.57	41	4.72	106	5.24
Brazil	77	4.32	79	3.38	70	3.20	91	3.97	52	6.72
Bulgaria	58	4.54	95	3.12	59	3.61	47	4.65	42	6.80
Cambodia	104	3.71	105	2.94	103	2.32	100	3.73	99	5.84
Cameroon	101	3.84	91	3.14	114	1.97	74	4.26	97	5.97
Canada	11	5.73	21	4.96	11	5.91	25	5.10	8	6.96
Chad	117	3.03	115	2.56	117	1.55	96	3.82	113	4.17
Chile	24	5.46	27	4.76	34	4.40	1	5.78	25	6.91
China	45	4.79	60	3.72	65	3.44	13	5.33	61	6.65
Colombia	63	4.52	69	3.57	71	3.19	51	4.54	48	6.76
Costa Rica	73	4.32	59	3.74	73	3.16	109	3.51	28	6.89
Croatia	67	4.46	72	3.44	54	3.67	86	4.10	67	6.62
Cyprus	36	5.05	30	4.65	30	4.59	81	4.20	49	6.75
Czech Republic	37	5.03	52	3.83	28	4.82	49	4.59	27	6.90
Denmark	1	6.15	2	5.91	1	6.48	16	5.29	23	6.91
Dominican Republic	97	3.91	111	2.83	94	2.58	107	3.59	65	6.63
East Timor	109	3.66	102	3.02	115	1.84	78	4.21	103	5.56
Ecuador	75	4.32	114	2.60	84	2.74	19	5.22	51	6.72
Egypt	53	4.64	49	3.91	55	3.66	50	4.57	79	6.42
El Salvador	50	4.67	57	3.75	52	3.72	59	4.46	46	6.77
Estonia	29	5.30	32	4.58	31	4.59	18	5.24	40	6.81
Ethiopia	115	3.19	80	3.36	105	2.31	101	3.71	116	3.36
Finland	2	6.05	3	5.77	10	6.02	10	5.46	10	6.95
France	16	5.65	20	4.96	3	6.28	61	4.40	6	6.96
Gambia	110	3.64	58	3.74	91	2.62	111	3.27	110	4.95
Georgia	88	4.05	82	3.32	83	2.76	87	4.07	91	6.06
Germany	8	5.79	11	5.33	2	6.44	54	4.49	24	6.91
Ghana	86	4.07	34	4.51	74	3.14	90	4.06	112	4.57
Greece	42	4.84	44	4.19	33	4.49	99	3.74	17	6.94
Guatemala	90	4.05	113	2.69	93	2.60	64	4.36	73	6.55
Guyana	111	3.64	110	2.83	109	2.11	113	3.14	78	6.47
Honduras	83	4.14	103	2.97	82	2.77	82	4.20	62	6.65
Hong Kong SAR	4	5.98	17	5.19	6	6.17	6	5.64	19	6.93
Hungary	49	4.68	43	4.19	45	4.02	105	3.64	33	6.85
Iceland	13	5.68	4	5.70	21	5.37	43	4.70	12	6.95
India	65	4.47	41	4.25	69	3.21	88	4.06	87	6.33
Indonesia	71	4.38	65	3.62	75	3.12	63	4.39	80	6.41
Ireland	22	5.52	14	5.27	32	4.58	15	5.31	21	6.93
Israel	31	5.18	33	4.57	27	4.86	67	4.35	7	6.96
Italy	44	4.79	55	3.77	39	4.18	76	4.23	5	6.97
Jamaica	72	4.33	68	3.59	56	3.64	112	3.25	35	6.83
Japan	25	5.43	26	4.78	9	6.02	93	3.93	1	6.98
Jordan	40	4.89	28	4.71	49	3.89	75	4.25	53	6.70
Kazakhstan	51	4.66	64	3.65	62	3.54	26	5.10	83	6.37
Kenya	108	3.67	90	3.20	89	2.63	104	3.69	107	5.16
Korea, Rep.	20	5.58	38	4.39	20	5.39	5	5.65	30	6.87
Kuwait	35	5.05	39	4.35	43	4.09	2	5.77	96	5.99
Kyrgyz Republic	106	3.69	109	2.85	106	2.31	115	3.03	71	6.58
Latvia	41	4.84	48	3.92	38	4.19	32	4.91	86	6.35
Lithuania	43	4.84	54	3.80	44	4.09	37	4.78	57	6.68
Luxembourg	10	5.77	12	5.32	16	5.54	14	5.33	29	6.88
Macedonia, FYR	69	4.42	100	3.06	79	2.93	22	5.14	72	6.56
Madagascar	102	3.75	84	3.30	104	2.32	110	3.45	98	5.94
Malawi	114	3.31	62	3.69	112	2.04	117	2.39	108	5.14
Malaysia	26	5.42	15	5.22	22	5.24	31	4.93	88	6.29
Mali	116	3.08	61	3.72	111	2.07	97	3.80	117	2.72
Malta	39	4.94	35	4.45	41	4.10	73	4.27	16	6.94

(cont'd.)

Table 10: Global Competitiveness Index: Basic Requirements *(cont'd.)*

Country	Basic requirements		1. Institutions		2. Infrastructure		3. Macroeconomy		4. Health and primary education	
	Rank	Score	Rank	Score	Rank	Score	Rank	Score	Rank	Score
Mauritius	64	4.51	53	3.83	46	3.97	89	4.06	89	6.18
Mexico	55	4.61	73	3.44	67	3.32	34	4.85	37	6.83
Moldova	93	3.98	94	3.12	78	2.94	80	4.21	102	5.65
Mongolia	98	3.89	96	3.10	107	2.28	102	3.70	76	6.50
Morocco	70	4.38	70	3.53	68	3.26	79	4.21	74	6.54
Mozambique	112	3.61	85	3.27	96	2.51	108	3.55	109	5.09
Namibia	66	4.46	50	3.87	40	4.15	57	4.46	104	5.35
Netherlands	9	5.77	13	5.27	7	6.12	39	4.75	14	6.94
New Zealand	15	5.66	7	5.47	23	5.07	21	5.17	18	6.93
Nicaragua	91	4.02	97	3.08	102	2.36	92	3.97	56	6.68
Nigeria	78	4.26	76	3.40	92	2.61	20	5.20	100	5.82
Norway	5	5.94	5	5.54	14	5.60	4	5.67	9	6.96
Pakistan	105	3.70	75	3.41	76	3.07	69	4.32	115	4.01
Panama	59	4.54	71	3.51	61	3.55	72	4.28	39	6.82
Paraguay	94	3.96	117	2.37	108	2.21	56	4.48	44	6.80
Peru	82	4.20	99	3.06	88	2.64	55	4.48	68	6.60
Philippines	81	4.20	89	3.21	90	2.62	58	4.46	77	6.49
Poland	57	4.60	66	3.61	50	3.80	83	4.14	38	6.83
Portugal	30	5.29	23	4.86	26	4.88	53	4.53	26	6.90
Qatar	27	5.34	19	5.04	47	3.96	8	5.58	45	6.78
Romania	76	4.32	83	3.32	66	3.43	95	3.88	64	6.64
Russian Federation	60	4.53	104	2.94	53	3.71	36	4.81	60	6.65
Serbia and Montenegro	92	3.98	93	3.12	97	2.50	106	3.64	58	6.67
Singapore	3	6.05	1	5.92	5	6.19	9	5.48	69	6.60
Slovak Republic	47	4.74	51	3.84	48	3.91	66	4.35	31	6.86
Slovenia	32	5.14	46	4.13	29	4.69	35	4.84	22	6.92
South Africa	46	4.77	36	4.42	35	4.33	48	4.61	101	5.73
Spain	28	5.33	37	4.40	25	4.95	29	5.01	11	6.95
Sri Lanka	84	4.13	88	3.22	81	2.87	103	3.70	50	6.72
Sweden	7	5.80	18	5.09	12	5.85	17	5.28	2	6.98
Switzerland	6	5.91	6	5.51	4	6.20	30	4.97	4	6.97
Taiwan	19	5.60	22	4.88	15	5.55	23	5.13	32	6.85
Tajikistan	85	4.11	81	3.32	99	2.45	71	4.29	81	6.39
Tanzania	103	3.75	47	4.01	86	2.67	84	4.14	114	4.16
Thailand	34	5.10	40	4.35	37	4.22	11	5.45	85	6.36
Trinidad and Tobago	56	4.60	78	3.39	72	3.19	24	5.13	55	6.69
Tunisia	33	5.13	25	4.80	36	4.28	38	4.78	59	6.65
Turkey	89	4.05	56	3.76	64	3.44	116	2.98	93	6.03
Uganda	107	3.67	87	3.24	113	1.98	77	4.22	105	5.25
Ukraine	74	4.32	92	3.13	58	3.63	65	4.36	90	6.16
United Arab Emirates	23	5.51	24	4.83	24	4.97	7	5.63	70	6.59
United Kingdom	17	5.63	10	5.35	17	5.52	42	4.72	15	6.94
United States	18	5.61	16	5.21	8	6.06	62	4.39	47	6.77
Uruguay	54	4.61	42	4.20	57	3.63	98	3.76	34	6.84
Venezuela	79	4.23	116	2.47	77	2.96	45	4.68	43	6.80
Vietnam	68	4.43	63	3.66	85	2.69	44	4.69	54	6.69
Zimbabwe	113	3.43	86	3.25	87	2.65	114	3.04	111	4.76

Table 11: Global Competitiveness Index: Efficiency Enhancers

Country	Efficiency enhancers		5. Higher education and training		6. Market efficiency		7. Technological readiness	
	Rank	Score	Rank	Score	Rank	Score	Rank	Score
Albania	95	3.02	93	3.19	100	3.43	98	2.44
Algeria	94	3.02	87	3.35	101	3.42	107	2.29
Argentina	57	3.81	35	4.68	84	3.65	62	3.11
Armenia	82	3.29	67	3.80	93	3.52	91	2.56
Australia	8	5.43	9	5.66	11	5.21	10	5.41
Austria	21	5.15	17	5.46	18	4.97	21	5.04
Azerbaijan	79	3.33	78	3.62	87	3.60	79	2.77
Bahrain	47	4.08	72	3.74	37	4.49	38	4.02
Bangladesh	100	2.95	103	2.68	76	3.85	106	2.31
Belgium	23	5.04	4	5.75	30	4.70	25	4.66
Benin	111	2.73	106	2.65	98	3.46	114	2.09
Bolivia	98	2.97	84	3.43	113	3.21	111	2.26
Bosnia and Herzegovina	91	3.14	81	3.57	91	3.53	105	2.33
Botswana	69	3.58	83	3.52	43	4.30	72	2.92
Brazil	51	3.89	50	4.19	55	4.14	51	3.35
Bulgaria	59	3.78	45	4.30	78	3.84	58	3.18
Cambodia	114	2.71	112	2.44	103	3.40	108	2.28
Cameroon	101	2.94	99	3.01	90	3.53	110	2.27
Canada	11	5.32	11	5.65	6	5.27	22	5.03
Chad	117	2.22	117	1.94	117	2.92	117	1.79
Chile	31	4.49	42	4.45	24	4.86	36	4.16
China	62	3.70	69	3.76	47	4.26	65	3.08
Colombia	67	3.63	64	3.83	53	4.19	75	2.86
Costa Rica	50	3.90	56	4.08	66	4.04	47	3.58
Croatia	60	3.75	54	4.10	77	3.85	54	3.31
Cyprus	40	4.26	39	4.53	51	4.21	37	4.05
Czech Republic	28	4.64	27	4.96	39	4.40	27	4.56
Denmark	3	5.60	3	5.82	5	5.31	2	5.69
Dominican Republic	85	3.26	94	3.18	96	3.49	63	3.10
East Timor	115	2.55	115	2.34	116	3.02	109	2.27
Ecuador	104	2.93	98	3.04	112	3.23	93	2.51
Egypt	68	3.59	66	3.82	68	3.99	70	2.95
El Salvador	73	3.53	86	3.38	50	4.21	69	2.99
Estonia	24	5.00	23	5.18	26	4.78	20	5.04
Ethiopia	116	2.48	116	2.25	114	3.15	116	2.03
Finland	5	5.54	1	6.13	12	5.10	12	5.40
France	18	5.18	5	5.75	20	4.91	24	4.86
Gambia	106	2.90	108	2.62	86	3.61	96	2.46
Georgia	88	3.23	80	3.60	83	3.69	100	2.41
Germany	19	5.16	15	5.48	22	4.90	16	5.11
Ghana	72	3.53	85	3.42	44	4.30	73	2.87
Greece	42	4.19	32	4.78	48	4.21	46	3.59
Guatemala	103	2.93	102	2.79	107	3.36	83	2.64
Guyana	102	2.93	95	3.16	105	3.39	112	2.25
Honduras	110	2.77	107	2.63	111	3.24	95	2.46
Hong Kong SAR	12	5.29	31	4.78	3	5.62	7	5.47
Hungary	30	4.50	30	4.79	36	4.54	35	4.17
Iceland	10	5.34	22	5.39	15	5.01	4	5.61
India	46	4.09	46	4.28	27	4.77	57	3.22
Indonesia	74	3.52	76	3.65	61	4.08	77	2.82
Ireland	14	5.23	21	5.40	13	5.08	13	5.20
Israel	22	5.11	20	5.41	21	4.90	23	5.00
Italy	36	4.35	33	4.69	59	4.10	33	4.26
Jamaica	52	3.87	71	3.75	54	4.15	42	3.71
Japan	17	5.19	16	5.46	16	5.00	17	5.09
Jordan	49	3.92	48	4.21	46	4.26	55	3.28
Kazakhstan	56	3.83	52	4.17	52	4.20	61	3.12
Kenya	83	3.29	90	3.23	75	3.86	78	2.79
Korea, Rep.	20	5.16	19	5.44	32	4.65	11	5.40
Kuwait	44	4.13	60	3.93	28	4.76	41	3.71
Kyrgyz Republic	92	3.08	75	3.69	92	3.52	115	2.03
Latvia	37	4.33	29	4.87	49	4.21	39	3.91
Lithuania	35	4.36	25	5.02	40	4.38	43	3.69
Luxembourg	26	4.76	51	4.19	19	4.92	14	5.17
Macedonia, FYR	81	3.32	62	3.91	97	3.47	88	2.58
Madagascar	109	2.79	110	2.52	94	3.50	103	2.36
Malawi	108	2.80	109	2.60	85	3.64	113	2.18
Malaysia	25	4.79	36	4.63	9	5.22	28	4.51
Mali	112	2.72	113	2.39	102	3.42	102	2.36
Malta	39	4.29	49	4.19	60	4.08	26	4.60

(cont'd.)

Table 11: Global Competitiveness Index: Efficiency Enhancers *(cont'd.)*

Country	Efficiency enhancers		5. Higher education and training		6. Market efficiency		7. Technological readiness	
	Rank	Score	Rank	Score	Rank	Score	Rank	Score
Mauritius	58	3.78	63	3.91	71	3.93	48	3.52
Mexico	61	3.73	68	3.79	62	4.08	53	3.32
Moldova	89	3.22	82	3.55	89	3.56	92	2.55
Mongolia	80	3.33	65	3.83	88	3.59	90	2.56
Morocco	84	3.27	89	3.24	80	3.80	80	2.76
Mozambique	113	2.71	111	2.44	110	3.25	97	2.44
Namibia	86	3.25	100	3.01	79	3.83	71	2.92
Netherlands	16	5.21	13	5.55	14	5.03	18	5.05
New Zealand	13	5.24	18	5.46	10	5.22	19	5.05
Nicaragua	97	2.99	91	3.20	108	3.34	99	2.42
Nigeria	90	3.17	96	3.08	70	3.95	94	2.47
Norway	15	5.22	14	5.54	17	5.00	15	5.12
Pakistan	87	3.25	104	2.68	41	4.34	82	2.73
Panama	65	3.64	70	3.75	63	4.06	64	3.10
Paraguay	107	2.80	101	2.99	115	3.08	104	2.35
Peru	70	3.57	74	3.70	69	3.98	68	3.03
Philippines	63	3.67	61	3.92	64	4.05	67	3.06
Poland	38	4.30	28	4.92	42	4.33	45	3.65
Portugal	32	4.47	37	4.61	34	4.57	34	4.21
Qatar	45	4.13	59	3.94	35	4.54	40	3.91
Romania	55	3.84	44	4.33	74	3.87	52	3.32
Russian Federation	53	3.87	34	4.69	65	4.04	74	2.87
Serbia and Montenegro	75	3.43	58	4.00	99	3.46	76	2.84
Singapore	2	5.70	8	5.68	4	5.59	1	5.82
Slovak Republic	34	4.40	40	4.47	38	4.42	32	4.29
Slovenia	29	4.52	24	5.08	58	4.11	31	4.38
South Africa	43	4.17	47	4.22	33	4.63	44	3.66
Spain	27	4.68	26	5.00	31	4.67	30	4.38
Sri Lanka	78	3.37	79	3.61	72	3.89	85	2.61
Sweden	9	5.40	7	5.69	25	4.85	3	5.67
Switzerland	7	5.44	10	5.65	7	5.23	8	5.43
Taiwan	6	5.50	6	5.69	8	5.22	6	5.59
Tajikistan	99	2.96	97	3.06	104	3.40	101	2.41
Tanzania	105	2.90	114	2.36	81	3.77	89	2.57
Thailand	41	4.22	43	4.45	29	4.72	49	3.50
Trinidad and Tobago	66	3.63	73	3.71	67	4.04	59	3.14
Tunisia	48	4.02	38	4.53	45	4.27	56	3.27
Turkey	54	3.86	55	4.10	57	4.11	50	3.38
Uganda	96	3.00	105	2.67	82	3.74	86	2.60
Ukraine	64	3.64	41	4.46	73	3.87	87	2.58
United Arab Emirates	33	4.42	57	4.00	23	4.87	29	4.39
United Kingdom	4	5.56	12	5.63	2	5.64	9	5.42
United States	1	5.85	2	6.04	1	5.91	5	5.61
Uruguay	71	3.53	53	4.15	106	3.38	66	3.07
Venezuela	76	3.42	77	3.63	95	3.49	60	3.13
Vietnam	77	3.39	88	3.32	56	4.12	81	2.74
Zimbabwe	93	3.05	92	3.19	109	3.34	84	2.62

Table 12: Global Competitiveness Index: Innovation Factors

Country	Innovation factors		8. Business sophistication		9. Innovation	
	Rank	Score	Rank	Score	Rank	Score
Albania	112	2.64	107	3.14	115	2.14
Algeria	97	3.01	102	3.24	90	2.78
Argentina	52	3.72	50	4.25	56	3.18
Armenia	80	3.35	81	3.69	73	3.01
Australia	23	4.75	24	5.18	22	4.31
Austria	13	5.25	5	5.85	17	4.65
Azerbaijan	64	3.55	71	3.89	53	3.21
Bahrain	83	3.30	62	4.03	102	2.57
Bangladesh	90	3.13	86	3.59	98	2.68
Belgium	15	5.19	10	5.74	18	4.64
Benin	100	2.94	105	3.19	95	2.69
Bolivia	114	2.57	116	2.90	112	2.24
Bosnia and Herzegovina	98	2.97	94	3.36	101	2.59
Botswana	77	3.37	84	3.60	61	3.15
Brazil	36	4.03	33	4.63	39	3.42
Bulgaria	74	3.39	79	3.76	72	3.01
Cambodia	113	2.61	115	2.91	110	2.32
Cameroon	84	3.29	87	3.56	70	3.03
Canada	16	5.14	17	5.35	12	4.92
Chad	116	2.50	114	2.92	116	2.09
Chile	32	4.09	31	4.77	41	3.41
China	48	3.83	58	4.11	35	3.56
Colombia	49	3.74	48	4.31	58	3.16
Costa Rica	37	4.01	38	4.54	37	3.49
Croatia	65	3.54	67	3.98	64	3.10
Cyprus	41	3.93	35	4.58	50	3.28
Czech Republic	27	4.44	29	4.92	26	3.95
Denmark	7	5.47	4	5.88	10	5.06
Dominican Republic	93	3.10	80	3.74	107	2.45
East Timor	117	2.39	117	2.61	114	2.17
Ecuador	101	2.94	91	3.41	106	2.47
Egypt	71	3.47	74	3.87	66	3.07
El Salvador	73	3.45	51	4.21	96	2.68
Estonia	34	4.05	40	4.51	34	3.59
Ethiopia	111	2.67	113	2.92	108	2.42
Finland	5	5.68	12	5.70	4	5.66
France	9	5.41	6	5.83	11	4.98
Gambia	108	2.78	103	3.22	109	2.35
Georgia	103	2.94	106	3.16	93	2.72
Germany	3	5.86	2	6.23	5	5.49
Ghana	53	3.70	65	3.99	40	3.42
Greece	47	3.84	47	4.32	45	3.36
Guatemala	94	3.08	83	3.64	103	2.52
Guyana	110	2.75	104	3.22	111	2.29
Honduras	104	2.93	93	3.37	105	2.48
Hong Kong SAR	21	4.80	14	5.40	24	4.20
Hungary	39	3.98	49	4.28	32	3.69
Iceland	18	4.99	21	5.29	16	4.68
India	26	4.48	27	5.02	27	3.94
Indonesia	55	3.63	70	3.93	47	3.32
Ireland	19	4.91	15	5.39	19	4.44
Israel	10	5.40	18	5.34	6	5.47
Italy	30	4.32	25	5.12	36	3.52
Jamaica	59	3.59	66	3.98	55	3.20
Japan	2	5.98	1	6.28	2	5.68
Jordan	50	3.73	60	4.04	42	3.41
Kazakhstan	58	3.59	63	4.03	59	3.16
Kenya	51	3.72	55	4.15	48	3.29
Korea, Rep.	17	5.06	19	5.31	15	4.81
Kuwait	61	3.58	53	4.19	78	2.97
Kyrgyz Republic	109	2.75	100	3.28	113	2.23
Latvia	62	3.57	54	4.16	74	2.99
Lithuania	40	3.94	37	4.55	46	3.34
Luxembourg	24	4.69	16	5.38	25	4.00
Macedonia, FYR	81	3.31	82	3.67	82	2.94
Madagascar	95	3.07	99	3.30	87	2.83
Malawi	99	2.97	95	3.34	100	2.60
Malaysia	25	4.67	28	4.98	21	4.37
Mali	91	3.13	98	3.31	81	2.95
Malta	70	3.47	59	4.09	85	2.86

(cont'd.)

Table 12: Global Competitiveness Index: Innovation Factors *(cont'd.)*

Country	Innovation factors		8. Business sophistication		9. Innovation	
	Rank	Score	Rank	Score	Rank	Score
Mauritius	46	3.85	36	4.57	63	3.12
Mexico	57	3.60	56	4.13	67	3.07
Moldova	96	3.05	97	3.33	92	2.76
Mongolia	105	2.89	112	2.99	89	2.79
Morocco	78	3.37	75	3.85	84	2.88
Mozambique	106	2.86	111	3.04	97	2.68
Namibia	89	3.15	85	3.59	94	2.71
Netherlands	12	5.26	11	5.71	14	4.81
New Zealand	22	4.75	22	5.24	23	4.25
Nicaragua	107	2.79	110	3.06	104	2.51
Nigeria	72	3.46	72	3.88	68	3.05
Norway	20	4.81	23	5.23	20	4.39
Pakistan	63	3.57	57	4.12	71	3.02
Panama	54	3.68	52	4.21	62	3.15
Paraguay	115	2.56	109	3.11	117	2.02
Peru	82	3.31	69	3.97	99	2.64
Philippines	56	3.61	43	4.36	86	2.85
Poland	45	3.87	45	4.34	44	3.40
Portugal	35	4.04	46	4.33	29	3.75
Qatar	67	3.52	73	3.88	60	3.15
Romania	76	3.37	78	3.76	75	2.98
Russian Federation	66	3.53	77	3.78	49	3.29
Serbia and Montenegro	85	3.19	90	3.41	79	2.96
Singapore	14	5.24	20	5.30	9	5.18
Slovak Republic	43	3.88	44	4.35	43	3.40
Slovenia	31	4.20	32	4.74	33	3.65
South Africa	29	4.32	30	4.80	28	3.85
Spain	28	4.41	26	5.11	31	3.71
Sri Lanka	68	3.52	64	3.99	69	3.04
Sweden	6	5.50	9	5.75	8	5.25
Switzerland	4	5.73	7	5.80	3	5.66
Taiwan	8	5.44	13	5.52	7	5.37
Tajikistan	102	2.94	108	3.12	91	2.77
Tanzania	88	3.16	96	3.34	77	2.98
Thailand	38	4.01	39	4.52	38	3.49
Trinidad and Tobago	69	3.49	61	4.04	80	2.95
Tunisia	33	4.08	42	4.45	30	3.72
Turkey	44	3.88	41	4.51	51	3.24
Uganda	86	3.18	101	3.28	65	3.08
Ukraine	60	3.59	68	3.97	54	3.21
United Arab Emirates	42	3.90	34	4.59	52	3.22
United Kingdom	11	5.33	8	5.77	13	4.88
United States	1	6.07	3	6.17	1	5.98
Uruguay	75	3.39	76	3.79	76	2.98
Venezuela	92	3.11	92	3.39	88	2.83
Vietnam	79	3.36	88	3.55	57	3.18
Zimbabwe	87	3.17	89	3.43	83	2.90

Table 13: Top performers in the nine pillars of the Global Competitiveness Index

Country	Institutions	Infrastructure	Macroeconomy	Health and primary education	Higher education and training	Market efficiency	Technological readiness	Business sophistication	Innovation
Singapore	1	5	9	69	8	4	1	20	9
Denmark	2	1	16	23	3	5	2	4	10
Chile	27	34	1	25	42	24	36	31	41
Japan	26	9	93	1	16	16	17	1	2
Finland	3	10	10	10	1	12	12	12	4
United States	16	8	62	47	2	1	5	3	1

Conclusions

This chapter has presented a detailed description of the 2005 results for the Growth Competitiveness Index, an indicator with which the Forum has been associated since 2001. This index represented a major step forward in the Forum's efforts to systematize its work in the area of competitiveness, capturing a broad range of factors seen to be essential to a better understanding of the determinants of growth.

The Global Competitiveness Index is a logical extension of the Forum's competitiveness work. It builds on the strengths of the work done by Sachs and McArthur (2002), by widening the scope of analysis through the introduction of concepts not previously considered, such as the role of gains in efficiency associated with the operation of goods, labor, and financial markets, the quality of a country's infrastructure, the state of its public health and human capital endowment, the degree of sophistication of its firms, among others. Our strategy—already announced last year upon publication of *The Global Competitiveness Report 2004–2005*—is to make the Global Competitiveness Index the centerpiece of our analytical work. The conceptual framework upon which this index has been built and its methodological underpinnings are strong, and its broader coverage of factors central to a proper study of the growth process is yet another attractive feature. Both the Growth and the Global indexes will co-exist for a while longer. The former, because it provides a useful link to the past; the latter, because it represents a deepening of the Forum's competitiveness work. However, the Global Competitiveness Index is expected to become the main analytical tool in our competitiveness work, and in 2006, it will be the results of this index that will be featured.

Notes

1 See Rogoff's contribution in Chapter 2.2 of this volume: "Rethinking Exchange Rate Competitiveness."

2 Indeed, few things make the importance of the exchange rate more evident than the central role it has played in any credible analysis of emerging market crises over the past decade. Unsustainable exchange rate policies, together with other structural and institutional factors, have contributed to major drops in output and income, from East Asia to Russia, Turkey, and Argentina, to name a few. On another front, it is difficult to analyze China's impressive growth performance during the past decade without reference to the key role played by the exchange rate in boosting the profitability of China's manufacturing sector.

3 See Chapter 2.2 in *The Global Competitiveness Report 2004–2005*, p. 51.

4 Acemoglu et al., 2001, p. 1369.

5 McArthur and Sachs, 2002.

6 According to Transparency International, Finland is the least corrupt country on earth. See www.transparency.org/surveys.

7 Daniel Pinto (2005) notes an interesting "French paradox": "While public officials, unions and the majority of the French population scream and shout to defend an antiquated version of capitalism, French companies have quietly been at the forefront of globalization, achieving world leading positions in a number of highly competitive sectors, from automotive to energy, food and banking."

8 The move of peasants from the countryside, where labor productivity is close to zero, into the cities, where it is much higher and captured in official statistics, has been central to the growth performance of the past 20 years.

9 Income per capita levels vary widely, from Egypt's US$1,049, to Qatar's US$46,641 (International Monetary Fund, 2005).

10 See World Bank (2003).

11 For more detailed analyses of the region's weaknesses and strong points, see *The Arab World Competitiveness Report 2005*, World Economic Forum.

12 Indeed, Jeffrey Sachs, author of *The End of Poverty* (2005) is painfully and eloquently aware of them.

13 Sala-i-Martin and Artadi, 2004, p. 52.

14 On this and related issues, see the excellent work by de Soto (2000).

15 See Kaufmann and Vishwanath (2001).

16 See, for instance, Fischer (1993).

17 See Lucas (1988) and Kremer (1993).

18 On some aspects of technological diffusion, see Basu and Weil (1998).

19 See Porter (2004) for a fuller discussion.

20 On the role of innovation in development and economic growth, see the works by Grossman and Helpman (1991), Krugman (1979), Romer (1987 and 1990), Barro and Sala-i-Martin (1995), and Schumpeter (1934).

21 Sala-i-Martin and Artadi, 2004, p. 72.

References

Acemoglu, D., S. Johnson, and J. A. Robinson. 2001. "The Colonial Origins of Comparative Development: An Empirical Investigation." *The American Economic Review.* December. 1369–1401.

Barro, R. and X. Sala-i-Martin. 1995. *Economic Growth.* Cambridge: MIT Press.

Basu, S. and D. Weil. 1998. "Appropriate Technology and Growth." *Quarterly Journal of Economics* 113(4):1025–1054.

The Economist. 2005. "The Real Sick Man of Europe." 21 May.

Fischer, S. 1993. "The Role of Macroeconomic Factors in Growth." *Journal of Monetary Economics* 32(3):1176–1196.

Grossman, G. and E. Helpman. 1991. *Innovation and Growth in the Global Economy.* Cambridge: MIT Press.

Heston, A., R. Summers, and B. Aten. 2002. Penn World Table Version 6.1. Center for International Comparisons at the University of Pennsylvania (CICUP). October.

International Monetary Fund. 2005. *World Economic Outlook Database.* April.

Kaufmann, D. and T. Vishwanath. 2001. "Toward Transparency: New Approaches and their Application to Financial Markets." *World Bank Observer* 16(1). Spring.

Kremer, M. 1993. "The O-Ring Theory of Economic Development." *Quarterly Journal of Economics* 108(3):551–75.

Krugman, P. 1979. "A Model of Innovation, Technological Transfer and the World Distribution of Income." *Journal of Political Economy* 87(2): 253–66.

The London Financial Times. 2005. Various issues. February-June.

Lucas, R. Jr. 1988. "On the Mechanics of Economic Development." *Journal of Monetary Economics* 21:3–42.

Organisation for Economic Co-operation and Development. 2005. Economic Outlook 77: Statistical Annex Tables. May.

Pinto, D. 2005. "Autistic Governments, Smart Companies." *The International Herald Tribune.* 27 July.

United States Patent and Trademark Office. 2005. Patent Counts by Country/State and Year. April.

Porter, M. 2004. "Building the Microeconomic Foundations of Prosperity: Findings from the Business Competitiveness Index." *The Global Competitiveness Report 2004–2005.* Hampshire: Palgrave Macmillan.

McArthur, J.W. and Sachs, J.D. 2002. "The Growth Competitiveness Index: Measuring Technological Advancement and the Stages of Development." *The Global Competitiveness Report 2001–2002.* New York: Oxford University Press, 28–51.

Romer, P. 1987. "Growth Based on Increasing Returns due to Specialization." *American Economic Review* 77(2):56–62.

———. 1990. "Endogenous Technological Change." *Journal of Political Economy* 98(5):71–102.

Sachs, J. 2005. *The End of Poverty.* New York: Penguin Press.

Sala-i-Martin, X. and E. V. Artadi, 2004. "The Global Competitiveness Index." *The Global Competitiveness Report 2004–2005.* Hampshire: Palgrave Macmillan. 51–80.

Schumpeter, J. A. 1934. *The Theory of Economic Development.* Cambridge, MA: Harvard University Press.

de Soto, H. 2000. *The Mystery of Capital: Why Capitalism Triumphs in the West and Fails Everywhere Else.* New York: Basic Books.

Transparency International, online at: www.transparency.org/surveys

World Bank. 2003. *Jobs, Growth, and Governance in the Middle East and North Africa: Unlocking the Potential for Prosperity.* New York.

World Economic Forum. 2004. *The Global Competitiveness Report 2004–2005.* Hampshire: Palgrave Macmillan.

———. 2005. *Global Information Technology Report 2004–2005.* New York: Palgrave Macmillan.

———. 2005. *The Arab World Competitiveness Report 2005.* New York: Palgrave MacMillan.

Appendix A: Composition of the Growth Competitiveness Index

The Growth Competitiveness Index is composed of three component indexes: the technology index, the public institutions index, and the macroeconomic environment index. These indexes are calculated on the basis of both "hard data" and "Survey data."

As explained in the chapter, the sample of countries is divided into two groups: the core innovators and the non-core innovators. Core innovators are countries with more than 15 US utility patents registered per million population; non-core innovators are all other countries.

For the core innovators, we place extra emphasis on the role of innovation and technology. The weightings for the core innovators are as follows:

Growth Competitiveness
Index for core innovators = 1/2 technology index
+ 1/4 public institutions index
+ 1/4 macroeconomic environment index

For the non-core innovators, we calculate the Growth Competitiveness Index values as a simple average of the three component indexes:

Growth Competitiveness
Index for non-core
innovators = 1/3 technology index
+ 1/3 public institutions index
+ 1/3 macroeconomic environment index

Technology index components

The technology index is calculated for the core and non-core innovators as follows:

technology index for
core innovators = 1/2 innovation subindex
+ 1/2 information and communication technology subindex

technology index for
non-core innovators = 1/8 innovation subindex
+ 3/8 technology transfer subindex
+ 1/2 information and communication technology subindex

Innovation subindex

innovation subindex = 1/4 Survey data
+ 3/4 hard data

Innovation Survey questions

3.01 What is your country's position in technology relative to world leaders'?

3.02 Are companies in your country unable/aggressive in absorbing new technology?

3.06 How much do companies in your country spend on R&D relative to other countries?

3.07 What is the extent of business collaboration in R&D with local universities?

Innovation hard data

3.17 US utility patents granted per million population

4.17 Gross tertiary enrollment rate

Technology transfer subindex

technology transfer
subindex = unweighted average of two technology transfer Survey questions

3.04 Is foreign direct investment in your country an important source of new technology?

3.03 Is foreign technology licensing in your country a common means of acquiring new technology?

Information and communication technology (ICT) subindex

information and
communication
technology subindex = 1/3 information and communication technology Survey data
+ 2/3 information and communication technology hard data

Information and communication technology Survey questions

3.11 How extensive is Internet access in schools?

3.12 Is there sufficient competition among ISPs in your country to ensure high quality, infrequent interruptions and low prices?

3.13 Is ICT an overall priority for the government?

3.14 Are government programs successful in promoting the use of ICT?

3.15 Are laws relating to ICT (electronic commerce, digital signatures, consumer protection) well developed and enforced?

Information and communication technology hard data

3.18 Cellular mobile subscribers per 100 inhabitants

3.19 Internet users per 10,000 inhabitants

3.20 Internet hosts per 10,000 inhabitants

5.08 Main telephone lines per 100 inhabitants

3.21 Personal computers per 100 inhabitants

(cont'd.)

Appendix A: Composition of the Growth Competitiveness Index *(cont'd.)*

Public institutions index components

public institutions index   = 1/2 contracts and law subindex
                                              + 1/2 corruption subindex

Contracts and law subindex

6.01 Is the judiciary in your country independent from political influences of members of government, citizens or firms?

6.03 Are financial assets and wealth clearly delineated and well protected by law?

6.08 Is your government neutral among bidders when deciding among public contracts?

6.16 Does organized crime impose significant costs on business?

Corruption subindex

6.19 How commonly are bribes paid in connection with import and export permits?

6.20 How commonly are bribes paid when getting connected with public utilities?

6.21 How commonly are bribes paid in connection with annual tax payments?

Macroeconomic environment index components

macroeconomic
environment index   = 1/2 macroeconomic stability subindex
                              + 1/4 country credit rating
                              + 1/4 government waste

Macroeconomic stability subindex

macroeconomic
stability subindex   = 5/7 macroeconomic stability hard data
                           + 2/7 macroeconomic stability Survey data

Macroeconomic stability Survey questions

2.01 Is your country's economy likely to be in a recession next year?

2.07 Has obtaining credit for your company become easier or more difficult over the past year?

Macroeconomic stability hard data

2.13 Government surplus/deficit

2.14 National savings rate

2.16 Inflation

2.15 Real effective exchange rate

2.17 Lending–borrowing interest rate spread

2.20 Government debt

2.21 **Institutional Investor country credit rating**

Government waste variable

6.06 Is the composition of public spending in your country wasteful, or does it provide necessary goods and services not provided by the market?

Appendix B: Composition of the Global Competitiveness Index

This appendix provides details on how the Global Competitiveness Index is constructed. All of the Survey and hard data variables used in this index can be found in the data tables section of this *Report* with more detailed descriptions.

1st Pillar: Institutions

A. Public institutions

1. Property rights
   - 6.03 Property rights

2. Ethics and corruption
   - 6.24 Diversion of public funds
   - 6.26 Public trust of politicians

3. Undue influence
   - 6.01 Judicial independence
   - 6.08 Favoritism in decisions of government officials

4. Government inefficiency (red tape, bureaucracy and waste)
   - 6.06 Wastefulness of government spending
   - 6.07 Burden of government regulation

5. Security
   - 2.02 Business costs of terrorism
   - 6.14 Reliability of police services
   - 6.15 Business costs of crime and violence
   - 6.16 Organized crime

B. Private institutions

1. Corporate ethics
   - 8.04 Ethical behavior of firms

2. Corporate accountability
   - 8.16 Efficacy of corporate boards
   - 8.21 Protection of minority shareholders' interests
   - 8.23 Strength of auditing and reporting standards

2nd Pillar: Infrastructure

- 5.01 Overall infrastructure quality
- 5.02 Railroad infrastructure development
- 5.03 Port infrastructure quality
- 5.04 Air transport infrastructure quality
- 5.05 Quality of electricity supply
- 5.08 Telephone lines (hard data)

3rd Pillar: Macroeconomy

- 2.13 Government surplus/deficit (hard data)
- 2.14 National savings rate (hard data)
- 2.16 Inflation (hard data)
- 2.17 Interest rate spread (hard data)
- 2.20 Government debt/GDP ratio (hard data)
- 2.15 Real effective exchange rate (hard data)

4th Pillar: Health and primary education

A. Health
- 4.04 Medium-term business impact of malaria
- 4.05 Medium-term business impact of tuberculosis
- 4.06 Medium-term business impact of HIV/AIDS
- 4.10 Infant mortality (hard data)
- 4.11 Life expectancy at birth (hard data)
- 4.12 Tuberculosis prevalence (hard data)
- 4.13 Malaria prevalence (hard data)
- 4.14 HIV/AIDS prevalence (hard data)

B. Primary education
- 4.15 Gross primary enrollment (hard data)

5th Pillar: Higher education and training

A. Quantity of education
- 4.16 Gross secondary enrollment (hard data)
- 4.17 Gross tertiary enrollment (hard data)

B. Quality of education system
- 4.01 Quality of the educational system
- 4.03 Quality of math and science education
- 8.15 Quality of management schools

C. On-the-job training
- 7.09 Local availability of specialized research and training services
- 8.11 Extent of staff training

6th Pillar: Market efficiency

A. Goods markets: distortions, competition and size

1. Distortions
   - 2.12 Agricultural policy costs
   - 6.02 Efficiency of legal framework
   - 6.11 Extent and effect of taxation
   - 7.10 Number of procedures to start business (hard data)
   - 7.11 Time required to start a business (hard data)

2. Competition
   Domestic competition
   - 7.01 Intensity of local competition
   - 7.02 Effectiveness of anti-trust policy
   Foreign competition
   - 2.19 Imports (hard data)
   - 2.09 Prevalence of trade barriers
   - 8.22 Foreign ownership restrictions

3. Size
   Local markets
   - GDP – exports + imports (hard data)
   Foreign markets (exports)
   - 2.18 Exports (hard data)

(cont'd.)

Appendix B: Composition of the Global Competitiveness Index *(cont'd.)*

B. **Labor markets: flexibility and efficiency**

1. Flexibility
   - 8.17 Hiring and firing practices
   - 8.18 Flexibility of wage determination
   - 8.19 Cooperation in labor/employer relations

2. Efficiency
   - 8.14 Reliance on professional management
   - 8.20 Pay and productivity
   - 4.08 Brain drain
   - 4.09 Private sector employment of women

C. **Financial markets: sophistication and openness**
   - 2.03 Financial market sophistication
   - 2.05 Ease of access to loans
   - 2.06 Venture capital availability
   - 2.04 Soundness of banks
   - 2.08 Local equity market access

7th Pillar: Technological readiness

- 3.01 Technological readiness
- 3.02 Firm-level technology absorption
- 3.15 Laws relating to ICT
- 3.04 FDI and technology transfer
- 3.18 Cellular telephones (hard data)
- 3.19 Internet users (hard data)
- 3.21 Personal computers (hard data)

8th Pillar: Business sophistication

A. **Networks and supporting industries**
   - 7.05 Local supplier quantity
   - 7.06 Local supplier quality

B. **Sophistication of firms operations and strategy**
   - 8.05 Production process sophistication
   - 8.06 Extent of marketing
   - 8.08 Control of international distribution
   - 8.12 Willingness to delegate authority
   - 8.01 Nature of competitive advantage
   - 8.02 Value chain presence

9th Pillar: Innovation

- 3.05 Quality of scientific research institutions
- 3.06 Company spending on research and development
- 3.07 University/industry research collaboration
- 3.08 Government procurement of advanced technology products
- 3.09 Availability of scientists and engineers
- 3.17 Utility patents (hard data)
- 6.04 Intellectual property protection
- 8.03 Capacity for innovation

42

Appendix C: Technical notes on the construction of the competitiveness indexes

Combining hard data and Survey data

The responses to the Executive Opinion Survey are what we refer to as Survey data, with responses ranging from 1 to 7; the hard data were collected from various sources, described in the Technical Notes and Sources at the end of the *Report*. All of the data used in the calculation of the Competitiveness Indexes can be found in the data tables section of the *Report*.

The standard formula for converting each hard data variable to the 1-to-7 scale is:

$$6 \times \frac{(\text{country value} - \text{sample minimum})}{(\text{sample maximum} - \text{sample minimum})} + 1$$

The sample minimum and sample maximum are the lowest and highest values of the overall sample, respectively.

For some variables, a higher value indicates a worse outcome. For example, high levels of budget deficits are bad. In this case, we "reverse" the series, by subtracting the newly created variable from 8.

In some instances, adjustments were made to account for extreme outliers in the data.

How we treat inflation

To capture the idea that both high inflation and deflation are detrimental to the economy, while no consensus yet exists in the literature on the specific threshold at which lower levels of inflation become detrimental, inflation enters the model in a U-shaped manner as follows: for values of inflation between 0 and 3 percent, a country receives the highest possible score of 7. Beyond this range, both inflation and deflation receive negative scores. Scores become more negative as they move away from these values, in a linear fashion. We use this treatment for inflation in both the Growth and Global Competitiveness Indexes.

How we measure the impact of disease

Within the 4th pillar of the Global Competitiveness Index, the impact of a disease on competitiveness depends not only on its incidence, but on how costly this incidence is for business. Therefore, to estimate the economic impact of disease, we combine hard data on incidence (on malaria, tuberculosis, and HIV) with Survey questions on the cost of these diseases to business.

To combine these data we first take the ratio of each country's disease prevalence, relative to the highest prevalence in the world. We then multiply the inverse of this ratio (to take into account that low values are "good") with the Survey average. This product is then normalized to a 1-to-7 scale. Note that counties with a zero prevalence rate will always obtain a 7 in the ranking, regardless of what the Survey data says.

How we measure domestic and foreign competition

Within the goods market efficiency subindex of the 6th pillar of the Global Competitiveness Index, the component called *competition* is weighted in a particular fashion. The Survey data provides an indication of the extent to which competition is distorted in both the domestic and the foreign market. The relative importance of these distortions depends, however, on the relative size of domestic versus foreign competition. In order to capture this interaction, we create two new variables that indicate this relative importance. Domestic competition is the sum of consumption (C), investment (I), government spending (G) and exports (X), while foreign competition is equal to imports (M). Thus, we assign a weight of $(C + I + G + X)/(C + I + G + X + M)$ to those Survey questions related to local competition, and $M/(C + I + G + X + M)$ to those related to foreign competition.

How we measure market size

Within the goods market efficiency subindex of the 6th pillar of the Global Competitiveness Index, the component called *size* measures the size of the market, to which local firms have access. This has two components: the size of the local market and the foreign market (exports). The local market should be the sum of consumption (C), investment (I), and government spending (G). Although we lack data on these three macro components, we do have data on exports (X), imports (M) and GDP. By definition, $GDP = C + I + G + (X - M)$. Therefore, we compute the local market as $GDP + M - X$.

CHAPTER 1.2

Building the Microeconomic Foundations of Prosperity: Findings from the Business Competitiveness Index[1]

MICHAEL E. PORTER, Harvard University

Introduction

Competitiveness has become a central preoccupation of both advanced and developing countries in an increasingly open and integrated world economy. Despite its acknowledged importance, the concept of competitiveness is often misunderstood. Here, we define competitiveness concretely, show its relationship to a nation's standard of living, outline a conceptual framework for understanding its causes, and compare the competitiveness of a large sample of countries.

The Business Competitiveness Index (BCI), based on this conceptual framework, provides a data-rich approach to measuring the fundamental competitiveness of a large number of countries in a comparative context. This year's BCI includes 116 countries, up thirteen from last year.[2] Our aim is to rank country competitiveness and identify each country's competitive strengths and weaknesses, while revealing competitiveness trends in the global economy, and extending our basic knowledge about the sources of competitiveness and the process of economic development.

Most discussion of competitiveness and economic development is still focused on the macroeconomic, political, legal, and social circumstances that underpin a successful economy. It is well understood that sound fiscal and monetary policies, a trusted and efficient legal system, a stable set of democratic institutions, and progress on social conditions contribute greatly to a healthy economy. However, these broader conditions are necessary, but not sufficient. They provide the opportunity to create wealth but do not themselves create wealth. Wealth is actually created at the microeconomic level of the economy, rooted in the capabilities of a nation's companies (both local and subsidiaries of multinationals), as well as in the quality of the microeconomic business environment in which these companies compete. Unless the microeconomic capabilities of a nation's companies improve, macroeconomic, political, legal, and social reforms will not bear full fruit in terms of prosperity.

Beginning in 1998, we began an effort to examine statistically the microeconomic foundations of competitiveness and prosperity across a wide array of countries. This work aims to move beyond the examination of broad, aggregate variables typical of most economic growth analyses, and provide a framework for countries and companies to understand their detailed competitive strengths and weaknesses. It also aims to be as rigorous as possible, verifying the importance of each measure statistically, and using statistical techniques to weight the contribution of individual variables.

The Business Competitiveness Index seeks to explore the underpinnings of a nation's prosperity, measured here by its level of GDP per capita, adjusted for purchasing power. The focus is on whether current prosperity is sustainable, and on the specific areas that must be addressed if

GDP per capita is to attain higher levels in the future. The sustainable level of current GDP per capita and the rate of growth in GDP per capita will be related in the long term, but each area requires its own distinctive policy agenda. The conceptual framework and statistical approach follow that of the previous reports and the findings are fully comparable with previous Microeconomic Competitiveness Index results.

The analysis here is pragmatic, making use of the best available data and econometric methods even though both are far from perfect. We also confront the challenge of establishing the direction of causality given limited time series data. However, even if definitive tests of causality are not possible, understanding the microeconomic correlates of prosperity clearly remains crucial. There may be a natural tendency for some microeconomic conditions to improve as GDP per capita increases. Yet the large observed differences across countries, even those at similar income levels, reveal that this improvement is far from automatic. Despite the statistical challenges, the statistical findings overall are remarkably stable and robust, compared with the *Global Competitiveness Report 2004–2005* (GCR) and earlier *Reports*.

The Business Competitiveness Index (BCI) accounts for 80 percent of the variation across countries in the level GDP per capita.[3] This level is remarkably high given the presence of so many unstable low income countries and the inherent imperfections in national income data. Once again, these findings reveal the crucial importance of microeconomic competitiveness for economic prosperity.

In developing countries, microeconomic failures nullify macroeconomic and social programs again and again. By accessing global capital markets, countries can engineer spurts of growth through macroeconomic stabilization and financial reforms that bring in floods of capital and create the illusion of progress. Without microeconomic improvement, however, growth will be snuffed out as exports and jobs fail to materialize, wages stagnate, and the return on investments proves disappointing. This disappointment and the austerity that results from such cycles remain at the heart of the backlash against globalization. And in advanced economies, microeconomic competitiveness is the missing link in countries that have achieved sufficient progress on the macro and social front.

Competitiveness, then, is the fundamental determinant of the level of prosperity a country can sustain. While macroeconomic shifts, political developments, resource price swings, and spurts of trade and foreign investment can drive growth in GDP per capita for periods of time, the only reliable basis of true prosperity is the productivity potential of a nation's economy. The central focus of public policy must be competitiveness, despite the constant tug on the causes and opportunities to engineer spurts of "success" in the short term. Similarly, national leaders must maintain a commitment to competitiveness even in difficult times, instead of undermining it for short term gain.

Competitiveness and its causes

What is competitiveness?

Competitiveness remains a concept that is not well understood, despite widespread acceptance of its importance. The most intuitive definition of competitiveness is a country's share of world markets for its products. This makes competitiveness a zero-sum game, because one country's gain comes at the expense of others. This view of competitiveness is used to justify intervention to skew market outcomes in a nation's favor (so-called strategic industrial policy). It also underpins policies intended to provide subsidies, hold down local wages and devalue the nation's currency, all aimed at expanding exports. In fact, it is still often said that lower wages or devaluation "make a nation more competitive."

Unfortunately, the most intuitive view of competitiveness is deeply flawed. The need for low wages reveals a lack of competitiveness and holds down prosperity. Subsidies drain national income and bias choices away from the most productive use of the nation's resources. Devaluation results in a collective national pay cut, by discounting the products and services sold in world markets, while raising the cost of the goods and services purchases abroad. Exports based on low wages or a cheap currency, then, do not support an attractive standard of living.

To understand competitiveness, the starting point must be the underlying sources of prosperity. A nation's standard of living is determined by the *productivity* of its economy, as measured by the value of goods and services produced per unit of the nation's human, capital, and natural resources. Productivity depends both on the value of a nation's products and services, measured by the prices they can command in open markets, and the efficiency with which they can be produced.

True competitiveness, then, is measured by productivity. Productivity allows a nation to support high wages, a strong currency, and attractive returns to capital—and with them a high standard of living. Productivity is the goal, not exports per se. Only if a nation increases exports of products or services that it can produce more productively than the average industry will national productivity rise. Also, productivity is the goal, not whether firms operating in the country are domestic or foreign-owned. What matters most is not ownership, but the nature and productivity of the business activities taking place in a particular country. Finally, purely local industries also matter for competitiveness, because their productivity not only sets their wages, but has a major influence on the cost of living, and on the cost of doing business in the country. The productivity of the entire economy matters for the standard of living, not just the traded sector.

The world economy is not a zero-sum game. Many nations can improve their prosperity if they can improve productivity. The central challenge in economic development, then, is how to create the conditions for rapid and sustained productivity growth.

Productivity depends on the ability of an economy to mobilize the available human resources. The overall productivity of the economy, measured by the real GDP generated per all potential employees available in the economy, is what determines overall prosperity. The productivity of employees actually working is only part of the story. Some European economies report high levels of productivity per hour worked, but the existence of high unemployment, sick leave, and limited working hours depress national income per capita.[4] Much of this underutilization of labor is not voluntary, but reflects a lack of employment alternatives.[5] Differences between economy-wide productivity and productivity of those that are working are often driven by inefficient labor markets, or other distortive interventions in factor input markets.

Microeconomic foundations of productivity

Stable political, legal, and social institutions and sound macroeconomic policies create the potential for productivity and national prosperity. But wealth is actually created at the microeconomic level—in the ability of firms to create valuable goods and services using efficient methods. Only in this way can a nation support high wages and the attractive returns to capital necessary to support sustained investment (see Figure 1). Only firms can create wealth, not government or other societal institutions.

The microeconomic foundations of productivity rest on two interrelated areas: (1) the sophistication (productivity) with which domestic companies or foreign subsidiaries compete in the country, and (2) the quality of the microeconomic business environment in which they operate.

Figure 1: Determinants of competitiveness

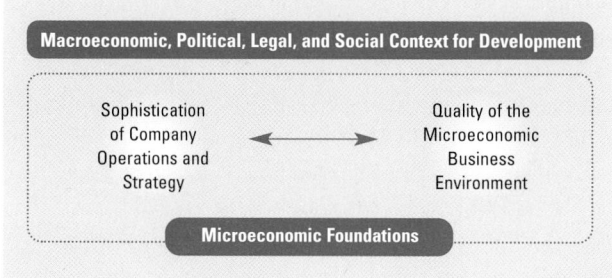

Figure 2: Company sophistication and economic development

Low-Income Countries	Middle-Income Countries	High-Income Countries
• Competitive advantages beyond cheap inputs • Production process sophistication • Broad value chain presence • Reliance on professional management	• Extent of regional sales • Control of international distribution • Extent of branding • Company spending on R&D • Prevalence of foreign technology licensing • Extent of staff training	• Capacity for innovation • Breadth of international markets • Extent of incentive compensation • Willingness to delegate authority

The productivity of a country is ultimately set by the productivity of its companies. An economy cannot be competitive unless companies operating there are competitive, whether they are domestic firms or subsidiaries of foreign companies. Economic policies affect prosperity, then, if they affect the productivity with which companies can operate. The sophistication and productivity of companies is inextricably intertwined with the quality of the national business environment. More productive company strategies and operating practices require more highly skilled people, better information, more efficient government processes, improved infrastructure, better suppliers, more advanced research institutions, and more intense competitive pressure, among other things.

The competitiveness of companies and the competitiveness of locations are different but related concepts. Locations compete based on their productivity as business locations. Companies also compete based on competitive advantages in terms of productivity, but can choose among locations. The competitiveness of a company, then, depends on both internal capabilities and the results of its choice of location.[6]

Companies in a nation must upgrade their ways of competing, if successful economic development is to occur. Broadly, companies must shift from competing on inherited endowments (comparative advantages such as low-cost labor or natural resources) to created competitive advantages arising from efficient and distinctive products and processes. Companies must move from tapping foreign distribution channels to building their own channels. These and other transitions in corporate strategies and operating practices required for successful economic development are shown in Figure 2.

What were strengths in competing at earlier stages of development become weaknesses at more advanced levels of development, because the level of productivity must be higher. Extensive technology licensing works for lower- and middle-income countries, but must give way to

Figure 3: The microeconomic business environment

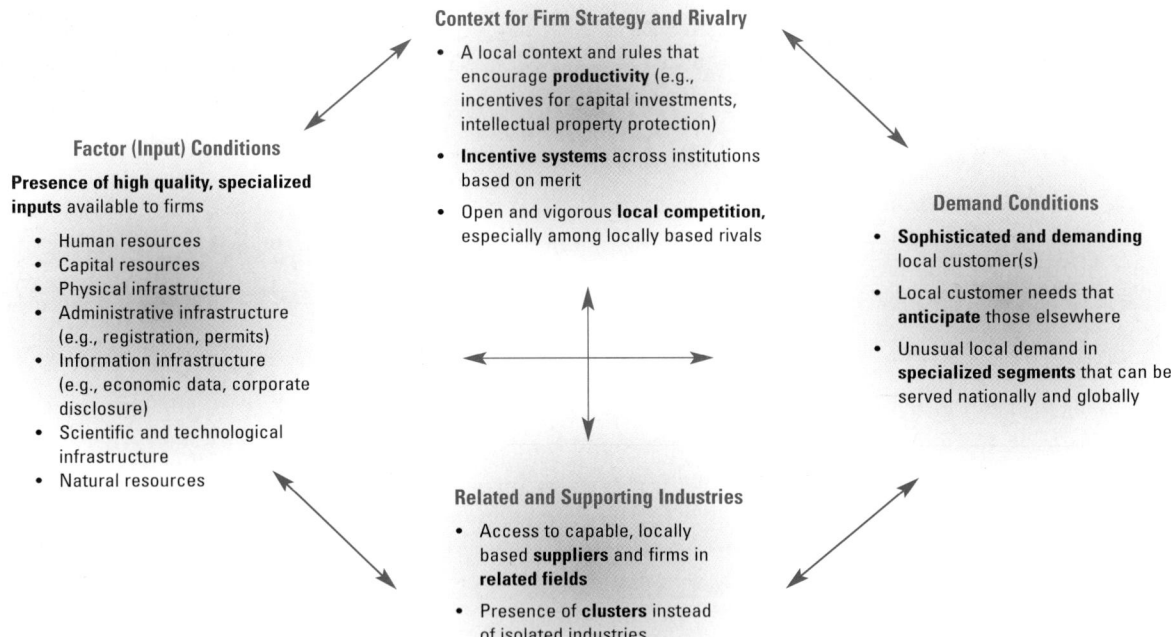

indigenous technology development. Necessary changes are often resisted by the corporate sector because past approaches were profitable and because old habits are deeply ingrained.

Moving to more sophisticated ways of competing depends on parallel changes in the microeconomic business environment. The business environment can be understood in terms of four interrelated areas: the quality of factor (input) conditions, the context for firm strategy and rivalry, the quality of local demand conditions, and the presence of the related and supporting industries. Because of their graphical representation (see Figure 3), the four areas have collectively become referred to as the *diamond*.

As the diamond framework reveals, almost everything matters for competitiveness. The schools matter, the roads matter, the financial markets matter, customer sophistication matters, among many other aspects of a nation's circumstances, many of which are deeply rooted in a nation's institutions, people, and culture. This makes improving competitiveness a special challenge, because there is no single policy or grand step that can create competitiveness, only many improvements in individual areas that, inevitably, take time to accomplish. Many parts of government have a role, as do universities, schools, and other societal institutions. Improving competitiveness is a marathon, not a sprint. How to sustain momentum in

improving competitiveness over time is among the greatest challenges facing countries.

Multiple geographic levels offset competitiveness: national, state, and local.[7] There are striking differences in economic performance within countries, not just across different countries. The crucial need for economic strategies for states, metropolitan regions, and even towns is among the most important new directions in competitiveness thinking and practice.

National productivity can also be offset by neighboring countries. Economic cooperation and coordination among neighbors is an important tool for expanding trade and improving the business environment.

Government plays an inevitable role in economic development because it affects many aspects of the business environment. The sophistication of home demand, for example, is affected by regulatory standards, consumer protection laws, government purchasing practices, and openness to imports. Many government departments and agencies impinge on competitiveness, as do government entities at the provincial, state, and city levels. The question is not whether government has a role, but what that role should be and how to coordinate policies across parts of government. Many countries have sought to limit the inappropriate roles of government while ignoring its positive roles. Government must set the right rules and

Figure 4: The Cairns (Australia) Tourism Cluster

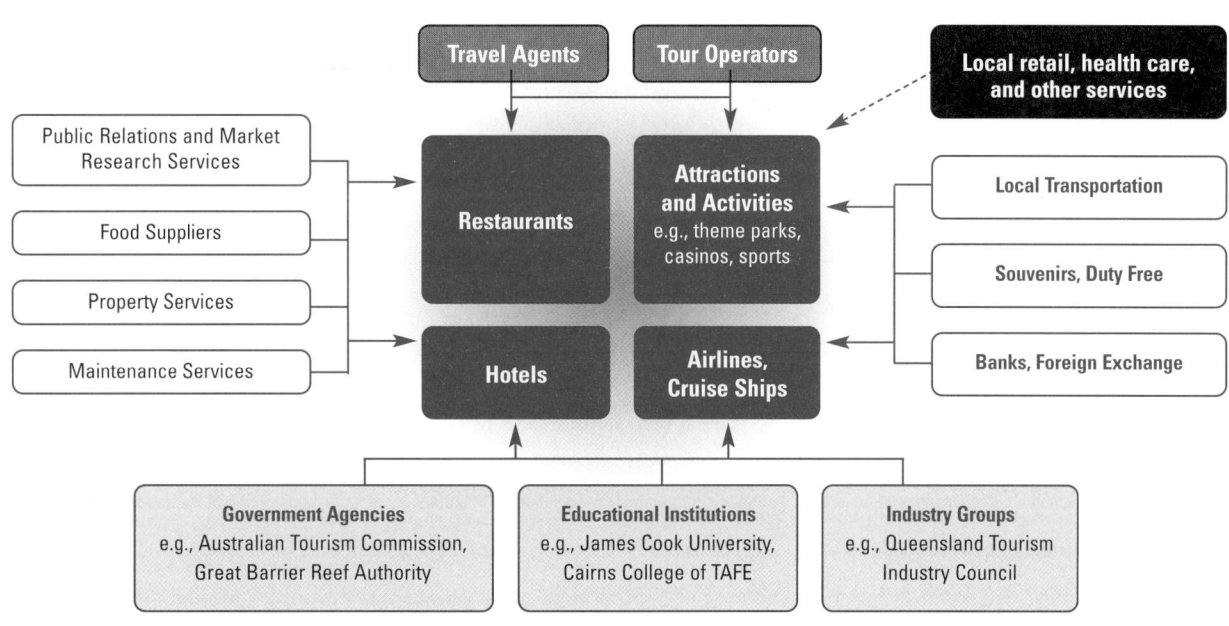

Source: Research by HBS Student Team, 2003.

incentives, and make the public investments needed for a productive economy.

Clusters and economic development

Clusters are geographically proximate groups of interconnected companies, suppliers, service providers, and associated institutions in a particular field, linked by commonalities and complementarities. Clusters such as software in India or high-performance cars in Germany are often concentrated in a particular region within a larger nation, and sometimes in a single town. Clusters are a natural manifestation of processes improving productivity and the enhancement of the business environment.

Clusters affect competitiveness in three broad ways: first, the presence of a cluster increases the productivity of constituent firms or industries. Within a cluster, firms have more efficient access to specialized suppliers, employees, information, and training than isolated firms who have to source from other locations. The presence of a wide range of available inputs, machinery, skills, and knowledge promotes greater efficiency and flexibility than vertical integration or relationships with distant suppliers. Second, the presence of a cluster increases the capacity for innovation and productivity growth. Opportunities for innovation are often perceived more easily within a cluster, and the assets, skills, and capital to realize innovation are present. Third, clusters stimulate and enable new business formation that

supports innovation and expands the cluster. Barriers to entry are lower if there are experienced workers and access to all the needed inputs and specialized services locally available.

The productivity benefits of clusters apply to virtually all parts of an economy, not only to knowledge intensive industries such as life sciences or information technology as is sometimes assumed. A good example is tourism: in the Cairns tourism cluster of Northwestern Australia, natural attractions such as proximity to the Great Barrier Reef and a tropical Rainforest will not be an advantage versus competing tourism destinations,[8] unless there are also high-quality hotels, restaurants, travel guides, and the many supporting activities important to offering an excellent experience for the tourist (see Figure 4).

National economies tend to specialize in a particular set of clusters, which account for a disproportionate share of their traded output. This specialization of economies is even more evident in subnational regions.

The nature and depth of clusters varies with the state of development of the economy. In developing countries, clusters normally lack many supporting industries and institutions. Firms compete based on cheap labor or local natural resources, and they depend heavily on imported components, machinery, and technology. Specialized local infrastructure and institutions are absent or inefficient.

Firms perform relatively less advanced activities in the cluster.

As economies advance, clusters develop and deepen to include suppliers of specialized inputs, components, machinery, and services, as well as specialized infrastructure, and institutions providing specialized training, education, information, research, and technical support.

It is rare that there is only a single cluster in the world in a given field, but an array of clusters in different locations, with different levels of sophistication and specialization. In a given field, only a small number of clusters tend to be true innovation centers, such as Silicon Valley and Japan in semiconductors. These innovation centers sometimes specialize in particular market segments; for example, Silicon Valley cluster is unusually strong in microprocessors. Other locations may be manufacturing centers. Still other clusters can be regional assembly and service clusters. An important trend in the modern economy is that clusters seem to be becoming more specialized in particular segments, or in particular layers of the value chain.

Firms based in the most advanced clusters often seed or enhance clusters in other locations as they disperse some activities to reduce risk, access lower cost inputs, or better serve particular regional markets. Intel, for example, has moved some assembly and testing, and some wafer fabrication to a number of non-US locations that have become regional clusters. The same development can be seen in a number of other areas, for example the offshoring of business services and manufacturing activities to locations with lower labor costs. Instead of spreading these activities across geography in less advanced economies, companies have found it advantageous to co-locate in newly-emerging clusters. This can be seen in outsourced business services in Bangalore, India, and in textile production in Timisoara, Romania.[9] These examples suggest that globalization does imply a readjustment of the global geographic patterns of clusters, not their demise. In fact, there is growing evidence that clusters are becoming more important, as regions increasingly specialize under the pressure of more intense competition across locations. Specialization occurs not only across clusters, but also within clusters, where different locations play increasingly different roles for overall value creation.

The challenge for an economy is to move from isolated firms to an array of clusters, and upgrade the sophistication of clusters to more advanced activities.

Stages of competitive development

Successful economic development is a process of successive upgrading, in which a nation's business environment evolves to support and encourage increasingly sophisticated and productive ways of competing by firms based

Figure 5: Stages of competitive development

Source: Porter (1990)

there. Nations at different levels of development face distinctly different challenges.

As nations develop, they progress in terms of their competitive advantages and modes of competing[10] (see Figure 5). In the *factor-driven* stage, basic factor conditions such as low-cost labor and unprocessed natural resources are the dominant sources of competitive advantage and exports. Firms produce commodities or relatively simple products designed in other, more-advanced countries. Technology is assimilated through imports, supply agreements, foreign direct investment, and imitation. In this stage, companies compete on price, and lack direct access to consumers. They have limited roles in the value chain, focusing on assembly, labor-intensive manufacturing, and resource extraction. A factor-driven economy is highly sensitive to world economic cycles, commodity prices, and exchange rate fluctuations.

In the *investment-driven* stage, efficiency in producing standard products and services becomes the dominant source of competitive advantage. Heavy investment in efficient infrastructure, business-friendly government administration, strong investment incentives, and better access to capital allow major improvements in productivity. The products and services produced become more sophisticated, but technology and designs still largely come from abroad. Technology is accessed through licensing, joint ventures, foreign direct investment, and imitation. However, nations at this stage not only assimilate foreign technology but also begin to develop the capacity to improve on it. Companies serve a mix of Original Equipment Manufacturer (OEM) customers and end users. Firms extend capabilities more widely in the value chain. An investment-driven economy is concentrated on manufacturing and on outsourced service exports. It is susceptible to financial crises and external, sector-specific demand shocks.

In the *innovation-driven* stage, the ability to produce innovative products and services at the global technology frontier, using the most advanced methods becomes the dominant source of competitive advantage. The national business environment is characterized by strengths in all areas, together with the presence of deep clusters. Institutions and incentives supporting innovation are well developed. Companies compete with unique strategies that are often global in scope. An innovation-driven economy has a high share of services in the economy and is resilient to external shocks.

Seeing economic development as a sequential process of building interdependent microeconomic capabilities, shifting company strategies, improving incentives, and increasing rivalry exposes important pitfalls in economic policy. The influence of one part of the microeconomic business environment depends on the state of others. Lack of improvement in any important area can lead to a plateau in productivity growth, and stalled development. Worse yet, it can undermine the whole economic reform process. When well-trained college graduates cannot find appropriate jobs because companies are still competing based on cheap labor, for example, a backlash against business is created.

This analysis also begins to reveal why countries find the transition to a new stage of development so difficult. Such inflection points require wholesale transformation of many interdependent aspects of competition.

Institutions and roles in economic development

While government is important to competitiveness, government alone also is less and less able to build a competitive economy. Many other national and local institutions have a role in competitiveness and economic development. The influence of universities and schools is growing as knowledge and technology become more and more central to competition. Universities and schools must not only improve the educational and research capabilities, but become better connected to the private sector.

The private sector has also become a crucial actor in improving competitiveness, and in setting economic policy. The private sector is not only a consumer of the business environment, but can and must play a role in shaping it. Individual firms, through steps such as establishing educational programs, attracting suppliers, or defining standards, not only benefit themselves but also improve the overall environment for competing. Collective industry bodies, such as trade associations and chambers of commerce, also have important roles to play in improving infrastructure, providing training, and developing export markets that are often overlooked. Collective efforts to enhance the capabilities of individual companies, such as quality certification programs and manufacturing assistance centers, are becoming more prominent. Engagement of the private sector in competitiveness is also important to provide the continuity of attention, necessary to sustain progress through changes of government, and to counteract the relatively short attention span of political leaders.

Finally, a whole class of institutions, which we term *institutions for collaboration* (IFCs), play an important role in competitiveness though they have been largely ignored in economic development thinking.[11] Neither government

agencies, educational institutions, nor firms, these organizations— for example, trade associations, entrepreneur networks, standard setting agencies, quality centers, technology networks, and many others—are common. They are especially prevalent in the most advanced economies, but are also crucial in developing countries. IFCs play an essential role in connecting the parts of the diamond, and fostering efficient collective activities in both advanced and developing countries.[12]

The relationship between macroeconomic and microeconomic policy

Our analysis makes it clear why the traditional focus on macroeconomic stabilization and market opening is insufficient. Macroeconomic policies fostering high rates of capital investment, for example, will not translate into rising productivity, unless the forms of investment are appropriate, the company skills and supporting industries are present to make the investments efficient, and strong competitive pressures and adequate corporate governance provide the needed market discipline. Sound monetary and fiscal policies and the removal of distortions in exchange rates and other prices will eliminate impediments to productivity, but microeconomic foundations must be in place if productivity is actually to increase.

Appropriate levels of foreign debt depend on microeconomic circumstances. The prudence of foreign debt levels depends on exactly where the foreign capital is invested, together with the microeconomic fundamentals surrounding its deployment and governance. Regulating overall debt levels is less important, in many ways, than improving the microeconomic foundations. The resilience of the US economy despite the existing serious macroeconomic imbalances might then have a lot to do with its impressive microeconomic strengths.

High rates of public investment in human capital will not pay off unless a nation's microeconomic circumstances create the demand for skills in companies. Privatization will not boost prosperity unless companies can improve efficiency and are pressured by local competition. For sound policies at the macroeconomic level to translate into an increasingly productive economy, then, parallel microeconomic improvements must take place.

The effects of trade agreements and other market-opening measures, a major focus in today's international economic policymaking, also depend on microeconomic policies. Market opening is good, but its benefits in terms of prosperity depend on microeconomic progress. If the local business environment does not become more efficient and local companies do not improve their productivity and sophistication, market opening will boost imports, but growth in exports and the attraction of foreign investment will be painfully slow. This lesson is particularly important for trade agreements between countries at very different stages of economic development, such as the Central American Free Trade Area (CAFTA). Microeconomic upgrading in the less developed, and efficient structural adjustment in the more advanced economies of such a free trade area is critical for the high potential economic benefits to materialize. The improvement in the microeconomic business environment has to begin *before* market opening measures are complete.

A greater focus on microeconomic reforms will pay another essential dividend. While macro reforms almost inevitability inflict hardship in the short and medium run, through raising interest rates and prices, while cutting public expenditures, micro reforms can produce tangible and visible benefits for citizens. Breaking up local cartels and monopolies, for example, lowers the cost of food, housing, electricity, telephone service, and other costs of living. Regulatory reform can rapidly begin to ease inefficiencies, reduce pollution, improve product quality, and end unsafe practices. Bold steps to improve the quality of education and training are particularly important, because they offer the hope of a better life for children. If citizens see businesses reforming themselves and having to confront tough competitive challenges, they themselves will be more willing to live with personal sacrifices, and less likely to side with anti-reform interest groups. The political will and public support to make real economic change is elevated.

Ranking competitiveness

Measures of competitiveness

The Business Competitiveness Index (BCI) is constructed from measures drawn primarily from the Survey of 10,961 senior business leaders in 116 countries, shown in Table 1.[13] Compared to last year 15 countries were added (Albania, Armenia, Azerbaijan, Benin, Cambodia, Cameroon, East Timor, Guyana, Kazakhstan, Kuwait, Kyrgyz Republic, Moldova, Mongolia, Qatar, and Tajikistan) and two countries (Angola, Zambia) were dropped.

Measuring competitiveness is challenging because of the sheer number and variety of influences that shape national productivity. Only through a detailed survey can textured measures of the competitive environment and company practices be assembled across many countries. The Survey questions aim to capture the circumstances in a nation, but do so in way that is meaningful for Survey respondents. For example, we get at the stock of basic human capital with a question on the quality of public schools, because this is something that respondents can more readily compare across countries. The quality of schools, a flow measure, will be highly correlated with the stock of basic skills.

The World Bank has in the last few years been working to systematically collect comparable data on governance and regulatory conditions across a wide number of countries.[14] World Bank data on corruption, regulatory quality, and the rule of law overlap with some of the areas covered in our Survey.[15] The correlation among our indicators and the World Bank data are regularly above 80 percent, even though the Survey questions address related, but usually different attributes. The World Bank also has a "Doing Business" data base, which covers such things as administrative procedures in starting a business, the availability of effective credit registers to enable loans to businesses, and the organization of bankruptcy procedures. Here, correlations with Survey data are relatively low. Given the differences in the attributes measured (for example, access to loans in the Survey versus cost of creating collateral in the World Bank data) these differences are not surprising. We rely mostly on the Survey data because they are available for all countries and Survey questions are designed to capture national conditions most meaningful for competitiveness.

Quantitative measures are utilized for patenting rates, Internet penetration, and cellular phone penetration. For all the other dimensions we measure, however, quantitative data are simply unavailable, especially for so many countries. The Survey not only offers many unique measures, but captures the informed judgments of the actual participants in the economies examined. The Survey responses are important in their own right, because they reflect the attitudes of the decision makers that ultimately determine economic activity. We test whether these judgments are affected by a country's general economic climate and find no significant relation between either a country's real growth rate, or the change in the growth rate to changes in the average level of responses across Survey questions.

Compared to previous years, we reduced the number of Survey questions from 67 to 57 to shrink the time needed to complete the Survey and expand the number of responses, in order to enable more business leaders to participate. The reduction has little effect on the overall rankings.[16]

As with last year, we examined the consistency of the Survey data to ensure that the sample used for statistical estimation is as valid as possible and to identify particular countries whose rankings may be less reliable. For each Survey question we compared the standard deviation of answers within a country to the standard deviation of answers across all countries. In those countries with high within-country variance of responses on many Survey questions it is hard to interpret the country averages, independently of the possible reasons for the variances.[17] We further analyzed within-country consensus in the subset of responses from executives from foreign companies operating in the country. We expect these respondents to have the best perspective on how the country compared to others.

Of the 116 countries surveyed this year, 110 passed our data consistency test.[18] These 110 countries are utilized in the estimation of our model, which we utilized to rank all 116 countries; however, the rankings of the six countries with data quality concerns should be interpreted with caution.

For the 110-country sample used in the regressions, and for computing the Index model, there is an average of more than 93 respondents per country, significantly up from 80 last year. The degree of within-country consensus is striking. For all measures, the proportion of variation due to country differences is statistically significant. As expected, the within-country consensus is higher for cross-cutting business environment indicators, and lower for measures where there would be variation within the country across companies and clusters. The country averages, then, capture meaningful differences across countries in competitive circumstances, while limiting idiosyncratic biases that would result if there were only a handful of responses per country.

The dependent variable used to develop the BCI is the level of GDP per capita in 2004, adjusted for purchasing power parity (PPP). GDP per capita is the broadest measure of national productivity and is strongly linked over time to a nation's standard of living. It is the best single, summary measure of microeconomic competitiveness available across all countries.[19] GDP per capita will reflect a country's structural fundamentals over the medium and long term. However, it is also influenced by a wide array of short-term and idiosyncratic factors such as natural disasters, macroeconomic shocks, and price movements in particular export industries. The proportion of the variation in GDP per capita across all countries that can be explained by microeconomic fundamentals is interesting in its own right.

To explore differences in the sources of competitiveness across countries at different levels of development, we divided countries into three groups based on income. There is no accepted division among low-, middle-, and high-income countries, and efforts to statistically define income cutoffs meet with data limitations. Instead, we proceed pragmatically, dividing countries using income cutoffs that yield logical divisions of countries in terms of aspirations and competitive position, and ensuring that there are enough countries in each group to allow meaningful statistical tests. We also attempt to ensure income-group stability from year to year. We use cutoff points at US$4,000 GDP per capita (PPP) in 2004 for low- to middle-income and US$17,000 GDP per capita (PPP) in 2004 for middle- to high-income, the same as in past years.

There were 28 low-income countries (seven new countries, net of three previous low-income countries that have moved into the middle-income group); 48 middle-income countries (four new, three previous low-income countries, less one previous middle-income country that moved to the high-income group); and 34 high-income countries (one new, one previously middle-income country). As will be reported, these groups exhibited quite different patterns of influence among variables, as we would expect.

Sources of competitiveness

To construct an overall index of competitiveness, we first validated the statistical relationship of each of the measures of microeconomic competitiveness suggested by our conceptual framework with GDP per capita. Variables are broadly grouped into those measuring the sophistication of company operations and strategy and those measuring the quality of the national business environment. A full list of Survey questions and available quantitative measures is given in Appendix A. For the construction of the index, a smaller number of measures would be statistically sufficient. However, the detailed pattern of individual strengths and weaknesses by country is interesting in its own right.

Appendix B gives bivariate regressions on GDP per capita in all variables. Included in the table is the mean response across all countries or groups of countries, the standard deviation, the slope of the regression relationship, a measure of the statistical significance of the relationship, and the adjusted R^2 (or proportion of variation in GDP per capita explained by the variable, adjusted for statistical degrees of freedom).[20] All the reported variables are highly statistically significant in the full sample of countries.[21] While the bivariate regressions are not meant to represent a fully specified model, they provide a basic test of whether the variables have a meaningful relationship with the level of GDP per capita across countries. A bilateral statistical correlation to GDP per capita does also not necessarily imply causation, but it does refute the hypothesis that microeconomic variables have no important relation to prosperity. Interestingly, prominent macroeconomic variables such as the national savings rate and the level of investment, as a percentage of GDP are either not significantly related to the level of GDP per capita in bilateral regressions, or are associated with only a minor share of its variation across countries.[22] These findings are highly consistent with results from earlier *Global Competitiveness Reports*.

Among the company variables, production process sophistication, the nature of competitive advantage, and the extent of staff training have the strongest bilateral association with per capita GDP. By itself, the nature of the competitive advantage of a nation's companies, whether it is based on cheap inputs or on unique products and

Table 1: The Business Competitiveness Index (BCI) Ranking

Country	BCI ranking								Company operations and strategy ranking								Quality of the national business environment ranking								2004 GDP per capita (PPP-adjusted)
	2005	2004	2003	2002	2001	2000	1999	1998	2005	2004	2003	2002	2001	2000	1999	1998	2005	2004	2003	2002	2001	2000	1999	1998	
United States	1	1	2	1	2	2	1	1	1	2	2	1	1	2	1	2	2	2	2	1	2	2	1	1	39,498
Finland	2	2	1	2	1	1	2	2	9	7	4	4	2	3	7	8	1	1	1	2	1	1	2	2	29,305
Germany	3	3	5	4	4	3	6	4	2	1	1	2	4	1	5	1	4	5	9	4	4	6	5	8	28,889
Denmark	4	7	4	8	8	6	7	8	4	9	7	9	9	8	9	10	3	3	3	9	10	4	6	7	33,089
Singapore	5	10	8	9	9	9	12	10	14	13	12	14	15	15	14	12	5	8	4	5	9	5	12	6	26,799
United Kingdom	6	6	6	3	7	8	10	5	6	8	8	3	7	11	13	9	6	4	6	3	8	9	8	5	28,968
Switzerland	7	5	7	5	5	5	5	9	5	4	5	5	5	5	2	3	7	7	8	6	5	10	9	10	31,690
Japan	8	8	13	11	10	14	14	18	3	3	6	7	8	4	4	7	10	11	20	17	16	19	19	19	29,906
Netherlands	9	9	9	7	3	4	3	3	8	6	10	8	3	7	8	5	8	9	11	10	3	3	3	4	29,253
Austria	10	16	17	12	11	13	11	16	11	14	13	12	11	12	10	11	9	17	18	12	12	12	13	17	31,406
France	11	12	10	15	13	15	9	11	10	10	9	10	10	9	6	6	11	16	14	21	13	15	11	13	27,913
Sweden	12	4	3	6	6	7	4	7	7	5	3	6	6	6	3	4	14	6	5	8	6	11	7	9	28,205
Canada	13	15	12	10	12	11	8	6	18	16	14	13	14	16	12	15	13	13	10	7	11	8	4	3	32,921
Taiwan	14	17	16	16	21	21	19	20	13	12	16	16	20	18	17	16	15	20	16	13	21	21	22	21	25,614
Australia	15	13	11	14	14	10	13	15	23	19	18	19	24	20	19	22	12	12	7	11	7	7	10	12	29,682
Belgium	16	14	15	13	15	12	15	19	12	11	11	11	12	10	11	13	17	19	17	15	14	13	15	18	30,062
Iceland	17	19	14	17	16	17	22	24	15	17	15	17	16	14	21	28	18	18	12	14	15	16	21	23	33,269
New Zealand	18	18	18	22	20	19	16	17	21	20	23	25	19	22	16	19	16	15	13	20	20	17	14	16	23,925
Ireland	19	22	21	20	22	22	17	13	16	22	17	15	17	19	20	18	20	22	22	22	22	22	17	14	31,263
Hong Kong SAR	20	11	19	19	18	16	21	12	20	15	22	24	21	23	24	17	19	10	15	16	17	14	18	11	30,558
Norway	21	20	22	21	19	20	18	14	22	23	21	23	23	21	23	14	21	14	21	19	19	18	16	15	40,005
Israel	22	21	20	18	17	18	20	21	19	18	20	20	18	13	18	21	22	21	19	18	18	20	20	20	22,077
Malaysia	23	23	26	26	37	30	27	27	24	28	26	27	37	30	25	34	23	23	24	26	37	30	31	26	10,423
Korea, Rep.	24	24	23	23	26	27	28	28	17	21	19	21	26	25	27	24	24	28	25	23	29	28	30	28	21,305
Spain	25	26	25	25	24	23	23	22	25	25	25	22	22	24	22	23	26	27	26	25	23	23	23	22	23,627
Estonia	26	27	28	30	28	—	—	—	33	34	36	36	32	—	—	—	25	24	27	28	26	—	—	—	15,217
Czech Republic	27	35	35	34	34	34	41	30	29	31	33	34	41	41	55	31	27	37	38	34	31	34	36	33	18,357
South Africa	28	25	27	29	25	25	26	25	26	24	28	31	25	26	28	33	30	25	28	33	27	25	25	25	10,603
Chile	29	29	32	31	29	26	24	23	31	33	34	35	30	27	26	25	29	29	30	31	30	24	24	24	10,869
Portugal	30	33	36	36	33	28	29	33	39	42	46	41	38	35	37	48	28	31	33	32	28	27	26	30	19,038
India	31	30	37	37	36	37	42	44	30	30	40	40	43	40	48	50	31	32	36	37	34	37	43	42	3,029
Slovenia	32	31	30	27	32	—	—	—	27	27	27	26	28	—	—	—	35	33	34	27	35	—	—	—	20,306
United Arab Emirates	33	28	—	—	—	—	—	—	36	32	—	—	—	—	—	—	33	26	—	—	—	—	—	—	23,818
Hungary	34	42	38	28	27	32	33	31	40	48	45	29	33	34	36	39	32	38	37	29	25	31	33	31	15,546
Tunisia	35	32	33	32	—	—	—	—	46	43	38	37	—	—	—	—	34	30	29	30	—	—	—	—	7,732
Cyprus	36	45	—	—	—	—	—	—	48	59	—	—	—	—	—	—	36	41	—	—	—	—	—	—	19,633
Thailand	37	37	31	35	38	40	39	37	35	36	31	33	42	47	43	37	37	36	32	35	39	40	39	36	7,901
Italy	38	34	24	24	23	24	25	26	28	26	24	18	13	17	15	20	39	43	23	24	24	26	27	27	28,172
Slovak Republic	39	39	43	42	40	36	48	36	47	41	44	43	57	31	51	40	38	39	43	40	36	36	47	37	15,066
Greece	40	41	39	43	46	33	36	38	42	40	39	47	51	32	45	32	40	42	40	41	43	33	34	38	20,362
Lithuania	41	36	40	40	50	—	—	—	41	37	41	39	47	—	—	—	41	35	41	39	47	—	—	—	12,919
Poland	42	57	47	46	42	41	37	41	43	47	43	46	55	36	38	38	46	64	45	45	40	41	38	40	12,244
Jordan	43	43	41	53	47	35	32	32	59	54	59	59	56	46	44	42	42	40	35	48	41	35	28	32	4,383
Qatar	44	—	—	—	—	—	—	—	64	—	—	—	—	—	—	—	43	—	—	—	—	—	—	—	28,919
Ghana	45	64	63	—	—	—	—	—	56	71	66	—	—	—	—	—	47	59	57	—	—	—	—	—	2,475
Malta	46	50	42	—	—	—	—	—	61	60	47	—	—	—	—	—	44	49	42	—	—	—	—	—	19,302
Kuwait	47	—	—	—	—	—	—	—	63	—	—	—	—	—	—	—	45	—	—	—	—	—	—	—	16,066
Latvia	48	49	29	45	41	—	—	—	51	51	29	48	35	—	—	—	48	48	31	42	42	—	—	—	11,845
Brazil	49	38	34	33	30	31	35	35	32	29	30	28	29	29	32	27	52	44	39	36	32	32	37	39	8,328
Costa Rica	50	48	45	39	48	43	38	—	34	35	32	32	34	39	35	—	53	50	47	47	51	42	41	—	9,887
Turkey	51	52	52	54	35	29	31	29	38	44	51	56	44	28	33	26	51	55	55	55	33	29	32	29	7,503
Mauritius	52	53	44	49	51	38	30	—	45	49	35	42	49	37	29	—	49	54	46	50	50	38	29	—	12,215
Jamaica	53	54	56	59	39	—	—	—	54	52	56	60	31	—	—	—	54	53	56	59	44	—	—	—	4,327
Bahrain	54	40	—	—	—	—	—	—	67	53	—	—	—	—	—	—	55	34	—	—	—	—	—	—	18,817
Botswana	55	62	54	57	—	—	—	—	76	73	67	64	—	—	—	—	50	52	50	51	—	—	—	—	10,169
Colombia	56	58	51	56	57	48	52	49	49	58	50	51	52	48	40	43	57	61	54	57	59	48	53	49	6,959
China	57	47	46	38	43	44	49	42	53	39	42	38	39	38	31	35	58	47	44	38	46	45	50	44	5,642
El Salvador	58	65	64	63	64	51	47	—	57	65	58	61	66	57	46	—	56	65	65	62	64	50	48	—	4,379
Indonesia	59	44	60	64	55	47	53	51	50	38	62	55	50	51	47	52	59	46	61	65	58	47	52	51	3,622
Mexico	60	55	48	55	52	42	34	39	55	46	37	45	46	42	30	29	62	56	51	60	52	43	35	41	9,666
Panama	61	60	59	50	49	—	—	—	37	66	60	54	40	—	—	—	68	58	60	52	49	—	—	—	6,997
Kazakhstan	62	—	—	—	—	—	—	—	72	—	—	—	—	—	—	—	60	—	—	—	—	—	—	—	7,418
Croatia	63	72	62	52	—	—	—	—	70	72	65	53	—	—	—	—	61	70	58	54	—	—	—	—	11,568
Argentina	64	74	69	65	54	45	40	34	52	68	63	57	53	45	39	30	64	78	73	68	53	44	40	34	12,468

(cont'd)

Table 1: The Business Competitiveness Index (BCI) Ranking *(cont'd.)*

Country	BCI ranking								Company operations and strategy ranking								Quality of the national business environment ranking								2004 GDP per capita (PPP-adjusted)
	2005	2004	2003	2002	2001	2000	1999	1998	2005	2004	2003	2002	2001	2000	1999	1998	2005	2004	2003	2002	2001	2000	1999	1998	
Trinidad and Tobago	65	59	53	44	31	—	—	—	62	55	54	44	27	—	—	—	63	62	53	44	38	—	—	—	12,794
Pakistan	66	73	75	—	—	—	—	—	68	67	81	—	—	—	—	—	65	75	70	—	—	—	—	—	2,404
Romania	67	56	76	67	61	—	—	—	69	61	84	69	63	—	—	—	67	57	71	64	60	—	—	—	7,641
Kenya	68	63	67	—	—	—	—	—	60	56	61	—	—	—	—	—	69	63	72	—	—	—	—	—	1,075
Philippines	69	70	65	61	53	46	44	45	44	50	48	49	45	43	34	41	78	77	74	67	54	46	46	45	4,561
Uruguay	70	77	71	62	45	—	—	—	79	80	77	63	48	—	—	—	66	76	68	61	45	—	—	—	9,107
Egypt	71	66	58	—	44	39	43	40	58	57	55	—	36	44	49	47	74	68	62	—	48	39	42	35	4,072
Sri Lanka	72	68	57	47	58	—	—	—	73	69	52	52	58	—	—	—	73	67	59	43	56	—	—	—	3,882
Namibia	73	51	55	51	—	—	—	—	75	63	64	58	—	—	—	—	72	51	52	49	—	—	—	—	6,449
Russian Federation	74	61	66	58	56	52	55	46	77	62	69	62	54	33	42	45	70	60	64	56	55	53	55	47	10,179
Ukraine	75	69	73	69	59	56	56	52	71	64	72	66	62	52	50	51	76	71	77	69	57	56	56	52	6,554
Nigeria	76	81	80	71	66	—	—	—	65	76	73	71	61	—	—	—	79	80	80	71	68	—	—	—	1,120
Azerbaijan	77	—	—	—	—	—	—	—	74	—	—	—	—	—	—	—	80	—	—	—	—	—	—	—	3,968
Bulgaria	78	75	77	68	68	55	54	—	82	86	85	72	70	54	52	—	71	72	75	63	65	54	54	—	8,500
Morocco	79	46	49	48	—	—	—	—	80	45	49	50	—	—	—	—	75	45	49	46	—	—	—	—	4,227
Vietnam	80	79	50	60	62	53	50	43	81	81	53	67	64	50	41	36	77	79	48	58	62	52	49	43	2,570
Peru	81	76	81	66	63	49	46	47	66	77	83	65	65	53	56	49	82	74	78	66	63	51	44	46	5,298
Tanzania	82	90	68	—	—	—	—	—	93	92	68	—	—	—	—	—	81	87	67	—	—	—	—	—	673
Macedonia, FYR	83	83	82	—	—	—	—	—	89	84	79	—	—	—	—	—	83	82	83	—	—	—	—	—	7,237
Zimbabwe	84	82	78	70	65	50	45	48	78	79	70	68	60	56	54	46	84	84	81	70	67	49	45	48	2,309
Uganda	*85*	—	—	—	—	—	—	—	*91*	—	—	—	—	—	—	—	*87*	—	—	—	—	—	—	—	*1,728*
Serbia and Montenegro	86	85	79	—	—	—	—	—	108	87	75	—	—	—	—	—	86	81	79	—	—	—	—	—	4,858
Mali	*87*	—	—	—	—	—	—	—	*109*	—	—	—	—	—	—	—	*85*	—	—	—	—	—	—	—	*1,024*
Armenia	88	—	—	—	—	—	—	—	87	—	—	—	—	—	—	—	90	—	—	—	—	—	—	—	3,806
Cameroon	*89*	—	—	—	—	—	—	—	*84*	—	—	—	—	—	—	—	*92*	—	—	—	—	—	—	—	*2,176*
Gambia	90	67	70	—	—	—	—	—	100	70	80	—	—	—	—	—	89	66	66	—	—	—	—	—	1,903
Malawi	91	84	72	—	—	—	—	—	86	83	71	—	—	—	—	—	93	85	76	—	—	—	—	—	569
Venezuela	92	88	85	72	67	54	51	50	85	82	74	73	67	49	53	44	97	91	87	72	66	55	51	50	5,571
Moldova	93	—	—	—	—	—	—	—	90	—	—	—	—	—	—	—	94	—	—	—	—	—	—	—	2,119
Bosnia and Herzegovina	94	93	—	—	—	—	—	—	101	96	—	—	—	—	—	—	91	92	—	—	—	—	—	—	5,504
Algeria	95	89	88	—	—	—	—	—	111	93	93	—	—	—	—	—	88	86	86	—	—	—	—	—	6,722
Georgia	96	92	—	—	—	—	—	—	94	89	—	—	—	—	—	—	95	93	—	—	—	—	—	—	2,774
Madagascar	97	87	90	—	—	—	—	—	102	88	88	—	—	—	—	—	96	88	90	—	—	—	—	—	854
Mozambique	98	96	93	—	—	—	—	—	97	94	90	—	—	—	—	—	99	98	95	—	—	—	—	—	1,247
Benin	*99*	—	—	—	—	—	—	—	*106*	—	—	—	—	—	—	—	*98*	—	—	—	—	—	—	—	*1,094*
Bangladesh	100	95	91	74	73	—	—	—	99	97	91	76	72	—	—	—	101	94	91	74	73	—	—	—	1,875
Dominican Republic	101	80	61	41	60	—	—	—	88	74	57	30	59	—	—	—	103	83	63	53	61	—	—	—	6,761
Tajikistan	102	—	—	—	—	—	—	—	107	—	—	—	—	—	—	—	100	—	—	—	—	—	—	—	1,246
Guatemala	103	86	86	73	69	—	—	—	83	78	76	70	69	—	—	—	104	90	88	73	69	—	—	—	4,009
Mongolia	104	—	—	—	—	—	—	—	98	—	—	—	—	—	—	—	102	—	—	—	—	—	—	—	1,918
Honduras	105	97	95	78	74	—	—	—	95	91	89	78	74	—	—	—	105	100	96	79	75	—	—	—	2,682
Nicaragua	106	100	94	75	71	—	—	—	110	100	92	75	73	—	—	—	106	99	93	76	70	—	—	—	2,677
Ecuador	107	94	89	77	72	57	57	—	96	90	87	74	71	55	57	—	108	95	92	77	72	58	57	—	3,819
Kyrgyz Republic	108	—	—	—	—	—	—	—	92	—	—	—	—	—	—	—	111	—	—	—	—	—	—	—	1,934
Cambodia	109	—	—	—	—	—	—	—	103	—	—	—	—	—	—	—	107	—	—	—	—	—	—	—	2,074
Guyana	110	—	—	—	—	—	—	—	105	—	—	—	—	—	—	—	109	—	—	—	—	—	—	—	4,579
Ethiopia	111	99	96	—	—	—	—	—	113	101	96	—	—	—	—	—	110	97	94	—	—	—	—	—	814
Albania	112	—	—	—	—	—	—	—	104	—	—	—	—	—	—	—	113	—	—	—	—	—	—	—	4,937
Bolivia	113	101	98	79	75	58	58	—	115	99	97	79	75	58	58	—	112	101	97	78	74	57	58	—	2,902
Paraguay	114	98	97	76	70	—	—	—	112	98	95	77	68	—	—	—	114	96	98	75	71	—	—	—	4,553
East Timor	*115*	—	—	—	—	—	—	—	*114*	—	—	—	—	—	—	—	*115*	—	—	—	—	—	—	—	*n/a*
Chad	*116*	—	—	—	—	—	—	—	*116*	—	—	—	—	—	—	—	*116*	—	—	—	—	—	—	—	*1,555*

Notes:
GNI per capita is used for Ireland.
Countries in bold italics did not pass the data consistency test and were not included in further analysis.

processes—explains a remarkable 69 percent of the variance in GDP per capita.

All four parts of the business environment prove important, with the influences of individual variables quite stable from previous years. Among the factor conditions are telecommunication access (cell phone and internet use), the quality of public schools, overall infrastructure quality, the quality of electricity supply, and the quality of financial markets (ease of access to loans, venture capital availability, and financial market sophistication).

Among local demand conditions, the presence of demanding regulatory standards, stringent environmental regulations, and the quality of laws relating to IT are strongly associated with the variation in GDP per capita. These results run counter to the perceived wisdom that local demand and local market conditions are less important in a global economy.

Cluster linkages, especially the quality of local suppliers and the presence of specialized local research and training providers, also prove significant and highlight the role of clusters in competitiveness. Finally, the incentives and rules governing local competition show a strong relationship to national productivity. Effective intellectual property protection, the absence of illegal or unfair activities (corruption), and the effectiveness of antitrust policy are particularly potent variables. The intensity of local competition is strongly and positively related to GDP per capita, alone explaining 50 percent of variations across countries in GDP per capita. The strong influence of local competition, supported in other recent studies,[23] is contrary to arguments made about the need to curb local competition in favor of creating national champions.

It is important to acknowledge that causality can be argued in both directions for some of the variables, although the Survey questions were worded to avoid spurious reverse causality. The quality of scientists and engineers or the sophistication of buyers, for example, could be partly the result of high per capita GDP, and not the cause. Note that the same causality issue applies with equal importance to macroeconomic and economic growth analyses. We provide some evidence of causality from microeconomic conditions to GDP per capita later in this chapter.

Competitiveness and economic development

As has been discussed, the appropriate company strategies and operating practices, as well as the influence of particular elements of the business environment will differ for countries at different levels of development. As noted earlier, the transition to entirely different stages of competitive development is particularly challenging.

To examine these issues, we explored the impact of measures of microeconomic competitiveness in the three country groups based on per capita GDP. While the

reported variables are statistically significant across the entire sample and strongly distinguish countries across groups, individual variables, as expected, differ in their influence within groups. Some variables will not yet be important for low income countries. Others may act via a threshold that a country must reach, but no longer explain income beyond this threshold.

The right side of Appendix B presents income subgroups regressions. We explore the differences in the mean Survey response, the differences in slope, as well as the pattern of statistical significance of each variable, with the caveat that limitations on subgroup sample size and the more limited variation of the dependent variable within versus across subgroups reduce statistical power.

It is notable that for all variables the mean Survey response increases as we compare low and high income countries. This confirms the fact that economic development is associated with improvement across many aspects of the business environment and company behavior. However, there are distinctive differences across income groups in the relative importance and trajectory of improvements of particular variables.

Low-income countries

For low-income countries at the factor-driven stage of development, the ability to move beyond competing solely on cheap labor or natural resources is the essential challenge, as reflected in the regressions. Company attributes such as production process sophistication and presence throughout the value chain have the strongest relationship to GDP per capita. With huge challenges in their surrounding business environment, other dimensions of company operations prove less significant.

Priorities for improving the business environment in low-income countries revealed in the regressions are upgrading weaknesses in the quality of infrastructure (including electricity, communications, and transportation networks) and improving the quality of schools. More complex dimensions of the business environment, such as updating regulatory standards, are not yet priorities at this stage of development.

Middle-income countries

For middle-income countries at the investment-driven stage of development, the key challenge is to improve their productivity in utilizing inputs, on the model of successful countries, which have invested in building up the stock of factor inputs. In the area of company operations, continuing to improve production process sophistication, and increasing the professionalism of management, are the most important corporate factors that distinguish more from less successful middle-income economies. The data also indicate that improving the quality of marketing, investing in staff training, and broadening the export base are also important corporate priorities in middle-income countries.

In terms of the business environment, the data reveal that middle-income countries need to continue to improve public schools while boosting the quality of telecommunication infrastructure and use of the Internet. These were priorities that were already important at the low-income stage. Our results also indicate new challenges in the business environment that were less relevant in the earlier stage: improving university-industry research collaboration, upgrading the quality of research institutions, and strengthening the judicial system become important differentiators of success among middle-income countries. Improving local demand conditions, for example through more stringent environmental and consumer protection laws, are also needed to pressure improvements in product quality at the middle-income level. Strengthening all aspects of cluster development becomes significant at the middle-income level, especially expanding the supplier base, and improving the availability of specialized research and training institutions. Finally, moving to greater levels of competition is essential for middle-income countries: liberalizing tariff and nontariff barriers, strengthening antitrust policy, and opening the market for corporate control.

High-income countries

To succeed as a high-income economy, assimilating quality and efficiency improvements from other locations is no longer sufficient. The hurdle is to move to the innovation-driven stage. Our regressions suggest that achieving high levels of innovation is not only a matter of companies spending more on R&D. It is also closely connected to their ability to transform technological advances into attractive new products and services, using flexible work organizations and the delegation of authority, combined with sophisticated marketing and advanced production processes. The quality of research-related institutions and the ease of collaboration with research institutions are important strengths of the most successful high-income economies.

High-income countries have all achieved strengths in many aspects of the business environment. However, we still find some areas of the business environment that distinguish the most successful high-income countries from their weaker peers, in particular the extent of bureaucratic red tape, quality of corporate governance, flexibility of labor markets, and the existence of any remaining barriers to foreign investment and local competition. Continuing to improve the stringency of regulation and the efficiency of the public sector institutions also remain important for success among high-income countries. Other distinguishing factors in successful high-income countries include the quality of financial markets (especially access to equity

and venture capital), the depth of cluster development (especially the improvement of local suppliers), and the quality of management education and business-related research.

Competitiveness trends in the global economy

Given that we have data for some measures since 1998, it is interesting to examine how the dynamics of competitiveness have changed over time (see Table 2). Between 1998 and 2001, the average responses across all questions (holding the set of questions and the sample of countries stable) increased most strongly in high-income economies, followed by middle- and low-income economies. As difficult economic times began in 2001, average responses from countries in all income groups fell by about the same absolute amount, with low- and middle-income economies falling behind their 1998 absolute response levels. Between 2002 and 2005, average responses rose across all income groups. However, low-income countries have improved the most (both in absolute and relative terms), followed by middle-income and then by high-income countries.

Looking at the entire 1998 to 2005 period, low-income countries narrowed the gap to middle-income countries, except in the area of factor conditions. Middle-income countries also lost ground relative to high-income countries, especially in company operations and strategy. While our data indicate that creating the conditions for a middle-income economy is within reach for many countries, it seems to be much harder to then prepare the ground for a high-income economy.

Ranking competitiveness

To derive an overall Business Competitiveness Index (BCI), we compute subindexes measuring the sophistication of company operations and strategy and the quality of the national business environment. The weighted average of the two subindexes is defined as the BCI. The weights are determined from the coefficients of a multiple regression of the subindexes on GDP per capita, using pooled data from 2002 to 2005 to smooth year-to-year variations. This procedure results in a weight of .8 for national business environment, and .2 for company operations and strategy, similar to last year. This suggests that business environment factors as a group are a greater discriminator of differences in competitiveness across countries than are corporate factors. This is perhaps not surprising, given that companies often operate across multiple locations, facilitating the spread of best practices. Also, there are other mechanisms for the spread of company best practices while business environment conditions are more caught up in local politics.

Table 2: Mean responses over time (stable sample of countries and questions)

	Low-income countries				Middle-income countries				High-income countries			
	1998	2001	2002	2005	1998	2001	2002	2005	1998	2001	2002	2005
I. COMPANY OPERATIONS & STRATEGY												
Breadth of international markets	4.54	3.57	3.42	3.84	4.90	5.41	3.70	4.15	5.33	5.41	5.29	5.49
Capacity for innovation	3.34	3.07	2.82	3.28	3.54	4.86	3.14	3.40	4.98	4.86	4.82	5.03
Control of international distribution	3.64	3.57	3.37	3.84	3.94	4.71	3.77	4.09	4.99	4.71	4.64	4.84
Degree of customer orientation	3.91	4.51	4.03	4.34	4.20	5.54	4.35	4.65	5.08	5.54	5.42	5.56
Extent of marketing	3.46	3.91	3.77	4.19	4.05	5.65	4.27	4.62	4.89	5.65	5.45	5.62
Extent of regional sales	3.76	4.48	4.31	4.47	4.46	5.83	4.63	4.92	5.34	5.83	5.68	5.72
Extent of staff training	3.54	3.70	3.45	3.81	3.74	5.20	3.66	3.82	4.80	5.20	5.08	5.15
Nature of competitive advantage	2.37	2.67	2.52	2.83	2.98	5.16	3.08	3.07	4.90	5.16	4.89	5.15
Prevalence of foreign technology licensing	4.61	5.02	4.85	4.35	4.67	5.29	4.70	4.56	5.08	5.29	5.03	5.21
Production process sophistication	3.41	3.72	2.82	3.17	3.99	5.73	3.53	3.82	5.41	5.73	5.34	5.45
Reliance on professional management	3.65	4.36	4.43	4.66	3.80	5.44	4.46	4.64	4.70	5.44	5.64	5.63
Value chain presence	4.49	3.29	3.06	3.43	4.76	5.17	3.33	3.64	5.42	5.17	5.25	5.45
II. NATIONAL BUSINESS ENVIRONMENT												
A. FACTOR (INPUT) CONDITIONS												
1. Physical Infrastructure												
Overall infrastructure quality	2.95	2.75	3.02	3.06	3.20	5.74	3.63	3.72	4.88	5.74	5.66	5.68
Railroad infrastructure development	3.60	3.54	3.34	3.09	2.60	5.00	2.98	2.94	4.49	5.00	4.85	4.92
Port infrastructure quality	3.15	2.90	2.69	2.87	3.42	5.56	3.60	3.57	5.14	5.56	5.44	5.43
Air transport infrastructure quality	3.90	3.73	3.96	3.86	4.04	5.95	4.39	4.53	5.67	5.95	5.80	5.87
Telephone/fax infrastructure quality	4.57	4.17	4.43	4.84	5.24	6.54	5.48	5.79	6.51	6.54	6.58	6.55
2. Administrative Infrastructure												
Reliability of police services	3.93	3.47	3.24	3.90	3.37	5.79	3.73	3.79	5.57	5.79	5.57	5.50
Judicial independence	4.24	3.60	3.22	3.51	4.02	5.78	3.43	3.38	5.79	5.78	5.50	5.35
Efficiency of legal framework	4.46	4.00	3.19	3.46	4.17	5.75	3.36	3.50	5.53	5.75	5.27	5.17
Extent of bureaucratic red tape	2.93	5.75	4.91	5.27	3.60	6.26	5.37	5.27	4.24	6.26	5.69	5.72
3. Human Resources												
Quality of management schools	3.85	3.91	3.87	4.03	4.17	5.37	4.27	4.46	4.92	5.37	5.20	5.33
Quality of public schools	3.76	2.83	2.65	2.92	3.88	5.65	3.33	3.41	5.11	5.65	5.49	5.40
Quality of math and science education	3.85	3.91	3.87	4.03	4.17	5.37	4.27	4.46	4.92	5.37	5.20	5.33
4. Technology Infrastructure												
Quality of scientific research institutions	3.09	4.21	4.02	3.95	3.46	5.53	3.94	3.88	4.83	5.53	5.14	5.13
University/industry research collaboration	3.12	3.52	3.24	3.06	3.36	4.88	3.33	3.30	4.59	4.88	4.56	4.46
5. Capital Markets												
Financial market sophistication	2.72	3.33	3.40	3.86	3.37	5.37	3.80	4.27	4.81	5.37	5.18	5.57
Venture capital availability	3.49	2.89	2.87	3.37	3.30	4.61	2.75	3.02	4.30	4.61	4.31	4.52
Local equity market access	4.74	5.19	5.08	5.69	4.55	5.95	4.31	4.98	5.67	5.95	5.64	5.91
B. DEMAND CONDITIONS												
Buyer sophistication	3.84	3.99	3.82	4.34	3.93	5.33	3.67	4.09	5.50	5.33	5.31	5.51
C. RELATED AND SUPPORTING INDUSTRIES												
Local supplier quality	3.54	4.15	4.09	4.10	3.95	5.57	4.26	4.55	5.31	5.57	5.55	5.70
Local supplier quantity	4.42	4.94	4.78	4.74	4.71	5.63	4.63	4.98	5.69	5.63	5.45	5.67
D. CONTEXT FOR FIRM STRATEGY AND RIVALRY												
1. Incentives												
Favoritism in decisions of government officials	2.93	2.73	2.62	3.03	3.14	4.35	2.95	2.88	3.88	4.35	4.22	4.17
Efficacy of corporate boards	3.46	3.75	3.63	4.51	3.82	4.73	3.89	4.64	4.44	4.73	4.50	5.25
Intellectual property protection	3.34	2.58	2.78	3.27	3.76	5.52	3.40	3.48	5.49	5.52	5.37	5.37
2. Competition												
Intensity of local competition	4.78	5.02	4.64	4.66	4.88	5.62	4.73	4.97	5.36	5.62	5.30	5.58
Effectiveness of antitrust policy	3.47	3.48	3.55	3.65	3.89	5.34	3.82	4.10	5.00	5.34	5.07	5.36
Prevalence of trade barriers	3.32	4.28	4.61	3.98	4.37	6.18	4.99	4.54	5.69	6.18	6.10	5.38

The correlation between the business environment subindex and the company operation subindex is positive, signifying that improvements in the two dimensions of competitiveness move together. However, when we include an interaction term in the regression on GDP per capita of the business environment and the company operations and strategy subindexes, it proves to be positive and significant. This means that the benefits of a better business environment for prosperity are increasing with the sophistication of local company operations and strategy, and vice versa. Countries that improve both the business environment and company sophistication in tandem reap disproportionate benefits, while countries where there is an imbalance bear disproportionate costs.

Figure 6 plots BCI against 2004 GDP per capita adjusted for purchasing power parity for each country in the sample of 110 countries used in building the model. The regression line is shown, together with bands above and below the regression line that delineates the 95 percent confidence forecast region.[24] Just five countries, Norway, Qatar, India, Malaysia, and Italy fall outside the forecast region. *Differences in BCI account for a remarkable 80 percent of the variation in GDP per capita across a widely disparate group of countries.*

In the regression we allow for a nonlinear relationship between the BCI and GDP per capita. The best fit proves to be the polynomial form, indicating a greater impact on GDP per capita of improvements in BCI for higher-income versus lower-income countries. This finding has a number of possible interpretations: First, we would expect improvements in microeconomic conditions to have positive spillovers, that is, an improvement in one part of the business environment has more impact, if other parts of the business environment are stronger. This interpretation is consistent with the positive interaction between company sophistication and the business environment previously reported. Second, lower-income countries may reap fewer productivity benefits from a given amount of microeconomic improvements, due to weaknesses in macroeconomic, political, legal, and social conditions.

We use our model, along with the data for each country, to calculate a Business Competitiveness Index score for each country, and then rank countries accordingly. The overall BCI rankings for 2005 are shown in Table 1, along with the rankings for the previous years where available. Also included are the separate subindex rankings. Because changes in the ranking can result from very small differences in the absolute value of the BCI score, we also graph the relation between rank and BCI score in Figure 7. BCI scores change smoothly with ranks for most parts of the ranking. However, between rank 25 and 20 at the transition between middle- and high-income countries, the gaps in BCI score become larger. Here, more significant changes in average responses are required for companies to

register changes in rank. Table 3 shows more detailed information on the changes of BCI score by country. The reader may refer to the country profiles section of the *Report* for detailed descriptions of the competitive advantages and disadvantages of each country.

The United States remains in the leading position in fundamental competitiveness, ahead of Finland; the two countries have been in the number one and two spots since 1998. The United States benefited in 2005 from improvements relative to its peers in telecommunication infrastructure, the quality of electricity supply, and, notably, the quality of the educational system. High-income nations improving their rankings the most include Cyprus (up 8 ranks, with all rank changes referring to a constant sample of countries), based especially on improvements in foreign ownership related to EU accession, the Czech Republic (up 7 ranks), which benefited from more effective corporate boards, less corruption and bureaucratic red tape, and better availability of scientists and engineers, Austria (up 6 ranks) based especially on improvements especially in the extent of bureaucratic red tape and several indicators of financial market strengths,[25] and Singapore (up 5 ranks), based especially on improvements in the intensity of local competition and the availability of scientists and engineers.

High-income countries which *fell* in the rankings include Hong Kong, Sweden, and Italy. Hong Kong (down 9 ranks) lost the ground it gained last year, especially due to increasing concerns over favoritism by government officials and growing bureaucracy. Sweden (down 8 ranks) dropped especially due to concerns over judicial independence, and erosion along a number of different measures of educational quality. Italy fell despite improvements in its absolute BCI score, overtaken by the Czech Republic, Cyprus, Hungary, and Thailand, all of which recorded a faster rate of improvement.

Middle-income nations improving their competitiveness ranking include Poland, Argentina, Croatia, Botswana, El Salvador, Hungary, and Bosnia-Herzegovina. Poland jumped by 5 ranks, driven by strong improvements in many areas of business environment quality; most pronounced in the effectiveness of antitrust policy and improving financial market sophistication. The country is now back at its 2001 level when it suffered a decline. Argentina, benefiting especially from improving measures of innovative capacity, and its neighbor Uruguay, with reductions in bureaucracy and improvements in the reliability of police services, rose by 13 and 10 ranks respectively. However, both are still below their 2001–02 levels. Finally, Croatia improved by 12 ranks, regaining the ground lost last year, based on a stronger assessment of the business environment, especially in the areas of fewer foreign ownership restrictions, better reliability of police services, and improved quality of overall infrastructure.

Figure 6: The relationship between business competitiveness and GDP per capita

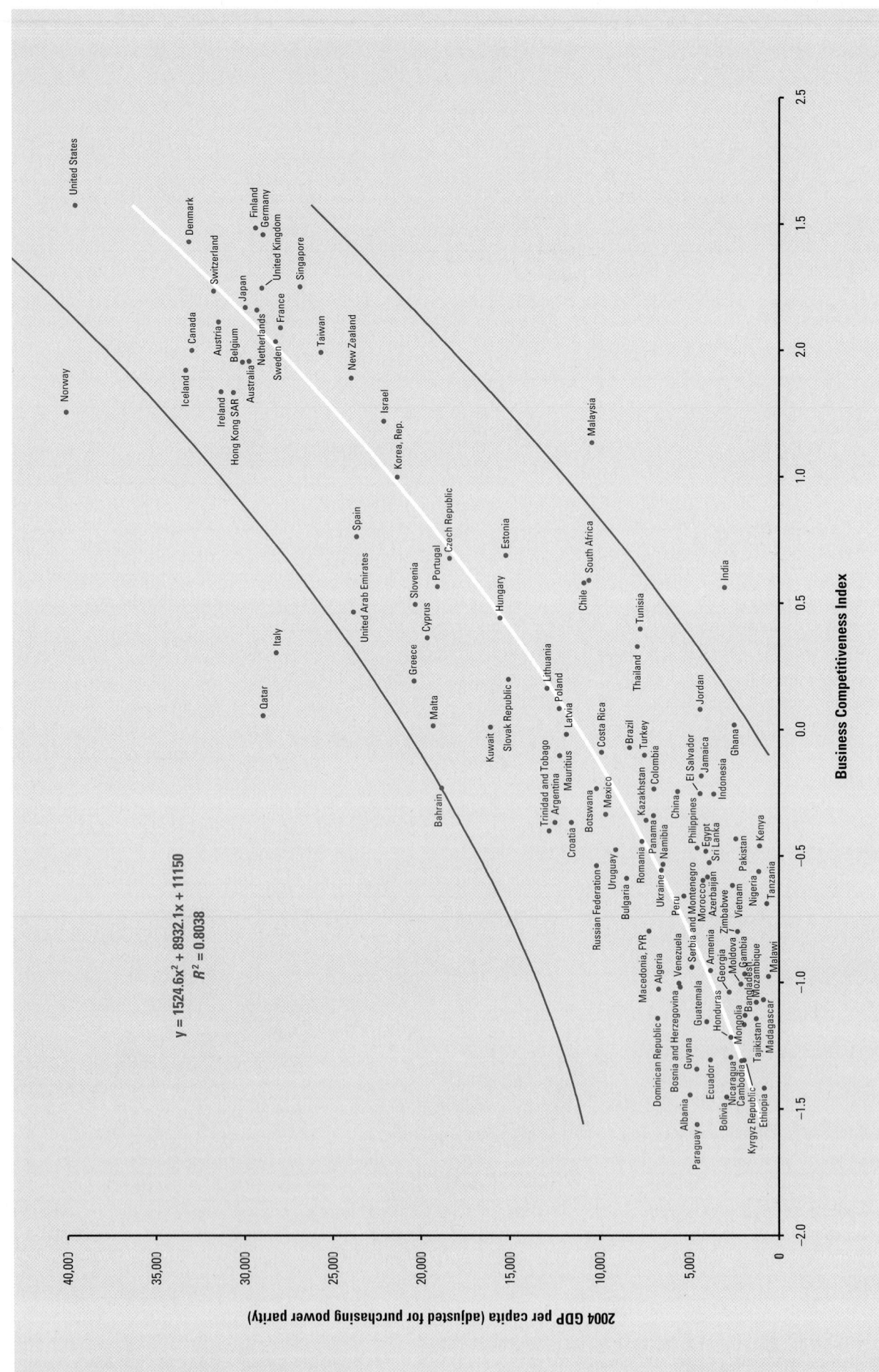

Figure 7: BCI rank and score by country

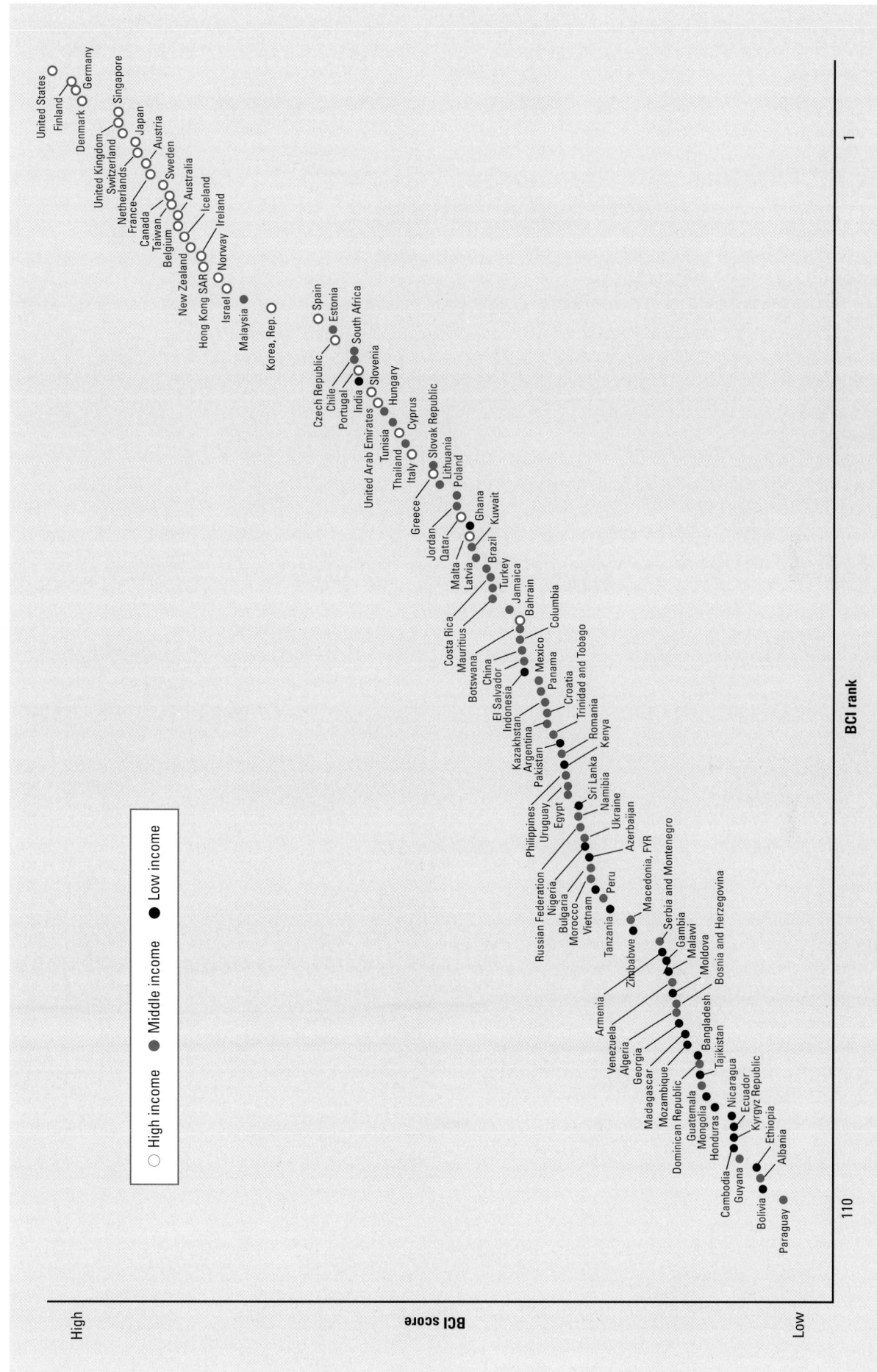

1.2: Building the Microeconomic Foundations of Prosperity

Source: Data exported from SAS program

Table 3: Decomposition of changes in Survey responses and BCI scores

	Change of		Change of		Change of NBE diamond elements				Income group
	BCI rank	BCI score	COS score	NBE score	FC mean score	DC mean score	RSI mean score	CFSR mean score	
ABSOLUTE									
All 110 Countries	**n/a**	**0.132**	**0.026**	**0.106**	**0.054**	**0.015**	**0.013**	**0.024**	
High income	n/a	0.161	0.031	0.130	0.067	0.018	0.012	0.034	
Middle income	n/a	0.092	0.021	0.072	0.036	0.011	0.010	0.015	
Low income	n/a	0.174	0.028	0.145	0.074	0.020	0.022	0.030	
RELATIVE TO INCOME GROUP									
Ghana	19	0.291	0.052	0.238	0.175	0.029	0.022	0.012	Low
Poland	14	0.449	0.038	0.411	0.181	0.039	0.027	0.163	Middle
Argentina	10	0.280	0.048	0.232	0.089	0.040	0.042	0.062	Middle
Botswana	9	0.061	0.009	0.052	0.051	−0.008	−0.013	0.022	Middle
Croatia	9	0.206	0.031	0.175	0.074	0.030	0.003	0.068	Middle
El Salvador	9	0.164	0.024	0.141	0.064	0.031	0.011	0.034	Middle
Tanzania	9	0.245	0.015	0.230	0.110	0.030	0.027	0.061	Low
Cyprus	8	0.215	0.043	0.172	0.042	0.043	0.031	0.056	High
Czech Republic	7	0.285	0.039	0.246	0.091	0.032	0.018	0.104	High
Hungary	7	0.249	0.053	0.195	0.078	0.020	0.007	0.091	Middle
Pakistan	7	0.239	−0.004	0.243	0.130	−0.002	0.013	0.101	Low
Uruguay	7	0.134	0.015	0.119	0.065	−0.001	0.018	0.037	Middle
Austria	6	0.150	0.053	0.097	0.024	0.010	0.008	0.056	High
Bosnia and Herzegovina	5	0.114	0.040	0.074	0.048	−0.014	−0.005	0.046	Middle
Singapore	5	0.103	0.005	0.098	0.035	0.003	0.018	0.042	High
Colombia	4	0.127	0.028	0.099	0.038	0.010	−0.008	0.059	Middle
Malta	4	−0.007	−0.013	0.006	−0.016	0.003	0.002	0.017	High
Mozambique	4	0.130	0.028	0.103	0.021	0.028	0.021	0.033	Low
Denmark	3	0.027	0.031	−0.004	−0.021	0.009	0.014	−0.007	High
Ireland	3	0.232	0.056	0.176	0.079	0.008	0.005	0.084	High
Nicaragua	3	0.033	0.021	0.012	0.017	−0.007	0.002	0.000	Low
Taiwan	3	0.070	0.010	0.060	0.060	0.015	−0.010	−0.005	High
Bangladesh	2	0.106	0.043	0.063	0.046	0.008	0.016	−0.006	Low
Canada	2	0.007	−0.008	0.015	0.019	0.004	0.000	−0.008	High
Georgia	2	0.038	−0.001	0.039	−0.005	0.003	−0.005	0.045	Low
Iceland	2	−0.051	0.026	−0.076	−0.014	0.003	−0.022	−0.044	High
Jamaica	2	0.047	0.005	0.042	0.022	−0.015	−0.015	0.049	Middle
Latvia	2	0.050	0.005	0.045	0.024	0.011	−0.011	0.021	Middle
Mauritius	2	0.122	0.039	0.083	0.017	0.013	0.023	0.029	Middle
Philippines	2	0.168	0.040	0.128	0.025	0.027	0.040	0.035	Middle
Portugal	2	0.126	0.004	0.122	0.074	0.018	−0.006	0.035	High
Turkey	2	0.195	0.036	0.159	0.077	0.030	0.011	0.040	Middle
Venezuela	2	−0.022	−0.023	0.001	−0.028	0.024	−0.004	0.009	Middle
Algeria	1	−0.086	−0.052	−0.033	−0.008	0.004	0.002	−0.032	Middle
Bolivia	1	−0.105	−0.035	−0.069	−0.032	−0.009	−0.004	−0.024	Low
Estonia	1	−0.009	−0.001	−0.007	−0.009	−0.015	0.009	0.008	Middle
France	1	0.031	−0.010	0.042	−0.011	0.003	0.013	0.037	High
Honduras	1	0.085	0.009	0.076	0.054	0.004	0.009	0.008	Low
Macedonia, FYR	1	−0.006	−0.019	0.013	0.071	−0.023	0.005	−0.039	Middle
Panama	1	0.025	0.106	−0.081	−0.038	−0.013	0.015	−0.045	Middle
Serbia and Montenegro	1	−0.071	−0.067	−0.003	−0.056	0.032	0.015	0.006	Middle
Spain	1	0.057	0.020	0.037	0.032	0.013	0.000	−0.008	High
Vietnam	1	0.064	−0.005	0.069	0.052	0.013	0.012	−0.008	Low
Bulgaria	0	0.032	0.006	0.026	0.046	0.002	0.002	−0.024	Middle
Ethiopia	0	−0.134	−0.012	−0.122	−0.058	−0.023	−0.027	−0.015	Low
Finland	0	−0.104	−0.049	−0.055	−0.013	−0.022	−0.005	−0.015	High
Germany	0	−0.004	−0.017	0.013	0.018	−0.016	−0.001	0.011	High
Greece	0	−0.049	0.000	−0.050	−0.030	−0.007	−0.017	0.004	High
Japan	0	−0.048	−0.012	−0.036	0.003	−0.021	0.008	−0.027	High
Korea, Rep.	0	0.274	0.040	0.234	0.136	0.014	0.007	0.077	High
Malaysia	0	0.288	0.072	0.216	0.115	0.032	0.008	0.061	Middle
Netherlands	0	−0.121	−0.047	−0.073	−0.039	−0.006	−0.004	−0.025	High
New Zealand	0	−0.066	−0.007	−0.058	−0.051	0.004	−0.002	−0.010	High
Slovak Republic	0	0.009	−0.019	0.028	−0.009	0.013	−0.006	0.030	Middle
Thailand	0	0.173	0.010	0.164	0.081	0.021	−0.003	0.065	Middle
United Kingdom	0	−0.093	−0.005	−0.089	−0.024	−0.020	−0.001	−0.044	High

(cont'd)

Table 3: Decomposition of changes in Survey responses and BCI scores *(cont'd.)*

	Change of		Change of		Change of NBE diamond elements				
	BCI rank	BCI score	COS score	NBE score	FC mean score	DC mean score	RSI mean score	CFSR mean score	Income group
RELATIVE TO INCOME GROUP *(cont'd.)*									
United States	0	0.030	0.011	0.020	0.028	0.003	−0.005	−0.007	High
Chile	−1	0.101	0.026	0.076	0.051	0.013	0.017	−0.005	Middle
Costa Rica	−1	−0.058	0.012	−0.070	−0.042	0.005	−0.001	−0.031	Middle
Israel	−1	0.041	0.015	0.026	0.022	0.023	−0.001	−0.019	High
Jordan	−1	−0.058	−0.002	−0.057	−0.023	−0.015	−0.009	−0.009	Middle
Malawi	−1	−0.175	−0.020	−0.156	−0.100	−0.033	−0.006	−0.017	Low
Norway	−1	−0.202	0.012	−0.214	−0.130	−0.018	0.004	−0.070	High
Zimbabwe	−1	−0.026	0.002	−0.028	−0.007	0.028	−0.038	−0.011	Low
Australia	−2	−0.155	−0.051	−0.104	−0.043	−0.031	−0.008	−0.022	High
Belgium	−2	−0.077	−0.011	−0.066	0.008	−0.023	−0.016	−0.034	High
India	−2	0.100	0.029	0.072	0.020	0.016	−0.011	0.047	Low
Kenya	−2	−0.140	−0.016	−0.125	−0.090	0.019	0.009	−0.062	Low
Peru	−2	0.067	0.050	0.018	−0.018	0.028	−0.005	0.013	Middle
Slovenia	−2	−0.004	0.004	−0.008	−0.021	−0.003	0.013	0.003	High
Sri Lanka	−2	−0.110	−0.013	−0.097	−0.044	−0.008	0.026	−0.071	Low
Switzerland	−2	−0.152	−0.046	−0.106	0.010	−0.017	−0.016	−0.082	High
Madagascar	−3	−0.175	−0.042	−0.134	−0.053	−0.027	−0.022	−0.031	Low
Mexico	−3	−0.052	−0.021	−0.031	0.003	0.006	−0.011	−0.029	Middle
Paraguay	−3	−0.214	−0.038	−0.177	−0.091	−0.016	−0.015	−0.055	Middle
South Africa	−3	−0.075	−0.003	−0.072	−0.025	−0.007	−0.004	−0.037	Middle
Trinidad and Tobago	−3	−0.056	−0.026	−0.031	−0.044	−0.007	0.008	0.012	Middle
Tunisia	−3	−0.051	−0.001	−0.050	−0.014	−0.010	−0.023	−0.004	Middle
Ecuador	−4	−0.131	0.007	−0.138	−0.055	−0.012	−0.022	−0.049	Low
Italy	−4	0.077	0.017	0.059	0.004	0.029	−0.012	0.039	High
Ukraine	−4	0.029	−0.008	0.037	0.036	0.004	−0.025	0.022	Middle
Lithuania	−5	−0.097	−0.015	−0.082	−0.021	−0.016	−0.008	−0.037	Middle
China	−8	−0.191	−0.045	−0.146	−0.062	−0.020	−0.017	−0.048	Middle
Guatemala	−8	−0.196	−0.037	−0.159	−0.063	−0.016	−0.009	−0.070	Middle
Romania	−8	−0.152	−0.021	−0.131	−0.059	−0.028	−0.004	−0.040	Middle
Sweden	−8	−0.347	−0.065	−0.282	−0.178	−0.035	−0.011	−0.059	High
Brazil	−9	−0.218	−0.023	−0.196	−0.117	−0.015	−0.016	−0.047	Middle
Hong Kong SAR	−9	−0.244	−0.045	−0.199	−0.094	−0.021	−0.005	−0.079	High
Russian Federation	−9	−0.146	−0.047	−0.100	−0.032	−0.016	−0.018	−0.033	Middle
Dominican Republic	−12	−0.367	−0.063	−0.305	−0.122	−0.048	−0.024	−0.111	Middle
Indonesia	−13	−0.335	−0.059	−0.276	−0.181	−0.059	−0.023	−0.013	Low
Namibia	−18	−0.347	−0.035	−0.312	−0.119	−0.048	0.007	−0.152	Middle
Morocco	−27	−0.618	−0.126	−0.492	−0.257	−0.083	−0.016	−0.135	Middle

Note: FC = Factor conditions, DC = Demand conditions, RSI = Related and supporting industries, CFSR = Context for firm strategy and rivalry

Middle-income countries falling in competitiveness rank include Morocco, Namibia, the Dominican Republic, Russia, Brazil, Romania, and China. Morocco registered a large drop (down 29 ranks), dragged down by lower assessments especially in bureaucracy, foreign ownership restrictions, and corruption. Namibia dropped by 19 ranks after having registered a stable ranking since entering the GCR in 2002, driven especially by lower assessments of bureaucracy, favoritism of government officials, and corruption. The Dominican Republic (down 11 places) continues its downward trend.

Among low-income countries, Ghana, Tanzania, and Pakistan made the largest improvements. Ghana benefited especially from improved public schools and less corruption, with Tanzania and Pakistan both reporting better labor-employer relations.

Gambia and Indonesia experienced the largest drops among low-income countries. Indonesia lost almost all the ground gained last year, when a change in government had created high expectations about imminent improvements. A sharply lower assessment of physical infrastructure and financial markets were key reasons for the drop.

Company competitiveness versus the quality of the business environment

To gain deeper insight into the competitive position of countries, normalized subindexes of company sophistication and the quality of the microeconomic business environment are plotted against each other in Figure 8. Countries near the 45-degree line enjoy the positive interaction of the two aspects of competitiveness, as noted previously. Countries lying above the line are those in which company sophistication is more advanced than the state of their business environment. Those below the line are countries whose business environment is more advanced than their companies.

Countries whose company development is ahead of the business environment include high-income economies such as Japan, Korea, Italy, Germany, and Sweden, middle-income countries such as the Philippines, Panama, Brazil, and Costa Rica, and low-income countries such as the Kyrgyz Republic, Kenya, and Ecuador. Significant changes in public policy are necessary in these countries to improve the platform for productivity. Unless the business environment improves, companies will be prone to *move*

operations or make new investments outside the country. Japan remains the advanced economy with the greatest gap between the business environment and the sophistication of its companies. The consequences of this weakness for Japan's economic growth have been severe, as Japanese corporate investment has fled the country.[26]

Countries whose business environment ranks ahead of current company sophistication include high-income countries Portugal, Qatar, and Australia, middle-income countries Algeria, Serbia, Tunisia, Botswana, Kuwait, and Estonia, and low-income countries Tanzania, Bolivia, Ethiopia, and Ghana. In these countries, many leading companies still rely on natural resource extraction (e.g., Qatar, Australia), OEM production, or local subsidiaries of foreign multinationals who compete heavily on the basis of low labor costs (e.g., Tunisia, Cyprus, and Portugal). In some countries, such as Estonia and Ghana, part of the gap results from rapid improvements in the business environment that have not yet been harnessed by companies, who remain focused on traditional ways of competing. Efforts to improve entrepreneurship, strategic thinking, managerial practice, and business education are high priorities in such countries.

Country overperformance and underperformance

We can gain further insights into the trajectory and sustainability of a country's prosperity by examining its level of microeconomic (business) competitiveness relative to its current level of per capita income. Table 4 lists countries in order of the absolute gap between *actual* GDP per capita and the *expected* GDP given microeconomic competitiveness. Countries where the level of actual GDP per capita is above the expected level are termed *overperformers*, countries below the expected level *underperformers*.

Overperformance is often a danger sign, because it indicates that the level of prosperity enjoyed in a country is not sustainable given its microeconomic fundamentals. For example, current prosperity can be based on speculative inflows of foreign capital or foreign aid.

Underperformance can be transitory, for example if improvements in the business environment are not yet fully reflected in company operations. However, underperformance can also be a sign of sustained structural challenges a country is facing in realizing its potential prosperity, due to political instability or an unfortunate location.

Figure 8: The relative development of companies and the microeconomic business environment

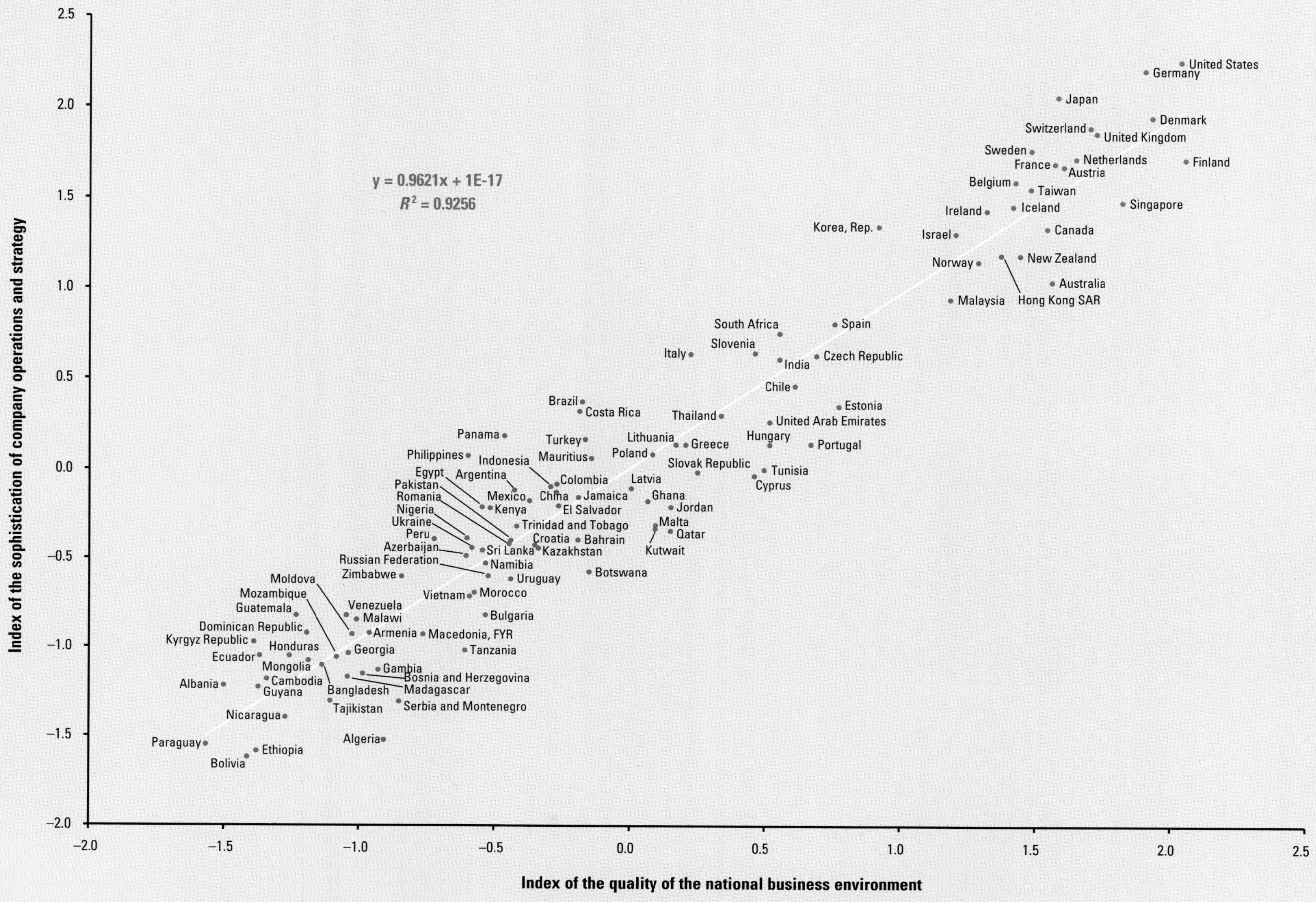

$y = 0.9621x + 1E-17$
$R^2 = 0.9256$

Index of the sophistication of company operations and strategy

Index of the quality of the national business environment

Table 4: Current GDP per capita relative to competitiveness

	High-income countries	Middle-income countries	Low-income countries
	UNDERPERFORMERS		
Competitiveness (measured by BCI) would support higher per capita income	Germany Finland Singapore New Zealand United Kingdom Taiwan Israel	Malaysia Jordan Tunisia South Africa Thailand Chile Jamaica El Salvador China Egypt Estonia Turkey Philippines Brazil Colombia Morocco	India Ghana Kenya Nigeria Indonesia Pakistan Tanzania Vietnam Malawi Sri Lanka Zimbabwe Azerbaijan Madagascar Mozambique Gambia Tajikistan Moldova
	NEUTRAL		
Competitiveness (measured by BCI) and per capita income are balanced	France Denmark Netherlands Japan Korea, Rep. Sweden Switzerland Czech Republic Austria	Panama Kazakhstan Peru Costa Rica Namibia Ukraine Romania Hungary Lithuania Poland Serbia and Montenegro Latvia Botswana Guatemala Mexico	Bangladesh Mongolia Georgia Ethiopia Armenia Kyrgyz Republic Cambodia Honduras Nicaragua
	OVERPERFORMERS		
Per capita income is high relative to competitiveness (measured by BCI)	Australia Portugal Belgium United States Slovenia Spain Hong Kong SAR Canada Cyprus Ireland Iceland Greece Malta United Arab Emirates Bahrain Italy Norway Qatar	Venezuela Uruguay Bosnia and Herzegovina Mauritius Bulgaria Slovak Republic Macedonia, FYR Guyana Algeria Russian Federation Croatia Albania Paraguay Dominican Republic Argentina Kuwait Trinidad and Tobago	Bolivia Ecuador

Political context

Our conceptual framework suggests that a country's political, governmental, and social context influences potential competitiveness. As with last year, we used a data set by Kaufmann et al. (2005) to explore this relationship. We find that Kaufmann's measures for "voice and accountability" and "government effectiveness" are significant in explaining the gap between actual and predicted GDP per capita in our model.[27] Table 5 shows the result of a joint regression of BCI score and the control variables on GDP per capita. The countries that benefit most from sound political conditions and governance are Switzerland, Denmark, Finland, New Zealand, the Netherlands, and Norway. Countries that suffer most from bad governance in terms of absolute GDP per capita reduction are Zimbabwe, Ethiopia, the Kyrgyz Republic, Nigeria, and Cambodia.

Location

A country's geographic location can affect its ability to achieve prosperity given its level of competitiveness. We examine two aspects of location: the neighborhood of a country—defined as neighbors with land border, a direct tunnel or bridge connection, and nearby countries for island nations—and its proximity to ocean transportation. Prosperous neighbors offer opportunities for trade and investment, and should enhance the prosperity of a given level of competitiveness. Access to ocean transport can enable the more effective integration of companies into global value chains, better leveraging competitiveness into trade and investment as well.

We find that the average income of neighboring countries is positive and significant in explaining the gap between predicted and actual GDP per capita. This is consistent with the interpretation that a good neighborhood enhances the prosperity resulting from a given level of competitiveness. We also find that the share of a country's population within 100 km of an ocean or rivers accessible from an ocean is positive and significant in explaining the gap between actual and predicted GDP per capita.[28] Countries that benefit most in terms of GDP per capita from geographic location are the Dominican Republic (because of its proximity to the United States), Canada, Mexico, Sweden, and Ireland (see Table 5). Countries that are most negatively affected by location in our regressions are Malawi, Ethiopia, Kenya, Tanzania, Nigeria, and Ghana.

Our competitiveness framework also suggests that there could be geographic spillovers of competitiveness across neighboring countries. The data confirm that the competitiveness of countries and their neighbors, as measured by BCI, is significantly correlated. The average BCI score of all neighbors explains about 29 percent of the cross-country variation in BCI. And a higher average BCI value of all neighbors translates into a 66 percent higher country BCI.

Natural resource endowments

Natural resources have played a prominent role in thinking about economic development. In last year's *Global Competitiveness Report* we discussed in more detail the often negative effect of natural resources on the ability to achieve fundamental microeconomic competitiveness.

As long as the natural resources are not exhausted and commodity price levels are maintained at high enough levels, natural resource exports have a direct positive effect on prosperity independent of competitiveness. Not surprisingly, we find oil exporters Norway and Kuwait benefiting most from natural resource exports in absolute terms, while Bangladesh, Gambia, and Pakistan benefit the least (see Table 5). As shown in Figure 9, looking at the share of GDP per capita accounted for by natural resource, Botswana, Nigeria, Kazakhstan, Algeria, Kuwait, Azerbaijan, and Venezuela are the leading countries (see Figure 8). Norway and Kuwait register a GDP per capita benefit significantly above the direct per capita value of the natural resource exports themselves, while the benefit for Kazakhstan and Botswana register a multiplier of their per capita natural resource exports of less than one. This is consistent with the hypothesis that a higher level of overall competitiveness enables an economy to derive more benefits from a given amount of natural resources.

Unexplained prosperity gaps

Controlling for political and governance conditions, geographic location, and natural resource endowments, competitiveness (BCI) explains more than 90 percent of the variation in GDP per capita across countries. There remains an unexplained residual between actual and predicted GDP per capita, which tends to be higher in absolute terms for high-income countries, but higher relative to GDP for low-income countries.

We find Italy, Hong Kong, the United States, and Argentina among the countries that register the highest positive residual in absolute terms, reflecting a GDP per capita above what our model suggests. We can only speculate about the reasons. For Italy, the current pessimism in the business community might be leading to an overly negative view of the business environment. Hong Kong could be benefiting from its unique position as port of access into China. The United States might reap benefits from its size and entrepreneurial culture. Argentina's position could be explained in either of two ways: continued pessimism in the business community in the aftermath of the economic meltdown, or a level of prosperity that is unsustainable in the long run, given the country's level of competitiveness. India, New Zealand, and Finland are among the countries that register the greatest absolute

Table 5: Effects on over- and underperformance

Country	GDP per capita explained by					Rank				
	Intercept and Quadratic form of BCI	Location	Governance	Natural resources	Unexplained residuals	Intercept and Quadratic form of BCI	Location	Governance	Natural resources	Unexplained residuals
United States	$22,222	$4,263	$5,998	$303	$6,712	1	23	11	38	4
Finland	$21,203	$3,953	$7,023	$791	−$3,664	2	28	3	18	93
Germany	$20,917	$5,272	$5,223	$369	−$2,892	3	13	16	34	87
Denmark	$20,596	$5,536	$7,364	$2,700	−$3,107	4	6	2	6	90
Singapore	$18,686	$1,900	$5,229	$426	$558	5	61	15	32	41
United Kingdom	$18,641	$5,393	$6,339	$857	−$2,261	6	10	10	16	81
Switzerland	$18,509	$4,810	$7,466	$302	$603	7	18	1	39	40
Japan	$17,855	$4,235	$4,262	$20	$3,535	8	24	20	90	9
Netherlands	$17,741	$5,439	$6,865	$2,216	−$3,009	9	9	5	9	89
Austria	$17,286	$5,016	$5,957	$693	$2,454	10	16	13	21	15
France	$17,057	$5,247	$5,126	$535	−$51	11	14	17	26	49
Sweden	$16,520	$5,981	$6,714	$799	−$1,809	12	4	7	17	73
Canada	$16,174	$6,715	$6,617	$3,018	$397	13	2	9	5	44
Australia	$15,773	$2,234	$6,620	$2,637	$2,418	14	44	8	7	16
Belgium	$15,743	$5,390	$5,975	$4,274	−$1,320	15	11	12	3	69
New Zealand	$15,151	$5,529	$6,957	$2,203	−$5,916	16	8	4	10	98
Ireland	$14,681	$5,708	$5,353	$1,294	$4,227	17	5	14	13	7
Hong Kong SAR	$14,638	$1,883	$3,871	$25	$10,141	18	62	24	85	2
Norway	$13,977	$4,171	$6,848	$14,202	$808	19	26	6	1	34
Israel	$13,654	$1,660	$2,991	$3,106	$666	20	71	31	4	36
Malaysia	$12,942	$2,311	$1,883	$742	−$7,455	21	42	39	19	100
Korea, Rep.	$11,852	$5,533	$3,292	$25	$605	22	7	25	86	38
Spain	$10,129	$4,751	$4,716	$591	$3,440	23	19	18	25	10
Estonia	$9,618	$3,003	$3,940	$685	−$2,029	24	34	23	22	76
Czech Republic	$9,539	$4,963	$2,937	$294	$625	25	17	33	40	37
South Africa	$8,979	$1,208	$2,966	$259	−$2,809	26	88	32	43	84
Chile	$8,917	$2,057	$4,558	$632	−$5,295	27	55	19	23	97
Portugal	$8,825	$4,526	$4,020	$166	$1,500	28	22	21	55	22
India	$8,803	$1,201	$277	$22	−$7,274	29	89	50	89	99
Slovenia	$8,399	$5,237	$3,998	$202	$2,469	30	15	22	47	13
Hungary	$8,086	$4,189	$3,236	$347	−$312	31	25	26	36	52
Tunisia	$7,833	$2,024	−$163	$102	−$2,065	32	56	54	63	77
Thailand	$7,444	$1,836	$1,245	$173	−$2,797	33	65	43	53	83
Italy	$7,313	$5,287	$2,858	$208	$12,506	34	12	34	46	1
Slovak Republic	$6,775	$3,799	$3,129	$194	$1,169	35	29	27	50	28
Greece	$6,740	$2,137	$3,035	$252	$8,198	36	51	28	44	3
Lithuania	$6,603	$2,511	$3,022	$334	$449	37	38	29	37	43
Poland	$6,229	$4,668	$2,690	$156	−$1,498	38	21	37	57	71
Jordan	$6,217	$2,499	−$386	$65	−$4,012	39	39	58	73	94
Ghana	$5,940	$653	$130	$14	−$4,262	40	95	52	93	95
Kuwait	$5,906	$2,912	$659	$6,736	−$148	41	35	46	2	50
Latvia	$5,790	$2,064	$2,768	$619	$604	42	54	35	24	39
Brazil	$5,570	$1,620	$518	$171	$449	43	72	48	54	42
Costa Rica	$5,498	$1,929	$2,711	$478	−$729	44	59	36	29	62
Turkey	$5,451	$2,571	−$183	$77	−$414	45	37	56	68	56
Jamaica	$5,143	$1,261	$1,058	$486	−$3,622	46	87	44	28	92
Botswana	$4,971	$1,567	$3,003	$2,252	−$1,624	47	77	30	8	72
Colombia	$4,965	$1,432	−$1,082	$198	$1,445	48	82	67	48	23
China	$4,930	$2,172	−$1,862	$23	$379	49	48	78	88	45
El Salvador	$4,903	$1,590	−$170	$11	−$1,955	50	74	55	94	75
Indonesia	$4,893	$4,711	−$1,473	$143	−$4,652	51	20	71	58	96
Mexico	$4,640	$6,303	$449	$369	−$2,095	52	3	49	35	79
Panama	$4,624	$2,156	$770	$123	−$676	53	50	45	60	61
Kazakhstan	$4,565	$1,035	−$3,185	$1,001	$4,003	54	92	94	15	8
Croatia	$4,541	$3,218	$1,404	$187	$2,217	55	33	41	51	17
Argentina	$4,541	$1,610	−$117	$428	$6,006	56	73	53	31	5
Trinidad and Tobago	$4,447	$1,874	$1,806	$1,884	$2,782	57	63	40	11	12
Pakistan	$4,357	$865	−$3,179	$5	$356	58	93	93	98	46
Romania	$4,332	$2,158	$137	$76	$939	59	49	51	69	32
Kenya	$4,282	$299	−$2,416	$29	−$1,118	60	98	85	81	68
Philippines	$4,258	$3,254	−$525	$20	−$2,446	61	32	61	91	82
Uruguay	$4,242	$2,214	$2,631	$446	−$425	62	45	38	30	57

(cont'd)

Table 5: Effects on over- and underperformance *(cont'd.)*

Country	GDP per capita explained by					Rank				
	Intercept and Quadratic form of BCI	Location	Governance	Natural resources	Unexplained residuals	Intercept and Quadratic form of BCI	Location	Governance	Natural resources	Unexplained residuals
Egypt	$4,223	$3,688	−$1,917	$28	−$1,950	63	31	79	83	74
Sri Lanka	$4,112	$1,475	−$870	$42	−$877	64	80	65	77	65
Namibia	$4,099	$1,531	$1,346	$278	−$804	65	79	42	42	64
Russian Federation	$4,086	$1,853	−$1,623	$716	$5,148	66	64	74	20	6
Ukraine	$4,044	$2,425	−$2,467	$95	$2,457	67	40	86	65	14
Nigeria	$4,033	$614	−$3,349	$290	−$467	68	96	97	41	58
Azerbaijan	$3,984	$1,362	−$3,286	$397	$1,510	69	84	95	33	21
Bulgaria	$3,972	$2,375	$609	$120	$1,425	70	41	47	62	24
Morocco	$3,952	$4,044	−$832	$45	−$2,984	71	27	64	76	88
Vietnam	$3,911	$1,788	−$2,872	$90	−$348	72	67	90	67	53
Peru	$3,827	$1,826	−$1,449	$121	$974	73	66	70	61	31
Tanzania	$3,772	$340	−$1,373	$19	−$2,085	74	97	69	92	78
Macedonia, FYR	$3,594	$2,769	−$436	$127	$1,183	75	36	59	59	27
Zimbabwe	$3,591	$1,542	−$4,928	$98	$2,006	76	78	100	64	18
Paraguay	$3,507	$1,946	−$2,890	$229	$1,761	77	58	91	45	19
Serbia and Montenegro	$3,420	$2,295	−$339	$50	−$569	78	43	57	75	60
Armenia	$3,408	$1,130	−$1,729	$180	$816	79	90	77	52	33
Gambia	$3,396	$1,300	−$1,993	$2	−$803	80	86	80	99	63
Bolivia	$3,394	$1,382	−$1,528	$159	−$505	81	83	73	56	59
Albania	$3,388	$3,716	−$824	$24	−$1,367	82	30	63	87	70
Malawi	$3,388	$132	−$2,637	$40	−$353	83	100	88	78	54
Venezuela	$3,368	$2,090	−$2,943	$1,357	$1,699	84	53	92	12	20
Ethiopia	$3,367	$275	−$3,840	$6	$1,007	85	99	99	95	30
Moldova	$3,365	$2,108	−$2,404	$70	−$1,020	86	52	84	72	66
Bosnia and Herzegovina	$3,357	$2,191	−$1,491	$72	$1,375	87	46	72	70	25
Algeria	$3,351	$1,710	−$2,362	$1,005	$3,018	88	70	82	14	11
Georgia	$3,344	$1,717	−$2,392	$32	$74	89	69	83	79	48
Madagascar	$3,328	$1,575	−$937	$28	−$3,139	90	75	66	82	91
Mozambique	$3,323	$1,907	−$1,117	$6	−$2,871	91	60	68	97	86
Cambodia	$3,309	$1,729	−$3,320	$6	$351	92	68	96	96	47
Kyrgyz Republic	$3,308	$860	−$3,459	$30	$1,194	93	94	98	80	26
Ecuador	$3,308	$1,568	−$2,306	$507	$742	94	76	81	27	35
Nicaragua	$3,304	$1,958	−$1,624	$64	−$1,026	95	57	75	74	67
Bangladesh	$3,303	$1,461	−$2,683	$1	−$207	96	81	89	100	51
Dominican Republic	$3,300	$7,031	−$733	$25	−$2,863	97	1	62	84	85
Guatemala	$3,297	$2,188	−$2,630	$93	$1,060	98	47	87	66	29
Mongolia	$3,295	$1,038	−$484	$195	−$2,127	99	91	60	49	80
Honduras	$3,292	$1,337	−$1,662	$70	−$355	100	85	76	71	55

Figure 9: Natural resource exports: Share of GDP vs. GDP per capita, (PPP adjusted)

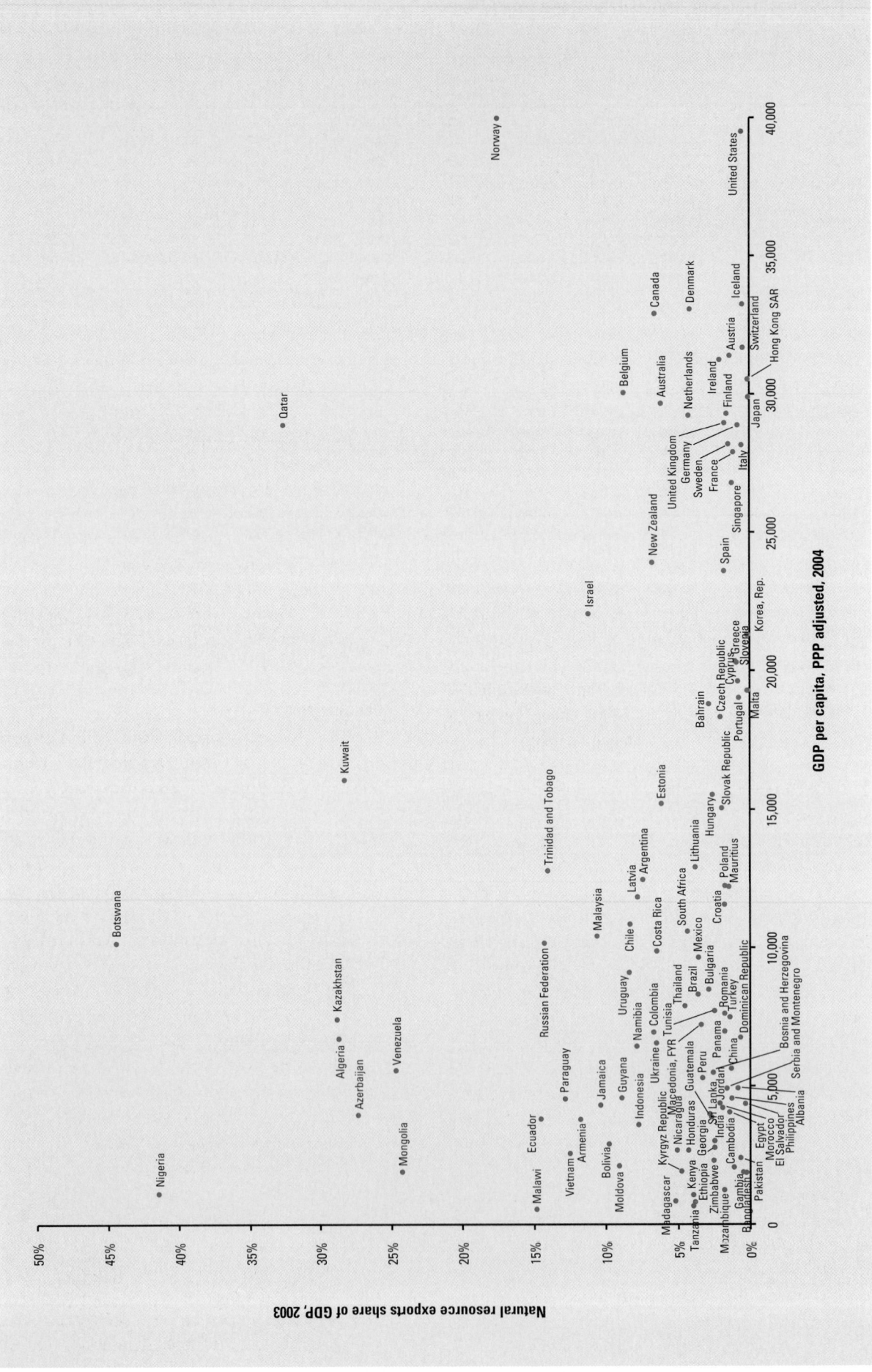

Note: Unprocessed only

gaps between actual GDP per capita and what our model suggests they could attain. For India, this might reflect the large regional heterogeneity of the country. Our Survey probably mirrors business conditions in the more prosperous regions of the country. For New Zealand, sheer distance from other advanced economies might play a role. Finland could suffer from the effects of inefficient labor market regulations[29] and a tax system that provides few incentives for entrepreneurship and innovation, so that Finland's potential is unfulfilled (see data table 6.11 in part 4.3 of this *Report*).

The link between microeconomic competitiveness and prosperity growth

If microeconomic capabilities are fundamental to prosperity, we should see a causal link between the two. To explore this, we examined whether countries that are improving or worsening their competitiveness ranking register corresponding trends in growth of GDP per capita. Changes in BCI rank should affect growth in GDP per capita as per capita income responds up or down to a new sustainable level. While macroeconomic adjustments and other shocks may also affect per capita income growth for periods of time, the relationship between shifts in BCI ranking and prosperity growth over the medium term provides a tentative indication of causality in the relationship between BCI and prosperity.

Regressing country GDP per capita growth between 1998 and 2004 on country BCI rank changes between 1999 and 2005, we find a positive and statistically significant relationship. About 17 percent of the total variation in the growth in GDP per capita across countries is explained by changes in BCI rank. The relationship is highly significant statistically. The coefficient of the relationship implies that an increase of 10 BCI ranks over the five-year time period is associated with a 1.6 percent higher growth rate in GDP per capita. This relationship has proved stable and significant each year that we have been calculating it. In this relationship, Zimbabwe falls outside the 95 percent significance interval around the main regression line. Zimbabwe's GDP per capita growth has dropped even more than predicted, not surprising given the political turmoil in this country.[30] Other countries that have grown GDP per capita much less than predicted by their improvement in BCI rank are Colombia, Venezuela, and Argentina, which have all suffered either political or macroeconomic crises in the period. The Ukraine, Russia, and China are on the other extreme, registering GDP per capita growth rates significantly ahead of what would be expected, given their BCI results over time. Positive changes in the macroeconomic and political context seem to have provided an additional boost to growth for these countries.

Clusters and export performance

This year, we report for the first time data from an analysis of international goods export data by cluster, and relate it to our data from the BCI Survey. The International Cluster Competitiveness Project[31] data set has been created from UNCTAD export data by industry. Using methodology drawn from earlier research, each industry code has been allocated to a particular subcluster and cluster. We have then calculated the overall share of goods exports by a country that occurred in clusters or subclusters in which the country had a revealed comparative advantage or export share higher than the country's average world export share. The BCI indicators on cluster development were expressed as a single measure, calculated as the first principal component of the Survey responses to the four cluster-related questions.

Table 6 shows the BCI Cluster Rank as well as the share of exports in clusters and subclusters in which a country has achieved a world market share above its average goods export market share. There is clear relationship between strong cluster conditions as registered in the BCI, and a high proportion of exports for strong clusters. Japan, Germany, and the United States particularly stand out, but the United Kingdom, France, Finland, Switzerland, Korea, and Italy are also countries where strong cluster conditions are consistent with exports concentrated in strong clusters.

69

Conclusions

National prosperity is strongly affected by competitiveness, which is defined by the productivity with which a nation utilizes its human, capital, and natural resources. Competitiveness is rooted in a nation's microeconomic fundamentals, manifested in the sophistication of its companies, and in the quality of its microeconomic business environment.

Stable institutions, sound macroeconomic policies, market opening, and privatization have long been considered the cornerstones for economic development. The results of this and previous years suggest that they are necessary but not sufficient. More than 80 percent of the variation of GDP per capita across countries is accounted for by microeconomic fundamentals. Other factors, including political governance, geography, natural resource deposits, also play a role and explain why a country's prosperity can deviate, sometimes for long time periods, from the level supported by its microeconomic fundamentals. However, the impact of these other factors is much less significant.

Without micro reforms, growth in GDP induced by sound macro policies, market opening, and privatization will be unsustainable or will not translate into improvements in GDP per capita. Conversely, appropriate micro reforms, which boost productivity and productivity growth, can greatly ease the challenge of meeting government's

Table 6: Goods export cluster performance (excluding natural resources)

Country	Cluster development		Share of goods exports								
			in clusters, with country's market share				in subclusters, with market share				
	BCI score	BCI rank	> overall market share	> overall market share +2.5%	> overall market share +5%	> overall market share +10%	> overall market share	> overall market share +2.5%	> overall market share +5%	> overall market share +10%	Year of data used
Japan	2.55	1	76.65%	67.22%	52.25%	8.88%	77.77%	66.45%	57.38%	14.62%	2003
Germany	2.44	2	69.18%	54.12%	31.86%	0.00%	65.57%	53.63%	38.29%	22.09%	2003
United States	2.34	3	44.36%	29.17%	18.98%	12.21%	55.32%	39.85%	30.44%	15.83%	2003
Denmark	1.73	4	41.24%	3.49%	0.00%	0.00%	49.26%	7.79%	1.58%	0.00%	2003
United Kingdom	1.72	5	36.69%	19.99%	16.58%	3.87%	47.33%	24.27%	12.28%	7.31%	2003
France	1.72	6	62.67%	19.10%	15.36%	8.04%	61.08%	28.38%	13.89%	11.28%	2003
Finland	1.70	7	55.81%	38.05%	16.23%	0.00%	59.12%	38.61%	15.73%	14.20%	2003
Austria	1.66	8	58.57%	3.14%	0.00%	0.00%	58.19%	13.75%	4.79%	3.19%	2003
Switzerland	1.63	9	73.84%	33.57%	28.80%	9.78%	75.63%	49.12%	36.09%	10.51%	2003
Netherlands	1.59	10	44.12%	27.74%	1.56%	1.56%	41.16%	27.09%	17.08%	3.24%	2003
Belgium	1.49	11	52.41%	24.39%	10.19%	0.00%	51.18%	30.93%	21.76%	1.43%	2003
Canada	1.48	12	36.67%	28.95%	3.61%	0.00%	38.62%	26.26%	4.91%	0.21%	2003
Sweden	1.42	13	63.83%	7.68%	7.68%	0.00%	64.78%	10.16%	8.92%	0.00%	2003
Taiwan	1.33	14	No data available								
Korea, Rep.	1.22	15	76.65%	40.22%	17.54%	5.80%	71.68%	54.98%	22.20%	7.37%	2003
Australia	1.19	16	2.45%	0.00%	0.00%	0.00%	4.12%	2.50%	2.50%	0.31%	2003
India	1.13	17	42.56%	16.78%	0.00%	0.00%	41.90%	23.49%	9.84%	0.00%	2003
Italy	1.02	18	62.94%	46.56%	18.33%	2.83%	64.68%	44.35%	34.29%	10.15%	2003
Spain	0.99	19	51.56%	26.66%	0.00%	0.00%	50.98%	28.35%	1.10%	0.00%	2003
Israel	0.98	20	36.06%	0.00%	0.00%	0.00%	38.72%	2.76%	0.32%	0.32%	2003
Czech Republic	0.98	21	68.40%	0.00%	0.00%	0.00%	72.65%	6.81%	0.15%	0.00%	2003
Hong Kong SAR	0.96	22	54.17%	42.08%	0.00%	0.00%	63.70%	44.07%	18.28%	0.00%	2003
New Zealand	0.95	23	11.60%	0.00%	0.00%	0.00%	14.64%	0.00%	0.00%	0.00%	2003
Malaysia	0.93	24	55.98%	45.00%	38.20%	0.00%	57.92%	45.50%	30.00%	0.00%	2003
Norway	0.92	25	3.72%	2.93%	0.00%	0.00%	7.38%	3.28%	0.00%	0.00%	2003
Singapore	0.89	26	64.95%	42.38%	42.38%	0.00%	66.93%	49.78%	44.90%	25.12%	2003
Ireland	0.84	27	74.30%	50.07%	43.05%	0.00%	73.85%	67.47%	51.00%	22.15%	2003
Brazil	0.84	28	12.19%	2.22%	0.00%	0.00%	18.63%	2.14%	0.11%	0.00%	2003
South Africa	0.78	29	21.16%	0.00%	0.00%	0.00%	28.25%	0.15%	0.00%	0.00%	2003
Iceland	0.60	30	2.65%	0.00%	0.00%	0.00%	5.95%	0.00%	0.00%	0.00%	2003
Chile	0.53	31	3.84%	0.00%	0.00%	0.00%	9.00%	3.34%	0.00%	0.00%	2003
China	0.52	32	70.37%	66.05%	63.30%	24.04%	71.93%	68.67%	62.27%	51.74%	2003
Slovenia	0.43	33	77.67%	0.00%	0.00%	0.00%	76.90%	0.37%	0.00%	0.00%	2003
Poland	0.41	34	57.16%	15.13%	0.00%	0.00%	59.08%	14.14%	3.98%	0.00%	2003
Turkey	0.39	35	70.21%	21.36%	0.00%	0.00%	67.29%	31.01%	12.66%	0.00%	2003
Lithuania	0.38	36	36.59%	0.00%	0.00%	0.00%	42.40%	0.00%	0.00%	0.00%	2003
Thailand	0.36	37	51.87%	0.00%	0.00%	0.00%	55.01%	7.22%	0.59%	0.22%	2003
Estonia	0.33	38	47.81%	0.00%	0.00%	0.00%	49.74%	0.00%	0.00%	0.00%	2003
Tunisia	0.23	39	62.21%	0.00%	0.00%	0.00%	70.20%	2.26%	0.00%	0.00%	2003
Argentina	0.22	40	2.73%	0.00%	0.00%	0.00%	10.34%	0.28%	0.28%	0.00%	2003
Cyprus	0.20	41	45.36%	0.00%	0.00%	0.00%	51.78%	0.00%	0.00%	0.00%	2003
Russian Federation	0.20	42	9.32%	0.00%	0.00%	0.00%	9.94%	2.45%	2.45%	0.60%	2003
Portugal	0.19	43	60.85%	5.11%	0.00%	0.00%	62.42%	10.47%	0.00%	0.00%	2003
Slovak Republic	0.16	44	67.08%	0.00%	0.00%	0.00%	69.52%	0.05%	0.00%	0.00%	2003
Ukraine	0.16	45	33.31%	0.00%	0.00%	0.00%	36.33%	21.43%	0.00%	0.00%	2002
Kenya	0.07	46	11.55%	0.00%	0.00%	0.00%	18.01%	0.00%	0.00%	0.00%	2003
Kazakhstan	0.01	47	8.46%	0.00%	0.00%	0.00%	9.81%	0.00%	0.00%	0.00%	2003
Hungary	0.01	48	58.78%	0.00%	0.00%	0.00%	65.66%	11.21%	1.28%	0.00%	2003
Costa Rica	0.00	49	55.00%	0.00%	0.00%	0.00%	59.85%	0.00%	0.00%	0.00%	2003
Kuwait	−0.04	50	4.32%	0.00%	0.00%	0.00%	4.70%	0.00%	0.00%	0.00%	2001
Mauritius	−0.07	51	58.86%	0.00%	0.00%	0.00%	62.44%	0.00%	0.00%	0.00%	2003
United Arab Emirates	−0.07	52	No data available								
Mexico	−0.11	53	66.78%	19.06%	0.00%	0.00%	67.97%	22.28%	13.84%	8.58%	2003
Latvia	−0.14	54	32.74%	0.00%	0.00%	0.00%	34.89%	0.00%	0.00%	0.00%	2003
Bulgaria	−0.14	55	43.49%	0.00%	0.00%	0.00%	48.37%	0.00%	0.00%	0.00%	2003
Pakistan	−0.15	56	75.91%	48.72%	0.00%	0.00%	78.55%	45.98%	25.53%	16.34%	2003
Panama	−0.16	57	3.98%	0.00%	0.00%	0.00%	5.69%	0.00%	0.00%	0.00%	2003
Sri Lanka	−0.17	58	58.66%	0.00%	0.00%	0.00%	61.74%	0.00%	0.00%	0.00%	2003
Greece	−0.22	59	46.70%	0.00%	0.00%	0.00%	49.19%	4.44%	1.91%	1.91%	2003
Jordan	−0.24	60	61.12%	0.00%	0.00%	0.00%	62.90%	0.00%	0.00%	0.00%	2003
Azerbaijan	−0.24	61	0.00%	0.00%	0.00%	0.00%	0.63%	0.00%	0.00%	0.00%	2003
Colombia	−0.24	62	16.21%	0.00%	0.00%	0.00%	19.72%	0.00%	0.00%	0.00%	2003

(cont'd)

Table 6: Goods export cluster performance (excluding natural resources) *(cont'd.)*

Country	Cluster development BCI score	Cluster development BCI rank	Share of goods exports in clusters, with country's market share > overall market share	> overall market share +2.5%	> overall market share +5%	> overall market share +10%	in subclusters, with market share > overall market share	> overall market share +2.5%	> overall market share +5%	> overall market share +10%	*Year of data used*
Morocco	−0.27	63	51.48%	0.00%	0.00%	0.00%	59.42%	0.00%	0.00%	0.00%	*2003*
Indonesia	−0.27	64	24.34%	0.00%	0.00%	0.00%	26.36%	5.40%	2.92%	0.88%	*2003*
Croatia	−0.27	65	45.56%	0.00%	0.00%	0.00%	58.49%	0.00%	0.00%	0.00%	*2003*
Philippines	−0.28	66	73.48%	63.09%	0.00%	0.00%	75.59%	48.39%	44.45%	0.00%	*2003*
Romania	−0.29	67	63.86%	8.06%	0.00%	0.00%	62.98%	10.66%	2.71%	0.00%	*2003*
El Salvador	−0.31	68	65.15%	0.00%	0.00%	0.00%	65.05%	0.00%	0.00%	0.00%	*2003*
Egypt	−0.41	69	18.73%	0.00%	0.00%	0.00%	23.26%	3.14%	0.00%	0.00%	*2003*
Ghana	−0.42	70	2.66%	0.00%	0.00%	0.00%	4.88%	0.00%	0.00%	0.00%	*2001*
Trinidad and Tobago	−0.43	71	14.27%	0.00%	0.00%	0.00%	17.69%	0.00%	0.00%	0.00%	*2003*
Nigeria	−0.45	72	1.49%	0.00%	0.00%	0.00%	1.49%	0.00%	0.00%	0.00%	*2003*
Vietnam	−0.51	73	*No data available*								
Peru	−0.54	74	8.26%	0.00%	0.00%	0.00%	12.19%	0.00%	0.00%	0.00%	*2003*
Macedonia, FYR	−0.54	75	59.80%	0.00%	0.00%	0.00%	61.31%	0.00%	0.00%	0.00%	*2003*
Serbia and Montenegro	−0.55	76	41.99%	0.00%	0.00%	0.00%	43.59%	0.00%	0.00%	0.00%	*2002*
Uruguay	−0.58	77	9.33%	0.00%	0.00%	0.00%	11.61%	0.00%	0.00%	0.00%	*2003*
Jamaica	−0.67	78	7.91%	0.00%	0.00%	0.00%	8.66%	0.00%	0.00%	0.00%	*2002*
Dominican Republic	−0.68	79	15.91%	0.00%	0.00%	0.00%	19.20%	0.00%	0.00%	0.00%	*2001*
Guatemala	−0.71	80	29.33%	0.00%	0.00%	0.00%	37.52%	0.00%	0.00%	0.00%	*2003*
Armenia	−0.73	81	19.16%	0.00%	0.00%	0.00%	20.88%	0.00%	0.00%	0.00%	*2003*
Malta	−0.74	82	88.67%	0.00%	0.00%	0.00%	89.67%	0.00%	0.00%	0.00%	*2001*
Bahrain	−0.75	83	13.63%	0.00%	0.00%	0.00%	18.75%	9.98%	9.98%	0.00%	*2003*
Bangladesh	−0.85	84	83.52%	0.00%	0.00%	0.00%	83.69%	30.40%	0.00%	0.00%	*2003*
Bosnia and Herzegovina	−0.86	85	33.25%	0.00%	0.00%	0.00%	42.37%	0.00%	0.00%	0.00%	*2003*
Qatar	−0.89	86	5.58%	0.00%	0.00%	0.00%	8.96%	0.00%	0.00%	0.00%	*2002*
Madagascar	−0.89	87	30.89%	0.00%	0.00%	0.00%	33.63%	0.00%	0.00%	0.00%	*2003*
Tanzania	−0.89	88	0.47%	0.00%	0.00%	0.00%	4.28%	0.00%	0.00%	0.00%	*2003*
Algeria	−0.92	89	0.00%	0.00%	0.00%	0.00%	0.00%	0.00%	0.00%	0.00%	*2003*
Botswana	−0.98	90	1.25%	0.00%	0.00%	0.00%	1.97%	1.08%	1.08%	0.00%	*2001*
Honduras	−1.06	91	12.77%	0.00%	0.00%	0.00%	19.09%	0.00%	0.00%	0.00%	*2003*
Namibia	−1.08	92	25.88%	0.00%	0.00%	0.00%	28.12%	0.00%	0.00%	0.00%	*2003*
Ecuador	−1.09	93	0.46%	0.00%	0.00%	0.00%	1.85%	0.00%	0.00%	0.00%	*2003*
Moldova	−1.10	94	52.70%	0.00%	0.00%	0.00%	55.98%	0.00%	0.00%	0.00%	*2003*
Zimbabwe	−1.11	95	15.58%	0.00%	0.00%	0.00%	20.54%	0.00%	0.00%	0.00%	*2002*
Tajikistan	−1.13	96	*No data available*								
Venezuela	−1.25	97	0.50%	0.00%	0.00%	0.00%	1.58%	0.00%	0.00%	0.00%	*2003*
Malawi	−1.25	98	8.62%	0.00%	0.00%	0.00%	9.76%	0.00%	0.00%	0.00%	*2003*
Gambia	−1.26	99	24.03%	0.00%	0.00%	0.00%	25.97%	0.00%	0.00%	0.00%	*2003*
Paraguay	−1.28	100	1.98%	0.00%	0.00%	0.00%	4.01%	0.00%	0.00%	0.00%	*2003*
Nicaragua	1.28	101	6.66%	0.00%	0.00%	0.00%	7.09%	0.00%	0.00%	0.00%	*2003*
Georgia	−1.33	102	36.36%	0.00%	0.00%	0.00%	36.92%	0.00%	0.00%	0.00%	*2003*
Guyana	−1.35	103	3.78%	0.00%	0.00%	0.00%	8.54%	0.00%	0.00%	0.00%	*2003*
Mozambique	−1.41	104	14.43%	0.00%	0.00%	0.00%	15.79%	0.00%	0.00%	0.00%	*2002*
Mongolia	−1.42	105	18.82%	0.00%	0.00%	0.00%	19.19%	0.00%	0.00%	0.00%	*2003*
Kyrgyz Republic	−1.45	106	10.22%	0.00%	0.00%	0.00%	15.41%	0.00%	0.00%	0.00%	*2003*
Bolivia	−1.47	107	3.78%	0.00%	0.00%	0.00%	9.42%	0.00%	0.00%	0.00%	*2003*
Ethiopia	−1.56	108	1.19%	0.00%	0.00%	0.00%	2.24%	0.00%	0.00%	0.00%	*2003*
Cambodia	−1.58	109	93.52%	0.00%	0.00%	0.00%	93.70%	0.00%	0.00%	0.00%	*2003*
Albania	−1.69	110	69.53%	0.00%	0.00%	0.00%	72.91%	0.00%	0.00%	0.00%	*2003*

Source: International Cluster Competitiveness Project, Harvard Business School.

fiscal obligations and reducing macroeconomic distortions. Microeconomic reforms can also reduce the political pressure on governments trying to defend macroeconomic stabilization and market opening against vested interests. Citizens who see monopolies losing their grip, businesses reforming themselves, and opportunities for employment and entrepreneurship increasing are much less likely to be seduced by the false promises of redistribution and government intervention.

Over time, many countries have realized that sustained prosperity growth can only be achieved through continuous improvements of microeconomic competitiveness. The European Union and the initiative it launched with the Lisbon Agenda in 2000 is, however, also a sign of how hard it is to move from stating principles to taking action. The experience of the EU indicates how critical it is to address competitiveness at the appropriate geographic level. Making cross-national institutions responsible for competitiveness will fail, if the most pressing barriers exist at the national level.

Our findings confirm the view that it is unwise to view micro reforms narrowly in terms of reducing the role of government and eliminating market distortions. Government has a range of positive roles that are fundamental to prosperity, such as investing in human resources, stimulating advanced demand via setting appropriate regulatory standards, and building innovative capacity. The private sector also has an important role in improving a nation's competitive platform through collective activities and cluster development initiatives.

Finally, our results again highlight the need to align a nation's economic priorities with its level of development. There is strong evidence that microeconomic upgrading is a sequential process in which countries at different levels of development face distinctly different challenges. Countries must address the weaknesses that are constraining productivity in their economy, not copy the policies of other countries.

Notes

1 I would like to thank Christian Ketels and Weifeng Weng for their major role in the analyses reported here. Lyn Pohl provided able supervision of the final production of the chapter.

2 In the 2004–2005 *Report*, we included 103 countries, about ten of which there were concerns about data consistency. For this reason, we included 93 countries in our 2004 analysis. This year, we have 116 countries in the overall sample, of which 6 are dropped from the full analysis because of concerns about data consistency.

3 The proportion has grown modestly over the last several years as the model has been improved.

4 See, for example, O'Mahony and van Ark (2003).

5 Accordingly, the European Union has made increasing labor participation one of the core goals of its Lisbon Agenda to improve competitiveness. See Lisbon European Council, 2000.

6 Economists point out another difference: companies go out of business when they fail to compete successfully; locations don't. Locations react, instead, by adjusting to a lower level of prosperity. While relevant in some contexts, this difference between companies and locations is less crucial here, where the level of prosperity a location can sustain is at the core of the analysis.

7 See the Porter, (2001); further reports on five US regions are available at www.compete.org.

8 Report by Harvard students Jean Hayden, Chai McConnell, Peter Tynan, and Alexandra West.

9 Reports by student teams at Harvard in 2003.

10 The stages were first introduced in Porter (1990).

11 The notion of *institutions for collaboration* has been developed further in joint work with Willis Emmons, Georgetown University. See Porter and Emmons (2003).

12 For a survey of cluster initiatives, a specific type of IFC with the explicit purpose to mobilize and upgrade a cluster, see Sölvell et al. (2003).

13 One surveyed economy, Luxembourg, was not included in the calculations because given its small size, functional concentration on a few sectors, and almost complete integration into the neighboring economies, it is better understood as regional economy.

14 See World Bank (2004), online at: http://rru.worldbank.org/doingbusiness

15 See Kaufmann et al., (2005), and the website http://www.worldbank.org/wbi/governance/pubs/govmatters4.html

16 We have recalculated the 2004 BCI ranking using only the set of questions used this year. The correlation between the revised 2004 ranking and the published 2004 ranking is above 99 percent.

17 These reasons could include larger actual heterogeneity within the country, as well as greater uncertainty by respondents about appropriate international benchmarks.

18 We test whether countries have at least 40 Survey questions out of the 57 with a lower within-country variance than cross-country variance. Countries that have more heterogeneous responses in the sample include some low-income countries added to the Survey process only this year (Benin, Cameroon, East Timor, and Tajikistan), but also some African countries (Chad, Mali, and Uganda), which were excluded from the BCI already last year because of the same data consistency issues.

19 In the case of Ireland, we used GNI per capita instead of GDP per capita, because of the size of dividend outflows to foreign investors. Ireland's GDP is about 20 percent higher than its GNP.

20 Statistical significance at ** = 5 percent and * = 10 percent (all two-tailed tests) is noted in the table.

21 Note that this approach leads us to not include the incentive effects of taxation in the analysis. Taxation has a nonlinear relationship with GDP per capita, being low for low-income economies but also some very successful high- and middle-income economies.

22 We conducted additional bivariate regressions (not reported here) using macroeconomic indicators collected for the *Global Competitiveness Report*. These regressions show no statistical relationship between GDP per capita and individual macroeconomic indicators. See also Easterly (2001), who finds similar results.

23 See Lewis (2004), and Porter and Sakakibara (2004).

24 The forecast region has wider bands than a 95 percent mean confidence region. The mean confidence region provides a confidence interval for a given level of competitiveness over repeated observations. The forecast region method, in contrast, reflects a higher degree of inherent uncertainty in predicting a single observation. As a result, interpretation of the proximity of data points to the regression line should be undertaken with appropriate caveats. Note that the forecast region widens slightly as it moves away from the "center" of the graph. The center is the point located at the intersection of the mean GDP per capita level and mean factor score.

25 Austria also registered a marked improvement in the incentive effects of its tax system, reflecting recent changes in corporate taxation rates. Note that the responses to this question are not included in the calculations of BCI score and rank, because it is not significantly related to GDP per capita across the entire country sample.

26 For a more detailed examination of Japan's competitive situation, see Porter et al. (2000).

27 This implies also a high correlation between these indicators and the BCI, providing a statistical challenge for distinguishing their independent effects.

28 See Gallup and Sachs (1999) for a discussion of the data on geographic location.

29 See World Bank (2004).

30 When Zimbabwe is dropped from the regression, the explanatory power of the equation falls to 12.8 percent and the coefficient falls to an increase of 1.2 percent annual GDP per capita growth for an increase of ten ranks in the BCI over five years.

31 Further information on this project is available at the Institute for Strategy and Competitiveness, www.isc.hbs.edu

References

Baumol, W. J. 2002. *The Free-Market Innovation Machine: Analyzing the Growth Miracle of Capitalism*. Princeton, NJ: Princeton University Press.

Barro, R. J. 1991. "Economic Growth in a Cross Section of Countries." *Quarterly Journal of Economics* 106(2):407–443.

Easterly, W. 2001.*The Elusive Quest for Growth: Economists' Adventures and Misadventures in the Tropics*. Cambridge, MA: MIT Press.

Easterly, W. and R. Levine. 2002. "Tropics, Germs, and Crops: How Endowments Influence Economic Development." NBER Working Paper 9106. Cambridge, MA: National Bureau of Economic Research.

Enright, M. J., A. Francés, and E. S. Saavadra. 1994. *Venezuela: El Reto de la Competitividad*. Caracas: Ediciones IESA.

Fairbanks, M. and S. Lindsay. 1997. *Plowing the Sea: The Challenge of Competitiveness in the Developing World*. Boston: Harvard Business School Press.

Gallup, J. L. and J. D. Sachs. 1999. *Geography and Economic Development*. Center for International Development (CID) Working Paper 1. Cambridge, MA: March 1999.

Glaeser, E., R. La Porta, F. Lopez-de-Silanes, and A Shleifer. 2004. *Do Institutions Cause Growth?*, NBER Working Paper 10568. Cambridge, MA: National Bureau of Economic Research.

Hall, R. E. and C. I. Jones. 1999. "Why Do Some Countries Produce So Much More Output per Worker than Others?" *Quarterly Journal of Economics*114(1):83–116.

Hirschman, A. O. 1958. *The Strategy of Economic Development*. New Haven, CT: Yale University Press.

Kaufmann, D., A. Kraay, and M. Mastruzzi. 2005. "Governance Matters IV: Governance Indicators for 1996–2004." Mimeo. Washington, D.C.: World Bank.

Lewis, W. W. 2004. *The Power of Productivity*. Chicago, IL: The University of Chicago Press.

Lisbon European Council. 2000. Presidency Conclusions. Lisbon. 23–24 March.

Lucas, R. E., Jr. 1988. "On the Mechanics of Economic Development." *Journal of Monetary Economics* 22. July. 3–42.

Mankiw, N. G. 1995. "The Growth of Nations." *Brookings Papers on Economic Activity* 1(1):275–310.

Mankiw, N. G., D. Romer, and D. N. Weil. 1992. "A Contribution to the Empirics of Economic Growth." *Quarterly Journal of Economics* 107(2):407–437.

Nickell, S. 1996. "Competition and Corporate Performance." *Journal of Political Economy* 104:724–746.

Nordhaus, W. D. 1994. "Climate and Economic Development." In *Proceedings of the World Bank Annual Conference on Development Economics 1993*. Washington, DC: The International Bank for Reconstruction and Development and World Bank.

North, D. C. 1990. *Institutions, Institutional Change and Economic Performance: Political Economy of Institutions and Decisions*. Cambridge: Cambridge University Press.

O'Mahony, M., B. van Ark, eds. 2003. *EU productivity and competitiveness: an industry perspective*. Brussels: European Commission.

Porter, M. E. 1990. *The Competitive Advantage of Nations*. New York: The Free Press.

———. 1995. "Comment on 'Interaction Between Regional and Industrial Policies: Evidence From Four Countries,' by J. Markusen." *Proceedings of The World Bank Annual Conference on Development Economics 1994*. Washington, DC: The International Bank for Reconstruction and Development and World Bank.

———. 1996. "What Is Strategy?" *Harvard Business Review* 74(6):61–78.

———. 1998a. "Introduction." In *The Competitive Advantage of Nations: With a New Introduction*. New York: The Free Press.

———. 1998b. "Clusters and Competition: New Agendas for Companies, Governments, and Institutions." In *On Competition*. Boston: Harvard Business School Press.

———. 2000a. "Attitudes, Values, Beliefs, and the Microeconomic of Prosperity." Harrison, L. E. and S. P. Huntington, eds. *Culture Matters*. New York: Basic Books, 2000: 14–28.

———. 2000b. "Locations, Clusters, and Company Strategy." in G. L. Clark, M. P. Feldman, and M. S. Gertler, eds. *The Oxford Handbook of Economic Geography*. New York: Oxford University Press, 2000: 253–274.

———. 2001. Council on Competitiveness, and Monitor Group. *Clusters of Innovation Initiative: Regional Foundations of U.S. Competitiveness*. Washington, DC: Council on Competitiveness.

———. 2003. "The Economic Performance of Regions." *Regional Studies* 37(6&7):549–678.

Porter, M. E. and M. Sakakibara. 2004. "Competition in Japan." *Journal of Economic Perspectives*. Winter.

Porter, M. E., C. Ketels, K. Miller, and R. Bryden. 2004. *Competitiveness in Rural U.S. Regions: Learning and Research Agenda*. Washington, D.C.: U.S. Economic Development Administration (EDA).

Porter, M. E. and W. Emmons. 2003. "Institutions for Collaboration: Overview". Harvard Business School case 9-703-436.

Porter, M. E. and T. Hirotaka, with M. Sakakibara. 2000. *Can Japan Compete?* Basingstoke, England, and New York: Macmillan and Basic Books.

Porter, M. E. and C. Ketels. 2003. *UK Competitiveness: Moving to the Next Stage*. DTI Economics Paper 3.

Porter, M. E. and C. van der Linde. 1995. "Toward a New Conception of the Environment-Competitiveness Relationship." *Journal of Economic Perspectives* 9(4):97–118.

Romer, P. M. 1990. "Endogenous Technological Change." *Journal of Political Economy* 98(5):S71–S102.

Sachs, J. D. and A. Warner. 1995. "Economic Reform and the Process of Global Integration." *Brookings Papers on Economic Activity* 1(1):1–118.

Sakakibara, M. and M. E. Porter. 1998. "Competing at Home to Win Abroad: Evidence from Japanese Industry." Harvard Business School Working Paper 99–036. Cambridge, MA: Harvard Business School Press.

Solow, R. M. 1956. "A Contribution to the Theory of Economic Growth." *Quarterly Journal of Economics* 70(1):65–94.

Sölvell, Ö., G. Lindqvist, and C. Ketels. 2003. "The Cluster Initiative Greenbook." Stockholm: November.

World Bank. 2004. *Doing Business in 2005: Removing Obstacles to Growth*. New York: Oxford University Press.

Appendix A: ANOVA analysis for Survey responses

I. COMPANY OPERATIONS & STRATEGY	R^2
Production process sophistication	0.467
Nature of competitive advantage	0.392
Extent of staff training	0.362
Extent of marketing	0.393
Willingness to delegate authority	0.282
Capacity for innovation	0.406
Company spending on research and development	0.363
Value chain presence	0.457
Breadth of international markets	0.461
Degree of customer orientation	0.240
Control of international distribution	0.182
Reliance on professional management	0.311
Extent of incentive compensation	0.274
Extent of regional sales	0.381
Prevalence of foreign technology licensing	0.237

II. NATIONAL BUSINESS ENVIRONMENT	R^2
A. FACTOR (INPUT) CONDITIONS	
1. Physical Infrastructure	
Overall infrastructure quality	0.594
Railroad infrastructure development	0.622
Port infrastructure quality	0.533
Air transport infrastructure quality	0.402
Quality of electricity supply	0.544
Telephone/fax infrastructure quality	0.396
2. Administrative Infrastructure	
Reliability of police services	0.381
Judicial independence	0.439
Efficiency of legal framework	0.409
Extent of bureaucratic red tape	0.088
3. Human Resources	
Quality of management schools	0.430
Quality of public schools	0.484
Quality of the educational system	0.310
Quality of math and science education	0.374
4. Technology Infrastructure	
Availability of scientists and engineers	0.301
Quality of scientific research institutions	0.376
University/industry research collaboration	0.331
5. Capital Markets	
Financial market sophistication	0.516
Venture capital availability	0.277
Ease of access to loans	0.262
Local equity market access	0.393

II. NATIONAL BUSINESS ENVIRONMENT *(Cont'd.)*	R^2
B. DEMAND CONDITIONS	
Buyer sophistication	0.361
Government procurement of advanced technology products	0.186
Presence of demanding regulatory standards	0.440
Laws relating to ICT	0.395
Stringency of environmental regulations	0.447
C. RELATED AND SUPPORTING INDUSTRIES	
Local supplier quality	0.382
Local availability of process machinery	0.327
Local availability of specialized research and training services	0.330
Local supplier quantity	0.247
D. CONTEXT FOR FIRM STRATEGY AND RIVALRY	
1. Incentives	
Favoritism in decisions of government officials	0.257
Cooperation in labor-employer relations	0.205
Efficacy of corporate boards	0.166
Intellectual property protection	0.468
Protection of minority shareholders' interests	0.277
2. Competition	
Intensity of local competition	0.228
Effectiveness of antitrust policy	0.369
Decentralization of corporate activity	0.314
Business costs of corruption	0.314
Prevalence of trade barriers	0.208
Centralization of economic policymaking	0.232
Foreign ownership restrictions	0.242

Appendix B: Bivariate regression results, dependent variable: 2004 GDP per capita (PPP-adjusted)

	All countries (N = 110)				Low-income countries GDP per capita < $4,000 (N = 28)				Middle-income countries GDP per capita > $4,000 and < $17,000 (N = 48)				High-income countries GDP per capita > $17,000 (N = 34)			
	Mean	STD	Slope	Adj. R²	Mean	STD	Slope	Adj. R²	Mean	STD	Slope	Adj. R²	Mean	STD	Slope	Adj. R²
I. COMPANY OPERATIONS & STRATEGY																
Production process sophistication	3.87	1.13	8704.2**	0.818	2.83	0.51	1025.7**	0.233	3.53	0.55	3851.8**	0.363	5.22	0.76	5212.6**	0.479
Nature of competitive advantage	3.60	1.09	8269.2**	0.688	2.85	0.44	463.3	0.003	3.11	0.44	230.8	−0.021	4.91	0.94	3245.7**	0.270
Extent of staff training	3.84	0.98	9152.0**	0.676	3.08	0.56	309.4	−0.009	3.54	0.57	2638.2**	0.174	4.90	0.81	4616.9**	0.417
Extent of marketing	4.41	0.98	8696.6**	0.620	3.52	0.68	519.9*	0.084	4.23	0.68	2277.4**	0.184	5.41	0.64	5112.9**	0.316
Willingness to delegate authority	3.72	0.92	9494.0**	0.648	3.11	0.51	197.9	−0.029	3.40	0.50	3073.0**	0.184	4.68	0.90	4452.7**	0.488
Capacity for innovation	3.52	1.08	7869.1**	0.608	2.82	0.45	1050.0**	0.177	3.11	0.54	1574.6*	0.041	4.67	1.11	2683.3**	0.254
Company spending on research and development	3.34	0.95	8568.8**	0.563	2.74	0.43	413.0	−0.007	3.02	0.47	2596.2**	0.105	4.30	1.06	2727.4**	0.240
Value chain presence	3.86	1.24	6653.3**	0.571	2.96	0.65	745.1**	0.193	3.45	0.75	1273.2*	0.056	5.17	1.09	1698.4*	0.079
Breadth of international markets	3.87	1.27	6715.6**	0.621	2.88	0.73	523.9*	0.103	3.50	0.91	1578.2**	0.153	5.19	0.96	3247.4**	0.286
Degree of customer orientation	4.65	0.76	10992.8**	0.583	4.09	0.54	106.2	−0.035	4.43	0.55	1843.3**	0.065	5.43	0.50	7194.1**	0.388
Control of international distribution	4.13	0.67	11432.9**	0.503	3.61	0.50	246.4	−0.024	3.98	0.48	1027.8	−0.001	4.78	0.52	5386.0**	0.221
Reliance on professional management	4.56	0.91	8688.1**	0.531	4.00	0.71	−389.3	0.037	4.28	0.66	2668.5**	0.247	5.41	0.75	4953.4**	0.418
Extent of incentive compensation	4.07	0.86	9607.9**	0.572	3.41	0.54	738.7**	0.116	3.89	0.66	2508.0**	0.209	4.88	0.69	5005.1**	0.350
Extent of regional sales	4.53	1.11	6978.1**	0.505	3.65	0.72	528.8*	0.102	4.35	0.91	1662.7**	0.173	5.51	0.88	3271.8**	0.236
Prevalence of foreign technology licensing	4.38	0.85	8466.9**	0.436	3.66	0.73	62.6	−0.036	4.26	0.73	1954.5**	0.151	5.14	0.37	1245.8	−0.024
II. NATIONAL BUSINESS ENVIRONMENT																
A. FACTOR (INPUT) CONDITIONS																
1. Physical Infrastructure																
Overall infrastructure quality	3.93	1.37	6744.4**	0.721	2.74	0.45	759.8*	0.076	3.52	0.94	1705.7**	0.196	5.50	0.88	3494.1**	0.275
Railroad infrastructure development	3.06	1.57	4438.8**	0.408	2.23	0.84	349.9	0.045	2.60	1.19	1155.4**	0.140	4.38	1.69	1231.2**	0.108
Port infrastructure quality	3.86	1.41	5946.2**	0.592	2.69	0.93	296.5	0.035	3.49	1.00	1198.3**	0.102	5.34	0.88	2603.5**	0.139
Air transport infrastructure quality	4.65	1.06	7795.7**	0.580	3.89	0.53	377.6	0.000	4.27	0.88	1045.6*	0.051	5.81	0.56	4321.2**	0.156
Quality of electricity supply	4.67	1.43	6331.8**	0.696	3.07	0.70	763.1**	0.238	4.54	1.01	1768.3**	0.249	6.19	0.59	6272.3**	0.404
Telephone/fax infrastructure quality	5.51	1.10	6712.3**	0.463	4.43	0.95	303.7	0.043	5.44	0.91	962.1*	0.043	6.51	0.30	7264.8**	0.124
Cell phones per 100 people (2003)	41.05	33.25	283.4**	0.754	5.87	5.08	113.2**	0.284	32.52	18.56	120.8**	0.408	82.07	15.79	−29.6	−0.024
Internet users per 10,000 people (2003)	1939	1920	5.0**	0.793	241	220	2.2**	0.187	1260	1029	2.2**	0.419	4295	1339	1.8**	0.154
2. Administrative Infrastructure																
Reliability of police services	4.17	1.16	7128.3**	0.580	3.44	0.71	85.0	−0.035	3.71	0.94	927.3*	0.043	5.42	0.65	5815.2**	0.425
Judicial independence	3.82	1.38	5874.1**	0.553	2.88	1.03	−267.2	0.035	3.37	1.08	1336.3**	0.157	5.22	0.82	3787.6**	0.282
Efficiency of legal framework	3.79	1.20	7012.0**	0.597	2.95	0.73	−134.8	−0.029	3.41	0.92	1573.6**	0.157	5.01	0.87	4309.5**	0.421
Extent of bureaucratic red tape	5.42	0.36	16120.8**	0.276	5.19	0.26	942.9	0.020	5.38	0.36	2462.7*	0.044	5.66	0.28	4795.5	0.027
3. Human Resources																
Quality of management schools	4.15	1.01	7618.8**	0.501	3.37	0.70	367.1	0.026	3.99	0.78	1751.7**	0.137	5.03	0.87	3810.7**	0.322
Quality of public schools	3.79	1.28	7201.0**	0.725	2.61	0.50	1009.3**	0.212	3.47	0.95	2460.3**	0.449	5.22	0.71	3713.8**	0.192
Quality of the educational system	3.70	0.98	8509.8**	0.586	3.04	0.62	30.4	−0.038	3.38	0.72	2500.2**	0.256	4.70	0.74	3882.5**	0.237
Quality of math and science education	4.13	1.01	6373.0**	0.346	3.49	0.77	525.1**	0.121	3.95	0.96	1716.1**	0.212	4.91	0.74	932.4	−0.016

(cont'd)

Appendix B: Bivariate regression results, dependent variable: 2004 GDP per capita (PPP-adjusted) *(cont'd.)*

	All countries (N = 110)				Low-income countries GDP per capita < $4,000 (N = 28)				Middle-income countries GDP per capita > $4,000 and < $17,000 (N = 48)				High-income countries GDP per capita > $17,000 (N = 34)			
	Mean	STD	Slope	Adj. R²	Mean	STD	Slope	Adj. R²	Mean	STD	Slope	Adj. R²	Mean	STD	Slope	Adj. R²
II. NATIONAL BUSINESS ENVIRONMENT *(cont'd.)*																
4. Technology Infrastructure																
Patents per million population (2004)	24.44	57.40	127.2**	0.449	0.10	0.21	1410.2	0.043	0.58	0.93	2150.3**	0.320	78.16	81.11	32.1**	0.187
Availability of scientists and engineers	4.58	0.90	7120.2**	0.347	4.06	0.88	412.7*	0.090	4.39	0.77	1697.5**	0.126	5.27	0.67	3064.8**	0.104
Quality of scientific research institutions	3.90	0.98	8039.2**	0.527	3.36	0.63	211.5	-0.021	3.57	0.67	3051.4**	0.340	4.81	0.99	3305.6**	0.311
University/industry research collaboration	3.18	0.95	8753.3**	0.588	2.54	0.41	424.7	-0.008	2.89	0.59	2586.8**	0.178	4.12	0.99	3357.2**	0.324
5. Capital Markets																
Financial market sophistication	4.06	1.25	7003.2**	0.646	3.01	0.73	418.6	0.053	3.76	0.94	1815.3**	0.225	5.35	0.81	4437.3**	0.390
Venture capital availability	3.33	0.95	9306.5**	0.658	2.63	0.53	598.6	0.061	3.04	0.66	2915.6**	0.290	4.32	0.75	4845.2**	0.398
Ease of access to loans	3.34	0.96	9169.3**	0.660	2.54	0.58	331.5	-0.002	3.07	0.66	2861.0**	0.284	4.37	0.65	4709.6**	0.271
Local equity market access	4.81	1.24	5265.9**	0.358	4.02	1.36	32.8	-0.037	4.57	1.08	998.8**	0.078	5.78	0.56	6516.2**	0.399
B. DEMAND CONDITIONS																
Buyer sophistication	4.14	1.07	8278.3**	0.665	3.31	0.79	381.8	0.050	3.80	0.69	2320.8**	0.197	5.32	0.63	5742.5**	0.395
Government procurement of advanced technology products	3.70	0.64	10206.4**	0.354	3.36	0.53	-191.2	-0.028	3.51	0.53	1678.5*	0.045	4.23	0.52	3304.0*	0.064
Presence of demanding regulatory standards	4.31	1.06	8938.0**	0.757	3.36	0.50	184.0	-0.030	4.02	0.70	3271.5**	0.421	5.51	0.64	5781.0**	0.405
Laws relating to ICT	3.81	1.09	8384.5**	0.703	2.82	0.47	518.4	0.019	3.53	0.77	2199.9**	0.224	5.02	0.66	4935.5**	0.308
Stringency of environmental regulations	4.00	1.21	7672.6**	0.728	3.06	0.49	112.1	-0.036	3.59	0.80	2527.1**	0.325	5.36	0.91	4089.9**	0.413
C. RELATED AND SUPPORTING INDUSTRIES																
Local supplier quality	4.45	0.96	9605.8**	0.727	3.53	0.58	639.5*	0.097	4.23	0.57	3664.5**	0.354	5.50	0.63	5741.2**	0.393
Local availability of process machinery	2.90	1.00	6872.2**	0.395	2.30	0.63	409.8	0.026	2.67	0.73	925.1	0.017	3.72	1.06	2343.4**	0.168
Local availability of specialized research and training services	4.05	0.96	8875.0**	0.612	3.27	0.54	799.8**	0.142	3.84	0.57	3182.1**	0.255	4.99	0.92	3467.4**	0.299
Local supplier quantity	4.80	0.76	10421.7**	0.527	4.16	0.64	256.8	-0.012	4.67	0.51	2905.4**	0.169	5.49	0.57	5456.9**	0.276
D. CONTEXT FOR FIRM STRATEGY AND RIVALRY																
1. Incentives																
Favoritism in decisions of government officials	3.22	0.87	8732.2**	0.491	2.71	0.52	-178.8	-0.030	2.90	0.68	1219.6	0.036	4.08	0.72	3554.3**	0.178
Cooperation in labor-employer relations	4.52	0.70	8574.2**	0.300	4.28	0.49	255.2	-0.023	4.31	0.59	1766.1**	0.071	5.02	0.75	3678.0**	0.213
Efficacy of corporate boards	4.58	0.61	12119.6**	0.455	4.25	0.43	-882.4*	0.100	4.40	0.48	3688.1**	0.250	5.09	0.58	6102.3**	0.367
Intellectual property protection	3.70	1.23	7744.8**	0.766	2.73	0.47	134.6	-0.035	3.21	0.76	2042.9**	0.186	5.17	0.78	5152.7**	0.486
Protection of minority shareholders' interests	4.41	0.87	8461.1**	0.461	3.94	0.71	-202.3	-0.019	4.10	0.71	1660.4**	0.097	5.23	0.62	4854.4**	0.259
2. Competition																
Intensity of local competition	4.79	0.76	10190.7**	0.505	4.18	0.64	103.9	-0.034	4.63	0.59	2549.5**	0.171	5.53	0.40	4072.8	0.053
Effectiveness of antitrust policy	3.99	1.04	8150.8**	0.614	3.20	0.59	-354.0	0.004	3.65	0.71	2017.8**	0.153	5.13	0.75	3182.5**	0.155
Decentralization of corporate activity	3.91	0.98	8615.2**	0.608	3.18	0.69	43.9	-0.038	3.60	0.59	1970.2**	0.093	4.94	0.79	4260.4**	0.337
Business costs of corruption	4.42	1.10	8298.5**	0.707	3.59	0.53	303.6	-0.014	4.00	0.75	1866.7**	0.144	5.71	0.66	5425.2**	0.379
Prevalence of trade barriers	4.59	0.85	8490.0**	0.441	3.91	0.56	-261.7	-0.017	4.40	0.67	2623.8**	0.242	5.42	0.58	-2898.5*	0.061
Centralization of economic policymaking	3.06	0.87	6942.8**	0.304	2.72	0.61	40.8	-0.038	2.82	0.67	1322.8*	0.046	3.68	0.98	2741.9**	0.203
Foreign ownership restrictions	5.01	0.73	6587.1**	0.192	4.77	0.65	71.1	-0.036	4.85	0.70	1606.5**	0.086	5.45	0.67	1986.4	0.026

* denotes $p < 0.10$, ** denotes $p < 0.05$.

Part 2

Selected Issues of Competitiveness

Myths and Realities of Governance and Corruption

DANIEL KAUFMANN,[1] World Bank

Governance and corruption remain controversial and misunderstood topics. But they are now given higher priority in development circles and by the corporate sector, including multinationals.

Indeed, some donors and international financial institutions (IFIs) increasingly work with emerging economies to help reduce corruption, and increase citizen voice, gender equality, and accountability. The 2005 World Economic Forum in Davos highlighted the agreement reached among 63 multinationals in key sectors to work within a set of principles to control corporate bribery. Further, with 29 countries having ratified already, and another handful of developing countries on the verge of doing so,[2] the UN convention against corruption signed almost two years ago is about to come into force, requiring, among other things, repatriation of looted assets stashed abroad by corrupt leaders.[3]

And when in July 2005 the Group of Eight countries announced their decision to double aid and debt relief to the poorest countries in Africa, governance concerns were prominent. As the recent joint report by the Africa Commission explicitly stated, "Good governance is the key.... Unless there are improvements in capacity, accountability, and reducing corruption ... other reforms will have only limited impact." Similar statements are voiced in other regions of the world, and there is also increasing scrutiny about corruption in OECD countries, and of multinationals.

But is good governance and controlling corruption really fundamental for growth, development, and security? The explosion of empirical research over the past decade, coupled with lessons from countries' own experience, have given us a more solid basis for judging many of the effects of governance on development, and the effectiveness—or lack thereof—of strategies to improve it. In our contributions to the *Global Competitiveness Reports* (GCR) in recent years[4] we have presented a number of selected governance topics. Insights derived from the analyses of the Executive Opinion Surveys (Survey) conducted by the World Economic Forum every year, and presented in previous GCR chapter contributions, include the study of determinants of governance at the city level, the anatomy of undue influence, state capture and bribery involving many domestic private firms, multinationals, and public officials, and the links between governance, corruption and security threats, and others.

Unfinished business

Yet in spite of the myriad contributions to the field by many authors, there are still serious unresolved questions and debates in the development community, not only about the importance of governance and corruption, but also about the willingness and ability of the international community, including the private sector, to help countries improve in these areas.

In this year's chapter, we provide a synthesis of the key challenges, many of which are unresolved or have become popularized notions. Some of them, we believe, are outright myths. At the risk of oversimplification, and for the sake of expositional clarity and generating debate, we present these unresolved or misunderstood issues as myths on governance and corruption, although we acknowledge at the outset that there is often a more nuanced reality. In each case, we present a "myth," with which we obviously disagree, and then discuss why we think it is mistaken. Following the eight myths, we present underemphasized interventions in the area of transparency reform, complemented by improvements in freedom of the press and gender equality. If implemented, such reforms could have a major impact on improving governance and anti-corruption in the next stage.

Myth #1: Definition: Governance and anti-corruption are one and the same.

We define *governance* as the traditions and institutions by which authority in a country is exercised for the common good. This includes:

- the process by which those in authority are selected, monitored, and replaced (the political dimension);
- the government's capacity to effectively manage its resources and implement sound policies (the economic dimension); and
- the respect of citizens and the state for the country's institutions (the institutional respect dimension).

By contrast, *corruption* is traditionally defined more narrowly as the "abuse of public office for private gain." In last year's GCR chapter on governance, we challenged this definition of corruption as placing too much emphasis on public office, and on the ostensible legality of the act. We analyzed the implications of viewing corruption as a broader phenomenon where private agents also share responsibility, and where many acts which are not ethical (and thus may be regarded as corrupt) may not necessarily be illegal. We presented empirical evidence of the extent to which many powerful private firms engage in undue influence, to shape state policies, laws and regulations, for their own benefit. Related to this, we also highlighted the extent to which they make campaign contributions, which may, in fact, be legal, but which unduly influences the rules of the game, for their benefit. Moreover, from the Survey results we showed that favoritism toward particular firms in the awarding of public procurement bids and contracts is widespread.

To generate debate, we offered an alternative, broader definition of what constitutes corruption, namely, "the privatization of public policy," in which public policy is seen as including access to public services. According to this more neutral definition, an act may not necessarily be illegal for it to be regarded as corrupt in a broader sense. Consider the situation in which legislative votes or executive decisions in sectoral policy-making—e.g., in telecommunications or energy—have been unduly influenced by either private campaign contributions to legislators, or by private favors provided to decision-makers. In such a case, corruption would be considered to have taken place, even if the act was not strictly illegal. And within such a broad definition, responsibility resides with *both those who exert undue influence, and those who are unduly influenced*. Based on the empirical results from the Survey last year, we also provided an illustrative index of corruption within this broader definition, which pays closer attention to the deeds of the private sector. We found that a number of rich OECD countries fare rather poorly when this more subtle, and not purely legalistic, definition of corruption is used in the analysis.

Such debates on alternative definitions of corruption notwithstanding, it is clear that the scope of the concept of governance is much broader than that of corruption. As we will see later, governance and corruption may be related, but they are distinct notions, and ought not to be regarded as one and the same.

Myth #2: Governance and corruption cannot be measured.

Less than a dozen years ago, few comparable, worldwide measures of governance or corruption existed. Yet in recent years, through the efforts of institutions such as the World Bank (the Governance Indicators), the World Economic Forum (the Executive Opinion Survey), Transparency International (Corruption Perception Index), Freedom House (political and civil liberties and freedom of the press), and numerous other institutions, we have sought to counteract this widespread perception.

At the World Bank, in order to more closely define and measure governance, we have constructed these aggregate Governance Indicators, which now cover more than 200 countries, based on more than 350 variables, obtained from dozens of institutions worldwide, including the Survey. The Governance Indicators capture six key dimensions of institutional quality or governance, and measure, through two indicators each, the political, economic, and institutional dimensions of governance described above. The following six dimensions are measured:

1. *Voice and accountability*—measuring political, civil and human rights

2. *Political instability and violence*—measuring the likelihood of violent threats to, or changes in, government, including terrorism

3. *Government effectiveness*—measuring the competence of the bureaucracy and the quality of public service delivery

4. *Regulatory burden*—measuring the incidence of market-unfriendly policies

5. *Rule of law*—measuring the quality of contract enforcement, the police, and the courts, as well as the likelihood of crime and violence

6. *Control of corruption*—measuring the exercise of public power for private gain, including both petty and grand corruption, and state capture

While the Governance Indicators may represent a big step forward, there are measurement challenges. Margins of error are not trivial, and caution in interpreting the results is warranted—i.e., countries cannot be precisely ranked. But these margins of error have declined, and are substantially lower than for any individual measure of corruption, governance, or the investment climate. As a result, these governance indicators are used worldwide for monitoring performance, country assessment, and research. These indicators have been available since 1996, and in recent months we released the last installment for 209 countries, with data up to the end of 2004.[5]

Myth #3: The importance of governance and anti-corruption efforts is overrated.

In order to give an approximation of the importance of corruption, one might pose the question: How large is the corruption "industry" worldwide? But it is very difficult to obtain even a rough estimate of the size of the corruption industry, given its hidden nature, for corruption and bribery typically operate in the dark. This makes official estimates virtually impossible to obtain, and, of course, unreliable. Nonetheless, thanks to the increasing availability of particular questions in enterprise and household surveys, which ask for quantitative estimates of bribery, it is possible, under certain conditions, to make calculations, and to extrapolate for the whole population.

In interpreting the results of this exercise, significant caution applies, given the margin of error in the data, the assumptions in the extrapolation exercise itself, and the fact that some forms of corruption are not quantified through this approach—e.g., budgetary leakages or asset theft within the public sector. Bearing such serious caveats in mind, an estimate of the extent of annual worldwide transactions that are tainted by corruption puts it close to US$1 trillion. The margin of error of this estimate being obviously large, it may well be as low as US$600 billion; or, at the other extreme of the spectrum, it could well exceed US$1.5 trillion.[6]

But even if a US$1 trillion estimate of the global size of bribery worldwide seems very large, it does not, in and of itself, give us much of a guide to the actual cost of corruption. Theoretically, it could be argued that all these bribes just grease the wheels of commerce, and no productive value added is lost to the economy. Therefore, to get a closer idea of the costs of corruption and poor governance, it is important to relate governance indicators with outcome variables, such as incomes or infant mortality, for instance.

Thanks to the advances in empirical measurement, a number of researchers have examined the impact of governance on development. The research generally shows that countries can derive a very large *development dividend,* as we have called it, from better governance. Indeed, there is now a growing consensus among both academics and policymakers that good governance provides the fundamental basis for economic development. Academic research has focused on the effects of institutional quality on growth in the very long run, noting that there is a strong causal impact of institutional quality on per capita incomes worldwide. These estimates of the development dividend of good governance suggest that a realistic one-standard-deviation improvement in governance would raise incomes in the long run by about two- to threefold.[7]

Such improvement in governance by one standard deviation is feasible, since it is only a fraction of the difference between the worst and best performers, and would correspond, for instance, to an improvement in the current ratings of voice and accountability from the lowest levels of Myanmar to that of Kazakhstan, or Kazakhstan to Georgia, or Georgia to Botswana. For improvements in *rule of law,* a one standard deviation difference would constitute the improvement from the level of Somalia to those of Laos, from Laos to Lebanon, Lebanon to Italy, or Italy to Canada; for *control of corruption* it is the improvement from the lowest levels of Equatorial Guinea to those of Cuba, Honduras, or Uganda, from Uganda to Lithuania or Mauritius, from Mauritius to Portugal, or from Portugal to the stellar standards of Finland, Iceland, or New Zealand. We also find that even over much shorter periods, such as the past 10 years, countries with better institutional quality have grown faster. And in our research, we have also found that good governance not only matters significantly for higher incomes per capita, but also for substantially reducing infant mortality and illiteracy.

Governance also matters significantly for a country's competitiveness. For this year's GCR, we performed a simple exercise, relating the recently released Governance Indicators (measuring country's ratings for the 2004 period), with the updated Growth Competitiveness Index

Figure 1: Better governance is associated with greater country competitiveness

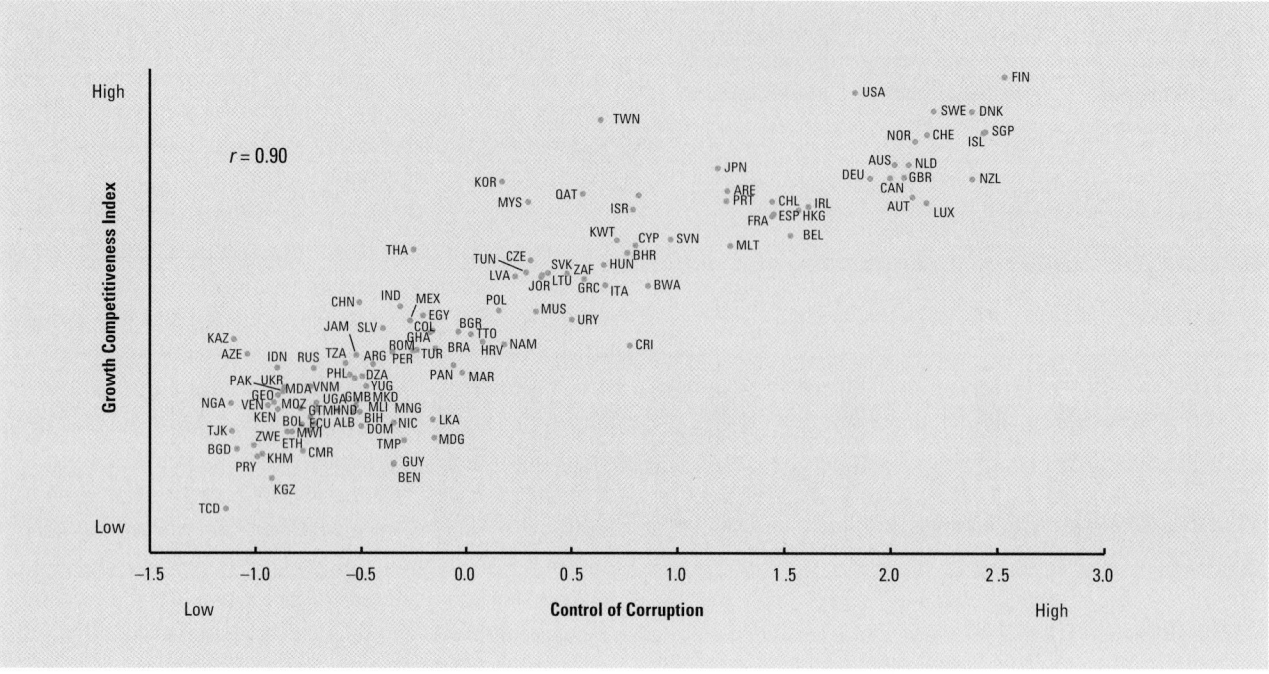

Sources: GCI is based on 2005 data of the World Economic Forum; *control of corruption* is for 2004, from Kaufmann et al. 2005.

(GCI) for 2005, which is featured in this *Report* (Part 1). It should be noted that the data used to compute the GCI this year (drawn in large measure from this year's Survey) did not feature in any of the calculations for the Governance Indicators, which utilized earlier data. Against such a background, it is noteworthy that the correlation between governance (measured through the Governance Indicators) and competitiveness (through the GCI) is extremely high. As we observe in Figure 1, for the case of one of the Governance Indicators, namely corruption control, the correlation is 0.9, i.e. an extremely tight fit. Obviously such a close correlation is highly significant statistically, and remains so after controls for income levels are included in econometric specifications which explain the country's competitiveness. On average, an improvement in control of corruption by only one standard deviation (which is realistic) is associated with a jump in the GCI for a country by almost 30 rank positions. Even after controlling for the income level of the country, improvement in corruption control can produce a very large jump in the competitiveness of a country, between 15 and 20 rank positions.

The most direct way to ascertain the importance of governance is to ask firms and households themselves. In the case of enterprises, insights can be derived from the synthesis question, at the end of the Survey, which asked firms to rank the most important constraints from a long list of 14 potential problems. The results are telling: firms in OECD countries rated labor regulations, bureaucracy, and taxes as the most problematic for their business, while firms in emerging economies considered that by far the largest constraints are bureaucracy and corruption. Finance and infrastructure are rated significantly lower than corruption and bureaucracy, but are still perceived by business executives worldwide as posing serious concerns for many enterprises. In terms of constraint severity, these dominate many of the other constraints.

It is important to disaggregate to the regional and country level, however, since averages for emerging economies mask significant variations. We see some of these in Figure 2, showing regional averages for some constraints. Bureaucracy is a serious constraint on governance everywhere, including in OECD countries. Corruption is also a serious impediment, especially in many emerging economies. Tax regulations constitute a severe constraint in OECD and in post-socialist transition countries, in contrast with regions such as South Asia, where it ranks low as an impediment, relative to the other constraints. Similarly, infrastructure is a major constraint in Africa and developing Asia, in contrast with the East Asian tigers, and, to an extent, Latin America and the transition economies (see Figure 2). This does not imply that in these regions it is unimportant to focus on infrastructure investments, since this type of question gives only a rela-

Figure 2: Some key constraints to business, by region: Responses from firms in Survey 2005

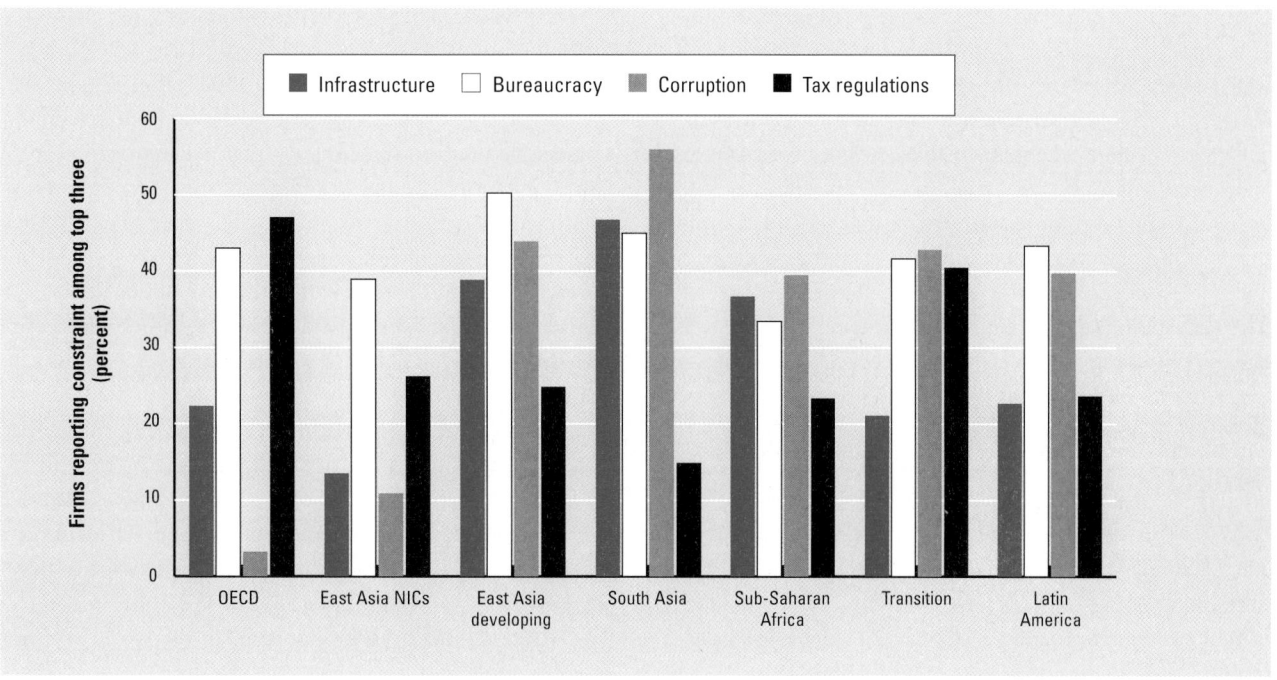

Source: Current Survey. The question posed to the firm was: "Select among the above 14 constraints the five most problematic factors for doing business in your country."

tive ranking across different constraints for each country. But the fact that infrastructure was not rated at the top in so many countries—in Latin America, Africa, transition, and others, which also suffer from infrastructure problems, and are in dire need of investments—is a sure sign of the extent to which some other factors—largely governance and corruption-related—impose even more severe constraints on business development.[8]

Regional averages always mask substantial variations across countries in each region. For instance, at only 3 percent, the percentage of firms reporting that corruption is one of the top three constraints across the 24 countries in the OECD (in the Survey) is very low. Yet this is only an average of varying country estimates ranging from zero—i.e., not a single enterprise ranking corruption as a constraint—in countries such as Finland, New Zealand, Norway, Iceland, and Australia, to a much higher 18 percent of the respondents mentioning corruption as a top impediment in Greece. In fact, there are a number of emerging economies in the various regions where the response rate is lower than for Greece, such as the cases of Uruguay (4 percent), Chile (7), Slovenia and South Africa (10), Botswana and Ghana (12), Estonia (13), and others. Yet the constraint posed by corruption to business, ranked much higher, on average, in the emerging economies, is the result of the prevalence of countries where over one-half of the respondents claim that corruption is one of the

top constraints to their business, such as Armenia, Azerbaijan, Bangladesh, Benin, Cambodia, Cameroon, Guatemala, Kazakhstan, Kenya, Morocco, Mozambique, Pakistan, Paraguay, Romania, Russia, Uganda, and Vietnam, among others.

The impact of poor governance and corruption is not limited to the corporate sector. In many countries, corruption represents a "regressive tax" on the household sector as well: as compared with higher-income groups, lower-income families pay a disproportionate share of their incomes in bribes to have access to public services, and end up with less access to such services because of corruption. Related, there is also the finding of research that corruption increases income inequality.[9]

Moreover, governance matters significantly for aid effectiveness. While some have challenged their findings, the widely known Burnside and Dollar[10] work on assessing aid effectiveness shows, on the basis of cross-country aggregate data, that the quality of policies and institutions of the aid recipient country is critical. It is at least as revealing, however, to explore these links at the microeconomic level, focusing, for instance, on the effectiveness of investment projects, which show that institutions matter for project effectiveness.[11] Also, our calculations of World Bank–funded projects suggests that if there is high corruption in an aid-recipient country, the probability of project success, of institutional development impact, and of long-term sustainability of the investment, is much lower than in countries with better governance.

These results are of particular relevance in the context of a corollary myth, the contention that donor agencies can "ringfence" projects in highly corrupt countries and sectors, and thus ensure that it is efficiently implemented, and that objectives are attained, even where other projects fail. This is unrealistic. With the possible exception of some humanitarian aid projects, the notion that the aid community can fully insulate projects from a country's overall corrupt environment is not borne out by the evidence. The data suggest that when a systemic approach to governance, civil liberties, rule of law, and control of corruption is absent, the likelihood of an aid-funded project being successful is greatly reduced.

Clearly, governance and corruption matter. Space constraints preclude an exhaustive presentation in this chapter of the literature on this topic, or a presentation of all the complex links between governance and other important factors and outcomes. For instance, the extent to which corruption and the absence of rule of law may undermine fledgling democracies is of critical importance, and worthy of deeper treatment elsewhere. Similarly, the links between misgovernance, corruption, and money laundering with such security threats as organized crime and terrorism require deeper analytical and empirical treatment.[12]

The answer to the myth that the importance of governance and anti-corruption is overrated would be incomplete without pointing out the obvious: governance is not the only important driver of development. Macroeconomic, trade, and sectoral policies are also important. But when governance is poor, policymaking in other areas is also, and often, compromised.

Myth #4: Good governance and corruption control is a luxury that only rich countries can afford.

Some claim that the link between governance and income does not mean that better governance *boosts* incomes, but, rather, the reverse, that higher incomes automatically translate into better governance. However, our research does not support this claim. It is misleading to suggest that corruption is due to low income, and thus, to invent a rationale for discounting bad governance in poor countries. In fact, the evidence points to better governance as being the *cause* of higher economic growth. Furthermore, a number of emerging economies, including the Baltics, Botswana, Chile, and Slovenia, have shown that it is possible to reach high standards of governance, without having yet joined the ranks of the wealthy nations.

While this finding applies across the globe, the recent focus on Africa by the international community makes this point particularly relevant for debates on aid effective-

ness, and about the priority the continent needs to give to improving governance to complement aid inflows. Indeed, in recent years, the international community has rightly turned its attention to the problems of underdevelopment in Africa. Not only is Africa poorer than other regions in the developing world, it also lags far behind other regions in terms of progress in achieving the Millennium Development Goals. If past trends continue, many countries in Africa will have to double their per capita incomes over the next decade, in order to attain the goal of halving poverty by 2015. There is widespread consensus that a combination of substantial aid inflows, together with concerted domestic policy effort, is necessary to meet this challenge.

In light of the strong positive effect of governance on development, and in light of its importance for effective aid delivery, it is then a matter of considerable concern that governance performance in sub-Saharan Africa is on average quite weak. Many countries in Africa are not only poor, but also poorly governed. Fully 38 out of 46 countries in the region are both poorer than the world average, and also exhibit worse governance than the world average. Some observers have argued that we should thus discount the poor governance performance of the region, based on the fact that these countries have very low income levels, thus arguing that good governance costs money. Yet, as described above, recent research provides very little evidence to support the proposition that poor governance (or corruption) in Africa is attributable to Africa's poverty. Rather, the direction of causality is largely in the opposite direction, from better governance to better development outcomes.[13]

Myth #5: It takes generations for governance to improve.

Reformers in many governments as well as investors, civil society leaders, and the international aid community increasingly view governance as being key to development, and to improving the investment climate. This, in turn, has increased the demand for monitoring the quality of governance in a country over time. Further, aid donors are also coming to the view that aid flows have a stronger impact on development in countries with good institutional quality. In light of this, it is important to measure trends over time, as well as levels of governance. Our new governance indicators now span an eight-year period from 1996 to 2004, a sufficiently long period to begin looking for meaningful trends in governance. As we have emphasized in our work, the presence of measurement error in all types of governance indicators, including our own, makes assessing trends in governance a challenging undertaking.

In the recently released paper "Governance Matters IV" (Kaufmann et al., 2005) we develop a formal statistical

Table 1: Significant changes in governance worldwide in short-term, 1998–2004

Selected countries based on aggregate indicators for 209 countries

Voice and accountability

Significantly worsened........Central African Republic, Nepal, Ivory Coast, Haiti, Zimbabwe, Russia, Kyrgyz Republic, Eritrea, Pakistan, Belarus, Solomon Islands, Venezuela, Kazakhstan, Bangladesh, Ecuador, Iran, Gabon

Significantly improved........Chile, Kenya, Bahrain, Gambia, Algeria, Mexico, Senegal, Peru, Turkey, Slovak Republic, Nigeria, Indonesia, Ghana, Croatia, Bosnia and Herzegovina, Sierra Leone, Serbia

Regulatory quality

Significantly worsened........Zimbabwe, Venezuela, Ivory Coast, Ethiopia, Bangladesh, Pakistan, Philippines, Lebanon, Egypt, Zambia, Myanmar, Guinea, Eritrea, Bolivia, Peru, Tunisia, Honduras, Guatemala, Ecuador, Kazakhstan, Cameroon, Cuba

Significantly improved........Cape Verde, Armenia, Tajikistan, Azerbaijan, Bosnia and Herzegovina, Serbia, Estonia, Zaire DRC, Equatorial Guinea, Iceland, Lithuania, Slovak Republic, Iraq

Rule of law

Significantly worsened........Zimbabwe, Argentina, Ivory Coast, Ethiopia, Moldova, Cuba, Venezuela, Nepal, Haiti, Lebanon, Papua New Guinea, Dominican Republic, Myanmar, Eritrea

Significantly improved........Mozambique, Slovak Republic, Estonia, Latvia, Lithuania, Madagascar

Control of corruption

Significantly worsened........Zimbabwe, Bangladesh, Eritrea, Ivory Coast, Swaziland, Ethiopia, Equatorial Guinea, Central African Republic, Sudan, Moldova

Significantly improved........Tanzania, Madagascar, Croatia, Serbia, Colombia, Bulgaria, Estonia, Latvia, Slovak Republic

Note: The significance level for the list of countries shown in this table was calculated at 75 percent confidence level. For the full list, including all governance components, and also at 90 percent confidence level, see Kaufmann et al., 2005. Source: Kaufmann et al., 2005.

ment among our many data sources about the direction of change in governance in these countries. Overall, this reminds us that, while changes in institutional quality are usually gradual, there are also countries which have achieved sharp improvements—or suffered rapid deterioration—over an eight-year period. This finding is of particular interest, given the common perception that, while deterioration in a particular country *can* take place rather quickly, improvements are of necessity slow and incremental.

Challenging the "institutional pessimists," Table 1 provides a list of countries that have improved markedly in selected dimensions of governance since the late 1990s. As we can see, this also challenges the "Afro-pessimists," since we can see in the same table that there are a number of countries in Africa which have improved in a rather short period of time, even if it is still the case that other countries have not. Generally, as shown in Table 1, it is found that roughly as many countries in Africa show declines in these particular governance dimensions as show improvements.

As Table 1 shows, there has been significant improvement since 1998 in *voice and accountability* in a number of countries, such as in Chile, Bosnia and Herzegovina, Croatia, Serbia, Ghana, Indonesia, Sierra Leone, Slovak Republic, and Peru, while a significant deterioration has taken place in countries such as Ivory Coast, Zimbabwe, Kyrgyz Republic, Russia, Venezuela, Pakistan, Belarus, Nepal, and Haiti. Similarly, a deterioration in *rule of law* during that period has taken place in a number of countries, such as Ethiopia, Namibia, and Argentina, while significant improvements in *government effectiveness* have taken place in South Africa and Bulgaria, among others.

We have also addressed the question of whether governance has been improving worldwide on average. We find that, in fact, there is no evidence that governance has improved since 1996 (or any period thereafter). It is quite sobering to see, from the review of these indicators, that, on average, the quality of governance worldwide has remained stagnant. Although, as pointed out earlier, there are a number of countries where significant improvement has taken place, there are also countries exhibiting significant deterioration, and many where little change has taken place.

In this context, it is telling that there are clusters of countries that have been improving, in comparison with others. For instance, there is some evidence of improved governance in a number of dimensions in some Caribbean countries, in contrast with much of Latin America. Particularly telling is the story of the post-socialist transition countries. As illustrated in Figure 3, those transition countries, which in the mid-1990s were promised potential entry to the European Union—upon fulfillment of an appropriate institutional and political path—exhibit an

methodology, as well as some simple rules of thumb, for identifying changes in governance that are likely to be statistically and practically significant. Over the eight-year period spanned by our governance indicators, we find that in about 10 percent of countries we can be fairly confident (at the 90 percent significance level) that governance has changed substantially, while at a lower (75 percent significance) level, roughly 20 percent of all observed changes stand out as significant. Similarly, in a nontrivial number of countries there have also been significant changes in the shorter six-year period from 1998 to 2004 (Table 1). Importantly, we show that there is a great deal of agree-

Figure 3: The tale of transition: Stagnating world average, but variation in trends across groups of countries

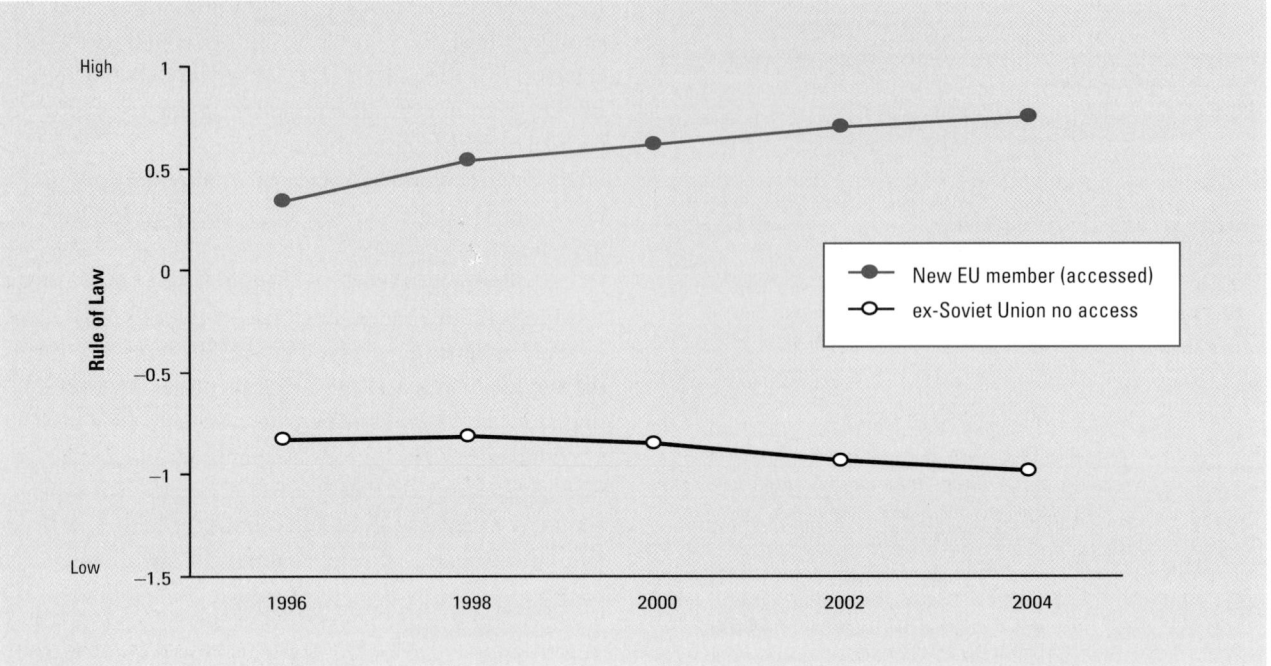

Source: Kaufmann et al., 2005.

improved trend in governance (shown in the figure on the rule-of-law variable), while those post-socialist countries which were not offered such a window of opportunity, stagnated or worsened.

Thus, while it is true that institutions tend to change only gradually, and that in many countries there has been little improvement in the short term, we can also see that in some countries there has been a sharp improvement during a short period of time. This defies the view that while governance may deteriorate quickly, improvements are always slow and incremental.

Myth #6: Fight corruption by fighting corruption.

A fallacy promoted by some in the field of anti-corruption, and at times also by the international community, is that the best way to fight corruption is by fighting corruption—that is, by means of yet another anti-corruption campaign, the creation of more anti-corruption commissions and ethics agencies, and the incessant drafting of new laws, decrees, and codes of conduct. Moreover, in some settings, the disproportionate emphasis on prosecutions—typically of a few corporations or individuals, and often of the political opposition—at the expense of a focus on prevention and incentives for integrity, has reduced the effectiveness of anticorruption efforts. An instinctive tendency to over-regulate, which may take place in the throes of a corruption scandal, is not infrequent, and can also be

counterproductive. Excessive regulations not only do not address the more fundamental causes of corruption, but often create further opportunities for bribery. Overall, these anti-corruption initiatives-by-fiat appear to have little impact, and often serve as politically expedient ways to react to the pressure to "do something" about corruption. Often, this results in neglect of more fundamental and systemic governance reforms.

Myth #7: The culprit in developing countries is the public sector, which is solely responsible for shaping the inadequate business environment.

A common fallacy is to focus solely on the failings of the public sector. The reality is much more complex, since powerful private interests often exert undue influence in shaping public policy, institutions, and state legislation. In extreme cases, so-called oligarchs capture state institutions. These are issues we have reviewed in some detail in the chapters on governance in previous *Reports,* presenting evidence from previous Surveys on the extent of undue influence, as well as outright capture of state institutions by corporate potentates. Contrary to conventional wisdom, the public sector is not the sole shaper of the investment climate faced by domestic firms and foreign investors in a country, and, similarly, the private sector is not the passive recipient of the investment climate. In reality, there is a complex interplay between corporate and public sector governance and policymaking, whereby powerful segments of the private sector also play a very important role in shaping key public policy, legislation, and regulations which constitute the rules of the game, and the business environment within which these corporations operate.[14]

Behind the conventional definition of corruption (as the abuse of public office for private gain) lies the image of a predatory state, seen as a huge outstretched hand, extorting firms for the benefit of politicians, high officials, and bureaucrats. The research carried out over the past six years argues for balancing the focus, to include the important role of private firms, since the evidence suggests that many firms collude with politicians for their mutual benefit. Even in strong states, such as in rich OECD countries, powerful conglomerates can have significant influence in shaping regulatory policy. Consequently, it is of paramount importance to revisit the traditional notions of the investment climate. More specifically, money in politics is at the heart of the interplay between the corporate and public sectors, in terms of policy and institutional outcomes, and within it, the role played by political finances in exerting undue influence.

The private-public sector governance challenge is not confined to the domestic players in a country. In spite of the fact that the OECD Anti Foreign Bribery Convention came into force over five years ago, many multinational corporations still bribe abroad, at times affecting public policy, and more generally undermining public governance in emerging economies. In the articles in previous *Reports* we codified in some detail the fact that there still appears to be considerable bribery by multinationals headquartered in OECD countries, but which operate outside of the OECD. While one ought not rule out that the OECD Convention may be effecting some progress—and there is an increase in the number of investigations in a few OECD countries—there appears to be little progress in most OECD signatory countries in actually bringing serious cases of bribery to court.

In fact, the data from the 2004 Survey illustrate the fact that domestic and multinational firms operating *within* the OECD may be behaving rather differently from those multinationals headquartered in the OECD and operating outside it. About 7 percent of firms were estimated to have bribed in public procurement contracts by multinationals headquartered in an OECD country and operating in another OECD country, which compares favorably with the estimate of about 10 percent of domestic firms bribing within their own OECD country. However, it does not compare well with the estimate exceeding 17 percent for multinationals that are also headquartered in an OECD country, but which operate outside of OECD.[15] We lack the same type of data from years past for precise comparison, and therefore it is not possible to indicate whether a downward trend is evident. Yet the existence of a significant gap between practices of multinationals within the OECD and outside of it in terms of bribery points to the need for tougher monitoring and enforcement of the Convention across the OECD, and of considering more effective complementary measures.

The fact that the private sector also plays a key role in governance and corruption has rather different implications for action. In fact, having ignored the private-public governance nexus for very long, the international community has often erred in its emphasis on conventional public sector interventions as a key instrument to help countries improve governance. Simply put, traditional public-sector management interventions have not worked, because they have focused on technocratic organizational "fixes," often supported through technical assistance, the importation of hardware, organizational templates, and visits by "experts" from rich countries.

Myth #8: Countries can do little to improve governance, and IFIs and the donor community can do even less.

Given the long list of interventions that have not worked, as well as the role often ascribed to historical and cultural factors in explaining governance, it is easy to fall into the pessimist camp. That would be a mistake. First, historical and cultural factors are far from deterministic—witness, for instance, the diverging governance paths of neighboring countries in the southern cone of Latin America, the Korean peninsula, the transition economies of Eastern Europe, and in southern Africa. Second, there are strategies that offer particular promise. The coupling of progress on improving voice and participation—freedom of expression and gender mainstreaming—with transparency reforms can be particularly effective, as seen in Figure 4.

Unfortunately, progress in these areas of political and institutional governance, such as freedom of the press, gender equality, and transparency, has been checkered in many countries in the world. This disappointing reality highlights the pitfalls of focusing only on formalistic political changes. For instance, over the past 20 years there has been a substantial increase in the number of electoral democracies across emerging economies, with dozens more countries joining the ranks of countries holding elections. However, improved formal polity has not always translated into improved freedoms for the press, increased citizen voice, or opportunities for women. For instance, out of the 121 countries which Freedom House classified as electoral democracies in 2002, 49 are in fact classified as *not* having a fully free press.[16]

The data for Africa are also telling. According to Freedom House, there has been significant progress in the area of political rights over the past two decades. Yet press freedoms, which it has been tracking since 1995, have not

Figure 4: Gender equality, freedom of the press, and transparency are associated with corruption control

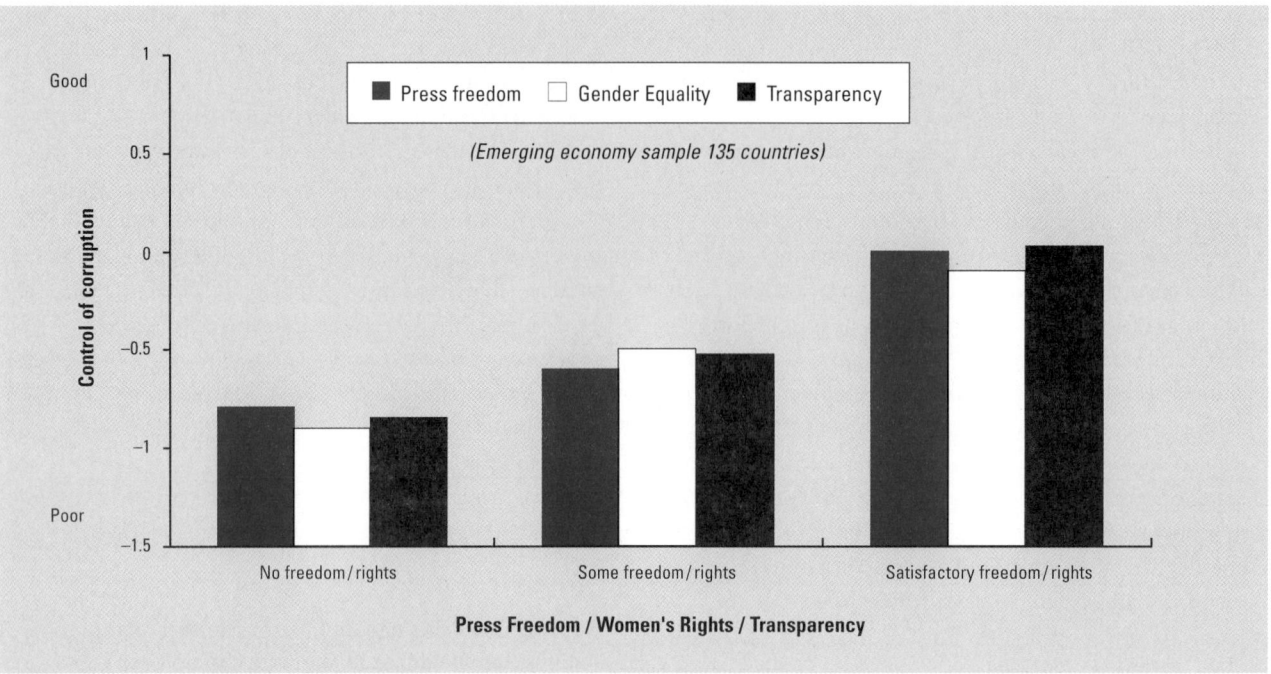

Note: Satisfactory Freedom/Rights reflect higher ratings in press freedom, gender equality, and transparency.

Sources: for *control of corruption:* Kaufmann et al., 2005; for *press freedom:* Freedom House, 2005, online at: http://www.freedomhouse.org ; for *gender equality:* World Bank, 2004; for *transparency:* Bellver and Kaufmann, 2005.

improved, as seen in Figure 5. There is evidence, in fact, that some deterioration may even have taken place in recent times in a number of countries in the continent, as suggested not only by the Freedom House evidence depicted here, but also by the responses by firms to the Survey questions. Over the past couple of years, an increasing number of respondents from the enterprise sector in Africa do report growing obstacles in terms of what media can report and print.[17]

In sum, while in many countries in the world there has been progress in selected political rights areas, this has not always been translated into enhanced media freedoms, gender equality, or political and institutional transparency. And this matters a great deal, because where there is progress in these areas, progress can also be expected in corruption control. There is nothing deterministic about corruption, yet difficult political and systemic institutional reforms are often needed.

Some argue that there is not much the IFIs can do about helping a country improve governance and controlling corruption, even if the country is not viewed as facing a historical or culturally deterministic fate to stay with poor governance for many generations to come. Some development experts are skeptical about the ability of IFIs and donors to help countries improve their governance, either because of a conviction that the "macro" matters more, a mistaken belief in historical determinism, or, the

more nuanced view, that because the interventions needed to improve governance are politically sensitive, they are very difficult for outsiders to encourage.

Indeed, there are areas that fall outside the mandate of IFIs, such as promotion of fair multiparty elections. But it may well be within the ability of IFIs and donors to do something about initiatives to encourage transparency, freedom of information and an independent media, participatory anti-corruption programs led by the country, and gender equality—all of which have been underemphasized so far in the fight against corruption.

The next stage of institutional reform: A strategy for transparency

Partly because there is a higher comfort level with technocratic "fixes," traditional themes such as Public Sector Management (including civil service reforms, codes of conduct, etc.) continue to be given significant prominence in the aid community. By contrast, transparency has been an underemphasized pillar of institutional reforms. That there has been relatively little progress on the ground in this area is regrettable, in view of the influential conceptual contributions of a number of Nobel-laureates, who have developed a framework linking the citizen's right to know and access to information with development outcomes.[18] Even popular lore subscribes to the importance

Figure 5: Press freedom in sub-Saharan Africa, 1995–2005

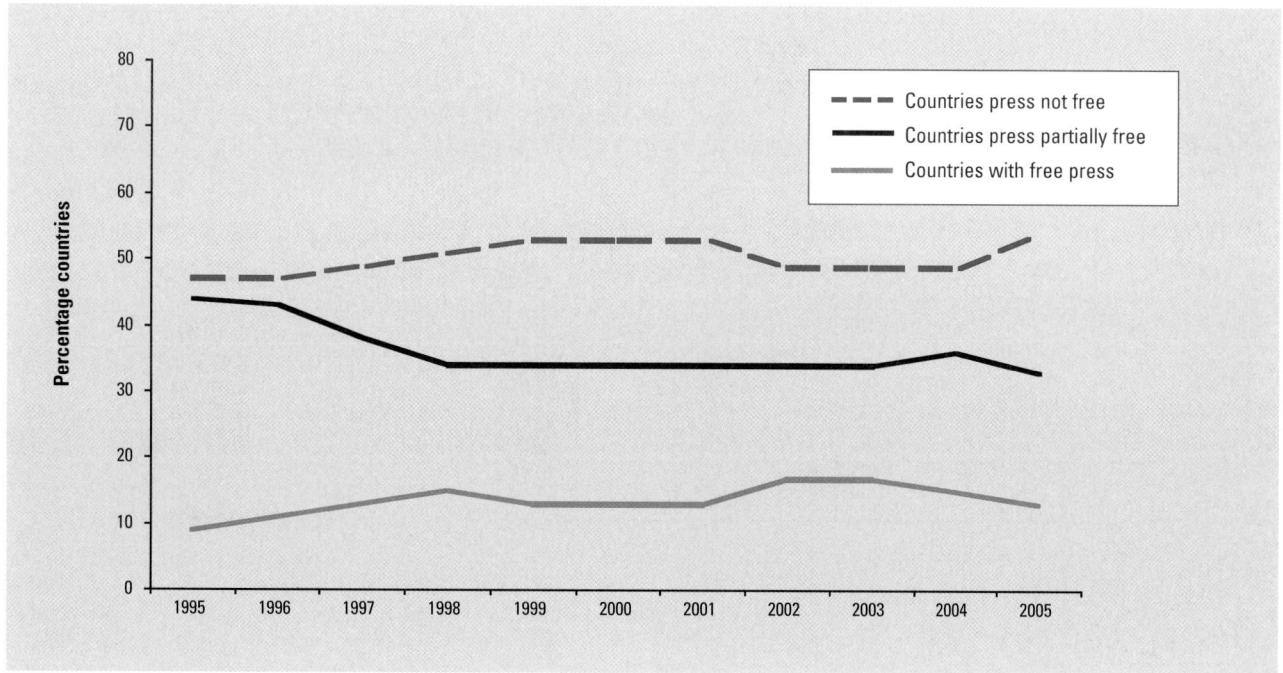

Note: Y-axis reports percentage of countries within the region with a free/partially free/not free rating, associated with scores in press freedom.

Source: Freedom House, 2005, online at: http://www.freedomhouse.org

of transparency, as illustrated by the old adage "sunlight is the best disinfectant."

Yet not only does the implementation of transparency-related reforms remain checkered on the ground virtually everywhere, but, in contrast with other dimensions of governance, such as the rule of law, corruption, and regulatory burden, there is a large gap between the extent of the conceptual contributions and the progress on its measurement and empirical analysis.[19]

Thus, we are attempting to contribute to the empirical understanding of various dimensions of transparency by undertaking construction of a transparency index for 194 countries, based on over 20 independent sources (including the Survey). Country ratings and their margins of error are generated, for an aggregate transparency index with two subcomponents: economic/institutional transparency and political transparency. The results suggest enormous variation across countries in the extent of their transparency. In fact, a high level of transparency is not the exclusive domain of a particular region, or of rich countries, and there are transparency-related challenges in countries in each region, as illustrated in Figure 6.[20] We find that transparency is associated with better socioeconomic and human development indicators, as well as with higher competitiveness and lower corruption. In presenting concrete policy initiatives, we suggest that much progress can be achieved without inordinate resources. In

fact, transparency reforms are substantial net *savers* of public resources, and can obviate the necessity for excessive regulations or rules. And transparency reforms need not remain abstractions at the level of rhetoric any longer. Some concrete examples of concrete reforms, which some countries have taken selectively, and which many more could consider undertaking comprehensively, are listed in the accompanying box.

Of course, transparency reforms are not the only institutional reform priorities. IFIs and donors can complement these reforms by continuing to support traditional core competencies, helping with capacity-building, sharing knowledge, and focused reforms in key institutions in emerging economies, such as in the judiciary, customs, and tax and procurement. Further, at the municipal level, and in the context of decentralization, the donor community can also help to further institutional progress and anti-corruption in emerging economies.

These targeted reforms supporting highly vulnerable institutions would have, however, to be adapted to the specific country realities, and thus might vary considerably from country to country in their priority and in specific design. In some countries, the first priority identified might be to support procurement reforms, strengthening accountability institutions in parliament, and freedom of the press; in others, it may be reforms in the judiciary, women's rights, and the revamping of customs. In-depth

Figure 6: Transparenting transparency: Toward an index of overall country transparency, selected countries

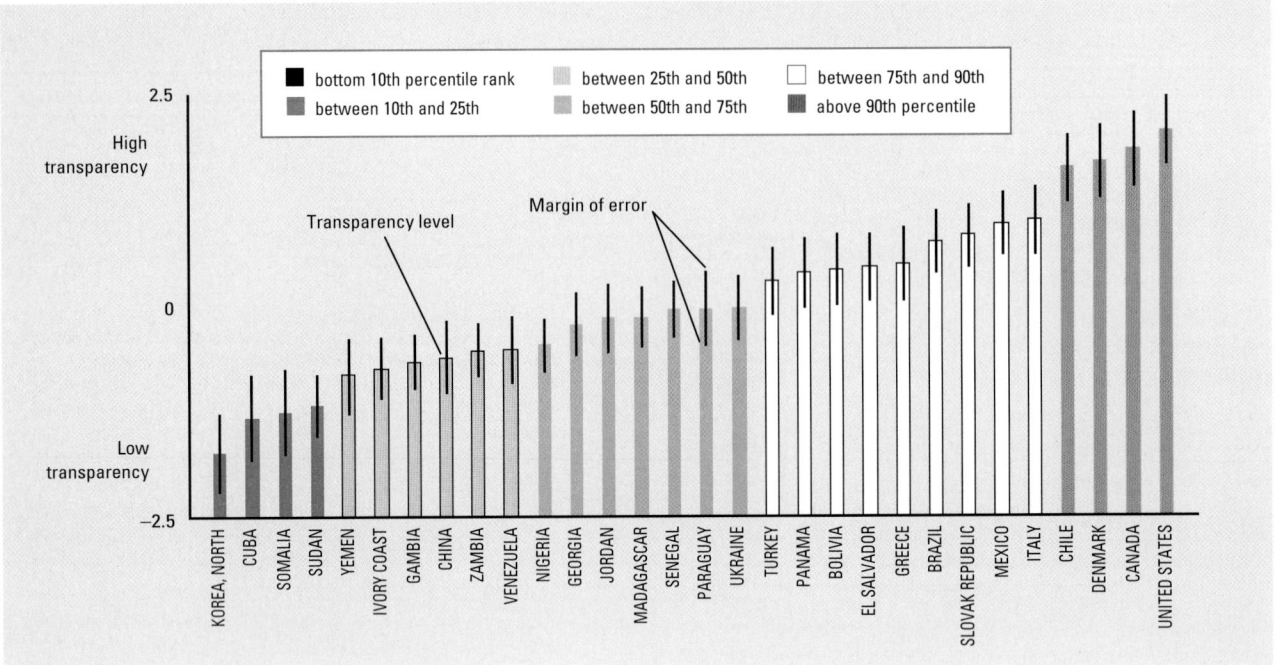

Note: Selected countries are presented for illustration, and due to margins of error, no precise ranking is warranted.
Source: Bellver and Kaufmann, 2005.

Box 1: Concrete Transparency Reforms

Since research shows clearly that transparency helps improve governance and reduce corruption—essential ingredients for better development and faster economic growth—the international community and individual countries must pay closer attention to this issue. Within a concerted, practical, and comprehensive pro-transparency strategy, a basic checklist of concrete reforms, which countries may use for self-assessment, a report-card of sorts, might include the following items:

- public disclosure of assets and incomes of candidates running for public office, public officials, politicians, legislators, judges, and their dependents;

- public disclosure of political campaign contributions by individuals and firms, and of campaign expenditures;

- public disclosure of all parliamentary votes, draft legislation, and parliamentary debates;

- effective implementation of conflict of interest laws, separating business, politics, legislation, and public service, and adoption of a law governing lobbying; publicly blacklisting firms that have been shown to bribe in public procurement (as done by the World Bank); and a requirement to "publish-what-you-pay" by multinationals working in extractive industries;

- effective implementation of freedom of information laws, with easy access for all to government information;

- freedom of the media (including the Internet);

- fiscal and public financial transparency of central and local budgets, adoption of the IMF's Reports on Standards and Codes framework of fiscal transparency, detailed government reporting of payments from multinationals in extractive industries, and open meetings involving the country's citizens;

- disclosure of actual ownership structure and financial status of domestic banks;

- transparent (Web-based) competitive procurement;

- periodic implementation and publicizing of country governance, anti-corruption and public expenditure tracking surveys, such as those supported by the World Bank;

- Transparency programs at the city level, including budget disclosure and open meetings.

governance diagnostics at the country level are thus required first,[21] working closely with experts and institutions within the country, which must, itself, take the lead in such reforms, allowing donors to play an important, but supportive, role.

Conclusions: A global compact on governance?

The challenge of governance and anti-corruption confronting the world today calls for something other than business-as-usual. A bolder approach is needed, and collective responsibility at the global level is called for. The myths discussed in this chapter highlight areas where the international community and individual countries may need to reconsider strategies and approaches. Improving governance and controlling corruption matter enormously for development, and countries can substantially improve, even in the short term, if the appropriate strategy and political resolve are present.

Whatever the strategy, it ought to benefit from the support of the international community, as well as the involvement of the private sector. Indeed, we emphasize that governance and corruption challenges are not the exclusive responsibility of the emerging economies (or poor world), nor are public institutions the only culprits. The rich world must not only deliver on its aid and trade liberalization promises, it must also lead by example. OECD countries, which are lagging behind, should ratify and effectively implement the 2003 UN Convention Against Corruption, and take concrete steps—as Switzerland is beginning to do—to repatriate assets looted and stashed abroad by corrupt officials.[22] It is also important that OECD countries address the daunting challenges of cross-border money laundering and arms trading.

Much more should be done to ensure that transnational corporations refrain from bribery abroad, and that they contribute to improved governance practices in host countries. Corporate initiatives promoting general principles against corruption, or voluntary codes of conduct, may raise awareness, and at times have a modest impact, but much tougher incentives and measures are called for, to encourage the private (including multinational) sector to refrain from engaging in bribery. Public disclosure and widespread dissemination of lists of offending firms could act as a serious deterrent. As for the IFIs and donors, there is a need to grapple with questions of selectivity and effectiveness in aid programs, rewarding countries which are making improvements in governance, and moving away from the notion that large scale financing to highly corrupt governments will benefit the poor. The notion that the donors can "ringfence" (or insulate) most projects from a generally corrupt environment ought to be abandoned.

It is clear that additional income flows alone will not improve governance. Indeed, we have learned that improved governance by a country *results* in higher incomes, not the other way around. Countries themselves must shoulder responsibility and take the lead in implementing often difficult political and institutional reforms.

Notes

1 The author is Director of Global Programs at the World Bank Institute. This chapter draws on collaborative research projects with Aart Kraay, Joel Hellman, Massimo Mastruzzi, and Ana Bellver, and has benefited from collaboration with Augusto Lopez-Claros and the Global Competitiveness team. I also thank Massimo Mastruzzi and Lorena Lenhart for their invaluable assistance. The views and errors expressed are the author's own. Neither those errors nor the data (which are subject to margins of error and do not imply precise country rankings) necessarily reflect the official views of the World Bank. An abridged version of some of the detailed material in this chapter is forthcoming in the fall issue of the IMF quarterly *Finance and Development*.

2 At the time of this writing, of the countries having already ratified the Convention only one is a rich OECD country, the remaining 28 being emerging economies, as is the next set of countries about to ratify. Well over 100 countries have signed the Convention, which requires ratification by 30 countries in order for it to come into force. Once the Convention is ratified—which is imminent—the central challenge will be its effective monitoring and implementation by the countries.

3 A precedent-setting concrete case is currently in the making, thanks to the imminent return by Switzerland to Nigeria of funds looted during the Abacha regime and stashed in Swiss banks.

4 Kaufmann, 2003 and 2004.

5 The updated set of aggregate governance indicators is available at: http://worldbank.org/wbi/governance The complete methodology, new findings, and data may be obtained in Kaufmann et al., 2005.

6 See Appendix for a methodological explanation of how these estimates were derived.

7 The estimates come from Alcala and Ciccone (2004), Acemoglu, Johnson and Robinson (2001), Kaufmann and Kraay (2002), and Rodrik, Subramanian and Trebbi (2004).

8 Caution in making precise comparisons across regional averages is warranted, since some regions are significantly underrepresented in the Survey. The Survey coverage has been steadily increasing over the years, and, with a current coverage of 117 countries in 2005, it is by far the broadest of any cross-country survey of firms. Yet it is typically those countries *not covered* in these surveys, such as some in the Middle East, Africa, and the CIS, which tend to rate lower in governance within their regions, compared with those surveyed.

9 Alonso-Terme et al., 1998.

10 Burnside and Dollar, 1999.

11 See Isham et al. (1997) and Dollar and Levin (2005).

12 See, for instance, the Report of the Commission on Weak States (2004), and Kaufmann (2004), each reporting on selected links between governance and security, areas which have typically been treated in isolation from each other. It is worth noting again the extent to which terrorism may often constitute the globalized result, in one country, of misgovernance in another.

13 See Kaufmann et al. (2005) for details.

14 Even the definitions and views as to what constitutes the investment climate tend to underestimate the importance of governance factors. Until very recently, the focus has been on a rather narrow and traditional set of factors comprising the investment climate, emphasizing economic, financial, and legal regulations by fiat, while divorced from the political dimensions of governance. A simple Web search illustrates the biases in how the investment climate is viewed and ana-

lyzed: of the almost 10,000 articles on investment climate since 1996 that come up in a search for prominent papers in the Factiva search engine (online at http://www.factiva.com) over 50 percent address issues related to economics or policy, 30 percent address monetary or financial factors, almost 20 percent address issues related to law or legal matters; yet less than 10 percent bring up issues related to corruption or governance. This means that in the literature, the treatment of the concept of the investment climate itself is not in tune with what the enterprises themselves report in surveys of what matters the most for their operations.

15 These are conservative estimates, and based on the sample of countries covered by the Survey. In countries not covered by the Survey, the prevalence of such bribes may be even higher, since there is a direct correlation between the propensity of multinationals to bribe, on the one hand, and the overall extent of domestic corruption in the host investment country, on the other.

16 Freedom House, online at: http://www.freedomhouse.org

17 For instance, the Survey reports that, while 29 percent of the respondent firms in 17 countries in sub-Saharan Africa reported very serious constraints in what the media could publish in their countries, the percentage of highly dissatisfied respondents in the same set of countries rose to 41 percent.

18 See Stiglitz (1999) and Sen (1981).

19 Further, there has been a particular paucity of literature on transparency which breaks down or unbundles transparency into its specific components, such that it becomes usable as policy advice and intervention. Our ongoing research attempts to partly fill these empirical and policy-related gaps. In a recent paper, we have reviewed the existing literature, and present various definitions of transparency, with a view to providing an empirical framework of worldwide indicators on various dimensions of transparency. These initial empirical results are intended to help bring about concrete policy and institutional innovations related to transparency reforms. See Bellver and Kaufmann (2005).

20 There is even significant variation in transparency within countries, such as differences in performance between the economic/institutional and political dimensions of transparency, or, related to this, differences in the way institutions within a country operate as regards transparency.

21 For details of participatory in-depth governance diagnostics at the country level, in which the country takes the lead in designing action programs, see http://www.worldbank.org/wbi/governance/capacity-build

22 It should be noted that there is more corruption in some of the richer OECD countries than in some emerging economies; thus the OECD must redouble its efforts among its own members.

References

Acemoglu D., S. Johnson, and J. A. Robinson. 2001. "The Colonial Origins of Comparative Development: An Empirical Investigation." *American Economic Review* 91(5):1369–1401.

Alcala, F. and A. Ciccone. 2004. " Trade and Productivity." *Quarterly Journal of Economics* 119(2):613–46.

Alonso-Terme, R., H. Davoodi, and S. Gupta. 1998. "Does Corruption Affect Income Inequality and Poverty?" IMF Working Papers 98/76. Washington, DC.

Bellver, A. and D. Kaufmann. 2005. "Transparenting Transparency: Initial Empirics and Policy Applications." World Bank Policy Research Working Paper. Washington, DC. Forthcoming.

Burnside, C. and D. Dollar. 1999. "Aid, Policies, and Growth." Policy Research Working Paper Series 1777. Washington, DC: World Bank.

Camdessus M. 1998. "Money Laundering: the Importance of International Countermeasures." Address by Michel Camdessus at the Plenary Meeting of the Financial Action Task Force on Money Laundering. Paris. 10 February.

Commission for Africa. 2005. *Our Common Interest: Report of the Commission for Africa.* London.

Center for Global Development. 2004. "On the Brink: Weak States and US National Security." Commission on Weak States and US National Security. Washington, DC.

Dollar, D. and V. Levin. 2005. "Sowing and Reaping: Institutional Quality and Project Outcomes in Developing Countries." Policy Research Working Paper Series 3524. Washington, DC: World Bank.

Factiva. Online at: http://www.factiva.com

Freedom House. 2005. "Freedom of the Press Indicators." Online at: http://www.freedomhouse.org

Friedman E., S. Johnson, and D. Kaufmann. 2000. "Dodging the Grabbing Hand: The Determinants of Unofficial Activity in 69 Countries." *Journal of Public Economics* 76(3):459–493.

Heston, A., R. Summers, and B. Aten. 2002. *Penn World Table Version 6.1.* Philadelphia: Center for International Comparisons at the University of Pennsylvania (CICUP).

Isham, J., D. Kaufmann, and L. Pritchett. 1997. "Civil Liberties, Democracy, and the Performance of Government Projects." *World Bank Economic Review* 11(2):219–2.

Kaufmann, D. 2002. "Governance Crossroads." *The Global Competitiveness Report 2002–2003.* World Economic Forum. New York: Oxford University Press

———. 2003. "Governance Redux: The Empirical Challenge." *The Global Competitiveness Report 2003–2004.* New York: Oxford University Press.

———. 2004. "Corruption, Governance and Security: Challenges for the Rich Countries and the World." *The Global Competitiveness Report 2004–2005.* World Economic Forum. New York: Oxford University Press.

Kaufmann, D., and A. Kraay. 2002. "Growth Without Governance." *Economia* 3(1):169–215.

Kaufmann, D. and M. Mastruzzi. 2005. "Corruption: A Trillion Dollar 'Industry'?" World Bank. Washington, DC. Forthcoming.

Kaufmann, D, A. Kraay and M. Mastruzzi. 2005. "Governance Matters IV: Governance Indicators for 1996–2004." World Bank Policy Research Working Paper 3630. Washington, DC.

Levin, M. and G. Satarov. 2000. "Corruption and Institutions in Russia." *European Journal of Political Economy* 16:113–32.

Organisation for Economic Co-operation and Development. 1998. "The Size of Government Procurement Markets." *OECD Journal on Budgeting* 1(4).

Rodrik, D., A. Subramanian, and F. Trebbi. 2004. "Institutions Rule: The Primacy of Institutions over Geography and Integration in Economic Development." *Journal of Economic Growth* 9(2):131–165.

Satarov G. and M. Levin. 2005. "Corruption in Russia: Dynamics and Perspectives." Moscow: INDEM.

Schneider, F. and D. Enste. 2002. "Shadow Economies Around the World: Size, Causes and Consequences." IMF WP/00/26.

Sen, A. 1981. *Poverty and Famines: An Essay on Entitlement and Deprivation.* Oxford: Oxford University Press.

Stiglitz, J. E. 1999. "On Liberty, the Right to Know, and Public Disclosure: The Role of Transparency in Public Life." Oxford Amnesty Lecture.

United States Central Agency. 2001. *The World Factbook.* Online at: http://www.cia.gov/cia/publications/factbook

United States Census Bureau. 2002. *Economic Census, Table 1. Advance Summary Statistics for the United States.* Washington, DC. Online at: http://www.census.gov/econ/censusU2/advance/TABLE1.HTM

Walker, J. 1999. "Measuring the Extent of International Crime and Money Laundering." Paper prepared for KriminalExpo Conference. Budapest. June.

World Bank. 1997. Governance Databank. Online at: http://www.worldbank.org/wbi/governance/govdata/unofficial_data.xls

94

———. 2004. *Country Policy and Institutional Assessments.* Washington, DC.

———. 2000. *World Business Environment Survey.* Washington, DC. Online at: http://www.worldbank.org/privatesector/ic/ic_ica_re-sources.htm

———. 2000–2003. Various diagnostics surveys for various countries. Online at: http://www.worldbank.org/wbi/governance/capacitybuild

World Bank Institute. 2002. "The Right to Tell: The Role of Mass Media in Economic Development." World Bank. Washington, DC.

———. Various years. Governance Databank. Online at: http://www.world-bank.org/wbi/governance/data.html

———. 2003. Governance Survey. Online at: http://www.wbigf.org/hague/hague_survey.php3

World Economic Forum. 2003. *The Global Competitiveness Report 2003–2004.* New York: Oxford University Press.

———. 2004. *The Global Competitiveness Report 2004–2005.* Hampshire: Palgrave Macmillan.

Appendix: The US$1 trillion estimate of worldwide bribery: Synthesis of the approach[1]

We present here, in brief, the method used to arrive at a rough estimate of the annual amount of worldwide bribery. Calculations are made under various scenarios and assumptions, which provide our range of estimates. A likely estimate derived from these calculations is roughly US$1 trillion, although the confidence range may be relatively wide, as will be suggested in the following. Nonetheless, even under very conservative assumptions, the estimate is highly unlikely to be less than about US$600 billion, while at the other extreme of the likely range of values it may well exceed an annual amount of US$1.5 billion.

Additionally, we reviewed the available literature and explored alternative estimation procedures, as a sort of external validation of this estimation exercise, simply by comparing the rough estimates derived from our method with independent proxies drawn from other sources or studies. Following is a description of the approach.

The strategy for estimating the annual amount of bribes is based on available data from surveys, in which firms and households report on average annual bribery payments as a share of sales (for enterprises), or incomes (households). Based on these, we made extrapolations for countries not covered in these surveys, and then also assumed that the overall population exhibits similar patterns to those of the sampled population.

We utilized various enterprise and household surveys for this estimation, including two different enterprise surveys: the World Bank Enterprise Survey (WBES) carried out in the year 2000 in 81 countries, and drawing on 10,033 responses from firms (WBES 2000), and on the Global Competitiveness Survey in 104 countries, drawing on 8,729 responses (Survey 2004). We also used the results from household surveys carried out by the World Bank in the context of 16 different Governance and Corruption Diagnostic Surveys. From these we extrapolate and compute estimates of bribery worldwide. Given the gaps, measurement errors and difficulty of data collection in the area of corruption, mentioned earlier, calculations were made under multiple scenarios, utilizing different assumptions, ranging from least to most conservative. Indeed, the main objective of this exercise was to arrive at a preliminary *likely* range of estimates, rather than a precise point estimate, which would be misleading.

Bribery paid by the household sector was computed by first obtaining the estimated share of bribes in total incomes from the diagnostic surveys, carried out between 1999 and 2003 in 16 countries. We mapped these available estimates of household bribery against the *control of corruption* indicator available worldwide from our aggregate Governance Indicators database (which is denominated in an ordinal scale), and regressed the reported bribe share from the household responses (dependent variable) against the control of corruption variable. The resulting coefficient from the regression and the actual values of the control of corruption variable was then used to have an estimate of the household bribe share for the countries, which did not have a direct measure from a country diagnostic report. This then gave an estimate of household bribery share in personal incomes for all countries. Each country estimate was multiplied by its GDP and then factored by 0.7, the estimate of the ratio of personal consumption to GDP.[2]

Estimates from corporate bribery were computed on the basis of two different surveys, utilized for alternative estimation scenarios, namely the WBES 2000 and the Survey 2004, respectively. In each scenario, we extrapolated worldwide bribe shares on the basis of quantitative responses of firms to the questions on the extent of administrative bribe share (in sales), as well as the bribe fees paid to secure public procurement contracts (as a share of the contract). Sensitivity analysis with multiple scenarios, under different assumptions, was done (including very conservative assumptions), in order to derive a broad-based range of likely bribery estimates.

In the case of WBES, worldwide administrative bribery was computed as the product of the world-weighted bribe share average and overall GDP (net of procurement), factored by 0.7, the assumed contribution of business to overall GDP. The bribe share average, in turn, was drawn from WBES 2000 findings, weighted by GDP per capita levels and converted using either midpoints (base scenario) or initial points (conservative case).

In the case of the alternative scenario based on the Survey, administrative bribery was computed as the product of the world-weighted bribe share average and overall GDP (net of procurement), factored by 0.7, i.e. contribution of business to overall GDP. The worldwide bribe and procurement shares, in turn, were drawn from Survey 2004 findings, weighted by GDP per capita levels.

The multiple scenarios, under many different assumptions, yielded multiple results and a range of estimates. Overall, 138 different scenarios were run, including 48 scenarios based on the WBES, and 90 scenarios based on the Survey, and within each, under many different scenarios and assumptions about different degrees of "conservatism" in the data analysis. For instance, under many scenarios, instead of deriving the bribe share estimate from a firm by computing the midpoint in the survey questionnaire range questions, the initial point of each range, given as the option in the question was used.

Utilizing the 48 estimations derived by adding household bribery estimates to those for corporate bribery, based on the survey of firms from the WBES, we obtained an average bribery estimate of US$1.25 trillion (with a median value of US$1.18 trillion). If, instead of the WBES, we use the Survey figures for the estimates for bribery by the corporate sector, we get a lower estimate for average bribery of about US$830 billion (median at US$820 billion).

From the 138 scenarios used, if one were to leave out the extreme "tails" (5 percent in each tail), the range of (reasonable) estimates would range from $604 billion to $1.76 trillion. In summary, based on this exercise, a reasonable *range* of estimates for annual bribery would appear to be between US$0.6 and well over US$1.5 trillion a year, with a reasonable *midpoint* being close to US$1 trillion. It should be noted that this rough estimate of around US$1 trillion did not include the extent of corrupt leakages from public budgets or theft of public assets—or other forms of corruption, such as nepotism—since the focus was on estimating bribery transactions.

External checks and validation

In order to obtain a reality check on these rough estimates, we searched the literature for existing estimates in related areas. There were no existing estimates of bribery worldwide, hence the search was broadened to estimates of related areas such as the unofficial economy, money laundering, and the like. For other proxies for corruption, or related to it, we did a literature and data review search, and provide calculations for the unofficial economy and money laundering, as well as other bribery estimates. For the size of the unofficial economy, we rely on studies by Schneider and Enste (2002) and Friedman et al. (2000). For money laundering, we use an IMF study (Camdessus, 1998), as well as a paper by John Walker (1999). And finally, for other bribery estimates, however unreliable, we look at the results of an online survey, and report on a recent survey of corruption in Russia.

Unofficial economy estimates ranging between US$3.4 to US$5.1 trillion worldwide

The first, and lower, estimate of the unofficial economy, based on the data in Friedman et al. and part of the World Bank governance databank[3] was computed as the sum of the products of individual unofficial country economy figures in 1997, and the associated GDP in 2002 (assuming no change in estimated shares in the last five years), adjusted by a factor of 1.19, on the assumption of a similar trend in unofficial economy shares in the countries missing from the database. A higher estimate was drawn from Schneider and Enste (2002), who provide estimates of the shadow economy in 76 developing and developed economies. Their findings highlight a large shadow economy. For 21 OECD economies they estimated the size of the underground economy as having moved from US$2 trillion (12.7 percent of GDP) in 1989, to US$3.4 trillion (16.7 percent of GDP) in 2001. It should be noted, however, that many unofficial economy transactions are not necessarily corrupt, and, conversely, many bribes and corrupt transactions do not necessarily take place in the unofficial economy.

Worldwide money laundering estimates: US$600 billion to US$2,800 billion

In a 1998 IMF study, it was estimated that the aggregate size of money laundering in the world could be somewhere between 2 and 5 percent of the world's gross domestic product, or between US$600 billion and US$1.5 trillion. In an unrelated study, conducted by John Walker (1999), the author provides an alternative estimate of money laundering of US$2.8 trillion. He does so by first estimating the numbers of crimes recorded by police in each country in each of eleven crime types, using data from United Nations Centre for International Crime Prevention database of recorded crime statistics, the UN Survey on Crime Trends, and the Operations of Criminal Justice Systems. The author then uses this model to estimate the total amount of money that is laundered within a country, or to a foreign country (per recorded crime). Such estimates are extrapolated for each country keeping accounts of corruption and income levels.

Other bribery estimates: US$1 trillion and higher

Further, and separately, a "Worldwide Bribe-Fee Commission in Tainted Procurement" was drawn from an online governance survey, carried out in 2003 by the World Bank Institute.[4] The estimate was computed as the sum of the products of regional procurement figures (using 1998 worldwide procurement figures of US$5.5 trillion) and the associated bribe shares in procurement. The latter was derived directly from the survey results, using midpoints. The resulting estimate from this independent Web source is about US$1 trillion. It should be noted that this estimate focuses on one area of bribery, namely procurement. Particular caveats apply to this exercise, given margins of error, and potentially large sample biases (through voluntary surveys on the Web).

Finally, a new study estimating bribery in Russia (Satarov and Levin, 2005), if validated, would hint at a vastly larger estimate of worldwide corruption. The report estimated an annual bribe amount exceed US$316 billion, or 73 percent of Russian GDP. Even if figures such as these are, in fact, substantial overestimates, and the actual figure is much smaller for Russia, the implications for worldwide bribery would suggest a global estimate that may vastly exceed an annual figure of US$1 trillion.

Notes

1 A more detailed description is available from the author upon request.

2 Many variations of the base scenario were performed, and are described in detail in Kaufmann and Mastruzzi (2005).

3 Online at: http://www.worldbank.org/wbi/governance/govdata/unofficial_data.xls

4 See http://www.wbigf.org/hague/hague_survey.php3

CHAPTER 2.2

Rethinking Exchange Rate Competitiveness

KENNETH ROGOFF,[1] Harvard University

Most governments care about the real exchange rate of their currency, that is, the value of prices (or wages) relative to world values, when translated into a common currency. For example, a high real exchange rate makes imports cheap relative to domestically produced goods. This is good not only for consumers, but for importers of foreign intermediate goods, such as capital equipment. But by the same token, a richly valued currency presents problems for exporters, whose goods become less competitive in global markets. Do the needs of exporters necessarily trump the interests of importers? If so, can macroeconomic policy do anything about it? Does export competitiveness depend mainly on microeconomic factors? These are fundamental and difficult questions, and the answers have never been as simple as some observers might have us believe.

In this short essay, I will try to explain some of the theoretical and practical problems in identifying severe exchange rate misalignments. This is particularly relevant, now that the vast majority of countries in the world have substantially unified their exchange rate systems, such that one can no longer simply point to a large black market exchange rate premium as a compelling sign of exchange rate misalignment.

Identifying situations of extreme real exchange rate under- or overvaluation used to be a lot simpler back in the not-so-distant past, when currency controls were rampant, often resulting in large discrepancies between the officially sanctioned exchange rate and the underground black (parallel) exchange rate. Indeed, such practices were the norm throughout most of the developing world until the past decade, with black market premia of 50 to 100 percent surprisingly common, especially in Africa, Latin America and, more recently, the CIS countries. A relatively unusual recent example is Myanmar where, at the beginning of 2003, the (active) black market price of foreign currency—in terms of domestic currency—exceeded the official rate by over 700 percent! Not surprisingly, with such pronounced market-based evidence of overvaluation, it is not difficult to find corroborating macroeconomic evidence, such as the fact that the county was experiencing high inflation with little offsetting exchange rate adjustment. (Myanmar's premium was hardly the modern record; the premium in pre-2002 Iraq was reported to be over 6,000 percent (see Reinhart and Rogoff, 2003)).

In principle, the black market premium, in and of itself, is not necessarily representative of underlying economic forces either, and can reflect many other factors, such as the severity of punishments for violating currency controls. In practice, however, large premia turn out to be very good indicators of underlying pressures, and strong predictors of the size and direction of future exchange rate movements (see Reinhart and Rogoff, 2003). Moreover, it was not the developing countries that invented the idea of using draconian exchange rate controls as a method of intervening into foreign trade. The same phenomenon plagued much of Europe for some 20 years after World War II.

Obviously, if governments are setting official exchange rates for their currencies far above observable market-determined rates, the spread constitutes prima facie evidence of exchange rate overvaluation, even if an exact measurement is still difficult. Today, however, these black and white cases of exchange rate misalignment are rarer than they used to be. Instead, analysts interested in assessing exchange rate misalignments are generally forced to rely more on other factors, such as comparisons of labor and product costs in different countries, and on trade imbalances. Unfortunately, each of these approaches poses problems. And we shall see that, even if they could be properly measured, it is very difficult to form appropriate quantitative benchmarks.

International measures of relative costs and prices are fraught with technical difficulties.[2] For one thing, non-traded goods form such a large part of GNP in so many countries today—estimated at over 75 percent in OECD countries (see Obstfeld and Rogoff, 2001)—that price developments can be very different across countries, without necessarily implying any misalignment. Nor are trade balances necessarily a clear marker of misalignment. Sustained trade imbalances can arise for many reasons—e.g., borrowing to finance new investment—which do not necessarily imply lack of long-run sustainability.

Sustained one-way currency interventions to either support or hold down the value of a country's currency are more meaningful, though they, too, may simply reflect asymmetries in a country's other capital controls. (Such is the case in contemporary China, where one-way intervention reflects, in part, a policy that is more open to capital inflows than outflows.)

In this essay, I will begin by focusing on the issue of measuring a country's real exchange rate, and then turn to some of the conceptual problems presented by other evidence. The main conclusion is that exchange misalignment—i.e., having an overly competitive or an uncompetitive exchange rate—remains an important practical problem in the global financial system. Because the global trend toward more unified exchange rate systems (free convertibility of currency) has eliminated many of the most obvious cases of misalignment, economists and policymakers must now think more deeply about the entire concept of exchange rate competitiveness.

Measurement

Measuring the so-called *real exchange rate* broadly aims at comparing the evolution of purchasing power across currencies. In principle, there are many alternative measures one could look at to compare costs, including, for example,

unit labor costs. I will concentrate on real exchange rate measures because we have by far the best and most comprehensive data available, while unit labor costs are only available on a comparable basis for a relatively select group of mostly richer countries. Also, many of the basic issues are the same, regardless of which metric one chooses.

Measuring the real exchange rate relative to trend

One problem with comparing real exchange rates is that different countries typically use different weights in constructing their consumer (or producer) price indices. Thus, comparisons of overall price levels are immediately clouded by the fact that we are often comparing apples and oranges. I will set this problem aside for the moment, not because it is unimportant, but because there is a deeper problem, one that is far more difficult to negotiate: price levels constructed by national statistical authorities are invariably *indices* rather than levels. What may seem a mundane distinction to the uninitiated, is actually quite significant, since comparisons of real exchange rates across two countries will show *changes* over time, while standard data make it difficult to say anything about *levels*. In other words, we may be able to compare two countries' price indices and exchange rates, and say that goods have become more expensive over time in, let us say, Poland, relative to Argentina. But national price level data can never tell us whether *levels* of exchange rate-adjusted prices are higher in one versus the other.

Consider Table 1, which lists average real "effective" (trade-weighted) exchange rates for 59 countries over the period 1990 to 2004, and compares these average levels with real exchange rates at the start of 2005. (In Table 1, the base year is 1990, so that 1990 = 100.)

At the top of the list, with the most competitive exchange rate by this measure, is Argentina. Relative to its 1990–2004 average, Argentina's real exchange rate is extraordinarily low, almost 50 percent below average, due, in part, to lingering effects of the currency's deep depreciation set off by the 2001 year-end default. Taiwan also has a low real exchange rate relative to the longer-term average, due partly to several recent years of deflation.[3] At the other end of the spectrum, the countries of Eastern Europe have experienced enormous exchange rate appreciation of 30 percent and more, due, in part, to high productivity growth, but also because of huge capital inflows, driven by the region's increasing integration with Western Europe. Interestingly, the real effective exchange rate of the United States dollar, for all its gyrations, was very near its 15-year average at the start of 2005, whereas China's effective real exchange rate was only 13.6 percent below its average.

Table 1: Effective real (CPI) exchange rates: Current versus 1990–2004 average

Country	1990–2004 average (1990 = 100)	Febuary 2005	Current over- (under-) valuation relative to 15-year average
Argentina	147.3	77.2	–47.6%
Paraguay	108.9	77.5	–28.9%
Egypt	123.9	92.7	–25.1%
Uganda	78.9	59.2	–25.0%
Algeria	62.0	46.8	–24.5%
Brazil	76.6	58.4	–23.8%
Taiwan	92.0	72.3	–21.4%
Uruguay	149.2	120.5	–19.3%
Saudi Arabia	96.0	78.3	–18.5%
Malaysia	95.4	78.5	–17.7%
Bolivia	102.6	84.8	–17.3%
Philippines	108.6	90.9	–16.3%
Israel	103.8	86.9	–16.3%
Pakistan	91.1	79.0	–13.3%
Indonesia	84.8	73.9	–12.9%
Thailand	92.7	80.9	–12.7%
Ukraine	110.4	96.6	–12.5%
Japan	118.3	106.9	–9.7%
Chile	117.1	108.4	–7.4%
Singapore	107.9	99.9	–7.4%
Sweden	88.0	82.2	–6.5%
Costa Rica	104.0	97.9	–5.9%
Nigeria	116.3	109.9	–5.4%
Finland	79.5	76.5	–3.8%
Jordan	112.4	108.4	–3.5%
United States	109.0	107.5	–1.4%
Kazakhstan	105.6	104.1	–1.4%
India	75.8	75.5	–0.4%
Venezuela	156.7	156.2	–0.3%
Morocco	112.9	112.7	–0.2%
Colombia	128.0	127.9	–0.1%
Germany	94.5	94.7	0.1%
Switzerland	104.4	105.0	0.6%
Norway	95.9	96.7	0.9%
France	98.2	99.2	1.0%
China	93.6	94.6	1.1%
Mexico	118.2	120.4	1.8%
Sri Lanka	112.9	117.0	3.7%
Spain	90.4	94.2	4.2%
Italy	88.3	91.9	4.2%
Korea	89.2	93.8	5.2%
Denmark	100.4	105.9	5.5%
Canada	84.1	89.0	5.9%
Netherlands	104.3	111.5	6.9%
Ireland	94.9	104.1	9.7%
United Kingdom	103.0	115.1	11.8%
Australia	88.7	101.7	14.7%
Kenya	117.2	136.2	16.2%
Lithuania	140.7	163.5	16.3%
New Zealand	96.2	113.3	17.8%
Russia	106.3	126.9	19.3%
Turkey	104.2	124.3	19.3%
Botswana	105.1	126.2	20.1%
Estonia	115.1	139.7	21.3%
Poland	208.5	272.4	30.6%
Czech Republic	106.9	140.4	31.3%
Hungary	138.0	188.0	36.2%
Bulgaria	112.8	155.2	37.6%
Romania	95.8	134.3	40.2%

Source: International Monetary Fund.

Does this mean that Argentina is the cheapest place in the world to do business and Eastern Europe the most expensive? Of course not. It only tells us that these regions have real exchange rates farthest from recent norms. Nevertheless, we should by no means dismiss the data in Table 1. Economists generally believe that transitory factors, such as financial shocks balance out over time, so long-run averages of any country's exchange rate are probably a fair measure of equilibrium, provided the country's current account performance over the extended period is reasonably stable. In principle, one can improve the measurement of underlying long-run equilibrium exchange rates by adjusting for factors such as differential growth or wealth effects (see Obstfeld and Rogoff, 1996). But even so, examining current deviations from long-term averages can be instructive, particularly for outliers.

Indeed, a cursory examination of the outliers in Table 1 confirms that, in the absence of a major productivity shock—such as a big rise in oil prices for an oil exporter—a high real exchange rate is usually a harbinger of current account weakness.[4] Argentina, with a very low exchange rate relative to recent norms, is, indeed, running a sizable current account surplus.[5] So, too, with Brazil, another country whose real exchange rate is also below trend. The countries of Eastern Europe, with sharply appreciated real exchange rates, are running epic current account deficits. For countries in the middle, however, the real exchange rate barometer does not send such a clear signal. For example, the United States today is running record current account deficits at roughly the same real exchange rate as it had in 1990, when the country's current account balance was tipping into surplus. (Of course, as former French President Charles de Gaulle pointed out, the United States dollar enjoys the "exorbitant privilege" of being the world's reserve currency and therefore, perhaps, is not representative.) Singapore, with an exchange rate only slightly more competitive than what it had in 1990, ran a current account surplus in excess of 25 percent of GDP in 2004.

But current account positions are only one manifestation of competitiveness, albeit one that captures a lot of attention. As we shall later discuss in detail, one cannot simply look at any one variable to determine if an exchange rate is under- or overvalued. A large current account deficit is often indicative of problems, but if, for example, a country is borrowing to finance productive investment in the export sector—or in infrastructure to support investment—this is far more likely to be sustainable that when it is borrowing to finance consumption.

Measuring the level of the real exchange rate

Another way to compare real exchange rates involves looking outside the data provided by national statistical authorities, and using specialized data sets to measure the absolute cost of identical baskets of goods in different countries. (The costs are "absolute" in that they measure exchange rate adjustment price *levels* at a point in time, rather than price level *changes* relative to a base year, where the real exchange rate might have been far from equilibrium.) From a methodological point of view, this approach is vastly superior to looking at conventional price indices; the main problem is that much of the data is constructed by small research teams commanding far less funding or manpower than a national statistical agency. The most important source for international comparisons of prices is the Penn World Table (Summers and Heston, 1991), from the University of Pennsylvania, and maintained also by the World Bank and the Organisation for Economic Cooperation and Development (OECD). These data, which the World Bank uses to compare incomes across countries, forms price indices by (essentially) looking at what it costs in each country to buy a specific item or group of items in the United States, known as a *consumption basket*. While there are many subtleties to such comparisons—it is difficult to ensure that one is measuring goods of similar quality, and the approach does not attach enough importance to variety—they at least give us a rough common denominator for comparing prices in different countries.

In Table 2, we see that by this purchasing power parity (PPP) metric, the former CIS countries (including Georgia, Belarus, and Ukraine) have among the lowest price levels in the world, even lower than those in Africa. But one should not press this nuance too far, since the data are relatively poor for these countries.

Japan and Switzerland are the world's most expensive countries, with Japan being almost 50 percent more expensive than the United States. The main practical problem with PPP data is that their availability tends to be very sparse. Comprehensive benchmark studies are available only at five-year intervals with the most recent being 1996. (Even data for 2001 are not available as of this writing.) The data in Table 2 for the year 2000 are derived by using various statistical techniques to extrapolate price developments from the last benchmark year.[6]

One other source of international price-level comparisons is *The Economist* magazine's "Big Mac" index,[7] which gives the cost of a Big Mac hamburger in different countries, translated into US dollars. Although this index is extremely narrow—perishable burgers are not exactly tradable—and there are huge differences in restaurant ambience across franchises, nonetheless, the index is updated annually, and is surprisingly informative. Table 3 (based on the most recent survey of June 2005) again shows Switzerland at the top with a cost of $5.05, compared to $3.06 in the United States, with China being the lowest-cost country (in the sample) at $1.27. (The table does not include all the former Soviet republics, although Russia itself is relatively cheap at $1.48.)

Table 2: International comparison of price levels

Country	Price level (US = 100)	Country	Price level (US = 100)
Kyrgyzstan	8.36	Hungary	41.78
Georgia	11.28	Poland	42.25
Ukraine	12.48	Chile	44.61
Kazakhstan	14.84	Brazil	45.13
India	17.07	Uruguay	58.47
Russia	17.25	Mexico	60.79
Indonesia	18.06	Korea, Republic of	64.75
Pakistan	19.93	Argentina	65.62
Zimbabwe	21.33	New Zealand	66.25
Sri Lanka	21.94	Venezuela	69.05
China	23.14	Spain	73.79
Bulgaria	23.29	Australia	74.57
Philippines	24.90	Canada	79.30
Uganda	24.95	Singapore	80.12
Kenya	26.32	Italy	81.32
Morocco	27.09	Netherlands	90.11
Algeria	28.71	France	90.70
Thailand	29.61	Israel	92.48
Estonia	31.97	Ireland	92.56
Romania	32.52	Germany	94.96
Colombia	33.10	Finland	95.99
Czech Republic	33.29	United Kingdom	98.50
Bolivia	33.93	United States	100.00
Egypt	34.43	Sweden	104.83
Lithuania	36.47	Denmark	106.83
South Africa	36.70	Norway	112.36
Nigeria	39.26	Syria	114.30
Jordan	39.85	Switzerland	118.14
Turkey	40.34	Japan	144.83
Malaysia	40.86		

(cont'd.)

Source: University of Pennsylvania, 2002. Online at: http://pwt.econ.upenn.edu/

Table 3: *The Economist* Big Mac Index of exchange rate under- and overvaluation

Switzerland	5.05	Brazil	2.39
Denmark	4.58	Japan	2.34
Sweden	4.46	Czech Republic	2.30
Euro area	3.58	Singapore	2.17
Britain	3.44	South Africa	2.10
New Zealand	3.17	Poland	1.96
United States	3.06	Argentina	1.64
Turkey	2.92	Egypt	1.55
Peru	2.76	Hong Kong	1.54
Canada	2.63	Indonesia	1.53
Hungary	2.60	Russia	1.48
Mexico	2.58	Thailand	1.48
Chile	2.53	Philippines	1.47
Australia	2.50	Malaysia	1.38
South Korea	2.49	China	1.27
Taiwan	2.41		

(cont'd.)

Source: *The Economist*, June 2005

Conceptual issues in interpreting real exchange rates and competitiveness indices

Of course, even with the measurement problems discussed in the previous section, there are still situations where we can speak of compelling evidence that exchange rates are overvalued. As mentioned at the outset, the clearest case is where a country has currency controls, and where there are large observable black market premia. Another is that of emerging markets, whose real exchange rate is very high relative to recent norms, and which are borrowing heavily to finance mainly consumption rather than productive investment. These examples are often marked by large capital flows which, if in the form of short-term debt, may be subject not only to a flattening, but to a sharp reversal. In these cases, a currency may be overvalued, in the sense that its current value is not sustainable according to any reasonable model. Unfortunately, the cases where one can make summary judgments are relatively rare.

When does productivity growth justify appreciation of the real exchange rate?

Real exchange rate growth, particularly slow steady real exchange rate growth does not always signal overvaluation. Countries experiencing rapid productivity growth may see rising real exchange rates, but it is generally difficult to rationalize trend changes of more than a couple of percentage points a year this way, mainly because productivity growth seldom exceeds world averages by more than a few percent, even in very rapidly growing economies. For example, many of the countries of Eastern Europe have experienced faster productivity growth than their neighbors in Western Europe, but not nearly at the same pace as their real exchange rates have appreciated. It is curious that, since its opening in 1979, China's real exchange rate has depreciated rather than appreciated in real terms. However, the significance of this is difficult to interpret, because producers have been able to draw on a large and underemployed rural population, thereby restraining price and wage pressures. Of course, this transition must ultimately slow at some point, as cities increasingly become congested and polluted.

Dutch disease

Another important related case to consider is that of oil exporters and other natural resource-rich countries. It is quite common for resource-rich countries to experience rapid rises in real exchange rates that hamper competitiveness in other industries, the so-called *Dutch disease.* For example, in New Zealand, Canada and Australia, all major commodity exporters, high commodity prices typically lead to a higher real exchange rate as wealth effects spill over into domestic demand for these countries' nontraded goods (see Chen and Rogoff, 2003). Although such effects

make manufactured exports less competitive, it would be wrong to conclude that the commodity-driven appreciations are necessarily making the overall economy uncompetitive since, of course, commodity production constitutes a major industry also. Instead, the interplay of high commodity prices and real exchange rates should be thought of as sending market signals for higher investment in commodities industries (when prices are up), while the high real exchange rates depress investment in other industries. In general, as long as the investment decisions are market driven, this is perfectly healthy, and should not be confused with a lack of competitiveness.

The situation is admittedly more problematic in countries where commodity production is dominated by state-run companies, and where investment decisions are driven as much by politics as by market considerations, such as Mexico's Pemex oil company, with its long history of problems along these lines. In the extreme, the "curse of natural resources," first identified by economic historian David Landau, may actually make a country worse off, by its corrupting influence on political management. In general, Dutch disease is far more likely to be a serious distortion in cases where heavy government intervention in an economy prevents price mechanisms from generating appropriate market responses to commodity price shocks.[8]

Problems of real exchange rate appreciation driven by aid inflows

The problem of managing exchange rate appreciations is not unique to rich countries, but can also affect very poor countries receiving aid flows. The problem could present itself some day in sub-Saharan Africa, particularly if rich countries ever step up to the plate and honor their promises to provide much higher levels of aid. If aid ever flows in earnest, African countries will likely see their currencies sharply appreciate as money flows in, bidding up demand for domestic goods, making export industries less competitive, and increasing the risk of aid dependency. This is not a reason to deny the aid, but it is a more significant complication than is the case of commodity exporters. For commodity exporters, high prices mean investment opportunities which, if well managed, lead to sustained profits in the commodities sector and overall increases in national growth rates even as manufacturing industries suffer and are forced to restructure. For African countries, the aid will be useful, but there is a risk that the exchange rate valuation effects may hamper growth.

Once again, it goes without saying that this is not an argument against giving aid, but, rather, is an effective argument for making such aid flows steadier and more dependable. It is no favor to a country to give large aid flows that hurt the competitiveness of its exports, and then withdraw them after the already poor country's export sector has dwindled. Dutch disease constitutes an additional argument for investing in education and infrastructure, so that exporters' productivity increases as the real exchange rate increases. Naturally, given the high levels of corruption in many poor countries, donors must beware that their donations do not simply end up in offshore bank accounts.

Are large trade imbalances prima facie evidence of misalignment?

What about trade imbalances? If a country has a large trade balance surplus or deficit, is that not clear evidence that it has an over- or undervalued exchange rate? Many politicians over the years have reached that conclusion. Perhaps they are right, but it is not so simple to prove. In a world with increasingly globalized capital markets, countries can run deficits and surpluses for macroeconomic reasons that have little or nothing to do with hypercompetitive exchange rates. For example, if a country's government is running a large deficit—let us say, to finance military expenditures or social welfare payments—it typically spills over into a country's overall current account deficit, which, for most countries can simply be thought of as a generalized version of the trade balance deficit. Indeed, it is a matter of simple accounting, that when the government runs a larger deficit, the country as a whole must also run a larger deficit—expressed in large part through a trade balance deficit—unless the private sector raises its savings rate or lowers its investment rate. The reverse holds when the government raises its surplus.

Many other macroeconomic factors can have an impact on the trade deficit. If, for example, a country scales back on domestic investment, perhaps because it over-invested in an earlier period, then, unless its savings rate is also reduced, it is going to have to run a larger trade surplus. In this case, the country's funds will flow abroad to advance investment in more productive regions elsewhere in the world. In this case, however, to assume that the country's trade balance surplus results from a highly competitive exchange rate is to completely misinterpret the situation. The trade balance surplus is a sign of weakness, rather than strength.

This does not mean that countries cannot benefit, in certain circumstances, by maintaining a low exchange rate, and this policy is viewed by many as the core of the Asian model. Still, it does not follow that a country's long-term growth necessarily benefits from having an undervalued exchange rate. For example, there is considerable evidence that capital goods imports are important for enhancing productivity growth (see, for example, the literature following from DeLong and Summers, 1991). But maintaining an undervalued real exchange rate makes capital goods imports expensive, affecting not only the traded goods sector but also nontraded goods, such as housing.

More fundamentally, export growth is not an end in itself. As was discussed in the introduction, consumers prefer a high real exchange rate that makes imports cheap, not a low real exchange rate that makes them expensive. If China's exchange rate is undervalued, this implies that its consumers are paying more than they would otherwise for imports, leading in turn to lower living standards. The notion that undervalued exchange rates are somehow more popular, and help maintain social stability must be challenged by the fact that in many democratic countries, popular pressure for higher consumption leads to overvalued exchange rates, not undervalued ones.

Does the United States, the world's dominant borrower, influence misalignment risks?

Last but not least, when one looks at exchange rate competitiveness today, there is another overarching issue that must be mentioned: in recent years, the United States has run increasingly massive current account deficits, Indeed, the United States so dominates global borrowing that its current account deficits accounted for roughly 70 percent of all the current account deficits of *all deficit countries in the world* in 2004! Correcting this phenomenon will almost surely bring about an eventual depreciation of the dollar, in real terms, broadly across most of the world, not least in emerging markets, which collectively ran a US$260 billion current account surplus in 2004. Thus, regardless of how they score on today's competitiveness indexes, most countries are likely to see significant further appreciation as the US current account and trade deficits close up.[9] Exchange rate competitiveness is a zero-sum game, and thanks to the United States, the world is in a bubble, where more countries are going to be looking more undervalued and more competitive than usual.

Conclusions

The idea that countries must maintain competitive exchange rates is enshrined in the Washington Consensus (Williamson, 1989), which firmly warns against grossly overvalued exchange rates. Ask any good international macroeconomist what key variables they most want to know in assessing a country's overall macroeconomic position, and the "real" exchange rate—the nominal exchange rate adjusted for price-level differences—will often be near the top of the list. It makes intuitive sense, even though any measure of real exchange rate overvaluation is of limited value in isolation from a broader assessment of the economy.

Nevertheless, throughout much of the world, the days are long gone when one could simply look at black market or parallel exchange rates and instantly have a sense of whether a country's exchange rate is overvalued. Today, with exchange rates increasingly driven by market forces—even in cases where countries peg, they increasingly use market-based instruments—measuring and assessing exchange rate overvaluation, and, relatedly, exchange rate competitiveness, has become more subtle. The notion that trade balance deficits or surpluses alone constitute evidence of exchange rate misalignment is wrong, simply because trade imbalances often reflect macroeconomic forces rather than trade policy, per se.

How, then, should policymakers address exchange rate competitiveness? The short answer is that, for most countries, it is not a macroeconomic issue until the exchange rate gets conspicuously out of line by historical standards, especially if this is caused by a dramatic change in monetary or fiscal policy, or in capital inflows. Otherwise, countries concerned with maintaining competitive exchange rates will generally be wise to pursue stable and transparent macroeconomic policies, and to ensure that those policies enhance competition and flexibility at the microeconomic level.

Notes

1 Professor of Economics and Thomas D. Cabot Professor of Public Policy, Harvard University. The author is grateful to Gian Maria Milesi-Ferretti and Jaewoo Lee for helpful advice, and to Augusto Lopez-Claros and Eyal Dvir for helpful comments on an earlier draft.

2 Witness how much difficulty Europe has had in aggregating inflation rates across its member states to form a euro-area inflation rate.

3 With the exchange rate against the dollar relatively stable, and with inflation in the United States, deflation in Taiwan means that goods are becoming cheaper relative to the United States, i.e., that the country's real exchange rate is declining.

4 Empirical evidence on real exchange rates suggests that they tend to be more predictable when deviations from trend are large; reversion to mean seems faster for large deviations; see Obstfeld and Rogoff, 2001.

5 Admittedly, running a deficit is not an option when a country is in default!

6 For a detailed description of the data, see Heston et al, 2002, online at http://pwt.econ.upenn.edu/

7 The Economist, June 2005.

8 An important issue, which cannot be addressed in such a brief article, is how resource rich countries may insulate themselves from commodity price volatility. In principle, this can be done through world capital markets, although in practice, political economic problems may interfere with optimal reserve management.

9 See Obstfeld and Rogoff, 2005, who estimate that if the US current account were to be cut in half from 6 percent to 3 percent of GDP over one to two years, the trade-weighted dollar would likely fall by roughly 15 percent, with Asian currencies rising by 18 percent and non-Asian currencies by 10 percent.

References

Chen, Y. and K. Rogoff. 2003. "Commodity Currencies." *Journal of International Economics* 60:133–160. February.

DeLong, B. and L. Summers. 1991. "Equipment Investment and Economic Growth." *Quarterly Journal of Economics* 106(2):445–502.

The Economist. June 2005.

Heston, A., R. Summers, and B. Aten. 2002. Penn World Table, Version 6.1. Philadelphia: Center for International Comparisons at the University of Pennsylvania (CICUP). October.

International Monetary Fund. No year. World Economic Outlook Database.

Kaminsky, G., S. Lizondo, and C. Reinhart. 1998. "Leading Indicators of Currency Crises." *International Monetary Fund Staff Papers*. March. 1–48.

Melitz, M. 2003. "The Impact of Trade on Intra-industry Reallocations and Aggregate Industry Productivity." *Econometrica* 71:1695–1725. November.

Obstfeld, M. and K. Rogoff. 1996. *Foundations of International Macroeconomics*. Cambridge: MIT Press.

——. 2001. "The Six Major Puzzles in International Macroeconomics: Is there a Common Cause?" Bernanke B. and K. Rogoff, eds. *NBER Macroeconomics Annual 2000*. Cambridge: MIT Press. 339–90.

——. 2005. "Global Current Account Imbalances and Exchange Rate Adjustments." Forthcoming in Brainard, W. and G. Perry, eds. *Brooking Papers on Economic Activity*. Washington: Brookings Institution Press.

Reinhart, C. and K. Rogoff. 2004. "The Modern History of Exchange Rate Arrangements: a Reinterpretation." *Quarterly Journal of Economics* 119(1):1–48. February.

Rogoff, K. 1996. "The Purchasing Power Parity Puzzle." *Journal of Economic Literature* 34:647–68. June.

Summers, R. and A. Heston. 1991. "The Penn World Table (Mark 5): An Expanded Set of International Comparisons, 1950–1988." *Quarterly Journal of Economics* 106:327–68. May.

University of Pennsylvania. 2002. Penn World Table. Philadelphia: Center for International Comparisons at the University of Pennsylvania (CICUP).

Williamson, J. 1989. "What Washington Means by Policy Reform." Institute for International Economics. Mimeo.

CHAPTER 2.3

Securing Land and Property Rights in Africa: Improving the Investment Climate

CAMILLA TOULMIN,[1] International Institute for Environment and Development

Introduction

Securing rights to land and property is of particular significance today, both for promoting investment, particularly in agriculture, and for the management of natural resources. This paper describes different approaches which have been taken to formalize rights to land, and establish new systems of tenure. It argues for a phased approach, tailored to the diverse social, economic and political environments across the continent, paying particular attention to questions of institutional design and procedures for securing land claims, to ensure that different groups can access their rights in practice.

The Commission for Africa has recognized the need for a more favorable climate to encourage investment, while the newly established High Level Commission on the Legal Empowerment of the Poor, building on the work of Hernando de Soto, plans to provide a framework for titling the property of millions of urban dwellers, farmers, and small-scale entrepreneurs across the continent. Titling programs have been tried in many African countries with little success, so analyzing and learning from past successes and failures is a useful first step.

At one time land seemed an almost inexhaustible asset in Africa, but now, population growth and market development are increasing the competition for land resources, especially close to towns and cities, and in productive, high-value areas. With such a high proportion of land undocumented in sub-Saharan Africa, the risks of dispossession for the poor majority from a major land grab are high.

Customary land management is under pressure, and the coverage of formal land institutions is generally very limited. As a result, land tenure and shelter are insecure for many ordinary Africans in both urban and rural areas. Historical experience suggests that in the evolution of oral to formal, written rights, certain interests tend to lose out (Clanchy, 1979).

Background: Land under increasing pressure and competition

Apart from its historical and spiritual significance, land is at the heart of social, political, and economic life in most African economies, which rely heavily on agriculture and natural resources for a significant share of GDP, national food needs, employment, and export revenue (Commission for Africa, 2005), and are likely to do so for the foreseeable future.

The family farm has been central to the economies of most African nations, and proven itself to be productive and responsive to new markets and opportunities, when conditions are right. Now, the challenge is how best to secure land rights, so as to enable the smallholder agricultural sector to address global competition more effectively.

107

Governments claim ownership of land, with customary use rights recognized, when land is not needed by others. This allows government to seize land for public and other purposes, such as roads or industrial estates, with minimal compensation given for standing crops or the value of buildings. Compensation is usually inadequate and late, with no provision for loss of the land itself. For example, recent estimates of unpaid compensation for land taken by the government in Ghana total many billions of cedis. Large land holdings in government hands constitute a valuable asset for gift to political allies, and foreign investors.

The growth of Africa's urban settlements, large and small, is having a major impact on peri-urban land values, creating insecurity for those living on and working such land. Squatter communities, unrecognized by the state, have no access to basic services. Their rights to the land and housing which may have sheltered them for many years are frequently swept aside when more powerful interests seek to acquire this land.

Women rarely have full rights to land, but must negotiate as secondary claimants through male relatives. On the death of a spouse, women usually cannot inherit the matrimonial home, a matter of growing concern, given the high death rate from AIDS. Women's rights are often affirmed unequivocally in constitutions, but custom usually wins out on the ground.

Farmers near urban areas, where land values are rising rapidly, face displacement from the conversion of agricultural to building land. Whether or not planning permission has been granted, land speculation is rampant.

In Africa, some 70 percent of the urban population live in slums, with squatter communities highly vulnerable to dispossession. For example, in July 2000, nearly one million people were evicted in Port Harcourt Nigeria. Recent mass evictions from informal settlements around Zimbabwe's capital, Harare, have led to more than 200,000 people losing their homes. The consequences of these evictions are severe: property destroyed, assets lost, social networks broken, and access to essential services lost (du Plessis, 2005).

Migrant farmers from Burkina Faso and Mali, working in the cocoa belt of Côte d'Ivoire, face particular challenges: sharecropping contracts have been central to the enormous growth in Ivorian cocoa and coffee over the last 40 years, yet as land becomes scarcer, such agreements are increasingly called into question.

Pastoral herders, who must move their animals, following seasonal changes in water and grazing cycles, have historically relied on longstanding secondary rights of use to stubble, water, and pasture resources, but find their passage blocked, with the ploughing up of cattle tracks and the enclosure of common grazing land.

Land rights in Africa: Multiple origins and overlapping systems

Rights to land in Africa stem from many different sources, such as first settlement, conquest, allocation by government, long occupation, or market transaction. In some cases these rights are transferable to heirs or through market transaction, while in others, consent must be sought from the underlying rights holder.

First settlement

Rights to land in many parts of rural Africa stem from the first settlers, who cleared the land, converting it from bush to field. Commonly, these rights pass down through the male or female line, so that current occupants can say: "this land belongs to me and my family because my great-great-great grandfather settled here and started farming."

Conquest

In the pre-colonial period, the great West African empires of the Hausa, Mossi, and Ashanti established control over extensive areas of land. Emperor Menelik's conquest and settlement of southern Ethiopia in the 19th century brought large tracts of land under feudal authority, to be allocated to loyal generals. Similarly, the colonial conquest enabled the British to acquire ownership of lands in eastern and southern Africa for settlement by white farmers. However, land claims based on conquest are subject to contest when political circumstances change.

Local or national government allocation

Governments grant rights to plots for housing, distributed as part of an urban planning scheme, for irrigation projects, and make grants of land to investors—allocations at grave risk of corrupt practices.

Long occupation and use

Investment of effort in the land may generate the basis for a claim. Such rights associated with "land to the tiller" policies[2] may contradict other rights, particularly those based on first settlement. Tensions sometimes arise between those who claim first settlement rights, and those claiming rights through long tenant occupation, an issue which arises mainly where there are substantial numbers of incoming migrant farmers, such as cash crop areas of Burkina Faso, Ghana, and Côte d'Ivoire. The Ashanti of Ghana say "long occupation can never ripen into ownership," and the Bambara of Mali that "a log may stay a long time in the water, but it never turns into a crocodile."[3]

Market transactions

Some observers claim that land is not bought and sold in customary African systems. However, in most parts of the continent, some forms of land transaction have a long history, even though they may not involve cash payments

(Lavigne Delville et al., 2004). A broad range of varied contracts allowing access to land is found in southern Benin, from the sale of full ownership rights, mortgage of land, rental, and sharecropping agreements, to temporary rights giving access for a season's cropping.[4] Similarly, in Sahelian Mali, Fulani cattle owners negotiate access to water and grazing in exchange for leaving their animals on the farmers' fields at night, thereby manuring the soil (Toulmin, 1992). But many contracts are increasingly contested, because of rapid changes in land values, differing attitudes on the part of the new generations following the death of those originally making the contract, and political shifts which have altered the balance of power between different groups.

Rights to land in Africa often involve a series of overlapping claims, dependent on customary use, season, and negotiation. The following example illustrates this complexity: cultivation rights to a millet field in Mali may be held by one household, with women from the wider family having rights to glean after harvest, and neighbors allowed to graze their animals on the stubble. Rights to dig a well on the field are held by the broader lineage of the household, while rights to tamarind fruit trees which shade the plot are given to those who have regularly pruned them. Where such a field has been let out to a tenant, however, rights are usually given for cultivation and harvesting of crops, but not to dig for water, plant trees, or make other investments in the land.[5] Tenants are often not permitted to pass a rented plot to their heirs.

Insecure rights to land stem from many sources, and affect different people and regions in diverse ways. The rapid pace of change is bringing new risks to formerly stable systems of property rights, since changing values bring a transformation in the authority claimed by different structures, whether family heads, customary chiefs, or district government. In many parts of the continent, this uncertainty stems in part from the high proportion of land for which no written paper exists, to document the rights held, or the terms on which these rights can be exercised. In the West African region as a whole, only 2 to 3 percent of land—confined largely to a few major cities and development areas, such as irrigation schemes—is held by written title. In Burundi, it is estimated that less than 1 percent of land is registered. In East and southern Africa, much higher levels of registration exist, given longstanding occupation of land by large commercial farmers. However, even the existence of paper title is not a sufficient condition for tenure security, as experience in Zimbabwe in recent years has clearly demonstrated.

Land management

Governments across the continent are revising their land tenure legislation, reforming institutions for the administration of rights, and experimenting with ways to register individual and collective rights to land and natural resources. Such new policy measures are of particular significance in countries seeking to re-establish peaceful relations between competing groups following civil war, such as Rwanda and Mozambique. With the recent issuing of the World Bank's policy research report on land (Deininger, 2003) and the publication in 2004 of the Guidelines of the European Union Task Force on Land Tenure, the donor community has also placed land issues higher up on their agenda.

The choice of structures to manage land rights and resolve land conflicts will have consequences for different groups of people. Some will lose, and others win. As the report of the Commission for Africa rightly notes, Africa's private sector is largely composed of family farms, and small and medium enterprises. Consequently, if investment and growth are to be promoted, design of land administration must consider carefully the needs of such smallholder farmers, traders, and entrepreneurs.

There are various ways to register rights to land, from short-term certificates of occupancy, to more formal registers and titling procedures. Rights can be secured at the level of the individual, the family, or the collective, such as the village or clan.

As we shall discuss in greater detail later, the state plays a fundamental role in managing or facilitating the process of checking and validating claims, either handling it centrally, or by devolving these functions to local institutions. Given the diversity of context and setting, there are strong arguments for developing locally appropriate initiatives and actions, rather than blueprint solutions.

Where tenure practices are evolving rapidly, writing things down is increasingly seen as an essential tool in managing relationships, even by rural people themselves. Faced with the risks of legal insecurity, small farmers try to amass documents, sometimes not knowing what they are for, and often hoping that they will have the right one when it is required (Lavigne Delville, 2004).

In South Africa, the Association for Rural Advancement (AFRA) has been working with communities in Kwa Zulu Natal to develop legal, affordable, and accessible records of household land rights, to both strengthen the communal system and give households more security over their holdings.[6] The absence of written evidence makes it very difficult for individuals to assert their rights to land, and has resulted in numerous requests for registration.

Multiple structures

Rights to land depend on different systems of authority for their validation. These include community councils, patrilineal hierarchy, local government, traditional leadership, irrigation authority, city council, or land agency. Different forms of power are exercised by each, and may rely on a combination of physical force, legal judgment, spiritual values, and moral authority. However, this multiplicity of structures brings contradictions and insecurity regarding whose rights count, whose will be supported in the event of contest, and which decision-making structures are paramount. It has led to what has been termed "institution shopping," whereby people seeking a judgment will try different options, to see which institution is more likely to rule in their favor (Lund, 2003; Benda-Beckmann, 1991). The rising competition for land, and the establishment of new systems of local government, leads to considerable uncertainty, frequent negotiation, and opportunism.

How are rights secured?

Securing property rights requires a combination of two forms of validation, at both the local and state level. At the local level, rights are secure if neighbors and others in the vicinity recognize a particular claim as legitimate, according to their knowledge and set of values. However, these rights have no legal validity, unless they also pass a second form of validation, i.e., recognition by the state. In practice, the lack of state recognition may not matter if land is not under particular pressure, and if local systems work reasonably well. But where land values are rising and there are significant outside interests, then clarity is needed on the status of local land rights. In the case of Burkina Faso, the government's claim of sole ownership puts the vast majority of the rural population in a situation of de facto illegality (Mathieu et al., 2003). But, in practice, the government recognizes that it must rely on traditional leaders for day-to-day management of land rights. At the same time, local government officials are increasingly involved in land disputes, and asked to provide judgment. Typically, these disputes pit incoming farmers against traditional rights holders. In some cases, the decision of the *préfet* supports traditional leaders, in others, they find in favor of incomers.

Thus, in the long-settled cotton lands of western Burkina Faso, land sales are now supported by three different documents, depending on circumstances:

- "Sales" backed by a local receipt (or *petit papier*), drawn up between the vendor and purchaser, but which has no formal rubber stamp from the local government officer; these documents typically mention the names of the parties, area and location of the plot, the rights granted, the sum involved in the transaction, identity of witnesses, signatures of parties and witnesses, and date;

- "Sales" supported by a deed (*papier*), registered by government, and having the certification of the local *préfet*;

- Grants of land supported by a *procès verbale de palabre*, involving the written minutes of a discussion between the transacting parties in the presence of a government official; this more formal deed of sale is sought by members of the urban elite, who want assured ownership rights to the land they are acquiring (Mathieu et al., 2003).

The role of government

Governments have been reluctant to transfer full property rights to their citizens, as large land holdings in government hands constitute a valuable asset for gift to political allies, and foreign investors.

In Tanzania, the President holds all rights to land in trust "in the name of the citizens." Long-term use rights are held by rural and urban dwellers, which can be registered and titled, and subsequently traded. In Senegal, Mali, and Burkina Faso the government claims ownership of most land, and attributes rights to customary occupants, as long as the land is not needed for some other purpose. Nigeria's Land Use Act of 1978 also asserts state control over land, to acquire it for public projects, such as roads and new urban developments. One of the stated aims of the Act was also to prevent land speculation, with all sales of land to be signed by the state governor. Similarly, the government of Ethiopia claims ultimate ownership of all land, with long-term use rights held by citizens. These use rights can be traded, so that, for instance, a widow owning land, but with neither household labor nor oxen, can lease her land to a neighbor to farm for a specified number of years.

By contrast, 80 percent of the land in Ghana is held in private hands, principally through the trusteeship of customary chiefs, who are charged with managing these lands for the benefit of their peoples, with the remainder owned by the state (Kasanga and Kotey, 2001). Yet there remains a long-standing struggle between government and customary chiefs over how land is actually used, involving the patronage usually associated with this asset, and the revenues gained from tenants. Since colonial times, power has shifted back and forth between government and chiefs. After Independence in 1957, Nkrumah's government used its power to acquire certain lands, by vesting them in the hands of government, as a means of bringing recalcitrant chiefs into line, and providing land for the development of cities and ports. The current government, by contrast, recognizes the strength of the customary chiefs, and is much more inclined to accommodate their interests in land, since their support at election time is critical.

In South Africa, the protection of private property rights is enshrined in the constitution. Yet land ownership remains a hot political issue, due to the very unequal pattern of land rights inherited from the former white regime. More than 85 percent of farmland is still in the hands of white commercial farmers (Ng'ong'ola, 2004). A process is now underway to transfer ownership gradually, by various means, to meet the target of placing 30 percent of farmland in the hands of black farmers by 2014.[7] Progress has not been as fast as might be hoped, and a nervous eye is often cast over the border toward Zimbabwe. Some parts of the commercial farming sector, such as the sugar industry, have launched plans to transfer 30 percent of land under sugar from white farmers to smaller scale black-held holdings by 2014.[8]

Governments have a rightful role to play in regulating and administering land rights, due to the significance of this asset for the economy, livelihoods, employment, and national stability. The degree and form of intervention must be balanced against the costs imposed on those owning or seeking land. Additionally, the design of such interventions and procedures requires careful thought to minimize the risks of corruption, and to ensure that the costs imposed are commensurate with the social good obtained.

Creating a favorable climate for investment

Ensuring a favorable climate for investors is vital to generate higher and more sustainable levels of growth (World Bank, 2005a). African governments have usually been far more interested in attracting foreign direct investment (FDI) through measures, such as advantageous tax regimes, than in promoting local enterprise, or preventing capital outflow. FDI is seen as bringing in new technology, training opportunities, access to markets, and competitive advantage. Yet, more than 90 percent of incomes in Africa come from small-scale domestic entrepreneurs.

A recent survey showed that 57 percent of firms in Ethiopia, and 25 percent in Kenya and Tanzania, reported access to land as their main obstacle (World Bank, 2005b). Both large and small investors need assured rights to the land and property in which they invest, not necessarily full ownership, but tenancy, sharecropping, and leases. While the law in many African countries does not allow for foreign ownership of land, foreign investors are often given leases of up to 99 years.

Many factors contribute to a favorable investment climate, including access to markets, price expectations, eliminating uncertainty and political risk, changes in technology, competition, and size of market. For some, constraints on investment may be the inability to access capital on reasonable terms, for others contractual uncertainty. Investment surveys, which expose the inefficiency of government bureaucracies, difficulties accessing credit, corruption, and policy instability (World Economic Forum, 2004) indicate that institutional factors are often as important as economic ones.

Table 1: Time and cost to register property

Number of days	Region	Percentage of property value
34	OECD high income	4.8
51	East Asia and Pacific	4.2
54	Middle East and North Africa	6.8
56	South Asia	6.1
62	Latin America and the Caribbean	5.6
133	Europe and Central Asia	3.2
116	Sub-Saharan Africa	14.4

Source: World Bank, 2005b.

Table 2: Time and costs for property transfers: Selected African countries

Number of days	Country	Percentage of property value
335	Angola	11.0
107	Burkina Faso	16.2
340	Côte d'Ivoire	10.2
382	Ghana	4.1
274	Nigeria	27.2
114	Senegal	34.0
69	Botswana	5.0
39	Kenya	4.0
20	South Africa	11.3
48	Uganda	5.5

Source: World Bank, 2005b.

Over the last 10 years, many African countries have reviewed their investment codes, to identify the barriers faced by both domestic and foreign investors. A number have set up Investment Promotion Agencies to attract FDI by providing services, such as help with company registration, customs clearance, and contacts with key officials (Wells, 1999). Surveys have also been carried out to identify and rate the investment climate of different countries, through comparative analysis of legal, institutional, and political constraints. The Foreign Investment Advisory Service lists 21 different surveys, which assess countries according to a range of criteria relevant to outside investors.

Table 1 summarizes the time and costs of registering property in sub-Saharan Africa, in comparison with other parts of the world, showing the wide disparity in cost, and uncertainty associated with securing access to land for business.

Although the hurdles in some African countries are extreme, others, such as Botswana, Kenya, South Africa, and Uganda, have shorter, less costly and more efficient procedures, as shown in Table 2.

It is widely asserted that a good investment climate benefits rich and poor alike, but will be of particular value to small-scale producers and entrepreneurs, who make up the bulk of local economic activity (Commission for Africa, 2005). However, small-scale entrepreneurs will typically have poorer access to the institutions and processes which can secure their rights. Support for local investors should ultimately encourage outside investment as well, since FDI will more likely be attracted into a sector where it sees good evidence of existing strong domestic activity.

Securing rights in practice

There are various ways to secure land and property rights, with claims dependent on contract terms, the funds individuals are able to mobilize, and on their recourse to state-backed institutions to back their claims.

The problem of bureaucracy

As shown in Table 2, many countries in sub-Saharan Africa have long, time-consuming, and difficult bureaucratic procedures, which also encourage corruption (de Soto, 2000; World Bank, 2005b). In the case of Ghana, registering a land purchase involves multiple visits to five government offices, to obtain the appropriate pieces of paper, confirming that a survey has been undertaken, the property appraised, taxes paid on the property transfer, and the presence or absence of rival claims ascertained. For many people, the process is so long and costly, that it is effectively inaccessible. Even those with excellent contacts in government and the judiciary report that the process can take more than 18 months from start to finish. Many give up before completing the process. Because many land registries are incomplete, local chiefs in a few areas have established their own, in an attempt to create order within their own locality. Such a locally based approach now provides the basis for Ghana's current Land Administration Project (LAP), which also aims to unify the different land sector agencies into a single administration, and establish a one-stop shop at the district government level.

Recognizing that long delays discourage investors, the Mozambique government has established a new shorter procedure for agreement between a local community and an outside investor seeking a land concession. The time period has now been cut to 90 days, with new rules aiming to ease access to land for FDI, giving rise to the concern that such a short period does not allow for adequate consultation with local people in advance of a land grant, and justified fears that government officials will reach agreement with local elites without taking account of the local population's interests.

Many have assumed that individual titling of full ownership rights represents the best focus, but, in fact, lesser forms of rights, such as occupancy and use, are possible and may provide adequate security (Quan and Toulmin, 2004). Rights can be registered by individuals, jointly by both spouses, by the family as a whole, or, in the

case of common property resources, such as woodland, grazing, and wetlands, by a community. In the latter case, management responsibility can be given fully or shared with government. Management and rule-making are carried out by a body on which different interests are represented.

What does experience tell us?

Evidence from other parts of the world shows that land titling can have a major impact on investment and productivity. For example, Feder presents data from Thailand, Indonesia, and Brazil which show a 30–80 percent increase in land values following titling. Investment levels show an increase of 40–115 percent in Brazil, Thailand, and Honduras with access to credit multiplying by 200–350 percent in Brazil and Thailand (Feder, 2002). De Soto's work in Lima, Peru, also shows the value of titling the land and housing assets of poor people, as a means of securing their rights and supporting subsequent economic growth and development.[9] The arguments of de Soto have now helped launch an inter-governmental commission on the Legal Empowerment of the Poor, due to begin work in September 2005 (Norwegian Ministry of Foreign Affairs, 2005).

Arguments in favor of registering title to land have been put forward for many years. They normally include the following perceived benefits:

1. Stimulates more efficient land use, by increasing tenure security and providing incentives to invest in the longer term management and productivity of the land;

2. Reduces transaction costs and enables the creation of a land market, allowing land transfers from less to more dynamic farmers and its consolidation into larger holdings;

3. Provides farmers with a title that can be offered as collateral to banks, improving farmers' access to credit, and allowing them to invest in land improvements;

4. Provides governments with information on landholders and size of plots, i.e., the foundation for a property tax system.

However, the evidence from research in Africa shows that many of the benefits assumed to stem from land titling are not automatic. In some circumstances, it may even have negative consequences. Land titles seem to make most sense in situations where customary systems have become extinct, where major tensions exist between different groups—which cannot be handled by local institutions for dispute management—in re-settlement areas, and where competition for land is fierce such as high-value urban or peri-urban areas (IIED, 1999).

While land registration is often proposed as a means of resolving disputes, the introduction of central registration systems may actually exacerbate them. Thus, for example, elite groups may assert claims to land which was not theirs under customary law, leaving local people to find that the land they thought was theirs has been registered to someone else. The high costs for registration, in money, time, and transport, make smallholders particularly vulnerable. Registration penalizes holders of secondary land rights—women and herders—as these rights often do not appear in the register, and are more easily dismissed. Registration alone may not be enough to improve farmers' access to credit, where the high transaction and other costs in rural areas hinder credit supply, and where an unpredictable and fluctuating environment makes farmers risk-averse and reluctant to apply for loans. Finally, where registering land transactions is expensive, transfers tend not to be recorded, with the result that the register becomes rapidly outdated, limiting its potentially positive effects (Shipton, 1988; Atwood, 1990; Migot-Adholla et al., 1994; Lund, 1998; Firmin-Sellers and Sellers, 1999; Platteau, 2000).

Tenure security is largely dependent on the right-holder's own perception of risk. Where farmers consider their rights under customary law sufficiently secure, registration may not result in higher investments, and research shows that there are simpler means of assuring farmers of security. For instance, in Cameroon, where land can be registered under the 1974 Land Ordinance, very few non-urban plots have been registered. Many farmers have initiated the procedure and abandoned it after the boundary demarcation phase. While demarcation, per se, had no force of law, village communities saw it as increasing tenure security, since other villagers were unlikely to contest land rights that had received official recognition (Firmin-Sellers and Sellers, 1999).

As a result of the recent research exposing the shortcomings of land titling, institutions, such as the World Bank, previously a vocal advocate, are now more cautious, and recognize that titling may not always be appropriate (Deininger, 2003).

Ghana

The Land Title Registration Law of 1986 provides for the registration of all interests in land, under customary law and common law. It also provides that land held by *stools* and *skins*[10] or families should be registered in the name of the corporate group. However, titling has only been initiated in the urban centers of Accra, Tema, and parts of Kumasi, and the registry had processed fewer than half the applications made to it by 2000. Its impact, after nearly two decades since its introduction, has been negligible.

Failure has been attributed to design and implementation defects, such as inadequate funding and human resources, the uncoordinated process, registration of individual interests when dispute remains at higher levels, and registration without the knowledge of other claimants, since insufficient care is taken to publicize these processes. Consequently, 30,000 disputed titles were in the courts in 2000 (Kasanga and Kotey, 2001).

Benin, Côte d'Ivoire, and Niger

There have been several programs aimed at registering land rights, such as the Rural Land Plans (*Plan Foncier Rural-PFR*) in Benin and Côte d'Ivoire, and titling by the Land Commissions in Niger. These examples demonstrate the high level of demand from rural dwellers in areas covered by such a project to get their land rights registered. But the process of issuing title is currently very slow. Other problems include increased insecurity stirred up by the registration of rights, the difficulties of registering complex and overlapping rights, and pressure on staff to achieve targets at the expense of accuracy.

The costs of establishing and maintaining an up-to-date register are also considerable. Estimates from Niger suggest an annual cost for running a Land Commission of around 40 million CFA francs (equivalent to US$74,000), with each plot registered costing roughly 1,000 CFA francs (US$1.85). Some consider this money well spent if it yields firm rights, and avoids further conflict with neighbors and kin (Yacouba, 1999). For the PFR in Côte d'Ivoire, costs averaged 4,700 CFA francs per hectare, the figure being lower in savannah areas and higher in the forest region, due to the larger holding sizes and easier survey work in the former (Okoin, 1999). Funds to cover the registration process could be sought by charging the land rights holder, at the risk of preventing poorer farmers from registering their land. Alternatively, countries must gain funding from western donors. This dependence may lead the country to accept a program which suits the donor, but is not necessarily appropriate to the country's needs, and loans from international banks must be repaid. Niger, for example, has been more than 90 percent reliant on funds from outside donors to establish the 11 pilot Land Commissions, and will need further major support to enable it to gain nation-wide coverage. Registers also require maintenance and updating, or they quickly lose their value as a record. Thus, it is not only necessary to find the capital sum involved in getting such registration systems established, but also the funds required to maintain them.

A recent initiative in Niger, building on the Land Commission structure (*Commissions Foncières*) shows a possible way forward and demonstrates the promise of decentralized, community-based systems for conferring rights over land. In the Mirriah region, 74 Village Land

Commissions (*Commissions Foncières de Base,* COFOB) have been established with NGO support, with authority to handle the great demand for registration of land rights which cannot be satisfied at the higher level—due to insufficient capacity to survey, map, and establish titles. In each village, a committee was established with five members (including one woman), responsible for receiving requests for registration, publicizing them and, where no contest is forthcoming, inscribing this claim in the village land register. The process is simple, inexpensive, and accessible to all. Registration at community level ensures the legitimacy of the claim, before it can be officially registered. Village committee members are trained to ensure they can manage the various tasks involved, and update the register, which includes other transactions, such as rentals, mortgages, and gifts (Lund, 2000).

Ethiopia

Here, several registration processes are underway. In Tigray, this is being done at the lowest level of government, the *tabia,* comprising one or several villages (Haile and Kassa, 2004). For each household, several plots of cultivated land held by the household are recorded in the local language on the pre-printed page of a record book in the *tabia* office. Each page lists each parcel of land, the approximate size of the plot, the type of land, and the names of the neighboring land holders. Certificates are then prepared and delivered to the land holder. This certification of land-use rights gives farmers greater confidence in the security of their claim, encourages investment in soil conservation, tree planting, and improvements to soil fertility.

In the Amhara region, the government is piloting two registration processes. In the traditional approach, farmers are trained to do the land measurement and complete registration documents. The land is measured and the boundaries of plots are identified. The information is then entered into an official form with a stamp, and a photo of the farmer and his wife are attached. By using this simple, inexpensive system, it is expected that 50 percent of land in 106 *woredas* (districts) will be registered by 2006. The second approach has adopted a modern, donor-funded *cadastral* survey[11] as the basis for registration and certification. Although too expensive to scale up to the regional level, this approach may be a useful model for the design of registration systems in higher-value urban and peri-urban areas.

Conserving the commons

While titling programs have focused on farmland, common property resources, such as grazing, woodlands, ponds, and fisheries, are vital for many groups, including mobile, pastoral herders, who produce much of Africa's meat and milk. There are growing pressures on these resources, and a trend toward privatization and enclosure.

But legal regimes often fail to protect collective rights. In many cases the breakdown or absence of access rules has led to a free-for-all, leading to unsustainable levels of use and degradation. Instead, an ad hoc series of by-laws provides some protection, but requires broader formalization.

Mobility is key for herders, who must move freely across both national and sub-regional borders. We hear calls for the pastoral herders to "modernize" and "settle down," but abandoning their way of life would jeopardize a sustainable pattern of life which has survived a harsh environment for millennia. Instead, ways should be found to reduce risks of conflict between herders, neighboring crop farmers, and other land users. This may involve rights of passage for animals along agreed pathways, access to water, and compensation for crop damage, as outlined in new legislation, such as the *Charte Pastorale* of Mali and Guinea (Touré, 2004).

Promising examples of common property management include local agreements "*conventions locales,*" for resource management in the West African Sahel, hillside enclosures in Ethiopia, and community land registration in Mozambique (Vogt and Vogt, 2000; Banzhaf et al., 2000; Toulmin et al. 2004; Gesellschaft für Technische Zusammenarbeit, 2000). Management of the commons works well when local people are assured secure legal rights over the common resources on which they depend, and can gain the technical support to manage these resources in an equitable and sustainable manner.

Options for securing rights to land and property

Given the steep costs of adjudication, and of maintaining a land register, other options to secure rights must be considered, especially in places where land is less valuable, and where titling and registration may be less important than working to strengthen local institutions responsible for managing land rights and related disputes. The recent shift toward decentralized government has helped to bring land rights management closer to the field. Methods of securing local rights seem to work best when they are based on tenure systems already known to the community concerned. The costs and techniques of land administration must also correspond to the value of land. New technologies, such as Global Positioning Systems, computerization of records, and Geographic Information Systems can help at some levels. For example, the large forest lands held by Ghana's customary chiefs could be mapped much more quickly and accurately using GPS, once agreement on the boundaries has been reached. But technology is no substitute for a locally legitimate process to adjudicate disputed claims. The knowledge of local neighbors is essential for clarifying rights and agreeing on boundaries before they are entered into a formal registry.

De Soto's (2000) approach to land titling, now being taken up by several African governments and donor

Table 3: Key choices in design of institutions for land administration

Attribute	Options and implications
Location	Central: closely coordinated with government, policy, and legislature, accessible to foreign investors and urban residents; Local: accessible to rural populations, monitored for accountability and efficiency.
Language	Local language ensures access to records and avoids mistranslation of rights, but prevents establishment of common national system.
Access to information	Restricted access, easier to manage, but risks poor governance; open access allows verification of land claims by neighbours and media; public scrutiny to reduce corrupt allocations.
Cost	Fees charged to applicants, purchasers, and sellers for registration and maintenance; steep fees prevent access by poor groups, and risk patchy maintenance of register.
Record-keeping system	Manual: only accessible at single location, unless copied systematically; computerized records allow multiple access, but not for most rural users and poor urban dwellers.
Adjudication process	Time is required to check rights claims with the testimony of neighbors and family members, and for a publicity process accessible to local people; reliance on government gazette for publicizing claims disadvantages non-literate and poor.
Systematic or on-demand registration	Systematic registration—simultaneous adjudication of all claims—more efficient, less open to fraud than on-demand titling.
Collective/individual	Recognition of land rights held by collective groups, as well as those held by individuals and households.

Source: Author.

agencies, is generating concern that it is being parachuted in from outside, rather than building on the substantial body of existing experience. Others object to de Soto's treatment of "the poor" as an undifferentiated group, rather than recognizing the diverse rights and claims of poor people, young and old, men and women, local and migrants. The complex, overlapping nature of property rights, together with the high risk of individual property title for secondary rights holders, and the vital importance of common property resources to many rural dwellers, make it imperative to find ways to register community title to land which is critical for their long-term survival. Although de Soto argues that titling is the central means of unlocking access to credit for poor people, consideration should be given to other means to achieve this end, such as building on the substantial experience with microfinance schemes.

Design of systems to secure land and property rights

Institutions are key to economic development, by establishing the rules, norms and governance systems within which resource flows take place (North, 1990; Ostrom, 1990; Easterly 2004). Rooted as they are in the social, political, and cultural landscape from which they grow, institutions take many different forms and cannot be simply transplanted from one setting to another. Design must consider such differences as high- or low-value areas, urban or rural environment, and should use a phased approach, in which priority areas are addressed first, with

less formal systems gradually integrated within the formal sector (Table 3).

Effective registration of land and property rights will take many decades in much of Africa, given current low levels of documentation. Setting up a single unified system may make sense as a long-term goal. In the meantime, it may be preferable to establish locally tailored procedures which can be upgraded over time. Priority areas should be identified for systematic registration. In areas of lower concern, reliance on less formal procedures—such as encouraging the use of simple contracts which can be validated by a village or district level official—is the best option.

Conclusions

The land issue in Africa raises major challenges related to the rapid economic and institutional change underway in both rural and urban contexts. These involve the formalization of existing informal processes, improving urban land security, and enabling Africa's farmers to modernize and compete in world markets.

Given the disappointing results of formal land titling programs in Africa, simpler, more diverse methods of securing land and property rights are urgently needed. Some recommended key elements include: strengthening local institutions for rights administration and just dispute resolution; identifying secondary rights and securing access for tenants, women, migrants, and herders; using a phased approach focused on priority areas, such as conserving the commons; introducing simple written contracts with agreed basic terms; and establishing property registers to serve as a base for property taxes, as revenue for services.

Innovative systems are needed in urban areas to strengthen rights and enable a negotiated solution to squatter tenure instead of forced evictions. Revised planning procedures would ensure affordable land on an adequate scale, and allow households to obtain basic services, irrespective of tenure status.

In the process of formalization, women are particularly vulnerable, with the rising incidence of HIV/AIDS exposing them to an even greater risk of being dispossessed. In addition to equitable policies and laws, practical measures to promote gender inclusion at all levels are needed. High-flown political statements in support of women's rights must be backed up by ensuring women's representation on land committees, informing local government staff of new legislation regarding women's rights, legal clinics, and encouraging community leaders to take women's rights seriously (International Food Policy Research Institute, 2005).

The High Level Commission on the Legal Empowerment of the Poor is focused on securing land rights and access to justice for the poor in Africa. What is needed is a careful, tailored approach, capitalizing on the wealth of experience of African professionals across the continent, recognizing the diversity and overlapping nature of land rights, and the importance of collective property. Such an approach would secure rights for poor and rich alike, and promote a better climate for long-term productive investment and competitiveness.

Notes

1 The author wishes to express appreciation to many colleagues for their collaboration, especially Hubert Ouédraogo, Thiendou Niang, Arlindo Chilundo, Ben Cousins, Mitiku Haile, Moussa Djire, Philippe Lavigne Delville, Jean-Pierre Chauveau, Julian Quan, David Brown, and colleagues Su Fei Tan, Lorenzo Cotula, Ced Hesse, and Nazneen Kanji.

2 Referred to as "la mise en valeur" in francophone systems.

3 *Jiri kuru be men ji la—a te ke bama ye.*

4 For further detail see Edja, 2000.

5 Such overlapping rights are not uncommon in developed countries, where different access rights to the same moor might be given to walkers, fishermen, mushroom gatherers, or bird and deer hunters. Even full owners may not claim water and mineral rights below the soil.

6 Hornby, 2004, online at: www.wits.ac.za/informalsettlements accessed July 2005.

7 South Africa Ministry for Agriculture and Land Affairs, (no date), online at: http://land.pwv.gov.za/redistribution/lrad.htm accessed July 2005.

8 Inkezo Land Company, 2005, online at: http://www.inkezo.co.za accessed July 2005.

9 However, new research suggests no unequivocal link between titling, investment, and access to credit, either in Lima (Buckley and Kalarickal, 2004; Calderon, 2004) or in Thailand (Leonard and Ayutthaya, 2003).

10 The customary land trustees, i.e. chiefs, who in the south sit on a ceremonial stool, and in the north on a ceremonial skin.

11 Showing and recording property boundaries.

References

Atwood, D.A. 1990. "Land Registration in Africa: The Impact on Agricultural Production." *World Development* 18(5):659–71.

Banzhaf, M., B. Drabo, and H. Grell. 2000. "From Conflict to Consensus: Towards Joint Management of Natural Resources by Pastoralists and Agro-Pastoralists in the Zone of Kishi Beiga, Burkina Faso." *Securing the Commons No 3.* London: IIED.

Benda-Beckmann, K. van. 1991. "Forum Shopping and Shopping Forums: Dispute Settlement in a Minangkabau Village, West Sumatra." *Journal of Legal Pluralism* 19:117–59.

Buckley, R. and Kalarickal, J. 2004. "Shelter Strategies for the Urban Poor: Idiosyncratic and Successful, but Hardly Mysterious." *World Bank Policy Research Working Paper 3427.* Washington, DC.

Calderon, J. 2002. "The Formalisation of Property in Peru 2001-2002: the Case of Lima." *Habitat International* 28:289–300.

Clanchy, M. T. 1979. *From Memory to Written Record, England 1066–1307.* Oxford: Blackwell.

Commission for Africa. 2005. *Our Common Interest: Report of the Commission for Africa.* London: Commission for Africa.

Deininger, K. 2003. *Land Policies for Growth and Poverty Reduction.* Oxford: World Bank and Oxford University Press.

Deininger, K. and L. Squire. 1998. "New Ways of Looking at Old Issues: Inequality and Growth." *Journal of Development Economics* 57(2):259–87.

Easterly, W. 2004. Can Foreign Aid Make Countries More Competitive? World Economic Forum. *The Global Competitiveness Report 2004–2005.* Hampshire: Palgrave Macmillan Forum, Geneva

Edja, H. 2000. *Land Rights Under Pressure: Access to Resources in Southern Benin.* IIED/GRET (Groupe de Recherche et d'Echanges Technologiques). London and Paris.

European Union. 2004. *Land Policy Guidelines: Guidelines for Support to Land Policy Design and Land Policy Reform Processes in Developing Countries.* Brussels.

Feder, G. 2002. "The Intricacies of Land Markets." Paper to the Conference of the International Federation of Surveyors. Washington. 19–26 April.

Firmin-Sellers, K., and P. Sellers. 1999. "Expected Failures and Unexpected Successes of Land Titling in Africa." *World Development* 27(7):1115–28.

Government of South Africa, Ministry for Agriculture and Land Affairs. no date. *Land Redistribution for Agricultural Development: A Sub-Program of the Land Redistribution Program* http://land.pwv.gov.za/redistribution/lrad.htm

Gesellschaft für Technische Zusammenarbeit (GTZ). 2000. *Codes locaux pour une gestion durable des ressources naturelles:Recueil des expériences de la Coopération technique allemande en Afrique francophone.* Eschborn.

Haile, M. and G. Kassa. 2004. "Formalising and Securing Land Rights: Diverse Approaches from Africa: the Case from Northern Ethiopia." Paper presented at the Land in Africa Conference. London. 8–9 November.

Horny, D. 2004. "Securing Tenure at Ekuthuleni." University of Witswatersrand or Kwa-Zulu Natal: Association for Rural Advancement.

Inkezo Land Company. 2005. Online at: http://www.inkezo.co.za

International Food Policy Research Institute (IFPRI). 2005. *Women: Still the Key to Food and Nutrition Security.* Washington.

International Institute for Environment and Development (IIED). 1999. *Land Tenure and Resource Access in West Africa: Issues and Opportunities for the Next Twenty Five Years.* London.

Kasanga, K. and N. A. Kotey. 2001. *Land Management in Ghana: Building on Tradition and Modernity.* London: IIED.

Land Equity. 2005. "Computerisation of Land Records: Building on Karnataka's Experience." Final draft. Wellington, Australia.

Lavigne Delville, P. 2004. "When Farmers Use 'Pieces of Paper' to Record Their Land Transactions in Francophone Rural Africa: Insights into the Dynamics of Institutional Innovation." Benjaminsen, T.A. and C. Lund, eds. *Securing Land Rights in Africa.* London: Frank Cass. 89–108.

Lavigne Delville, P., C. Toulmin, J. P. Colin, and J. P. Chauveau. 2002. *Negotiating Access to Land in West Africa: A Synthesis of Findings from Research on Derived Rights to Land.* London: IIED.

Leonard, R. and K. Ayutthaya. 2003. "Taking Land From the Poor, Giving to the Rich." *Watershed—People's Forum onEecology* 8(2):14–25.

Lund, C. 1998. *Law, Power and Politics in Niger—Land Struggles and the Rural Code.* Hamburg: LIT Verlag.

Lund, C. 2000. «Rapport d'évaluation des activités des commissions foncières de base (COFOB) du projet d'application de la législation foncière et de la gestion durable des ressources naturelles. Mirriah Niger.» Consultant's report. Denmark: University of Roskilde.

Lund, C. 2003. "Questioning Some Assumptions About Land Tenure." Benjaminsen, T.A. and C Lund eds. *Politics, property and production in the West African Sahel.* Uppsala: Nordic African Institute. 144–62.

Mathieu, P., P. Lavigne Delville, L. Paré, M. Zongo, H. Ouédraogo, with J. Baud, E. Bologo, N. Koné, and K. Triollet. 2003. "Making Land Transactions More Secure in the West of Burkina Faso." Drylands Issue Paper 117. London: IIED.

Mighot-Adholla, S. and J. Bruce. 1994. "Are Indigenous African Tenure Systems Insecure?" J. Bruce and S. E. Mighot-Adholla, eds. *Searching for Land Tenure Security in Africa.* Iowa: Kendall-Hunt. 1–13.

Mingay, G.E. 1997. *Parliamentary Enclosure in England:An Introduction to its Causes, Incidence and Impact 1975–1850.* London: Longman.

Ng'ong'ola, C. 2004. "Constitutional Protection of Property and Contemporary Land Problems in Southern Africa." Saruchera, M., ed. *Securing Land and Resource Rights in Africa: Pan-African Perspectives.* Pretoria: PLASS. 60–74.

North, D. 1990. *Institutions, Institutional Change and Economic Performance.* Cambridge: Cambridge University Press.

Norwegian Ministry of Foreign Affairs. 2005. "High Level Commission on Legal Empowerment of the Poor. Poverty Reduction Through Improved Asset Security, Formalisation of Property Rights and the Rule of Law." Concept paper. Oslo.

Okoin, J. R. M. 1999. "Cote d'Ivoire's Rural Land Use Plan: An Innovative Approach Toward an Appropriate Rural Land Tenure Code." Paper presented at the Conference on Land Rights and Sustainable Development in Sub-Saharan Africa: Lessons and Ways Forward in Land Tenure Policy. Sunningdale: UK. 16–19 February.

Ostrom, E. 1990. *Governing the Commons: The Evolution of Institutions for Collective Action.* Cambridge: Cambridge University Press.

Ouédraogo, M. 2003. "New Stakeholders and the Promotion of Agro-Silvo-Pastoral Activities in Southern Burkina Faso." Drylands Issue Paper 118. London: IIED.

Platteau, J. P. 2000. "Does Africa Need Land Reform?" Toulmin C. and J. Quan, eds. *Evolving Land Rights, Policy and Tenure in Africa.* London: DFID/IIED. 51–73.

du Plessis, J. 2005. "The Growing Problem of Forced Evictions and the Crucial Importance of Community-Based, Locally-Appropriate Alternatives." *Environment and Urbanisation* 17(1):123–34.

Quan J. and C. Toulmin. 2004. "Formalizing and Securing Land Rights in Africa: Overview." Paper presented at the Land in Africa Conference. London. 8–9 November.

Shipton, P. 1988. *The Kenya Land Tenure Reform: Misunderstandings in the Public Creation of Private Property.* Downs, R. E. and S. P. Reyna, eds. Land and Society in Contemporary Africa. Hanover and London: University Press of New England. 91–135.

Shitarek, T., S. Manaye and B. Abebe. 2001. *Strengthening User Rights over Local Resources in Wollo, Ethiopia.* Drylands Issue Paper 103. London: IIED.

de Soto, H. 2000. *The Mystery of Capital:Why Capitalism Triumphs in the West and Fails Everywhere Else.* London: Bantam Press.

South Africa Ministry for Agriculture and Land Affairs. No date. "Land Redistribution for Agricultural Development." Pretoria.

Stamm, V. 2000. "The Rural Land Plan: An Innovate Approach from Côte d'Ivoire." Drylands Issue Paper 91. London: IIED.

Tibaijuka, A. 2004. "Security of Tenure in Urban Africa: Where Are We, and Where Do We Go From Here." Paper presented at the IIED/NRI/RAS Conference on Land in Africa. London. 8–9 November.

Toulmin, C. 1992. *Cattle, Women, and Wells: Managing Household Survival in the Sahel.* Oxford: Clarendon Press.

Toulmin, C. and J. Quan, eds. 2000. *Evolving Land Rights, Policy and Tenure in Africa.* London: DFID/IIED/NRI.

Toulmin, C., L. Cotula, and C. Hesse. 2004. "Pastoral Common Sense: Lessons from Recent Development in Policy, Law and Practice for the Management of Grazing Lands." *Forests, Trees and Livelihood* 14:243–62.

Touré, O. 2004. "The Impact of Pastoral Legislation on Equitable and Sustainable Natural Resource Management in Guinea." Drylands Issue Paper 126. London: IIED.

Vogt, G. and K. Vogt. 2000. "Hannu Biyu Ke Tchuda Juna – Strength in Unity: Shared Management of Common Property Resources. A Case Study from Takiéta, Niger." Securing the Commons 2. London: IIED.

Wells, L. T. 1999. *Revisiting Marketing a Country: Promotion as a Tool for Attracting Foreign Investment.* Washington: Foreign Investment Advisory Service (FIAS).

World Bank. 2005a. *World Development Report: A Better Investment Climate for Everyone.* Washington, D.C.

World Bank. 2005b. *Doing Business 2005: Removing Obstacles to Growth.* Oxford: Oxford University Press.

World Economic Forum. 2004. *The Africa Competitiveness Report 2004.* Geneva: World Economic Forum.

Yacouba, M. 1999. "Niger's Experience in Decentralized Management of Natural Resources." Paper presented at the Conference on Land Rights and Sustainable Development in Sub-Saharan Africa: Lessons and Ways Forward in Land Tenure Policy. Sunningdale: UK. 16–19 February.

CHAPTER 2.4

The Environment as a Source of Competitive Advantage

ALLEN L. HAMMOND,[1] World Resources Institute

Environmental regulations have long been understood as a potential constraint or risk for business. Increasingly, however, environmental and social/developmental issues are also coming to be understood as a source of opportunity—for new products and services, new technology, and new markets. It is only when both risk and opportunity are taken into account, that the full implications for business can be evaluated. This chapter offers that broader perspective on environment and sustainable development as a source of competitive advantage, drawing on a number of analyses, surveys, reports, and examples, including the results of the World Economic Forum's 2005 Executive Opinion Survey (Survey).

In addition to the Survey, this chapter will look at some of the areas of opportunity for business presented by global environmental problems—principally climate change and ecosystem degradation—and by critical global social and sustainable development challenges—principally poverty. It will examine in more detail recent analyses bearing on the competitiveness implications of climate policies, and new scientific evidence on the scope of the challenge to competitiveness posed by ecosystem degradation.

Global environmental challenges as business opportunities

The world's escalating demand for energy propels economic development, but it also threatens the earth's climate. Likewise, while the world's growing demand for food, fresh water, wood, and fiber meets human and economic needs, it is also degrading the ecosystems which provide these and other essential services, and on which all human life ultimately depends. These conflicts are real, but they are not the whole story.

Increasingly, businesses, large and small, are finding new and more environment-friendly ways to meet these demands. These innovative approaches include greater industrial efficiency, low or zero-pollution processes, and renewable energy sources. They also include processes and technologies that use less water, as well as novel ways to provide clean water where it is needed, new approaches to produce food and fiber in more sustainable ways, and ecosystem management techniques to capture carbon through reforestation. A third approach focuses on developing new technologies and business models that meet the needs of low-income communities, empowering them through access to information and improved productivity, so that, ultimately, they can build livelihoods and create wealth, not from the finite resources of the earth, but from the limitless resources of human knowledge.

The need for new approaches is hardly in doubt. World energy production rose 42 percent between 1980 and 2000, and has continued to climb rapidly. In 2005, oil prices reached new highs, reflecting rising demand, capacity constraints, and growing uncertainty. The environmental effects of rising energy production and use—especially the risk of significant climate change—and the entry into force of the Kyoto Protocol are also introducing uncertainty to many industries. Together these factors have changed the competitiveness landscape, forced many sectors to re-examine their vulnerabilities and basic business strategies, and generated new interest in energy efficiency, in renewable energy sources, and in a possible transition to a hydrogen economy.

What might tomorrow's energy markets look like? Renewable energy sources including geothermal, solar, wind, and biomass now contribute about 12 percent of world energy consumption. Wind is the world's fastest growing energy source, and shipments of photovoltaic solar cells are also accelerating. But inevitably, as the world continues to use large amounts of coal, oil, and natural gas, learning to burn it more efficiently and more cleanly is also becoming important. All of these markets present significant business opportunities, which, not surprisingly, are attracting new investment from entrepreneurs and established companies alike, including some of the world's largest firms. For example, General Electric has launched a major new initiative that includes doubling R&D investments to US$2 billion a year on more efficient gas turbines, aircraft engines, locomotives, and other energy-using equipment. Toyota leads the market in efficient hybrid automobiles, and is investing heavily in fuel cell technology.

The situation is equally clear as regards ecosystem services. The four-year Millennium Ecosystems Assessment, conducted by 1,360 scientists around the world,[2] found that human activities have changed ecosystems rapidly and extensively over the past 50 years to meet growing demands for food, fresh water, timber, fiber, and fuel. These benefits have come at a cost of the increased degradation of ecosystem services, which is expected to accelerate unless there is significant institutional change. These changes are important to business because, as the World Business Council for Sustainable Development put it: "Business cannot function if ecosystems and the services they provide—like water, biodiversity, fiber, food, and climate—are degraded or out of balance."[3] Businesses may face increasing competition for water, for example, higher operating costs or reduced flexibility from diminished supplies of natural materials or products, as well as increasing scrutiny of their role in depleting forests and fisheries, or contributing to the degradation of other ecosystem service.

As a result, the competitive landscape is changing. As Antony Burgmans, Chairman of Unilever, says, "The solutions of the past are often not robust enough under the conditions of global change and need to be re-thought and re-implemented."[4] That means new business opportunities for companies able to produce natural resources more sustainably, or to reduce, or mitigate ecosystem degradation.

Poverty is not only a cancer on the human condition and the focus of increasing development efforts, but it also contributes to ecosystem degradation when low income communities—disproportionately dependent on ecosystem services—can not afford, or do not have the capacity and tools, to use these services sustainably. So a third challenge is to lift low-income communities—a majority of the world's population—out of poverty, by empowering people, and by raising their productivity through access to information and energy, basic social services, and financial services. "If we stop thinking of the poor as victims or as a burden and start recognizing them as resilient and creative entrepreneurs and value-conscious consumers, a whole new world of opportunity will open up," says Professor C.K. Prahalad in his book, *The Fortune at the Bottom of the Pyramid*.[5] Increasingly, businesses of all sizes are discovering significant new opportunities to serve the poor, by meeting basic needs in affordable ways, providing infrastructural and financial services, and creating new products and new business models that address the real circumstances of the poor. Indeed, low-income communities constitute perhaps the largest untapped market available today, introducing new avenues for growth and a new factor in the competitive landscape. Already, Indian companies such as India Tobacco Company and ICICI, the country's largest bank, are focusing on the huge market of rural India as central to their future.

Business perceptions: The World Economic Forum Executive Opinion Survey

The 2005 Survey included 19 questions dealing with business perceptions in four broad areas. Five questions dealt with the governance climate surrounding environmental issues, including questions on the stringency of environmental regulations, the consistency of enforcement, the degree of required transparency regarding pollution emissions and other business activities, the perceived impact of regulation on competitiveness, and the impact of privatization. Another six questions covered business attitudes toward global and local environmental problems and solutions: climate change, the Kyoto Protocol, renewable energy sources, clean water, other ecosystem-based natural resources, and environmental disasters. Four questions addressed corporate social responsibility attitudes concerning environment and sustainable development practices, covering such topics as codes of conduct, environmental reporting, environmental risk assessment, and the relevance of multilateral standards. A final four questions probed corporate environmental management practices, from compliance to eco-efficiency, to stakeholder consultation. All questions offered a seven point scale for response.

Responses were tabulated separately for businesses in each country, providing a basis for some generalized comparisons among countries, as well as insights into business attitudes globally.

To be largely consistent with the Environment Chapter of last year's *Global Competitiveness Report,* we have analyzed overall responses by averaging responses for each question by country. On each question, countries were assigned to one of four categories: high (5–7), marginally positive (4–5), marginally negative (3–4), and low (1–3). Each country was scored for the number of questions rated in each of these categories, with very high or low ratings weighted twice the more marginal values. The resulting ranking of countries (Table 1) can be interpreted as reflecting an evaluation by business leaders of the climate for decision-making within their respective countries on environmental and social responsibility issues—hence, a reflection on the performance of both government and business with respect to environmental and social responsibility. The rankings do not necessarily reflect either the environmental quality or the broader competitiveness climate of the country.

In all, 49 countries ranked positive for at least half of the topics surveyed, a slightly higher number than in the previous year. Of the 69 with overall negative scores on balance, more than one-third were making progress in some areas. The results generally show that, in the opinion of business leaders, economic development and performance in environmental and social responsibility are reasonably well correlated. Wealthier countries can afford more environmental action. Nonetheless, a number of less wealthy countries ranked very high—Malaysia in the first tier, and South Africa, Brazil, and Ghana in the second tier—suggesting that a positive climate can be achieved at many levels of development. Moreover, there is some evidence that growing and competitive business sectors correlate well with positive responses to this part of the survey.

The Survey makes clear that there is much room for improvement. Fewer than 42 percent of the countries responding described environmental regulations in their country as stringent; only about 35 percent thought that regulations were enforced in a stable and consistent manner, or reported that government-mandated environmental disclosures were wide-spread and effective. At the same time, a regression analysis suggests a significant link between broader negative factors, such as perception of widespread corruption, and the consistency with which environmental regulations are enforced. Clearly, as shown in Table 1, environmental and social responsibility do not exist apart from the overall business climate.

Strikingly, however, a majority of business leaders in 70 percent of the countries responding agreed that com-

plying with environmental standards improves long-term competitiveness. Even more striking was the consensus—76 percent of countries with a positive response—on the extent to which lack of clean water or clear air has an impact on company operations or inhibits business expansion. This finding resonates with new evidence of ecosystem degradation discussed in more detail later. Only slightly fewer countries, 63 percent of those reporting, agreed that the incidence of environmental disasters had a significant impact on operations or expansion. Business leaders in only about one third of the countries viewed climate, the Kyoto Protocol, renewable energy, or ecosystem degradation as a priority. Apparently, business leaders in the vast majority of countries do not yet see a link between ecosystem degradation and flooding, or between climate change and droughts or severe storms.

Performance on environmental management was mixed. In only about one-third of the countries was the financial impact of non-compliance considered important, or environmental management systems valued apart from regulatory necessity. At the same time, business leaders in more than 55 percent of countries viewed consultation with affected communities as a necessary part of development, and more than 80 percent thought cleaner production and waste reduction important for their companies.

Understanding the competitive implications of climate policies

Policies to regulate greenhouse gas (GHG) emissions caused by human activity are increasingly being developed and implemented in major markets around the world. These new policies will likely change cost structures, create new markets and product opportunities, affect competition, and alter demand patterns in a variety of industries. The structure and design of these policies will shape companies' competitive responses, which will ultimately define the impact on company finances.

Assessing the competitive implications of climate policies goes beyond simply determining which companies will, or will not, be regulated. Climate policies could affect different sectors in varying forms and over different time frames. For instance, the power sector will likely face limits on GHG emissions. Other large point emitters and the transport sector will also likely have GHG emissions capped (as in the EU).

Even within a given policy framework, decisions regarding implementation and design can have quite different financial effects. For instance, in a cap-and-trade system, decisions on allowance allocation—which can be highly political—can have different economic consequences. Moreover, a carbon tax scenario could have different implications from an emissions trading system.

Table 1: Country performance in environmental and social responsibility as assessed in the 2005 Executive Opinion Survey.

High performance	Some weak areas	Positive with major weakness	Progress by on balance negative	Some progress but mostly negative	Negative, not yet started
1. Finland	21. South Africa	32. Thailand	49. China	71. Croatia	101. Georgia
2. Denmark	22. Belgium	33. Hungary	50. Turkey	72. Indonesia	102. Guatemala
3. Germany	23. Korea, Rep.	34. Slovak Republic	51. Namibia	73. Pakistan	103. Guyana
4. Norway	24. Slovenia	35. Tunisia	52. Egypt	74. Mali	104. Honduras
5. Netherlands	25. Israel	36. Chile	53. Latvia	75. Argentina	105. Russian Federation
6. Singapore	26. Luxembourg	37. Lithuania	54. Jordan	76. Bahrain	106. Bolivia
7. Sweden	27. Spain	38. Colombia	55. Poland	77. Azerbaijan	107. East Timor
8. United Kingdom	28. Portugal	39. Estonia	56. Botswana	78. Malta	108. Ethiopia
9. New Zealand	29. Czech Republic	40. Hong Kong SAR	57. Jamaica	79. Ukraine	109. Nicaragua
10. Japan	30. Brazil	41. United Arab Emirates	58. Kenya	80. Bangladesh	110. Bosnia and Herzegovina
11. Australia	31. Ghana	42. India	59. Uruguay	81. Kazakhstan	111. Albania
12. Canada		43. Cyprus	60. Gambia	82. Kuwait	112. Dominican Republic
13. Iceland		44. Italy	61. Philippines	83. Malawi	113. Algeria
14. Switzerland		45. Costa Rica	62. Romania	84. Serbia and Montenegro	114. Chad
15. Taiwan		46. Mauritius	63. Zimbabwe	85. Tajikistan	115. Ecuador
16. Austria		47. Qatar	64. Mexico	86. Trinidad and Tobago	116. Kyrgyz Republic
17. France		48. Greece	65. Nigeria	87. Cameroon	117. Paraguay
18. Ireland			66. Panama	88. Morocco	
19. Malaysia			67. Peru	89. Vietnam	
20. United States			68. Tanzania	90. Sri Lanka	
			69. Uganda	91. Benin	
			70. El Salvador	92. Bulgaria	
				93. Madagascar	
				94. Moldova	
				95. Mongolia	
				96. Mozambique	
				97. Armenia	
				98. Cambodia	
				99. Macedonia, FYR	
				100. Venezuela	

Source: World Economic Forum, 2004.

The impact of climate policies goes beyond direct regulatory costs[6]

To assess more accurately the competitive impact of climate policies on companies, one must go beyond simple measures of GHG emissions, and refer to cash flow analyses, which take into consideration the different forms of GHG constraints, and their impact throughout the value chain. Analyzing the competitive and financial implications of climate policies at the company level is the best way to pick the winners and losers. Most of the literature on climate risk has focused on direct regulatory cost, but in order to fully capture the impact of climate policies on investments, one should also assess:

- *The effects of climate risk throughout the value chain:* the use or consumption of some goods and services, which may result in additional GHG emissions beyond those associated with production. Policies to limit GHG emissions may affect these sectors indirectly, by reducing or increasing demand for the goods and services produced. Moreover, the degree to which climate policies affect a company's supply chain might affect input costs.

- *The scope for passing on costs to consumers:* the demand for certain GHG-intensive goods and services may be inelastic because they are considered necessities, or because short-term substitution opportunities are limited, or both. Hence, even if a climate policy seeks to limit GHG emissions from certain sectors, the immediate impact may be small, and the costs of long-term change may be passed on to consumers.

- *The strategic response to climate policy:* for most industries affected by climate policies, each company's strategic response to GHG regulations could entail various options such as investments in low-carbon technology, emissions trading, investments in GHG-offset projects, or lobbying and legal efforts to head off GHG regulations, to name a few. These options involve different costs, different financial outcomes, and competitive issues.

Table 2: Opportunities and risk in the auto sector

Financial driver	Risk	Opportunity
Cost structure	Carbon constraints could raise costs, from R&D to design to production.	More efficient OEMs could have a relative costs advantage.
Brand	Lagging behind in development of cleaner technologies could harm brand.	Being viewed as a leader on climate change could enhance brand equity.
Innovation	Carbon constraints puts pressure on innovation capacity.	Leadership in low carbon technologies could translate into first-mover advantages.
Product segmentation	OEMs that depend on carbon-intensive segments could see sales and profits fall.	OEMs producing lower-carbon vehicles could see sales and profits grow.

Source: World Resources Institute, Capital Markets research, published and unpublished data.

Climate competitiveness will influence corporate profitability

How climate policies can affect company profitability might not be entirely clear. Climate risk can potentially change cash flows and profitability. How much cash flows will be affected depends on companies' skill in managing their strategic response to climate policy, innovating around new product and market opportunities, mitigating regulatory costs, investing their capital, and managing their supply chain.

Climate polices can affect both operating and non-operating expenses. Indeed, the costs of some climate policy scenarios might entail only non-operating costs, in the form of taxes or capital expenditures (and the possible impact on debt costs). Other policies might offer opportunities to increase operating profit through different pricing structures or emissions trading. Following, are some examples of ways in which climate policies can affect profitability.

- *Revenues:* changes in demand patterns, pricing structures, new product and market opportunities
- *Cost of goods sold:* changes in pricing structures throughout the supply chain
- *Operating costs:* changes in production cost structures, emission trading expenses
- *Capital expenditures:* investments in new capital assets to reduce GHG emissions
- *Taxes:* possible effects on tax expense

Case study: The global automotive sector[7]

The automotive industry is increasingly influenced by constraints on oil consumption and climate change. The confluence of energy security concerns and growing awareness of climate change are fueling more stringent and widespread regulations on carbon dioxide (CO_2) emissions and fuel economy. These regulations will have a profound impact on the competitiveness of companies operating within the sector. Companies will increasingly consider how these new parameters shape opportunities to capitalize on cleaner technology and less carbon emission.

Although energy security concerns and climate change have largely been regulated separately, there is a trend toward convergence. As this occurs, the effects will be felt by the world's largest consumer of oil: personal transportation, over both the near and long term. In this section, we discuss how regulations around the world are driving competition in the auto sector.

As shown in Table 2, carbon constraints constitute new sources of risk and opportunity, which investors and managers will have to consider alongside existing industry fundamentals. In particular, carbon constraints could influence OEM[8] competitiveness and profitability by affecting the industry's traditional value drivers. Conventional valuation models will have to be updated to reflect these new pressures.

The traditional value model for the automotive industry is based on supply and demand forces, which in turn determine sales volumes, pricing, margins, and profitability.[8] In addition to these *tangible* value drivers, a number of *intangible* ones, such as brand, innovation, and product quality are increasingly viewed as important sources of competitive advantage and value creation. Intangible assets may represent as much as 50 percent of an automobile company's market value.[10]

In mature, low-growth markets, companies can increase sales only by taking market share from another firm. In this zero-sum-game environment, competitive advantages tend to be temporary. An important means of securing short-term advantage is through innovation. Successful innovation, in the form of new models or technologies, allows first-mover advantages, such as pricing power and higher margins. As a result, maintaining innovation capacity is essential for competitiveness in the automotive industry.

Momentum has been gathering around the world on policies to regulate GHG emissions, including CO_2. Companies in the auto sector will be subject to regulations and standards in the European Union (EU), Canada, Japan, Australia, and some United States regional markets. Also, regulations on fuel economy in China have recently been enacted. Because CO_2 emissions are directly proportional to fossil fuel consumption, it is difficult to separate policies motivated by climate change concerns from those motivated by energy security benefits. Regardless of the motivation, these regulations place pressure on the industry to produce vehicles with higher fuel economy and lower emissions. This will stimulate demand for cleaner technologies and fuels as companies begin to compete around these new parameters.

In addition to fuel economy and GHG standards, air pollution regulations are increasing in scope and stringency, particularly in the major auto markets. These regulations set emissions standards that are particularly relevant for diesel engines, which emit higher levels of particulate matter (causing respiratory illnesses and haze), and nitrogen oxides (precursors to smog) than petrol engines. Historically, Europe had lower air quality standards, which along with preferential tax treatment, allowed for the growth of diesel engines in the market. In Europe, automobile companies were able to meet the latest round of air quality regulations (Euro 4) through efficiency improvements to diesel engines (including direct injection). It remains unclear whether efficiency improvements alone will be enough to meet the next phase of air emissions standards (Euro 5), or if filters and after-treatments will be necessary. The answer to this question will also inform diesel growth in the United States, where standards are currently being phased in to approximate the same level as Euro 5 by 2009.

Clearly, there is a discernable trend toward regulating emissions of carbon dioxide and other tailpipe emissions from the burning of fossil fuels. As the causes of human-induced climate change become more generally understood and accepted, policies to reduce GHG emissions will continue to proliferate. Higher oil prices and energy security concerns are pushing governments around the world to enact new, or to tighten existing, fuel economy requirements in the auto sector.

Ecosystem services and economic competitiveness

The Millennium Ecosystem Assessment Report[11] examined how changes in the following ecosystem services affect human well-being: a) food, water, and timber; b) regulatory services affecting climate, floods, disease, wastes, and water quality; c) cultural services providing recreational, aesthetic, and spiritual benefits; d) support services, such as soil formation, photosynthesis, and nutrient cycling. The Assessment concluded that:

- Human activity has changed ecosystems extensively over the past 50 years.
- These changes have often benefited human well-being and economic development but have also degraded many ecosystem services, exacerbating poverty and risking reduced benefits for future generations.
- Ecosystem degradation could intensify in the next 50 years to such an extent as to prevent achievement of the Millennium Development Goals.
- Reversing these trends would require significant change in policies, institutions, and practices.

The ecosystem changes documented by the Assessment have the potential, in the extreme, to disrupt and even undermine whole economies. They can lead to net declines in wealth, especially in the natural resource-dependent economies of most developing countries, to an increase in floods and other environmental disasters, to the spread of disease, and to constraints on the supply of food, fiber, firewood, and fresh water. These changes will have a serious impact on business as well, and represent an important new factor in the competitiveness equation.

The Assessment found extensive declines in provisioning services, including capture fisheries, wild foods, wood fuel, fresh water supplies, and the genetic resources represented by biodiversity. Supplies of timber and fiber were mixed, expanding in some regions, declining in others.

Regulating services also showed widespread decline in air quality regulation, water purification, pest regulation, pollination, and natural hazard regulation, among others. In addition, the Assessment found rapid decline in sacred groves, decline in quantity and quality of lands with aesthetic values, and a mixed picture regarding recreation and ecotourism.

Cutting forests for their timber, clearing and draining wetlands for farms, and similar practices may be very short-sighted business practices. In most countries, the Assessment found that the value of timber and fuel-wood production was less than one-third the total value, including the potential value of such services as carbon sequestration, watershed protection, and recreation—services that are normally unmarketed. The Assessment also found the value of sustainably managed intact ecosystems—Canadian wetlands, Thai mangrove swamps, Cameroon tropical forests—to be significantly higher than those ecosystems converted to intensive farming, shrimp farming, or small-scale farming, respectively. These disparities suggest new business opportunities in capturing more of the unmarketed value of ecosystems, or in managing intact systems sustainably, so as to maximize their value.

Of particular importance to business is the impending scarcity of fresh water in many regions, which may increase competition and raise costs, force recycling, and require introduction of technologies or processes to reduce overall water use per unit of output. At the same time, selling clean water or water purification equipment looks to be a growth business. Likewise the over-exploitation of capture fisheries may limit supplies of fish as food or feed, or force cessation of fishing operations in specific areas, with consequent cost to many businesses. As ecosystems are stressed, abrupt changes can occur—such as the sudden collapse of the Newfoundland cod fishery—posing new challenges for business strategies and potentially higher insurance premiums in some industries. These risks also suggest new business opportunities, such as finding alternative to fish meal for animal feed.

The pattern of ecosystem degradation found by the Assessment can have a potential impact on businesses in a number of ways. Growing concern about ecosystem degradation can limit the license to operate for businesses that do not meet growing stakeholder expectations. These growing expectations for corporate performance may, in turn, require increased adherence to standards and the use of third-party certification to protect corporate reputations. At the same time, the spread of market mechanisms to reduce the cost of compliance is creating new opportunities—the trading of carbon offsets reached US$300 million in 2003, according to the Assessment, and the use of payments for land set-asides is growing. Shifting tastes are expanding the market for organic agriculture in many affluent countries, and continued demand for seafood worldwide may mean big opportunities in environmentally appropriate aquaculture. More broadly, commercializing unmarketed ecosystem services is a huge opportunity, one which can bring wealth to low-income communities as well as to businesses, and which may represent a powerful force for sustainable practices.

Conclusions: Serving the poor profitably

Enabling several billion low-income people to participate in and benefit from the global economy could transform the human condition. Such a transformation also represents a vast array of business opportunities—to provide basic goods and services, to build the energy, communications, and physical infrastructure that most rural areas of the developing world now lack, to supply financial services such as credit, insurance, and secure transactions, even to provide health and education services where public systems are failing.

The case for a much greater private sector role in alleviating poverty and related social issues rests on several observations. The needed scale of job creation, infrastructure deployment, and service delivery dwarfs the capacity of either civil society or government in most developing countries. The private sector has a distinct advantage in management skill, technology, and market discipline. And its financial capacity to invest is much greater than available or likely development aid.

Why should businesses attempt to serve low-income markets in developing countries? Because—as a growing number of businesses can attest—these markets can be a source of profitable growth. Contrary to conventional wisdom and the rhetoric of the development agencies, low-income communities have, in aggregate, very substantial and growing purchasing power: because of vigorous informal sectors and huge remittance flows, the poor are a lot less poor than official statistics suggest.

The challenges and the risks of these new markets are significant: products and services must be re-invented to meet new circumstances, new business models and distribution systems developed, and extensive market development undertaken. But the potential rewards, public and private, are equally significant. Businesses can gain large new markets, and, because the unmet demand is so large, growth can be rapid. Countries where this transformation occurs are also likely to benefit from larger and more competitive domestic markets, greater foreign direct investment, more rapid economic growth, and the alleviation of serious social problems which breed instability. It is hard to escape the conclusion that business approaches to poverty, such as climate change and degradation of ecosystem services, could be significant competitiveness factors in the years ahead.

Notes

1 The author is Vice President for Innovation at the World Resources Institute.

2 World Resources Institute, 2005a and 2005b.

3 World Resources Institute, 2005b, p2.

4 Ibid.

5 Prahalad, 2004, p.1

6 Adapted from Wellington and Sauer, 2005, online at: http://capitalmarkets.wri.org accessed 15 July 2005.

7 This section draws on several reports by the Capital Markets Research team of the World Resources Institute and its partners, including Merrill Lynch, Sustainable Asset Management, and the Pew Center on Global Climate Change.

8 OEM = Original equipment manufacturer.

9 See, for example, Deutsche Bank AG, 2002, p. 14.

10 Kalafut, 2003.

11 What follows is adapted from World Resources Institute, 2005a and 2005b.

References

Deutsche Bank AG. 2002. *The Drivers: How to Navigate the Auto Industry.* Frankfurt. July.

Kalafut, P. C. 2003. *Invisible Advantage: How Intangibles Are Driving Business Performance*. Cambridge, MA: Perseus Publishing.

Prahalad, C. K. 2004. *The Fortune at the Bottom of the Pyramid*. Upper Saddle River, NJ: Wharton School Publishing.

Wellington, F. and A. Sauer. 2005. "Framing Climate Risk in Portfolio Management." CERES and World Resources Institute. May.

World Economic Forum. 2004. *The Global Competitiveness Report 2004–2005*. Hampshire: Palgrave Macmillan.

World Resources Institute. 2005a. *Ecosystems and Human Well-Being Synthesis Report, Millennium Ecosystem Assessment*. Washington.

———. 2005b. *Ecosystems and Human Well-Being, Opportunities and Challenges for Business and Industry, Millennium Ecosystem Assessment*. Washington.

CHAPTER 2.5

Can Europe Compete? The International and Technological Competitiveness of Europe

BEATRICE WEDER di MAURO, University of Mainz, and Centre
for Economic Policy Research

Introduction

These days it has become popular to paint Europe in dark colors. The French and Dutch rejection of the European Constitution has called into question the legitimacy of European institutions, including the European Monetary Union. At the mid-term review of the Lisbon strategy, European leaders have been forced to acknowledge quietly that the goals were not reachable, that Europe does not seem to be coping well with the challenge from East Asia and from globalization. The consensus suggests that Europe—in particular Old Europe—cannot compete. These statements reflect the prevailing thinking about Europe. But is it correct?

This paper argues that Europe is competing very successfully in international markets, as documented by evidence on market shares and the pricing power of European exporters. This positive view contradicts the notion that Europe is falling behind in terms of technological performance. It suggests that a possible answer to this puzzle lies in the fact that industrial structure may matter more than country factors. Using micro data from the World Economic Forum's Executive Opinion Survey (Survey), I show that the differences in perceived technological performance between the EU and the United States can be explained largely by firm characteristics such as size and industrial affiliation. Some structural factors, mainly relating to the labor market, also help to explain the gap.

Before getting to the meat of my subject, I would like to begin by discussing the different meanings of *competitiveness,* as it applies to countries.

Defining competitiveness of countries

Everyone agrees on the importance of competitiveness; political leaders as well as corporations worry about it, especially in the context of the associated concerns about an ever-globalizing world, outsourcing, and manufacturing relocation. However, it is much less clear what is actually meant by competitiveness. The term is used loosely to describe different, sometimes conflicting, and often unrelated concepts. Here are three distinct approaches to the definition of competitiveness:

1. **International competitiveness:** the ability to sell in international markets. This view of competitiveness focuses on relative price and market share performance in international trade, possibly related to a high growth rate at home, but not necessarily.

2. **Technological or growth competitiveness:** synonymous with growth performance, or growth potential. This is probably the most common meaning of the term when applied to countries. If competitiveness means growth, then the measures of competitiveness can be derived from a growth model, and the focus

Box 1: A country is not a company

Business people are often inclined to translate competitive strategies directly from the company to the country level. Innovative technology increases productivity, and boosts the firm's income. So, surely the same applies at the level of the country.

Economists are distinctly uncomfortable applying the term competitiveness to a country. They will be especially wary of extrapolating strategic management to the industry level. Some analogies from the firm level simply do not carry over to the country level.

Take, for example, the thesis: *"A country is competitive when it exports more than it imports."* At the firm level this statement makes sense, if one interprets it as *"A firm is competitive when revenue growth exceeds the growth of cost."* However, the translation to the country level does not work. When exports exceed imports, the country is running a trade surplus, which could be interpreted as a sign of strength. However, a trade surplus can just as easily result from strong export growth as from weak import demand. The implications for present and future consumption of the country of these two underlying causes are certainly different. A trade—or more accurately a current account—surplus means that current consumption is lower than current production. If one is concerned only about current consumption, a trade deficit is clearly preferable to a trade surplus. On the other hand, a trade deficit implies incurring debts vis-à-vis the rest of the world, thereby reducing future consumption possibilities.

There are many other instances, where the application of firm-level strategies has different consequences at the country level. Paul Krugman describes some of these arguments in his article "A Country Is Not a Company,"[1] in which he also explains why great business leaders do not necessarily make great economic policymakers.

Note

1 Krugman, 1996.

---

will be on growth factors, namely technology, productivity, human and physical capital. The summary indicators of *The Global Competitiveness Report* follow this logic.

3. **Competitiveness as the ability to attract mobile factors of production.** This view of competitiveness suggests a different priority of relevant factors. For instance, the decision of a firm where to locate its headquarters may depend on the overall dynamism of a country, but is more likely to be influenced by more immediate considerations, such as the level of corporate taxes or business regulations.

In this paper we focus on the first two definitions, and begin by looking at Europe's international competitiveness. Following this will be an explanation of the gap in technological competitiveness.

How is Europe doing in international competitiveness?

Very well, indeed. In fact, Europe dominates in world trade, in which it has by far the largest market share, and over the past decade has clearly outperformed its main competitors, the United States and Japan. Moreover, Europe's strong export performance is *not* due to a favorable exchange rate.

Figure 1 shows the export market share of the euro area and its competitors. Euro area exports account for almost a quarter of world trade, as compared with about 15 percent for the United States, and less than 9 percent for Japan. This makes the euro area the largest exporter in the world. Moreover, euro area exports have outperformed those of its main competitors in the face of rising Chinese exports. Both the United States and Japan have experienced significant losses both in value and in terms of volume.[1] By contrast, the share of the euro area has remained very high.

How can we explain the better performance of European exports, as compared with its main competitors? Certainly one factor to consider would be price competitiveness. Is it possible that the strong export performance is simply the result of the sharp depreciation of the euro vis-á-vis the dollar—at least from 1999 until 2002? Moreover, the euro depreciated, not only in nominal terms, but also in real terms (accounting for price differences between countries), and even real effective terms (accounting for the weight of different trading partners). Thus, one might assume that the relatively strong performance of the euro area—at least until 2001—might be due to exchange rate depreciation. It turns out that exchange rate changes are not as important for price competitiveness as one might assume. The more important measure of price competitiveness is relative export prices. And they point to another story.

Prices of extra-euro area exports as compared to those of its competitors remained more or less flat through the large swings in nominal and real exchange rates. If anything, they increased slightly vis-à-vis competitors, which would indicate a small loss in price competitiveness.[2] In other words, increases in prices of euro area exports offset the potential gains resulting from a real depreciation of almost 30 percent between 1992 and 2001. And after 2001, export prices of the euro area did not decrease in line with the euro appreciation. Apparently European firms were able to absorb the appreciation in their margins, and did not pass on the cost increase to cus-

Figure 1: Export market shares as percent of world trade

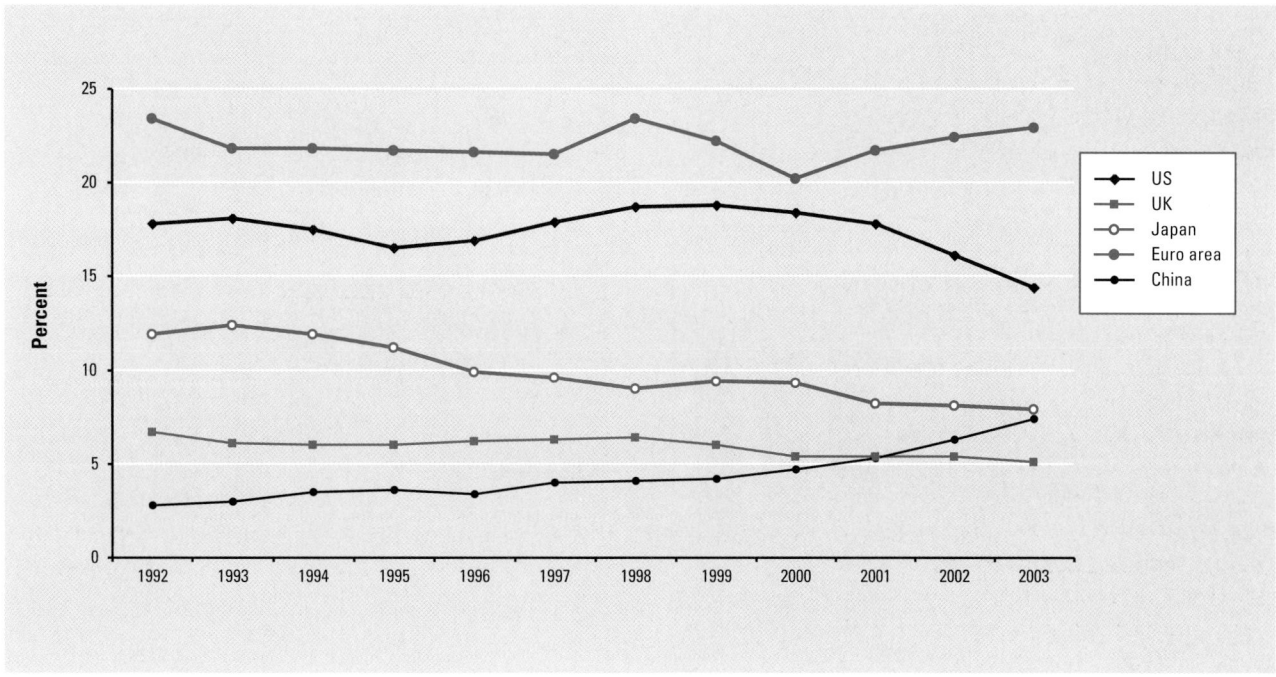

Source: European Central Bank, 2005.

tomers, just as before 2001, they had not passed on the profits from more favorable cost relations.

The upshot of all this is that the good performance of European exports is not due to lowering export prices, since, in relative terms, these did not change appreciably. This also means that European firms are not competing primarily on prices, but, rather, have some pricing power, and the ability to adjust margins to their changes in cost and demand. Prima facie, such pricing power contrasts with the view that European products are not up to the mark on the technological frontier.

How is Europe doing in technological competitiveness?

As measured by most indicators of technological performance, Europe is lagging behind both the United States and Japan. However, as I show later, it is industry composition, rather than country characteristics, which explains a good part of the differences in performance. The remaining difference can be attributed to structural factors, such as labor market rigidities.

One of the motivations for the Lisbon strategy was to improve Europe's innovation performance. The European Innovation Scoreboard (2004)[3] comes to a sobering conclusion: the innovation gap between the United States, Japan, and the EU still exists, and is even widening slightly. Figure 2a shows the summary innovation index, a composite of 20 indicators of innovation, human capital and

R&D investment, which ranges from 0 to 1. In 2004, Japan surpassed the United States, and now receives the highest score (0.77), while the United States scores 0.70, and the EU15 reaches only a low of 0.44. Within the EU, however, there are considerable differences. Some Nordic countries outperform both the United States and Japan. Most of the new EU members are clearly below average, although they have made very strong improvements.

As shown in Figure 2b, the main areas of divergence are patenting (which explains 50 percent of the gap in the summary indicator), working population with tertiary education (26 percent of the gap), and public R&D expenditure (11 percent of the gap). Another common indicator of patenting performance is the number of utility patents registered in the United States.[4] Although these figures refer to patents registered in the United States, and are therefore biased toward US companies, nevertheless, because of the importance of the US market, the data are frequently used to compare the level of technological competitiveness across countries. In 2003, the United States registered 299 utility patents per million population, closely followed by Japan with 278 per million. The best EU performers on this score are Finland and Germany, with 166 and 138 per million, respectively.

In addition to these hard data, the Global Competitiveness Report offers a firm level perspective on technological competitiveness. In compiling the summary

Figure 2a: Summary innovation index 2004

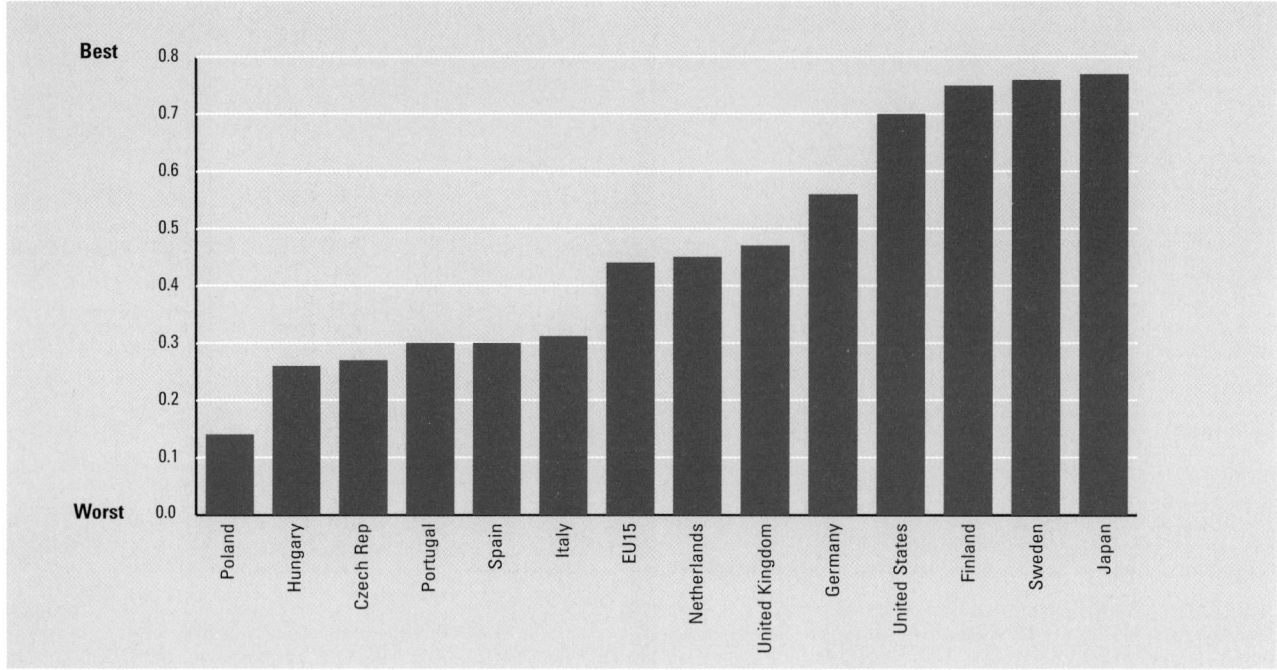

Source: Commission of the European Communities, 2004.

Figure 2b: Selected indicators

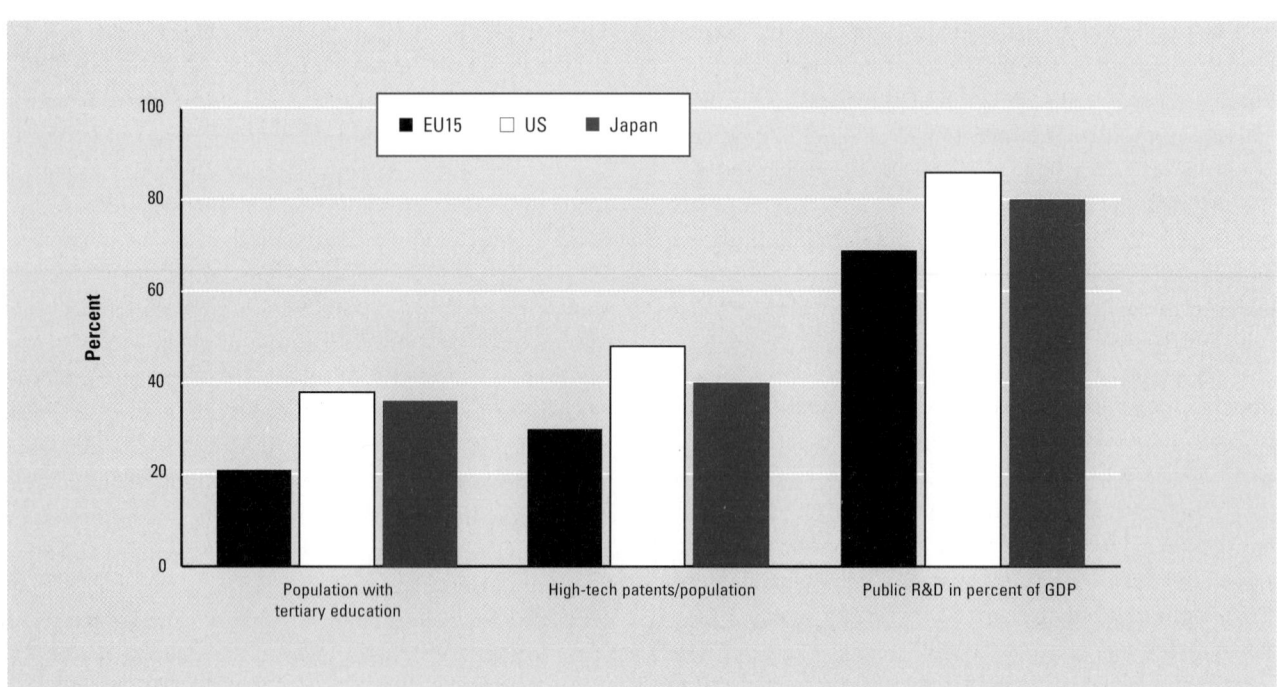

Source: Commission of the European Communities, 2004; author's calculations.

Figure 3: Opinions of business executives on technology and productivity

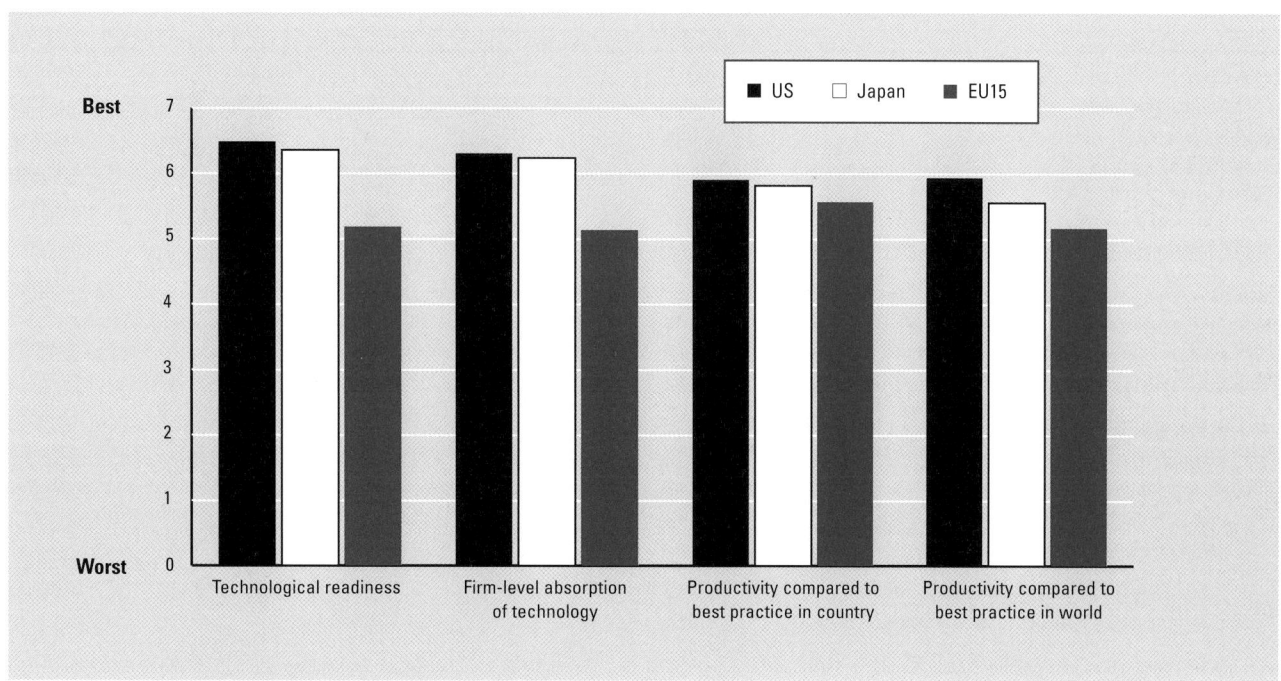

Source: Executive Opinion Survey 2005; author's calculations.

indicators of competitiveness, the *Report* uses both hard and soft data, the latter coming from the Executive Opinion Survey. One of the categories in the survey is the level of technology. Executives are asked to rank the level of technological preparedness of their country, and to estimate the extent of firm-level technology absorption, productivity relative to best practice in the country, and productivity relative to best practice in the world. Above I show the mean responses to these questions for the United States, Japan, and the EU. Since the report does not offer an aggregate European score, I calculate the indicator for the EU15 as a weighted average of individual country means, using GDP weights. As Figure 3 shows, the opinions of business executives corroborate the results from the hard data: the EU underperforms relative to the United States and Japan.

Results from other Survey questions show a similar pattern. Table 1 shows the average results for Japan, the United States, the EU15, and the EU25. Again, the EU indicators are constructed by using GDP as a weighting scheme. Generally, the EU15 receives somewhat higher average scores than the EU25 on technology and human resources, indicating that the new member countries of the EU still lag behind on these scores. This is not the case, however, when it comes to barriers to higher productivity. Here the scores of the EU25 tend to be very similar to those of the EU15 or even slightly higher. On

average, executives rate Japan higher than the EU, and lower than the United States.

It should be borne in mind that the observations underlying these averages differ substantially in number. Since the Forum collects information for every single European country, the average EU25 score is calculated from over 2000 individual responses, whereas the US and Japanese scores are based on 75 and 158 responses respectively. This could bias the results. One possible source of bias is that the sample of US and Japanese companies might include mainly the largest and most successful ones, whereas in Europe, in order to achieve a sufficient coverage for every country, the sample might include smaller, local firms. To test this hypothesis, one could draw a sample of 150 companies that are comparable to the US respondents from the European surveys and calculate the scores on that basis.

This observation carries over to many other indicators of relative performance between the United States and Europe: whereas for Europe it is common to discuss country data, and therefore highlight differences within Europe, for the United States we tend to have only one number. This certainly does not mean that there are no differences across regions and states within the United States, but they tend to receive little attention.

So far all evidence points to an affirmative answer to the question whether Europe is falling behind in the

**Table 1: Comparing the EU with its main competitors:
Selected questions from the Executive Opinion Survey, 2004 and 2005**

	Japan	US	EU25	EU15
Technology				
Technological readiness	6.35	6.48	5.14	5.19
Firm-level absorption of technology	6.23	6.30	5.13	5.14
Licensing of foreign technology	5.45	5.15	5.04	5.05
FDI as source of technology	4.58	4.44	4.76	4.74
Quality of scientific research institutions	5.57	6.44	5.05	5.09
Firm-level R&D spending	5.81	5.91	4.58	4.64
Human resources and labor market				
Ease of hiring and firing	3.63	5.29	3.01	2.98
Effort of hourly worker	5.67	5.31	4.69	4.71
Effort of salaried worker	5.82	5.86	5.03	5.04
Barriers to higher productivity*				
Poor labor practices	2.75	3.29	3.43	3.43
Business regulations	3.81	3.55	4.02	4.02
Poor labor skills/lack of training	3.52	4.05	3.56	3.54
Poor capital and infrastructure	2.93	2.91	3.10	3.05
Productivity compared to best practice in country	5.81	5.90	5.55	5.57
Productivity compared to best practice in world	5.55	5.93	5.14	5.17
Intensity of competition in local market	5.87	6.27	5.69	5.72
Number of observations, 2005	75	158	2,130	1,142

Sources: Executive Opinion Survey 2004 and 2005.

* EU15 and EU25 are weighted averages using GDP weights of member countries. A higher score indicates a lower barrier to productivity.

132

technological race. But this is puzzling, in the light of the very strong external performance of Europe. In what follows, I explore different possible explanations of why this is so.

A first explanation is that industry composition matters more for performance than country conditions. This is a result that has been found in the international finance literature, where stock market performance can be explained by industry, rather than country factors. The industrial structure of European exports is strongly concentrated in the medium-technology products. About 50 percent of exports from the euro area are in chemical products, manufacture of transport equipment, and agricultural/industrial machinery. Low-tech exports make up about 30 percent and high-tech account for about 20 percent of European exports (in 2000–2001). In world exports these shares are about one-third each. It follows that the euro area's relative specialization is clearly in medium-tech products.

Figure 4 shows the relative product specialization at the industry level. The indicator is the difference between the shares of each industry in euro area exports, in relation to the share in world exports. A value higher than zero indicates that the euro area is relatively specialized in this industry, whereas a value lower than zero indicates relative

non-specialization. The graph shows that Europe is specialized in medium-tech products, and not specialized in either high- or in most low-tech industries. Moreover, the specialization in the medium-tech industries has remained relatively constant. The manufacturing of transport equipment in Europe has gained relative specialization. The reverse is true for high-tech industries: in this area, Europe started from a position of relative under-specialization, and has lost over time.

Prima facie, specialization seems less desirable in medium-tech than in high-tech products. There is a view that high-tech products have greater spillover and higher growth effects, and a higher growth in demand. However, in many cases medium-tech products are rich in high-tech research and technology. Consider how much high technology goes into a high-end car. Moreover, the growth of world demand for medium-tech products has expanded at the same rate as overall trade. In other words, exporters of medium-tech products did not fall behind, and this relative specialization of Europe may help explain why the export performance was strong. Of course, this does not necessarily mean that demand for medium-tech products will continue to be buoyant ad infinitum. However, so far Europe has specialized in the right markets and products.

Figure 4: Euro area: Relative product specialization

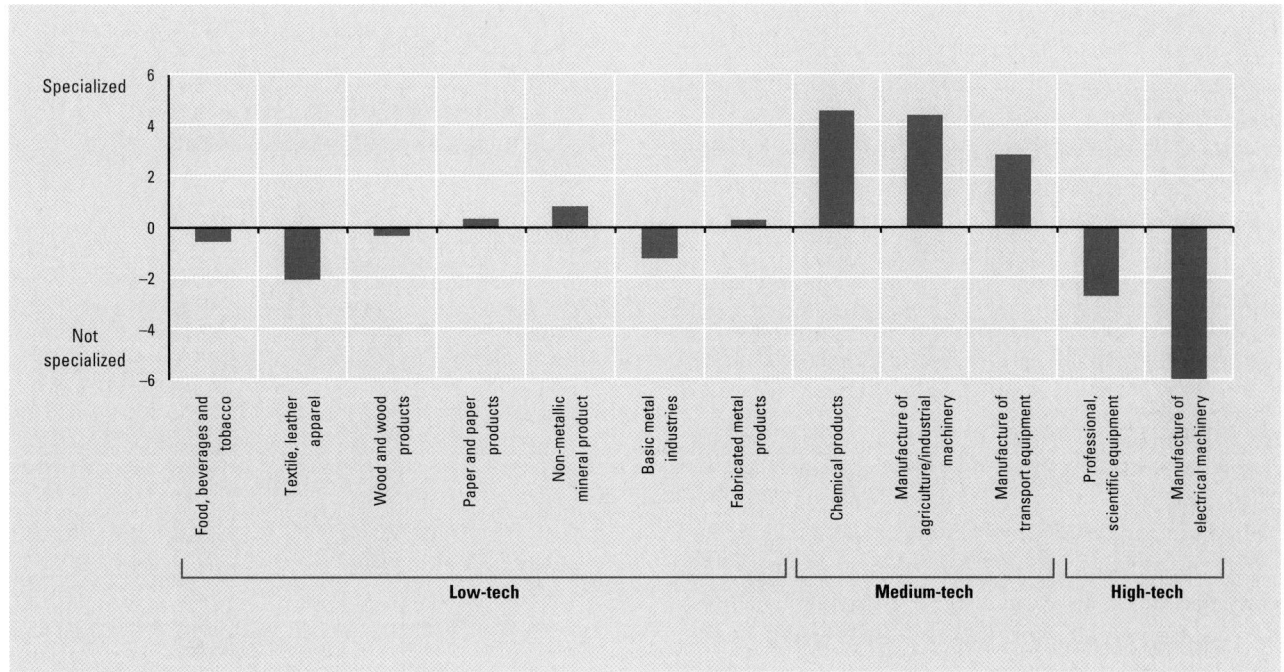

Note: Relative product specialization is defined as a difference of the share of the sector in the euro area exports from the share of the sector in world exports. A value higher than zero indicates the relative specialization of euro area exports in this sector.

Source: European Central Bank, 2005.

Next, let us explore the question of country-versus-industry factors further, by using the micro data from the Survey. So far, I have only made use of mean responses, neglecting much information that is available at the micro level. For instance, we can check whether industry affiliation has an influence on executives' opinions of country productivity and technological performance, while also controlling for other firm characteristics, such as size. This is done through probit analysis: the executives' responses regarding country performance on technological readiness and productivity form the qualitative dependent variables, while industry, size, and regional factors form the independent variables. The analysis shows estimates of the probability that a specific executive would express a positive opinion on technology readiness and productivity contingent on its location (region), industry affiliation and firm size. The full equation output is presented in Appendix A, but the overall results are as follows: using only firm size and industry type as independent variables, both are found to be positive and significant in explaining executives' perceptions of their country's performance on technological readiness and relative productivity. That is, larger firms will generally have a more positive view of their country's performance. Similarly, industry affiliation also has an influence on the perceived country performance.

However, since these factors cannot account fully for differences between Europe, Japan, and the United States, I next include independent variables for regions to the equations above. Regional indicators for the EU15 and the new EU members remain negative and significant, indicating that being in the EU lowers the probability of a good evaluation, even if we take into account differences in industry and in size. That is, even when firm size and industry affiliation are taken into account, there still appears to be a gap between the perceived performance of the EU and that of the United States. The Japan indicator is not statistically significant, indicating that firm size and industry affiliation go a long way to explaining differences in perception between US and Japanese managers.

Finally, the differences were analyzed by focusing only on the manufacturing sector, that is, by isolating the responses to the Survey that belong to manufacturing firms. As shown above, Europe's relative specialization is in the manufacturing sector. Therefore, it is interesting to investigate how these questions play out in this particular sector. The results show that firm size still matters: even among manufacturers, the larger ones will have a more positive view—the industry variable evidently cannot be applied here, since we are looking at one "industry" only, the manufacturing sector. However, the EU15 indicator, although negative, is only borderline significant; the EU's new members are negatively significant, that is, lower than the United States, and Japan is insignificant. We can conclude, therefore, that in the manufacturing sector, differences between the perceptions of the EU15 and the US performance are much less pronounced than those in an aggregate of all sectors. This supports the earlier discussion on Europe's relative specialization in manufacturing.

Next, we turn to providing a structural explanation of the perceived productivity gap between the EU, Japan, and the United States. Once more, the detailed equation outputs are reported in Appendix B, with the basic results as follows: first, I use the difference in perceived productivity between the United States and EU15 (in all industries) as the dependent variable, and various indicators of obstacles to higher productivity as the independent variables. The results show that differences in industrial affiliation, perceived work effort, poor labor practices, ease of hiring and firing, and capital infrastructure can explain the difference between the performance of the EU15 and the United States. The indicator of the EU15 is statistically insignificant, after taking into account these structural differences between the two economies. Second, I analyzed the same question for the manufacturing sector, with the sample now including the new EU member countries and Japan. Again, work effort and labor practices can explain differences in productivity, while the country indicators are not significant. The conclusion is that industry composition and labor market practices explain the technological gap between the United States and the EU15.

It is also interesting to take note of the "dogs that did not bark," at least in this Survey. Namely, differences in business regulation and in labor skills are *not* significantly associated with differences in productivity, and, therefore, are not to blame for the lower levels of perceived productivity in Europe.

Finally, I would like to point out an interesting observation with regard to differences between the United States and Europe in the Survey: a large share of US firms surveyed actually have their headquarters in Europe. Figure 5 shows that more than one-third of the US firms in the sample have their headquarters abroad (mostly in Europe), while this share is much smaller for the EU, e.g. for Germany. In other words, many of the firms assessing the United States are actually European. The pattern could simply be the result of the large acquisitions of European firms in the United States, which were done precisely because of higher expected returns. It shows that European firms are profiting from the dynamics in the United States through acquisitions and investment there. To the extent that these global players repatriate earnings, they are contributing to raising European GNP.

Figure 5: Share of foreign and domestic firms in the US and German samples

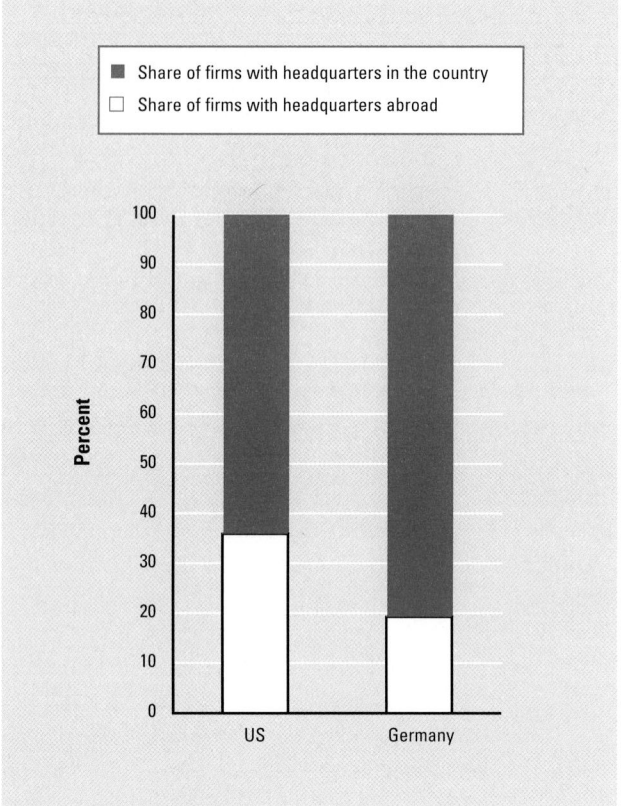

Source: Executive Opinion Survey.

Conclusions

This paper first shows that it is a myth that Europe cannot compete. In terms of international competitiveness, Europe is outperforming its main competitors. This is documented by evidence on market shares and the pricing power of European exporters. Second, is the matter of technological competitiveness. The indicators of competitiveness for the group of EU15 and EU25 were calculated and compared to the United States and Japan, showing that Europe lags behind. This gap is explored using micro evidence from the World Economic Forum's Survey. The first finding—rather good news for Europe—suggests that the technological gap may be overstated, since perceived technological differences between the EU and the United States can be largely explained by industrial affiliation. Europe specializes in chemical products, machinery and cars, which are classified as medium-tech products, even if they embody much high technology. Experience over the past several years has shown that worldwide demand for these products is robust, explaining the strong performance of European exports and the market power of European firms. A further positive result is that European firms have bought into the American market, and should therefore be able to profit from the dynamics and knowledge production there. The second finding highlights the weak spots of Europe's competitiveness. I find that structural factors—in particular labor market rigidities and ease of hiring and firing—contribute significantly to the better performance of the United States vis-à-vis Europe. This underlines the widely acknowledged importance of making the reform of labor markets a priority for the EU15.

Notes

1 See European Central Bank (2005) for the comparison in terms of volumes.

2 Ibid., p. 15.

3 The European Innovation Scoreboard is an instrument developed under the Lisbon Strategy for monitoring and comparing the innovation performance of EU Member states.

4 See World Economic Forum (2004), p. 482.

References

Commission of the European Communities. 2004. European Innovation Scoreboard, Comparative Analysis of Innovation Performance. Online at: http://register.consilium.eu.int/pdf/en/04/st15/st15189.en04.pdf

European Central Bank. 2005. Competitiveness and the Export Performance of the Euro Area. Occasional Paper Series 30. Frankurt.

Krugman, P. 1996. "A Country Is Not a Company." Harvard Business Review. January/February. 40–51.

World Economic Forum. 2003. The Global Competitiveness Report 2003–2004. New York: Oxford University Press.

———. 2004. The Global Competitiveness Report 2004–2005. Hampshire: Palgrave Macmillan.

———. 2005. The Global Information Technology Report 2004–2005. Hampshire: Palgrave Macmillan.

135

Appendix A: Ordered probit explaining differences in technological and productivity performance: Sample EU25, Japan, and United States

	(1) Technological readiness	(2) Technological readiness	(3) Relative productivity	(4) Relative productivity	(5) Relative productivity in manufacturing
Firm size	0.18 *12.22*	0.07 *4.74*	0.11 *7.69*	0.04 *2.63*	0.13 *3.77*
Industry	0.02 *3.66*	0.01 *1.85*	0.03 *4.70*	0.02 *3.10*	— —
EU15	— —	−1.46 *−10.17*	— —	−0.55 *−3.89*	−0.45 *−1.84*
New EU Members	— —	−2.16 *−14.36*	— —	−1.09 *−7.35*	−1.03 *−3.99*
Japan	— —	−0.32 *−1.66*	— —	−0.26 *−1.30*	−0.20 *−0.67*
Number of observations	1,604	1,604	1,556	1,556	462

Source: Author's calculations based on Executive Opinion Survey 2004.

Notes: Z-statistics are in italics. Indicators for the EU15, the new EU member countries, and Japan reflect the position relative to the United States, which is the comparator country.

Appendix B: Ordered probit explaining differences in technological and productivity performance

	(1) Relative productivity EU15 and US	(2) Relative productivity in manufacturing EU, Japan, and US
Firm size	0.03 *1.15*	0.05 *1.28*
Industry	0.02 *2.41*	— —
Effort of hourly worker	0.15 *3.46*	0.26 *4.78*
Effort of salaried worker	0.27 *5.88*	0.23 *4.10*
Ease of hiring and firing	0.09 *3.26*	0.05 *1.53*
Poor labor practices	−0.07 *−2.94*	−0.06 *−1.78*
Business regulations	−0.01 *−0.33*	0.01 *0.36*
Poor labor skills/lack of training	−0.03 *−1.16*	−0.01 *−0.25*
Poor capital and infrastructure	−0.09 *−3.04*	−0.13 *−3.64*
EU15	−0.24 *−1.50*	−0.11 *−0.39*
New EU Members	— —	−0.48 *−1.65*
Japan	— —	−0.42 *−1.22*
Number of observations	664	412

Source: Author's calculations based on Executive Opinion Survey 2004.

Note: Z-statistics are in italics.

Russia: Competitiveness, Growth, and the Next Stage of Development

AUGUSTO LOPEZ-CLAROS, World Economic Forum[1]

In a recent article in the *International Herald Tribune*, entitled "And Now, Command Capitalism," the Russian writer Viktor Erofeyev refers to the difficulties associated with building the institutions of capitalism in Russia while hindered by a "lack of competitiveness."[2] Erofeyev's essay is mainly about the contradictions of government attempts at building a market economy—the essence of which is increasing its flexibility by giving a larger role to market forces—while at the same time exercising a growing degree of bureaucratic control. But it indirectly addresses the broader question of the policy and institutional requirements for boosting the Russian economy's long-term growth prospects.

In this chapter we will examine the factors that are likely to play a key role in enhancing the productivity of the Russian economy, and improving its levels of competitiveness. As noted elsewhere in this volume, productivity is the main driver of the rates of return on investment, which, in turn, determine the growth rates of an economy. A more competitive economy is one that is likely to grow faster over the medium to long term,[3] so the natural question is whether these factors are likely to sustain high growth rates in Russia over the next decade.

We then turn our attention to a broader institutional question: to what extent can Russia anchor its future economic development in a significant strengthening of its relations with the European Union? Can the EU play in Russia, in some fashion, the critical role it has played in the development of Central and Eastern Europe during the past decade and a half? If so, how?

The need for convergence

The question of the pace of economic growth in Russia was put at the centre of the economic policy debate by President Putin himself in his State of the Nation address of May 2003, when he called for a doubling of Russian GDP within the next ten years. With all its imperfections as an indicator of human welfare, the evolution of GDP per capita is still seen by officials, academia, the media, and the development community as an appropriate measure of a government's success in implementing good economic policies, supportive of private sector development. Nowhere is this measure more relevant than in those countries coming out of long periods of stagnation or crisis, in which the need to "catch up" with neighbors and trade partners is seen as of the utmost importance. As shown in Figure 1 and Table 1, the question acquires an additional layer of urgency in Russia because of the heavy costs borne by the population during the period 1992–98, when output contracted by a cumulative 40 percent, leading to a calamitous decline in living standards.[4]

Figure 1: Russia: Gross domestic product, constant prices, annual percent change

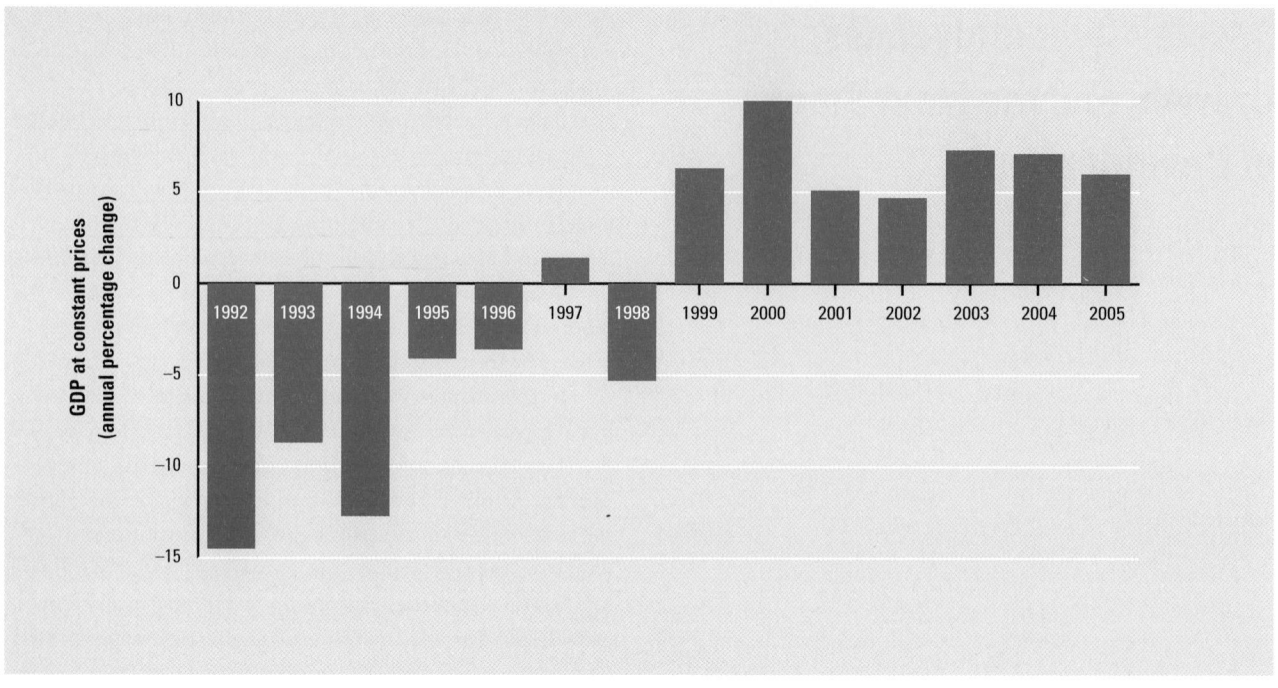

Source: IMF, 2005b.

Table 1: Russia: Selected economic indicators

	1992	1993	1994	1995	1996	1997	1998	1999	2000	2001	2002	2003	2004	2005
Inflation[1]	1734.7	878.8	307.5	198.0	47.7	14.8	27.7	85.7	20.8	21.5	15.8	13.7	10.9	11.8
GDP growth[2]	−14.5	−8.7	−12.7	−4.1	−3.6	1.4	−5.3	6.3	10.0	5.1	4.7	7.3	7.1	6.0
Fiscal balance[3]	−44.3	−15.6	−10.6	−6.1	−8.9	−7.4	−5.0	−1.3	1.2	3.0	1.4	1.7	4.4	6.1
Public debt[4]	—	63.8	48.8	41.7	40.7	50.7	57.5	92.1	61.3	46.9	40.8	34.0	24.8	—
Current account balance[5]	−1.4	1.4	1.9	1.4	2.1	−0.6	−0.8	11.3	17.2	10.9	9.0	8.2	10.2	11.4
Interest rate (percent)[6]	80	210	180	160	48	28	60	55	25	25	21	16	13	13

Sources:
[1] Inflation, annual percent change, IMF, 2005b.
[2] Gross domestic product, constant prices, annual percent change, IMF, 2005b.
[3] Federal budget, as a percentage of GDP, Russian Federation, 2005.
[4] Total foreign and domestic currency public debt, as a percentage of GDP. IMF, 2003; EIU, 2005.
[5] Current account balance in percent of GDP, IMF 2005b.
[6] Refinancing rate of the Central Bank, end of year values in percent, Russian Federation, Central Bank, as of end July 2005.

Much of this decline was probably inevitable, reflecting the need to eliminate the mindless distortions of central planning, such as the undue emphasis on propping up the military industrial complex; the ubiquitous presence of overt and hidden subsidization of consumers and producers (without regard to the associated opportunity costs), and the overwhelming presence of the state as producer, distributor and regulator of the economy. However, the fact remains that it brought with it a period of economic divergence between Russia and the rest of the world. For instance, as shown in Figure 2, on a PPP-adjusted basis

Russian per capita GDP was higher in 1992 than in Brazil, China and India, but by 1998, Brazil had overtaken it by a significant margin, and China (and to a lesser extent India) had considerably narrowed the gap. By the late 1990s no economic policy question in Russia was more pressing than how to reverse the decline and set the economy on a path of recovery and convergence with the rest of the world.

Russia does not fare well in the competitiveness indicators assembled by the World Economic Forum, attaining a rank of 75 among 117 economies in the 2005 version of

Figure 2: Russia and selected economies: GDP per capita 1992–2005

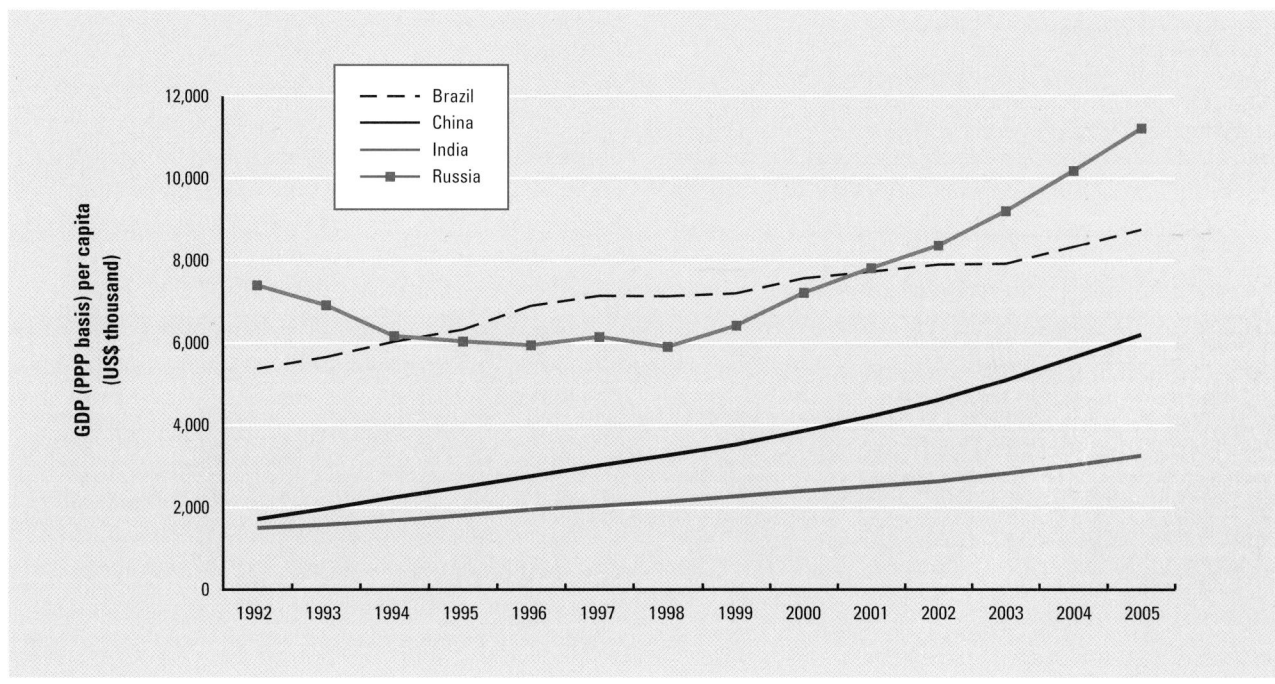

Source: IMF, 2005b.

the Growth Competitiveness Index, a position well below that of China and India (49th and 50th respectively), Poland (51st), Mexico (55th), Brazil (65th), Turkey (66th), and Argentina (72nd).[5] At the same time, Russia has enjoyed several years of relatively strong growth since 1999, reflecting significant gains in the terms of trade, the introduction of some structural reforms, particularly during the early part of the first Putin administration, and the generally more cautious approach to management of the public finances pursued by the authorities in the aftermath of the 1998 financial crisis. However, these growth rates have not been high enough to match those of China, or even India during the last three years, and have been accompanied by an increase in the relative importance of the energy sector as the mainstay of the Russian economy—beneficial during periods of buoyant oil markets, dangerous during the bust phase of the cycle. In parallel, there has been a significant deterioration in a number of indicators which track aspects of the country's institutional environment. More importantly, the growth rates themselves are not high enough to ensure rapid convergence to the levels of income per capita attained in other transition economies in the region, to say nothing of the average levels within the EU.

A narrowing of the per capita income gap with the likes of Poland, Hungary, and other new EU members will require substantially higher real growth rates than the

6 percent average rate seen during the last three years. The goal is likely to remain a challenging one for the government, because most countries want to "converge" to the levels of income per capita seen in the wealthier economies. The transition economies of Central and Eastern Europe, for instance—a useful comparator group for Russia given their common central planning past and geographical proximity—are expected to continue to grow rapidly in coming years. This will reflect the beneficial effects of the institutional and policy improvements required for full participation within the EU—including the adoption of the euro, which is likely to act as the new disciplining mechanism within the new member states—and continued inflows of foreign direct investment, brought about by the attractive combination of a skilled labor force, low labor costs, and political and social stability. As Ireland has done so effectively during the past 20 years, the new EU member states—already growing at close to three times the average of the EU15—are well set on a path of convergence. As shown in Table 2, Russia, on the other hand, is far behind in terms of GDP per capita levels, and does not benefit from the institutional incentives which made it possible for the EU accession states in the 1990s to push ahead with ambitious macroeconomic and institutional reforms.

Table 2: Gross Domestic Product per capita, 2004 (US$)

	Nominal dollars	PPP-adjusted
Russian Federation	**4,093**	**10,179**
Spain	24,144	23,627
Israel	17,695	22,077
Portugal	16,375	19,038
Korea	14,098	21,305
Taiwan	13,260	25,614
Czech Republic	10,480	18,357
Hungary	10,129	15,546
Mexico	6,506	9,666
Poland	6,227	12,244
Malaysia	4,625	10,423
South Africa	4,500	10,603
Turkey	4,251	7,503
Argentina	3,912	12,468
Brazil	3,417	8,328
China	1,269	5,642
Indonesia	1,165	3,622
Nigeria	500	1,120
India	608	3,029

Source: IMF, 2005b.

Russia's long-term growth

There are at least four sets of factors which are likely to play a prominent role in determining Russia's growth path over the longer term, say, the next ten years: the economy's structural endowments, the nature of the external environment, the content of macroeconomic and structural policies, and the evolution of the country's potential for technological innovation. We now look at each of these factors in turn, with particular reference to the ways in which they can be perceived as strengths, that is, able to fuel the growth process in important ways, or as weaknesses, dragging the economy down, and preventing improvements in the efficiency of resource utilization and factor productivity.

Structural endowments

This concept refers to the structural inheritance of Russia, as it emerged from several decades of central planning under the Soviet Union. There are several components to this set of factors, some which work to Russia's advantage, and some of which do not. The economic distortions of the Soviet era were far more pervasive in Russia than in other centrally planned economies, many of which, by the early 1990s, had thriving private sectors. In contrast, Russia did not even have the rudiments of a price and tax system, and there was pervasive and widespread subsidization of production through the exchange rate, interest rates, and the price of raw materials. All this, exacerbated by an unhealthy emphasis on boosting the prominence of military output, had made its industrial sector glaringly uncompetitive. In the early stages, broadly through 1995–96, the phasing out of many of these distortions had

an adverse impact on measured output. As the privileged access by various sectors in the economy to resources, such as cheap credit, hard currency, and commodities at a fraction of the world price, were withdrawn, and as the country moved gradually to a more rational system of resource allocation—based on a decentralized structure of market-determined prices—the economy entered a period of severe contraction, with drastically reduced levels of profitability at the enterprise level, major cutbacks in investment and employment, and associated social dislocations.[6]

However, the ongoing dismantling of these distortions is expected to have a potentially large impact on existing supply constraints, and could tangibly boost potential output. Two examples of this process make the point clear. First, the gradual elimination of restrictions on the ownership of agricultural land, and the beneficial impact this could eventually have on the ability of farmers to mortgage their land to finance planting and harvesting, as is done routinely in more developed economies. The agricultural sector is emerging from decades of neglect; the territory of the Russian Federation is by a huge margin the largest land mass in the planet, spanning 11 time zones, yet the country imports a large share of its food requirements. The potential for growth in the agricultural sector is, therefore, clearly enormous, if supported by the appropriate policy framework. Second, the emergence of a broad array of private schools, universities, and training centers far more attuned to the needs of the private sector. These new institutions are better able to deliver to the market a labor force with a vastly improved set of skills and capabilities, as compared with the early stages of the transition, when education and training were state funded, and in which virtually no effort was made to match skills with needs. Both could have potentially huge implications for the future evolution of total factor productivity and, therefore, potential output. Both highlight the scope for improved resource utilization as a key driver of growth in Russia, in contrast with early episodes of growth in the Soviet economy, which were largely driven by heavy investment and higher labor force participation rates.[7]

A related aspect is the extent to which repressed demand for consumer and durable goods seems to be fuelling the growth of investment, particularly in the construction sector, where the potential benefits of modernization of the entire stock of residential and commercial real estate could spur growth significantly in coming years. Unlike China, Russia is not likely to benefit much from a process of urbanization, whereby a large peasant population moves from the country side—where labor productivity is close to zero—to the cities, where it is much higher and captured in the official statistics. However, Russia does have an unusually old and dilapidated capital stock: a full 67 percent of capital equipment is at least 15 years old. Again, the potential here for major gains in factor productivity are large. As with tapping the potential of Russian agriculture, the extent to which the country will benefit from this process will depend on the content of policies—in the case of the renewal of the capital stock, a marked improvement in the investment climate (see below). Similar comments apply to the country's decaying infrastructure.

Yet another feature which enhances Russia's long-term growth potential is its natural resource base. At a time of increasing pressures on world reserves Russia is quickly emerging as a major power in the international oil markets.[8] Partly reflecting sizeable investments by the oil companies during the last several years, Russian oil output (Table 3) has expanded by close to 42 percent in the period 2000–04 and the country is now the world's number two oil producer, after Saudi Arabia, and well ahead of the United States.[9] If account is taken of gas exports—where Russia is by far the largest supplier in world markets (Table 4), accounting for a 27 percent global share—then Russia may well be the world's largest *energy* exporter.

The government's past reluctance to submit to requests from OPEC for production cuts reflects a combination of factors, including the setting of ambitious medium-term production targets by Russian private producers, concerns about the establishment of a precedent which could then lead to future OPEC demands on the government and producers, and the fact that the government appears to have made a deliberate strategic choice to present itself to other trade partners as a reliable, alternative supplier. While some of these plans may have suffered a blow in the wake of the clumsy re-nationalization of Yukos (see below), the fact remains that Russia continues to maintain a number of important strategic advantages. (in oil)

First, the Russian oil companies are engaged in a major process of restructuring and modernization, reinvesting their large profits to expand capacity and enhance efficiency. Unlike their peers in many of the OPEC member countries—often dominated by state monopoly companies that bar or sharply limit foreign investment in the oil sector—Russia's oil companies are seeking to establish a presence among the world's oil industry leaders, and are doing so against the background of a much stronger macroeconomic situation.

Second, and more important, there are a number of questions about the long-term political outlook for those countries in the Middle East which have been major suppliers of oil to the United States and other markets in the industrial world. In particular, Saudi Arabia (the world's largest oil exporter) and other countries in the Middle East may well be on the threshold of major political changes in the next decade or so. The countries in the Gulf region have the highest rates of population growth in the world and, hence, the most rapidly expanding labor

Table 3: Oil production, 2004 (million tons)

	Million tons	Share of total (percent)	Rank
United States	329.8	8.5	3
Canada	147.6	3.8	9
Mexico	190.7	4.9	5
Venezuela	153.5	4.0	7
Norway	149.9	3.9	8
United Kingdom	95.4	2.5	14
Russian Federation	**458.7**	**11.9**	**2**
Iran	202.6	5.2	4
Iraq	99.7	2.6	13
Kuwait	119.8	3.1	12
Saudi Arabia	505.9	13.1	1
United Arab Emirates	125.8	3.3	10
Nigeria	122.2	3.2	11
China	174.5	4.5	6
Total World	**3,867.9**		

Source: British Petroleum, 2005.

Table 4: Natural gas exports, 2004 (billion cubic meters)[1]

	Billion cubic meters	Share of total (percent)	Rank	World rank
United States	21.4	2.6%	7	10
Canada	102.1	12.6%	2	2
Argentina	7.8	1.0%	10	20
Denmark	4.1	0.5%	11	24
Germany	12.1	1.5%	8	15
Netherlands	49.2	6.1%	5	5
Norway	74.9	9.2%	3	3
United Kingdom	9.8	1.2%	9	17
Russian Federation	**215.0**	**26.5%**	**1**	**1**
Turkmenistan	43.9	5.4%	6	6
Algeria	60.9	7.5%	4	4
Other	210.0	25.9%	—	—
Total	**811.2**	**100.0%**		

[1] Provisional
Source: Cedigaz, 2005.

forces. Unemployment rates have reached historically high levels, and serious structural rigidities in their economies have resulted in anemic economic growth rates, and falling per capita incomes.[10] Rising social tensions in countries with unreformed political institutions and no ostensible experience of democracy could well result in instability. Whether these emerging tensions will lead to evolutionary and largely peaceful changes—as happened in Central and Eastern Europe in the late 1980s and early 1990s—or will be more destabilizing in nature is not yet clear. The point is that, from a strategic point of view—Yukos notwithstanding—the new geopolitics of energy may, indeed, create an opportunity for Moscow to "assume a far more significant position in the world petroleum sector than ever before," as noted in an insightful article by Morse and Richard (2002). This would mean potentially larger inflows of FDI to the energy sector, with the associated beneficial repercussions for technological diffusion, modernization, and growth.

The extent to which the country's *human* capital endowment is likely to spur growth in coming years is more difficult to assess. The redeployment of labor from the military-industrial complex and other heavy and inefficient industries to the private non-defense sector has probably run most of its course, and has led to improvements in labor productivity, as Russia's generally educated labor force has continued to move to light manufacturing, services and other industries long neglected under central planning. However, the Russian labor force continues to suffer from skills mismatches, which are particularly acute in the public sector. Submerged in a centuries-old deeply authoritarian tradition, the capacity of Russia's civil service to formulate and implement policy reforms is woefully inadequate, and this, in turn, has limited the ability of the government to efficiently utilize surplus revenues in ways that might contribute to enhancing factor productivity and boosting competitiveness.

Two examples illustrate the dilemmas this sometimes creates. The social expenditure reforms introduced in early 2005 met with fierce opposition on the part of the population, had to be partially abandoned, and ended up being far more costly in financial terms than initially envisaged. A key aspect of this was lack of proper preparation during the formulation stage. The public sector was just not up to the task of effectively tackling reforms in Russia's complex system of social benefits. On another front: having amortized, ahead of schedule, all of its obligations to the IMF, the government has just prepaid some US$15 billion of debt to Paris Club official bilateral creditors. While it is possible to come up with good reasons to justify this use of public resources, one cannot help noting that Moscow's main international airport (Sheremetyevo 2) remains a third-rate facility. Fifteen years into the transition, with a bountiful surplus in the budget, an efficient mechanism has not been found to deliver an essential facility to a G8 capital: a large modern international airport.

Furthermore, Russia's long-term demographic trends are not particularly favorable, as is persuasively argued by Nicholas Eberstadt elsewhere in this volume (Chapter 3.2). Thus, the expansion of the labor force is unlikely to be an engine of economic growth in coming years. However, the scope for progress in innovation and improvements in the productivity of the factors of production is considerably larger (see below). Although it is difficult to quantify the impact on long-term growth of these structural endowments, they are expected to play a supportive role, particularly if accompanied by a favorable external environment, and by the structural and institutional reforms noted below.

The external environment

The external environment has played a key role in the evolution of the Russian economy, with the most recent examples being the collapse of oil prices in 1997–98 and in 1986. As Figure 3 implies, both precipitated a fiscal implosion, although the effects of the more recent episode were more readily apparent, owing to the substantial opening up of the economy that had taken place in the intervening decade.

Some recent progress notwithstanding, the Russian economy remains strongly dependent on the energy sector. According to an IMF study released in 2002,[11] the energy sector contributes some 17 percent of Russia's total value added: oil and gas extraction account for 6 percent of GDP; energy-related transportation and pipelines account for 9 percent of GDP; and other fuels and products make up the remaining 2 percent of GDP. Furthermore, the energy sector contributes about a quarter of total revenues for the consolidated government budget.[12] It has also accounted for 40 percent of total investment in recent years and energy exports account for nearly 60 percent of total exports. The IMF also reports on some oil price sensitivity analysis, the results of which suggest that a US$1/barrel drop in the price of oil translates into a 0.5 percent GDP contraction; a 0.3 percent reduction in federal revenues and a US$1 billion drop in exports.[13]

The authorities have been generally aware of the vulnerabilities implicit in the above "facts" about the Russian economy, and have gone about mitigating the undue influence of oil in two ways: first, to encourage the growth of exports and to gear taxation of the energy sector with a view to generating a higher level of revenues for the federal budget for a given level of prices. Their efforts in this area have met a measure of success, as the interests of the state and the oil companies have broadly converged. In this scenario—provided the federal budget continues to be implemented in the cautious fashion seen in recent years—the growth in the volume of exports would far exceed the real rate of expenditure growth, and, hence, the demands made by the budget on oil revenues. Implicit is the assumption that existing pipeline capacity constraints on exports would be gradually relieved through additional construction.

A second component of this strategy has been the creation of a Norwegian-style Stabilization Fund in early 2004, to reduce the country's vulnerability to external shocks linked to terms of trade losses.[14] This important initiative—arguably the most important piece of economic legislation approved during the past two years—has made an important contribution to reducing investor perceptions that the country is nothing more than "an oil play." Incidentally, it has also been used by the authorities as a monetary sterilization mechanism, at a time of considerable

Figure 3: Urals oil price (US$ per barrel)

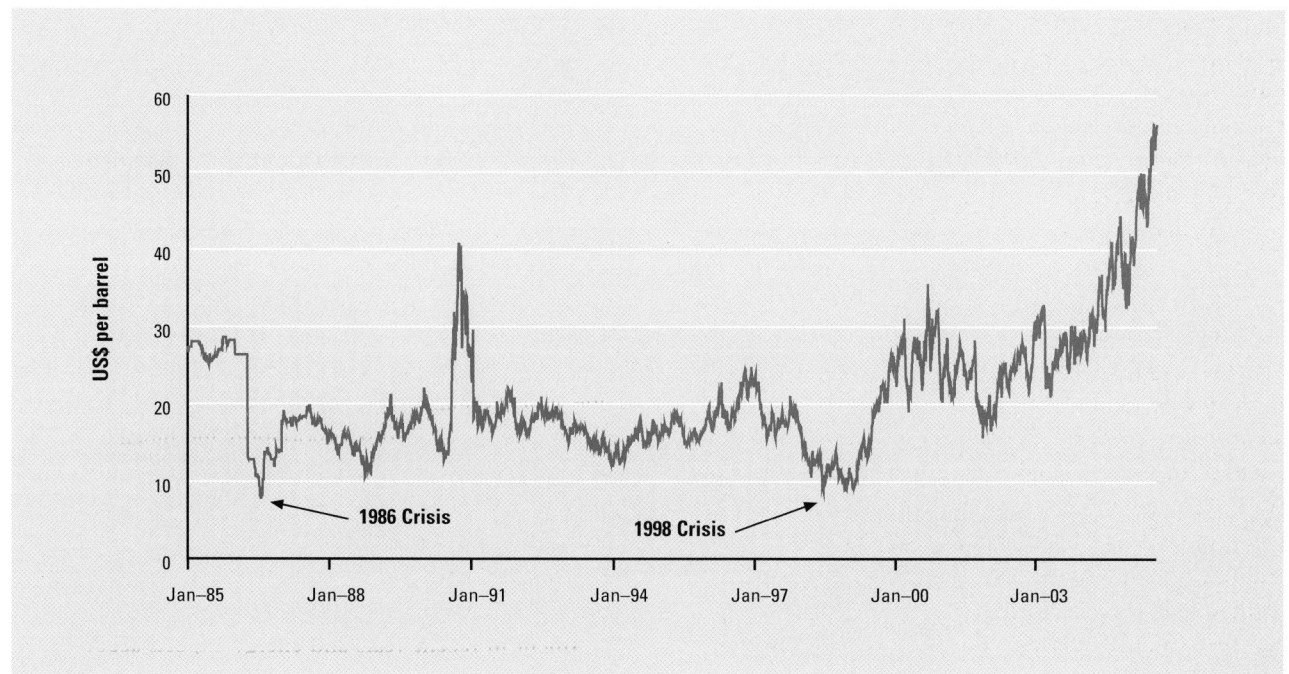

Source: Bloomberg.

upward pressure on the ruble, associated with massive inflows of liquidity through the balance of payments. Of course, the budget and the balance of payments continue to be strongly determined by commodity prices, but the circumstances under which the country used to enter a financial danger zone have been radically altered. To the extent that a major share of the proceeds of the Stabilization Fund continue to be allocated to prepayment of external debt, it is not inconceivable that within a few years Russia's debt-to-GDP ratio may have fallen to some 10 percent, significantly enhancing the capacity of the government to precipitate major shifts in the composition of spending, away from debt service toward education, health, investment in infrastructure, and other competitiveness-enhancing areas.

The external environment has other features which could have a bearing on Russia's ability to sustain high growth rates. Global demand prospects, the timing and conditions under which Russia would enter the WTO, the patterns of trade flows and the extent to which these are likely to be affected by the increasingly global reach of Russia's energy sector (e.g., in China). On balance, as shown in Figure 4, the combination of an unusually strong balance of payments position—the current account in 2005 should amount to some US$70 billion and reserves at the Central Bank of Russia reach some US$170 billion, equivalent to about a year and a half of imports—and a

strong medium-term outlook for energy prices, is expected to provide favorable conditions for continued economic growth.[15]

Policy content: structural and institutional reforms
Real growth rates in the 7–9 percent range are needed to make a tangible difference in the pace of "catch-up." Such rates are not impossible, but would require a much more aggressive stance as regards structural reforms and improvements in the institutional environment. We take it as given that the government will continue to show credible commitment to a stable macroeconomic framework, and that the budget indiscipline—the defining characteristic of Russian economic policy during much of the 1990s—is long gone. The actual evolution of the fiscal accounts during the last six years, shown in Figure 5, would suggest this to be a reasonable assumption.

Indeed, since coming into office in early 2000, the government of President Vladimir Putin has shown remarkable fiscal restraint, largely avoiding the sort of relaxation of policies that have come to be associated with countries experiencing significant improvements in the terms of trade. Instead, the government has been running budget surpluses—for the sixth consecutive year in 2005—having used the excess revenues stemming from higher-than-assumed oil prices in successive annual budgets, to reduce the stock of external debt, to build up a

Figure 4: Russia: Gross international reserves, US$ billion

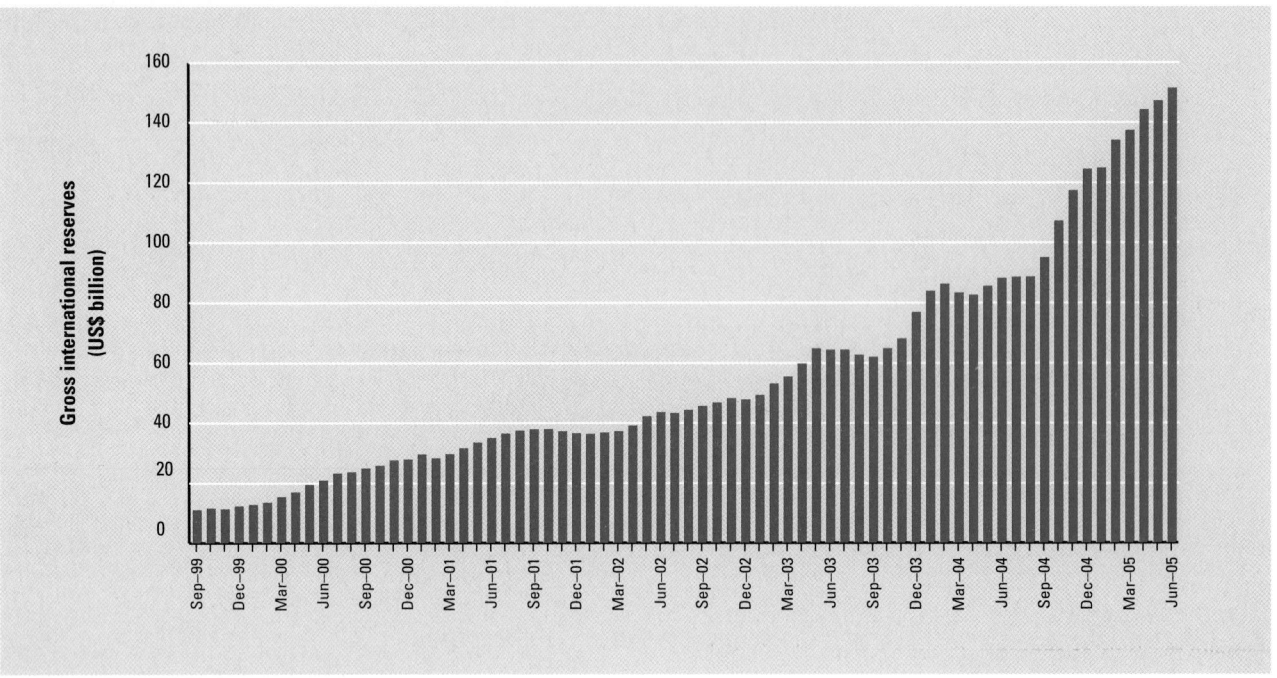

Source: Central Bank of Russia, online at: http://www.cbr.ru/eng/

Figure 5: Russia: Government budget balance (percent of GDP)

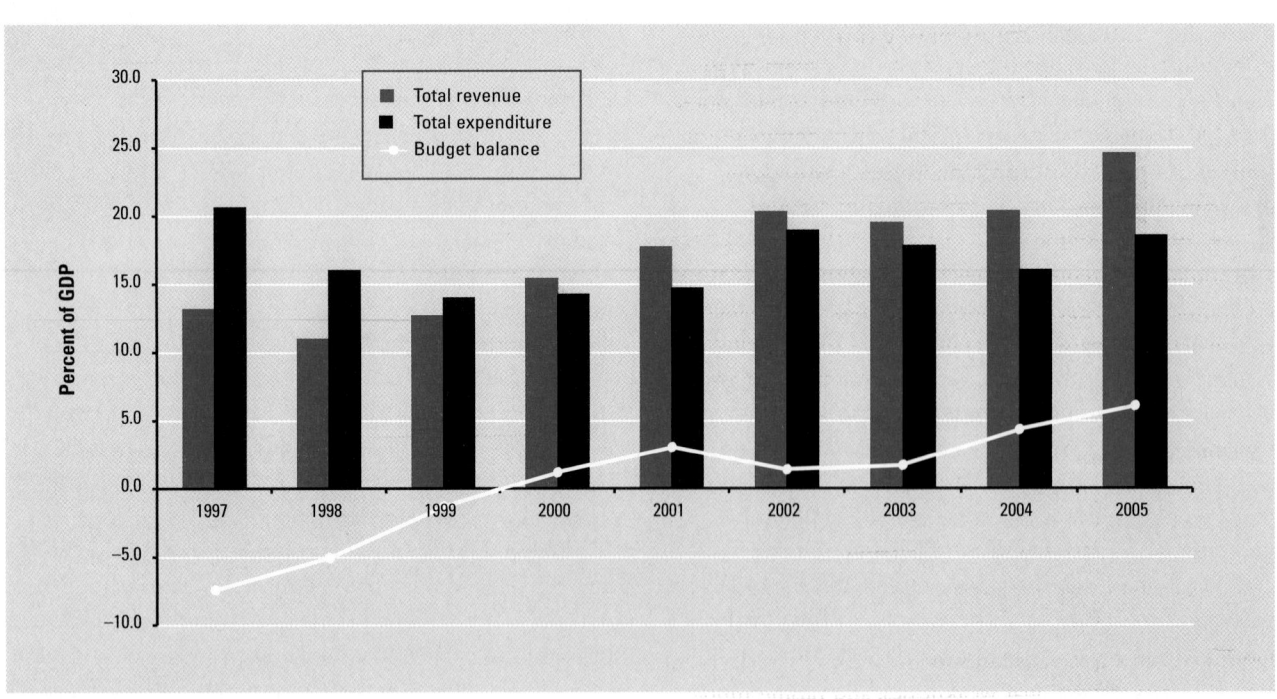

Source: Russian Federation, 2005.

large cushion of cash reserves at the central bank, and to boost pensions and public sector wages, as well as selected components of expenditure. In this respect, in the remarkably benign external environment of the last few years created by buoyant oil markets, the Russian government's behavior in the area of fiscal policy can be characterized as being closer in spirit to that of Norway, than to that of Venezuela and Nigeria, where oil revenues in the past have tended to fall victim to a combination of inefficiency and venality. However, a solid budget and cautious monetary policies will clearly not be enough.

Temporarily setting aside the management of the fiscal accounts (see below), particular attention would have to be given to measures aimed at creating a friendlier environment for small- to medium-sized enterprises, the bedrock of output and employment growth in the more successful transition economies in the region. In particular, the authorities must urgently concentrate on the task of enhancing the intermediation role of Russia's banking sector by addressing some of its most glaring weaknesses, namely: the lack of appropriate supervision, the fact that it is dominated by state banks which do not always operate on a commercial basis, its sprawling nature, and the absence of international accounting standards (IAS) reporting, to name a few.

But this is not all. The authorities must do much more to improve the legal and regulatory environment. The big conglomerates have no difficulty lobbying the government and parliament to ensure that the system works for them, just as they have had no problem financing expansion plans out of retained earnings, or via "pocket" banks. Indeed, the extent to which they dominate the economic and political landscape is itself a worrisome development, suggesting the emergence of a South Korean–style *chaebol* form of capitalism.[16] But, at the other end, potential entrepreneurs face a labyrinthine regulatory environment, corrupt officialdom, and have few chances to gain access to bank credit. There was a time, a few years back, when the government seemed to be aware of these weaknesses, and appeared intent on doing something about them. Indeed, much of the push in the area of structural reforms seen during the first Putin administration appears to have been motivated by a desire to remedy them. But remaining problems are glaring.

The Forum's 2005 Executive Opinion Survey of more than 470 enterprises in Russia shows extremely poor rankings in a number of critical areas, highlighting several serious institutional weaknesses, and raising fundamental questions about the quality of the investment climate. Table 5 shows a comprehensive summary of these indicators for 2004 and 2005.

The private sector in Russia has serious misgivings about the independence of the judiciary, and about the way justice is administered. Legal redress in Russia is not

Table 5: Russia's macroeconomic and structural environment: An international perspective

Variable	Rank 2005 (out of 117 countries)	Rank 2004 (out of 104 countries)
Macroeconomic and financial environment		
Level of financial market sophistication	86	72
Soundness of banks	101	91
Ease of access to loans	91	67
Venture capital availability	66	49
Local equity market access for raising money	69	74
Government encouragement of FDI	109	97
Prevalence of trade barriers	91	95
Technological innovation and diffusion		
Technological readiness	77	69
Firm level technology absorption	63	56
Prevalence of foreign technology licensing	101	87
Extent to which FDI brings new technology into the country	98	87
Quality of science and math education	21	23
University/industry research collaboration	42	40
Quality of research institutions	31	19
Information and communication technology (ICT)		
Cellular mobile subscribers per 100 inhabitants	65	74
Internet users per 10,000 inhabitants	66	72
Government prioritization of ICT	91	68
Personal computers per 100 inhabitants	52	47
General infrastructure		
Overall infrastructure quality	79	64
Air transport quality	64	66
Railroad infrastructure development	24	26
Fixed telephone lines	46	50
Public institutions-contracts and law		
Judicial independence	102	84
Efficiency of legal framework	95	80
Protection of property rights	108	88
Intellectual property protection	105	84
Favoritism in decisions of government officials	106	85
Effectiveness of law-making bodies	80	63
Extent of bureaucratic red tape	90	89
Reliability of police services	99	90
Business costs of organized crime	101	88
Strength of auditing and accounting standards	89	81
Impact of taxes on the incentives to work or invest	81	73
Freedom of the press	96	84
Public institutions-corruption		
Irregular payments in:		
Exports and imports	83	91
Tax collection	69	69
Public contracts	82	75
Judicial decisions	76	83
Diversion of public funds	87	69
Business costs of corruption	109	100
Public trust of politicians	94	76

Source: World Economic Forum, 2004 and 2005.

Table 6: Russia: Doing business in 2005

	Starting a business			Enforcing a contract		
	Number of procedures	Time[1]	Cost[2]	Number of procedures	Time[1]	Cost[3]
Argentina	15	32	15.7	33	520	15.0
Brazil	17	152	11.7	25	566	15.5
China	12	41	14.5	25	241	25.5
Czech Republic	10	40	10.8	22	300	9.6
Hungary	6	52	22.9	21	365	8.1
India	11	89	49.5	40	425	43.1
Indonesia	12	151	130.7	34	570	126.5
Israel	5	34	5.5	27	585	22.1
Korea	12	22	17.7	29	75	5.4
Malaysia	9	30	25.1	31	300	20.2
Mexico	8	58	16.7	37	421	20.0
Nigeria	10	44	95.2	23	730	37.2
Poland	10	31	20.6	41	1000	8.7
Portugal	11	78	13.5	24	320	17.5
Russian Federation	**9**	**36**	**6.7**	**29**	**330**	**20.3**
South Africa	9	38	9.1	26	277	11.5
Spain	6	108	16.5	23	169	14.1
Taiwan	8	48	6.3	22	210	7.7
Turkey	8	9	26.4	22	330	12.5
Sample Average	10	57	27.1	28	407	23.2

Notes:
[1] Time measured in days
[2] Cost measured as percent income per capita
[3] Percent of debt

Source: World Bank, 2005

expeditious, transparent, or inexpensive, as it is in the most competitive economies in the world. A ranking of 102 among 117 countries in 2005 suggests that it is time consuming, unpredictable, and a burden on the cost structure of enterprises. Partly because of this, the environment for the protection of property rights is extremely poor and worsening. Russia's ranking in this indicator this year has suffered a precipitous decline with respect to 2004, from 88 to 108, among the worst in the world. The heavy-handed, arbitrary handling of the Yukos case has, no doubt, been a contributing factor.[17]

What foreign investment has come in has been largely directed to the energy sector, characterized by a high risk/high reward tradeoff. In this respect, Russia is not unlike China, where property rights and a poor judicial climate are also a serious concern, but where the growth of FDI has been fuelled by the country's large and expanding market, offering the promise of high returns on such investments. The opportunity costs associated with the poor property rights climate are huge for the country, as Russian flight capital—well in excess of US$200 billion by conservative estimates during the past decade—remains parked abroad, waiting for a better day.[18] Russia is afflicted with insufferable levels of red tape and needless bureaucracy, a particularly heavy burden for potential startups, as shown, in Table 6, by the unremittingly mediocre scores in the World Bank study on the costs of doing business

(number of procedures and cost to start a new business, etc.).

But there is more. Public officials in general are not perceived as impartial arbitrators of government policy, but rather as active supporters of particular interests. Lack of security remains a heavy burden on businesses as well, reflecting a combination of the high prevalence of crime and the unreliability of police services. The incidence of crime and corruption imposes heavy costs on business, and, therefore, adversely affects the international competitiveness of Russian companies. Accounting and auditing standards are weak, raising yet another set of concerns about the investment climate. Increasing restraints on freedom of the press highlight the risks for the abuse of power, and the difficulties for civil society to emerge as a constructive counterweight to the power of the state.

Technology and innovation

The speed with which a country can utilize new technologies and the extent to which it can itself be part of the process of scientific and technological innovation are key drivers of productivity growth. The Growth Competitiveness Index captures this by looking at two specific aspects of technology that foster sustained growth: innovation and technology transfer, on the one hand, and the use that is made of information and communications technologies (ICT), on the other. Technological improvements may be made through the introduction of new technologies—that is, innovation—or by adopting those technologies already developed abroad through technology transfer. The second process is generally seen to be particularly important for developing economies, where it is cheaper to import and adapt technologies from outside, than to develop them from the outset.

Russia finds itself in a unique position along the technology frontier. On the one hand, it is a country that has a century-long history of distinguished contributions to basic scientific research.[19] Innovation as a concept—the process of scientific inquiry and application, leading to an expansion of the frontiers of knowledge—is an integral part of the country's cultural and educational heritage. The collapse of the Soviet Union, however, precipitated a massive brain drain. Faced with sharp cutbacks in resources allocated to basic scientific research and an unsettled political situation, many of Russia's best scientists emigrated, enriching the universities and research establishments in other parts of the world. Thus, the various indicators used to construct the technology index of the Growth Competitiveness Index convey an ambiguous picture. Some examples will suffice to illustrate Russia's mixed picture. First, not surprisingly, and reflecting the country's still impressive scientific endowment, Russia gets a very good ranking of 29 on the innovation subindex; its extremely high tertiary enrollment rates and relatively high number of patent registrations, as well as good levels of university/industry collaboration help explain this.[20] Its innovation ranking would be even higher, were it not for relatively weak scores in the area of "technological sophistication" captured by the Survey, broadly reflecting the antiquated state of the capital stock, as noted earlier.

Second, Russia does not have particularly impressive penetration rates for the latest technologies. Even in the area of mobile telephony—where notable progress has been made in recent years in terms of expanding coverage—cellular telephone use per 100 inhabitants is about 25, putting Russia in 65th place in the world, better than its 74th rank in 2004, but still not quite in the top half among the 117 economies covered in the GCR. Similar results are obtained for Internet use: improvements with respect to 2004 but absolute levels that are not high enough to put Russia above its 66th place in the world. The results of the Survey also suggest that the government does not appear to give high priority to the promotion and dissemination of information and communications technologies (ICT) policies, in contrast to other countries, where the government plays a leading role in promoting the use of the latest technologies in the public sector, encourages their adoption and use in the private sector, and continuously updates the legal environment underlying the ICT sector. The importance of this cannot be underestimated. ICT continues to be regarded as a key driver for productivity and sustained growth. It acts as a catalyst for organizational transformation, improving the way people work in an economy, facilitating the flow of information, and increasing the efficiency and speed needed to accomplish tasks. For developing countries in particular, ICT is further seen as a means of leapfrogging to a greatly improved economic and business environment.[21]

However, Russia gets its *lowest* ranking in the area of technology transfer, whether as regards the role of FDI as a source of new technologies, or the prevalence of foreign technology licensing as a means of acquiring new technologies. This may be due, in part, to the fact that with a commodity-based export structure, Russia may be less adept at absorbing foreign technologies than a country with a strong technology-based export sector. In addition to this, there seems to be broad consensus that Russian attitudes toward FDI may contain an element of ambivalence. Throughout much of the past decade the government has remained publicly committed to encouraging foreign direct investment and, at least formally, Russia has managed to create a fairly liberal regulatory framework. The authorities seem to recognize that the benefits of FDI could be great, involving much-needed technology transfers, improving managerial skills in the enterprise sector, as well as helping to reduce, through diversification, the dependence of the balance of payments and the budget on primary commodities. However, in practice, the authorities have sometimes displayed a more ambivalent attitude toward foreign ownership, one characterized by the somewhat old-fashioned view that there are sectors that should remain "strategic," largely under national control. This has been reflected in a number of ways in recent years: in the consolidation of the aluminium sector, in the relatively low levels of foreign participation in the banking sector,[22] in sharp contrast with what has happened in other transition economies in the region—particularly in Central and Eastern Europe—and, more recently, in government attempts—clumsy but largely effective—in reasserting control over the energy sector. Not surprisingly, FDI inflows have been relatively small in Russia over the past decade, rarely above 2 percent of GDP on an annual basis.

Summary

The above picture is decidedly mixed. It consists of good resource and structural endowments, the pursuit, in recent years, of broadly cautious macro policies, buttressed by a benign external environment, one that is likely to remain so in coming years. It includes much unfulfilled potential in the area of technological innovation—against a background of impressive past achievements in the area of basic scientific research. It is marred, however, by disturbing institutional deficiencies across a broad range of areas, essential for the creation of a more investor-friendly environment. This would suggest that to ensure high growth

Figure 6: Russia and selected economies: GDP per capita 1992 to 2005

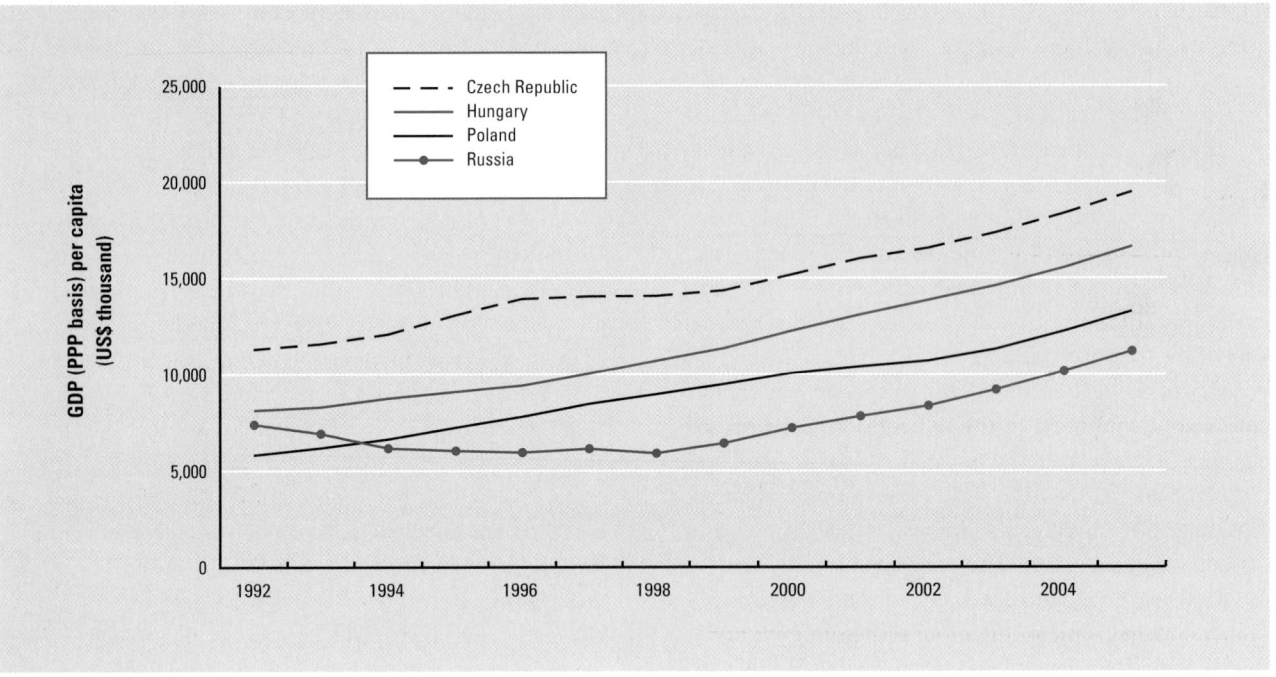

Source: IMF, 2005b.

rates in coming years, a multi-pronged strategy should be adopted. First and foremost, deliberate and ambitious reforms are needed to tackle rule of law, property rights and transparency issues. The government will also have to continue to pursue cautious macroeconomic policies—in particular, it will have to strive not to yield to the temptation to simply convert buoyant oil revenues into higher public sector wages and pensions. In this respect, the Concluding Statement of the 2005 IMF Mission, with its warning that "the oil wealth is not being harnessed in support of reforms that could raise potential GDP" is a troubling development.[23] Only as these deficiencies are addressed will Russia be able to capitalize on its strengths to move the economy's growth profile to a higher level, consistent with the government's desire to converge to income per capita levels seen elsewhere in Central and Eastern Europe. As noted in Figure 6, the gap in PPP-adjusted Russian GDP per capita with respect to Poland, Hungary, and the Czech Republic is actually wider in 2005 than it was in 1992. Russia has, in fact, *diverged*.

The EU: An institutional anchor for Russian development?

The future of Russia's relations with the EU has been the subject of frequent consultations between the EU and successive Russian governments.[24] Discussions have addressed issues both of economic integration and the associated institutional mechanisms that would gradually remove barriers to the flow of goods and services and facilitate factor mobility, as well as aspects of political cooperation. The dialogue has stretched for more than a decade now, and various decisions taken along the way have at times fallen victim to the somewhat disorderly nature of Russia's transition to the market, and to the accompanying introduction of democratic processes and institutions. To a lesser extent in recent years, the EU enlargement process has also at times acted as a temporary distraction.

More recently, the dialogue has intensified, and has merged with the broader agenda that seeks to identify what Russia's future role will be in the international community. This agenda includes the formulation of new cooperative arrangements with NATO, under the umbrella of an established Russia-NATO Council, the decision to put WTO accession negotiations on a fast track,[25] and plans for the creation of a Common European Economic Area, initially called for in 1999 and reaffirmed on several subsequent occasions. We now consider some aspects of the evolving Russia-EU relationship.

Russia–EU facts

It is useful to set out some basic structural parameters that will have a bearing on the future of Russia-EU relations. Russia has a population of some 145 million, compared with the EU's 457 million. Its population is thus 80 percent higher than that of Germany, the largest of the EU states. Russia's population is twice that of the 10 new members of the EU who joined on 1 May 2004. It has a landmass of 17.1 million square kilometers, 5.3 times that of the EU15. Russia had a *per capita* GDP of US$4,093 in 2004, compared with a weighted average for the EU25 of US$28,058. On a PPP-adjusted basis, the gap is smaller: according to the IMF World Economic Outlook database, GDP *per capita* in Russia in 2004 was $10,179, as compared with US$25,791 for the EU25 and US$19,038 for Portugal. On a PPP-adjusted basis, the Russian economy is roughly the size of Brazil's, and about 40 to 50 percent larger than that of Canada, Korea, Mexico, and Spain. Russia's main macroeconomic indicators do not compare unfavorably with those in the EU: inflation is higher, but Russia has a large budget surplus, lower public indebtedness, a stronger current account, and GDP growth rates during the past three years more than three times the EU average.

In terms of structural and institutional reforms, Russia still lags behind some of the more successful transition economies in the region, most of which had a considerable head start in terms of private sector development. The EU is a far more important trade partner to Russia than the other way around (Table 7). In 2004, Russian merchandise exports amounted to US$183 billion, of which roughly 31 percent were sold to EU15 countries. The share rises to 50 percent if the 10 EU enlargement candidates are added. On the import side, some 32 percent of goods originate in EU25 countries.

About 50 percent of Russia's exports to the EU15 are energy products. This figure rises to close to 70 percent, if the combined EU25 is considered, because many of the new EU member states import up to 100 percent of their energy needs from Russia, including gas, oil, and nuclear fuels. In contrast, Russia accounts only for some 2–3 percent of total EU exports and imports. It is the fourth largest market for EU exporters, after the United States, Switzerland, and China.

Russia's international political weight far exceeds its economic importance. This stems as much from the Cold War, as from the fact that Russia emerged as the legal successor state to the Soviet Union. It is a permanent member of the United Nations Security Council, has been made a full member of the G8, and is presently a member of the "Quartet" (with the United States, the EU, and the UN), holding discussions on a possible peace settlement in the Middle East. A not insignificant share of Russia's perceived political weight stems from the desire by G7 partners during the 1990s to encourage a peaceful transition, at a time of severe internal tensions associated with the collapse of the central planning system. A key element of this was tacit recognition of Russia's earlier status as a global nuclear power.

Table 7: Russia: Exports and imports 2004 (US$ billion)[1]

	Exports	Imports	Share of exports (percent)	Share of imports (percent)
World	183.5	96.3	100	100
EU25	91.6	30.7	49.9	31.8
Of which				
France	4.7	2.7	2.6	2.8
Germany	14.0	9.4	7.7	9.7
Italy	11.4	2.8	6.2	2.9
United Kingdom	6.5	1.7	3.6	1.7
Finland	5.8	2.1	3.2	2.2
Netherlands	11.7	1.5	6.4	1.5
Poland	6.3	2.0	3.4	2.1
Hungary	3.9	0.7	2.1	0.7
Czech Republic	2.6	0.8	1.4	0.9
United States	8.3	3.5	4.5	3.6
Japan	3.3	2.1	1.8	2.2
Switzerland	7.8	0.6	4.3	0.7
China	11.1	3.9	6.1	4.0
India	3.7	0.7	2.0	0.7
Belarus	10.3	5.8	5.6	6.0
Cyprus	6.0	0.0	3.2	0.0
Kazakhstan	4.5	3.1	2.4	3.3
Ukraine	10.3	5.2	5.6	5.4
Other	26.6	40.8	14.5	42.3

[1] Country levels corresponded to 2003 totals.
Source: IMF, 2005a.

Russia–EU cooperation

One of the first initiatives in the area of Russia-EU cooperation was the 1994 Agreement on Partnership and Cooperation (APC), a comprehensive document containing 112 articles, various annexes and protocols, covering trade in goods, investment, intellectual protection, and understandings in the areas of energy, agriculture, the environment, transport, and so on. The agreement, which came into force on 1 December 1997, contains various provisions aimed at strengthening cooperation in the political and security areas as well. Its avowed goal is to prepare the groundwork for the eventual establishment of a free trade area.[26] This vision has been reinforced a number of times in subsequent summits, and in 1999 the EU called for the creation of a Common Economic Space, a goal which presupposes tangible steps in the direction of harmonization of legislation and the regulatory framework. The Common Economic Space figured prominently in the discussions at the May 2005 summit. Russia has not been a passive party in this process: in late 1999 it set out its own vision of the future of Russia-EU relations, proposing, in a medium-term framework, some of the priority areas for cooperation. Implicit in this document is the notion of the voluntary and gradual incorporation by Russia of the EU's *acquis communautaire*. This particular interpretation of future relations has been reiterated by President Putin, including in his annual addresses to the Federal Assembly, in which he has stated that the Russian government would "continue the vigorous work with the European Union aimed at forming a single economic space."

Options for the future

A reading of these policy statements suggests that, at least over the next decade, Russian membership of the EU is not on the agenda. Indeed, it is not clear whether, because of its size and other structural characteristics, Russian membership could ever be seriously contemplated, at least under the EU's present legal and institutional structure. Russia is simply too large for the EU to absorb, in the way it has absorbed 10 countries in 2004, with (together) half the population of Russia, a small fraction of the land mass, no strategic nuclear weapons, or the associated political weight (inherited or otherwise) that comes with having a permanent seat in the UN's Security Council.

Paradoxically, it is not the *stage* of Russia's development that is likely to be the binding constraint. The EU has agreed to start accession negotiations with Turkey later in 2005, although when it agreed to do so, it had serious concerns about the strength of its democracy, the treatment of its Kurdish minority, its treatment of women, and its unwillingness to recognize Cyprus, an EU member. While negotiations with Turkey could be delayed and will, in any event, take at least a decade to complete, the prospect of these getting off the ground at some point and actually being successfully concluded, cannot be totally ruled out. In contrast, even if Russia were to continue to solidify its democratic credentials, sort out the conflict in Chechnya, and achieve macroeconomic and financial indicators comparable to the likes of Estonia and Hungary, it is unlikely to be invited. On the doorsteps of China and Japan, spanning 11 time zones, Russia inside the EU would change the EU as much, if not more, than it would change Russia.

So, a more promising approach might be to continue to work in those areas of common interest, with the APC surely providing a broad enough agenda. Russia could gain much from a voluntary incorporation of those elements of the *acquis* which have a bearing on improved competitiveness and efficiency, and which might facilitate EU trade with, and investment in, Russia. Russia is still in the early stages of private sector development. It has only been five years since it approved a revised version of the Land Code, which allows, for the first time since the earliest days of the Communist revolution, the private ownership of agricultural land. It has a banking system which does not yet efficiently intermediate financial resources for investment by small and medium-sized companies, and has thereby become a drag on growth rather than a propeller of it. While much progress has been made in recent years in laying the foundation of a sounder macroeconomic environment, the Russian economy remains saddled with

many rigidities and inefficiencies: from extensive subsidization of energy consumption to the household and business sector, to a (still) labyrinthine regulatory environment, to enormous deficiencies in the legal framework, as noted above, and highlighted in the World Economic Forum's Executive Opinion Survey.

Progress in all of these areas need not be held captive to a political decision whether or not to pursue EU membership as a long-term goal. The above deficiencies will have to be addressed *in any event,* if Russia is to be able to catch up to the per capita income levels of the more successful transition economies in the region. Unlike Estonia—which has had to *introduce* agricultural subsidies and *raise* its overall level of tariff protection to the EU's common external tariff in order to ensure EU accession—or Poland and Hungary—which negotiated with the EU from a position of weakness—Russia could pick and choose those elements of the *acquis* which were in its national interest.

Thus, going it alone, it would not introduce the grossly distorting features of the EU's Common Agricultural Policy, but would definitely seek to reform its banking sector to meet the regulatory and prudential requirements of the EU's Banking Directives. In the same spirit, it would have to make its bankruptcy legislation conform to EU norms and actively cooperate with the EU in such areas as law enforcement, the environment, energy—where Russia is expected to continue to be a major supplier to the EU—and a broad range of security issues where Russia is a global player. In parallel, Russia could seek to play a stabilizing role vis-à-vis the 11 other members of the former Soviet Union, many of them highly dependant on Russian trade (including energy), fostering among them the kind of policy and institutional innovations that have been the basis for the early phases of the EU's development. In due course, say, after a decade of further political and economic consolidation in Russia, with the EU having successfully dealt with the challenges of possible further waves of enlargement, the Russian government and its counterparts in Brussels could re-examine the broad parameters and supporting institutions of a future Russia-EU relationship.

Risk factors and conclusions

There is no intrinsic reason why the Russian economy could not enter a period of high, sustained growth in coming years. It has a number of structural features which create the conditions for rapid growth: it is likely to benefit from gains in efficiency associated with the continued elimination of remaining distortions from its central planning past; it has an impressive natural resource endowment which is likely to spur continued and growing interest among foreign investors, particularly in the all-important energy sector. The human capital stock is, likewise, on balance, a competitive advantage, and remaining skills shortages—while sharply limiting in many ways in the public sector—are gradually being addressed. Russia has an impressive tradition of world-class research in the basic sciences, including seminal contributions to mathematics and physics. But the brain drain has been a blow to the country's ability to quickly move back to the outer limits of the technology frontier. The basic machinery to do so, in the form of higher education establishments that support scientific research, and the commitment to excellence that was the distinguishing feature of Russian culture and science during much of the past century will have to be revamped.

Tight conditions in the global oil markets suggest that the external environment is likely to remain favorable to Russia, creating an ideal opportunity to push ahead with structural and institutional reforms. A strong budgetary position provides the cushion, in political economy terms, for implementing ambitious reforms. The alternative is to pursue these in the middle of an economic downturn or a crisis, a scenario that is traditionally more difficult. Particular attention will have to be paid to reforms to improve Russia's woefully inadequate public institutions, to improve the judicial and legal climate, to safeguard property rights, to reduce the prevalence of corruption and crime. It is to be hoped that the arbitrary and amateur behavior which characterized the Yukos case are behind us, a lesson for the future on how *not* to go about enhancing the rule of law and creating a better investment climate.

Russian policymakers will have their hands full in the period ahead. The large inflows from record high energy prices create opportunities, but they also pose important challenges. Liquidity management—not a central concern of policymakers in the past—is now very much at the center of macroeconomic policy, particularly as regards the evolution of the real exchange rate for the ruble. The IMF is certainly correct in suggesting that a loosening of fiscal policy—particularly one aimed at boosting public sector wages and pensions, not investments in education, public health, and infrastructure, all of which would boost productivity and thus enhance the permissible level of real appreciation of the ruble—will "exacerbate tensions between exchange rate and inflation objectives." But beyond these issues, it is incumbent on the authorities to broaden their focus, and deal with a broad range of emerging stresses. Foremost among these are how to arrest the disturbing demographic trends, how to better utilize surplus public resources to enhance the economy's capacity for innovation, and how to put the country back on a path of world-class scientific and technological achievement, so that Russia may join the ranks of the most competitive economies in the world.

Notes

1 The author would like to thank Sergey Alexashenko, Evgeny Gavrilenkov, Kristalina I. Georgieva, Andrew Kutchins, Yaroslav Lissovolik, John Litwack, Natalia Ivanova, Thierry Malleret, Alexei Mozhin, Tatyana V. Paramonova, Alexander Pumpyansky, Alan Rousso, Charles Ryan, and Mikhail M. Zadornov. He also thanks Ibrahim Cotran, Justina Roberts, and Shubhra Saxena for able research assistance during the preparation of this chapter.

2 Erofeyev, 2005.

3 See Chapter 1.1 in this volume.

4 On Russia's output collapse during the early phase of the transition and other related policy issues, see Gavrilenkov and Koen (1995) and Koen and Phillips (1993). Tanzi (1993) provides an excellent perspective on fiscal issues in transition economies.

5 Russia's ranking in the newly formulated Global Competitiveness Index (to be used by the Forum as of 2006) is likely to be higher, because the country will get credit for certain factors on which the country does well, and for which our present competitiveness indicators do not give it enough credit (e.g., excellent levels of higher education).

6 On this and related topics see Lipton and Sachs (1992), Aslund (1994, 1995), Layard and Parker (1996), and Lopez-Claros and Alexashenko (1998).

7 On this point see Dolinskaya (2001).

8 See the analysis by Kenneth S. Deffeyes (2001), and Lopez-Claros (2003a).

9 Crude oil output growth rates during the four-year period ending in 2004 were 7.7, 8.9, 11.0, and 8.9 percent, respectively, for a cumulative growth rate of 41.8 percent.

10 See, for instance, World Bank (2003).

11 IMF, 2002.

12 Russia, however, is considerably less energy dependent than Saudi Arabia, where 83 percent of total revenues and 88 percent of total exports are linked to oil (IMF, 2005c).

13 These estimates should now be updated, to reflect oil prices roughly twice as high as those which prevailed in 2002. Nevertheless, the broad thrust of the conclusion is unlikely to have changed fundamentally.

14 As of the end of 2005, the Stabilization Fund will have accumulated close to US$45 billion, a significant relaxation of Russia's external constraint.

15 Merchandise exports from Russia in 2005 could amount to some US$220 billion, more than double 2002 levels, and nearly triple 1999 levels. This represents an annual rate of growth of 20 percent in dollar terms.

16 *Chaebol*, the Korean term for a conglomerate of many companies clustered around one parent company. The companies usually hold shares in each other and are often run by one family.

17 This is not to suggest that the "loans-for-shares" privatization schemes of the mid-1990s were not intrinsically corrupt. One cannot help thinking, however, that if the intent of the government in 2003 was to revisit these old transactions in an attempt to extract, post facto, greater value for the original owner (the state), this could have been done in a less amateurish way, one which did not convey to outsiders the impression—rightly or wrongly—that there were other agendas at play. The handling of the Yukos case has done much to undermine investor confidence, and this is reflected, as noted above, in the terrible competitiveness rankings on rule of law and transparency indicators.

18 Estimates of capital flight in Russia—a combination of non-receipt of export earnings, unredeemed import advances, and errors and omissions—are subject to large margins of uncertainty. For a careful discussion of the issues, see Grigoryev and Kosarev (2000).

19 Particularly noteworthy are Russia's 10 Nobel Prize winners in physics: Pavel Cherenkov, Ilya Frank, Igor Tamm, Leo Landau, Alexander Prokhorov, Nikolay Basov, Petr Kapitsa, Zhores Alferov, Vitaly Ginzburg, and Alexei Abrikosov. Even more impressive is its list of mathematicians, a veritable pantheon that includes such 20th century superstars as Lyapunov, Steklov, Kolmogorov, Pontryagin, Vinogradov, Kantorovich, Markov, Sobolev, Krein, and many others. Soviet and Russian mathematicians have greatly enriched the field of mathematics during the past 100 years.

20 Russian patents for inventions registered at the US Patent and Trademark Office during the last few years have averaged about 200 or so per year. However, patents registered in 2002 (the latest year for which such information is available) with Russia's own patents office were closer to 20,000.

21 I am indebted to Jennifer Blanke for the latter observations. For a fuller discussion see Blanke et al., (2003).

22 The share of bank capital in Russia controlled by non-residents is about 7 percent, as compared to well over 60 percent in much of Central and Eastern Europe.

23 See IMF (2005d).

24 The EU and Russia had their 15th summit in Moscow on 10 May 2005.

25 European support for Russia's bid to join the WTO was facilitated in 2004 by Russian agreement to endorse the Kyoto Protocol on Global Warming.

26 For the full text, see: http://www.eur.ru

References

Aslund, A. 1994. "Russia's Success Story." *Foreign Affairs* 73:58–71.

———. 1995. *How Russia Became a Market Economy.* The Brookings Institution, Washington, DC.

Blanke, J., A. Lopez-Claros, and T. Malleret. 2003. "Enhancing Russian Competitiveness in an Interdependent World." Geneva: World Economic Forum.

Bloomberg. 2005. Online at: http://www.bloomberg.com

British Petroleum. 2005. Statistical Review of World Energy. June.

CEDIGAZ. 2005. *Natural Gas in the World.* Paris.

Dolinskaya, I. 2002. "Explaining Russia's Output Collapse: Aggregate Sources and Regional Evidence." *IMF Working Papers* 49. Washington, DC.

Deffeyes, K. S. 2001. *Hubbert's Peak: The Impending World Oil Shortage.* Princeton, NJ: Princeton University Press.

Economist Intelligence Unit. 2005. *Country Data.*

Erofeyev, V. 2005. "And Now, Command Capitalism." *International Herald Tribune,* 27 July.

Gavrilenkov, E. and V. Koen. 1995. "How Large Was the Output Collapse in Russia? Alternative Estimates and Welfare Implications." *Staff Studies for the World Economic Outlook.* World Economic and Financial Surveys. Washington, DC: International Monetary Fund.

Grigoryev, L. and A. Kosarev. 2000. "Capital Flight: Scale and Nature." International Monetary Fund.

International Monetary Fund. 2002. Staff Report for the 2001 Article IV Consultation, Country Report 02/74, Washington, DC.

———. 2005a. *Direction of Trade Statistics Yearbook 2004.* Washington, DC.

———. 2005b. World Economic Outlook Database. Washington, DC. April.

———. 2005c. Public Information Notice: 2004 Article IV Consultation with Saudi Arabia. 12 January. Online at: www.imf.org

———. 2005d. "Russia: Concluding Statement of the 2005 IMF Mission." Online at: www.imf.org

Koen, V. and S. Phillips. 1993. "Price Liberalization in Russia: Behavior of Prices, Household Incomes, and Consumption During the First Year." *International Monetary Fund, Occasional Paper 104.* Washington, DC.

Kornai, J. 1986. "The Soft Budget Constraint." *Kyklos* 39:3–30.

Kovalev, S. 1997. "Russia after Chechnya." *New York Review of Books* 44:27–31.

Lambeth, B. 1995. "Russia's Wounded Military." *Foreign Affairs* 74:86–98.

Layard, R. and J. Parker. 1996. "The Coming Russian Boom: A Guide to New Markets and Politics." New York: The Free Press.

Landell-Mills, P. and I. Serageldin. 1991. "Governance and the Development Process." *Finance & Development* 29. 14–17.

Lipton, D. and J. Sachs. 1992. "Prospects for Russia's Economic Reforms." *Brookings Papers in Economic Activity* 2:213–83.

Lopez-Claros, A. 2001. "Bringing Stability to Russia." Personal View. *London Financial Times.* 18 December.

———. 2002a. "Economic Reforms: Steady As She Goes." A Decade of Russian Economic Reforms (with Mikhail M. Zadornov). *The Washington Quarterly* 25.

———. 2002b. "Swapping Soviet Debt for Russian Progress." *The Wall Street Journal* 23 August.

———. 2003a. "The Risks and Rewards of BP's Russia Gamble." *The Wall Street Journal* 17 February.

———. 2004. "Varieties of Economic Experience in the Developing World." *The Global Competitiveness Report 2003–2004.* New York: Oxford University Press.

Lopez-Claros, A. and S. Alexashenko. 1998. "Fiscal Policy Issues During the Transition in Russia." *International Monetary Fund, Occasional Paper 155.* Washington, DC..

Matlock J. Jr. 1996. "Dealing with a Russia in Turmoil." *Foreign Affairs* 75:38–51.

Morse, E. and J. Richard. 2002. "The Battle for Energy Dominance." *Foreign Affairs* 81:16–31.

Owen, D. and D. Robinson. 2003. *Russia Rebounds.* International Monetary Fund. Washington, DC.

Plessix Gray, F. 1989. *Soviet Women: Walking the Tightrope.* New York: Doubleday.

Remmick, D. 1997. "Can Russia Change?" *Foreign Affairs* 76:35–49.

Russian Federation. 2005. Economic Expert Group Estimates. Ministry of Finance, Economic Expert Group. January–June.

Sachs, J. and K. Pistor, eds. 1997. *The Rule of Law and Economic Reform in Russia.* Boulder, CO: Westview Press.

Summers, L. and V. Thomas. 1993. "Recent Lessons of Development." *World Bank Research Observer* 8: 241–54.

Tanzi, V. 1993. *Transition to Market: Studies in Fiscal Reform.* Washington, DC: International Monetary Fund.

———. 1997. "The Changing Role of the State in the Economy: A Historical Perspective." *IMF Working Paper* 97/114. Washington, DC: International Monetary Fund.

Williamson, J. 1991. "Current Issues in Transition Economics." Frenkel J. and M. Goldstein, eds. *International Financial Policy: Essays in Honor of Jacques J. Polak.* Washington, DC: International Monetary Fund and Netherlands Bank. 350–370.

World Bank. 2003. *Jobs, Growth, and Governance in the Middle East and North Africa: Unlocking the Potential for Prosperity.* New York.

———. 2005. *Doing Business in 2005.* World Bank and International Finance Corporation. Oxford University Press.

World Economic Forum. 2004. *The Global Competitiveness Report 2004–2005.* Hampshire: Palgrave Macmillan.

Part 3

Special Topics

CHAPTER 3.1

Should There Be a Development Consensus?

JOHN WILLIAMSON, Senior Fellow, Institute for International Economics

In 1989, just after the Berlin Wall fell, when history was supposedly ending, I wrote a background paper for a conference, devoted to examining the extent to which Latin America was abandoning the encrusted economic policies that some of us thought had led it into the lost decade of the 1980s.

This paper laid out ten policies, which, I argued, most people in Washington—at least, those who thought about these issues at all—believed were needed in most Latin American countries, if they were to have a chance of modernizing. The purpose was to provide a common set of questions on which the authors of the country papers could focus.

However, this list—which I dubbed the *Washington Consensus*—was widely interpreted as a policy manifesto for the region, indeed, for the developing world as a whole. The conference concluded that many countries had already experienced a sea change in their economic policies, in the direction of the Washington Consensus, and in subsequent years a number of others made similar policy changes. Yet the recovery in economic growth in the region in the 1990s was distinctly modest, a fact which has led some economists to question whether the policy changes were a mistake.

Perhaps the most thoughtful such critic is Dani Rodrik (2002, 2003). He accepts that the policies espoused by the Washington-based international financial institutions (IFIs) around 1989 could be summarized by the Washington Consensus as I had described it. However, in the following years, these were augmented by a series of additional policies. He also argued that this augmented Washington Consensus was equally bound to disappoint— as the original supposedly had done—because what development needs is not a cookbook, nor a description of what advanced countries look like, but, rather, a strategy for kick-starting growth and a series of institutional reforms that will keep a country growing.

I have a certain sympathy with the Rodrik critique. I am no more enthusiastic about laundry lists and cookbooks than he is, and I do not believe that we do developing countries a service if we give the impression that growth is just a matter of following a list of rules. Policymakers need to know that they are hired to think, not to act by rote. However, I also believe that we would be failing developing countries if we did not discuss what sort of policies they should normally follow, and lay out such generalizations as we believe to be possible. It is for this reason that some colleagues and I have written a book (Kuczynski and Williamson, 2003), which, in some ways, represents a sequel to the Washington Consensus. It is the substance of this thinking, which I am attempting to convey in this article.

155

If we are to assess whether the policies laid out in the Washington Consensus are desirable, then we must start by identifying what those policies may be. This is necessary, because at least three different interpretations have been given to the term. It is not conducive to clarity in debate to use an ambiguous term, unless one specifies the meaning one is attaching to it. I have no wish to defend some of the ideas which have at times been described as part of the Washington Consensus, but I remain convinced of the usefulness of the three basic ideas that underlay my version of the consensus, namely, macroeconomic discipline, market liberalization, and globalization. I continue to wish for these ideas to command a consensus, although nowadays I am doubtful whether they do. To say that they are useful is not, of course, to claim that they constitute a complete agenda, and this paper fills in the elements of a more complete program.

Meanings of the Washington Consensus

My own usage referred to the following ten reforms:

1. **Fiscal discipline:** in a region where almost all countries had run large deficits that led to balance-of-payment crises and high inflation, the poor suffered the most, while the rich could protect their money—e.g. by parking it abroad;

2. **Reordering public expenditure priorities:** this entailed switching expenditures to promote growth and protect the poor, away from nonmerit subsidies toward basic health and education, and infrastructure. It did not propose that the challenge of fiscal discipline should be achieved entirely by cutting expenditures. On the contrary, the intention was to be strictly neutral about the desirable size of the public sector, since even a hopeless consensus-seeker like myself did not imagine that resolution of the historical battle between capitalism and socialism implied agreement on the ideal size of the state;

3. **Tax reform:** the aim was a tax system that would combine a broad tax base with moderate marginal tax rates;

4. **Liberalizing interest rates:** I subsequently reformulated this idea more broadly to mean financial liberalization, and stressed that views differed on how quickly it should be achieved. I wish I had recognized at the outset the importance of emphasizing that financial liberalization must be accompanied by prudent supervision, and that I had made it clear that only domestic financial liberalization was envisioned, not the abolition of all capital controls;

5. **A competitive exchange rate:**[1] I fear I indulged in wishful thinking when I maintained that there was a consensus in favor of ensuring a competitive exchange rate, more or less implying an intermediate regime; in fact, Washington was already beginning to edge toward the two-corner doctrine, which holds that a country must either fix firmly, or else float "cleanly";

6. **Trade liberalization:** I acknowledged that there were differing views as to how quickly trade should be liberalized, but everyone agreed on this as being the appropriate direction in which to move;

7. **Liberalization of inward foreign direct investment:** I specifically excluded comprehensive capital account liberalization, because I did not believe that it did, or should, command a consensus in Washington;

8. **Privatization:** we have since been made acutely aware that it matters a great deal how privatization is done: it can be a highly corrupt process, resulting in the transfer of assets to a privileged elite for a fraction of their true value. However, it is evident that privatization brings benefits when it is carried out properly—especially in terms of increased efficiency and improved service coverage for utilities—and when the privatized enterprise either sells into a competitive market or, if that is not practicable, is properly regulated;

9. **Deregulation:** this focused specifically on easing barriers to entry and exit, not on abolishing regulations designed to promote safety or protect the environment, or to govern prices in a non-competitive industry;

10. **Property rights:** this was inspired by Hernando de Soto's analysis, and was primarily concerned with ensuring property rights for the informal sector, at an acceptable cost.

One alternative meaning in widespread use employs the phrase *Washington Consensus* to refer to the policies the Bretton Woods institutions apply to their client countries—or perhaps the attitude of the Bretton Woods institutions in combination with the United States government.[2] This seems to me a reasonable, well-defined usage, which Dani Rodrik has sought to spell out explicitly (see Table 1). In the early days after 1989, there was not much difference between my concept and this one, but, over time, some substantive differences emerged. For instance, as regards the exchange rate, the Bretton Woods institutions increasingly came to espouse the so-called *bipolar doctrine*—at least until the Argentine economy imploded in 2001, as a direct result of applying one of the supposedly crisis-free

Table 1: Rodrik's augmented Washington Consensus

The original Washington Consensus	The augmented Washington Consensus
	The original list plus:
• Fiscal discipline • Reorientation of public expenditures • Tax reform • Financial liberalization • Unified and competitive exchange rates • Trade liberalization • Openness to FDI • Privatization • Deregulation • Secure property rights	• Legal/political reform • Regulatory institutions • Anti-corruption • Labor market flexibility • WTO agreements • Financial codes and standards • "Prudent" capital-account opening • Non-intermediate exchange rate regimes • Social safety nets • Poverty reduction

Source: Rodrik, 2002.

regimes, according to which countries should either float their exchange rate "cleanly" or else fix it firmly by adopting an institutional device, such as a currency board. As pointed out above, this runs directly counter to my version of the Washington Consensus, which called for a *competitive exchange rate,* i.e. an intermediate regime, since either fixed or floating rates can easily become overvalued.

Again, in the mid-1990s, the Bretton Woods institutions—or at least the IMF—were urging countries to liberalize their capital accounts, whereas my version had deliberately limited the call for liberalization of capital flows to FDI. Both of those deviations from the original version were, in my opinion, disastrous, the second one being the principal cause of the Asian crisis of 1997.

But there were also some highly positive differences, as the World Bank and the IMF began to take up particular institutional issues that I had not judged sufficiently important in Latin America in 1989 to justify inclusion. I am referring here to governance and corruption (in the case of the World Bank), and financial sector reform as reflected in standards and codes (in the case of the IMF). By the late 1990s, both institutions had replaced their earlier indifference to issues of income distribution by a recognition that it matters profoundly who gains or loses income.

The third interpretation of the term *Washington Consensus* uses it as a synonym for neoliberalism or market fundamentalism.[3] This I regard as a far more dramatic deviation from my original intent, and a thoroughly objectionable perversion of the original meaning. Whatever else the term Washington Consensus may mean, it should surely refer to a set of policies that command, or commanded, a consensus in some significant segment of Washington—either the US government or the IFIs, or both, or perhaps both along with some other group. Even in the early years of the Reagan administration, or during

that of George W. Bush, it would be difficult to contend that any of the distinctively neoliberal policies, such as supply-side economics, monetarism, or minimal government, commanded any sort of consensus—certainly not in the IFIs. And it would be preposterous to associate any of those policies with the Clinton administration. Yet most of the diatribes against the Washington Consensus have been directed against this third concept, with those using the term in this way apparently unconcerned with the need to establish that there actually was a consensus in favor of the policies they love to hate.[4]

How could the term have come to be used in such different ways? I find it easy enough to see why the second usage emerged. The term initially provided a reasonable description of the policies of the Bretton Woods institutions, the list having been constructed as an attempt to portray the essence of what they were preaching. And as these policies evolved, the term continued to refer to what they actually were at a given time.

What puzzles me is how the third usage became so popular. One possible hypothesis is that this was an attempt to discredit economic reform by bundling a raft of ideas that deserve to be consigned to oblivion, along with the list of common-sense pro-reform proposals that constituted my original list. No doubt, the name that I had bestowed on my list gave anyone who disliked the policies or attitudes of the US government or the IFIs an incentive to join in misrepresenting the policies associated with them. But an alternative hypothesis is that some people really do believe that the IFIs—or at least the IMF (and perhaps the US Treasury too)—promote market fundamentalism and minimal government. Stiglitz (2002) certainly writes as though he believes this, and therefore treats the second and third interpretations as synonymous. I must say I find this preposterous: I have often found the IMF's positions to be more conservative than my own views, but have never believed that its policy positions were based on the far-fetched notion that markets work perfectly. Only academics—and not many of them—believe such things. Stiglitz's view that the IMF has a theological belief in market fundamentalism is pure assertion, unsupported by a single citation.

Three big ideas that deserve adoption

As I see it, the three historic changes that underlay my version of the Washington Consensus are the commitment to macroeconomic discipline, the choice of the market as the basic social instrument for allocating resources, and opening up the economy for trade and FDI—now usually called globalization. In all three respects, Latin America—and, to a somewhat lesser extent, many other developing countries as well—made fundamental policy changes in the late 1980s or early 1990s.

Stabilization policy

The first of these areas concerns stabilization policy. In the earlier postwar years, many Latin American economists accepted a measure of inflation as desirable, because it generated forced savings that could add to investment. Even many of those who declined to welcome inflation nevertheless believed that it was caused by structural forces, and was therefore more or less unavoidable. All this changed in the 1980s, as inflation accelerated—as monetarist critics of the structural inflation school predicted it would—and as that part of the fiscal deficits which had been financed abroad generated the debt crisis. Efforts to adjust the balance of payments in response to the debt crisis involved, inter alia, achieving real devaluations, which served to worsen inflation. When I drew up the Washington Consensus, the overwhelming need—at least in Latin America—was to conquer inflation, so that was the macroeconomic objective I emphasized.

Had my list been intended as a manifesto for the policies to be applied at all times and in all places, as it has sometimes been parodied, it would have been a sad oversight if I had restricted the subject matter in this way. There are many situations in which counter-cyclical policies are needed. There are many things governments can do to reduce the risk of a capital account crisis. The failure of many Latin American governments to apply such policies in the 1990s was a direct cause of the crises that began exploding in 1994, leading to the subsequent dismal half-decade. When Pedro Pablo Kuczynski and I (2003) edited a volume that aimed at producing an updated development agenda for the region, we duly emphasized the need for more proactive policies to keep the economy on an even keel. But it is hopeless to imagine that anyone could anticipate all the situations demanding a policy response in future years. The world is a complex place, and

policymakers will continue to need to think, not just to apply formulae from a policy cookbook.

This in no way precludes the recognition that the decision to pursue disciplined macroeconomic policies in the late 1980s marked an important turning point for economic thought in the region. Nor does it mean that there are not going to be important and controversial issues regarding the design of future macroeconomic policy. One current example concerns Brazilian interest rate policy. During the latter part of 2004 and the early months of 2005, the Brazilian overnight interest rate (the SELIC) was raised from an already high 15.75 percent (about 9 percent real) to 19.5 percent, in order to combat an uptick of inflation. No doubt, there are those who would denounce this policy as another example of neoliberal determination to sabotage economic growth and benefit the rentiers at the expense of the productive classes (entrepreneurs and workers). But it is also possible to believe that a central bank whose policy remit is to control inflation would see its credibility undermined if it acquiesced in accelerating inflation. One can hold the view that it is precisely the establishment of such credibility that creates the most promising circumstances for a subsequent major cut in interest rates.

Liberalization

A second historic development that occurred in Latin America in the late 1980s, which was reflected in the Washington Consensus, was the decision to use markets as the basic social mechanism for allocating resources. The region had, of course, never experimented in a major way with central planning on the Soviet model. Nonetheless, there existed an element of ambiguity in attitudes, captured well by José Antonio Ocampo's phrase "state-led development." While many industries were privately owned, the state offered protection to encourage import substitution, directed credit to favored sectors, founded state companies where private entrepreneurs were not entering an industry that the state felt was necessary, and deliberately made it difficult to establish private companies which did not fit into state plans.

This was not such a bad system for initiating the move away from the traditional export-oriented, overwhelmingly rural economies of Latin America, toward industrialization. Except for Argentina, the region prospered as never before—nor since—in the years 1950–1980, when this system was in place. The question is not whether this system was a grand historical error at the time that its elements were invented by the Economic Commission for Latin America and the Caribbean (ECLAC) around 1950, but, rather, whether it had outlived its social usefulness by the late 1980s. The first "easy stage" of import substitution had long since been achieved. The financial system had grown in sophistication to the point where directed credit was less efficient than lending by a competitive banking system. While there were still some efficient state-run firms, many had succumbed to the temptations of the easy life inherent in a noncompetitive environment. Entry into a new industry was absurdly difficult. Thus, when growth collapsed after the onset of the debt crisis, it seemed natural to switch to a more competitive system, in the style of those countries, which have successfully made the transition to a mature industrial economy.

In the Washington Consensus, I recognized five aspects of this decision to switch unambiguously to a market economy: financial liberalization, trade liberalization (discussed in the next section), privatization, deregulation, and property rights. It is the adoption of these reforms that critics deride as *neoliberalism,* and which some of us would prefer to call simply *liberalization*. It is important to understand that they do not imply the state's withdrawal from an economic role: rather, the state's role must change to one that will support the market, rather than seeking to replace it.

Take financial liberalization as perhaps the best example. In a survey we once wrote of financial liberalization, Molly Mahar and I[5] distinguished six aspects:

1. allowing private lenders rather than government to determine who gets credit

2. abolishing interest rate controls

3. lifting entry barriers to the financial industry

4. eliminating government controls of commercial decisions, such as who is hired and at what salary

5. privatizing financial firms

6. eliminating capital controls in the foreign exchange market

In my initial statement of the Washington Consensus, I focused only on the second of those aspects, which I soon realized was a mistake. When I therefore broadened the agenda, and described the objective as "financial liberalization," I omitted to say that I was thinking only of domestic liberalization, and did not include capital account liberalization. That was also a mistake, as, in my view, capital account liberalization is very different and far more dangerous.

But the fundamental point is different. When the government abandons its right to decide who will get credit and at what price, and allows those decisions to be made by, for example, a private bank, it should have in place an adequate supervisory mechanism to ensure that bankers try to allocate credit where the risk/return tradeoff is best, rather than giving it to their friends, or to those who pay

them the biggest bribes. In other words, financial liberalization does not imply that the government ceases to have any role in the financial sector; it implies a different role: one in which the government, rather than being the one which itself decides who will get the credit, tries to ensure that certain rules or practices are followed.

Since the idea was first broached in 1973, financial liberalization has come a long way, both in Latin America and in other parts of the developing world. Most countries in the region now have a mixed system, with active financial markets and profit-making banks mixed in with a residue of state banks. Accordingly, a number of studies of the impact of financial liberalization have come to three basic conclusions:[6]

1. It has no perceptible effect on the level of saving, although it tends to increase the proportion of savings that are intermediated by the financial system;

2. It makes the system dangerously more crisis-prone;

3. It leads to a significantly better allocation of saving, which raises the productivity of investment and reduces the incremental capital output ratio (ICOR).

It follows that liberalization involves a tradeoff between an increased danger of crisis, versus an increased growth potential if crisis is averted. The obvious policy implication is that much greater emphasis should be placed on improving supervision and other measures to reduce the probability of a crisis. I do feel somewhat guilty that in early statements of the Washington Consensus I did not emphasize this need; however, in my own defense I must say that I did not think of myself as providing a cookbook of economic policy.

My reason for skepticism about capital account liberalization is that it increases the danger of crisis, in return for minimal—perhaps zero—benefits in terms of faster growth. Countries that borrow heavily are clearly more vulnerable to sudden stops, especially if they borrow short term in foreign currency denominations. Capital controls do not prevent a country from borrowing abroad, if there is indeed a real benefit to be had from domestic investment exceeding saving. The empirical record provides no persuasive evidence that growth is faster under free capital mobility. (There is evidence that inward FDI, and inward portfolio equity investment, increase growth, but not that complete opening—including to the free inflow and outflow of short-term loans—accelerates growth.) Eventually the day will come when an economy is so integrated into the world economy that continuing controls will be ineffective; but by then, it is probable that an economy will be able to borrow even in difficult times—not true today for emerging economies—such that sudden stops will have become history. When that happy day dawns, it will be sensible to liberalize the capital account. The point is that it can be dangerous to hurry the process along.

Privatization is probably an even more controversial recommendation than financial liberalization. It is certainly a distinctly unpopular policy in Latin America, as Latinobarómetro has found. Economists ask themselves why it is so unpopular, given that most studies have suggested that its effects are on the whole fairly benign. For example, empirical studies have mostly found that privatization has raised efficiency and profitability, and that when utilities are privatized, the access to services has increased, while its impact on prices, employment, and income distribution has varied capriciously from one place to another.[7] The most persuasive explanation for its unpopularity is that the process of privatization has sometimes been perceived to be corrupt, and corruption seems to be despised by the public, even when people do not perceive themselves to be suffering personally as a result. This much seems to be clear from experience with the calamitous "loans for shares" privatization scheme in Russia. If that is inzdeed correct, then it is crucial that future privatizations be squeaky clean.

The other main failing of privatization programs in Latin America has been that in some cases privatized firms that do not sell into a competitive market have been allowed to escape a coherent regulatory system. Many economists would doubt whether a process of privatizing a public monopoly that leaves its monopoly position unchallenged can be expected to enhance consumer welfare: while it may enhance efficiency because of the more focused objective of the principal, the owner has both the ability and the incentive to raise prices. This is yet another instance of the phenomenon noted before: getting the government out of its ownership position does not necessarily involve its abdication from any policy role at all. That role must be adapted to a market economy, in this instance, not by absenting itself altogether, but by creating an appropriate regulator.

Privatization has become rather uncommon in Latin America today, although the process has not quite ground to a halt. This is only partly because the low-hanging fruit—telecoms, firms in the tradable sector, mines—have been exhausted. It is also because utilities investors have been demoralized by what happened to them in Argentina, and even those who draw a sharp distinction between what happens in that dysfunctional polity and the rest of the continent are bound to worry about the possibility of contagion. Finally, precisely because privatization has become so unpopular, it requires a courageous politician to push it. But there still exist quite substantial state-owned sectors in most countries—usually a large chunk of the banking system, some energy industries, most utilities, and a number of national champions. Under present circumstances one may doubt the wisdom of investing a lot of

political capital in privatization—especially in the case of the national champions—although perhaps one day the Brazilian public will realize the significance of the fact that Embraer has done even better since being privatized. But who knows, circumstances may change in the future.

Another element in the program for building a competitive market economy is deregulation. As mentioned already, this refers to the elimination of regulations that impede entry and exit, rather than to those that are needed to safeguard safety or quality. The outstanding example of this in many countries—especially in Latin America—concerns labor market regulation. Most econometric studies of the labor market have concluded that one effect of restrictions on firing is to discourage hiring, and thus to limit the number of persons employed, at least in the formal sector. In addition, formal labor contracts confer a variety of benefits, including lengthy holidays, which a large portion of the workforce appear not to appreciate as much as they would higher wages. However, these legal requirements are so costly to fulfill that they discourage many employers from operating in the formal sector of the economy. The result is that some workers get a generous supplementary social wage, while others forego even the most basic social protections, such as health insurance, pension rights, and unemployment protection. In Kuczynski and Williamson (2003), we argue that it would be better to strip down the social requirements to the basics, and make them widely available, so that virtually all workers would get the really important benefits.

The final element of my version of the Washington Consensus, in support of constructing a market economy—following the analysis of Hernando de Soto (1989, 2000)—involves making property rights easily and cheaply available to the informal sector. Secure property rights are fundamental to the operation of a market economy, since assurance that the investor will retain the fruits of his or her efforts is fundamental to the willingness to invest. In Latin America, there is little need to worry about the property rights of the elite: these are securely entrenched. The concern is that large numbers of the entrepreneurially inclined, who until now have operated in the informal sector, have little or nothing in the way of formal property rights. This situation vastly diminishes the value of what they de facto own. It is expensive to defend property without the benefit of legal property title; property cannot be used as collateral to get a loan; it cannot be insured; and so on. Hence the importance of titling programs.

Globalization

For a long time after the Washington Consensus was created, I thought of its third major theme as being the opening up of an economy. Nowadays, this is referred to as globalization. It should be distinguished from the old Latin idea about how countries are *inserted* into the world economy. In the modern conception, governments do not *insert* their countries into the world economy; they stand aside, while their citizens gain the benefits of inserting *themselves* into the world economy.

In the original Washington Consensus, I focused on the need to liberalize trade and inward FDI, both of which are overwhelmingly desirable. That is not to claim that they will solve all problems: in particular, freer trade does not help resolve the problem of a concentrated income distribution, as was once hoped. The reason is that South America is not particularly labor-abundant by world standards, and the extractive industries which constitute its main global comparative advantage are not particularly labor-intensive. Similarly, we have seen how questionable government policies thwarted the benefits of trade liberalization. By welcoming excessive capital inflows, exchange rates became overvalued. As a result, workers were dismissed from import-substituting industries and forced to enter the nontraded sector. Worse still, many lost their jobs entirely.

But if macroeconomic policy avoids such overvaluation, the presumption is that trade liberalization will be beneficial. Similarly, provided that excessive protection does not create an incentive for foreign capital to flow into uneconomic import-competing industries, then FDI is likely to bring net benefits.

My own view is that countries are not only likely to benefit from allowing free access to foreign portfolio investment, but from also allowing their own pension funds to diversify internationally. While long-term borrowing from abroad is also likely to be beneficial, I have never heard any remotely convincing argument that there are advantages in allowing free entry and exit for short-term capital. Moreover, there is the obvious danger of turning national financial and foreign-exchange markets into new gambling casinos for the investment banks. It may be that one day there will be little to lose by giving these forces free rein, once the markets are convinced that an emerging market is so closely integrated into the world economy that a sudden stop to capital inflows becomes inconceivable. At that point there will be no point in maintaining restrictions, which, after all, do lead to the danger of abuse by corruption, and may also seduce policymakers into attempting the impossible. But one suspects that this point is still a long way away for most emerging markets, and until then, a willingness to restrict short-term capital flows seems sensible.

Other ideas that merit consensus

So I believe that the ideas contained in my original statement of the Washington Consensus continue to resonate. But they do not constitute a complete program. In a recent publication of the Institute for International

Economics, a group of economists—primarily Latin Americans—attempted to delineate a set of ideas that we thought should guide economic policy in the region in the coming years (Kuczynski and Williamson, 2003). We identified four major thrusts that policy should pursue.

First, we argued that macroeconomic policy should pay much more attention to crisis avoidance than it has in the past, since it was primarily the outbreak of crises in the second half of the 1990s that had led to such a bleak half-decade for the region. We sketched a range of policies that could contribute to avoiding crises, or at least mitigating them if they nevertheless occurred. These might include counter-cyclical fiscal policies, accumulating a stabilization fund when exports are cyclically strong, avoiding excessive capital inflows when capital is available, and avoiding currency mismatching.

Second, rather than stalling—or worse, reversing gears—we urged a continuation of microeconomic liberalization. As presented above, we argued that the major priority in most countries should be the liberalization of the labor market.

Third, we joined the currently dominant trend by arguing the importance of strengthening institutions, rather than simply relying on good policies. The point is really rather obvious: for example, a good tax code is not going to guarantee a satisfactory tax regime, if the tax authority is hopelessly corrupt. Good outcomes depend on having both a sensible policy *and* an efficient institutional mechanism for implementing the policy. We did not attempt to go one stage further and say which particular institutions we thought needed to be strengthened, since we judged that this is a question that would differ enormously from one country to another.

Fourth, we argued that the economic agenda should focus on improving the distribution of income as well as accelerating the rate of economic growth. Traditionally, this is done through the fiscal system: raising taxes that are paid in the main by the relatively affluent, in order to finance expenditures that disproportionately benefit the poor. Since the scope for raising taxes is fairly limited in Latin America—inter alia, because of the ease of shifting money offshore—we argued that it would be a good idea to pay particular attention to expenditures that would allow the poor to increase their acquisition of earning assets, notably by improving the educational system. This means that an improvement in income distribution may come about only gradually, but it is far more likely to occur in the long run than under the traditional populist policies.

Conclusion

I hope that the agenda sketched above does not give the impression of a laundry list, or carry the false promise of instant prosperity, if only these actions are undertaken. The world is not like that. It is always necessary to figure out priorities in a particular country at a given moment of history, and to identify the adaptations that are needed, given the specific situation. There is no country so normal in its functioning, that it can deduce an action agenda from some list, without its policymakers having to think about making adaptations to local circumstances. But it is equally true, that there is no country that is so atypical, that it cannot learn from the experiences of others. I have argued in this paper that it makes sense to use experience to identify the general thrust of those policies that will promote prosperity. If Rodrik had argued that some crucial issues—such as how to initiate growth in a country suffering from a failure to grow—had been given inadequate attention in this agenda, he might have had a point. But to dismiss the value of attempting to distill the lessons of experience is not persuasive.

Notes

1 It has been asserted that a competitive exchange rate is the same as an undervalued rate. Not so. A competitive rate is one which is not overvalued, i.e. which is either undervalued or correctly valued. This fifth point reflects a conviction that overvalued exchange rates are worse than undervalued rates; better still is a rate that is neither overvalued nor undervalued.

2 For years I was oblivious to this obvious interpretation, and owe my enlightenment to Yaw Ansu of the World Bank. The fact that it is widespread was brought home to me vividly at a conference in Havana in 2004, where I presented a paper, going to considerable lengths to distinguish three concepts: my original and the two variants described above in this article. In his summary of my presentation, Fidel Castro told the assembled throng that I disagreed with the Washington Consensus in two ways: exchange rate policy and capital account liberalization, namely, the two ways in which I regard the IFIs' version of the Washington Consensus as inferior to mine!

3 For example, Stiglitz (2002, p. 74) writes: "The Washington Consensus policies … were based on a simplistic version of the market economy, the competitive equilibrium model, in which Adam Smith's invisible hand works, and works perfectly. Because in this model there is no need for government—that is, free, unfettered, 'liberal' markets work perfectly—the Washington Consensus policies are sometimes referred to as 'neo-liberal', based on 'market fundamentalism'…"

4 I find it ironic that a chairman of President Clinton's Council of Economic Advisers should have adopted this usage, since the definition of the word *consensus* surely precludes a Washington consensus on a view to which he took serious objection while in office as chairman of the US Council of Economic Advisers or as Chief Economist at the World Bank.

5 Williamson and Mahar, 1998.

6 See, in particular, Caprio and Honohan (2001), Rajan and Zingales (2003), and Williamson and Mahar (1998).

7 See, for example, Birdsall and Nevis (2002).

References

Birdsall, N. and J. Nellis. 2002. *Winners and Losers: Assessing the Distributional Impacts of Privatization*. CGD Working Paper 6. Washington: Center for Global Development.

Caprio, G. and P. Honohan. 2001. *Finance for Growth: Policy Choices in a Volatile World*. Washington: World Bank.

De Soto, H. 1989. *The Other Path: The Invisible Revolution in the Third World*. New York: Harper and Row.

———. 2000. *The Mystery of Capital: Why Capitalism Triumphs in the West and Fails Everywhere Else*. London: Black Swan.

Kuczysnki, P. P. and J. Williamson, eds. 2003. *After the Washington Consensus: Restarting Growth and Reform in Latin America*. Washington: Institute for International Economics.

Rajan, R. G. and L. Zingales. 2003. *Saving Capitalism from the Capitalists*. New York: Crown Business.

Rodrik, D. 2002. "After Neoliberalism, What? Remarks at the BNDES Seminar on New Paths of Development." Rio de Janeiro, September 12–13.

———. 2003. Growth Strategies. Harvard University, processed.

Stiglitz, J. E. 2002. *Globalization and its Discontents*. New York: Norton.

Williamson, J. and M. Mahar. 1998. *A Survey of Financial Liberalization*. Princeton: Essays in International Finance (211).

CHAPTER 3.2

Aging in Low-Income Countries: Looking to 2025

NICHOLAS EBERSTADT,[1] American Enterprise Institute

The other global aging crisis

Over the past decade and a half, the phenomenon of population aging in the already-affluent OECD societies has become a topic of sustained policy analysis and concern.[2] The reasons for this growing attention—and apprehension—are clear enough.

By such measures as median age or proportion of total population above the age of 65, virtually every developed society today is more elderly than practically any human society ever surveyed before the year 1950. And every one of today's developed societies is slated to experience further population aging in the decades immediately ahead. In all of the affluent OECD societies, the proportion of what is customarily called the retirement-age population (65 years of age or older) will steadily swell, with the most rapid expansion occurring among those aged 80 or more. Simultaneously, the ratio of people of working age—the cohort, by arbitrary though not entirely unreasonable custom, designated at 15–64 years—to those of retirement age will relentlessly shrink. Within the working-age grouping, more youthful adults will account for a steadily dwindling share of overall manpower.

Whether these impending revolutionary transformations of national population structure constitute a crisis for the economies and societies in the industrialized world is, let us emphasize, still a matter of dispute. To be sure, this literal upending of the familiar population pyramid—characteristic of all humanity until just yesterday—will surely have direct consequences for economic institutions and structures in the world's more affluent societies, and could have a potentially major impact on their macroeconomic performance.

Left unaddressed, the mounting pressures that population aging in today's affluent OECD societies will place on pension outlays, health care expenditures, fiscal discipline, savings levels, manpower availability, and workforce attainment can only have adverse domestic implications for productivity and economic growth, to say nothing of their negative impact on the global outlook for innovation, entrepreneurship, and competitiveness. However, a host of possible policy interventions and orderly changes in existing institutional arrangements offer the now-rich countries the possibility of "maintaining prosperity in an aging society"—to borrow a phrase from the OECD—and even of steadily *enhancing* prosperity for graying populations. Today's rich countries may succeed in meeting the coming challenges, and in grasping the potential opportunities inherent in population aging. Then again, they may fail to do so. The point is that an aging crisis is theirs to avert, and they have considerable scope for doing so.

In contrast to the intense interest currently devoted to the issue of population aging in developed countries, the topic of aging in the low-income regions has attracted relatively little attention as yet. This neglect is somewhat

163

surprising, for over the coming decades a parallel, dramatic graying of much of the third world also lies in store. Furthermore, the burdens of pronounced population aging are unlikely to be born as easily by poor countries as by rich ones. Simply stated, societies and governments have fewer options for dealing with the problems imposed by population aging when income levels are low, and the available options are distinctly less attractive than if income levels were higher.

It seems entirely likely—indeed, all but inevitable—that over the next generation, a large proportion of the populations in what are often termed emerging market economies will be coping with the phenomenon of population aging, but on income levels far lower than those yet witnessed in any society with comparable degrees of graying. For such countries, the social and economic consequences of aging could be harsh, and the options for mitigating the adverse effects of population aging may be limited. In some of these countries, in certain circumstances, aging could potentially emerge as a factor appreciably constraining long-term growth and development. As we will show in detail, rapid and pronounced population aging represents a highly uneven, largely unappreciated, and, as yet, almost entirely undiscounted long-term risk for the world's emerging markets.

Population aging in low-income areas to 2025: Dynamics and dimensions

Venturing predictions about the world outlook 20 years hence is a hazardous enterprise. Nevertheless, at this juncture, we can state quite confidently that a tremendous wave of population aging is virtually certain to sweep through the developing regions between now and 2025, and that population aging over the coming decades in that vast expanse can only be forestalled by a cataclysm of biblical proportions.

How can we talk so boldly and categorically about events that have yet to unfold? The answers lie in the simple arithmetic of demographic projections and the unforgiving demography of aging.

Given that a country's economic or political circumstances can change tremendously over the course of two decades, plausible future political/economic scenarios could vary widely. By contrast, demographic evolution tends to be gradual, contingent on previous developments, and tightly bound by existing social tendencies. Therefore, in light of the stubborn and unyielding realities of population change, there is inherently less leeway among plausible alternative demographic scenarios 20 years hence. In fact, barring only utter catastrophe, we already have a fairly good picture of the population profile of the low-income regions in 2025. About five sixths of the roughly 5.3 billion people alive today in the less developed regions

are still likely to be around in 2025. As of 2025, something like two thirds of the projected 6.7 billion population of those areas will comprise people alive now.[3]

Since tomorrow's elderly are already with us now, we can foresee their future numbers without much conjecture. Between 2005 and 2025, current projections anticipate the population of the less developed regions to increase by about one fourth. The most rapidly growing cohort within that population, however, will be the 65-plus group. Thus, barring only catastrophe, the third world's seniors citizens will roughly double in numbers over those years, to about 570 million person, or about 8.5 percent of the total for 2025.

While the less developed regions in 2025 would meet the United Nations definition of an aging population—i.e., where persons 65 and older account for over 7 percent of total population—its overall population profile would nevertheless be roughly as youthful as that of Europe from the late 1950s or Japan in the mid-1970s. But the extent and tempo of population aging varies tremendously within the less developed regions: some territories are slated to experience practically no population aging over the coming two decades, while others will become markedly aged. The demography of aging explains this difference.

As a matter of pure arithmetic (and perhaps somewhat counter-intuitively), the scope and scale of population aging in any typical human society is determined primarily by changes in its fertility levels, not by changes in mortality.[4] It is low birth rates, rather than long life expectancies, that drive population aging, and in much of the third world, fertility levels are already very low. In fact, today, the majority of humanity probably already lives in countries with sub-replacement fertility regimes, that is to say, childbearing patterns which, if continued, would ultimately result in indefinite population decline, in the absence of immigration.[5]

Since the world's more developed regions account for less than a fifth (19 percent) of the current global population, this means that the great majority of the planet's sub-replacement populations today are found in low-income regions. And since fertility levels in low-income areas continue to drop, even in places where sub-replacement is already the norm, the momentum for rapid population aging continues to build.

Not, to be sure, in sub-Saharan Africa, where the median age is likely to remain a mere 20 years some two decades from now, and certainly not in those parts of the Arab/Islamic expanse, where total fertility rates still apparently exceed five births-per-lifetime for each woman, as in Yemen, Oman, and Afghanistan. But in much of East Asia, South Asia, the Middle East, Eastern Europe,[6] and Latin America, sub-replacement fertility is now the norm. This means that those areas of the developing world presently

Figure 1: Percentage of the population aged 65-plus vs. per capita GDP: Developed countries 1950–2000.

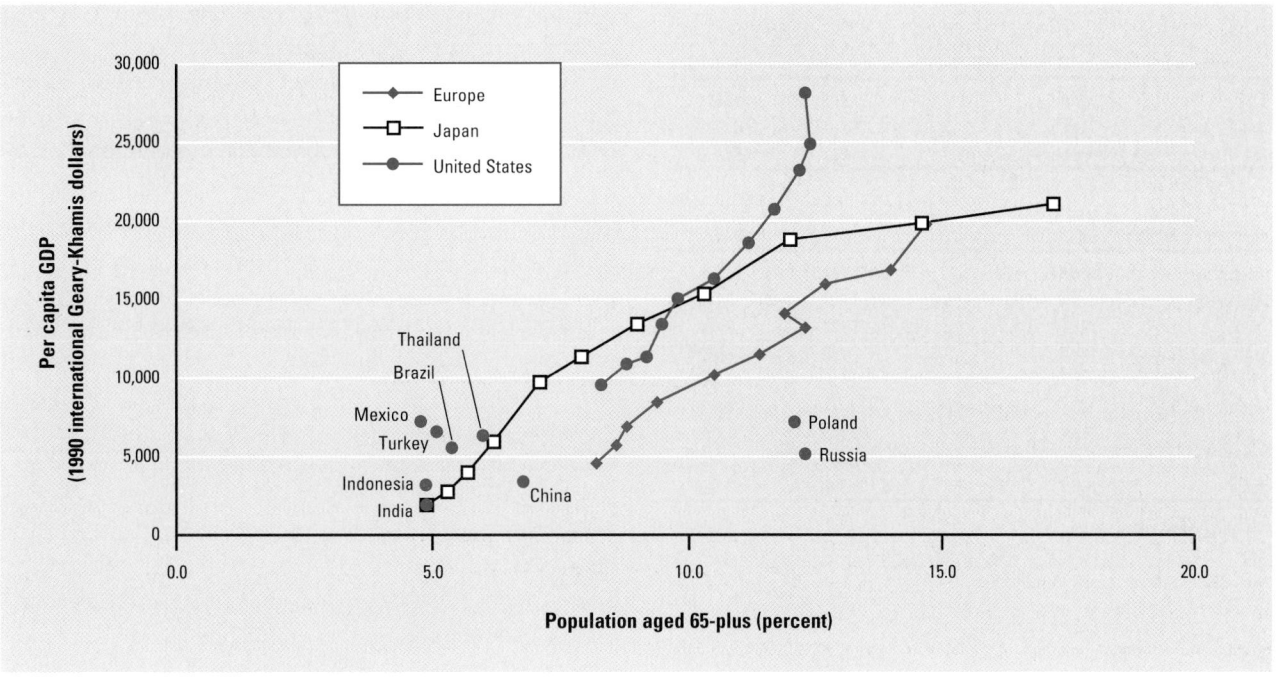

Sources: United Nations, 2004; Maddison, 2003, pp. 65, 89, 101, 111, 144, 184, 187, online at: http://www.un.org/esa

set on a trajectory for rapid population aging are precisely the ones encompassing today's most promising emerging market economies.

Population aging and economic development in international perspective

In order to see the population aging phenomenon of the low-income regions in an international economic perspective, we must begin by comparing the correspondence between graying and income levels in today's major emerging market economies with the old-age-to-income trajectories charted by the major western economies over the course of their postwar development.

As we see in Figure 1, the picture in the emerging economies today is highly varied. On the one hand, some developing economies appear to be much more youthful today than Western Europe, the United States, or Japan, at comparable levels of per capita income. For example, Turkey, Brazil, and Mexico presently support barely half as many senior citizens as Western Europe did at those levels of per capita output, the plausible explanation for this contradistinction being that Brazil, Mexico, and Turkey all had much higher birth rates than the western countries, when all were approaching the US$5000 GDP per capita threshold.

Some other emerging market economies appear to be at virtually the same age-to-income coordinates as those

traced by western countries during their economic ascent: India and Thailand, for example, are each located at points earlier delineated by Japan on its postwar aging/growth path.

But some emerging market economies already have distinctly higher old age burdens than those borne by western countries at similar stages of development. As of the year 2000, China's 65-plus cohort accounted for about the same share of population as Japan in 1970; but per capita output was three times higher for Japan in 1970 than for China in 2000. By the same token, at the point when Western Europe and the United States had the same ratio of elderly to total population as Russia in 2000, their per capita income levels were, respectively, three and six times higher than that of Russia.

Turning from the relatively recent past to the immediate future, Table 1 indicates the prospective dimensions of the coming wave of population aging for nine of the largest emerging market economies.

By UN criteria, all nine will count as aging societies by 2025, although, not surprisingly, the degree of population aging differs greatly from one country to the next. For example, India, Indonesia, and Mexico will be likely to have more youthful age profiles in 2025 than the United States in 2003. On the other hand, by 2025, Turkey and Brazil will be roughly as gray as the United States is today, but not as gray as Japan or Western Europe

Table 1: Population aging in developed countries today vs. emerging market economies tomorrow

Country/region	Median age, years (2003)	Percentage of population 65+ (2003)	GDP per capita PPP, USD (2003)	GDP per capita exchange rate, USD (2003)
USA	35.8	12.4	37,562	37,648
Japan	42.0	18.5	27,967	33,713
EU15	39.5	16.9	26,640	26,710[1]

Country/region	Median age, years (2025)	Percentage of population 65+ (2025)	GDP per capita PPP, (2003)	GDP per capita exchange rate, USD (2003)
Poland	44.2	21.6	11,379	5,280
Russia	43.4	19.8	9,230	2,120
Mexico	32.1	9.8	9,168	6,230
Brazil	36.1	11.0	7,790	2,670
Thailand	39.7	14.6	7,595	2,190
Turkey	36.4	10.8	6,772	2,800
China	39.1	13.7	5,003	1,100
Indonesia	32.8	9.2	3,361	810
India	30.8	7.8	2,892	540

[1] European Monetary Union only.

Sources: World Economic Forum, 2004, Annex Tables 1.01–1.03; World Bank, 2004; United States Census Bureau, 2004.

today. By 2025, China and Thailand will likely have population profiles almost as elderly as the original EU15. Russia and Poland, for their part, will likely have populations more aged in 2025 than Japan's today, grayer than any population yet seen in human history.

Although most of these emerging market economies will have age profiles similar to, or in some cases, even more extreme than, today's developed economies, their income levels are far lower than those of the affluent OECD societies today. And two decades from now, in almost every case, they will almost certainly remain below today's OECD levels.

Over a 22-year interim (i.e., 2003 to 2025), Poland could reach today's EU15 Purchasing Power Parity (PPP)-adjusted per capita output levels, if it grew at a steady 4 percent per capita per annum—an ambitious though not utterly impossible hope. To hit *current* Japanese PPP-adjusted income levels, however, per capita Russian growth would have to be maintained at 5 percent per year for nearly a quarter century. Attaining current EU PPP-adjusted income levels by 2025 would require annualized per capita growth rates of 8 percent for China, and over 10 percent for India. One need not be a Russo-, Sino-, or an Indo-pessimist to suggest that such tempos may be out of reach.[7]

The following closer examinations of the Chinese, Russian, and Indian aging problems provides a clear picture of the constraints for each of these economies over the coming decades.

China: A tightening triple bind

China's impending aging wave is illustrated by Figure 2, which compares the country's actual population structure in 2000 with its projected profile for 2025.

China has evidently experienced sub-replacement fertility levels since the early 1990s.[8] Consequently, as may be seen from these projections, every age group under 35 years of age is anticipated to be smaller in China in 2025 than it was in 2000, while all of the older groups are expected to be larger. China's coercive population control program may have succeeded in limiting numbers for the country's rising contingents of young people, but its elderly population will be exploding in the years ahead, increasing at an annual pace of something like 3.5 percent per year. Between 2005 and 2025, approximately two-thirds of China's aggregate population growth will occur in the 65-plus grouping. That cohort will likely double in size, to roughly 200 million people. By 2025, according to current United Nation Population Division (UNDP) and United States Census (USCB) projections, China would account for less than one fifth of the world's population, but almost a fourth of the world's senior citizens.

China is a vast land with much regional variation. As regards aging and economic development, the country's provinces are characterized both by notable differences in provincial demographic profiles, and tremendous variation in the levels of per capita output. For example, in 2001, local per capita GDP was 13 times as high in bustling Shanghai as in isolated Guizhou. While there is a broad overall correlation between graying and income levels in China's provinces today, the correspondence is not a tight one. Over the next two decades, some of China's most dramatic aging trends are set to unfold in areas that are the poorest today.

Currently (2005), Japan reports the world's highest proportion of persons 65 and older, at about 19.5 percent of total population. By 2025, however, the 65-plus cohort is projected to account for 21 percent of total population in one part of China, that place not being relatively prosperous Beijing or booming Shanghai, but, rather, Heilongjiang, in China's Manchurian rustbelt, where per capita provincial output (at current exchange rates) was just over US$1100 in 2001.

Currently Japan also reports the world's highest median age, at about 42.5 years. Yet, as of 2025, nine of China's 31 provinces and major municipalities are projected to have higher median ages than contemporary Japan: among them, Liaoning (where the exchange-rate-based GDP per capita was around US$1450 in 2001), Jilin (around US$925), and Chongqing (under US$690). (Heilongjiang province, for its part, looks to be positively ancient by 2025, with a projected median age of 51 years.) PPP adjustments of these exchange-rate-based figures do not alter the basic picture conveyed: in just 20 years, large parts

Figure 2: Estimated and projected population structure of China: 2000 vs. 2025

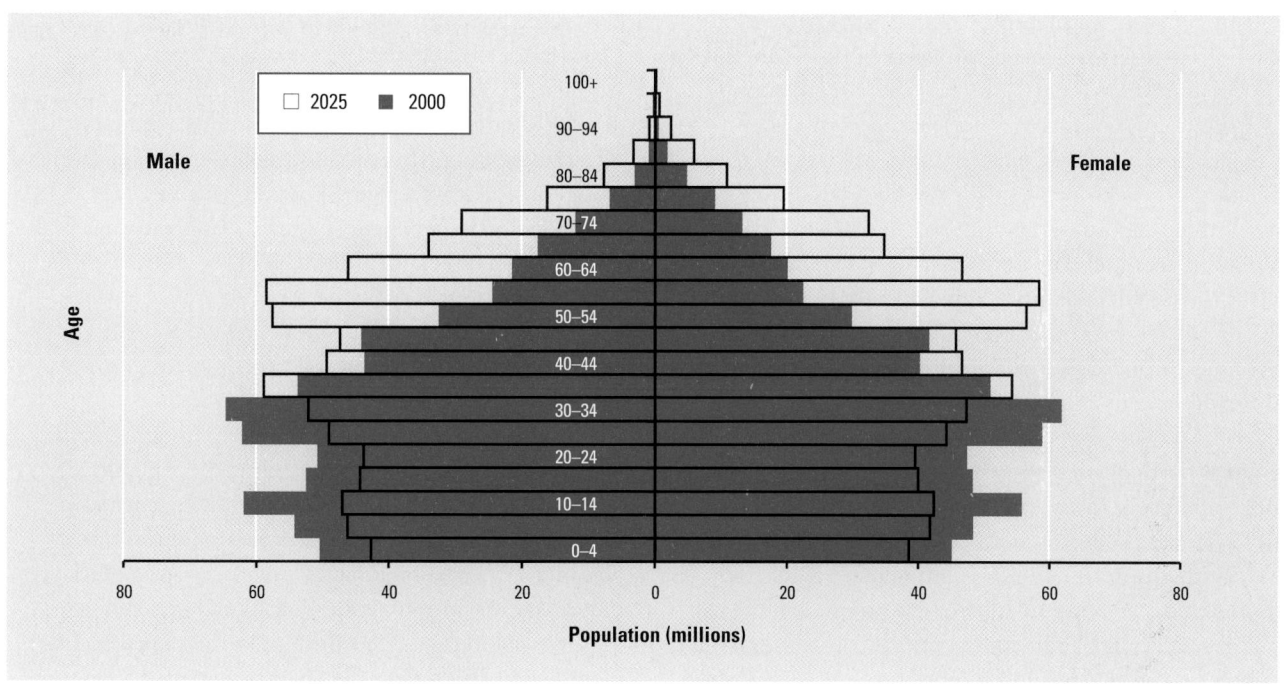

Source: USCB, 2004, online at: http://www.census.gov/ipc/www/

of China will have to support very aged populations on low average income levels.

How will China's elderly population be sustained financially two decades hence? All uncertainties about the future notwithstanding, we can be fairly confident in surmising that these prospective pensioners are not going to be supported through the country's existing state pension arrangements. Table 2 outlines the dilemma.

For all the justifiable anxiety about the current actuarial health of national pension systems in various OECD countries, the financial disarray of China's official pension apparatus is in a league of its own. The present net value of the unfunded liabilities of this patchwork—covering perhaps a sixth of the total Chinese workforce—is estimated to exceed current GDP, perhaps substantially. China's pension system is clearly unsustainable, and despite the better part of a decade of high-level policy deliberations in Beijing on the national pension problem—the issue has been addressed by directives at the highest levels of government since 1997— no alternative formula has as yet been officially offered.[9] Nor is promulgation of legislation for a new and unified social security system anywhere evident on China's policy horizon today.[10]

Thus China's national pension system as of 2025 promises today to be more or less the same one that has traditionally provided for the country's elderly and infirm: namely, the family unit. But there is a problem here: the

Table 2: Coverage and actuarial balances of current public pension systems: USA, Japan, China (percent)

	Coverage	Net present value unfunded/GDP
USA 2004	87%[1]	32%
Japan 2001	c. 100%[2]	60–70%[3]
China 2003	c. 16%	125–150%

Notes:

[1] Proportion of fully insured persons 20+ in OASDI, 2003.

[2] Mandatory participation of persons 20+ in basic plan.

[3] Estimates for burden post-2000 round of reforms.

Sources: For China: West and Goodkind, 2003; for Japan: Faruqee and Muehleiser, 2001, online at: http://www.imf.org/external/pubs/ft/wp /2001/wp0140.pdf; for USA: United States Social Security Administration, 2004a, Table 4.c5, online at: http://www.ssa.gov/policy/docs/statcomps/supplement/2003/4c.pdf, United States Social Security Administration, 2004b, Table VI.F5 Chapter II.D, online at: http://www.ssa.gov/OACT/TR/TR04/

"success" of the Chinese government's continuing anti-natal population drive will inevitably translate in coming decades into a plummeting ratio of working-age children to elderly parents. Whereas the average Chinese woman who celebrated her 60th birthday in the early 1990s had borne five children during her lifetime, her counterpart in 2025 will have had fewer than two.

No less important is the fact that, over the next 20 years, China's rising cohorts of prospective retirees face a growing "son deficit." In Chinese cultural tradition, sons have the primary duty of supporting aged parents, while daughters are obliged to care for her husband's parents as well as her own. In the early 1990s, about 7 percent of China's 60-year-old women had never borne a son. Today that proportion is about 10 percent. By 2025, the figure will shoot up to roughly 30 percent.

Furthermore, some male children will not live to adulthood to help support their parents. Thus, taking both fertility and survival trends into account, it seem likely that a third or more of Chinese women approaching retirement age two decades from now will have no living sons. When tens of millions of aged Chinese just 20 years from now seek financial and material help from their children, they will have to compete for resources with the parents of their sons-in-law, presuming that China's longstanding cultural norm of near-universal marriage for women continues. Suffice it to say that such a niche is not promising from the perspective of social ecology.

With government pension guarantees a distinctly more limited and problematic set of options than official policy might wish, and with the traditional social security system known as the family a more fragile construct than at any time in the recent past, the grim reality may be that a great many elderly Chinese men and women in the coming decades will be forced to sustain themselves by continuing to work. Paradoxically, despite China's tremendous material progress over the half century beginning 1975, the nation's elderly will face a continuing need—quite possibly, a growing need—to support themselves in old age through their own labor. To make matters worse, China's elderly population is not ideally placed to compete in their country's labor markets, either today or tomorrow. And here we come to the second constraint of China's tightening triple bind.

China's elderly workers occupy a decidedly unfavorable position in the country's labor force today. At the start of the new century, in comparison with China's overall workforce, workers 65 or older were six times more likely to be illiterate or semi-literate, and only a tenth as likely to have a high school or college diploma. They are also much more likely to be toiling in the agricultural sector; in the year 2000, 87 percent of China's elderly workers were engaged in farming, as opposed to 66 percent for the workforce as a whole.[11] Consigned to the low-income sector of the economy, and laboring with low levels of human capital, China's older labor force provides a virtual textbook definition of the working poor.

From the already available data on the educational attainment of the people who will make up China's elderly cohorts 20 years from now, we already know that, despite China's educational advances, its older population will still be seriously disadvantaged in the year 2025.

Research by Bauman and Graf (2003) shows the age groups from 2000 that will correspond to future elderly cohorts in 2025; i.e., the number of 35-year-olds as of 2000 who will be 60 in 2025. According to these numbers, some two-fifths of China's senior citizens would have a primary school education or less as of 2025. That circumstance contrasts starkly with prospects for today's developed countries: in both Japan and the United States, for example, nearly five-sixths of the 65-plus population would have at least a high school diploma in 2025.

In 2025, despite rapid structural transformation in the Chinese economy, agriculture will likely still remain the largest single source of employment in China, and the country's poorly educated, low-skilled older workers will be over-represented in, and still primarily consigned to, field work.

It should be borne in mind that farming in China is not only low-paid work, but entails endless, physically demanding, strenuous activity. Even those occupations, which people in the West do not commonly associate with physical exertion, routinely require stamina and muscle-power for job performance in China. This is so, quite simply, because China still lacks the capital investment per worker to provide labor saving alternatives to brute human strength in the production process. With mechanization so much more limited in China than in western economies, the machines powering much of Chinese economic activity today are human bodies, and this circumstance is unlikely to change appreciably over the next 20 years.

Perversely, because China's older workers suffer from lower levels of education and training than the general labor force, they are precisely the cohort most directly obliged to rely upon physical effort to earn its living. This will hold true tomorrow as well as today.

And that brings us to the third strand of the triple bind, characterizing China's looming aging problem: in the years ahead, China's senior citizens are not only likely to face real and perhaps mounting pressures to support themselves through paid labor, principally in low-paying, physically demanding jobs, but they are also likely to be less healthy and more fragile than their counterparts in other countries, where the physical demands of employment are much less forbidding for the elderly and non-elderly alike.

Upon reflection, the proposition that the health of senior citizens in China is more tenuous than that of older populations in western countries should not surprise us. After all, over their life histories, older people in China have, on average, been exposed to more in the way of health and nutritional risk, and have less scope for protecting and/or recovering from illness and injury, than older people in affluent societies. Overall, the availability and quality of food, housing, education, and health services in China—not to mention many other factors influencing health status—do not compare favorably with OECD levels. Consequently, China's senior citizens live shorter lives than old people in OECD countries, and their remaining years are more heavily compromised by serious health problems.

Estimates of disability-free life expectancy in China and Japan at age 65 make the point.

Table 3: Life expectancy and disability-free life expectancy at age 65: Japan 1990 vs. China 1987

	LE (years)	DFLE (years)	Difference (years)	DFLE/LE (percent)
Males, China 1987	12.5	8.9	3.6	71
Males, Japan 1990	16.2	13.8	3.4	85
Females, China 1987	14.6	9.9	4.7	68
Females, Japan 1990	20.0	15.9	4.1	80

Source: Saito et al., 2003, pp. 289–317.

Although these particular data come from c. 1990, the patterns they reveal still hold. For men and women alike, overall life expectancy at age 65 was over 50 percent longer in Japan than in China. Twice the fraction of Chinese as Japanese men can reportedly expect to be burdened with disability for nearly a third of their remaining years. Likewise, Chinese women can reportedly expect to spend a third of their final years afflicted with disabilities, whereas the corresponding fraction for Japanese women was one fifth. Moreover, Table 3 may considerably understate the extent of health impairment in later life for China's elderly, since, for one thing, the table only refers to disability, and not to the broader matter of potentially serious health problems; secondly, the data on disability in Table 3 come from self-assessments, and, as is well known, subjective expectations regarding health tend to be lower for populations with lower income and educational levels.

In summary, China's outlook for population aging can in some respects be likened to a slow-motion humanitarian tragedy already underway. On the current trajectory, the graying of China—despite the context of an increasingly successful emerging market—threatens tens of millions of future senior citizens with a penurious and uncertain livelihood, compounded by the necessity of hard physical labor, illness, and disability. The incidence of individual misfortune implied by current trends is sufficiently widespread as to suggest that impoverished aging may emerge as a major social problem for China in the years ahead. The impending fault lines for impoverished aging, furthermore, promise to magnify yet further the social inequalities with which China is already struggling.

How the country will deal with the social and political tensions generated by impoverished aging remains to be seen. Since 1997, Beijing's policy makers have recognized the question, but have been deferring the response

to it. Quite predictably, feasible policy options have narrowed over these years of indecision, with the remaining alternatives becoming steadily more expensive.

The Russian Federation: Graying with unhealthy aging

In some respects, Russia's outlook for population aging can be regarded as an ordinary European tale, with prospective changes in the country's population structure, by themselves, conveying just such an impression.

Between 2000 and 2025, Russia's total population is expected to decline, while the number of its citizens 65 and above is slated to grow substantially (Figure 3). Consequently, Russia's population support ratio (PSR)—a metric that relates the working age population (15–64 years) to the retirement age population (65-plus)—falls by USCB projections over this quarter century from 5.5:1 to 3.3:1.

To be sure, the implied burden of potential pensioners on the potential Russian workforce of 2025 is high by contemporary standards, but such ratios look unexceptional for the Europe that awaits in 2025. By Census Bureau projections, the PSR for all of Europe would be about 3.0:1 in 2025, indicating the Russia would have a slightly higher working age population to retirement age population than the rest of the continent. For 2025, in fact, the proportion of Russia's population 65 and older promises to be slightly higher than America's and slightly lower than that of Western Europe (Figure 4).

It would be tempting to describe Russia's prospective aging profile as that of a typical developed society, with the expectation that Russia's aging problem will be similar to that of OECD Europe. However, the weight of the aging burden that Russian society will have to bear in coming years cannot be measured adequately by population pyramids or population support ratios alone. Russia's particular vulnerabilities in population aging pivot not so much on the size of nation's prospective elderly population, as on the exceptional fragility of the workforce that will be expected to support it.

Pronounced long-term *deterioration* of public health for an industrialized society during peacetime is a highly anomalous—indeed counter-intuitive—proposition for the modern sensibility. Nevertheless, over the four decades between 1961–1962 and 2003, life expectancy at birth in Russia fell by nearly five years for males, and also fell slightly for females, making for an overall drop in life expectancy of nearly three years over the past four decades.

Between the mid-1960s and the start of the 21st century, Russia's age-standardized death rates climbed by over 15 percent for women, and by a shocking 40 percent for men. This upswing in mortality was especially concentrated among the working age group, where the upsurges in

169

Figure 3: Estimated and projected population structure of Russia: 2000 vs. 2025

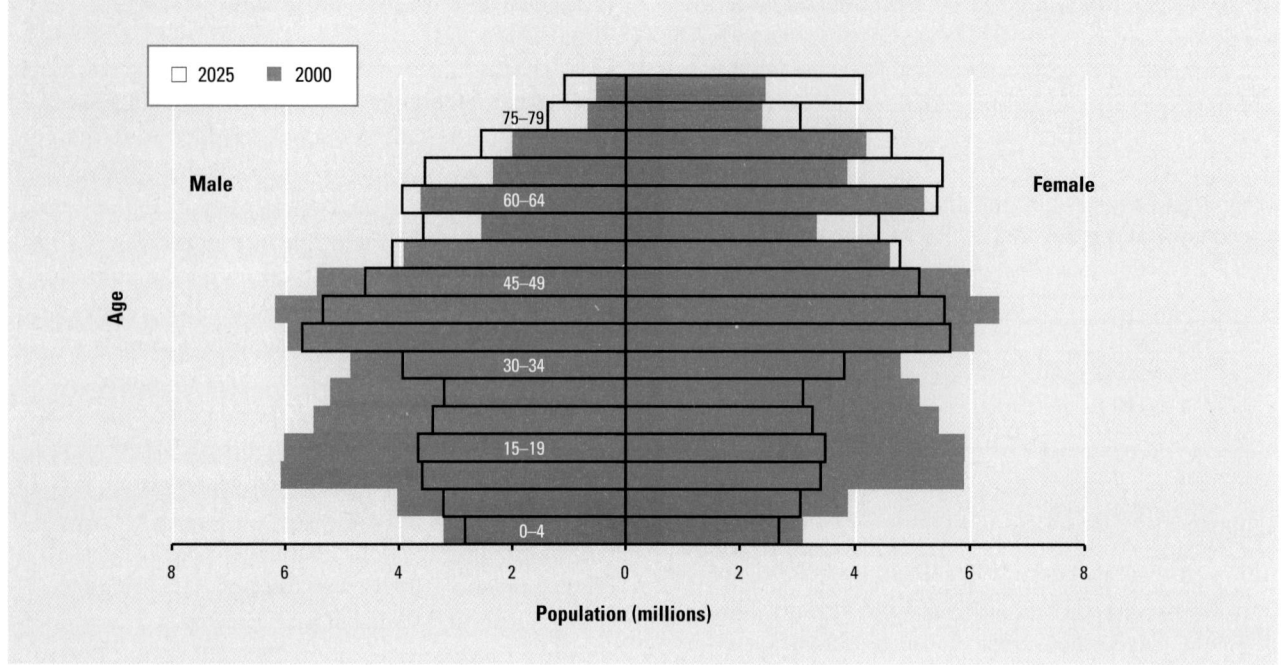

Source: United Nations, 2004, online at http://esa.un.org/unpp/index.asp?panel=2 accessed 4 March 2005.

170

Figure 4: Estimated and projected percentage of population aged 65-plus: United States, Russia, Western Europe, 1975–2025

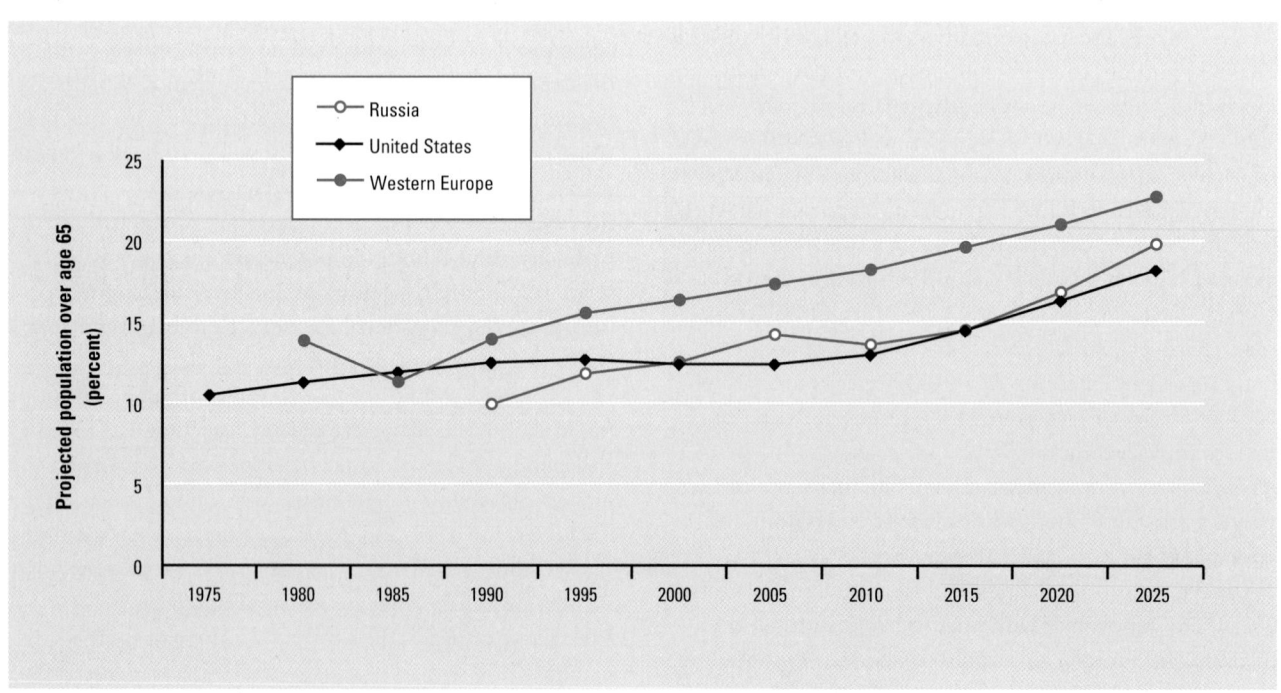

Source: United States Census Bureau, 2004, online at: http://www.census.gov/ipc/www/idbnew.html accessed 10 May 2005.

Figure 5: Male life expectancy at birth: Russia vs. Indian subcontinent, 1989–2025

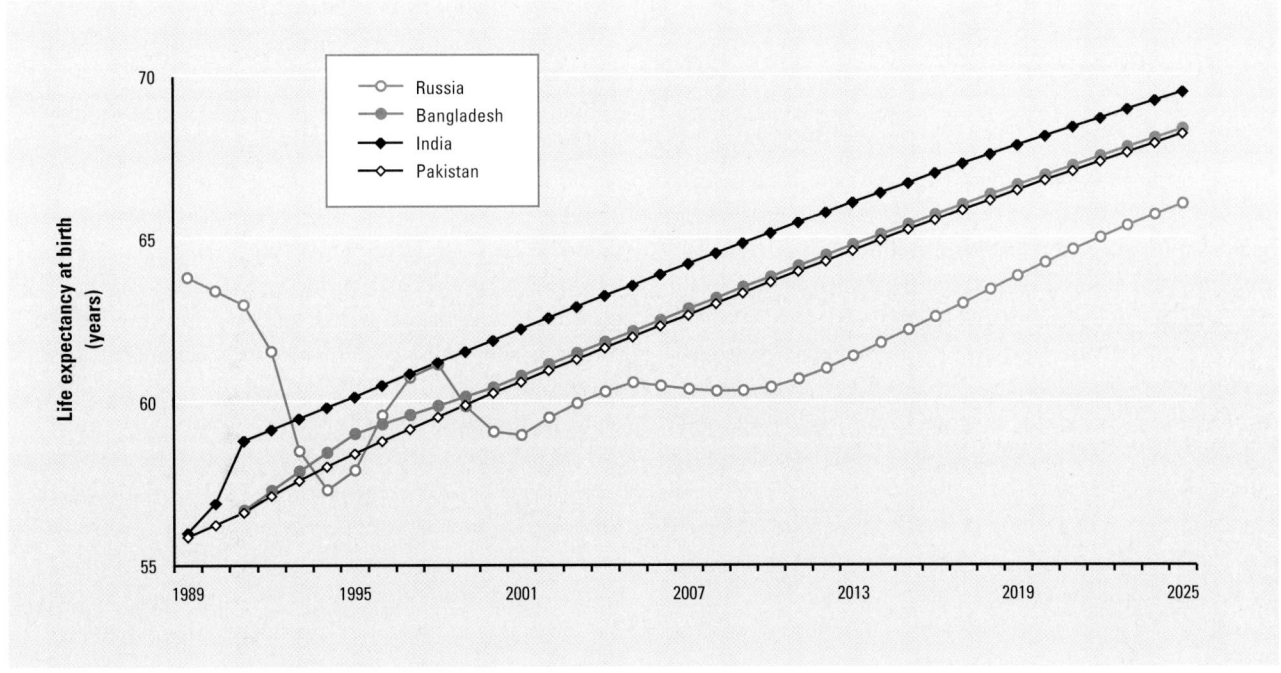

Source: United States Census Bureau, 2004, online at http://www.census.gov/ipc/www/idbnew.html accessed 19 January 2005.

death rates were breathtaking. For example, between 1970–71 and 2003, every female cohort between the ages of 25 and 59 suffered at least a 40 percent increase in death rates; for men between the ages of 30 and 64, the corresponding figures reached a uniform 50 percent, in some cases exceeding 80 percent.[12]

To get a sense of just how bad current health and mortality conditions are for Russian adults, we can compare survival rates for Swiss men with their Russian counterparts for 1999, thanks to information compiled by the Human Mortality Database.[13] In Switzerland, a 20-year-old man had a five-out-of-six chance of making it to 65 years of age; in Russia, he stood less than even odds.[14]

If Russia's adult mortality levels are so abnormally high today, won't more normal levels more or less automatically reassert themselves in the coming decades? The disappointing answer is: not necessarily, for in Russia's demography the abnormal seems to have become the new norm. Unlike other parts of the industrialized world, Russia's health trends are characterized by a heavy measure of what we might call negative momentum, that is to say, an unfavorable accumulation of immunological insults and health risks in today's adult population, by comparison with their parents' generation. To the extent that death rates provide evidence about general health conditions, modern Russia's mortality data strongly suggest that each new cohort is more fragile than its predecessor.

In other industrialized western societies in the post-war era, younger generations have routinely come to enjoy better survival rates than their predecessors. For example, in contemporary Japan men born in 1950 have thus far, over the course of their adult life, experienced age-specific death rates 30 percent to 80 percent lower than those recorded for the cohort born 20 years before them.

By contrast, there has been no improvement in survival schedules among the two generations of Russian men born between the late 1920s and 1970. On the contrary: over the life course, each rising cohort of Russian men seems to be charting out a slightly more dismal mortality trajectory than the one traced by its immediate predecessors, the same pattern being evident among Russian females.

This negative momentum makes the objective of major, sustained improvements in public health especially problematic. Partly for this reason, demographers have generally low expectations for health progress in Russia in the years immediately ahead. The USCB, for example, suggests that male life expectancy in Russia will be consistently lower that that of India, Pakistan, or even Bangladesh through the year 2025 (Figure 5).[15]

Russia's lingering health and mortality crisis promises to be a significant impediment to rapid economic development, frustrating the country's efforts to move onto a path of swift and sustained material advancement. It is difficult to see how Russia can expect, in some imagined future, to achieve an Irish standard of living, if its labor force still faces an Indian schedule of survival, or worse. Widespread debilitation and premature mortality among working age cohorts depresses economic potential directly and immediately, but also has adverse and far-reaching effects on longer-term productivity. The expectation of a seriously foreshortened working life alters the cost-benefit calculus for higher education and technical training, lowering investment in human capital. And since Russian working-age adults appear far older than western counterparts of the same age,[16] the scope for economically active aging—that is, for enhancing the labor force participation and economic contributions of persons in middle age and beyond—will be far more constrained for Russia than for OECD Europe.

Population aging in the context of unhealthy aging poses additional particular economic and social challenges for Russia. Given the country's steep and forbidding age-specific health gradient today, and the limited prospects for health improvements over the coming two decades, the prospective aging of Russia's working-age population—given a median age of the population within the 15–64 grouping of about 42 years in 2025, three and a half years higher than today—means that the health and mortality outlook for Russian manpower could actually be less favorable than today, perhaps even appreciably so. Second, the specter of a swelling population of elderly pensioners,[17] dependent for support on an unhealthy and diminishing population of low-income workers suggests some particularly unattractive tradeoffs between welfare and growth.

This unpromising outlook begs a sinister question: would Russian resources be best allocated to capital accumulation, or to consumption for the unproductive elderly? Given Russia's population structure, the question cannot be finessed. As of the year 2002, Russia had only 1.7 workers for every pensioner,[18] and that ratio will only fall in the years ahead. Though the government officially embarked upon pension reform in 2002, the process threatens to be a long and complicated one. What the eventual arrangements will presage, on the one hand, for the availability of investable funds, and, on the other, for the living conditions of Russia's steadily growing ranks of elderly and the infirm, is, as yet, an open question.

Aging in India: A tale of two countries

India's population profile will age over the coming 20 years, but will, nevertheless, remain relatively youthful. This fact is widely understood by informed readers and policymakers, and is reinforced by prospective changes in the country's population structure.

Although projections indicate that India's 65-plus cohort is slated to double in size between 2005 and 2025, those elders will account for less than 8 percent of the overall population 20 years hence; the country's median age is barely over 30, and the PSR is almost 9:1, a level last witnessed in today's more developed countries only before the Second World War (Figure 6).

But just as vast India is in many ways a sort of arithmetic expression, averaging the sum of its many diverse components, so it is, too, with population aging. Closer examination reveals that, as regards population aging there are in reality two Indias, with very different aging prospects and challenges: one that stays remarkably youthful over the next 20 years, and the other already embarked on a very rapid graying.

As already noted, the pace and scale of future aging is largely determined by current local levels of fertility. India's total fertility rate has dropped by more than two-fifths over the past three decades, from about 5.4 births per woman per lifetime in the early 1970s, to approximately 3.1 today. But the pace of change has varied strikingly from one region and setting to the next. It will surprise some readers to learn that sub-replacement fertility today prevails in many of India's huge urban centers, including New Delhi, Mumbai (Bombay), Kolkata (Calcutta), Chennai (Madras).[19] Even more surprising is the fact that, throughout much of rural India—especially rural south India—fertility levels today are also near, or already below, replacement.

Dr. P. N. Mari Bhat of Delhi University's Institute for Economic Growth has laid out the implications of these discrepant patterns for future aging in the supra-state regions he labels "north" India and "south" India.[20] Current (2005) fertility levels for the roughly half-billion population of this northern region are almost twice as high as for the near quarter billion people of the southern region.[21] By 2025, north India's population would still be very young.

India's projected median age would be just 26, and the 65-plus group would account for less than 6 percent of the total population. On the other hand, south India's population structure in 2025 would bear unmistakable signs of population aging.

In the south, the median age would be about 34—a level comparable to Europe's in the late 1980s—and 9 percent of the population would be 65 or older—about the same share as Japan's in 1980.

Mari Bhat does not break down his 2025 projections to the state level, but Professor Tim Dyson of the London School of Economics has done so for India for the year 2026.[22] His projections differ from those of Mari Bhat in some particulars, most importantly in positing a slightly faster pace of fertility decline over the next generation. But his calculations depict a similar growing aging gap

Figure 6: Estimated and projected population structure of India: 2000 vs. 2025

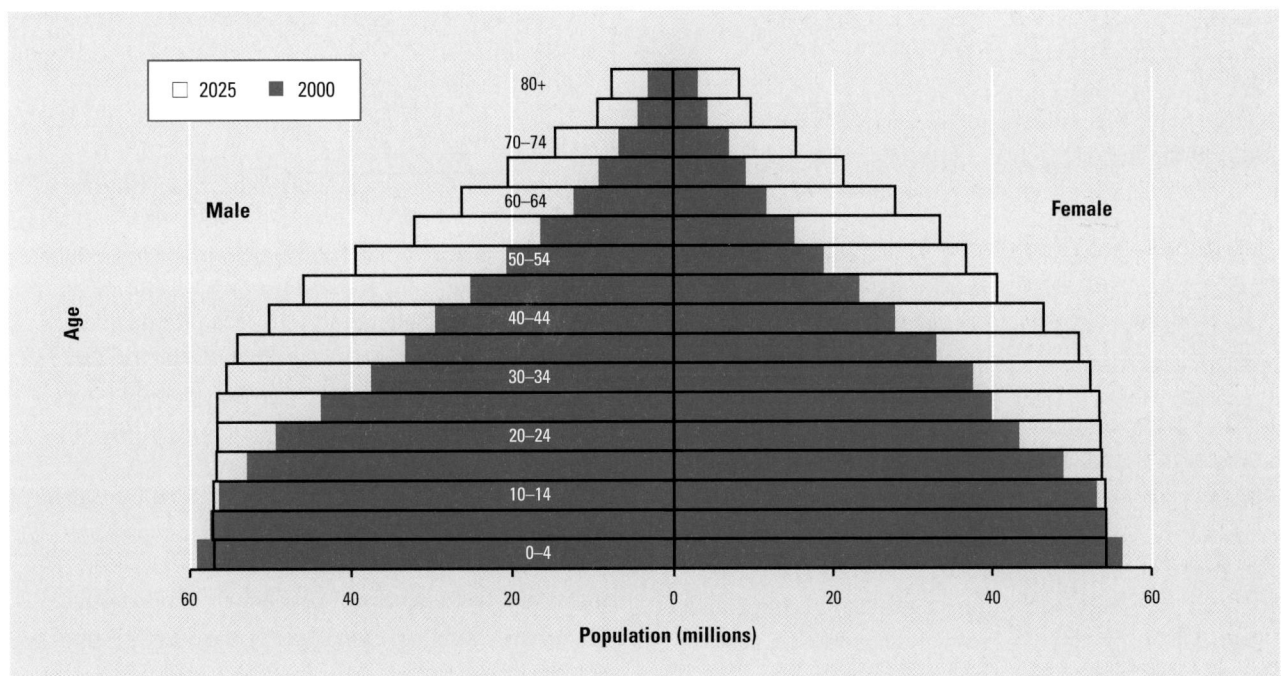

Source: USCB, 2004, online at: http://www.census.gov/ipc/www/

between north and south India, with aging by 2026 already having progressed considerably in a number of southern states. In each of India's four southernmost states, median age would be over 35—and over 37 in both Kerala and Tamil Nadu. (These figures compare with those of Western Europe around 1990.) In these projections, the proportion of persons 65 and older in Kerala and Tamil Nadu both exceeded 10 percent by 2025. (Here, the figures compare with Japan in the mid-1980s.)

It must be borne in mind, however, that a generation before the median age reached 35, Western Europe's GDP per capita was in the range of US$6000–$8000 (at year 2000 prices and exchange rates); likewise, a generation before Japan's share of 65-plus to total population hit the 10 percent mark, the country's per capita GDP (at constant 2000 exchange rates and prices) was around US$7000.[23] In 2001—that is to say, 25 years before the two states in question are projected to reflect those same demographic specifics—exchange-rate-based GDP per capita was less than US$450 a year in both Kerala and Tamil Nadu. By any international or historical benchmark, indeed, many areas of India are facing the onset of rapid population aging on current levels of per capita output that are alarmingly low.

At the moment, India has nothing resembling society-wide old-age pension coverage. On the contrary, only about 11 percent of India's workforce participate in any

sort of guaranteed retirement income system. (An emergency, needs-based monthly stipend is publicly available for persons over 60 in India, but this mechanism offers less than US$2 a month to its beneficiaries, and is not guaranteed to be available to all who apply for it, and who meet its hardship qualifications.) Although Indian policymakers and academics have been discussing alternative potential paths to universal old-age income protection with a reasonable measure of seriousness in recent years, no plans for national coverage are even remotely on the national policy agenda.[24] Lacking a tangible comprehensive national retirement pension policy, India's implicit strategy for meeting its coming aging challenge is, at least for now, to muddle its way through it. Like many unspoken—and thus unexamined—game-plans, this one looks highly problematic. Even if India, like the Japan of an earlier day, were poised to grow at a 5.5 percent per capita per annum over the coming generation, significant parts of India would be approaching the advent of an aged society on income levels almost an order of magnitude lower than those of Japan in the mid-1980s.

Furthermore, it can hardly be taken for granted at the moment that India is going to experience a sustained 5.5 percent per capita growth rate over the next generation. In the period since its 1991 economic crisis, India has averaged a highly respectable 4.0 percent annual rate of per capita growth, and has become a presence in the global IT economy, through its enclaves in places like Bangalore. But Bangalore—like the rest of the Indian south—is part of what may soon be known as "old" India, that is, with an available source of relatively skilled, but older, manpower, which will soon peak and begin to shrink. By contrast, other parts of India will have abundant and growing supplies of manpower, but a disproportionate share of it will be either entirely unschooled or only barely literate.

Profs. Anne Goujon of the Vienna Insitute for Demography and Kirtsy McNay of Oxford compared the projected 2026 age, sex, and education pyramids for the Indian states of Kerala and Bihar.[25] The extreme contrast is intentional. Kerala is India's most educated state, while Bihar is its least schooled. In the Kerala of 2026, almost everyone of working age (15 to 64) will have some schooling, and the majority of the economically active manpower would have a high school diploma or better. The largest population cohort would be people in their 40s, with every successive cohort a little bit smaller. In the Bihar of 2026, on the other hand, each new birth cohort entering the labor pool will be larger than the one before—but less than one third of the economically active population (15 to 64 years) would have even completed grade school. Well over two-fifths of the economically active age population would be illiterate, with no schooling whatsoever. (These projections, one is compelled to note, assume further continuation into the future of the progress achieved over the 1990s in expanding access to education in India.)

To appreciate how seriously disadvantaged India stands to be educationally a generation hence, we may compare the Goujon-McNay projections with earlier work by Robert J. Barro and Jong-Wha Lee on historical patterns of worldwide educational attainment.[26] By the Goujon-McNay projections, in 2026 nearly one-third (32 percent) of Indians 25 years of age or older will be illiterate, with no formal schooling. By contrast, as of 1960—that is to say, nearly three generations earlier—the illiteracy rate for the 25-plus group in 23 OECD countries would have been about 6 percent. Perhaps even more telling are comparisons with educational levels from other developing regions. According to the Goujon-McNay projections and the Barro-Lee estimates, India's rate of adult 25-plus illiteracy in 2026 will be roughly comparable to the levels in Latin America and the Caribbean or East Asia around 1970 (35 and 31 percent, respectively), two generations earlier. Indeed, surprising as this may sound, India's future adult illiteracy rates will probably not be that much lower than the current (2000) levels prevailing in sub-Saharan Africa (43 percent).

Educated and aging, or untutored and fertile: this looks to be the contradiction for India's development in the years immediately ahead. Human resources are the foundation for economic growth for the coming century, but while Russia's Achilles heel is the poor health of its human resource base, India's is surely the grossly inadequate educational opportunity offered to a large segment of that country's population.

Waiting for the demographic dividend, or waiting for Godot?

Clearly, not all emerging markets are poised to try to provide for their aging populations on a base of income levels so low as to be without historical precedent. Such middle-income economies as Mexico, Brazil and Turkey, among others, promise to have relatively youthful populations in 2025.

Moreover, given current productivity levels and reasonable future economic prospects, a number of these countries promise to fall well within the western age-income experience over their presumed ascent in the coming decades. They may even remain more youthful than the western economies were at similar levels of per capita income.

Is there a special economic benefit to be had from relatively youthful development? One hardy strand of thought in the economics literature, reaching back nearly half a century, suggests that the answer depends not only upon graying, but upon the ratio of all dependents, young and old, to economically productive workers.

According to this argument, the lower the dependency ratio of children and elderly to working age people, the higher the rates of capital accumulation and growth. Some contemporary economists argue that there is a special moment in the demographic transition, namely, when birth rates are low and elderly populations are not yet burgeoning, which provides a sort of ideal circumstance for very rapid economic growth. According to this view, societies that have recently made the transition from high to low birthrates, but which have yet to experience significant graying, are positioned to reap a *demographic dividend*. In this telling, crucial shifts in demographic structure are integral to the modern era's great development success stories, from East Asia's remarkable economic ascent over the past generation and a half, to Ireland's more recent transformation into Europe's Celtic tiger.[27]

The picture of the demographic dividend is certainly compelling, and it may be heartening for those low-income societies whose dependency ratios are now about to begin a long-term decline. But is the story correct? Are dependency ratios, in fact, critical to a given population's prospects for sustained and rapid material advance?

It is surely incontestable that, all else being equal, per capita output will be higher in the society where people of working age account for the greater share of total population. And variations in dependency ratios may be

Figure 7: Age dependency ratios*: East Asia and the Pacific vs. Latin America and the Caribbean, 1960–2000

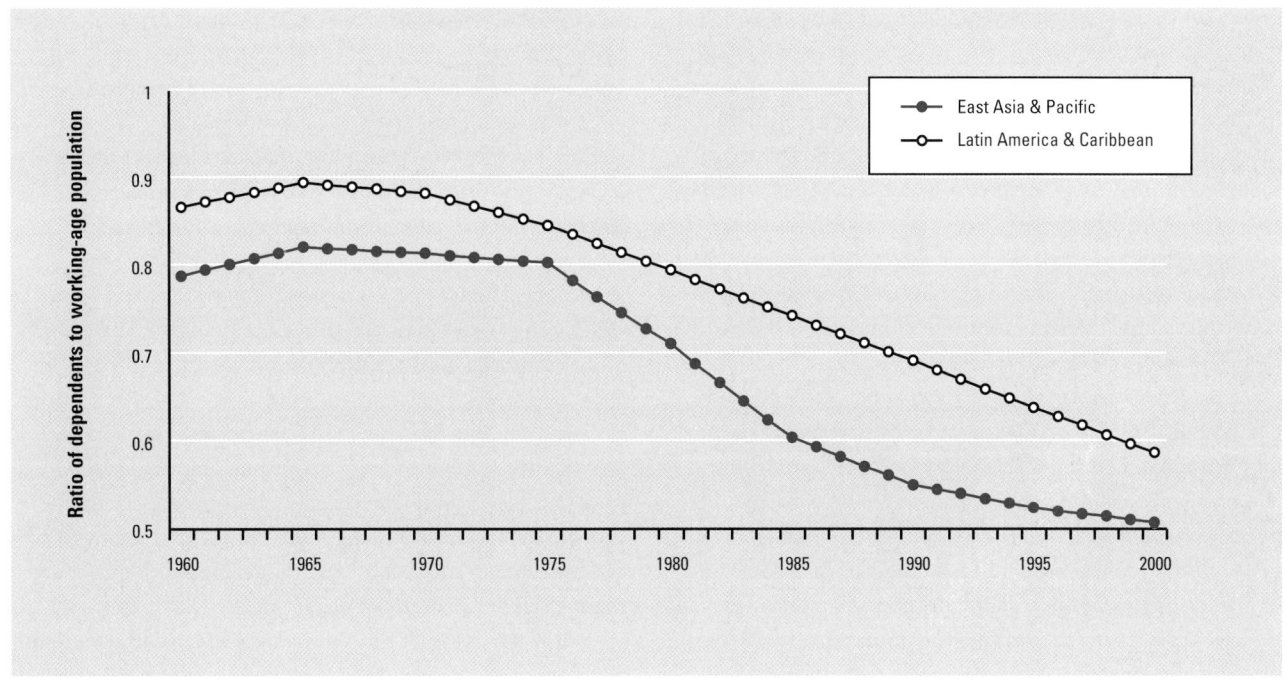

* The age dependency ratio is the proportion of the population under 15 and 65-plus to the population 15–64 years of age; data are for developing countries only.
Source: World Bank, 2003.

**Figure 8: Demographic dividend? GDP per capita (PPP):
East Asia and the Pacific vs. Latin America and the Caribbean, 1975–2003**

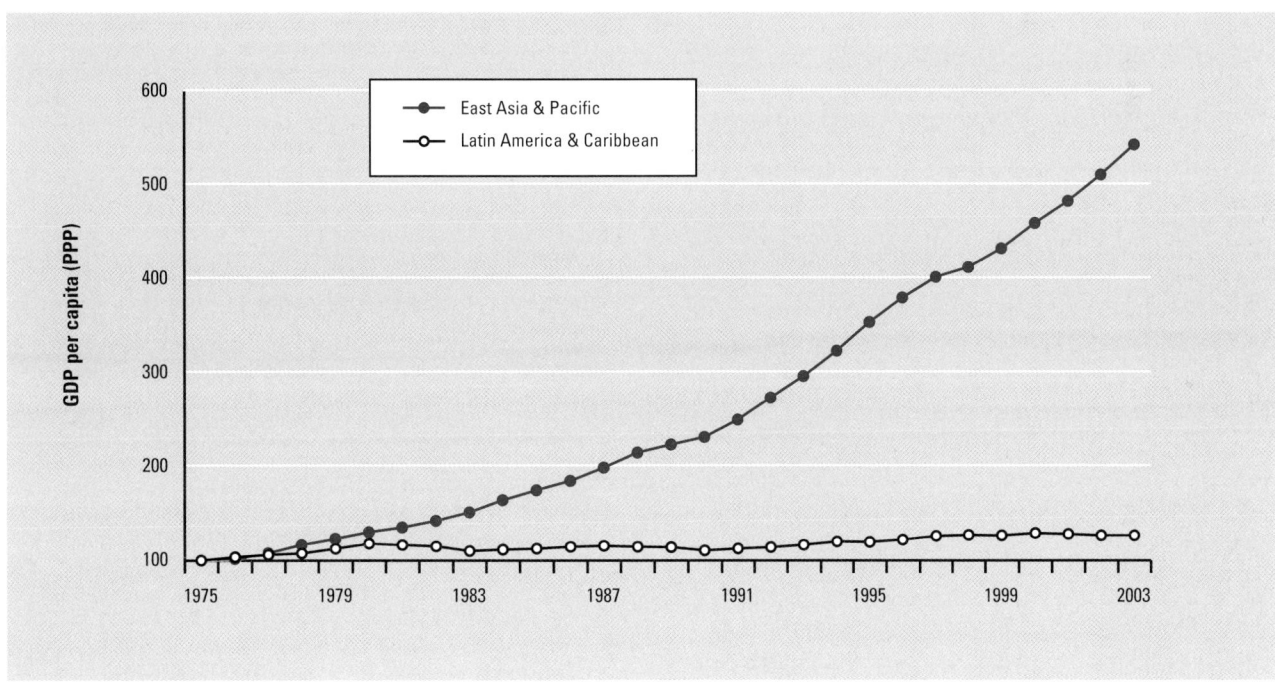

Source: World Bank, 2003.

plausibly expected to correspond with variations in savings ratios—or more strictly speaking, with differences in a population's disposition to save, and the ease with which it tries to accumulate savings. But in an era of truly global capital markets, relatively low savings rates in any given locale do not necessarily constitute a binding constraint on that area's development. Postwar economic history would seem to demonstrate that dependency ratios are not a decisive influence of long run economic performance in our increasingly globalized times, viz. the developmental records of two major global regions: East Asia, on the one hand, and Latin America and the Caribbean, on the other. Figures 8 and 9 present the evidence.

Over the 40 years between 1960 and 2000, dependency ratios for the low-income countries in East Asia and Latin America and the Caribbean traced quite similar trajectories—although dependency ratios were always somewhat lower in East Asia. Despite the close correspondence between the indicators for the two regions over the course of the past four decades, economic results in the two areas have been anything but similar: per capita output septupled for East Asia, whereas it rose by about 85 percent for Latin America and the Caribbean. Moreover, in both regions the dependency ratio commenced a steady decline around 1975. But while the pace of growth accelerated in East Asia in the quarter century following this drop, Latin America suffered a growth slowdown. In the high dependency ratio era (1960–75) Latin America's per capita output growth averaged almost 3 percent a year, whereas in the years of steadily falling dependency ratios (1975–2003), annual per capita growth was under 1 percent. Clearly, other factors, including government policy, are more important in determining prospects for material progress.

Mari Bhat's cautious assessment of the possible influence of the demographic dividend on economic growth for India could be extended to other low-income areas as well:

> ...during the next 10–20 years demographic conditions would be favorable for growth... However, as Bloom and Williamson note, their effect is by no means inevitable. To realize the effect, it is necessary to support it with appropriate economic, social and political institutions and policies. Otherwise it would only lead to higher levels of unemployment.[28]

Countries with declining dependency ratios may enjoy some potential for economic advantage, given the right cultural, institutional, and policy conditions. But demographic dividends are nothing to bank on.

Global implications

All other things being equal—without proactive policy and institutional adjustments—the pronounced population aging that awaits the affluent OECD countries over the generation ahead can be expected to have a depressing effect on both local savings rates and local rates of economic growth. Much the same may also be said of the aging trends that are due to have a serious impact on some of the major emerging markets in the next few decades. The conjunction of population aging in the world's developed economies and important parts of the developing world naturally raises the question of potential global impact. Global capital markets may be efficient in allocating investment to promising countries, corporations, and projects, but the availability of capital will affect the cost of capital, and thus the profitability or attractiveness of undertakings worldwide. By the same token, economic slowdowns in one major region can be expected to have spillover effects on growth in other regions, in an environment of liberalized global trade.

Will the aging of the third world have such unanticipated effects on the world economy? The answer is not yet clear, but it is none to early to begin asking the question.

Notes

1 With special thanks to Ms. Courtney Richard and Ms. Assia Dosseva of the American Enterprise Institute for their assistance with figures and tables in this chapter. Special gratitude is also due Prof. Tim Dyson of the London School of Economics, Dr. Anne Goujon of the Vienna Institute of Demography, and Drs. Loraine West and Daniel Goodkind of the United States Census Bureau (USCB) for generously sharing their detailed projections of regional population trends for India, India by educational status, and China, respectively. I am also indebted to Dennis J. Donahue of the USCB for some thoughtful cautionary comments about the limitations of demographic projections. Any remaining errors are those of the author.

2 A select representation of this voluminous and diverse analytical literature might include: Auerbach et al., 1989; Cutler et al., 1990, pp. 1–56; Disney, 1996; OECD, 1998; United Nations Population Division, 2000; Heller, 2003; MacKellar et al.,.2004; Poterba, 2004; International Monetary Fund, 2004; popularized presentations include Peterson, 1999; England, 2002; Longman, 2004; Kotlikoff and Burns, 2004.

3 Demographers today generally use global population projections by the United Nations Population Division (UNPD) and the United States Census Bureau (USCB) as their reference standard; the UNPD's *World Population Prospects* are available online at http://www.un.org/News/Press/docs/2005/pop918.doc.html; USCB's "International Data Base" can be accessed at http://www.census.gov/ipc/www/idbnew.html ; either set of projections can be used to support the calculations above.

4 An example illustrates the point: in a high-mortality society where female life expectancy stayed forever at 50 years and an average of six births-per-lifetime for each woman, the median age would eventually stabilize at around 16 years. On the other hand, if female life expectancy was 50, but births-per-lifetime averaged two instead of six, the median age would stabilize at close to 40! Thus, with an average of two children and a female life expectancy of only 50, the 65-plus group would ultimately account for over 15 percent of the total population, a level roughly comparable to that of the OECD countries today.

5 Wilson and Pison, 2004.

6 Technically, in the UN's global taxonomy, Eastern Europe is defined as "more developed" rather than "less developed." But because these "more developed" countries are nonetheless relatively low-income societies, we have included them for consideration in this chapter.

7 It should be noted that the task of reaching today's OECD per capita income levels may be even more daunting than those numbers suggest, since China, Russia, and India all enjoy extremely generous PPP-adjustments in this table, each of which scales up the country's actual exchange-rate-based per capita output level by a factor of four or more. By actual exchange-rate-based estimates, Russia's per capita GDP is only one-fifteenth that of Western Europe, and China's less than one-twentieth that of Japan.

8 The UNDP currently suggests that China's *total fertility rate* (TFR) was about 1.92 in 1990–1995—a level roughly 16 percent below that required for long-term population replacement—and that China's TFR has subsequently declined to slightly more than 1.7 today. The USCB reading is quite similar: for 2005, it projects a TFR of 1.72 for China. It must be borne in mind that these estimates may be somewhat unreliable, given the lack of complete annual vital registration data for China, and the unknown degree of under-reporting of infants and children in the country's census and demographic surveys. For background, see Goodkind, 2004, pp. 281–295, and Zhang and Zhao, 2005.

9 For background, see World Bank, 1997; Song, 2001; Huang, 2003, pp.171–198; and Wang, 2004, pp. 3–16.

10 Professor Mark W. Frazier of Lawrence University may have pinpointed a critical factor in this continuing delay: "Until the fundamental question of what the state owes its citizens in terms of guaranteed basic pension benefits is resolved, the debate over the necessity of pension legislation to supplant the current patchwork of national and local regulatory controls is largely academic;" see Frazier, 2005, pp. 108–130.

11 Data taken from People's Republic of China, 2002b, Tables 1-43, 1-51; and People's Republic of China, 2000, Tables 4-4, 4-4c.

12 How are we to explain modern Russia's awful health tragedy? Demographers and public health specialists do not fully understand the reasons behind these gruesome statistics. Diet, smoking, sedentary lifestyles, and poor health care all play their part. Russia's romance with vodka is certainly deeply implicated here. Part of the mystery of the ongoing Russian health disaster, however, is that the problem looks to be worse than the sum of its parts; i.e. death rates are significantly higher than one would predict on the basis of observed risk factors alone.

13 Online at http://www.mortality.org accessed 14 January, 2005.

14 It should be noted that in 1999 Russian adult survival schedules were slightly better than they are today.

15 Furthermore, those USCB projections do not take into account the possibility that additional and perhaps severe new health setbacks may be in store for the Russian Federation. Yet precisely such problems are almost certainly on the horizon today; one has only to think of the country's still-gathering storm of HIV/AIDS and drug-resistant tuberculosis epidemics.

16 A single example: in 1999—by no means the worst year for health in post-Communist Russia—the same death rates experienced by 40-year-old Russians were matched in Italy by women at age 55, and by men at age 60, respectively; estimates from the Human Mortality Database, online at: www.mortality.org.

17 Given Russia's grim health problems, it may seem paradoxical that the population should be aging so rapidly. However, it should be remembered from our earlier discussion that population aging is driven much more by fertility patterns than by mortality, and Russia's fertility levels today are far below replacement levels.

18 From Aron, 2004, p.2, a penetrating overview and analysis of the Russian pension situation.

19 Cf. Guilmoto and Rajan, 2002, pp. 665–672; data from Table A-1. For a more comprehensive treatment, see Guilmoto and Rajan, eds. 2005.

20 Mari Bhat, 2003, online at: http://planningcommission.nic.in/reports/sereport/er/vision2025/demogra.pdf accessed 1 May 2005.

21 India's remaining 350 million people live in states and union territories not included in Mari Bhat's north-south analysis.

22 Dyson, 2004, pp. 74–107, online at: http://indiabudget.nic.in/es2004-05/chapt2005/tab18.pdf accessed 1 May 2005. Professor Dyson also generously shared with me some of the additional unpublished details from this same series of projections.

23 Derived from *World Development Indicators 2004 CD-ROM*; estimates for Western Europe are for the 12 countries of the European Monetary Union for 1960–65; estimates for Japan are for the year 1960.

24 For background, see India, Ministry of Social Justice and Empowerment, 1999; World Bank, 2001; Purohil, 2003, pp. 49–79; Palacios, 2004, pp. 282–300.

25 Goujon and McNay, 2003, pp. 25–35. The discussion below benefits from additional unpublished projections from that effort, kindly transmitted to me by Dr. Goujon. The discussion refers to the Goujon-McNay "Scenario One" projections.

26 Barro and Lee, 2000.

27 See, for example: Coale and Hoover, 1958; Enke, 1966; Bloom and Williamson, 1998; Bloom et al., 2003.

28 Mari Bhat, 2003, p. 9.

References

Aron, L. 2004. "Privatizing Pensions." *AEI Russian Outlook*. Summer.

Auerbach A., J. Auerbach, L. J. Kotlikoff, and R. Hageman. 1989. "The Dynamics of an Aging Population: The Case of Four OECD Countries." *NBER Working Papers* 2797.

Barro, R. J. and J. W. Lee. 2000. "International Data on Educational Attainment: Updates and Implications." *Harvard University Center for International Development Working Papers* 42. April.

Baurman, K. J. and N. L. Graf. 2003. "Educational Attainment, 2000." *Census 2000 Brief*, August. United States Department of Commerce and United States Census Bureau.

Bloom, D. and J. Williamson. 1998. "Demographic Transitions and Economic Miracles in Emerging Asia." *World Bank Economic Review* 12:419–56.

Bloom, D., D. Canning, and J. Sevilla. 2003. *The Demographic Dividend: A New Perspective on the Economic Consequences of Population Change*. Santa Monica, CA: Rand.

Coale, A. J. and E. M. Hoover. 1958. *Population Growth and Economic Development in Low-Income Countries*. Princeton, NJ: Princeton University Press.

Coale, A. J., P. Demeny, and B. Vaughan. 1983. *Regional Model Life Tables and Stable Populations*. New York: Academic Press.

Cutler, D., J. M. Poterba, L. M. Sheiner, and L. H. Summers. 1990. "An Aging Society: Opportunity or Challenge?" *Brookings Papers on Economic Activity* 1:1–56.

Disney R. 1996. *Can We Afford To Grow Older? A Perspective on the Economics of Aging*. Cambridge, MA: MIT Press.

Dyson, T. 2004. "India's Population—The Future." T. Dyson, Robert Casses and Leela Visaria, eds. *Twenty-First Century India: Population, Economy, Human Development, and the Environment*. New York: Oxford University Press. 74–107.

England, R. S. 2002. *Global Aging and Financial Markets: Hard Landings Ahead?* Washington, DC: CSIS Press.

Enke, S. 1966. "The Economic Aspects of Slowing Population Growth." *Economic Journal* 76:44–56.

Faruqee H. and M. Muehleiser. 2001. "Population Aging in Japan: Demographic and Fiscal Sustainability." *IMF Working Paper* WP/01/40. April.

Feeney, G., N. Y. Luther, Q. Meng, and Y. Sun. 1993. "Recent Fertility Trends for China: Results from the 1990 Census." 1990 Population Census of China: Proceedings of International Seminar. Beijing: State Statistical Bureau. Online at: http://www.gfeeney.com/pubs/1992-rft-china/1992-rft-china.pdf

Frazier, M. W. 2005. "What's in a Law? China's Pension Reform and its Discontents." N. J. Diamant, S. J. Lubman, and K. J. O'Brien, eds. *Engaging the Law In China: State, Society and Possibilities for Justice*. Stanford, CA: Stanford University Press.108–30.

Goodkind, D. 2004. "China's Missing Children: The 2000 Census Underreporting Surprise." *Population Studies* 58(3):281–95.

Goujon A. and K. McNay. 2003. "Projecting the Educational Composition of the Population of India: Selected State-Level Perspectives." *Applied Population and Policy* 1(1):25–35.

Guilmoto, C. Z. and S. I. Rajan. 2002. "District Level Estimates of Fertility from India's 2001 Census." *Economic and Political Weekly*. 16 February. 665–72.

Guilmoto, C. Z. and S. I. Rajan, eds. 2005. *Fertility Transition in South India*. New Delhi: Sage Publications.

Heller P. 2003. *Who Will Pay? Coping with Aging Societies, Climate Change and Other Long-Term Fiscal Challenges*. Washington, DC: IMF.

Huang, J. 2003. "Economic Restructuring, Social Safety-Net and Old-Age Pension Reform in China." *American Asian Review* 21(2):171–98.

Human Mortality Database. 2005. Online at: www.mortality.org

India Ministry of Social Justice and Empowerment. 1999. *First Report of Project OASIS (Old Age Social and Income Security)*. 1 February. Online at: http://seniorindian.com/oasis_.htm accessed 1 May 2005.

International Monetary Fund. 2004. *World Economic Outlook: The Global Demographic Transition*. Washington, DC: IMF. September.

Japan Ministry of Internal Affairs and Communications. 2004. *Japan Statistical Yearbook 2004*. ed. Statistical Training Institute. Tokyo: Statistics Bureau.

Kotlikoff, L. J. and S. Burns. 2004. *The Coming Generational Storm: What You Need to Know About America's Economic Future*. Cambridge, MA: MIT Press.

Longman, P. 2004. *The Empty Cradle: How Falling Birth Rates Threaten World Prosperity and What to Do About It*. New York: Basic Books.

MacKellar L., T. Ermolieva, D. Horlacher, and L. Mayhew. 2004. *The Economic Impacts of Population Ageing in Japan*. Northampton, MA: Elgar.

Maddison, A. 2003. *The World Economy: Historical Statistics*. Paris: OECD Development Centre Studies.

Mari Bhat, P. N. 2003. "Demographic Scenario, 2025." Study #S-15, Research Projects on India- 2025. New Delhi: Centre for Policy Research. July.

Organisation for Economic Co-operation and Development. 1998. *Maintaining Prosperity in an Ageing Society*. Paris: OECD.

Palacios, R. 2004. "The Challenge of Pension Reform in India." E. M. Favaro and A. K. Lahiri, eds. *Fiscal Policies and Sustainable Growth in India*. New Delhi: Oxford University Press. 282–300.

People's Republic of China. 2000. *Tabulation of the 2000 Population Census of the People's Republic of China* Vol. 2. National Bureau of Statistics.

———. 2002a. *China Statistical Yearbook*.

———. 2002b. *Tabulation on the 2000 Population Census of the People's Republic of China* 2 (Tables 4–4, 4–4c).

———. 2002c. *Tabulation of the 2000 Population Census of the People's Republic of China*. 3. Beijing: National Bureau of Statistics.

———. 2003. *China Labour Statistical Yearbook 2003*. Beijing: Ministry of Labor and Social Security.

Peterson, P. G. 1999. *Gray Dawn: How the Coming Age Wave Will Transform America—and the World*. New York: Times Books.

Proterba, J. 2004. "The Impact of Population Aging on Financial Markets." *NBER Working Papers* 10851.

Purohil, B. C. 2003. "Policymaking for Diversity among the Aged in India." *Journal of Aging and Social Policy* 15(4): 49–79.

Saito Y., X. Qiao, and S. Jitapunkul. 2003. "Health Expectancy in Asian Countries." J. M. Robine, C. Jagger, C. D. Mathers, E. M. Crimmins, and R. M. Suzman, eds. *Determining Health Expectancies*. Chichester: John Wiley & Sons. 289–317.

Song Xiaowu, ed. 2001. *Perfect the Pension System*. Beijing: Enterprise Management Publishing House. [in Chinese]

United Nations. 2000. *Replacement Migration: Is It a Solution to Declining and Aging Populations?* New York: ECOSOC Population Division. March.

———. 2003. World Population Prospects: the 2003 Revision and World Urbanization Prospects. New York: ECOSOC Population Division. Online at: http://esa.un.org/unpp accessed 19 April 2005.

———. 2004. World Population Prospects: the 2004 Revision and World Urbanization Prospects. New York: ECOSOC Population Division.

United States Social Security Administration. 2004a. Annual Statistical Supplement 2003. March.

———. 2004b. Old Age Survivor and Disability Insurance (OASDI) Trustees Report. 24 March.

United States Census Bureau. 2004. International Data Base.

Wang, X. 2004. "China's Pension Reform and Capital Market Development." *China and World Economy* 12(3):3–16.

West, L. A. and D. Goodkind. 2003. "Population Aging and Social Safety Nets in China: Factors and Trends Affecting Policy Trade-Offs." Unpublished paper. USCB, International Programs Center. April.

Wilson, C. and G. Pison. 2004. "La majorité de l'humanité vit dans un pays où la fécondité est basse." *Population et Sociétés* 405. October.

World Bank. 1997. *Old Age Security: Pension Reform in China*. Washington.

———. 2001. *India: The Challenge of Old Age Insurance Security*. Report 22034-IN. 5 April.

———. 2003. *World Development Indicators 2003 CD-ROM*. Washington.

———. 2004. *World Development Indicators 2004 CD-ROM*. Washington.

World Economic Forum. 2004. *The Global Competitiveness Report 2004–2005*. Hampshire: Palgrave Macmillan.

Zhang, G. and Z. Zhao. 2005. "China's Fertility Puzzle: Data Collection and Data Use in the Last Two Decades." Paper presented at Annual Meeting of Population Association of America. Philadelpia, PA. 1 April.

CHAPTER 3.3

Emerging Market Crises and Crisis Resolution: A Decade of Experience

NOURIEL ROUBINI, Stern School of Business, New York University, and Roubini Global Economics

BRAD SETSER, Global Economic Governance Programme, Oxford University

Introduction

Severe crises in emerging market economies have been a recurring feature of the last ten years. The trail begins in Mexico at the end of 1994, and ends in Brazil in 2002, with stops in Thailand, Korea, Indonesia, Malaysia, Russia, Brazil, Turkey, and Argentina along the way. And that list does not include the crises in smaller economies, such as Ecuador, Ukraine, Uruguay, and the Dominican Republic.

A floating currency is no guarantee against crisis. Ask anyone in Brazil in 2002. But it is also true that most recent crises have been marked by the collapse of an exchange rate peg, whether a soft peg or a currency board. Industrial countries have often been able to let their currencies float, reduce domestic interest rates, and move on after being forced off a peg. Consider the United Kingdom's experience in 1992, after the pound was forced out of Europe's exchange rate mechanism. Emerging economies are not so lucky, as currency crises in emerging economies have usually been associated with severe banking, corporate, or sovereign payment crises.

By the standards of advanced economies, the output contractions that typically accompanied these crises were extraordinarily steep: falls of 5 percent of GDP were common, and falls of 10 percent of GDP or more occurred in the worst crises. Repeated financial crises and sharp drops in output are the antithesis of sustained economic growth. Large falls in output also led to sharp increases in poverty. In some cases, financial ties with the rest of the world were interrupted, with an enduring impact on the country's capacity to attract foreign capital to finance future development. In other cases, the domestic financial system shut down temporarily—an enormously disruptive effect. Countries often avoided a domestic financial system meltdown only by means of costly government bailouts, which continue to be a substantial drain on the country's public finances. That is why it is important that countries avoid policies which contribute to the risk of a financial crisis, and why the international community must strive to encourage countries to operate with large enough financial cushions to absorb shocks.

But it would be unrealistic to expect crises to simply disappear. Emerging economies, almost by definition, often finance themselves in ways that generate an ongoing risk of crisis, whether from dependence on short maturity debt, foreign currency debt, external debt, or all three. They lack the deep reserves of policy credibility that allow advanced economies to follow irresponsible policies for a while, and then to make the needed adjustments gradually, without precipitating a deep crisis. Thus, the international community must be prepared to respond effectively when a crisis does arise.

When a country has lost access to international capital markets and, in some cases, is close to running out of foreign exchange reserves, the International Monetary

179

Fund (IMF)—and the G7 countries that put up the lion's share of the IMF's financial resources—face two broad choices: the first takes the form of a rescue loan—typically from the IMF—enabling the country to make payments on at least those hard currency debts which fall due immediately, with the hope that the country will use the reprieve to take steps to correct its underlying macroeconomic problems. If all goes well, money starts flowing into the country again, allowing the country to rebuild its reserves and repay the IMF quickly. The second choice is to encourage the country to ask its creditors to roll over, or reschedule, their maturing claims, reducing the pressure on the country's foreign exchange reserves. The maturing claims can be obligations of the government (e.g. a sovereign bond) or cross-border loans to private borrowers (most often banks) in the crisis country. In either case, convincing private creditors to defer payment typically requires at least the implicit threat of default.[1]

There is no magic bullet. No attractive option for providing a country with emergency financing while it takes steps to right itself. IMF loans—termed *bailouts* by their critics—are given to help the country honor its contractual commitment to pay its debts. But they also help the country's creditors, particularly those who are lucky enough to have claims coming due soon after the country gets the rescue loan. Former Treasury Secretary Robert Rubin has said that he would have preferred not to lend even a nickel (five US cents) to bail out private creditors. He also commented that it is often hard to help a country—or to avoid a default that spills over and damages other countries—without helping the country's lenders as well. In the section of his memoirs describing the decision to lend to Mexico, Rubin wrote "Alan [Greenspan], Larry [Summers] and I all opposed making the holders of tesobonos[2] whole. But we concluded—I think rightly—that Mexico couldn't be rescued without the side effect of helping some investors."[3]

A *bail-in*—either an agreement by creditors to roll over their short-term claims, or a formal debt restructuring—can also give a country some time to right itself. But this requires that the country, with the implicit backing of the IMF, break its contractual promise to pay creditors in full and on time. Nothing guarantees that the country will be able to reach agreement with its creditors on a consensual rollover agreement or restructuring to avoid an outright default. Even a successful debt restructuring risks triggering a broader loss of confidence in the country's currency and in its banking system. And to those opposing any official intervention, it should be borne in mind that IMF or G7 efforts to catalyze a consensual restructuring constitute a form of market interference that is just as bad, if not worse, than large bailouts.

Many look to the corporate bond market and dream of a world where sovereign governments—or, for that matter, the banking system of a major emerging-market economy—can go under without drawing the IMF into either the country's decision to default or the often messy restructuring process that follows. Letting nature take its course is an alternative to both an IMF bailout and an IMF-sanctioned bail-in.

However, such an approach is hardly realistic. It is difficult to limit access to IMF financing unless you are willing to have bad things happen, and in large countries which are of global financial importance (such as Brazil), or which are of strategic importance to key G7 countries (such as Turkey). As Table 1 shows, it has proven far easier for the official sector to say that it intends to limit access to *large amounts* of IMF financing, than to carry through with its calls to *stop* large IMF loans to crisis countries altogether. IMF lending peaked in 2003, after the Bush Administration approved large loans to Argentina, Turkey, Brazil, and Uruguay, not after the Asian crisis (see Figure 1).

Crisis prevention is a bit like motherhood and apple pie: it is hard not to like. But it is unlikely to offer a true alternative to continued work on crisis resolution. Unless emerging market crises are truly and simply a product of initial growing pains—associated with the first stage of financial integration into modern global financial markets—it behooves the IMF, the G7, and others, who have a stake in the health of the global financial system, to expect that emerging economies will continue to get into trouble and seek help, plan accordingly, and constantly ask if the right policies and institutions are in place to handle future crises.

Our critique of the current policy approach and our suggestions for improvement are grounded in our assessment of the reasons why emerging economies have gotten into trouble, and the reasons why some IMF rescues—bailouts—have worked better than others. It is to this experience that we now turn.

Have emerging economies put crises behind them?

Few emerging economies have fond memories of the years between 1995 and 2002. Almost every major emerging economy had to turn to the IMF for help during this time. Two of the biggest issuers of international bonds, Argentina and Russia, defaulted on at least some of their international debt. Mexico, Korea, Brazil, and Turkey were only spared default on their domestic dollar bonds, their international bonds, and cross-border bank loans through large loans from the IMF, and, in the case of Mexico, from the United States government as well. These financial crises had serious economic consequences. As Table 2 shows, only two countries, Russia in 1998 and Brazil in 1999, avoided sharp falls in output.[4]

Most emerging economies experienced a crisis. But that does not mean that all countries experience exactly

Table 1: IMF financing[1]

	Amount agreed			Total disbursed			In the first year		
	as percent of quota	in US$ billion	as percent of GDP	as percent of quota	in US$ billion	as percent of GDP	as percent of quota	in US$ billion	as percent of GDP
Mexico	688	18.0	4.4	500	13.1	3.2	500	13.1	3.2
Thailand	505	3.9	2.2	470	3.7	2.0	366	2.8	1.6
Indonesia	557	11.3	5.0	555	11.3	5.0	245	5.0	2.2
Korea[2]	1,938	20.8	4.0	1,802	19.4	3.7	1,757	18.9	3.6
Brazil 1998	600	18.4	2.3	436	13.4	1.7	363	11.1	1.4
Russia	186	15.1	3.5	63	5.1	1.2	63	5.1	1.2
Argentina	800	22.1	7.8	461	12.7	4.5	461	12.7	4.5
Brazil 2001	400	15.6	3.1	375	14.6	2.9	261	10.2	2.0
Brazil 2002	752	29.3	5.7	567	22.1	4.3	566	22.1	4.3
Brazil combined[3]	900	35.1	6.9	770	30.1	5.9	340	13.3	2.3
Uruguay	694	2.7	14.5	560	2.2	11.7	434	1.7	9.1
Turkey 1999–01	1,560	20.7	10.4	1,218	16.2	8.1	900	11.9	6.0
Turkey 2002	1,330	17.6	8.9	1,154	14.8	7.7	1,030	13.7	6.9
Turkey combined[3]	2,548	33.8	17.0	1,709	23.1	11.4	900	11.9	6.0

Notes:

[1] Special Drawing Rights (SDR) are converted into dollars at the SDR/US$ exchange rate at the time of the initial program.

[2] Korea's quota was unusually small in relation to its GDP.

[3] Combined programs = outstanding disbursement plus new commitment; however, some of the new program was intended to refinance the IMF's existing exposure.

Source: IMF, 2005, online at: http://www.imf.org/external/fin.htm

Figure 1: IMF loans outstanding in US$ billion

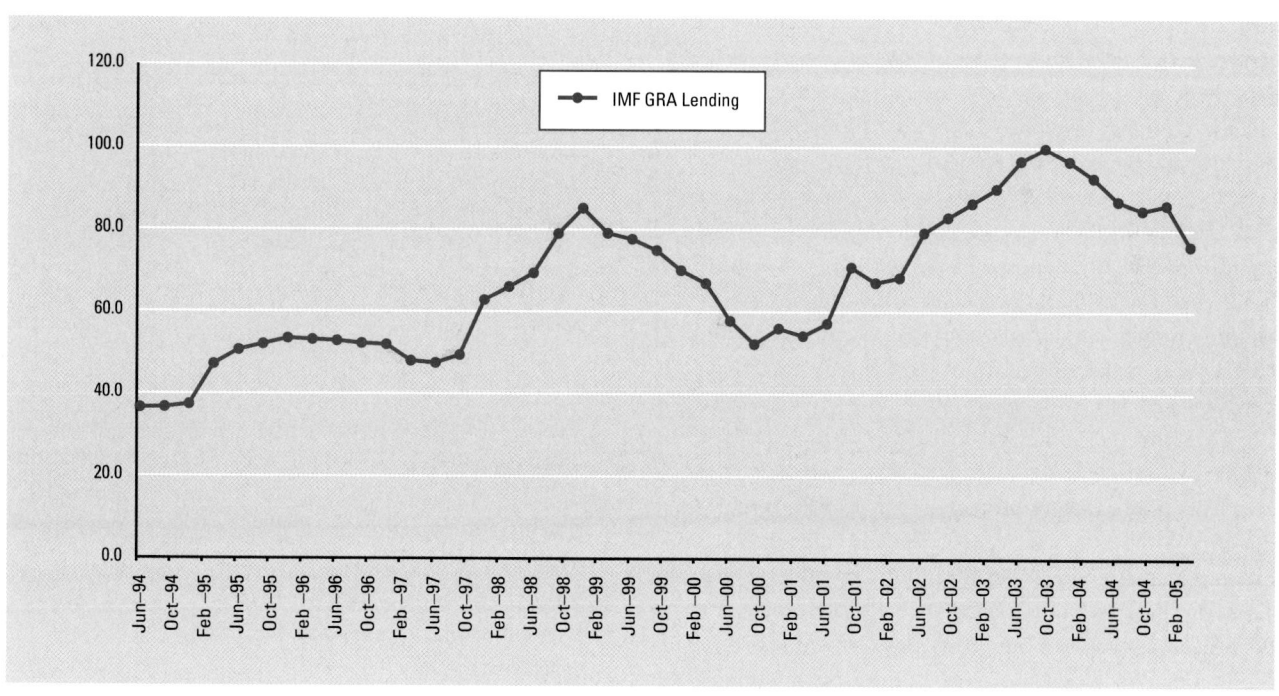

Source: IMF, 2005, online at http://www.imf.org/external/fin.htm and http://www.imf.org/external/np/tre/tad/extcred1.cfm

Table 2: Output contraction during financial crises

Country	Date crisis began	Change in real GDP (percent)
Argentina	Dec 01	−12.8
Brazil	Jan 99	3.8
Ecuador	Sep 98	−6.9
Indonesia	Aug 97	−16.5
Korea	Nov 97	−8.4
Malaysia	Aug 97	−8.9
Mexico	Dec 94	−8.0
Russia	Aug 98	−2.3
Thailand	Jul 97	−13.4
Turkey	Feb 01	−7.4

Note: Definition of real GDP change: a) For countries with output contraction, it is the percent change of the lowest output level during the two-year post-crisis period from the pre-crisis output level; b) For countries without a post-crisis output contraction, it is the percent increase in the output level one year after the crisis from the pre-crisis output level.

Sources: Data Resources Inc (2005); IMF (2005), online at: http://www.imf.org/external/fin.htm

the same kind of crisis. In Thailand, Korea, and Indonesia, private banks, financial institutions, and corporations experienced the most acute payment difficulties when their crisis struck. This is the mirror image of the fact that the external borrowing of private banks and firms, not the government, had financed current account deficits in Asia before the crisis. In Mexico, Russia, Brazil, Ecuador, Argentina, and Turkey, the government's own borrowing—often in conjunction with current account deficits linked in part to overvalued pegged exchange rates—was an important element of their financial difficulties. In some cases, the country had difficulty paying its domestic debt, often held principally by the local banking system. In other cases, the problem was a country's international bonds. Uruguay combined a banking system vulnerable to cross border and domestic runs with a heavily indebted government.

By any standard, and particularly in comparison with the preceding five or six years, the past two years have been very good for most emerging economies. Apart from the Dominican Republic, no country has fallen into crisis. Emerging economies are growing quite rapidly, in many cases for the first time in a long time. Private capital is once again seeking out opportunities in emerging economies. In the spring of 2005, spreads on emerging market debt are very low, suggesting that the financial markets believe that there is little risk of default.

No doubt, many countries have learned from their crises and taken important steps to reduce their financial vulnerabilities:

- Most emerging economies outside central Europe now have current account surpluses. Emerging economies with high levels of debt are generally run-

ning substantial primary surpluses, and their overall fiscal deficits have started to fall.

- Emerging economies have recognized the risks of holding too few reserves. Almost all emerging economies now have more reserves than short-term external debt. Few are likely to repeat Thailand's mistake by trying to finance persistent current account deficits exclusively with short-term external borrowing. If anything, many emerging economies are now adding to their already substantial reserves at too rapid a pace.[5] Rapid reserve growth risks leading to rapid domestic credit growth, and eventually a domestic financial crisis.

- Most emerging economies recognize that access to external capital markets is neither a given nor a constant; emerging economies are more likely to have access to external financing in good times than in bad. They have, in general, not responded to current low spreads by embarking on a new borrowing spree. Latin America, for example, has historically made up for a shortage of domestic savings by importing savings from abroad, and has run chronic current account deficits. Good times have coincided with easy access to financing. Yet today, Latin America as a whole is running a substantial current account surplus, helped in no small measure by the surge in commodity prices. Right now, only emerging economies in central Europe are running large current account deficits. In some cases, those deficits are financed largely by direct investment from the rest of Europe, but other transition economies also have large fiscal deficits, creating concerns about the sustainability of their "twin deficits."

- Many emerging economies have recognized that fixed exchange rates are risky, not least because expectations that the exchange rate will not change lead to over-reliance on foreign currency denominated debt. Or they may have concluded that overvalued fixed exchange rates are risky. Those emerging economies now intervening heavily in the foreign exchange markets generally have current account surpluses, not deficits, and they are buying foreign currency to try to keep their exchange rate from appreciating.

- Greater emphasis has been placed on developing markets for local currency denominated debt. Just as Thailand illustrates the dangers of short-term external borrowing, Argentina serves as an important cautionary tale, illustrating the dangers of domestic dollarization.

On the other hand, it is difficult for any emerging economy to get into trouble in the favorable environment of combined strong global growth, strong commodity prices—not just for oil—and very low interest rates in the United States, Europe, and Japan. While real improvements have been made over the past few years, real risks still remain.

It is certain that, as a group, emerging economies now have more reserves than they need. Yet not every individual country has all the reserves it needs. Some countries with little external debt and little domestic liability dollarization have large reserves, while other countries with high external debt and substantial liability dollarization have relatively small reserves. Both Brazil and Turkey, for example, retain large stocks of external debt relative to the reserves, especially since a meaningful portion of their reported reserves are borrowed from the IMF. Some smaller economies, such as Lebanon and the Philippines, also have significant external debts in relation to their reserves.

More importantly, even though emerging economies have brought their external debt loads down, the same cannot be said of their domestic debts. Domestic debt levels of emerging economies remain high across the board. Indeed, domestic debt levels remain too high in crisis-prone economies, such as Brazil, Turkey, Argentina, and Uruguay, and they are rising elsewhere. Brazil and Turkey still have large amounts of short-term domestic debt that they must continuously rollover.

Recent sobering work by the IMF suggests that emerging economies often default or seek to restructure their debt, at levels well below those that can be sustained by advanced industrial economies. That is the core conclusion of Rogoff, Reinhardt, and Savastano's work on *debt intolerance*.[6] Doubts about the borrower's capacity and willingness to pay can be self-reinforcing: investors demand high real rates, lend for short-term, or lend only foreign currency. In turn, high real rates increase the real burden of the debt, making it harder to sustain political support for the demanding adjustments required for full payment. The debt levels of many key economies will have to fall further, before they can be taken off the watch list.

Nor have all emerging markets learned the lesson that it is dangerous to stuff their banking systems with government paper. India, for example, continues to finance large deficits—close to 10 percent of GDP in recent years—by selling significant amounts of debt to domestic banks. Even in countries where the risks for the banking system of large holdings of government debt are obvious and well-known, as in Turkey and Lebanon, it takes time to change the government's creditor base.

Even countries with reserves to protect against anything, to use the words of the IMF's chief economist, "short of the apocalypse,"[7] often have other kinds of problems. China's government, for example, has yet to foot

the bill to clean up the legacy of bad loans that its state-owned banks made in the 1990s. Those costs could be massive. Standard & Poor's recently estimated that the cost of cleaning up two of the big four—admittedly, the two in the worst shape—could total US$190 billion.[8] More importantly, that calculation focused primarily on the cost of cleaning up past bad loans. If a substantial share of the loans extended in the 2003–04 credit boom ends up going bad, as history suggests is likely, the costs of cleaning up these two banks—and the banking system more generally—could be much higher.[9]

China's extensive foreign exchange reserves will not do much to reduce the bill her taxpayers will have to pay to clean up the banking system. Indeed, China's extensive foreign exchange reserves could well be the source of additional losses for the country's taxpayers. To prevent rising reserves from leading to an even more rapid expansion of its money base, China's central bank, the People's Bank of China, has to sell large sums of domestic renminbi-denominated debt. This process is called sterilization. But it, too, comes at a cost. Once the renminbi[10] is revalued, the central bank's dollar holdings will be worth less, in renminbi terms, while its liabilities, which are in remninbi, will remain constant. Since China's reserves are quite large in relation to its GDP, the potential losses are significant, particularly since China is now adding more than 10 percent of GDP to its reserves annually.

This is one example of how risks evolve over time. China's domestic financial system has many of the same vulnerabilities found elsewhere in Asia before 1997: a massive credit and real estate boom, and over-investment. But unlike the Asian economies that got into trouble in 1997, China has large reserves, and relatively little short-term foreign currency debt and capital controls. Unlike East Asia in 1997–98, a financial crisis in China would not take the form of an external debt payment crisis. Capital inflows into China have not been used to finance current account deficits, but rather to finance an exceptionally rapid increase in reserves. Yet, like many Asian crisis economies, China has experienced a domestic credit boom. It has the domestic vulnerabilities of many of the Asian crisis economies, but without the external vulnerability.

Similarly, emerging economies, as a whole, face a different set of risks from those of the halcyon days of the mid 1990s. On the one hand, they have less direct exposure to global capital markets. On the other, they continue to be exposed to changes in the global economic cycle, as well as to sharp swings in commodity prices. A global slowdown could make continuing high levels of domestic debt feel like a greater burden, thereby testing the country's domestic political commitment to the kind of sustained adjustment needed to pay off large amounts of high-yielding debt. Nor can runs on vulnerable and still fragile banking systems be ruled out.

Fair or unfair, emerging economies have to hold themselves to a higher standard of economic policy than advanced economies, at least until their institutions have matured and their credibility built up. They are more exposed to global shocks. But in many ways this only increases the rewards of sound economic management. Chile steered clear of large fiscal deficits, paid attention to the composition of its external debt, avoided too much short-term debt, and developed institutions to help manage the boom-bust cycle in copper, its main export. Asia's crisis led copper prices to tumble and led to a slowdown in Chile, but it did not lead to a sharp crisis.

Lessons learned from 21st century financial crises

Larry Summers liked to call Mexico the first "21st century financial crisis." He was picking up on a phrase first used by Newt Gingrich,[11] marking a relatively rare instance of bipartisan agreement in the United States, if only on the right name for a new phenomenon. To Summers, the term "21st century crisis" referred to Mexico's difficulties paying traded securities (tesobonos) rather than syndicated bank loans, and also to the risk that a sudden shift in investor sentiment could trigger a cascading collapse of confidence. Prior to its crisis, Mexico had attracted large capital inflows from private investors to finance a large and growing current account deficit. Yet in late 1994 and early 1995, it faced massive capital outflows, which overwhelmed the country's reserves, and would have led to a massive default, but for the US-led rescue loan.

Mexico's crisis did not prove to be an isolated event. It was followed by crises in Asia, Russia, and Brazil. The largely unexpected collapse of previously high-flying Asian economies made the reform of the international financial architecture the subject du jour. And the attention paid to emerging market crises only intensified after Russia's default triggered a chain of market reactions, humbling an enormous hedge fund, Long-Term Capital Management, and, at least for a short period, seeming to threaten the basic stability of almost every major financial market.

The first set of financial crises that actually occurred in the 21st century—beginning in late 2000 with IMF programs in Argentina and Turkey, and continuing in Brazil and Uruguay in 2002—attracted far less attention. Unlike Clinton's, the Bush administration has not put forward its handling of financial crisis as a central part of its foreign policy legacy. But that does not mean that the era of large bailouts has disappeared. If anything, the countries that have had difficulties since 2001 have tended to receive more IMF money than the countries that got into trouble before. As Figure 1 shows, overall IMF lending peaked in 2003.

We think it is possible to draw several lessons from the international community's experience managing 21st century financial crises:

- Large rescue packages can work, in the right circumstances;
- The odds of success are greater when initial debt is modest;
- Sometimes it is better to use money borrowed from the IMF to soften the blow associated with a debt restructuring, rather than trying to avoid it altogether;
- Crisis resolution has not been all bailout and no bail-in.

Large IMF rescue packages can work, but only in the right circumstances

This is the lesson of Mexico, which received more money than had previously been the norm. The money was needed, because Mexico blew its reserves defending an untenable exchange rate peg, and had enormous sums of dollar-linked debt coming due. Rather than restructure this debt, it used the funds from the IMF to pay off the debt. This strategy worked. Mexico was not spared a recession, but it was spared the more severe recession and cascading domestic financial failure, which would have ensued had it defaulted altogether. Capital soon returned, and Mexico was able to repay its large loan quite quickly. That is how it should be: the basic theory behind lender-of-last-resort-style IMF lending is that in the face of a confidence crisis, countries need more money than before, but for less time.

Mexico, Korea and Brazil all received relatively large IMF loans—or bailouts. All had relatively low levels of debt, both domestic and external. All got into trouble because they held onto a fixed exchange rate for too long, running down their reserves in the process, leaving themselves too few reserves relative to their remaining dollar-denominated debts. Their fundamental financial problem was too few reserves, not too much debt—although Brazil had slightly more debt than the others, even in 1998. All repaid the IMF relatively quickly.

The odds of success are greater if countries receiving bailouts have modest initial debt

As Table 3 shows, Argentina, Brazil in 2001–2002, Turkey, and Uruguay all had much higher levels of debt than Mexico, Korea, and even Brazil in 1998. The difficulties facing these countries went beyond simple illiquidity, that is, too few reserves relative to their short-term debt. There was a significant risk that all four had too much debt relative to their capacity to sustain the kinds of policy adjustments required for payment. All four countries were illiquid without an immediate infusion of foreign exchange, but also potentially insolvent without sustained adjustment. In

Table 3: How quickly IMF (and bilateral first line) loans were disbursed and repaid

	Peak disbursement US$ billion (percent of GDP)		Quarters to reach peak	Quarters to repay half of peak disbursement	External debt pre-crisis (percent of GDP)	Fiscal debt pre-crisis (percent of GDP)
Mexico	27.6	(6.8)	4	9	34	31
Thailand	11.2	(6.2)	12	17*	60	5
Indonesia	10.8	(4.7)	13	—	43	24
Korea	19.4	(3.7)	4	8	32	12
Russia	5.1	(1.2)	2	4	35	52
Brazil (1998–99)	17.5	(2.2)	3	7	25	40
Turkey (2000–02)	23.1	(11.6)	13	—	57	56
Argentina	13.7	(4.8)	4	—	51	45
Uruguay	2.1	(11.3)	8	—	81	38
Brazil (2001–02)	30.1	(5.9)	9	—	44	65

* Thailand IMF exposure peaked after nine quarters, and it repaid half of that exposure after 17 quarters, by which time, it had not repaid half of its bilateral lending; we do not have data indicating Thailand's bilateral repayments after the end of 2001.

Notes: Moody's debt numbers for Brazil are higher than other sources; the IMF shows Brazil's 1997 (pre-crisis) debt to GDP as 35 percent rather than 40 percent, and its 2000 (pre-crisis) debt to GDP at 49 percent rather than 65 percent.

Sources: IMF, 2005, online at: http://www.imf.org/external/fin.htm; United States Treasury, various years; Moody's, 2004

these cases, large-scale IMF loans were used not only to cover a temporary shortage of liquidity, but to buy the time needed for the country to grow out of its debt trouble.

To date, this strategy has worked in some cases, notably in Brazil and Turkey, but not in others, notably in Argentina. It failed in Argentina, at least in part, because the country was trying to avoid exchange rate adjustment as well as default, while Brazil and Turkey were trying to avoid default but not exchange rate adjustment. Moreover, since Argentina's debts were almost all in dollars and its exchange rate was significantly overvalued, Argentina was in much deeper trouble than many had realized, if they only looked at its debt-to-GDP ratio in 2000 or 2001. But even those countries in which the strategy has worked have generally needed large sums, and have not been able to repay the IMF very rapidly. Turkey received far more money from the IMF than did Mexico from the IMF and the US combined (relative to its GDP). And, as shown in Figure 2, it is paying those funds back much more slowly. Four and a half years after first receiving large-scale support from the IMF, Turkey still owed the IMF roughly US$20 billion (nearly 10 percent of its pre-crisis GDP). Realistically, Turkey will not fully repay the IMF before 2009. Rather than getting a very large short-term loan, Turkey received a very large medium- to long-term loan.

In some cases, the IMF should try to soften the blow associated with a debt restructuring, rather than trying to avoid one altogether

Most crisis countries have received a substantial IMF loan—some more substantial than others—and were given a chance to see if the combination of money and

economic policy changes allowed the country to avoid a major, potentially disruptive debt restructuring. Indeed, in many, though not all, cases, the official sector has often responded to a failed first program with a much larger second infusion of funds. In some cases, the combination of policy adjustment and IMF financing worked, and the country was able to avoid a debt restructuring. But in other cases, notably in Russia and Argentina, it did not.

However, there is an important difference between Russia in 1998 and Argentina in 2001. In the case of Russia, lending was cut off rather quickly in 1998, well before most of the IMF's funds had actually been disbursed. In Argentina, however, the official sector hesitated to pull the plug. IMF money kept flowing in long after it was clear that the initial approach was not working. The decision to augment the IMF's initial US$15 billion loan to Argentina with another US$8 billion loan in late summer 2001 was an obvious mistake.[12] The small augmentation of summer 2001 had no chance of working, left the IMF with additional exposure when Argentina collapsed, and damaged the IMF's credibility inside Argentina, by signaling continued IMF support for policies that failed.

Indeed, the initial decision to lend to Argentina in the absence of any exchange rate adjustment can certainly be questioned. Politically, it was probably impossible to insist that Argentina move off its currency board from the very beginning. But it almost certainly would have been better to have pulled the plug on the initial loan, and adopt a different strategy in the spring of 2001, once it became clear that Argentina was mired in a deep economic slump. The IMF had plenty of opportunities to stop lending without a change of strategy. Argentina consistently missed its fiscal targets in the spring of 2001.

Figure 2: IMF and US bilateral (ESF) loans outstanding: Mexico and Turkey

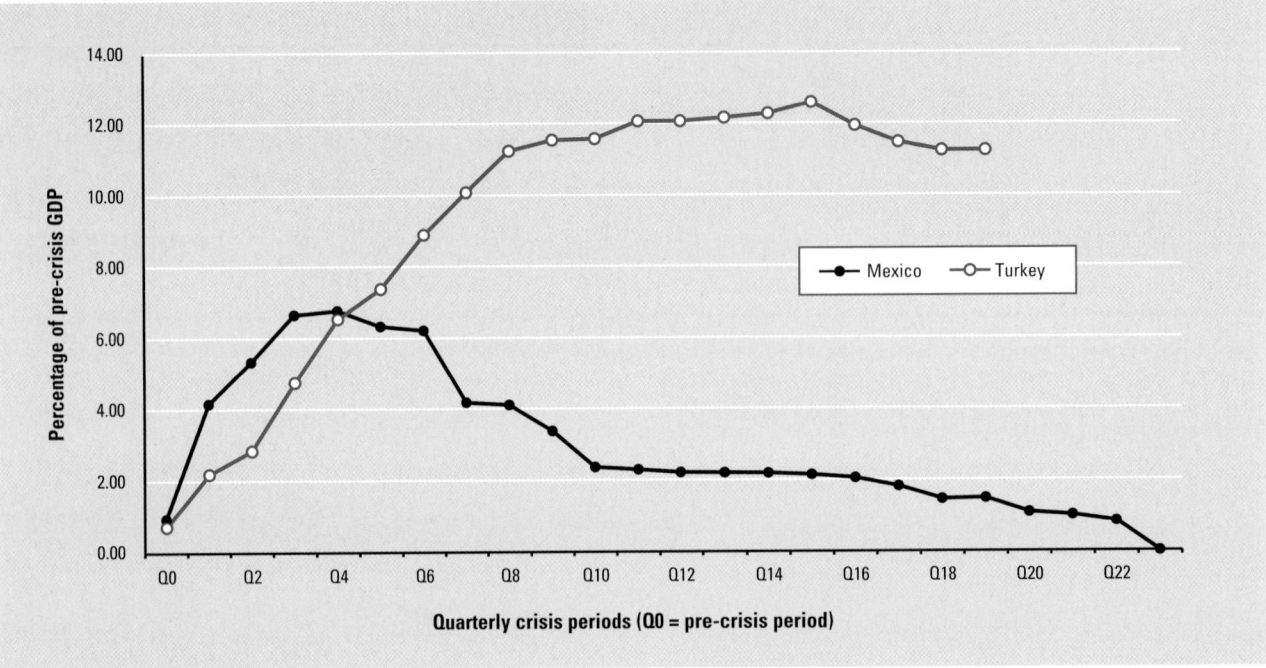

Sources: IMF (2005), online at: http://www.imf.org/external/np/tre/tad/exfin1.cfm; United States Treasury, various dates, including 1997, online at: http://www.federalreserve.gov/pubs/bulletin/1997/1997032.pdf and http://www.federalreserve.gov/pubs/bulletin/1998/199803forex.pdf.

No option available to Argentina in 2000 could have avoided a significant fall in output. Recognizing reality and letting the exchange rate adjust was going to be painful no matter what. Argentina's overvalued exchange rate had masked its true debt burden. But instead, Argentina ended up receiving a significant loan to support an attempt to avoid both real debt restructuring and any exchange rate adjustment, but nothing to support the transition to a sustainable real exchange rate and a more sustainable debt profile. A better policy would have used the IMF's lending capacity to limit the negative fallout from exiting the currency board, and from the unavoidable debt restructuring. The IMF's funds—along with any of Argentina's own remaining reserves—could have been used to try to avoid a bank run, and to limit the overshooting of the peso.

Such an approach would also have left the IMF in a stronger position to negotiate a framework to guide the macroeconomic policies that Argentina adopted after its default, and to push the country to put forward a restructuring plan quickly. Instead, the IMF was forced to try to link its conditionality in 2002 and 2003 to loans that did nothing more than prevent Argentina from falling into arrears on the IMF, the World Bank and the Inter-American Development Bank. Partially, as a result, the IMF ended up settling for a program that failed to set a fiscal policy path to guide the subsequent debt restructuring.

This is not just a theoretical option. After several small loans failed to restore confidence, Uruguay received a large loan from the IMF that allowed the central bank to act as a lender-of-last-resort in dollars to the banking system. It therefore helped Uruguay to avoid both a domestic and an external bank holiday. After the bank run subsided, the government's own debt was restructured through a maturity-extending bond exchange. One important caution though: Uruguay received a loan equal to about 15 percent of its GDP. That is far more than the IMF can provide to major emerging economies. And it is far more than the IMF should have provided to a country as indebted as Uruguay.

Crisis resolution is not all bailout and no bail-in
The shift from syndicated bank loans to securities traded on the open market has not precluded successful debt restructuring. Most countries in crisis have received an initial jolt of cash, allowing those creditors lucky enough to have claims coming due at the right moment to get out scot-free. However, the official sector has never put nearly enough money on the table to let all private creditors off the hook, recognizing that the citizens of the crisis country typically have far more money invested in the crisis country than do international investors.

In Korea, the IMF's initial program failed to prevent banks from continuing to withdraw credit. But rather than responding simply by lending Korea more money, the IMF and the G7 developed a new approach, and helped Korea to organize a coordinated rollover or maturing short-term debt. They then drew up a formal rescheduling plan that extended over the full term of maturity of Korea's debt. In cases like that of Korea, the initial IMF program was all bailout and no-bail-in, but the initial program was quickly superseded by a new program, built around a debt rescheduling. In other cases, when the initial IMF program failed, it was not necessarily replaced by a new IMF program built around a debt restructuring. But since the amount of financing available from the IMF fell far short of what would have been needed for all private creditors to get out, private creditors retained substantial exposure to the country when the IMF program failed. In those cases too, private creditors and investors ended up restructuring their claims, often on terms that implied large losses.

Argentina, for example, drew on IMF funds—along with its own reserves—to help repay US$6 billion of principal on its international sovereign bonds during the course of 2001.[13] But it still had nearly US$90 billion of bonds outstanding at the end of the year—or would have, had it not converted some of the bonds held by Argentina's domestic banking system into loans. A sizable share of those loans were converted into pesos, and effectively restructured immediately after the default. But Argentina still had US$80 billion of bonds to restructure in its 2005 exchange. Clearly, IMF financing did not let most investors get out of Argentina without taking losses.

Although syndicated bank loans remain important in other forms of cross-border financing, they have been superseded by bonds as the dominant vehicle for providing unsecured financing to emerging market sovereigns. Fortunately, bonds proved easier to restructure than many expected. Fears that dispersed bondholders would never be persuaded to give up their legal claims, and would tie down a sovereign seeking a restructuring in lengthy court battles have, by and large, not been borne out.[14] Pakistan, Ecuador, Ukraine, and Uruguay all convinced more than 90 percent of their bondholders to participate in their restructurings, and all but Uruguay obtained participation rates of well over 95 percent. Argentina initially attracted only about 75 percent of its bondholders into its exchange—a combination of poorly advised Italian retail investors and a few more sophisticated "vulture" investors held out. But recent court decisions suggest that those holdouts, who are intent on testing the court system will have trouble stopping payments on the new bonds, as their initial efforts to holdup the restructuring were rejected by the US courts.

Just because you say so (over and over) does not make it true

Recent crises have pushed the IMF into new roles and led it to disburse large sums to more heavily indebted countries—in relation to their GDP—than has been typical in the past. But we cannot look to recent policy statements from the G7 or the IMF's formal policy-making body, the International Monetary and Financial Committee, for any substantive discussion, illuminating how the international financial policy making elite will wrestle with such crises in the future.

The G7 has preferred to use its statements to signal that the era of big lending is over. Brazil may be a success story, but the G7 does not intend to replicate it. Rather, they have called on the IMF to return to its old lending limits. These limits would rule out Mexico- or Brazil-sized, let alone Turkey-sized rescues. The 2002 G7 statement is typical: "We are prepared to limit official lending to normal access limits, except when circumstances justify an exception … it is becoming clearer that official sector support is being limited. Limiting official sector lending and developing private lending are essential parts of our action plan."[15] The thrust is pretty clear, even with the poorly defined "exceptional circumstances" loophole. G7 policy statements also reflect a belief, expressed most strongly by former US Treasury Undersecretary John Taylor,[16] that collective action clauses in international bonds will both help to eliminate the need for large IMF bailouts, and reduce the need for the IMF to guide a country through a major sovereign debt restructuring.

Unfortunately, both the call for a return to traditional lending limits and the belief that bond clauses will let the official sector successfully disengage from sovereign debt restructuring represent attempts to escape reality. Bond clauses will not reduce demand for IMF bailouts. Why? Because bond payments have not been the main source of financial pressure in the major bailout cases. Bonds were at the center of only one out of the eight crises that have led to "exceptional" IMF lending. Even in Argentina—the bond crisis par excellence—a domestic bank run put far more pressure on the country's reserves than payments on maturing long-term bonds. Shorter-term debts usually cause more trouble. Nor will bond clauses make a sovereign restructuring smooth and financially uneventful. Such clauses will not magically eliminate the risk that a restructuring will trigger a run on the banks or a run on the currency, nor will they help the country and its creditors reach agreement on the amount of fiscal effort the country should make to pay interest on its bonds.

For all the talk of the need to limit the IMF's role, it has, in practice, expanded, since IMF bailouts are used to address a range of problems well beyond a short-term need for liquidity created by the withdrawal of external credit. IMF bailouts are being used increasingly to try to save indebted economies from the pain of any government debt restructuring—often, to be fair, in return for very significant fiscal effort. Increasingly, the IMF is being used not only to address financial difficulties from the country's external debt, but to manage the pressures created by a large stock of domestic debt. Turkey and Brazil both have far larger stocks of domestic government debt than international bonds. And international bonds are not always held only by external investors: domestic Argentines held 50 percent or more of Argentina's "international" bonds at the end of 2001. In Turkey, the IMF is effectively bailing out Turkish bank depositors, as well as international investors. In Argentina and Uruguay, the IMF provided the hard currency needed to enable those countries to act as a domestic lender of last resort to a dollarized domestic banking system. Using the IMF to provide support for domestic debt markets, and also of the domestic financial system of many emerging markets is not inconsistent with its broad mandate: in a world of integrated capital markets and open capital accounts, domestic restructuring—let alone domestic default—would quickly give rise to an external payments crisis. But it does imply that the IMF's de facto role is evolving.

Talk of limiting IMF financing and returning to normal access limits has become a way of avoiding serious debate about the proper role of the IMF in a range of financial crises. Rather than assessing options for how to use the IMF's financial capacity, the official sector has preferred to pretend that the IMF's financial capacity will be taken off the table. Recent lending decisions have broadened the IMF's role in responding to emerging-market crises almost as significantly as the Clinton administration's decision to encourage the IMF to act as a surrogate lender of last resort in Mexico in 1995. Yet no effort has been made to define whether the IMF should expect to assume these roles in other crises.

This is unfortunate. After the IMF was stretched in new directions in Mexico, the United States worked with the rest of the G7 to articulate when larger than normal IMF lending was appropriate. As a result, new facilities were created, which were adapted to this kind of lending, and the resources available to the IMF expanded, so that it could play this role in future crises. No comparable effort has been made to articulate how the new uses of the IMF in countries like Turkey and Uruguay fit into a broader policy framework, or whether the IMF's response to these crises should be repeated, in the event that other countries encounter similar problems.

We need real, not fake, solutions

There are a few seductive siren songs that must be dismissed before we lay out the principles that we think should guide the world's approach to financial crises.

Limiting IMF financing to countries that pre-qualify because of their good policies

If the bar is set too high for qualifying for IMF financing, the countries that qualify will not want or need the IMF backstop. If the bar is set too low, the IMF will be on the hook to provide countries with almost unconditional financing in a crisis. Yet our knowledge of the sources of financial vulnerabilities is still not perfect. Remember that Argentina was considered something of a model reformer as recently as 1998, if not 1999. Most countries that get into trouble must change some key policies in order to get out of trouble. Pre-qualification suffers a second problem: it assumes that if the IMF sets out in advance a list of countries that are good and bad, the IMF and its political masters in the G7 countries can turn their back on "bad" countries. That is unrealistic, for we now know that no country is too big or too nuclear to fail: Argentina had more bonds than anyone else and it was allowed to default; Russia had more bombs than anyone else, and it too defaulted. But there are many countries that are too important not to at least try to help.

Adopting a policy of bailing bond markets rather than countries

Some have proposed that the IMF—or another agency—should offer to buy bonds in the secondary market in order to limit volatility in market prices. A few influential economists even proposed buying Argentina's bonds at 60 cents on the dollar in 2001.[17] This is not a good idea.

Countries in crisis need cold hard cash, not a floor under the price of their long-term debt. Rather than worrying much about the price of their long-term debt, troubled countries need cash to stabilize the foreign exchange market, to backstop the domestic banking system, and to make payments on short-term debt as it comes due. Sharp falls in the secondary market price of sovereign bonds are problems for the investors who bought the debt, but as long as the bonds are not about to come due, they are not an immediate problem for the country. Brazil's long-term bonds traded as low as 50 cents on the dollar in 2002. Their price recovered when Brazil recovered. Spending money to buy bonds from international investors, so they can get out of their losing positions does not do much to help the country in crisis. And it potentially exposes the agency buying the bonds—the IMF or other—to enormous risks. Buying Argentina's US$90 billion in international bonds at 60 cents on the dollar, as some suggested, would have cost US$54 billion, far more than the US$15 billion (US$10 billion net) the IMF actually lent to Argentina.

At the same time, the right approach to crisis is not simply to continue with the current de facto approach, and to institutionalize a policy of giving every country a lot of money to try to avoid exchange rate adjustment, debt restructuring, or both. That policy approach leads to the mistake that was made in Argentina: too much money was wasted trying to save the currency board, and to avoid a debt restructuring, leaving no money to try to soften the blow—particularly to the domestic financial system—that came with the necessary devaluation and restructuring.

Building blocks for a more sensible approach toward crisis resolution

What principles should guide a better approach to resolving emerging market crises? In our judgment, the core problems lie more in the system's software than in its hardware. That is good news. It is far easier to upgrade the software of the international system than to build the political support needed to create new hardware. The basic tools needed to respond to a wide range of crises generally exist. The core challenge is to use those tools better and to do a better job of adapting the available tools to different types of crises.

The current hardware can be divided into two types: hardware for providing emergency financing, and hardware for restructuring debts. The IMF is at the center of the architecture for providing financial support. Bilateral financing from the G7 fell by the wayside after the IMF's resources were increased in 1998. The absence of private sources of emergency financing is quite understandable: countries typically need official financing precisely because private creditors want to reduce their exposure to the crisis country. At present (2005), the IMF has the resources needed to provide rescue loans of about 5 percent of GDP to even large emerging economies like Brazil. That is about right: there should be a financial backstop behind countries, but it should not be so big that it protects both countries and investors from all risks.

The hardware for debt restructuring is a bit like the British constitution. It is not found in one place or in one single document. But the needed institutions are there. Multi-instrument debt-exchanges stand at the center of the debt restructuring architecture. These exchanges perform the core task of coordinating the restructuring of different instruments: every bondholder knows the terms offered to other bondholders in the exchange, which is supported by the evolving legal norms used to document sovereign bonds. The institutions for restructuring bonds and other traded securities are complemented by the official sector's capacity—a capacity that recently has been underused—to insist that a crisis country get agreement from its cross border bank creditors to rollover their claims. Such deals work best when the banks know that the official sector is monitoring their commitment. Particularly when the goal is to buy a country enough time to start to get its own house in order, the ability to limit the roll-off of short-term external debt can be central to crisis resolution.

But what about the software? The IMF should not try to treat all countries in the same way, whether by denying all countries access to large amounts of emergency financing, or by providing all countries with large amounts of financing to try to maintain their chosen exchange rate regime, and to make full payments on their debt. Rather, policymakers should strive to treat countries *in similar circumstances* in the same way.

Consequently, we recommend the following six building blocks as a framework for addressing modern emerging market financial crises:

1. *Recognition that not all emerging market crises—not even all crises marked by sudden swings in capital flows—are alike.* There is a huge difference between bailing out countries with modest debt levels, which have blown their reserves in defense of a fixed exchange rate (Mexico), and bailing out countries with large debt loads, which are on the verge of spiraling into a deep debt crisis (Turkey). If all goes well, countries like Mexico, which start off in a relatively strong position can repay the IMF relatively quickly. Yet even when everything goes well, countries like Turkey that go into their crisis with high levels of debt typically cannot repay the IMF quickly.

2. *The biggest problems in emerging market financial crises arise not from litigation by external creditors, but rather from spillovers between external financial distress and the domestic financial system.* The amount of attention that has been directed at reducing litigation from international sovereign bondholders during a debt restructuring has been disproportionate to the actual threat posed by such litigation.[18]

3. *Cash—foreign exchange borrowed from IMF—remains the most powerful tool at the disposal of the international community, both for trying to help countries with modest debt to avoid the risks intrinsic to any form of restructuring, and for helping to soften the blow associated with a debt restructuring when the latter is unavoidable.* The IMF is not going to return to its traditional lending limits the next time a major emerging economy encounters a crisis. It should adjust its policy framework accordingly. However, cash from the IMF only really works when it is backed by a real commitment from the crisis country to make necessary policy changes. Often those necessary changes include a change in exchange rate regime.

189

4. *Although IMF money is sometimes best used to help countries avoid any form of debt restructuring, it is sometimes better to use IMF money as a complement to, not a substitute for, a debt restructuring.* The IMF should select from three different responses:

- Acting as lender-of-last-resort-style financing to avoid any form of debt restructuring. The IMF is not a true lender-of-last-resort, but it can act as a surrogate. The hope is that by paying off some debt as it matures, the country will be able to quickly regain market confidence—so called "catalytic" financing. This kind of financing is most appropriate when a country's problems stem primarily from having run down its reserves, when its debt levels are low, and when its leadership has a (perhaps belated) commitment to the needed policy adjustments. Mexico is an example.

- Financing to backstop a maturity-extending debt restructuring. The restructuring buys the country time without letting creditors off the hook. The financing helps to prevent the restructuring from triggering runs out of the domestic banking system and the local currency. This kind of approach is most appropriate when it is clear that it will take several years for the country to dig itself out of its hole. Uruguay is a current example: its ability to carry off a successful sovereign restructuring hinged on its ability to draw on the IMF to provide a credible backstop for its domestic banking system.

- Financing to back a deep debt restructuring, when it is clear virtually from the outset that a restructuring is necessary to restore financial health. This is the approach that we believe should have been adopted in Argentina in early 2001.

Obviously, choosing between these options requires making hard up-front judgments, and it means telling some countries that the IMF will only help them if they are willing to seek a debt restructuring. Currently, the IMF usually tends to try lender-of-last-resort-style financing, i.e., providing a country with liquidity and hoping that the problem proves to be one of illiquidity. That is fine when it works. But it also means that the IMF will exhaust its lending capacity trying to avoid some unavoidable restructurings, leaving itself with limited influence over the debt-restructuring process.

5. *The IMF should not step aside when a debt restructuring is the right way through a crisis.* IMF lending during a debt restructuring does not need to be a giveaway to bondholders. There is a range of other possible uses of IMF funds during a debt restructuring: IMF lending can, with appropriate safeguards, be used to help backstop the domestic banking system, as happened in Uruguay, or to finance limited intervention in the foreign exchange market to avoid excessive falls in the currency. By putting money on the table—providing the analogue to debtor-in-possession (DIP) financing in the US corporate context—the IMF gains the leverage needed to help the country define a sensible macroeconomic course, and to push the country to quickly resolve its payments difficulties. Like climbers on Mount Everest, most countries going through debt restructuring need a Sherpa.

6. *The IMF's political masters should remember that the IMF is not the right tool for protecting the geopolitical interests of the G7.* If Turkey is not too strategically important to fail, it is at least too strategically important not to try to help. But that alone does not make it a good candidate for a large IMF bailout. At present, the IMF is simply not set up to lend 10 percent or more of GDP for 5 or more years to every country with debt-to-GDP ratios of around 80 percent and budget deficits of 10 percent of GDP. If a country requires large amounts of medium to long-term money—as Turkey clearly did in 2001—most of that money should come from the G7, not from the IMF.

Conclusions

To paraphrase Deep Throat's famous line during the Watergate scandal, we should "follow the money," in order to understand the key issues facing the IMF.[19] The IMF also has gone beyond helping countries manage a collapse of external confidence. It is now helping to backstop domestic banking systems, and finance domestic budget deficits, and increasingly provides emerging economies with medium- to long-term financing, as they undertake not only short-term financing, but adopt programs of medium- to long-term fiscal adjustment. These roles did not arise by accident; they emerged in response to real needs.

Looking ahead, it is not unrealistic to expect that the IMF will confront more crises of domestic confidence. Domestic debt levels remain high in many emerging economies. Open capital markets make it easier not only for foreign investors to pull their financing in times of stress, but also for domestic residents to shift their savings abroad.

Moreover, the IMF is likely to continue to have to make difficult calls about how best to deploy its financial resources. Larger debts usually translate directly or indirectly into large needs for emergency financing. IMF lending on the order of 5 or even 10 percent of a country's GDP brings more financial force to bear, if a country's debt to GDP ratio is around 30 percent than if it is around 60, 70, or 80 percent. Both lending large sums and not lending large sums can be risky. Not putting enough money on the table risks tying down the IMF's lending capacity without catalyzing a clear change in market sentiment. Yet upping the IMF's lending in face of rising financing needs ceases at some point to be a sensible option. Quite aside from the risks it poses to the IMF, it also gives rise to moral hazard, that is, the expectation that the IMF backstop would protect the country and its creditors from poor policies and bad investments.

In a world of volatile international capital flows, sustained and stable growth in emerging market economies depends, above all, on the ability of emerging economies themselves to maintain sound macroeconomic policies and debt structures that protect them against sudden shifts in global markets. But the international community must also be ready to help countries through occasional crisis, and to try to help to reduce their economic and social costs.

Finding the right balance between lending too much and lending too little is always a critical challenge. We suspect that the IMF has tended to lend a bit too much in its efforts to give every country a chance to avoid a debt restructuring, and a bit too little when helping certain countries through a debt restructuring. We are certain, however, that stale calls for the IMF to return to its traditional lending limits—calls which are always forgotten in a crisis—are not moving the debate forward. Instead, the lull created by current favorable macroeconomic and financial conditions allows the opportunity for a serious discussion of the set of problems that should, and should not, be addressed by large-scale IMF lending.

Notes

1 This article draws heavily on the authors' recent book, *Bailouts or Bailins? Responding to Financial Crises in Emerging Economies*, 2004.

2 Mexican dollar-denominated bonds.

3 Rubin and Weisberg, 2003 and Rubin, 1998.

4 While many emerging economies were booming prior to 1997, Russia's economy had been consistently *contracting* during the early years of its transition. After stabilizing in 1997, Russian output contracted further in 1998. However, the devaluation of the rouble, combined with the rebound in oil prices, proved to be a tonic for the Russian economy. In 1999, it entered a period of sustained growth. In 1999, Brazil, with the help from the IMF, was able to devalue and eventually float the real without experiencing a sovereign or private-sector payments crisis. Growth slowed significantly, but Brazil at least avoided a fall in output.

5 In the process, they are providing substantial amounts of financing to the United States, which now runs a substantial current account deficit, financed significantly by the growth in the dollar holdings of the world's central banks.

6 See Rogoff et al., 2003. Manasse, Roubini, and Schimmelpfenning (2003) found that emerging market economies are at risk of default at significantly lower levels of debt than advanced economies.

7 Raghuran Rajan, cited in Balls, 2005, online at: http://news.ft.com/cms/s/b64d1dda-ac36-11d9-bb67-00000e2511c8.html

8 Standard & Poor's, 2005, as reported by the Associated Press.

9 See Goldstein, 2004, and Roubini and Setser, 2005.

10 *Renminbi* means "people's currency."

11 Former Speaker of the United States House of Representatives.

12 Mussa, 2002.

13 A domestic bank run generated more pressure on Argentina's reserves during the course of 2001 than payments on its international sovereign bonds. During the course of 2001, domestic depositors and external creditors withdrew US$24 billion from the Argentine banking system. See IMF, 2004.

14 It is difficult to make a definitive judgment until various holdout creditors test Argentina in the courts.

15 Group of Seven, 2002, Online at: www.treas.gov/press/releases/po3015.htm

16 Taylor, 2002. Online at: www.treas.gov/press/releases/po2056.htm

17 Lerrick and Meltzer, 2001.

18 The expanded use of collective action clauses, i.e., provisions that allow a supermajority of bondholders to vote to make the restructuring terms binding on all bondholders, clearly is a good thing. But clauses alone will not make debt restructuring easy or painless, nor will it do much to limit the risk that a restructuring will trigger a bank run, or a run on the currency.

19 Former IMF Chief Economist Michael Mussa first used this expression in this context.

References

Balls A. 2005. "IMF Takes Rich Nations to Task on Imbalances." *Financial Times*. April.

Data Resources Inc. 2005. Macroeconomic Data Base. Stern Business School library.

Dornbusch, R. 2001. "A Primer on Emerging Market Crises." NBER Working Paper 8326. Cambridge: National Bureau of Economic Research.

Goldstein, M. 2004. "Adjusting China's Exchange Rate Policies." Institute for International Economics Working Paper 04-1. Washington. June.

Goldstein, M. and N. Lardy. 2004. "What Kind of Landing for the Chinese Economy?" Institute for International Economics Policy Brief 04-7. Washington. November.

Group of Seven. 2002. Statement of G7 Finance Ministers and Central Bank Governors and Action Plan. Washington. 20 April.

International Monetary Fund. 2004. Debt-related Vulnerabilities and Financial Crises: An Application of the Balance Sheet Approach to Emerging Market Economies. Washington. July.

International Monetary Fund. 2005. *International Financial Statistics*. Washington.

Lerrick, A. and A. Meltzer. 2001. "Blueprint for an International Lender of Last Resort." Photocopy. Carnegie Mellon University. October.

Manasse, P., N. Roubini, and A. Schimmelpfenning. 2003. "Predicting Sovereign Debt Crises." Working Paper 03/221. Washington: International Monetary Fund. November.

Moody's. 2004. Annual statistical publication.

Mussa, M. 2002. "Argentina and the Fund: From Triumph to Tragedy." *Policy Analyses in International Economics* 67. Washington: Institute for International Economics.

Pettis. M. 2001. *The Volatility Machine.* Oxford: Oxford University Press.

Rogoff, K., C. Reinhardt, and M. Savastano. 2003. "Debt Intolerance." *Brookings Papers on Economic Activity* 1:1–74. Washington: Brookings Institution.

Roubini, N. and B. Setser. 2004. "Bailouts or Bail-ins? Responding to Financial Crises in Emerging Economies." Institute for International Economics. Washington. August.

Roubini, N and B. Setser. 2005. China Trip Report. Unpublished manuscript. Online at: www.rgemonitor.com

Rubin, R. E. 1998. Statement at the Special Meeting of Finance Ministers and Central Bank Governors, April. Washington: United States Treasury.

Rubin, R. E. and J. Weisberg. 2003. *In an Uncertain World: Tough Choices from Wall Street to Washington.* New York: Random House.

Standard and Poor's. 2005.

Taylor, J. 2002. "Sovereign Debt Restructuring: A US Perspective." Remarks at a Conference on Sovereign Debt Workouts: Hopes and Hazards. Institute for International Economics, Washington. April 1.

United States Treasury. Various dates, including 1997. *Federal Reserve Bulletin.* Washington.

CHAPTER 3.4

Full Employment for Europe

RICHARD LAYARD,[1] London School of Economics

Unemployment, not productivity, is the problem in Europe.[2]

Europe's four largest countries have unemployment rates far higher than the United States (see Table 1). As I shall show, this is a specific problem, having specific causes, and for which there are specific remedies.

Unemployment does not reflect some general weakness of the European economy. If it did, we would also see poor secular productivity growth, which is not the case (see Table 2).[3] Moreover, many European countries have reduced their unemployment rates to US levels or below, including some, such as Denmark, which have very high tax rates, and others, such as the Netherlands, which have tax rates typical of the European Union as a whole. So there is no general European unemployment problem. It is precisely the variation of experience among the different countries, which helps us to understand what must be done by those countries where unemployment remains so shockingly high.

Table 1: Unemployment rate (percent)

	1993	2004
USA	7	5.5
REFORMED		
Britain	10	4.8
Denmark	10	5.4
Netherlands	6	4.6
DID NOT REFORM		
France	11	9.7
Germany	8	9.5
Italy	10	8.0
Spain	17	10.8

Source: United Kingdom, 2005b.

Table 2: Productivity per hour worked in United States and Europe (growth percent per annum)

	1980–2004	1990–2004
United States	1.8	2.0
Europe (15)	2.0	1.8

Source: Groningen Growth and Development Centre, no year given.

The required remedies were advocated by many writers as early as 1990 (for example, Layard et al.,1991). Some countries pursued these remedies and others did not—yielding a perfect natural experiment. Those countries which implemented the remedies have halved their unemployment, while in those countries which did not: France, Germany and Italy, unemployment remains almost as high as ever.

In what follows, I begin by assessing the importance of reducing unemployment. I then discuss the main factors

193

affecting unemployment rates, and how these explain the experience of different countries. I end by discussing what specific policy changes are needed, if there is to be real progress.

The cost of unemployment

The present level of unemployment in some European countries is totally unacceptable, for the simple reason that unemployment is one of the clearest sources of human misery, and one which we already know how to reduce.

The high cost of unemployment is less a matter of the loss of output and income than of the pain of rejection. We can see this from the numerous studies of human happiness carried out in the last ten years, using Eurobarometer, the United States General Social Survey, or the World Values Survey.

Table 3 reports the results of the World Values Survey, as analyzed by John Helliwell (2003a).[4] In this survey of 46 countries, individuals report their happiness on a scale from 1 to 10, as well as various other features of their life. These features are then used to explain happiness. To avoid incorrect inferences, the effect of each feature is examined, while holding the other features constant. Some of the effects are given in Table 3, which shows that a one third drop in family income reduces happiness by 0.2 points. But if, in addition, a person is unemployed, happiness falls much more steeply: by a further 0.6 points—equal to the effect of divorce. In both cases, the person ceases to be needed.

Table 3: Effects on happiness

	Fall in happiness (points)
Family income falls by one third	0.2
Unemployed	0.6
Divorced	0.5
Separated	0.8

Source: Helliwell, 2003a. For the other variables which are held constant, see Helliwell, 2003a, or Layard et al., 2005, p. 64.

In further work, Helliwell (2003b) has investigated the factors affecting the difference between nations in average happiness and in suicide rates. Again, the unemployment rate shows up as an important factor. Clearly, unemployment really does matter. And, a reasonable corollary to Table 3 would be that a job at almost any wage is better than no job at all, even if unemployed people do not always foresee this.

Expanding the number of jobs

But how is the number of jobs determined? In the medium term, it depends on the number of people actively seeking work. Many people find this difficult to believe, and it should be stressed that many policy mistakes arise from a failure to understand it. Before the Pilgrim Fathers landed in New England, there were no jobs; but after they landed, jobs sprang up. Or, to take a less obvious example, the labor force in Britain has grown by 212 percent since 1851.[5] Over the same period, the number of jobs has grown by 212 percent. So, a market economy—ignoring the business cycle—always provides more jobs, if there are more people actively seeking work.

The same point emerges if we compare countries. Since 1960, the labor force has grown at very different rates in different countries, mainly due to demographic factors. If jobs were determined independently of the supply of labor, this would have caused massive problems in countries with the fastest growing labor forces: the United States, Ireland, and Japan. Yet, as Figure 1 shows, wherever the number of job-seekers has grown faster, the number of jobs has grown at a roughly corresponding rate. Similarly, countries which have artificially reduced their labor forces by requiring early retirement have simultaneously reduced the number of jobs, with no change in the unemployment rate.[6]

Thus, in the medium term, the number of jobs is not determined independently of the supply of labor. It is determined by two factors: a) the size of the labor force, and b) the equilibrium unemployment rate, which is itself influenced by how hard unemployed people look for work.

In the short run, of course, things are completely different: the number of jobs is determined by the level of aggregate demand. Since it is easy to expand the level of aggregate demand by fiscal and monetary policy, one has to ask why unemployment cannot always be diminished. The answer is that inflation would eventually set in. The labor market would become too tight, due to the excess of unfilled vacancies. This is, in fact, exactly what happened in Europe in 2000, forcing the European Central Bank (ECB) to raise interest rates, and dampen the boom. So the key to reducing unemployment is to mobilize the unemployed to fill emerging vacancies as quickly as possible.

Figure 1: Percentage growth in the labor force and employment 1960–2000

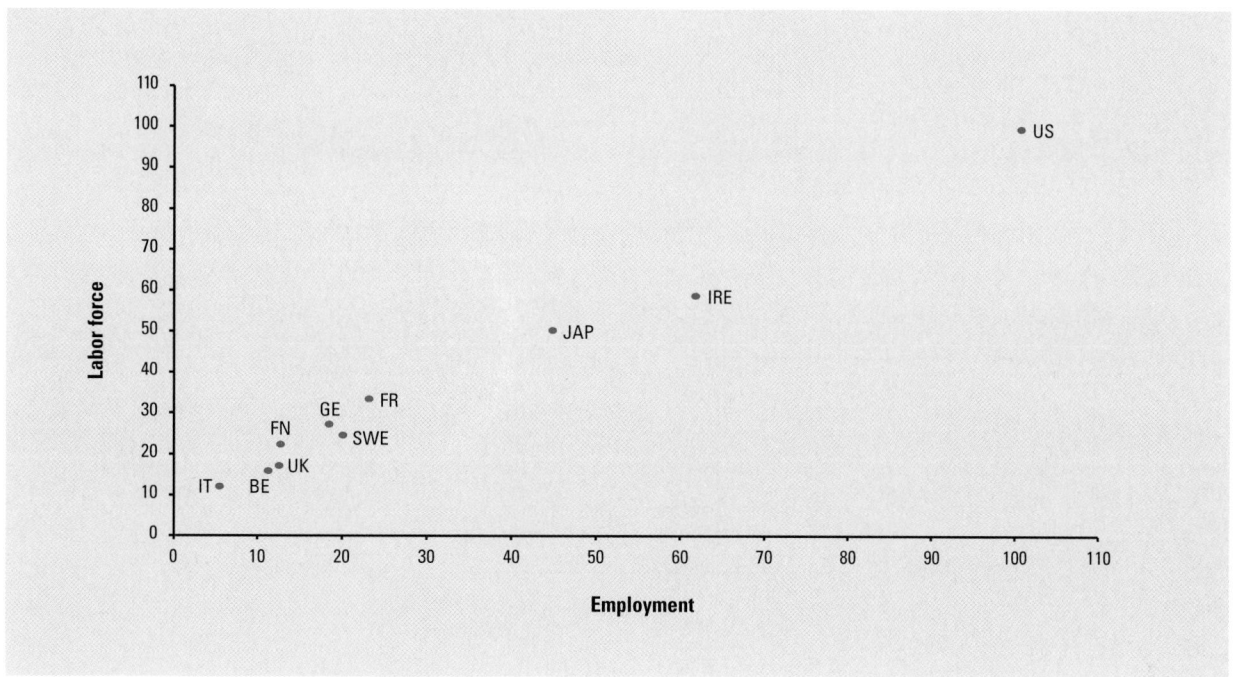

Source: OECD Labour Force Statistics, European Economy.

Unemployment and vacancies

According to the simplest theory of unemployment, inflation will rise when a specific level of vacancies has been reached. This is the *non-inflationary* vacancy rate (see Figure 2).[7] In addition, there is an inverse relation between vacancies and unemployment (see Figure 3): the higher the vacancy rate, the lower the unemployment rate.[8] Thus, equilibrium unemployment is whatever level of unemployment is consistent with the non-inflationary level of vacancies.

This rate depends on human institutions. It can be reduced by mobilizing the unemployed, so that they are better at filling vacancies, thus moving the Vacancy/Unemployment (VU) curve to the left.

At least six factors have been suggested as possible influences on equilibrium unemployment rates:

1. how unemployed people are treated
2. the flexibility of wages
3. the flexibility of employment (i.e. firing)
4. the size of the labor force
5. hours of work
6. taxes on labor

But by 1990, the evidence supported the overriding importance of the first two, and this still remains the case. Layard et al. (2005) show that institutional changes in these first two variables explained nearly half the variance in unemployment change across OECD countries between the 1960s and the early 1990s, and similarly between the 1980s and 2000–2001. There is still no consistent evidence that any of the other four variables have any major influence on the unemployment rate (see Layard et al. 1991, and Nickell and Layard 1999). Thus reform is needed mainly in the first two areas, which are the focus of my argument.

How unemployed people are treated

If unemployed people are more actively looking for work, and being helped in their efforts, there will be fewer unfilled vacancies at any level of unemployment. So the equilibrium level of unemployment will be lower. Therefore, one key issue has to do with how unemployed people are treated.

Countries differ to an astonishing degree in how they treat unemployed people (OECD, 2001). Although the level of actual benefits is significant, the following are more important:

1. how long people may receive benefits without working
2. what job search is required, with what intensity, and what kind of jobs must be accepted
3. what help is provided with job search and employability

Figure 2: Vacancies and inflation

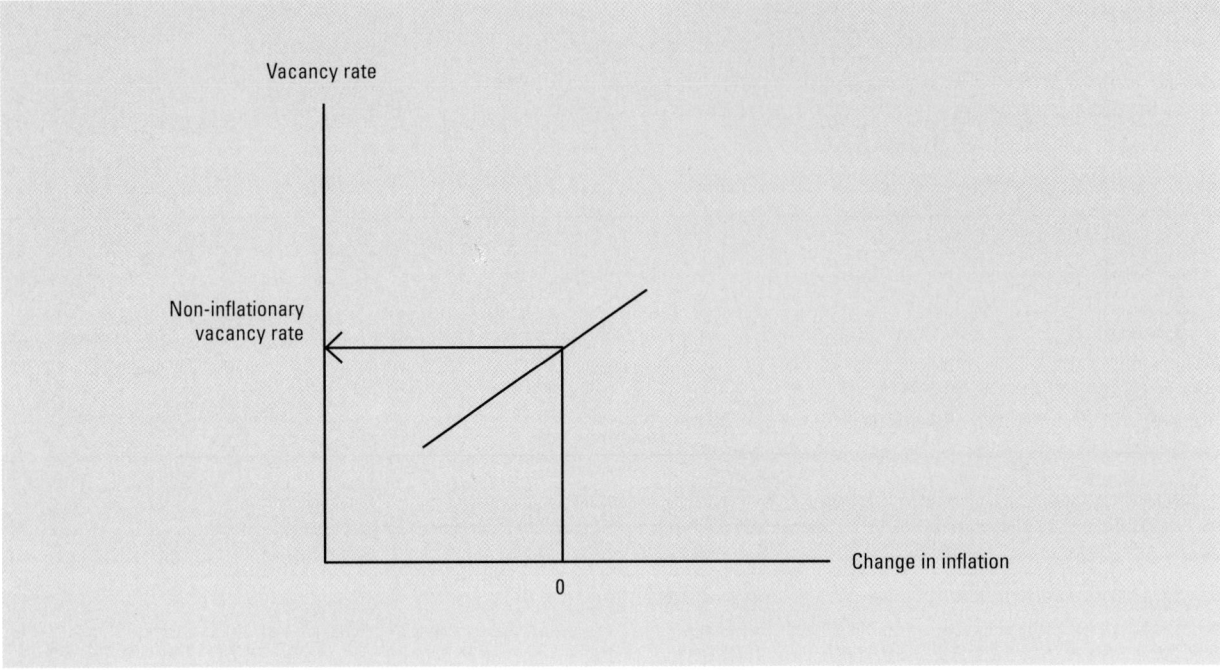

Source: Author.

Figure 3: Vacancies and unemployment

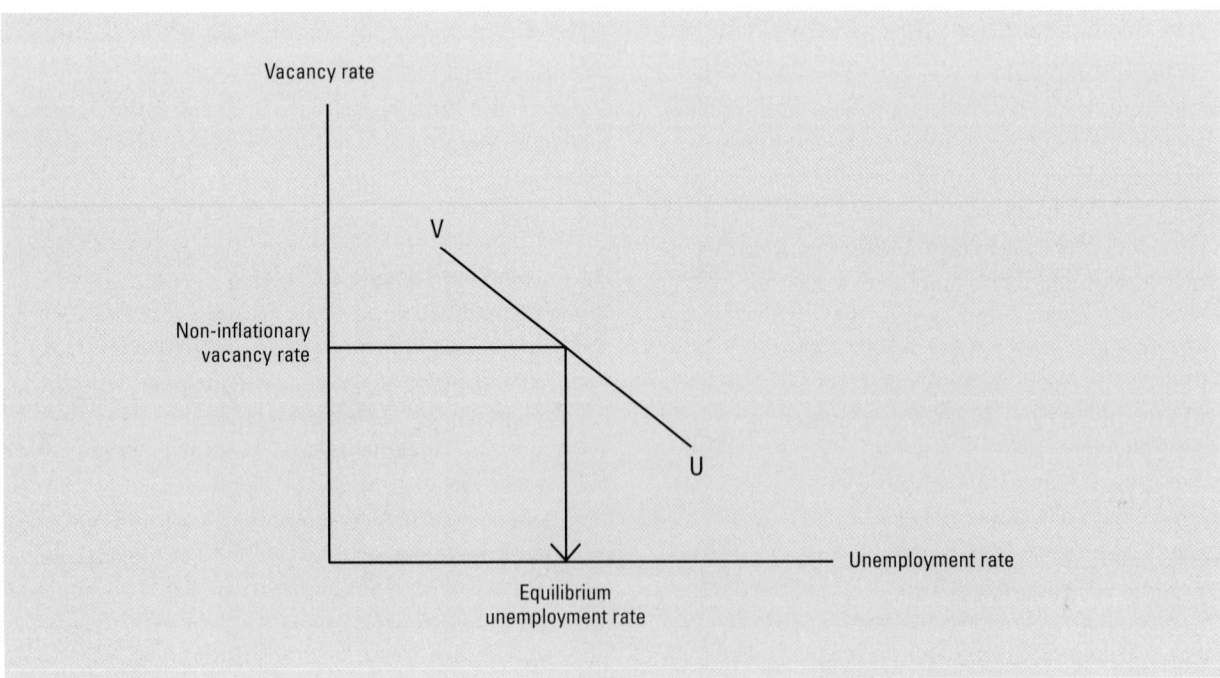

Source: Author.

Figure 4: Long-term unemployment and the duration of benefits

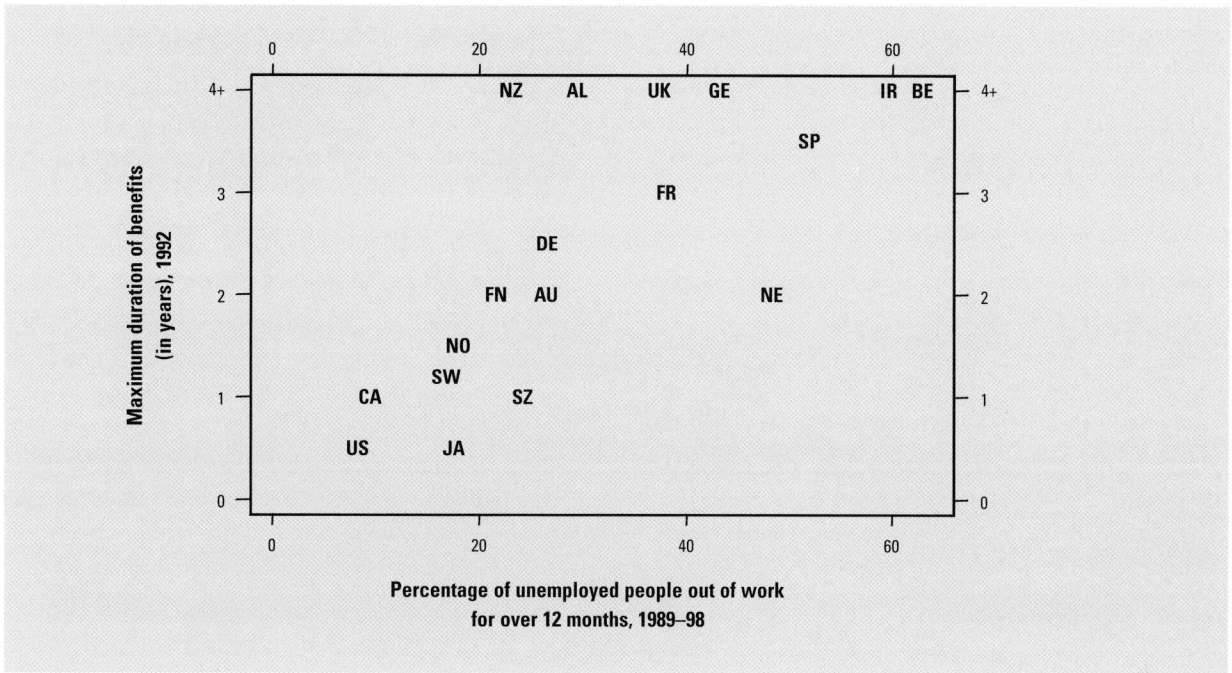

Source: Nickell and Layard, 1999.

The importance of the duration of benefits can be seen from Figure 4. The longer you pay people for doing nothing, the longer they will do just that.

But conditionality is also vital. In some countries, an unemployed person must visit the employment office every two weeks, report on the job search done; at this time, he or she will receive a list of possible vacancies to approach in the following two weeks. In some other countries, the unemployed have only to call the benefit office every three months to confirm that they are still out of work. In Britain, once a person has been unemployed for 13 weeks, he or she must accept any type of job within one hour's traveling time to work. In Germany, even after the Hartz reforms, such a requirement comes into effect only after a year.

Needless to say, conditionality is impossible, unless the employment service is actively providing job-search assistance. But even in that case, it is not easy to enforce: if a person doesn't actually want a job, he is not likely to be offered one. For this reason—and on humanitarian grounds—many countries have concluded that the employment service, within the first year, should offer each unemployed person some sort of activity. This activation principle was included in the 1997 Employment Guidelines adopted by the EU heads of government. But it has so far been implemented by only a few countries, especially Denmark and the Netherlands.

The case of Denmark is the most striking. As Figure 5a shows, in 1993, despite its 10 percent unemployment, the level of vacancies was at a record high. After concluding that the problem was a failure to mobilize the unemployed to fill available job vacancies, they adopted the principle of activation after a specified period of time, which is now one year. The results were remarkable: unemployment dropped by 6 percentage points, and the employment rate increased by 6 percentage points, with the number of people actually working in activation positions no higher than before activation became compulsory. The policy has worked, because people have become more willing to fill the existing vacancies. Thus, despite the huge increase in labor demand, there has been no increase at all in the number of vacancies.

Similar policies have been adopted in Britain and the Netherlands, with similar results. (In the Netherlands the high vacancies in the boom of 2000 were not inflationary, due to a policy of wage restraint.) In each of the three countries discussed so far, the policies have included: more active help with job search, stricter conditionality, more active sanctions for non-compliance, more use of job subsidies, and, after a period of time, the guarantee of activation, along with the corresponding responsibility to comply. In addition, the policies depend on a unified administration of benefits and active labor market assistance, which ensures that benefits act as an aid to job search, and

Figure 5: Three countries with low unemployment
(During the 1990s unemployment at given vacancies fell.)

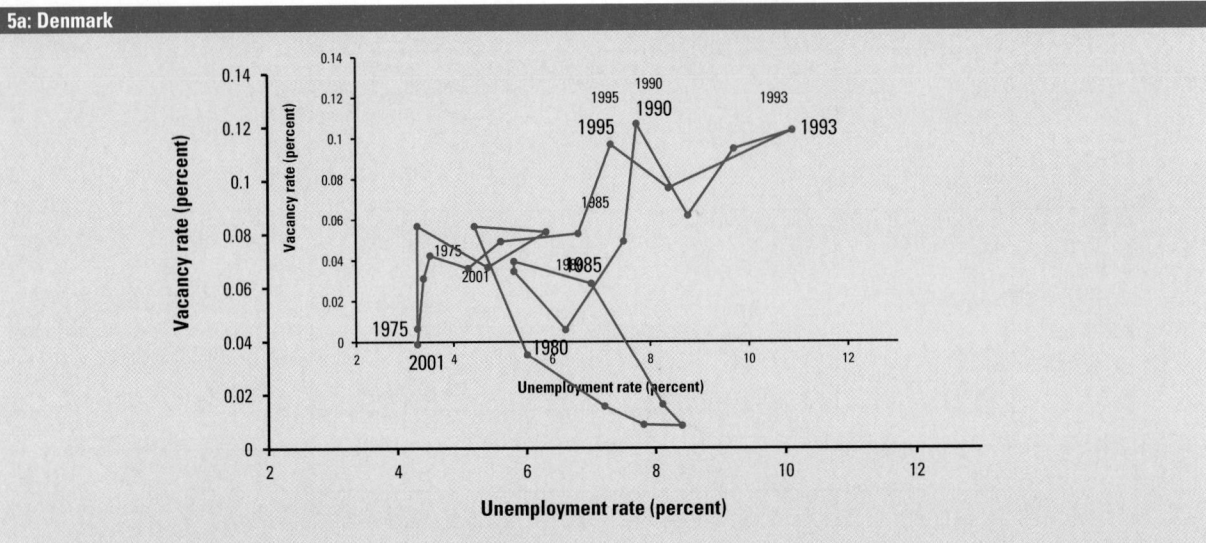

5a: Denmark

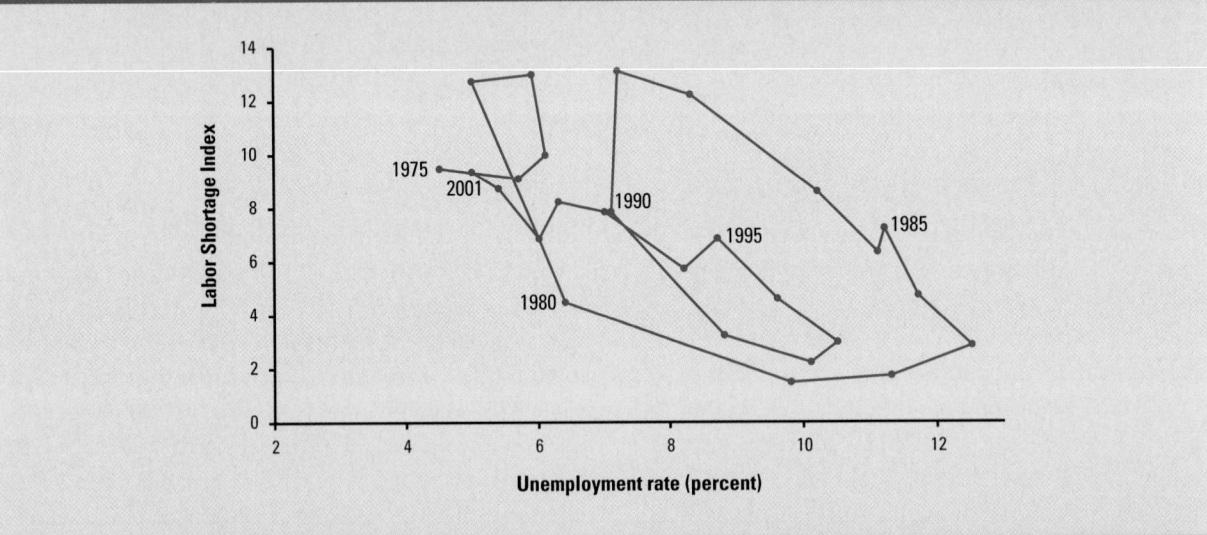

5b: Britain

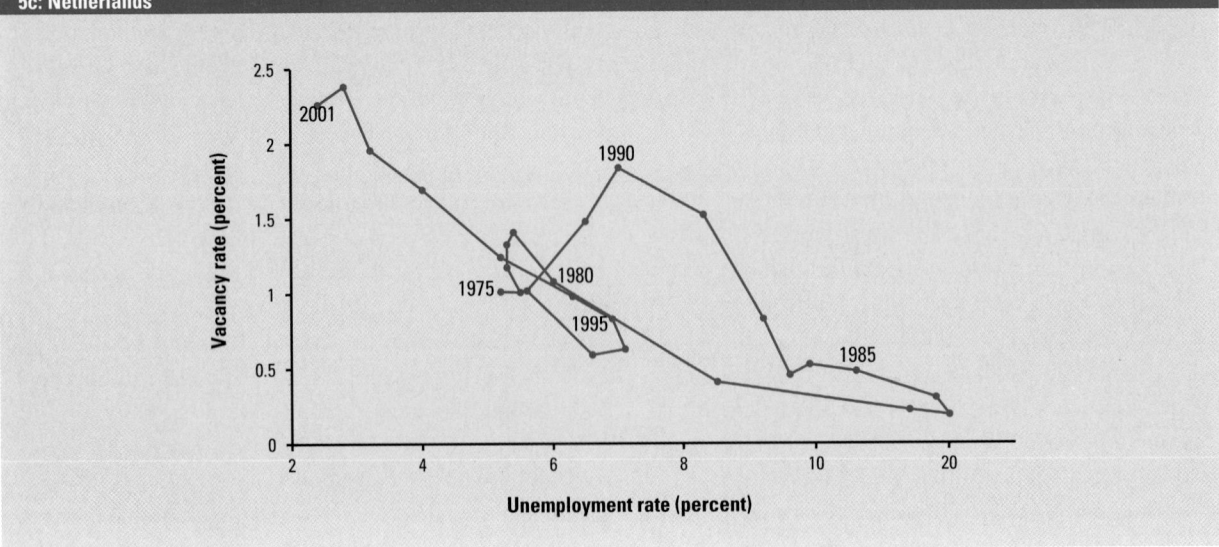

5c: Netherlands

Source: de Koning et al., 2004. p. 47–8.

not as a deterrent. In Britain, these policy changes were introduced gradually throughout the 1990s, first by a Conservative government (with a somewhat punitive slant), and then by a Labour government (with a more positive slant).

The contrast between these successful experiences and those of France and Germany is striking, and provides social scientists with a rare natural experiment which can confirm or disprove their predictions. It, indeed, confirms all the predictions of the 1990 view of mainstream labor economists.

During the 1990s, neither France nor Germany introduced any of the above-mentioned reforms. The result was as predicted (see Figure 6). In the European boom of 1997

to 2001, unemployment fell only 2 percentage points in Germany and 3 in France, but vacancies rose to record levels, despite high unemployment. Clearly there had been a failure to mobilize the unemployed.

In both countries, public opinion has been unwilling to accept the idea that the behavior of the unemployed could have any affect on the number of jobs. This has been due partly to inappropriate theories—of the kind criticized at the beginning of this paper—and partly to a compassionate regard for the unemployed.

But respect requires understanding as well as compassion. Unemployment is quite difficult to understand using traditional theories; most scientific theories conclude that, because unemployment makes people miserable, the

Figure 6: Two countries with high unemployment
(During the 1990s unemployment at given vacancies did **not** fall.)

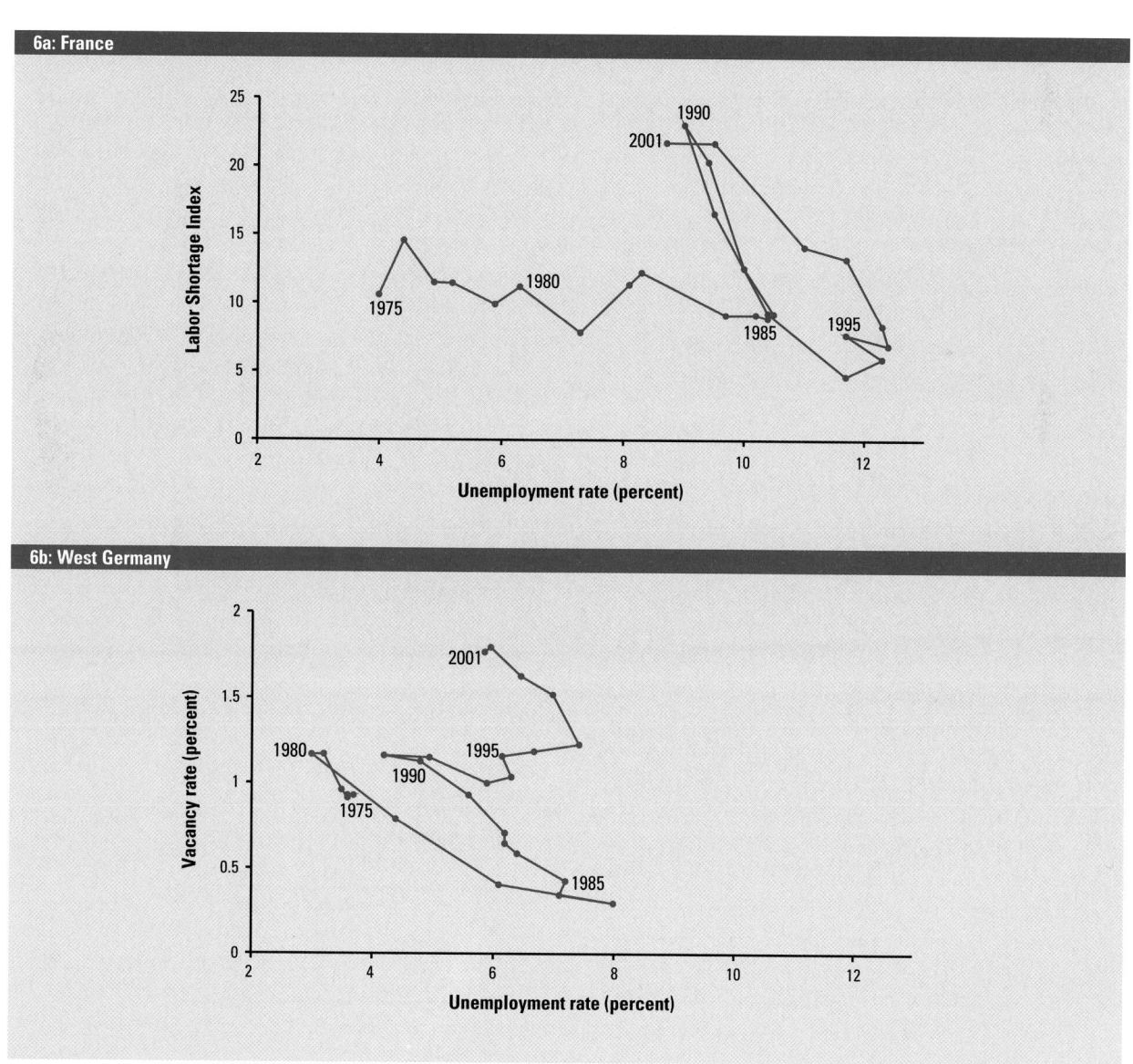

Source: de Koning et al., 2004, pp. 47–8.

unemployed must be doing all they can to escape from it. But modern psychology explains that, even though unemployment causes great unhappiness, unemployed people often reject opportunities which would make them happier.

This is explained by the fact that people a) adapt, to some extent, to almost anything and fear further change (Frederick and Loewenstein, 1999), and b) do not, as a rule, do well at predicting how they would actually feel in changed circumstances (Loewenstein and Schkade, 1999).

Therefore, in the interests of the unemployed themselves, employment services should introduce them to something that will make them feel better. That is the justification for a policy that is both tough and tender: it is on the side of the unemployed, but against unemployment as any form of solution.

Unfortunately, such arguments are still not widely understood in France.[9] In Germany, political leaders now understand these points quite well, and the Hartz reforms passed by the German legislature are an important and courageous step in the right direction. They include a unified set of benefits (with a means test after a year), stricter conditions about job search, more job opportunities through temporary work agencies, and application of the "activation principle" to all people under 25. In addition, the administration of benefits is to be integrated with active labor market assistance.

But, as is well known, it is one thing to pass a law and quite another to implement it on the ground. Unless the workers in the Labor Ministry and the Employment Agency are convinced that these measures make sense, they will not be properly implemented. There is still a long way to go in establishing that consensus.

Regional wage flexibility

However, mobilizing the unemployed through the Employment Service is not the answer everywhere. It cannot significantly increase employment in those parts of a country where wages are too high relative to productivity. This is the case in eastern Germany, in southern Italy, and southern Spain. In those regions, trade unions, often with strong political support, have tried to hold wages close to the levels in the more productive parts of the country, giving rise to higher unit labor costs in the low-productivity regions, and giving employers every incentive to generate their vacancies elsewhere. As a result, a mismatch arises between the pattern of vacancies and unemployment, with a disproportionate share of vacancies appearing in the high-productivity regions and a disproportionate share of unemployment in the low-productivity regions. Such a mismatch inevitably shifts the VU relationship shown in Figure 3 to the right and increases the equilibrium unemployment rate.

The only remedy is to lower the relative unit-labor costs in the high-unemployment regions. In principle, this could be achieved either by raising relative productivity, or by lowering relative wages. The problem with the former approach is that employers are simply not willing to make the necessary investment until relative wages are low enough to raise relative rates of return on capital. (This situation is particularly acute in the former East Germany, because it is so uncompetitive compared with the neighbouring East European countries and with the former West Germany.)

Thus, the burden of adjustment falls on wages. In some cases, there is the possibility of achieving a relative wage adjustment by negotiation, or through the political process. But it is highly unlikely that this will happen without some greater decentralization of wages. In Britain, this was achieved in the 1980s, as a result of the weakened power of the trade unions. As a consequence, local wages became more responsive to local unemployment rates, and relative wages in the north of England fell by 12 percent in the 1980s. This had the effect, in the 1990s, of halting the age-old drift of jobs from the north to the south of England. Clearly, each country must find its own way towards a more flexible structure of regional wages.

Transition countries

The analysis so far has concentrated on the countries of Western Europe. But, in fact, it applies equally to the countries of the former communist bloc. In the early days of the transition, it was widely believed that high unemployment would be a temporary phenomenon—while the workforce was redeployed—and that it would subsequently decline.

However a number of writers observed quite quickly that unemployment in those countries could be explained by the same factors as in Western Europe, and that the situation would be unlikely to change unless those factors also changed (Burda, 1994; Layard and Richter, 1995). Thus, with the exception of Hungary, unemployment in Eastern Europe has remained high (see Table 4).

Table 4: Unemployment rates (percent) in some transition countries

	1993	2003
Poland	16.4	19.2
Hungary	14.5	5.9
Czech Republic	3.5	7.8
Slovak Republic	14.4	17.4

Source: EBRD Transition Reports.

In fact, the redeployment of labor has occurred largely because people moved from one job to another, while inflow rates to unemployment were not particularly high. Therefore, the reason for high unemployment, as in Western Europe, was the low rate of outflow from unemployment. Thus, it can be seen that the lessons discussed earlier in this paper apply equally to the transition countries: high unemployment will only be reduced by having more flexible relative wages across regions, and better policies toward the unemployed.

Conclusion

Unemployment, and not productivity, is the key economic problem facing Europe. Since it is a major source of misery, it requires urgent attention, but that attention must be based on the evidence of what works. This means reform in two difficult areas: how unemployed people are treated—the principle should be tough and tender—and greater flexibility in wage differentials between regions.

It took courage and understanding to tackle inflation, now a thing of the past. In the end, politicians in every country will find similar courage to tackle high unemployment in ways that work, so that it too will become a thing of the past.

Notes

1 Richard Layard is Professor of Economics (Emeritus), and founder and former Director of the Centre for Economic Performance.

2 This paper draws heavily on Layard et al., 2005, which evaluates the experience of the 1990s; also on de Koning et al., 2004, which examines in detail the experiences of Britain, Denmark, and the Netherlands.

3 See also Blanchard, 2004. As regards levels, productivity per hour worked in northern Europe is broadly similar to the United States.

4 See also Layard, 2005, pp. 63–68.

5 Mitchell, 1992, p. 81, and United Kingdom, 2005, Table A.11.

6 de Koning et al., 2004, Figure 3, and related discussion.

7 See, for example, Layard et al., 1991, p. 275.

8 This assumes a fixed degree of turnover in the market.

9 Notable exceptions are a) the report, written in 2000–2001 for M. Jospin by his Council of Economic Analysis, and b) the example set by the negotiators of the Patronat and the unions (especially Mme Nicole Notat, Director General of VIGEO) in 2000–2001, who, unfortunately, were unable to secure effective government backing for their proposals.

References

Blanchard, O. 2004. "The Economic Future of Europe." *The Journal of Economic Perspectives* 18(4): 3–26.

Burda, M. 1994. "Unemployment, Labour Markets and Structural Changes in Eastern Europe." *Economic Policy* 16: 101–138.

de Koning, J., R. Layard, S. Nickell, and N. Westergaard-Nielsen. 2004. "Policies for Full Employment." UK Department for Work and Pensions. Online at www.dwp.gov.uk.

European Bank for Reconstruction and Development (EBRD). Various Years. Transition Reports. London: EBRD.

Frederick, S. and G. Loewenstein. 1999. "Hedonic adaptation." D. Kahneman, E. Diener, and N. Schwarz, eds. *Well-Being: The Foundations of Hedonic Psychology*. New York: Russell Sage Foundation. 302–329.

Groningen Growth and Development Centre. No Year Given. Conference Board. Groningen: Rijksuniversiteit.

Helliwell, J. 2003a. "How's Life? Combining Individual and National Variables to Explain Subjective Well-Being." *Economic Modelling* 20:331–60.

Helliwell, J. 2003b. "Well-Being and Social Capital: Does Suicide Pose a Puzzle?" University of British Columbia. Mimeo.

Layard, R. 2005. *Happiness: Lessons from a New Science*. New York: Penguin Press.

Layard, R., Nickell, S., and Jackman, R. 1991. *Unemployment: Macroeconomic Performance and the Labour Market*. Oxford: Oxford University Press.

———. 2005. *Unemployment: Macroeconomic Performance and the Labour Market*. 2nd ed. Oxford: Oxford University Press.

Layard, R. and Richter, A. 1995. "How Much Unemployment Is Needed for Restructuring? The Russian Experience." *Economics of Transition* 3(1):39–58.

Loewenstein, G. and Schkade, D. 1999. "Wouldn't It Be Nice? Predicting Future Feelings." D. Kahneman, E. Diener, and N. Schwarz, eds. *Well-Being: The Foundations of Hedonic Psychology*. New York: Russell Sage Foundation. 85–108.

Mitchell, B. 1992. *International Historical Statistics: Europe 1750–1988*. Basingstoke: Macmillan.

Nickell, S. and Layard, R. 1999. "Labor Market Institutions and Economic Performance." O. Ashenfelter and D. Card, eds. *Handbook of Labor Economics 3C*. Amsterdam: Elsevier. 3029–84.

OECD. 2001. *Labour Market Policies and the Public Employment Service*. Paris: Conference.

Organisation for Economic Co-operation and Development (OECD). Various Years. Labour Force Statistics, European Economy. OECD: Paris.

United Kingdom. 2005a. National Statistics: *Labour Market Trends,* Table A.11. HM Stationery Office. March.

———. 2005b. Her Majesty's Treasury Pocket Databank. 24 May.

CHAPTER 3.5

Globalization as an Agent of Prosperity

JAGDISH BHAGWATI,[1] Columbia University

In the race to be the most competitive among nations, economic globalization is certainly a winner. Pro-globalization policies are part of the complex of economic policies that promise to make a nation more prosperous. Before I say why, let me enter a couple of caveats.

First, it is important to remember that, even if we confine our attention to economic globalization, as opposed to cultural globalization—such as greater flows of students or the export of films and music, to name only two forms—we run into the fallacy of aggregation. Economic globalization embraces many different forms: trade, multinationals, foreign direct investment, short-term capital flows, international flows of humanity, and technology diffusion, involving patent rights. Of these, trade and foreign investment are sure winners.

But, while freer capital mobility certainly offers advantages under fair weather conditions, the downside risks of free capital flows are quite dramatic, as illustrated by the Asian financial crisis beginning in 1997. Experience and first principles demonstrate this quite well. As noted in my 1998 article in *Foreign Affairs,*[2] the asymmetry between free trade and capital flow attracted worldwide attention, simply because many assumed—erroneously—that a free trader must necessarily be a supporter of the free flow of capital. The IMF has now recognized the error of its haste, and become more cautious about pushing nations into free capital mobility in the form of capital account convertibility. Even *The Economist* fell in line with this view.[3]

Second, policies that produce prosperity must produce it in a sustainable fashion. Of course, the phrase "sustainable development" is used indiscriminately to characterize whatever one desires. I was amused to read about a United Nations Committee on "Sustainable Business," since the essence of efficiency in business life is that the inefficient are *not* sustained but allowed to disappear! But, in the present context, it is easy to see, for example, that the Soviet Union and the other "socialist" countries registered high growth rates for over a decade, but finally slowed down and even crashed. I am reminded of a story where my radical teacher at Cambridge, Joan Robinson, was overheard agreeing with the "neoliberal" economist Gus Ranis of Yale, that Korea was doing fantastically well, the paradox of their "agreement" being that she was referring to North Korea and he was talking about South Korea! And, of course, we know now which country had the sustainable miracle.

I believe that globalization, defined in this article as integration into the world economy on the dimensions of trade and direct foreign investment, is a benign force, not a malign one, on *both* economic and social dimensions. Since economic prosperity is directly served by globalization, and because social agendas—of particular interest to today's anti-globalization critics—are also advanced, it should be possible to contain the social discord often attributed, indiscriminately, to globalization. In my book *In Defense of Globalization,* I argue that globalization should help to *promote* sustained development. But before we consider each of these two dimensions of globalization, social and economic, a few words about the sources of anti-globalization thinking.

The sources of anti-globalization thought

Why are the critics of globalization agitated? What bothers them? There are two main groups that must be distinguished: first, there are the hard-core protesters, who have deep-seated antipathy, coming from different intellectual and ideological directions, and not all sharing the same ideas or sentiments. But many buy into a linked trilogy of discontents, characterized by an anti-capitalist, anti-globalization, and acutely anti-corporation mind-set. Globalization is seen by them as the extension of capitalism throughout the world, with multinational corporations seen as the B-52s of its global reach. There is little one can do to dialogue with this group.

Second, there are critics of globalization whose discontents are well within the parameters of mainstream dissent and discourse. Their critique focuses on globalization as the cause of social ills, such as poverty in poor countries, and the deterioration of the environment. However ill-founded their argumentation, or implacable their opposition, they are, nonetheless, susceptible to reasoned engagement, and their criticisms require extended and careful response. Many NGOs fall into this category.

Far too many among the young see capitalism as a system that cannot meaningfully address questions of social justice. That capitalism may be viewed instead as a system that can paradoxically destroy privilege and open up economic opportunity to the many is still an uncommon thought. The number of well-meaning, admirable socialists who cling to the erroneous belief that controls and direct allocations are an appropriate answer to inequality is astonishing. The deconstructionism of Derrida and the anti-rationalism of Michel Foucault, have combined with post-colonial theorists, such as Edward Said, in nurturing a profound suspicion of western scholarship as an objective source of interpretation and conceptualization of the colonial societies that were part of the global polity that European expansion created. That suspicion breeds hostility both to disciplines such as economics, and to the threat they perceive to the cultures of the communities and nations that have succeeded colonial rule.

Much hostility is focused against multinational corporations, who are often described—and sometimes targeted directly—as being the heart of the problem: an exploitative force that delays the doomsday for capitalism at home, and harms those abroad, a force that embodies the evils of

globalization because they are perceived to be its principal beneficiaries. Multinationals must necessarily be bad in a global economy because global integration without globally shared regulations must surely amount to an advantageous playing field for multinationals, who seek profits by searching for the most likely locations to exploit workers and nations, putting intolerable pressure on their home states to abandon their gains in social legislation in a so-called "race to the bottom."

Also propelling the young into anti-capitalist attitudes is the dissonance—ironically created by modern communications technology—that now exists between empathy for others elsewhere for their misery, and the inadequate intellectual grasp of what can be done to ameliorate that distress. The resulting tension spills over into unhappiness with the capitalist system in which they live, and, hence, anger at its apparent callousness. Today, we have the inverse of philosopher David Hume's concentric circles of reducing loyalty and empathy.[4] Each of us feels diminishing empathy as we go from our nuclear family to the extended family, to the local community, to the state or country, to the world. What Internet and CNN have done is to take Hume's outermost circle and turn it inwards. So the young see, and are anguished by, the poverty, civil wars, and famines in remote areas of the world, but often have no intellectual training to cope with their anguish and follow it through rationally in terms of appropriate action.

Added to this heady mixture is the general presumption that the proponents of capitalism are engaged, as Edward Said claims, in a "dominant discourse [whose goal] is to fashion the merciless logic of corporate profit-making and political power into a normal state of affairs."[5] However, the distracting debate over "conservative" vs. "radical," misses the central issue, which is not about conservative counterrevolution and the supposedly enlightened past order. It is rather about shifting the center of gravity in public action more toward the use of markets and less toward dirigisme. It is not about "whether markets," but about where the "limits to markets" must be drawn. The present-day turn toward reform in the developing countries is prompted by excessive and knee-jerk dirigisme. Their turn to economic reforms is to be attributed not to the rise of "conservatism" but to a pragmatic reaction on the part of many to the failure of what a number of us once considered to be "progressive" policies, aimed at lifting us out of poverty, illiteracy, and injustice.

Thus, the chief task before those who favor globalization, is to confront the fears that, while globalization may be economically benign, in the sense of increasing the pie, it is socially malign. These fears relate to several areas, among them accentuation of poverty in both rich and poor countries, erosion of unionization and other labor rights, creation of a democratic deficit, harming of women, imperiling of local mainstream and indigenous cultures, and damage to the environment. At first blush, these fears often appear to be plausible. But the key task is to consider whether, on closer analytical and empirical examination, they are well-founded.

Social dimensions: Why globalization *has* a human face

While the favorable effects on social dimensions are partly based on benign effects on economic prosperity—as when peasants earning more incomes from the opening of foreign markets also take more children out of work and put them into school instead—let us consider the social dimensions first, as they are the ones that animate the most articulate and disruptive anti-globalizers.

Indeed, with the noise made by the vast numbers of anti-globalization protesters, most politicians can be forgiven for thinking that here is a phenomenon that, indeed, imperils the social agendas that we value. Thus, Prime Minister Tony Blair, former President Bill Clinton, and Chancellor Gerhard Schroeder, the social-democratic proponents of the "Third Way," lament the phenomenon of economic globalization, even as they pursue it, saying that it "needs a human face." Logic tells us that if it needs one, it lacks one. Former Prime Minister of Ireland, Mary Robinson, having finished her term as United Nations Commissioner for Human Rights, seeks an "ethical globalization," implying that it is not so.

Indeed, in the anti-globalization circles, there is a general tendency to blame globalization for all shortfalls in social agendas. Typically, many reports in international agencies observe that globalization has increased, that social ills such as poverty exist or have increased, and therefore the former is the cause of the latter. But, like Tina Turner's famous song "What's love got to do with it?" we must ask: what has globalization got to do with it?

The contrary view, which I develop and defend in my book, is that economic globalization *has* a human face. In fact, it advances, instead of inhibiting, the achievement of social agendas as wide-ranging as the promotion of gender equality, the reduction of poverty in poor countries, the shifting of children from work to schools, and the spread of democracy.

The choice between the two contradicting assessments of economic globalization is a matter of the utmost importance. It also has immediate implications for what I call "appropriate governance." For, if you believe that globalization lacks a human face, then appropriate governance will encourage policy interventions to restrain globalization. But if you believe, as I now do, that globalization *has* a human face, then you will want very different policy interventions, ones which preserve, celebrate, and enhance the good effects that globalization generally brings, but which address its occasional downsides. For example, if you believe that multinationals do social harm—that they

exploit their workers abroad—you will want corporate social responsibility to be mandatory, uniform, and regulatory, so as to *reduce that harm,* even if their effects on host-country economic prosperity are beneficial. But if you believe, as I do, that multinationals in truth *advance* social agendas as well—for example by increasing the demand for local labor, they help to promote higher wages and actually benefit workers—then corporate social responsibility would be defined in terms of doing greater good, in which case the prescriptions would be for voluntary actions, much like altruism-based charity by different people with different ideas and convictions. Corporate social responsibility then would be voluntary, diverse, and non-regulatory.

This contrast between the prescriptions for appropriate governance that follow from the two contrasting theses, that globalization *lacks* a human face, and that globalization *has* a human face is seen even better in relation to the effects of globalization on child labor in the poor countries. So, if globalization brings increased incomes to parents, will parents, in fact, be more inclined to send children out to work, to augment their already improving incomes, or less inclined, because they do not need the income from the children's work and can send them to school instead? If the former, then clearly globalization creates a trade-off between increased prosperity and the reduction of child labor, and policies that inhibit globalization become sensible. But if the latter, then we are likely to ask: what can we do to *accelerate* the pace at which child labor will be reduced by globalization?

Consider then just two examples of the effect of globalization on gender equality and on child labor. In both cases, the effects can be argued to be benign rather than malign.

Gender equality

Growth is a powerful mechanism that brings to life social legislation aimed at helping the poor and peripheral groups. Thus, rights and benefits for women may be guaranteed by legislation that prohibits dowry, proscribes polygamy, mandates primary school enrollment for all children (including girls), and much else. But it will often amount to a row of beans unless a growing economy gives women the economic independence to leave abusive situations, and even to sue at the risk of being discarded. A battered wife who cannot find a new job is less likely to take advantage of legislation that says a husband cannot beat his wife. And no matter what the legislation says, an impoverished parent is unlikely to send a child to school, if the economy is stagnant and his prospects of finding a job are dismal. In short, empowerment—today's fancy word for what we development economists have long understood and written about—proceeds from both political democracy and economic prosperity, the principal tools for aiding the poor.

Take the infamous issue of unequal pay, with women earning less than men. There are several ways in which gender pay inequality may be defined: in the same firm for the same professional occupation, a woman may be getting a fraction of the pay that a similarly qualified man receives. Alternatively, a pay commission (as in some European countries) may try to compare pay across occupations: a professor of economics with a Ph.D. may be compared with an economist in a consulting firm, or even with one in industry. Inferring gender pay inequality from such comparisons is arbitrary and therefore cockeyed, to say the least. Or, we may take a "mega" approach and say that, while within specific occupations there is no significant gender pay inequality, women are conditioned, or directed by custom, to accept low-paying occupations, such as secretarial, teaching and nursing, whereas men typically go into higher-paying occupations.

It may surprise some to learn that inequality at the firm level can be shown to have been reduced *faster* when the industry is part of a globalized industry, as distinct from being a non-traded one. For their Harvard dissertation, two brilliant economists, Elizabeth Brainerd and Sandra Black, hypothesized that if competition is fierce, the gender differential will reduce faster because the prejudice which leads to paying men more than equally productive women will become more difficult to indulge. Indeed, their analysis of recent United States data on pay inequality finds that, over two decades, increased competition through trade contributed to the relative improvement in female wages in competitive, traded industries, suggesting that, trade may benefit women by reducing firms' ability to discriminate. Thus, globalization helped, not harmed, the women's cause.[6]

Globalization also helps by welcoming multinationals from different countries with diverse practices. Host country NGOs, citizens, politicians, and firms are thus exposed to the diversity, and, if they are behind on the escalator, gradually propelled to break down the traditions that hold women back from high-paying occupations in their countries. I would argue, for example, that gender equality was advanced in Japan itself by the spread of Japanese multinationals abroad in the 1980s, when the country was enormously successful; typically, their executives abroad were exclusively Japanese men, but were accompanied by their wives and young children, who saw how differently women were treated, and how they had greater economic opportunities than in Japan; these women became agents of change on return; the children also acquired different— in this case western—values at school; all of which has helped Japan to make progress in the area of women's rights, although the West, and even some developing countries, have moved ahead faster.

What is the role of social policy? Antiglobalization groups have expressed outrage at the fact that in some traditional societies, women produce crops for home consumption and men produce cash crops. The claim has been made, for example, that "in sub-Saharan Africa … a switch to export-promotion crops … has often diverted resources from domestic consumption. Men have controlled the extra cash earned from this strategy and the nutritional status of women and children declined."[7] What the author is saying is that intra-family decision-making can lead to increased incomes being spent on frills, rather than on food. Indeed, it can. But, instead of bypassing the opportunity to bring increased income—thereby empowering women by providing them with the economic opportunities of a growing and prosperous economy—here is a prime case for social policy to accompany the increased prosperity, to counter the untoward effects of the men's behavior on the nutrition and health of women and children.

Finally, a number of women's groups are obsessed with export processing zones (EPZs), seeing them as the brutal face of globalization and the source of much of the devastation that they say it wreaks on women in the poor countries. First, it must be remembered that, although the EPZs have played a part in the outward-oriented strategy of several countries, they are rarely as dominant as critics imagine. In fact, their relative importance in overall exports often diminishes over time because the advantages offered by EPZs gradually become available nationwide. Thus, Taiwan's exports from its three EPZs were no more than 10 percent of her overall exports in the 1960s, but by the 1980s, their share had fallen to 6 percent. But the crux of the counter-argument in this complex issue[8] comes from a study done by two New York Times journalists, Nicholas Kristof and Sheryl WuDunn, who, in an effort to investigate the charge that EPZs exploited their mostly female workers, visited many sites in China. They reported[9] that the young women they interviewed *wanted* to accumulate money, worked hard, long hours (sometimes seven days a week!) *by choice*, and returned home *by choice*. In fact, some sought particular factories because they offered the opportunity to earn more, leading one factory manager to lament that they wanted to work so hard that the owners had additional concerns about security, and had to have a supervisor constantly present!

Child labor

The conclusions are equally encouraging for child labor. Poor parents, no less than rich ones, generally want the best for their children. Poverty is what drives many to put children to work rather than into school. Parents will choose to feed their children instead of schooling them, if forced to make a choice. Several NGOs have argued that, when incomes increase, wicked parents will take a child away from schools and put them to work. But then there is the virtuous parent hypothesis: that parents who are earning more money will make sure that more of their children go to school. Economics also reinforces the virtuous parent hypothesis. Why? Because many studies show that the returns to primary education are usually very high, but that credit-constrained parents are unable to send their children to school because they cannot borrow against the expected high returns. But when parents earn more, the credit-constraint is indented, quite obviously. Economists Priya Ranjan, Jean-Marie Baland, and James Robinson have argued[10] that the returns to primary education have been so attractive in many poor countries with high levels of child labor, that the most likely hypothesis to explain why children are not being sent to school is that poor parents are unable to borrow the money needed to send them, and later to repay their loans. In short, credit markets are imperfect. So the growth of parental income, and hence the easing of credit constraint—which can certainly follow from improved incomes following globalization—should lead to greater school enrollment and reduced child labor. So, by now, we have an increasing number of studies, showing that when incomes improve thanks to globalization (among other factors), schooling also goes up and child labor declines.

Of particular interest in this regard are pioneering studies by a husband-wife team of economists at Dartmouth College[11] on how Vietnamese peasants responded after experiencing an over 30 percent improvement in their incomes after rice exports were liberalized. The government had gradually liberalized its export regime, allowing rice exports to more than double—to about 3 million tons in 1996. By 1997, Vietnam's export quota was no longer binding, and Vietnam was fully exposed to the international price of rice. Vietnam happens to be a country where 26 percent of children ages six through fifteen work in agriculture, and about 7 percent work elsewhere, providing an ideal opportunity to study how globalization might affect the use of child labor. It turned out that households that earned an extra income from higher rice prices substituted these extra earnings for the money their children would have made, and sent them to school instead. Interestingly, the extra income appeared to benefit older girls, who experienced the largest declines in child labor and the largest increases in school enrollment.

And one can go down the line, examining the concerns of the anti-globalizers about the dire consequences of globalization on social agendas. Over and over again, we find the effects to be benign rather than malign. Many of the concerned anti-globalizers are young. I talk to many of them on campuses, and find that they are eager to learn to think about the issues, instead of receiving packaged anti-globalization conclusions from their lectures. The fact that my book sold almost 50,000 copies in English hardback in just over a year, even though it does not offer inflammatory assertions against globalization, is clear evidence that one does not have to write anti-globalization nonsense to get great sales! And I have recently decided to repeat a course on globalization at Columbia—which I had dropped last year—because many students expressed discontent with the propagandistic anti-trade and anti-globalization courses offered on the subject in our School of International Affairs.

Appropriate governance

If the effects of economic globalization on several social dimensions are, on balance, benign rather than malign, then we must ask: what institutional and policy framework is necessary to *improve* on the benign outcomes that globalization produces?

Evidently, three types of issues matter. First, even if the effect is benign, it is not always so. Therefore, we must devise institutions to deal with downsides, as and when they arise. I have argued that the developing countries often lack adjustment assistance programs of the kind that the developed countries have evolved over time.[12] But how can the poor countries finance such programs? Evidently, aid agencies such as the World Bank can be mobilized to provide funds to support trade liberalization.

Second, we need to ensure that we do not repeat the mistake made by the reformers in Russia, where shock therapy was tried and failed. Maximal speed is not necessarily the optimal speed, as both economics and politics require cautious adjustment. When a leading economist insisted on shock therapy in Russia, using the analogy that "you cannot cross a chasm in two leaps," Soviet expert Padma Desai replied: "You cannot cross it in one leap either unless you are Indiana Jones; it is better to drop a bridge." Events proved her right.

Finally, supplementary policies are needed to accelerate the pace at which the social agendas are advanced. If it is true that child labor will be reduced by the prosperity enhanced by globalization, what more can we do to reduce it even further? Here, the unions in the rich countries have taken the view that only trade sanctions have "teeth." This is a myopic and counterproductive view. It is far better, as many intellectuals from the developing countries argue, to use moral suasion today. After all, God gave us a tongue, and in today's world, with democratic regimes worldwide, with CNN and with well-functioning and responsible NGOs, consultation, argumentation—even a good tongue-lashing—are far more powerful tools than sanctions imposed by governments whose own credentials are not always unblemished.

Economic prosperity and globalization

I shall conclude with a brief set of arguments about the economic benefits that follow from freer trade, in combination with benign policies toward the inflow of direct foreign investment.

First, however, let me say that the objections to freer trade are mostly ill-informed, particularly when they come from hugely endowed and media-connected NGOs like Oxfam, who like to wander in an ever-expanding search for "policy markets" into fields that they know nothing about.

Thus, they argue that the poor countries should not be asked to lower their trade barriers but the rich countries should lower theirs. This ignores the practical lesson we have learned from decades of non-reciprocity, and of the automatic extension of the status of *most favored nation* (MFN) to the developing countries: that reciprocity has its usefulness, when it enables a country's administration to face down the import-competing lobbies by motivating countervailing export-oriented ones. But then these misguided critics have the temerity to advise the poor-country governments that it is good for them to have high tariffs, presumably on infant-industry grounds. In fact, most of the poor countries have used these tariffs and other trade barriers quite freely in the last six decades, and have little to show for it! They also forget that, even to access foreign markets, it is important that one's producers also find it profitable to do so. When rich-country foreign tariffs and subsidies fall, and the metaphorical foreign door opens, the poor country will find that its exporters do not get past their own door, because their own tariffs create a bias in favor of the home market and a flip-side "bias against exports." This is the inescapable conclusion of numerous post-war studies of trade and developmental policies at the Organisation for Economic Co-operation and Development, the National Bureau of Economic Research, and the World Bank in the late 1960s and 1970s.

Since it has become fashionable to say that "one (shoe) size doesn't fit all," protectionism should be allowed whenever a country says it needs it. And this nonsensical cliché is reinforced by another: that the poor countries must have "ownership" of their trade and developmental programs. But surely we need to decide whether we want to go barefoot or wear shoes! In other words, do we move toward freer trade, or do we move toward protectionism? Once you have decided to wear shoes, the shoe size will naturally vary. Thus, every country engaged in WTO negotiations[13] can say that certain sectors will not be freed: the General Agreement on Trade and Services (GATS) negotiations do just that, and even in manufacturing and agriculture, such freedom exists, even though negotiation puts pressure on everyone to make compromises. And as for IMF and World Bank conditionalities,

one would have to be exceedingly naïve not to know that they are often disregarded and even reversed. The shoe size is therefore often adjusted to your feet, have no fear!

Trade enhances growth and growth reduces poverty

What does the evidence show about the relationship between trade and growth? I have argued, as have others, that India and China, two big countries with almost 3 billion people today, grew disappointingly until the mid-1980s, when autarkic[14] policies were followed: in India because of bad economic ideas, and in China because of communist ideas and political realities. Both countries turned around to embrace globalization, and have since experienced dramatic increases in their growth rates. Most importantly, they have both radically reduced poverty. This is the essence of what I argued in the early 1960s, when I described growth not as a passive "trickle down" strategy, but as an active "pull up" strategy, by which growth would pull large numbers of the poor into gainful employment. The problem was that, until the 1980s, autarky in trade and foreign investment, along with other bad policies, meant that India grew abysmally!

India and China have the largest pool of world poverty. Both shifted to an outward orientation roughly two decades ago, and this contributed to their higher growth in the 1980s and 1990s. China adopted aggressively outward-oriented economic policies in 1978. India also began opening its insular economy in a limited fashion in the 1980s, then more systematically and boldly in the 1990s. According to World Bank estimates, real income (GDP) grew at an annual average rate of 10 percent in China and 6 percent in India during the two decades ending in 2000. No country in the world had growth as rapid as China's, and fewer than ten countries—except for China, none with poverty rates and population size comparable to India's—had a growth rate exceeding India's during these years. What happened to their poverty? Just what common sense suggests: it declined. According to the Asian Development Bank, poverty declined from an estimated 28 percent in 1978 to 9 percent in 1998 in China. Official Indian estimates report that poverty fell from 51 percent in 1977–78 to 26 percent in 1999–2000.

Thus, when we move away from the anti-globalization rhetoric and look at fears—even convictions—dispassionately, armed with the available empirical evidence, we can see conclusively that globalization, in the form of trade and direct equity investment, *helps,* not harms, the cause of poverty reduction in the poor countries.

The Swedish journalist Thomas Larsson in his new book, *The Race to the Top: The Real Story of Globalization,*[15] has written from his firsthand experiences in Asia and described with telling stories and portraits from the ground how poverty has been licked by globalization.

One particularly vivid example stayed with me long after I had read the book.

> Betting on poultry (cockfighting) wasn't what I had in mind when I came to Navanakorn, an industrial area in the northern outskirts of Bangkok. I'd taken the afternoon off from the UNCTAD conference to find out for myself what globalization looks like up close. The combined chicken farm and gambling den is right next door to a Lucent factory that manufactures microelectronics components—the factory floor of the broadband revolution and the knowledge economy.

> The work is done in large square buildings that look like giant sugar cubes. At the entrance stands a shrine honoring Brahma with yellow garlands and small wooden elephants. … Inside are thousands of Thai laborers.

> "When they started, the workers came on foot. Then they got motorbikes. Now they drive cars," says the rooster guardian. "Everyone wants to work there, but it is hard to get in."

> … On my way back into town I amble through the industrial estate in search of a ride. A shift is ending. Thousands of women (for it is mostly women who work in the foreign-owned electronics factories) pour through the factory gates. I pass restaurants, drugstores, supermarkets, jewelers, tailors, film shops, vendors of automatic washing machines."[16]

Most policymakers in the poor countries, despite the ill-considered blandishments of Oxfam and a handful of populist economists, do understand the benefits of globalization. Many of us are beginning to write actively to dispel the dangerous misinformation which is being peddled to these poor countries, aimed at undermining their resolve to join globalization and prosper from it.

A real problem now lies in the protectionism, which seems to be plaguing some of the leading rich countries. The fears about outsourcing are a case in point. The United States and France, often opposed in their policies, are both victims of the same fear: the United States foolishly so, and France wisely so, given its failing economic model—which amplifies the risks from globalization and dampens the possibility of gaining from it. To the "yellow peril," they have both added the "brown peril" from India. Neither makes sense, and it is possible to expose these fears as groundless.[17] But then, as the Russian proverb goes, fear has big eyes. I would add: it sometimes also has deaf ears.

The critics of globalization think of themselves as waking us from what they see as our complacency and disturbing our comfort with the process of globalization. However, public action will not succeed unless it reflects not only passions, but also reason. Reason and analysis require that we abandon the conviction that globalization lacks a human face, an assertion that is tantamount to a false alarm, and in its place, recognize that it has one, and improve on it. It can be done.

Notes

1 Jagdish Bhagwati is University Professor at Columbia University, Senior Fellow at the Council on Foreign Relations, New York, and author of the book *In Defense of Globalization,* 2004.

2 Bhagwati, 1998.

3 *The Economist,* 2003; see also Baghwati, 2004, Chapter 13.

4 Hume, 1983, p.49.

5 Said, 2001.

6 Brainerd and Black, 2000, online at: http://econpapers.repec.org/paper/izaizadps/dp556.htm ; for more detail and additional arguments, see Bhagwati, 2004, Chapter 7.

7 White, 1999.

8 See Bhagwati, 2004, pp. 83–86.

9 Their report, published in the New York Times Magazine, and provocatively titled "Two Cheers for Sweatshops," was based on their book *Thunder From the East* (2000).

10 Ranjan, 2001.

11 Edmonds and Pavcnik, 2002, online at: http://www.nber.org/papers/w8760

12 Contrary to Oxfam's ill-informed talk about "double standards" in trade, the developed countries have liberalized trade far more than people realize.

13 More arguments against the most fashionable objections to freer trade today are offered in the report on the Future of the World Trading System, submitted to the Director General of the WTO this year, by the expert group headed by Peter Sutherland, of which I was a member. There is much concern today about the functioning of the WTO, and its distortion by heavy-weight lobbies. For example, many economists (myself included) believe that, while the optimal length of patents is non-zero, the industrial lobbies that push for intellectual property (IP) protection have succeeded in creating patent rights for far too many years. Many trade economists have also raised objections that these lobbies have managed to put IP protection into the WTO, via the agreements on *trade-related aspects of international property rights,* known as TRIPs. They argue that the WTO is a trade organization, that collection of royalties does not belong to it, and that introducing an extraneous issue such as IP protection into the WTO has now opened the floodgates to others, such as labor and environment lobbies—and doubtless many others in the near future—to muscle their way into the WTO, destroying its essential functions and character.

14 Policies fostering national and economic self-sufficiency and independence.

15 Larsson, 2001.

16 Ibid., pp.133–34.

17 See, for instance, Bhagwati, et al., 2005.

References

Bhagwati, J. 2004. *In Defense of Globalization.* New York: Oxford University Press.

———. 1998. "The Capital Myth: The Difference Between Trade in Widgets and Dollars." *Foreign Affairs.* May–June.

Bhagwati, J., A. Panagariya, and T. N. Srinivasan. 2005. "Muddles Over Outsourcing." *Journal of Economic Perspectives* 18(4). American Economic Association. Winter.

Brainerd, E. and S. Black. 2000. "Importing Equality? The Impact of Globalization on Gender Discrimination." EconPapers 556. Institute for the Study of Labor.

The Economist. 2003. "A Place for Capital Controls." Editorial. 3 May.

Edmonds, E. and N. Pavcnik. 2002. "Does Globalization Increase Child Labor? Evidence from Vietnam." National Bureau of Economic Research Working Paper 8760. Cambridge.

Hume, D. 1983. *An Enquiry Concerning the Principles of Morals.* J.B. Schneewind, ed. Indianapolis: Hackett.

Kristof, N. and S. WuDunn. 2000. *Thunder from the East: Portrait of a Rising Asia.* New York: Alfred Knopf.

Larsson, T. 2001. *The Race to the Top: The Real Story of Globalization.* Washington, D.C.: Cato Institute.

Oxfam. 2002. *Rigged Rules and Double Standards: Trade, Globalization and the Fight Against Poverty.* Oxford: Oxfam.

Ranjan, P. 2001. "Credit Constraints and the Phenomenon of Child Labor." *Journal of Development Economics* 64:81–102.

Said, E. 2001. "The Public Role of Writers and Intellectuals." *The Nation* 8(273):27. September.

White, M. 1999. "Women and Trade." Testimony for Hill Briefing on Women and the WTO. Women's Edge. 28 June.

World Trade Organization. 2005. *Future of the World Trading System.* Geneva.

Part 4

Country Profiles and Data Presentation

CHAPTER 4.1

The Executive Opinion Survey: An Essential Tool for Measuring Country Competitiveness

JENNIFER BLANKE

EMMA LOADES[1]

at the World Economic Forum

In today's world, public opinion has become a critical factor in shaping government policies, and in guiding investment and other business-related decisions. It should not surprise us, then, that the opinions and insights of those having first-hand experience of the inner workings of an economy have proven to be invaluable for determining and refining the strategies needed to improve it. When people have the opportunity to voice their opinions on important issues, their sense of responsibility and involvement in the process of change increases, facilitating policy reform. The true value of such opinions—responsibly collected, and using well-defined and respected methodology—is fast becoming recognized by governments and business communities alike as a key element in strategic planning.

The World Economic Forum conducted its first Executive Opinion Survey (Survey) in 1979, with the goal of developing a tool to measure the growth potential of nations. Now carried out annually among thousands of top executives from a cross-section of firms worldwide, the Survey is designed to capture the expert opinions of business leaders on the most important issues affecting their working environment. The questionnaire has been carefully crafted to gather information on a range of variables for which hard data sources are scarce or nonexistent. For example, one of the three main components of the Growth Competitiveness Index (presented in Chapter 1.1 of this *Report*) measures the quality of a nation's public institutions, a fundamental factor in a nation's sustainable economic growth. Quantitative measurement of such important concepts as the independence of the judiciary, the prevalence of bribery in public/private transactions, or the perception of waste in the use of public resources is difficult to obtain. Thus, the Survey serves as an instrument for gathering *qualitative* data, valuable for in-depth research and analysis.

The data collected from the responses to the Survey questionnaire constitute a key ingredient of *The Global Competitiveness Report,* in its function as an annual measure of the quality of a nation's economic environment, and its ability to achieve sustained growth. The result is probably the most accurate portrayal available of the current and prospective health of a nation's economic and business environment, and how it relates to the global economy. This chapter describes the Executive Opinion Survey process, and the increasingly central role played by our Partner Institutes in each of the countries featured in the *Report*. It also contains a detailed look at the characteristics of this year's Survey respondents, some of the methods introduced recently to improve the quantity and quality of the data collected, and the results of several tests measuring the robustness and reliability of the Survey data itself.

The Executive Opinion Survey questionnaire

Structured around eleven issue areas, each relevant to the current state of an economy's business environment, the questionnaire asks participants to respond to 150 questions, on the basis of their own business experience. The questions cover such areas as the general state of the economy, the level and extent of use of technology by individuals, business and government, the effectiveness of the government and public sector, the quality of public institutions, general infrastructure, human resources, finance and openness, domestic competition, company operations and strategy, and, last but not least, the extent of environmental and social responsibility. The results for each variable are presented in the data tables section of this *Report* and are categorized by issue area. The final question in the Survey asks participants to select from a list of 14 the five which they see as being the most problematic for doing business in their country. The results for this particular question are presented in the country profiles section of this *Report*.

To facilitate analysis of the data, and for comparative purposes, the structure of most questions in the Survey is the same. The participant is asked to assess the condition of their own business environment, and then rank their perception on a scale of 1 to 7, where 1 typically represents the worst-case scenario, and 7 represents the best. Box 1 shows an example of a typical Survey question.

Box 1: Example of a Typical Survey Question

Intellectual property protection in your country:

Is weak or non-existent   **1 2 3 4 5 6 7**   Is equal to the world's most stringent

Circling 1.....means you agree completely with the answer on the left-hand side

Circling 2.....means you largely agree with the left-hand side

Circling 3.....means you somewhat agree with the left-hand side

Circling 4.....means your opinion is indifferent between the two answers

Circling 5.....means you somewhat agree with the right-hand side

Circling 6.....means you largely agree with the right-hand side

Circling 7.....means you agree completely with the answer on the right-hand side

---

It is important to ensure that the Survey questionnaire can be applied across the entire range of countries featured in the *Report*. Not only are the questions worded carefully so as to meet this requirement, but they are presented to participants in over 30 language versions. Though most participants use the English version, four other main language versions, Arabic, French, German and Spanish are prepared. Our Partner Institutes (see below)

lead the Survey process at the national level. They are given the option of translating the questionnaire into their local language. Countries which chose that option this year are Albania, Angola, Armenia, Azerbaijan, Bosnia and Herzegovina, Brazil, China, Croatia, Cyprus, Czech Republic, Estonia, Italy, Japan, Latvia, Lithuania, Macedonia, Moldova, Mongolia, Mozambique, Portugal, Romania, Russia, Serbia and Montenegro, Slovakia, Slovenia, Tajikistan, and Ukraine. In order to avoid distorting the meaning of any of the Survey questions, the translations are closely monitored by the respective Partner Institutes (see below).

In keeping with the expanded outreach of this year's Survey, the Forum has developed an interactive, user-friendly, online version of the questionnaire, as an option for participants in completing the Survey. Given the increased worldwide access to the Internet, this innovation has been very well-received, and we decided to introduce a French-language online option, to supplement the existing English and Spanish versions. Although there is still a preference for the hard copy, the online version of the Survey saw a 17.7 percent increase in use this year. Interestingly, 83 percent of the total online responses (1,011) used English. This year, our Partner Institute in Finland, the Research Institute of the Finnish Economy (ETLA), moved entirely to the online version. We will encourage this more cost- and environment-friendly alternative, and expect a number of other countries to follow suit. Because the completed questionnaire results are automatically collected in a database system, status reports can be generated at any point during the process.

Methodology

The Executive Opinion Survey is supervised by the World Economic Forum's Global Competitiveness Programme, which distributes it to the approximately 8,000 executives, who represent the Forum's community of member and partner companies worldwide. In order to ensure that the methods used to conduct the survey are consistent across the entire set of countries included in the *Report*, the Forum has developed detailed guidelines for Partner Institutes, who administer the Survey on the ground. The Partner Institute is offered guidance on how to conduct the Survey and asked to select a sample of business executives (preferably those having some international experience) to take part. The selected executive must hold the position of Chief Executive Officer, or equivalent, within the company, unless it has over 500 employees, in which case the participant may hold any of the company's top five management positions. The companies sampled should represent the main sectors of the economy, in proportion to its percentage share of GDP in each country. In order to guide Partner Institutes in this process, the Forum provides a detailed breakdown of the percentage share of GDP by sector from the World Bank's 2004 *World Development Indicators.* In many cases, this is supplemented by more detailed information from national sources about the distribution of enterprises in a particular country.

A stratified sample of companies to be interviewed is then drawn from a master list, which most closely represents the spectrum of companies in the country. Sometimes the master list is obtained from a list of companies registered for a telephone line, or other widely used public service. Alternatively, the selection process starts with a list of all companies registered with the national statistical office or tax authorities. The master list of companies in each country is then grouped by economic sector, geographical region, and size. We further recommend selecting from within these groups a final sample representing the national distribution of the country's firms. The selection of firms to be interviewed within each grouping cannot be completely random, in part because there is a preference for interviewing business executives, who have an international perspective; this often means choosing relatively large companies. However, subject to these considerations, we ask that the Partner Institutes use the guidelines to come as close as possible to a fair and representative sample.

The sample of respondents should include at least some of the following:

- Domestic firms that sell in foreign markets
- Units of foreign firms that operate in the domestic market
- Enterprises with significant government ownership (where applicable)

Partner Institutes are advised to try to visit more than 50 percent of the enterprises to participate in the Survey. Where this is not possible, direct contact by telephone is preferred, as a follow-up to direct mail. Not all Partner Institutes choose to use this method for carrying out the Survey, however, and adapt their approach according to the size, structure, and condition of their respective business sectors.

The role of Partner Institutes[2]

The Global Competitiveness Programme has established a network of 122 Partner Institutes located in the 117 countries featured in this year's *Report.* These typically consist of leading research or academic institutes, business organizations, national competitiveness councils, or any other recognized professional entity, committed to improving the competitiveness condition of their economy. In some of the larger countries featured in our *Report,* it has become necessary to establish a partnership with more than one Institute. For example, in Russia, we collaborate with three: the Academy of National Economy (under the Government of Russian Federation), and the Institute for Private Sector Development and Socio-Economic Analysis (IPSSA), both of which are based in Moscow, and the Stockholm School of Economics, based in St. Petersburg.

The main responsibility of the Partner Institutes is to conduct the Executive Opinion Survey in accordance with the guidelines set by the World Economic Forum. The high response rates to the Survey, and the overall quality of responses both testify to the efforts of our Partners, and to the strength of their local relationships. The relationship between the Partner Institutes and the Forum is designed to be strong and mutually beneficial, enabling the Partner Institute not only to be associated with one of the world's most comprehensive assessments of national competitiveness, but to receive exclusive access to data relevant to their own research projects. In order to maximize outreach, the Forum also encourages the Partner Institutes to assist in the dissemination of the results of the *Report* at the national level, with the underlying goal of making a positive contribution to the policy debate and overall development of the economy.

Geographic coverage and survey response rate

This year's *Report* features 15 new countries: Albania, Armenia, Azerbaijan, Benin, Cambodia, Cameroon, East Timor, Guyana, Kazakhstan, Kuwait, Kyrgyzstan, Moldova, Mongolia, Qatar, and Tajikistan, bringing total country coverage up from 104 last year to a record 117. Unfortunately, due to difficult local conditions, Angola and Zambia were unable to conduct the Survey this year, and are therefore not included in this edition. Total country coverage is equivalent to 98.2 percent of the world's Gross Domestic Product. The map of the world shown in Figure 1 illustrates the extent of country coverage. The dark blue-shaded areas on the map show those countries which are included for the first time this year, the gray-shaded areas show existing coverage and the white areas show many countries we hope to be able to feature in our Report in years to come.

The response rate of the Survey has reached an all-time high this year, up from 8,729 last year to 10,993—a 26 percent increase. This corresponds to an average of 94 responses per country. The Forum continues to make efforts to improve the response rate and the quality of the Survey data each year. A number of improvements (see below) have been introduced to this year's Survey process, which is clearly reflected in the increased quantity of responses collected.

Table 1: Distribution of respondents by sector

Country	Sample size	Agriculture (%)	Industry (%)	Services (%)	Not classifiable (%)	No response (%)	Country	Sample size	Agriculture (%)	Industry (%)	Services (%)	Not classifiable (%)	No response (%)
Albania	93	4	51	37	5	3	Malawi	43	16	23	44	0	16
Algeria	64	8	34	22	6	30	Malaysia	85	1	38	49	8	4
Argentina	97	6	41	38	10	4	Mali	63	21	29	16	3	32
Armenia	102	23	33	35	5	4	Malta	53	2	21	55	8	15
Australia	91	2	44	41	8	5	Mauritius	22	9	18	68	5	0
Austria	117	2	38	37	18	5	Mexico	135	4	39	33	16	7
Azerbaijan	66	3	42	48	5	2	Moldova	91	22	27	44	7	0
Bahrain	38	0	8	42	16	34	Mongolia	103	11	37	45	4	4
Bangladesh	96	4	43	25	15	14	Morocco	73	7	30	55	8	0
Belgium	62	3	37	50	8	2	Mozambique	70	6	13	64	9	9
Benin	143	8	27	63	2	0	Namibia	39	8	15	59	8	10
Bolivia	79	0	29	43	16	11	Netherlands	87	2	18	64	10	5
Bosnia and Herzegovina	75	7	41	28	13	11	New Zealand	47	23	38	32	6	0
Botswana	62	2	31	56	5	6	Nicaragua	66	8	20	47	9	17
Brazil	212	2	36	45	14	3	Nigeria	153	1	42	48	7	2
Bulgaria	156	8	41	50	1	0	Norway	63	0	54	35	10	2
Cambodia	95	6	41	53	0	0	Pakistan	55	9	51	25	11	4
Cameroon	90	31	21	28	10	10	Panama	62	0	11	69	16	3
Canada	126	2	43	40	10	4	Paraguay	91	5	16	52	15	11
Chad	216	6	13	70	9	2	Peru	71	4	56	27	8	4
Chile	164	6	41	38	9	6	Philippines	43	7	26	37	21	9
China	299	7	40	47	5	1	Poland	109	2	20	66	8	4
Colombia	53	11	64	21	4	0	Portugal	42	0	45	43	7	5
Costa Rica	81	12	36	42	10	0	Qatar	63	0	19	33	13	35
Croatia	103	8	36	50	7	0	Romania	107	7	42	36	15	0
Cyprus	78	3	35	59	4	0	Russian Federation	473	6	47	42	3	3
Czech Republic	99	0	22	54	18	6	Serbia and Montenegro	98	17	36	39	7	1
Denmark	50	0	36	54	10	0	Singapore	151	0	50	36	11	3
Dominican Republic	70	1	30	54	3	11	Slovak Republic	69	4	57	23	9	7
East Timor	61	5	31	57	7	0	Slovenia	128	0	53	39	0	8
Ecuador	87	3	22	59	13	3	South Africa	96	2	40	44	13	2
Egypt	119	13	38	35	13	1	Spain	82	4	37	41	15	4
El Salvador	49	2	29	47	8	14	Sri Lanka	90	19	28	52	1	0
Estonia	88	1	35	53	10	0	Sweden	44	0	34	45	11	9
Ethiopia	89	9	24	39	18	10	Switzerland	101	1	41	39	14	6
Finland	36	0	72	25	0	3	Taiwan	82	0	61	30	6	2
France	163	2	25	48	17	9	Tajikistan	90	20	36	41	0	3
Gambia	80	0	26	60	11	3	Tanzania	102	40	15	39	5	1
Georgia	77	18	21	53	8	0	Thailand	64	3	42	39	9	6
Germany	78	0	40	40	15	5	Trinidad and Tobago	108	6	24	52	11	7
Ghana	83	17	36	36	6	5	Tunisia	74	22	31	26	14	8
Greece	73	3	40	32	11	15	Turkey	125	2	57	28	10	3
Guatemala	261	7	23	52	12	7	Uganda	90	31	20	48	1	0
Guyana	49	12	37	47	2	2	Ukraine	101	4	54	38	4	0
Honduras	82	10	23	49	11	7	United Arab Emirates	54	0	52	37	4	7
Hong Kong SAR	56	0	27	55	11	7	United Kingdom	97	0	28	54	16	2
Hungary	59	0	69	27	3	0	United States	158	0	39	42	16	3
Iceland	30	10	40	43	3	3	Uruguay	79	8	27	48	14	4
India	100	2	53	23	17	5	Venezuela	35	0	26	49	26	0
Indonesia	93	8	69	16	8	0	Vietnam	157	7	20	35	22	16
Ireland	38	5	50	42	3	0	Zimbabwe	28	11	54	32	4	0
Israel	37	3	68	22	5	3	**TOTAL**	**10,993**					
Italy	141	1	35	35	13	16							
Jamaica	70	4	23	54	17	1							
Japan	75	0	51	37	12	0							
Jordan	88	1	18	41	14	26							
Kazakhstan	82	5	45	45	4	1							
Kenya	101	11	22	62	4	1							
Korea, Rep.	190	1	47	48	2	2							
Kuwait	62	0	2	23	6	69							
Kyrgyz Republic	100	26	38	35	0	1							
Latvia	170	4	29	51	11	5							
Lithuania	135	10	38	50	1	1							
Luxembourg	32	0	38	50	9	3							
Macedonia, FYR	87	10	37	49	3	0							
Madagascar	83	37	18	29	8	7							

Note: Categories are taken from the World Bank (2004); *No response* refers to the share of respondents who did not answer this particular question in the Survey.

(cont'd.)

216

Figure 1: Country coverage of the Executive Opinion Survey

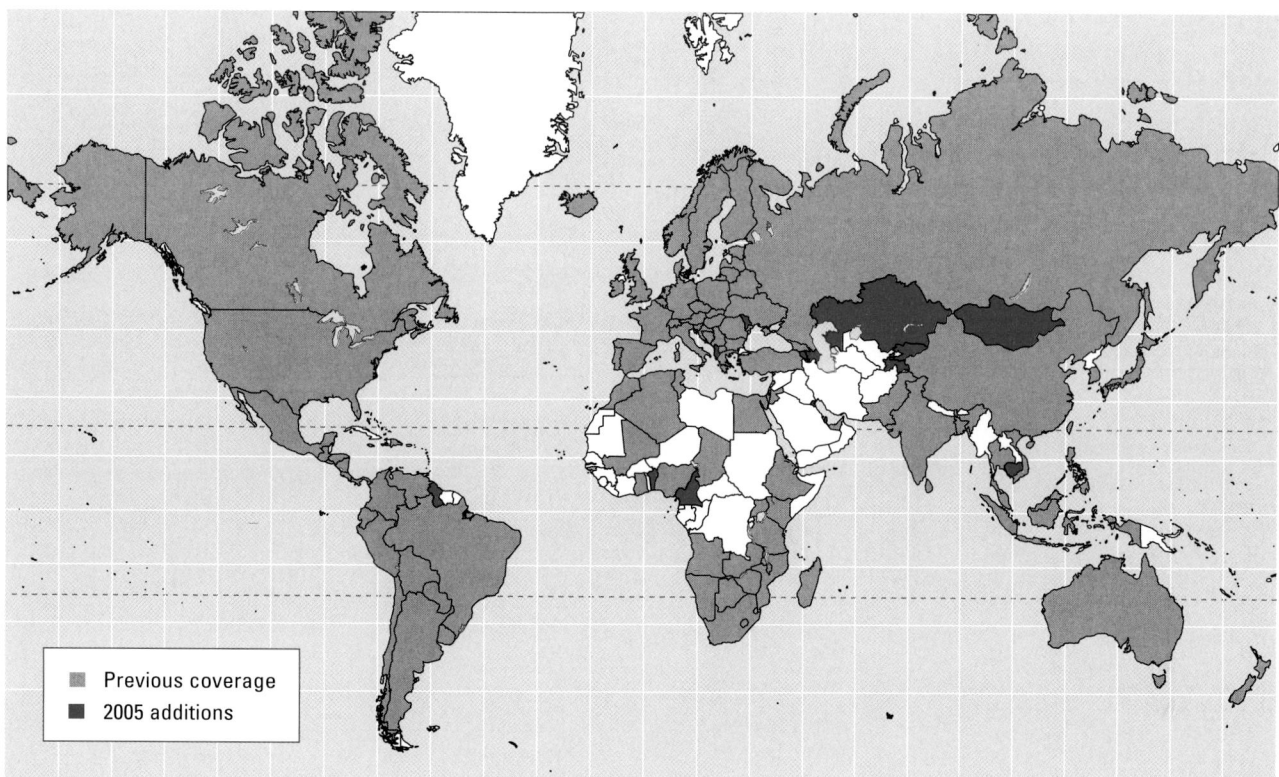

Previous coverage

2005 additions

Characteristics of respondents

Table 1 provides the actual distribution of respondents by industry sector (agriculture, industry, services), as well as the sample size for each country.

The distribution of most responses across sectors reflects reasonably well the actual structure of the respective business sectors. Shown in Table 2 is a comparison between the actual distribution of GDP by sector in Croatia and the percentage of Survey respondents from each corresponding sector, providing a reasonably clear picture of Croatia's business sector.

Table 3 presents the detailed characteristics of each country's respondents surveyed this year. The left part of the table analyzes the distribution of respondents by size of firm (number of employees), while the right part examines the sample structure by firm type (domestic, foreign, state-owned, or mixed).

This year's Executive Opinion Survey was carried out between January and May 2005. The completed surveys were retrieved by the World Economic Forum, and outsourced for data entry by a Geneva-based, professional data processing company.

Table 2: Comparison of Survey response sample with the underlying economic structure

Sector	Actual percent of GDP	Percent of respondents
Agriculture (agriculture, forestry, and fishing)	8	8
Industry (manufacturing, mining, construction, electricity, water and gas)	30	36
Services (transport and communications, retailing and hotels, financial services and real estate, other services)	62	50
Not classifiable	—	7

Table 3: Distribution of respondents by firm size (number of employees) and type

	Sample size (# of respondents)	Distribution of respondents by firm size (# employees in country)						Distribution of respondents by firm type				
		<101 (%)	101–500 (%)	501–5,000 (%)	5,001–20,000 (%)	>20,000 (%)	No response (%)	Dom[1] >50%	Gov[2] >50%	Fgn[3] >50%	D, G, F[4] ≤50%	No response (%)
Albania	93	66	26	8	1	0	0	66	3	24	5	2
Algeria	64	58	14	14	6	3	5	47	33	2	8	11
Argentina	97	26	31	37	3	0	3	61	2	34	0	3
Armenia	102	58	25	15	2	0	1	59	3	24	6	9
Australia	91	21	19	45	9	7	0	53	10	30	4	3
Austria	117	5	42	44	7	2	0	65	3	25	6	1
Azerbaijan	66	65	21	11	0	0	3	67	18	8	0	8
Bahrain	38	39	37	21	0	0	3	47	5	24	11	13
Bangladesh	96	21	34	34	4	3	3	77	1	13	1	8
Belgium	62	52	18	16	6	6	2	68	5	16	5	6
Benin	143	87	8	3	0	0	1	78	5	12	0	6
Bolivia	79	75	20	4	0	0	1	75	5	15	1	4
Bosnia and Herzegovina	75	35	35	27	0	1	3	59	21	16	0	4
Botswana	62	65	27	8	0	0	0	45	10	34	2	10
Brazil	212	32	13	36	13	5	0	71	5	17	1	6
Bulgaria	156	73	15	8	2	0	2	73	10	8	0	10
Cambodia	95	31	36	26	4	0	3	37	0	59	4	0
Cameroon	90	54	38	7	1	0	0	54	11	18	2	14
Canada	126	19	44	30	5	2	0	65	14	17	1	3
Chad	216	93	6	1	0	0	1	76	3	8	1	11
Chile	164	27	30	33	7	0	2	60	8	26	2	4
China	299	8	22	57	9	4	0	41	48	7	2	2
Colombia	53	25	34	30	9	2	0	60	6	30	0	4
Costa Rica	81	38	42	17	2	0	0	60	7	30	1	1
Croatia	103	44	35	16	4	2	0	53	22	17	1	6
Cyprus	78	51	36	12	1	0	0	88	5	1	1	4
Czech Republic	99	48	18	24	5	0	4	37	16	28	3	15
Denmark	50	38	20	30	10	2	0	62	4	28	0	6
Dominican Republic	70	49	26	26	0	0	0	70	0	17	3	10
East Timor	61	90	8	2	0	0	0	44	2	34	11	8
Ecuador	87	36	43	17	2	0	2	75	7	15	0	3
Egypt	119	38	35	24	1	0	2	64	11	21	2	3
El Salvador	49	20	37	41	0	0	2	73	6	12	0	8
Estonia	88	78	17	3	0	1	0	60	7	31	1	1
Ethiopia	89	52	26	18	1	1	2	62	22	4	0	11
Finland	36	3	53	36	6	3	0	50	11	28	8	3
France	163	23	21	29	10	17	0	50	9	31	6	4
Gambia	80	79	13	3	0	0	6	70	4	18	1	8
Georgia	77	53	30	14	0	0	3	58	1	32	4	4
Germany	78	13	15	21	27	24	0	64	6	15	5	9
Ghana	83	36	49	11	1	1	1	53	4	33	0	11
Greece	73	18	25	45	10	0	3	63	5	21	3	8
Guatemala	261	65	20	11	2	1	2	78	2	10	3	7
Guyana	49	63	18	14	2	0	2	61	12	14	2	10
Honduras	82	50	28	17	4	0	1	89	5	2	0	4
Hong Kong SAR	56	34	18	30	9	9	0	43	5	43	4	5
Hungary	59	24	41	29	7	0	0	53	3	39	0	5
Iceland	30	50	43	7	0	0	0	77	17	7	0	0
India	100	9	16	47	19	8	1	65	2	18	4	11
Indonesia	93	39	38	15	4	4	0	65	9	16	3	8
Ireland	38	24	26	37	11	3	0	45	11	39	0	5
Israel	37	35	46	14	5	0	0	76	0	16	3	5
Italy	141	37	24	19	11	9	0	52	1	32	5	10
Jamaica	70	61	19	16	1	0	3	69	0	26	1	4
Japan	75	11	12	35	23	19	1	73	3	11	0	13
Jordan	88	43	31	22	0	0	5	60	15	11	1	13
Kazakhstan	82	44	39	12	2	2	0	80	17	2	0	0
Kenya	101	54	30	13	1	0	2	71	5	12	1	11
Korea, Rep.	190	14	29	41	10	6	1	78	4	13	2	4
Kuwait	62	48	26	23	3	0	0	65	11	0	2	23
Kyrgyz Republic	100	51	38	10	0	0	1	73	14	7	3	3
Latvia	170	69	17	9	2	0	2	66	8	20	2	4
Lithuania	135	10	57	30	2	0	1	50	32	16	1	0
Luxembourg	32	34	22	38	6	0	0	56	3	38	0	3

(cont'd.)

Table 3: Distribution of respondents by firm size (number of employees) and type *(cont'd.)*

	Sample size (# of respondents)	Distribution of respondents by firm size (# employees in country)						Distribution of respondents by firm type				
		<101 (%)	101–500 (%)	501–5,000 (%)	5,001–20,000 (%)	>20,000 (%)	No response (%)	Dom[1] >50%	Gov[2] >50%	Fgn[3] >50%	D, G, F[4] ≤50%	No response (%)
Macedonia, FYR	87	61	24	11	3	0	0	77	13	9	0	1
Madagascar	83	76	18	5	0	0	1	70	2	11	0	17
Malawi	43	44	28	16	5	0	7	44	7	30	9	9
Malaysia	85	25	27	38	6	4	1	58	13	15	1	13
Mali	63	54	33	8	0	0	5	56	14	16	5	10
Malta	53	57	26	15	0	0	2	60	6	28	2	4
Mauritius	22	36	18	45	0	0	0	73	9	14	5	0
Mexico	135	27	19	29	16	7	2	63	6	22	4	5
Moldova	91	32	37	29	2	0	0	59	21	19	1	0
Mongolia	103	53	28	17	1	0	1	69	8	16	3	5
Morocco	73	67	22	8	3	0	0	85	3	5	1	5
Mozambique	70	61	29	7	0	0	3	61	4	27	1	6
Namibia	39	49	21	23	0	3	5	56	13	21	5	5
Netherlands	87	20	17	36	15	13	0	46	13	31	1	9
New Zealand	47	11	45	36	6	2	0	47	13	36	2	2
Nicaragua	66	58	27	12	0	0	3	58	15	15	5	8
Nigeria	153	46	26	25	2	0	1	82	0	15	1	3
Norway	63	19	43	27	10	0	2	29	2	60	6	3
Pakistan	55	33	25	29	9	2	2	78	7	7	2	5
Panama	62	58	23	11	3	0	5	74	3	10	0	13
Paraguay	91	62	26	9	0	0	3	85	0	9	1	5
Peru	71	20	44	31	4	0	1	59	7	30	1	3
Philippines	43	16	28	40	12	0	5	65	5	21	0	9
Poland	109	39	20	19	4	6	12	39	4	46	1	11
Portugal	42	12	26	52	10	0	0	40	31	14	5	10
Qatar	63	38	22	33	2	0	5	62	8	8	6	16
Romania	107	56	24	20	0	0	0	84	1	14	0	1
Russian Federation	473	32	29	27	5	3	3	70	18	6	2	4
Serbia and Montenegro	98	44	29	23	2	1	1	61	16	19	1	2
Singapore	151	30	32	32	5	1	1	13	7	69	4	7
Slovak Republic	69	23	23	41	10	0	3	54	6	36	1	3
Slovenia	128	37	34	24	2	0	3	61	9	23	4	2
South Africa	96	20	20	29	22	9	0	58	5	29	3	4
Spain	82	24	17	35	11	12	0	65	5	24	6	0
Sri Lanka	90	46	33	17	4	0	0	78	6	13	2	1
Sweden	44	41	20	14	18	7	0	61	7	30	2	0
Switzerland	101	38	24	24	10	4	1	63	8	24	2	3
Taiwan	82	6	24	54	12	4	0	62	10	23	1	4
Tajikistan	90	61	23	12	0	0	3	62	24	7	7	0
Tanzania	102	63	21	15	0	0	2	61	6	26	4	3
Thailand	64	3	25	38	23	9	2	56	22	9	6	6
Trinidad and Tobago	108	44	28	23	1	1	4	62	19	14	0	6
Tunisia	74	69	18	11	0	0	3	77	3	8	3	9
Turkey	125	33	3	43	7	13	1	71	6	14	6	2
Uganda	90	68	19	10	1	1	1	82	2	12	2	1
Ukraine	101	40	42	14	1	3	1	65	21	5	1	8
United Arab Emirates	54	17	30	39	9	2	4	57	20	17	0	6
United Kingdom	97	27	15	29	19	10	0	57	2	27	5	9
United States	158	30	8	27	19	16	0	83	2	8	3	5
Uruguay	79	59	37	4	0	0	0	61	8	24	3	5
Venezuela	35	46	20	26	6	3	0	77	0	23	0	0
Vietnam	157	43	26	23	4	3	1	41	26	22	4	6
Zimbabwe	28	11	7	64	18	0	0	57	18	21	0	4
TOTAL	**10.993**											

Notes:

[1] Companies majority-owned by the domestic private sector (more than 50%)

[2] Companies majority-owned by the government (more than 50%)

[3] Companies majority-owned by foreign groups (more than 50%)

[4] Mixed companies (not more than 50% owned by any one of the three sectors)

No response refers to the share of respondents who did not answer this particular question in the Survey.

Improvements, innovations, and quality control

Early in the process, Gallup International, a leader in the field of survey research and public opinion polling, acted as advisor to our program. They provided a comprehensive methodological and technical review of the Survey, which resulted in many improvements to both the quantity and quality of the data collected this year. The majority of the recommendations made by Gallup were implemented, including the use of a professional firm to ensure error-free data entry. A new set of documents was crafted for Partner Institutes with clear instructions on procedures and Survey administration guidelines. The content of the Survey was shortened by one third this year, making it much less onerous for respondents to complete. Feedback from the new Survey record sheet was introduced, to monitor the methods used by each Partner Institute. These will be carefully evaluated to help us explore ways to make further improvements to next year's Survey.

Members of the Global Competitiveness Programme team also made a number of field trips to some of the new countries featured this year. The trips involved debriefing sessions with the Partner Institute to discuss the obstacles in first-time conduct of the Survey, and to explore ways to overcome them in future. These trips added to our knowledge by introducing us, first hand, to the general condition of the economy.

Results of the Survey

As explained earlier, the data from the Survey serve to gain insight into the perspective of the average business person in a given economy on a wide range of issues. Therefore, it is important to take into account the degree of consensus on these issues among respondents within each economy. To this end, in Figure 2, we provide the standard deviations of the responses from each country to each Survey question within the survey data tables, which can be found to the right of the bars showing the average country responses. The standard deviations measure the degree of agreement among respondents in each country on each question, showing how closely or widely the individual responses are spread over respondents.

Figure 2 provides a graphic representation of the relationship between the mean responses and the standard deviations for a typical Executive Opinion Survey question (8.23) about the strength of auditing and accounting standards. The thick bars show the average score for each country to this question, while the thin black lines to the right of each bar represent the standard deviations. We have arranged the figure in the same order as shown in the data tables, with the best-rated responses (the highest scores) at the top, and the lowest-rated responses (the lowest scores) at the bottom. As the figure shows, the countries ranked highest (that is, with the highest scores) have

relatively low standard deviations. The countries ranked in the top 10 percent have standard deviations that are generally significantly below 1. This indicates a relatively high degree of consensus among respondents, indicating that auditing and accounting standards are strong in their respective countries. As might be expected, the level of agreement is lower for respondents in countries ranked lower on this question, showing that consensus is more difficult to obtain as the quality of accounting standards gets weaker.

Another question often raised regarding the Survey results, and the Survey data in general, is the extent to which Survey respondents suffer from what has been called "perception bias"—i.e., a systematic positive or negative bias found among all respondents in a given country; for example, some might believe that people in a certain country are more generally positive about their own economic environment than people in another country, who might be more pessimistic. If this were the case, such a bias might be expected to skew all of the Survey results in favor of the country with the more positive overall outlook.

While a certain degree of bias is inevitable, we have made great efforts to reduce it by phrasing Survey questions in such a way that asks respondents to compare their own environment to a world standard, rather than thinking in national terms. While it is difficult to test for perception bias, one method of measuring the extent to which it does exist is to compare results from the Survey data with hard data on similar issues. While comparable hard data does not exist for most of the Survey questions, which are primarily qualitative in nature, it is possible to carry out such comparisons for a few of the more technical and scientific questions. Figure 3 shows the relationship between hard data variable 4.12 and Survey question 4.05. The estimated number of tuberculosis cases in each country, appears in log form on the horizontal axis, and the question, concerning the expected impact of the disease on business, appears on the vertical axis.

The figure shows that there is a very strong relationship between the two variables, with higher prevalence rates corresponding, on average, to higher expected costs for business.

Figure 4 plots a similar comparison, this time between hard data question 3.19 and Survey question 3.16: the per capita number of Internet users (in log form) is seen on the horizontal axis, and the perceived extent of Internet use by businesses on the vertical axis. The graph shows a strong relationship between the two variables, with a large group of countries falling in the lower right-hand quadrant. Although Internet penetration rates are relatively high among individuals in these countries, it has not yet been widely adopted for business use. However, the graph does show that, in general, there is a relatively close relationship

Figure 2: Country means and standard deviations for a typical Executive Opinion Survey question:

"Financial auditing and reporting standards regarding company financial performance in your country are (1 = extremely weak, 7 = extremely strong—the best in the world)."

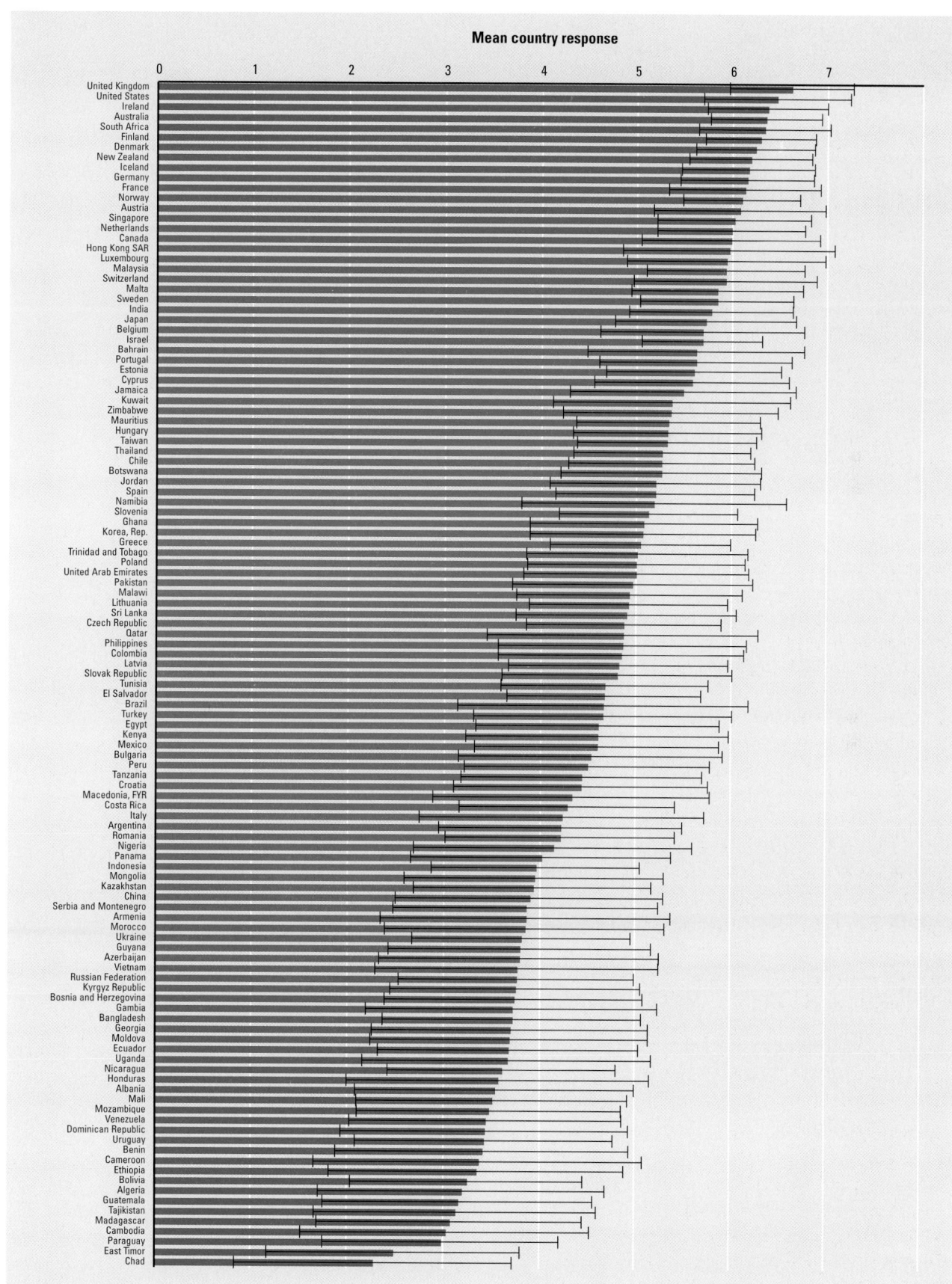

Note: Thick bars indicate scores; thin lines indicate standard deviations.

Figure 3: Hard versus Survey data on tuberculosis

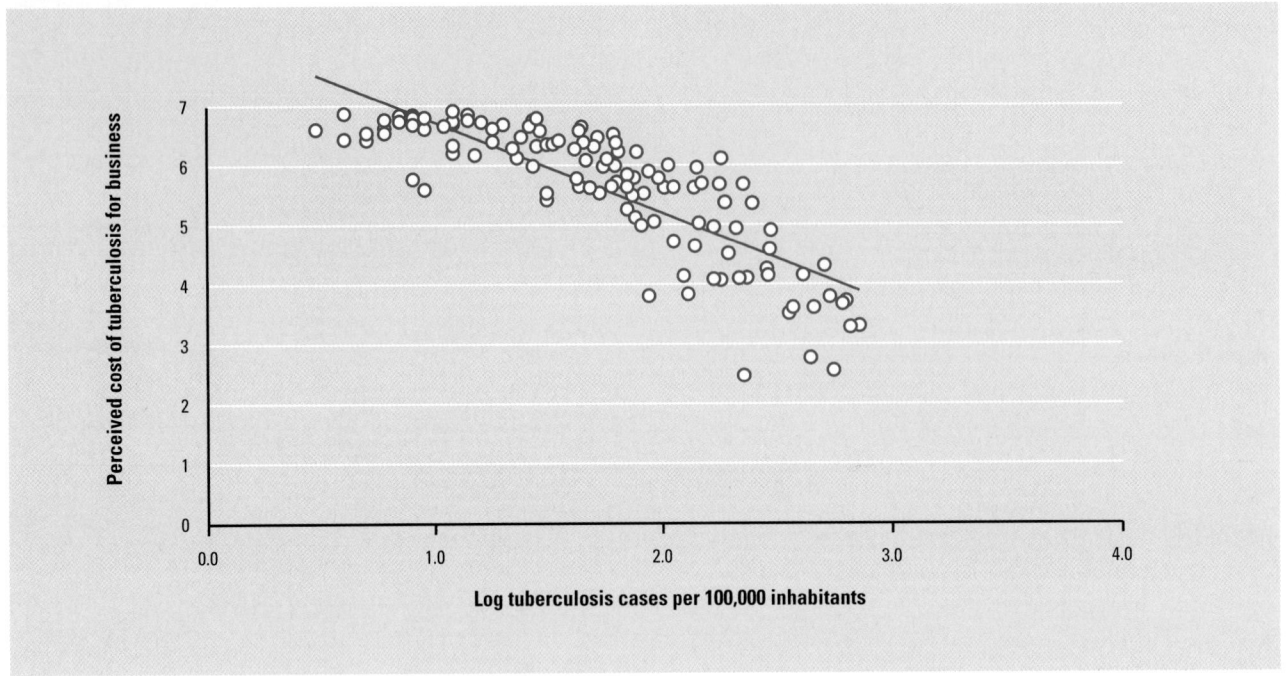

Figure 4: Hard versus Survey data on Internet use by business

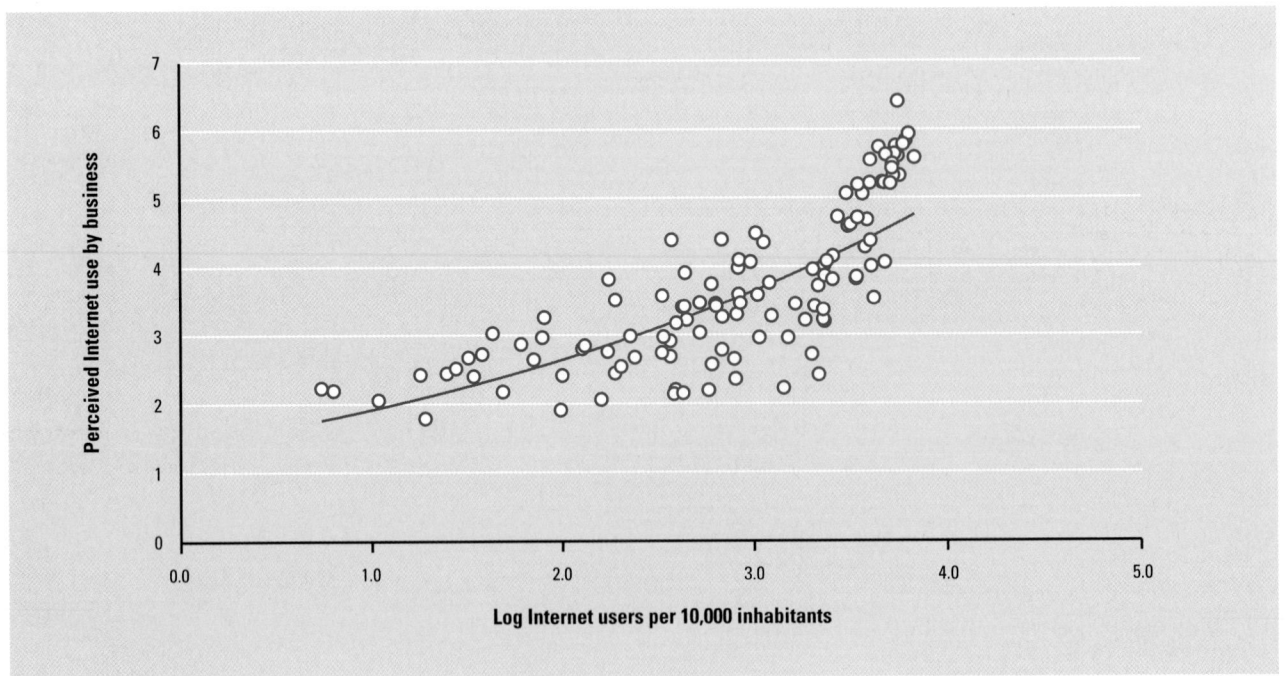

between perceived use of the Internet by business, and actual Internet use by businesses in the country.

Given the importance of measuring qualitative issues for which no hard data exists, these graphs provide evidence that the Survey is, in fact, capturing an underlying reality in the economies covered.

Summary

The Executive Opinion Survey generates a valuable set of data that complements hard data collected from publicly available sources. By soliciting the views of leading business executives worldwide on issues that affect their work environment, the Survey provides unique insight into concerns which are otherwise difficult to measure, but which are essential to the achievement of sustained economic growth.

The Executive Opinion Survey remains a vitally important instrument in the calculation of the Growth, Global, and Business Competitiveness Indexes presented in this *Report*. In addition, the data accumulated by the Survey is also widely used by a range of international organizations and development agencies, including the World Bank, USAID, government agencies, businesses, and academic institutions. It also yields a wealth of information, used by the Forum's Global Competitiveness Programme to produce other publications, supplementary to the present *Report,* such as *The Global Information Technology Report, The Arab World Competitiveness Report,* and new research projects, such as the recently released study *Women's Empowerment: Measuring the Gender Gap.*

Notes

1 The authors would like to thank Justina Roberts for her valuable research assistance and preparation of Tables 1 and 3 in this chapter.

2 Refer to page v of this *Report* for a complete list of Partner Institutes.

References

World Bank. 2004. *World Development Indicators 2004*. Washington: The International Bank for Reconstruction and Development and World Bank.

World Economic Forum. 2004. *The Global Information Technology Report*. Hampshire: Palgrave Macmillan.

———. 2005. *The Arab World Competitiveness Report*. Hampshire: Palgrave Macmillan.

———. 2005. *Women's Empowerment: Measuring the Global Gender Gap*. http://www.weforum.org/gendergap

4.2: Country Profiles

How country profiles work

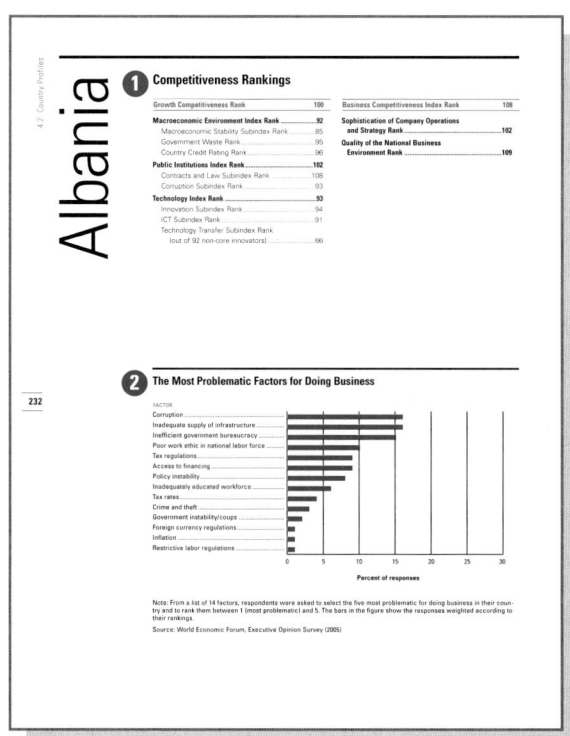

.The Country Profiles section presents a two-page profile with selected data for each individual economy included in the *Global Competitiveness Report 2005–2006*.

Left-hand page

The **left-hand page** gives each country's ranks in the *Global Competitiveness Report* indexes (the GCI and the BCI), as well as information on the issues perceived as most problematic for doing business in each country. The page is divided into the following two sections:

1 Competitiveness rankings

Overall Growth Competitiveness Index (GCI) rankings (out of 117 countries), and the Business Competitiveness Index (BCI) rankings (out of 110 countries) are listed in the upper right-hand side of the page, along with results for the composite subindex rankings.

2 Chart of most problematic factors for doing business

This chart summarizes those factors seen by CEOs and top executives as the most problematic for doing business in their country. The information is drawn from a question from the Executive Opinion Survey 2005. Respondents were presented with 14 different factors and were asked to rank from 1 (most problematic) to 5 those they considered the most problematic for doing business in their country. The results were then tabulated and weighted according to the ranking assigned by the respondents.

(continued on next page)

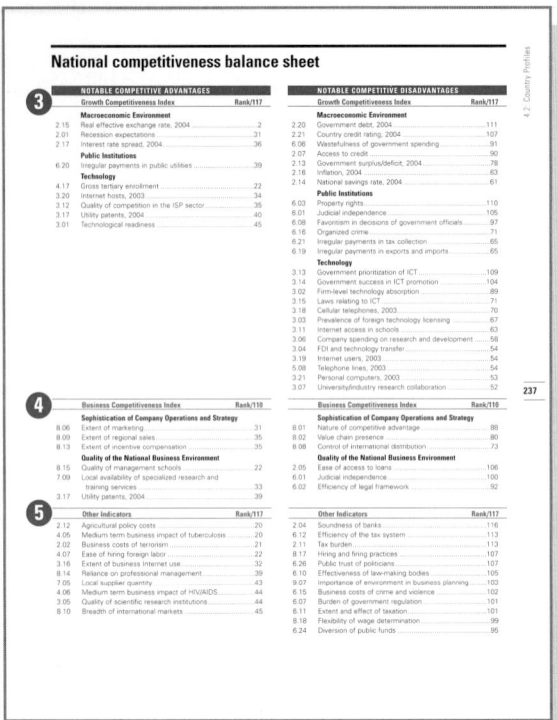

Right-hand page

The **right-hand page** of each profile forms a competitiveness balance sheet, providing detailed information on the relative strengths and weaknesses of each economy. The balance sheet is broken into two main sections, one on growth competitiveness, and one on business competitiveness, reflecting the complementary perspectives on competitiveness presented in Chapters 1.1 and 1.2, respectively. It also includes a list of other noteworthy indicators about the economic environment of each specific country.

Advantages and disadvantages are calculated based on an economy's overall rankings on individual variables. The left-hand side of the page includes those variables that at present reflect competitive advantages relative to other economies at similar levels of development. The right-hand side includes those variables indicating competitive disadvantages. It is important to note that what constitutes a strength or weakness is relative to each country's overall situation.

❸ Growth Competitiveness Index section
Variable rankings for the GCI section are based on data from 117 countries; the details of these variables and their associated rankings can be found in the data tables section of the *Report*.

The variables are selected as advantages or disadvantages as follows. Top-ranked countries such as the United States and Finland, for example, list no criterion with a rank lower than 10 as an advantage. For those countries ranked from 11 to 50 overall in the GCI, any variables ranked higher than the country's own rank are considered as advantages. For those countries ranked lower than 50 overall in the GCI, any variables ranked equal to or higher than 50 are considered as advantages.

❹ Business Competitiveness Index section
Variable rankings for the BCI section are based on the data set for the 110 countries used for calculating the BCI; see Chapter 1.2 for further information on this data set.

The variables are selected as advantages or disadvantages using the following decision rule: For each of the two categories: "Sophistication of company operations and strategy" and "Quality of the national business environment," for each country the variables with the top three rankings are selected as advantages, and variables with the bottom three rankings are selected as disadvantages. However, when the three lowest-ranked variables have ranking better than 15, they are automatically eliminated from the disadvantage list. Conversely, when the three highest rankings are lower than 95, they are eliminated from the advantage list. The result is that some countries have no advantages or disadvantages.

❺ Other indicators section

Variable rankings for the other indicators section are based on data from 117 countries; the details of these variables and their associated rankings can be found in the data tables section of the *Report*. The variables are selected as advantages or disadvantages using the same decision rule described in the GCI section above.

List of countries

Albania

Competitiveness Rankings

Growth Competitiveness Index Rank	100

Macroeconomic Environment Index Rank 92
    Macroeconomic Stability Subindex Rank 85
    Government Waste Rank 95
    Country Credit Rating Rank 96

Public Institutions Index Rank 102
    Contracts and Law Subindex Rank 108
    Corruption Subindex Rank....................................93

Technology Index Rank 93
    Innovation Subindex Rank 94
    ICT Subindex Rank 91
    Technology Transfer Subindex Rank
      (out of 92 non-core innovators) 66

Business Competitiveness Index Rank	108

**Sophistication of Company Operations
and Strategy Rank** 102
**Quality of the National Business
Environment Rank** 109

232

The Most Problematic Factors for Doing Business

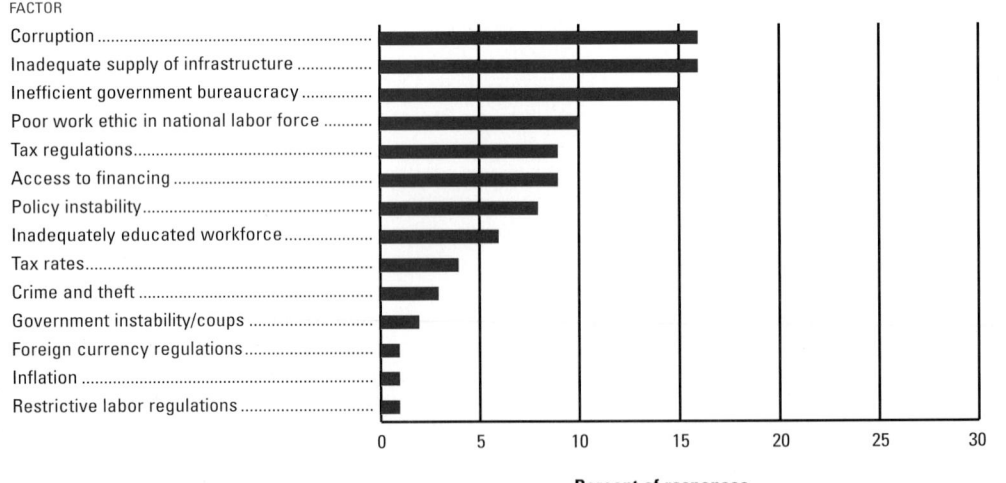

FACTOR
Corruption
Inadequate supply of infrastructure
Inefficient government bureaucracy
Poor work ethic in national labor force
Tax regulations
Access to financing
Policy instability
Inadequately educated workforce
Tax rates
Crime and theft
Government instability/coups
Foreign currency regulations
Inflation
Restrictive labor regulations

Percent of responses

Note: From a list of 14 factors, respondents were asked to select the five most problematic for doing business in their country and to rank them between 1 (most problematic) and 5. The bars in the figure show the responses weighted according to their rankings.

Source: World Economic Forum, Executive Opinion Survey (2005)

National competitiveness balance sheet

NOTABLE COMPETITIVE ADVANTAGES		
Growth Competitiveness Index		**Rank/117**
	Macroeconomic Environment	
2.16	Inflation, 2004	45

NOTABLE COMPETITIVE DISADVANTAGES		
Growth Competitiveness Index		**Rank/117**
	Macroeconomic Environment	
2.15	Real effective exchange rate, 2004	110
2.13	Government surplus/deficit, 2004	100
2.21	Country credit rating, 2004	96
6.06	Wastefulness of government spending	95
2.01	Recession expectations	92
2.14	National savings rate, 2004	85
2.07	Access to credit	63
2.20	Government debt, 2004	61
2.17	Interest rate spread, 2004	54
	Public Institutions	
6.08	Favoritism in decisions of government officials	111
6.16	Organized crime	108
6.21	Irregular payments in tax collection	100
6.03	Property rights	100
6.20	Irregular payments in public utilities	96
6.01	Judicial independence	82
6.19	Irregular payments in exports and imports	77
	Technology	
3.07	University/industry research collaboration	117
3.14	Government success in ICT promotion	113
3.15	Laws relating to ICT	110
3.06	Company spending on research and development	109
3.01	Technological readiness	109
3.12	Quality of competition in the ISP sector	108
3.11	Internet access in schools	108
3.02	Firm-level technology absorption	103
3.19	Internet users, 2003	101
3.20	Internet hosts, 2003	100
3.21	Personal computers, 2003	95
3.04	FDI and technology transfer	91
4.17	Gross tertiary enrollment	84
3.17	Utility patents, 2004	81
5.08	Telephone lines, 2003	80
3.13	Government prioritization of ICT	80
3.03	Prevalence of foreign technology licensing	79
3.18	Cellular telephones, 2003	53

Business Competitiveness Index		Rank/110
	Sophistication of Company Operations and Strategy	
8.08	Control of international distribution	53
8.01	Nature of competitive advantage	55
3.03	Prevalence of foreign technology licensing	77
	Quality of the National Business Environment	
8.19	Cooperation in labor-employer relations	39
4.03	Quality of math and science education	56

Business Competitiveness Index		Rank/110
	Sophistication of Company Operations and Strategy	
8.03	Capacity for innovation	110
8.10	Breadth of international markets	110
8.09	Extent of regional sales	110
	Quality of the National Business Environment	
3.08	Government procurement of advanced technology products	110
6.25	Business costs of corruption	110
2.08	Local equity market access	110

Other Indicators		Rank/117
4.07	Ease of hiring foreign labor	11
8.17	Hiring and firing practices	16
8.18	Flexibility of wage determination	26
8.20	Pay and productivity	29
4.09	Private sector employment of women	30
2.11	Tax burden	36
4.06	Medium term business impact of HIV/AIDS	41
4.05	Medium term business impact of tuberculosis	50

Other Indicators		Rank/117
9.10	Grass-roots involvement in development projects	117
9.08	Protection of ecosystems by business	117
9.02	Clarity and stability of regulations	117
9.01	Stringency of environmental regulations	117
7.09	Local availability of specialized research and training services	116
7.08	Local availability of process machinery	116
7.02	Effectiveness of antitrust policy	116
3.16	Extent of business Internet use	116
3.05	Quality of scientific research institutions	116

233

Note: The Business Competitiveness Index applies different criteria for selecting a country's competitive advantages and disadvantages. Please refer to the section "How Country Profiles Work" for further details.

Algeria

Competitiveness Rankings

Growth Competitiveness Index Rank	78

Macroeconomic Environment Index Rank **44**
    Macroeconomic Stability Subindex Rank 12
    Government Waste Rank 51
    Country Credit Rating Rank 68

Public Institutions Index Rank..**81**
    Contracts and Law Subindex Rank 67
    Corruption Subindex Rank...................................91

Technology Index Rank **114**
    Innovation Subindex Rank...................................84
    ICT Subindex Rank 110
    Technology Transfer Subindex Rank
    (out of 92 non-core innovators).........................89

Business Competitiveness Index Rank	92

**Sophistication of Company Operations
  and Strategy Rank** **107**
**Quality of the National Business
  Environment Rank** **86**

The Most Problematic Factors for Doing Business

Percent of responses

Note: From a list of 14 factors, respondents were asked to select the five most problematic for doing business in their country and to rank them between 1 (most problematic) and 5. The bars in the figure show the responses weighted according to their rankings.

Source: World Economic Forum, Executive Opinion Survey (2005)

234

National competitiveness balance sheet

NOTABLE COMPETITIVE ADVANTAGES	
Growth Competitiveness Index	**Rank/117**

Macroeconomic Environment
- 2.14 National savings rate, 2004 5
- 2.13 Government surplus/deficit, 2004 8
- 2.01 Recession expectations 20
- 2.15 Real effective exchange rate, 2004 24
- 2.20 Government debt, 2004 29

Public Institutions
- 6.08 Favoritism in decisions of government officials 35

Business Competitiveness Index	**Rank/110**

Sophistication of Company Operations and Strategy
- 8.14 Reliance on professional management 82
- 8.08 Control of international distribution 93

Quality of the National Business Environment
- 3.09 Availability of scientists and engineers 27
- 6.08 Favoritism in decisions of government officials 34
- 6.14 Reliability of police services 42

Other Indicators	**Rank/117**
7.03 Extent of market dominance 48	
3.08 Government procurement of advanced technology products 48	

NOTABLE COMPETITIVE DISADVANTAGES	
Growth Competitiveness Index	**Rank/117**

Macroeconomic Environment
- 2.07 Access to credit 103
- 2.21 Country credit rating, 2004 68
- 2.17 Interest rate spread, 2004 57
- 2.16 Inflation, 2004 52
- 6.06 Wastefulness of government spending 51

Public Institutions
- 6.20 Irregular payments in public utilities 100
- 6.21 Irregular payments in tax collection 97
- 6.03 Property rights 89
- 6.01 Judicial independence 79
- 6.19 Irregular payments in exports and imports 73
- 6.16 Organized crime 60

Technology
- 3.04 FDI and technology transfer 115
- 3.15 Laws relating to ICT 108
- 3.20 Internet hosts, 2003 107
- 3.07 University/industry research collaboration 106
- 3.03 Prevalence of foreign technology licensing 106
- 3.11 Internet access in schools 102
- 3.06 Company spending on research and development 101
- 3.12 Quality of competition in the ISP sector 100
- 3.19 Internet users, 2003 97
- 3.21 Personal computers, 2003 97
- 3.18 Cellular telephones, 2003 96
- 3.13 Government prioritization of ICT 89
- 3.01 Technological readiness 85
- 5.08 Telephone lines, 2003 85
- 3.17 Utility patents, 2004 76
- 4.17 Gross tertiary enrollment 75
- 3.14 Government success in ICT promotion 67
- 3.02 Firm-level technology absorption 55

Business Competitiveness Index	**Rank/110**

Sophistication of Company Operations and Strategy
- 8.02 Value chain presence 110
- 8.13 Extent of incentive compensation 110
- 8.09 Extent of regional sales 109

Quality of the National Business Environment
- 2.03 Financial market sophistication 109
- 8.16 Efficacy of corporate boards 108
- 3.15 Laws relating to ICT 102

Other Indicators	**Rank/117**
3.16 Extent of business Internet use 114	
8.07 Degree of customer orientation 114	
8.12 Willingness to delegate authority 113	
8.01 Nature of competitive advantage 113	
8.03 Capacity for innovation 112	
2.02 Business costs of terrorism 112	
8.06 Extent of marketing 112	
9.10 Grass-roots involvement in development projects 110	
8.23 Strength of auditing and accounting standards 110	
9.02 Clarity and stability of regulations 109	

235

Note: The Business Competitiveness Index applies different criteria for selecting a country's competitive advantages and disadvantages. Please refer to the section "How Country Profiles Work" for further details.

Argentina

Competitiveness Rankings

Growth Competitiveness Index Rank	72

Macroeconomic Environment Index Rank **86**
    Macroeconomic Stability Subindex Rank 50
    Government Waste Rank 91
    Country Credit Rating Rank 107

Public Institutions Index Rank..**74**
    Contracts and Law Subindex Rank 100
    Corruption Subindex Rank....................................57

Technology Index Rank **59**
    Innovation Subindex Rank....................................34
    ICT Subindex Rank 59
    Technology Transfer Subindex Rank
        (out of 92 non-core innovators) 39

Business Competitiveness Index Rank	64

**Sophistication of Company Operations
and Strategy Rank** **52**

**Quality of the National Business
Environment Rank** **64**

The Most Problematic Factors for Doing Business

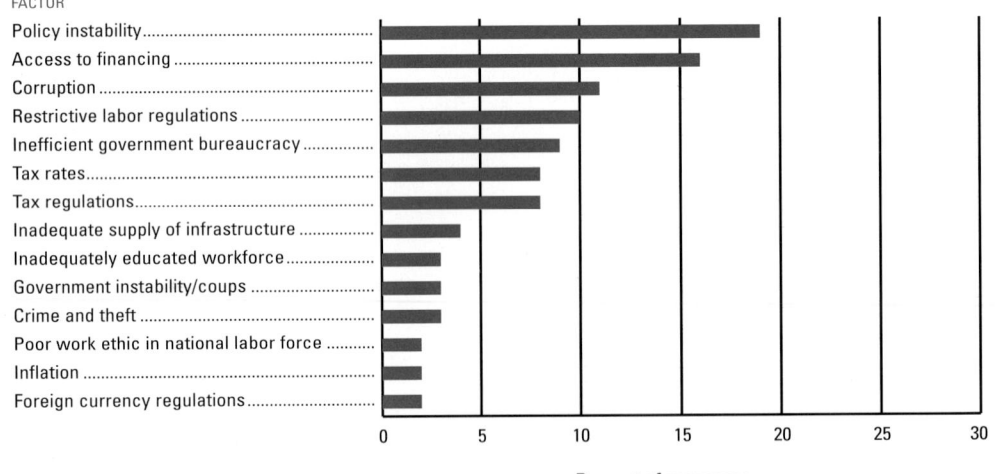

Note: From a list of 14 factors, respondents were asked to select the five most problematic for doing business in their country and to rank them between 1 (most problematic) and 5. The bars in the figure show the responses weighted according to their rankings.

Source: World Economic Forum, Executive Opinion Survey (2005)

236

National competitiveness balance sheet

NOTABLE COMPETITIVE ADVANTAGES	
Growth Competitiveness Index	**Rank/117**

	Macroeconomic Environment	
2.15	Real effective exchange rate, 2004	2
2.01	Recession expectations	31
2.17	Interest rate spread, 2004	36
	Public Institutions	
6.20	Irregular payments in public utilities	39
	Technology	
4.17	Gross tertiary enrollment	22
3.20	Internet hosts, 2003	34
3.12	Quality of competition in the ISP sector	35
3.17	Utility patents, 2004	40
3.01	Technological readiness	45

NOTABLE COMPETITIVE DISADVANTAGES	
Growth Competitiveness Index	**Rank/117**

	Macroeconomic Environment	
2.20	Government debt, 2004	111
2.21	Country credit rating, 2004	107
6.06	Wastefulness of government spending	91
2.07	Access to credit	90
2.13	Government surplus/deficit, 2004	78
2.16	Inflation, 2004	63
2.14	National savings rate, 2004	61
	Public Institutions	
6.03	Property rights	110
6.01	Judicial independence	105
6.08	Favoritism in decisions of government officials	97
6.16	Organized crime	71
6.21	Irregular payments in tax collection	65
6.19	Irregular payments in exports and imports	65
	Technology	
3.13	Government prioritization of ICT	109
3.14	Government success in ICT promotion	104
3.02	Firm-level technology absorption	89
3.15	Laws relating to ICT	71
3.18	Cellular telephones, 2003	70
3.03	Prevalence of foreign technology licensing	67
3.11	Internet access in schools	63
3.06	Company spending on research and development	58
3.04	FDI and technology transfer	54
3.19	Internet users, 2003	54
5.08	Telephone lines, 2003	54
3.21	Personal computers, 2003	53
3.07	University/industry research collaboration	52

237

Business Competitiveness Index	Rank/110

	Sophistication of Company Operations and Strategy	
8.06	Extent of marketing	31
8.09	Extent of regional sales	35
8.13	Extent of incentive compensation	35
	Quality of the National Business Environment	
8.15	Quality of management schools	22
7.09	Local availability of specialized research and training services	33
3.17	Utility patents, 2004	39

Business Competitiveness Index	Rank/110

	Sophistication of Company Operations and Strategy	
8.01	Nature of competitive advantage	88
8.02	Value chain presence	80
8.08	Control of international distribution	73
	Quality of the National Business Environment	
2.05	Ease of access to loans	106
6.01	Judicial independence	100
6.02	Efficiency of legal framework	92

Other Indicators	Rank/117
2.12	Agricultural policy costs	20
4.05	Medium term business impact of tuberculosis	20
2.02	Business costs of terrorism	21
4.07	Ease of hiring foreign labor	22
3.16	Extent of business Internet use	32
8.14	Reliance on professional management	39
7.05	Local supplier quantity	43
4.06	Medium term business impact of HIV/AIDS	44
3.05	Quality of scientific research institutions	44
8.10	Breadth of international markets	45

Other Indicators	Rank/117
2.04	Soundness of banks	116
6.12	Efficiency of the tax system	113
2.11	Tax burden	113
8.17	Hiring and firing practices	107
6.26	Public trust of politicians	107
6.10	Effectiveness of law-making bodies	105
9.07	Importance of environment in business planning	103
6.15	Business costs of crime and violence	102
6.07	Burden of government regulation	101
6.11	Extent and effect of taxation	101
8.18	Flexibility of wage determination	99
6.24	Diversion of public funds	95

Note: The Business Competitiveness Index applies different criteria for selecting a country's competitive advantages and disadvantages. Please refer to the section "How Country Profiles Work" for further details.

Armenia

Competitiveness Rankings

Growth Competitiveness Index Rank	**79**

Macroeconomic Environment Index Rank **77**
    Macroeconomic Stability Subindex Rank 55
    Government Waste Rank 63
    Country Credit Rating Rank 98

Public Institutions Index Rank...........................**66**
    Contracts and Law Subindex Rank 72
    Corruption Subindex Rank...................................61

Technology Index Rank **94**
    Innovation Subindex Rank 71
    ICT Subindex Rank 97
    Technology Transfer Subindex Rank
    (out of 92 non-core innovators).........................70

Business Competitiveness Index Rank	**86**

**Sophistication of Company Operations
and Strategy Rank** **86**

**Quality of the National Business
Environment Rank** **88**

The Most Problematic Factors for Doing Business

FACTOR

Percent of responses

Note: From a list of 14 factors, respondents were asked to select the five most problematic for doing business in their country and to rank them between 1 (most problematic) and 5. The bars in the figure show the responses weighted according to their rankings.

Source: World Economic Forum, Executive Opinion Survey (2005)

National competitiveness balance sheet

NOTABLE COMPETITIVE ADVANTAGES		
Growth Competitiveness Index		**Rank/117**
	Macroeconomic Environment	
2.15	Real effective exchange rate, 2004	28
2.01	Recession expectations	29
2.20	Government debt, 2004	30
2.07	Access to credit	32
2.13	Government surplus/deficit, 2004	45
	Public Institutions	
6.16	Organized crime	38
	Technology	
3.02	Firm-level technology absorption	49

NOTABLE COMPETITIVE DISADVANTAGES		
Growth Competitiveness Index		**Rank/117**
	Macroeconomic Environment	
2.17	Interest rate spread, 2004	104
2.21	Country credit rating, 2004	98
2.16	Inflation, 2004	87
6.06	Wastefulness of government spending	63
2.14	National savings rate, 2004	63
	Public Institutions	
6.01	Judicial independence	108
6.08	Favoritism in decisions of government officials	102
6.21	Irregular payments in tax collection	67
6.19	Irregular payments in exports and imports	66
6.03	Property rights	65
6.20	Irregular payments in public utilities	56
	Technology	
3.12	Quality of competition in the ISP sector	109
3.18	Cellular telephones, 2003	103
3.03	Prevalence of foreign technology licensing	103
3.11	Internet access in schools	100
3.01	Technological readiness	96
3.15	Laws relating to ICT	95
3.06	Company spending on research and development	91
3.21	Personal computers, 2003	88
3.19	Internet users, 2003	86
3.14	Government success in ICT promotion	84
3.07	University/industry research collaboration	82
3.20	Internet hosts, 2003	81
3.04	FDI and technology transfer	66
4.17	Gross tertiary enrollment	66
5.08	Telephone lines, 2003	65
3.13	Government prioritization of ICT	64
3.17	Utility patents, 2004	57

Business Competitiveness Index		Rank/110
	Sophistication of Company Operations and Strategy	
8.01	Nature of competitive advantage	41
8.03	Capacity for innovation	47
8.02	Value chain presence	48
	Quality of the National Business Environment	
3.09	Availability of scientists and engineers	25
8.19	Cooperation in labor-employer relations	28
4.03	Quality of math and science education	36

Other Indicators		Rank/117
4.07	Ease of hiring foreign labor	1
8.17	Hiring and firing practices	12
6.15	Business costs of crime and violence	29
9.06	Prioritization of energy efficiency	31
8.18	Flexibility of wage determination	31
8.20	Pay and productivity	32
2.12	Agricultural policy costs	39
4.09	Private sector employment of women	45
2.10	Impact of rules on FDI	45

Business Competitiveness Index		Rank/110
	Sophistication of Company Operations and Strategy	
8.06	Extent of marketing	107
8.14	Reliance on professional management	105
3.03	Prevalence of foreign technology licensing	99
	Quality of the National Business Environment	
5.03	Port infrastructure quality	109
7.03	Decentralization of corporate activity	108
7.01	Intensity of local competition	107

Other Indicators		Rank/117
3.10	Availability of mobile or cellular telephones	117
7.03	Extent of market dominance	115
8.24	Importance of corporate social responsibility	112
7.02	Effectiveness of antitrust policy	110
2.03	Financial market sophistication	110
9.05	Effects of privatization on competition and the environment	109
6.04	Intellectual property protection	109
9.08	Protection of ecosystems by business	109
2.08	Local equity market access	108
8.21	Protection of minority shareholders' interests	106
5.07	Telephone/fax infrastructure quality	105
9.04	Effects of compliance on business	104

239

Note: The Business Competitiveness Index applies different criteria for selecting a country's competitive advantages and disadvantages.
Please refer to the section "How Country Profiles Work" for further details.

Australia

Competitiveness Rankings

Growth Competitiveness Index Rank	10

Macroeconomic Environment Index Rank **14**
    Macroeconomic Stability Subindex Rank 25
    Government Waste Rank 16
    Country Credit Rating Rank 18

Public Institutions Index Rank..**10**
    Contracts and Law Subindex Rank 10
    Corruption Subindex Rank....................................10

Technology Index Rank **14**
    Innovation Subindex Rank 15
    ICT Subindex Rank 9

Business Competitiveness Index Rank	15

**Sophistication of Company Operations
  and Strategy Rank** **23**
**Quality of the National Business
  Environment Rank** **12**

The Most Problematic Factors for Doing Business

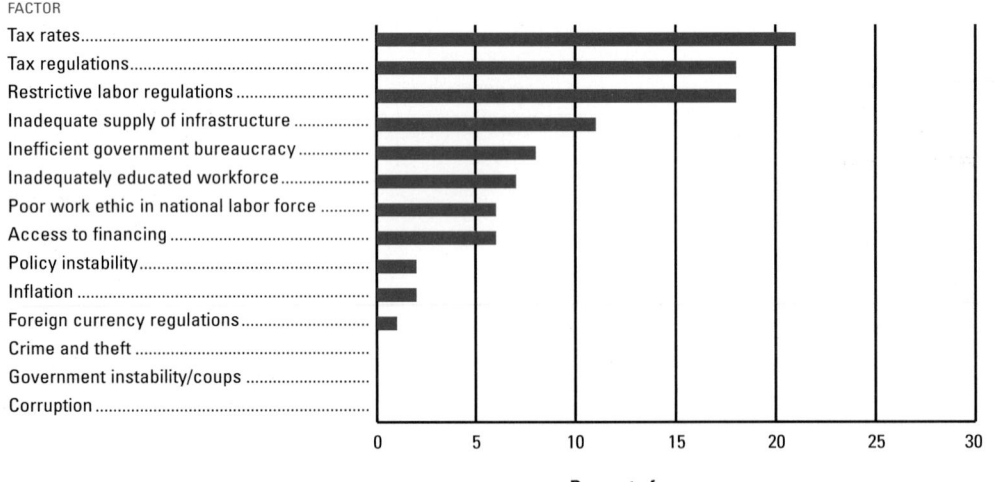

Note: From a list of 14 factors, respondents were asked to select the five most problematic for doing business in their country and to rank them between 1 (most problematic) and 5. The bars in the figure show the responses weighted according to their rankings.

Source: World Economic Forum, Executive Opinion Survey (2005)

National competitiveness balance sheet

NOTABLE COMPETITIVE ADVANTAGES		NOTABLE COMPETITIVE DISADVANTAGES	
Growth Competitiveness Index	**Rank/117**	**Growth Competitiveness Index**	**Rank/117**

Growth Competitiveness Index — Advantages

Public Institutions

6.01	Judicial independence	4
6.20	Irregular payments in public utilities	9
6.03	Property rights	9
6.21	Irregular payments in tax collection	9

Technology

3.19	Internet users, 2003	5
4.17	Gross tertiary enrollment	6
3.20	Internet hosts, 2003	6
3.21	Personal computers, 2003	6
3.15	Laws relating to ICT	8

Growth Competitiveness Index — Disadvantages

Macroeconomic Environment

2.15	Real effective exchange rate, 2004	113
2.14	National savings rate, 2004	75
2.17	Interest rate spread, 2004	53
2.01	Recession expectations	45
2.16	Inflation, 2004	32
2.13	Government surplus/deficit, 2004	23
2.07	Access to credit	23
2.21	Country credit rating, 2004	18
6.06	Wastefulness of government spending	16
2.20	Government debt, 2004	12

Public Institutions

6.16	Organized crime	21
6.08	Favoritism in decisions of government officials	18
6.19	Irregular payments in exports and imports	12

Technology

3.13	Government prioritization of ICT	62
3.14	Government success in ICT promotion	53
3.18	Cellular telephones, 2003	29
3.06	Company spending on research and development	28
3.07	University/industry research collaboration	23
3.17	Utility patents, 2004	21
3.02	Firm-level technology absorption	21
3.12	Quality of competition in the ISP sector	19
3.01	Technological readiness	19
5.08	Telephone lines, 2003	16
3.11	Internet access in schools	12

Business Competitiveness Index	**Rank/110**	**Business Competitiveness Index**	**Rank/110**

Business Competitiveness Index — Advantages

Sophistication of Company Operations and Strategy

8.14	Reliance on professional management	6
8.06	Extent of marketing	10
8.13	Extent of incentive compensation	13

Quality of the National Business Environment

7.02	Effectiveness of antitrust policy	2
8.16	Efficacy of corporate boards	3
6.01	Judicial independence	4

Business Competitiveness Index — Disadvantages

Sophistication of Company Operations and Strategy

8.02	Value chain presence	74
8.08	Control of international distribution	48
8.01	Nature of competitive advantage	29

Quality of the National Business Environment

8.19	Cooperation in labor-employer relations	45
3.08	Government procurement of advanced technology products	43
6.09	Extent of bureaucratic red tape	31

Other Indicators	**Rank/117**	**Other Indicators**	**Rank/117**

Other Indicators — Advantages

9.10	Grass-roots involvement in development projects	2
8.23	Strength of auditing and accounting standards	4
6.10	Effectiveness of law-making bodies	4
2.12	Agricultural policy costs	5
2.03	Financial market sophistication	5
8.24	Importance of corporate social responsibility	5
7.01	Intensity of local competition	5
6.23	Irregular payments in judicial decisions	6
6.13	Centralization of economic policymaking	6
8.21	Protection of minority shareholders' interests	6
2.08	Local equity market access	6
6.22	Irregular payments in public contracts	7

Other Indicators — Disadvantages

6.12	Efficiency of the tax system	109
4.07	Ease of hiring foreign labor	108
2.11	Tax burden	85
8.18	Flexibility of wage determination	77
8.17	Hiring and firing practices	75
6.11	Extent and effect of taxation	72
6.07	Burden of government regulation	52
4.06	Medium term business impact of HIV/AIDS	46
3.10	Availability of mobile or cellular telephones	41
2.02	Business costs of terrorism	38
4.08	Brain drain	37

241

Note: The Business Competitiveness Index applies different criteria for selecting a country's competitive advantages and disadvantages. Please refer to the section "How Country Profiles Work" for further details.

Austria

Competitiveness Rankings

Growth Competitiveness Index Rank	21

Macroeconomic Environment Index Rank **22**
  Macroeconomic Stability Subindex Rank 38
  Government Waste Rank 22
  Country Credit Rating Rank 12

Public Institutions Index Rank...**11**
  Contracts and Law Subindex Rank 13
  Corruption Subindex Rank......................................9

Technology Index Rank **21**
  Innovation Subindex Rank 21
  ICT Subindex Rank 18

Business Competitiveness Index Rank	10

**Sophistication of Company Operations
  and Strategy Rank** **11**
**Quality of the National Business
  Environment Rank** **9**

The Most Problematic Factors for Doing Business

Note: From a list of 14 factors, respondents were asked to select the five most problematic for doing business in their country and to rank them between 1 (most problematic) and 5. The bars in the figure show the responses weighted according to their rankings.

Source: World Economic Forum, Executive Opinion Survey (2005)

National competitiveness balance sheet

NOTABLE COMPETITIVE ADVANTAGES		
Growth Competitiveness Index		**Rank/117**

Macroeconomic Environment

| 2.17 | Interest rate spread, 2004 | 7 |
| 2.21 | Country credit rating, 2004 | 12 |

Public Institutions

6.20	Irregular payments in public utilities	4
6.03	Property rights	8
6.01	Judicial independence	13
6.21	Irregular payments in tax collection	13
6.19	Irregular payments in exports and imports	14
6.16	Organized crime	14

Technology

3.12	Quality of competition in the ISP sector	5
3.11	Internet access in schools	7
3.02	Firm-level technology absorption	12
3.17	Utility patents, 2004	15
3.19	Internet users, 2003	17
3.20	Internet hosts, 2003	17
3.18	Cellular telephones, 2003	17
3.15	Laws relating to ICT	18
3.07	University/industry research collaboration	19
3.06	Company spending on research and development	19

Business Competitiveness Index		**Rank/110**

Sophistication of Company Operations and Strategy

8.07	Degree of customer orientation	2
8.09	Extent of regional sales	4
8.02	Value chain presence	5

Quality of the National Business Environment

9.01	Stringency of environmental regulations	3
7.07	Presence of demanding regulatory standards	3
7.05	Local supplier quantity	4

Other Indicators		**Rank/117**

3.10	Availability of mobile or cellular telephones	2
4.06	Medium term business impact of HIV/AIDS	2
4.05	Medium term business impact of tuberculosis	3
7.06	Local supplier quality	4
7.03	Extent of market dominance	5
8.19	Cooperation in labor-employer relations	5
8.04	Ethical behavior of firms	6
8.05	Production process sophistication	6
8.11	Extent of staff training	6

NOTABLE COMPETITIVE DISADVANTAGES		
Growth Competitiveness Index		**Rank/117**

Macroeconomic Environment

2.15	Real effective exchange rate, 2004	81
2.20	Government debt, 2004	76
2.07	Access to credit	75
2.01	Recession expectations	60
2.14	National savings rate, 2004	58
2.13	Government surplus/deficit, 2004	43
2.16	Inflation, 2004	27
6.06	Wastefulness of government spending	22

Public Institutions

| 6.08 | Favoritism in decisions of government officials | 23 |

Technology

3.13	Government prioritization of ICT	43
4.17	Gross tertiary enrollment	33
3.14	Government success in ICT promotion	32
3.01	Technological readiness	25
5.08	Telephone lines, 2003	23
3.21	Personal computers, 2003	22

Business Competitiveness Index		**Rank/110**

Sophistication of Company Operations and Strategy

3.06	Company spending on research and development	19
8.14	Reliance on professional management	18
8.08	Control of international distribution	18

Quality of the National Business Environment

5.03	Port infrastructure quality	34
4.03	Quality of math and science education	33
3.05	Quality of scientific research institutions	24

Other Indicators		**Rank/117**

8.18	Flexibility of wage determination	116
4.07	Ease of hiring foreign labor	102
6.12	Efficiency of the tax system	82
2.11	Tax burden	63
4.09	Private sector employment of women	56
8.17	Hiring and firing practices	55
8.20	Pay and productivity	38
6.07	Burden of government regulation	32
6.10	Effectiveness of law-making bodies	32
9.07	Importance of environment in business planning	27
6.18	Government effectiveness in reducing poverty and inequality	26
6.11	Extent and effect of taxation	25
3.08	Government procurement of advanced technology products	24
2.12	Agricultural policy costs	23

243

Note: The Business Competitiveness Index applies different criteria for selecting a country's competitive advantages and disadvantages.
Please refer to the section "How Country Profiles Work" for further details.

Azerbaijan

Competitiveness Rankings

Growth Competitiveness Index Rank	69

Macroeconomic Environment Index Rank **56**
    Macroeconomic Stability Subindex Rank 18
    Government Waste Rank 57
    Country Credit Rating Rank 78
Public Institutions Index Rank............................**67**
    Contracts and Law Subindex Rank 61
    Corruption Subindex Rank....................................72
Technology Index Rank **87**
    Innovation Subindex Rank 81
    ICT Subindex Rank 78
    Technology Transfer Subindex Rank
       (out of 92 non-core innovators).......................72

Business Competitiveness Index Rank	77

**Sophistication of Company Operations
  and Strategy Rank**...**74**
**Quality of the National Business
  Environment Rank** **80**

The Most Problematic Factors for Doing Business

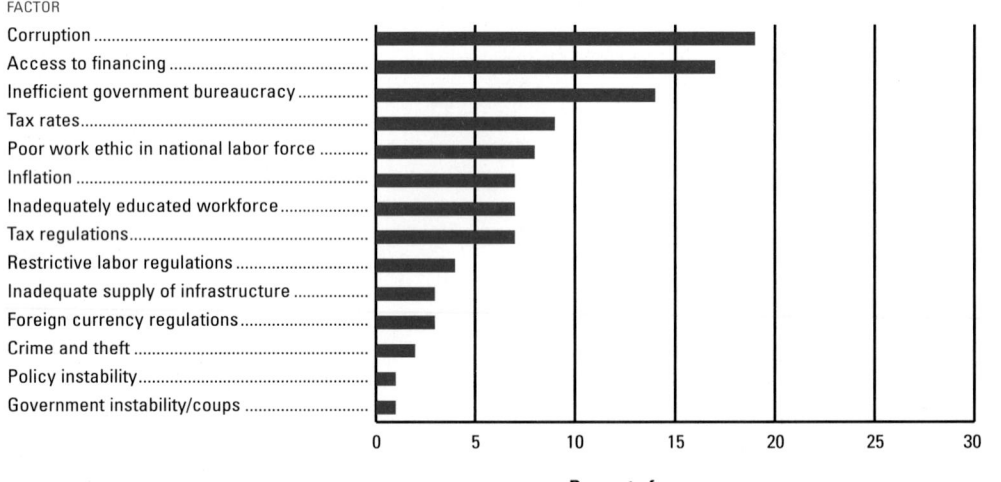

Note: From a list of 14 factors, respondents were asked to select the five most problematic for doing business in their country and to rank them between 1 (most problematic) and 5. The bars in the figure show the responses weighted according to their rankings.

Source: World Economic Forum, Executive Opinion Survey (2005)

244

National competitiveness balance sheet

NOTABLE COMPETITIVE ADVANTAGES				NOTABLE COMPETITIVE DISADVANTAGES		
Growth Competitiveness Index		**Rank/117**		**Growth Competitiveness Index**		**Rank/117**

Macroeconomic Environment

2.20	Government debt, 2004	9		2.16	Inflation, 2004	94
2.15	Real effective exchange rate, 2004	9		2.07	Access to credit	89
2.13	Government surplus/deficit, 2004	21		2.21	Country credit rating, 2004	78
2.14	National savings rate, 2004	22		2.17	Interest rate spread, 2004	69
2.01	Recession expectations	36		6.06	Wastefulness of government spending	57

Public Institutions (left) / **Public Institutions** (right)

6.08	Favoritism in decisions of government officials	47		6.01	Judicial independence	80
				6.03	Property rights	77
				6.19	Irregular payments in exports and imports	75
				6.21	Irregular payments in tax collection	73
				6.20	Irregular payments in public utilities	69
				6.16	Organized crime	53

Technology (left) / **Technology** (right)

3.13	Government prioritization of ICT	29		3.20	Internet hosts, 2003	101
3.14	Government success in ICT promotion	38		3.03	Prevalence of foreign technology licensing	93
3.06	Company spending on research and development	41		3.04	FDI and technology transfer	93
				3.21	Personal computers, 2003	89
				3.18	Cellular telephones, 2003	83
				3.12	Quality of competition in the ISP sector	83
				4.17	Gross tertiary enrollment	81
				3.19	Internet users, 2003	80
				3.11	Internet access in schools	77
				5.08	Telephone lines, 2003	73
				3.01	Technological readiness	72
				3.17	Utility patents, 2004	70
				3.15	Laws relating to ICT	64
				3.07	University/industry research collaboration	53
				3.02	Firm-level technology absorption	51

Business Competitiveness Index		**Rank/110**		**Business Competitiveness Index**		**Rank/110**

Sophistication of Company Operations and Strategy

8.01	Nature of competitive advantage	37		8.14	Reliance on professional management	108
3.06	Company spending on research and development	40		8.06	Extent of marketing	92
8.03	Capacity for innovation	44		3.03	Prevalence of foreign technology licensing	90

Quality of the National Business Environment

5.02	Railroad infrastructure development	25		2.05	Ease of access to loans	107
7.08	Local availability of process machinery	27		2.09	Prevalence of trade barriers	102
6.09	Extent of bureaucratic red tape	39		8.15	Quality of management schools	101

Other Indicators		**Rank/117**		**Other Indicators**		**Rank/117**
8.17	Hiring and firing practices	20		2.04	Soundness of banks	107
6.12	Efficiency of the tax system	26		6.27	Pervasiveness of money laundering through banks	106
6.07	Burden of government regulation	27		7.02	Effectiveness of antitrust policy	105
2.11	Tax burden	28		9.05	Effects of privatization on competition and the environment	104
8.20	Pay and productivity	31		9.04	Effects of compliance on business	102
4.09	Private sector employment of women	34		2.08	Local equity market access	101
4.07	Ease of hiring foreign labor	37		7.01	Intensity of local competition	101
6.11	Extent and effect of taxation	38		8.16	Efficacy of corporate boards	100
3.05	Quality of scientific research institutions	46		8.24	Importance of corporate social responsibility	93
8.05	Production process sophistication	49		5.05	Quality of electricity supply	93
6.13	Centralization of economic policymaking	50				

245

Note: The Business Competitiveness Index applies different criteria for selecting a country's competitive advantages and disadvantages.
Please refer to the section "How Country Profiles Work" for further details.

Bahrain

Competitiveness Rankings

Growth Competitiveness Index Rank	37

Macroeconomic Environment Index Rank	**32**
Macroeconomic Stability Subindex Rank	20
Government Waste Rank	36
Country Credit Rating Rank	47
Public Institutions Index Rank	**38**
Contracts and Law Subindex Rank	39
Corruption Subindex Rank	34
Technology Index Rank	**41**
Innovation Subindex Rank	52
ICT Subindex Rank	42
Technology Transfer Subindex Rank (out of 92 non-core innovators)	19

Business Competitiveness Index Rank	54

Sophistication of Company Operations and Strategy Rank	**67**
Quality of the National Business Environment Rank	**55**

The Most Problematic Factors for Doing Business

FACTOR

| Inadequately educated workforce |
| Inefficient government bureaucracy |
| Restrictive labor regulations |
| Poor work ethic in national labor force |
| Access to financing |
| Inadequate supply of infrastructure |
| Corruption |
| Policy instability |
| Foreign currency regulations |
| Inflation |
| Crime and theft |
| Government instability/coups |
| Tax regulations |
| Tax rates |

Percent of responses

Note: From a list of 14 factors, respondents were asked to select the five most problematic for doing business in their country and to rank them between 1 (most problematic) and 5. The bars in the figure show the responses weighted according to their rankings.

Source: World Economic Forum, Executive Opinion Survey (2005)

National competitiveness balance sheet

NOTABLE COMPETITIVE ADVANTAGES

Growth Competitiveness Index	Rank/117

Macroeconomic Environment

2.13	Government surplus/deficit, 2004	6
2.01	Recession expectations	14
2.07	Access to credit	28
2.15	Real effective exchange rate, 2004	29
6.06	Wastefulness of government spending	36

Public Institutions

6.16	Organized crime	18
6.21	Irregular payments in tax collection	23
6.19	Irregular payments in exports and imports	34

Technology

3.03	Prevalence of foreign technology licensing	20
3.01	Technological readiness	30
3.02	Firm-level technology absorption	32
3.18	Cellular telephones, 2003	36

Business Competitiveness Index	Rank/110

Sophistication of Company Operations and Strategy

8.08	Control of international distribution	7
8.01	Nature of competitive advantage	48
8.14	Reliance on professional management	58

Quality of the National Business Environment

2.03	Financial market sophistication	19
2.09	Prevalence of trade barriers	23
5.04	Air transport infrastructure quality	25

Other Indicators	Rank/117

6.12	Efficiency of the tax system	3
2.11	Tax burden	3
6.11	Extent and effect of taxation	3
8.18	Flexibility of wage determination	6
6.27	Pervasiveness of money laundering through banks	14
2.04	Soundness of banks	17
6.17	Informal sector	18
2.12	Agricultural policy costs	19
9.05	Effects of privatization on competition and the environment	20
8.23	Strength of auditing and accounting standards	27
5.07	Telephone/fax infrastructure quality	29
2.10	Impact of rules on FDI	31

NOTABLE COMPETITIVE DISADVANTAGES

Growth Competitiveness Index	Rank/117

Macroeconomic Environment

2.20	Government debt, 2004	74
2.17	Interest rate spread, 2004	73
2.16	Inflation, 2004	70
2.14	National savings rate, 2004	53
2.21	Country credit rating, 2004	47

Public Institutions

6.01	Judicial independence	56
6.20	Irregular payments in public utilities	55
6.03	Property rights	44
6.08	Favoritism in decisions of government officials	40

Technology

3.06	Company spending on research and development	115
3.12	Quality of competition in the ISP sector	113
3.07	University/industry research collaboration	112
3.17	Utility patents, 2004	81
3.20	Internet hosts, 2003	60
3.14	Government success in ICT promotion	59
4.17	Gross tertiary enrollment	55
3.04	FDI and technology transfer	49
3.13	Government prioritization of ICT	46
3.19	Internet users, 2003	43
3.11	Internet access in schools	43
5.08	Telephone lines, 2003	43
3.21	Personal computers, 2003	39
3.15	Laws relating to ICT	38

Business Competitiveness Index	Rank/110

Sophistication of Company Operations and Strategy

3.06	Company spending on research and development	109
8.03	Capacity for innovation	109
8.02	Value chain presence	82

Quality of the National Business Environment

6.13	Centralization of economic policymaking	107
3.07	University/industry research collaboration	107
3.05	Quality of scientific research institutions	107

Other Indicators	Rank/117

9.10	Grass-roots involvement in development projects	107
9.07	Importance of environment in business planning	106
8.16	Efficacy of corporate boards	105
7.08	Local availability of process machinery	105
8.15	Quality of management schools	102
3.16	Extent of business Internet use	102
6.09	Extent of bureaucratic red tape	102
7.09	Local availability of specialized research and training services	100
4.07	Ease of hiring foreign labor	100
6.05	Freedom of the press	94
9.06	Prioritization of energy efficiency	94
3.09	Availability of scientists and engineers	94

247

Note: The Business Competitiveness Index applies different criteria for selecting a country's competitive advantages and disadvantages. Please refer to the section "How Country Profiles Work" for further details.

Bangladesh

Competitiveness Rankings

Growth Competitiveness Index Rank	110

Macroeconomic Environment Index Rank **83**
    Macroeconomic Stability Subindex Rank 67
    Government Waste Rank 85
    Country Credit Rating Rank..................................86

Public Institutions Index Rank..**117**
    Contracts and Law Subindex Rank 104
    Corruption Subindex Rank...................................117

Technology Index Rank **101**
    Innovation Subindex Rank 105
    ICT Subindex Rank 112
    Technology Transfer Subindex Rank
       (out of 92 non-core innovators).......................59

Business Competitiveness Index Rank	96

**Sophistication of Company Operations
and Strategy Rank** **97**

**Quality of the National Business
Environment Rank** **97**

The Most Problematic Factors for Doing Business

FACTOR

Factor	
Corruption	
Inefficient government bureaucracy	
Inadequate supply of infrastructure	
Policy instability	
Crime and theft	
Access to financing	
Government instability/coups	
Inadequately educated workforce	
Tax regulations	
Poor work ethic in national labor force	
Foreign currency regulations	
Tax rates	
Inflation	
Restrictive labor regulations	

Percent of responses

Note: From a list of 14 factors, respondents were asked to select the five most problematic for doing business in their country and to rank them between 1 (most problematic) and 5. The bars in the figure show the responses weighted according to their rankings.

Source: World Economic Forum, Executive Opinion Survey (2005)

248

National competitiveness balance sheet

NOTABLE COMPETITIVE ADVANTAGES		
Growth Competitiveness Index		**Rank/117**
	Macroeconomic Environment	
2.15	Real effective exchange rate, 2004	34
2.14	National savings rate, 2004	41
2.20	Government debt, 2004	48

NOTABLE COMPETITIVE DISADVANTAGES		
Growth Competitiveness Index		**Rank/117**
	Macroeconomic Environment	
2.21	Country credit rating, 2004	86
6.06	Wastefulness of government spending	85
2.13	Government surplus/deficit, 2004	81
2.17	Interest rate spread, 2004	80
2.16	Inflation, 2004	78
2.01	Recession expectations	68
2.07	Access to credit	52
	Public Institutions	
6.20	Irregular payments in public utilities	117
6.21	Irregular payments in tax collection	117
6.19	Irregular payments in exports and imports	116
6.08	Favoritism in decisions of government officials	110
6.16	Organized crime	105
6.03	Property rights	91
6.01	Judicial independence	84
	Technology	
3.20	Internet hosts, 2003	117
3.19	Internet users, 2003	114
3.15	Laws relating to ICT	114
3.18	Cellular telephones, 2003	114
5.08	Telephone lines, 2003	110
3.07	University/industry research collaboration	105
3.11	Internet access in schools	104
3.14	Government success in ICT promotion	100
3.06	Company spending on research and development	99
4.17	Gross tertiary enrollment	98
3.21	Personal computers, 2003	98
3.01	Technological readiness	95
3.04	FDI and technology transfer	83
3.03	Prevalence of foreign technology licensing	83
3.17	Utility patents, 2004	81
3.02	Firm-level technology absorption	76
3.12	Quality of competition in the ISP sector	59
3.13	Government prioritization of ICT	57

Business Competitiveness Index		Rank/110
	Sophistication of Company Operations and Strategy	
8.07	Degree of customer orientation	64
8.10	Breadth of international markets	78
8.02	Value chain presence	79
	Quality of the National Business Environment	
2.08	Local equity market access	38
8.22	Foreign ownership restrictions	42
3.09	Availability of scientists and engineers	59

Business Competitiveness Index		Rank/110
	Sophistication of Company Operations and Strategy	
8.01	Nature of competitive advantage	110
8.11	Extent of staff training	106
8.09	Extent of regional sales	105
	Quality of the National Business Environment	
5.07	Telephone/fax infrastructure quality	110
6.14	Reliability of police services	108
3.15	Laws relating to ICT	108

Other Indicators		Rank/117
2.10	Impact of rules on FDI	23
2.12	Agricultural policy costs	34
6.11	Extent and effect of taxation	37
9.05	Effects of privatization on competition and the environment	42
8.17	Hiring and firing practices	44
8.22	Foreign ownership restrictions	45

Other Indicators		Rank/117
6.22	Irregular payments in public contracts	117
4.09	Private sector employment of women	114
6.13	Centralization of economic policymaking	113
4.07	Ease of hiring foreign labor	113
6.25	Business costs of corruption	113
7.09	Local availability of specialized research and training services	112
6.09	Extent of bureaucratic red tape	111
6.04	Intellectual property protection	111
8.16	Efficacy of corporate boards	110
7.03	Extent of market dominance	109

249

Note: The Business Competitiveness Index applies different criteria for selecting a country's competitive advantages and disadvantages. Please refer to the section "How Country Profiles Work" for further details.

Belgium

Competitiveness Rankings

Growth Competitiveness Index Rank	31

Macroeconomic Environment Index Rank **29**
    Macroeconomic Stability Subindex Rank 52
    Government Waste Rank 50
    Country Credit Rating Rank..................................16

Public Institutions Index Rank..**28**
    Contracts and Law Subindex Rank 23
    Corruption Subindex Rank..................................35

Technology Index Rank **28**
    Innovation Subindex Rank 19
    ICT Subindex Rank 26

Business Competitiveness Index Rank	16

**Sophistication of Company Operations
and Strategy Rank** **12**
**Quality of the National Business
Environment Rank** **17**

The Most Problematic Factors for Doing Business

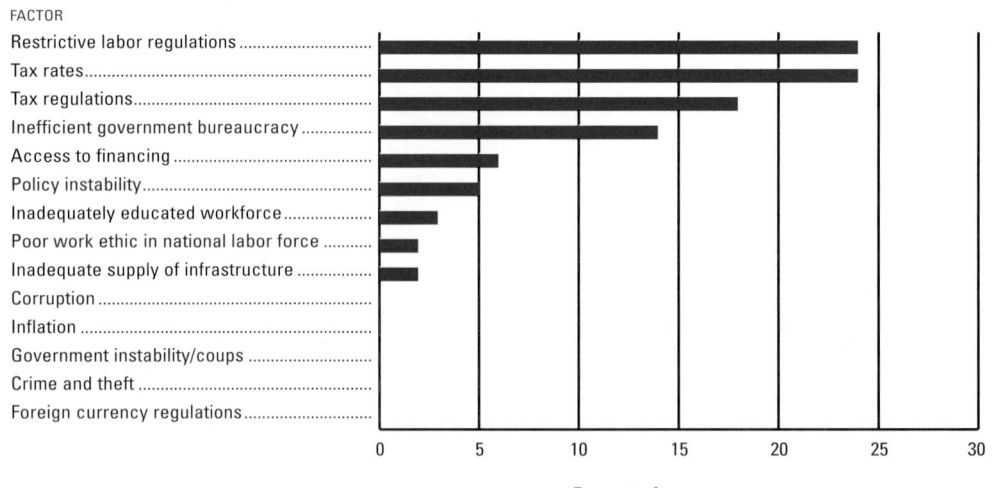

Note: From a list of 14 factors, respondents were asked to select the five most problematic for doing business in their country and to rank them between 1 (most problematic) and 5. The bars in the figure show the responses weighted according to their rankings.

Source: World Economic Forum, Executive Opinion Survey (2005)

National competitiveness balance sheet

NOTABLE COMPETITIVE ADVANTAGES	
Growth Competitiveness Index	**Rank/117**

Macroeconomic Environment

2.21	Country credit rating, 2004	16
2.16	Inflation, 2004	26
2.13	Government surplus/deficit, 2004	30

Public Institutions

6.03	Property rights	24
6.16	Organized crime	24
6.01	Judicial independence	28
6.08	Favoritism in decisions of government officials	28

Technology

3.07	University/industry research collaboration	14
3.06	Company spending on research and development	15
3.12	Quality of competition in the ISP sector	17
3.17	Utility patents, 2004	17
4.17	Gross tertiary enrollment	20
3.18	Cellular telephones, 2003	20
5.08	Telephone lines, 2003	21
3.11	Internet access in schools	22
3.01	Technological readiness	23
3.19	Internet users, 2003	24
3.21	Personal computers, 2003	25

Business Competitiveness Index	**Rank/110**

Sophistication of Company Operations and Strategy

8.01	Nature of competitive advantage	6
8.12	Willingness to delegate authority	7
8.03	Capacity for innovation	9

Quality of the National Business Environment

4.03	Quality of math and science education	2
6.13	Centralization of economic policymaking	3
7.01	Intensity of local competition	4

Other Indicators	**Rank/117**

7.06	Local supplier quality	6
7.03	Extent of market dominance	8
7.05	Local supplier quantity	9
8.02	Value chain presence	9
8.15	Quality of management schools	9
7.07	Presence of demanding regulatory standards	9
8.11	Extent of staff training	9
4.05	Medium term business impact of tuberculosis	10
8.05	Production process sophistication	10
5.05	Quality of electricity supply	10

NOTABLE COMPETITIVE DISADVANTAGES	
Growth Competitiveness Index	**Rank/117**

Macroeconomic Environment

2.20	Government debt, 2004	103
2.15	Real effective exchange rate, 2004	84
2.01	Recession expectations	78
2.07	Access to credit	77
2.17	Interest rate spread, 2004	55
6.06	Wastefulness of government spending	50
2.14	National savings rate, 2004	40

Public Institutions

6.21	Irregular payments in tax collection	41
6.19	Irregular payments in exports and imports	37
6.20	Irregular payments in public utilities	31

Technology

3.13	Government prioritization of ICT	66
3.14	Government success in ICT promotion	56
3.20	Internet hosts, 2003	33
3.02	Firm-level technology absorption	33
3.15	Laws relating to ICT	32

Business Competitiveness Index	**Rank/110**

Sophistication of Company Operations and Strategy

8.08	Control of international distribution	35
8.10	Breadth of international markets	21
8.14	Reliance on professional management	19

Quality of the National Business Environment

8.19	Cooperation in labor-employer relations	72
3.08	Government procurement of advanced technology products	56
2.08	Local equity market access	46

Other Indicators	**Rank/117**

6.12	Efficiency of the tax system	115
6.11	Extent and effect of taxation	115
8.18	Flexibility of wage determination	113
8.17	Hiring and firing practices	110
6.07	Burden of government regulation	109
2.11	Tax burden	107
8.20	Pay and productivity	84
9.04	Effects of compliance on business	84
2.12	Agricultural policy costs	77
4.07	Ease of hiring foreign labor	75
6.10	Effectiveness of law-making bodies	57
2.10	Impact of rules on FDI	57
2.02	Business costs of terrorism	48

Note: The Business Competitiveness Index applies different criteria for selecting a country's competitive advantages and disadvantages. Please refer to the section "How Country Profiles Work" for further details.

Benin

Competitiveness Rankings

Growth Competitiveness Index Rank	114

Macroeconomic Environment Index Rank **101**
    Macroeconomic Stability Subindex Rank 92
    Government Waste Rank 104
    Country Credit Rating Rank 101

Public Institutions Index Rank **110**
    Contracts and Law Subindex Rank 95
    Corruption Subindex Rank..................................113

Technology Index Rank **116**
    Innovation Subindex Rank 113
    ICT Subindex Rank 104
    Technology Transfer Subindex Rank
    (out of 92 non-core innovators).......................91

Business Competitiveness Index Rank	n/a

**Sophistication of Company Operations
and Strategy Rank** ....**n/a**

**Quality of the National Business
Environment Rank**..**n/a**

The Most Problematic Factors for Doing Business

FACTOR

Access to financing ....
Corruption ....
Tax regulations..
Inefficient government bureaucracy ....
Tax rates...
Inadequate supply of infrastructure ....
Policy instability...
Inflation ....
Inadequately educated workforce...................
Poor work ethic in national labor force ....
Restrictive labor regulations ....
Crime and theft ....
Foreign currency regulations.............................
Government instability/coups ....

Percent of responses

Note: From a list of 14 factors, respondents were asked to select the five most problematic for doing business in their country and to rank them between 1 (most problematic) and 5. The bars in the figure show the responses weighted according to their rankings.

Source: World Economic Forum, Executive Opinion Survey (2005)

National competitiveness balance sheet

NOTABLE COMPETITIVE ADVANTAGES

Growth Competitiveness Index	Rank/117
Macroeconomic Environment	
2.20 Government debt, 2004	36
2.16 Inflation, 2004	39
Technology	
3.13 Government prioritization of ICT	38

Other Indicators	Rank/117
6.09 Extent of bureaucratic red tape	9
6.13 Centralization of economic policymaking	25
4.07 Ease of hiring foreign labor	32
9.04 Effects of compliance on business	40
2.04 Soundness of banks	41
8.17 Hiring and firing practices	42
7.03 Extent of market dominance	47

NOTABLE COMPETITIVE DISADVANTAGES

Growth Competitiveness Index	Rank/117
Macroeconomic Environment	
2.07 Access to credit	114
2.01 Recession expectations	112
6.06 Wastefulness of government spending	104
2.15 Real effective exchange rate, 2004	102
2.21 Country credit rating, 2004	101
2.17 Interest rate spread, 2004	83
2.14 National savings rate, 2004	81
2.13 Government surplus/deficit, 2004	51
Public Institutions	
6.20 Irregular payments in public utilities	115
6.21 Irregular payments in tax collection	110
6.19 Irregular payments in exports and imports	104
6.03 Property rights	97
6.01 Judicial independence	95
6.08 Favoritism in decisions of government officials	92
6.16 Organized crime	77
Technology	
3.04 FDI and technology transfer	116
3.11 Internet access in schools	116
3.03 Prevalence of foreign technology licensing	115
3.07 University/industry research collaboration	115
3.01 Technological readiness	114
3.06 Company spending on research and development	113
3.21 Personal computers, 2003	109
5.08 Telephone lines, 2003	104
4.17 Gross tertiary enrollment	104
3.15 Laws relating to ICT	102
3.19 Internet users, 2003	100
3.18 Cellular telephones, 2003	100
3.20 Internet hosts, 2003	94
3.02 Firm-level technology absorption	88
3.17 Utility patents, 2004	81
3.12 Quality of competition in the ISP sector	72
3.14 Government success in ICT promotion	55

Other Indicators	Rank/117
2.05 Ease of access to loans	117
5.07 Telephone/fax infrastructure quality	117
6.11 Extent and effect of taxation	116
8.11 Extent of staff training	116
6.22 Irregular payments in public contracts	115
6.17 Informal sector	115
6.24 Diversion of public funds	115
2.06 Venture capital availability	115
8.10 Breadth of international markets	115
3.10 Availability of mobile or cellular telephones	114
6.25 Business costs of corruption	114
6.18 Government effectiveness in reducing poverty and inequality	114
6.23 Irregular payments in judicial decisions	113
7.04 Buyer sophistication	113
8.12 Willingness to delegate authority	112

253

Note: This country is not included in the coverage of the Business Competitiveness Index 2005–2006.

Bolivia

Competitiveness Rankings

Growth Competitiveness Index Rank	101

Macroeconomic Environment Index Rank **103**
    Macroeconomic Stability Subindex Rank 105
    Government Waste Rank 97
    Country Credit Rating Rank 87

Public Institutions Index Rank **84**
    Contracts and Law Subindex Rank 97
    Corruption Subindex Rank....................................75

Technology Index Rank **108**
    Innovation Subindex Rank 59
    ICT Subindex Rank 106
    Technology Transfer Subindex Rank
      (out of 92 non-core innovators).......................86

Business Competitiveness Index Rank	109

**Sophistication of Company Operations
   and Strategy Rank** **110**
**Quality of the National Business
   Environment Rank** **108**

The Most Problematic Factors for Doing Business

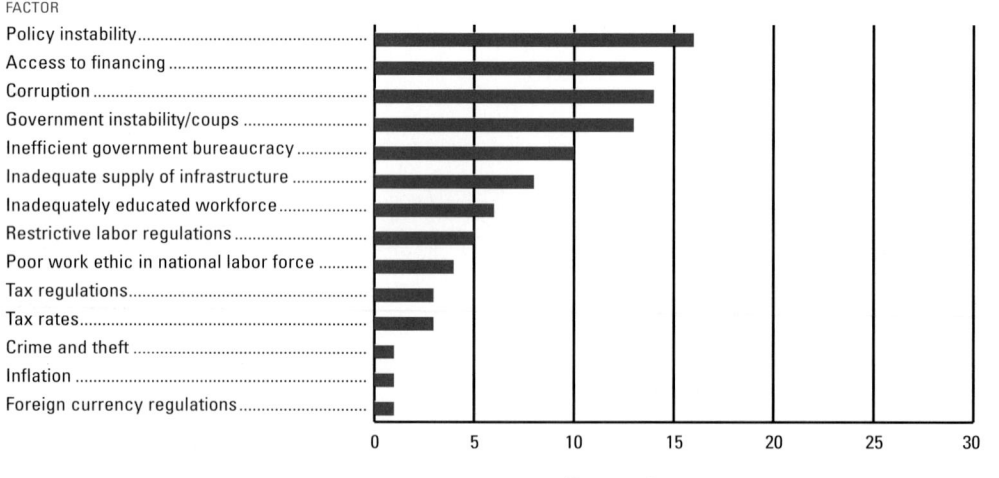

Note: From a list of 14 factors, respondents were asked to select the five most problematic for doing business in their country and to rank them between 1 (most problematic) and 5. The bars in the figure show the responses weighted according to their rankings.

Source: World Economic Forum, Executive Opinion Survey (2005)

National competitiveness balance sheet

NOTABLE COMPETITIVE ADVANTAGES

Growth Competitiveness Index		Rank/117
Macroeconomic Environment		
2.15	Real effective exchange rate, 2004	21
Technology		
4.17	Gross tertiary enrollment	41

Business Competitiveness Index		Rank/110
Sophistication of Company Operations and Strategy		
8.09	Extent of regional sales	93
Quality of the National Business Environment		
5.05	Quality of electricity supply	65
6.09	Extent of bureaucratic red tape	68
5.07	Telephone/fax infrastructure quality	74

Other Indicators		Rank/117
4.07	Ease of hiring foreign labor	19
6.05	Freedom of the press	25
6.12	Efficiency of the tax system	41
8.18	Flexibility of wage determination	45
2.12	Agricultural policy costs	48

NOTABLE COMPETITIVE DISADVANTAGES

Growth Competitiveness Index		Rank/117
Macroeconomic Environment		
2.01	Recession expectations	111
2.13	Government surplus/deficit, 2004	109
2.07	Access to credit	108
2.14	National savings rate, 2004	103
6.06	Wastefulness of government spending	97
2.20	Government debt, 2004	92
2.21	Country credit rating, 2004	87
2.17	Interest rate spread, 2004	74
2.16	Inflation, 2004	63
Public Institutions		
6.08	Favoritism in decisions of government officials	108
6.03	Property rights	107
6.01	Judicial independence	106
6.21	Irregular payments in tax collection	82
6.19	Irregular payments in exports and imports	76
6.20	Irregular payments in public utilities	68
6.16	Organized crime	59
Technology		
3.15	Laws relating to ICT	115
3.14	Government success in ICT promotion	115
3.13	Government prioritization of ICT	115
3.03	Prevalence of foreign technology licensing	113
3.06	Company spending on research and development	110
3.07	University/industry research collaboration	109
3.02	Firm-level technology absorption	109
3.04	FDI and technology transfer	100
3.01	Technological readiness	94
3.11	Internet access in schools	89
3.19	Internet users, 2003	85
3.21	Personal computers, 2003	84
5.08	Telephone lines, 2003	84
3.18	Cellular telephones, 2003	81
3.17	Utility patents, 2004	81
3.20	Internet hosts, 2003	76
3.12	Quality of competition in the ISP sector	75

Business Competitiveness Index		Rank/110
Sophistication of Company Operations and Strategy		
8.07	Degree of customer orientation	110
8.08	Control of international distribution	109
8.14	Reliance on professional management	109
Quality of the National Business Environment		
7.04	Buyer sophistication	110
3.15	Laws relating to ICT	109
8.16	Efficacy of corporate boards	109

Other Indicators		Rank/117
9.07	Importance of environment in business planning	117
6.17	Informal sector	116
6.04	Intellectual property protection	116
8.01	Nature of competitive advantage	116
8.12	Willingness to delegate authority	115
7.05	Local supplier quantity	114
8.24	Importance of corporate social responsibility	114
3.08	Government procurement of advanced technology products	114
2.05	Ease of access to loans	113
4.09	Private sector employment of women	113

255

Note: The Business Competitiveness Index applies different criteria for selecting a country's competitive advantages and disadvantages. Please refer to the section "How Country Profiles Work" for further details.

Bosnia and Herzegovina

Competitiveness Rankings

Growth Competitiveness Index Rank	**95**

Macroeconomic Environment Index Rank **91**
    Macroeconomic Stability Subindex Rank 70
    Government Waste Rank 110
    Country Credit Rating Rank 89

Public Institutions Index Rank..**86**
    Contracts and Law Subindex Rank 101
    Corruption Subindex Rank.....................................74

Technology Index Rank **99**
    Innovation Subindex Rank 82
    ICT Subindex Rank 76
    Technology Transfer Subindex Rank
        (out of 92 non-core innovators).......................84

Business Competitiveness Index Rank	**91**

**Sophistication of Company Operations
and Strategy Rank** **99**
**Quality of the National Business
Environment Rank** **89**

The Most Problematic Factors for Doing Business

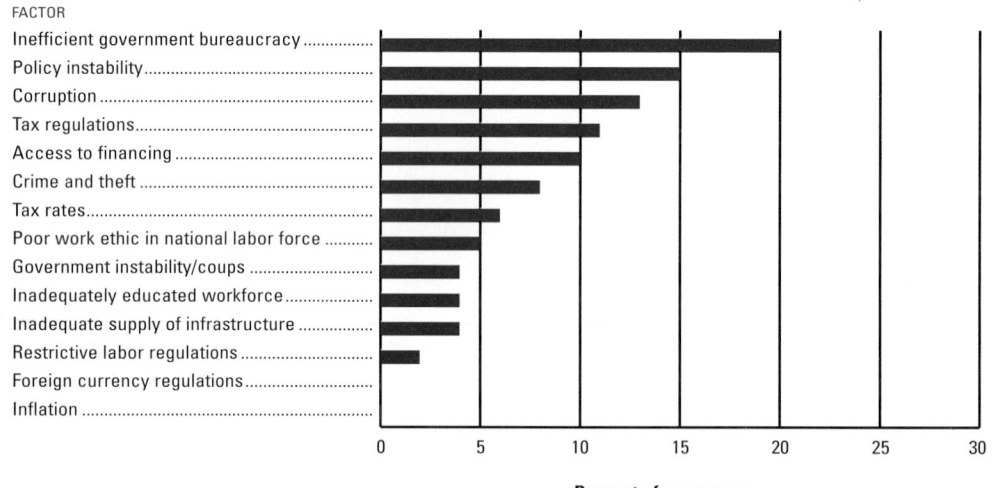

FACTOR
Inefficient government bureaucracy
Policy instability
Corruption
Tax regulations
Access to financing
Crime and theft
Tax rates
Poor work ethic in national labor force
Government instability/coups
Inadequately educated workforce
Inadequate supply of infrastructure
Restrictive labor regulations
Foreign currency regulations
Inflation

Percent of responses

Note: From a list of 14 factors, respondents were asked to select the five most problematic for doing business in their country and to rank them between 1 (most problematic) and 5. The bars in the figure show the responses weighted according to their rankings.

Source: World Economic Forum, Executive Opinion Survey (2005)

National competitiveness balance sheet

NOTABLE COMPETITIVE ADVANTAGES

Growth Competitiveness Index	Rank/117

Macroeconomic Environment

2.16	Inflation, 2004	11
2.13	Government surplus/deficit, 2004	34

Technology

5.08	Telephone lines, 2003	49

NOTABLE COMPETITIVE DISADVANTAGES

Growth Competitiveness Index	Rank/117

Macroeconomic Environment

2.01	Recession expectations	114
2.14	National savings rate, 2004	114
6.06	Wastefulness of government spending	110
2.21	Country credit rating, 2004	89
2.17	Interest rate spread, 2004	70
2.20	Government debt, 2004	66
2.07	Access to credit	65
2.15	Real effective exchange rate, 2004	61

Public Institutions

6.03	Property rights	113
6.16	Organized crime	91
6.19	Irregular payments in exports and imports	87
6.08	Favoritism in decisions of government officials	84
6.01	Judicial independence	83
6.21	Irregular payments in tax collection	78
6.20	Irregular payments in public utilities	61

Technology

3.02	Firm-level technology absorption	114
3.04	FDI and technology transfer	114
3.14	Government success in ICT promotion	110
3.12	Quality of competition in the ISP sector	107
3.15	Laws relating to ICT	105
3.06	Company spending on research and development	105
3.01	Technological readiness	102
3.03	Prevalence of foreign technology licensing	100
3.13	Government prioritization of ICT	88
3.19	Internet users, 2003	82
3.17	Utility patents, 2004	81
3.07	University/industry research collaboration	76
3.11	Internet access in schools	70
4.17	Gross tertiary enrollment	69
3.20	Internet hosts, 2003	62
3.21	Personal computers, 2003	60
3.18	Cellular telephones, 2003	59

Business Competitiveness Index	Rank/110

Sophistication of Company Operations and Strategy

8.03	Capacity for innovation	62
8.08	Control of international distribution	72
8.02	Value chain presence	81

Quality of the National Business Environment

6.09	Extent of bureaucratic red tape	6
6.13	Centralization of economic policymaking	16
2.05	Ease of access to loans	50

Other Indicators	Rank/117

8.18	Flexibility of wage determination	19
4.06	Medium term business impact of HIV/AIDS	37
2.11	Tax burden	39
2.02	Business costs of terrorism	45

Business Competitiveness Index	Rank/110

Sophistication of Company Operations and Strategy

8.06	Extent of marketing	104
8.13	Extent of incentive compensation	104
8.09	Extent of regional sales	102

Quality of the National Business Environment

5.04	Air transport infrastructure quality	110
9.01	Stringency of environmental regulations	108
5.03	Port infrastructure quality	108

Other Indicators	Rank/117

6.07	Burden of government regulation	117
8.24	Importance of corporate social responsibility	116
2.12	Agricultural policy costs	116
9.06	Prioritization of energy efficiency	115
9.10	Grass-roots involvement in development projects	114
6.04	Intellectual property protection	113
6.18	Government effectiveness in reducing poverty and inequality	112
9.09	Prevalence of corporate environmental reporting	112
9.07	Importance of environment in business planning	111
6.14	Reliability of police services	111
9.03	Extent of government mandated environmental reporting	111
3.08	Government procurement of advanced technology products	110
7.02	Effectiveness of antitrust policy	109
6.02	Efficiency of legal framework	109

Note: The Business Competitiveness Index applies different criteria for selecting a country's competitive advantages and disadvantages. Please refer to the section "How Country Profiles Work" for further details.

Botswana

Competitiveness Rankings

Growth Competitiveness Index Rank	48

Macroeconomic Environment Index Rank **36**
   Macroeconomic Stability Subindex Rank 53
   Government Waste Rank 15
   Country Credit Rating Rank 43

Public Institutions Index Rank **39**
   Contracts and Law Subindex Rank 30
   Corruption Subindex Rank...................................48

Technology Index Rank **76**
   Innovation Subindex Rank 98
   ICT Subindex Rank 75
   Technology Transfer Subindex Rank
     (out of 92 non-core innovators)........................46

Business Competitiveness Index Rank	55

**Sophistication of Company Operations
  and Strategy Rank** **76**
**Quality of the National Business
  Environment Rank** **50**

The Most Problematic Factors for Doing Business

FACTOR

Percent of responses

Note: From a list of 14 factors, respondents were asked to select the five most problematic for doing business in their country and to rank them between 1 (most problematic) and 5. The bars in the figure show the responses weighted according to their rankings.

Source: World Economic Forum, Executive Opinion Survey (2005)

National competitiveness balance sheet

NOTABLE COMPETITIVE ADVANTAGES	
Growth Competitiveness Index	**Rank/117**

Macroeconomic Environment

2.14	National savings rate, 2004	4
2.20	Government debt, 2004	5
6.06	Wastefulness of government spending	15
2.21	Country credit rating, 2004	43
2.13	Government surplus/deficit, 2004	47

Public Institutions

6.01	Judicial independence	24
6.08	Favoritism in decisions of government officials	25
6.03	Property rights	34
6.21	Irregular payments in tax collection	40
6.16	Organized crime	40

Technology

3.13	Government prioritization of ICT	39

NOTABLE COMPETITIVE DISADVANTAGES	
Growth Competitiveness Index	**Rank/117**

Macroeconomic Environment

2.15	Real effective exchange rate, 2004	116
2.01	Recession expectations	88
2.16	Inflation, 2004	81
2.17	Interest rate spread, 2004	71
2.07	Access to credit	62

Public Institutions

6.19	Irregular payments in exports and imports	53
6.20	Irregular payments in public utilities	53

Technology

4.17	Gross tertiary enrollment	102
3.12	Quality of competition in the ISP sector	93
3.19	Internet users, 2003	91
5.08	Telephone lines, 2003	83
3.17	Utility patents, 2004	81
3.02	Firm-level technology absorption	80
3.11	Internet access in schools	79
3.20	Internet hosts, 2003	73
3.15	Laws relating to ICT	70
3.04	FDI and technology transfer	69
3.01	Technological readiness	69
3.07	University/industry research collaboration	69
3.21	Personal computers, 2003	69
3.03	Prevalence of foreign technology licensing	66
3.06	Company spending on research and development	59
3.14	Government success in ICT promotion	57
3.18	Cellular telephones, 2003	57

Business Competitiveness Index	Rank/110

Sophistication of Company Operations and Strategy

8.14	Reliance on professional management	27
8.01	Nature of competitive advantage	27
8.11	Extent of staff training	47

Quality of the National Business Environment

6.01	Judicial independence	23
6.02	Efficiency of legal framework	23
6.08	Favoritism in decisions of government officials	24

Other Indicators	Rank/117

2.02	Business costs of terrorism	4
6.12	Efficiency of the tax system	7
6.11	Extent and effect of taxation	14
6.10	Effectiveness of law-making bodies	17
2.11	Tax burden	19
6.26	Public trust of politicians	19
6.07	Burden of government regulation	26
2.04	Soundness of banks	28
2.06	Venture capital availability	30
3.08	Government procurement of advanced technology products	30
2.12	Agricultural policy costs	32
8.19	Cooperation in labor-employer relations	34

Business Competitiveness Index	Rank/110

Sophistication of Company Operations and Strategy

8.08	Control of international distribution	102
8.09	Extent of regional sales	101
8.07	Degree of customer orientation	95

Quality of the National Business Environment

7.05	Local supplier quantity	100
5.07	Telephone/fax infrastructure quality	90
3.19	Internet users, 2003	90

Other Indicators	Rank/117

4.06	Medium term business impact of HIV/AIDS	114
4.05	Medium term business impact of tuberculosis	108
8.02	Value chain presence	98
8.10	Breadth of international markets	96
3.09	Availability of scientists and engineers	91
4.07	Ease of hiring foreign labor	90
8.03	Capacity for innovation	90
7.09	Local availability of specialized research and training services	85
6.09	Extent of bureaucratic red tape	85
7.08	Local availability of process machinery	84

259

Note: The Business Competitiveness Index applies different criteria for selecting a country's competitive advantages and disadvantages. Please refer to the section "How Country Profiles Work" for further details.

Brazil

Competitiveness Rankings

Growth Competitiveness Index Rank	65

Macroeconomic Environment Index Rank **79**
    Macroeconomic Stability Subindex Rank 81
    Government Waste Rank 111
    Country Credit Rating Rank 62

Public Institutions Index Rank **70**
    Contracts and Law Subindex Rank 77
    Corruption Subindex Rank....................................62

Technology Index Rank **50**
    Innovation Subindex Rank 68
    ICT Subindex Rank 52
    Technology Transfer Subindex Rank
      (out of 92 non-core innovators) 18

Business Competitiveness Index Rank	49

**Sophistication of Company Operations
    and Strategy Rank** **32**

**Quality of the National Business
    Environment Rank** **52**

The Most Problematic Factors for Doing Business

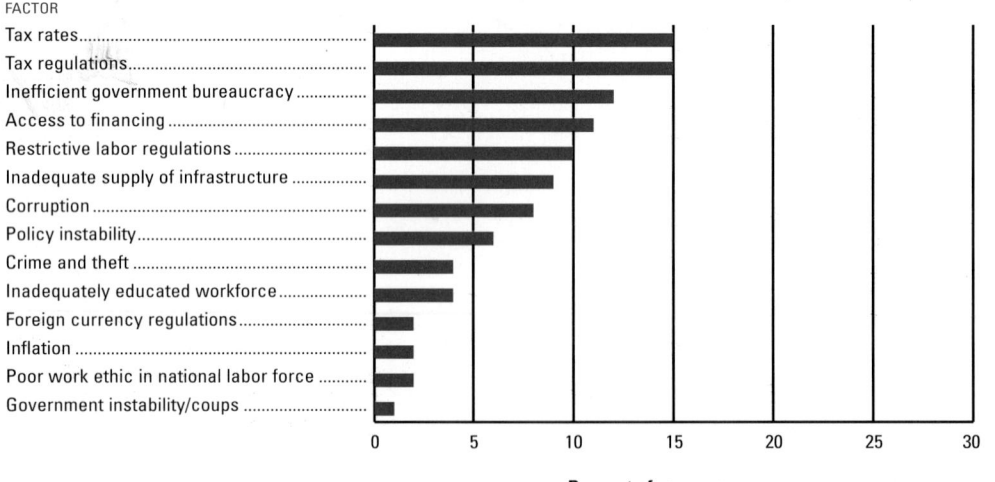

FACTOR

Tax rates
Tax regulations
Inefficient government bureaucracy
Access to financing
Restrictive labor regulations
Inadequate supply of infrastructure
Corruption
Policy instability
Crime and theft
Inadequately educated workforce
Foreign currency regulations
Inflation
Poor work ethic in national labor force
Government instability/coups

0   5   10   15   20   25   30

Percent of responses

Note: From a list of 14 factors, respondents were asked to select the five most problematic for doing business in their country and to rank them between 1 (most problematic) and 5. The bars in the figure show the responses weighted according to their rankings.

Source: World Economic Forum, Executive Opinion Survey (2005)

National competitiveness balance sheet

NOTABLE COMPETITIVE ADVANTAGES	
Growth Competitiveness Index	**Rank/117**

Macroeconomic Environment

2.15	Real effective exchange rate, 2004	8
2.01	Recession expectations	42
2.14	National savings rate, 2004	43

Technology

3.12	Quality of competition in the ISP sector	27
3.06	Company spending on research and development	29
3.04	FDI and technology transfer	31
3.20	Internet hosts, 2003	36
3.03	Prevalence of foreign technology licensing	37
3.07	University/industry research collaboration	40
3.15	Laws relating to ICT	44
3.02	Firm-level technology absorption	46
3.17	Utility patents, 2004	50

NOTABLE COMPETITIVE DISADVANTAGES	
Growth Competitiveness Index	**Rank/117**

Macroeconomic Environment

2.17	Interest rate spread, 2004	115
6.06	Wastefulness of government spending	111
2.16	Inflation, 2004	83
2.07	Access to credit	69
2.13	Government surplus/deficit, 2004	68
2.21	Country credit rating, 2004	62
2.20	Government debt, 2004	59

Public Institutions

6.16	Organized crime	99
6.21	Irregular payments in tax collection	74
6.01	Judicial independence	72
6.08	Favoritism in decisions of government officials	69
6.03	Property rights	60
6.19	Irregular payments in exports and imports	58
6.20	Irregular payments in public utilities	58

Technology

3.13	Government prioritization of ICT	75
4.17	Gross tertiary enrollment	74
3.11	Internet access in schools	64
3.18	Cellular telephones, 2003	64
3.14	Government success in ICT promotion	58
3.19	Internet users, 2003	57
3.21	Personal computers, 2003	57
3.01	Technological readiness	56
5.08	Telephone lines, 2003	55

Business Competitiveness Index	Rank/110

Sophistication of Company Operations and Strategy

8.06	Extent of marketing	25
3.06	Company spending on research and development	28
8.10	Breadth of international markets	30

Quality of the National Business Environment

7.08	Local availability of process machinery	18
9.01	Stringency of environmental regulations	24
7.09	Local availability of specialized research and training services	24

Business Competitiveness Index	Rank/110

Sophistication of Company Operations and Strategy

8.01	Nature of competitive advantage	71
8.02	Value chain presence	55
8.07	Degree of customer orientation	52

Quality of the National Business Environment

4.03	Quality of math and science education	97
4.02	Quality of public schools	97
4.01	Quality of the educational system	91

Other Indicators	Rank/117

2.02	Business costs of terrorism	13
9.06	Prioritization of energy efficiency	25
2.12	Agricultural policy costs	27
2.03	Financial market sophistication	27
7.05	Local supplier quantity	27
3.16	Extent of business Internet use	28
9.05	Effects of privatization on competition and the environment	29
9.07	Importance of environment in business planning	30
5.06	Postal efficiency	32
9.09	Prevalence of corporate environmental reporting	32

Other Indicators	Rank/117

6.11	Extent and effect of taxation	117
6.12	Efficiency of the tax system	117
6.07	Burden of government regulation	115
6.15	Business costs of crime and violence	107
6.17	Informal sector	104
4.07	Ease of hiring foreign labor	103
6.24	Diversion of public funds	99
8.18	Flexibility of wage determination	98
6.26	Public trust of politicians	93
2.11	Tax burden	93
6.10	Effectiveness of law-making bodies	92
2.06	Venture capital availability	91
8.17	Hiring and firing practices	89
6.14	Reliability of police services	89
2.09	Prevalence of trade barriers	88

261

Note: The Business Competitiveness Index applies different criteria for selecting a country's competitive advantages and disadvantages. Please refer to the section "How Country Profiles Work" for further details.

Bulgaria

Competitiveness Rankings

Growth Competitiveness Index Rank	58

Macroeconomic Environment Index Rank **62**
    Macroeconomic Stability Subindex Rank 51
    Government Waste Rank 89
    Country Credit Rating Rank.................................56

Public Institutions Index Rank........................**62**
    Contracts and Law Subindex Rank 103
    Corruption Subindex Rank...................................38

Technology Index Rank **61**
    Innovation Subindex Rank 50
    ICT Subindex Rank 48
    Technology Transfer Subindex Rank
       (out of 92 non-core innovators).......................58

Business Competitiveness Index Rank	78

**Sophistication of Company Operations
   and Strategy Rank** **82**

**Quality of the National Business
   Environment Rank** **71**

The Most Problematic Factors for Doing Business

FACTOR

Inefficient government bureaucracy ....
Access to financing ....
Corruption ....
Tax regulations...
Inadequate supply of infrastructure ....
Tax rates..
Restrictive labor regulations ....
Crime and theft ....
Policy instability..
Government instability/coups ....
Poor work ethic in national labor force ....
Inadequately educated workforce...................
Inflation ....
Foreign currency regulations...........................

Percent of responses

Note: From a list of 14 factors, respondents were asked to select the five most problematic for doing business in their country and to rank them between 1 (most problematic) and 5. The bars in the figure show the responses weighted according to their rankings.

Source: World Economic Forum, Executive Opinion Survey (2005)

National competitiveness balance sheet

<table>
<tr><td colspan="3">NOTABLE COMPETITIVE ADVANTAGES</td></tr>
<tr><td colspan="2">Growth Competitiveness Index</td><td>Rank/117</td></tr>
</table>

Macroeconomic Environment

| 2.13 | Government surplus/deficit, 2004 | 16 |
| 2.20 | Government debt, 2004 | 41 |

Public Institutions

6.21	Irregular payments in tax collection	33
6.19	Irregular payments in exports and imports	38
6.20	Irregular payments in public utilities	46

Technology

5.08	Telephone lines, 2003	33
4.17	Gross tertiary enrollment	43
3.18	Cellular telephones, 2003	44
3.19	Internet users, 2003	45
3.15	Laws relating to ICT	46
3.20	Internet hosts, 2003	47

<table>
<tr><td colspan="3">NOTABLE COMPETITIVE DISADVANTAGES</td></tr>
<tr><td colspan="2">Growth Competitiveness Index</td><td>Rank/117</td></tr>
</table>

Macroeconomic Environment

2.15	Real effective exchange rate, 2004	114
6.06	Wastefulness of government spending	89
2.14	National savings rate, 2004	89
2.16	Inflation, 2004	78
2.01	Recession expectations	63
2.17	Interest rate spread, 2004	62
2.21	Country credit rating, 2004	56
2.07	Access to credit	53

Public Institutions

6.16	Organized crime	110
6.08	Favoritism in decisions of government officials	101
6.01	Judicial independence	88
6.03	Property rights	85

Technology

3.02	Firm-level technology absorption	100
3.14	Government success in ICT promotion	91
3.13	Government prioritization of ICT	90
3.01	Technological readiness	90
3.03	Prevalence of foreign technology licensing	89
3.07	University/industry research collaboration	86
3.06	Company spending on research and development	79
3.04	FDI and technology transfer	65
3.21	Personal computers, 2003	64
3.12	Quality of competition in the ISP sector	64
3.11	Internet access in schools	59
3.17	Utility patents, 2004	54

| **Business Competitiveness Index** | | **Rank/110** |

Sophistication of Company Operations and Strategy

8.02	Value chain presence	65
8.07	Degree of customer orientation	72
8.03	Capacity for innovation	74

Quality of the National Business Environment

4.03	Quality of math and science education	20
3.09	Availability of scientists and engineers	30
7.08	Local availability of process machinery	35

| **Business Competitiveness Index** | | **Rank/110** |

Sophistication of Company Operations and Strategy

8.14	Reliance on professional management	97
8.12	Willingness to delegate authority	93
8.11	Extent of staff training	87

Quality of the National Business Environment

8.21	Protection of minority shareholders' interests	103
8.22	Foreign ownership restrictions	97
5.04	Air transport infrastructure quality	97

263

| **Other Indicators** | | **Rank/117** |

8.17	Hiring and firing practices	28
6.22	Irregular payments in public contracts	32
8.18	Flexibility of wage determination	33
8.20	Pay and productivity	41
4.09	Private sector employment of women	44
6.23	Irregular payments in judicial decisions	47
2.05	Ease of access to loans	47

| **Other Indicators** | | **Rank/117** |

2.12	Agricultural policy costs	115
9.08	Protection of ecosystems by business	114
9.05	Effects of privatization on competition and the environment	113
4.08	Brain drain	110
2.10	Impact of rules on FDI	108
6.18	Government effectiveness in reducing poverty and inequality	107
6.27	Pervasiveness of money laundering through banks	103
6.24	Diversion of public funds	100
9.07	Importance of environment in business planning	100
9.10	Grass-roots involvement in development projects	99
2.03	Financial market sophistication	98
6.12	Efficiency of the tax system	97

Note: The Business Competitiveness Index applies different criteria for selecting a country's competitive advantages and disadvantages. Please refer to the section "How Country Profiles Work" for further details.

Cambodia

Competitiveness Rankings

Growth Competitiveness Index Rank	**112**

Macroeconomic Environment Index Rank **104**
    Macroeconomic Stability Subindex Rank 100
    Government Waste Rank 70
    Country Credit Rating Rank 107

Public Institutions Index Rank...**114**
    Contracts and Law Subindex Rank 102
    Corruption Subindex Rank..................................115

Technology Index Rank **105**
    Innovation Subindex Rank 110
    ICT Subindex Rank 113
    Technology Transfer Subindex Rank
        (out of 92 non-core innovators).........................68

Business Competitiveness Index Rank	**105**

**Sophistication of Company Operations
  and Strategy Rank** **101**
**Quality of the National Business
  Environment Rank** **103**

The Most Problematic Factors for Doing Business

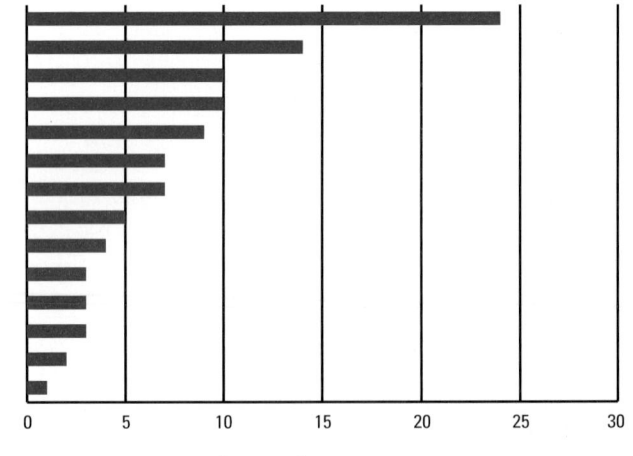

FACTOR

Corruption
Inefficient government bureaucracy
Inadequately educated workforce
Inadequate supply of infrastructure
Access to financing
Government instability/coups
Policy instability
Poor work ethic in national labor force
Tax regulations
Crime and theft
Restrictive labor regulations
Tax rates
Foreign currency regulations
Inflation

Percent of responses

Note: From a list of 14 factors, respondents were asked to select the five most problematic for doing business in their country and to rank them between 1 (most problematic) and 5. The bars in the figure show the responses weighted according to their rankings.

Source: World Economic Forum, Executive Opinion Survey (2005)

National competitiveness balance sheet

NOTABLE COMPETITIVE ADVANTAGES		
Growth Competitiveness Index		**Rank/117**
	Macroeconomic Environment	
2.16	Inflation, 2004	27
2.15	Real effective exchange rate, 2004	44

NOTABLE COMPETITIVE DISADVANTAGES		
Growth Competitiveness Index		**Rank/117**
	Macroeconomic Environment	
2.13	Government surplus/deficit, 2004	110
2.17	Interest rate spread, 2004	109
2.21	Country credit rating, 2004	107
2.07	Access to credit	94
2.14	National savings rate, 2004	79
2.01	Recession expectations	73
6.06	Wastefulness of government spending	70
2.20	Government debt, 2004	55
	Public Institutions	
6.19	Irregular payments in exports and imports	117
6.21	Irregular payments in tax collection	112
6.03	Property rights	111
6.20	Irregular payments in public utilities	110
6.01	Judicial independence	101
6.08	Favoritism in decisions of government officials	94
6.16	Organized crime	88
	Technology	
5.08	Telephone lines, 2003	114
3.19	Internet users, 2003	112
3.21	Personal computers, 2003	111
3.15	Laws relating to ICT	111
3.12	Quality of competition in the ISP sector	106
4.17	Gross tertiary enrollment	105
3.01	Technological readiness	104
3.06	Company spending on research and development	104
3.20	Internet hosts, 2003	102
3.11	Internet access in schools	101
3.03	Prevalence of foreign technology licensing	98
3.18	Cellular telephones, 2003	98
3.02	Firm-level technology absorption	97
3.07	University/industry research collaboration	96
3.14	Government success in ICT promotion	87
3.17	Utility patents, 2004	81
3.13	Government prioritization of ICT	78
3.04	FDI and technology transfer	68

Business Competitiveness Index		Rank/110
	Sophistication of Company Operations and Strategy	
8.07	Degree of customer orientation	71
8.11	Extent of staff training	84
8.02	Value chain presence	85
	Quality of the National Business Environment	
8.22	Foreign ownership restrictions	69
8.16	Efficacy of corporate boards	70
6.13	Centralization of economic policymaking	77

Business Competitiveness Index		Rank/110
	Sophistication of Company Operations and Strategy	
8.08	Control of international distribution	108
8.05	Production process sophistication	107
8.06	Extent of marketing	106
	Quality of the National Business Environment	
7.05	Local supplier quantity	109
3.09	Availability of scientists and engineers	109
2.08	Local equity market access	109

Other Indicators		Rank/117
2.11	Tax burden	15
6.11	Extent and effect of taxation	33
6.12	Efficiency of the tax system	39
4.08	Brain drain	41
4.07	Ease of hiring foreign labor	44
4.09	Private sector employment of women	48
8.20	Pay and productivity	50

Other Indicators		Rank/117
8.23	Strength of auditing and accounting standards	114
6.23	Irregular payments in judicial decisions	114
2.03	Financial market sophistication	112
7.06	Local supplier quality	112
8.04	Ethical behavior of firms	111
8.15	Quality of management schools	111
3.05	Quality of scientific research institutions	111
6.22	Irregular payments in public contracts	111
2.04	Soundness of banks	110

265

Note: The Business Competitiveness Index applies different criteria for selecting a country's competitive advantages and disadvantages.
Please refer to the section "How Country Profiles Work" for further details.

Cameroon

Competitiveness Rankings

Growth Competitiveness Index Rank	111

Macroeconomic Environment Index Rank **100**
    Macroeconomic Stability Subindex Rank 87
    Government Waste Rank 102
    Country Credit Rating Rank 100

Public Institutions Index Rank..**111**
    Contracts and Law Subindex Rank 91
    Corruption Subindex Rank..................................114

Technology Index Rank **110**
    Innovation Subindex Rank..................................106
    ICT Subindex Rank 107
    Technology Transfer Subindex Rank
        (out of 92 non-core innovators)........................85

Business Competitiveness Index Rank	n/a

**Sophistication of Company Operations
and Strategy Rank** ....n/a
**Quality of the National Business
Environment Rank**...n/a

The Most Problematic Factors for Doing Business

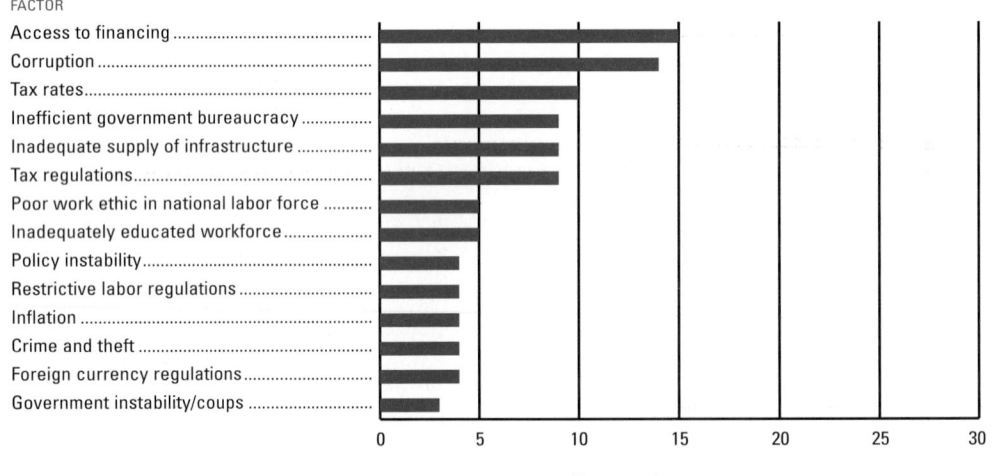

Note: From a list of 14 factors, respondents were asked to select the five most problematic for doing business in their country and to rank them between 1 (most problematic) and 5. The bars in the figure show the responses weighted according to their rankings.

Source: World Economic Forum, Executive Opinion Survey (2005)

National competitiveness balance sheet

NOTABLE COMPETITIVE ADVANTAGES	
Growth Competitiveness Index	**Rank/117**
Macroeconomic Environment	
2.16 Inflation, 2004	8
2.13 Government surplus/deficit, 2004	34
Technology	
3.14 Government success in ICT promotion	41

NOTABLE COMPETITIVE DISADVANTAGES	
Growth Competitiveness Index	**Rank/117**
Macroeconomic Environment	
2.17 Interest rate spread, 2004	102
6.06 Wastefulness of government spending	102
2.21 Country credit rating, 2004	100
2.01 Recession expectations	99
2.07 Access to credit	96
2.14 National savings rate, 2004	95
2.15 Real effective exchange rate, 2004	89
2.20 Government debt, 2004	73
Public Institutions	
6.21 Irregular payments in tax collection	113
6.20 Irregular payments in public utilities	113
6.19 Irregular payments in exports and imports	108
6.01 Judicial independence	107
6.16 Organized crime	89
6.03 Property rights	82
6.08 Favoritism in decisions of government officials	75
Technology	
3.11 Internet access in schools	114
3.04 FDI and technology transfer	113
3.19 Internet users, 2003	108
5.08 Telephone lines, 2003	107
3.20 Internet hosts, 2003	105
3.03 Prevalence of foreign technology licensing	104
3.21 Personal computers, 2003	102
3.01 Technological readiness	102
4.17 Gross tertiary enrollment	100
3.15 Laws relating to ICT	98
3.18 Cellular telephones, 2003	93
3.07 University/industry research collaboration	87
3.06 Company spending on research and development	83
3.17 Utility patents, 2004	81
3.02 Firm-level technology absorption	78
3.12 Quality of competition in the ISP sector	77
3.13 Government prioritization of ICT	69

Other Indicators	Rank/117
3.09 Availability of scientists and engineers	25
8.22 Foreign ownership restrictions	40
2.02 Business costs of terrorism	47
2.09 Prevalence of trade barriers	48

Other Indicators	Rank/117
5.06 Postal efficiency	115
5.07 Telephone/fax infrastructure quality	114
6.24 Diversion of public funds	112
6.13 Centralization of economic policymaking	112
7.07 Presence of demanding regulatory standards	111
6.25 Business costs of corruption	111
7.08 Local availability of process machinery	111
6.23 Irregular payments in judicial decisions	110
8.08 Control of international distribution	110
6.22 Irregular payments in public contracts	110
6.11 Extent and effect of taxation	110
2.06 Venture capital availability	109
2.11 Tax burden	109
3.10 Availability of mobile or cellular telephones	108
6.09 Extent of bureaucratic red tape	108

267

Note: This country is not included in the coverage of the Business Competitiveness Index 2005–2006.

Canada

Competitiveness Rankings

Growth Competitiveness Index Rank	14

Macroeconomic Environment Index Rank 16
    Macroeconomic Stability Subindex Rank 23
    Government Waste Rank 33
    Country Credit Rating Rank 13

Public Institutions Index Rank...21
    Contracts and Law Subindex Rank 24
    Corruption Subindex Rank.....................................17

Technology Index Rank 15
    Innovation Subindex Rank 11
    ICT Subindex Rank 16

Business Competitiveness Index Rank	13

**Sophistication of Company Operations
  and Strategy Rank** 18

**Quality of the National Business
  Environment Rank** 13

The Most Problematic Factors for Doing Business

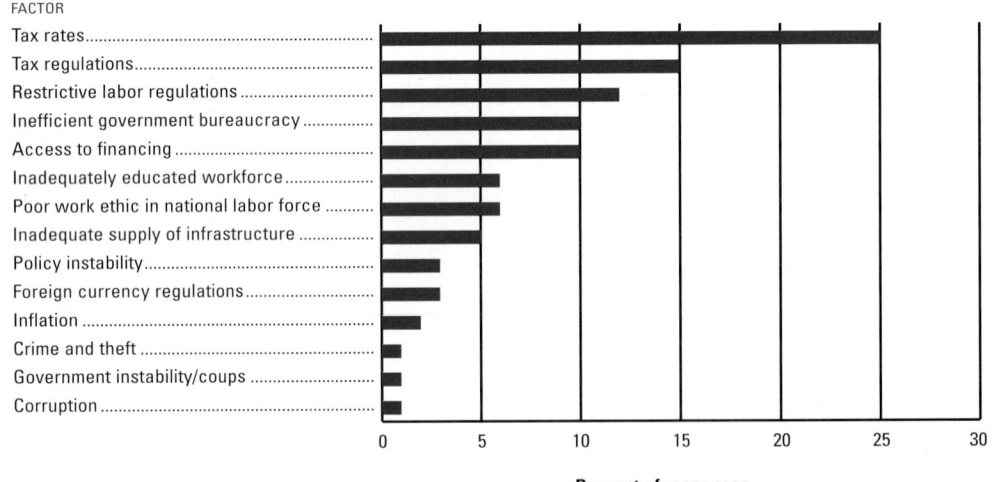

Note: From a list of 14 factors, respondents were asked to select the five most problematic for doing business in their country and to rank them between 1 (most problematic) and 5. The bars in the figure show the responses weighted according to their rankings.

Source: World Economic Forum, Executive Opinion Survey (2005)

National competitiveness balance sheet

NOTABLE COMPETITIVE ADVANTAGES	
Growth Competitiveness Index	**Rank/117**

Macroeconomic Environment

2.21 Country credit rating, 2004 13

Technology

3.19 Internet users, 2003...7
5.08 Telephone lines, 2003 8
3.12 Quality of competition in the ISP sector 9
3.17 Utility patents, 2004 9
3.21 Personal computers, 2003 11
3.07 University/industry research collaboration 13
3.20 Internet hosts, 2003..13

NOTABLE COMPETITIVE DISADVANTAGES	
Growth Competitiveness Index	**Rank/117**

Macroeconomic Environment

2.15 Real effective exchange rate, 2004 105
2.20 Government debt, 2004...84
2.14 National savings rate, 2004 46
2.07 Access to credit 35
6.06 Wastefulness of government spending 33
2.01 Recession expectations 32
2.16 Inflation, 2004 23
2.17 Interest rate spread, 2004 21
2.13 Government surplus/deficit, 2004...................................17

Public Institutions

6.08 Favoritism in decisions of government officials..............45
6.16 Organized crime 37
6.19 Irregular payments in exports and imports 19
6.20 Irregular payments in public utilities 18
6.03 Property rights..18
6.21 Irregular payments in tax collection 17
6.01 Judicial independence..16

Technology

3.13 Government prioritization of ICT 50
3.18 Cellular telephones, 2003...47
3.14 Government success in ICT promotion 42
4.17 Gross tertiary enrollment 24
3.02 Firm-level technology absorption 22
3.01 Technological readiness 18
3.06 Company spending on research and development 16
3.15 Laws relating to ICT 15
3.11 Internet access in schools 14

269

Business Competitiveness Index	Rank/110

Sophistication of Company Operations and Strategy

8.13 Extent of incentive compensation 6
8.09 Extent of regional sales..7
8.07 Degree of customer orientation..9

Quality of the National Business Environment

8.15 Quality of management schools 4
6.13 Centralization of economic policymaking.........................5
3.19 Internet users, 2003...7

Business Competitiveness Index	Rank/110

Sophistication of Company Operations and Strategy

8.02 Value chain presence 37
8.10 Breadth of international markets......................................28
8.01 Nature of competitive advantage 28

Quality of the National Business Environment

8.19 Cooperation in labor-employer relations.........................46
3.18 Cellular telephones, 2003...46
6.08 Favoritism in decisions of government officials..............43

Other Indicators	Rank/117

9.10 Grass-roots involvement in development projects 5
2.04 Soundness of banks...5
8.24 Importance of corporate social responsibility 6
3.09 Availability of scientists and engineers 8
2.03 Financial market sophistication 8
7.09 Local availability of specialized research and
     training services 9
8.06 Extent of marketing 9
9.08 Protection of ecosystems by business.............................9
3.16 Extent of business Internet use..9
9.07 Importance of environment in business planning...........10

Other Indicators	Rank/117

2.02 Business costs of terrorism 74
6.12 Efficiency of the tax system 73
4.07 Ease of hiring foreign labor 67
6.11 Extent and effect of taxation...63
2.11 Tax burden..55
2.12 Agricultural policy costs 50
4.06 Medium term business impact of HIV/AIDS.................48
2.10 Impact of rules on FDI 42
8.18 Flexibility of wage determination 37
8.17 Hiring and firing practices 36
6.17 Informal sector 31
3.10 Availability of mobile or cellular telephones...................29
6.07 Burden of government regulation 29

Note: The Business Competitiveness Index applies different criteria for selecting a country's competitive advantages and disadvantages.
Please refer to the section "How Country Profiles Work" for further details.

Chad

Competitiveness Rankings

Growth Competitiveness Index Rank	117

Macroeconomic Environment Index Rank **114**
    Macroeconomic Stability Subindex Rank 110
    Government Waste Rank 114
    Country Credit Rating Rank 104

Public Institutions Index Rank..**116**
    Contracts and Law Subindex Rank 113
    Corruption Subindex Rank..................................116

Technology Index Rank **117**
    Innovation Subindex Rank 117
    ICT Subindex Rank 117
    Technology Transfer Subindex Rank
      (out of 92 non-core innovators).........................92

Business Competitiveness Index Rank	n/a

**Sophistication of Company Operations
and Strategy Rank** ....**n/a**

**Quality of the National Business
Environment Rank**...**n/a**

The Most Problematic Factors for Doing Business

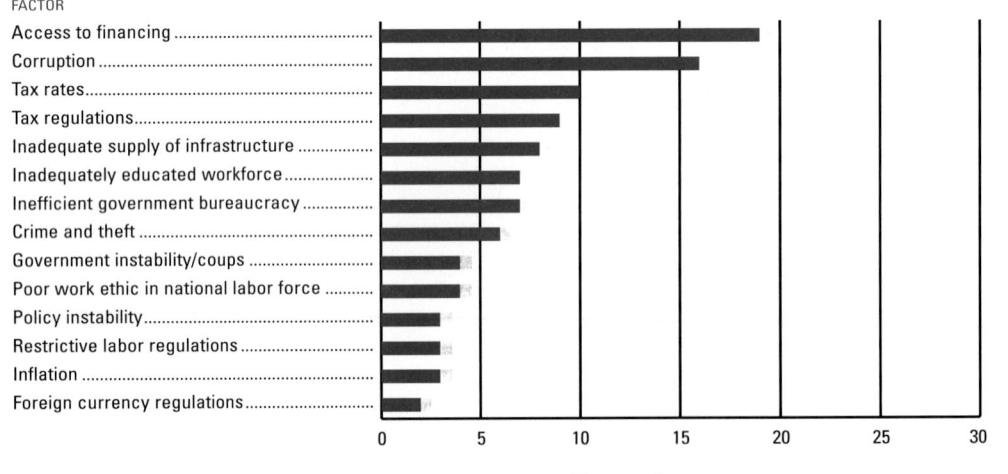

FACTOR

Access to financing
Corruption
Tax rates
Tax regulations
Inadequate supply of infrastructure
Inadequately educated workforce
Inefficient government bureaucracy
Crime and theft
Government instability/coups
Poor work ethic in national labor force
Policy instability
Restrictive labor regulations
Inflation
Foreign currency regulations

Percent of responses

Note: From a list of 14 factors, respondents were asked to select the five most problematic for doing business in their country and to rank them between 1 (most problematic) and 5. The bars in the figure show the responses weighted according to their rankings.

Source: World Economic Forum, Executive Opinion Survey (2005)

National competitiveness balance sheet

NOTABLE COMPETITIVE ADVANTAGES	
Growth Competitiveness Index	**Rank/117**

Macroeconomic Environment

2.16	Inflation, 2004	1

NOTABLE COMPETITIVE DISADVANTAGES	
Growth Competitiveness Index	**Rank/117**

Macroeconomic Environment

2.07	Access to credit	117
6.06	Wastefulness of government spending	114
2.21	Country credit rating, 2004	104
2.15	Real effective exchange rate, 2004	103
2.17	Interest rate spread, 2004	102
2.01	Recession expectations	94
2.20	Government debt, 2004	88
2.14	National savings rate, 2004	68
2.13	Government surplus/deficit, 2004	53

Public Institutions

6.03	Property rights	115
6.19	Irregular payments in exports and imports	114
6.20	Irregular payments in public utilities	114
6.21	Irregular payments in tax collection	111
6.01	Judicial independence	111
6.16	Organized crime	109
6.08	Favoritism in decisions of government officials	90

Technology

3.04	FDI and technology transfer	117
3.03	Prevalence of foreign technology licensing	117
3.01	Technological readiness	117
3.11	Internet access in schools	117
5.08	Telephone lines, 2003	117
3.06	Company spending on research and development	116
3.15	Laws relating to ICT	116
3.18	Cellular telephones, 2003	115
4.17	Gross tertiary enrollment	115
3.20	Internet hosts, 2003	115
3.14	Government success in ICT promotion	114
3.07	University/industry research collaboration	114
3.12	Quality of competition in the ISP sector	114
3.13	Government prioritization of ICT	113
3.21	Personal computers, 2003	113
3.19	Internet users, 2003	113
3.02	Firm-level technology absorption	111
3.17	Utility patents, 2004	81

Other Indicators	
Other Indicators	**Rank/117**

8.18	Flexibility of wage determination	46
6.09	Extent of bureaucratic red tape	47

Other Indicators	
Other Indicators	**Rank/117**

4.06	Medium term business impact of HIV/AIDS	117
4.05	Medium term business impact of tuberculosis	117
8.11	Extent of staff training	117
6.23	Irregular payments in judicial decisions	117
8.23	Strength of auditing and accounting standards	117
7.07	Presence of demanding regulatory standards	117
7.01	Intensity of local competition	117
7.04	Buyer sophistication	117
8.14	Reliance on professional management	117
8.16	Efficacy of corporate boards	117
3.16	Extent of business Internet use	117
8.06	Extent of marketing	117
8.07	Degree of customer orientation	117
2.03	Financial market sophistication	117
8.13	Extent of incentive compensation	117

271

Note: This country is not included in the coverage of the Business Competitiveness Index 2005–2006.

Chile

Competitiveness Rankings

Growth Competitiveness Index Rank	23

Macroeconomic Environment Index Rank **15**
    Macroeconomic Stability Subindex Rank 3
    Government Waste Rank 19
    Country Credit Rating Rank 32

Public Institutions Index Rank.........................**22**
    Contracts and Law Subindex Rank 34
    Corruption Subindex Rank...................................13

Technology Index Rank **35**
    Innovation Subindex Rank...................................38
    ICT Subindex Rank 37
    Technology Transfer Subindex Rank
    (out of 92 non-core innovators)........................17

Business Competitiveness Index Rank	29

**Sophistication of Company Operations
  and Strategy Rank** **31**
**Quality of the National Business
  Environment Rank** **29**

The Most Problematic Factors for Doing Business

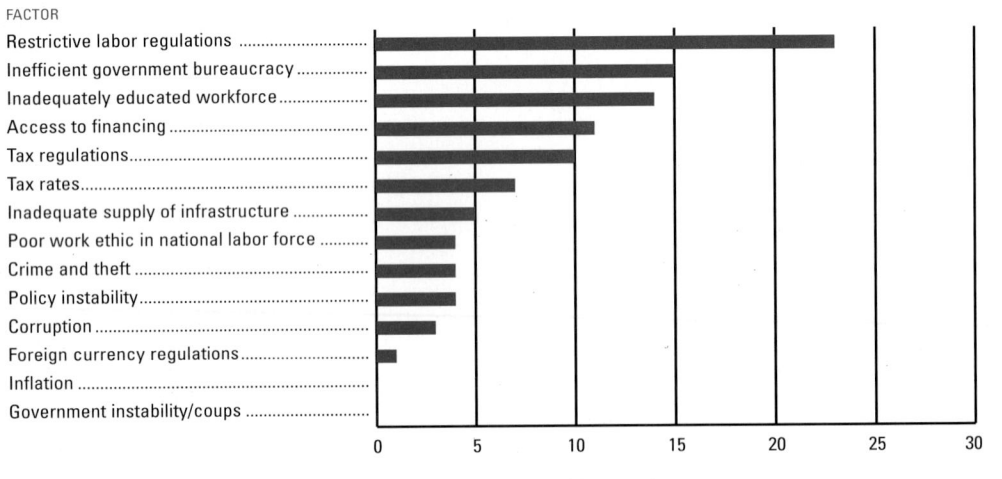

Note: From a list of 14 factors, respondents were asked to select the five most problematic for doing business in their country and to rank them between 1 (most problematic) and 5. The bars in the figure show the responses weighted according to their rankings.

Source: World Economic Forum, Executive Opinion Survey (2005)

National competitiveness balance sheet

NOTABLE COMPETITIVE ADVANTAGES	
Growth Competitiveness Index	**Rank/117**

Macroeconomic Environment
2.20	Government debt, 2004	7
2.01	Recession expectations	11
2.16	Inflation, 2004	13
2.13	Government surplus/deficit, 2004	13
6.06	Wastefulness of government spending	19
2.17	Interest rate spread, 2004	20

Public Institutions
6.19	Irregular payments in exports and imports	7
6.20	Irregular payments in public utilities	12
6.08	Favoritism in decisions of government officials	20
6.16	Organized crime	22

Technology
| 3.12 | Quality of competition in the ISP sector | 14 |
| 3.04 | FDI and technology transfer | 18 |

NOTABLE COMPETITIVE DISADVANTAGES	
Growth Competitiveness Index	**Rank/117**

Macroeconomic Environment
2.14	National savings rate, 2004	45
2.21	Country credit rating, 2004	32
2.07	Access to credit	27
2.15	Real effective exchange rate, 2004	26

Public Institutions
6.01	Judicial independence	47
6.03	Property rights	31
6.21	Irregular payments in tax collection	24

Technology
5.08	Telephone lines, 2003	56
3.03	Prevalence of foreign technology licensing	47
3.06	Company spending on research and development	47
3.07	University/industry research collaboration	45
3.18	Cellular telephones, 2003	43
3.21	Personal computers, 2003	42
3.20	Internet hosts, 2003	41
3.17	Utility patents, 2004	41
3.02	Firm-level technology absorption	40
4.17	Gross tertiary enrollment	38
3.14	Government success in ICT promotion	37
3.19	Internet users, 2003	34
3.11	Internet access in schools	33
3.13	Government prioritization of ICT	31
3.01	Technological readiness	26
3.15	Laws relating to ICT	26

Business Competitiveness Index	Rank/110

Sophistication of Company Operations and Strategy
8.10	Breadth of international markets	14
8.06	Extent of marketing	23
8.14	Reliance on professional management	25

Quality of the National Business Environment
7.01	Intensity of local competition	7
8.22	Foreign ownership restrictions	7
5.07	Telephone/fax infrastructure quality	14

Other Indicators	Rank/117
9.05	Effects of privatization on competition and the environment	5
8.18	Flexibility of wage determination	7
2.12	Agricultural policy costs	8
4.08	Brain drain	8
3.10	Availability of mobile or cellular telephones	8
4.05	Medium term business impact of tuberculosis	14
6.17	Informal sector	15
8.15	Quality of management schools	15
2.10	Impact of rules on FDI	16
2.02	Business costs of terrorism	18
6.07	Burden of government regulation	18

Business Competitiveness Index	Rank/110

Sophistication of Company Operations and Strategy
8.01	Nature of competitive advantage	66
8.02	Value chain presence	63
8.09	Extent of regional sales	48

Quality of the National Business Environment
4.03	Quality of math and science education	85
4.02	Quality of public schools	81
4.01	Quality of the educational system	71

Other Indicators	Rank/117
4.09	Private sector employment of women	101
8.17	Hiring and firing practices	82
9.07	Importance of environment in business planning	67
7.03	Extent of market dominance	58
7.08	Local availability of process machinery	53
3.09	Availability of scientists and engineers	52
6.15	Business costs of crime and violence	50
3.05	Quality of scientific research institutions	48
6.04	Intellectual property protection	45
9.03	Extent of government mandated environmental reporting	45
6.10	Effectiveness of law-making bodies	44
6.13	Centralization of economic policymaking	44

273

Note: The Business Competitiveness Index applies different criteria for selecting a country's competitive advantages and disadvantages. Please refer to the section "How Country Profiles Work" for further details.

China

Competitiveness Rankings

Growth Competitiveness Index Rank	49

Macroeconomic Environment Index Rank **33**
    Macroeconomic Stability Subindex Rank 27
    Government Waste Rank 44
    Country Credit Rating Rank 37

Public Institutions Index Rank **56**
    Contracts and Law Subindex Rank 62
    Corruption Subindex Rank 50

Technology Index Rank **64**
    Innovation Subindex Rank 75
    ICT Subindex Rank 60
    Technology Transfer Subindex Rank
      (out of 92 non-core innovators)........................43

Business Competitiveness Index Rank	57

**Sophistication of Company Operations
  and Strategy Rank** **53**
**Quality of the National Business
  Environment Rank** **58**

The Most Problematic Factors for Doing Business

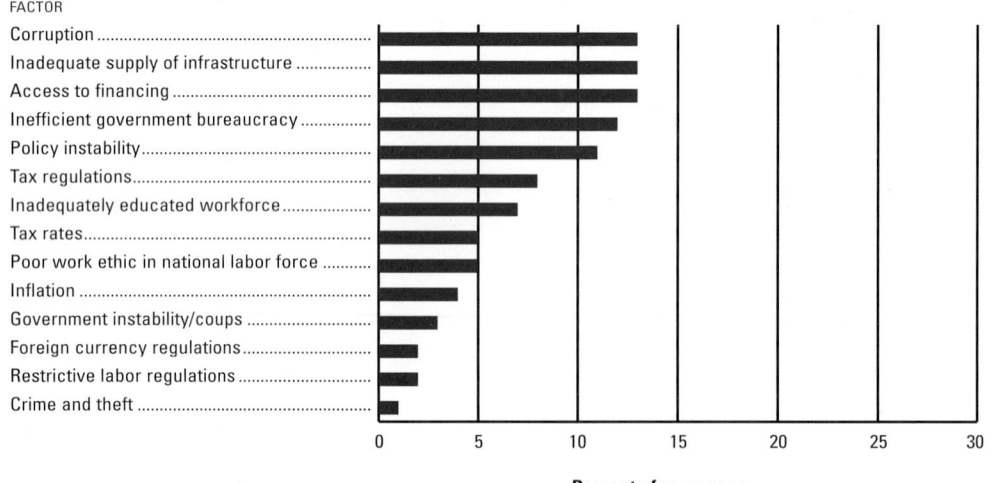

Note: From a list of 14 factors, respondents were asked to select the five most problematic for doing business in their country and to rank them between 1 (most problematic) and 5. The bars in the figure show the responses weighted according to their rankings.

Source: World Economic Forum, Executive Opinion Survey (2005)

274

National competitiveness balance sheet

NOTABLE COMPETITIVE ADVANTAGES		NOTABLE COMPETITIVE DISADVANTAGES	
Growth Competitiveness Index	**Rank/117**	**Growth Competitiveness Index**	**Rank/117**

Macroeconomic Environment (Advantages)

2.14	National savings rate, 2004	2
2.17	Interest rate spread, 2004	22
2.01	Recession expectations	26
2.20	Government debt, 2004	28
2.21	Country credit rating, 2004	37
6.06	Wastefulness of government spending	44

Public Institutions

6.19	Irregular payments in exports and imports	47

Technology

3.07	University/industry research collaboration	26
3.06	Company spending on research and development	31
3.02	Firm-level technology absorption	37
3.12	Quality of competition in the ISP sector	40
3.14	Government success in ICT promotion	40

Macroeconomic Environment (Disadvantages)

2.07	Access to credit	105
2.16	Inflation, 2004	59
2.13	Government surplus/deficit, 2004	57
2.15	Real effective exchange rate, 2004	54

Public Institutions

6.03	Property rights	71
6.01	Judicial independence	65
6.16	Organized crime	65
6.21	Irregular payments in tax collection	59
6.08	Favoritism in decisions of government officials	59
6.20	Irregular payments in public utilities	52

Technology

3.20	Internet hosts, 2003	93
4.17	Gross tertiary enrollment	85
3.21	Personal computers, 2003	80
3.03	Prevalence of foreign technology licensing	71
3.19	Internet users, 2003	70
3.18	Cellular telephones, 2003	69
3.01	Technological readiness	68
5.08	Telephone lines, 2003	58
3.17	Utility patents, 2004	58
3.04	FDI and technology transfer	57
3.13	Government prioritization of ICT	56
3.15	Laws relating to ICT	56
3.11	Internet access in schools	54

Business Competitiveness Index	**Rank/110**	**Business Competitiveness Index**	**Rank/110**

Sophistication of Company Operations and Strategy (Advantages)

3.06	Company spending on research and development	30
8.03	Capacity for innovation	33
8.10	Breadth of international markets	36

Quality of the National Business Environment

7.08	Local availability of process machinery	7
3.08	Government procurement of advanced technology products	11
6.13	Centralization of economic policymaking	25

Sophistication of Company Operations and Strategy (Disadvantages)

8.14	Reliance on professional management	75
8.06	Extent of marketing	73
3.03	Prevalence of foreign technology licensing	69

Quality of the National Business Environment

6.09	Extent of bureaucratic red tape	110
8.21	Protection of minority shareholders' interests	101
8.16	Efficacy of corporate boards	96

Other Indicators	**Rank/117**	**Other Indicators**	**Rank/117**

(Advantages)

8.20	Pay and productivity	13
2.12	Agricultural policy costs	15
6.10	Effectiveness of law-making bodies	26
8.17	Hiring and firing practices	26
9.06	Prioritization of energy efficiency	27
6.26	Public trust of politicians	29
6.18	Government effectiveness in reducing poverty and inequality	29
6.07	Burden of government regulation	30
7.01	Intensity of local competition	31
7.09	Local availability of specialized research and training services	36

(Disadvantages)

6.05	Freedom of the press	114
2.04	Soundness of banks	113
2.11	Tax burden	100
9.05	Effects of privatization on competition and the environment	97
3.10	Availability of mobile or cellular telephones	95
2.05	Ease of access to loans	89
9.01	Stringency of environmental regulations	88
2.03	Financial market sophistication	87
2.08	Local equity market access	85
2.09	Prevalence of trade barriers	83
8.23	Strength of auditing and accounting standards	81
5.05	Quality of electricity supply	80

275

Note: The Business Competitiveness Index applies different criteria for selecting a country's competitive advantages and disadvantages. Please refer to the section "How Country Profiles Work" for further details.

Colombia

Competitiveness Rankings

Growth Competitiveness Index Rank	57

Macroeconomic Environment Index Rank **61**
    Macroeconomic Stability Subindex Rank 48
    Government Waste Rank 66
    Country Credit Rating Rank 65

Public Institutions Index Rank..........................**49**
    Contracts and Law Subindex Rank 83
    Corruption Subindex Rank...................................30

Technology Index Rank **74**
    Innovation Subindex Rank 67
    ICT Subindex Rank 71
    Technology Transfer Subindex Rank
      (out of 92 non-core innovators)........................53

Business Competitiveness Index Rank	56

**Sophistication of Company Operations
and Strategy Rank** **49**
**Quality of the National Business
Environment Rank** **57**

The Most Problematic Factors for Doing Business

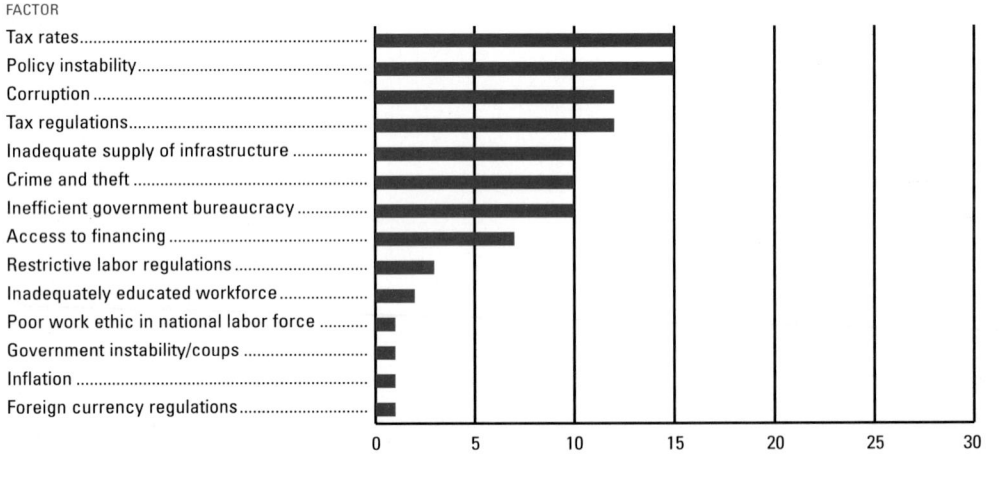

Note: From a list of 14 factors, respondents were asked to select the five most problematic for doing business in their country and to rank them between 1 (most problematic) and 5. The bars in the figure show the responses weighted according to their rankings.

Source: World Economic Forum, Executive Opinion Survey (2005)

National competitiveness balance sheet

NOTABLE COMPETITIVE ADVANTAGES		NOTABLE COMPETITIVE DISADVANTAGES	
Growth Competitiveness Index	**Rank/117**	**Growth Competitiveness Index**	**Rank/117**

	Macroeconomic Environment			**Macroeconomic Environment**	
2.07	Access to credit	22	2.14	National savings rate, 2004	81
2.15	Real effective exchange rate, 2004	23	2.16	Inflation, 2004	76
2.13	Government surplus/deficit, 2004	49	2.17	Interest rate spread, 2004	76
	Public Institutions		6.06	Wastefulness of government spending	66
6.19	Irregular payments in exports and imports	29	2.21	Country credit rating, 2004	65
6.21	Irregular payments in tax collection	32	2.01	Recession expectations	62
6.20	Irregular payments in public utilities	35	2.20	Government debt, 2004	56
	Technology			**Public Institutions**	
3.07	University/industry research collaboration	30	6.16	Organized crime	115
3.06	Company spending on research and development	39	6.08	Favoritism in decisions of government officials	80
			6.01	Judicial independence	66
			6.03	Property rights	51
				Technology	
			3.13	Government prioritization of ICT	97
			3.02	Firm-level technology absorption	92
			3.14	Government success in ICT promotion	80
			3.03	Prevalence of foreign technology licensing	78
			3.18	Cellular telephones, 2003	78
			3.19	Internet users, 2003	74
			4.17	Gross tertiary enrollment	70
			3.01	Technological readiness	70
			3.04	FDI and technology transfer	70
			3.11	Internet access in schools	67
			3.21	Personal computers, 2003	65
			3.17	Utility patents, 2004	63
			5.08	Telephone lines, 2003	62
			3.20	Internet hosts, 2003	55
			3.15	Laws relating to ICT	55
			3.12	Quality of competition in the ISP sector	54

Business Competitiveness Index	**Rank/110**	**Business Competitiveness Index**	**Rank/110**

	Sophistication of Company Operations and Strategy			**Sophistication of Company Operations and Strategy**	
8.07	Degree of customer orientation	30	8.13	Extent of incentive compensation	87
3.06	Company spending on research and development	38	3.03	Prevalence of foreign technology licensing	76
8.09	Extent of regional sales	40	8.11	Extent of staff training	65
	Quality of the National Business Environment			**Quality of the National Business Environment**	
8.16	Efficacy of corporate boards	25	2.06	Venture capital availability	103
8.19	Cooperation in labor-employer relations	27	5.02	Railroad infrastructure development	96
3.07	University/industry research collaboration	30	7.08	Local availability of process machinery	91

Other Indicators	**Rank/117**	**Other Indicators**	**Rank/117**

4.07	Ease of hiring foreign labor	15	2.02	Business costs of terrorism	117
8.24	Importance of corporate social responsibility	32	2.11	Tax burden	115
4.05	Medium term business impact of tuberculosis	32	6.12	Efficiency of the tax system	103
8.04	Ethical behavior of firms	34	6.11	Extent and effect of taxation	100
4.09	Private sector employment of women	36	6.15	Business costs of crime and violence	97
9.05	Effects of privatization on competition and the environment	36	6.27	Pervasiveness of money laundering through banks	93
6.22	Irregular payments in public contracts	38	8.20	Pay and productivity	90
8.18	Flexibility of wage determination	38	7.03	Extent of market dominance	89
8.15	Quality of management schools	39	2.05	Ease of access to loans	87
9.01	Stringency of environmental regulations	41	3.09	Availability of scientists and engineers	87
2.04	Soundness of banks	42	2.12	Agricultural policy costs	85
			6.10	Effectiveness of law-making bodies	84

Note: The Business Competitiveness Index applies different criteria for selecting a country's competitive advantages and disadvantages. Please refer to the section "How Country Profiles Work" for further details.

Costa Rica

Competitiveness Rankings

Growth Competitiveness Index Rank	64

Macroeconomic Environment Index Rank **82**
    Macroeconomic Stability Subindex Rank 109
    Government Waste Rank 83
    Country Credit Rating Rank 60

Public Institutions Index Rank **58**
    Contracts and Law Subindex Rank 49
    Corruption Subindex Rank...................................68

Technology Index Rank **56**
    Innovation Subindex Rank 72
    ICT Subindex Rank 58
    Technology Transfer Subindex Rank
        (out of 92 non-core innovators).......................22

Business Competitiveness Index Rank	50

**Sophistication of Company Operations
and Strategy Rank** **34**
**Quality of the National Business
Environment Rank** **53**

The Most Problematic Factors for Doing Business

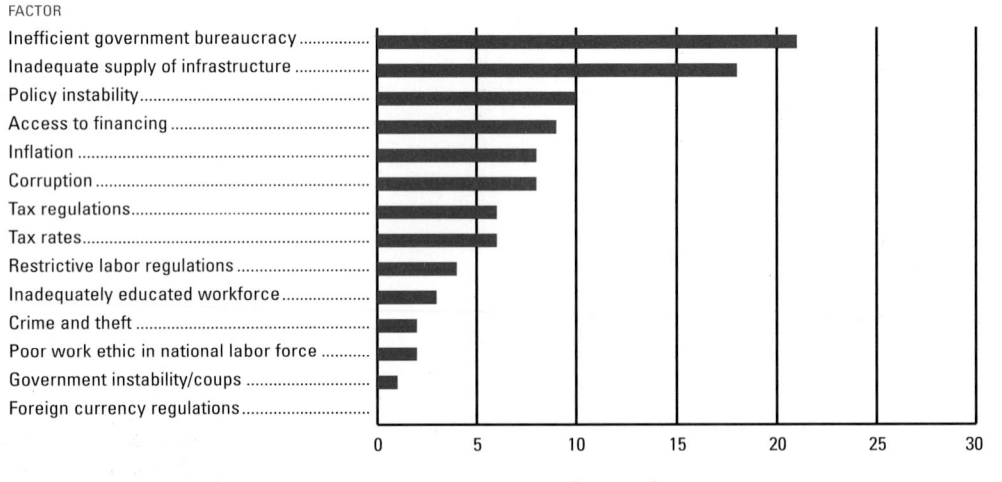

Note: From a list of 14 factors, respondents were asked to select the five most problematic for doing business in their country and to rank them between 1 (most problematic) and 5. The bars in the figure show the responses weighted according to their rankings.

Source: World Economic Forum, Executive Opinion Survey (2005)

National competitiveness balance sheet

NOTABLE COMPETITIVE ADVANTAGES		
Growth Competitiveness Index		**Rank/117**

Macroeconomic Environment
2.15	Real effective exchange rate, 2004	41

Public Institutions
6.01	Judicial independence	32

Technology
3.04	FDI and technology transfer	5
3.21	Personal computers, 2003	31
3.07	University/industry research collaboration	33
3.06	Company spending on research and development	34
5.08	Telephone lines, 2003	42
3.19	Internet users, 2003	44
3.01	Technological readiness	48

NOTABLE COMPETITIVE DISADVANTAGES		
Growth Competitiveness Index		**Rank/117**

Macroeconomic Environment
2.16	Inflation, 2004	108
2.17	Interest rate spread, 2004	105
2.01	Recession expectations	105
2.13	Government surplus/deficit, 2004	88
2.14	National savings rate, 2004	83
6.06	Wastefulness of government spending	83
2.07	Access to credit	73
2.20	Government debt, 2004	70
2.21	Country credit rating, 2004	60

Public Institutions
6.20	Irregular payments in public utilities	77
6.16	Organized crime	75
6.19	Irregular payments in exports and imports	69
6.21	Irregular payments in tax collection	66
6.08	Favoritism in decisions of government officials	60
6.03	Property rights	54

Technology
3.12	Quality of competition in the ISP sector	114
3.13	Government prioritization of ICT	111
3.14	Government success in ICT promotion	93
3.11	Internet access in schools	85
3.17	Utility patents, 2004	81
4.17	Gross tertiary enrollment	76
3.18	Cellular telephones, 2003	73
3.03	Prevalence of foreign technology licensing	70
3.15	Laws relating to ICT	69
3.02	Firm-level technology absorption	56
3.20	Internet hosts, 2003	56

279

Business Competitiveness Index		Rank/110

Sophistication of Company Operations and Strategy
8.12	Willingness to delegate authority	28
8.09	Extent of regional sales	29
8.11	Extent of staff training	29

Quality of the National Business Environment
8.19	Cooperation in labor-employer relations	13
8.22	Foreign ownership restrictions	19
8.15	Quality of management schools	21

Other Indicators		Rank/117
2.02	Business costs of terrorism	25
4.08	Brain drain	29
8.13	Extent of incentive compensation	30
8.01	Nature of competitive advantage	31
6.05	Freedom of the press	32
8.02	Value chain presence	33
8.03	Capacity for innovation	33
4.07	Ease of hiring foreign labor	34
3.05	Quality of scientific research institutions	34

Business Competitiveness Index		Rank/110

Sophistication of Company Operations and Strategy
3.03	Prevalence of foreign technology licensing	68
8.08	Control of international distribution	63
8.14	Reliance on professional management	53

Quality of the National Business Environment
5.07	Telephone/fax infrastructure quality	108
2.09	Prevalence of trade barriers	105
5.02	Railroad infrastructure development	101

Other Indicators		Rank/117
3.10	Availability of mobile or cellular telephones	116
6.10	Effectiveness of law-making bodies	114
6.13	Centralization of economic policymaking	106
6.15	Business costs of crime and violence	92
5.06	Postal efficiency	92
8.18	Flexibility of wage determination	88
6.07	Burden of government regulation	87
3.08	Government procurement of advanced technology products	86
6.26	Public trust of politicians	85
6.18	Government effectiveness in reducing poverty and inequality	83
2.08	Local equity market access	81
2.05	Ease of access to loans	80
9.05	Effects of privatization on competition and the environment	80

Note: The Business Competitiveness Index applies different criteria for selecting a country's competitive advantages and disadvantages. Please refer to the section "How Country Profiles Work" for further details.

Croatia

Competitiveness Rankings

Growth Competitiveness Index Rank	62

Macroeconomic Environment Index Rank **68**
   Macroeconomic Stability Subindex Rank.............90
   Government Waste Rank.......................................74
   Country Credit Rating Rank.................................55

Public Institutions Index Rank...........................**73**
   Contracts and Law Subindex Rank 80
   Corruption Subindex Rank...................................65

Technology Index Rank **51**
   Innovation Subindex Rank...................................48
   ICT Subindex Rank 40
   Technology Transfer Subindex Rank
     (out of 92 non-core innovators).......................56

Business Competitiveness Index Rank	63

**Sophistication of Company Operations
and Strategy Rank** **70**

**Quality of the National Business
Environment Rank** **61**

The Most Problematic Factors for Doing Business

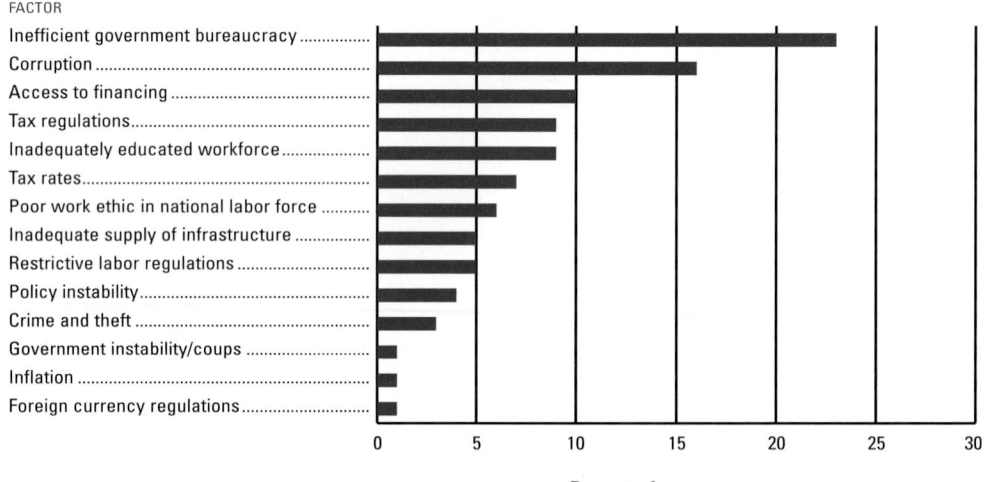

FACTOR

Inefficient government bureaucracy................
Corruption...
Access to financing ....
Tax regulations...
Inadequately educated workforce....................
Tax rates..
Poor work ethic in national labor force ....
Inadequate supply of infrastructure ....
Restrictive labor regulations ....
Policy instability..
Crime and theft ....
Government instability/coups ....
Inflation ....
Foreign currency regulations...........................

Percent of responses

Note: From a list of 14 factors, respondents were asked to select the five most problematic for doing business in their country and to rank them between 1 (most problematic) and 5. The bars in the figure show the responses weighted according to
their rankings.

Source: World Economic Forum, Executive Opinion Survey (2005)

National competitiveness balance sheet

	NOTABLE COMPETITIVE ADVANTAGES	

Growth Competitiveness Index — Rank/117

Macroeconomic Environment
| 2.16 | Inflation, 2004 | 30 |
| 2.14 | National savings rate, 2004 | 32 |

Technology
5.08	Telephone lines, 2003	32
3.17	Utility patents, 2004	33
3.21	Personal computers, 2003	35
3.18	Cellular telephones, 2003	38
3.19	Internet users, 2003	40
4.17	Gross tertiary enrollment	42
3.20	Internet hosts, 2003	46
3.11	Internet access in schools	50

Business Competitiveness Index — Rank/110

Sophistication of Company Operations and Strategy
| 8.01 | Nature of competitive advantage | 39 |
| 8.13 | Extent of incentive compensation | 53 |

Quality of the National Business Environment
6.09	Extent of bureaucratic red tape	4
3.17	Utility patents, 2004	32
3.18	Cellular telephones, 2003	37

Other Indicators — Rank/117
2.02	Business costs of terrorism	16
4.06	Medium term business impact of HIV/AIDS	16
4.05	Medium term business impact of tuberculosis	26
2.11	Tax burden	26
3.10	Availability of mobile or cellular telephones	40
6.12	Efficiency of the tax system	42
9.04	Effects of compliance on business	45
5.06	Postal efficiency	47
7.09	Local availability of specialized research and training services	48
5.07	Telephone/fax infrastructure quality	48
6.24	Diversion of public funds	49

NOTABLE COMPETITIVE DISADVANTAGES

Growth Competitiveness Index — Rank/117

Macroeconomic Environment
2.01	Recession expectations	108
2.13	Government surplus/deficit, 2004	103
2.17	Interest rate spread, 2004	87
2.15	Real effective exchange rate, 2004	80
6.06	Wastefulness of government spending	74
2.20	Government debt, 2004	64
2.07	Access to credit	58
2.21	Country credit rating, 2004	55

Public Institutions
6.03	Property rights	86
6.16	Organized crime	85
6.08	Favoritism in decisions of government officials	77
6.01	Judicial independence	76
6.19	Irregular payments in exports and imports	67
6.21	Irregular payments in tax collection	64
6.20	Irregular payments in public utilities	62

Technology
3.04	FDI and technology transfer	109
3.02	Firm-level technology absorption	94
3.01	Technological readiness	87
3.12	Quality of competition in the ISP sector	80
3.06	Company spending on research and development	78
3.14	Government success in ICT promotion	76
3.13	Government prioritization of ICT	67
3.07	University/industry research collaboration	59
3.15	Laws relating to ICT	57
3.03	Prevalence of foreign technology licensing	52

Business Competitiveness Index — Rank/110

Sophistication of Company Operations and Strategy
8.10	Breadth of international markets	86
8.11	Extent of staff training	81
8.07	Degree of customer orientation	77

Quality of the National Business Environment
2.06	Venture capital availability	96
8.19	Cooperation in labor-employer relations	90
8.21	Protection of minority shareholders' interests	89

Other Indicators — Rank/117
2.12	Agricultural policy costs	112
9.05	Effects of privatization on competition and the environment	99
6.07	Burden of government regulation	97
2.10	Impact of rules on FDI	97
9.06	Prioritization of energy efficiency	95
9.07	Importance of environment in business planning	93
8.15	Quality of management schools	92
6.18	Government effectiveness in reducing poverty and inequality	87
7.02	Effectiveness of antitrust policy	86
8.24	Importance of corporate social responsibility	86
8.16	Efficacy of corporate boards	83

281

4.2: Country Profiles

Note: The Business Competitiveness Index applies different criteria for selecting a country's competitive advantages and disadvantages. Please refer to the section "How Country Profiles Work" for further details.

Cyprus

Competitiveness Rankings

Growth Competitiveness Index Rank	34

Macroeconomic Environment Index Rank **45**
  Macroeconomic Stability Subindex Rank 76
  Government Waste Rank 30
  Country Credit Rating Rank 36

Public Institutions Index Rank **27**
  Contracts and Law Subindex Rank 25
  Corruption Subindex Rank 31

Technology Index Rank **36**
  Innovation Subindex Rank 51
  ICT Subindex Rank 29
  Technology Transfer Subindex Rank
    (out of 92 non-core innovators).........................50

Business Competitiveness Index Rank	36

**Sophistication of Company Operations
  and Strategy Rank** **48**
**Quality of the National Business
  Environment Rank** **36**

The Most Problematic Factors for Doing Business

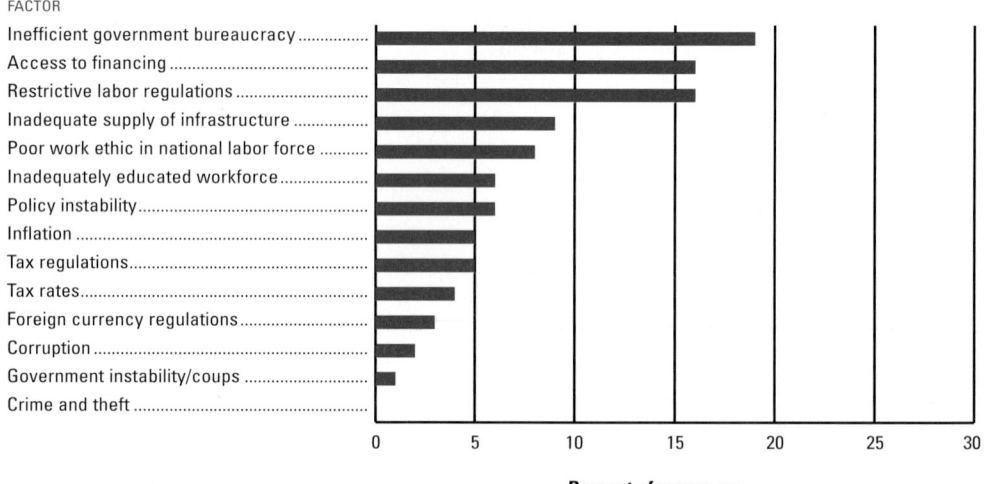

Note: From a list of 14 factors, respondents were asked to select the five most problematic for doing business in their country and to rank them between 1 (most problematic) and 5. The bars in the figure show the responses weighted according to their rankings.

Source: World Economic Forum, Executive Opinion Survey (2005)

National competitiveness balance sheet

NOTABLE COMPETITIVE ADVANTAGES

Growth Competitiveness Index	Rank/117

Macroeconomic Environment

2.17	Interest rate spread, 2004	28
6.06	Wastefulness of government spending	30
2.16	Inflation, 2004	32

Public Institutions

6.01	Judicial independence	18
6.03	Property rights	22
6.16	Organized crime	25
6.20	Irregular payments in public utilities	29
6.19	Irregular payments in exports and imports	31

Technology

5.08	Telephone lines, 2003	13
3.21	Personal computers, 2003	26
3.18	Cellular telephones, 2003	26
3.19	Internet users, 2003	30
3.11	Internet access in schools	32
3.12	Quality of competition in the ISP sector	33

Business Competitiveness Index	Rank/110

Sophistication of Company Operations and Strategy

8.01	Nature of competitive advantage	22
8.07	Degree of customer orientation	27
8.06	Extent of marketing	32

Quality of the National Business Environment

6.09	Extent of bureaucratic red tape	10
2.09	Prevalence of trade barriers	17
6.01	Judicial independence	17

Other Indicators	Rank/117

2.11	Tax burden	8
6.11	Extent and effect of taxation	11
6.12	Efficiency of the tax system	12
6.15	Business costs of crime and violence	18
6.07	Burden of government regulation	19
5.07	Telephone/fax infrastructure quality	21
7.02	Effectiveness of antitrust policy	21
5.06	Postal efficiency	22
5.05	Quality of electricity supply	22
6.02	Efficiency of legal framework	22
6.24	Diversion of public funds	23
3.09	Availability of scientists and engineers	24

NOTABLE COMPETITIVE DISADVANTAGES

Growth Competitiveness Index	Rank/117

Macroeconomic Environment

2.15	Real effective exchange rate, 2004	98
2.14	National savings rate, 2004	96
2.13	Government surplus/deficit, 2004	90
2.20	Government debt, 2004	85
2.07	Access to credit	72
2.01	Recession expectations	70
2.21	Country credit rating, 2004	36

Public Institutions

6.08	Favoritism in decisions of government officials	44
6.21	Irregular payments in tax collection	34

Technology

3.04	FDI and technology transfer	94
3.07	University/industry research collaboration	78
3.06	Company spending on research and development	74
3.13	Government prioritization of ICT	74
3.14	Government success in ICT promotion	62
4.17	Gross tertiary enrollment	56
3.02	Firm-level technology absorption	54
3.03	Prevalence of foreign technology licensing	54
3.15	Laws relating to ICT	51
3.01	Technological readiness	46
3.20	Internet hosts, 2003	45
3.17	Utility patents, 2004	37

Business Competitiveness Index	Rank/110

Sophistication of Company Operations and Strategy

8.14	Reliance on professional management	89
8.10	Breadth of international markets	74
8.13	Extent of incentive compensation	73

Quality of the National Business Environment

5.02	Railroad infrastructure development	109
8.16	Efficacy of corporate boards	91
8.22	Foreign ownership restrictions	80

Other Indicators	Rank/117

8.18	Flexibility of wage determination	96
4.07	Ease of hiring foreign labor	88
8.17	Hiring and firing practices	83
2.12	Agricultural policy costs	81
2.08	Local equity market access	77
8.20	Pay and productivity	76
3.05	Quality of scientific research institutions	74
8.09	Extent of regional sales	71
8.12	Willingness to delegate authority	70
8.03	Capacity for innovation	69

283

Note: The Business Competitiveness Index applies different criteria for selecting a country's competitive advantages and disadvantages. Please refer to the section "How Country Profiles Work" for further details.

Czech Republic

Competitiveness Rankings

Growth Competitiveness Index Rank	38

Macroeconomic Environment Index Rank **46**
    Macroeconomic Stability Subindex Rank 44
    Government Waste Rank 78
    Country Credit Rating Rank 34

Public Institutions Index Rank...........................**48**
    Contracts and Law Subindex Rank 50
    Corruption Subindex Rank...................................49

Technology Index Rank **22**
    Innovation Subindex Rank 39
    ICT Subindex Rank 31
    Technology Transfer Subindex Rank
        (out of 92 non-core innovators)..........................2

Business Competitiveness Index Rank	27

**Sophistication of Company Operations
and Strategy Rank** **29**
**Quality of the National Business
Environment Rank** **27**

The Most Problematic Factors for Doing Business

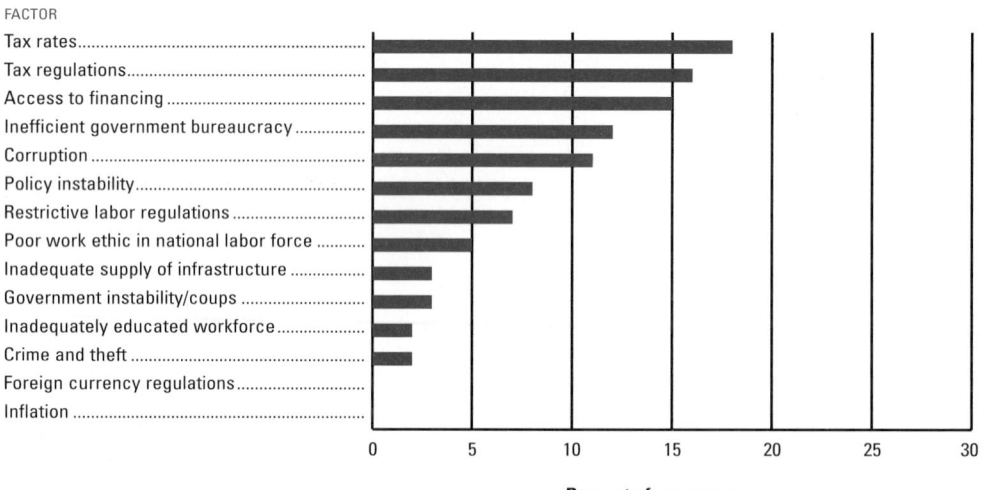

FACTOR

Tax rates
Tax regulations
Access to financing
Inefficient government bureaucracy
Corruption
Policy instability
Restrictive labor regulations
Poor work ethic in national labor force
Inadequate supply of infrastructure
Government instability/coups
Inadequately educated workforce
Crime and theft
Foreign currency regulations
Inflation

Percent of responses

Note: From a list of 14 factors, respondents were asked to select the five most problematic for doing business in their country and to rank them between 1 (most problematic) and 5. The bars in the figure show the responses weighted according to their rankings.

Source: World Economic Forum, Executive Opinion Survey (2005)

National competitiveness balance sheet

NOTABLE COMPETITIVE ADVANTAGES	
Growth Competitiveness Index	**Rank/117**

Macroeconomic Environment

| 2.20 | Government debt, 2004 | 26 |
| 2.21 | Country credit rating, 2004 | 34 |

Technology

3.04	FDI and technology transfer	3
3.18	Cellular telephones, 2003	7
3.03	Prevalence of foreign technology licensing	18
3.02	Firm-level technology absorption	25
3.06	Company spending on research and development	25
3.11	Internet access in schools	26
3.20	Internet hosts, 2003	26
3.07	University/industry research collaboration	27
3.01	Technological readiness	29
3.17	Utility patents, 2004	30
3.19	Internet users, 2003	32
5.08	Telephone lines, 2003	34
3.21	Personal computers, 2003	34

Business Competitiveness Index	
Business Competitiveness Index	**Rank/110**

Sophistication of Company Operations and Strategy

8.02	Value chain presence	21
8.03	Capacity for innovation	23
3.06	Company spending on research and development	24

Quality of the National Business Environment

3.18	Cellular telephones, 2003	6
4.03	Quality of math and science education	6
3.09	Availability of scientists and engineers	6

Other Indicators	
Other Indicators	**Rank/117**

6.09	Extent of bureaucratic red tape	10
3.10	Availability of mobile or cellular telephones	16
8.20	Pay and productivity	16
6.13	Centralization of economic policymaking	19
5.05	Quality of electricity supply	20
7.09	Local availability of specialized research and training services	21
4.09	Private sector employment of women	22
2.02	Business costs of terrorism	22
8.22	Foreign ownership restrictions	22
7.07	Presence of demanding regulatory standards	23
7.08	Local availability of process machinery	23
7.05	Local supplier quantity	23
9.01	Stringency of environmental regulations	23

NOTABLE COMPETITIVE DISADVANTAGES	
Growth Competitiveness Index	**Rank/117**

Macroeconomic Environment

2.15	Real effective exchange rate, 2004	108
2.13	Government surplus/deficit, 2004	81
6.06	Wastefulness of government spending	78
2.14	National savings rate, 2004	52
2.17	Interest rate spread, 2004	46
2.07	Access to credit	45
2.16	Inflation, 2004	44
2.01	Recession expectations	43

Public Institutions

6.03	Property rights	62
6.16	Organized crime	58
6.08	Favoritism in decisions of government officials	56
6.20	Irregular payments in public utilities	51
6.21	Irregular payments in tax collection	49
6.19	Irregular payments in exports and imports	49
6.01	Judicial independence	41

Technology

3.13	Government prioritization of ICT	73
3.14	Government success in ICT promotion	69
3.12	Quality of competition in the ISP sector	56
4.17	Gross tertiary enrollment	49
3.15	Laws relating to ICT	40

Business Competitiveness Index	
Business Competitiveness Index	**Rank/110**

Sophistication of Company Operations and Strategy

8.08	Control of international distribution	60
8.13	Extent of incentive compensation	47
8.12	Willingness to delegate authority	37

Quality of the National Business Environment

8.21	Protection of minority shareholders' interests	68
2.03	Financial market sophistication	65
2.08	Local equity market access	64

Other Indicators	
Other Indicators	**Rank/117**

6.12	Efficiency of the tax system	83
8.17	Hiring and firing practices	77
2.04	Soundness of banks	73
6.10	Effectiveness of law-making bodies	69
6.11	Extent and effect of taxation	67
2.11	Tax burden	67
6.26	Public trust of politicians	66
6.07	Burden of government regulation	64
6.22	Irregular payments in public contracts	63
6.14	Reliability of police services	61
2.05	Ease of access to loans	60

285

Note: The Business Competitiveness Index applies different criteria for selecting a country's competitive advantages and disadvantages. Please refer to the section "How Country Profiles Work" for further details.

Denmark

Competitiveness Rankings

Growth Competitiveness Index Rank	4

Macroeconomic Environment Index Rank 3
    Macroeconomic Stability Subindex Rank 11
    Government Waste Rank 4
    Country Credit Rating Rank 8

Public Institutions Index Rank 2
    Contracts and Law Subindex Rank 1
    Corruption Subindex Rank......................................4

Technology Index Rank 5
    Innovation Subindex Rank 10
    ICT Subindex Rank 1

Business Competitiveness Index Rank	4

**Sophistication of Company Operations
and Strategy Rank** 4

**Quality of the National Business
Environment Rank** 3

The Most Problematic Factors for Doing Business

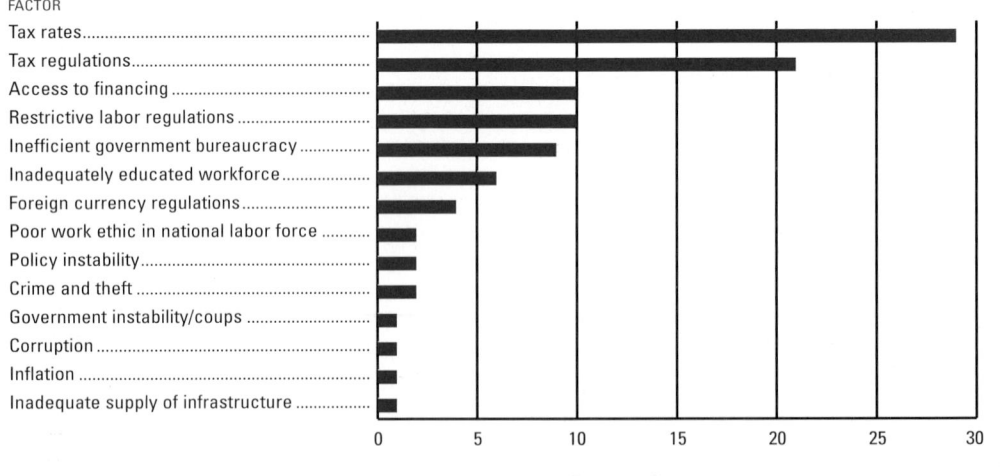

Note: From a list of 14 factors, respondents were asked to select the five most problematic for doing business in their country and to rank them between 1 (most problematic) and 5. The bars in the figure show the responses weighted according to their rankings.

Source: World Economic Forum, Executive Opinion Survey (2005)

National competitiveness balance sheet

NOTABLE COMPETITIVE ADVANTAGES		NOTABLE COMPETITIVE DISADVANTAGES	
Growth Competitiveness Index	**Rank/117**	**Growth Competitiveness Index**	**Rank/117**

Macroeconomic Environment

6.06	Wastefulness of government spending	4
2.21	Country credit rating, 2004	8
2.07	Access to credit	9

Public Institutions

6.08	Favoritism in decisions of government officials	1
6.01	Judicial independence	2
6.21	Irregular payments in tax collection	4
6.16	Organized crime	4
6.03	Property rights	5
6.19	Irregular payments in exports and imports	6
6.20	Irregular payments in public utilities	6

Technology

3.15	Laws relating to ICT	2
3.11	Internet access in schools	3
3.13	Government prioritization of ICT	3
3.20	Internet hosts, 2003	4
3.01	Technological readiness	5
5.08	Telephone lines, 2003	5
3.21	Personal computers, 2003	7
3.19	Internet users, 2003	8
3.14	Government success in ICT promotion	8
3.02	Firm-level technology absorption	9
3.06	Company spending on research and development	9
3.07	University/industry research collaboration	9

Macroeconomic Environment

2.15	Real effective exchange rate, 2004	88
2.14	National savings rate, 2004	48
2.20	Government debt, 2004	47
2.17	Interest rate spread, 2004	25
2.13	Government surplus/deficit, 2004	18
2.01	Recession expectations	18
2.16	Inflation, 2004	15

Technology

3.12	Quality of competition in the ISP sector	23
3.18	Cellular telephones, 2003	15
4.17	Gross tertiary enrollment	14
3.17	Utility patents, 2004	14

Business Competitiveness Index	**Rank/110**	**Business Competitiveness Index**	**Rank/110**

Sophistication of Company Operations and Strategy

8.12	Willingness to delegate authority	1
8.11	Extent of staff training	2
8.07	Degree of customer orientation	4

Quality of the National Business Environment

6.08	Favoritism in decisions of government officials	1
6.02	Efficiency of legal framework	1
5.01	Overall infrastructure quality	1

Quality of the National Business Environment

2.08	Local equity market access	36
6.09	Extent of bureaucratic red tape	34
4.03	Quality of math and science education	30

Other Indicators	**Rank/117**	**Other Indicators**	**Rank/117**

9.03	Extent of government mandated environmental reporting	1
9.02	Clarity and stability of regulations	1
9.09	Prevalence of corporate environmental reporting	1
9.04	Effects of compliance on business	1
9.06	Prioritization of energy efficiency	1
6.18	Government effectiveness in reducing poverty and inequality	1
8.04	Ethical behavior of firms	1
6.24	Diversion of public funds	1
4.09	Private sector employment of women	2
9.01	Stringency of environmental regulations	2
8.19	Cooperation in labor-employer relations	2
6.14	Reliability of police services	2

6.11	Extent and effect of taxation	105
6.12	Efficiency of the tax system	101
8.18	Flexibility of wage determination	95
2.11	Tax burden	66
2.02	Business costs of terrorism	51
4.07	Ease of hiring foreign labor	45
2.10	Impact of rules on FDI	27
6.17	Informal sector	24
8.22	Foreign ownership restrictions	24
4.08	Brain drain	23
7.01	Intensity of local competition	22
3.05	Quality of scientific research institutions	15
2.03	Financial market sophistication	14

Note: The Business Competitiveness Index applies different criteria for selecting a country's competitive advantages and disadvantages. Please refer to the section "How Country Profiles Work" for further details.

Dominican Republic

288

Competitiveness Rankings

Growth Competitiveness Index Rank	102

Macroeconomic Environment Index Rank **112**
    Macroeconomic Stability Subindex Rank 108
    Government Waste Rank 115
    Country Credit Rating Rank 92

Public Institutions Index Rank...**105**
    Contracts and Law Subindex Rank 106
    Corruption Subindex Rank.....................................99

Technology Index Rank **67**
    Innovation Subindex Rank 55
    ICT Subindex Rank 65
    Technology Transfer Subindex Rank
        (out of 92 non-core innovators).......................47

Business Competitiveness Index Rank	97

**Sophistication of Company Operations
   and Strategy Rank** **87**
**Quality of the National Business
   Environment Rank** **99**

The Most Problematic Factors for Doing Business

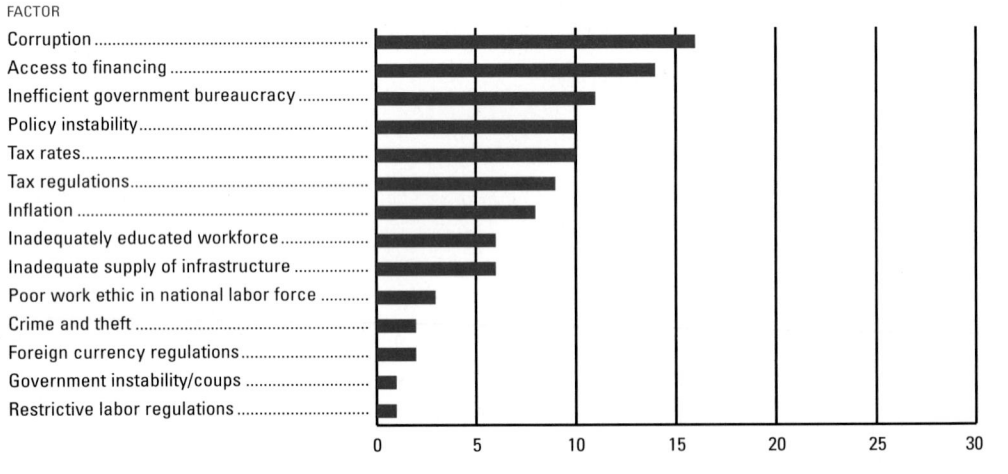

Note: From a list of 14 factors, respondents were asked to select the five most problematic for doing business in their country and to rank them between 1 (most problematic) and 5. The bars in the figure show the responses weighted according to their rankings.

Source: World Economic Forum, Executive Opinion Survey (2005)

National competitiveness balance sheet

NOTABLE COMPETITIVE ADVANTAGES	
Growth Competitiveness Index	**Rank/117**

Macroeconomic Environment

2.15	Real effective exchange rate, 2004	19
2.14	National savings rate, 2004	30

Technology

3.20	Internet hosts, 2003	44
3.21	Personal computers, 2003	46
3.04	FDI and technology transfer	48

NOTABLE COMPETITIVE DISADVANTAGES	
Growth Competitiveness Index	**Rank/117**

Macroeconomic Environment

2.16	Inflation, 2004	116
6.06	Wastefulness of government spending	115
2.07	Access to credit	110
2.17	Interest rate spread, 2004	95
2.21	Country credit rating, 2004	92
2.01	Recession expectations	71
2.13	Government surplus/deficit, 2004	68
2.20	Government debt, 2004	60

Public Institutions

6.08	Favoritism in decisions of government officials	117
6.21	Irregular payments in tax collection	106
6.01	Judicial independence	98
6.03	Property rights	95
6.19	Irregular payments in exports and imports	94
6.20	Irregular payments in public utilities	91
6.16	Organized crime	86

Technology

3.07	University/industry research collaboration	108
3.06	Company spending on research and development	97
3.14	Government success in ICT promotion	96
3.15	Laws relating to ICT	91
3.11	Internet access in schools	83
3.17	Utility patents, 2004	81
3.03	Prevalence of foreign technology licensing	77
5.08	Telephone lines, 2003	72
3.02	Firm-level technology absorption	71
3.13	Government prioritization of ICT	65
3.18	Cellular telephones, 2003	61
3.19	Internet users, 2003	61
3.12	Quality of competition in the ISP sector	58
4.17	Gross tertiary enrollment	53
3.01	Technological readiness	53

Business Competitiveness Index	
Business Competitiveness Index	**Rank/110**

Sophistication of Company Operations and Strategy

8.06	Extent of marketing	60
8.13	Extent of incentive compensation	65

Quality of the National Business Environment

6.09	Extent of bureaucratic red tape	16
8.19	Cooperation in labor-employer relations	29
8.22	Foreign ownership restrictions	41

Business Competitiveness Index	
Business Competitiveness Index	**Rank/110**

Sophistication of Company Operations and Strategy

8.14	Reliance on professional management	104
8.01	Nature of competitive advantage	100
8.03	Capacity for innovation	97

Quality of the National Business Environment

2.09	Prevalence of trade barriers	110
4.02	Quality of public schools	110
5.05	Quality of electricity supply	110

Other Indicators	
Other Indicators	**Rank/117**

4.07	Ease of hiring foreign labor	3
3.10	Availability of mobile or cellular telephones	18
2.02	Business costs of terrorism	24
2.10	Impact of rules on FDI	40
6.07	Burden of government regulation	41
5.07	Telephone/fax infrastructure quality	44
8.17	Hiring and firing practices	50

Other Indicators	
Other Indicators	**Rank/117**

7.02	Effectiveness of antitrust policy	117
5.06	Postal efficiency	117
9.09	Prevalence of corporate environmental reporting	117
9.03	Extent of government mandated environmental reporting	117
6.27	Pervasiveness of money laundering through banks	116
8.24	Importance of corporate social responsibility	115
9.04	Effects of compliance on business	115
3.05	Quality of scientific research institutions	114
6.26	Public trust of politicians	114
9.02	Clarity and stability of regulations	114
9.07	Importance of environment in business planning	113
6.18	Government effectiveness in reducing poverty and inequality	113
6.22	Irregular payments in public contracts	112

Note: The Business Competitiveness Index applies different criteria for selecting a country's competitive advantages and disadvantages. Please refer to the section "How Country Profiles Work" for further details.

East Timor

Competitiveness Rankings

Growth Competitiveness Index Rank	108

Macroeconomic Environment Index Rank **93**
    Macroeconomic Stability Subindex Rank 93
    Government Waste Rank 61
    Country Credit Rating Rank 113

Public Institutions Index Rank **108**
    Contracts and Law Subindex Rank 96
    Corruption Subindex Rank 107

Technology Index Rank **109**
    Innovation Subindex Rank 103
    ICT Subindex Rank 115
    Technology Transfer Subindex Rank
      (out of 92 non-core innovators).......................74

Business Competitiveness Index Rank	n/a

**Sophistication of Company Operations
and Strategy Rank** ....**n/a**

**Quality of the National Business
Environment Rank**..**n/a**

The Most Problematic Factors for Doing Business

FACTOR

Note: From a list of 14 factors, respondents were asked to select the five most problematic for doing business in their country and to rank them between 1 (most problematic) and 5. The bars in the figure show the responses weighted according to their rankings.

Source: World Economic Forum, Executive Opinion Survey (2005)

National competitiveness balance sheet

NOTABLE COMPETITIVE ADVANTAGES		
Growth Competitiveness Index		**Rank/117**
	Macroeconomic Environment	
2.15	Government debt, 2004	1

NOTABLE COMPETITIVE DISADVANTAGES		
Growth Competitiveness Index		**Rank/117**
	Macroeconomic Environment	
2.01	National savings rate, 2004	117
2.07	Country credit rating, 2004	113
2.16	Recession expectations	109
6.06	Access to credit	87
2.13	Inflation, 2004	61
2.20	Wastefulness of government spending	61
2.17	Government surplus/deficit, 2004	57
	Public Institutions	
6.03	Property rights	114
6.20	Irregular payments in public utilities	112
6.19	Irregular payments in exports and imports	109
6.21	Irregular payments in tax collection	102
6.08	Favoritism in decisions of government officials	86
6.01	Judicial independence	81
6.16	Organized crime	76
	Technology	
3.19	Internet users, 2003	117
5.08	Telephone lines, 2003	116
3.02	Firm-level technology absorption	116
3.11	Internet access in schools	115
3.01	Technological readiness	115
3.06	Company spending on research and development	111
3.12	Quality of competition in the ISP sector	110
3.18	Cellular telephones, 2003	105
3.07	University/industry research collaboration	104
3.14	Government success in ICT promotion	102
3.15	Laws relating to ICT	99
3.04	FDI and technology transfer	96
3.13	Government prioritization of ICT	93
3.20	Internet hosts, 2003	92
3.03	Prevalence of foreign technology licensing	91
4.17	Gross tertiary enrollment	90
3.17	Utility patents, 2004	81

Other Indicators		Rank/117
2.11	Tax burden	41
6.17	Informal sector	41
6.12	Efficiency of the tax system	45
2.05	Ease of access to loans	47

Other Indicators		Rank/117
3.09	Availability of scientists and engineers	117
8.09	Extent of regional sales	117
8.15	Quality of management schools	117
8.08	Control of international distribution	117
7.06	Local supplier quality	117
6.09	Extent of bureaucratic red tape	117
8.04	Ethical behavior of firms	116
7.07	Presence of demanding regulatory standards	116
8.23	Strength of auditing and accounting standards	116
2.03	Financial market sophistication	116
4.05	Medium term business impact of tuberculosis	116
8.06	Extent of marketing	116
3.05	Quality of scientific research institutions	115
7.01	Intensity of local competition	115
7.04	Buyer sophistication	115

Note: This country is not included in the coverage of the Business Competitiveness Index 2005–2006.

Ecuador

Competitiveness Rankings

Growth Competitiveness Index Rank	103

Macroeconomic Environment Index Rank	**80**
Macroeconomic Stability Subindex Rank	33
Government Waste Rank	113
Country Credit Rating Rank	84

Public Institutions Index Rank	**113**
Contracts and Law Subindex Rank	115
Corruption Subindex Rank	101

Technology Index Rank	**100**
Innovation Subindex Rank	87
ICT Subindex Rank	95
Technology Transfer Subindex Rank (out of 92 non-core innovators)	73

Business Competitiveness Index Rank	103

Sophistication of Company Operations and Strategy Rank	**94**
Quality of the National Business Environment Rank	**104**

The Most Problematic Factors for Doing Business

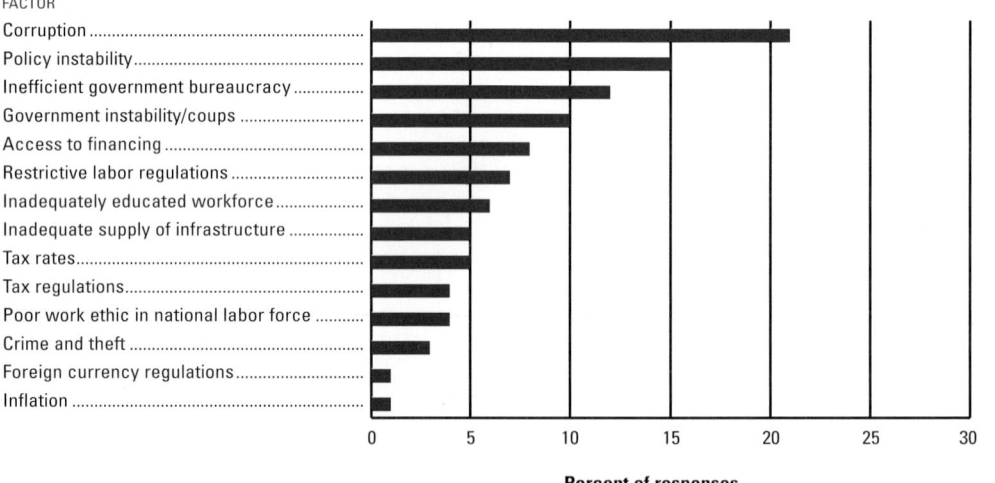

FACTOR

Corruption
Policy instability
Inefficient government bureaucracy
Government instability/coups
Access to financing
Restrictive labor regulations
Inadequately educated workforce
Inadequate supply of infrastructure
Tax rates
Tax regulations
Poor work ethic in national labor force
Crime and theft
Foreign currency regulations
Inflation

Percent of responses

Note: From a list of 14 factors, respondents were asked to select the five most problematic for doing business in their country and to rank them between 1 (most problematic) and 5. The bars in the figure show the responses weighted according to their rankings.

Source: World Economic Forum, Executive Opinion Survey (2005)

National competitiveness balance sheet

NOTABLE COMPETITIVE ADVANTAGES	
Growth Competitiveness Index	**Rank/117**

Macroeconomic Environment

2.13	Government surplus/deficit, 2004	12
2.14	National savings rate, 2004	26
2.16	Inflation, 2004	40

NOTABLE COMPETITIVE DISADVANTAGES	
Growth Competitiveness Index	**Rank/117**

Macroeconomic Environment

6.06	Wastefulness of government spending	113
2.01	Recession expectations	96
2.15	Real effective exchange rate, 2004	96
2.21	Country credit rating, 2004	84
2.07	Access to credit	83
2.17	Interest rate spread, 2004	58
2.20	Government debt, 2004	52

Public Institutions

6.01	Judicial independence	115
6.08	Favoritism in decisions of government officials	114
6.20	Irregular payments in public utilities	111
6.03	Property rights	109
6.16	Organized crime	107
6.19	Irregular payments in exports and imports	105
6.21	Irregular payments in tax collection	86

Technology

3.13	Government prioritization of ICT	117
3.14	Government success in ICT promotion	116
3.02	Firm-level technology absorption	107
3.07	University/industry research collaboration	98
3.04	FDI and technology transfer	95
3.03	Prevalence of foreign technology licensing	92
3.11	Internet access in schools	91
3.06	Company spending on research and development	90
3.15	Laws relating to ICT	89
3.20	Internet hosts, 2003	89
3.12	Quality of competition in the ISP sector	85
3.01	Technological readiness	84
4.17	Gross tertiary enrollment	78
3.21	Personal computers, 2003	76
3.19	Internet users, 2003	76
3.18	Cellular telephones, 2003	72
5.08	Telephone lines, 2003	69
3.17	Utility patents, 2004	62

Business Competitiveness Index	**Rank/110**

Sophistication of Company Operations and Strategy

8.06	Extent of marketing	69
8.09	Extent of regional sales	77
8.10	Breadth of international markets	81

Quality of the National Business Environment

5.04	Air transport infrastructure quality	61

Business Competitiveness Index	**Rank/110**

Sophistication of Company Operations and Strategy

8.07	Degree of customer orientation	109
8.11	Extent of staff training	98
8.14	Reliance on professional management	98

Quality of the National Business Environment

7.03	Decentralization of corporate activity	110
2.09	Prevalence of trade barriers	108
6.01	Judicial independence	108

Other Indicators	**Rank/117**

6.10	Effectiveness of law-making bodies	117
7.03	Extent of market dominance	117
9.06	Prioritization of energy efficiency	116
6.23	Irregular payments in judicial decisions	116
9.07	Importance of environment in business planning	116
6.26	Public trust of politicians	116
6.18	Government effectiveness in reducing poverty and inequality	115
7.02	Effectiveness of antitrust policy	115
6.02	Efficiency of legal framework	115
9.04	Effects of compliance on business	114
6.24	Diversion of public funds	114
2.10	Impact of rules on FDI	113
3.08	Government procurement of advanced technology products	113

Note: The Business Competitiveness Index applies different criteria for selecting a country's competitive advantages and disadvantages. Please refer to the section "How Country Profiles Work" for further details.

Egypt

Competitiveness Rankings

Growth Competitiveness Index Rank	**53**

Macroeconomic Environment Index Rank **55**
    Macroeconomic Stability Subindex Rank 59
    Government Waste Rank 34
    Country Credit Rating Rank.................................64

Public Institutions Index Rank..**53**
    Contracts and Law Subindex Rank 45
    Corruption Subindex Rank...................................67

Technology Index Rank **58**
    Innovation Subindex Rank...................................64
    ICT Subindex Rank 68
    Technology Transfer Subindex Rank
      (out of 92 non-core innovators).......................14

Business Competitiveness Index Rank	**71**

**Sophistication of Company Operations
  and Strategy Rank** **58**
**Quality of the National Business
  Environment Rank** **74**

The Most Problematic Factors for Doing Business

Note: From a list of 14 factors, respondents were asked to select the five most problematic for doing business in their country and to rank them between 1 (most problematic) and 5. The bars in the figure show the responses weighted according to
their rankings.

Source: World Economic Forum, Executive Opinion Survey (2005)

National competitiveness balance sheet

NOTABLE COMPETITIVE ADVANTAGES		NOTABLE COMPETITIVE DISADVANTAGES	
Growth Competitiveness Index	**Rank/117**	**Growth Competitiveness Index**	**Rank/117**

Macroeconomic Environment

2.15	Real effective exchange rate, 2004 4
6.06	Wastefulness of government spending 34
2.01	Recession expectations 40
2.14	National savings rate, 2004 50

Public Institutions

| 6.16 | Organized crime ....42 |
| 6.08 | Favoritism in decisions of government officials.............42 |

Technology

3.13	Government prioritization of ICT 10
3.14	Government success in ICT promotion 20
3.04	FDI and technology transfer....................................22
3.12	Quality of competition in the ISP sector 39
3.03	Prevalence of foreign technology licensing 40
3.02	Firm-level technology absorption 50

Macroeconomic Environment

2.20	Government debt, 2004 102
2.07	Access to credit 95
2.16	Inflation, 2004 94
2.21	Country credit rating, 2004 64
2.13	Government surplus/deficit, 2004 64
2.17	Interest rate spread, 2004...59

Public Institutions

6.21	Irregular payments in tax collection 77
6.20	Irregular payments in public utilities 70
6.19	Irregular payments in exports and imports 62
6.03	Property rights...57

Technology

3.20	Internet hosts, 2003.....................................103
3.18	Cellular telephones, 2003................................89
3.15	Laws relating to ICT 83
3.07	University/industry research collaboration 81
3.19	Internet users, 2003...78
3.21	Personal computers, 2003 77
3.11	Internet access in schools 74
3.06	Company spending on research and development 73
3.17	Utility patents, 2004 73
5.08	Telephone lines, 2003 68
4.17	Gross tertiary enrollment 62
3.01	Technological readiness 61

Business Competitiveness Index	**Rank/110**	**Business Competitiveness Index**	**Rank/110**

Sophistication of Company Operations and Strategy

8.07	Degree of customer orientation...7
3.03	Prevalence of foreign technology licensing 40
8.12	Willingness to delegate authority....................................43

Quality of the National Business Environment

3.09	Availability of scientists and engineers 31
6.14	Reliability of police services 37
6.08	Favoritism in decisions of government officials..............41

Sophistication of Company Operations and Strategy

8.09	Extent of regional sales.................................84
8.06	Extent of marketing.......................................81
8.10	Breadth of international markets.................................76

Quality of the National Business Environment

6.09	Extent of bureaucratic red tape....................................104
7.04	Buyer sophistication.....................................103
2.09	Prevalence of trade barriers 99

Other Indicators	**Rank/117**	**Other Indicators**	**Rank/117**

8.18	Flexibility of wage determination 13
4.06	Medium term business impact of HIV/AIDS..................15
9.04	Effects of compliance on business 33
6.23	Irregular payments in judicial decisions 33
9.06	Prioritization of energy efficiency....................................34
6.22	Irregular payments in public contracts 39
2.12	Agricultural policy costs 41
9.05	Effects of privatization on competition and the environment...41
4.05	Medium term business impact of tuberculosis 42
2.11	Tax burden...43
6.27	Pervasiveness of money laundering through banks 43
9.07	Importance of environment in business planning...........43

2.02	Business costs of terrorism 109
9.10	Grass-roots involvement in development projects 105
2.04	Soundness of banks...98
3.08	Government procurement of advanced technology products 93
4.08	Brain drain 92
7.06	Local supplier quality...85
9.02	Clarity and stability of regulations 81
7.07	Presence of demanding regulatory standards 81
3.10	Availability of mobile or cellular telephones...................80
8.15	Quality of management schools 80

Note: The Business Competitiveness Index applies different criteria for selecting a country's competitive advantages and disadvantages. Please refer to the section "How Country Profiles Work" for further details.

El Salvador

Competitiveness Rankings

Growth Competitiveness Index Rank	56

Macroeconomic Environment Index Rank **57**
    Macroeconomic Stability Subindex Rank 63
    Government Waste Rank 35
    Country Credit Rating Rank 62

Public Institutions Index Rank.............................**54**
    Contracts and Law Subindex Rank 70
    Corruption Subindex Rank....................................44

Technology Index Rank **70**
    Innovation Subindex Rank 85
    ICT Subindex Rank 66
    Technology Transfer Subindex Rank
        (out of 92 non-core innovators).......................45

Business Competitiveness Index Rank	58

**Sophistication of Company Operations
   and Strategy Rank** **57**
**Quality of the National Business
   Environment Rank** **56**

The Most Problematic Factors for Doing Business

FACTOR

Note: From a list of 14 factors, respondents were asked to select the five most problematic for doing business in their country and to rank them between 1 (most problematic) and 5. The bars in the figure show the responses weighted according to their rankings.

Source: World Economic Forum, Executive Opinion Survey (2005)

296

National competitiveness balance sheet

Growth Competitiveness Index	Rank/117

Macroeconomic Environment

2.17	Interest rate spread, 2004	15
6.06	Wastefulness of government spending	35
2.07	Access to credit	35
2.20	Government debt, 2004	44

Public Institutions

6.08	Favoritism in decisions of government officials	38
6.20	Irregular payments in public utilities	38
6.19	Irregular payments in exports and imports	44

Technology

3.12	Quality of competition in the ISP sector	29

Growth Competitiveness Index	Rank/117

Macroeconomic Environment

2.14	National savings rate, 2004	106
2.01	Recession expectations	98
2.13	Government surplus/deficit, 2004	75
2.16	Inflation, 2004	66
2.21	Country credit rating, 2004	62
2.15	Real effective exchange rate, 2004	60

Public Institutions

6.16	Organized crime	100
6.01	Judicial independence	69
6.03	Property rights	67
6.21	Irregular payments in tax collection	54

Technology

3.07	University/industry research collaboration	100
4.17	Gross tertiary enrollment	80
3.20	Internet hosts, 2003	78
3.14	Government success in ICT promotion	78
3.13	Government prioritization of ICT	76
3.21	Personal computers, 2003	75
3.06	Company spending on research and development	75
5.08	Telephone lines, 2003	75
3.18	Cellular telephones, 2003	74
3.04	FDI and technology transfer	74
3.17	Utility patents, 2004	68
3.02	Firm-level technology absorption	68
3.03	Prevalence of foreign technology licensing	64
3.01	Technological readiness	63
3.19	Internet users, 2003	62
3.11	Internet access in schools	61
3.15	Laws relating to ICT	54

Business Competitiveness Index	Rank/110

Sophistication of Company Operations and Strategy

8.01	Nature of competitive advantage	31
8.07	Degree of customer orientation	44
8.13	Extent of incentive compensation	45

Quality of the National Business Environment

5.07	Telephone/fax infrastructure quality	20
5.04	Air transport infrastructure quality	23
8.19	Cooperation in labor-employer relations	23

Other Indicators	Rank/117

3.10	Availability of mobile or cellular telephones	11
8.17	Hiring and firing practices	13
6.11	Extent and effect of taxation	20
7.01	Intensity of local competition	28
2.12	Agricultural policy costs	30
8.20	Pay and productivity	30
2.10	Impact of rules on FDI	33
6.12	Efficiency of the tax system	33
6.13	Centralization of economic policymaking	34
2.04	Soundness of banks	35
6.27	Pervasiveness of money laundering through banks	38
6.18	Government effectiveness in reducing poverty and inequality	38

Business Competitiveness Index	Rank/110

Sophistication of Company Operations and Strategy

8.10	Breadth of international markets	79
8.08	Control of international distribution	78
3.06	Company spending on research and development	73

Quality of the National Business Environment

3.09	Availability of scientists and engineers	107
3.05	Quality of scientific research institutions	105
3.07	University/industry research collaboration	96

Other Indicators	Rank/117

6.15	Business costs of crime and violence	105
6.10	Effectiveness of law-making bodies	103
9.04	Effects of compliance on business	98
9.03	Extent of government mandated environmental reporting	94
9.07	Importance of environment in business planning	94
6.23	Irregular payments in judicial decisions	92
4.06	Medium term business impact of HIV/AIDS	87
9.09	Prevalence of corporate environmental reporting	85
2.08	Local equity market access	83
9.02	Clarity and stability of regulations	82
2.02	Business costs of terrorism	79

297

Note: The Business Competitiveness Index applies different criteria for selecting a country's competitive advantages and disadvantages. Please refer to the section "How Country Profiles Work" for further details.

Estonia

Competitiveness Rankings

Growth Competitiveness Index Rank	20

Macroeconomic Environment Index Rank **30**
    Macroeconomic Stability Subindex Rank 14
    Government Waste Rank 43
    Country Credit Rating Rank 38

Public Institutions Index Rank **25**
    Contracts and Law Subindex Rank 35
    Corruption Subindex Rank 21

Technology Index Rank **18**
    Innovation Subindex Rank 27
    ICT Subindex Rank 21
    Technology Transfer Subindex Rank
      (out of 92 non-core innovators).......................15

Business Competitiveness Index Rank	26

**Sophistication of Company Operations
  and Strategy Rank** **33**
**Quality of the National Business
  Environment Rank** **25**

298

The Most Problematic Factors for Doing Business

Note: From a list of 14 factors, respondents were asked to select the five most problematic for doing business in their country and to rank them between 1 (most problematic) and 5. The bars in the figure show the responses weighted according to their rankings.

Source: World Economic Forum, Executive Opinion Survey (2005)

National competitiveness balance sheet

NOTABLE COMPETITIVE ADVANTAGES		
Growth Competitiveness Index		**Rank/117**

Macroeconomic Environment

| 2.20 | Government debt, 2004 | 3 |
| 2.07 | Access to credit | 7 |

Public Institutions

| 6.20 | Irregular payments in public utilities | 15 |
| 6.21 | Irregular payments in tax collection | 18 |

Technology

3.11	Internet access in schools	5
3.15	Laws relating to ICT	7
3.14	Government success in ICT promotion	12
3.04	FDI and technology transfer	13
4.17	Gross tertiary enrollment	15
3.21	Personal computers, 2003	17
3.12	Quality of competition in the ISP sector	18
3.19	Internet users, 2003	18

NOTABLE COMPETITIVE DISADVANTAGES		
Growth Competitiveness Index		**Rank/117**

Macroeconomic Environment

2.15	Real effective exchange rate, 2004	101
2.14	National savings rate, 2004	71
2.16	Inflation, 2004	46
6.06	Wastefulness of government spending	43
2.21	Country credit rating, 2004	38
2.17	Interest rate spread, 2004	24
2.01	Recession expectations	23
2.13	Government surplus/deficit, 2004	22

Public Institutions

6.01	Judicial independence	38
6.08	Favoritism in decisions of government officials	34
6.16	Organized crime	27
6.03	Property rights	27
6.19	Irregular payments in exports and imports	25

Technology

3.03	Prevalence of foreign technology licensing	46
3.06	Company spending on research and development	36
5.08	Telephone lines, 2003	36
3.17	Utility patents, 2004	35
3.02	Firm-level technology absorption	35
3.07	University/industry research collaboration	34
3.01	Technological readiness	27
3.18	Cellular telephones, 2003	23
3.20	Internet hosts, 2003	21
3.13	Government prioritization of ICT	21

Business Competitiveness Index		**Rank/110**

Sophistication of Company Operations and Strategy

8.07	Degree of customer orientation	25
8.14	Reliance on professional management	26
8.13	Extent of incentive compensation	28

Quality of the National Business Environment

2.09	Prevalence of trade barriers	6
3.15	Laws relating to ICT	7
6.13	Centralization of economic policymaking	9

Business Competitiveness Index		**Rank/110**

Sophistication of Company Operations and Strategy

8.08	Control of international distribution	61
8.01	Nature of competitive advantage	60
8.10	Breadth of international markets	46

Quality of the National Business Environment

7.08	Local availability of process machinery	67
8.19	Cooperation in labor-employer relations	50
7.03	Decentralization of corporate activity	49

Other Indicators		**Rank/117**

8.18	Flexibility of wage determination	4
3.10	Availability of mobile or cellular telephones	6
6.12	Efficiency of the tax system	6
3.16	Extent of business Internet use	6
8.20	Pay and productivity	7
2.10	Impact of rules on FDI	8
6.07	Burden of government regulation	8
6.05	Freedom of the press	10
4.09	Private sector employment of women	10
6.11	Extent and effect of taxation	13
6.17	Informal sector	17
7.01	Intensity of local competition	18
8.22	Foreign ownership restrictions	19

Other Indicators		**Rank/117**

9.07	Importance of environment in business planning	83
6.18	Government effectiveness in reducing poverty and inequality	64
8.24	Importance of corporate social responsibility	62
9.05	Effects of privatization on competition and the environment	53
4.07	Ease of hiring foreign labor	52
7.03	Extent of market dominance	51
3.09	Availability of scientists and engineers	50
4.06	Medium term business impact of HIV/AIDS	49
3.08	Government procurement of advanced technology products	49
7.05	Local supplier quantity	49
5.05	Quality of electricity supply	48

299

Note: The Business Competitiveness Index applies different criteria for selecting a country's competitive advantages and disadvantages.
Please refer to the section "How Country Profiles Work" for further details.

Ethiopia

Competitiveness Rankings

Growth Competitiveness Index Rank	106

Macroeconomic Environment Index Rank	**108**
Macroeconomic Stability Subindex Rank	106
Government Waste Rank	59
Country Credit Rating Rank	114
Public Institutions Index Rank	**79**
Contracts and Law Subindex Rank	75
Corruption Subindex Rank	84
Technology Index Rank	**115**
Innovation Subindex Rank	116
ICT Subindex Rank	116
Technology Transfer Subindex Rank (out of 92 non-core innovators)	83

Business Competitiveness Index Rank	107

Sophistication of Company Operations and Strategy Rank	**109**
Quality of the National Business Environment Rank	**106**

The Most Problematic Factors for Doing Business

FACTOR

Access to financing	
Inefficient government bureaucracy	
Inadequate supply of infrastructure	
Corruption	
Policy instability	
Tax regulations	
Poor work ethic in national labor force	
Tax rates	
Inadequately educated workforce	
Foreign currency regulations	
Government instability/coups	
Inflation	
Restrictive labor regulations	
Crime and theft	

Percent of responses

Note: From a list of 14 factors, respondents were asked to select the five most problematic for doing business in their country and to rank them between 1 (most problematic) and 5. The bars in the figure show the responses weighted according to their rankings.

Source: World Economic Forum, Executive Opinion Survey (2005)

300

National competitiveness balance sheet

NOTABLE COMPETITIVE ADVANTAGES	
Growth Competitiveness Index	**Rank/117**
Macroeconomic Environment	
2.17 Interest rate spread, 2004	27
2.15 Real effective exchange rate, 2004	33
Public Institutions	
6.16 Organized crime	36

NOTABLE COMPETITIVE DISADVANTAGES	
Growth Competitiveness Index	**Rank/117**
Macroeconomic Environment	
2.21 Country credit rating, 2004	114
2.20 Government debt, 2004	112
2.07 Access to credit	111
2.16 Inflation, 2004	98
2.01 Recession expectations	95
2.13 Government surplus/deficit, 2004	95
2.14 National savings rate, 2004	91
6.06 Wastefulness of government spending	59
Public Institutions	
6.03 Property rights	112
6.21 Irregular payments in tax collection	93
6.01 Judicial independence	92
6.20 Irregular payments in public utilities	80
6.19 Irregular payments in exports and imports	68
6.08 Favoritism in decisions of government officials	66
Technology	
3.18 Cellular telephones, 2003	117
3.12 Quality of competition in the ISP sector	117
3.01 Technological readiness	116
3.20 Internet hosts, 2003	116
3.19 Internet users, 2003	115
3.15 Laws relating to ICT	113
3.11 Internet access in schools	113
3.06 Company spending on research and development	112
3.02 Firm-level technology absorption	112
3.21 Personal computers, 2003	112
3.03 Prevalence of foreign technology licensing	111
4.17 Gross tertiary enrollment	111
5.08 Telephone lines, 2003	108
3.07 University/industry research collaboration	107
3.13 Government prioritization of ICT	98
3.14 Government success in ICT promotion	97
3.04 FDI and technology transfer	90
3.17 Utility patents, 2004	81

Business Competitiveness Index	Rank/110
Sophistication of Company Operations and Strategy	
8.08 Control of international distribution	64
8.14 Reliance on professional management	94
Quality of the National Business Environment	
6.14 Reliability of police services	60
6.13 Centralization of economic policymaking	61
5.04 Air transport infrastructure quality	62

Business Competitiveness Index	Rank/110
Sophistication of Company Operations and Strategy	
8.05 Production process sophistication	110
8.06 Extent of marketing	110
8.13 Extent of incentive compensation	109
Quality of the National Business Environment	
3.18 Cellular telephones, 2003	110
2.06 Venture capital availability	110
8.22 Foreign ownership restrictions	109

Other Indicators	Rank/117
8.18 Flexibility of wage determination	29
6.15 Business costs of crime and violence	44
6.07 Burden of government regulation	47

Other Indicators	Rank/117
4.09 Private sector employment of women	117
8.01 Nature of competitive advantage	115
7.09 Local availability of specialized research and training services	115
3.16 Extent of business Internet use	115
3.10 Availability of mobile or cellular telephones	115
8.02 Value chain presence	114
2.05 Ease of access to loans	114
2.11 Tax burden	114
7.06 Local supplier quality	113
2.03 Financial market sophistication	113

301

Note: The Business Competitiveness Index applies different criteria for selecting a country's competitive advantages and disadvantages. Please refer to the section "How Country Profiles Work" for further details.

Finland

Competitiveness Rankings

The Most Problematic Factors for Doing Business

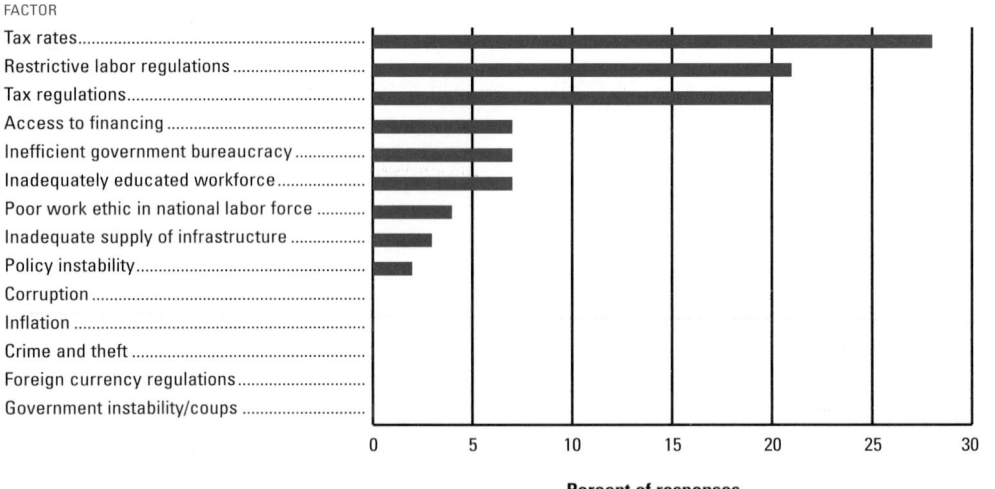

FACTOR

Tax rates
Restrictive labor regulations
Tax regulations
Access to financing
Inefficient government bureaucracy
Inadequately educated workforce
Poor work ethic in national labor force
Inadequate supply of infrastructure
Policy instability
Corruption
Inflation
Crime and theft
Foreign currency regulations
Government instability/coups

Percent of responses

Note: From a list of 14 factors, respondents were asked to select the five most problematic for doing business in their country and to rank them between 1 (most problematic) and 5. The bars in the figure show the responses weighted according to their rankings.

Source: World Economic Forum, Executive Opinion Survey (2005)

National competitiveness balance sheet

NOTABLE COMPETITIVE ADVANTAGES	
Growth Competitiveness Index	**Rank/117**

Macroeconomic Environment

2.21	Country credit rating, 2004	4
2.16	Inflation, 2004	7
6.06	Wastefulness of government spending	10

Public Institutions

6.16	Organized crime	2
6.19	Irregular payments in exports and imports	4
6.08	Favoritism in decisions of government officials	5
6.21	Irregular payments in tax collection	7
6.20	Irregular payments in public utilities	8

Technology

4.17	Gross tertiary enrollment	1
3.07	University/industry research collaboration	2
3.11	Internet access in schools	2
3.20	Internet hosts, 2003	3
3.01	Technological readiness	3
3.13	Government prioritization of ICT	4
3.17	Utility patents, 2004	5
3.02	Firm-level technology absorption	5
3.06	Company spending on research and development	6
3.15	Laws relating to ICT	6
3.12	Quality of competition in the ISP sector	6
3.14	Government success in ICT promotion	9
3.19	Internet users, 2003	9
3.18	Cellular telephones, 2003	10

NOTABLE COMPETITIVE DISADVANTAGES	
Growth Competitiveness Index	**Rank/117**

Macroeconomic Environment

2.15	Real effective exchange rate, 2004	76
2.01	Recession expectations	59
2.20	Government debt, 2004	38
2.14	National savings rate, 2004	34
2.07	Access to credit	19
2.13	Government surplus/deficit, 2004	15
2.17	Interest rate spread, 2004	13

Public Institutions

6.03	Property rights	13
6.01	Judicial independence	12

Technology

5.08	Telephone lines, 2003	19
3.21	Personal computers, 2003	16

Business Competitiveness Index	**Rank/110**

Sophistication of Company Operations and Strategy

8.12	Willingness to delegate authority	4
8.01	Nature of competitive advantage	4
8.05	Production process sophistication	5

Quality of the National Business Environment

2.05	Ease of access to loans	1
4.02	Quality of public schools	1
3.07	University/industry research collaboration	2

Business Competitiveness Index	**Rank/110**

Sophistication of Company Operations and Strategy

8.06	Extent of marketing	30
8.08	Control of international distribution	29
8.10	Breadth of international markets	16

Quality of the National Business Environment

2.08	Local equity market access	20
8.15	Quality of management schools	18
7.06	Local supplier quality	17

Other Indicators	**Rank/117**

6.24	Diversion of public funds	2
9.07	Importance of environment in business planning	2
3.09	Availability of scientists and engineers	2
9.08	Protection of ecosystems by business	2
2.06	Venture capital availability	2
6.14	Reliability of police services	3
6.26	Public trust of politicians	3
2.02	Business costs of terrorism	3
6.23	Irregular payments in judicial decisions	3
6.09	Extent of bureaucratic red tape	3
8.04	Ethical behavior of firms	3
5.07	Telephone/fax infrastructure quality	3
6.15	Business costs of crime and violence	4
6.27	Pervasiveness of money laundering through banks	4

Other Indicators	**Rank/117**

8.18	Flexibility of wage determination	117
6.11	Extent and effect of taxation	106
8.17	Hiring and firing practices	66
8.20	Pay and productivity	65
2.12	Agricultural policy costs	65
4.07	Ease of hiring foreign labor	43
6.12	Efficiency of the tax system	36
4.06	Medium term business impact of HIV/AIDS	23
2.11	Tax burden	22
4.05	Medium term business impact of tuberculosis	22
2.04	Soundness of banks	18

303

Note: The Business Competitiveness Index applies different criteria for selecting a country's competitive advantages and disadvantages. Please refer to the section "How Country Profiles Work" for further details.

France

Competitiveness Rankings

Growth Competitiveness Index Rank	30

Macroeconomic Environment Index Rank **27**	
Macroeconomic Stability Subindex Rank **61**	
Government Waste Rank **29**	
Country Credit Rating Rank **7**	
Public Institutions Index Rank...........................**20**	
Contracts and Law Subindex Rank **18**	
Corruption Subindex Rank...................................**22**	
Technology Index Rank **24**	
Innovation Subindex Rank **20**	
ICT Subindex Rank **22**	

Business Competitiveness Index Rank	11

Sophistication of Company Operations and Strategy Rank **10**	
Quality of the National Business Environment Rank **11**	

The Most Problematic Factors for Doing Business

FACTOR

Percent of responses

Note: From a list of 14 factors, respondents were asked to select the five most problematic for doing business in their country and to rank them between 1 (most problematic) and 5. The bars in the figure show the responses weighted according to their rankings.

Source: World Economic Forum, Executive Opinion Survey (2005)

304

National competitiveness balance sheet

NOTABLE COMPETITIVE ADVANTAGES		
Growth Competitiveness Index		**Rank/117**
	Macroeconomic Environment	
2.21	Country credit rating, 2004	7
6.06	Wastefulness of government spending	29
	Public Institutions	
6.03	Property rights	16
6.20	Irregular payments in public utilities	17
6.16	Organized crime	19
6.08	Favoritism in decisions of government officials	21
6.21	Irregular payments in tax collection	21
6.19	Irregular payments in exports and imports	24
6.01	Judicial independence	29
	Technology	
3.01	Technological readiness	13
3.06	Company spending on research and development	13
5.08	Telephone lines, 2003	14
3.14	Government success in ICT promotion	15
3.15	Laws relating to ICT	16
3.12	Quality of competition in the ISP sector	16
3.07	University/industry research collaboration	17
3.17	Utility patents, 2004	19
3.21	Personal computers, 2003	19
3.20	Internet hosts, 2003	22
3.13	Government prioritization of ICT	25
3.19	Internet users, 2003	26
3.11	Internet access in schools	27
3.02	Firm-level technology absorption	27
4.17	Gross tertiary enrollment	28

Business Competitiveness Index		**Rank/110**
	Sophistication of Company Operations and Strategy	
8.06	Extent of marketing	3
8.08	Control of international distribution	4
8.03	Capacity for innovation	5
	Quality of the National Business Environment	
8.15	Quality of management schools	2
5.02	Railroad infrastructure development	3
7.09	Local availability of specialized research and training services	4

Other Indicators		**Rank/117**
3.08	Government procurement of advanced technology products	4
3.09	Availability of scientists and engineers	5
5.05	Quality of electricity supply	6
7.05	Local supplier quantity	6
6.27	Pervasiveness of money laundering through banks	7
7.02	Effectiveness of antitrust policy	7
7.07	Presence of demanding regulatory standards	7
8.02	Value chain presence	7
8.13	Extent of incentive compensation	7
7.06	Local supplier quality	7

NOTABLE COMPETITIVE DISADVANTAGES		
Growth Competitiveness Index		**Rank/117**
	Macroeconomic Environment	
2.15	Real effective exchange rate, 2004	86
2.13	Government surplus/deficit, 2004	86
2.20	Government debt, 2004	79
2.01	Recession expectations	71
2.14	National savings rate, 2004	67
2.07	Access to credit	40
2.17	Interest rate spread, 2004	38
2.16	Inflation, 2004	32
	Technology	
3.18	Cellular telephones, 2003	31

Business Competitiveness Index		**Rank/110**
	Sophistication of Company Operations and Strategy	
8.07	Degree of customer orientation	23
8.12	Willingness to delegate authority	21
	Quality of the National Business Environment	
8.19	Cooperation in labor-employer relations	108
8.22	Foreign ownership restrictions	36
3.18	Cellular telephones, 2003	30

Other Indicators		**Rank/117**
8.17	Hiring and firing practices	112
2.11	Tax burden	105
6.11	Extent and effect of taxation	91
6.12	Efficiency of the tax system	91
8.18	Flexibility of wage determination	76
4.07	Ease of hiring foreign labor	72
6.07	Burden of government regulation	68
2.02	Business costs of terrorism	61
2.12	Agricultural policy costs	46
8.20	Pay and productivity	43
4.09	Private sector employment of women	42
2.10	Impact of rules on FDI	36
4.08	Brain drain	35

305

Note: The Business Competitiveness Index applies different criteria for selecting a country's competitive advantages and disadvantages. Please refer to the section "How Country Profiles Work" for further details.

Gambia

Competitiveness Rankings

Growth Competitiveness Index Rank	94

Macroeconomic Environment Index Rank **107**
    Macroeconomic Stability Subindex Rank 113
    Government Waste Rank 45
    Country Credit Rating Rank 106

Public Institutions Index Rank...**77**
    Contracts and Law Subindex Rank 55
    Corruption Subindex Rank...................................97

Technology Index Rank **97**
    Innovation Subindex Rank 112
    ICT Subindex Rank 93
    Technology Transfer Subindex Rank
    (out of 92 non-core innovators) 65

Business Competitiveness Index Rank	87

**Sophistication of Company Operations
and Strategy Rank** **98**

**Quality of the National Business
Environment Rank** **87**

The Most Problematic Factors for Doing Business

FACTOR

Note: From a list of 14 factors, respondents were asked to select the five most problematic for doing business in their country and to rank them between 1 (most problematic) and 5. The bars in the figure show the responses weighted according to their rankings.

Source: World Economic Forum, Executive Opinion Survey (2005)

National competitiveness balance sheet

NOTABLE COMPETITIVE ADVANTAGES		
Growth Competitiveness Index		**Rank/117**
	Macroeconomic Environment	
2.15	Real effective exchange rate, 2004	3
6.06	Wastefulness of government spending	45
	Public Institutions	
6.16	Organized crime	35
6.08	Favoritism in decisions of government officials	46
	Technology	
3.13	Government prioritization of ICT	42
3.14	Government success in ICT promotion	43

NOTABLE COMPETITIVE DISADVANTAGES		
Growth Competitiveness Index		**Rank/117**
	Macroeconomic Environment	
2.20	Government debt, 2004	116
2.16	Inflation, 2004	113
2.17	Interest rate spread, 2004	107
2.21	Country credit rating, 2004	106
2.07	Access to credit	98
2.13	Government surplus/deficit, 2004	84
2.14	National savings rate, 2004	71
2.01	Recession expectations	69
	Public Institutions	
6.20	Irregular payments in public utilities	104
6.21	Irregular payments in tax collection	96
6.19	Irregular payments in exports and imports	92
6.03	Property rights	76
6.01	Judicial independence	61
	Technology	
4.17	Gross tertiary enrollment	113
3.07	University/industry research collaboration	110
3.06	Company spending on research and development	106
3.15	Laws relating to ICT	101
5.08	Telephone lines, 2003	99
3.11	Internet access in schools	98
3.12	Quality of competition in the ISP sector	98
3.19	Internet users, 2003	94
3.21	Personal computers, 2003	93
3.18	Cellular telephones, 2003	91
3.01	Technological readiness	91
3.02	Firm-level technology absorption	90
3.03	Prevalence of foreign technology licensing	87
3.20	Internet hosts, 2003	82
3.17	Utility patents, 2004	81
3.04	FDI and technology transfer	80

Business Competitiveness Index		**Rank/110**
	Sophistication of Company Operations and Strategy	
8.14	Reliance on professional management	50
8.01	Nature of competitive advantage	81
8.07	Degree of customer orientation	83
	Quality of the National Business Environment	
8.22	Foreign ownership restrictions	16
8.19	Cooperation in labor-employer relations	34
2.09	Prevalence of trade barriers	36

Business Competitiveness Index		**Rank/110**
	Sophistication of Company Operations and Strategy	
8.05	Production process sophistication	108
8.13	Extent of incentive compensation	107
8.06	Extent of marketing	105
	Quality of the National Business Environment	
3.09	Availability of scientists and engineers	110
7.07	Presence of demanding regulatory standards	109
5.05	Quality of electricity supply	105

Other Indicators		**Rank/117**
6.12	Efficiency of the tax system	16
6.07	Burden of government regulation	17
8.18	Flexibility of wage determination	25
4.07	Ease of hiring foreign labor	28
2.11	Tax burden	31
8.17	Hiring and firing practices	35
2.10	Impact of rules on FDI	38
9.10	Grass-roots involvement in development projects	40
6.15	Business costs of crime and violence	40
4.09	Private sector employment of women	40
9.07	Importance of environment in business planning	45
9.02	Clarity and stability of regulations	47

Other Indicators		**Rank/117**
6.05	Freedom of the press	113
7.09	Local availability of specialized research and training services	110
5.06	Postal efficiency	108
8.10	Breadth of international markets	108
2.03	Financial market sophistication	107
8.03	Capacity for innovation	107
4.08	Brain drain	106
8.02	Value chain presence	103
4.05	Medium term business impact of tuberculosis	101

307

Note: The Business Competitiveness Index applies different criteria for selecting a country's competitive advantages and disadvantages. Please refer to the section "How Country Profiles Work" for further details.

Georgia

Competitiveness Rankings

Growth Competitiveness Index Rank	86

Macroeconomic Environment Index Rank **90**
   Macroeconomic Stability Subindex Rank 74
   Government Waste Rank 69
   Country Credit Rating Rank 111

Public Institutions Index Rank **87**
   Contracts and Law Subindex Rank 84
   Corruption Subindex Rank 87

Technology Index Rank **84**
   Innovation Subindex Rank 60
   ICT Subindex Rank 87
   Technology Transfer Subindex Rank
     (out of 92 non-core innovators) 62

Business Competitiveness Index Rank	93

**Sophistication of Company Operations
  and Strategy Rank** **92**
**Quality of the National Business
  Environment Rank** **92**

The Most Problematic Factors for Doing Business

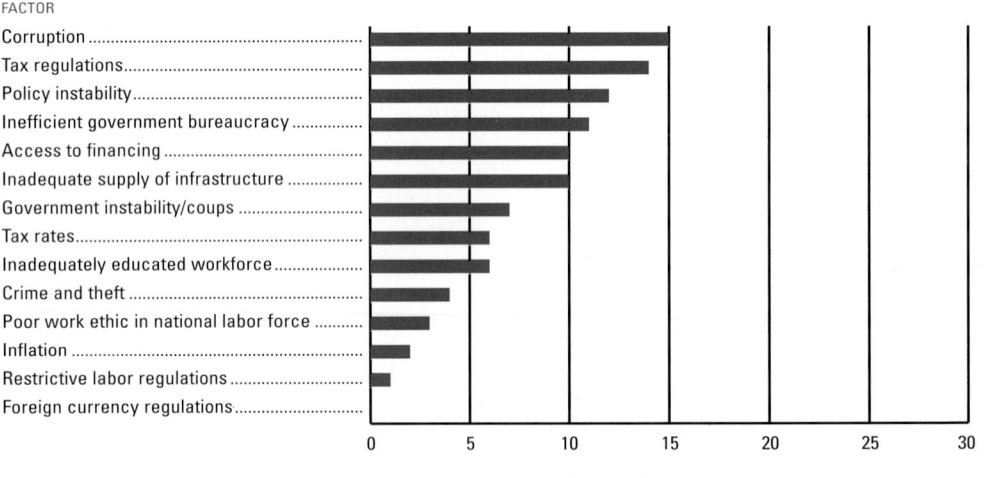

Note: From a list of 14 factors, respondents were asked to select the five most problematic for doing business in their country and to rank them between 1 (most problematic) and 5. The bars in the figure show the responses weighted according to their rankings.

Source: World Economic Forum, Executive Opinion Survey (2005)

National competitiveness balance sheet

NOTABLE COMPETITIVE ADVANTAGES		
Growth Competitiveness Index		**Rank/117**
	Macroeconomic Environment	
2.07	Access to credit	11
2.13	Government surplus/deficit, 2004	23
2.20	Government debt, 2004	50
	Technology	
3.12	Quality of competition in the ISP sector	42
4.17	Gross tertiary enrollment	44
3.17	Utility patents, 2004	45

NOTABLE COMPETITIVE DISADVANTAGES		
Growth Competitiveness Index		**Rank/117**
	Macroeconomic Environment	
2.17	Interest rate spread, 2004	113
2.21	Country credit rating, 2004	111
2.14	National savings rate, 2004	99
2.01	Recession expectations	90
2.16	Inflation, 2004	75
6.06	Wastefulness of government spending	69
2.15	Real effective exchange rate, 2004	55
	Public Institutions	
6.19	Irregular payments in exports and imports	100
6.01	Judicial independence	100
6.03	Property rights	92
6.21	Irregular payments in tax collection	87
6.08	Favoritism in decisions of government officials	74
6.20	Irregular payments in public utilities	72
6.16	Organized crime	70
	Technology	
3.13	Government prioritization of ICT	107
3.15	Laws relating to ICT	106
3.14	Government success in ICT promotion	106
3.02	Firm-level technology absorption	105
3.06	Company spending on research and development	102
3.07	University/industry research collaboration	101
3.01	Technological readiness	101
3.19	Internet users, 2003	90
3.03	Prevalence of foreign technology licensing	90
3.11	Internet access in schools	80
3.18	Cellular telephones, 2003	77
3.20	Internet hosts, 2003	75
3.21	Personal computers, 2003	73
3.04	FDI and technology transfer	71
5.08	Telephone lines, 2003	67

Business Competitiveness Index		Rank/110
Sophistication of Company Operations and Strategy		
8.01	Nature of competitive advantage	69
8.14	Reliance on professional management	69
8.02	Value chain presence	69
Quality of the National Business Environment		
8.19	Cooperation in labor-employer relations	44
3.17	Utility patents, 2004	44
5.02	Railroad infrastructure development	47

Other Indicators		Rank/117
4.07	Ease of hiring foreign labor	2
4.09	Private sector employment of women	8
8.18	Flexibility of wage determination	10
8.17	Hiring and firing practices	14
3.10	Availability of mobile or cellular telephones	44
2.02	Business costs of terrorism	46
4.06	Medium term business impact of HIV/AIDS	47

Business Competitiveness Index		Rank/110
Sophistication of Company Operations and Strategy		
8.12	Willingness to delegate authority	106
8.10	Breadth of international markets	106
8.11	Extent of staff training	101
Quality of the National Business Environment		
5.05	Quality of electricity supply	108
7.07	Presence of demanding regulatory standards	107
7.05	Local supplier quantity	107

Other Indicators		Rank/117
9.07	Importance of environment in business planning	114
9.08	Protection of ecosystems by business	112
9.09	Prevalence of corporate environmental reporting	111
2.08	Local equity market access	110
7.06	Local supplier quality	109
6.04	Intellectual property protection	108
9.04	Effects of compliance on business	107
3.08	Government procurement of advanced technology products	106
8.24	Importance of corporate social responsibility	106

Note: The Business Competitiveness Index applies different criteria for selecting a country's competitive advantages and disadvantages. Please refer to the section "How Country Profiles Work" for further details.

Germany

Competitiveness Rankings

Growth Competitiveness Index Rank	15

Macroeconomic Environment Index Rank **28**
Macroeconomic Stability Subindex Rank 65
Government Waste Rank 37
Country Credit Rating Rank 10

Public Institutions Index Rank..**8**
Contracts and Law Subindex Rank 6
Corruption Subindex Rank....................................20

Technology Index Rank **16**
Innovation Subindex Rank 9
ICT Subindex Rank 20

Business Competitiveness Index Rank	3

**Sophistication of Company Operations
and Strategy Rank** 2

**Quality of the National Business
Environment Rank** 4

The Most Problematic Factors for Doing Business

FACTOR

Percent of responses

Note: From a list of 14 factors, respondents were asked to select the five most problematic for doing business in their country and to rank them between 1 (most problematic) and 5. The bars in the figure show the responses weighted according to their rankings.

Source: World Economic Forum, Executive Opinion Survey (2005)

310

National competitiveness balance sheet

NOTABLE COMPETITIVE ADVANTAGES

Growth Competitiveness Index	Rank/117

Macroeconomic Environment

2.21	Country credit rating, 2004	10

Public Institutions

6.03	Property rights	1
6.01	Judicial independence	1
6.16	Organized crime	13
6.08	Favoritism in decisions of government officials	13

Technology

3.06	Company spending on research and development	3
3.07	University/industry research collaboration	4
5.08	Telephone lines, 2003	7
3.12	Quality of competition in the ISP sector	8
3.17	Utility patents, 2004	8
3.01	Technological readiness	9
3.15	Laws relating to ICT	9
3.21	Personal computers, 2003	12
3.02	Firm-level technology absorption	14

Business Competitiveness Index	Rank/110

Sophistication of Company Operations and Strategy

8.03	Capacity for innovation	1
8.10	Breadth of international markets	1
8.11	Extent of staff training	1

Quality of the National Business Environment

9.01	Stringency of environmental regulations	1
7.02	Effectiveness of antitrust policy	1
7.07	Presence of demanding regulatory standards	1

Other Indicators	Rank/117

3.10	Availability of mobile or cellular telephones	1
5.07	Telephone/fax infrastructure quality	1
6.05	Freedom of the press	1
9.05	Effects of privatization on competition and the environment	1
8.09	Extent of regional sales	1
8.02	Value chain presence	2
8.01	Nature of competitive advantage	2
7.01	Intensity of local competition	2
9.06	Prioritization of energy efficiency	2

NOTABLE COMPETITIVE DISADVANTAGES

Growth Competitiveness Index	Rank/117

Macroeconomic Environment

2.01	Recession expectations	93
2.13	Government surplus/deficit, 2004	86
2.15	Real effective exchange rate, 2004	82
2.20	Government debt, 2004	78
2.07	Access to credit	68
2.14	National savings rate, 2004	59
6.06	Wastefulness of government spending	37
2.17	Interest rate spread, 2004	23
2.16	Inflation, 2004	23

Public Institutions

6.20	Irregular payments in public utilities	21
6.21	Irregular payments in tax collection	20
6.19	Irregular payments in exports and imports	18

Technology

3.13	Government prioritization of ICT	53
3.14	Government success in ICT promotion	49
4.17	Gross tertiary enrollment	31
3.11	Internet access in schools	30
3.20	Internet hosts, 2003	25
3.19	Internet users, 2003	22
3.18	Cellular telephones, 2003	22

Business Competitiveness Index	Rank/110

Quality of the National Business Environment

4.03	Quality of math and science education	46
6.09	Extent of bureaucratic red tape	40
8.19	Cooperation in labor-employer relations	34

Other Indicators	Rank/117

6.12	Efficiency of the tax system	116
8.18	Flexibility of wage determination	115
8.17	Hiring and firing practices	114
2.11	Tax burden	103
2.12	Agricultural policy costs	96
4.07	Ease of hiring foreign labor	85
6.11	Extent and effect of taxation	83
6.07	Burden of government regulation	80
4.09	Private sector employment of women	61
8.20	Pay and productivity	56
2.02	Business costs of terrorism	55
2.04	Soundness of banks	39
6.10	Effectiveness of law-making bodies	34

311

Note: The Business Competitiveness Index applies different criteria for selecting a country's competitive advantages and disadvantages. Please refer to the section "How Country Profiles Work" for further details.

Ghana

Competitiveness Rankings

Growth Competitiveness Index Rank	59

Macroeconomic Environment Index Rank **66**
    Macroeconomic Stability Subindex Rank 66
    Government Waste Rank 21
    Country Credit Rating Rank..............................83

Public Institutions Index Rank..**51**
    Contracts and Law Subindex Rank 36
    Corruption Subindex Rank....................................77

Technology Index Rank **69**
    Innovation Subindex Rank...................................96
    ICT Subindex Rank 82
    Technology Transfer Subindex Rank
    (out of 92 non-core innovators) 21

Business Competitiveness Index Rank	45

**Sophistication of Company Operations
   and Strategy Rank** **56**

**Quality of the National Business
   Environment Rank** **47**

The Most Problematic Factors for Doing Business

FACTOR

Percent of responses

Note: From a list of 14 factors, respondents were asked to select the five most problematic for doing business in their country and to rank them between 1 (most problematic) and 5. The bars in the figure show the responses weighted according to their rankings.

Source: World Economic Forum, Executive Opinion Survey (2005)

National competitiveness balance sheet

NOTABLE COMPETITIVE ADVANTAGES		
Growth Competitiveness Index		**Rank/117**
	Macroeconomic Environment	
2.01	Recession expectations	19
2.15	Real effective exchange rate, 2004	20
6.06	Wastefulness of government spending	21
2.07	Access to credit	30
	Public Institutions	
6.16	Organized crime	23
6.08	Favoritism in decisions of government officials	29
6.01	Judicial independence	31
	Technology	
3.13	Government prioritization of ICT	18
3.04	FDI and technology transfer	20
3.14	Government success in ICT promotion	28

NOTABLE COMPETITIVE DISADVANTAGES		
Growth Competitiveness Index		**Rank/117**
	Macroeconomic Environment	
2.16	Inflation, 2004	110
2.20	Government debt, 2004	100
2.21	Country credit rating, 2004	83
2.14	National savings rate, 2004	68
2.17	Interest rate spread, 2004	66
2.13	Government surplus/deficit, 2004	57
	Public Institutions	
6.20	Irregular payments in public utilities	106
6.21	Irregular payments in tax collection	70
6.03	Property rights	55
6.19	Irregular payments in exports and imports	54
	Technology	
3.20	Internet hosts, 2003	108
3.21	Personal computers, 2003	108
4.17	Gross tertiary enrollment	106
3.19	Internet users, 2003	103
5.08	Telephone lines, 2003	102
3.18	Cellular telephones, 2003	97
3.17	Utility patents, 2004	81
3.11	Internet access in schools	76
3.02	Firm-level technology absorption	67
3.15	Laws relating to ICT	66
3.07	University/industry research collaboration	57
3.06	Company spending on research and development	57
3.01	Technological readiness	55
3.03	Prevalence of foreign technology licensing	54
3.12	Quality of competition in the ISP sector	53

313

Business Competitiveness Index		Rank/110
	Sophistication of Company Operations and Strategy	
8.14	Reliance on professional management	29
8.08	Control of international distribution	44
8.06	Extent of marketing	46
	Quality of the National Business Environment	
8.22	Foreign ownership restrictions	9
3.08	Government procurement of advanced technology products	17
2.08	Local equity market access	23

Business Competitiveness Index		Rank/110
	Sophistication of Company Operations and Strategy	
8.13	Extent of incentive compensation	86
8.03	Capacity for innovation	83
8.02	Value chain presence	73
	Quality of the National Business Environment	
3.19	Internet users, 2003	101
3.18	Cellular telephones, 2003	95
6.09	Extent of bureaucratic red tape	89

Other Indicators		Rank/117
2.10	Impact of rules on FDI	6
6.10	Effectiveness of law-making bodies	6
2.02	Business costs of terrorism	8
6.07	Burden of government regulation	16
4.07	Ease of hiring foreign labor	18
6.05	Freedom of the press	20
6.11	Extent and effect of taxation	21
6.12	Efficiency of the tax system	21
4.09	Private sector employment of women	23
6.15	Business costs of crime and violence	24
2.12	Agricultural policy costs	24
8.19	Cooperation in labor-employer relations	26

Other Indicators		Rank/117
8.18	Flexibility of wage determination	104
2.11	Tax burden	96
6.17	Informal sector	96
6.22	Irregular payments in public contracts	96
5.07	Telephone/fax infrastructure quality	91
4.05	Medium term business impact of tuberculosis	90
4.06	Medium term business impact of HIV/AIDS	90
8.20	Pay and productivity	89
3.16	Extent of business Internet use	79
7.08	Local availability of process machinery	79
3.10	Availability of mobile or cellular telephones	77
5.05	Quality of electricity supply	75

Note: The Business Competitiveness Index applies different criteria for selecting a country's competitive advantages and disadvantages. Please refer to the section "How Country Profiles Work" for further details.

Greece

Competitiveness Rankings

Growth Competitiveness Index Rank	46

Macroeconomic Environment Index Rank **51**
   Macroeconomic Stability Subindex Rank 96
   Government Waste Rank 60
   Country Credit Rating Rank.................................25

Public Institutions Index Rank...**43**
   Contracts and Law Subindex Rank 40
   Corruption Subindex Rank...................................54

Technology Index Rank **37**
   Innovation Subindex Rank...................................24
   ICT Subindex Rank 38
   Technology Transfer Subindex Rank
      (out of 92 non-core innovators).......................35

Business Competitiveness Index Rank	40

**Sophistication of Company Operations
and Strategy Rank** 42

**Quality of the National Business
Environment Rank** 40

The Most Problematic Factors for Doing Business

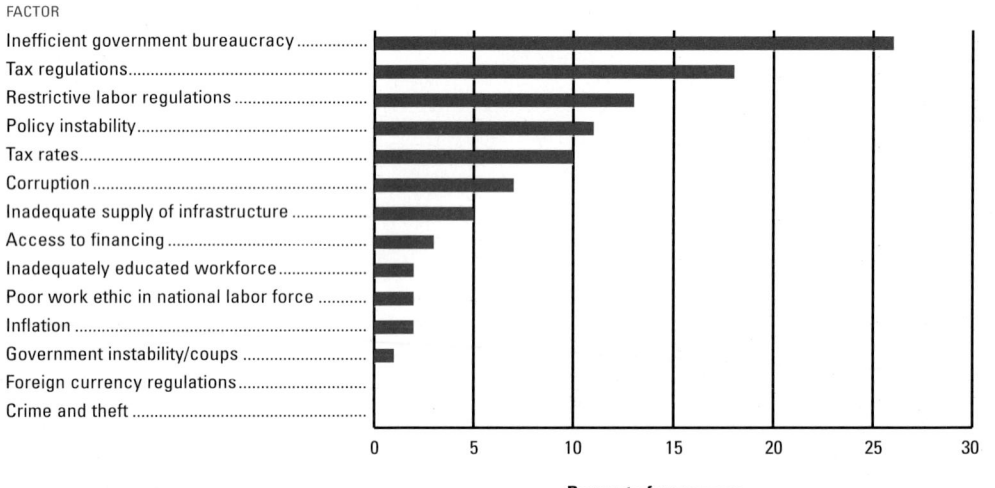

FACTOR

Inefficient government bureaucracy
Tax regulations
Restrictive labor regulations
Policy instability
Tax rates
Corruption
Inadequate supply of infrastructure
Access to financing
Inadequately educated workforce
Poor work ethic in national labor force
Inflation
Government instability/coups
Foreign currency regulations
Crime and theft

Percent of responses

Note: From a list of 14 factors, respondents were asked to select the five most problematic for doing business in their country and to rank them between 1 (most problematic) and 5. The bars in the figure show the responses weighted according to their rankings.

Source: World Economic Forum, Executive Opinion Survey (2005)

National competitiveness balance sheet

NOTABLE COMPETITIVE ADVANTAGES		
Growth Competitiveness Index		**Rank/117**
	Macroeconomic Environment	
2.21	Country credit rating, 2004	25
2.17	Interest rate spread, 2004	34
2.07	Access to credit	39
	Public Institutions	
6.16	Organized crime	26
6.03	Property rights	39
6.19	Irregular payments in exports and imports	43
6.20	Irregular payments in public utilities	44
	Technology	
4.17	Gross tertiary enrollment	7
3.18	Cellular telephones, 2003	13
5.08	Telephone lines, 2003	26
3.03	Prevalence of foreign technology licensing	33
3.17	Utility patents, 2004	38
3.20	Internet hosts, 2003	39
3.12	Quality of competition in the ISP sector	44
3.11	Internet access in schools	44

Business Competitiveness Index		Rank/110
	Sophistication of Company Operations and Strategy	
8.06	Extent of marketing	35
8.01	Nature of competitive advantage	35
8.13	Extent of incentive compensation	39
	Quality of the National Business Environment	
3.18	Cellular telephones, 2003	12
2.09	Prevalence of trade barriers	21
3.09	Availability of scientists and engineers	21

Other Indicators		Rank/117
4.06	Medium term business impact of HIV/AIDS	10
4.05	Medium term business impact of tuberculosis	16
6.15	Business costs of crime and violence	20
6.05	Freedom of the press	23
8.21	Protection of minority shareholders' interests	24
2.05	Ease of access to loans	29
5.06	Postal efficiency	30
6.14	Reliability of police services	33
7.02	Effectiveness of antitrust policy	34
2.02	Business costs of terrorism	35
9.10	Grass-roots involvement in development projects	35

NOTABLE COMPETITIVE DISADVANTAGES		
Growth Competitiveness Index		**Rank/117**
	Macroeconomic Environment	
2.20	Government debt, 2004	110
2.13	Government surplus/deficit, 2004	110
2.01	Recession expectations	97
2.15	Real effective exchange rate, 2004	90
6.06	Wastefulness of government spending	60
2.14	National savings rate, 2004	53
2.16	Inflation, 2004	47
	Public Institutions	
6.21	Irregular payments in tax collection	81
6.08	Favoritism in decisions of government officials	54
6.01	Judicial independence	48
	Technology	
3.04	FDI and technology transfer	87
3.14	Government success in ICT promotion	81
3.13	Government prioritization of ICT	71
3.02	Firm-level technology absorption	70
3.01	Technological readiness	65
3.15	Laws relating to ICT	62
3.07	University/industry research collaboration	58
3.21	Personal computers, 2003	54
3.06	Company spending on research and development	52
3.19	Internet users, 2003	50

Business Competitiveness Index		Rank/110
	Sophistication of Company Operations and Strategy	
8.14	Reliance on professional management	57
8.12	Willingness to delegate authority	57
8.03	Capacity for innovation	57
	Quality of the National Business Environment	
8.16	Efficacy of corporate boards	86
6.13	Centralization of economic policymaking	78
8.19	Cooperation in labor-employer relations	70

Other Indicators		Rank/117
8.18	Flexibility of wage determination	107
8.17	Hiring and firing practices	100
2.11	Tax burden	99
2.12	Agricultural policy costs	95
6.12	Efficiency of the tax system	94
2.10	Impact of rules on FDI	90
3.16	Extent of business Internet use	81
8.20	Pay and productivity	80
3.08	Government procurement of advanced technology products	74
9.04	Effects of compliance on business	70
6.07	Burden of government regulation	69
7.08	Local availability of process machinery	67

315

Note: The Business Competitiveness Index applies different criteria for selecting a country's competitive advantages and disadvantages. Please refer to the section "How Country Profiles Work" for further details.

Guatemala

Competitiveness Rankings

Growth Competitiveness Index Rank	97

Macroeconomic Environment Index Rank **81**
    Macroeconomic Stability Subindex Rank 73
    Government Waste Rank 106
    Country Credit Rating Rank 72

Public Institutions Index Rank...........................**107**
    Contracts and Law Subindex Rank 114
    Corruption Subindex Rank....................................89

Technology Index Rank **96**
    Innovation Subindex Rank 95
    ICT Subindex Rank 100
    Technology Transfer Subindex Rank
        (out of 92 non-core innovators)........................61

Business Competitiveness Index Rank	99

**Sophistication of Company Operations
   and Strategy Rank** **83**
**Quality of the National Business
   Environment Rank** **100**

The Most Problematic Factors for Doing Business

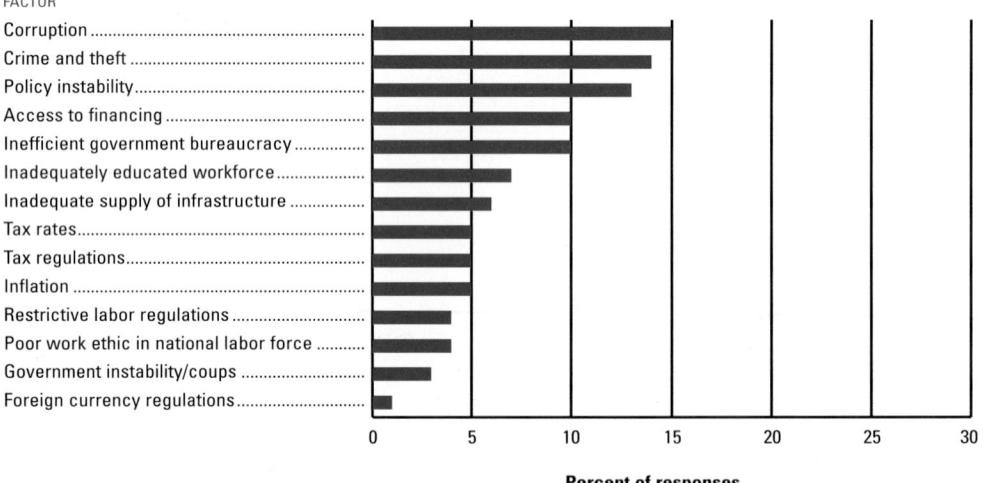

FACTOR

Corruption
Crime and theft
Policy instability
Access to financing
Inefficient government bureaucracy
Inadequately educated workforce
Inadequate supply of infrastructure
Tax rates
Tax regulations
Inflation
Restrictive labor regulations
Poor work ethic in national labor force
Government instability/coups
Foreign currency regulations

Percent of responses

Note: From a list of 14 factors, respondents were asked to select the five most problematic for doing business in their country and to rank them between 1 (most problematic) and 5. The bars in the figure show the responses weighted according to their rankings.

Source: World Economic Forum, Executive Opinion Survey (2005)

National competitiveness balance sheet

NOTABLE COMPETITIVE ADVANTAGES		
Growth Competitiveness Index		**Rank/117**
	Macroeconomic Environment	
2.20	Government debt, 2004	21
2.13	Government surplus/deficit, 2004	42

NOTABLE COMPETITIVE DISADVANTAGES		
Growth Competitiveness Index		**Rank/117**
	Macroeconomic Environment	
6.06	Wastefulness of government spending	106
2.14	National savings rate, 2004	92
2.07	Access to credit	91
2.16	Inflation, 2004	87
2.17	Interest rate spread, 2004	85
2.01	Recession expectations	77
2.15	Real effective exchange rate, 2004	74
2.21	Country credit rating, 2004	72
	Public Institutions	
6.16	Organized crime	117
6.08	Favoritism in decisions of government officials	105
6.03	Property rights	105
6.21	Irregular payments in tax collection	92
6.01	Judicial independence	90
6.19	Irregular payments in exports and imports	89
6.20	Irregular payments in public utilities	79
	Technology	
3.13	Government prioritization of ICT	114
3.14	Government success in ICT promotion	112
3.15	Laws relating to ICT	96
3.11	Internet access in schools	96
3.03	Prevalence of foreign technology licensing	95
4.17	Gross tertiary enrollment	94
3.02	Firm-level technology absorption	93
3.07	University/industry research collaboration	92
3.21	Personal computers, 2003	91
3.06	Company spending on research and development	88
3.19	Internet users, 2003	88
3.12	Quality of competition in the ISP sector	88
3.17	Utility patents, 2004	81
5.08	Telephone lines, 2003	81
3.01	Technological readiness	75
3.18	Cellular telephones, 2003	75
3.20	Internet hosts, 2003	65
3.04	FDI and technology transfer	58

Business Competitiveness Index		Rank/110
	Sophistication of Company Operations and Strategy	
8.03	Capacity for innovation	63
8.09	Extent of regional sales	66
8.01	Nature of competitive advantage	67
	Quality of the National Business Environment	
6.09	Extent of bureaucratic red tape	48
8.15	Quality of management schools	67
7.09	Local availability of specialized research and training services	72

Business Competitiveness Index		Rank/110
	Sophistication of Company Operations and Strategy	
8.14	Reliance on professional management	99
8.11	Extent of staff training	93
3.03	Prevalence of foreign technology licensing	92
	Quality of the National Business Environment	
6.14	Reliability of police services	110
4.03	Quality of math and science education	109
4.01	Quality of the educational system	109

Other Indicators		Rank/117
2.11	Tax burden	45

Other Indicators		Rank/117
6.15	Business costs of crime and violence	117
2.09	Prevalence of trade barriers	114
6.27	Pervasiveness of money laundering through banks	113
9.04	Effects of compliance on business	112
8.21	Protection of minority shareholders' interests	112
3.08	Government procurement of advanced technology products	111
4.09	Private sector employment of women	111
9.02	Clarity and stability of regulations	111
8.23	Strength of auditing and accounting standards	111
2.10	Impact of rules on FDI	110
9.09	Prevalence of corporate environmental reporting	110
6.10	Effectiveness of law-making bodies	110

317

Note: The Business Competitiveness Index applies different criteria for selecting a country's competitive advantages and disadvantages. Please refer to the section "How Country Profiles Work" for further details.

Guyana

Competitiveness Rankings

Growth Competitiveness Index Rank	115

Macroeconomic Environment Index Rank **113**
  Macroeconomic Stability Subindex Rank 115
  Government Waste Rank 86
  Country Credit Rating Rank 92

Public Institutions Index Rank.......................................**109**
  Contracts and Law Subindex Rank 110
  Corruption Subindex Rank..................................105

Technology Index Rank **112**
  Innovation Subindex Rank 111
  ICT Subindex Rank 94
  Technology Transfer Subindex Rank
    (out of 92 non-core innovators).......................88

Business Competitiveness Index Rank	106

**Sophistication of Company Operations
  and Strategy Rank** **103**
**Quality of the National Business
  Environment Rank** **105**

The Most Problematic Factors for Doing Business

FACTOR

Access to financing ....
Inadequate supply of infrastructure ....
Inefficient government bureaucracy ....
Corruption ....
Crime and theft ....
Poor work ethic in national labor force ....
Policy instability...
Inadequately educated workforce.....................
Government instability/coups ....
Tax rates..
Inflation ....
Tax regulations...
Foreign currency regulations............................
Restrictive labor regulations ....

Percent of responses

Note: From a list of 14 factors, respondents were asked to select the five most problematic for doing business in their country and to rank them between 1 (most problematic) and 5. The bars in the figure show the responses weighted according to their rankings.

Source: World Economic Forum, Executive Opinion Survey (2005)

National competitiveness balance sheet

NOTABLE COMPETITIVE ADVANTAGES		
Growth Competitiveness Index		**Rank/117**
	Macroeconomic Environment	
2.15	Real effective exchange rate, 2004	36
2.14	National savings rate, 2004	43

NOTABLE COMPETITIVE DISADVANTAGES		
Growth Competitiveness Index		**Rank/117**
	Macroeconomic Environment	
2.01	Recession expectations	116
2.13	Government surplus/deficit, 2004	115
2.20	Government debt, 2004	115
2.07	Access to credit	106
2.17	Interest rate spread, 2004	96
2.21	Country credit rating, 2004	92
6.06	Wastefulness of government spending	86
2.16	Inflation, 2004	68
	Public Institutions	
6.08	Favoritism in decisions of government officials	113
6.19	Irregular payments in exports and imports	110
6.20	Irregular payments in public utilities	108
6.16	Organized crime	102
6.03	Property rights	99
6.01	Judicial independence	96
6.21	Irregular payments in tax collection	95
	Technology	
3.15	Laws relating to ICT	117
3.03	Prevalence of foreign technology licensing	114
3.02	Firm-level technology absorption	113
3.11	Internet access in schools	111
3.07	University/industry research collaboration	111
3.01	Technological readiness	111
3.13	Government prioritization of ICT	108
3.14	Government success in ICT promotion	105
3.06	Company spending on research and development	103
3.04	FDI and technology transfer	101
4.17	Gross tertiary enrollment	99
3.12	Quality of competition in the ISP sector	92
3.18	Cellular telephones, 2003	86
3.21	Personal computers, 2003	81
3.17	Utility patents, 2004	81
5.08	Telephone lines, 2003	79
3.20	Internet hosts, 2003	77
3.19	Internet users, 2003	51

Business Competitiveness Index		Rank/110
	Sophistication of Company Operations and Strategy	
8.01	Nature of competitive advantage	73
8.08	Control of international distribution	77
8.14	Reliance on professional management	84
	Quality of the National Business Environment	
2.09	Prevalence of trade barriers	53
6.25	Business costs of corruption	55

Business Competitiveness Index		Rank/110
	Sophistication of Company Operations and Strategy	
3.03	Prevalence of foreign technology licensing	109
8.05	Production process sophistication	106
8.06	Extent of marketing	102
	Quality of the National Business Environment	
2.03	Financial market sophistication	110
6.04	Intellectual property protection	110
3.15	Laws relating to ICT	110

Other Indicators		Rank/117
8.17	Hiring and firing practices	27
6.12	Efficiency of the tax system	27
4.07	Ease of hiring foreign labor	29
2.12	Agricultural policy costs	42
2.04	Soundness of banks	49

Other Indicators		Rank/117
6.27	Pervasiveness of money laundering through banks	117
4.08	Brain drain	117
6.14	Reliability of police services	116
6.13	Centralization of economic policymaking	115
6.22	Irregular payments in public contracts	114
8.15	Quality of management schools	114
6.15	Business costs of crime and violence	113
6.02	Efficiency of legal framework	113
8.19	Cooperation in labor-employer relations	113
8.20	Pay and productivity	112
8.04	Ethical behavior of firms	112
5.07	Telephone/fax infrastructure quality	112
3.09	Availability of scientists and engineers	111

319

Note: The Business Competitiveness Index applies different criteria for selecting a country's competitive advantages and disadvantages. Please refer to the section "How Country Profiles Work" for further details.

Honduras

Competitiveness Rankings

Growth Competitiveness Index Rank	93

Macroeconomic Environment Index Rank **89**
    Macroeconomic Stability Subindex Rank 84
    Government Waste Rank 94
    Country Credit Rating Rank 88

Public Institutions Index Rank...**88**
    Contracts and Law Subindex Rank 107
    Corruption Subindex Rank....................................73

Technology Index Rank **95**
    Innovation Subindex Rank 90
    ICT Subindex Rank 101
    Technology Transfer Subindex Rank
      (out of 92 non-core innovators)........................60

Business Competitiveness Index Rank	101

**Sophistication of Company Operations
  and Strategy Rank** 93
**Quality of the National Business
  Environment Rank** 101

The Most Problematic Factors for Doing Business

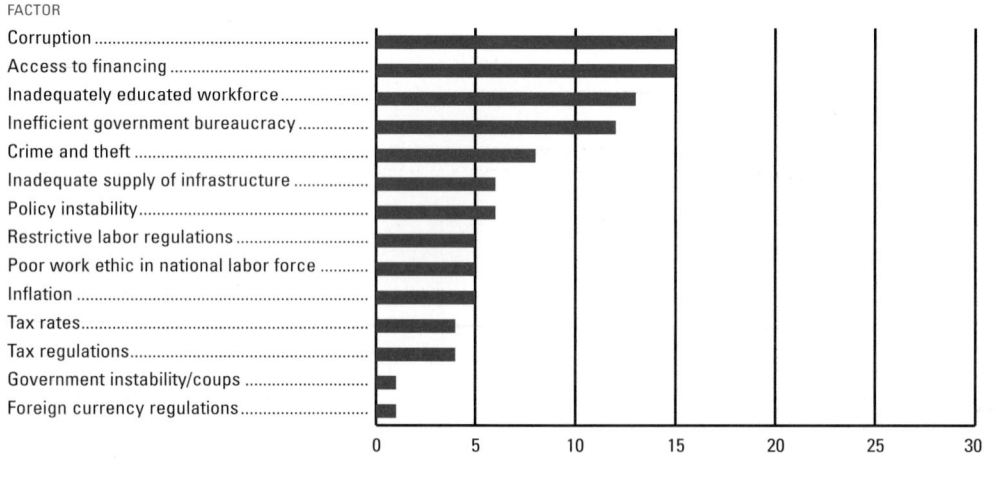

Note: From a list of 14 factors, respondents were asked to select the five most problematic for doing business in their country and to rank them between 1 (most problematic) and 5. The bars in the figure show the responses weighted according to their rankings.

Source: World Economic Forum, Executive Opinion Survey (2005)

National competitiveness balance sheet

NOTABLE COMPETITIVE ADVANTAGES	
Growth Competitiveness Index	**Rank/117**

Macroeconomic Environment

2.14	National savings rate, 2004	33

NOTABLE COMPETITIVE DISADVANTAGES	
Growth Competitiveness Index	**Rank/117**

Macroeconomic Environment

6.06	Wastefulness of government spending	94
2.16	Inflation, 2004	94
2.07	Access to credit	88
2.21	Country credit rating, 2004	88
2.01	Recession expectations	87
2.20	Government debt, 2004	83
2.17	Interest rate spread, 2004	82
2.15	Real effective exchange rate, 2004	67
2.13	Government surplus/deficit, 2004	51

Public Institutions

6.16	Organized crime	106
6.08	Favoritism in decisions of government officials	103
6.01	Judicial independence	97
6.03	Property rights	94
6.20	Irregular payments in public utilities	92
6.21	Irregular payments in tax collection	71
6.19	Irregular payments in exports and imports	56

Technology

3.06	Company spending on research and development	107
3.15	Laws relating to ICT	104
3.13	Government prioritization of ICT	104
3.02	Firm-level technology absorption	102
3.03	Prevalence of foreign technology licensing	99
3.07	University/industry research collaboration	99
3.14	Government success in ICT promotion	98
3.18	Cellular telephones, 2003	94
3.11	Internet access in schools	92
5.08	Telephone lines, 2003	91
3.21	Personal computers, 2003	90
3.01	Technological readiness	89
4.17	Gross tertiary enrollment	88
3.20	Internet hosts, 2003	87
3.17	Utility patents, 2004	81
3.19	Internet users, 2003	81
3.12	Quality of competition in the ISP sector	74
3.04	FDI and technology transfer	53

Business Competitiveness Index	
	Rank/110

Sophistication of Company Operations and Strategy

8.13	Extent of incentive compensation	61
8.09	Extent of regional sales	73
8.02	Value chain presence	78

Quality of the National Business Environment

5.03	Port infrastructure quality	50
9.01	Stringency of environmental regulations	59
8.22	Foreign ownership restrictions	59

Other Indicators	
	Rank/117

2.11	Tax burden	34

Business Competitiveness Index	
	Rank/110

Sophistication of Company Operations and Strategy

8.14	Reliance on professional management	107
3.06	Company spending on research and development	103
8.08	Control of international distribution	101

Quality of the National Business Environment

4.03	Quality of math and science education	110
4.01	Quality of the educational system	108
2.08	Local equity market access	108

Other Indicators	
	Rank/117

7.02	Effectiveness of antitrust policy	114
9.05	Effects of privatization on competition and the environment	114
5.06	Postal efficiency	112
5.07	Telephone/fax infrastructure quality	111
7.03	Extent of market dominance	111
7.01	Intensity of local competition	109
3.08	Government procurement of advanced technology products	109
6.15	Business costs of crime and violence	108
8.04	Ethical behavior of firms	108
3.09	Availability of scientists and engineers	107
3.05	Quality of scientific research institutions	107
9.04	Effects of compliance on business	106
2.09	Prevalence of trade barriers	106

Note: The Business Competitiveness Index applies different criteria for selecting a country's competitive advantages and disadvantages. Please refer to the section "How Country Profiles Work" for further details.

Hong Kong SAR

Competitiveness Rankings

Growth Competitiveness Index Rank	28

Macroeconomic Environment Index Rank 8
   Macroeconomic Stability Subindex Rank 6
   Government Waste Rank 11
   Country Credit Rating Rank 26

Public Institutions Index Rank..23
   Contracts and Law Subindex Rank 22
   Corruption Subindex Rank...................................26

Technology Index Rank 26
   Innovation Subindex Rank 32
   ICT Subindex Rank 10

Business Competitiveness Index Rank	20

**Sophistication of Company Operations
   and Strategy Rank** 20
**Quality of the National Business
   Environment Rank** 19

The Most Problematic Factors for Doing Business

FACTOR

Percent of responses

Note: From a list of 14 factors, respondents were asked to select the five most problematic for doing business in their country and to rank them between 1 (most problematic) and 5. The bars in the figure show the responses weighted according to their rankings.

Source: World Economic Forum, Executive Opinion Survey (2005)

322

National competitiveness balance sheet

NOTABLE COMPETITIVE ADVANTAGES

Growth Competitiveness Index		Rank/117

Macroeconomic Environment

2.20	Government debt, 2004	2
2.16	Inflation, 2004	3
6.06	Wastefulness of government spending	11
2.14	National savings rate, 2004	13
2.01	Recession expectations	13
2.15	Real effective exchange rate, 2004	16
2.07	Access to credit	24
2.21	Country credit rating, 2004	26

Public Institutions

6.03	Property rights	15
6.20	Irregular payments in public utilities	24
6.01	Judicial independence	25
6.21	Irregular payments in tax collection	26

Technology

3.18	Cellular telephones, 2003	3
3.21	Personal computers, 2003	9
3.11	Internet access in schools	9
3.12	Quality of competition in the ISP sector	10
3.20	Internet hosts, 2003	14
5.08	Telephone lines, 2003	15
3.19	Internet users, 2003	16
3.02	Firm-level technology absorption	18
3.01	Technological readiness	21
3.14	Government success in ICT promotion	21
3.15	Laws relating to ICT	21
3.17	Utility patents, 2004	23
3.07	University/industry research collaboration	24
3.13	Government prioritization of ICT	24
3.06	Company spending on research and development	26

Business Competitiveness Index		Rank/110

Sophistication of Company Operations and Strategy

8.09	Extent of regional sales	6
8.10	Breadth of international markets	7
8.07	Degree of customer orientation	10

Quality of the National Business Environment

8.22	Foreign ownership restrictions	1
3.18	Cellular telephones, 2003	2
7.04	Buyer sophistication	3

Other Indicators		Rank/117

6.11	Extent and effect of taxation	1
8.18	Flexibility of wage determination	1
8.20	Pay and productivity	1
6.12	Efficiency of the tax system	2
6.07	Burden of government regulation	2
8.17	Hiring and firing practices	2
2.10	Impact of rules on FDI	5
3.10	Availability of mobile or cellular telephones	5
4.09	Private sector employment of women	5
2.05	Ease of access to loans	5
2.03	Financial market sophistication	6
8.19	Cooperation in labor-employer relations	6

NOTABLE COMPETITIVE DISADVANTAGES

Growth Competitiveness Index		Rank/117

Macroeconomic Environment

| 2.17 | Interest rate spread, 2004 | 50 |
| 2.13 | Government surplus/deficit, 2004 | 36 |

Public Institutions

6.08	Favoritism in decisions of government officials	32
6.16	Organized crime	28
6.19	Irregular payments in exports and imports	28

Technology

| 4.17 | Gross tertiary enrollment | 58 |

Business Competitiveness Index		Rank/110

Sophistication of Company Operations and Strategy

8.14	Reliance on professional management	28
8.03	Capacity for innovation	28
8.05	Production process sophistication	27

Quality of the National Business Environment

6.09	Extent of bureaucratic red tape	64
7.02	Effectiveness of antitrust policy	45
9.01	Stringency of environmental regulations	41

Other Indicators		Rank/117

9.08	Protection of ecosystems by business	71
9.07	Importance of environment in business planning	64
9.06	Prioritization of energy efficiency	51
9.09	Prevalence of corporate environmental reporting	50
4.05	Medium term business impact of tuberculosis	47
6.10	Effectiveness of law-making bodies	47
6.05	Freedom of the press	47
6.27	Pervasiveness of money laundering through banks	42
8.16	Efficacy of corporate boards	42
7.08	Local availability of process machinery	40
9.03	Extent of government mandated environmental reporting	38
4.06	Medium term business impact of HIV/AIDS	38

323

Note: The Business Competitiveness Index applies different criteria for selecting a country's competitive advantages and disadvantages. Please refer to the section "How Country Profiles Work" for further details.

Hungary

Competitiveness Rankings

Growth Competitiveness Index Rank	39

Macroeconomic Environment Index Rank **63**
    Macroeconomic Stability Subindex Rank 95
    Government Waste Rank 73
    Country Credit Rating Rank 40

Public Institutions Index Rank..........................**34**
    Contracts and Law Subindex Rank 43
    Corruption Subindex Rank...................................29

Technology Index Rank **30**
    Innovation Subindex Rank 36
    ICT Subindex Rank 35
    Technology Transfer Subindex Rank
        (out of 92 non-core innovators).........................8

Business Competitiveness Index Rank	34

**Sophistication of Company Operations
  and Strategy Rank** **40**

**Quality of the National Business
  Environment Rank** **32**

The Most Problematic Factors for Doing Business

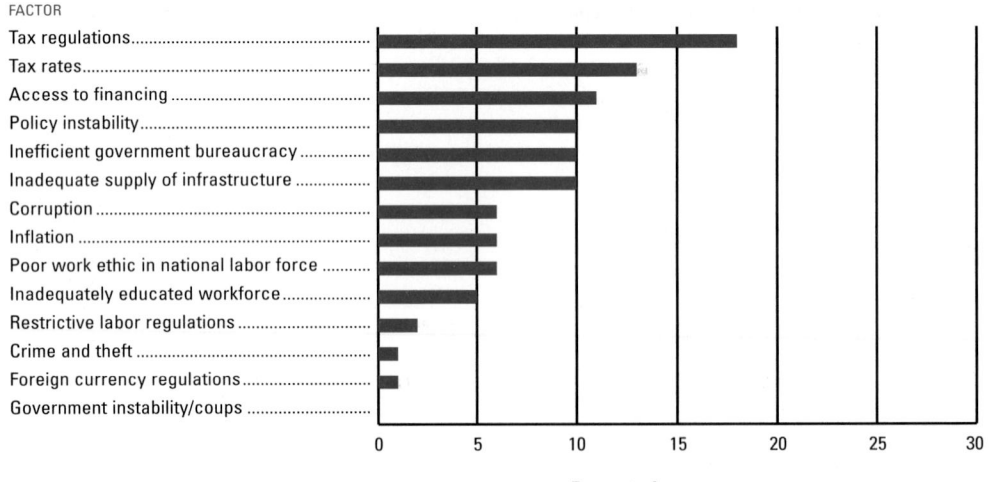

FACTOR
Tax regulations
Tax rates
Access to financing
Policy instability
Inefficient government bureaucracy
Inadequate supply of infrastructure
Corruption
Inflation
Poor work ethic in national labor force
Inadequately educated workforce
Restrictive labor regulations
Crime and theft
Foreign currency regulations
Government instability/coups

Percent of responses

Note: From a list of 14 factors, respondents were asked to select the five most problematic for doing business in their country and to rank them between 1 (most problematic) and 5. The bars in the figure show the responses weighted according to their rankings.

Source: World Economic Forum, Executive Opinion Survey (2005)

National competitiveness balance sheet

NOTABLE COMPETITIVE ADVANTAGES		
Growth Competitiveness Index		**Rank/117**
	Macroeconomic Environment	
2.17	Interest rate spread, 2004	29
	Public Institutions	
6.03	Property rights	28
6.21	Irregular payments in tax collection	28
6.20	Irregular payments in public utilities	30
6.19	Irregular payments in exports and imports	33
	Technology	
3.04	FDI and technology transfer	7
3.18	Cellular telephones, 2003	24
3.20	Internet hosts, 2003	24
3.02	Firm-level technology absorption	28
3.17	Utility patents, 2004	28
3.11	Internet access in schools	29
4.17	Gross tertiary enrollment	30
3.15	Laws relating to ICT	33
5.08	Telephone lines, 2003	35
3.07	University/industry research collaboration	38
3.03	Prevalence of foreign technology licensing	38

NOTABLE COMPETITIVE DISADVANTAGES		
Growth Competitiveness Index		**Rank/117**
	Macroeconomic Environment	
2.15	Real effective exchange rate, 2004	115
2.13	Government surplus/deficit, 2004	107
2.14	National savings rate, 2004	93
2.16	Inflation, 2004	85
6.06	Wastefulness of government spending	73
2.20	Government debt, 2004	71
2.01	Recession expectations	57
2.07	Access to credit	46
2.21	Country credit rating, 2004	40
	Public Institutions	
6.08	Favoritism in decisions of government officials	73
6.16	Organized crime	50
6.01	Judicial independence	42
	Technology	
3.13	Government prioritization of ICT	80
3.12	Quality of competition in the ISP sector	79
3.14	Government success in ICT promotion	61
3.06	Company spending on research and development	49
3.21	Personal computers, 2003	48
3.01	Technological readiness	43
3.19	Internet users, 2003	39

Business Competitiveness Index		Rank/110
	Sophistication of Company Operations and Strategy	
8.02	Value chain presence	26
8.14	Reliance on professional management	32
8.10	Breadth of international markets	33
	Quality of the National Business Environment	
6.09	Extent of bureaucratic red tape	2
2.09	Prevalence of trade barriers	8
8.22	Foreign ownership restrictions	8

Business Competitiveness Index		Rank/110
	Sophistication of Company Operations and Strategy	
8.08	Control of international distribution	82
8.07	Degree of customer orientation	66
8.06	Extent of marketing	59
	Quality of the National Business Environment	
5.03	Port infrastructure quality	73
6.08	Favoritism in decisions of government officials	71
7.04	Buyer sophistication	65

Other Indicators		Rank/117
4.06	Medium term business impact of HIV/AIDS	1
2.02	Business costs of terrorism	9
2.10	Impact of rules on FDI	12
3.09	Availability of scientists and engineers	17
2.11	Tax burden	18
3.05	Quality of scientific research institutions	21
9.09	Prevalence of corporate environmental reporting	21
9.10	Grass-roots involvement in development projects	24
9.01	Stringency of environmental regulations	24
8.20	Pay and productivity	25
8.21	Protection of minority shareholders' interests	25
8.16	Efficacy of corporate boards	25

Other Indicators		Rank/117
6.12	Efficiency of the tax system	106
2.12	Agricultural policy costs	100
9.07	Importance of environment in business planning	94
4.09	Private sector employment of women	89
8.24	Importance of corporate social responsibility	84
6.11	Extent and effect of taxation	82
6.18	Government effectiveness in reducing poverty and inequality	80
9.06	Prioritization of energy efficiency	67
8.04	Ethical behavior of firms	63
9.05	Effects of privatization on competition and the environment	61
7.09	Local availability of specialized research and training services	59

Note: The Business Competitiveness Index applies different criteria for selecting a country's competitive advantages and disadvantages. Please refer to the section "How Country Profiles Work" for further details.

Iceland

Competitiveness Rankings

The Most Problematic Factors for Doing Business

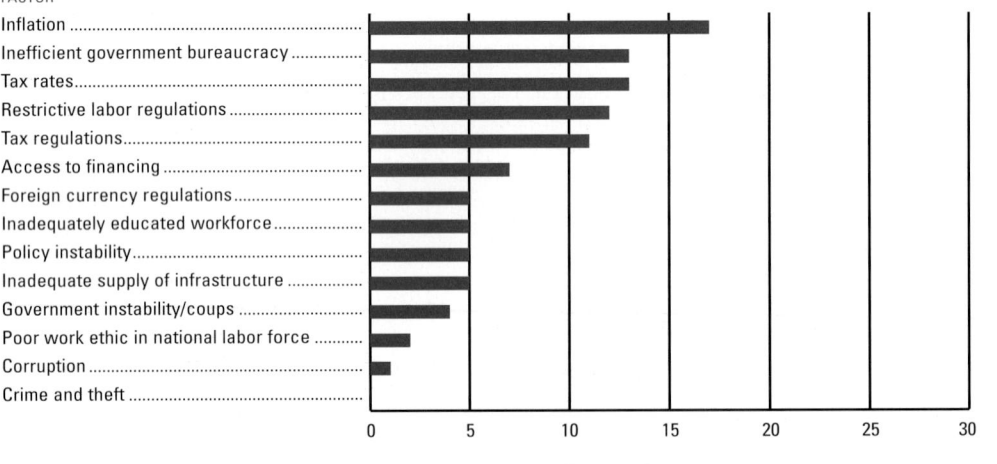

Note: From a list of 14 factors, respondents were asked to select the five most problematic for doing business in their country and to rank them between 1 (most problematic) and 5. The bars in the figure show the responses weighted according to their rankings.

Source: World Economic Forum, Executive Opinion Survey (2005)

326

National competitiveness balance sheet

Growth Competitiveness Index		Rank/117

Macroeconomic Environment

2.07	Access to credit	2
2.01	Recession expectations	4
6.06	Wastefulness of government spending	6

Public Institutions

6.20	Irregular payments in public utilities	1
6.19	Irregular payments in exports and imports	1
6.16	Organized crime	1
6.21	Irregular payments in tax collection	2
6.03	Property rights	3

Technology

3.11	Internet access in schools	1
3.19	Internet users, 2003	1
3.20	Internet hosts, 2003	2
3.02	Firm-level technology absorption	3
3.15	Laws relating to ICT	5
3.18	Cellular telephones, 2003	6
5.08	Telephone lines, 2003	6
3.01	Technological readiness	6

Business Competitiveness Index		Rank/110

Sophistication of Company Operations and Strategy

| 8.08 | Control of international distribution | 1 |
| 8.07 | Degree of customer orientation | 5 |

Quality of the National Business Environment

3.19	Internet users, 2003	1
6.25	Business costs of corruption	1
2.08	Local equity market access	1

Other Indicators		Rank/117

5.05	Quality of electricity supply	1
9.08	Protection of ecosystems by business	1
6.23	Irregular payments in judicial decisions	1
6.27	Pervasiveness of money laundering through banks	1
5.06	Postal efficiency	1
6.05	Freedom of the press	2
6.17	Informal sector	2
2.05	Ease of access to loans	2
6.22	Irregular payments in public contracts	2
9.05	Effects of privatization on competition and the environment	2
6.24	Diversion of public funds	3
8.17	Hiring and firing practices	3

Growth Competitiveness Index		Rank/117

Macroeconomic Environment

2.14	National savings rate, 2004	104
2.15	Real effective exchange rate, 2004	93
2.17	Interest rate spread, 2004	75
2.16	Inflation, 2004	47
2.20	Government debt, 2004	41
2.13	Government surplus/deficit, 2004	27
2.21	Country credit rating, 2004	23

Public Institutions

| 6.08 | Favoritism in decisions of government officials | 15 |
| 6.01 | Judicial independence | 11 |

Technology

3.13	Government prioritization of ICT	37
3.14	Government success in ICT promotion	22
3.12	Quality of competition in the ISP sector	21
3.07	University/industry research collaboration	18
4.17	Gross tertiary enrollment	17
3.21	Personal computers, 2003	15
3.17	Utility patents, 2004	15
3.06	Company spending on research and development	14

Business Competitiveness Index		Rank/110

Sophistication of Company Operations and Strategy

8.10	Breadth of international markets	25
8.02	Value chain presence	23
8.01	Nature of competitive advantage	20

Quality of the National Business Environment

8.22	Foreign ownership restrictions	89
5.02	Railroad infrastructure development	79
7.08	Local availability of process machinery	46

Other Indicators		Rank/117

2.12	Agricultural policy costs	99
8.18	Flexibility of wage determination	84
2.10	Impact of rules on FDI	71
4.07	Ease of hiring foreign labor	48
7.03	Extent of market dominance	46
2.09	Prevalence of trade barriers	39
7.05	Local supplier quantity	38
7.01	Intensity of local competition	35
7.09	Local availability of specialized research and training services	31
3.08	Government procurement of advanced technology products	28
3.05	Quality of scientific research institutions	27
8.15	Quality of management schools	25

327

Note: The Business Competitiveness Index applies different criteria for selecting a country's competitive advantages and disadvantages. Please refer to the section "How Country Profiles Work" for further details.

India

Competitiveness Rankings

Growth Competitiveness Index Rank	50

Macroeconomic Environment Index Rank	**50**
Macroeconomic Stability Subindex Rank	41
Government Waste Rank	63
Country Credit Rating Rank	53
Public Institutions Index Rank	**52**
Contracts and Law Subindex Rank	37
Corruption Subindex Rank	78
Technology Index Rank	**55**
Innovation Subindex Rank	76
ICT Subindex Rank	67
Technology Transfer Subindex Rank (out of 92 non-core innovators)	6

Business Competitiveness Index Rank	31

Sophistication of Company Operations and Strategy Rank	**30**
Quality of the National Business Environment Rank	**31**

The Most Problematic Factors for Doing Business

FACTOR

Percent of responses

Note: From a list of 14 factors, respondents were asked to select the five most problematic for doing business in their country and to rank them between 1 (most problematic) and 5. The bars in the figure show the responses weighted according to their rankings.

Source: World Economic Forum, Executive Opinion Survey (2005)

National competitiveness balance sheet

NOTABLE COMPETITIVE ADVANTAGES		**NOTABLE COMPETITIVE DISADVANTAGES**	
Growth Competitiveness Index	**Rank/117**	**Growth Competitiveness Index**	**Rank/117**

Macroeconomic Environment

2.07	Access to credit	1
2.01	Recession expectations	3
2.14	National savings rate, 2004	38

Public Institutions

6.01	Judicial independence	23
6.03	Property rights	32
6.16	Organized crime	43

Technology

3.03	Prevalence of foreign technology licensing	7
3.13	Government prioritization of ICT	9
3.14	Government success in ICT promotion	11
3.02	Firm-level technology absorption	19
3.12	Quality of competition in the ISP sector	24
3.06	Company spending on research and development	27
3.01	Technological readiness	28
3.04	FDI and technology transfer	34
3.07	University/industry research collaboration	36
3.15	Laws relating to ICT	43
3.11	Internet access in schools	49

Macroeconomic Environment

2.13	Government surplus/deficit, 2004	116
2.20	Government debt, 2004	69
2.15	Real effective exchange rate, 2004	63
6.06	Wastefulness of government spending	63
2.17	Interest rate spread, 2004	60
2.16	Inflation, 2004	57
2.21	Country credit rating, 2004	53

Public Institutions

6.20	Irregular payments in public utilities	83
6.21	Irregular payments in tax collection	75
6.19	Irregular payments in exports and imports	72
6.08	Favoritism in decisions of government officials	53

Technology

3.18	Cellular telephones, 2003	108
3.21	Personal computers, 2003	99
3.20	Internet hosts, 2003	99
5.08	Telephone lines, 2003	95
3.19	Internet users, 2003	95
4.17	Gross tertiary enrollment	91
3.17	Utility patents, 2004	56

Business Competitiveness Index	**Rank/110**	**Business Competitiveness Index**	**Rank/110**

Sophistication of Company Operations and Strategy

3.03	Prevalence of foreign technology licensing	7
8.02	Value chain presence	25
8.10	Breadth of international markets	26

Quality of the National Business Environment

3.09	Availability of scientists and engineers	1
2.08	Local equity market access	2
7.05	Local supplier quantity	5

Sophistication of Company Operations and Strategy

8.01	Nature of competitive advantage	63
8.09	Extent of regional sales	50
8.07	Degree of customer orientation	42

Quality of the National Business Environment

3.18	Cellular telephones, 2003	103
3.19	Internet users, 2003	94
5.05	Quality of electricity supply	93

Other Indicators	**Rank/117**	**Other Indicators**	**Rank/117**

8.15	Quality of management schools	6
9.05	Effects of privatization on competition and the environment	9
7.01	Intensity of local competition	11
3.05	Quality of scientific research institutions	17
7.03	Extent of market dominance	17
6.05	Freedom of the press	18
6.13	Centralization of economic policymaking	18
6.10	Effectiveness of law-making bodies	21
6.11	Extent and effect of taxation	22
7.08	Local availability of process machinery	22
8.23	Strength of auditing and accounting standards	23
6.15	Business costs of crime and violence	25

8.17	Hiring and firing practices	111
4.06	Medium term business impact of HIV/AIDS	94
4.05	Medium term business impact of tuberculosis	89
2.12	Agricultural policy costs	78
2.11	Tax burden	78
4.09	Private sector employment of women	77
6.07	Burden of government regulation	76
2.02	Business costs of terrorism	75
6.17	Informal sector	75
6.26	Public trust of politicians	69
6.22	Irregular payments in public contracts	68
4.07	Ease of hiring foreign labor	66
6.09	Extent of bureaucratic red tape	60

329

Note: The Business Competitiveness Index applies different criteria for selecting a country's competitive advantages and disadvantages. Please refer to the section "How Country Profiles Work" for further details.

Indonesia

Competitiveness Rankings

Growth Competitiveness Index Rank	74

Macroeconomic Environment Index Rank **64**
    Macroeconomic Stability Subindex Rank 56
    Government Waste Rank 40
    Country Credit Rating Rank 75

Public Institutions Index Rank..**89**
    Contracts and Law Subindex Rank 66
    Corruption Subindex Rank..................................103

Technology Index Rank...**66**
    Innovation Subindex Rank 80
    ICT Subindex Rank 85
    Technology Transfer Subindex Rank
       (out of 92 non-core innovators).........................23

Business Competitiveness Index Rank	59

**Sophistication of Company Operations
  and Strategy Rank**..**50**

**Quality of the National Business
  Environment Rank** **59**

The Most Problematic Factors for Doing Business

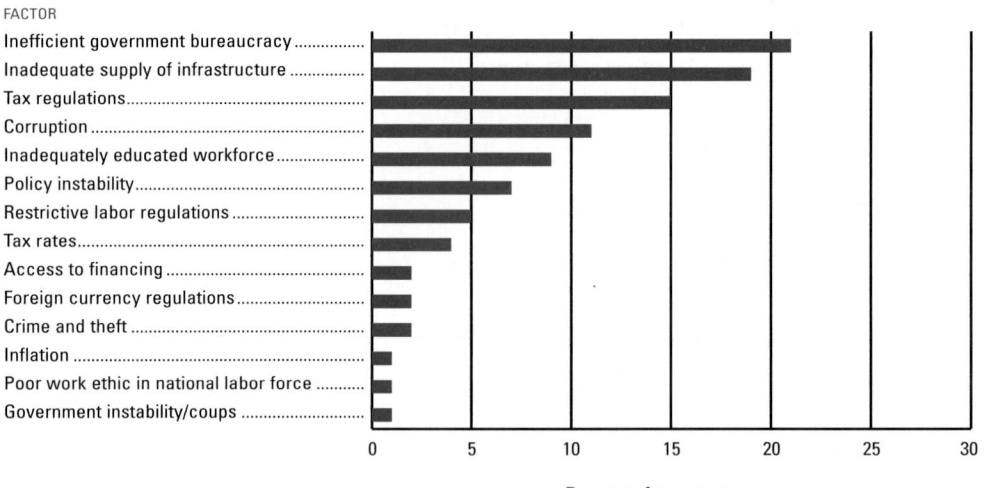

FACTOR

Inefficient government bureaucracy ....
Inadequate supply of infrastructure ....
Tax regulations...
Corruption ....
Inadequately educated workforce....................
Policy instability..
Restrictive labor regulations ....
Tax rates..
Access to financing ....
Foreign currency regulations............................
Crime and theft ....
Inflation ....
Poor work ethic in national labor force ....
Government instability/coups ....

Percent of responses

Note: From a list of 14 factors, respondents were asked to select the five most problematic for doing business in their country and to rank them between 1 (most problematic) and 5. The bars in the figure show the responses weighted according to their rankings.

Source: World Economic Forum, Executive Opinion Survey (2005)

National competitiveness balance sheet

NOTABLE COMPETITIVE ADVANTAGES		NOTABLE COMPETITIVE DISADVANTAGES	
Growth Competitiveness Index	**Rank/117**	**Growth Competitiveness Index**	**Rank/117**

Macroeconomic Environment		**Macroeconomic Environment**	
2.01	Recession expectations 15	2.15	Real effective exchange rate, 2004 99
2.14	National savings rate, 2004 39	2.17	Interest rate spread, 2004 78
6.06	Wastefulness of government spending 40	2.16	Inflation, 2004 78
2.13	Government surplus/deficit, 2004 40	2.21	Country credit rating, 2004 75
Public Institutions		2.07	Access to credit 70
6.08	Favoritism in decisions of government officials...............30	2.20	Government debt, 2004 65
Technology		**Public Institutions**	
3.03	Prevalence of foreign technology licensing 35	6.19	Irregular payments in exports and imports 106
3.07	University/industry research collaboration 35	6.21	Irregular payments in tax collection 104
3.12	Quality of competition in the ISP sector 37	6.20	Irregular payments in public utilities 94
3.04	FDI and technology transfer...............43	6.03	Property rights...............88
3.06	Company spending on research and development 45	6.16	Organized crime 79
		6.01	Judicial independence 68
		Technology	
		3.13	Government prioritization of ICT 101
		5.08	Telephone lines, 2003 96
		3.21	Personal computers, 2003 94
		3.18	Cellular telephones, 2003...............87
		3.20	Internet hosts, 2003 86
		3.19	Internet users, 2003 84
		4.17	Gross tertiary enrollment 83
		3.02	Firm-level technology absorption 82
		3.14	Government success in ICT promotion 82
		3.17	Utility patents, 2004 77
		3.15	Laws relating to ICT 67
		3.01	Technological readiness 67
		3.11	Internet access in schools 62

331

Business Competitiveness Index	**Rank/110**	**Business Competitiveness Index**	**Rank/110**
Sophistication of Company Operations and Strategy		**Sophistication of Company Operations and Strategy**	
3.03	Prevalence of foreign technology licensing 35	8.14	Reliance on professional management...............77
8.10	Breadth of international markets...............43	8.05	Production process sophistication 72
3.06	Company spending on research and development 44	8.11	Extent of staff training 66
Quality of the National Business Environment		**Quality of the National Business Environment**	
6.13	Centralization of economic policymaking...............17	5.07	Telephone/fax infrastructure quality 88
6.08	Favoritism in decisions of government officials...............29	3.18	Cellular telephones, 2003...............86
3.07	University/industry research collaboration 35	3.19	Internet users, 2003...............83

Other Indicators	**Rank/117**	**Other Indicators**	**Rank/117**
2.11	Tax burden...............7	6.27	Pervasiveness of money laundering through banks 111
6.11	Extent and effect of taxation...............24	2.04	Soundness of banks...............109
3.16	Extent of business Internet use...............30	3.10	Availability of mobile or cellular telephones...............101
4.08	Brain drain 32	6.23	Irregular payments in judicial decisions 99
6.12	Efficiency of the tax system 35	4.05	Medium term business impact of tuberculosis 97
4.07	Ease of hiring foreign labor 35	8.18	Flexibility of wage determination 94
7.08	Local availability of process machinery 36	4.06	Medium term business impact of HIV/AIDS...............92
7.04	Buyer sophistication...............38	8.04	Ethical behavior of firms 87
3.08	Government procurement of advanced technology products 39	5.05	Quality of electricity supply...............84
4.09	Private sector employment of women 41	2.02	Business costs of terrorism 84
6.26	Public trust of politicians 42	6.22	Irregular payments in public contracts...............84
6.18	Government effectiveness in reducing poverty and inequality 44	7.06	Local supplier quality...............83
2.12	Agricultural policy costs 44	7.05	Local supplier quantity 81

Note: The Business Competitiveness Index applies different criteria for selecting a country's competitive advantages and disadvantages. Please refer to the section "How Country Profiles Work" for further details.

Ireland

Competitiveness Rankings

Growth Competitiveness Index Rank	26

Macroeconomic Environment Index Rank **7**
   Macroeconomic Stability Subindex Rank 7
   Government Waste Rank 28
   Country Credit Rating Rank 14
Public Institutions Index Rank...**13**
   Contracts and Law Subindex Rank 11
   Corruption Subindex Rank....................................18
Technology Index Rank **31**
   Innovation Subindex Rank 22
   ICT Subindex Rank 24

Business Competitiveness Index Rank	19

**Sophistication of Company Operations
  and Strategy Rank** **16**
**Quality of the National Business
  Environment Rank** **20**

The Most Problematic Factors for Doing Business

Note: From a list of 14 factors, respondents were asked to select the five most problematic for doing business in their country and to rank them between 1 (most problematic) and 5. The bars in the figure show the responses weighted according to their rankings.

Source: World Economic Forum, Executive Opinion Survey (2005)

National competitiveness balance sheet

NOTABLE COMPETITIVE ADVANTAGES	
Growth Competitiveness Index	**Rank/117**

Macroeconomic Environment

2.07	Access to credit	4
2.01	Recession expectations	5
2.21	Country credit rating, 2004	14
2.13	Government surplus/deficit, 2004	18

Public Institutions

6.01	Judicial independence	5
6.08	Favoritism in decisions of government officials	10
6.03	Property rights	10
6.21	Irregular payments in tax collection	12
6.19	Irregular payments in exports and imports	16
6.20	Irregular payments in public utilities	23

Technology

3.02	Firm-level technology absorption	10
3.15	Laws relating to ICT	13
3.18	Cellular telephones, 2003	16
3.21	Personal computers, 2003	18
3.07	University/industry research collaboration	20
3.01	Technological readiness	20
5.08	Telephone lines, 2003	20
3.13	Government prioritization of ICT	20
3.06	Company spending on research and development	21
3.17	Utility patents, 2004	22
3.20	Internet hosts, 2003	23

Business Competitiveness Index	**Rank/110**

Sophistication of Company Operations and Strategy

8.09	Extent of regional sales	2
8.12	Willingness to delegate authority	11
8.13	Extent of incentive compensation	11

Quality of the National Business Environment

8.22	Foreign ownership restrictions	2
4.01	Quality of the educational system	3
4.02	Quality of public schools	3

Other Indicators	**Rank/117**

2.10	Impact of rules on FDI	2
2.04	Soundness of banks	2
8.23	Strength of auditing and accounting standards	3
2.06	Venture capital availability	4
2.05	Ease of access to loans	6
6.25	Business costs of corruption	9
8.16	Efficacy of corporate boards	9
2.11	Tax burden	10
6.11	Extent and effect of taxation	10
8.21	Protection of minority shareholders' interests	10
8.24	Importance of corporate social responsibility	10
6.10	Effectiveness of law-making bodies	11

NOTABLE COMPETITIVE DISADVANTAGES	
Growth Competitiveness Index	**Rank/117**

Macroeconomic Environment

2.15	Real effective exchange rate, 2004	106
2.17	Interest rate spread, 2004	35
2.14	National savings rate, 2004	35
2.16	Inflation, 2004	32
6.06	Wastefulness of government spending	28
2.20	Government debt, 2004	27

Public Institutions

6.16	Organized crime	30

Technology

3.12	Quality of competition in the ISP sector	55
3.11	Internet access in schools	37
3.19	Internet users, 2003	31
4.17	Gross tertiary enrollment	29
3.14	Government success in ICT promotion	29

Business Competitiveness Index	**Rank/110**

Sophistication of Company Operations and Strategy

8.03	Capacity for innovation	22
3.06	Company spending on research and development	20
8.05	Production process sophistication	19

Quality of the National Business Environment

6.13	Centralization of economic policymaking	84
5.02	Railroad infrastructure development	55
5.07	Telephone/fax infrastructure quality	50

Other Indicators	**Rank/117**

8.18	Flexibility of wage determination	110
8.17	Hiring and firing practices	79
3.10	Availability of mobile or cellular telephones	67
8.20	Pay and productivity	44
7.01	Intensity of local competition	43
6.15	Business costs of crime and violence	34
3.08	Government procurement of advanced technology products	34
9.06	Prioritization of energy efficiency	32
7.08	Local availability of process machinery	32
6.27	Pervasiveness of money laundering through banks	31
9.05	Effects of privatization on competition and the environment	27
9.09	Prevalence of corporate environmental reporting	27
7.05	Local supplier quantity	26

333

Note: The Business Competitiveness Index applies different criteria for selecting a country's competitive advantages and disadvantages. Please refer to the section "How Country Profiles Work" for further details.

Israel

Competitiveness Rankings

Growth Competitiveness Index Rank	27

Macroeconomic Environment Index Rank **48**
   Macroeconomic Stability Subindex Rank 62
   Government Waste Rank 41
   Country Credit Rating Rank 44

Public Institutions Index Rank **30**
   Contracts and Law Subindex Rank 27
   Corruption Subindex Rank....................................33

Technology Index Rank **12**
   Innovation Subindex Rank 6
   ICT Subindex Rank 23

Business Competitiveness Index Rank	22

**Sophistication of Company Operations
  and Strategy Rank** **19**

**Quality of the National Business
  Environment Rank** **22**

The Most Problematic Factors for Doing Business

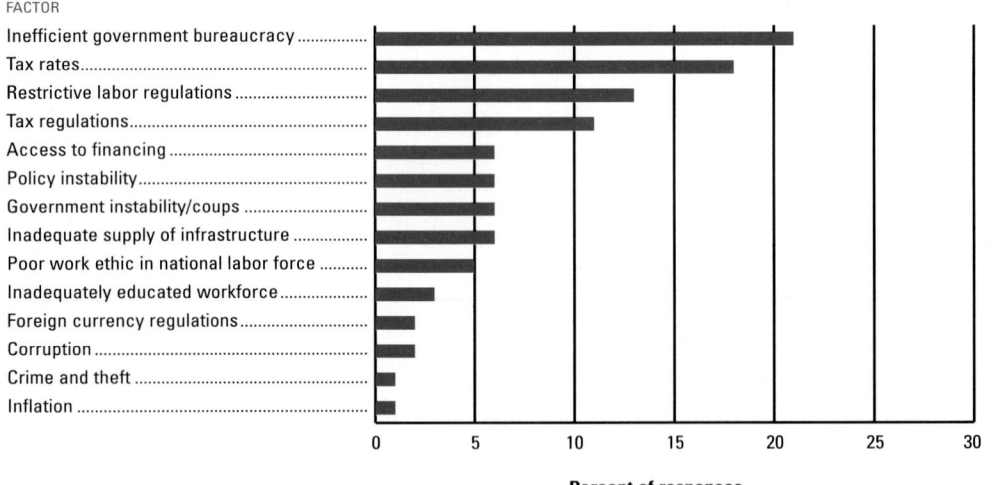

FACTOR

Inefficient government bureaucracy
Tax rates
Restrictive labor regulations
Tax regulations
Access to financing
Policy instability
Government instability/coups
Inadequate supply of infrastructure
Poor work ethic in national labor force
Inadequately educated workforce
Foreign currency regulations
Corruption
Crime and theft
Inflation

Percent of responses

Note: From a list of 14 factors, respondents were asked to select the five most problematic for doing business in their country and to rank them between 1 (most problematic) and 5. The bars in the figure show the responses weighted according to their rankings.

Source: World Economic Forum, Executive Opinion Survey (2005)

National competitiveness balance sheet

NOTABLE COMPETITIVE ADVANTAGES	
Growth Competitiveness Index	**Rank/117**

Macroeconomic Environment

2.16	Inflation, 2004	3
2.15	Real effective exchange rate, 2004	17

Public Institutions

6.01	Judicial independence	14
6.03	Property rights	26
6.19	Irregular payments in exports and imports	26

Technology

3.01	Technological readiness	4
3.02	Firm-level technology absorption	5
3.06	Company spending on research and development	5
3.17	Utility patents, 2004	6
3.18	Cellular telephones, 2003	8
3.07	University/industry research collaboration	11
3.12	Quality of competition in the ISP sector	11
3.14	Government success in ICT promotion	17
3.20	Internet hosts, 2003	18
3.11	Internet access in schools	19
3.15	Laws relating to ICT	23
5.08	Telephone lines, 2003	25
4.17	Gross tertiary enrollment	25

Business Competitiveness Index	Rank/110

Sophistication of Company Operations and Strategy

8.03	Capacity for innovation	2
3.06	Company spending on research and development	5
8.01	Nature of competitive advantage	13

Quality of the National Business Environment

3.05	Quality of scientific research institutions	4
3.09	Availability of scientists and engineers	4
2.06	Venture capital availability	5

Other Indicators	Rank/117

3.10	Availability of mobile or cellular telephones	3
3.08	Government procurement of advanced technology products	5
4.05	Medium term business impact of tuberculosis	6
4.06	Medium term business impact of HIV/AIDS	6
7.01	Intensity of local competition	9
7.09	Local availability of specialized research and training services	10
9.05	Effects of privatization on competition and the environment	13
5.07	Telephone/fax infrastructure quality	13
8.15	Quality of management schools	14
8.10	Breadth of international markets	15

NOTABLE COMPETITIVE DISADVANTAGES	
Growth Competitiveness Index	**Rank/117**

Macroeconomic Environment

2.20	Government debt, 2004	106
2.13	Government surplus/deficit, 2004	93
2.14	National savings rate, 2004	78
2.07	Access to credit	58
2.01	Recession expectations	47
2.21	Country credit rating, 2004	44
6.06	Wastefulness of government spending	41
2.17	Interest rate spread, 2004	31

Public Institutions

6.08	Favoritism in decisions of government officials	49
6.20	Irregular payments in public utilities	42
6.21	Irregular payments in tax collection	42
6.16	Organized crime	32

Technology

3.13	Government prioritization of ICT	34
3.19	Internet users, 2003	33
3.21	Personal computers, 2003	28

Business Competitiveness Index	Rank/110

Sophistication of Company Operations and Strategy

8.09	Extent of regional sales	107
8.14	Reliance on professional management	30
8.07	Degree of customer orientation	29

Quality of the National Business Environment

6.09	Extent of bureaucratic red tape	53
8.19	Cooperation in labor-employer relations	49
6.08	Favoritism in decisions of government officials	47

Other Indicators	Rank/117

4.07	Ease of hiring foreign labor	116
2.02	Business costs of terrorism	115
2.11	Tax burden	104
6.11	Extent and effect of taxation	75
6.12	Efficiency of the tax system	71
6.18	Government effectiveness in reducing poverty and inequality	66
8.18	Flexibility of wage determination	57
4.09	Private sector employment of women	53
2.10	Impact of rules on FDI	47
6.26	Public trust of politicians	40
6.14	Reliability of police services	39
6.07	Burden of government regulation	38

Note: The Business Competitiveness Index applies different criteria for selecting a country's competitive advantages and disadvantages. Please refer to the section "How Country Profiles Work" for further details.

Italy

Competitiveness Rankings

Growth Competitiveness Index Rank	47

Macroeconomic Environment Index Rank **47**
    Macroeconomic Stability Subindex Rank 89
    Government Waste Rank 87
    Country Credit Rating Rank 20

Public Institutions Index Rank **46**
    Contracts and Law Subindex Rank 68
    Corruption Subindex Rank 32

Technology Index Rank **44**
    Innovation Subindex Rank 30
    ICT Subindex Rank 28

Business Competitiveness Index Rank	38

**Sophistication of Company Operations
   and Strategy Rank** **28**
**Quality of the National Business
   Environment Rank** **39**

The Most Problematic Factors for Doing Business

FACTOR

Tax rates
Inadequate supply of infrastructure
Inefficient government bureaucracy
Access to financing
Tax regulations
Restrictive labor regulations
Corruption
Inadequately educated workforce
Crime and theft
Policy instability
Inflation
Poor work ethic in national labor force
Government instability/coups
Foreign currency regulations

Percent of responses

Note: From a list of 14 factors, respondents were asked to select the five most problematic for doing business in their country and to rank them between 1 (most problematic) and 5. The bars in the figure show the responses weighted according to their rankings.

Source: World Economic Forum, Executive Opinion Survey (2005)

336

National competitiveness balance sheet

NOTABLE COMPETITIVE ADVANTAGES	
Growth Competitiveness Index	**Rank/117**

Macroeconomic Environment
2.21	Country credit rating, 2004	20
2.16	Inflation, 2004	32
2.17	Interest rate spread, 2004	32

Public Institutions
6.20	Irregular payments in public utilities	28
6.19	Irregular payments in exports and imports	35
6.21	Irregular payments in tax collection	37
6.03	Property rights	41

Technology
3.18	Cellular telephones, 2003	4
3.19	Internet users, 2003	19
5.08	Telephone lines, 2003	22
3.17	Utility patents, 2004	25
4.17	Gross tertiary enrollment	26
3.21	Personal computers, 2003	30
3.15	Laws relating to ICT	37
3.12	Quality of competition in the ISP sector	38
3.01	Technological readiness	42
3.20	Internet hosts, 2003	43

Business Competitiveness Index	**Rank/110**

Sophistication of Company Operations and Strategy
8.02	Value chain presence	8
8.01	Nature of competitive advantage	14
8.03	Capacity for innovation	19

Quality of the National Business Environment
3.18	Cellular telephones, 2003	3
7.08	Local availability of process machinery	6
6.09	Extent of bureaucratic red tape	19

Other Indicators	**Rank/117**
4.05	Medium term business impact of tuberculosis	5
4.06	Medium term business impact of HIV/AIDS	20
8.13	Extent of incentive compensation	21
2.09	Prevalence of trade barriers	23
8.10	Breadth of international markets	24
7.05	Local supplier quantity	24
8.05	Production process sophistication	25
4.07	Ease of hiring foreign labor	27
8.06	Extent of marketing	28
9.01	Stringency of environmental regulations	28

NOTABLE COMPETITIVE DISADVANTAGES	
Growth Competitiveness Index	**Rank/117**

Macroeconomic Environment
2.01	Recession expectations	110
2.20	Government debt, 2004	109
2.15	Real effective exchange rate, 2004	92
6.06	Wastefulness of government spending	87
2.07	Access to credit	76
2.13	Government surplus/deficit, 2004	73
2.14	National savings rate, 2004	71

Public Institutions
6.16	Organized crime	103
6.08	Favoritism in decisions of government officials	72
6.01	Judicial independence	59

Technology
3.02	Firm-level technology absorption	91
3.13	Government prioritization of ICT	85
3.06	Company spending on research and development	71
3.07	University/industry research collaboration	66
3.14	Government success in ICT promotion	63
3.11	Internet access in schools	48

Business Competitiveness Index	**Rank/110**

Sophistication of Company Operations and Strategy
8.14	Reliance on professional management	87
3.06	Company spending on research and development	69
8.11	Extent of staff training	52

Quality of the National Business Environment
8.19	Cooperation in labor-employer relations	91
8.22	Foreign ownership restrictions	86
8.21	Protection of minority shareholders' interests	79

Other Indicators	**Rank/117**
6.12	Efficiency of the tax system	114
6.07	Burden of government regulation	113
2.11	Tax burden	112
8.18	Flexibility of wage determination	109
6.11	Extent and effect of taxation	108
8.17	Hiring and firing practices	108
2.10	Impact of rules on FDI	94
8.20	Pay and productivity	85
9.07	Importance of environment in business planning	84
4.09	Private sector employment of women	82
2.12	Agricultural policy costs	79

337

Note: The Business Competitiveness Index applies different criteria for selecting a country's competitive advantages and disadvantages. Please refer to the section "How Country Profiles Work" for further details.

Jamaica

Competitiveness Rankings

Growth Competitiveness Index Rank	70

Macroeconomic Environment Index Rank **99**
    Macroeconomic Stability Subindex Rank 107
    Government Waste Rank 88
    Country Credit Rating Rank 80

Public Institutions Index Rank............................**65**
    Contracts and Law Subindex Rank 74
    Corruption Subindex Rank...................................58

Technology Index Rank **45**
    Innovation Subindex Rank 78
    ICT Subindex Rank 46
    Technology Transfer Subindex Rank
        (out of 92 non-core innovators).......................16

Business Competitiveness Index Rank	53

**Sophistication of Company Operations
  and Strategy Rank**...**54**
**Quality of the National Business
  Environment Rank** **54**

The Most Problematic Factors for Doing Business

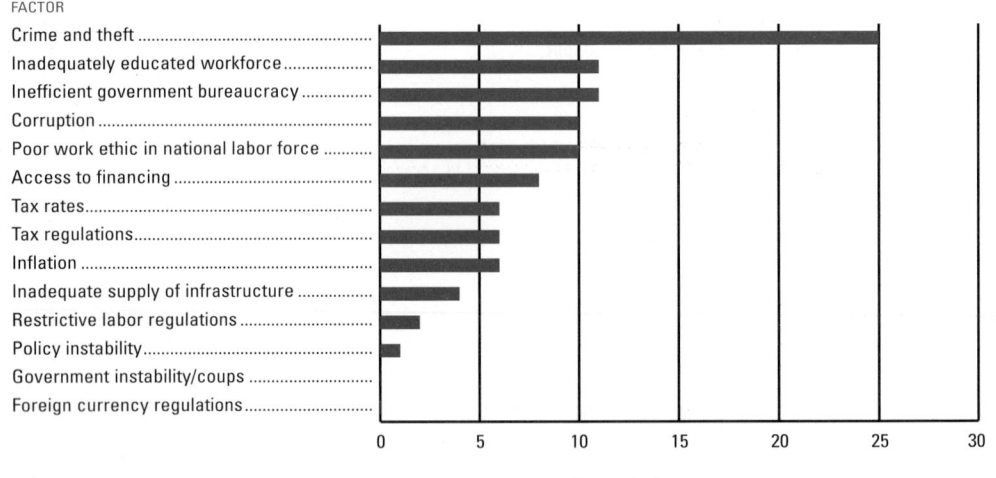

Note: From a list of 14 factors, respondents were asked to select the five most problematic for doing business in their country and to rank them between 1 (most problematic) and 5. The bars in the figure show the responses weighted according to their rankings.

Source: World Economic Forum, Executive Opinion Survey (2005)

338

National competitiveness balance sheet

NOTABLE COMPETITIVE ADVANTAGES	
Growth Competitiveness Index	**Rank/117**
Macroeconomic Environment	
2.15 Real effective exchange rate, 2004	30
2.01 Recession expectations	50
Public Institutions	
6.03 Property rights	47
6.01 Judicial independence	49
Technology	
3.04 FDI and technology transfer	17
3.13 Government prioritization of ICT	30
3.18 Cellular telephones, 2003	33
3.14 Government success in ICT promotion	35
3.19 Internet users, 2003	41
3.12 Quality of competition in the ISP sector	41
3.07 University/industry research collaboration	43
3.03 Prevalence of foreign technology licensing	45
3.01 Technological readiness	49
3.06 Company spending on research and development	50

NOTABLE COMPETITIVE DISADVANTAGES	
Growth Competitiveness Index	**Rank/117**
Macroeconomic Environment	
2.20 Government debt, 2004	113
2.16 Inflation, 2004	104
2.13 Government surplus/deficit, 2004	103
2.17 Interest rate spread, 2004	89
6.06 Wastefulness of government spending	88
2.21 Country credit rating, 2004	80
2.07 Access to credit	57
2.14 National savings rate, 2004	56
Public Institutions	
6.16 Organized crime	116
6.08 Favoritism in decisions of government officials	79
6.19 Irregular payments in exports and imports	64
6.21 Irregular payments in tax collection	58
6.20 Irregular payments in public utilities	57
Technology	
3.20 Internet hosts, 2003	80
4.17 Gross tertiary enrollment	79
3.11 Internet access in schools	69
3.02 Firm-level technology absorption	65
5.08 Telephone lines, 2003	63
3.21 Personal computers, 2003	62
3.15 Laws relating to ICT	61
3.17 Utility patents, 2004	55

Business Competitiveness Index	Rank/110
Sophistication of Company Operations and Strategy	
8.01 Nature of competitive advantage	24
8.14 Reliance on professional management	35
8.06 Extent of marketing	40
Quality of the National Business Environment	
2.08 Local equity market access	17
6.09 Extent of bureaucratic red tape	21
5.03 Port infrastructure quality	25

Business Competitiveness Index	Rank/110
Sophistication of Company Operations and Strategy	
8.09 Extent of regional sales	85
8.07 Degree of customer orientation	76
8.08 Control of international distribution	74
Quality of the National Business Environment	
5.02 Railroad infrastructure development	104
6.14 Reliability of police services	94
4.03 Quality of math and science education	93

Other Indicators	Rank/117
4.09 Private sector employment of women	16
8.22 Foreign ownership restrictions	26
3.10 Availability of mobile or cellular telephones	27
8.23 Strength of auditing and accounting standards	31
2.03 Financial market sophistication	35
6.25 Business costs of corruption	37
2.10 Impact of rules on FDI	37
3.05 Quality of scientific research institutions	38
7.01 Intensity of local competition	40
2.09 Prevalence of trade barriers	41

Other Indicators	Rank/117
6.15 Business costs of crime and violence	116
2.11 Tax burden	108
6.27 Pervasiveness of money laundering through banks	105
6.17 Informal sector	102
4.06 Medium term business impact of HIV/AIDS	98
6.18 Government effectiveness in reducing poverty and inequality	97
7.08 Local availability of process machinery	97
9.03 Extent of government mandated environmental reporting	96
7.05 Local supplier quantity	96
6.13 Centralization of economic policymaking	91
6.07 Burden of government regulation	89
3.09 Availability of scientists and engineers	89
9.09 Prevalence of corporate environmental reporting	89

339

Note: The Business Competitiveness Index applies different criteria for selecting a country's competitive advantages and disadvantages. Please refer to the section "How Country Profiles Work" for further details.

Japan

Competitiveness Rankings

Growth Competitiveness Index Rank	**12**

Macroeconomic Environment Index Rank **42**
    Macroeconomic Stability Subindex Rank 78
    Government Waste Rank 68
    Country Credit Rating Rank 19

Public Institutions Index Rank **14**
    Contracts and Law Subindex Rank 21
    Corruption Subindex Rank 8

Technology Index Rank **8**
    Innovation Subindex Rank 5
    ICT Subindex Rank 17

Business Competitiveness Index Rank	**8**

**Sophistication of Company Operations
and Strategy Rank** **3**

**Quality of the National Business
Environment Rank** **10**

The Most Problematic Factors for Doing Business

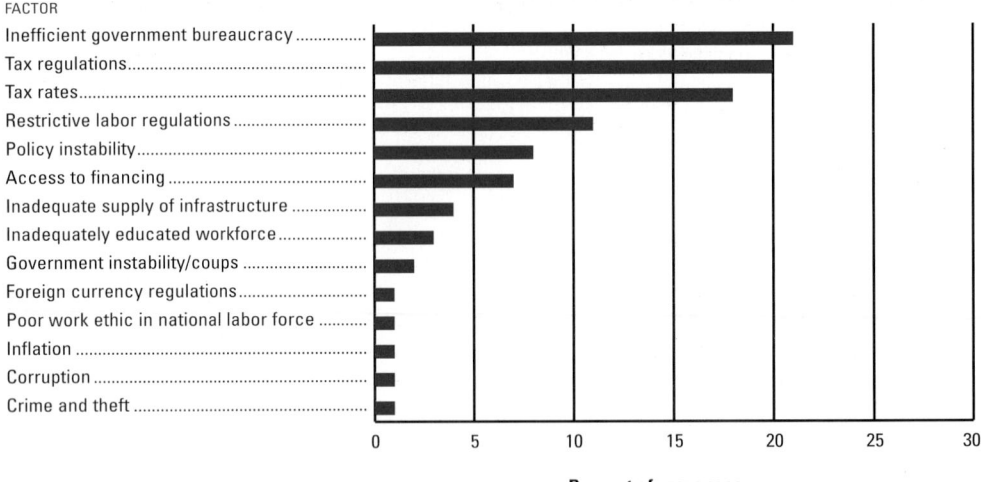

FACTOR

Inefficient government bureaucracy ....
Tax regulations..
Tax rates..
Restrictive labor regulations ....
Policy instability..
Access to financing ....
Inadequate supply of infrastructure ....
Inadequately educated workforce....................
Government instability/coups ....
Foreign currency regulations............................
Poor work ethic in national labor force ....
Inflation ....
Corruption ....
Crime and theft ....

Percent of responses

Note: From a list of 14 factors, respondents were asked to select the five most problematic for doing business in their country and to rank them between 1 (most problematic) and 5. The bars in the figure show the responses weighted according to their rankings.

Source: World Economic Forum, Executive Opinion Survey (2005)

National competitiveness balance sheet

NOTABLE COMPETITIVE ADVANTAGES		
Growth Competitiveness Index		**Rank/117**

Macroeconomic Environment
2.17	Interest rate spread, 2004	3
2.16	Inflation, 2004	6

Public Institutions
6.19	Irregular payments in exports and imports	5
6.21	Irregular payments in tax collection	7

Technology
3.12	Quality of competition in the ISP sector	2
3.01	Technological readiness	2
3.06	Company spending on research and development	2
3.17	Utility patents, 2004	2
3.02	Firm-level technology absorption	2

NOTABLE COMPETITIVE DISADVANTAGES		
Growth Competitiveness Index		**Rank/117**

Macroeconomic Environment
2.20	Government debt, 2004	114
2.13	Government surplus/deficit, 2004	113
6.06	Wastefulness of government spending	68
2.01	Recession expectations	52
2.15	Real effective exchange rate, 2004	48
2.07	Access to credit	31
2.14	National savings rate, 2004	23
2.21	Country credit rating, 2004	19

Public Institutions
6.16	Organized crime	39
6.01	Judicial independence	22
6.08	Favoritism in decisions of government officials	19
6.03	Property rights	17
6.20	Irregular payments in public utilities	14

Technology
3.18	Cellular telephones, 2003	34
4.17	Gross tertiary enrollment	32
3.15	Laws relating to ICT	30
5.08	Telephone lines, 2003	24
3.21	Personal computers, 2003	23
3.14	Government success in ICT promotion	23
3.11	Internet access in schools	21
3.07	University/industry research collaboration	15
3.19	Internet users, 2003	14
3.13	Government prioritization of ICT	13
3.20	Internet hosts, 2003	12

Business Competitiveness Index		Rank/110

Sophistication of Company Operations and Strategy
8.01	Nature of competitive advantage	1
8.05	Production process sophistication	1
8.02	Value chain presence	1

Quality of the National Business Environment
7.08	Local availability of process machinery	1
7.05	Local supplier quantity	1
5.02	Railroad infrastructure development	1

Business Competitiveness Index		Rank/110

341

Sophistication of Company Operations and Strategy
8.13	Extent of incentive compensation	48
8.12	Willingness to delegate authority	17

Quality of the National Business Environment
8.22	Foreign ownership restrictions	73
2.09	Prevalence of trade barriers	60
2.05	Ease of access to loans	52

Other Indicators		Rank/117
7.06	Local supplier quality	1
9.07	Importance of environment in business planning	1
7.07	Presence of demanding regulatory standards	2
9.04	Effects of compliance on business	2
8.10	Breadth of international markets	2
5.07	Telephone/fax infrastructure quality	2
8.08	Control of international distribution	2
5.06	Postal efficiency	2
8.03	Capacity for innovation	3
8.11	Extent of staff training	3

Other Indicators		Rank/117
2.12	Agricultural policy costs	105
2.04	Soundness of banks	99
2.11	Tax burden	94
2.02	Business costs of terrorism	86
4.09	Private sector employment of women	86
2.10	Impact of rules on FDI	82
4.07	Ease of hiring foreign labor	79
8.17	Hiring and firing practices	64
6.12	Efficiency of the tax system	59
6.13	Centralization of economic policymaking	55
8.21	Protection of minority shareholders' interests	42

Note: The Business Competitiveness Index applies different criteria for selecting a country's competitive advantages and disadvantages. Please refer to the section "How Country Profiles Work" for further details.

Jordan

Competitiveness Rankings

Growth Competitiveness Index Rank	45

Macroeconomic Environment Index Rank **52**
    Macroeconomic Stability Subindex Rank 57
    Government Waste Rank 23
    Country Credit Rating Rank 70

Public Institutions Index Rank **31**
    Contracts and Law Subindex Rank 26
    Corruption Subindex Rank......................................40

Technology Index Rank **52**
    Innovation Subindex Rank 47
    ICT Subindex Rank 53
    Technology Transfer Subindex Rank
        (out of 92 non-core innovators).......................31

Business Competitiveness Index Rank	43

**Sophistication of Company Operations
and Strategy Rank** **59**

**Quality of the National Business
Environment Rank** **42**

The Most Problematic Factors for Doing Business

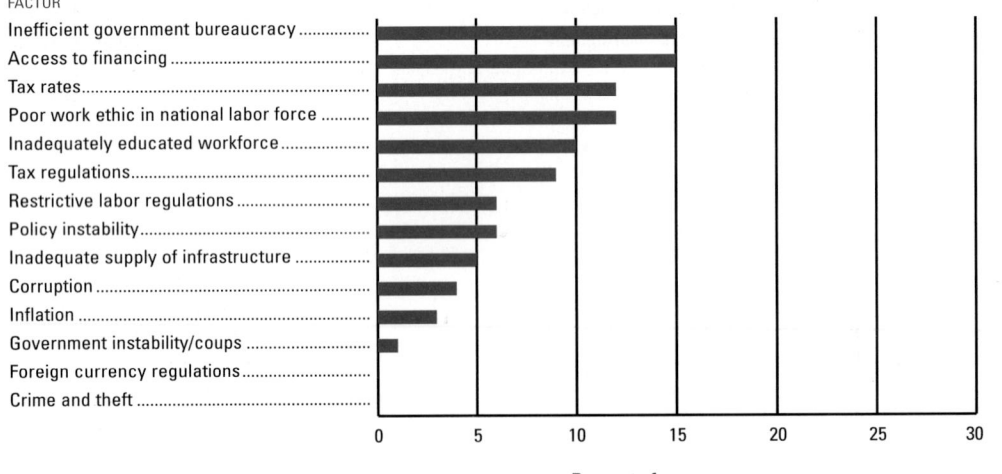

FACTOR

Inefficient government bureaucracy
Access to financing
Tax rates
Poor work ethic in national labor force
Inadequately educated workforce
Tax regulations
Restrictive labor regulations
Policy instability
Inadequate supply of infrastructure
Corruption
Inflation
Government instability/coups
Foreign currency regulations
Crime and theft

Percent of responses

Note: From a list of 14 factors, respondents were asked to select the five most problematic for doing business in their country and to rank them between 1 (most problematic) and 5. The bars in the figure show the responses weighted according to their rankings.

Source: World Economic Forum, Executive Opinion Survey (2005)

342

National competitiveness balance sheet

NOTABLE COMPETITIVE ADVANTAGES		NOTABLE COMPETITIVE DISADVANTAGES	
Growth Competitiveness Index	**Rank/117**	**Growth Competitiveness Index**	**Rank/117**

Macroeconomic Environment		
2.01	Recession expectations	22
6.06	Wastefulness of government spending	23
2.07	Access to credit	33
Public Institutions		
6.16	Organized crime	5
6.08	Favoritism in decisions of government officials	31
6.19	Irregular payments in exports and imports	32
6.03	Property rights	35
6.20	Irregular payments in public utilities	36
6.01	Judicial independence	39
Technology		
3.13	Government prioritization of ICT	12
3.14	Government success in ICT promotion	18
3.12	Quality of competition in the ISP sector	28
3.01	Technological readiness	35
3.03	Prevalence of foreign technology licensing	39
3.11	Internet access in schools	42

Macroeconomic Environment		
2.20	Government debt, 2004	95
2.13	Government surplus/deficit, 2004	78
2.14	National savings rate, 2004	77
2.21	Country credit rating, 2004	70
2.17	Interest rate spread, 2004	61
2.16	Inflation, 2004	50
2.15	Real effective exchange rate, 2004	47
Public Institutions		
6.21	Irregular payments in tax collection	52
Technology		
3.20	Internet hosts, 2003	79
5.08	Telephone lines, 2003	74
3.06	Company spending on research and development	69
3.18	Cellular telephones, 2003	67
3.17	Utility patents, 2004	67
3.21	Personal computers, 2003	66
3.07	University/industry research collaboration	65
3.19	Internet users, 2003	63
3.04	FDI and technology transfer	52
3.15	Laws relating to ICT	52
4.17	Gross tertiary enrollment	51
3.02	Firm-level technology absorption	45

Business Competitiveness Index	**Rank/110**	**Business Competitiveness Index**	**Rank/110**

Sophistication of Company Operations and Strategy		
8.08	Control of international distribution	20
8.09	Extent of regional sales	34
3.03	Prevalence of foreign technology licensing	39
Quality of the National Business Environment		
6.14	Reliability of police services	10
3.09	Availability of scientists and engineers	14
8.22	Foreign ownership restrictions	15

Sophistication of Company Operations and Strategy		
8.13	Extent of incentive compensation	93
8.14	Reliance on professional management	83
8.12	Willingness to delegate authority	78
Quality of the National Business Environment		
6.09	Extent of bureaucratic red tape	103
8.16	Efficacy of corporate boards	83
8.15	Quality of management schools	74

Other Indicators	**Rank/117**	**Other Indicators**	**Rank/117**

6.15	Business costs of crime and violence	8
6.07	Burden of government regulation	12
8.18	Flexibility of wage determination	16
9.05	Effects of privatization on competition and the environment	17
6.27	Pervasiveness of money laundering through banks	19
2.10	Impact of rules on FDI	19
6.24	Diversion of public funds	20
2.11	Tax burden	20
4.06	Medium term business impact of HIV/AIDS	21
6.17	Informal sector	23
5.07	Telephone/fax infrastructure quality	24

6.05	Freedom of the press	98
4.07	Ease of hiring foreign labor	92
4.08	Brain drain	87
8.17	Hiring and firing practices	81
6.13	Centralization of economic policymaking	77
9.07	Importance of environment in business planning	75
8.06	Extent of marketing	73
7.05	Local supplier quantity	71
9.09	Prevalence of corporate environmental reporting	70

343

Note: The Business Competitiveness Index applies different criteria for selecting a country's competitive advantages and disadvantages. Please refer to the section "How Country Profiles Work" for further details.

Kazakhstan

Competitiveness Rankings

Growth Competitiveness Index Rank	61

Macroeconomic Environment Index Rank **41**
    Macroeconomic Stability Subindex Rank 24
    Government Waste Rank 39
    Country Credit Rating Rank 57

Public Institutions Index Rank **76**
    Contracts and Law Subindex Rank 71
    Corruption Subindex Rank...................................81

Technology Index Rank **77**
    Innovation Subindex Rank 41
    ICT Subindex Rank 74
    Technology Transfer Subindex Rank
      (out of 92 non-core innovators) 64

Business Competitiveness Index Rank	62

**Sophistication of Company Operations
  and Strategy Rank** **72**
**Quality of the National Business
  Environment Rank** **60**

The Most Problematic Factors for Doing Business

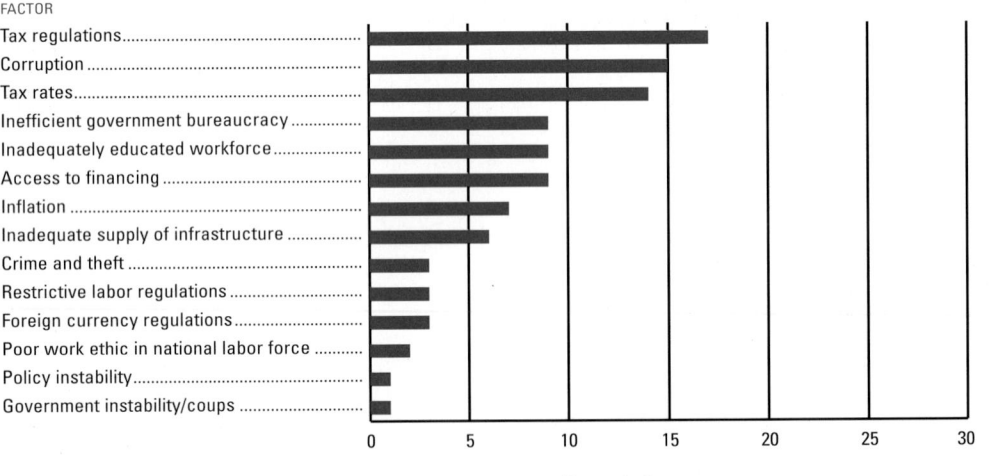

Note: From a list of 14 factors, respondents were asked to select the five most problematic for doing business in their country and to rank them between 1 (most problematic) and 5. The bars in the figure show the responses weighted according to their rankings.

Source: World Economic Forum, Executive Opinion Survey (2005)

National competitiveness balance sheet

NOTABLE COMPETITIVE ADVANTAGES	
Growth Competitiveness Index	**Rank/117**

Macroeconomic Environment

2.20	Government debt, 2004	6
2.13	Government surplus/deficit, 2004	11
2.01	Recession expectations	17
2.14	National savings rate, 2004	27
6.06	Wastefulness of government spending	39
2.15	Real effective exchange rate, 2004	46
2.07	Access to credit	47

Technology

4.17	Gross tertiary enrollment	36
3.13	Government prioritization of ICT	40
3.06	Company spending on research and development	44
3.15	Laws relating to ICT	50

NOTABLE COMPETITIVE DISADVANTAGES	
Growth Competitiveness Index	**Rank/117**

Macroeconomic Environment

2.17	Interest rate spread, 2004	90
2.16	Inflation, 2004	86
2.21	Country credit rating, 2004	57

Public Institutions

6.19	Irregular payments in exports and imports	86
6.21	Irregular payments in tax collection	80
6.20	Irregular payments in public utilities	76
6.01	Judicial independence	74
6.16	Organized crime	74
6.03	Property rights	73
6.08	Favoritism in decisions of government officials	55

Technology

3.19	Internet users, 2003	93
3.18	Cellular telephones, 2003	90
3.12	Quality of competition in the ISP sector	90
3.04	FDI and technology transfer	89
3.03	Prevalence of foreign technology licensing	82
3.20	Internet hosts, 2003	70
3.17	Utility patents, 2004	69
5.08	Telephone lines, 2003	66
3.01	Technological readiness	64
3.02	Firm-level technology absorption	59
3.11	Internet access in schools	56
3.07	University/industry research collaboration	54
3.14	Government success in ICT promotion	54

Business Competitiveness Index	Rank/110

Sophistication of Company Operations and Strategy

8.08	Control of international distribution	40
3.06	Company spending on research and development	43
8.05	Production process sophistication	47

Quality of the National Business Environment

7.08	Local availability of process machinery	26
5.02	Railroad infrastructure development	31
8.16	Efficacy of corporate boards	37

Business Competitiveness Index	Rank/110

Sophistication of Company Operations and Strategy

8.02	Value chain presence	88
8.14	Reliance on professional management	85
8.13	Extent of incentive compensation	83

Quality of the National Business Environment

8.22	Foreign ownership restrictions	96
3.19	Internet users, 2003	92
3.18	Cellular telephones, 2003	89

Other Indicators	Rank/117

8.17	Hiring and firing practices	4
8.20	Pay and productivity	17
9.09	Prevalence of corporate environmental reporting	29
8.18	Flexibility of wage determination	35
6.10	Effectiveness of law-making bodies	36
6.13	Centralization of economic policymaking	39
7.04	Buyer sophistication	40
8.19	Cooperation in labor-employer relations	41
3.08	Government procurement of advanced technology products	45
2.06	Venture capital availability	45
6.07	Burden of government regulation	48

Other Indicators	Rank/117

9.05	Effects of privatization on competition and the environment	107
6.27	Pervasiveness of money laundering through banks	101
6.05	Freedom of the press	99
4.07	Ease of hiring foreign labor	99
8.21	Protection of minority shareholders' interests	90
9.04	Effects of compliance on business	89
3.09	Availability of scientists and engineers	88
4.05	Medium term business impact of tuberculosis	87
3.10	Availability of mobile or cellular telephones	86
6.25	Business costs of corruption	85
2.10	Impact of rules on FDI	85

345

Note: The Business Competitiveness Index applies different criteria for selecting a country's competitive advantages and disadvantages. Please refer to the section "How Country Profiles Work" for further details.

Kenya

Competitiveness Rankings

Growth Competitiveness Index Rank	92

Macroeconomic Environment Index Rank **106**
    Macroeconomic Stability Subindex Rank 99
    Government Waste Rank 105
    Country Credit Rating Rank 94

Public Institutions Index Rank..........................**94**
    Contracts and Law Subindex Rank 90
    Corruption Subindex Rank..................................94

Technology Index Rank **71**
    Innovation Subindex Rank 97
    ICT Subindex Rank 108
    Technology Transfer Subindex Rank
    (out of 92 non-core innovators).......................12

Business Competitiveness Index Rank	68

**Sophistication of Company Operations
  and Strategy Rank** **60**
**Quality of the National Business
  Environment Rank** **69**

The Most Problematic Factors for Doing Business

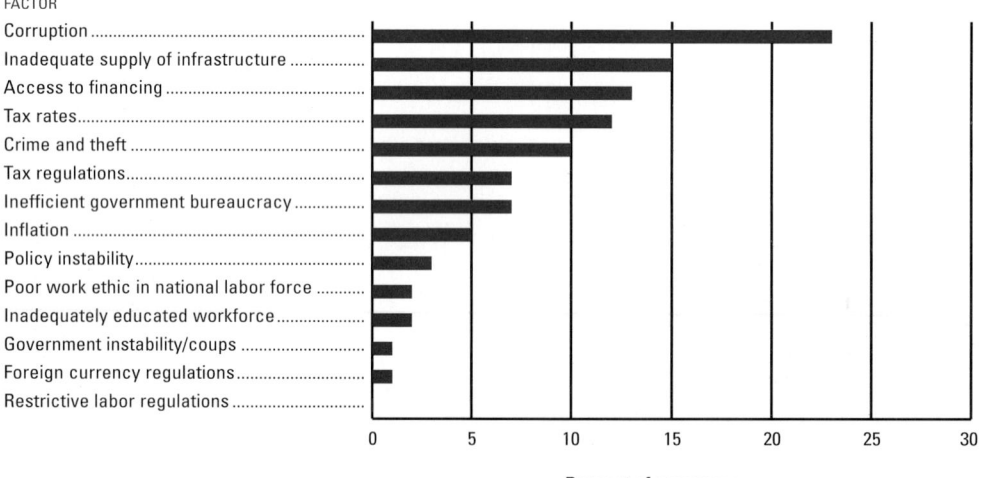

Note: From a list of 14 factors, respondents were asked to select the five most problematic for doing business in their country and to rank them between 1 (most problematic) and 5. The bars in the figure show the responses weighted according to their rankings.

Source: World Economic Forum, Executive Opinion Survey (2005)

National competitiveness balance sheet

NOTABLE COMPETITIVE ADVANTAGES		
Growth Competitiveness Index		**Rank/117**

Technology

3.04	FDI and technology transfer	9
3.06	Company spending on research and development	33
3.07	University/industry research collaboration	41
3.03	Prevalence of foreign technology licensing	43

NOTABLE COMPETITIVE DISADVANTAGES		
Growth Competitiveness Index		**Rank/117**

Macroeconomic Environment

2.14	National savings rate, 2004	111
6.06	Wastefulness of government spending	105
2.16	Inflation, 2004	104
2.21	Country credit rating, 2004	94
2.17	Interest rate spread, 2004	88
2.07	Access to credit	81
2.20	Government debt, 2004	81
2.01	Recession expectations	74
2.15	Real effective exchange rate, 2004	64
2.13	Government surplus/deficit, 2004	57

Public Institutions

6.08	Favoritism in decisions of government officials	109
6.20	Irregular payments in public utilities	103
6.16	Organized crime	96
6.21	Irregular payments in tax collection	89
6.19	Irregular payments in exports and imports	84
6.01	Judicial independence	75
6.03	Property rights	69

Technology

3.11	Internet access in schools	109
4.17	Gross tertiary enrollment	108
5.08	Telephone lines, 2003	103
3.21	Personal computers, 2003	101
3.19	Internet users, 2003	99
3.18	Cellular telephones, 2003	95
3.13	Government prioritization of ICT	92
3.20	Internet hosts, 2003	88
3.14	Government success in ICT promotion	83
3.01	Technological readiness	80
3.15	Laws relating to ICT	77
3.12	Quality of competition in the ISP sector	73
3.17	Utility patents, 2004	65
3.02	Firm-level technology absorption	57

Business Competitiveness Index		**Rank/110**

Sophistication of Company Operations and Strategy

3.06	Company spending on research and development	32
8.01	Nature of competitive advantage	34
8.07	Degree of customer orientation	38

Quality of the National Business Environment

3.05	Quality of scientific research institutions	32
7.05	Local supplier quantity	38
8.16	Efficacy of corporate boards	38

Business Competitiveness Index		**Rank/110**

Sophistication of Company Operations and Strategy

8.05	Production process sophistication	99
8.08	Control of international distribution	88
8.13	Extent of incentive compensation	85

Quality of the National Business Environment

6.08	Favoritism in decisions of government officials	102
5.07	Telephone/fax infrastructure quality	101
5.01	Overall infrastructure quality	100

Other Indicators		**Rank/117**

8.17	Hiring and firing practices	15
9.07	Importance of environment in business planning	24
9.04	Effects of compliance on business	30
8.09	Extent of regional sales	40
7.06	Local supplier quality	47
8.21	Protection of minority shareholders' interests	49
9.10	Grass-roots involvement in development projects	50

Other Indicators		**Rank/117**

2.02	Business costs of terrorism	114
6.15	Business costs of crime and violence	110
4.05	Medium term business impact of tuberculosis	109
4.06	Medium term business impact of HIV/AIDS	106
6.24	Diversion of public funds	106
6.14	Reliability of police services	105
8.19	Cooperation in labor-employer relations	105
6.11	Extent and effect of taxation	104
6.13	Centralization of economic policymaking	103
6.18	Government effectiveness in reducing poverty and inequality	101
6.10	Effectiveness of law-making bodies	100
5.05	Quality of electricity supply	98
6.26	Public trust of politicians	97

Note: The Business Competitiveness Index applies different criteria for selecting a country's competitive advantages and disadvantages. Please refer to the section "How Country Profiles Work" for further details.

Korea, Rep.

Competitiveness Rankings

Growth Competitiveness Index Rank	17

Macroeconomic Environment Index Rank **25**	
Macroeconomic Stability Subindex Rank 8	
Government Waste Rank 32	
Country Credit Rating Rank 28	
Public Institutions Index Rank...**42**	
Contracts and Law Subindex Rank 41	
Corruption Subindex Rank....................................52	
Technology Index Rank **7**	
Innovation Subindex Rank 8	
ICT Subindex Rank 11	

Business Competitiveness Index Rank	24

Sophistication of Company Operations	
and Strategy Rank **17**	
Quality of the National Business	
Environment Rank **24**	

The Most Problematic Factors for Doing Business

FACTOR

Policy instability...
Inefficient government bureaucracy...............
Access to financing ....
Restrictive labor regulations ....
Tax regulations...
Corruption ....
Tax rates...
Inadequate supply of infrastructure ....
Government instability/coups ....
Inadequately educated workforce...................
Inflation ....
Poor work ethic in national labor force ....
Foreign currency regulations...........................
Crime and theft ....

0   5   10   15   20   25   30

Percent of responses

Note: From a list of 14 factors, respondents were asked to select the five most problematic for doing business in their country and to rank them between 1 (most problematic) and 5. The bars in the figure show the responses weighted according to their rankings.

Source: World Economic Forum, Executive Opinion Survey (2005)

National competitiveness balance sheet

NOTABLE COMPETITIVE ADVANTAGES		NOTABLE COMPETITIVE DISADVANTAGES	
Growth Competitiveness Index	**Rank/117**	**Growth Competitiveness Index**	**Rank/117**

Growth Competitiveness Index — Advantages

Macroeconomic Environment

2.17	Interest rate spread, 2004	6
2.14	National savings rate, 2004	10
2.20	Government debt, 2004	11
2.13	Government surplus/deficit, 2004	14

Technology

4.17	Gross tertiary enrollment	2
3.12	Quality of competition in the ISP sector	3
3.19	Internet users, 2003	3
3.14	Government success in ICT promotion	6
3.11	Internet access in schools	6
3.13	Government prioritization of ICT	7
3.06	Company spending on research and development	8
3.02	Firm-level technology absorption	8
3.21	Personal computers, 2003	8
3.07	University/industry research collaboration	10
3.15	Laws relating to ICT	10
3.17	Utility patents, 2004	11
3.20	Internet hosts, 2003	15
3.01	Technological readiness	16

Growth Competitiveness Index — Disadvantages

Macroeconomic Environment

2.15	Real effective exchange rate, 2004	85
2.16	Inflation, 2004	52
2.07	Access to credit	48
2.01	Recession expectations	46
6.06	Wastefulness of government spending	32
2.21	Country credit rating, 2004	28

Public Institutions

6.21	Irregular payments in tax collection	61
6.16	Organized crime	55
6.19	Irregular payments in exports and imports	51
6.20	Irregular payments in public utilities	49
6.01	Judicial independence	45
6.03	Property rights	36
6.08	Favoritism in decisions of government officials	26

Technology

3.18	Cellular telephones, 2003	30
5.08	Telephone lines, 2003	17

Business Competitiveness Index	**Rank/110**	**Business Competitiveness Index**	**Rank/110**

Business Competitiveness Index — Advantages

Sophistication of Company Operations and Strategy

3.06	Company spending on research and development	8
8.03	Capacity for innovation	14
8.13	Extent of incentive compensation	14

Quality of the National Business Environment

3.19	Internet users, 2003	3
7.08	Local availability of process machinery	5
3.07	University/industry research collaboration	10

Business Competitiveness Index — Disadvantages

Sophistication of Company Operations and Strategy

8.14	Reliance on professional management	36
8.09	Extent of regional sales	27
8.06	Extent of marketing	24

Quality of the National Business Environment

8.19	Cooperation in labor-employer relations	77
8.22	Foreign ownership restrictions	57
8.16	Efficacy of corporate boards	51

Other Indicators	**Rank/117**	**Other Indicators**	**Rank/117**

Other Indicators — Advantages

3.16	Extent of business Internet use	3
3.08	Government procurement of advanced technology products	10
9.06	Prioritization of energy efficiency	13
6.07	Burden of government regulation	14
9.07	Importance of environment in business planning	15
8.01	Nature of competitive advantage	16
8.07	Degree of customer orientation	16
7.04	Buyer sophistication	16
8.08	Control of international distribution	16

Other Indicators — Disadvantages

4.09	Private sector employment of women	96
4.07	Ease of hiring foreign labor	89
2.04	Soundness of banks	71
2.10	Impact of rules on FDI	62
4.05	Medium term business impact of tuberculosis	59
4.06	Medium term business impact of HIV/AIDS	55
6.23	Irregular payments in judicial decisions	54
6.05	Freedom of the press	54
3.10	Availability of mobile or cellular telephones	49
6.10	Effectiveness of law-making bodies	48
2.08	Local equity market access	48
6.27	Pervasiveness of money laundering through banks	47

349

Note: The Business Competitiveness Index applies different criteria for selecting a country's competitive advantages and disadvantages. Please refer to the section "How Country Profiles Work" for further details.

Kuwait

Competitiveness Rankings

Growth Competitiveness Index Rank	33

Macroeconomic Environment Index Rank **21**
   Macroeconomic Stability Subindex Rank 1
   Government Waste Rank 38
   Country Credit Rating Rank 31

Public Institutions Index Rank **37**
   Contracts and Law Subindex Rank 31
   Corruption Subindex Rank 45

Technology Index Rank **48**
   Innovation Subindex Rank 69
   ICT Subindex Rank 45
   Technology Transfer Subindex Rank
      (out of 92 non-core innovators) 33

Business Competitiveness Index Rank	47

**Sophistication of Company Operations
  and Strategy Rank** 63

**Quality of the National Business
  Environment Rank** 45

The Most Problematic Factors for Doing Business

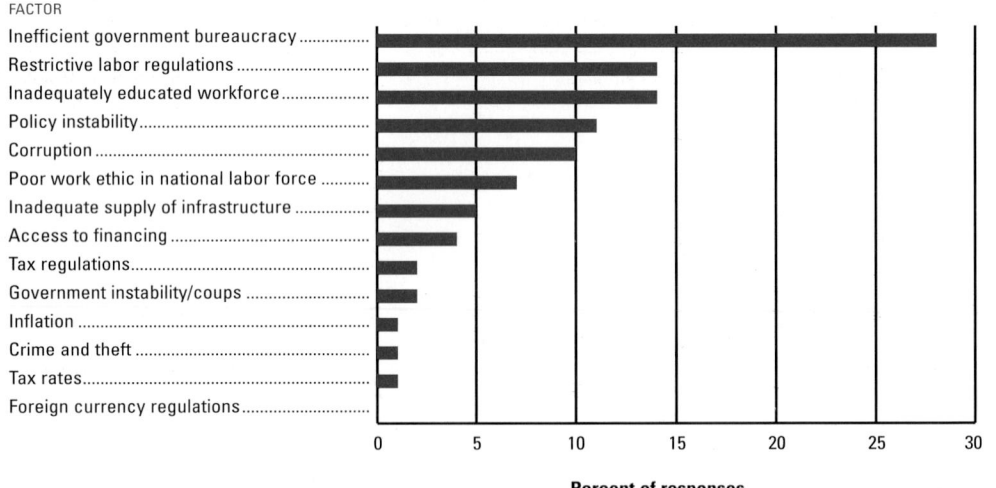

Note: From a list of 14 factors, respondents were asked to select the five most problematic for doing business in their country and to rank them between 1 (most problematic) and 5. The bars in the figure show the responses weighted according to their rankings.

Source: World Economic Forum, Executive Opinion Survey (2005)

National competitiveness balance sheet

NOTABLE COMPETITIVE ADVANTAGES	
Growth Competitiveness Index	**Rank/117**

Macroeconomic Environment

2.13	Government surplus/deficit, 2004	1
2.01	Recession expectations	8
2.14	National savings rate, 2004	15
2.17	Interest rate spread, 2004	16
2.07	Access to credit	20
2.16	Inflation, 2004	23
2.20	Government debt, 2004	25
2.21	Country credit rating, 2004	31

Public Institutions

6.16	Organized crime	16
6.01	Judicial independence	27
6.21	Irregular payments in tax collection	31

Technology

3.03	Prevalence of foreign technology licensing	28
3.02	Firm-level technology absorption	31

Business Competitiveness Index	Rank/110

Sophistication of Company Operations and Strategy

8.08	Control of international distribution	11
3.03	Prevalence of foreign technology licensing	28
8.13	Extent of incentive compensation	40

Quality of the National Business Environment

5.05	Quality of electricity supply	19
2.06	Venture capital availability	24
2.05	Ease of access to loans	24

Other Indicators	Rank/117

2.11	Tax burden	2
4.08	Brain drain	5
6.11	Extent and effect of taxation	6
8.18	Flexibility of wage determination	8
4.07	Ease of hiring foreign labor	9
6.12	Efficiency of the tax system	10
6.17	Informal sector	12
2.12	Agricultural policy costs	17
6.27	Pervasiveness of money laundering through banks	18
6.15	Business costs of crime and violence	19
8.17	Hiring and firing practices	24
2.08	Local equity market access	24

NOTABLE COMPETITIVE DISADVANTAGES	
Growth Competitiveness Index	**Rank/117**

Macroeconomic Environment

2.15	Real effective exchange rate, 2004	43
6.06	Wastefulness of government spending	38

Public Institutions

6.20	Irregular payments in public utilities	54
6.19	Irregular payments in exports and imports	52
6.03	Property rights	48
6.08	Favoritism in decisions of government officials	36

Technology

3.06	Company spending on research and development	94
3.15	Laws relating to ICT	84
3.04	FDI and technology transfer	79
3.13	Government prioritization of ICT	79
3.20	Internet hosts, 2003	74
4.17	Gross tertiary enrollment	73
3.14	Government success in ICT promotion	70
5.08	Telephone lines, 2003	60
3.07	University/industry research collaboration	60
3.12	Quality of competition in the ISP sector	45
3.19	Internet users, 2003	42
3.18	Cellular telephones, 2003	39
3.21	Personal computers, 2003	38
3.01	Technological readiness	36
3.17	Utility patents, 2004	35
3.11	Internet access in schools	34

Business Competitiveness Index	Rank/110

Sophistication of Company Operations and Strategy

8.03	Capacity for innovation	107
8.02	Value chain presence	93
3.06	Company spending on research and development	90

Quality of the National Business Environment

8.22	Foreign ownership restrictions	110
6.09	Extent of bureaucratic red tape	99
6.13	Centralization of economic policymaking	98

Other Indicators	Rank/117

9.10	Grass-roots involvement in development projects	115
9.06	Prioritization of energy efficiency	114
2.10	Impact of rules on FDI	112
3.08	Government procurement of advanced technology products	100
2.02	Business costs of terrorism	97
8.16	Efficacy of corporate boards	94
9.09	Prevalence of corporate environmental reporting	92
8.14	Reliance on professional management	90
9.07	Importance of environment in business planning	88
9.04	Effects of compliance on business	86

Note: The Business Competitiveness Index applies different criteria for selecting a country's competitive advantages and disadvantages. Please refer to the section "How Country Profiles Work" for further details.

Kyrgyz Republic

Competitiveness Rankings

The Most Problematic Factors for Doing Business

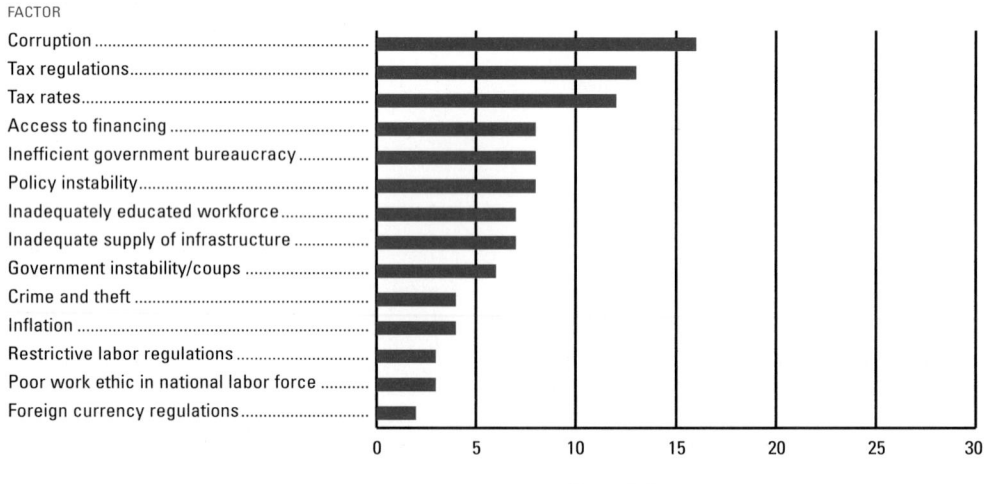

Note: From a list of 14 factors, respondents were asked to select the five most problematic for doing business in their country and to rank them between 1 (most problematic) and 5. The bars in the figure show the responses weighted according to their rankings.

Source: World Economic Forum, Executive Opinion Survey (2005)

National competitiveness balance sheet

NOTABLE COMPETITIVE ADVANTAGES	
Growth Competitiveness Index	**Rank/117**

Technology

4.17	Gross tertiary enrollment	39
3.13	Government prioritization of ICT	41

NOTABLE COMPETITIVE DISADVANTAGES	
Growth Competitiveness Index	**Rank/117**

Macroeconomic Environment

2.17	Interest rate spread, 2004	111
2.21	Country credit rating, 2004	109
2.14	National savings rate, 2004	108
6.06	Wastefulness of government spending	107
2.01	Recession expectations	106
2.20	Government debt, 2004	104
2.13	Government surplus/deficit, 2004	90
2.07	Access to credit	79
2.15	Real effective exchange rate, 2004	68
2.16	Inflation, 2004	61

Public Institutions

6.19	Irregular payments in exports and imports	115
6.08	Favoritism in decisions of government officials	112
6.01	Judicial independence	112
6.21	Irregular payments in tax collection	109
6.03	Property rights	104
6.20	Irregular payments in public utilities	102
6.16	Organized crime	80

Technology

3.06	Company spending on research and development	117
3.02	Firm-level technology absorption	117
3.03	Prevalence of foreign technology licensing	116
3.07	University/industry research collaboration	113
3.04	FDI and technology transfer	112
3.01	Technological readiness	112
3.15	Laws relating to ICT	109
3.18	Cellular telephones, 2003	106
3.14	Government success in ICT promotion	95
3.12	Quality of competition in the ISP sector	94
3.21	Personal computers, 2003	92
3.19	Internet users, 2003	83
5.08	Telephone lines, 2003	82
3.17	Utility patents, 2004	81
3.11	Internet access in schools	81
3.20	Internet hosts, 2003	72

Business Competitiveness Index	Rank/110

Sophistication of Company Operations and Strategy

8.07	Degree of customer orientation	40
8.08	Control of international distribution	46
8.12	Willingness to delegate authority	51

Quality of the National Business Environment

8.16	Efficacy of corporate boards	43
8.19	Cooperation in labor-employer relations	43
4.01	Quality of the educational system	73

Business Competitiveness Index	Rank/110

Sophistication of Company Operations and Strategy

3.06	Company spending on research and development	110
3.03	Prevalence of foreign technology licensing	110
8.10	Breadth of international markets	108

Quality of the National Business Environment

7.09	Local availability of specialized research and training services	110
5.03	Port infrastructure quality	110
3.08	Government procurement of advanced technology products	109

Other Indicators	Rank/117

8.20	Pay and productivity	8
8.17	Hiring and firing practices	11
8.18	Flexibility of wage determination	18
4.09	Private sector employment of women	24

Other Indicators	Rank/117

9.05	Effects of privatization on competition and the environment	117
6.17	Informal sector	117
9.09	Prevalence of corporate environmental reporting	116
9.01	Stringency of environmental regulations	116
6.25	Business costs of corruption	116
7.03	Extent of market dominance	116
2.09	Prevalence of trade barriers	116
2.04	Soundness of banks	115
8.04	Ethical behavior of firms	114
6.11	Extent and effect of taxation	114
9.04	Effects of compliance on business	113
8.10	Breadth of international markets	113

353

Note: The Business Competitiveness Index applies different criteria for selecting a country's competitive advantages and disadvantages. Please refer to the section "How Country Profiles Work" for further details.

Latvia

Competitiveness Rankings

The Most Problematic Factors for Doing Business

FACTOR

Factor	
Corruption	
Inefficient government bureaucracy	
Access to financing	
Tax regulations	
Tax rates	
Inadequately educated workforce	
Inflation	
Inadequate supply of infrastructure	
Government instability/coups	
Policy instability	
Poor work ethic in national labor force	
Restrictive labor regulations	
Crime and theft	
Foreign currency regulations	

Percent of responses

Note: From a list of 14 factors, respondents were asked to select the five most problematic for doing business in their country and to rank them between 1 (most problematic) and 5. The bars in the figure show the responses weighted according to their rankings.

Source: World Economic Forum, Executive Opinion Survey (2005)

354

National competitiveness balance sheet

NOTABLE COMPETITIVE ADVANTAGES	
Growth Competitiveness Index	**Rank/117**

Macroeconomic Environment

2.20	Government debt, 2004	8
2.07	Access to credit	13
2.01	Recession expectations	27
2.13	Government surplus/deficit, 2004	37
2.17	Interest rate spread, 2004	37

Technology

4.17	Gross tertiary enrollment	9
3.19	Internet users, 2003	20
3.21	Personal computers, 2003	33
3.20	Internet hosts, 2003	38
3.11	Internet access in schools	38
5.08	Telephone lines, 2003	40
3.18	Cellular telephones, 2003	42
3.17	Utility patents, 2004	43

NOTABLE COMPETITIVE DISADVANTAGES	
Growth Competitiveness Index	**Rank/117**

Macroeconomic Environment

2.16	Inflation, 2004	81
2.14	National savings rate, 2004	65
2.15	Real effective exchange rate, 2004	59
6.06	Wastefulness of government spending	49
2.21	Country credit rating, 2004	48

Public Institutions

6.08	Favoritism in decisions of government officials	63
6.21	Irregular payments in tax collection	60
6.01	Judicial independence	58
6.19	Irregular payments in exports and imports	57
6.03	Property rights	53
6.20	Irregular payments in public utilities	48
6.16	Organized crime	44

Technology

3.14	Government success in ICT promotion	89
3.13	Government prioritization of ICT	87
3.03	Prevalence of foreign technology licensing	68
3.07	University/industry research collaboration	61
3.01	Technological readiness	60
3.15	Laws relating to ICT	59
3.02	Firm-level technology absorption	52
3.04	FDI and technology transfer	50
3.12	Quality of competition in the ISP sector	49
3.06	Company spending on research and development	48

Business Competitiveness Index	
Business Competitiveness Index	**Rank/110**

Sophistication of Company Operations and Strategy

8.12	Willingness to delegate authority	39
8.14	Reliance on professional management	46
8.02	Value chain presence	47

Quality of the National Business Environment

3.19	Internet users, 2003	20
6.13	Centralization of economic policymaking	23
5.02	Railroad infrastructure development	30

Business Competitiveness Index	
Business Competitiveness Index	**Rank/110**

Sophistication of Company Operations and Strategy

8.08	Control of international distribution	71
3.03	Prevalence of foreign technology licensing	67
8.10	Breadth of international markets	59

Quality of the National Business Environment

3.09	Availability of scientists and engineers	94
3.08	Government procurement of advanced technology products	89
8.21	Protection of minority shareholders' interests	83

Other Indicators	
Other Indicators	**Rank/117**

8.20	Pay and productivity	22
8.18	Flexibility of wage determination	24
6.07	Burden of government regulation	33
6.11	Extent and effect of taxation	35
6.15	Business costs of crime and violence	37
6.12	Efficiency of the tax system	37
4.09	Private sector employment of women	38
6.09	Extent of bureaucratic red tape	38
7.07	Presence of demanding regulatory standards	40
2.02	Business costs of terrorism	40
9.02	Clarity and stability of regulations	40
3.16	Extent of business Internet use	40
6.17	Informal sector	42

Other Indicators	
Other Indicators	**Rank/117**

6.27	Pervasiveness of money laundering through banks	104
9.07	Importance of environment in business planning	99
9.05	Effects of privatization on competition and the environment	91
7.05	Local supplier quantity	80
6.18	Government effectiveness in reducing poverty and inequality	78
2.08	Local equity market access	76
8.24	Importance of corporate social responsibility	74
3.05	Quality of scientific research institutions	73
6.22	Irregular payments in public contracts	73
6.23	Irregular payments in judicial decisions	72
2.11	Tax burden	69

Note: The Business Competitiveness Index applies different criteria for selecting a country's competitive advantages and disadvantages. Please refer to the section "How Country Profiles Work" for further details.

Lithuania

Competitiveness Rankings

Growth Competitiveness Index Rank	43

Macroeconomic Environment Index Rank **39**
    Macroeconomic Stability Subindex Rank 29
    Government Waste Rank 46
    Country Credit Rating Rank...................................46

Public Institutions Index Rank...**44**
    Contracts and Law Subindex Rank 58
    Corruption Subindex Rank....................................36

Technology Index Rank **42**
    Innovation Subindex Rank 26
    ICT Subindex Rank 41
    Technology Transfer Subindex Rank
        (out of 92 non-core innovators).......................41

Business Competitiveness Index Rank	41

**Sophistication of Company Operations
and Strategy Rank** **41**
**Quality of the National Business
Environment Rank** **41**

The Most Problematic Factors for Doing Business

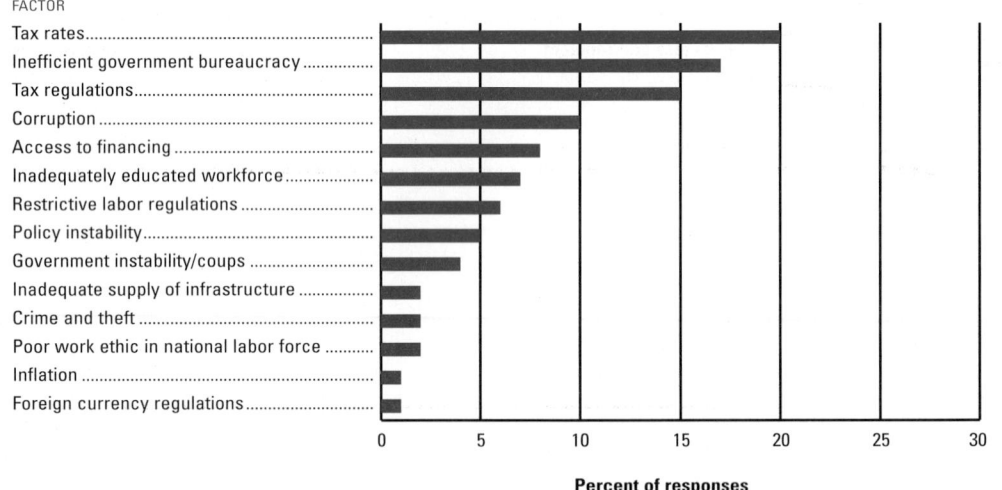

FACTOR

Note: From a list of 14 factors, respondents were asked to select the five most problematic for doing business in their country and to rank them between 1 (most problematic) and 5. The bars in the figure show the responses weighted according to their rankings.

Source: World Economic Forum, Executive Opinion Survey (2005)

National competitiveness balance sheet

NOTABLE COMPETITIVE ADVANTAGES	
Growth Competitiveness Index	**Rank/117**

Macroeconomic Environment
2.07	Access to credit	5
2.20	Government debt, 2004	14
2.16	Inflation, 2004	15
2.01	Recession expectations	39
2.17	Interest rate spread, 2004	42

Public Institutions
6.20	Irregular payments in public utilities	32
6.21	Irregular payments in tax collection	35
6.19	Irregular payments in exports and imports	41

Technology
4.17	Gross tertiary enrollment	11
3.20	Internet hosts, 2003	35
3.11	Internet access in schools	36
3.18	Cellular telephones, 2003	37
3.02	Firm-level technology absorption	41
3.15	Laws relating to ICT	41

NOTABLE COMPETITIVE DISADVANTAGES	
Growth Competitiveness Index	**Rank/117**

Macroeconomic Environment
2.15	Real effective exchange rate, 2004	95
2.14	National savings rate, 2004	87
2.13	Government surplus/deficit, 2004	53
6.06	Wastefulness of government spending	46
2.21	Country credit rating, 2004	46

Public Institutions
6.01	Judicial independence	78
6.16	Organized crime	63
6.08	Favoritism in decisions of government officials	57
6.03	Property rights	45

Technology
3.04	FDI and technology transfer	73
3.13	Government prioritization of ICT	68
3.01	Technological readiness	66
3.14	Government success in ICT promotion	65
3.03	Prevalence of foreign technology licensing	61
3.17	Utility patents, 2004	59
5.08	Telephone lines, 2003	52
3.12	Quality of competition in the ISP sector	51
3.07	University/industry research collaboration	47
3.21	Personal computers, 2003	47
3.06	Company spending on research and development	46
3.19	Internet users, 2003	46

Business Competitiveness Index	**Rank/110**

Sophistication of Company Operations and Strategy
8.02	Value chain presence	27
8.07	Degree of customer orientation	28
8.10	Breadth of international markets	38

Quality of the National Business Environment
2.05	Ease of access to loans	10
4.03	Quality of math and science education	18
2.06	Venture capital availability	27

Business Competitiveness Index	**Rank/110**

Sophistication of Company Operations and Strategy
8.13	Extent of incentive compensation	72
3.03	Prevalence of foreign technology licensing	60
8.11	Extent of staff training	57

Quality of the National Business Environment
8.21	Protection of minority shareholders' interests	80
6.14	Reliability of police services	79
6.01	Judicial independence	75

Other Indicators	**Rank/117**
6.17	Informal sector	20
8.18	Flexibility of wage determination	21
8.20	Pay and productivity	26
9.06	Prioritization of energy efficiency	28
9.09	Prevalence of corporate environmental reporting	28
9.03	Extent of government mandated environmental reporting	30
2.02	Business costs of terrorism	31
9.08	Protection of ecosystems by business	34
7.09	Local availability of specialized research and training services	35
7.05	Local supplier quantity	35
3.09	Availability of scientists and engineers	35

Other Indicators	**Rank/117**
6.12	Efficiency of the tax system	96
2.12	Agricultural policy costs	93
9.07	Importance of environment in business planning	87
8.17	Hiring and firing practices	87
6.18	Government effectiveness in reducing poverty and inequality	86
6.24	Diversion of public funds	79
4.08	Brain drain	77
6.02	Efficiency of legal framework	75
9.05	Effects of privatization on competition and the environment	74
7.04	Buyer sophistication	73
6.26	Public trust of politicians	72
6.04	Intellectual property protection	69

Note: The Business Competitiveness Index applies different criteria for selecting a country's competitive advantages and disadvantages. Please refer to the section "How Country Profiles Work" for further details.

Luxembourg

Competitiveness Rankings

Growth Competitiveness Index Rank	**25**

Macroeconomic Environment Index Rank 9
    Macroeconomic Stability Subindex Rank 26
    Government Waste Rank 18
    Country Credit Rating Rank 3

Public Institutions Index Rank..**7**
    Contracts and Law Subindex Rank 9
    Corruption Subindex Rank 7

Technology Index Rank **29**
    Innovation Subindex Rank 37
    ICT Subindex Rank 13

Business Competitiveness Index Rank	n/a

**Sophistication of Company Operations
   and Strategy Rank** ....n/a
**Quality of the National Business
   Environment Rank**...n/a

The Most Problematic Factors for Doing Business

FACTOR

Inadequately educated workforce...................
Restrictive labor regulations ....
Inefficient government bureaucracy ....
Inadequate supply of infrastructure ....
Access to financing ....
Tax rates...
Inflation ....
Tax regulations...
Poor work ethic in national labor force ....
Policy instability...
Government instability/coups ....
Crime and theft ....
Foreign currency regulations...........................
Corruption ....

Percent of responses

Note: From a list of 14 factors, respondents were asked to select the five most problematic for doing business in their country and to rank them between 1 (most problematic) and 5. The bars in the figure show the responses weighted according to their rankings.

Source: World Economic Forum, Executive Opinion Survey (2005)

National competitiveness balance sheet

NOTABLE COMPETITIVE ADVANTAGES	
Growth Competitiveness Index	**Rank/117**

Macroeconomic Environment
2.21	Country credit rating, 2004	3
2.20	Government debt, 2004	4
2.17	Interest rate spread, 2004	4
6.06	Wastefulness of government spending	18

Public Institutions
6.20	Irregular payments in public utilities	3
6.08	Favoritism in decisions of government officials	7
6.16	Organized crime	9
6.01	Judicial independence	10
6.21	Irregular payments in tax collection	11
6.19	Irregular payments in exports and imports	11
6.03	Property rights	20

Technology
3.18	Cellular telephones, 2003	1
5.08	Telephone lines, 2003	1
3.21	Personal computers, 2003	5
3.17	Utility patents, 2004	12
3.11	Internet access in schools	17
3.20	Internet hosts, 2003	19
3.06	Company spending on research and development	20

Other Indicators	**Rank/117**
2.09	Prevalence of trade barriers	1
8.22	Foreign ownership restrictions	1
4.05	Medium term business impact of tuberculosis	1
7.04	Buyer sophistication	2
2.04	Soundness of banks	4
2.10	Impact of rules on FDI	4
6.26	Public trust of politicians	4
4.07	Ease of hiring foreign labor	6
2.03	Financial market sophistication	7
6.17	Informal sector	8
9.01	Stringency of environmental regulations	8
8.01	Nature of competitive advantage	8
6.18	Government effectiveness in reducing poverty and inequality	8
8.02	Value chain presence	9
8.12	Willingness to delegate authority	9

NOTABLE COMPETITIVE DISADVANTAGES	
Growth Competitiveness Index	**Rank/117**

Macroeconomic Environment
2.15	Real effective exchange rate, 2004	79
2.07	Access to credit	67
2.01	Recession expectations	64
2.13	Government surplus/deficit, 2004	43
2.16	Inflation, 2004	31
2.14	National savings rate, 2004	30

Technology
4.17	Gross tertiary enrollment	89
3.07	University/industry research collaboration	73
3.12	Quality of competition in the ISP sector	60
3.01	Technological readiness	47
3.13	Government prioritization of ICT	45
3.02	Firm-level technology absorption	42
3.14	Government success in ICT promotion	36
3.15	Laws relating to ICT	29
3.19	Internet users, 2003	25

Other Indicators	**Rank/117**
8.15	Quality of management schools	109
8.18	Flexibility of wage determination	91
8.21	Protection of minority shareholders' interests	89
8.17	Hiring and firing practices	86
3.05	Quality of scientific research institutions	84
6.13	Centralization of economic policymaking	83
3.09	Availability of scientists and engineers	78
2.11	Tax burden	75
7.08	Local availability of process machinery	66
7.01	Intensity of local competition	58
8.20	Pay and productivity	54
2.08	Local equity market access	50
9.05	Effects of privatization on competition and the environment	49
7.09	Local availability of specialized research and training services	49
9.04	Effects of compliance on business	44

359

Note: This country is not included in the coverage of the Business Competitiveness Index 2005–2006.

Macedonia, FYR

Competitiveness Rankings

Growth Competitiveness Index Rank	85

Macroeconomic Environment Index Rank **75**
   Macroeconomic Stability Subindex Rank 46
   Government Waste Rank 84
   Country Credit Rating Rank 81

Public Institutions Index Rank **96**
   Contracts and Law Subindex Rank 111
   Corruption Subindex Rank....................................82

Technology Index Rank **91**
   Innovation Subindex Rank 77
   ICT Subindex Rank 70
   Technology Transfer Subindex Rank
     (out of 92 non-core innovators).......................82

Business Competitiveness Index Rank	83

**Sophistication of Company Operations
  and Strategy Rank** **88**

**Quality of the National Business
  Environment Rank** **83**

The Most Problematic Factors for Doing Business

FACTOR

Percent of responses

Note: From a list of 14 factors, respondents were asked to select the five most problematic for doing business in their country and to rank them between 1 (most problematic) and 5. The bars in the figure show the responses weighted according to their rankings.

Source: World Economic Forum, Executive Opinion Survey (2005)

National competitiveness balance sheet

NOTABLE COMPETITIVE ADVANTAGES		
Growth Competitiveness Index		**Rank/117**
	Macroeconomic Environment	
2.16	Inflation, 2004	5
2.20	Government debt, 2004	20
2.13	Government surplus/deficit, 2004	28
	Technology	
5.08	Telephone lines, 2003	47

NOTABLE COMPETITIVE DISADVANTAGES		
Growth Competitiveness Index		**Rank/117**
	Macroeconomic Environment	
2.01	Recession expectations	113
2.07	Access to credit	97
2.14	National savings rate, 2004	90
6.06	Wastefulness of government spending	84
2.21	Country credit rating, 2004	81
2.17	Interest rate spread, 2004	65
2.15	Real effective exchange rate, 2004	57
	Public Institutions	
6.16	Organized crime	114
6.01	Judicial independence	104
6.03	Property rights	102
6.19	Irregular payments in exports and imports	88
6.21	Irregular payments in tax collection	88
6.08	Favoritism in decisions of government officials	76
6.20	Irregular payments in public utilities	63
	Technology	
3.02	Firm-level technology absorption	110
3.14	Government success in ICT promotion	108
3.01	Technological readiness	107
3.04	FDI and technology transfer	106
3.03	Prevalence of foreign technology licensing	105
3.12	Quality of competition in the ISP sector	105
3.13	Government prioritization of ICT	105
3.11	Internet access in schools	90
3.06	Company spending on research and development	85
3.15	Laws relating to ICT	81
3.17	Utility patents, 2004	81
3.07	University/industry research collaboration	77
3.19	Internet users, 2003	71
4.17	Gross tertiary enrollment	65
3.20	Internet hosts, 2003	64
3.21	Personal computers, 2003	61
3.18	Cellular telephones, 2003	51

361

Business Competitiveness Index		**Rank/110**
	Sophistication of Company Operations and Strategy	
8.03	Capacity for innovation	55
8.08	Control of international distribution	65
8.12	Willingness to delegate authority	66
	Quality of the National Business Environment	
2.06	Venture capital availability	41
3.09	Availability of scientists and engineers	44
4.01	Quality of the educational system	46

Other Indicators		**Rank/117**
8.18	Flexibility of wage determination	40

Business Competitiveness Index		**Rank/110**
	Sophistication of Company Operations and Strategy	
8.14	Reliance on professional management	103
3.03	Prevalence of foreign technology licensing	100
8.07	Degree of customer orientation	96
	Quality of the National Business Environment	
9.01	Stringency of environmental regulations	102
7.01	Intensity of local competition	101
5.03	Port infrastructure quality	100

Other Indicators		**Rank/117**
2.02	Business costs of terrorism	111
4.08	Brain drain	109
9.02	Clarity and stability of regulations	108
8.04	Ethical behavior of firms	107
9.06	Prioritization of energy efficiency	105
6.02	Efficiency of legal framework	105
6.18	Government effectiveness in reducing poverty and inequality	105
8.22	Foreign ownership restrictions	105
8.19	Cooperation in labor-employer relations	102
2.04	Soundness of banks	102
9.04	Effects of compliance on business	101

Note: The Business Competitiveness Index applies different criteria for selecting a country's competitive advantages and disadvantages. Please refer to the section "How Country Profiles Work" for further details.

Madagascar

Competitiveness Rankings

Growth Competitiveness Index Rank	**107**

Macroeconomic Environment Index Rank **109**
    Macroeconomic Stability Subindex Rank 112
    Government Waste Rank 47
    Country Credit Rating Rank 112

Public Institutions Index Rank **99**
    Contracts and Law Subindex Rank 88
    Corruption Subindex Rank 100

Technology Index Rank **106**
    Innovation Subindex Rank 108
    ICT Subindex Rank 102
    Technology Transfer Subindex Rank
      (out of 92 non-core innovators)........................77

Business Competitiveness Index Rank	**94**

**Sophistication of Company Operations
  and Strategy Rank** **100**
**Quality of the National Business
  Environment Rank** **93**

The Most Problematic Factors for Doing Business

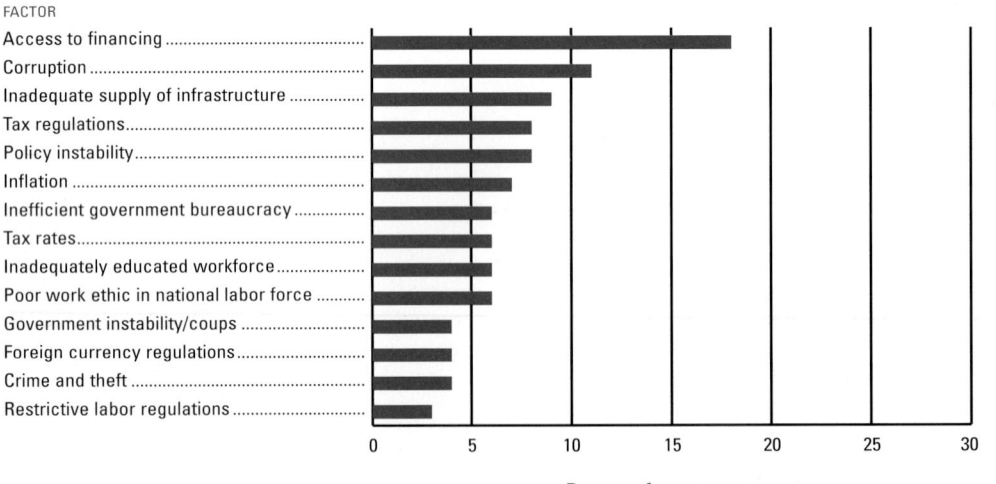

Note: From a list of 14 factors, respondents were asked to select the five most problematic for doing business in their country and to rank them between 1 (most problematic) and 5. The bars in the figure show the responses weighted according to their rankings.

Source: World Economic Forum, Executive Opinion Survey (2005)

National competitiveness balance sheet

NOTABLE COMPETITIVE ADVANTAGES	
Growth Competitiveness Index	**Rank/117**

Macroeconomic Environment

2.15	Real effective exchange rate, 2004	12
6.06	Wastefulness of government spending	47

Technology

3.14	Government success in ICT promotion	30
3.13	Government prioritization of ICT	48

NOTABLE COMPETITIVE DISADVANTAGES	
Growth Competitiveness Index	**Rank/117**

Macroeconomic Environment

2.07	Access to credit	112
2.21	Country credit rating, 2004	112
2.16	Inflation, 2004	112
2.14	National savings rate, 2004	110
2.20	Government debt, 2004	99
2.17	Interest rate spread, 2004	97
2.01	Recession expectations	81
2.13	Government surplus/deficit, 2004	81

Public Institutions

6.21	Irregular payments in tax collection	105
6.20	Irregular payments in public utilities	99
6.19	Irregular payments in exports and imports	95
6.16	Organized crime	93
6.03	Property rights	84
6.08	Favoritism in decisions of government officials	78
6.01	Judicial independence	77

Technology

5.08	Telephone lines, 2003	113
4.17	Gross tertiary enrollment	112
3.18	Cellular telephones, 2003	112
3.04	FDI and technology transfer	108
3.19	Internet users, 2003	107
3.20	Internet hosts, 2003	104
3.21	Personal computers, 2003	104
3.11	Internet access in schools	103
3.15	Laws relating to ICT	100
3.01	Technological readiness	97
3.07	University/industry research collaboration	95
3.03	Prevalence of foreign technology licensing	93
3.12	Quality of competition in the ISP sector	84
3.06	Company spending on research and development	84
3.17	Utility patents, 2004	81
3.02	Firm-level technology absorption	58

Business Competitiveness Index	Rank/110

Sophistication of Company Operations and Strategy

8.06	Extent of marketing	84
8.14	Reliance on professional management	88

Quality of the National Business Environment

6.13	Centralization of economic policymaking	52
6.09	Extent of bureaucratic red tape	54
3.08	Government procurement of advanced technology products	55

Other Indicators	Rank/117

4.09	Private sector employment of women	43
2.11	Tax burden	48
8.18	Flexibility of wage determination	49

Business Competitiveness Index	Rank/110

Sophistication of Company Operations and Strategy

8.05	Production process sophistication	104
8.08	Control of international distribution	103
8.13	Extent of incentive compensation	101

Quality of the National Business Environment

7.04	Buyer sophistication	109
3.18	Cellular telephones, 2003	106
7.07	Presence of demanding regulatory standards	104

Other Indicators	Rank/117

8.23	Strength of auditing and accounting standards	113
3.10	Availability of mobile or cellular telephones	110
6.17	Informal sector	109
2.08	Local equity market access	107
5.07	Telephone/fax infrastructure quality	107
6.22	Irregular payments in public contracts	106
7.03	Extent of market dominance	105
8.07	Degree of customer orientation	104
8.01	Nature of competitive advantage	104
6.23	Irregular payments in judicial decisions	104
8.12	Willingness to delegate authority	104

363

Note: The Business Competitiveness Index applies different criteria for selecting a country's competitive advantages and disadvantages. Please refer to the section "How Country Profiles Work" for further details.

Malawi

Competitiveness Rankings

Growth Competitiveness Index Rank	**105**

Macroeconomic Environment Index Rank **116**
    Macroeconomic Stability Subindex Rank 117
    Government Waste Rank 92
    Country Credit Rating Rank 110

Public Institutions Index Rank..**68**
    Contracts and Law Subindex Rank 56
    Corruption Subindex Rank....................................83

Technology Index Rank **107**
    Innovation Subindex Rank 115
    ICT Subindex Rank 114
    Technology Transfer Subindex Rank
        (out of 92 non-core innovators).........................71

Business Competitiveness Index Rank	**88**

**Sophistication of Company Operations
  and Strategy Rank** **85**
**Quality of the National Business
  Environment Rank** **90**

364

The Most Problematic Factors for Doing Business

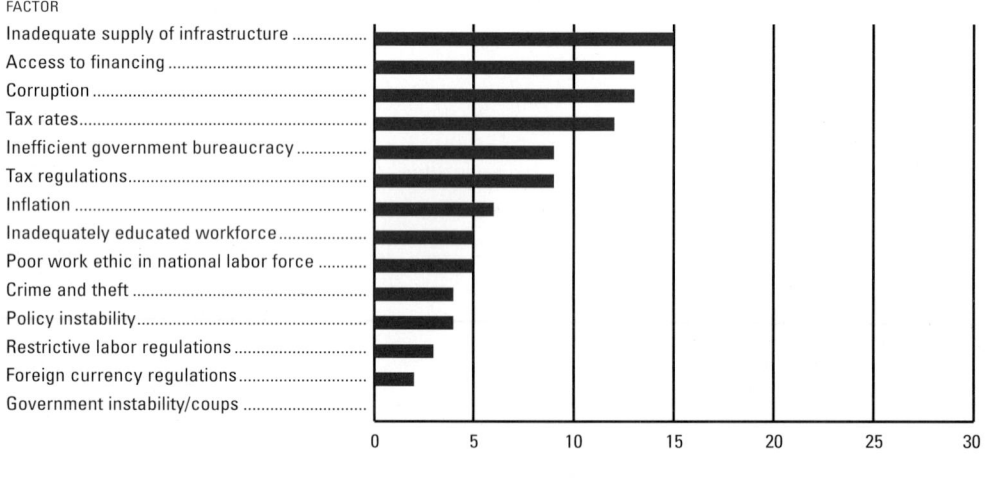

Note: From a list of 14 factors, respondents were asked to select the five most problematic for doing business in their country and to rank them between 1 (most problematic) and 5. The bars in the figure show the responses weighted according to their rankings.

Source: World Economic Forum, Executive Opinion Survey (2005)

National competitiveness balance sheet

NOTABLE COMPETITIVE ADVANTAGES	
Growth Competitiveness Index	**Rank/117**

Macroeconomic Environment

2.15	Real effective exchange rate, 2004	7

Public Institutions

6.01	Judicial independence	43

Business Competitiveness Index	Rank/110

Sophistication of Company Operations and Strategy

8.14	Reliance on professional management	37
8.11	Extent of staff training	69

Quality of the National Business Environment

8.16	Efficacy of corporate boards	27
6.01	Judicial independence	42
8.22	Foreign ownership restrictions	44

Other Indicators	Rank/117

6.12	Efficiency of the tax system	29
2.02	Business costs of terrorism	30
2.12	Agricultural policy costs	36
2.04	Soundness of banks	36
6.07	Burden of government regulation	42
8.21	Protection of minority shareholders' interests	46

NOTABLE COMPETITIVE DISADVANTAGES	
Growth Competitiveness Index	**Rank/117**

Macroeconomic Environment

2.20	Government debt, 2004	117
2.14	National savings rate, 2004	115
2.17	Interest rate spread, 2004	112
2.21	Country credit rating, 2004	110
2.16	Inflation, 2004	106
2.13	Government surplus/deficit, 2004	105
2.01	Recession expectations	101
6.06	Wastefulness of government spending	92
2.07	Access to credit	71

Public Institutions

6.20	Irregular payments in public utilities	98
6.08	Favoritism in decisions of government officials	81
6.21	Irregular payments in tax collection	79
6.03	Property rights	70
6.19	Irregular payments in exports and imports	63
6.16	Organized crime	57

Technology

4.17	Gross tertiary enrollment	117
3.20	Internet hosts, 2003	114
3.21	Personal computers, 2003	114
3.18	Cellular telephones, 2003	113
3.19	Internet users, 2003	109
3.02	Firm-level technology absorption	108
3.11	Internet access in schools	107
5.08	Telephone lines, 2003	105
3.01	Technological readiness	105
3.13	Government prioritization of ICT	103
3.04	FDI and technology transfer	97
3.07	University/industry research collaboration	97
3.12	Quality of competition in the ISP sector	95
3.14	Government success in ICT promotion	94
3.15	Laws relating to ICT	93
3.03	Prevalence of foreign technology licensing	85
3.17	Utility patents, 2004	81
3.06	Company spending on research and development	66

Business Competitiveness Index	Rank/110

Sophistication of Company Operations and Strategy

8.05	Production process sophistication	105
8.09	Extent of regional sales	100
8.06	Extent of marketing	96

Quality of the National Business Environment

4.02	Quality of public schools	109
7.08	Local availability of process machinery	108
2.06	Venture capital availability	107

Other Indicators	Rank/117

2.11	Tax burden	117
4.06	Medium term business impact of HIV/AIDS	116
4.05	Medium term business impact of tuberculosis	115
6.11	Extent and effect of taxation	113
4.09	Private sector employment of women	112
7.03	Extent of market dominance	110
5.05	Quality of electricity supply	110
5.07	Telephone/fax infrastructure quality	109
4.07	Ease of hiring foreign labor	107
7.09	Local availability of specialized research and training services	105
3.16	Extent of business Internet use	104
3.09	Availability of scientists and engineers	104

365

Note: The Business Competitiveness Index applies different criteria for selecting a country's competitive advantages and disadvantages. Please refer to the section "How Country Profiles Work" for further details.

Malaysia

Competitiveness Rankings

Growth Competitiveness Index Rank	24

Macroeconomic Environment Index Rank **19**
    Macroeconomic Stability Subindex Rank 19
    Government Waste Rank 2
    Country Credit Rating Rank 35

Public Institutions Index Rank..**29**
    Contracts and Law Subindex Rank 17
    Corruption Subindex Rank....................................43

Technology Index Rank **25**
    Innovation Subindex Rank 40
    ICT Subindex Rank 33
    Technology Transfer Subindex Rank
        (out of 92 non-core innovators).........................1

Business Competitiveness Index Rank	23

**Sophistication of Company Operations
   and Strategy Rank** **24**
**Quality of the National Business
   Environment Rank** **23**

The Most Problematic Factors for Doing Business

FACTOR

Access to financing
Foreign currency regulations
Inefficient government bureaucracy
Tax regulations
Poor work ethic in national labor force
Corruption
Restrictive labor regulations
Inadequately educated workforce
Tax rates
Policy instability
Inflation
Crime and theft
Inadequate supply of infrastructure
Government instability/coups

Percent of responses

Note: From a list of 14 factors, respondents were asked to select the five most problematic for doing business in their country and to rank them between 1 (most problematic) and 5. The bars in the figure show the responses weighted according to their rankings.

Source: World Economic Forum, Executive Opinion Survey (2005)

National competitiveness balance sheet

NOTABLE COMPETITIVE ADVANTAGES	
Growth Competitiveness Index	**Rank/117**

Macroeconomic Environment

6.06	Wastefulness of government spending	2
2.14	National savings rate, 2004	7
2.01	Recession expectations	9
2.07	Access to credit	18
2.16	Inflation, 2004	18
2.17	Interest rate spread, 2004	19

Public Institutions

6.08	Favoritism in decisions of government officials	11
6.01	Judicial independence	20
6.03	Property rights	23

Technology

3.14	Government success in ICT promotion	2
3.13	Government prioritization of ICT	2
3.04	FDI and technology transfer	6
3.03	Prevalence of foreign technology licensing	9
3.07	University/industry research collaboration	12
3.15	Laws relating to ICT	14
3.01	Technological readiness	15
3.02	Firm-level technology absorption	16
3.06	Company spending on research and development	18

Business Competitiveness Index	**Rank/110**

Sophistication of Company Operations and Strategy

3.03	Prevalence of foreign technology licensing	9
3.06	Company spending on research and development	18
8.10	Breadth of international markets	19

Quality of the National Business Environment

3.08	Government procurement of advanced technology products	3
8.19	Cooperation in labor-employer relations	8
2.08	Local equity market access	9

Other Indicators	**Rank/117**

2.12	Agricultural policy costs	2
6.07	Burden of government regulation	3
4.09	Private sector employment of women	3
6.10	Effectiveness of law-making bodies	5
6.18	Government effectiveness in reducing poverty and inequality	5
8.20	Pay and productivity	5
6.12	Efficiency of the tax system	8
6.11	Extent and effect of taxation	9
6.26	Public trust of politicians	10
9.04	Effects of compliance on business	13
8.16	Efficacy of corporate boards	14
2.06	Venture capital availability	14

NOTABLE COMPETITIVE DISADVANTAGES	
Growth Competitiveness Index	**Rank/117**

Macroeconomic Environment

2.13	Government surplus/deficit, 2004	96
2.20	Government debt, 2004	49
2.21	Country credit rating, 2004	35
2.15	Real effective exchange rate, 2004	32

Public Institutions

6.20	Irregular payments in public utilities	47
6.19	Irregular payments in exports and imports	45
6.21	Irregular payments in tax collection	36
6.16	Organized crime	31

Technology

4.17	Gross tertiary enrollment	63
5.08	Telephone lines, 2003	61
3.20	Internet hosts, 2003	51
3.18	Cellular telephones, 2003	46
3.21	Personal computers, 2003	36
3.17	Utility patents, 2004	29
3.19	Internet users, 2003	28
3.11	Internet access in schools	25
3.12	Quality of competition in the ISP sector	25

Business Competitiveness Index	**Rank/110**

Sophistication of Company Operations and Strategy

8.01	Nature of competitive advantage	54
8.06	Extent of marketing	33
8.02	Value chain presence	28

Quality of the National Business Environment

6.09	Extent of bureaucratic red tape	101
6.13	Centralization of economic policymaking	80
3.18	Cellular telephones, 2003	45

Other Indicators	**Rank/117**

6.05	Freedom of the press	83
4.05	Medium term business impact of tuberculosis	54
3.10	Availability of mobile or cellular telephones	54
4.06	Medium term business impact of HIV/AIDS	51
2.04	Soundness of banks	48
5.07	Telephone/fax infrastructure quality	45
8.17	Hiring and firing practices	43
9.05	Effects of privatization on competition and the environment	39
2.09	Prevalence of trade barriers	38
6.17	Informal sector	37
6.14	Reliability of police services	37
8.22	Foreign ownership restrictions	37

367

Note: The Business Competitiveness Index applies different criteria for selecting a country's competitive advantages and disadvantages. Please refer to the section "How Country Profiles Work" for further details.

Mali

Competitiveness Rankings

Growth Competitiveness Index Rank	**90**

Macroeconomic Environment Index Rank **97**
    Macroeconomic Stability Subindex Rank 104
    Government Waste Rank 56
    Country Credit Rating Rank 102

Public Institutions Index Rank **72**
    Contracts and Law Subindex Rank 51
    Corruption Subindex Rank....................................90

Technology Index Rank **103**
    Innovation Subindex Rank 109
    ICT Subindex Rank 88
    Technology Transfer Subindex Rank
    (out of 92 non-core innovators).........................80

Business Competitiveness Index Rank	**n/a**

**Sophistication of Company Operations
  and Strategy Rank** ....**n/a**

**Quality of the National Business
  Environment Rank**..**n/a**

The Most Problematic Factors for Doing Business

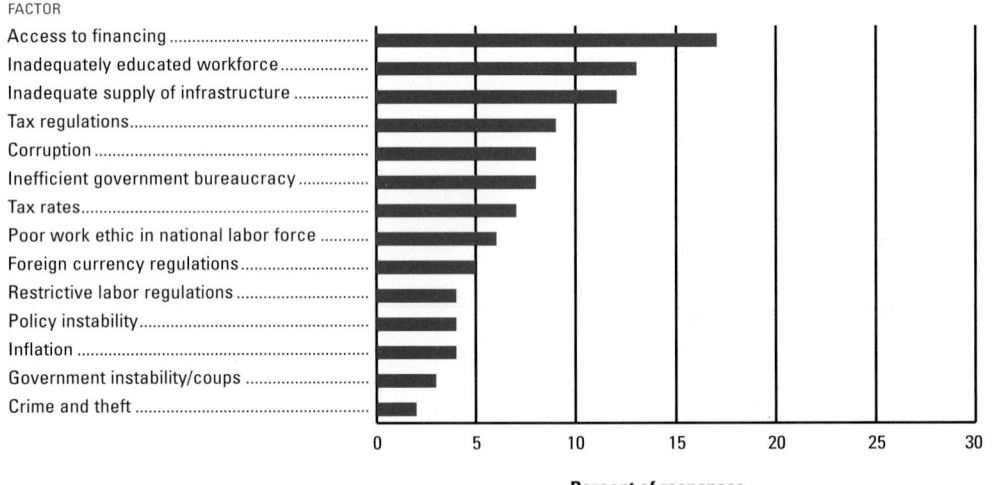

FACTOR

Access to financing
Inadequately educated workforce
Inadequate supply of infrastructure
Tax regulations
Corruption
Inefficient government bureaucracy
Tax rates
Poor work ethic in national labor force
Foreign currency regulations
Restrictive labor regulations
Policy instability
Inflation
Government instability/coups
Crime and theft

Percent of responses

Note: From a list of 14 factors, respondents were asked to select the five most problematic for doing business in their country and to rank them between 1 (most problematic) and 5. The bars in the figure show the responses weighted according to their rankings.

Source: World Economic Forum, Executive Opinion Survey (2005)

National competitiveness balance sheet

NOTABLE COMPETITIVE ADVANTAGES	
Growth Competitiveness Index	**Rank/117**

Macroeconomic Environment

2.16	Inflation, 2004	2

Public Institutions

6.08	Favoritism in decisions of government officials	43
6.16	Organized crime	49

Technology

3.13	Government prioritization of ICT	11
3.14	Government success in ICT promotion	25
3.12	Quality of competition in the ISP sector	46

NOTABLE COMPETITIVE DISADVANTAGES	
Growth Competitiveness Index	**Rank/117**

Macroeconomic Environment

2.07	Access to credit	113
2.21	Country credit rating, 2004	102
2.14	National savings rate, 2004	101
2.17	Interest rate spread, 2004	93
2.13	Government surplus/deficit, 2004	89
2.01	Recession expectations	85
2.20	Government debt, 2004	79
2.15	Real effective exchange rate, 2004	65
6.06	Wastefulness of government spending	56

Public Institutions

6.21	Irregular payments in tax collection	101
6.20	Irregular payments in public utilities	92
6.03	Property rights	74
6.19	Irregular payments in exports and imports	70
6.01	Judicial independence	52

Technology

4.17	Gross tertiary enrollment	110
3.18	Cellular telephones, 2003	110
3.21	Personal computers, 2003	110
3.19	Internet users, 2003	110
3.11	Internet access in schools	110
3.04	FDI and technology transfer	110
5.08	Telephone lines, 2003	109
3.20	Internet hosts, 2003	109
3.03	Prevalence of foreign technology licensing	97
3.01	Technological readiness	93
3.07	University/industry research collaboration	91
3.06	Company spending on research and development	89
3.02	Firm-level technology absorption	85
3.15	Laws relating to ICT	85
3.17	Utility patents, 2004	81

Other Indicators		Rank/117
9.04	Effects of compliance on business	27
3.08	Government procurement of advanced technology products	31
2.11	Tax burden	33
9.07	Importance of environment in business planning	37
9.06	Prioritization of energy efficiency	39
6.07	Burden of government regulation	40
6.10	Effectiveness of law-making bodies	45
9.10	Grass-roots involvement in development projects	45
8.21	Protection of minority shareholders' interests	47
6.13	Centralization of economic policymaking	47
6.27	Pervasiveness of money laundering through banks	48

Other Indicators		Rank/117
8.11	Extent of staff training	115
8.20	Pay and productivity	115
8.13	Extent of incentive compensation	114
8.12	Willingness to delegate authority	114
8.06	Extent of marketing	113
8.05	Production process sophistication	113
7.04	Buyer sophistication	111
2.05	Ease of access to loans	109
4.09	Private sector employment of women	109
2.06	Venture capital availability	108
6.17	Informal sector	107
8.09	Extent of regional sales	105
9.02	Clarity and stability of regulations	105
6.23	Irregular payments in judicial decisions	102
8.07	Degree of customer orientation	102

369

Note: This country is not included in the coverage of the Business Competitiveness Index 2005–2006.

Malta

Competitiveness Rankings

Growth Competitiveness Index Rank	**35**

Macroeconomic Environment Index Rank **54**
    Macroeconomic Stability Subindex Rank 80
    Government Waste Rank 79
    Country Credit Rating Rank..............................30
Public Institutions Index Rank...**32**
    Contracts and Law Subindex Rank 29
    Corruption Subindex Rank................................41
Technology Index Rank **23**
    Innovation Subindex Rank 58
    ICT Subindex Rank 25
    Technology Transfer Subindex Rank
        (out of 92 non-core innovators)........................26

Business Competitiveness Index Rank	**46**

**Sophistication of Company Operations
  and Strategy Rank** **61**
**Quality of the National Business
  Environment Rank** **44**

The Most Problematic Factors for Doing Business

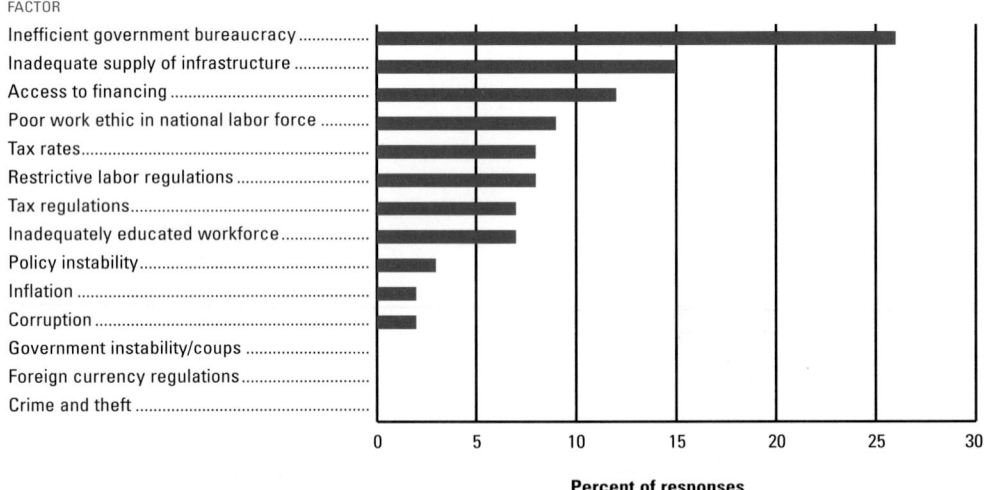

Note: From a list of 14 factors, respondents were asked to select the five most problematic for doing business in their country and to rank them between 1 (most problematic) and 5. The bars in the figure show the responses weighted according to their rankings.

Source: World Economic Forum, Executive Opinion Survey (2005)

National competitiveness balance sheet

NOTABLE COMPETITIVE ADVANTAGES	
Growth Competitiveness Index	**Rank/117**

Macroeconomic Environment

2.17	Interest rate spread, 2004	8
2.21	Country credit rating, 2004	30

Public Institutions

6.16	Organized crime	11
6.01	Judicial independence	30
6.03	Property rights	30

Technology

3.14	Government success in ICT promotion	10
3.13	Government prioritization of ICT	14
3.19	Internet users, 2003	15
5.08	Telephone lines, 2003	18
3.04	FDI and technology transfer	19
3.11	Internet access in schools	23
3.15	Laws relating to ICT	25
3.21	Personal computers, 2003	27
3.18	Cellular telephones, 2003	28
3.12	Quality of competition in the ISP sector	31
3.17	Utility patents, 2004	31
3.01	Technological readiness	34

Business Competitiveness Index	**Rank/110**

Sophistication of Company Operations and Strategy

8.01	Nature of competitive advantage	32
8.02	Value chain presence	35
8.11	Extent of staff training	42

Quality of the National Business Environment

6.09	Extent of bureaucratic red tape	14
3.19	Internet users, 2003	15
2.09	Prevalence of trade barriers	16

Other Indicators	**Rank/117**

2.02	Business costs of terrorism	2
6.15	Business costs of crime and violence	12
2.04	Soundness of banks	16
6.12	Efficiency of the tax system	18
6.18	Government effectiveness in reducing poverty and inequality	19
8.23	Strength of auditing and accounting standards	21
4.06	Medium term business impact of HIV/AIDS	22
6.10	Effectiveness of law-making bodies	23
6.27	Pervasiveness of money laundering through banks	25
2.10	Impact of rules on FDI	25
6.14	Reliability of police services	25
6.25	Business costs of corruption	26
8.22	Foreign ownership restrictions	27

NOTABLE COMPETITIVE DISADVANTAGES	
Growth Competitiveness Index	**Rank/117**

Macroeconomic Environment

2.01	Recession expectations	104
2.13	Government surplus/deficit, 2004	99
2.14	National savings rate, 2004	97
2.20	Government debt, 2004	87
6.06	Wastefulness of government spending	79
2.07	Access to credit	78
2.15	Real effective exchange rate, 2004	78
2.16	Inflation, 2004	40

Public Institutions

6.08	Favoritism in decisions of government officials	61
6.21	Irregular payments in tax collection	44
6.20	Irregular payments in public utilities	40
6.19	Irregular payments in exports and imports	36

Technology

3.07	University/industry research collaboration	102
3.06	Company spending on research and development	96
3.03	Prevalence of foreign technology licensing	62
4.17	Gross tertiary enrollment	59
3.02	Firm-level technology absorption	53
3.20	Internet hosts, 2003	37

Business Competitiveness Index	**Rank/110**

Sophistication of Company Operations and Strategy

3.06	Company spending on research and development	92
8.08	Control of international distribution	87
8.13	Extent of incentive compensation	79

Quality of the National Business Environment

7.08	Local availability of process machinery	107
3.05	Quality of scientific research institutions	101
3.07	University/industry research collaboration	98

Other Indicators	**Rank/117**

9.06	Prioritization of energy efficiency	107
8.19	Cooperation in labor-employer relations	103
9.07	Importance of environment in business planning	102
6.07	Burden of government regulation	99
8.20	Pay and productivity	98
7.09	Local availability of specialized research and training services	97
8.17	Hiring and firing practices	96
9.09	Prevalence of corporate environmental reporting	96
6.13	Centralization of economic policymaking	94
9.08	Protection of ecosystems by business	92
9.03	Extent of government mandated environmental reporting	89
9.02	Clarity and stability of regulations	88

371

Note: The Business Competitiveness Index applies different criteria for selecting a country's competitive advantages and disadvantages. Please refer to the section "How Country Profiles Work" for further details.

Mauritius

Competitiveness Rankings

Growth Competitiveness Index Rank	52

Macroeconomic Environment Index Rank 59
  Macroeconomic Stability Subindex Rank 86
  Government Waste Rank 41
  Country Credit Rating Rank 51

Public Institutions Index Rank 55
  Contracts and Law Subindex Rank 53
  Corruption Subindex Rank 59

Technology Index Rank 47
  Innovation Subindex Rank 79
  ICT Subindex Rank 47
  Technology Transfer Subindex Rank
    (out of 92 non-core innovators).........................25

Business Competitiveness Index Rank	52

**Sophistication of Company Operations
  and Strategy Rank** 45
**Quality of the National Business
  Environment Rank** 49

The Most Problematic Factors for Doing Business

FACTOR

Inefficient government bureaucracy ....
Corruption ....
Inadequately educated workforce ....
Access to financing ....
Poor work ethic in national labor force ....
Inadequate supply of infrastructure ....
Inflation ....
Policy instability ....
Tax rates ....
Restrictive labor regulations ....
Crime and theft ....
Government instability/coups ....
Tax regulations ....
Foreign currency regulations ....

Percent of responses

Note: From a list of 14 factors, respondents were asked to select the five most problematic for doing business in their country and to rank them between 1 (most problematic) and 5. The bars in the figure show the responses weighted according to their rankings.

Source: World Economic Forum, Executive Opinion Survey (2005)

National competitiveness balance sheet

NOTABLE COMPETITIVE ADVANTAGES		
Growth Competitiveness Index		**Rank/117**
	Macroeconomic Environment	
2.14	National savings rate, 2004	21
2.20	Government debt, 2004	23
6.06	Wastefulness of government spending	41
	Public Institutions	
6.03	Property rights	40
6.21	Irregular payments in tax collection	47
	Technology	
3.13	Government prioritization of ICT	6
3.14	Government success in ICT promotion	18
3.03	Prevalence of foreign technology licensing	25
3.15	Laws relating to ICT	36
3.01	Technological readiness	38
5.08	Telephone lines, 2003	39
3.21	Personal computers, 2003	40
3.02	Firm-level technology absorption	44

NOTABLE COMPETITIVE DISADVANTAGES		
Growth Competitiveness Index		**Rank/117**
	Macroeconomic Environment	
2.13	Government surplus/deficit, 2004	107
2.17	Interest rate spread, 2004	100
2.01	Recession expectations	86
2.07	Access to credit	63
2.16	Inflation, 2004	63
2.15	Real effective exchange rate, 2004	56
2.21	Country credit rating, 2004	51
	Public Institutions	
6.19	Irregular payments in exports and imports	82
6.01	Judicial independence	64
6.16	Organized crime	61
6.20	Irregular payments in public utilities	60
6.08	Favoritism in decisions of government officials	51
	Technology	
4.17	Gross tertiary enrollment	86
3.12	Quality of competition in the ISP sector	82
3.17	Utility patents, 2004	81
3.18	Cellular telephones, 2003	63
3.07	University/industry research collaboration	62
3.06	Company spending on research and development	59
3.04	FDI and technology transfer	55
3.20	Internet hosts, 2003	54
3.19	Internet users, 2003	52
3.11	Internet access in schools	51

Business Competitiveness Index		**Rank/110**
	Sophistication of Company Operations and Strategy	
8.08	Control of international distribution	9
8.02	Value chain presence	24
3.03	Prevalence of foreign technology licensing	25
	Quality of the National Business Environment	
5.03	Port infrastructure quality	26
7.04	Buyer sophistication	28
7.05	Local supplier quantity	29

Business Competitiveness Index		**Rank/110**
	Sophistication of Company Operations and Strategy	
8.03	Capacity for innovation	78
8.10	Breadth of international markets	67
8.14	Reliance on professional management	66
	Quality of the National Business Environment	
6.13	Centralization of economic policymaking	103
2.09	Prevalence of trade barriers	103
7.08	Local availability of process machinery	97

Other Indicators		**Rank/117**
6.12	Efficiency of the tax system	23
2.12	Agricultural policy costs	25
6.11	Extent and effect of taxation	29
6.10	Effectiveness of law-making bodies	30
8.24	Importance of corporate social responsibility	31
8.23	Strength of auditing and accounting standards	34
8.07	Degree of customer orientation	34
2.11	Tax burden	35
6.17	Informal sector	36
8.16	Efficacy of corporate boards	37
2.08	Local equity market access	37

Other Indicators		**Rank/117**
6.07	Burden of government regulation	112
8.18	Flexibility of wage determination	112
4.09	Private sector employment of women	106
4.07	Ease of hiring foreign labor	105
6.26	Public trust of politicians	96
3.09	Availability of scientists and engineers	95
8.20	Pay and productivity	92
7.03	Extent of market dominance	92
8.22	Foreign ownership restrictions	81
4.08	Brain drain	79
6.14	Reliability of police services	77

373

Note: The Business Competitiveness Index applies different criteria for selecting a country's competitive advantages and disadvantages. Please refer to the section "How Country Profiles Work" for further details.

Mexico

Competitiveness Rankings

Growth Competitiveness Index Rank	55

Macroeconomic Environment Index Rank **43**
  Macroeconomic Stability Subindex Rank 36
  Government Waste Rank 55
  Country Credit Rating Rank 45

Public Institutions Index Rank **71**
  Contracts and Law Subindex Rank 79
  Corruption Subindex Rank...................................60

Technology Index Rank **57**
  Innovation Subindex Rank 73
  ICT Subindex Rank 57
  Technology Transfer Subindex Rank
    (out of 92 non-core innovators) 27

Business Competitiveness Index Rank	60

**Sophistication of Company Operations
  and Strategy Rank** **55**
**Quality of the National Business
  Environment Rank** **62**

The Most Problematic Factors for Doing Business

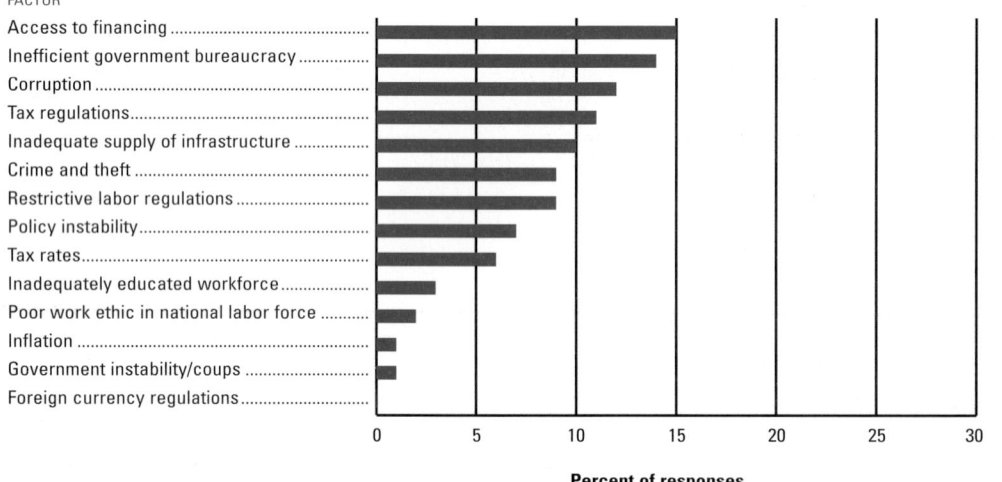

Percent of responses

Note: From a list of 14 factors, respondents were asked to select the five most problematic for doing business in their country and to rank them between 1 (most problematic) and 5. The bars in the figure show the responses weighted according to their rankings.

Source: World Economic Forum, Executive Opinion Survey (2005)

National competitiveness balance sheet

Growth Competitiveness Index	Rank/117

Macroeconomic Environment

2.20	Government debt, 2004	15
2.17	Interest rate spread, 2004	43
2.21	Country credit rating, 2004	45
2.13	Government surplus/deficit, 2004	49
2.15	Real effective exchange rate, 2004	50
2.07	Access to credit	50

Technology

3.04	FDI and technology transfer	29
3.20	Internet hosts, 2003	42
3.17	Utility patents, 2004	44
3.15	Laws relating to ICT	49
3.21	Personal computers, 2003	50
3.07	University/industry research collaboration	50

Business Competitiveness Index	Rank/110

Sophistication of Company Operations and Strategy

8.09	Extent of regional sales	31
8.13	Extent of incentive compensation	38
8.02	Value chain presence	49

Quality of the National Business Environment

8.15	Quality of management schools	36
2.03	Financial market sophistication	39
8.22	Foreign ownership restrictions	39

Other Indicators	Rank/117

2.02	Business costs of terrorism	34
4.05	Medium term business impact of tuberculosis	39
6.05	Freedom of the press	41
6.13	Centralization of economic policymaking	43
3.16	Extent of business Internet use	49

Growth Competitiveness Index	Rank/117

Macroeconomic Environment

2.16	Inflation, 2004	68
2.14	National savings rate, 2004	62
2.01	Recession expectations	61
6.06	Wastefulness of government spending	55

Public Institutions

6.16	Organized crime	113
6.20	Irregular payments in public utilities	74
6.08	Favoritism in decisions of government officials	71
6.03	Property rights	66
6.19	Irregular payments in exports and imports	61
6.01	Judicial independence	60
6.21	Irregular payments in tax collection	57

Technology

3.13	Government prioritization of ICT	80
3.14	Government success in ICT promotion	79
3.02	Firm-level technology absorption	75
4.17	Gross tertiary enrollment	71
3.12	Quality of competition in the ISP sector	67
5.08	Telephone lines, 2003	64
3.06	Company spending on research and development	63
3.11	Internet access in schools	60
3.18	Cellular telephones, 2003	58
3.01	Technological readiness	58
3.19	Internet users, 2003	53
3.03	Prevalence of foreign technology licensing	53

Business Competitiveness Index	Rank/110

Sophistication of Company Operations and Strategy

8.14	Reliance on professional management	74
8.11	Extent of staff training	71
8.10	Breadth of international markets	71

Quality of the National Business Environment

6.09	Extent of bureaucratic red tape	102
6.14	Reliability of police services	96
2.06	Venture capital availability	91

Other Indicators	Rank/117

6.15	Business costs of crime and violence	115
6.12	Efficiency of the tax system	112
4.09	Private sector employment of women	108
6.10	Effectiveness of law-making bodies	108
2.12	Agricultural policy costs	107
5.06	Postal efficiency	100
6.17	Informal sector	99
8.17	Hiring and firing practices	97
6.07	Burden of government regulation	96
9.06	Prioritization of energy efficiency	96
6.27	Pervasiveness of money laundering through banks	95
3.09	Availability of scientists and engineers	92

Note: The Business Competitiveness Index applies different criteria for selecting a country's competitive advantages and disadvantages. Please refer to the section "How Country Profiles Work" for further details.

Moldova

Competitiveness Rankings

Growth Competitiveness Index Rank	**82**

Macroeconomic Environment Index Rank **96**
    Macroeconomic Stability Subindex Rank 75
    Government Waste Rank 80
    Country Credit Rating Rank..............................115

Public Institutions Index Rank...**63**
    Contracts and Law Subindex Rank 93
    Corruption Subindex Rank...................................47

Technology Index Rank **89**
    Innovation Subindex Rank 74
    ICT Subindex Rank 72
    Technology Transfer Subindex Rank
        (out of 92 non-core innovators).......................78

Business Competitiveness Index Rank	**90**

**Sophistication of Company Operations
   and Strategy Rank** **89**
**Quality of the National Business
   Environment Rank** **91**

The Most Problematic Factors for Doing Business

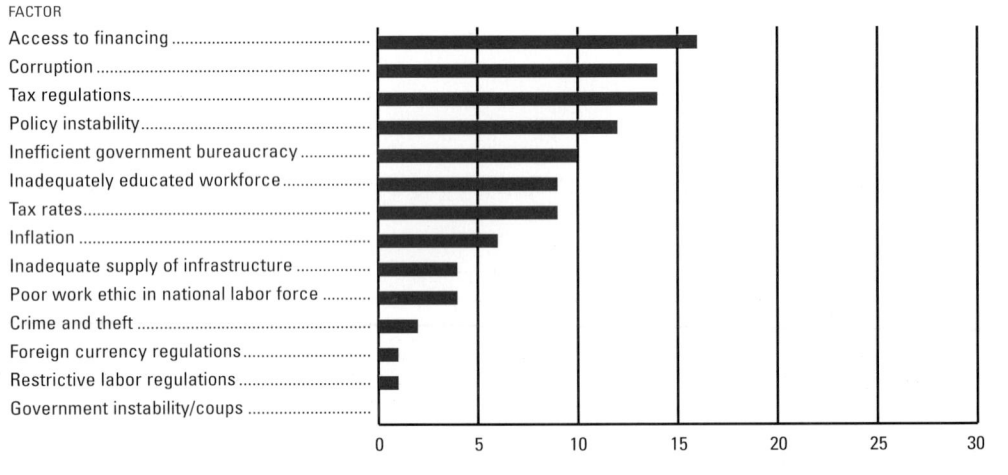

FACTOR

Access to financing
Corruption
Tax regulations
Policy instability
Inefficient government bureaucracy
Inadequately educated workforce
Tax rates
Inflation
Inadequate supply of infrastructure
Poor work ethic in national labor force
Crime and theft
Foreign currency regulations
Restrictive labor regulations
Government instability/coups

0   5   10   15   20   25   30

Percent of responses

Note: From a list of 14 factors, respondents were asked to select the five most problematic for doing business in their country and to rank them between 1 (most problematic) and 5. The bars in the figure show the responses weighted according to their rankings.

Source: World Economic Forum, Executive Opinion Survey (2005)

National competitiveness balance sheet

NOTABLE COMPETITIVE ADVANTAGES			NOTABLE COMPETITIVE DISADVANTAGES		
Growth Competitiveness Index		**Rank/117**	**Growth Competitiveness Index**		**Rank/117**
	Macroeconomic Environment			**Macroeconomic Environment**	
2.13	Government surplus/deficit, 2004	37	2.21	Country credit rating, 2004	115
	Public Institutions		2.16	Inflation, 2004	108
6.20	Irregular payments in public utilities	45	2.07	Access to credit	84
6.19	Irregular payments in exports and imports	46	2.15	Real effective exchange rate, 2004	83
6.21	Irregular payments in tax collection	50	2.20	Government debt, 2004	82
	Technology		6.06	Wastefulness of government spending	80
3.17	Utility patents, 2004	46	2.17	Interest rate spread, 2004	63
			2.14	National savings rate, 2004	60
			2.01	Recession expectations	58
				Public Institutions	
			6.03	Property rights	96
			6.01	Judicial independence	94
			6.16	Organized crime	83
			6.08	Favoritism in decisions of government officials	83
				Technology	
			3.03	Prevalence of foreign technology licensing	110
			3.01	Technological readiness	108
			3.06	Company spending on research and development	98
			3.02	Firm-level technology absorption	96
			3.07	University/industry research collaboration	94
			3.04	FDI and technology transfer	88
			3.12	Quality of competition in the ISP sector	86
			3.21	Personal computers, 2003	85
			3.11	Internet access in schools	82
			3.18	Cellular telephones, 2003	80
			3.15	Laws relating to ICT	76
			3.14	Government success in ICT promotion	73
			3.19	Internet users, 2003	64
			4.17	Gross tertiary enrollment	61
			5.08	Telephone lines, 2003	57
			3.13	Government prioritization of ICT	53
			3.20	Internet hosts, 2003	53

Business Competitiveness Index		**Rank/110**	**Business Competitiveness Index**		**Rank/110**
	Sophistication of Company Operations and Strategy			**Sophistication of Company Operations and Strategy**	
8.03	Capacity for innovation	58	3.03	Prevalence of foreign technology licensing	105
8.12	Willingness to delegate authority	64	8.06	Extent of marketing	103
8.02	Value chain presence	64	8.10	Breadth of international markets	101
	Quality of the National Business Environment			**Quality of the National Business Environment**	
8.19	Cooperation in labor-employer relations	31	7.01	Intensity of local competition	110
3.17	Utility patents, 2004	45	8.22	Foreign ownership restrictions	107
4.03	Quality of math and science education	48	8.21	Protection of minority shareholders' interests	106

Other Indicators		**Rank/117**	**Other Indicators**		**Rank/117**
8.20	Pay and productivity	12	4.08	Brain drain	114
4.09	Private sector employment of women	21	7.05	Local supplier quantity	109
6.22	Irregular payments in public contracts	30	6.12	Efficiency of the tax system	108
8.17	Hiring and firing practices	34	6.07	Burden of government regulation	108
9.09	Prevalence of corporate environmental reporting	45	8.24	Importance of corporate social responsibility	108
8.18	Flexibility of wage determination	50	6.27	Pervasiveness of money laundering through banks	107
9.07	Importance of environment in business planning	50	2.06	Venture capital availability	107
			8.15	Quality of management schools	107
			9.10	Grass-roots involvement in development projects	106
			2.03	Financial market sophistication	106
			8.04	Ethical behavior of firms	105

Note: The Business Competitiveness Index applies different criteria for selecting a country's competitive advantages and disadvantages. Please refer to the section "How Country Profiles Work" for further details.

Mongolia

Competitiveness Rankings

Growth Competitiveness Index Rank	96

Macroeconomic Environment Index Rank **105**
    Macroeconomic Stability Subindex Rank 94
    Government Waste Rank 109
    Country Credit Rating Rank 97

Public Institutions Index Rank..**93**
    Contracts and Law Subindex Rank 81
    Corruption Subindex Rank....................................96

Technology Index Rank **81**
    Innovation Subindex Rank.....................................53
    ICT Subindex Rank 81
    Technology Transfer Subindex Rank
      (out of 92 non-core innovators)........................55

Business Competitiveness Index Rank	100

**Sophistication of Company Operations
  and Strategy Rank**...**96**

**Quality of the National Business
  Environment Rank** **98**

The Most Problematic Factors for Doing Business

FACTOR

Percent of responses

Note: From a list of 14 factors, respondents were asked to select the five most problematic for doing business in their country and to rank them between 1 (most problematic) and 5. The bars in the figure show the responses weighted according to their rankings.

Source: World Economic Forum, Executive Opinion Survey (2005)

National competitiveness balance sheet

NOTABLE COMPETITIVE ADVANTAGES	
Growth Competitiveness Index	**Rank/117**

Macroeconomic Environment

| 2.15 | Real effective exchange rate, 2004 | 31 |
| 2.07 | Access to credit | 35 |

Technology

| 3.13 | Government prioritization of ICT | 22 |
| 4.17 | Gross tertiary enrollment | 47 |

NOTABLE COMPETITIVE DISADVANTAGES	
Growth Competitiveness Index	**Rank/117**

Macroeconomic Environment

6.06	Wastefulness of government spending	109
2.13	Government surplus/deficit, 2004	100
2.20	Government debt, 2004	98
2.21	Country credit rating, 2004	97
2.17	Interest rate spread, 2004	92
2.16	Inflation, 2004	71
2.01	Recession expectations	67
2.14	National savings rate, 2004	65

Public Institutions

6.08	Favoritism in decisions of government officials	107
6.19	Irregular payments in exports and imports	107
6.01	Judicial independence	99
6.21	Irregular payments in tax collection	90
6.20	Irregular payments in public utilities	84
6.03	Property rights	83
6.16	Organized crime	52

Technology

3.20	Internet hosts, 2003	110
3.15	Laws relating to ICT	107
3.12	Quality of competition in the ISP sector	103
3.01	Technological readiness	98
5.08	Telephone lines, 2003	88
3.02	Firm-level technology absorption	87
3.11	Internet access in schools	87
3.04	FDI and technology transfer	86
3.18	Cellular telephones, 2003	82
3.17	Utility patents, 2004	81
3.06	Company spending on research and development	80
3.19	Internet users, 2003	73
3.03	Prevalence of foreign technology licensing	72
3.07	University/industry research collaboration	67
3.14	Government success in ICT promotion	64
3.21	Personal computers, 2003	56

Business Competitiveness Index	
	Rank/110

Sophistication of Company Operations and Strategy

| 8.03 | Capacity for innovation | 66 |
| 8.01 | Nature of competitive advantage | 78 |

Quality of the National Business Environment

6.13	Centralization of economic policymaking	48
5.02	Railroad infrastructure development	56
4.03	Quality of math and science education	62

Business Competitiveness Index	
	Rank/110

Sophistication of Company Operations and Strategy

8.02	Value chain presence	109
8.10	Breadth of international markets	107
8.07	Degree of customer orientation	106

Quality of the National Business Environment

7.05	Local supplier quantity	110
5.04	Air transport infrastructure quality	108
5.03	Port infrastructure quality	105

Other Indicators	
	Rank/117

8.18	Flexibility of wage determination	14
2.02	Business costs of terrorism	15
8.17	Hiring and firing practices	22
8.20	Pay and productivity	27
4.09	Private sector employment of women	39

Other Indicators	
	Rank/117

9.04	Effects of compliance on business	117
9.08	Protection of ecosystems by business	116
9.03	Extent of government mandated environmental reporting	115
9.09	Prevalence of corporate environmental reporting	114
9.10	Grass-roots involvement in development projects	113
9.05	Effects of privatization on competition and the environment	112
8.21	Protection of minority shareholders' interests	111
6.02	Efficiency of legal framework	111
3.10	Availability of mobile or cellular telephones	111
9.01	Stringency of environmental regulations	110
8.04	Ethical behavior of firms	109

379

Note: The Business Competitiveness Index applies different criteria for selecting a country's competitive advantages and disadvantages.
Please refer to the section "How Country Profiles Work" for further details.

Morocco

Competitiveness Rankings

Growth Competitiveness Index Rank	76

Macroeconomic Environment Index Rank **67**
    Macroeconomic Stability Subindex Rank 88
    Government Waste Rank 54
    Country Credit Rating Rank 58

Public Institutions Index Rank **85**
    Contracts and Law Subindex Rank 60
    Corruption Subindex Rank...................................98

Technology Index Rank **78**
    Innovation Subindex Rank...................................93
    ICT Subindex Rank 83
    Technology Transfer Subindex Rank
        (out of 92 non-core innovators).......................38

Business Competitiveness Index Rank	79

**Sophistication of Company Operations
and Strategy Rank** **80**

**Quality of the National Business
Environment Rank** **75**

The Most Problematic Factors for Doing Business

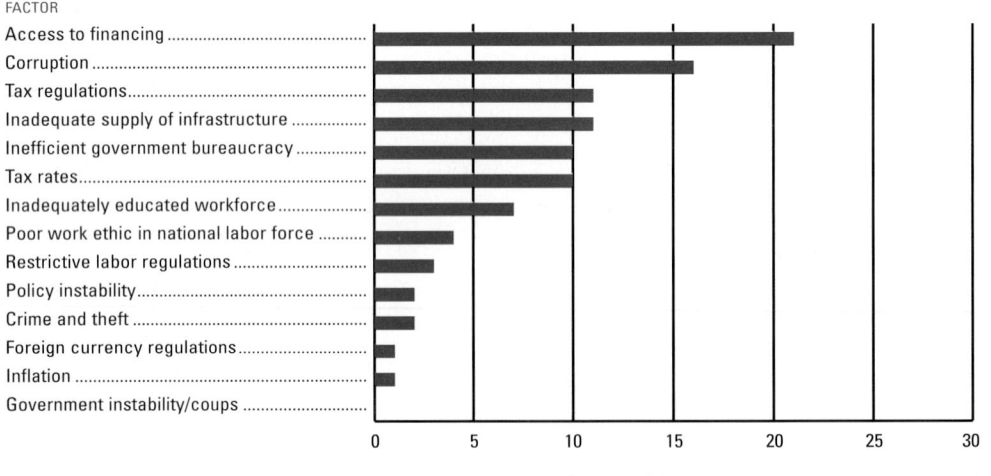

Note: From a list of 14 factors, respondents were asked to select the five most problematic for doing business in their country and to rank them between 1 (most problematic) and 5. The bars in the figure show the responses weighted according to their rankings.

Source: World Economic Forum, Executive Opinion Survey (2005)

National competitiveness balance sheet

NOTABLE COMPETITIVE ADVANTAGES	
Growth Competitiveness Index	**Rank/117**
Macroeconomic Environment	
2.16 Inflation, 2004	27
2.14 National savings rate, 2004	36
Public Institutions	
6.08 Favoritism in decisions of government officials	48
Technology	
3.14 Government success in ICT promotion	48

NOTABLE COMPETITIVE DISADVANTAGES	
Growth Competitiveness Index	**Rank/117**
Macroeconomic Environment	
2.07 Access to credit	100
2.13 Government surplus/deficit, 2004	96
2.20 Government debt, 2004	91
2.01 Recession expectations	84
2.17 Interest rate spread, 2004	79
2.21 Country credit rating, 2004	58
2.15 Real effective exchange rate, 2004	58
6.06 Wastefulness of government spending	54
Public Institutions	
6.21 Irregular payments in tax collection	107
6.19 Irregular payments in exports and imports	97
6.20 Irregular payments in public utilities	88
6.03 Property rights	72
6.01 Judicial independence	70
6.16 Organized crime	62
Technology	
3.12 Quality of competition in the ISP sector	103
3.07 University/industry research collaboration	103
3.20 Internet hosts, 2003	95
5.08 Telephone lines, 2003	94
4.17 Gross tertiary enrollment	92
3.19 Internet users, 2003	89
3.15 Laws relating to ICT	88
3.21 Personal computers, 2003	86
3.13 Government prioritization of ICT	83
3.01 Technological readiness	81
3.17 Utility patents, 2004	75
3.11 Internet access in schools	73
3.02 Firm-level technology absorption	72
3.06 Company spending on research and development	70
3.18 Cellular telephones, 2003	66
3.03 Prevalence of foreign technology licensing	65
3.04 FDI and technology transfer	61

Business Competitiveness Index	Rank/110
Sophistication of Company Operations and Strategy	
8.08 Control of international distribution	55
8.02 Value chain presence	59
8.01 Nature of competitive advantage	61
Quality of the National Business Environment	
6.14 Reliability of police services	30
8.15 Quality of management schools	43
6.08 Favoritism in decisions of government officials	46

Other Indicators	Rank/117
4.09 Private sector employment of women	31
9.07 Importance of environment in business planning	33
9.06 Prioritization of energy efficiency	46
5.07 Telephone/fax infrastructure quality	49
5.06 Postal efficiency	50

Business Competitiveness Index	Rank/110
Sophistication of Company Operations and Strategy	
8.12 Willingness to delegate authority	100
8.14 Reliance on professional management	100
8.13 Extent of incentive compensation	95
Quality of the National Business Environment	
3.07 University/industry research collaboration	99
2.09 Prevalence of trade barriers	97
6.25 Business costs of corruption	96

Other Indicators	Rank/117
4.08 Brain drain	104
6.11 Extent and effect of taxation	102
8.19 Cooperation in labor-employer relations	101
6.22 Irregular payments in public contracts	100
6.05 Freedom of the press	100
6.17 Informal sector	100
2.02 Business costs of terrorism	100
8.16 Efficacy of corporate boards	99
6.23 Irregular payments in judicial decisions	97
9.02 Clarity and stability of regulations	96

381

Note: The Business Competitiveness Index applies different criteria for selecting a country's competitive advantages and disadvantages. Please refer to the section "How Country Profiles Work" for further details.

Mozambique

Competitiveness Rankings

Growth Competitiveness Index Rank	**91**

Macroeconomic Environment Index Rank **98**
    Macroeconomic Stability Subindex Rank 102
    Government Waste Rank 72
    Country Credit Rating Rank 95

Public Institutions Index Rank **92**
    Contracts and Law Subindex Rank 86
    Corruption Subindex Rank 92

Technology Index Rank **83**
    Innovation Subindex Rank 114
    ICT Subindex Rank 105
    Technology Transfer Subindex Rank
       (out of 92 non-core innovators) 28

Business Competitiveness Index Rank	**95**

**Sophistication of Company Operations
  and Strategy Rank** **95**
**Quality of the National Business
  Environment Rank** **95**

The Most Problematic Factors for Doing Business

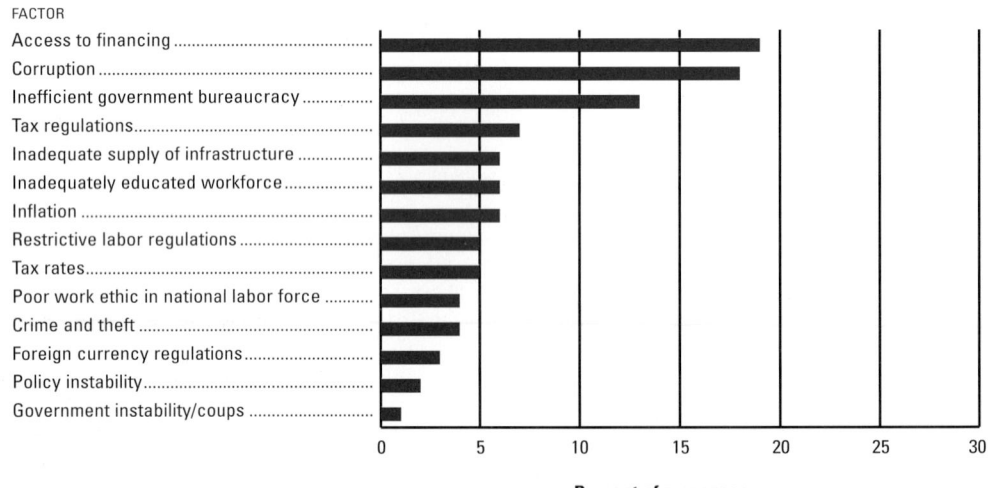

FACTOR

Note: From a list of 14 factors, respondents were asked to select the five most problematic for doing business in their country and to rank them between 1 (most problematic) and 5. The bars in the figure show the responses weighted according to their rankings.

Source: World Economic Forum, Executive Opinion Survey (2005)

National competitiveness balance sheet

NOTABLE COMPETITIVE ADVANTAGES	
Growth Competitiveness Index	**Rank/117**

Macroeconomic Environment
2.14	National savings rate, 2004	6
2.01	Recession expectations	33

Technology
3.04	FDI and technology transfer	24
3.14	Government success in ICT promotion	34

NOTABLE COMPETITIVE DISADVANTAGES	
Growth Competitiveness Index	**Rank/117**

Macroeconomic Environment
2.16	Inflation, 2004	110
2.07	Access to credit	101
2.20	Government debt, 2004	101
2.13	Government surplus/deficit, 2004	100
2.17	Interest rate spread, 2004	98
2.21	Country credit rating, 2004	95
6.06	Wastefulness of government spending	72
2.15	Real effective exchange rate, 2004	53

Public Institutions
6.21	Irregular payments in tax collection	99
6.01	Judicial independence	93
6.16	Organized crime	92
6.20	Irregular payments in public utilities	90
6.19	Irregular payments in exports and imports	85
6.03	Property rights	81
6.08	Favoritism in decisions of government officials	65

Technology
4.17	Gross tertiary enrollment	116
5.08	Telephone lines, 2003	112
3.19	Internet users, 2003	111
3.01	Technological readiness	110
3.18	Cellular telephones, 2003	109
3.21	Personal computers, 2003	105
3.06	Company spending on research and development	100
3.02	Firm-level technology absorption	99
3.11	Internet access in schools	95
3.12	Quality of competition in the ISP sector	91
3.20	Internet hosts, 2003	90
3.15	Laws relating to ICT	90
3.07	University/industry research collaboration	85
3.17	Utility patents, 2004	81
3.13	Government prioritization of ICT	77
3.03	Prevalence of foreign technology licensing	62

Business Competitiveness Index	
Business Competitiveness Index	**Rank/110**

Sophistication of Company Operations and Strategy
8.01	Nature of competitive advantage	82
8.11	Extent of staff training	82

Quality of the National Business Environment
6.09	Extent of bureaucratic red tape	30
3.08	Government procurement of advanced technology products	50
6.13	Centralization of economic policymaking	50

Business Competitiveness Index	
Business Competitiveness Index	**Rank/110**

Sophistication of Company Operations and Strategy
8.02	Value chain presence	104
8.07	Degree of customer orientation	102
8.08	Control of international distribution	100

Quality of the National Business Environment
2.05	Ease of access to loans	110
7.06	Local supplier quality	109
7.01	Intensity of local competition	109

Other Indicators	
Other Indicators	**Rank/117**

6.18	Government effectiveness in reducing poverty and inequality	36
6.07	Burden of government regulation	43
2.12	Agricultural policy costs	48

Other Indicators	
Other Indicators	**Rank/117**

4.05	Medium term business impact of tuberculosis	111
4.06	Medium term business impact of HIV/AIDS	109
3.09	Availability of scientists and engineers	109
8.20	Pay and productivity	108
7.04	Buyer sophistication	107
7.05	Local supplier quantity	107
5.06	Postal efficiency	107
7.09	Local availability of specialized research and training services	106
2.06	Venture capital availability	105
8.03	Capacity for innovation	104

383

Note: The Business Competitiveness Index applies different criteria for selecting a country's competitive advantages and disadvantages. Please refer to the section "How Country Profiles Work" for further details.

Namibia

Competitiveness Rankings

Growth Competitiveness Index Rank	63

Macroeconomic Environment Index Rank **65**
    Macroeconomic Stability Subindex Rank 71
    Government Waste Rank 52
    Country Credit Rating Rank 66

Public Institutions Index Rank...**57**
    Contracts and Law Subindex Rank 54
    Corruption Subindex Rank....................................63

Technology Index Rank **79**
    Innovation Subindex Rank 91
    ICT Subindex Rank 80
    Technology Transfer Subindex Rank
       (out of 92 non-core innovators).......................42

Business Competitiveness Index Rank	73

**Sophistication of Company Operations
  and Strategy Rank** **75**
**Quality of the National Business
  Environment Rank** **72**

The Most Problematic Factors for Doing Business

FACTOR

Percent of responses

Note: From a list of 14 factors, respondents were asked to select the five most problematic for doing business in their country and to rank them between 1 (most problematic) and 5. The bars in the figure show the responses weighted according to their rankings.

Source: World Economic Forum, Executive Opinion Survey (2005)

National competitiveness balance sheet

NOTABLE COMPETITIVE ADVANTAGES

Growth Competitiveness Index	Rank/117

Macroeconomic Environment
- 2.14 National savings rate, 2004 16
- 2.20 Government debt, 2004 40

Public Institutions
- 6.01 Judicial independence 35
- 6.03 Property rights 50

Technology
- 3.21 Personal computers, 2003 49

NOTABLE COMPETITIVE DISADVANTAGES

Growth Competitiveness Index	Rank/117

Macroeconomic Environment
- 2.15 Real effective exchange rate, 2004 107
- 2.01 Recession expectations 89
- 2.07 Access to credit 86
- 2.13 Government surplus/deficit, 2004 78
- 2.16 Inflation, 2004 73
- 2.21 Country credit rating, 2004 66
- 2.17 Interest rate spread, 2004 52
- 6.06 Wastefulness of government spending 52

Public Institutions
- 6.08 Favoritism in decisions of government officials 85
- 6.19 Irregular payments in exports and imports 74
- 6.16 Organized crime 73
- 6.20 Irregular payments in public utilities 64
- 6.21 Irregular payments in tax collection 55

Technology
- 3.13 Government prioritization of ICT 102
- 4.17 Gross tertiary enrollment 97
- 3.14 Government success in ICT promotion 92
- 3.07 University/industry research collaboration 88
- 5.08 Telephone lines, 2003 87
- 3.19 Internet users, 2003 87
- 3.04 FDI and technology transfer 85
- 3.18 Cellular telephones, 2003 84
- 3.17 Utility patents, 2004 81
- 3.15 Laws relating to ICT 72
- 3.12 Quality of competition in the ISP sector 69
- 3.11 Internet access in schools 68
- 3.20 Internet hosts, 2003 66
- 3.06 Company spending on research and development 64
- 3.02 Firm-level technology absorption 62
- 3.01 Technological readiness 54
- 3.03 Prevalence of foreign technology licensing 51

Business Competitiveness Index	Rank/110

Sophistication of Company Operations and Strategy
- 8.01 Nature of competitive advantage 43
- 8.11 Extent of staff training 45
- 8.12 Willingness to delegate authority 48

Quality of the National Business Environment
- 5.03 Port infrastructure quality 22
- 8.21 Protection of minority shareholders' interests 31
- 6.01 Judicial independence 34

Business Competitiveness Index	Rank/110

Sophistication of Company Operations and Strategy
- 8.08 Control of international distribution 96
- 8.07 Degree of customer orientation 90
- 8.02 Value chain presence 89

Quality of the National Business Environment
- 8.15 Quality of management schools 110
- 3.09 Availability of scientists and engineers 103
- 7.05 Local supplier quantity 103

Other Indicators	Rank/117

- 6.12 Efficiency of the tax system 25
- 9.08 Protection of ecosystems by business 31
- 6.11 Extent and effect of taxation 32
- 2.12 Agricultural policy costs 37
- 2.02 Business costs of terrorism 42
- 8.23 Strength of auditing and accounting standards 42
- 9.02 Clarity and stability of regulations 43
- 6.02 Efficiency of legal framework 43
- 6.07 Burden of government regulation 44
- 8.24 Importance of corporate social responsibility 47
- 2.04 Soundness of banks 47
- 9.04 Effects of compliance on business 48

Other Indicators	Rank/117

- 4.07 Ease of hiring foreign labor 115
- 4.05 Medium term business impact of tuberculosis 113
- 4.06 Medium term business impact of HIV/AIDS 110
- 7.09 Local availability of specialized research and training services 107
- 8.20 Pay and productivity 102
- 6.15 Business costs of crime and violence 101
- 6.14 Reliability of police services 98
- 8.17 Hiring and firing practices 98
- 6.09 Extent of bureaucratic red tape 97
- 8.19 Cooperation in labor-employer relations 96
- 3.05 Quality of scientific research institutions 96

385

Note: The Business Competitiveness Index applies different criteria for selecting a country's competitive advantages and disadvantages. Please refer to the section "How Country Profiles Work" for further details.

Netherlands

Competitiveness Rankings

Growth Competitiveness Index Rank	11

Macroeconomic Environment Index Rank **10**
    Macroeconomic Stability Subindex Rank 39
    Government Waste Rank 9
    Country Credit Rating Rank...................................9

Public Institutions Index Rank............................**16**
    Contracts and Law Subindex Rank 14
    Corruption Subindex Rank....................................23

Technology Index Rank **11**
    Innovation Subindex Rank 17
    ICT Subindex Rank 7

Business Competitiveness Index Rank	9

**Sophistication of Company Operations
   and Strategy Rank** **8**
**Quality of the National Business
   Environment Rank** **8**

The Most Problematic Factors for Doing Business

FACTOR

Note: From a list of 14 factors, respondents were asked to select the five most problematic for doing business in their country and to rank them between 1 (most problematic) and 5. The bars in the figure show the responses weighted according to their rankings.

Source: World Economic Forum, Executive Opinion Survey (2005)

National competitiveness balance sheet

NOTABLE COMPETITIVE ADVANTAGES		NOTABLE COMPETITIVE DISADVANTAGES	
Growth Competitiveness Index	**Rank/117**	**Growth Competitiveness Index**	**Rank/117**

Macroeconomic Environment (Advantages)

6.06	Wastefulness of government spending	9
2.17	Interest rate spread, 2004	9
2.21	Country credit rating, 2004	9

Public Institutions (Advantages)

6.01	Judicial independence	6
6.08	Favoritism in decisions of government officials	6

Technology (Advantages)

3.12	Quality of competition in the ISP sector	4
3.20	Internet hosts, 2003	5
3.11	Internet access in schools	8
5.08	Telephone lines, 2003	10

Macroeconomic Environment (Disadvantages)

2.15	Real effective exchange rate, 2004	94
2.13	Government surplus/deficit, 2004	64
2.20	Government debt, 2004	63
2.01	Recession expectations	56
2.07	Access to credit	54
2.14	National savings rate, 2004	48
2.16	Inflation, 2004	18

Public Institutions (Disadvantages)

6.16	Organized crime	45
6.19	Irregular payments in exports and imports	22
6.20	Irregular payments in public utilities	22
6.21	Irregular payments in tax collection	22
6.03	Property rights	12

Technology (Disadvantages)

3.14	Government success in ICT promotion	51
3.13	Government prioritization of ICT	49
3.02	Firm-level technology absorption	36
3.18	Cellular telephones, 2003	25
4.17	Gross tertiary enrollment	23
3.01	Technological readiness	23
3.15	Laws relating to ICT	20
3.06	Company spending on research and development	17
3.07	University/industry research collaboration	16
3.21	Personal computers, 2003	14
3.17	Utility patents, 2004	13
3.19	Internet users, 2003	11

Business Competitiveness Index	**Rank/110**	**Business Competitiveness Index**	**Rank/110**

Sophistication of Company Operations and Strategy (Advantages)

8.13	Extent of incentive compensation	3
8.10	Breadth of international markets	5
8.12	Willingness to delegate authority	6

Quality of the National Business Environment (Advantages)

5.03	Port infrastructure quality	2
2.06	Venture capital availability	6
6.08	Favoritism in decisions of government officials	6

Sophistication of Company Operations and Strategy (Disadvantages)

8.07	Degree of customer orientation	20
3.06	Company spending on research and development	17
8.08	Control of international distribution	16

Quality of the National Business Environment (Disadvantages)

6.09	Extent of bureaucratic red tape	60
3.09	Availability of scientists and engineers	36
2.08	Local equity market access	29

Other Indicators	**Rank/117**	**Other Indicators**	**Rank/117**

Other Indicators (Advantages)

6.05	Freedom of the press	5
6.02	Efficiency of legal framework	6
6.18	Government effectiveness in reducing poverty and inequality	6
9.07	Importance of environment in business planning	6
6.17	Informal sector	6
7.01	Intensity of local competition	6
8.24	Importance of corporate social responsibility	7
5.05	Quality of electricity supply	7
6.04	Intellectual property protection	7
6.26	Public trust of politicians	8
6.25	Business costs of corruption	8

Other Indicators (Disadvantages)

8.18	Flexibility of wage determination	111
8.17	Hiring and firing practices	103
2.02	Business costs of terrorism	87
4.07	Ease of hiring foreign labor	86
8.20	Pay and productivity	83
2.11	Tax burden	72
4.09	Private sector employment of women	52
6.07	Burden of government regulation	49
6.15	Business costs of crime and violence	46
6.11	Extent and effect of taxation	46
9.05	Effects of privatization on competition and the environment	40
2.12	Agricultural policy costs	40
6.12	Efficiency of the tax system	40

387

Note: The Business Competitiveness Index applies different criteria for selecting a country's competitive advantages and disadvantages. Please refer to the section "How Country Profiles Work" for further details.

New Zealand

Competitiveness Rankings

Growth Competitiveness Index Rank	16

Macroeconomic Environment Index Rank **20**
   Macroeconomic Stability Subindex Rank 22
   Government Waste Rank 25
   Country Credit Rating Rank 21

Public Institutions Index Rank..**1**
   Contracts and Law Subindex Rank 2
   Corruption Subindex Rank.....................................2

Technology Index Rank **19**
   Innovation Subindex Rank 18
   ICT Subindex Rank 19

Business Competitiveness Index Rank	18

**Sophistication of Company Operations
and Strategy Rank** **21**

**Quality of the National Business
Environment Rank** **16**

The Most Problematic Factors for Doing Business

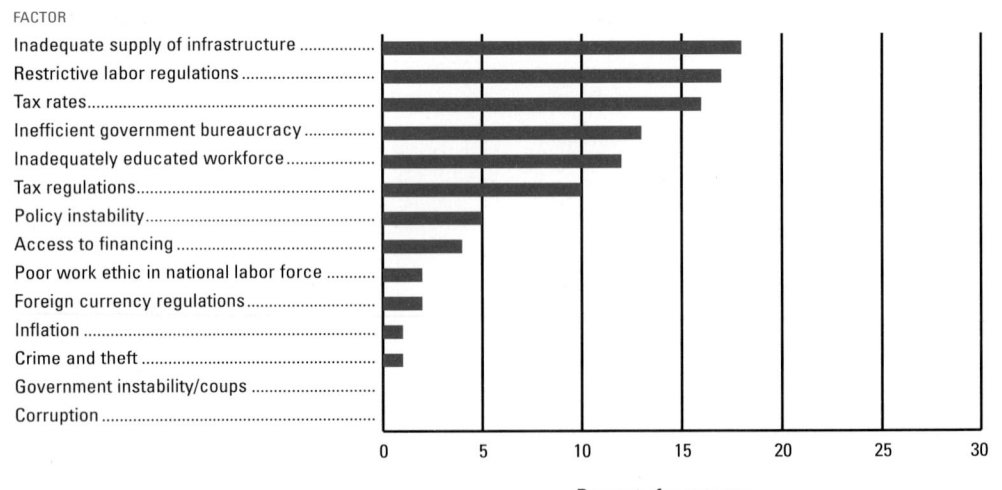

Note: From a list of 14 factors, respondents were asked to select the five most problematic for doing business in their country and to rank them between 1 (most problematic) and 5. The bars in the figure show the responses weighted according to their rankings.

Source: World Economic Forum, Executive Opinion Survey (2005)

National competitiveness balance sheet

NOTABLE COMPETITIVE ADVANTAGES

Growth Competitiveness Index		Rank/117

Macroeconomic Environment

| 2.13 | Government surplus/deficit, 2004 | 10 |

Public Institutions

6.21	Irregular payments in tax collection	1
6.08	Favoritism in decisions of government officials	2
6.20	Irregular payments in public utilities	2
6.19	Irregular payments in exports and imports	2
6.01	Judicial independence	7
6.03	Property rights	11
6.16	Organized crime	12

Technology

4.17	Gross tertiary enrollment	8
3.20	Internet hosts, 2003	9
3.19	Internet users, 2003	10
3.15	Laws relating to ICT	12

Business Competitiveness Index		Rank/110

Sophistication of Company Operations and Strategy

8.14	Reliance on professional management	2
8.07	Degree of customer orientation	8
8.09	Extent of regional sales	8

Quality of the National Business Environment

2.09	Prevalence of trade barriers	1
6.08	Favoritism in decisions of government officials	2
6.02	Efficiency of legal framework	2

Other Indicators		Rank/117

6.22	Irregular payments in public contracts	1
9.10	Grass-roots involvement in development projects	1
2.12	Agricultural policy costs	1
6.23	Irregular payments in judicial decisions	2
6.27	Pervasiveness of money laundering through banks	2
8.21	Protection of minority shareholders' interests	2
6.25	Business costs of corruption	3
2.08	Local equity market access	3
9.08	Protection of ecosystems by business	4
8.16	Efficacy of corporate boards	4
8.04	Ethical behavior of firms	4
7.02	Effectiveness of antitrust policy	5

NOTABLE COMPETITIVE DISADVANTAGES

Growth Competitiveness Index		Rank/117

Macroeconomic Environment

2.15	Real effective exchange rate, 2004	112
2.14	National savings rate, 2004	83
2.01	Recession expectations	51
2.17	Interest rate spread, 2004	44
2.16	Inflation, 2004	32
2.07	Access to credit	25
6.06	Wastefulness of government spending	25
2.21	Country credit rating, 2004	21
2.20	Government debt, 2004	18

Technology

3.14	Government success in ICT promotion	60
3.13	Government prioritization of ICT	52
3.18	Cellular telephones, 2003	35
3.12	Quality of competition in the ISP sector	32
5.08	Telephone lines, 2003	28
3.07	University/industry research collaboration	25
3.06	Company spending on research and development	24
3.17	Utility patents, 2004	24
3.01	Technological readiness	22
3.02	Firm-level technology absorption	20
3.21	Personal computers, 2003	20
3.11	Internet access in schools	18

Business Competitiveness Index		Rank/110

Sophistication of Company Operations and Strategy

8.08	Control of international distribution	31
8.02	Value chain presence	31
8.13	Extent of incentive compensation	30

Quality of the National Business Environment

3.09	Availability of scientists and engineers	56
6.13	Centralization of economic policymaking	52
7.08	Local availability of process machinery	39

Other Indicators		Rank/117

2.11	Tax burden	87
4.07	Ease of hiring foreign labor	60
3.10	Availability of mobile or cellular telephones	58
4.08	Brain drain	55
8.17	Hiring and firing practices	54
6.11	Extent and effect of taxation	44
6.07	Burden of government regulation	39
6.14	Reliability of police services	36
5.05	Quality of electricity supply	34

389

Note: The Business Competitiveness Index applies different criteria for selecting a country's competitive advantages and disadvantages. Please refer to the section "How Country Profiles Work" for further details.

Nicaragua

Competitiveness Rankings

Growth Competitiveness Index Rank	99

Macroeconomic Environment Index Rank **110**
   Macroeconomic Stability Subindex Rank 97
   Government Waste Rank 101
   Country Credit Rating Rank..............................105

Public Institutions Index Rank...**82**
   Contracts and Law Subindex Rank 98
   Corruption Subindex Rank...................................70

Technology Index Rank **102**
   Innovation Subindex Rank...................................86
   ICT Subindex Rank 109
   Technology Transfer Subindex Rank
     (out of 92 non-core innovators).......................75

Business Competitiveness Index Rank	102

**Sophistication of Company Operations
  and Strategy Rank** **106**
**Quality of the National Business
  Environment Rank** **102**

The Most Problematic Factors for Doing Business

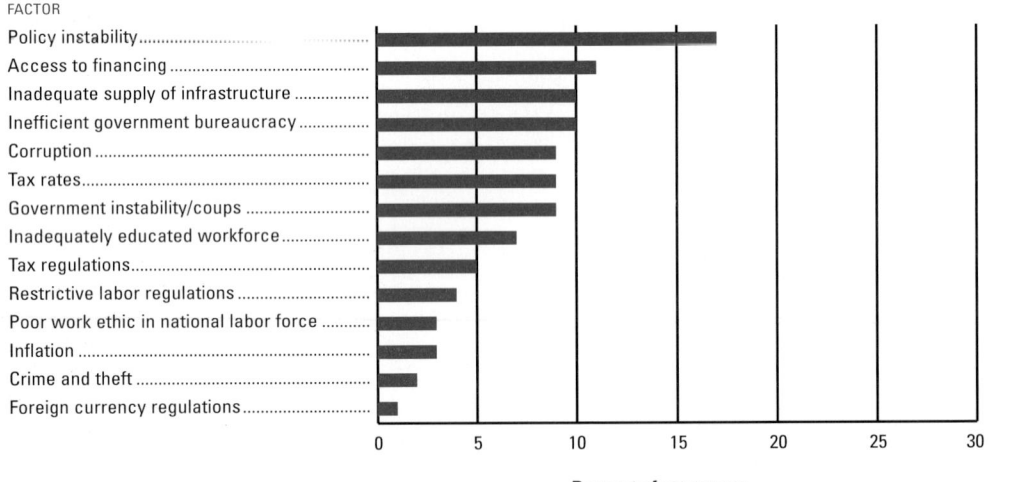

Note: From a list of 14 factors, respondents were asked to select the five most problematic for doing business in their country and to rank them between 1 (most problematic) and 5. The bars in the figure show the responses weighted according to their rankings.

Source: World Economic Forum, Executive Opinion Survey (2005)

390

National competitiveness balance sheet

NOTABLE COMPETITIVE ADVANTAGES		
Growth Competitiveness Index		**Rank/117**
	Macroeconomic Environment	
2.15	Real effective exchange rate, 2004	27

NOTABLE COMPETITIVE DISADVANTAGES		
Growth Competitiveness Index		**Rank/117**
	Macroeconomic Environment	
2.14	National savings rate, 2004	107
2.21	Country credit rating, 2004	105
2.07	Access to credit	104
6.06	Wastefulness of government spending	101
2.16	Inflation, 2004	97
2.20	Government debt, 2004	97
2.01	Recession expectations	91
2.17	Interest rate spread, 2004	81
2.13	Government surplus/deficit, 2004	56
	Public Institutions	
6.01	Judicial independence	116
6.03	Property rights	93
6.20	Irregular payments in public utilities	86
6.08	Favoritism in decisions of government officials	82
6.21	Irregular payments in tax collection	72
6.19	Irregular payments in exports and imports	59
6.16	Organized crime	56
	Technology	
3.06	Company spending on research and development	108
3.03	Prevalence of foreign technology licensing	107
3.02	Firm-level technology absorption	106
3.14	Government success in ICT promotion	101
3.11	Internet access in schools	99
5.08	Telephone lines, 2003	98
3.13	Government prioritization of ICT	96
3.12	Quality of competition in the ISP sector	96
3.19	Internet users, 2003	96
3.15	Laws relating to ICT	94
3.07	University/industry research collaboration	90
3.18	Cellular telephones, 2003	88
3.01	Technological readiness	86
3.04	FDI and technology transfer	81
3.17	Utility patents, 2004	81
3.21	Personal computers, 2003	78
4.17	Gross tertiary enrollment	77
3.20	Internet hosts, 2003	71

Business Competitiveness Index		Rank/110
	Sophistication of Company Operations and Strategy	
8.03	Capacity for innovation	93
	Quality of the National Business Environment	
6.14	Reliability of police services	46
8.15	Quality of management schools	51
6.13	Centralization of economic policymaking	51

Business Competitiveness Index		Rank/110
	Sophistication of Company Operations and Strategy	
8.08	Control of international distribution	110
3.06	Company spending on research and development	104
8.07	Degree of customer orientation	104
	Quality of the National Business Environment	
2.06	Venture capital availability	109
6.02	Efficiency of legal framework	109
6.01	Judicial independence	109

Other Indicators		Rank/117
4.07	Ease of hiring foreign labor	13
6.05	Freedom of the press	37
8.18	Flexibility of wage determination	41

Other Indicators		Rank/117
6.10	Effectiveness of law-making bodies	116
8.21	Protection of minority shareholders' interests	115
7.03	Extent of market dominance	114
6.26	Public trust of politicians	113
2.09	Prevalence of trade barriers	113
7.02	Effectiveness of antitrust policy	112
2.11	Tax burden	110
9.05	Effects of privatization on competition and the environment	110
4.09	Private sector employment of women	110
2.05	Ease of access to loans	110
7.04	Buyer sophistication	110
9.08	Protection of ecosystems by business	110

391

Note: The Business Competitiveness Index applies different criteria for selecting a country's competitive advantages and disadvantages. Please refer to the section "How Country Profiles Work" for further details.

Nigeria

Competitiveness Rankings

Growth Competitiveness Index Rank	88

Macroeconomic Environment Index Rank **76**
    Macroeconomic Stability Subindex Rank 45
    Government Waste Rank 81
    Country Credit Rating Rank..................................91

Public Institutions Index Rank...**98**
    Contracts and Law Subindex Rank 69
    Corruption Subindex Rank...................................109

Technology Index Rank **90**
    Innovation Subindex Rank....................................99
    ICT Subindex Rank 103
    Technology Transfer Subindex Rank
        (out of 92 non-core innovators).......................51

Business Competitiveness Index Rank	76

Sophistication of Company Operations
  and Strategy Rank 65
Quality of the National Business
  Environment Rank 79

The Most Problematic Factors for Doing Business

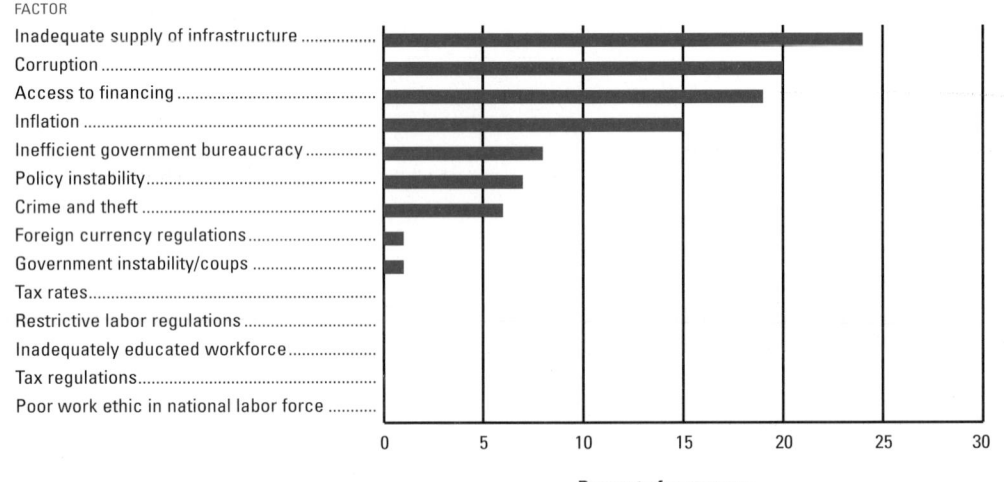

Note: From a list of 14 factors, respondents were asked to select the five most problematic for doing business in their country and to rank them between 1 (most problematic) and 5. The bars in the figure show the responses weighted according to their rankings.

Source: World Economic Forum, Executive Opinion Survey (2005)

National competitiveness balance sheet

NOTABLE COMPETITIVE ADVANTAGES	
Growth Competitiveness Index	**Rank/117**

Macroeconomic Environment

2.13	Government surplus/deficit, 2004	5
2.20	Government debt, 2004	13
2.14	National savings rate, 2004	17
2.15	Real effective exchange rate, 2004	22

NOTABLE COMPETITIVE DISADVANTAGES	
Growth Competitiveness Index	**Rank/117**

Macroeconomic Environment

2.07	Access to credit	116
2.16	Inflation, 2004	114
2.01	Recession expectations	100
2.21	Country credit rating, 2004	91
6.06	Wastefulness of government spending	81
2.17	Interest rate spread, 2004	56

Public Institutions

6.20	Irregular payments in public utilities	116
6.19	Irregular payments in exports and imports	102
6.21	Irregular payments in tax collection	98
6.16	Organized crime	97
6.03	Property rights	75
6.08	Favoritism in decisions of government officials	67
6.01	Judicial independence	51

Technology

3.20	Internet hosts, 2003	112
3.18	Cellular telephones, 2003	107
5.08	Telephone lines, 2003	106
3.19	Internet users, 2003	105
3.21	Personal computers, 2003	100
3.02	Firm-level technology absorption	98
4.17	Gross tertiary enrollment	96
3.13	Government prioritization of ICT	95
3.11	Internet access in schools	94
3.01	Technological readiness	92
3.17	Utility patents, 2004	80
3.03	Prevalence of foreign technology licensing	76
3.12	Quality of competition in the ISP sector	76
3.14	Government success in ICT promotion	74
3.15	Laws relating to ICT	74
3.07	University/industry research collaboration	71
3.06	Company spending on research and development	68
3.04	FDI and technology transfer	64

Business Competitiveness Index	
	Rank/110

Sophistication of Company Operations and Strategy

8.12	Willingness to delegate authority	34
8.01	Nature of competitive advantage	38
8.11	Extent of staff training	46

Quality of the National Business Environment

6.13	Centralization of economic policymaking	27
3.08	Government procurement of advanced technology products	35
7.02	Effectiveness of antitrust policy	46

Business Competitiveness Index	
	Rank/110

Sophistication of Company Operations and Strategy

8.07	Degree of customer orientation	82
8.08	Control of international distribution	80
8.09	Extent of regional sales	78

Quality of the National Business Environment

6.09	Extent of bureaucratic red tape	109
6.14	Reliability of police services	105
5.05	Quality of electricity supply	103

Other Indicators	
	Rank/117

4.07	Ease of hiring foreign labor	23
8.17	Hiring and firing practices	25
9.05	Effects of privatization on competition and the environment	32
6.07	Burden of government regulation	35
6.11	Extent and effect of taxation	36
9.10	Grass-roots involvement in development projects	39
8.24	Importance of corporate social responsibility	41
9.07	Importance of environment in business planning	42
9.09	Prevalence of corporate environmental reporting	44
7.08	Local availability of process machinery	47

Other Indicators	
	Rank/117

5.06	Postal efficiency	113
2.12	Agricultural policy costs	109
8.19	Cooperation in labor-employer relations	106
2.04	Soundness of banks	105
4.06	Medium term business impact of HIV/AIDS	102
3.10	Availability of mobile or cellular telephones	102
6.27	Pervasiveness of money laundering through banks	102
2.05	Ease of access to loans	101
2.02	Business costs of terrorism	99
2.09	Prevalence of trade barriers	97
4.05	Medium term business impact of tuberculosis	94
8.15	Quality of management schools	93

393

Note: The Business Competitiveness Index applies different criteria for selecting a country's competitive advantages and disadvantages. Please refer to the section "How Country Profiles Work" for further details.

Norway

Competitiveness Rankings

The Most Problematic Factors for Doing Business

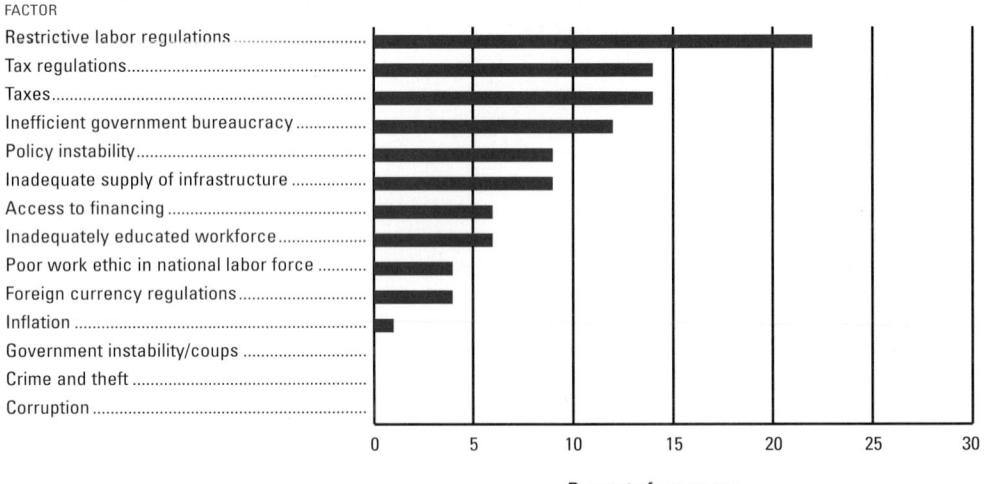

Note: From a list of 14 factors, respondents were asked to select the five most problematic for doing business in their country and to rank them between 1 (most problematic) and 5. The bars in the figure show the responses weighted according to their rankings.

Source: World Economic Forum, Executive Opinion Survey (2005)

National competitiveness balance sheet

NOTABLE COMPETITIVE ADVANTAGES	
Growth Competitiveness Index	**Rank/117**

Macroeconomic Environment

2.21	Country credit rating, 2004	2
2.13	Government surplus/deficit, 2004	3
2.07	Access to credit	6
6.06	Wastefulness of government spending	8
2.16	Inflation, 2004	9
2.17	Interest rate spread, 2004	10

Public Institutions

6.21	Irregular payments in tax collection	6
6.20	Irregular payments in public utilities	7
6.01	Judicial independence	8
6.08	Favoritism in decisions of government officials	8
6.19	Irregular payments in exports and imports	8
6.16	Organized crime	10

Technology

5.08	Telephone lines, 2003	4
4.17	Gross tertiary enrollment	5
3.20	Internet hosts, 2003	7
3.21	Personal computers, 2003	10

Business Competitiveness Index	**Rank/110**

Sophistication of Company Operations and Strategy

8.12	Willingness to delegate authority	3
8.14	Reliance on professional management	7
8.11	Extent of staff training	10

Quality of the National Business Environment

6.25	Business costs of corruption	2
9.01	Stringency of environmental regulations	5
6.08	Favoritism in decisions of government officials	7

Other Indicators	**Rank/117**

9.09	Prevalence of corporate environmental reporting	2
9.03	Extent of government mandated environmental reporting	3
4.06	Medium term business impact of HIV/AIDS	3
9.04	Effects of compliance on business	4
4.08	Brain drain	4
9.07	Importance of environment in business planning	5
9.02	Clarity and stability of regulations	5
6.26	Public trust of politicians	5
6.24	Diversion of public funds	5
6.22	Irregular payments in public contracts	5
6.17	Informal sector	5

NOTABLE COMPETITIVE DISADVANTAGES	
Growth Competitiveness Index	**Rank/117**

Macroeconomic Environment

2.15	Real effective exchange rate, 2004	72
2.20	Government debt, 2004	32
2.01	Recession expectations	16
2.14	National savings rate, 2004	12

Public Institutions

6.03	Property rights	14

Technology

3.13	Government prioritization of ICT	51
3.14	Government success in ICT promotion	46
3.19	Internet users, 2003	27
3.11	Internet access in schools	24
3.06	Company spending on research and development	23
3.12	Quality of competition in the ISP sector	22
3.07	University/industry research collaboration	22
3.17	Utility patents, 2004	20
3.02	Firm-level technology absorption	17
3.18	Cellular telephones, 2003	12
3.01	Technological readiness	12
3.15	Laws relating to ICT	11

Business Competitiveness Index	**Rank/110**

Sophistication of Company Operations and Strategy

8.10	Breadth of international markets	40
8.02	Value chain presence	40
8.13	Extent of incentive compensation	34

Quality of the National Business Environment

2.09	Prevalence of trade barriers	82
4.03	Quality of math and science education	74
7.01	Intensity of local competition	38

Other Indicators	**Rank/117**

2.12	Agricultural policy costs	114
8.18	Flexibility of wage determination	101
8.17	Hiring and firing practices	99
2.11	Tax burden	95
6.12	Efficiency of the tax system	61
8.20	Pay and productivity	55
2.10	Impact of rules on FDI	54
6.11	Extent and effect of taxation	48
4.07	Ease of hiring foreign labor	40
6.13	Centralization of economic policymaking	37
3.09	Availability of scientists and engineers	36

395

Note: The Business Competitiveness Index applies different criteria for selecting a country's competitive advantages and disadvantages. Please refer to the section "How Country Profiles Work" for further details.

Pakistan

Competitiveness Rankings

Growth Competitiveness Index Rank	83

Macroeconomic Environment Index Rank	69
Macroeconomic Stability Subindex Rank	49
Government Waste Rank	48
Country Credit Rating Rank	82

Public Institutions Index Rank	103
Contracts and Law Subindex Rank	87
Corruption Subindex Rank	106

Technology Index Rank	80
Innovation Subindex Rank	100
ICT Subindex Rank	77
Technology Transfer Subindex Rank (out of 92 non-core innovators)	49

Business Competitiveness Index Rank	66

Sophistication of Company Operations and Strategy Rank	68
Quality of the National Business Environment Rank	65

The Most Problematic Factors for Doing Business

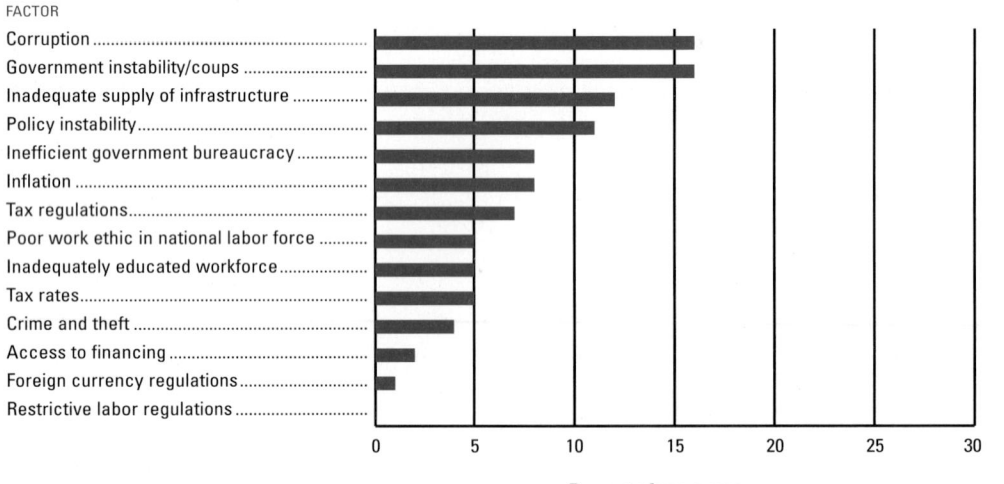

FACTOR

Corruption
Government instability/coups
Inadequate supply of infrastructure
Policy instability
Inefficient government bureaucracy
Inflation
Tax regulations
Poor work ethic in national labor force
Inadequately educated workforce
Tax rates
Crime and theft
Access to financing
Foreign currency regulations
Restrictive labor regulations

Percent of responses

Note: From a list of 14 factors, respondents were asked to select the five most problematic for doing business in their country and to rank them between 1 (most problematic) and 5. The bars in the figure show the responses weighted according to their rankings.

Source: World Economic Forum, Executive Opinion Survey (2005)

National competitiveness balance sheet

NOTABLE COMPETITIVE ADVANTAGES	
Growth Competitiveness Index	**Rank/117**

Macroeconomic Environment

2.07	Access to credit 8
2.01	Recession expectations 24
2.15	Real effective exchange rate, 2004 38
6.06	Wastefulness of government spending 48

Technology

3.14	Government success in ICT promotion 7
3.13	Government prioritization of ICT 17
3.12	Quality of competition in the ISP sector 20
3.04	FDI and technology transfer 40
3.02	Firm-level technology absorption 47

NOTABLE COMPETITIVE DISADVANTAGES	
Growth Competitiveness Index	**Rank/117**

Macroeconomic Environment

2.14	National savings rate, 2004 88
2.16	Inflation, 2004 84
2.21	Country credit rating, 2004 82
2.20	Government debt, 2004 68
2.17	Interest rate spread, 2004 67
2.13	Government surplus/deficit, 2004 64

Public Institutions

6.20	Irregular payments in public utilities 109
6.21	Irregular payments in tax collection 108
6.19	Irregular payments in exports and imports 96
6.16	Organized crime 90
6.03	Property rights 87
6.01	Judicial independence 87
6.08	Favoritism in decisions of government officials 68

Technology

3.18	Cellular telephones, 2003 111
4.17	Gross tertiary enrollment 109
3.21	Personal computers, 2003 106
3.19	Internet users, 2003 102
5.08	Telephone lines, 2003 100
3.20	Internet hosts, 2003 96
3.03	Prevalence of foreign technology licensing 88
3.17	Utility patents, 2004 78
3.15	Laws relating to ICT 78
3.01	Technological readiness 74
3.07	University/industry research collaboration 72
3.11	Internet access in schools 66
3.06	Company spending on research and development 59

Business Competitiveness Index	**Rank/110**

Sophistication of Company Operations and Strategy

8.08	Control of international distribution 22
8.07	Degree of customer orientation 41
8.10	Breadth of international markets 48

Quality of the National Business Environment

8.21	Protection of minority shareholders' interests 27
2.05	Ease of access to loans 30
7.03	Decentralization of corporate activity 30

Business Competitiveness Index	**Rank/110**

Sophistication of Company Operations and Strategy

8.11	Extent of staff training 103
8.12	Willingness to delegate authority 99
3.03	Prevalence of foreign technology licensing 86

Quality of the National Business Environment

8.16	Efficacy of corporate boards 110
3.18	Cellular telephones, 2003 105
6.14	Reliability of police services 101

Other Indicators	**Rank/117**
2.10	Impact of rules on FDI 14
8.18	Flexibility of wage determination 23
8.17	Hiring and firing practices 29
2.08	Local equity market access 30
6.11	Extent and effect of taxation 30
7.03	Extent of market dominance 31
8.22	Foreign ownership restrictions 31
2.12	Agricultural policy costs 35
8.19	Cooperation in labor-employer relations 39
7.02	Effectiveness of antitrust policy 40
2.04	Soundness of banks 40
7.05	Local supplier quantity 40

Other Indicators	**Rank/117**
4.09	Private sector employment of women 115
8.20	Pay and productivity 109
6.02	Efficiency of legal framework 106
6.13	Centralization of economic policymaking 105
9.08	Protection of ecosystems by business 104
6.22	Irregular payments in public contracts 102
2.02	Business costs of terrorism 101
6.23	Irregular payments in judicial decisions 98
9.03	Extent of government mandated environmental reporting 95
6.07	Burden of government regulation 94
9.02	Clarity and stability of regulations 94

397

Note: The Business Competitiveness Index applies different criteria for selecting a country's competitive advantages and disadvantages. Please refer to the section "How Country Profiles Work" for further details.

Panama

Competitiveness Rankings

Growth Competitiveness Index Rank	**73**

Macroeconomic Environment Index Rank **74**
    Macroeconomic Stability Subindex Rank 91
    Government Waste Rank 99
    Country Credit Rating Rank 59

Public Institutions Index Rank **75**
    Contracts and Law Subindex Rank 63
    Corruption Subindex Rank 86

Technology Index Rank **65**
    Innovation Subindex Rank 42
    ICT Subindex Rank 73
    Technology Transfer Subindex Rank
      (out of 92 non-core innovators).......................37

Business Competitiveness Index Rank	**61**

**Sophistication of Company Operations
  and Strategy Rank** **37**
**Quality of the National Business
  Environment Rank** **68**

The Most Problematic Factors for Doing Business

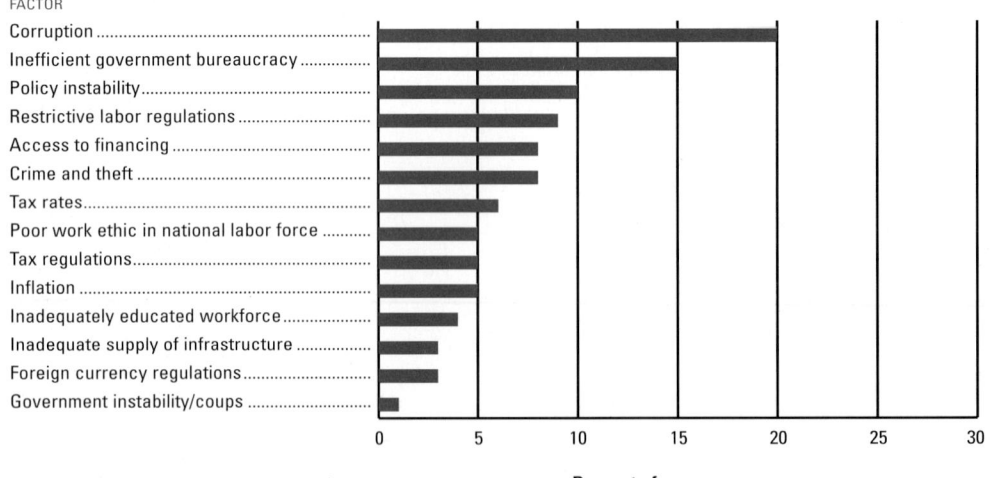

Note: From a list of 14 factors, respondents were asked to select the five most problematic for doing business in their country and to rank them between 1 (most problematic) and 5. The bars in the figure show the responses weighted according to their rankings.

Source: World Economic Forum, Executive Opinion Survey (2005)

National competitiveness balance sheet

NOTABLE COMPETITIVE ADVANTAGES

Growth Competitiveness Index	Rank/117

Macroeconomic Environment

2.16	Inflation, 2004	10
2.15	Real effective exchange rate, 2004	42

Public Institutions

6.08	Favoritism in decisions of government officials	41
6.03	Property rights	46

Technology

3.04	FDI and technology transfer	35
4.17	Gross tertiary enrollment	37
3.17	Utility patents, 2004	49

NOTABLE COMPETITIVE DISADVANTAGES

Growth Competitiveness Index	Rank/117

Macroeconomic Environment

2.01	Recession expectations	115
6.06	Wastefulness of government spending	99
2.13	Government surplus/deficit, 2004	96
2.20	Government debt, 2004	86
2.07	Access to credit	82
2.17	Interest rate spread, 2004	72
2.14	National savings rate, 2004	64
2.21	Country credit rating, 2004	59

Public Institutions

6.19	Irregular payments in exports and imports	101
6.20	Irregular payments in public utilities	89
6.01	Judicial independence	89
6.16	Organized crime	78
6.21	Irregular payments in tax collection	68

Technology

3.13	Government prioritization of ICT	106
3.14	Government success in ICT promotion	103
3.03	Prevalence of foreign technology licensing	74
3.02	Firm-level technology absorption	73
3.21	Personal computers, 2003	72
5.08	Telephone lines, 2003	70
3.18	Cellular telephones, 2003	68
3.11	Internet access in schools	65
3.15	Laws relating to ICT	63
3.19	Internet users, 2003	60
3.20	Internet hosts, 2003	58
3.01	Technological readiness	57
3.07	University/industry research collaboration	54
3.12	Quality of competition in the ISP sector	52
3.06	Company spending on research and development	51

Business Competitiveness Index	Rank/110

Sophistication of Company Operations and Strategy

8.13	Extent of incentive compensation	19
8.08	Control of international distribution	21
8.03	Capacity for innovation	26

Quality of the National Business Environment

2.06	Venture capital availability	19
2.05	Ease of access to loans	34
6.13	Centralization of economic policymaking	36

Other Indicators	Rank/117

2.11	Tax burden	16
9.07	Importance of environment in business planning	28
4.09	Private sector employment of women	28
8.02	Value chain presence	30
2.04	Soundness of banks	32
8.06	Extent of marketing	35
3.16	Extent of business Internet use	35
8.10	Breadth of international markets	38
2.03	Financial market sophistication	38

Business Competitiveness Index	Rank/110

Sophistication of Company Operations and Strategy

8.12	Willingness to delegate authority	88
3.03	Prevalence of foreign technology licensing	72
8.14	Reliance on professional management	67

Quality of the National Business Environment

8.19	Cooperation in labor-employer relations	107
7.01	Intensity of local competition	106
4.01	Quality of the educational system	103

Other Indicators	Rank/117

4.07	Ease of hiring foreign labor	110
2.02	Business costs of terrorism	104
8.16	Efficacy of corporate boards	103
8.18	Flexibility of wage determination	100
6.10	Effectiveness of law-making bodies	98
8.22	Foreign ownership restrictions	98
5.06	Postal efficiency	95
8.17	Hiring and firing practices	94
3.05	Quality of scientific research institutions	93
6.26	Public trust of politicians	90
9.10	Grass-roots involvement in development projects	90
3.08	Government procurement of advanced technology products	90

Note: The Business Competitiveness Index applies different criteria for selecting a country's competitive advantages and disadvantages. Please refer to the section "How Country Profiles Work" for further details.

Paraguay

Competitiveness Rankings

Growth Competitiveness Index Rank	113

Macroeconomic Environment Index Rank **102**
    Macroeconomic Stability Subindex Rank 79
    Government Waste Rank 117
    Country Credit Rating Rank 85

Public Institutions Index Rank..**112**
    Contracts and Law Subindex Rank 117
    Corruption Subindex Rank.....................................95

Technology Index Rank **111**
    Innovation Subindex Rank 83
    ICT Subindex Rank 111
    Technology Transfer Subindex Rank
       (out of 92 non-core innovators).........................87

Business Competitiveness Index Rank	110

**Sophistication of Company Operations
and Strategy Rank** **108**

**Quality of the National Business
Environment Rank** **110**

The Most Problematic Factors for Doing Business

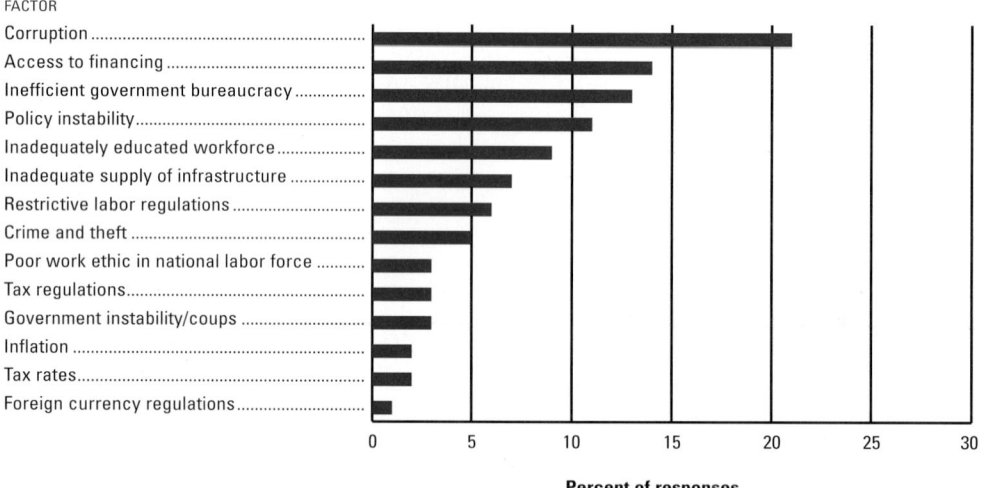

Note: From a list of 14 factors, respondents were asked to select the five most problematic for doing business in their country and to rank them between 1 (most problematic) and 5. The bars in the figure show the responses weighted according to their rankings.

Source: World Economic Forum, Executive Opinion Survey (2005)

National competitiveness balance sheet

NOTABLE COMPETITIVE ADVANTAGES	
Growth Competitiveness Index	**Rank/117**

Macroeconomic Environment

2.15	Real effective exchange rate, 2004	11
2.13	Government surplus/deficit, 2004	23
2.20	Government debt, 2004	39

NOTABLE COMPETITIVE DISADVANTAGES	
Growth Competitiveness Index	**Rank/117**

Macroeconomic Environment

6.06	Wastefulness of government spending	117
2.17	Interest rate spread, 2004	114
2.07	Access to credit	109
2.01	Recession expectations	107
2.21	Country credit rating, 2004	85
2.16	Inflation, 2004	72
2.14	National savings rate, 2004	55

Public Institutions

6.03	Property rights	116
6.08	Favoritism in decisions of government officials	115
6.01	Judicial independence	113
6.16	Organized crime	112
6.20	Irregular payments in public utilities	101
6.21	Irregular payments in tax collection	94
6.19	Irregular payments in exports and imports	90

Technology

3.14	Government success in ICT promotion	117
3.13	Government prioritization of ICT	116
3.07	University/industry research collaboration	116
3.02	Firm-level technology absorption	115
3.06	Company spending on research and development	114
3.03	Prevalence of foreign technology licensing	112
3.15	Laws relating to ICT	112
3.11	Internet access in schools	106
3.04	FDI and technology transfer	105
3.12	Quality of competition in the ISP sector	101
3.01	Technological readiness	99
5.08	Telephone lines, 2003	92
3.19	Internet users, 2003	92
3.17	Utility patents, 2004	81
3.21	Personal computers, 2003	74
3.20	Internet hosts, 2003	68
4.17	Gross tertiary enrollment	67
3.18	Cellular telephones, 2003	56

Business Competitiveness Index	Rank/110

Sophistication of Company Operations and Strategy

8.09	Extent of regional sales	80
8.06	Extent of marketing	94

Quality of the National Business Environment

6.09	Extent of bureaucratic red tape	37
2.09	Prevalence of trade barriers	75

Business Competitiveness Index	Rank/110

Sophistication of Company Operations and Strategy

8.12	Willingness to delegate authority	110
8.14	Reliance on professional management	110
8.02	Value chain presence	108

Quality of the National Business Environment

4.01	Quality of the educational system	110
3.05	Quality of scientific research institutions	110
3.07	University/industry research collaboration	109

Other Indicators	Rank/117

4.07	Ease of hiring foreign labor	30
6.11	Extent and effect of taxation	47
2.11	Tax burden	49

Other Indicators	Rank/117

8.04	Ethical behavior of firms	117
6.18	Government effectiveness in reducing poverty and inequality	117
8.20	Pay and productivity	117
9.10	Grass-roots involvement in development projects	116
6.24	Diversion of public funds	116
9.04	Effects of compliance on business	116
9.03	Extent of government mandated environmental reporting	116
4.09	Private sector employment of women	116
6.26	Public trust of politicians	115
3.08	Government procurement of advanced technology products	115
9.09	Prevalence of corporate environmental reporting	115
8.23	Strength of auditing and accounting standards	115

Note: The Business Competitiveness Index applies different criteria for selecting a country's competitive advantages and disadvantages. Please refer to the section "How Country Profiles Work" for further details.

Peru

Competitiveness Rankings

Growth Competitiveness Index Rank	68

Macroeconomic Environment Index Rank **70**
    Macroeconomic Stability Subindex Rank 54
    Government Waste Rank 103
    Country Credit Rating Rank 67

Public Institutions Index Rank..**59**
    Contracts and Law Subindex Rank 99
    Corruption Subindex Rank....................................39

Technology Index Rank **75**
    Innovation Subindex Rank 62
    ICT Subindex Rank 84
    Technology Transfer Subindex Rank
      (out of 92 non-core innovators).........................40

Business Competitiveness Index Rank	81

Sophistication of Company Operations
    and Strategy Rank 66
Quality of the National Business
    Environment Rank 82

The Most Problematic Factors for Doing Business

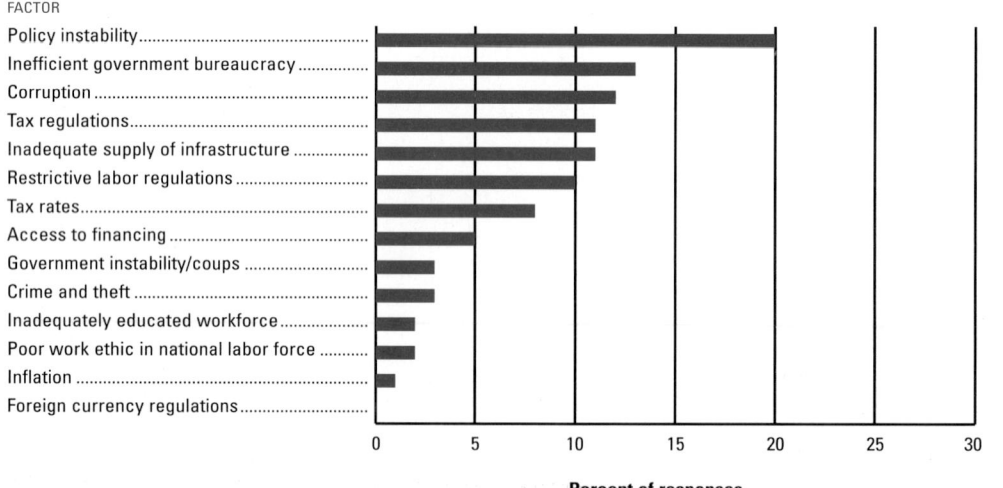

FACTOR

Note: From a list of 14 factors, respondents were asked to select the five most problematic for doing business in their country and to rank them between 1 (most problematic) and 5. The bars in the figure show the responses weighted according to their rankings.

Source: World Economic Forum, Executive Opinion Survey (2005)

National competitiveness balance sheet

NOTABLE COMPETITIVE ADVANTAGES

Growth Competitiveness Index	Rank/117

Macroeconomic Environment

2.15	Real effective exchange rate, 2004	39
2.13	Government surplus/deficit, 2004	40
2.01	Recession expectations	44
2.20	Government debt, 2004	45

Public Institutions

6.19	Irregular payments in exports and imports	39
6.21	Irregular payments in tax collection	39
6.20	Irregular payments in public utilities	41

Technology

3.04	FDI and technology transfer	30

NOTABLE COMPETITIVE DISADVANTAGES

Growth Competitiveness Index	Rank/117

Macroeconomic Environment

6.06	Wastefulness of government spending	103
2.17	Interest rate spread, 2004	94
2.14	National savings rate, 2004	74
2.21	Country credit rating, 2004	67
2.07	Access to credit	60
2.16	Inflation, 2004	56

Public Institutions

6.01	Judicial independence	110
6.03	Property rights	98
6.08	Favoritism in decisions of government officials	89
6.16	Organized crime	84

Technology

3.14	Government success in ICT promotion	111
3.13	Government prioritization of ICT	110
3.06	Company spending on research and development	93
3.07	University/industry research collaboration	89
5.08	Telephone lines, 2003	86
3.18	Cellular telephones, 2003	85
3.02	Firm-level technology absorption	84
3.03	Prevalence of foreign technology licensing	84
3.12	Quality of competition in the ISP sector	78
3.11	Internet access in schools	75
3.21	Personal computers, 2003	68
3.17	Utility patents, 2004	64
3.01	Technological readiness	62
3.15	Laws relating to ICT	60
3.20	Internet hosts, 2003	57
4.17	Gross tertiary enrollment	57
3.19	Internet users, 2003	56

Business Competitiveness Index	Rank/110

Sophistication of Company Operations and Strategy

8.07	Degree of customer orientation	47
8.06	Extent of marketing	50
8.10	Breadth of international markets	53

Quality of the National Business Environment

5.07	Telephone/fax infrastructure quality	34
8.15	Quality of management schools	44
2.03	Financial market sophistication	49

Business Competitiveness Index	Rank/110

Sophistication of Company Operations and Strategy

3.06	Company spending on research and development	89
3.03	Prevalence of foreign technology licensing	82
8.03	Capacity for innovation	79

Quality of the National Business Environment

4.02	Quality of public schools	108
4.03	Quality of math and science education	105
4.01	Quality of the educational system	104

Other Indicators	Rank/117

4.07	Ease of hiring foreign labor	20
8.18	Flexibility of wage determination	28
6.05	Freedom of the press	33
3.10	Availability of mobile or cellular telephones	45

Other Indicators	Rank/117

6.10	Effectiveness of law-making bodies	115
6.17	Informal sector	114
6.07	Burden of government regulation	114
6.26	Public trust of politicians	110
6.02	Efficiency of legal framework	107
6.18	Government effectiveness in reducing poverty and inequality	106
3.05	Quality of scientific research institutions	104
3.08	Government procurement of advanced technology products	104
6.15	Business costs of crime and violence	104
2.12	Agricultural policy costs	98
6.14	Reliability of police services	97
3.09	Availability of scientists and engineers	96
9.07	Importance of environment in business planning	96
6.23	Irregular payments in judicial decisions	96
5.06	Postal efficiency	94

Note: The Business Competitiveness Index applies different criteria for selecting a country's competitive advantages and disadvantages. Please refer to the section "How Country Profiles Work" for further details.

Philippines

Competitiveness Rankings

Growth Competitiveness Index Rank	77

Macroeconomic Environment Index Rank **71**
  Macroeconomic Stability Subindex Rank 58
  Government Waste Rank 100
  Country Credit Rating Rank 71

Public Institutions Index Rank..**104**
  Contracts and Law Subindex Rank 82
  Corruption Subindex Rank................................108

Technology Index Rank **54**
  Innovation Subindex Rank 65
  ICT Subindex Rank 63
  Technology Transfer Subindex Rank
    (out of 92 non-core innovators).........................11

Business Competitiveness Index Rank	69

**Sophistication of Company Operations
  and Strategy Rank** **44**
**Quality of the National Business
  Environment Rank** **78**

The Most Problematic Factors for Doing Business

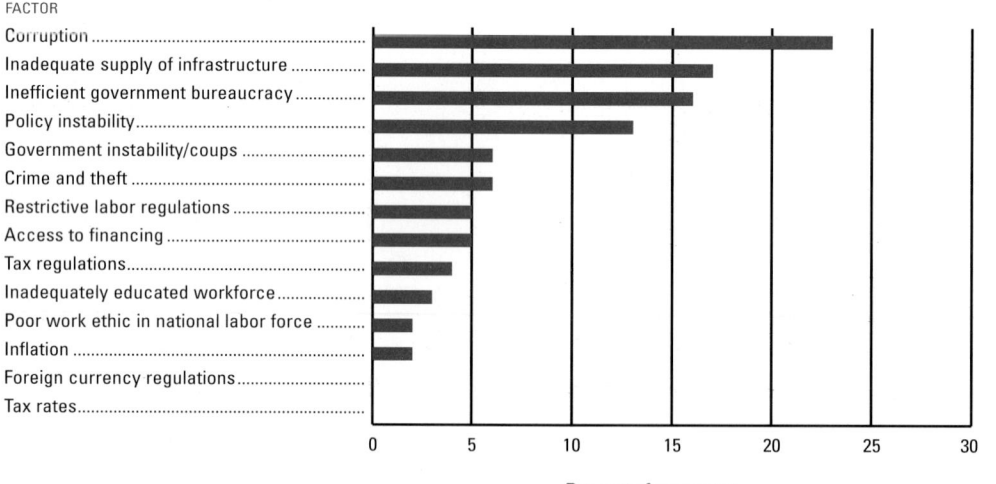

FACTOR

Corruption
Inadequate supply of infrastructure
Inefficient government bureaucracy
Policy instability
Government instability/coups
Crime and theft
Restrictive labor regulations
Access to financing
Tax regulations
Inadequately educated workforce
Poor work ethic in national labor force
Inflation
Foreign currency regulations
Tax rates

Percent of responses

Note: From a list of 14 factors, respondents were asked to select the five most problematic for doing business in their country and to rank them between 1 (most problematic) and 5. The bars in the figure show the responses weighted according to their rankings.

Source: World Economic Forum, Executive Opinion Survey (2005)

National competitiveness balance sheet

NOTABLE COMPETITIVE ADVANTAGES	
Growth Competitiveness Index	**Rank/117**

Macroeconomic Environment

2.15	Real effective exchange rate, 2004	18
2.17	Interest rate spread, 2004	33

Technology

3.03	Prevalence of foreign technology licensing	19
3.12	Quality of competition in the ISP sector	26
3.04	FDI and technology transfer	37
3.15	Laws relating to ICT	42
3.13	Government prioritization of ICT	44
3.14	Government success in ICT promotion	44

NOTABLE COMPETITIVE DISADVANTAGES	
Growth Competitiveness Index	**Rank/117**

Macroeconomic Environment

6.06	Wastefulness of government spending	100
2.20	Government debt, 2004	93
2.13	Government surplus/deficit, 2004	84
2.16	Inflation, 2004	73
2.21	Country credit rating, 2004	71
2.14	National savings rate, 2004	57
2.07	Access to credit	55
2.01	Recession expectations	55

Public Institutions

6.21	Irregular payments in tax collection	115
6.19	Irregular payments in exports and imports	111
6.08	Favoritism in decisions of government officials	98
6.01	Judicial independence	85
6.20	Irregular payments in public utilities	85
6.16	Organized crime	82
6.03	Property rights	64

Technology

5.08	Telephone lines, 2003	93
3.20	Internet hosts, 2003	84
3.21	Personal computers, 2003	79
3.19	Internet users, 2003	77
3.01	Technological readiness	76
3.07	University/industry research collaboration	68
3.06	Company spending on research and development	66
3.02	Firm-level technology absorption	64
3.18	Cellular telephones, 2003	62
3.17	Utility patents, 2004	61
4.17	Gross tertiary enrollment	60
3.11	Internet access in schools	52

Business Competitiveness Index	**Rank/110**

Sophistication of Company Operations and Strategy

3.03	Prevalence of foreign technology licensing	19
8.12	Willingness to delegate authority	31
8.02	Value chain presence	33

Quality of the National Business Environment

8.15	Quality of management schools	29
2.08	Local equity market access	32
3.15	Laws relating to ICT	41

Business Competitiveness Index	**Rank/110**

Sophistication of Company Operations and Strategy

8.05	Production process sophistication	79
8.03	Capacity for innovation	75
3.06	Company spending on research and development	64

Quality of the National Business Environment

4.03	Quality of math and science education	107
4.02	Quality of public schools	100
8.22	Foreign ownership restrictions	100

Other Indicators	**Rank/117**

4.09	Private sector employment of women	7
3.10	Availability of mobile or cellular telephones	23
6.05	Freedom of the press	28
6.11	Extent and effect of taxation	31
9.10	Grass-roots involvement in development projects	33
8.13	Extent of incentive compensation	38
8.24	Importance of corporate social responsibility	38
2.11	Tax burden	38
2.12	Agricultural policy costs	38
8.11	Extent of staff training	39
8.06	Extent of marketing	40

Other Indicators	**Rank/117**

2.02	Business costs of terrorism	116
6.22	Irregular payments in public contracts	116
6.23	Irregular payments in judicial decisions	115
6.26	Public trust of politicians	109
8.17	Hiring and firing practices	109
4.07	Ease of hiring foreign labor	109
6.24	Diversion of public funds	107
5.06	Postal efficiency	103
4.08	Brain drain	101
8.19	Cooperation in labor-employer relations	100
9.02	Clarity and stability of regulations	98
6.14	Reliability of police services	96
6.25	Business costs of corruption	96
6.07	Burden of government regulation	95

405

Note: The Business Competitiveness Index applies different criteria for selecting a country's competitive advantages and disadvantages. Please refer to the section "How Country Profiles Work" for further details.

Poland

Competitiveness Rankings

Growth Competitiveness Index Rank	51

Macroeconomic Environment Index Rank **53**
   Macroeconomic Stability Subindex Rank 68
   Government Waste Rank 77
   Country Credit Rating Rank 39

Public Institutions Index Rank **64**
   Contracts and Law Subindex Rank 65
   Corruption Subindex Rank....................................66

Technology Index Rank **39**
   Innovation Subindex Rank 31
   ICT Subindex Rank 43
   Technology Transfer Subindex Rank
      (out of 92 non-core innovators) 24

Business Competitiveness Index Rank	42

**Sophistication of Company Operations
and Strategy Rank** **43**

**Quality of the National Business
Environment Rank** **46**

The Most Problematic Factors for Doing Business

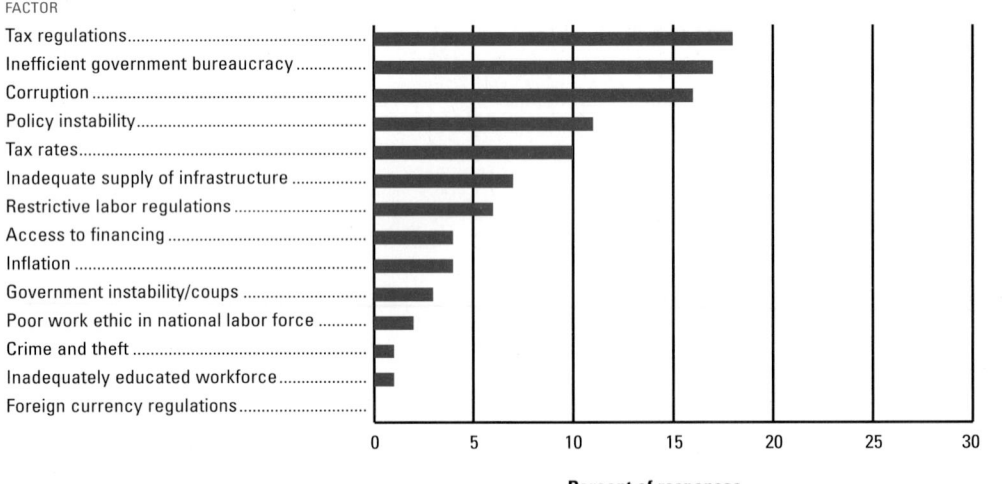

FACTOR
Tax regulations
Inefficient government bureaucracy
Corruption
Policy instability
Tax rates
Inadequate supply of infrastructure
Restrictive labor regulations
Access to financing
Inflation
Government instability/coups
Poor work ethic in national labor force
Crime and theft
Inadequately educated workforce
Foreign currency regulations

Percent of responses

Note: From a list of 14 factors, respondents were asked to select the five most problematic for doing business in their country and to rank them between 1 (most problematic) and 5. The bars in the figure show the responses weighted according to their rankings.

Source: World Economic Forum, Executive Opinion Survey (2005)

National competitiveness balance sheet

NOTABLE COMPETITIVE ADVANTAGES

Growth Competitiveness Index		Rank/117

Macroeconomic Environment

2.17	Interest rate spread, 2004	30
2.21	Country credit rating, 2004	39
2.01	Recession expectations	41
2.07	Access to credit	44

Technology

4.17	Gross tertiary enrollment	21
3.20	Internet hosts, 2003	32
3.06	Company spending on research and development	35
3.04	FDI and technology transfer	36
5.08	Telephone lines, 2003	37
3.19	Internet users, 2003	38
3.07	University/industry research collaboration	39
3.21	Personal computers, 2003	41
3.03	Prevalence of foreign technology licensing	42
3.18	Cellular telephones, 2003	45
3.15	Laws relating to ICT	47
3.11	Internet access in schools	47

Business Competitiveness Index		Rank/110

Sophistication of Company Operations and Strategy

3.06	Company spending on research and development	34
8.06	Extent of marketing	36
8.12	Willingness to delegate authority	40

Quality of the National Business Environment

6.13	Centralization of economic policymaking	22
4.03	Quality of math and science education	24
7.03	Decentralization of corporate activity	25

Other Indicators		Rank/117

7.08	Local availability of process machinery	25
7.03	Extent of market dominance	26
3.09	Availability of scientists and engineers	29
7.09	Local availability of specialized research and training services	32
2.06	Venture capital availability	36
6.09	Extent of bureaucratic red tape	37
7.06	Local supplier quality	39
7.02	Effectiveness of antitrust policy	39
9.09	Prevalence of corporate environmental reporting	40
2.05	Ease of access to loans	41
8.13	Extent of incentive compensation	42
8.03	Capacity for innovation	42

NOTABLE COMPETITIVE DISADVANTAGES

Growth Competitiveness Index		Rank/117

Macroeconomic Environment

2.13	Government surplus/deficit, 2004	112
6.06	Wastefulness of government spending	77
2.14	National savings rate, 2004	76
2.15	Real effective exchange rate, 2004	66
2.20	Government debt, 2004	51
2.16	Inflation, 2004	51

Public Institutions

6.08	Favoritism in decisions of government officials	88
6.19	Irregular payments in exports and imports	71
6.16	Organized crime	66
6.20	Irregular payments in public utilities	65
6.21	Irregular payments in tax collection	63
6.01	Judicial independence	62
6.03	Property rights	59

Technology

3.13	Government prioritization of ICT	99
3.14	Government success in ICT promotion	90
3.12	Quality of competition in the ISP sector	66
3.02	Firm-level technology absorption	61
3.01	Technological readiness	59
3.17	Utility patents, 2004	52

Business Competitiveness Index		Rank/110

Sophistication of Company Operations and Strategy

8.08	Control of international distribution	69
8.01	Nature of competitive advantage	68
8.07	Degree of customer orientation	58

Quality of the National Business Environment

8.19	Cooperation in labor-employer relations	92
6.08	Favoritism in decisions of government officials	84
3.08	Government procurement of advanced technology products	78

Other Indicators		Rank/117

4.07	Ease of hiring foreign labor	98
6.12	Efficiency of the tax system	90
3.10	Availability of mobile or cellular telephones	88
2.12	Agricultural policy costs	87
4.09	Private sector employment of women	84
6.07	Burden of government regulation	81
2.10	Impact of rules on FDI	81
9.07	Importance of environment in business planning	80
4.05	Medium term business impact of tuberculosis	78
6.10	Effectiveness of law-making bodies	77
6.22	Irregular payments in public contracts	76
8.04	Ethical behavior of firms	76
5.07	Telephone/fax infrastructure quality	76

407

Note: The Business Competitiveness Index applies different criteria for selecting a country's competitive advantages and disadvantages. Please refer to the section "How Country Profiles Work" for further details.

Portugal

Competitiveness Rankings

Growth Competitiveness Index Rank	22

Macroeconomic Environment Index Rank	**37**
Macroeconomic Stability Subindex Rank	64
Government Waste Rank	58
Country Credit Rating Rank	22

Public Institutions Index Rank	**15**
Contracts and Law Subindex Rank	16
Corruption Subindex Rank	19

Technology Index Rank	**20**
Innovation Subindex Rank	35
ICT Subindex Rank	30
Technology Transfer Subindex Rank (out of 92 non-core innovators)	3

Business Competitiveness Index Rank	30

Sophistication of Company Operations and Strategy Rank	**39**
Quality of the National Business Environment Rank	**28**

The Most Problematic Factors for Doing Business

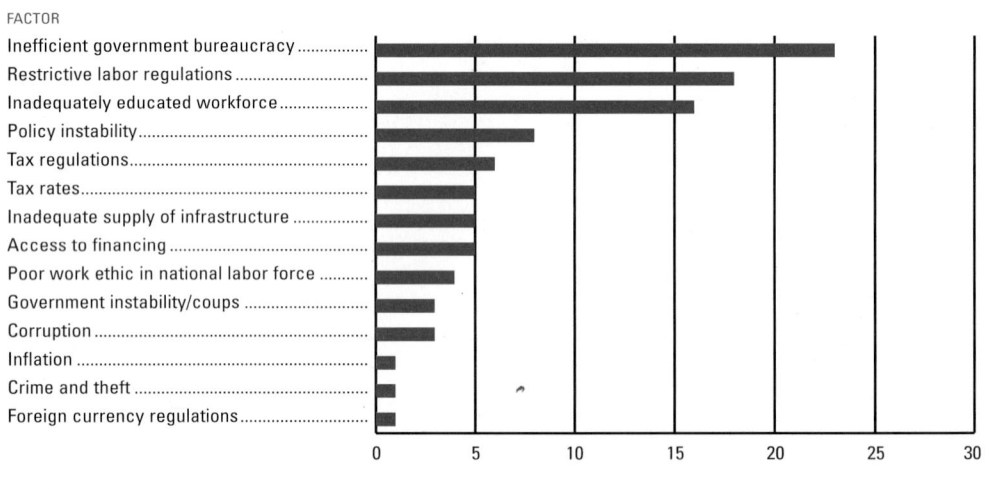

FACTOR / Percent of responses

Note: From a list of 14 factors, respondents were asked to select the five most problematic for doing business in their country and to rank them between 1 (most problematic) and 5. The bars in the figure show the responses weighted according to their rankings.

Source: World Economic Forum, Executive Opinion Survey (2005)

National competitiveness balance sheet

<table>
<tr><td colspan="3">NOTABLE COMPETITIVE ADVANTAGES</td></tr>
<tr><td colspan="2">Growth Competitiveness Index</td><td>Rank/117</td></tr>
</table>

Macroeconomic Environment

2.17	Interest rate spread, 2004	11

Public Institutions

6.16	Organized crime	7
6.19	Irregular payments in exports and imports	9
6.01	Judicial independence	15
6.20	Irregular payments in public utilities	19

Technology

3.03	Prevalence of foreign technology licensing	4
3.14	Government success in ICT promotion	13
3.04	FDI and technology transfer	14
3.18	Cellular telephones, 2003	14
3.13	Government prioritization of ICT	16

<table>
<tr><td colspan="2">Business Competitiveness Index</td><td>Rank/110</td></tr>
</table>

Sophistication of Company Operations and Strategy

8.13	Extent of incentive compensation	31
8.03	Capacity for innovation	36
8.02	Value chain presence	38

Quality of the National Business Environment

2.09	Prevalence of trade barriers	7
3.18	Cellular telephones, 2003	13
6.01	Judicial independence	14

<table>
<tr><td colspan="2">Other Indicators</td><td>Rank/117</td></tr>
</table>

2.02	Business costs of terrorism	1
6.05	Freedom of the press	4
4.07	Ease of hiring foreign labor	8
3.10	Availability of mobile or cellular telephones	9
6.15	Business costs of crime and violence	14
2.05	Ease of access to loans	17
2.11	Tax burden	17
6.23	Irregular payments in judicial decisions	20
8.21	Protection of minority shareholders' interests	21
5.06	Postal efficiency	21
6.25	Business costs of corruption	21

<table>
<tr><td colspan="3">NOTABLE COMPETITIVE DISADVANTAGES</td></tr>
<tr><td colspan="2">Growth Competitiveness Index</td><td>Rank/117</td></tr>
</table>

Macroeconomic Environment

2.01	Recession expectations	103
2.14	National savings rate, 2004	94
2.15	Real effective exchange rate, 2004	91
2.20	Government debt, 2004	72
2.13	Government surplus/deficit, 2004	71
6.06	Wastefulness of government spending	58
2.07	Access to credit	51
2.16	Inflation, 2004	38
2.21	Country credit rating, 2004	22

Public Institutions

6.21	Irregular payments in tax collection	28
6.03	Property rights	25
6.08	Favoritism in decisions of government officials	22

Technology

3.01	Technological readiness	50
3.02	Firm-level technology absorption	48
3.21	Personal computers, 2003	43
3.06	Company spending on research and development	42
3.11	Internet access in schools	39
3.19	Internet users, 2003	35
3.12	Quality of competition in the ISP sector	34
3.17	Utility patents, 2004	34
3.07	University/industry research collaboration	31
5.08	Telephone lines, 2003	30
3.20	Internet hosts, 2003	29
3.15	Laws relating to ICT	28
4.17	Gross tertiary enrollment	27

<table>
<tr><td colspan="2">Business Competitiveness Index</td><td>Rank/110</td></tr>
</table>

409

Sophistication of Company Operations and Strategy

8.08	Control of international distribution	68
8.07	Degree of customer orientation	61
8.11	Extent of staff training	59

Quality of the National Business Environment

4.03	Quality of math and science education	81
6.09	Extent of bureaucratic red tape	77
6.13	Centralization of economic policymaking	70

<table>
<tr><td colspan="2">Other Indicators</td><td>Rank/117</td></tr>
</table>

8.17	Hiring and firing practices	104
8.18	Flexibility of wage determination	86
8.20	Pay and productivity	70
8.19	Cooperation in labor-employer relations	55
8.10	Breadth of international markets	55
8.12	Willingness to delegate authority	55
8.01	Nature of competitive advantage	54
7.04	Buyer sophistication	51
9.04	Effects of compliance on business	50
3.09	Availability of scientists and engineers	49

Note: The Business Competitiveness Index applies different criteria for selecting a country's competitive advantages and disadvantages. Please refer to the section "How Country Profiles Work" for further details.

Qatar

Competitiveness Rankings

Growth Competitiveness Index Rank	19

Macroeconomic Environment Index Rank **6**
    Macroeconomic Stability Subindex Rank 4
    Government Waste Rank 3
    Country Credit Rating Rank 33

Public Institutions Index Rank............................**19**
    Contracts and Law Subindex Rank 15
    Corruption Subindex Rank....................................27

Technology Index Rank **40**
    Innovation Subindex Rank 70
    ICT Subindex Rank 44
    Technology Transfer Subindex Rank
       (out of 92 non-core innovators)...........................7

Business Competitiveness Index Rank	44

Sophistication of Company Operations
    and Strategy Rank **64**
Quality of the National Business
    Environment Rank **43**

The Most Problematic Factors for Doing Business

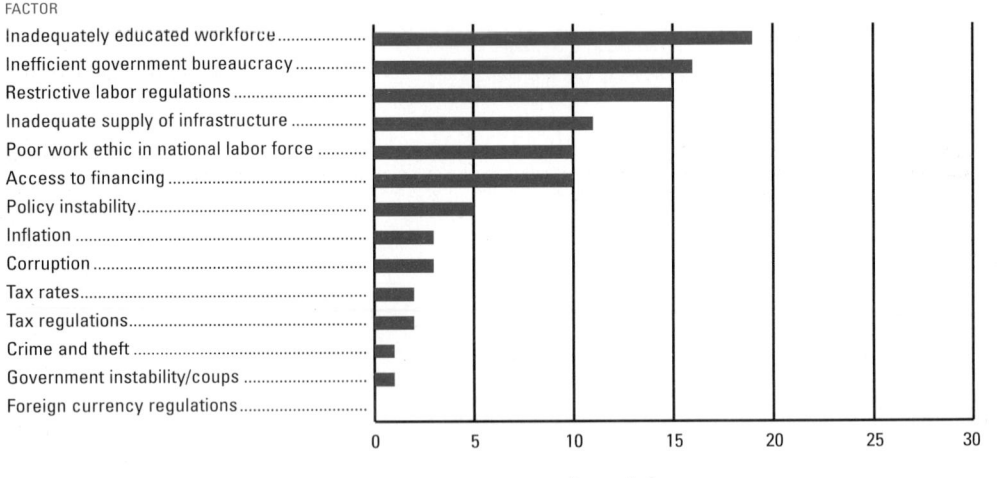

Note: From a list of 14 factors, respondents were asked to select the five most problematic for doing business in their country and to rank them between 1 (most problematic) and 5. The bars in the figure show the responses weighted according to their rankings.

Source: World Economic Forum, Executive Opinion Survey (2005)

National competitiveness balance sheet

NOTABLE COMPETITIVE ADVANTAGES		
Growth Competitiveness Index		**Rank/117**

Macroeconomic Environment

2.14	National savings rate, 2004	1
2.01	Recession expectations	1
6.06	Wastefulness of government spending	3
2.13	Government surplus/deficit, 2004	3

Public Institutions

6.16	Organized crime	3
6.08	Favoritism in decisions of government officials	4
6.21	Irregular payments in tax collection	14

Technology

| 3.04 | FDI and technology transfer | 8 |
| 3.14 | Government success in ICT promotion | 14 |

NOTABLE COMPETITIVE DISADVANTAGES		
Growth Competitiveness Index		**Rank/117**

Macroeconomic Environment

2.16	Inflation, 2004	90
2.15	Real effective exchange rate, 2004	62
2.20	Government debt, 2004	57
2.17	Interest rate spread, 2004	51
2.07	Access to credit	42
2.21	Country credit rating, 2004	33

Public Institutions

6.03	Property rights	38
6.20	Irregular payments in public utilities	37
6.19	Irregular payments in exports and imports	27
6.01	Judicial independence	21

Technology

3.12	Quality of competition in the ISP sector	116
3.06	Company spending on research and development	94
3.20	Internet hosts, 2003	85
3.17	Utility patents, 2004	81
3.07	University/industry research collaboration	74
4.17	Gross tertiary enrollment	72
3.15	Laws relating to ICT	53
3.19	Internet users, 2003	47
5.08	Telephone lines, 2003	45
3.02	Firm-level technology absorption	43
3.11	Internet access in schools	41
3.18	Cellular telephones, 2003	41
3.21	Personal computers, 2003	37
3.01	Technological readiness	32
3.03	Prevalence of foreign technology licensing	32
3.13	Government prioritization of ICT	28

411

Business Competitiveness Index		Rank/110

Sophistication of Company Operations and Strategy

8.05	Production process sophistication	29
8.08	Control of international distribution	37
8.10	Breadth of international markets	45

Quality of the National Business Environment

6.08	Favoritism in decisions of government officials	4
6.14	Reliability of police services	14
8.19	Cooperation in labor-employer relations	16

Other Indicators		Rank/117
6.15	Business costs of crime and violence	2
4.08	Brain drain	2
6.17	Informal sector	3
2.11	Tax burden	4
2.12	Agricultural policy costs	4
6.27	Pervasiveness of money laundering through banks	5
6.11	Extent and effect of taxation	5
6.12	Efficiency of the tax system	5
6.26	Public trust of politicians	11
6.18	Government effectiveness in reducing poverty and inequality	11
4.06	Medium term business impact of HIV/AIDS	11
4.07	Ease of hiring foreign labor	12
8.18	Flexibility of wage determination	12
6.24	Diversion of public funds	17

Business Competitiveness Index		Rank/110

Sophistication of Company Operations and Strategy

8.03	Capacity for innovation	100
8.02	Value chain presence	91
3.06	Company spending on research and development	90

Quality of the National Business Environment

6.09	Extent of bureaucratic red tape	106
8.22	Foreign ownership restrictions	102
7.09	Local availability of specialized research and training services	96

Other Indicators		Rank/117
4.09	Private sector employment of women	102
7.08	Local availability of process machinery	98
9.10	Grass-roots involvement in development projects	96
7.05	Local supplier quantity	92
6.13	Centralization of economic policymaking	90
3.16	Extent of business Internet use	90
8.12	Willingness to delegate authority	84
8.15	Quality of management schools	82
8.09	Extent of regional sales	81
7.02	Effectiveness of antitrust policy	80

Note: The Business Competitiveness Index applies different criteria for selecting a country's competitive advantages and disadvantages. Please refer to the section "How Country Profiles Work" for further details.

Romania

Competitiveness Rankings

Growth Competitiveness Index Rank	67

Macroeconomic Environment Index Rank **73**
   Macroeconomic Stability Subindex Rank 83
   Government Waste Rank 90
   Country Credit Rating Rank 61

Public Institutions Index Rank...........................**78**
   Contracts and Law Subindex Rank 85
   Corruption Subindex Rank...................................71

Technology Index Rank **49**
   Innovation Subindex Rank 54
   ICT Subindex Rank 50
   Technology Transfer Subindex Rank
     (out of 92 non-core innovators).......................20

Business Competitiveness Index Rank	67

**Sophistication of Company Operations
  and Strategy Rank**..**69**

**Quality of the National Business
  Environment Rank** **67**

The Most Problematic Factors for Doing Business

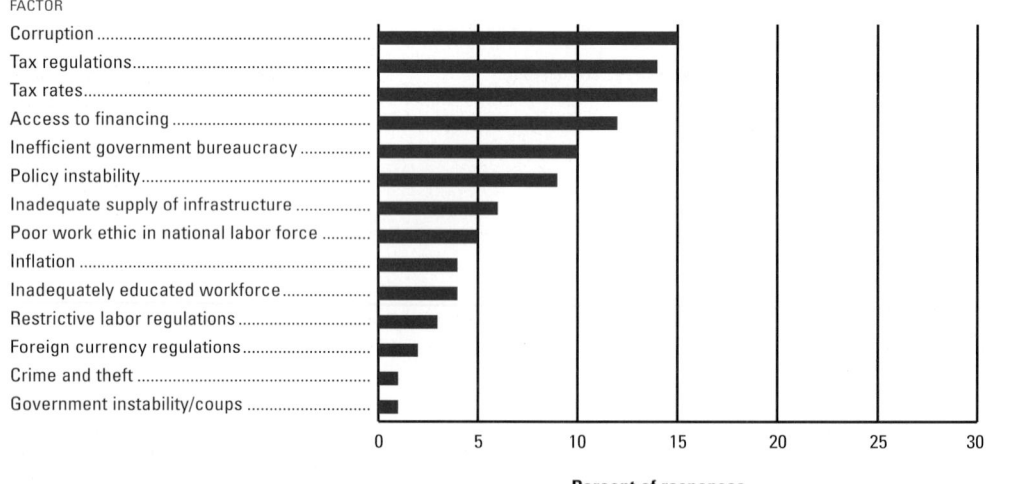

FACTOR

Corruption
Tax regulations
Tax rates
Access to financing
Inefficient government bureaucracy
Policy instability
Inadequate supply of infrastructure
Poor work ethic in national labor force
Inflation
Inadequately educated workforce
Restrictive labor regulations
Foreign currency regulations
Crime and theft
Government instability/coups

Percent of responses

Note: From a list of 14 factors, respondents were asked to select the five most problematic for doing business in their country and to rank them between 1 (most problematic) and 5. The bars in the figure show the responses weighted according to their rankings.

Source: World Economic Forum, Executive Opinion Survey (2005)

National competitiveness balance sheet

NOTABLE COMPETITIVE ADVANTAGES		
Growth Competitiveness Index		**Rank/117**
	Macroeconomic Environment	
2.20	Government debt, 2004	16
2.13	Government surplus/deficit, 2004	37
2.07	Access to credit	43
2.01	Recession expectations	48
	Technology	
3.04	FDI and technology transfer	12
3.19	Internet users, 2003	48
3.14	Government success in ICT promotion	50
4.17	Gross tertiary enrollment	50

NOTABLE COMPETITIVE DISADVANTAGES		
Growth Competitiveness Index		**Rank/117**
	Macroeconomic Environment	
2.16	Inflation, 2004	107
2.17	Interest rate spread, 2004	106
2.15	Real effective exchange rate, 2004	104
6.06	Wastefulness of government spending	90
2.14	National savings rate, 2004	86
2.21	Country credit rating, 2004	61
	Public Institutions	
6.19	Irregular payments in exports and imports	93
6.08	Favoritism in decisions of government officials	93
6.01	Judicial independence	86
6.16	Organized crime	80
6.03	Property rights	78
6.20	Irregular payments in public utilities	73
6.21	Irregular payments in tax collection	56
	Technology	
3.07	University/industry research collaboration	93
3.01	Technological readiness	73
3.06	Company spending on research and development	72
3.02	Firm-level technology absorption	69
3.12	Quality of competition in the ISP sector	65
3.15	Laws relating to ICT	65
3.13	Government prioritization of ICT	60
3.20	Internet hosts, 2003	59
5.08	Telephone lines, 2003	59
3.03	Prevalence of foreign technology licensing	58
3.18	Cellular telephones, 2003	55
3.17	Utility patents, 2004	53
3.11	Internet access in schools	53
3.21	Personal computers, 2003	51

Business Competitiveness Index		Rank/110
	Sophistication of Company Operations and Strategy	
8.12	Willingness to delegate authority	45
8.13	Extent of incentive compensation	49
	Quality of the National Business Environment	
6.09	Extent of bureaucratic red tape	1
4.03	Quality of math and science education	8
4.02	Quality of public schools	35

Business Competitiveness Index		Rank/110
	Sophistication of Company Operations and Strategy	
8.01	Nature of competitive advantage	102
8.07	Degree of customer orientation	80
8.09	Extent of regional sales	76
	Quality of the National Business Environment	
8.19	Cooperation in labor-employer relations	110
6.25	Business costs of corruption	102
3.07	University/industry research collaboration	89

Other Indicators		Rank/117
8.20	Pay and productivity	23
8.18	Flexibility of wage determination	34
7.03	Extent of market dominance	37
3.09	Availability of scientists and engineers	40
7.09	Local availability of specialized research and training services	41
2.02	Business costs of terrorism	43
6.13	Centralization of economic policymaking	48
7.08	Local availability of process machinery	48
6.07	Burden of government regulation	50

Other Indicators		Rank/117
2.11	Tax burden	116
9.07	Importance of environment in business planning	109
4.08	Brain drain	108
6.12	Efficiency of the tax system	104
2.12	Agricultural policy costs	103
6.27	Pervasiveness of money laundering through banks	99
6.22	Irregular payments in public contracts	95
3.10	Availability of mobile or cellular telephones	94
8.21	Protection of minority shareholders' interests	94
6.11	Extent and effect of taxation	94
6.24	Diversion of public funds	93
6.10	Effectiveness of law-making bodies	90

413

Note: The Business Competitiveness Index applies different criteria for selecting a country's competitive advantages and disadvantages. Please refer to the section "How Country Profiles Work" for further details.

Russian Federation

Competitiveness Rankings

Growth Competitiveness Index Rank	75

Macroeconomic Environment Index Rank **58**
   Macroeconomic Stability Subindex Rank 42
   Government Waste Rank 93
   Country Credit Rating Rank 54

Public Institutions Index Rank **91**
   Contracts and Law Subindex Rank 109
   Corruption Subindex Rank...................................76

Technology Index Rank **73**
   Innovation Subindex Rank 29
   ICT Subindex Rank 62
   Technology Transfer Subindex Rank
     (out of 92 non-core innovators).........................76

Business Competitiveness Index Rank	74

**Sophistication of Company Operations
and Strategy Rank** **77**
**Quality of the National Business
Environment Rank** **70**

The Most Problematic Factors for Doing Business

Note: From a list of 14 factors, respondents were asked to select the five most problematic for doing business in their country and to rank them between 1 (most problematic) and 5. The bars in the figure show the responses weighted according to their rankings.

Source: World Economic Forum, Executive Opinion Survey (2005)

National competitiveness balance sheet

NOTABLE COMPETITIVE ADVANTAGES	
Growth Competitiveness Index	**Rank/117**

Macroeconomic Environment

2.13	Government surplus/deficit, 2004	9
2.20	Government debt, 2004	19
2.14	National savings rate, 2004	20

Technology

4.17	Gross tertiary enrollment	12
3.17	Utility patents, 2004	39
3.07	University/industry research collaboration	42
3.06	Company spending on research and development	43
5.08	Telephone lines, 2003	46

NOTABLE COMPETITIVE DISADVANTAGES	
Growth Competitiveness Index	**Rank/117**

Macroeconomic Environment

2.15	Real effective exchange rate, 2004	111
2.16	Inflation, 2004	103
6.06	Wastefulness of government spending	93
2.01	Recession expectations	83
2.17	Interest rate spread, 2004	77
2.07	Access to credit	61
2.21	Country credit rating, 2004	54

Public Institutions

6.03	Property rights	108
6.08	Favoritism in decisions of government officials	106
6.01	Judicial independence	102
6.16	Organized crime	101
6.19	Irregular payments in exports and imports	83
6.20	Irregular payments in public utilities	78
6.21	Irregular payments in tax collection	69

Technology

3.03	Prevalence of foreign technology licensing	101
3.14	Government success in ICT promotion	99
3.04	FDI and technology transfer	98
3.13	Government prioritization of ICT	91
3.12	Quality of competition in the ISP sector	81
3.15	Laws relating to ICT	79
3.01	Technological readiness	77
3.19	Internet users, 2003	66
3.18	Cellular telephones, 2003	65
3.02	Firm-level technology absorption	63
3.11	Internet access in schools	55
3.20	Internet hosts, 2003	52
3.21	Personal computers, 2003	52

Business Competitiveness Index	Rank/110

Sophistication of Company Operations and Strategy

8.03	Capacity for innovation	42
3.06	Company spending on research and development	42
8.13	Extent of incentive compensation	57

Quality of the National Business Environment

7.08	Local availability of process machinery	20
4.03	Quality of math and science education	21
5.02	Railroad infrastructure development	23

Other Indicators	Rank/117

8.17	Hiring and firing practices	8
3.05	Quality of scientific research institutions	31
8.18	Flexibility of wage determination	36
8.16	Efficacy of corporate boards	36
8.20	Pay and productivity	37
3.09	Availability of scientists and engineers	44
7.09	Local availability of specialized research and training services	50

Business Competitiveness Index	Rank/110

Sophistication of Company Operations and Strategy

8.02	Value chain presence	103
3.03	Prevalence of foreign technology licensing	97
8.01	Nature of competitive advantage	92

Quality of the National Business Environment

8.21	Protection of minority shareholders' interests	109
8.22	Foreign ownership restrictions	106
6.25	Business costs of corruption	105

Other Indicators	Rank/117

9.05	Effects of privatization on competition and the environment	115
6.27	Pervasiveness of money laundering through banks	114
9.10	Grass-roots involvement in development projects	111
4.07	Ease of hiring foreign labor	111
9.07	Importance of environment in business planning	110
6.07	Burden of government regulation	110
6.18	Government effectiveness in reducing poverty and inequality	109
2.10	Impact of rules on FDI	109
2.12	Agricultural policy costs	106
9.08	Protection of ecosystems by business	106
6.17	Informal sector	106

415

Note: The Business Competitiveness Index applies different criteria for selecting a country's competitive advantages and disadvantages. Please refer to the section "How Country Profiles Work" for further details.

Serbia and Montenegro

Competitiveness Rankings

Growth Competitiveness Index Rank	80

Macroeconomic Environment Index Rank **111**
    Macroeconomic Stability Subindex Rank 101
    Government Waste Rank 108
    Country Credit Rating Rank 98

Public Institutions Index Rank...**69**
    Contracts and Law Subindex Rank 92
    Corruption Subindex Rank.....................................55

Technology Index Rank **68**
    Innovation Subindex Rank 61
    ICT Subindex Rank 64
    Technology Transfer Subindex Rank
        (out of 92 non-core innovators).......................48

Business Competitiveness Index Rank	85

**Sophistication of Company Operations
  and Strategy Rank**..**105**
**Quality of the National Business
  Environment Rank** **85**

The Most Problematic Factors for Doing Business

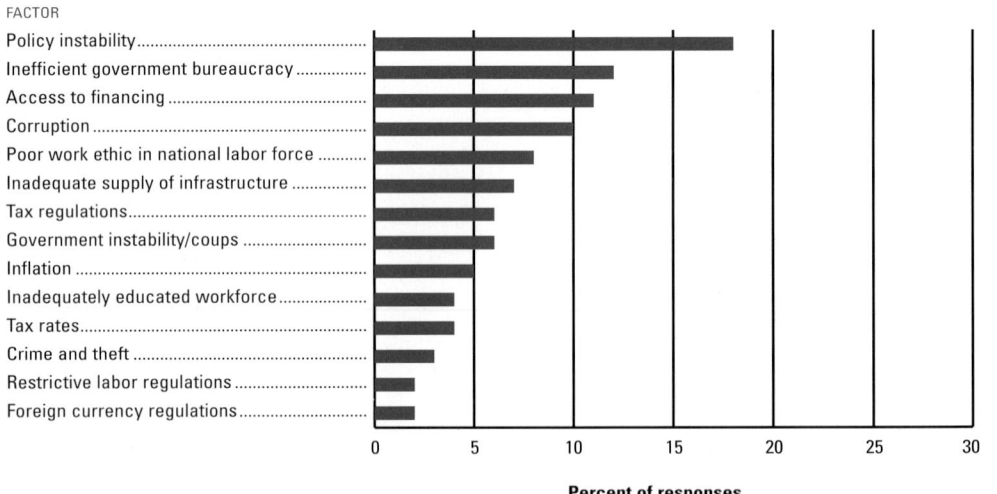

Note: From a list of 14 factors, respondents were asked to select the five most problematic for doing business in their country and to rank them between 1 (most problematic) and 5. The bars in the figure show the responses weighted according to their rankings.

Source: World Economic Forum, Executive Opinion Survey (2005)

National competitiveness balance sheet

NOTABLE COMPETITIVE ADVANTAGES

Growth Competitiveness Index	Rank/117

Macroeconomic Environment

2.13	Government surplus/deficit, 2004	31
2.07	Access to credit	49

Public Institutions

6.21	Irregular payments in tax collection	45

Technology

3.04	FDI and technology transfer	10
4.17	Gross tertiary enrollment	48
5.08	Telephone lines, 2003	50

NOTABLE COMPETITIVE DISADVANTAGES

Growth Competitiveness Index	Rank/117

Macroeconomic Environment

2.14	National savings rate, 2004	116
6.06	Wastefulness of government spending	108
2.01	Recession expectations	102
2.16	Inflation, 2004	101
2.17	Interest rate spread, 2004	99
2.21	Country credit rating, 2004	98
2.20	Government debt, 2004	94
2.15	Real effective exchange rate, 2004	70

Public Institutions

6.03	Property rights	103
6.08	Favoritism in decisions of government officials	95
6.01	Judicial independence	91
6.16	Organized crime	67
6.20	Irregular payments in public utilities	66
6.19	Irregular payments in exports and imports	55

Technology

3.01	Technological readiness	113
3.03	Prevalence of foreign technology licensing	102
3.02	Firm-level technology absorption	101
3.12	Quality of competition in the ISP sector	99
3.06	Company spending on research and development	92
3.14	Government success in ICT promotion	86
3.13	Government prioritization of ICT	86
3.11	Internet access in schools	84
3.21	Personal computers, 2003	82
3.17	Utility patents, 2004	81
3.15	Laws relating to ICT	73
3.19	Internet users, 2003	65
3.20	Internet hosts, 2003	63
3.18	Cellular telephones, 2003	54
3.07	University/industry research collaboration	51

417

Business Competitiveness Index	Rank/110

Sophistication of Company Operations and Strategy

8.10	Breadth of international markets	85
8.08	Control of international distribution	90

Quality of the National Business Environment

4.03	Quality of math and science education	28
3.09	Availability of scientists and engineers	45
3.08	Government procurement of advanced technology products	47

Other Indicators	Rank/117

4.06	Medium term business impact of HIV/AIDS	25
4.07	Ease of hiring foreign labor	33
6.12	Efficiency of the tax system	34
4.05	Medium term business impact of tuberculosis	35
6.22	Irregular payments in public contracts	46
6.15	Business costs of crime and violence	48

Business Competitiveness Index	Rank/110

Sophistication of Company Operations and Strategy

8.07	Degree of customer orientation	107
8.14	Reliance on professional management	106
8.12	Willingness to delegate authority	105

Quality of the National Business Environment

5.01	Overall infrastructure quality	109
8.21	Protection of minority shareholders' interests	107
5.04	Air transport infrastructure quality	107

Other Indicators	Rank/117

6.07	Burden of government regulation	116
9.02	Clarity and stability of regulations	113
4.08	Brain drain	113
8.19	Cooperation in labor-employer relations	111
6.04	Intellectual property protection	110
9.09	Prevalence of corporate environmental reporting	109
8.01	Nature of competitive advantage	108
8.11	Extent of staff training	108
8.16	Efficacy of corporate boards	108
9.08	Protection of ecosystems by business	107
8.13	Extent of incentive compensation	106

Note: The Business Competitiveness Index applies different criteria for selecting a country's competitive advantages and disadvantages. Please refer to the section "How Country Profiles Work" for further details.

Singapore

Competitiveness Rankings

Growth Competitiveness Index Rank	6

Macroeconomic Environment Index Rank 1
    Macroeconomic Stability Subindex Rank 10
    Government Waste Rank 1
    Country Credit Rating Rank 15

Public Institutions Index Rank..4
    Contracts and Law Subindex Rank 5
    Corruption Subindex Rank 3

Technology Index Rank 10
    Innovation Subindex Rank 13
    ICT Subindex Rank 8

Business Competitiveness Index Rank	5

**Sophistication of Company Operations
and Strategy Rank** 14

**Quality of the National Business
Environment Rank** 5

The Most Problematic Factors for Doing Business

FACTOR

Restrictive labor regulations ....
Access to financing ....
Inadequately educated workforce ....
Tax regulations..
Tax rates..
Poor work ethic in national labor force ....
Inefficient government bureaucracy ....
Inflation ....
Inadequate supply of infrastructure ....
Foreign currency regulations............................
Policy instability...
Government instability/coups ....
Crime and theft ....
Corruption ....

0   5   10   15   20   25   30

Percent of responses

Note: From a list of 14 factors, respondents were asked to select the five most problematic for doing business in their country and to rank them between 1 (most problematic) and 5. The bars in the figure show the responses weighted according to their rankings.

Source: World Economic Forum, Executive Opinion Survey (2005)

418

National competitiveness balance sheet

Growth Competitiveness Index		Rank/117

Macroeconomic Environment

6.06	Wastefulness of government spending	1
2.14	National savings rate, 2004	3
2.13	Government surplus/deficit, 2004	7

Public Institutions

6.21	Irregular payments in tax collection	3
6.19	Irregular payments in exports and imports	3
6.08	Favoritism in decisions of government officials	3
6.20	Irregular payments in public utilities	5
6.16	Organized crime	6
6.03	Property rights	6

Technology

3.15	Laws relating to ICT	1
3.13	Government prioritization of ICT	1
3.14	Government success in ICT promotion	1
3.21	Personal computers, 2003	3
3.11	Internet access in schools	4
3.07	University/industry research collaboration	5
3.02	Firm-level technology absorption	7
3.01	Technological readiness	7
3.20	Internet hosts, 2003	10
3.17	Utility patents, 2004	10
3.06	Company spending on research and development	10

Business Competitiveness Index		Rank/110

Sophistication of Company Operations and Strategy

8.11	Extent of staff training	7
8.05	Production process sophistication	9
8.13	Extent of incentive compensation	9

Quality of the National Business Environment

4.01	Quality of the educational system	1
3.08	Government procurement of advanced technology products	1
8.19	Cooperation in labor-employer relations	1

Other Indicators		Rank/117

8.17	Hiring and firing practices	1
6.17	Informal sector	1
6.10	Effectiveness of law-making bodies	1
6.14	Reliability of police services	1
6.26	Public trust of politicians	1
4.09	Private sector employment of women	1
2.10	Impact of rules on FDI	1
6.07	Burden of government regulation	1
8.20	Pay and productivity	2
6.18	Government effectiveness in reducing poverty and inequality	2
9.02	Clarity and stability of regulations	2
6.22	Irregular payments in public contracts	3
6.15	Business costs of crime and violence	3

Growth Competitiveness Index		Rank/117

Macroeconomic Environment

2.20	Government debt, 2004	107
2.17	Interest rate spread, 2004	48
2.15	Real effective exchange rate, 2004	40
2.01	Recession expectations	30
2.07	Access to credit	29
2.16	Inflation, 2004	22
2.21	Country credit rating, 2004	15

Public Institutions

| 6.01 | Judicial independence | 19 |

Technology

4.17	Gross tertiary enrollment	35
5.08	Telephone lines, 2003	27
3.18	Cellular telephones, 2003	21
3.12	Quality of competition in the ISP sector	15
3.19	Internet users, 2003	13

Business Competitiveness Index		Rank/110

Sophistication of Company Operations and Strategy

8.08	Control of international distribution	45
8.09	Extent of regional sales	21
8.03	Capacity for innovation	21

Quality of the National Business Environment

6.13	Centralization of economic policymaking	95
7.08	Local availability of process machinery	37
7.05	Local supplier quantity	32

Other Indicators		Rank/117

6.05	Freedom of the press	109
2.02	Business costs of terrorism	80
4.05	Medium term business impact of tuberculosis	45
4.06	Medium term business impact of HIV/AIDS	45
7.02	Effectiveness of antitrust policy	24
8.12	Willingness to delegate authority	21
9.08	Protection of ecosystems by business	21
9.10	Grass-roots involvement in development projects	21
7.01	Intensity of local competition	21

419

Note: The Business Competitiveness Index applies different criteria for selecting a country's competitive advantages and disadvantages. Please refer to the section "How Country Profiles Work" for further details.

Slovak Republic

Competitiveness Rankings

Growth Competitiveness Index Rank	41

Macroeconomic Environment Index Rank **49**
    Macroeconomic Stability Subindex Rank 40
    Government Waste Rank 82
    Country Credit Rating Rank 41

Public Institutions Index Rank **45**
    Contracts and Law Subindex Rank 57
    Corruption Subindex Rank....................................37

Technology Index Rank **34**
    Innovation Subindex Rank 46
    ICT Subindex Rank 36
    Technology Transfer Subindex Rank
        (out of 92 non-core innovators)..........................9

Business Competitiveness Index Rank	39

**Sophistication of Company Operations
   and Strategy Rank** **47**

**Quality of the National Business
   Environment Rank** **38**

The Most Problematic Factors for Doing Business

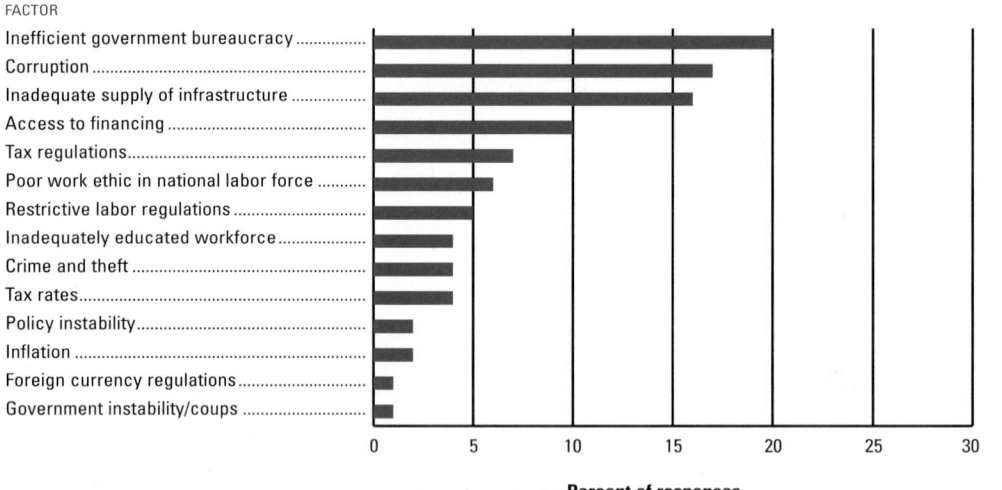

FACTOR

- Inefficient government bureaucracy
- Corruption
- Inadequate supply of infrastructure
- Access to financing
- Tax regulations
- Poor work ethic in national labor force
- Restrictive labor regulations
- Inadequately educated workforce
- Crime and theft
- Tax rates
- Policy instability
- Inflation
- Foreign currency regulations
- Government instability/coups

Percent of responses

Note: From a list of 14 factors, respondents were asked to select the five most problematic for doing business in their country and to rank them between 1 (most problematic) and 5. The bars in the figure show the responses weighted according to their rankings.

Source: World Economic Forum, Executive Opinion Survey (2005)

National competitiveness balance sheet

NOTABLE COMPETITIVE ADVANTAGES		
Growth Competitiveness Index		**Rank/117**
Macroeconomic Environment		
2.07	Access to credit	10
2.01	Recession expectations	12
Public Institutions		
6.20	Irregular payments in public utilities	34
6.21	Irregular payments in tax collection	38
6.19	Irregular payments in exports and imports	40
Technology		
3.04	FDI and technology transfer	4
3.02	Firm-level technology absorption	24
3.21	Personal computers, 2003	29
3.07	University/industry research collaboration	29
3.11	Internet access in schools	31
3.20	Internet hosts, 2003	31
3.18	Cellular telephones, 2003	32
3.19	Internet users, 2003	36
3.15	Laws relating to ICT	39

NOTABLE COMPETITIVE DISADVANTAGES		
Growth Competitiveness Index		**Rank/117**
Macroeconomic Environment		
2.16	Inflation, 2004	90
6.06	Wastefulness of government spending	82
2.13	Government surplus/deficit, 2004	76
2.15	Real effective exchange rate, 2004	73
2.17	Interest rate spread, 2004	49
2.14	National savings rate, 2004	47
2.20	Government debt, 2004	46
2.21	Country credit rating, 2004	41
Public Institutions		
6.08	Favoritism in decisions of government officials	91
6.01	Judicial independence	67
6.16	Organized crime	64
6.03	Property rights	42
Technology		
3.14	Government success in ICT promotion	66
3.13	Government prioritization of ICT	63
3.03	Prevalence of foreign technology licensing	57
3.12	Quality of competition in the ISP sector	57
3.06	Company spending on research and development	56
4.17	Gross tertiary enrollment	54
5.08	Telephone lines, 2003	51
3.17	Utility patents, 2004	42
3.01	Technological readiness	41

	Business Competitiveness Index	**Rank/110**
	Sophistication of Company Operations and Strategy	
8.09	Extent of regional sales	25
8.10	Breadth of international markets	35
8.11	Extent of staff training	39
	Quality of the National Business Environment	
8.22	Foreign ownership restrictions	4
2.09	Prevalence of trade barriers	9
6.13	Centralization of economic policymaking	13

	Business Competitiveness Index	**Rank/110**
	Sophistication of Company Operations and Strategy	
8.08	Control of international distribution	91
8.01	Nature of competitive advantage	89
8.13	Extent of incentive compensation	66
	Quality of the National Business Environment	
5.04	Air transport infrastructure quality	104
2.08	Local equity market access	89
6.08	Favoritism in decisions of government officials	86

	Other Indicators	**Rank/117**
2.10	Impact of rules on FDI	3
6.11	Extent and effect of taxation	7
6.12	Efficiency of the tax system	9
2.11	Tax burden	9
4.06	Medium term business impact of HIV/AIDS	9
8.20	Pay and productivity	10
4.07	Ease of hiring foreign labor	10
3.09	Availability of scientists and engineers	16
8.17	Hiring and firing practices	18
8.19	Cooperation in labor-employer relations	23
9.03	Extent of government mandated environmental reporting	23
7.07	Presence of demanding regulatory standards	24

	Other Indicators	**Rank/117**
6.26	Public trust of politicians	88
9.07	Importance of environment in business planning	82
6.22	Irregular payments in public contracts	81
6.23	Irregular payments in judicial decisions	79
9.06	Prioritization of energy efficiency	78
8.21	Protection of minority shareholders' interests	75
2.12	Agricultural policy costs	73
6.07	Burden of government regulation	73
7.04	Buyer sophistication	72
3.05	Quality of scientific research institutions	71
9.05	Effects of privatization on competition and the environment	69
6.02	Efficiency of legal framework	68

Note: The Business Competitiveness Index applies different criteria for selecting a country's competitive advantages and disadvantages. Please refer to the section "How Country Profiles Work" for further details.

Slovenia

Competitiveness Rankings

Growth Competitiveness Index Rank	32

Macroeconomic Environment Index Rank **35**	
Macroeconomic Stability Subindex Rank 35	
Government Waste Rank 62	
Country Credit Rating Rank 27	
Public Institutions Index Rank **35**	
Contracts and Law Subindex Rank 48	
Corruption Subindex Rank 25	
Technology Index Rank **32**	
Innovation Subindex Rank 23	
ICT Subindex Rank 27	
Technology Transfer Subindex Rank	
(out of 92 non-core innovators) 54	

Business Competitiveness Index Rank	32

Sophistication of Company Operations	
and Strategy Rank **27**	
Quality of the National Business	
Environment Rank **35**	

The Most Problematic Factors for Doing Business

FACTOR

Tax regulations	
Inefficient government bureaucracy	
Tax rates	
Restrictive labor regulations	
Access to financing	
Inadequately educated workforce	
Inflation	
Inadequate supply of infrastructure	
Poor work ethic in national labor force	
Corruption	
Policy instability	
Crime and theft	
Foreign currency regulations	
Government instability/coups	

Percent of responses

Note: From a list of 14 factors, respondents were asked to select the five most problematic for doing business in their country and to rank them between 1 (most problematic) and 5. The bars in the figure show the responses weighted according to their rankings.

Source: World Economic Forum, Executive Opinion Survey (2005)

422

National competitiveness balance sheet

NOTABLE COMPETITIVE ADVANTAGES		
Growth Competitiveness Index		**Rank/117**

Macroeconomic Environment

2.20	Government debt, 2004	24
2.07	Access to credit	26
2.21	Country credit rating, 2004	27
2.14	National savings rate, 2004	28

Public Institutions

6.19	Irregular payments in exports and imports	21
6.20	Irregular payments in public utilities	27
6.21	Irregular payments in tax collection	30

Technology

4.17	Gross tertiary enrollment	13
3.18	Cellular telephones, 2003	18
3.11	Internet access in schools	20
3.19	Internet users, 2003	21
3.21	Personal computers, 2003	24
3.17	Utility patents, 2004	26
3.20	Internet hosts, 2003	30
3.06	Company spending on research and development	30
3.15	Laws relating to ICT	31
5.08	Telephone lines, 2003	31

Business Competitiveness Index		**Rank/110**

Sophistication of Company Operations and Strategy

8.03	Capacity for innovation	20
8.02	Value chain presence	20
8.07	Degree of customer orientation	22

Quality of the National Business Environment

3.18	Cellular telephones, 2003	17
2.09	Prevalence of trade barriers	20
3.19	Internet users, 2003	21

Other Indicators		**Rank/117**

5.06	Postal efficiency	15
9.09	Prevalence of corporate environmental reporting	15
4.06	Medium term business impact of HIV/AIDS	18
9.03	Extent of government mandated environmental reporting	19
9.02	Clarity and stability of regulations	22
9.01	Stringency of environmental regulations	22
4.05	Medium term business impact of tuberculosis	23
9.07	Importance of environment in business planning	23
8.08	Control of international distribution	24
8.01	Nature of competitive advantage	24
2.11	Tax burden	25

NOTABLE COMPETITIVE DISADVANTAGES		
Growth Competitiveness Index		**Rank/117**

Macroeconomic Environment

2.15	Real effective exchange rate, 2004	77
2.01	Recession expectations	75
6.06	Wastefulness of government spending	62
2.16	Inflation, 2004	52
2.13	Government surplus/deficit, 2004	47
2.17	Interest rate spread, 2004	47

Public Institutions

6.08	Favoritism in decisions of government officials	50
6.01	Judicial independence	50
6.03	Property rights	49
6.16	Organized crime	46

Technology

3.04	FDI and technology transfer	99
3.14	Government success in ICT promotion	68
3.02	Firm-level technology absorption	60
3.13	Government prioritization of ICT	59
3.03	Prevalence of foreign technology licensing	59
3.12	Quality of competition in the ISP sector	50
3.01	Technological readiness	44
3.07	University/industry research collaboration	32

Business Competitiveness Index		**Rank/110**

Sophistication of Company Operations and Strategy

8.14	Reliance on professional management	47
8.06	Extent of marketing	43
8.13	Extent of incentive compensation	43

Quality of the National Business Environment

8.22	Foreign ownership restrictions	85
3.09	Availability of scientists and engineers	78
2.08	Local equity market access	65

Other Indicators		**Rank/117**

8.17	Hiring and firing practices	102
2.10	Impact of rules on FDI	99
6.12	Efficiency of the tax system	98
6.11	Extent and effect of taxation	95
2.12	Agricultural policy costs	82
6.07	Burden of government regulation	79
8.18	Flexibility of wage determination	78
4.07	Ease of hiring foreign labor	76
4.09	Private sector employment of women	74
9.05	Effects of privatization on competition and the environment	65
8.19	Cooperation in labor-employer relations	62
3.08	Government procurement of advanced technology products	60

423

Note: The Business Competitiveness Index applies different criteria for selecting a country's competitive advantages and disadvantages. Please refer to the section "How Country Profiles Work" for further details.

South Africa

Competitiveness Rankings

Growth Competitiveness Index Rank	42

Macroeconomic Environment Index Rank **31**
    Macroeconomic Stability Subindex Rank 30
    Government Waste Rank 14
    Country Credit Rating Rank 49

Public Institutions Index Rank...**47**
    Contracts and Law Subindex Rank 46
    Corruption Subindex Rank....................................56

Technology Index Rank **46**
    Innovation Subindex Rank 66
    ICT Subindex Rank 55
    Technology Transfer Subindex Rank
       (out of 92 non-core innovators).........................4

Business Competitiveness Index Rank	28

**Sophistication of Company Operations
  and Strategy Rank** **26**
**Quality of the National Business
  Environment Rank** **30**

The Most Problematic Factors for Doing Business

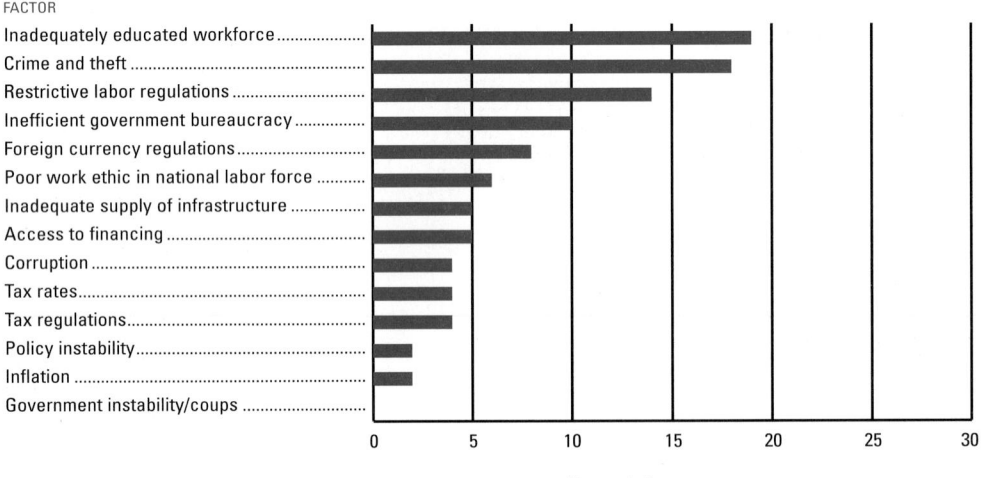

FACTOR

Note: From a list of 14 factors, respondents were asked to select the five most problematic for doing business in their country and to rank them between 1 (most problematic) and 5. The bars in the figure show the responses weighted according to their rankings.

Source: World Economic Forum, Executive Opinion Survey (2005)

National competitiveness balance sheet

NOTABLE COMPETITIVE ADVANTAGES		
Growth Competitiveness Index		**Rank/117**

Macroeconomic Environment

2.01	Recession expectations	7
6.06	Wastefulness of government spending	14
2.16	Inflation, 2004	18
2.07	Access to credit	21
2.20	Government debt, 2004	34

Public Institutions

6.03	Property rights	19
6.01	Judicial independence	33

Technology

3.03	Prevalence of foreign technology licensing	3
3.07	University/industry research collaboration	21
3.06	Company spending on research and development	22
3.15	Laws relating to ICT	23
3.02	Firm-level technology absorption	30
3.17	Utility patents, 2004	32
3.13	Government prioritization of ICT	32
3.01	Technological readiness	33
3.14	Government success in ICT promotion	39
3.04	FDI and technology transfer	39

Business Competitiveness Index		**Rank/110**

Sophistication of Company Operations and Strategy

3.03	Prevalence of foreign technology licensing	3
8.13	Extent of incentive compensation	8
8.14	Reliance on professional management	12

Quality of the National Business Environment

8.16	Efficacy of corporate boards	8
2.03	Financial market sophistication	11
2.08	Local equity market access	11

Other Indicators		**Rank/117**
8.23	Strength of auditing and accounting standards	5
8.24	Importance of corporate social responsibility	8
9.10	Grass-roots involvement in development projects	12
6.10	Effectiveness of law-making bodies	13
2.12	Agricultural policy costs	13
7.02	Effectiveness of antitrust policy	14
8.21	Protection of minority shareholders' interests	15
2.04	Soundness of banks	15
8.15	Quality of management schools	16
8.09	Extent of regional sales	18

NOTABLE COMPETITIVE DISADVANTAGES		
Growth Competitiveness Index		**Rank/117**

Macroeconomic Environment

2.15	Real effective exchange rate, 2004	100
2.14	National savings rate, 2004	100
2.13	Government surplus/deficit, 2004	53
2.21	Country credit rating, 2004	49
2.17	Interest rate spread, 2004	45

Public Institutions

6.16	Organized crime	98
6.20	Irregular payments in public utilities	71
6.19	Irregular payments in exports and imports	59
6.08	Favoritism in decisions of government officials	58
6.21	Irregular payments in tax collection	43

Technology

4.17	Gross tertiary enrollment	87
5.08	Telephone lines, 2003	78
3.12	Quality of competition in the ISP sector	71
3.19	Internet users, 2003	67
3.21	Personal computers, 2003	58
3.11	Internet access in schools	57
3.18	Cellular telephones, 2003	52
3.20	Internet hosts, 2003	48

Business Competitiveness Index		**Rank/110**

Sophistication of Company Operations and Strategy

8.02	Value chain presence	68
8.07	Degree of customer orientation	51
8.01	Nature of competitive advantage	45

Quality of the National Business Environment

4.03	Quality of math and science education	100
8.19	Cooperation in labor-employer relations	97
3.09	Availability of scientists and engineers	86

Other Indicators		**Rank/117**
8.17	Hiring and firing practices	115
4.07	Ease of hiring foreign labor	114
4.06	Medium term business impact of HIV/AIDS	113
4.05	Medium term business impact of tuberculosis	107
8.18	Flexibility of wage determination	106
6.15	Business costs of crime and violence	106
2.11	Tax burden	90
6.14	Reliability of police services	85
8.20	Pay and productivity	81
5.06	Postal efficiency	81
5.07	Telephone/fax infrastructure quality	79
6.09	Extent of bureaucratic red tape	69

425

Note: The Business Competitiveness Index applies different criteria for selecting a country's competitive advantages and disadvantages.
Please refer to the section "How Country Profiles Work" for further details.

Spain

Competitiveness Rankings

Growth Competitiveness Index Rank	29

Macroeconomic Environment Index Rank **24**
    Macroeconomic Stability Subindex Rank 31
    Government Waste Rank 24
    Country Credit Rating Rank.................................17

Public Institutions Index Rank...**36**
    Contracts and Law Subindex Rank 47
    Corruption Subindex Rank....................................28

Technology Index Rank **27**
    Innovation Subindex Rank 28
    ICT Subindex Rank 32
    Technology Transfer Subindex Rank
        (out of 92 non-core innovators).........................13

Business Competitiveness Index Rank	25

**Sophistication of Company Operations
  and Strategy Rank** **25**
**Quality of the National Business
  Environment Rank** **26**

The Most Problematic Factors for Doing Business

FACTOR

Percent of responses

Note: From a list of 14 factors, respondents were asked to select the five most problematic for doing business in their country and to rank them between 1 (most problematic) and 5. The bars in the figure show the responses weighted according to their rankings.

Source: World Economic Forum, Executive Opinion Survey (2005)

National competitiveness balance sheet

NOTABLE COMPETITIVE ADVANTAGES	
Growth Competitiveness Index	**Rank/117**

Macroeconomic Environment

2.17	Interest rate spread, 2004	2
2.21	Country credit rating, 2004	17
6.06	Wastefulness of government spending	24

Public Institutions

| 6.20 | Irregular payments in public utilities | 25 |
| 6.21 | Irregular payments in tax collection | 27 |

Technology

3.18	Cellular telephones, 2003	11
4.17	Gross tertiary enrollment	18
3.03	Prevalence of foreign technology licensing	24
3.15	Laws relating to ICT	27
3.17	Utility patents, 2004	27
3.20	Internet hosts, 2003	28

NOTABLE COMPETITIVE DISADVANTAGES	
Growth Competitiveness Index	**Rank/117**

Macroeconomic Environment

2.15	Real effective exchange rate, 2004	97
2.01	Recession expectations	65
2.20	Government debt, 2004	53
2.16	Inflation, 2004	47
2.14	National savings rate, 2004	42
2.07	Access to credit	41
2.13	Government surplus/deficit, 2004	31

Public Institutions

6.01	Judicial independence	55
6.08	Favoritism in decisions of government officials	52
6.16	Organized crime	51
6.03	Property rights	33
6.19	Irregular payments in exports and imports	30

Technology

3.14	Government success in ICT promotion	72
3.13	Government prioritization of ICT	61
3.12	Quality of competition in the ISP sector	43
3.02	Firm-level technology absorption	39
3.04	FDI and technology transfer	38
3.19	Internet users, 2003	37
3.07	University/industry research collaboration	37
3.11	Internet access in schools	35
3.21	Personal computers, 2003	32
3.06	Company spending on research and development	32
3.01	Technological readiness	31
5.08	Telephone lines, 2003	29

Business Competitiveness Index	**Rank/110**

Sophistication of Company Operations and Strategy

8.13	Extent of incentive compensation	17
8.06	Extent of marketing	19
8.02	Value chain presence	22

Quality of the National Business Environment

6.13	Centralization of economic policymaking	8
8.15	Quality of management schools	8
3.18	Cellular telephones, 2003	10

Business Competitiveness Index	**Rank/110**

Sophistication of Company Operations and Strategy

8.08	Control of international distribution	39
8.09	Extent of regional sales	37
8.07	Degree of customer orientation	32

Quality of the National Business Environment

4.03	Quality of math and science education	67
2.08	Local equity market access	52
6.01	Judicial independence	52

427

Other Indicators	**Rank/117**

4.05	Medium term business impact of tuberculosis	11
7.08	Local availability of process machinery	16
7.05	Local supplier quantity	19
9.06	Prioritization of energy efficiency	21
7.06	Local supplier quality	22
2.04	Soundness of banks	23
8.14	Reliance on professional management	24
7.03	Extent of market dominance	24
8.05	Production process sophistication	24
7.01	Intensity of local competition	24

Other Indicators	**Rank/117**

4.09	Private sector employment of women	103
8.17	Hiring and firing practices	101
2.02	Business costs of terrorism	82
2.11	Tax burden	81
8.18	Flexibility of wage determination	72
8.20	Pay and productivity	58
6.15	Business costs of crime and violence	53
9.04	Effects of compliance on business	53
2.12	Agricultural policy costs	53
5.07	Telephone/fax infrastructure quality	50
8.19	Cooperation in labor-employer relations	49
8.21	Protection of minority shareholders' interests	44
3.05	Quality of scientific research institutions	43
5.06	Postal efficiency	41

Note: The Business Competitiveness Index applies different criteria for selecting a country's competitive advantages and disadvantages. Please refer to the section "How Country Profiles Work" for further details.

Sri Lanka

Competitiveness Rankings

The Most Problematic Factors for Doing Business

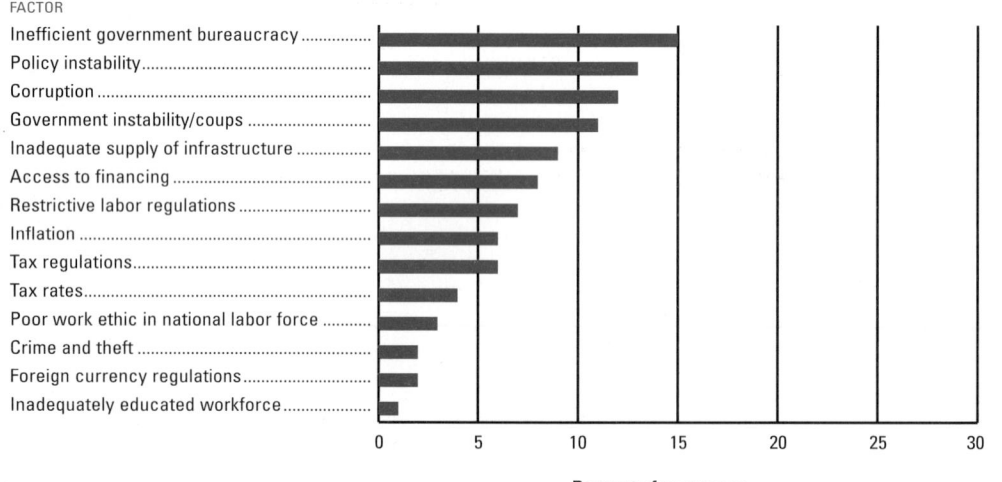

Note: From a list of 14 factors, respondents were asked to select the five most problematic for doing business in their country and to rank them between 1 (most problematic) and 5. The bars in the figure show the responses weighted according to their rankings.

Source: World Economic Forum, Executive Opinion Survey (2005)

National competitiveness balance sheet

NOTABLE COMPETITIVE ADVANTAGES		
Growth Competitiveness Index		**Rank/117**
Macroeconomic Environment		
2.15	Real effective exchange rate, 2004	37
2.17	Interest rate spread, 2004	39
Technology		
3.12	Quality of competition in the ISP sector	48

NOTABLE COMPETITIVE DISADVANTAGES		
Growth Competitiveness Index		**Rank/117**
Macroeconomic Environment		
2.13	Government surplus/deficit, 2004	114
2.20	Government debt, 2004	107
6.06	Wastefulness of government spending	98
2.07	Access to credit	93
2.16	Inflation, 2004	92
2.01	Recession expectations	82
2.14	National savings rate, 2004	80
2.21	Country credit rating, 2004	79
Public Institutions		
6.19	Irregular payments in exports and imports	112
6.08	Favoritism in decisions of government officials	100
6.20	Irregular payments in public utilities	97
6.16	Organized crime	94
6.21	Irregular payments in tax collection	91
6.03	Property rights	79
6.01	Judicial independence	73
Technology		
4.17	Gross tertiary enrollment	101
3.19	Internet users, 2003	98
3.20	Internet hosts, 2003	98
3.11	Internet access in schools	93
3.18	Cellular telephones, 2003	92
5.08	Telephone lines, 2003	90
3.21	Personal computers, 2003	87
3.15	Laws relating to ICT	87
3.13	Government prioritization of ICT	84
3.07	University/industry research collaboration	83
3.03	Prevalence of foreign technology licensing	80
3.01	Technological readiness	79
3.02	Firm-level technology absorption	77
3.06	Company spending on research and development	77
3.14	Government success in ICT promotion	75
3.17	Utility patents, 2004	74
3.04	FDI and technology transfer	62

Business Competitiveness Index		Rank/110
Sophistication of Company Operations and Strategy		
8.10	Breadth of international markets	50
8.02	Value chain presence	50
8.06	Extent of marketing	51
Quality of the National Business Environment		
7.01	Intensity of local competition	34
7.04	Buyer sophistication	36
2.08	Local equity market access	39

Business Competitiveness Index		Rank/110
Sophistication of Company Operations and Strategy		
8.05	Production process sophistication	93
8.13	Extent of incentive compensation	90
8.01	Nature of competitive advantage	87
Quality of the National Business Environment		
8.19	Cooperation in labor-employer relations	109
6.09	Extent of bureaucratic red tape	100
3.19	Internet users, 2003	97

Other Indicators		Rank/117
2.10	Impact of rules on FDI	17
2.11	Tax burden	23
4.09	Private sector employment of women	37
8.22	Foreign ownership restrictions	43
6.12	Efficiency of the tax system	50

Other Indicators		Rank/117
8.20	Pay and productivity	114
2.02	Business costs of terrorism	113
6.22	Irregular payments in public contracts	107
8.17	Hiring and firing practices	106
6.26	Public trust of politicians	102
6.17	Informal sector	98
6.24	Diversion of public funds	97
6.14	Reliability of police services	94
4.08	Brain drain	94
2.09	Prevalence of trade barriers	93
6.18	Government effectiveness in reducing poverty and inequality	93

Note: The Business Competitiveness Index applies different criteria for selecting a country's competitive advantages and disadvantages. Please refer to the section "How Country Profiles Work" for further details.

429

Sweden

Competitiveness Rankings

The Most Problematic Factors for Doing Business

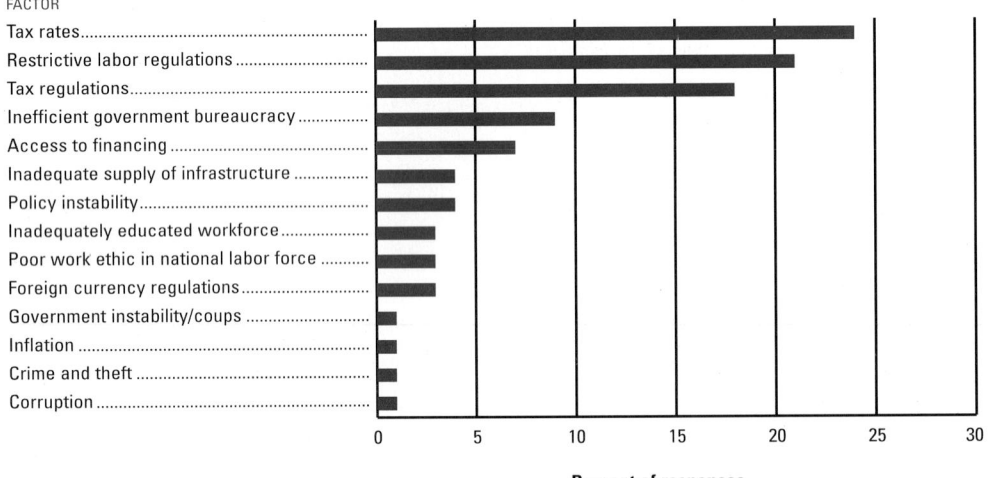

FACTOR
Tax rates
Restrictive labor regulations
Tax regulations
Inefficient government bureaucracy
Access to financing
Inadequate supply of infrastructure
Policy instability
Inadequately educated workforce
Poor work ethic in national labor force
Foreign currency regulations
Government instability/coups
Inflation
Crime and theft
Corruption

0   5   10   15   20   25   30

Percent of responses

Note: From a list of 14 factors, respondents were asked to select the five most problematic for doing business in their country and to rank them between 1 (most problematic) and 5. The bars in the figure show the responses weighted according to their rankings.

Source: World Economic Forum, Executive Opinion Survey (2005)

National competitiveness balance sheet

NOTABLE COMPETITIVE ADVANTAGES	
Growth Competitiveness Index	**Rank/117**

Public Institutions

| 6.08 | Favoritism in decisions of government officials | 9 |
| 6.19 | Irregular payments in exports and imports | 10 |

Technology

5.08	Telephone lines, 2003	2
3.19	Internet users, 2003	2
4.17	Gross tertiary enrollment	3
3.21	Personal computers, 2003	4
3.18	Cellular telephones, 2003	5
3.07	University/industry research collaboration	6
3.17	Utility patents, 2004	7
3.06	Company spending on research and development	7
3.01	Technological readiness	8
3.11	Internet access in schools	10

NOTABLE COMPETITIVE DISADVANTAGES	
Growth Competitiveness Index	**Rank/117**

Macroeconomic Environment

2.15	Real effective exchange rate, 2004	69
2.20	Government debt, 2004	58
2.14	National savings rate, 2004	36
2.07	Access to credit	35
2.01	Recession expectations	35
6.06	Wastefulness of government spending	31
2.13	Government surplus/deficit, 2004	23
2.17	Interest rate spread, 2004	17
2.16	Inflation, 2004	13
2.21	Country credit rating, 2004	11

Public Institutions

6.01	Judicial independence	36
6.03	Property rights	21
6.16	Organized crime	17
6.21	Irregular payments in tax collection	16
6.20	Irregular payments in public utilities	11

Technology

3.13	Government prioritization of ICT	36
3.14	Government success in ICT promotion	27
3.15	Laws relating to ICT	22
3.12	Quality of competition in the ISP sector	13
3.20	Internet hosts, 2003	11
3.02	Firm-level technology absorption	11

Business Competitiveness Index	
****	**Rank/110**

Sophistication of Company Operations and Strategy

8.12	Willingness to delegate authority	2
8.11	Extent of staff training	5
3.06	Company spending on research and development	7

Quality of the National Business Environment

3.19	Internet users, 2003	2
3.18	Cellular telephones, 2003	4
6.09	Extent of bureaucratic red tape	5

Business Competitiveness Index	
****	**Rank/110**

Sophistication of Company Operations and Strategy

| 8.13 | Extent of incentive compensation | 24 |
| 8.09 | Extent of regional sales | 19 |

Quality of the National Business Environment

4.03	Quality of math and science education	42
6.01	Judicial independence	35
6.13	Centralization of economic policymaking	33

Other Indicators	
****	**Rank/117**

4.05	Medium term business impact of tuberculosis	2
3.16	Extent of business Internet use	2
4.06	Medium term business impact of HIV/AIDS	4
9.09	Prevalence of corporate environmental reporting	4
9.07	Importance of environment in business planning	4
9.03	Extent of government mandated environmental reporting	5
2.02	Business costs of terrorism	5
9.01	Stringency of environmental regulations	6
6.05	Freedom of the press	6
9.06	Prioritization of energy efficiency	7
9.08	Protection of ecosystems by business	7
8.10	Breadth of international markets	8

Other Indicators	
****	**Rank/117**

8.17	Hiring and firing practices	113
6.11	Extent and effect of taxation	109
8.18	Flexibility of wage determination	108
6.12	Efficiency of the tax system	102
2.11	Tax burden	81
8.20	Pay and productivity	73
4.07	Ease of hiring foreign labor	73
3.08	Government procurement of advanced technology products	35
9.05	Effects of privatization on competition and the environment	35
6.17	Informal sector	33
2.12	Agricultural policy costs	33
8.15	Quality of management schools	27
5.05	Quality of electricity supply	26
7.03	Extent of market dominance	25

Note: The Business Competitiveness Index applies different criteria for selecting a country's competitive advantages and disadvantages. Please refer to the section "How Country Profiles Work" for further details.

Switzerland

Competitiveness Rankings

Growth Competitiveness Index Rank	8

Business Competitiveness Index Rank	7

Macroeconomic Environment Index Rank **13**
    Macroeconomic Stability Subindex Rank 37
    Government Waste Rank 13
    Country Credit Rating Rank 1

Public Institutions Index Rank...**9**
    Contracts and Law Subindex Rank 8
    Corruption Subindex Rank....................................15

Technology Index Rank **6**
    Innovation Subindex Rank 7
    ICT Subindex Rank 12

**Sophistication of Company Operations
    and Strategy Rank** **5**

**Quality of the National Business
    Environment Rank** **7**

The Most Problematic Factors for Doing Business

FACTOR

Percent of responses

Note: From a list of 14 factors, respondents were asked to select the five most problematic for doing business in their country and to rank them between 1 (most problematic) and 5. The bars in the figure show the responses weighted according to their rankings.

Source: World Economic Forum, Executive Opinion Survey (2005)

National competitiveness balance sheet

Growth Competitiveness Index	Rank/117

Macroeconomic Environment

| 2.21 | Country credit rating, 2004 | 1 |

Public Institutions

6.01	Judicial independence	3
6.03	Property rights	4
6.20	Irregular payments in public utilities	10

Technology

3.21	Personal computers, 2003	1
5.08	Telephone lines, 2003	3
3.07	University/industry research collaboration	3
3.17	Utility patents, 2004	4
3.06	Company spending on research and development	4
3.01	Technological readiness	10

Business Competitiveness Index	Rank/110

Sophistication of Company Operations and Strategy

8.01	Nature of competitive advantage	3
8.02	Value chain presence	3
3.06	Company spending on research and development	4

Quality of the National Business Environment

6.13	Centralization of economic policymaking	1
5.02	Railroad infrastructure development	2
3.05	Quality of scientific research institutions	2

Other Indicators	Rank/117
2.04	Soundness of banks	1
2.03	Financial market sophistication	3
6.04	Intellectual property protection	3
8.15	Quality of management schools	3
9.01	Stringency of environmental regulations	4
8.10	Breadth of international markets	4
8.05	Production process sophistication	4
8.19	Cooperation in labor-employer relations	4
6.17	Informal sector	4
9.08	Protection of ecosystems by business	5

Growth Competitiveness Index	Rank/117

Macroeconomic Environment

2.01	Recession expectations	79
2.15	Real effective exchange rate, 2004	75
2.07	Access to credit	66
2.20	Government debt, 2004	62
2.13	Government surplus/deficit, 2004	57
2.14	National savings rate, 2004	14
2.17	Interest rate spread, 2004	14
6.06	Wastefulness of government spending	13
2.16	Inflation, 2004	11

Public Institutions

6.21	Irregular payments in tax collection	19
6.19	Irregular payments in exports and imports	17
6.16	Organized crime	15
6.08	Favoritism in decisions of government officials	12

Technology

3.14	Government success in ICT promotion	45
4.17	Gross tertiary enrollment	34
3.13	Government prioritization of ICT	33
3.12	Quality of competition in the ISP sector	30
3.19	Internet users, 2003	23
3.18	Cellular telephones, 2003	19
3.15	Laws relating to ICT	17
3.20	Internet hosts, 2003	16
3.11	Internet access in schools	15
3.02	Firm-level technology absorption	13

Business Competitiveness Index	Rank/110

Sophistication of Company Operations and Strategy

| 8.14 | Reliance on professional management | 20 |

Quality of the National Business Environment

2.09	Prevalence of trade barriers	94
7.01	Intensity of local competition	62
8.21	Protection of minority shareholders' interests	34

Other Indicators	Rank/117
2.12	Agricultural policy costs	104
4.09	Private sector employment of women	66
4.07	Ease of hiring foreign labor	39
6.12	Efficiency of the tax system	32
7.02	Effectiveness of antitrust policy	31
8.22	Foreign ownership restrictions	28
6.27	Pervasiveness of money laundering through banks	27
4.06	Medium term business impact of HIV/AIDS	27
2.06	Venture capital availability	23
2.05	Ease of access to loans	23
8.16	Efficacy of corporate boards	22

Note: The Business Competitiveness Index applies different criteria for selecting a country's competitive advantages and disadvantages.
Please refer to the section "How Country Profiles Work" for further details.

Taiwan

Competitiveness Rankings

Growth Competitiveness Index Rank	5

Macroeconomic Environment Index Rank **17**
    Macroeconomic Stability Subindex Rank 17
    Government Waste Rank 12
    Country Credit Rating Rank 24

Public Institutions Index Rank..........................**26**
    Contracts and Law Subindex Rank 33
    Corruption Subindex Rank...................................24

Technology Index Rank **3**
    Innovation Subindex Rank 3
    ICT Subindex Rank 6

Business Competitiveness Index Rank	14

**Sophistication of Company Operations
  and Strategy Rank** **13**
**Quality of the National Business
  Environment Rank** **15**

The Most Problematic Factors for Doing Business

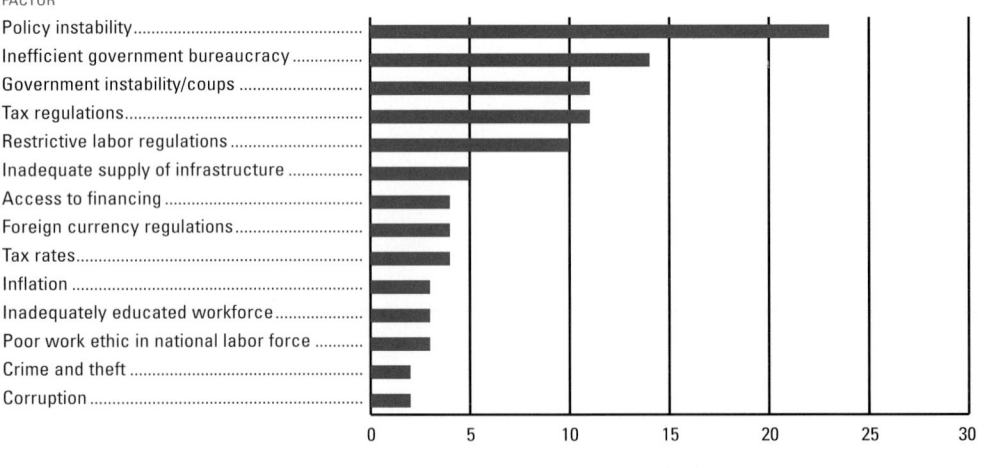

FACTOR

Policy instability
Inefficient government bureaucracy
Government instability/coups
Tax regulations
Restrictive labor regulations
Inadequate supply of infrastructure
Access to financing
Foreign currency regulations
Tax rates
Inflation
Inadequately educated workforce
Poor work ethic in national labor force
Crime and theft
Corruption

Percent of responses

Note: From a list of 14 factors, respondents were asked to select the five most problematic for doing business in their country and to rank them between 1 (most problematic) and 5. The bars in the figure show the responses weighted according to their rankings.

Source: World Economic Forum, Executive Opinion Survey (2005)

National competitiveness balance sheet

NOTABLE COMPETITIVE ADVANTAGES	
Growth Competitiveness Index	**Rank/117**

Macroeconomic Environment
2.07	Access to credit	3
2.17	Interest rate spread, 2004	5

Technology
3.18	Cellular telephones, 2003	2
3.17	Utility patents, 2004	3
3.14	Government success in ICT promotion	3
3.02	Firm-level technology absorption	4
3.13	Government prioritization of ICT	5
3.07	University/industry research collaboration	8
3.20	Internet hosts, 2003	8
4.17	Gross tertiary enrollment	10

NOTABLE COMPETITIVE DISADVANTAGES	
Growth Competitiveness Index	**Rank/117**

Macroeconomic Environment
2.13	Government surplus/deficit, 2004	76
2.01	Recession expectations	53
2.20	Government debt, 2004	31
2.15	Real effective exchange rate, 2004	25
2.14	National savings rate, 2004	25
2.21	Country credit rating, 2004	24
2.16	Inflation, 2004	21
6.06	Wastefulness of government spending	12

Public Institutions
6.01	Judicial independence	44
6.16	Organized crime	41
6.03	Property rights	29
6.20	Irregular payments in public utilities	26
6.21	Irregular payments in tax collection	25
6.19	Irregular payments in exports and imports	20
6.08	Favoritism in decisions of government officials	17

Technology
3.15	Laws relating to ICT	19
3.01	Technological readiness	14
3.21	Personal computers, 2003	13
3.12	Quality of competition in the ISP sector	12
3.19	Internet users, 2003	12
3.06	Company spending on research and development	12
5.08	Telephone lines, 2003	12
3.11	Internet access in schools	11

Business Competitiveness Index	Rank/110

Sophistication of Company Operations and Strategy
8.07	Degree of customer orientation	6
8.10	Breadth of international markets	9

Quality of the National Business Environment
3.18	Cellular telephones, 2003	1
3.08	Government procurement of advanced technology products	2
3.17	Utility patents, 2004	3

Business Competitiveness Index	Rank/110

Sophistication of Company Operations and Strategy
8.14	Reliance on professional management	24
8.06	Extent of marketing	22
8.13	Extent of incentive compensation	20

Quality of the National Business Environment
6.01	Judicial independence	43
8.21	Protection of minority shareholders' interests	39
8.22	Foreign ownership restrictions	32

Other Indicators	Rank/117

8.20	Pay and productivity	3
6.07	Burden of government regulation	4
8.18	Flexibility of wage determination	5
9.04	Effects of compliance on business	6
2.11	Tax burden	6
2.12	Agricultural policy costs	7
7.03	Extent of market dominance	9
9.10	Grass-roots involvement in development projects	10
3.09	Availability of scientists and engineers	10

Other Indicators	Rank/117

2.04	Soundness of banks	74
4.07	Ease of hiring foreign labor	54
3.10	Availability of mobile or cellular telephones	52
2.02	Business costs of terrorism	44
6.10	Effectiveness of law-making bodies	42
4.05	Medium term business impact of tuberculosis	38
8.23	Strength of auditing and accounting standards	36
6.05	Freedom of the press	36
6.23	Irregular payments in judicial decisions	35
6.17	Informal sector	34
9.08	Protection of ecosystems by business	33
6.27	Pervasiveness of money laundering through banks	32
6.18	Government effectiveness in reducing poverty and inequality	32

435

Note: The Business Competitiveness Index applies different criteria for selecting a country's competitive advantages and disadvantages. Please refer to the section "How Country Profiles Work" for further details.

Tajikistan

Competitiveness Rankings

Growth Competitiveness Index Rank	104

Macroeconomic Environment Index Rank **95**
    Macroeconomic Stability Subindex Rank 72
    Government Waste Rank 71
    Country Credit Rating Rank 116

Public Institutions Index Rank..**101**
    Contracts and Law Subindex Rank 76
    Corruption Subindex Rank..................................110

Technology Index Rank **104**
    Innovation Subindex Rank 89
    ICT Subindex Rank 92
    Technology Transfer Subindex Rank
        (out of 92 non-core innovators).......................81

Business Competitiveness Index Rank	98

**Sophistication of Company Operations
  and Strategy Rank** **104**
**Quality of the National Business
  Environment Rank** **96**

The Most Problematic Factors for Doing Business

FACTOR

Access to financing
Corruption
Inadequately educated workforce
Tax regulations
Tax rates
Inadequate supply of infrastructure
Inefficient government bureaucracy
Poor work ethic in national labor force
Inflation
Restrictive labor regulations
Crime and theft
Foreign currency regulations
Policy instability
Government instability/coups

Percent of responses

Note: From a list of 14 factors, respondents were asked to select the five most problematic for doing business in their country and to rank them between 1 (most problematic) and 5. The bars in the figure show the responses weighted according to their rankings.

Source: World Economic Forum, Executive Opinion Survey (2005)

436

National competitiveness balance sheet

	NOTABLE COMPETITIVE ADVANTAGES	
	Growth Competitiveness Index	**Rank/117**

Macroeconomic Environment
2.15 Real effective exchange rate, 2004 13
2.01 Recession expectations 28
2.20 Government debt, 2004 37

Technology
3.14 Government success in ICT promotion 31
3.13 Government prioritization of ICT 35

	Business Competitiveness Index	**Rank/110**

Sophistication of Company Operations and Strategy
8.08 Control of international distribution 43
8.03 Capacity for innovation 80

Quality of the National Business Environment
7.08 Local availability of process machinery 34
5.02 Railroad infrastructure development 53

	Other Indicators	**Rank/117**
8.17 Hiring and firing practices 19
8.20 Pay and productivity 36
6.10 Effectiveness of law-making bodies 38
9.07 Importance of environment in business planning..........46
6.26 Public trust of politicians 47
9.06 Prioritization of energy efficiency 48
6.18 Government effectiveness in reducing poverty
and inequality 49

	NOTABLE COMPETITIVE DISADVANTAGES	
	Growth Competitiveness Index	**Rank/117**

Macroeconomic Environment
2.21 Country credit rating, 2004 116
2.14 National savings rate, 2004...102
2.07 Access to credit 102
2.17 Interest rate spread, 2004..91
2.16 Inflation, 2004 89
6.06 Wastefulness of government spending..........................71
2.13 Government surplus/deficit, 2004..................................68

Public Institutions
6.21 Irregular payments in tax collection 116
6.20 Irregular payments in public utilities 107
6.19 Irregular payments in exports and imports...................103
6.03 Property rights..90
6.16 Organized crime 72
6.01 Judicial independence...71
6.08 Favoritism in decisions of government officials..............62

Technology
3.19 Internet users, 2003..116
3.18 Cellular telephones, 2003..116
3.20 Internet hosts, 2003...111
3.03 Prevalence of foreign technology licensing 108
3.01 Technological readiness 106
3.02 Firm-level technology absorption 104
3.15 Laws relating to ICT..97
5.08 Telephone lines, 2003...97
3.04 FDI and technology transfer..92
3.12 Quality of competition in the ISP sector 89
3.11 Internet access in schools 88
3.07 University/industry research collaboration 84
4.17 Gross tertiary enrollment 82
3.06 Company spending on research and development 81
3.17 Utility patents, 2004 81

	Business Competitiveness Index	**Rank/110**

Sophistication of Company Operations and Strategy
8.11 Extent of staff training 110
8.10 Breadth of international markets....................................109
8.06 Extent of marketing..109

Quality of the National Business Environment
3.19 Internet users, 2003..110
3.18 Cellular telephones, 2003..109
8.15 Quality of management schools 108

	Other Indicators	**Rank/117**
8.09 Extent of regional sales..114
8.23 Strength of auditing and accounting standards 112
7.05 Local supplier quantity 112
2.04 Soundness of banks..111
6.05 Freedom of the press 111
5.05 Quality of electricity supply..111
9.05 Effects of privatization on competition and the
environment..111
8.24 Importance of corporate social responsibility 110
3.16 Extent of business Internet use....................................110
9.04 Effects of compliance on business...............................110
8.13 Extent of incentive compensation 109

437

Note: The Business Competitiveness Index applies different criteria for selecting a country's competitive advantages and disadvantages. Please refer to the section "How Country Profiles Work" for further details.

Tanzania

Competitiveness Rankings

Growth Competitiveness Index Rank	**71**

Macroeconomic Environment Index Rank **72**
    Macroeconomic Stability Subindex Rank 77
    Government Waste Rank 26
    Country Credit Rating Rank 89

Public Institutions Index Rank..........................**60**
    Contracts and Law Subindex Rank 44
    Corruption Subindex Rank...................................85

Technology Index Rank **86**
    Innovation Subindex Rank 107
    ICT Subindex Rank 96
    Technology Transfer Subindex Rank
        (out of 92 non-core innovators).......................44

Business Competitiveness Index Rank	**82**

**Sophistication of Company Operations
  and Strategy Rank** **91**
**Quality of the National Business
  Environment Rank** **81**

438

The Most Problematic Factors for Doing Business

FACTOR

Note: From a list of 14 factors, respondents were asked to select the five most problematic for doing business in their country and to rank them between 1 (most problematic) and 5. The bars in the figure show the responses weighted according to their rankings.

Source: World Economic Forum, Executive Opinion Survey (2005)

National competitiveness balance sheet

NOTABLE COMPETITIVE ADVANTAGES	
Growth Competitiveness Index	**Rank/117**

	Macroeconomic Environment	
2.15	Real effective exchange rate, 2004	6
6.06	Wastefulness of government spending	26
2.01	Recession expectations	38
	Public Institutions	
6.01	Judicial independence	34
6.08	Favoritism in decisions of government officials	37
6.16	Organized crime	47
	Technology	
3.14	Government success in ICT promotion	33
3.04	FDI and technology transfer	41
3.13	Government prioritization of ICT	47

NOTABLE COMPETITIVE DISADVANTAGES	
Growth Competitiveness Index	**Rank/117**

	Macroeconomic Environment	
2.14	National savings rate, 2004	112
2.20	Government debt, 2004	96
2.21	Country credit rating, 2004	89
2.17	Interest rate spread, 2004	86
2.07	Access to credit	85
2.13	Government surplus/deficit, 2004	72
2.16	Inflation, 2004	67
	Public Institutions	
6.21	Irregular payments in tax collection	85
6.20	Irregular payments in public utilities	82
6.19	Irregular payments in exports and imports	80
6.03	Property rights	68
	Technology	
4.17	Gross tertiary enrollment	114
5.08	Telephone lines, 2003	111
3.11	Internet access in schools	105
3.19	Internet users, 2003	104
3.18	Cellular telephones, 2003	104
3.21	Personal computers, 2003	103
3.20	Internet hosts, 2003	91
3.01	Technological readiness	88
3.15	Laws relating to ICT	85
3.06	Company spending on research and development	82
3.02	Firm-level technology absorption	81
3.17	Utility patents, 2004	81
3.03	Prevalence of foreign technology licensing	75
3.12	Quality of competition in the ISP sector	68
3.07	University/industry research collaboration	54

Business Competitiveness Index	**Rank/110**

	Sophistication of Company Operations and Strategy	
8.14	Reliance on professional management	39
8.12	Willingness to delegate authority	75
	Quality of the National Business Environment	
3.08	Government procurement of advanced technology products	24
6.01	Judicial independence	33
6.08	Favoritism in decisions of government officials	36

Business Competitiveness Index	**Rank/110**

	Sophistication of Company Operations and Strategy	
8.08	Control of international distribution	105
8.13	Extent of incentive compensation	103
8.02	Value chain presence	102
	Quality of the National Business Environment	
3.19	Internet users, 2003	102
3.18	Cellular telephones, 2003	100
5.05	Quality of electricity supply	99

Other Indicators	**Rank/117**

6.10	Effectiveness of law-making bodies	22
6.07	Burden of government regulation	23
6.18	Government effectiveness in reducing poverty and inequality	33
9.07	Importance of environment in business planning	39
2.11	Tax burden	40
9.04	Effects of compliance on business	41
9.10	Grass-roots involvement in development projects	42
8.16	Efficacy of corporate boards	43
6.12	Efficiency of the tax system	43
6.11	Extent and effect of taxation	43
2.10	Impact of rules on FDI	44
6.02	Efficiency of legal framework	45
9.05	Effects of privatization on competition and the environment	45

Other Indicators	**Rank/117**

4.06	Medium term business impact of HIV/AIDS	112
4.05	Medium term business impact of tuberculosis	110
8.01	Nature of competitive advantage	106
8.11	Extent of staff training	104
8.05	Production process sophistication	102
8.06	Extent of marketing	101
8.10	Breadth of international markets	99
8.15	Quality of management schools	99
7.06	Local supplier quality	97
8.20	Pay and productivity	97
2.03	Financial market sophistication	96

439

Note: The Business Competitiveness Index applies different criteria for selecting a country's competitive advantages and disadvantages. Please refer to the section "How Country Profiles Work" for further details.

Thailand

Competitiveness Rankings

Growth Competitiveness Index Rank	36

Macroeconomic Environment Index Rank **26**
   Macroeconomic Stability Subindex Rank 9
   Government Waste Rank 17
   Country Credit Rating Rank 42

Public Institutions Index Rank **41**
   Contracts and Law Subindex Rank 42
   Corruption Subindex Rank.....................................46

Technology Index Rank **43**
   Innovation Subindex Rank 43
   ICT Subindex Rank 51
   Technology Transfer Subindex Rank
     (out of 92 non-core innovators).........................5

Business Competitiveness Index Rank	37

**Sophistication of Company Operations
and Strategy Rank** **35**
**Quality of the National Business
Environment Rank** **37**

The Most Problematic Factors for Doing Business

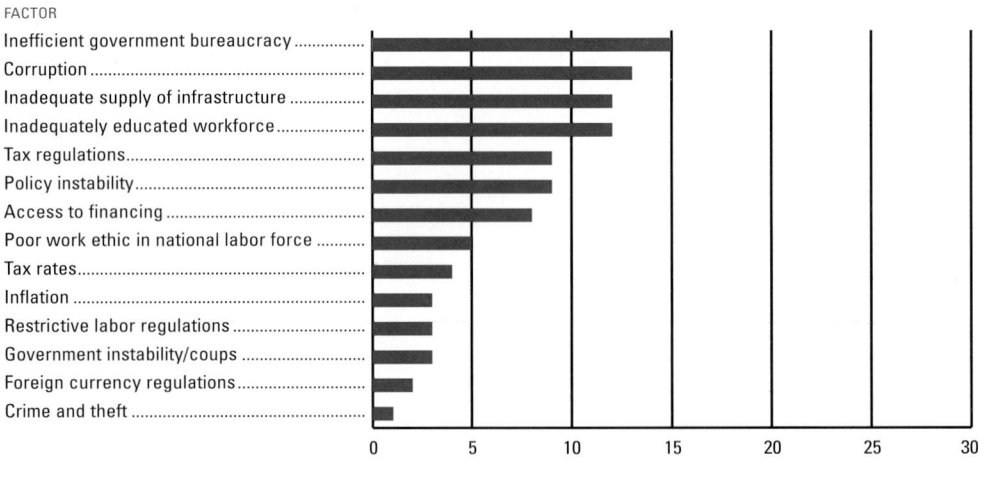

Note: From a list of 14 factors, respondents were asked to select the five most problematic for doing business in their country and to rank them between 1 (most problematic) and 5. The bars in the figure show the responses weighted according to their rankings.

Source: World Economic Forum, Executive Opinion Survey (2005)

National competitiveness balance sheet

Growth Competitiveness Index — Rank/117

Macroeconomic Environment
2.07	Access to credit	12
6.06	Wastefulness of government spending	17
2.14	National savings rate, 2004	19
2.13	Government surplus/deficit, 2004	29
2.20	Government debt, 2004	35

Technology
3.14	Government success in ICT promotion	16
3.03	Prevalence of foreign technology licensing	16
3.04	FDI and technology transfer	23
3.13	Government prioritization of ICT	23
3.07	University/industry research collaboration	28

Business Competitiveness Index — Rank/110

Sophistication of Company Operations and Strategy
3.03	Prevalence of foreign technology licensing	16
8.09	Extent of regional sales	22
8.11	Extent of staff training	28

Quality of the National Business Environment
2.08	Local equity market access	15
8.19	Cooperation in labor-employer relations	18
3.08	Government procurement of advanced technology products	22

Other Indicators — Rank/117
4.09	Private sector employment of women	9
2.12	Agricultural policy costs	10
6.07	Burden of government regulation	11
4.08	Brain drain	17
6.11	Extent and effect of taxation	19
6.12	Efficiency of the tax system	20
6.10	Effectiveness of law-making bodies	24
9.06	Prioritization of energy efficiency	26
6.18	Government effectiveness in reducing poverty and inequality	27
8.20	Pay and productivity	28
9.07	Importance of environment in business planning	29

Growth Competitiveness Index — Rank/117

Macroeconomic Environment
2.15	Real effective exchange rate, 2004	45
2.21	Country credit rating, 2004	42
2.17	Interest rate spread, 2004	41
2.16	Inflation, 2004	40
2.01	Recession expectations	37

Public Institutions
6.19	Irregular payments in exports and imports	50
6.16	Organized crime	48
6.21	Irregular payments in tax collection	46
6.20	Irregular payments in public utilities	43
6.03	Property rights	43
6.01	Judicial independence	40
6.08	Favoritism in decisions of government officials	39

Technology
5.08	Telephone lines, 2003	77
3.21	Personal computers, 2003	71
3.20	Internet hosts, 2003	67
3.17	Utility patents, 2004	60
3.19	Internet users, 2003	58
3.18	Cellular telephones, 2003	50
4.17	Gross tertiary enrollment	45
3.11	Internet access in schools	45
3.15	Laws relating to ICT	45
3.01	Technological readiness	39
3.02	Firm-level technology absorption	38
3.06	Company spending on research and development	37
3.12	Quality of competition in the ISP sector	36

Business Competitiveness Index — Rank/110

Sophistication of Company Operations and Strategy
8.03	Capacity for innovation	60
8.08	Control of international distribution	56
8.05	Production process sophistication	52

Quality of the National Business Environment
6.09	Extent of bureaucratic red tape	87
3.09	Availability of scientists and engineers	68
6.13	Centralization of economic policymaking	68

Other Indicators — Rank/117
4.07	Ease of hiring foreign labor	101
4.06	Medium term business impact of HIV/AIDS	81
8.18	Flexibility of wage determination	74
2.02	Business costs of terrorism	73
2.04	Soundness of banks	70
6.05	Freedom of the press	69
8.22	Foreign ownership restrictions	66
2.09	Prevalence of trade barriers	65
6.27	Pervasiveness of money laundering through banks	61
4.05	Medium term business impact of tuberculosis	58

Note: The Business Competitiveness Index applies different criteria for selecting a country's competitive advantages and disadvantages. Please refer to the section "How Country Profiles Work" for further details.

Trinidad and Tobago

Competitiveness Rankings

Growth Competitiveness Index Rank	**60**

Macroeconomic Environment Index Rank **40**
   Macroeconomic Stability Subindex Rank 15
   Government Waste Rank 75
   Country Credit Rating Rank 50

Public Institutions Index Rank...**83**
   Contracts and Law Subindex Rank 78
   Corruption Subindex Rank....................................88

Technology Index Rank **62**
   Innovation Subindex Rank 92
   ICT Subindex Rank 61
   Technology Transfer Subindex Rank
     (out of 92 non-core innovators).......................30

Business Competitiveness Index Rank	**65**

**Sophistication of Company Operations
  and Strategy Rank** 62
**Quality of the National Business
  Environment Rank** 63

The Most Problematic Factors for Doing Business

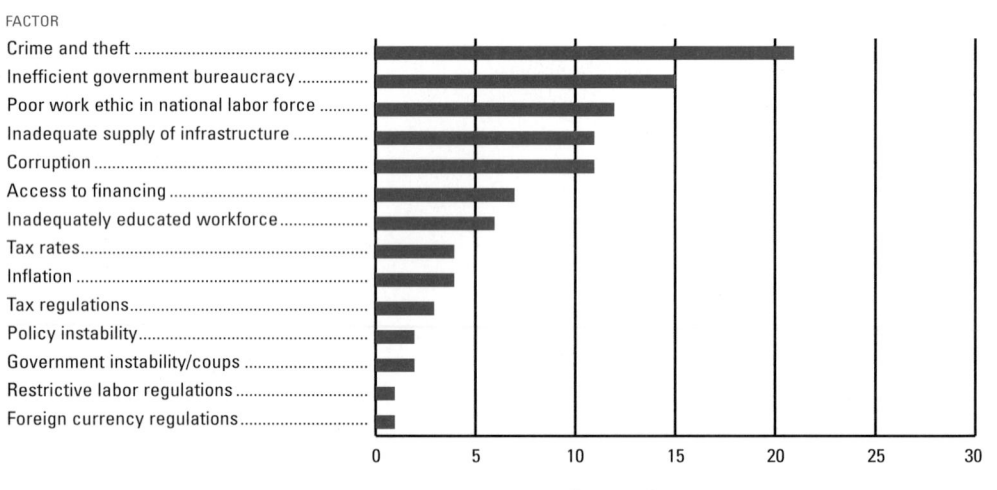

FACTOR

Crime and theft
Inefficient government bureaucracy
Poor work ethic in national labor force
Inadequate supply of infrastructure
Corruption
Access to financing
Inadequately educated workforce
Tax rates
Inflation
Tax regulations
Policy instability
Government instability/coups
Restrictive labor regulations
Foreign currency regulations

Percent of responses

Note: From a list of 14 factors, respondents were asked to select the five most problematic for doing business in their country and to rank them between 1 (most problematic) and 5. The bars in the figure show the responses weighted according to their rankings.

Source: World Economic Forum, Executive Opinion Survey (2005)

National competitiveness balance sheet

NOTABLE COMPETITIVE ADVANTAGES	
Growth Competitiveness Index	**Rank/117**

Macroeconomic Environment

2.01	Recession expectations	6
2.14	National savings rate, 2004	17
2.13	Government surplus/deficit, 2004	20
2.07	Access to credit	34
2.21	Country credit rating, 2004	50

Technology

3.04	FDI and technology transfer	32
3.18	Cellular telephones, 2003	48
5.08	Telephone lines, 2003	48
3.20	Internet hosts, 2003	49

NOTABLE COMPETITIVE DISADVANTAGES	
Growth Competitiveness Index	**Rank/117**

Macroeconomic Environment

6.06	Wastefulness of government spending	75
2.15	Real effective exchange rate, 2004	71
2.17	Interest rate spread, 2004	68
2.16	Inflation, 2004	59
2.20	Government debt, 2004	53

Public Institutions

6.16	Organized crime	111
6.19	Irregular payments in exports and imports	91
6.20	Irregular payments in public utilities	87
6.08	Favoritism in decisions of government officials	87
6.21	Irregular payments in tax collection	83
6.03	Property rights	63
6.01	Judicial independence	53

Technology

3.12	Quality of competition in the ISP sector	111
4.17	Gross tertiary enrollment	95
3.13	Government prioritization of ICT	94
3.15	Laws relating to ICT	92
3.17	Utility patents, 2004	81
3.07	University/industry research collaboration	80
3.11	Internet access in schools	78
3.14	Government success in ICT promotion	77
3.06	Company spending on research and development	76
3.02	Firm-level technology absorption	74
3.01	Technological readiness	71
3.03	Prevalence of foreign technology licensing	56
3.21	Personal computers, 2003	55
3.19	Internet users, 2003	55

Business Competitiveness Index	**Rank/110**

Sophistication of Company Operations and Strategy

8.09	Extent of regional sales	30
8.14	Reliance on professional management	41
8.13	Extent of incentive compensation	44

Quality of the National Business Environment

2.06	Venture capital availability	36
2.08	Local equity market access	42
2.09	Prevalence of trade barriers	44

Other Indicators	**Rank/117**

6.12	Efficiency of the tax system	18
6.11	Extent and effect of taxation	28
2.04	Soundness of banks	29
2.10	Impact of rules on FDI	35
8.17	Hiring and firing practices	45
2.03	Financial market sophistication	46
3.08	Government procurement of advanced technology products	47
7.04	Buyer sophistication	47
8.23	Strength of auditing and accounting standards	47

Business Competitiveness Index	**Rank/110**

Sophistication of Company Operations and Strategy

8.07	Degree of customer orientation	91
8.03	Capacity for innovation	90
8.01	Nature of competitive advantage	84

Quality of the National Business Environment

8.19	Cooperation in labor-employer relations	102
6.14	Reliability of police services	102
6.13	Centralization of economic policymaking	101

Other Indicators	**Rank/117**

6.15	Business costs of crime and violence	114
9.06	Prioritization of energy efficiency	106
3.10	Availability of mobile or cellular telephones	105
4.06	Medium term business impact of HIV/AIDS	103
8.20	Pay and productivity	103
2.02	Business costs of terrorism	98
9.03	Extent of government mandated environmental reporting	98
6.27	Pervasiveness of money laundering through banks	97
5.07	Telephone/fax infrastructure quality	95
7.02	Effectiveness of antitrust policy	95

443

Note: The Business Competitiveness Index applies different criteria for selecting a country's competitive advantages and disadvantages. Please refer to the section "How Country Profiles Work" for further details.

Tunisia

Competitiveness Rankings

Growth Competitiveness Index Rank	40

Macroeconomic Environment Index Rank **34**
    Macroeconomic Stability Subindex Rank 43
    Government Waste Rank 7
    Country Credit Rating Rank 52

Public Institutions Index Rank..**40**
    Contracts and Law Subindex Rank 28
    Corruption Subindex Rank....................................51

Technology Index Rank **60**
    Innovation Subindex Rank 57
    ICT Subindex Rank 56
    Technology Transfer Subindex Rank
      (out of 92 non-core innovators) 34

Business Competitiveness Index Rank	35

**Sophistication of Company Operations
  and Strategy Rank** **46**
**Quality of the National Business
  Environment Rank** **34**

444

The Most Problematic Factors for Doing Business

FACTOR

Note: From a list of 14 factors, respondents were asked to select the five most problematic for doing business in their country and to rank them between 1 (most problematic) and 5. The bars in the figure show the responses weighted according to their rankings.

Source: World Economic Forum, Executive Opinion Survey (2005)

National competitiveness balance sheet

NOTABLE COMPETITIVE ADVANTAGES		
Growth Competitiveness Index		**Rank/117**

Macroeconomic Environment
6.06	Wastefulness of government spending	7
2.17	Interest rate spread, 2004	17
2.15	Real effective exchange rate, 2004	35

Public Institutions
6.08	Favoritism in decisions of government officials	14
6.16	Organized crime	34
6.01	Judicial independence	37
6.03	Property rights	37

Technology
3.14	Government success in ICT promotion	4
3.13	Government prioritization of ICT	15
3.02	Firm-level technology absorption	34
3.15	Laws relating to ICT	34

NOTABLE COMPETITIVE DISADVANTAGES		
Growth Competitiveness Index		**Rank/117**

Macroeconomic Environment
2.07	Access to credit	80
2.20	Government debt, 2004	67
2.13	Government surplus/deficit, 2004	57
2.01	Recession expectations	54
2.21	Country credit rating, 2004	52
2.16	Inflation, 2004	52
2.14	National savings rate, 2004	51

Public Institutions
6.21	Irregular payments in tax collection	62
6.20	Irregular payments in public utilities	50
6.19	Irregular payments in exports and imports	48

Technology
3.20	Internet hosts, 2003	106
3.04	FDI and technology transfer	74
3.17	Utility patents, 2004	71
5.08	Telephone lines, 2003	71
3.18	Cellular telephones, 2003	71
3.21	Personal computers, 2003	70
3.19	Internet users, 2003	69
4.17	Gross tertiary enrollment	68
3.12	Quality of competition in the ISP sector	63
3.07	University/industry research collaboration	44
3.03	Prevalence of foreign technology licensing	44
3.11	Internet access in schools	40
3.06	Company spending on research and development	40
3.01	Technological readiness	40

Business Competitiveness Index		**Rank/110**

Sophistication of Company Operations and Strategy
| 8.02 | Value chain presence | 30 |
| 8.11 | Extent of staff training | 35 |

Quality of the National Business Environment
4.03	Quality of math and science education	11
3.08	Government procurement of advanced technology products	7
3.09	Availability of scientists and engineers	11

Other Indicators		**Rank/117**
4.09	Private sector employment of women	4
6.18	Government effectiveness in reducing poverty and inequality	4
2.12	Agricultural policy costs	6
6.07	Burden of government regulation	10
2.10	Impact of rules on FDI	13
6.26	Public trust of politicians	14
6.12	Efficiency of the tax system	15
6.11	Extent and effect of taxation	17
9.06	Prioritization of energy efficiency	17
6.14	Reliability of police services	19
9.04	Effects of compliance on business	21
7.03	Extent of market dominance	21
8.15	Quality of management schools	24

Business Competitiveness Index		**Rank/110**

Sophistication of Company Operations and Strategy
8.13	Extent of incentive compensation	78
8.14	Reliance on professional management	78
8.07	Degree of customer orientation	69

Quality of the National Business Environment
8.16	Efficacy of corporate boards	90
2.03	Financial market sophistication	71
3.18	Cellular telephones, 2003	70

Other Indicators		**Rank/117**
8.18	Flexibility of wage determination	105
4.07	Ease of hiring foreign labor	104
6.05	Freedom of the press	97
2.04	Soundness of banks	84
2.09	Prevalence of trade barriers	64
3.16	Extent of business Internet use	62
7.01	Intensity of local competition	61
2.05	Ease of access to loans	61
8.23	Strength of auditing and accounting standards	60
2.08	Local equity market access	60

445

Note: The Business Competitiveness Index applies different criteria for selecting a country's competitive advantages and disadvantages. Please refer to the section "How Country Profiles Work" for further details.

Turkey

Competitiveness Rankings

Growth Competitiveness Index Rank	66

Macroeconomic Environment Index Rank **87**
   Macroeconomic Stability Subindex Rank 111
   Government Waste Rank 76
   Country Credit Rating Rank 69

Public Institutions Index Rank..........................**61**
   Contracts and Law Subindex Rank 59
   Corruption Subindex Rank...................................64

Technology Index Rank **53**
   Innovation Subindex Rank 56
   ICT Subindex Rank 54
   Technology Transfer Subindex Rank
   (out of 92 non-core innovators).........................29

Business Competitiveness Index Rank	51

**Sophistication of Company Operations
and Strategy Rank** **38**
**Quality of the National Business
Environment Rank** **51**

The Most Problematic Factors for Doing Business

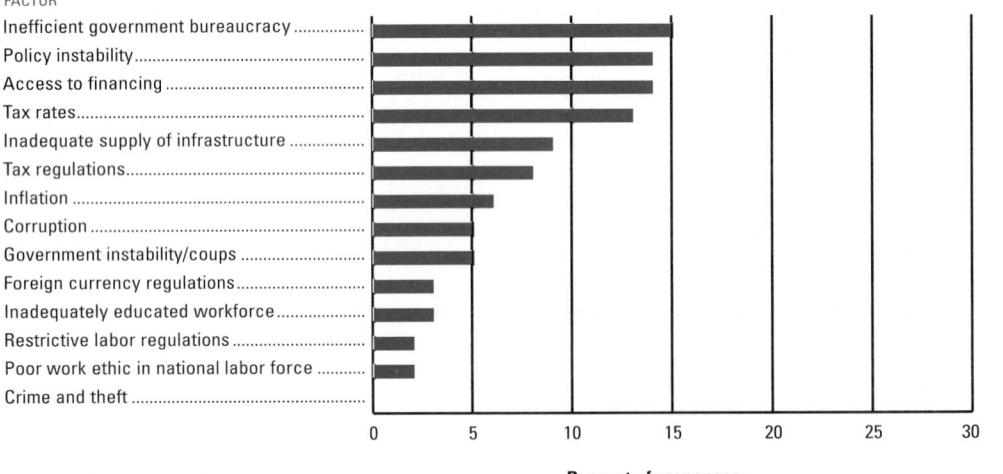

Note: From a list of 14 factors, respondents were asked to select the five most problematic for doing business in their country and to rank them between 1 (most problematic) and 5. The bars in the figure show the responses weighted according to their rankings.

Source: World Economic Forum, Executive Opinion Survey (2005)

National competitiveness balance sheet

NOTABLE COMPETITIVE ADVANTAGES	
Growth Competitiveness Index	**Rank/117**

Macroeconomic Environment

2.07	Access to credit	14
2.14	National savings rate, 2004	29
2.01	Recession expectations	49

Technology

3.02	Firm-level technology absorption	29
3.03	Prevalence of foreign technology licensing	29
5.08	Telephone lines, 2003	44
3.12	Quality of competition in the ISP sector	47
3.15	Laws relating to ICT	48
3.07	University/industry research collaboration	49
3.18	Cellular telephones, 2003	49
3.20	Internet hosts, 2003	50

Business Competitiveness Index	**Rank/110**

Sophistication of Company Operations and Strategy

8.10	Breadth of international markets	20
8.08	Control of international distribution	26
3.03	Prevalence of foreign technology licensing	29

Quality of the National Business Environment

2.08	Local equity market access	26
7.08	Local availability of process machinery	29
7.05	Local supplier quantity	33

Other Indicators	**Rank/117**

4.06	Medium term business impact of HIV/AIDS	14
4.05	Medium term business impact of tuberculosis	19
9.05	Effects of privatization on competition and the environment	26
6.10	Effectiveness of law-making bodies	27
7.01	Intensity of local competition	33
8.02	Value chain presence	37
7.02	Effectiveness of antitrust policy	37
7.06	Local supplier quality	37
8.09	Extent of regional sales	37
8.07	Degree of customer orientation	38

NOTABLE COMPETITIVE DISADVANTAGES	
Growth Competitiveness Index	**Rank/117**

Macroeconomic Environment

2.13	Government surplus/deficit, 2004	117
2.17	Interest rate spread, 2004	110
2.15	Real effective exchange rate, 2004	109
2.16	Inflation, 2004	102
2.20	Government debt, 2004	89
6.06	Wastefulness of government spending	76
2.21	Country credit rating, 2004	69

Public Institutions

6.19	Irregular payments in exports and imports	81
6.16	Organized crime	68
6.08	Favoritism in decisions of government officials	64
6.20	Irregular payments in public utilities	59
6.03	Property rights	58
6.01	Judicial independence	57
6.21	Irregular payments in tax collection	51

Technology

3.13	Government prioritization of ICT	72
3.14	Government success in ICT promotion	71
3.21	Personal computers, 2003	67
3.17	Utility patents, 2004	66
4.17	Gross tertiary enrollment	64
3.04	FDI and technology transfer	59
3.19	Internet users, 2003	59
3.11	Internet access in schools	58
3.06	Company spending on research and development	54
3.01	Technological readiness	51

Business Competitiveness Index	**Rank/110**

Sophistication of Company Operations and Strategy

8.13	Extent of incentive compensation	81
8.01	Nature of competitive advantage	79
8.14	Reliance on professional management	65

Quality of the National Business Environment

6.13	Centralization of economic policymaking	96
2.06	Venture capital availability	83
2.05	Ease of access to loans	80

Other Indicators	**Rank/117**

2.04	Soundness of banks	114
6.17	Informal sector	105
6.11	Extent and effect of taxation	103
2.12	Agricultural policy costs	102
6.12	Efficiency of the tax system	93
9.10	Grass-roots involvement in development projects	88
2.11	Tax burden	86
6.05	Freedom of the press	84
8.22	Foreign ownership restrictions	82
8.19	Cooperation in labor-employer relations	80

447

Note: The Business Competitiveness Index applies different criteria for selecting a country's competitive advantages and disadvantages. Please refer to the section "How Country Profiles Work" for further details.

Uganda

Competitiveness Rankings

Growth Competitiveness Index Rank	87

Macroeconomic Environment Index Rank **88**
    Macroeconomic Stability Subindex Rank 82
    Government Waste Rank 65
    Country Credit Rating Rank 102

Public Institutions Index Rank..........................**95**
    Contracts and Law Subindex Rank 73
    Corruption Subindex Rank...................................102

Technology Index Rank **82**
    Innovation Subindex Rank 104
    ICT Subindex Rank 98
    Technology Transfer Subindex Rank
      (out of 92 non-core innovators).......................32

Business Competitiveness Index Rank	n/a

**Sophistication of Company Operations
and Strategy Rank** ....**n/a**

**Quality of the National Business
Environment Rank**..**n/a**

The Most Problematic Factors for Doing Business

FACTOR

Percent of responses

Note: From a list of 14 factors, respondents were asked to select the five most problematic for doing business in their country and to rank them between 1 (most problematic) and 5. The bars in the figure show the responses weighted according to their rankings.

Source: World Economic Forum, Executive Opinion Survey (2005)

National competitiveness balance sheet

NOTABLE COMPETITIVE ADVANTAGES	
Growth Competitiveness Index	**Rank/117**

Macroeconomic Environment

2.15	Real effective exchange rate, 2004	14
2.13	Government surplus/deficit, 2004	45

Technology

3.04	FDI and technology transfer	15
3.14	Government success in ICT promotion	47
3.07	University/industry research collaboration	48

NOTABLE COMPETITIVE DISADVANTAGES	
Growth Competitiveness Index	**Rank/117**

Macroeconomic Environment

2.21	Country credit rating, 2004	102
2.17	Interest rate spread, 2004	101
2.07	Access to credit	99
2.20	Government debt, 2004	90
2.16	Inflation, 2004	76
2.14	National savings rate, 2004	70
2.01	Recession expectations	66
6.06	Wastefulness of government spending	65

Public Institutions

6.20	Irregular payments in public utilities	105
6.08	Favoritism in decisions of government officials	104
6.21	Irregular payments in tax collection	103
6.19	Irregular payments in exports and imports	99
6.16	Organized crime	87
6.03	Property rights	80
6.01	Judicial independence	54

Technology

5.08	Telephone lines, 2003	115
3.11	Internet access in schools	112
3.21	Personal computers, 2003	107
4.17	Gross tertiary enrollment	107
3.19	Internet users, 2003	106
3.18	Cellular telephones, 2003	102
3.01	Technological readiness	100
3.20	Internet hosts, 2003	97
3.02	Firm-level technology absorption	83
3.17	Utility patents, 2004	81
3.15	Laws relating to ICT	80
3.12	Quality of competition in the ISP sector	70
3.03	Prevalence of foreign technology licensing	69
3.13	Government prioritization of ICT	55
3.06	Company spending on research and development	53

Other Indicators	
	Rank/117

8.18	Flexibility of wage determination	2
8.17	Hiring and firing practices	10
9.07	Importance of environment in business planning	19
9.05	Effects of privatization on competition and the environment	21
4.07	Ease of hiring foreign labor	21
2.10	Impact of rules on FDI	22
3.08	Government procurement of advanced technology products	25
2.12	Agricultural policy costs	26
9.04	Effects of compliance on business	28
6.13	Centralization of economic policymaking	30
8.22	Foreign ownership restrictions	34
3.05	Quality of scientific research institutions	36
6.07	Burden of government regulation	37
9.09	Prevalence of corporate environmental reporting	41
7.09	Local availability of specialized research and training services	45

Other Indicators	
	Rank/117

8.20	Pay and productivity	116
7.03	Extent of market dominance	113
5.05	Quality of electricity supply	112
3.16	Extent of business Internet use	111
6.24	Diversion of public funds	111
2.03	Financial market sophistication	111
8.06	Extent of marketing	111
2.02	Business costs of terrorism	110
7.06	Local supplier quality	110
4.06	Medium term business impact of HIV/AIDS	108
8.05	Production process sophistication	107
6.25	Business costs of corruption	106
7.04	Buyer sophistication	106
8.13	Extent of incentive compensation	105
6.22	Irregular payments in public contracts	105

Note: This country is not included in the coverage of the Business Competitiveness Index 2005–2006.

Ukraine

Competitiveness Rankings

Growth Competitiveness Index Rank	84

Macroeconomic Environment Index Rank **78**	
Macroeconomic Stability Subindex Rank 69	
Government Waste Rank 96	
Country Credit Rating Rank 76	
Public Institutions Index Rank..**90**	
Contracts and Law Subindex Rank 105	
Corruption Subindex Rank....................................79	
Technology Index Rank **85**	
Innovation Subindex Rank 33	
ICT Subindex Rank 79	
Technology Transfer Subindex Rank	
(out of 92 non-core innovators) 79	

Business Competitiveness Index Rank	75

Sophistication of Company Operations	
and Strategy Rank **71**	
Quality of the National Business	
Environment Rank **76**	

The Most Problematic Factors for Doing Business

Note: From a list of 14 factors, respondents were asked to select the five most problematic for doing business in their country and to rank them between 1 (most problematic) and 5. The bars in the figure show the responses weighted according to their rankings.

Source: World Economic Forum, Executive Opinion Survey (2005)

National competitiveness balance sheet

4, 4.2: Country Profiles

NOTABLE COMPETITIVE ADVANTAGES

Growth Competitiveness Index	Rank/117

Macroeconomic Environment

2.15	Real effective exchange rate, 2004	15
2.20	Government debt, 2004	17
2.14	National savings rate, 2004	24

Technology

4.17	Gross tertiary enrollment	19
3.06	Company spending on research and development	38
3.07	University/industry research collaboration	46

NOTABLE COMPETITIVE DISADVANTAGES

Growth Competitiveness Index	Rank/117

Macroeconomic Environment

2.16	Inflation, 2004	98
6.06	Wastefulness of government spending	96
2.13	Government surplus/deficit, 2004	93
2.17	Interest rate spread, 2004	84
2.21	Country credit rating, 2004	76
2.01	Recession expectations	76
2.07	Access to credit	74

Public Institutions

6.01	Judicial independence	103
6.03	Property rights	101
6.08	Favoritism in decisions of government officials	96
6.16	Organized crime	95
6.21	Irregular payments in tax collection	84
6.19	Irregular payments in exports and imports	78
6.20	Irregular payments in public utilities	75

Technology

3.04	FDI and technology transfer	111
3.12	Quality of competition in the ISP sector	102
3.03	Prevalence of foreign technology licensing	96
3.11	Internet access in schools	86
3.02	Firm-level technology absorption	86
3.14	Government success in ICT promotion	85
3.21	Personal computers, 2003	83
3.15	Laws relating to ICT	82
3.18	Cellular telephones, 2003	79
3.01	Technological readiness	78
3.19	Internet users, 2003	75
3.13	Government prioritization of ICT	70
3.20	Internet hosts, 2003	61
5.08	Telephone lines, 2003	53
3.17	Utility patents, 2004	51

451

Business Competitiveness Index	Rank/110

Sophistication of Company Operations and Strategy

8.08	Control of international distribution	25
8.03	Capacity for innovation	34
3.06	Company spending on research and development	37

Quality of the National Business Environment

7.08	Local availability of process machinery	11
5.02	Railroad infrastructure development	19
4.03	Quality of math and science education	35

Other Indicators	Rank/117

8.17	Hiring and firing practices	17
9.09	Prevalence of corporate environmental reporting	33
2.02	Business costs of terrorism	33
8.20	Pay and productivity	40
8.16	Efficacy of corporate boards	41
6.13	Centralization of economic policymaking	42
8.07	Degree of customer orientation	45
3.05	Quality of scientific research institutions	47
6.22	Irregular payments in public contracts	47
4.07	Ease of hiring foreign labor	49

Business Competitiveness Index	Rank/110

Sophistication of Company Operations and Strategy

8.09	Extent of regional sales	95
3.03	Prevalence of foreign technology licensing	93
8.11	Extent of staff training	85

Quality of the National Business Environment

8.21	Protection of minority shareholders' interests	110
8.22	Foreign ownership restrictions	108
6.25	Business costs of corruption	104

Other Indicators	Rank/117

2.10	Impact of rules on FDI	116
9.05	Effects of privatization on competition and the environment	116
6.27	Pervasiveness of money laundering through banks	115
2.12	Agricultural policy costs	113
6.17	Informal sector	112
6.11	Extent and effect of taxation	111
8.24	Importance of corporate social responsibility	111
6.12	Efficiency of the tax system	110
2.11	Tax burden	106
4.09	Private sector employment of women	105
3.10	Availability of mobile or cellular telephones	103

Note: The Business Competitiveness Index applies different criteria for selecting a country's competitive advantages and disadvantages. Please refer to the section "How Country Profiles Work" for further details.

United Arab Emirates

Competitiveness Rankings

Growth Competitiveness Index Rank	18

Macroeconomic Environment Index Rank **5**
   Macroeconomic Stability Subindex Rank 2
   Government Waste Rank 5
   Country Credit Rating Rank 29

Public Institutions Index Rank...**24**
   Contracts and Law Subindex Rank 38
   Corruption Subindex Rank...................................16

Technology Index Rank **33**
   Innovation Subindex Rank...................................44
   ICT Subindex Rank 34
   Technology Transfer Subindex Rank
     (out of 92 non-core innovators).......................10

Business Competitiveness Index Rank	33

**Sophistication of Company Operations
  and Strategy Rank** **36**
**Quality of the National Business
  Environment Rank** **33**

The Most Problematic Factors for Doing Business

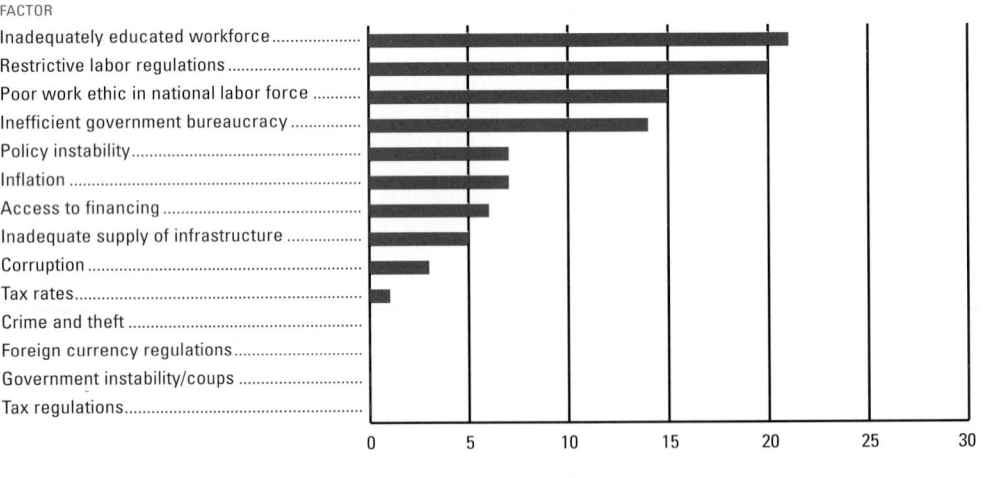

FACTOR

Inadequately educated workforce
Restrictive labor regulations
Poor work ethic in national labor force
Inefficient government bureaucracy
Policy instability
Inflation
Access to financing
Inadequate supply of infrastructure
Corruption
Tax rates
Crime and theft
Foreign currency regulations
Government instability/coups
Tax regulations

Percent of responses

Note: From a list of 14 factors, respondents were asked to select the five most problematic for doing business in their country and to rank them between 1 (most problematic) and 5. The bars in the figure show the responses weighted according to their rankings.

Source: World Economic Forum, Executive Opinion Survey (2005)

National competitiveness balance sheet

Growth Competitiveness Index	Rank/117
Macroeconomic Environment	
2.01 Recession expectations	2
2.13 Government surplus/deficit, 2004	2
6.06 Wastefulness of government spending	5
2.14 National savings rate, 2004	8
2.20 Government debt, 2004	10
2.07 Access to credit	16
Public Institutions	
6.21 Irregular payments in tax collection	5
6.16 Organized crime	8
Technology	
3.14 Government success in ICT promotion	5
3.13 Government prioritization of ICT	8
3.02 Firm-level technology absorption	15
3.03 Prevalence of foreign technology licensing	15
3.01 Technological readiness	17

Business Competitiveness Index	Rank/110
Sophistication of Company Operations and Strategy	
8.09 Extent of regional sales	26
8.08 Control of international distribution	28
8.07 Degree of customer orientation	33
Quality of the National Business Environment	
2.09 Prevalence of trade barriers	3
5.04 Air transport infrastructure quality	4
5.03 Port infrastructure quality	7

Other Indicators	Rank/117
6.15 Business costs of crime and violence	1
2.11 Tax burden	1
6.12 Efficiency of the tax system	1
6.11 Extent and effect of taxation	2
8.18 Flexibility of wage determination	3
4.08 Brain drain	3
6.18 Government effectiveness in reducing poverty and inequality	3
4.07 Ease of hiring foreign labor	7
6.07 Burden of government regulation	7
8.17 Hiring and firing practices	9
6.26 Public trust of politicians	9
2.12 Agricultural policy costs	9
6.17 Informal sector	10
6.14 Reliability of police services	11

Growth Competitiveness Index	Rank/117
Macroeconomic Environment	
2.16 Inflation, 2004	57
2.15 Real effective exchange rate, 2004	52
2.17 Interest rate spread, 2004	40
2.21 Country credit rating, 2004	29
Public Institutions	
6.03 Property rights	56
6.01 Judicial independence	46
6.08 Favoritism in decisions of government officials	24
6.19 Irregular payments in exports and imports	23
6.20 Irregular payments in public utilities	20
Technology	
3.12 Quality of competition in the ISP sector	112
3.07 University/industry research collaboration	75
3.06 Company spending on research and development	62
4.17 Gross tertiary enrollment	52
3.17 Utility patents, 2004	48
3.21 Personal computers, 2003	45
3.04 FDI and technology transfer	44
5.08 Telephone lines, 2003	41
3.20 Internet hosts, 2003	40
3.15 Laws relating to ICT	35
3.19 Internet users, 2003	29
3.11 Internet access in schools	28
3.18 Cellular telephones, 2003	27

Business Competitiveness Index	Rank/110
Sophistication of Company Operations and Strategy	
8.03 Capacity for innovation	73
8.12 Willingness to delegate authority	68
3.06 Company spending on research and development	60
Quality of the National Business Environment	
8.22 Foreign ownership restrictions	95
8.15 Quality of management schools	84
5.02 Railroad infrastructure development	83

Other Indicators	Rank/117
6.05 Freedom of the press	110
4.09 Private sector employment of women	98
9.10 Grass-roots involvement in development projects	87
7.09 Local availability of specialized research and training services	86
3.09 Availability of scientists and engineers	80
3.05 Quality of scientific research institutions	79
9.06 Prioritization of energy efficiency	71
7.08 Local availability of process machinery	71
7.02 Effectiveness of antitrust policy	69
2.10 Impact of rules on FDI	65
6.09 Extent of bureaucratic red tape	62

Note: The Business Competitiveness Index applies different criteria for selecting a country's competitive advantages and disadvantages. Please refer to the section "How Country Profiles Work" for further details.

United Kingdom

Competitiveness Rankings

Growth Competitiveness Index Rank	**13**

Macroeconomic Environment Index Rank **18**
    Macroeconomic Stability Subindex Rank 32
    Government Waste Rank 27
    Country Credit Rating Rank.................................4

Public Institutions Index Rank...**12**
    Contracts and Law Subindex Rank 12
    Corruption Subindex Rank...................................12

Technology Index Rank **17**
    Innovation Subindex Rank 16
    ICT Subindex Rank 15

Business Competitiveness Index Rank	**6**

**Sophistication of Company Operations
and Strategy Rank** 6
**Quality of the National Business
Environment Rank** 6

The Most Problematic Factors for Doing Business

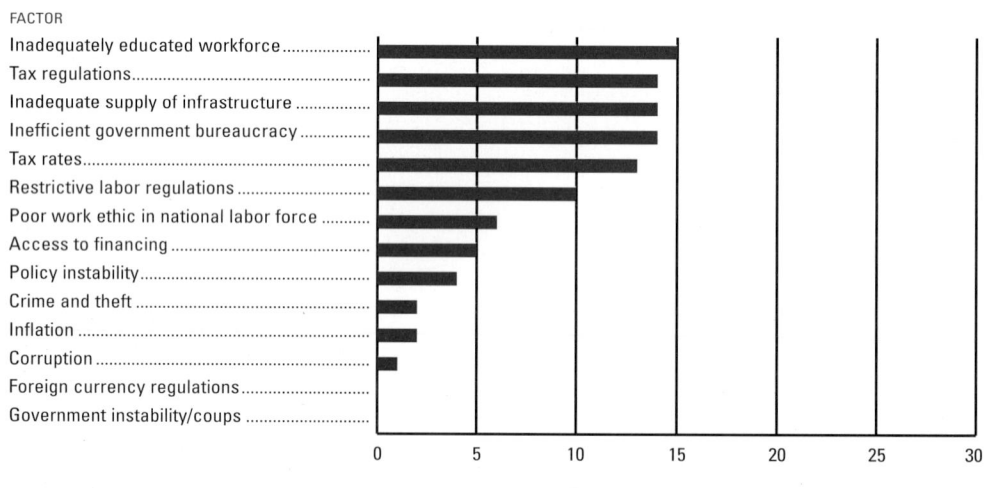

FACTOR

Inadequately educated workforce ....
Tax regulations...
Inadequate supply of infrastructure ....
Inefficient government bureaucracy ....
Tax rates...
Restrictive labor regulations ....
Poor work ethic in national labor force ....
Access to financing ....
Policy instability..
Crime and theft ....
Inflation ....
Corruption ....
Foreign currency regulations...........................
Government instability/coups ....

Percent of responses

Note: From a list of 14 factors, respondents were asked to select the five most problematic for doing business in their country and to rank them between 1 (most problematic) and 5. The bars in the figure show the responses weighted according to their rankings.

Source: World Economic Forum, Executive Opinion Survey (2005)

National competitiveness balance sheet

NOTABLE COMPETITIVE ADVANTAGES	
Growth Competitiveness Index	**Rank/117**

Macroeconomic Environment

2.17	Interest rate spread, 2004	1
2.21	Country credit rating, 2004	4

Public Institutions

6.03	Property rights	7
6.01	Judicial independence	9
6.21	Irregular payments in tax collection	10

Technology

3.19	Internet users, 2003	4
3.15	Laws relating to ICT	4
3.07	University/industry research collaboration	7
3.12	Quality of competition in the ISP sector	7
3.18	Cellular telephones, 2003	9
3.01	Technological readiness	11
5.08	Telephone lines, 2003	11
3.06	Company spending on research and development	11

NOTABLE COMPETITIVE DISADVANTAGES	
Growth Competitiveness Index	**Rank/117**

Macroeconomic Environment

2.14	National savings rate, 2004	98
2.15	Real effective exchange rate, 2004	87
2.13	Government surplus/deficit, 2004	73
2.20	Government debt, 2004	41
6.06	Wastefulness of government spending	27
2.01	Recession expectations	25
2.16	Inflation, 2004	17
2.07	Access to credit	15

Public Institutions

6.16	Organized crime	29
6.08	Favoritism in decisions of government officials	16
6.19	Irregular payments in exports and imports	13
6.20	Irregular payments in public utilities	13

Technology

3.14	Government success in ICT promotion	52
3.13	Government prioritization of ICT	27
3.02	Firm-level technology absorption	23
3.21	Personal computers, 2003	21
3.20	Internet hosts, 2003	20
3.17	Utility patents, 2004	18
4.17	Gross tertiary enrollment	16
3.11	Internet access in schools	16

Business Competitiveness Index	Rank/110

Sophistication of Company Operations and Strategy

8.13	Extent of incentive compensation	2
8.06	Extent of marketing	2
8.14	Reliance on professional management	3

Quality of the National Business Environment

8.16	Efficacy of corporate boards	1
2.03	Financial market sophistication	1
8.21	Protection of minority shareholders' interests	1

Business Competitiveness Index	Rank/110

Sophistication of Company Operations and Strategy

8.07	Degree of customer orientation	19
8.05	Production process sophistication	17

Quality of the National Business Environment

4.03	Quality of math and science education	47
6.13	Centralization of economic policymaking	46
3.09	Availability of scientists and engineers	40

Other Indicators	Rank/117

8.23	Strength of auditing and accounting standards	1
8.24	Importance of corporate social responsibility	1
8.04	Ethical behavior of firms	2
7.09	Local availability of specialized research and training services	2
7.01	Intensity of local competition	3
2.06	Venture capital availability	3
2.04	Soundness of banks	3
6.10	Effectiveness of law-making bodies	3
7.03	Extent of market dominance	3

Other Indicators	Rank/117

2.02	Business costs of terrorism	105
6.12	Efficiency of the tax system	67
2.12	Agricultural policy costs	55
2.11	Tax burden	54
6.07	Burden of government regulation	51
4.05	Medium term business impact of tuberculosis	41
6.15	Business costs of crime and violence	41
4.06	Medium term business impact of HIV/AIDS	36
3.08	Government procurement of advanced technology products	36
8.17	Hiring and firing practices	32
2.09	Prevalence of trade barriers	32
5.06	Postal efficiency	28
5.07	Telephone/fax infrastructure quality	26

455

Note: The Business Competitiveness Index applies different criteria for selecting a country's competitive advantages and disadvantages. Please refer to the section "How Country Profiles Work" for further details.

United States

Competitiveness Rankings

Growth Competitiveness Index Rank	2

Macroeconomic Environment Index Rank **23**
    Macroeconomic Stability Subindex Rank 47
    Government Waste Rank 20
    Country Credit Rating Rank....................................6

Public Institutions Index Rank...**18**
    Contracts and Law Subindex Rank 20
    Corruption Subindex Rank...................................14

Technology Index Rank **1**
    Innovation Subindex Rank 1
    ICT Subindex Rank 3

Business Competitiveness Index Rank	1

**Sophistication of Company Operations
   and Strategy Rank** 1

**Quality of the National Business
   Environment Rank** 2

The Most Problematic Factors for Doing Business

FACTOR

Note: From a list of 14 factors, respondents were asked to select the five most problematic for doing business in their country and to rank them between 1 (most problematic) and 5. The bars in the figure show the responses weighted according to their rankings.

Source: World Economic Forum, Executive Opinion Survey (2005)

National competitiveness balance sheet

NOTABLE COMPETITIVE ADVANTAGES	
Growth Competitiveness Index	**Rank/117**

Macroeconomic Environment

2.21	Country credit rating, 2004	6

Public Institutions

6.03	Property rights	2

Technology

3.07	University/industry research collaboration	1
3.12	Quality of competition in the ISP sector	1
3.01	Technological readiness	1
3.06	Company spending on research and development	1
3.17	Utility patents, 2004	1
3.20	Internet hosts, 2003	1
3.02	Firm-level technology absorption	1
3.21	Personal computers, 2003	2
3.15	Laws relating to ICT	3
4.17	Gross tertiary enrollment	4
3.19	Internet users, 2003	6
5.08	Telephone lines, 2003	9

Business Competitiveness Index	Rank/110

Sophistication of Company Operations and Strategy

3.06	Company spending on research and development	1
8.13	Extent of incentive compensation	1
8.06	Extent of marketing	1

Quality of the National Business Environment

3.17	Utility patents, 2004	1
2.06	Venture capital availability	1
3.07	University/industry research collaboration	1

Other Indicators	Rank/117

7.09	Local availability of specialized research and training services	1
7.01	Intensity of local competition	1
8.14	Reliance on professional management	1
7.03	Extent of market dominance	1
3.05	Quality of scientific research institutions	1
6.04	Intellectual property protection	1
3.16	Extent of business Internet use	1
8.15	Quality of management schools	1
7.04	Buyer sophistication	1
4.08	Brain drain	1
8.07	Degree of customer orientation	1
2.03	Financial market sophistication	2

NOTABLE COMPETITIVE DISADVANTAGES	
Growth Competitiveness Index	**Rank/117**

Macroeconomic Environment

2.14	National savings rate, 2004	109
2.13	Government surplus/deficit, 2004	92
2.20	Government debt, 2004	76
2.15	Real effective exchange rate, 2004	49
2.16	Inflation, 2004	40
2.01	Recession expectations	34
6.06	Wastefulness of government spending	20
2.07	Access to credit	17
2.17	Interest rate spread, 2004	12

Public Institutions

6.16	Organized crime	33
6.08	Favoritism in decisions of government officials	33
6.01	Judicial independence	17
6.20	Irregular payments in public utilities	16
6.19	Irregular payments in exports and imports	15
6.21	Irregular payments in tax collection	15

Technology

3.18	Cellular telephones, 2003	40
3.14	Government success in ICT promotion	24
3.13	Government prioritization of ICT	19
3.11	Internet access in schools	13

Business Competitiveness Index	Rank/110

Sophistication of Company Operations and Strategy

8.09	Extent of regional sales	16

Quality of the National Business Environment

4.03	Quality of math and science education	39
3.18	Cellular telephones, 2003	39
6.09	Extent of bureaucratic red tape	33

Other Indicators	Rank/117

2.02	Business costs of terrorism	107
6.12	Efficiency of the tax system	107
4.06	Medium term business impact of HIV/AIDS	69
4.07	Ease of hiring foreign labor	64
2.11	Tax burden	59
2.12	Agricultural policy costs	52
9.07	Importance of environment in business planning	47
6.18	Government effectiveness in reducing poverty and inequality	42
9.06	Prioritization of energy efficiency	37
6.15	Business costs of crime and violence	30
2.09	Prevalence of trade barriers	28
4.05	Medium term business impact of tuberculosis	27
3.10	Availability of mobile or cellular telephones	22
6.07	Burden of government regulation	20

457

Note: The Business Competitiveness Index applies different criteria for selecting a country's competitive advantages and disadvantages. Please refer to the section "How Country Profiles Work" for further details.

Uruguay

Competitiveness Rankings

Growth Competitiveness Index Rank	54

Macroeconomic Environment Index Rank **84**
    Macroeconomic Stability Subindex Rank 98
    Government Waste Rank 67
    Country Credit Rating Rank................................77

Public Institutions Index Rank..**33**
    Contracts and Law Subindex Rank 32
    Corruption Subindex Rank..................................42

Technology Index Rank **63**
    Innovation Subindex Rank 49
    ICT Subindex Rank 49
    Technology Transfer Subindex Rank
      (out of 92 non-core innovators)........................63

Business Competitiveness Index Rank	70

**Sophistication of Company Operations
   and Strategy Rank** **79**
**Quality of the National Business
   Environment Rank** **66**

The Most Problematic Factors for Doing Business

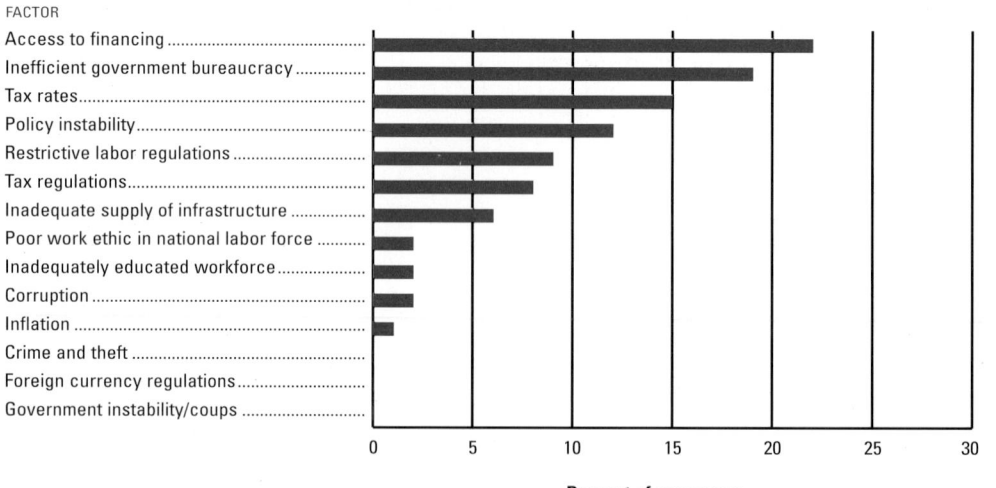

Note: From a list of 14 factors, respondents were asked to select the five most problematic for doing business in their country and to rank them between 1 (most problematic) and 5. The bars in the figure show the responses weighted according to their rankings.

Source: World Economic Forum, Executive Opinion Survey (2005)

458

National competitiveness balance sheet

459

Note: The Business Competitiveness Index applies different criteria for selecting a country's competitive advantages and disadvantages. Please refer to the section "How Country Profiles Work" for further details.

Venezuela

Competitiveness Rankings

Growth Competitiveness Index Rank	89

Macroeconomic Environment Index Rank **85**
   Macroeconomic Stability Subindex Rank 60
   Government Waste Rank 116
   Country Credit Rating Rank 74

Public Institutions Index Rank......................................**106**
   Contracts and Law Subindex Rank 116
   Corruption Subindex Rank...................................80

Technology Index Rank **72**
   Innovation Subindex Rank 45
   ICT Subindex Rank 69
   Technology Transfer Subindex Rank
     (out of 92 non-core innovators).......................57

Business Competitiveness Index Rank	89

**Sophistication of Company Operations
  and Strategy Rank** **84**

**Quality of the National Business
  Environment Rank** **94**

The Most Problematic Factors for Doing Business

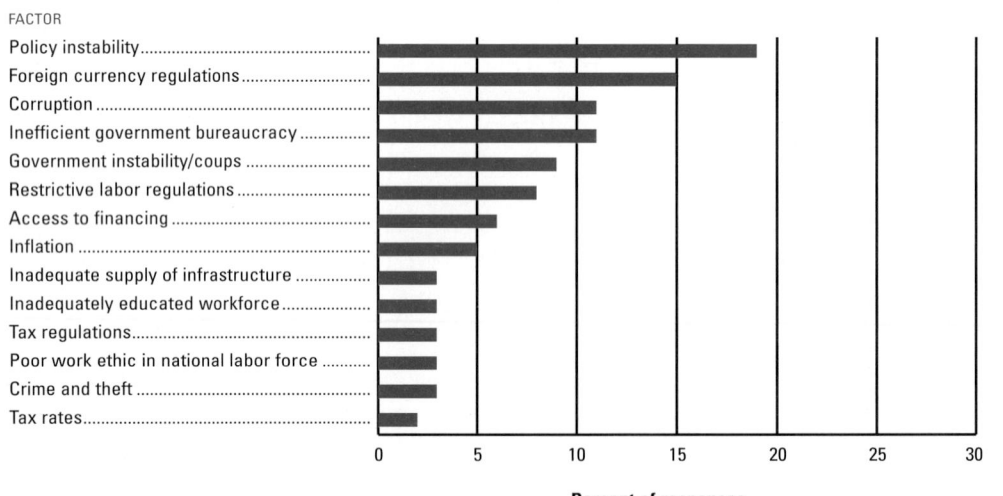

FACTOR

Policy instability
Foreign currency regulations
Corruption
Inefficient government bureaucracy
Government instability/coups
Restrictive labor regulations
Access to financing
Inflation
Inadequate supply of infrastructure
Inadequately educated workforce
Tax regulations
Poor work ethic in national labor force
Crime and theft
Tax rates

Percent of responses

Note: From a list of 14 factors, respondents were asked to select the five most problematic for doing business in their country and to rank them between 1 (most problematic) and 5. The bars in the figure show the responses weighted according to their rankings.

Source: World Economic Forum, Executive Opinion Survey (2005)

National competitiveness balance sheet

Growth Competitiveness Index	Rank/117
Macroeconomic Environment	
2.14 National savings rate, 2004	9
2.15 Real effective exchange rate, 2004	10
2.13 Government surplus/deficit, 2004	33
2.20 Government debt, 2004	33
Technology	
3.01 Technological readiness	37
4.17 Gross tertiary enrollment	40
3.17 Utility patents, 2004	47

Business Competitiveness Index	Rank/110
Sophistication of Company Operations and Strategy	
8.14 Reliance on professional management	48
8.13 Extent of incentive compensation	54
8.06 Extent of marketing	58
Quality of the National Business Environment	
3.17 Utility patents, 2004	46
3.09 Availability of scientists and engineers	53
8.15 Quality of management schools	55

Other Indicators	Rank/117
4.09 Private sector employment of women	20
3.10 Availability of mobile or cellular telephones	39
3.16 Extent of business Internet use	50

Growth Competitiveness Index	Rank/117
Macroeconomic Environment	
6.06 Wastefulness of government spending	116
2.16 Inflation, 2004	115
2.07 Access to credit	92
2.01 Recession expectations	80
2.21 Country credit rating, 2004	74
2.17 Interest rate spread, 2004	64
Public Institutions	
6.03 Property rights	117
6.08 Favoritism in decisions of government officials	116
6.01 Judicial independence	114
6.16 Organized crime	104
6.19 Irregular payments in exports and imports	98
6.21 Irregular payments in tax collection	76
6.20 Irregular payments in public utilities	67
Technology	
3.14 Government success in ICT promotion	107
3.06 Company spending on research and development	87
3.03 Prevalence of foreign technology licensing	81
3.04 FDI and technology transfer	81
5.08 Telephone lines, 2003	76
3.19 Internet users, 2003	72
3.11 Internet access in schools	71
3.20 Internet hosts, 2003	69
3.02 Firm-level technology absorption	66
3.07 University/industry research collaboration	63
3.12 Quality of competition in the ISP sector	61
3.18 Cellular telephones, 2003	60
3.21 Personal computers, 2003	59
3.13 Government prioritization of ICT	58
3.15 Laws relating to ICT	58

Business Competitiveness Index	Rank/110
Sophistication of Company Operations and Strategy	
8.08 Control of international distribution	106
8.10 Breadth of international markets	105
8.07 Degree of customer orientation	105
Quality of the National Business Environment	
6.13 Centralization of economic policymaking	110
6.02 Efficiency of legal framework	110
6.08 Favoritism in decisions of government officials	109

Other Indicators	Rank/117
9.06 Prioritization of energy efficiency	117
8.17 Hiring and firing practices	117
6.24 Diversion of public funds	117
5.06 Postal efficiency	116
6.18 Government effectiveness in reducing poverty and inequality	116
9.07 Importance of environment in business planning	115
2.10 Impact of rules on FDI	115
6.05 Freedom of the press	115
6.09 Extent of bureaucratic red tape	114
6.14 Reliability of police services	113
6.26 Public trust of politicians	112
9.04 Effects of compliance on business	111

461

Note: The Business Competitiveness Index applies different criteria for selecting a country's competitive advantages and disadvantages. Please refer to the section "How Country Profiles Work" for further details.

Vietnam

Competitiveness Rankings

Growth Competitiveness Index Rank	81

Macroeconomic Environment Index Rank **60**
    Macroeconomic Stability Subindex Rank 34
    Government Waste Rank 52
    Country Credit Rating Rank 73

Public Institutions Index Rank **97**
    Contracts and Law Subindex Rank 64
    Corruption Subindex Rank 111

Technology Index Rank **92**
    Innovation Subindex Rank 88
    ICT Subindex Rank 86
    Technology Transfer Subindex Rank
    (out of 92 non-core innovators) 69

Business Competitiveness Index Rank	80

**Sophistication of Company Operations
  and Strategy Rank** **81**
**Quality of the National Business
  Environment Rank** **77**

The Most Problematic Factors for Doing Business

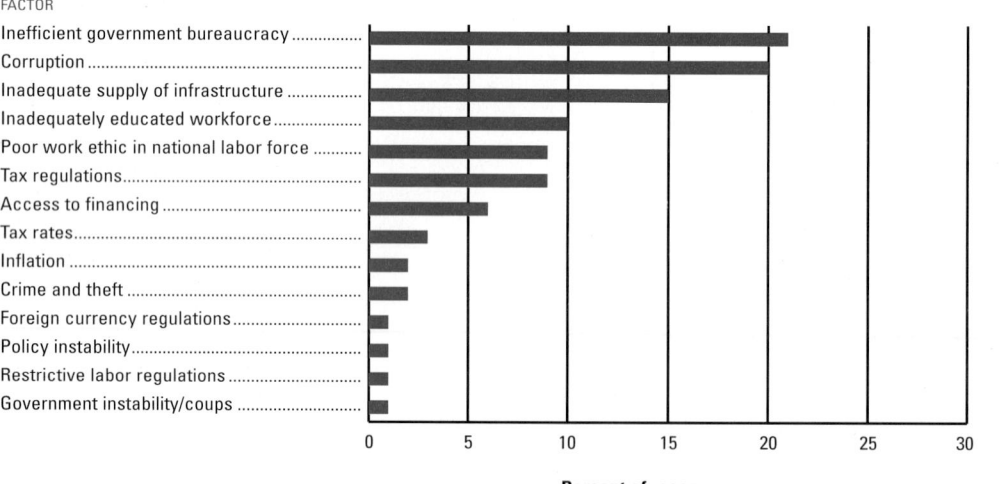

FACTOR

Inefficient government bureaucracy
Corruption
Inadequate supply of infrastructure
Inadequately educated workforce
Poor work ethic in national labor force
Tax regulations
Access to financing
Tax rates
Inflation
Crime and theft
Foreign currency regulations
Policy instability
Restrictive labor regulations
Government instability/coups

Percent of responses

Note: From a list of 14 factors, respondents were asked to select the five most problematic for doing business in their country and to rank them between 1 (most problematic) and 5. The bars in the figure show the responses weighted according to their rankings.

Source: World Economic Forum, Executive Opinion Survey (2005)

National competitiveness balance sheet

NOTABLE COMPETITIVE ADVANTAGES	
Growth Competitiveness Index	**Rank/117**

Macroeconomic Environment
2.01	Recession expectations	10
2.14	National savings rate, 2004	11
2.17	Interest rate spread, 2004	25

Technology
3.13	Government prioritization of ICT	26
3.02	Firm-level technology absorption	26
3.14	Government success in ICT promotion	26
3.04	FDI and technology transfer	46

NOTABLE COMPETITIVE DISADVANTAGES	
Growth Competitiveness Index	**Rank/117**

Macroeconomic Environment
2.16	Inflation, 2004	93
2.20	Government debt, 2004	75
2.21	Country credit rating, 2004	73
2.13	Government surplus/deficit, 2004	57
2.07	Access to credit	56
6.06	Wastefulness of government spending	52
2.15	Real effective exchange rate, 2004	51

Public Institutions
6.21	Irregular payments in tax collection	114
6.19	Irregular payments in exports and imports	113
6.20	Irregular payments in public utilities	95
6.08	Favoritism in decisions of government officials	70
6.16	Organized crime	69
6.01	Judicial independence	63
6.03	Property rights	61

Technology
3.20	Internet hosts, 2003	113
3.03	Prevalence of foreign technology licensing	109
3.15	Laws relating to ICT	103
3.18	Cellular telephones, 2003	99
3.12	Quality of competition in the ISP sector	97
3.21	Personal computers, 2003	96
4.17	Gross tertiary enrollment	93
5.08	Telephone lines, 2003	89
3.01	Technological readiness	82
3.19	Internet users, 2003	79
3.17	Utility patents, 2004	79
3.11	Internet access in schools	72
3.07	University/industry research collaboration	70
3.06	Company spending on research and development	55

Business Competitiveness Index	**Rank/110**

Sophistication of Company Operations and Strategy
| 8.03 | Capacity for innovation | 40 |
| 8.09 | Extent of regional sales | 57 |

Quality of the National Business Environment
3.08	Government procurement of advanced technology products	18
6.13	Centralization of economic policymaking	34
7.03	Decentralization of corporate activity	35

Business Competitiveness Index	**Rank/110**

Sophistication of Company Operations and Strategy
8.08	Control of international distribution	104
3.03	Prevalence of foreign technology licensing	104
8.01	Nature of competitive advantage	103

Quality of the National Business Environment
8.15	Quality of management schools	105
8.22	Foreign ownership restrictions	104
2.09	Prevalence of trade barriers	101

Other Indicators	**Rank/117**
2.11	Tax burden	12
2.12	Agricultural policy costs	14
6.18	Government effectiveness in reducing poverty and inequality	20
8.20	Pay and productivity	21
9.05	Effects of privatization on competition and the environment	31
5.06	Postal efficiency	35
7.03	Extent of market dominance	36
8.17	Hiring and firing practices	37
3.09	Availability of scientists and engineers	39
2.06	Venture capital availability	40
6.10	Effectiveness of law-making bodies	40
6.14	Reliability of police services	42

Other Indicators	**Rank/117**
3.16	Extent of business Internet use	112
6.22	Irregular payments in public contracts	108
7.02	Effectiveness of antitrust policy	107
6.05	Freedom of the press	104
6.07	Burden of government regulation	102
6.23	Irregular payments in judicial decisions	100
9.01	Stringency of environmental regulations	95
6.04	Intellectual property protection	92
8.06	Extent of marketing	92
7.07	Presence of demanding regulatory standards	91

463

Note: The Business Competitiveness Index applies different criteria for selecting a country's competitive advantages and disadvantages. Please refer to the section "How Country Profiles Work" for further details.

Zimbabwe

Competitiveness Rankings

Growth Competitiveness Index Rank	**109**

Macroeconomic Environment Index Rank **117**
    Macroeconomic Stability Subindex Rank 116
    Government Waste Rank 112
    Country Credit Rating Rank 117

Public Institutions Index Rank **80**
    Contracts and Law Subindex Rank 94
    Corruption Subindex Rank 69

Technology Index Rank **98**
    Innovation Subindex Rank 102
    ICT Subindex Rank 99
    Technology Transfer Subindex Rank
        (out of 92 non-core innovators).......................67

Business Competitiveness Index Rank	**84**

**Sophistication of Company Operations
  and Strategy Rank** **78**
**Quality of the National Business
  Environment Rank** **84**

The Most Problematic Factors for Doing Business

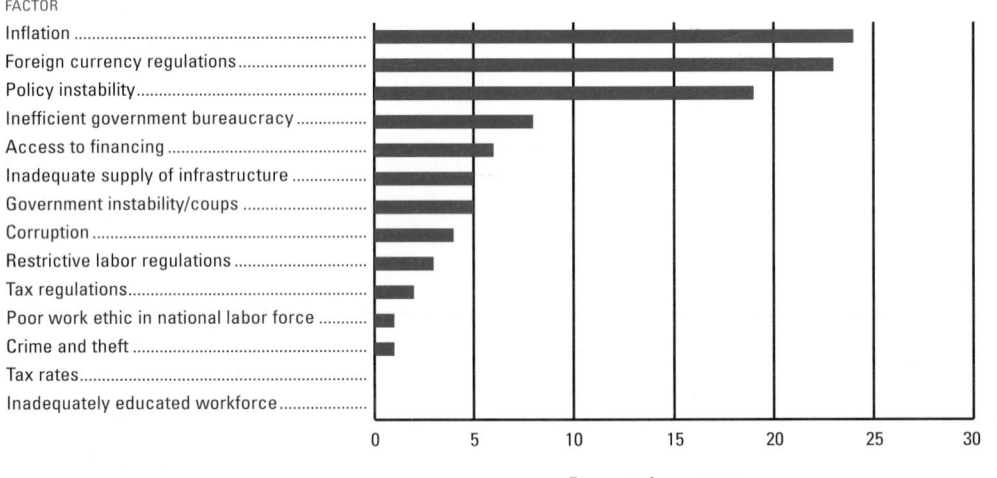

Note: From a list of 14 factors, respondents were asked to select the five most problematic for doing business in their country and to rank them between 1 (most problematic) and 5. The bars in the figure show the responses weighted according to their rankings.

Source: World Economic Forum, Executive Opinion Survey (2005)

National competitiveness balance sheet

NOTABLE COMPETITIVE ADVANTAGES	
Growth Competitiveness Index	**Rank/117**

Macroeconomic Environment

2.15	Real effective exchange rate, 2004	1
2.20	Government debt, 2004	21

NOTABLE COMPETITIVE DISADVANTAGES	
Growth Competitiveness Index	**Rank/117**

Macroeconomic Environment

2.16	Inflation, 2004	117
2.21	Country credit rating, 2004	117
2.01	Recession expectations	117
2.17	Interest rate spread, 2004	116
2.14	National savings rate, 2004	113
6.06	Wastefulness of government spending	112
2.07	Access to credit	107
2.13	Government surplus/deficit, 2004	106

Public Institutions

6.01	Judicial independence	109
6.03	Property rights	106
6.08	Favoritism in decisions of government officials	99
6.20	Irregular payments in public utilities	81
6.19	Irregular payments in exports and imports	78
6.16	Organized crime	54
6.21	Irregular payments in tax collection	53

Technology

3.13	Government prioritization of ICT	112
3.14	Government success in ICT promotion	109
4.17	Gross tertiary enrollment	103
3.04	FDI and technology transfer	102
3.18	Cellular telephones, 2003	101
5.08	Telephone lines, 2003	101
3.11	Internet access in schools	97
3.12	Quality of competition in the ISP sector	87
3.20	Internet hosts, 2003	83
3.01	Technological readiness	83
3.02	Firm-level technology absorption	79
3.03	Prevalence of foreign technology licensing	73
3.17	Utility patents, 2004	72
3.15	Laws relating to ICT	68
3.19	Internet users, 2003	68
3.06	Company spending on research and development	65
3.07	University/industry research collaboration	64
3.21	Personal computers, 2003	63

Business Competitiveness Index	
Business Competitiveness Index	**Rank/110**

Sophistication of Company Operations and Strategy

8.14	Reliance on professional management	21
8.13	Extent of incentive compensation	27
8.12	Willingness to delegate authority	30

Quality of the National Business Environment

8.21	Protection of minority shareholders' interests	20
2.08	Local equity market access	25
8.16	Efficacy of corporate boards	29

Other Indicators	
Other Indicators	**Rank/117**

2.02	Business costs of terrorism	14
8.24	Importance of corporate social responsibility	28
6.12	Efficiency of the tax system	29
8.23	Strength of auditing and accounting standards	33
8.11	Extent of staff training	37
9.08	Protection of ecosystems by business	44
9.10	Grass-roots involvement in development projects	48

Business Competitiveness Index	
Business Competitiveness Index	**Rank/110**

Sophistication of Company Operations and Strategy

8.05	Production process sophistication	109
8.01	Nature of competitive advantage	106
8.02	Value chain presence	106

Quality of the National Business Environment

7.08	Local availability of process machinery	110
6.13	Centralization of economic policymaking	109
5.07	Telephone/fax infrastructure quality	109

Other Indicators	
Other Indicators	**Rank/117**

2.04	Soundness of banks	117
4.07	Ease of hiring foreign labor	117
2.10	Impact of rules on FDI	117
2.12	Agricultural policy costs	117
6.05	Freedom of the press	116
4.08	Brain drain	116
8.17	Hiring and firing practices	116
4.06	Medium term business impact of HIV/AIDS	115
4.05	Medium term business impact of tuberculosis	114
8.18	Flexibility of wage determination	114

465

Note: The Business Competitiveness Index applies different criteria for selecting a country's competitive advantages and disadvantages. Please refer to the section "How Country Profiles Work" for further details.

How data pages work

The following pages provide detailed data for all 117 economies included in the *Global Competitiveness Report 2005–2006*. The data are organized into nine categories:

I	Aggregate Country Performance Indicators
II	Macroeconomic Environment
III	Technology: Innovation and Diffusion
IV	Human Resources: Education, Health, and Labor
V	General Infrastructure
VI	Public Institutions
VII	Domestic Competition and Cluster Development
VIII	Company Operations and Strategy
IX	Environment

Two types of variables are presented in these tables: (1) average country responses to questions included in the World Economic Forum's Executive Opinion Survey, conducted in the early months of 2005; and (2) "hard data" obtained from a variety of sources.

❶ Survey data

Data yielded from the Executive Opinion Survey are presented with blue-colored bar graphs. In sections including both hard and Survey data, the Survey data are presented first. For each Survey variable, the original question is included in the description at the top of the page, with minor abbreviations made in some instances due to space constraints. As outlined in Chapter 4.1 of this *Report*, in most cases questions asked for responses on a scale of 1 to 7, where an answer of 1 corresponds to one end of a spectrum of responses and an answer of 7 corresponds to the other end. We report the average response for each country. Variable 2.01, for example, asks about respondents' recession expectations at the time of the Survey, with higher scores corresponding to a lower perceived likelihood of recession. The score noted for Qatar is 6.8, indicating the arithmetic mean of responses to this question from executives in Qatar, and a low average expectation of recession.

❷ A dotted line on the graph indicates the mean score across the sample of 117 countries. We report country responses rounded to a single decimal point, but use the exact figures to determine rankings and for graphs. In the case of variable 2.01, for example, Trinidad and Tobago's average score was 5.9150, South Africa's was 5.9052, and Kuwait's was 5.8833. These economies are therefore ranked sixth through eighth respectively, even though they are all listed with the same rounded score of 5.9. In other cases, ties are true, so shared rankings are indicated accordingly. For example, still in the case of variable 2.01, the average scores for Dominican Republic and France are the same down to 14 decimal points, so here both countries are ranked 71st.

❸ Just to the right of each country's mean score, we have also included the standard deviation of the responses. This gives an indication of how closely or widely the individual responses are spread around the mean country score. In other words, this provides information on the extent of agreement or disagreement on the question within the given country. Still looking at variable 2.01, we see that the standard deviation of the responses from Qatar is 0.4, a measure of the fluctuation of the responses around the mean score of 6.8.

(continued on next page)

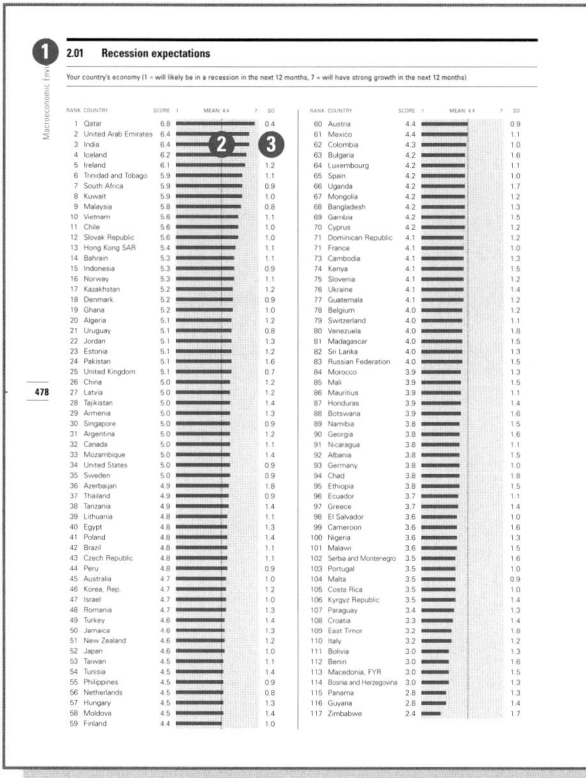

Hard data

Data originating not from the Executive Opinion Survey but from other publicly available sources are presented in gray-shaded bar graphs and are followed on each page with a brief reference to the source from which they were obtained. More detailed citation information can be found in the Technical Notes and Sources section at the end of the *Report*. Here again, true ties are indicated by shared rankings where relevant.

Many of these variables, although presented as hard data, still depend to a great extent on surveying techniques. Indeed, even GDP statistics rely heavily on surveying methodologies.

Index of tables

471

Section VII. Domestic Competition and Cluster Development

Section VIII. Company Operations and Strategy

Section IX. Environment

1.01   Total GDP, 2004

Gross Domestic Product in billions of US Dollars, 2004

RANK	COUNTRY	HARD DATA
1	United States	11,733.48
2	Japan	4,668.42
3	Germany	2,706.67
4	United Kingdom	2,125.51
5	France	2,018.08
6	Italy	1,680.69
7	China	1,649.39
8	Canada	995.83
9	Spain	992.99
10	Korea	681.47
11	Mexico	676.50
12	India	661.05
13	Australia	617.61
14	Brazil	599.73
15	Russian Federation	582.73
16	Netherlands	577.99
17	Switzerland	358.00
18	Belgium	352.00
19	Sweden	346.53
20	Taiwan	305.20
21	Turkey	300.09
22	Austria	289.72
23	Indonesia	257.87
24	Norway	250.44
25	Denmark	242.34
26	Poland	241.77
27	South Africa	212.90
28	Greece	205.49
29	Finland	186.18
30	Ireland	181.52
31	Portugal	167.24
32	Hong Kong SAR	164.55
33	Thailand	163.49
34	Argentina	151.94
35	Malaysia	117.78
36	Israel	116.34
37	Venezuela	107.49
38	Czech Republic	107.05
39	Singapore	106.82
40	Hungary	99.35
41	New Zealand	96.97
42	United Arab Emirates	95.72
43	Colombia	95.19
44	Chile	93.65
45	Philippines	85.14
46	Pakistan	82.61
47	Algeria	81.46
48	Egypt	77.03
49	Nigeria	71.33
50	Romania	71.32
51	Peru	67.86
52	Ukraine	65.04
53	Bangladesh	56.16
54	Kuwait	51.80
55	Morocco	49.82
56	Vietnam	43.89
57	Slovak Republic	41.09
58	Kazakhstan	40.75
59	Croatia	33.20

RANK	COUNTRY	HARD DATA
60	Slovenia	32.79
61	Luxembourg	31.78
62	Ecuador	29.88
63	Tunisia	28.57
64	Qatar	28.45
65	Guatemala	26.12
66	Serbia and Montenegro	24.13
67	Bulgaria	23.91
68	Lithuania	22.17
69	Sri Lanka	20.13
70	Dominican Republic	19.45
71	Costa Rica	18.51
72	El Salvador	15.80
73	Kenya	15.62
74	Cyprus	15.42
75	Cameroon	14.43
76	Panama	13.79
77	Latvia	13.66
78	Iceland	12.78
79	Trinidad and Tobago	12.54
80	Uruguay	12.04
81	Estonia	11.20
82	Jordan	10.97
83	Tanzania	10.83
84	Bahrain	10.75
85	Bolivia	9.36
86	Botswana	9.13
87	Ghana	8.83
88	Jamaica	8.71
89	Azerbaijan	8.54
90	Bosnia and Herzegovina	8.28
91	Ethiopia	8.21
92	Albania	7.51
93	Honduras	7.43
94	Paraguay	7.00
95	Uganda	6.84
96	Mauritius	5.90
97	Zimbabwe	5.82
98	Mozambique	5.55
99	Malta	5.39
100	Mali	4.93
101	Macedonia, FYR	4.73
102	Namibia	4.68
103	Georgia	4.45
104	Nicaragua	4.43
105	Cambodia	4.43
106	Madagascar	4.36
107	Chad	4.32
108	Benin	4.09
109	Armenia	3.55
110	Moldova	2.58
111	Kyrgyz Republic	2.17
112	Tajikistan	2.07
113	Malawi	1.86
114	Mongolia	1.29
115	Guyana	0.77
116	Gambia	0.41
117	East Timor	0.33

474

SOURCE: IMF *World Economic Outlook Database*, April 2005

1.02 Total population, 2004

Population in millions, 2004

RANK	COUNTRY	HARD DATA
1	China	1,313.3
2	India	1,081.2
3	United States	297.0
4	Indonesia	222.6
5	Brazil	180.7
6	Pakistan	157.3
7	Bangladesh	149.7
8	Russian Federation	142.4
9	Japan	127.8
10	Nigeria	127.1
11	Mexico	104.9
12	Germany	82.5
12	Vietnam	82.5
14	Philippines	81.4
15	Egypt	73.4
16	Ethiopia	72.4
17	Turkey	72.3
18	Thailand	63.5
19	France	60.4
20	United Kingdom	59.4
21	Italy	57.3
22	Ukraine	48.2
23	Korea	48.0
24	South Africa	45.2
25	Colombia	44.9
26	Spain	41.1
27	Argentina	38.9
28	Poland	38.6
29	Tanzania	37.7
30	Kenya	32.4
31	Algeria	32.3
32	Canada	31.7
33	Morocco	31.1
34	Peru	27.6
35	Uganda	26.7
36	Venezuela	26.2
37	Malaysia	24.9
38	Taiwan	22.5
39	Romania	22.3
40	Ghana	21.4
41	Australia	19.9
42	Mozambique	19.2
42	Sri Lanka	19.2
44	Madagascar	17.9
45	Cameroon	16.3
46	Netherlands	16.2
47	Chile	16.0
48	Kazakhstan	15.4
49	Cambodia	14.5
50	Mali	13.4
51	Ecuador	13.2
52	Zimbabwe	12.9
53	Guatemala	12.7
54	Malawi	12.3
55	Greece	11.0
56	Serbia and Montenegro	10.5
57	Belgium	10.3
58	Czech Republic	10.2
59	Portugal	10.1

RANK	COUNTRY	HARD DATA
60	Tunisia	9.9
61	Hungary	9.8
62	Bolivia	9.0
63	Chad	8.9
63	Dominican Republic	8.9
63	Sweden	8.9
66	Azerbaijan	8.4
67	Austria	8.1
68	Bulgaria	7.8
69	Switzerland	7.2
70	Honduras	7.1
70	Hong Kong SAR	7.1
72	Benin	6.9
73	El Salvador	6.6
73	Israel	6.6
75	Tajikistan	6.3
76	Paraguay	6.0
77	Jordan	5.6
77	Nicaragua	5.6
79	Denmark	5.4
79	Slovak Republic	5.4
81	Finland	5.2
81	Kyrgyz Republic	5.2
83	Georgia	5.1
84	Norway	4.6
85	Croatia	4.4
86	Costa Rica	4.3
86	Moldova	4.3
86	Singapore	4.3
89	Bosnia and Herzegovina	4.2
90	Ireland	4.0
91	New Zealand	3.9
92	Lithuania	3.4
92	Uruguay	3.4
94	Albania	3.2
94	Panama	3.2
96	Armenia	3.1
96	United Arab Emirates	3.1
98	Jamaica	2.7
99	Kuwait	2.6
99	Mongolia	2.6
101	Latvia	2.3
102	Macedonia, FYR	2.1
103	Namibia	2.0
103	Slovenia	2.0
105	Botswana	1.8
106	Gambia	1.5
107	Estonia	1.3
107	Trinidad and Tobago	1.3
109	Mauritius	1.2
110	East Timor	0.9
111	Guyana	0.8
112	Bahrain	0.7
112	Cyprus	0.7
112	Qatar	0.7
115	Luxembourg	0.5
116	Malta	0.4
117	Iceland	0.3

475

SOURCES: UNFPA *State of World Population 2004*, Economist Intelligence Unit, and national sources

Aggregate Country Performance Indicators

1.03　GDP per capita (PPP), 2004

Gross Domestic Product per capita in US dollars, measured at Purchasing Power Parity, 2004

RANK	COUNTRY	HARD DATA
1	Luxembourg	63,609
2	Norway	40,005
3	United States	39,498
4	Ireland	37,663
5	Iceland	33,269
6	Denmark	33,089
7	Canada	32,921
8	Switzerland	31,690
9	Austria	31,406
10	Hong Kong SAR	30,558
11	Belgium	30,062
12	Japan	29,906
13	Australia	29,682
14	Finland	29,305
15	Netherlands	29,253
16	United Kingdom	28,968
17	Qatar	28,919
18	Germany	28,889
19	Sweden	28,205
20	Italy	28,172
21	France	27,913
22	Singapore	26,799
23	Taiwan	25,614
24	New Zealand	23,925
25	United Arab Emirates	23,818
26	Spain	23,627
27	Israel	22,077
28	Korea	21,305
29	Greece	20,362
30	Slovenia	20,306
31	Cyprus	19,633
32	Malta	19,302
33	Portugal	19,038
34	Bahrain	18,817
35	Czech Republic	18,357
36	Kuwait	16,066
37	Hungary	15,546
38	Estonia	15,217
39	Slovak Republic	15,066
40	Lithuania	12,919
41	Trinidad and Tobago	12,794
42	Argentina	12,468
43	Poland	12,244
44	Mauritius	12,215
45	Latvia	11,845
46	Croatia	11,568
47	Chile	10,869
48	South Africa	10,603
49	Malaysia	10,423
50	Russian Federation	10,179
51	Botswana	10,169
52	Costa Rica	9,887
53	Mexico	9,666
54	Uruguay	9,107
55	Bulgaria	8,500
56	Brazil	8,328
57	Thailand	7,901
58	Tunisia	7,732
59	Romania	7,641

RANK	COUNTRY	HARD DATA
60	Turkey	7,503
61	Kazakhstan	7,418
62	Macedonia, FYR	7,237
63	Panama	6,997
64	Colombia	6,959
65	Dominican Republic	6,761
66	Algeria	6,722
67	Ukraine	6,554
68	Namibia	6,449
69	China	5,642
70	Venezuela	5,571
71	Bosnia and Herzegovina	5,504
72	Peru	5,298
73	Albania	4,937
74	Serbia and Montenegro	4,858
75	Guyana	4,579
76	Philippines	4,561
77	Paraguay	4,553
78	Jordan	4,383
79	El Salvador	4,379
80	Jamaica	4,327
81	Morocco	4,227
82	Egypt	4,072
83	Guatemala	4,009
84	Azerbaijan	3,968
85	Sri Lanka	3,882
86	Ecuador	3,819
87	Armenia	3,806
88	Indonesia	3,622
89	India	3,029
90	Bolivia	2,902
91	Georgia	2,774
92	Honduras	2,682
93	Nicaragua	2,677
94	Vietnam	2,570
95	Ghana	2,475
96	Pakistan	2,404
97	Zimbabwe	2,309
98	Cameroon	2,176
99	Moldova	2,119
100	Cambodia	2,074
101	Kyrgyz Republic	1,934
102	Mongolia	1,918
103	Gambia	1,903
104	Bangladesh	1,875
105	Uganda	1,728
106	Chad	1,555
107	Mozambique	1,247
108	Tajikistan	1,246
109	Nigeria	1,120
110	Benin	1,094
111	Kenya	1,075
112	Mali	1,024
113	Madagascar	854
114	Ethiopia	814
115	Tanzania	673
116	Malawi	569
	East Timor	n/a

SOURCE: IMF *World Economic Outlook Database*, April 2005

476

2.01 Recession expectations

Your country's economy (1 = will likely be in a recession in the next 12 months, 7 = will have strong growth in the next 12 months)

RANK	COUNTRY	SCORE	1 MEAN: 4.4 7	SD
1	Qatar	6.8		0.4
2	United Arab Emirates	6.4		1.0
3	India	6.4		0.8
4	Iceland	6.2		1.0
5	Ireland	6.1		1.2
6	Trinidad and Tobago	5.9		1.1
7	South Africa	5.9		0.9
8	Kuwait	5.9		1.0
9	Malaysia	5.8		0.8
10	Vietnam	5.6		1.1
11	Chile	5.6		1.0
12	Slovak Republic	5.6		1.0
13	Hong Kong SAR	5.4		1.1
14	Bahrain	5.3		1.1
15	Indonesia	5.3		0.9
16	Norway	5.3		1.1
17	Kazakhstan	5.2		1.2
18	Denmark	5.2		0.9
19	Ghana	5.2		1.0
20	Algeria	5.1		1.2
21	Uruguay	5.1		0.8
22	Jordan	5.1		1.3
23	Estonia	5.1		1.2
24	Pakistan	5.1		1.6
25	United Kingdom	5.1		0.7
26	China	5.0		1.2
27	Latvia	5.0		1.2
28	Tajikistan	5.0		1.4
29	Armenia	5.0		1.3
30	Singapore	5.0		0.9
31	Argentina	5.0		1.2
32	Canada	5.0		1.1
33	Mozambique	5.0		1.4
34	United States	5.0		0.9
35	Sweden	5.0		0.9
36	Azerbaijan	4.9		1.8
37	Thailand	4.9		0.9
38	Tanzania	4.9		1.4
39	Lithuania	4.8		1.1
40	Egypt	4.8		1.3
41	Poland	4.8		1.4
42	Brazil	4.8		1.1
43	Czech Republic	4.8		1.1
44	Peru	4.8		0.9
45	Australia	4.7		1.0
46	Korea, Rep.	4.7		1.2
47	Israel	4.7		1.0
48	Romania	4.7		1.3
49	Turkey	4.6		1.4
50	Jamaica	4.6		1.3
51	New Zealand	4.6		1.2
52	Japan	4.6		1.0
53	Taiwan	4.5		1.1
54	Tunisia	4.5		1.4
55	Philippines	4.5		0.9
56	Netherlands	4.5		0.8
57	Hungary	4.5		1.3
58	Moldova	4.5		1.4
59	Finland	4.4		1.0

RANK	COUNTRY	SCORE	1 MEAN: 4.4 7	SD
60	Austria	4.4		0.9
61	Mexico	4.4		1.1
62	Colombia	4.3		1.0
63	Bulgaria	4.2		1.6
64	Luxembourg	4.2		1.1
65	Spain	4.2		1.0
66	Uganda	4.2		1.7
67	Mongolia	4.2		1.2
68	Bangladesh	4.2		1.3
69	Gambia	4.2		1.5
70	Cyprus	4.2		1.2
71	Dominican Republic	4.1		1.2
71	France	4.1		1.0
73	Cambodia	4.1		1.3
74	Kenya	4.1		1.5
75	Slovenia	4.1		1.2
76	Ukraine	4.1		1.4
77	Guatemala	4.1		1.2
78	Belgium	4.0		1.2
79	Switzerland	4.0		1.1
80	Venezuela	4.0		1.8
81	Madagascar	4.0		1.5
82	Sri Lanka	4.0		1.3
83	Russian Federation	4.0		1.5
84	Morocco	3.9		1.3
85	Mali	3.9		1.5
86	Mauritius	3.9		1.1
87	Honduras	3.9		1.4
88	Botswana	3.9		1.6
89	Namibia	3.8		1.5
90	Georgia	3.8		1.6
91	Nicaragua	3.8		1.1
92	Albania	3.8		1.5
93	Germany	3.8		1.0
94	Chad	3.8		1.8
95	Ethiopia	3.8		1.5
96	Ecuador	3.7		1.1
97	Greece	3.7		1.4
98	El Salvador	3.6		1.0
99	Cameroon	3.6		1.6
100	Nigeria	3.6		1.3
101	Malawi	3.6		1.5
102	Serbia and Montenegro	3.5		1.6
103	Portugal	3.5		1.0
104	Malta	3.5		0.9
105	Costa Rica	3.5		1.0
106	Kyrgyz Republic	3.5		1.4
107	Paraguay	3.4		1.3
108	Croatia	3.3		1.4
109	East Timor	3.2		1.8
110	Italy	3.2		1.2
111	Bolivia	3.0		1.3
112	Benin	3.0		1.6
113	Macedonia, FYR	3.0		1.5
114	Bosnia and Herzegovina	3.0		1.3
115	Panama	2.8		1.3
116	Guyana	2.8		1.4
117	Zimbabwe	2.4		1.7

2.02   Business costs of terrorism

The threat of terrorism in your country (1 = imposes significant costs on business, 7 = does not impose significant costs on business)

RANK	COUNTRY	SCORE	1 MEAN: 5.0 7	SD		RANK	COUNTRY	SCORE	1 MEAN: 5.0 7	SD
1	Portugal	6.5		1.0		60	Jordan	5.1		1.9
2	Malta	6.4		1.1		61	France	5.1		1.6
3	Finland	6.3		1.5		62	Armenia	5.0		2.1
4	Botswana	6.3		1.2		63	Bulgaria	5.0		2.0
5	Sweden	6.3		1.2		64	Gambia	5.0		2.1
6	Austria	6.2		1.2		65	Guyana	5.0		1.7
7	Iceland	6.2		1.6		66	China	4.9		1.4
8	Ghana	6.2		1.2		67	Ethiopia	4.9		1.8
9	Hungary	6.1		1.6		68	Turkey	4.9		1.7
10	Luxembourg	6.1		1.3		69	Bolivia	4.9		2.0
11	Uruguay	6.1		1.8		70	Tanzania	4.9		1.9
12	Norway	5.9		1.5		71	Kazakhstan	4.8		1.8
13	Brazil	5.9		1.8		72	Mozambique	4.8		2.0
14	Zimbabwe	5.8		1.7		73	Thailand	4.8		1.6
15	Mongolia	5.8		1.8		74	Canada	4.8		1.7
16	Croatia	5.8		1.6		75	India	4.8		1.7
17	Ireland	5.8		1.5		76	Moldova	4.8		1.9
18	Chile	5.7		1.9		77	Azerbaijan	4.8		2.1
19	Switzerland	5.7		1.6		78	Chad	4.7		1.9
20	Malaysia	5.7		1.2		79	El Salvador	4.7		1.8
21	Argentina	5.7		1.6		80	Singapore	4.7		1.7
22	Czech Republic	5.7		1.5		81	Jamaica	4.6		1.8
23	Estonia	5.7		2.1		82	Spain	4.6		1.9
24	Dominican Republic	5.7		1.7		83	Peru	4.6		1.8
25	Costa Rica	5.6		1.8		84	Indonesia	4.6		1.5
26	New Zealand	5.6		1.6		85	Madagascar	4.6		1.9
27	Hong Kong SAR	5.6		1.5		86	Japan	4.5		1.8
28	Slovenia	5.6		1.9		87	Netherlands	4.5		1.7
29	Slovak Republic	5.6		1.8		88	Venezuela	4.5		2.0
30	Malawi	5.5		1.6		89	Bahrain	4.5		2.1
31	Lithuania	5.5		1.9		89	Cambodia	4.5		2.1
32	South Africa	5.5		1.6		91	Ecuador	4.5		1.9
33	Ukraine	5.5		1.6		92	Kyrgyz Republic	4.5		2.0
34	Mexico	5.5		1.5		93	East Timor	4.4		2.0
35	Greece	5.5		1.7		93	Paraguay	4.4		1.9
36	Korea, Rep.	5.4		1.5		95	Guatemala	4.3		2.1
37	Qatar	5.4		1.9		96	Albania	4.2		2.0
38	Australia	5.4		1.4		97	Kuwait	4.2		2.0
39	Tunisia	5.4		1.8		98	Trinidad and Tobago	4.2		1.7
40	Latvia	5.4		1.9		99	Nigeria	4.2		1.7
41	Mauritius	5.4		1.9		100	Morocco	4.1		2.1
42	Namibia	5.4		2.1		101	Pakistan	4.1		1.9
43	Romania	5.4		2.0		102	Honduras	4.0		2.0
44	Taiwan	5.3		1.9		103	Russian Federation	4.0		1.9
45	Bosnia and Herzegovina	5.3		2.1		104	Panama	4.0		2.3
46	Georgia	5.3		1.7		105	United Kingdom	4.0		1.5
47	Cameroon	5.3		1.9		106	Tajikistan	3.9		2.2
48	Belgium	5.3		1.9		107	United States	3.7		1.7
49	United Arab Emirates	5.3		1.6		108	Bangladesh	3.6		2.0
50	Italy	5.2		1.7		109	Egypt	3.6		2.3
51	Denmark	5.2		2.1		110	Uganda	3.6		2.1
52	Benin	5.2		2.1		111	Macedonia, FYR	3.6		2.1
53	Vietnam	5.2		2.0		112	Algeria	3.6		2.2
54	Serbia and Montenegro	5.2		2.0		113	Sri Lanka	3.3		1.7
55	Germany	5.2		1.7		114	Kenya	3.3		2.0
56	Mali	5.1		2.1		115	Israel	3.2		2.0
57	Cyprus	5.1		1.9		116	Philippines	3.0		1.5
58	Poland	5.1		1.7		117	Colombia	2.4		1.5
59	Nicaragua	5.1		1.9						

2.03 Financial market sophistication

The level of sophistication of financial markets in your country is (1 = lower than international norms, 7 = higher than international norms)

RANK	COUNTRY	SCORE	1 MEAN: 4.0 7	SD
1	United Kingdom	6.7		0.6
2	United States	6.7		0.6
3	Switzerland	6.4		1.0
4	Germany	6.1		0.9
5	Australia	6.0		0.9
6	Hong Kong SAR	6.0		1.4
7	Luxembourg	6.0		1.2
8	Canada	6.0		1.0
9	Finland	5.9		0.7
10	Singapore	5.9		0.8
11	Netherlands	5.8		1.0
12	South Africa	5.8		0.9
13	Sweden	5.8		0.9
14	Denmark	5.8		1.0
15	Belgium	5.7		0.9
16	France	5.7		1.0
17	New Zealand	5.7		1.1
18	Ireland	5.7		1.0
19	Iceland	5.7		1.0
20	Bahrain	5.5		1.6
21	Austria	5.5		1.3
22	Japan	5.4		1.3
23	Norway	5.4		0.9
24	Malaysia	5.4		1.1
25	Israel	5.3		1.0
26	Chile	5.3		1.0
27	Brazil	5.3		1.4
28	Portugal	5.2		1.3
29	Spain	5.2		1.1
30	Kuwait	5.0		1.3
31	Taiwan	5.0		1.0
32	India	5.0		1.0
33	Estonia	4.9		1.0
34	Hungary	4.8		1.1
35	Jamaica	4.7		1.0
36	Korea, Rep.	4.6		1.3
37	Ghana	4.5		1.4
38	Panama	4.5		1.7
39	Greece	4.5		1.1
40	Mexico	4.4		1.2
41	Thailand	4.3		1.1
42	El Salvador	4.3		1.5
43	Italy	4.3		1.5
44	Colombia	4.3		1.2
45	Cyprus	4.3		1.3
46	Trinidad and Tobago	4.3		1.4
47	United Arab Emirates	4.3		1.4
48	Jordan	4.2		1.3
49	Poland	4.2		1.0
50	Peru	4.1		1.2
51	Turkey	4.1		1.3
52	Lithuania	4.1		1.2
53	Slovak Republic	4.1		1.4
54	Mauritius	4.0		1.3
55	Philippines	4.0		1.2
56	Zimbabwe	4.0		1.3
57	Slovenia	4.0		1.1
58	Malta	3.9		1.4
59	Argentina	3.9		1.2
60	Qatar	3.9		1.4
61	Venezuela	3.9		1.4
62	Kazakhstan	3.9		1.5
63	Namibia	3.8		1.5
64	Nigeria	3.8		1.3
65	Latvia	3.8		1.3
66	Czech Republic	3.8		0.9
67	Costa Rica	3.7		1.3
68	Botswana	3.6		1.3
69	Kenya	3.6		1.4
70	Indonesia	3.6		1.1
71	Pakistan	3.6		1.5
72	Tunisia	3.6		1.2
73	Sri Lanka	3.6		1.4
74	Croatia	3.5		1.4
75	Uruguay	3.4		1.3
76	Romania	3.2		1.2
77	Honduras	3.2		1.5
78	Egypt	3.2		1.3
79	Ecuador	3.2		1.2
80	Guatemala	3.1		1.2
81	Morocco	3.1		1.4
82	Azerbaijan	3.1		1.4
83	Dominican Republic	3.1		1.3
84	Ukraine	3.1		1.2
85	Nicaragua	3.0		1.2
86	Russian Federation	3.0		1.2
87	China	2.9		1.1
88	Vietnam	2.9		1.4
89	Bangladesh	2.8		1.3
90	Macedonia, FYR	2.8		1.5
91	Madagascar	2.8		1.5
92	Mali	2.8		1.7
93	Kyrgyz Republic	2.8		1.2
94	Mongolia	2.7		1.2
95	Bolivia	2.6		1.4
96	Tanzania	2.6		1.3
97	Benin	2.5		1.4
98	Bulgaria	2.5		1.2
99	Malawi	2.5		1.2
100	Mozambique	2.5		1.1
101	Georgia	2.5		1.3
102	Bosnia and Herzegovina	2.4		1.1
103	Tajikistan	2.4		1.2
104	Cameroon	2.4		1.6
105	Serbia and Montenegro	2.4		1.1
106	Moldova	2.4		1.3
107	Gambia	2.4		1.3
108	Paraguay	2.3		1.0
109	Albania	2.3		1.0
110	Armenia	2.2		1.2
111	Uganda	2.2		1.2
112	Cambodia	2.1		1.2
113	Ethiopia	2.0		1.1
114	Algeria	1.9		1.0
115	Guyana	1.9		0.8
116	East Timor	1.9		1.2
117	Chad	1.7		1.2

2.04 Soundness of banks

Banks in your country are (1 = insolvent and may require government bailout, 7 = generally healthy with sound balance sheets)

RANK	COUNTRY	SCORE	MEAN: 5.4	SD
1	Switzerland	6.8		0.6
2	Ireland	6.8		0.6
3	United Kingdom	6.8		0.6
4	Luxembourg	6.8		0.4
5	Canada	6.7		0.6
6	Denmark	6.7		0.6
7	New Zealand	6.7		0.5
8	France	6.7		0.6
9	Australia	6.7		0.5
10	United States	6.7		0.6
11	Belgium	6.6		0.7
12	Austria	6.6		0.6
13	Netherlands	6.6		0.7
14	Norway	6.5		0.6
15	South Africa	6.5		0.6
16	Malta	6.5		0.6
17	Bahrain	6.5		0.6
18	Finland	6.5		0.5
19	Singapore	6.5		0.7
20	Iceland	6.4		0.6
21	Sweden	6.4		0.7
22	Chile	6.4		0.7
23	Spain	6.4		0.7
24	Hong Kong SAR	6.4		1.4
25	Kuwait	6.4		0.9
26	Portugal	6.3		0.7
27	Estonia	6.3		0.8
28	Botswana	6.2		0.8
29	Trinidad and Tobago	6.2		1.0
30	Slovak Republic	6.1		0.8
31	United Arab Emirates	6.1		0.9
32	Panama	6.1		1.1
33	Qatar	6.1		1.1
34	Israel	6.0		0.9
35	El Salvador	6.0		0.6
36	Malawi	6.0		1.1
37	Jordan	6.0		0.8
38	Cyprus	5.9		0.8
39	Germany	5.9		1.0
40	Pakistan	5.9		0.9
41	Benin	5.8		1.2
42	Colombia	5.8		1.0
43	Greece	5.8		0.9
44	Lithuania	5.8		1.0
45	Brazil	5.8		1.5
46	Ghana	5.7		0.9
47	Namibia	5.7		1.1
48	Malaysia	5.7		0.9
49	Guyana	5.7		1.1
50	Mauritius	5.7		1.3
51	Hungary	5.7		1.3
52	Latvia	5.7		1.0
53	India	5.6		0.9
54	Croatia	5.6		1.4
55	Jamaica	5.5		1.0
56	Slovenia	5.5		1.0
57	Peru	5.5		1.0
58	Tanzania	5.5		1.1
59	Cameroon	5.4		1.2
60	Gambia	5.4		1.3
61	Mexico	5.4		1.3
62	Costa Rica	5.4		0.9
63	Sri Lanka	5.4		1.1
64	Italy	5.4		1.3
65	Madagascar	5.3		1.4
66	Moldova	5.3		1.4
67	Mali	5.2		1.4
68	Kazakhstan	5.2		1.0
69	Bulgaria	5.2		1.4
70	Thailand	5.2		1.1
71	Korea, Rep.	5.2		1.2
72	Poland	5.1		1.2
73	Czech Republic	5.1		1.1
74	Taiwan	5.1		1.1
75	Romania	5.1		1.0
76	Philippines	5.1		1.1
77	Georgia	5.1		1.1
78	Kenya	5.0		1.3
79	Bangladesh	4.9		1.3
80	Albania	4.9		1.5
81	Morocco	4.8		1.7
82	Bosnia and Herzegovina	4.8		1.4
83	Mongolia	4.7		1.3
84	Tunisia	4.7		1.3
85	Vietnam	4.7		1.4
86	Nicaragua	4.7		1.3
87	Uganda	4.7		1.5
88	Honduras	4.6		1.4
89	Venezuela	4.6		1.2
90	Armenia	4.6		1.4
91	East Timor	4.6		1.7
92	Algeria	4.5		1.6
93	Ethiopia	4.5		1.7
94	Guatemala	4.5		1.4
95	Ukraine	4.4		1.1
96	Mozambique	4.4		1.4
97	Dominican Republic	4.4		1.4
98	Egypt	4.4		1.5
99	Japan	4.3		1.4
100	Bolivia	4.2		1.4
101	Russian Federation	4.2		1.2
102	Macedonia, FYR	4.2		1.8
103	Serbia and Montenegro	4.2		1.5
104	Chad	4.1		1.9
105	Nigeria	4.1		1.3
106	Ecuador	4.1		1.4
107	Azerbaijan	4.0		1.4
108	Paraguay	4.0		1.4
109	Indonesia	4.0		1.2
110	Cambodia	3.9		1.3
111	Tajikistan	3.9		1.6
112	Uruguay	3.9		1.3
113	China	3.8		1.3
114	Turkey	3.8		1.4
115	Kyrgyz Republic	3.7		1.3
116	Argentina	3.5		1.2
117	Zimbabwe	3.0		1.3

481

2.05 Ease of access to loans

How easy is it to obtain a bank loan in your country with only a good business plan and no collateral? (1 = impossible, 7 = easy)

RANK	COUNTRY	SCORE	1 MEAN: 3.3 7	SD
1	Finland	5.4		1.7
2	Iceland	5.4		1.8
3	Denmark	5.4		1.4
4	United Kingdom	5.2		1.4
5	Hong Kong SAR	5.0		1.6
6	Ireland	5.0		1.6
7	United States	4.9		1.6
8	Norway	4.9		1.3
9	Netherlands	4.9		1.5
10	Lithuania	4.9		1.4
11	Australia	4.8		1.5
12	Luxembourg	4.8		1.4
13	New Zealand	4.8		1.6
14	Sweden	4.7		1.6
15	Taiwan	4.7		1.5
16	Singapore	4.6		1.5
17	Portugal	4.5		1.6
18	Belgium	4.5		1.6
19	Malaysia	4.4		1.4
20	United Arab Emirates	4.4		1.6
21	Austria	4.4		1.6
22	France	4.4		1.5
23	Switzerland	4.2		1.7
24	Canada	4.2		1.6
25	Kuwait	4.2		1.9
26	India	4.1		1.5
27	Qatar	4.1		1.5
28	Germany	4.1		1.4
29	Greece	4.0		1.6
30	Slovenia	4.0		1.7
31	Pakistan	3.9		2.0
32	Chile	3.9		1.8
33	Israel	3.9		1.6
34	Spain	3.9		1.8
35	Panama	3.9		1.9
36	South Africa	3.9		1.6
37	Cyprus	3.8		1.7
38	Estonia	3.8		1.9
39	Bahrain	3.8		1.8
40	Thailand	3.8		1.5
41	Poland	3.7		1.4
42	Slovak Republic	3.7		2.0
43	Malta	3.7		1.7
44	Latvia	3.6		1.7
45	Botswana	3.5		1.8
46	Korea, Rep.	3.5		1.9
47	Bulgaria	3.5		1.9
47	East Timor	3.5		1.9
49	El Salvador	3.5		1.8
50	Namibia	3.5		1.6
51	Hungary	3.5		1.6
52	Bosnia and Herzegovina	3.4		1.8
53	Mauritius	3.4		1.7
54	Japan	3.4		1.5
55	Trinidad and Tobago	3.3		1.7
56	Croatia	3.3		1.8
57	Kazakhstan	3.2		1.7
58	Sri Lanka	3.2		1.9
59	Peru	3.2		1.6
60	Czech Republic	3.2		1.4
61	Tunisia	3.2		1.5
62	Kenya	3.1		1.7
63	Jordan	3.1		1.7
64	Ghana	3.0		1.5
65	Indonesia	3.0		1.6
66	Romania	3.0		1.6
67	Ukraine	3.0		1.5
68	Uganda	2.9		1.8
69	Gambia	2.8		1.6
70	Philippines	2.8		1.3
71	Brazil	2.8		1.6
72	Egypt	2.8		1.7
73	Italy	2.8		1.5
74	Malawi	2.8		1.6
75	Vietnam	2.7		1.7
76	Serbia and Montenegro	2.6		1.6
76	Zimbabwe	2.6		1.1
78	Georgia	2.6		1.5
79	Venezuela	2.6		1.6
80	Costa Rica	2.6		1.4
81	Mexico	2.6		1.4
82	Jamaica	2.6		1.6
83	Turkey	2.5		1.4
84	Bangladesh	2.5		1.4
85	Tanzania	2.5		1.8
86	Dominican Republic	2.5		1.5
87	Colombia	2.5		1.3
88	Tajikistan	2.5		1.7
89	China	2.4		1.4
90	Macedonia, FYR	2.4		1.9
91	Russian Federation	2.4		1.3
92	Morocco	2.4		1.4
93	Guatemala	2.4		1.4
94	Moldova	2.4		1.7
95	Paraguay	2.3		1.3
96	Cambodia	2.3		1.3
97	Honduras	2.3		1.4
98	Guyana	2.3		1.5
99	Algeria	2.3		1.4
100	Armenia	2.2		1.5
101	Nigeria	2.2		1.1
102	Uruguay	2.2		1.1
103	Madagascar	2.2		1.6
104	Ecuador	2.2		1.0
105	Mongolia	2.1		1.4
106	Cameroon	2.1		1.4
107	Albania	2.1		1.4
108	Kyrgyz Republic	2.1		1.4
109	Mali	2.1		1.4
110	Nicaragua	2.1		1.3
111	Argentina	2.1		1.0
112	Azerbaijan	2.0		1.3
113	Bolivia	2.0		1.2
114	Ethiopia	1.7		1.2
115	Mozambique	1.7		1.1
116	Chad	1.6		1.1
117	Benin	1.6		1.2

2.06 Venture capital availability

Entrepreneurs with innovative but risky projects can generally find venture capital in your country (1 = not true, 7 = true)

RANK	COUNTRY	SCORE	1 MEAN: 3.3 7	SD
1	United States	5.9		1.2
2	Finland	5.4		1.3
3	United Kingdom	5.4		1.3
4	Ireland	5.3		1.4
5	Israel	5.1		1.2
6	Netherlands	5.0		1.3
7	Hong Kong SAR	4.9		1.4
8	Denmark	4.9		1.3
9	Australia	4.9		1.3
10	Canada	4.8		1.5
11	Taiwan	4.7		1.2
12	Norway	4.7		1.2
13	Luxembourg	4.6		1.5
14	Malaysia	4.6		1.3
15	Singapore	4.6		1.3
16	France	4.5		1.5
17	Sweden	4.5		1.3
18	Iceland	4.4		1.7
19	New Zealand	4.4		1.5
20	Panama	4.4		1.6
21	Belgium	4.4		1.7
22	Austria	4.3		1.5
23	Switzerland	4.3		1.7
24	Germany	4.3		1.5
25	Kuwait	4.3		1.6
26	United Arab Emirates	4.2		1.5
27	Spain	4.2		1.4
28	Lithuania	4.2		1.4
29	India	4.2		1.4
30	Botswana	4.1		1.7
31	Korea, Rep.	4.0		1.8
32	Portugal	3.9		1.5
33	Japan	3.9		1.4
34	Estonia	3.9		1.4
35	South Africa	3.8		1.5
36	Poland	3.6		1.3
37	Trinidad and Tobago	3.6		1.5
38	Hungary	3.6		1.4
39	Greece	3.6		1.6
40	Vietnam	3.5		1.8
41	Tunisia	3.5		1.5
42	Macedonia, FYR	3.5		1.8
43	Chile	3.5		1.5
44	Pakistan	3.4		1.7
45	Kazakhstan	3.4		1.5
46	Bahrain	3.4		1.6
47	Qatar	3.4		1.7
48	Cyprus	3.3		1.3
49	Slovak Republic	3.3		1.4
50	Slovenia	3.3		1.3
51	Bulgaria	3.3		1.6
52	Mauritius	3.3		1.8
53	Thailand	3.3		1.4
54	Czech Republic	3.3		1.4
55	Latvia	3.2		1.5
56	Costa Rica	3.1		1.5
57	Indonesia	3.1		1.4
58	Italy	3.1		1.6
59	East Timor	3.0		1.8

RANK	COUNTRY	SCORE	1 MEAN: 3.3 7	SD
60	Jordan	3.0		1.7
61	El Salvador	3.0		1.6
61	Namibia	3.0		1.4
63	Nigeria	3.0		1.4
64	Peru	3.0		1.6
65	Sri Lanka	3.0		1.6
66	Russian Federation	2.9		1.5
67	Tajikistan	2.9		1.8
68	Ukraine	2.9		1.4
69	China	2.9		1.1
70	Ghana	2.9		1.4
71	Kenya	2.8		1.6
72	Egypt	2.8		1.7
73	Romania	2.8		1.4
74	Madagascar	2.8		1.8
75	Bosnia and Herzegovina	2.8		1.6
76	Uganda	2.8		1.8
77	Albania	2.7		1.6
78	Serbia and Montenegro	2.7		1.7
79	Zimbabwe	2.6		1.2
80	Azerbaijan	2.6		1.4
81	Cambodia	2.6		1.7
82	Malta	2.6		1.3
83	Philippines	2.6		1.3
84	Jamaica	2.6		1.4
85	Turkey	2.5		1.4
86	Tanzania	2.5		1.6
87	Morocco	2.5		1.5
88	Georgia	2.5		1.4
89	Honduras	2.5		1.7
90	Argentina	2.5		1.3
91	Brazil	2.4		1.4
92	Guatemala	2.4		1.4
93	Mexico	2.4		1.2
94	Bangladesh	2.3		1.5
95	Mongolia	2.3		1.5
96	Dominican Republic	2.3		1.5
97	Algeria	2.3		1.7
98	Croatia	2.3		1.3
99	Gambia	2.3		1.3
100	Armenia	2.3		1.5
101	Venezuela	2.3		1.2
102	Ecuador	2.3		1.2
103	Guyana	2.2		1.4
104	Kyrgyz Republic	2.2		1.6
105	Mozambique	2.2		1.3
106	Colombia	2.2		1.1
107	Moldova	2.2		1.4
108	Mali	2.1		1.6
109	Cameroon	2.1		1.5
110	Bolivia	2.1		1.3
111	Uruguay	2.1		1.1
112	Malawi	2.0		1.2
113	Paraguay	2.0		1.2
114	Nicaragua	1.9		1.2
115	Benin	1.9		1.4
116	Chad	1.9		1.4
117	Ethiopia	1.7		1.2

2.07 Access to credit

During the past year, obtaining credit for your company has become (1 = more difficult, 7 = easier)

RANK	COUNTRY	SCORE	1 MEAN: 4.5 7	SD
1	India	6.1		0.9
2	Iceland	6.0		1.1
3	Taiwan	5.8		1.1
4	Ireland	5.7		1.2
5	Lithuania	5.6		1.3
6	Norway	5.6		1.1
7	Estonia	5.6		1.2
8	Pakistan	5.6		1.3
9	Denmark	5.5		1.3
10	Slovak Republic	5.5		1.6
11	Georgia	5.5		1.1
12	Thailand	5.4		1.3
13	Latvia	5.4		1.2
14	Turkey	5.4		1.4
15	United Kingdom	5.4		1.2
16	United Arab Emirates	5.4		1.1
17	United States	5.3		1.3
18	Malaysia	5.3		1.0
19	Finland	5.3		1.2
20	Kuwait	5.3		1.5
21	South Africa	5.3		1.2
22	Colombia	5.2		1.4
23	Australia	5.2		1.3
24	Hong Kong SAR	5.2		1.4
25	New Zealand	5.2		1.3
26	Slovenia	5.2		1.4
27	Chile	5.1		1.5
28	Bahrain	5.1		1.6
29	Singapore	5.1		1.3
30	Ghana	5.1		1.2
31	Japan	5.1		1.3
32	Armenia	5.1		1.5
33	Jordan	5.1		1.7
34	Trinidad and Tobago	5.0		1.5
35	Canada	5.0		1.4
35	El Salvador	5.0		1.6
35	Mongolia	5.0		1.6
35	Sweden	5.0		1.2
39	Greece	4.9		1.4
40	France	4.9		1.4
41	Spain	4.8		1.3
42	Qatar	4.8		1.6
43	Romania	4.8		1.4
44	Poland	4.8		1.4
45	Czech Republic	4.8		1.5
46	Hungary	4.8		1.4
47	Kazakhstan	4.7		1.5
48	Korea, Rep.	4.7		1.4
49	Serbia and Montenegro	4.7		1.7
50	Mexico	4.7		1.7
51	Portugal	4.6		1.6
52	Bangladesh	4.6		1.7
53	Bulgaria	4.6		1.7
54	Netherlands	4.6		1.3
55	Philippines	4.6		1.5
56	Vietnam	4.5		1.7
57	Jamaica	4.5		1.5
58	Croatia	4.5		1.7
58	Israel	4.5		1.7

RANK	COUNTRY	SCORE	1 MEAN: 4.5 7	SD
60	Peru	4.5		1.5
61	Russian Federation	4.5		1.6
62	Botswana	4.5		1.4
63	Albania	4.4		1.6
63	Mauritius	4.4		1.9
65	Bosnia and Herzegovina	4.4		1.8
66	Switzerland	4.4		1.6
67	Luxembourg	4.4		1.2
68	Germany	4.4		1.3
69	Brazil	4.4		1.9
70	Indonesia	4.3		1.2
71	Malawi	4.3		1.8
72	Cyprus	4.3		1.6
73	Costa Rica	4.3		1.8
74	Ukraine	4.3		1.3
75	Austria	4.2		1.5
76	Italy	4.2		1.4
77	Belgium	4.2		1.7
78	Malta	4.2		1.5
79	Kyrgyz Republic	4.1		1.6
80	Tunisia	4.1		1.4
81	Kenya	4.1		1.8
82	Panama	4.0		1.5
83	Ecuador	4.0		1.7
84	Moldova	4.0		1.8
85	Tanzania	3.9		1.8
86	Namibia	3.9		1.6
87	East Timor	3.9		1.8
88	Honduras	3.9		1.8
89	Azerbaijan	3.8		1.7
90	Argentina	3.8		1.8
91	Guatemala	3.8		1.7
92	Venezuela	3.8		1.7
93	Sri Lanka	3.7		1.8
94	Cambodia	3.7		1.6
95	Egypt	3.7		1.8
96	Cameroon	3.7		1.7
97	Macedonia, FYR	3.6		1.8
98	Gambia	3.6		1.7
99	Uganda	3.6		1.8
100	Morocco	3.6		1.6
101	Mozambique	3.6		1.5
102	Tajikistan	3.5		1.9
103	Algeria	3.5		1.8
104	Nicaragua	3.4		1.7
105	China	3.4		1.3
106	Guyana	3.4		1.6
107	Zimbabwe	3.4		1.7
108	Bolivia	3.3		1.8
109	Paraguay	3.3		1.7
110	Dominican Republic	3.3		1.8
111	Ethiopia	3.3		1.8
112	Madagascar	3.2		1.5
113	Mali	3.1		1.7
114	Benin	3.1		1.8
115	Uruguay	3.0		1.8
116	Nigeria	2.8		1.2
117	Chad	2.1		1.4

2.08   Local equity market access

Raising money by issuing shares on the local stock market is (1 = nearly impossible, 7 = quite possible for a good company)

RANK	COUNTRY	SCORE	1 MEAN: 4.7 7	SD
1	Iceland	6.6		0.6
2	India	6.5		0.8
3	New Zealand	6.5		0.6
4	United Kingdom	6.5		0.9
5	United States	6.4		0.9
6	Australia	6.4		0.7
7	Japan	6.4		0.9
8	Hong Kong SAR	6.4		1.2
9	Malaysia	6.3		0.7
10	Norway	6.3		0.7
11	South Africa	6.3		1.1
12	Taiwan	6.2		0.7
13	Austria	6.1		1.1
14	Singapore	6.1		0.9
15	Thailand	6.1		1.0
16	Switzerland	6.1		1.0
17	Jamaica	6.0		1.2
18	France	6.0		1.2
19	Canada	6.0		1.1
20	Finland	6.0		1.3
21	Ireland	5.9		1.4
22	Sweden	5.9		1.3
23	Ghana	5.9		1.1
24	Kuwait	5.9		1.3
25	Zimbabwe	5.9		1.1
26	Turkey	5.8		1.2
27	Germany	5.8		1.1
27	Israel	5.8		1.2
29	Netherlands	5.8		1.1
30	Pakistan	5.8		0.8
31	Bahrain	5.8		1.4
32	Philippines	5.8		1.3
33	Chile	5.8		1.2
34	Estonia	5.8		0.9
35	Jordan	5.7		1.1
36	Denmark	5.7		1.1
37	Mauritius	5.7		1.1
38	Bangladesh	5.6		1.5
39	Sri Lanka	5.5		1.5
40	Portugal	5.5		1.5
41	United Arab Emirates	5.5		1.3
42	Trinidad and Tobago	5.4		1.6
43	Malta	5.4		1.3
44	Italy	5.4		1.5
45	Poland	5.3		1.5
46	Belgium	5.3		1.5
47	Botswana	5.3		1.4
48	Korea, Rep.	5.3		1.4
49	Qatar	5.3		1.7
50	Luxembourg	5.3		1.7
51	Indonesia	5.2		1.2
52	Nigeria	5.2		1.4
53	Spain	5.2		1.5
54	Greece	5.2		1.4
55	Vietnam	5.2		1.6
56	Hungary	5.1		1.5
57	Lithuania	5.1		1.4
58	Colombia	5.0		1.8
59	Brazil	5.0		1.8

RANK	COUNTRY	SCORE	1 MEAN: 4.7 7	SD
60	Tunisia	4.9		1.3
61	Tanzania	4.9		1.7
62	Egypt	4.9		1.6
63	Panama	4.9		1.3
64	Malawi	4.9		1.6
65	Czech Republic	4.8		1.5
66	Slovenia	4.7		1.5
67	Namibia	4.7		1.9
68	Kenya	4.6		1.7
69	Russian Federation	4.6		1.5
70	Peru	4.6		1.6
71	Morocco	4.5		1.9
72	Mexico	4.5		1.7
73	Guyana	4.5		1.8
74	Romania	4.4		1.7
75	Croatia	4.4		1.7
76	Latvia	4.4		1.6
77	Cyprus	4.3		1.7
78	Serbia and Montenegro	4.3		1.7
79	Macedonia, FYR	4.2		1.9
80	Uganda	4.2		1.9
81	Costa Rica	4.2		1.8
82	Kazakhstan	4.2		1.7
83	El Salvador	4.1		1.9
84	Argentina	4.1		1.7
85	China	4.0		1.7
86	Bulgaria	4.0		1.6
87	Benin	3.8		2.0
88	Ukraine	3.7		1.4
89	Mongolia	3.6		2.4
90	Kyrgyz Republic	3.6		2.1
91	Bosnia and Herzegovina	3.5		1.9
92	Mali	3.5		1.8
93	Slovak Republic	3.5		1.7
94	Venezuela	3.4		2.0
95	Paraguay	3.4		1.9
96	Nicaragua	3.4		1.7
97	Cameroon	3.4		2.0
98	Bolivia	3.4		1.6
99	Gambia	3.2		2.0
100	Moldova	3.2		1.9
101	Azerbaijan	3.2		1.6
102	Ecuador	3.2		1.9
103	Tajikistan	3.2		1.7
104	Mozambique	3.2		1.7
105	Guatemala	3.1		1.6
106	Algeria	2.9		2.0
107	Madagascar	2.8		1.9
108	Armenia	2.7		1.8
109	East Timor	2.7		1.8
110	Georgia	2.7		1.7
111	Dominican Republic	2.6		1.7
112	Ethiopia	2.3		1.8
113	Uruguay	2.1		1.4
114	Chad	2.1		1.7
115	Honduras	1.9		1.4
116	Cambodia	1.7		1.3
117	Albania	1.5		1.1

2.09 Prevalence of trade barriers

In your country, tariff and nontariff barriers significantly reduce the ability of imported goods to compete in the domestic market (1 = strongly agree, 7 = strongly disagree)

RANK	COUNTRY	SCORE	1 MEAN: 4.6 7	SD	RANK	COUNTRY	SCORE	1 MEAN: 4.6 7	SD
1	Luxembourg	6.5		0.7	60	Mali	4.5		1.9
2	New Zealand	6.3		1.3	61	Georgia	4.5		1.9
3	Singapore	6.2		1.0	62	Panama	4.5		1.6
4	United Arab Emirates	6.2		0.9	63	Japan	4.5		1.6
5	Finland	6.2		1.1	64	Tunisia	4.5		1.6
6	Hong Kong SAR	6.1		1.5	65	Thailand	4.5		1.5
7	Estonia	5.9		1.3	66	Ethiopia	4.4		1.9
8	Portugal	5.9		1.4	67	Bosnia and Herzegovina	4.4		2.1
9	Hungary	5.9		1.1	68	Jordan	4.4		1.7
10	Slovak Republic	5.8		1.1	69	Bangladesh	4.4		1.9
11	Sweden	5.8		1.2	70	Romania	4.3		1.7
12	Denmark	5.8		1.5	71	Colombia	4.2		1.8
13	France	5.7		1.4	72	Albania	4.2		2.0
14	Austria	5.7		1.5	73	Madagascar	4.2		1.9
15	Germany	5.7		1.2	74	Peru	4.2		1.5
16	Ireland	5.7		1.4	75	Benin	4.2		2.1
17	Malta	5.7		1.3	76	Malawi	4.2		2.2
18	Cyprus	5.6		1.2	77	Uruguay	4.1		1.7
19	Chile	5.6		1.9	78	Algeria	4.1		1.7
20	Australia	5.6		1.4	79	Paraguay	4.1		2.0
21	Slovenia	5.5		1.3	80	Kazakhstan	4.1		1.4
22	Greece	5.5		1.2	81	Pakistan	4.1		1.5
23	Italy	5.5		1.5	82	Mozambique	4.0		1.8
24	Bahrain	5.4		1.6	83	China	4.0		1.4
25	Canada	5.4		1.4	84	Macedonia, FYR	4.0		2.0
26	Qatar	5.4		1.6	85	Armenia	4.0		1.8
27	Ghana	5.4		1.4	86	Argentina	4.0		1.7
28	United States	5.3		1.7	87	Norway	3.9		1.5
29	Netherlands	5.3		1.3	88	Brazil	3.9		1.7
30	Taiwan	5.3		1.4	89	Uganda	3.9		2.2
31	Belgium	5.3		1.6	90	Moldova	3.9		2.0
32	United Kingdom	5.3		1.6	91	Russian Federation	3.8		1.7
33	Czech Republic	5.2		1.2	92	Ukraine	3.8		1.4
34	Israel	5.2		1.5	93	Sri Lanka	3.8		1.7
35	Kuwait	5.1		1.6	94	Kenya	3.8		1.9
36	Botswana	5.1		1.5	95	Tanzania	3.8		1.8
37	Gambia	5.0		1.6	96	Venezuela	3.8		1.9
38	Malaysia	4.9		1.5	97	Nigeria	3.7		1.4
39	Iceland	4.9		1.7	98	East Timor	3.7		2.1
40	Spain	4.9		1.7	99	Cambodia	3.7		1.7
41	Jamaica	4.9		1.7	100	Switzerland	3.6		1.6
42	Korea, Rep.	4.9		1.3	101	Tajikistan	3.6		1.6
43	El Salvador	4.8		1.5	102	Mongolia	3.5		1.9
44	Philippines	4.8		1.7	103	Morocco	3.5		1.7
45	Trinidad and Tobago	4.8		1.5	104	Bolivia	3.5		1.9
46	Turkey	4.8		1.9	105	Egypt	3.5		2.0
47	Poland	4.7		1.3	106	Honduras	3.5		1.9
48	Cameroon	4.7		1.9	107	Vietnam	3.4		1.7
49	Lithuania	4.7		1.5	108	Azerbaijan	3.4		1.5
50	Latvia	4.7		1.5	109	Mauritius	3.4		1.3
51	Serbia and Montenegro	4.7		1.9	110	Chad	3.4		2.0
52	Namibia	4.7		1.6	111	Zimbabwe	3.4		1.7
53	Croatia	4.7		1.6	112	Costa Rica	3.3		1.7
54	India	4.6		1.5	113	Nicaragua	3.2		1.7
55	Guyana	4.6		1.7	114	Guatemala	3.1		1.7
56	South Africa	4.6		1.7	115	Ecuador	3.1		1.6
57	Bulgaria	4.5		1.9	116	Kyrgyz Republic	3.0		1.9
58	Indonesia	4.5		1.4	117	Dominican Republic	2.8		1.9
59	Mexico	4.5		1.8					

2.10 Impact of rules on FDI

In your country, rules governing foreign direct investment are (1 = damaging and discourage foreign direct investment, 7 = beneficial and encourage foreign direct investment)

RANK	COUNTRY	SCORE	1 MEAN: 5.0 7	SD		RANK	COUNTRY	SCORE	1 MEAN: 5.0 7	SD
1	Singapore	6.6		0.8		60	Lithuania	4.9		1.0
2	Ireland	6.6		0.9		61	Egypt	4.9		1.5
3	Slovak Republic	6.5		0.6		62	Korea, Rep.	4.9		1.2
4	Luxembourg	6.5		0.7		63	Qatar	4.9		1.4
5	Hong Kong SAR	6.3		0.9		64	Uruguay	4.9		1.3
6	Ghana	6.2		1.0		65	United Arab Emirates	4.9		1.5
7	United Kingdom	6.1		1.1		66	Indonesia	4.8		1.1
8	Estonia	6.0		0.9		67	Mozambique	4.8		1.3
9	Austria	5.9		1.0		68	China	4.8		1.3
10	United States	5.9		1.1		69	Cameroon	4.8		1.6
11	Finland	5.9		0.8		70	Malawi	4.8		1.6
12	Hungary	5.9		0.9		71	Iceland	4.8		1.7
13	Tunisia	5.8		1.2		72	Romania	4.7		1.3
14	Pakistan	5.8		1.1		73	Honduras	4.7		1.6
15	Switzerland	5.8		1.0		74	Cambodia	4.7		1.6
16	Chile	5.8		0.9		75	Colombia	4.7		1.4
17	Sri Lanka	5.7		1.3		76	Georgia	4.7		1.2
18	Malaysia	5.7		0.8		77	Turkey	4.7		1.3
19	Jordan	5.7		1.1		78	Namibia	4.7		1.5
20	Sweden	5.7		1.0		79	Philippines	4.7		1.5
21	Netherlands	5.7		1.0		80	Brazil	4.6		1.3
22	Uganda	5.7		1.3		81	Poland	4.6		1.2
23	Bangladesh	5.7		1.4		82	Japan	4.6		1.3
24	Taiwan	5.6		1.0		83	Azerbaijan	4.6		1.4
25	Malta	5.6		1.3		83	Panama	4.6		1.5
26	India	5.6		1.0		85	Kazakhstan	4.5		1.1
27	Denmark	5.6		1.1		86	Mongolia	4.5		1.8
28	Germany	5.6		1.1		87	Kenya	4.5		1.7
29	Portugal	5.6		1.1		88	Tajikistan	4.5		1.6
30	New Zealand	5.6		0.9		89	Guyana	4.5		1.2
31	Bahrain	5.6		1.4		90	Greece	4.5		1.4
32	Spain	5.6		0.9		91	Morocco	4.4		1.9
33	El Salvador	5.6		1.1		92	Algeria	4.4		1.8
34	Australia	5.6		1.0		93	Argentina	4.4		1.4
35	Trinidad and Tobago	5.5		1.1		94	Italy	4.3		1.6
36	France	5.5		1.2		95	Benin	4.2		1.9
37	Jamaica	5.5		1.3		96	Macedonia, FYR	4.2		1.7
38	Gambia	5.5		1.4		97	Croatia	4.2		1.3
39	Thailand	5.4		1.3		98	Madagascar	4.2		1.4
40	Dominican Republic	5.4		1.2		99	Slovenia	4.1		1.1
41	Botswana	5.4		1.4		100	Albania	4.1		1.6
42	Canada	5.4		1.1		101	Ethiopia	4.1		1.7
43	Czech Republic	5.4		1.2		102	Serbia and Montenegro	4.0		1.6
44	Tanzania	5.4		1.2		103	Chad	4.0		2.0
45	Armenia	5.3		1.4		104	Paraguay	3.9		1.6
46	Vietnam	5.3		1.5		105	Moldova	3.9		1.6
47	Israel	5.2		1.4		106	Bosnia and Herzegovina	3.9		1.3
48	Costa Rica	5.2		1.3		107	Kyrgyz Republic	3.8		1.5
49	Nigeria	5.1		1.3		108	Bulgaria	3.8		1.6
50	Cyprus	5.1		1.2		109	Russian Federation	3.8		1.3
51	Mexico	5.1		1.3		110	Guatemala	3.8		1.6
52	Peru	5.1		1.1		111	Bolivia	3.6		1.7
53	Mauritius	5.1		1.2		112	Kuwait	3.5		1.5
54	Norway	5.1		0.9		113	Ecuador	3.5		1.2
55	Latvia	5.0		1.1		114	East Timor	3.5		1.9
56	Mali	5.0		1.6		115	Venezuela	3.4		1.5
57	Belgium	5.0		1.4		116	Ukraine	3.3		1.4
58	South Africa	5.0		1.4		117	Zimbabwe	3.1		1.5
59	Nicaragua	4.9		1.2						

2.11   Tax burden

The overall tax burden on your enterprise, including all associated costs (tax rates plus administrative and time costs, penalties, etc.), is estimated as (in percent of net revenues) (1 = 0–4%, 2 = 5–15%, 3 = 16–25%, 7 = 81–100%)

RANK	COUNTRY	SCORE	MEAN: 3.6	SD
1	United Arab Emirates	1.6		1.0
2	Kuwait	1.7		1.2
3	Bahrain	1.7		0.7
4	Qatar	1.8		1.0
5	Singapore	2.3		1.0
6	Taiwan	2.4		1.0
7	Indonesia	2.4		1.2
8	Cyprus	2.4		0.9
9	Slovak Republic	2.7		1.2
10	Ireland	2.7		1.0
11	Hong Kong SAR	2.7		0.8
12	Vietnam	2.7		1.3
13	Iceland	2.9		0.8
14	Switzerland	2.9		1.2
15	Cambodia	3.0		1.6
16	Panama	3.0		1.9
17	Portugal	3.1		1.0
18	Hungary	3.1		1.4
19	Botswana	3.2		1.0
20	Jordan	3.2		1.4
21	Chile	3.2		1.1
22	Finland	3.2		1.3
23	Sri Lanka	3.3		1.2
24	Korea, Rep.	3.3		1.1
25	Slovenia	3.3		1.4
26	Croatia	3.3		1.5
27	Estonia	3.3		1.5
28	Azerbaijan	3.3		1.8
29	Malaysia	3.3		0.9
30	Malta	3.4		1.5
31	Gambia	3.4		1.7
32	Uruguay	3.4		1.5
33	Mali	3.4		1.4
34	Honduras	3.4		1.7
35	Mauritius	3.4		1.0
36	Albania	3.4		1.5
37	Lithuania	3.4		1.7
38	Philippines	3.4		1.4
39	Bosnia and Herzegovina	3.5		1.9
40	Tanzania	3.5		1.6
41	East Timor	3.5		1.4
42	Tunisia	3.5		1.5
43	Egypt	3.5		1.6
44	Thailand	3.5		1.7
45	Guatemala	3.5		1.7
46	El Salvador	3.5		1.2
47	Nigeria	3.6		1.4
48	Madagascar	3.6		1.4
49	Paraguay	3.6		1.5
50	Trinidad and Tobago	3.6		1.6
51	Kazakhstan	3.6		1.4
52	Poland	3.6		1.3
53	Bulgaria	3.6		1.7
54	United Kingdom	3.6		1.2
55	Canada	3.6		1.5
56	Serbia and Montenegro	3.6		1.6
57	Bolivia	3.6		1.3
58	Benin	3.6		1.9
59	United States	3.7		1.3

RANK	COUNTRY	SCORE	MEAN: 3.6	SD
60	Mozambique	3.7		1.3
61	Algeria	3.7		1.9
62	Costa Rica	3.7		1.5
63	Austria	3.7		1.2
64	Pakistan	3.7		1.2
65	Russian Federation	3.7		1.4
66	Denmark	3.7		1.3
67	Czech Republic	3.8		1.3
68	Armenia	3.8		1.5
69	Latvia	3.8		1.5
70	Venezuela	3.8		1.5
71	Uganda	3.8		1.8
72	Netherlands	3.9		1.2
73	Mexico	3.9		1.4
74	Bangladesh	3.9		1.5
75	Luxembourg	3.9		0.9
76	Moldova	3.9		1.6
77	Kyrgyz Republic	4.0		1.8
78	India	4.0		1.3
79	Kenya	4.0		1.5
80	Dominican Republic	4.0		1.3
81	Namibia	4.0		1.3
81	Spain	4.0		1.2
81	Sweden	4.0		1.3
84	Guyana	4.0		1.4
85	Australia	4.0		1.2
86	Turkey	4.0		1.9
87	New Zealand	4.0		1.2
88	Tajikistan	4.1		1.4
89	Peru	4.1		1.3
90	South Africa	4.2		1.3
91	Morocco	4.2		1.4
92	Ecuador	4.2		1.6
93	Brazil	4.2		1.3
94	Japan	4.2		1.6
95	Norway	4.2		1.4
96	Ghana	4.2		1.1
97	Mongolia	4.2		1.7
98	Macedonia, FYR	4.3		1.9
99	Greece	4.3		1.1
100	China	4.3		1.6
101	Zimbabwe	4.3		1.3
102	Georgia	4.3		1.4
103	Germany	4.3		1.3
104	Israel	4.4		1.4
105	France	4.4		1.2
106	Ukraine	4.4		1.7
107	Belgium	4.4		1.3
108	Jamaica	4.4		1.3
109	Cameroon	4.4		1.7
110	Nicaragua	4.4		1.8
111	Chad	4.4		1.7
112	Italy	4.5		1.7
113	Argentina	4.5		1.1
114	Ethiopia	4.5		1.5
115	Colombia	4.6		1.6
116	Romania	4.7		1.7
117	Malawi	5.1		1.1

2.12 Agricultural policy costs

Agricultural policy in your country (1 = is excessively burdensome for the economy, 7 = balances the interests of taxpayers, consumers, and producers)

RANK	COUNTRY	SCORE	SD
1	New Zealand	5.6	1.2
2	Malaysia	5.3	0.9
3	Singapore	4.9	1.4
4	Qatar	4.8	1.5
5	Australia	4.7	1.4
6	Tunisia	4.6	1.3
7	Taiwan	4.6	1.2
8	Chile	4.6	1.2
9	United Arab Emirates	4.5	1.4
10	Thailand	4.5	1.3
11	Hong Kong SAR	4.4	1.1
12	Denmark	4.4	1.5
13	South Africa	4.4	1.3
14	Vietnam	4.3	1.3
15	China	4.3	1.4
16	Luxembourg	4.3	1.1
17	Kuwait	4.3	1.6
18	Ireland	4.3	1.4
19	Bahrain	4.3	1.5
20	Argentina	4.2	1.7
21	Estonia	4.2	1.3
22	Israel	4.1	1.3
23	Austria	4.1	1.4
24	Ghana	4.1	1.1
25	Mauritius	4.1	1.6
26	Uganda	4.1	1.6
27	Brazil	4.0	1.6
28	Uruguay	4.0	1.4
29	Malta	4.0	0.8
30	El Salvador	3.9	0.9
31	Korea, Rep.	3.9	1.4
32	Botswana	3.9	1.3
33	Sweden	3.9	1.4
34	Bangladesh	3.8	1.4
35	Pakistan	3.8	1.5
36	Malawi	3.8	1.2
37	Namibia	3.8	1.5
38	Philippines	3.8	1.3
39	Armenia	3.8	1.8
40	Netherlands	3.8	1.3
41	Egypt	3.8	1.4
42	Guyana	3.8	1.3
43	Portugal	3.7	1.0
44	Indonesia	3.7	1.1
45	Jamaica	3.7	1.1
46	France	3.7	1.5
47	Jordan	3.7	1.4
48	Bolivia	3.7	1.4
48	Mozambique	3.7	1.4
50	Canada	3.7	1.3
51	Tanzania	3.7	1.7
52	United States	3.7	1.5
53	Spain	3.7	1.3
54	Cameroon	3.6	1.3
55	Serbia and Montenegro	3.6	1.6
55	United Kingdom	3.6	1.4
57	Mali	3.6	1.7
58	Czech Republic	3.6	1.1
59	Costa Rica	3.6	1.2
60	Latvia	3.6	1.3
61	Madagascar	3.6	1.6
62	Gambia	3.6	1.5
63	Panama	3.6	1.5
64	Cambodia	3.6	1.5
65	Finland	3.6	1.6
66	Kazakhstan	3.5	1.3
67	Kenya	3.5	1.7
68	Algeria	3.5	1.6
69	Benin	3.5	1.7
70	Paraguay	3.5	1.4
71	Albania	3.4	1.3
72	Macedonia, FYR	3.4	1.3
73	Slovak Republic	3.4	1.3
74	Mongolia	3.4	1.3
75	Morocco	3.4	1.6
76	Nicaragua	3.4	1.3
77	Belgium	3.4	1.4
78	India	3.4	1.4
79	Italy	3.4	1.3
80	Trinidad and Tobago	3.4	1.3
81	Cyprus	3.4	1.2
82	Slovenia	3.3	1.1
83	Sri Lanka	3.3	1.3
84	Dominican Republic	3.3	1.2
85	Colombia	3.3	1.2
86	East Timor	3.3	1.5
87	Poland	3.3	1.2
88	Guatemala	3.3	1.3
89	Ecuador	3.2	1.1
90	Azerbaijan	3.2	1.6
91	Honduras	3.2	1.3
92	Georgia	3.2	1.2
93	Lithuania	3.2	1.2
94	Chad	3.1	1.8
95	Greece	3.1	0.9
96	Germany	3.1	1.3
97	Tajikistan	3.0	1.6
98	Peru	3.0	1.1
99	Iceland	2.9	1.4
100	Hungary	2.9	1.2
101	Moldova	2.9	1.6
102	Turkey	2.9	1.2
103	Romania	2.9	1.2
104	Switzerland	2.9	1.4
105	Japan	2.9	1.4
106	Russian Federation	2.8	1.3
107	Mexico	2.8	1.1
108	Ethiopia	2.8	1.6
109	Nigeria	2.8	1.5
110	Venezuela	2.8	1.3
111	Kyrgyz Republic	2.8	1.4
112	Croatia	2.7	1.1
113	Ukraine	2.7	1.2
114	Norway	2.7	1.4
115	Bulgaria	2.7	1.4
116	Bosnia and Herzegovina	2.3	1.1
117	Zimbabwe	2.0	1.3

489

2.13   Government surplus/deficit, 2004

Government fiscal surplus/deficit as a percentage of GDP, 2004

RANK	COUNTRY	HARD DATA
1	Kuwait	23.0
2	United Arab Emirates	18.5
3	Norway	11.5
3	Qatar	11.5
5	Nigeria	7.4
6	Bahrain	7.3
7	Singapore	5.2
8	Algeria[1]	4.7
9	Russian Federation	4.5
10	New Zealand	3.5
11	Kazakhstan	3.2
12	Ecuador	2.3
13	Chile	2.2
14	Korea[1]	2.0
15	Finland	1.9
16	Bulgaria	1.8
17	Canada	1.4
18	Denmark	1.3
18	Ireland	1.3
20	Trinidad and Tobago	1.1
21	Azerbaijan	1.0
22	Estonia	0.8
23	Australia	0.7
23	Georgia	0.7
23	Paraguay	0.7
23	Sweden	0.7
27	Iceland	0.5
28	Macedonia, FYR	0.4
29	Thailand	0.3
30	Belgium	0.0
31	Serbia and Montenegro	−0.3
31	Spain	−0.3
33	Venezuela	−0.5
34	Bosnia and Herzegovina	−0.7
34	Cameroon	−0.7
36	Hong Kong SAR	−0.9
37	Latvia	−1.1
37	Moldova	−1.1
37	Romania	−1.1
40	Indonesia	−1.2
40	Peru	−1.2
42	Guatemala	−1.3
43	Austria	−1.4
43	Luxembourg	−1.4
45	Armenia	−1.7
45	Uganda	−1.7
47	Botswana	−1.9
47	Slovenia	−1.9
49	Colombia	−2.0
49	Mexico	−2.0
51	Benin	−2.1
51	Honduras	−2.1
53	Chad	−2.2
53	Lithuania	−2.2
53	South Africa	−2.2
56	Nicaragua	−2.3
57	China	−2.4
57	East Timor[1]	−2.4
57	Ghana[1]	−2.4

RANK	COUNTRY	HARD DATA
57	Kenya	−2.4
57	Switzerland	−2.4
57	Tunisia	−2.4
57	Vietnam	−2.4
64	Egypt	−2.5
64	Netherlands	−2.5
64	Pakistan	−2.5
64	Uruguay	−2.5
68	Brazil	−2.7
68	Dominican Republic	−2.7
68	Tajikistan	−2.7
71	Portugal	−2.9
72	Tanzania	−3.0
73	Italy	−3.0
73	United Kingdom	−3.0
75	El Salvador	−3.1
76	Slovak Republic	−3.3
76	Taiwan	−3.3
78	Argentina	−3.4
78	Jordan	−3.4
78	Namibia	−3.4
81	Bangladesh[1]	−3.5
81	Czech Republic	−3.5
81	Madagascar	−3.5
84	Gambia	−3.6
84	Philippines	−3.6
86	France	−3.7
86	Germany	−3.7
88	Costa Rica	−4.0
89	Mali	−4.1
90	Cyprus	−4.2
90	Kyrgyz Republic	−4.2
92	United States	−4.3
93	Israel	−4.4
93	Ukraine	−4.4
95	Ethiopia	−4.5
96	Malaysia	−4.6
96	Morocco	−4.6
96	Panama	−4.6
99	Malta	−4.7
100	Albania	−4.9
100	Mongolia	−4.9
100	Mozambique	−4.9
103	Croatia	−5.0
103	Jamaica	−5.0
105	Malawi	−5.2
106	Zimbabwe	−5.3
107	Hungary	−5.4
107	Mauritius	−5.4
109	Bolivia	−5.9
110	Cambodia	−6.1
110	Greece	−6.1
112	Poland	−6.5
113	Japan	−7.1
114	Sri Lanka	−7.7
115	Guyana	−8.3
116	India	−9.5
117	Turkey	−9.8

SOURCES: IMF *World Economic Outlook*, Winter 2005 published version
[1] Central Government Balance

2.14 National savings rate, 2004

National savings rate as a percentage of GDP, 2004

RANK	COUNTRY	HARD DATA
1	Qatar	56.8
2	China	49.7
3	Singapore	46.7
4	Botswana	43.0
5	Algeria	39.2
6	Mozambique	36.1
7	Malaysia	35.0
8	United Arab Emirates	34.6
9	Venezuela	34.4
10	Korea	34.2
11	Vietnam	33.1
12	Norway	32.8
13	Hong Kong SAR	32.7
14	Switzerland	32.3
15	Kuwait	32.0
16	Namibia	31.7
17	Nigeria	31.6
17	Trinidad and Tobago	31.6
19	Thailand	31.4
20	Russian Federation	31.4
21	Mauritius	30.0
22	Azerbaijan	28.9
23	Japan	27.6
24	Ukraine	27.0
25	Taiwan	26.9
26	Ecuador	26.8
27	Kazakhstan	26.8
28	Slovenia	26.1
29	Turkey	25.7
30	Dominican Republic	25.6
30	Luxembourg	25.6
32	Croatia	25.3
33	Honduras	25.2
34	Finland	24.7
35	Ireland	24.6
36	Morocco	24.1
36	Sweden	24.1
38	India	24.0
39	Indonesia	23.9
40	Belgium	23.7
41	Bangladesh	23.7
42	Spain	23.3
43	Brazil	23.2
43	Guyana	23.2
45	Chile	23.2
46	Canada	23.1
47	Slovak Republic	22.8
48	Denmark	22.8
48	Netherlands	22.8
50	Egypt	22.8
51	Tunisia	22.7
52	Czech Republic	22.6
53	Bahrain	22.6
53	Greece	22.6
55	Paraguay	22.5
56	Jamaica	22.2
57	Philippines	21.7
58	Austria	21.5
59	Germany	21.0

RANK	COUNTRY	HARD DATA
60	Moldova	21.0
61	Argentina	20.8
62	Mexico	20.4
63	Armenia	20.1
64	Panama	20.0
65	Latvia	19.6
65	Mongolia	19.6
67	France	19.4
68	Chad	18.9
68	Ghana	18.9
70	Uganda	18.8
71	Estonia	18.7
71	Gambia	18.7
71	Italy	18.7
74	Peru	18.5
75	Australia	18.5
76	Poland	18.5
77	Jordan	18.4
78	Israel	18.1
79	Cambodia	18.1
80	Sri Lanka	17.9
81	Benin	17.6
81	Colombia	17.6
83	Costa Rica	17.5
83	New Zealand	17.5
85	Albania	17.2
86	Romania	17.0
87	Lithuania	16.9
88	Pakistan	16.2
89	Bulgaria	16.0
90	Macedonia, FYR	15.9
91	Ethiopia[1]	15.8
92	Guatemala	15.5
93	Hungary	15.4
94	Portugal	15.2
95	Cameroon	15.1
96	Cyprus	15.0
97	Malta	14.8
98	United Kingdom	14.8
99	Georgia	14.7
100	South Africa	14.5
101	Mali	14.3
102	Tajikistan	14.0
103	Bolivia	13.6
104	Iceland	13.5
105	Uruguay	12.5
106	El Salvador	11.5
107	Nicaragua	11.3
108	Kyrgyz Republic	10.8
109	United States	10.7
110	Madagascar	9.7
111	Kenya	9.3
112	Tanzania	8.9
113	Zimbabwe	7.0
114	Bosnia and Herzegovina	4.6
115	Malawi	2.2
116	Serbia and Montenegro	–1.0
117	East Timor[1]	–32.0

SOURCES: Economist Intelligence Unit; IMF Country Reports, and national sources

[1] 2003

491

2.15   Real effective exchange rate, 2004

Real effective exchange rate 2004 relative to the 1997–2003 average

RANK	COUNTRY	HARD DATA		RANK	COUNTRY	HARD DATA
1	Zimbabwe	−53.3		60	El Salvador	−2.4
2	Argentina	−49.4		61	Bosnia and Herzegovina	−1.7
3	Gambia	−43.1		62	Qatar	−1.7
4	Egypt	−37.2		63	India	−1.3
5	Uruguay	−33.8		64	Kenya	−1.2
6	Tanzania	−29.1		65	Mali	−0.8
7	Malawi	−27.7		66	Poland	−0.8
8	Brazil	−26.8		67	Honduras	−0.8
9	Azerbaijan	−25.2		68	Kyrgyz Republic	0.0
10	Venezuela	−23.9		69	Sweden	0.4
11	Paraguay	−22.0		70	Serbia and Montenegro	0.7
12	Madagascar	−21.8		71	Trinidad and Tobago	0.7
13	Tajikistan	−20.3		72	Norway	0.9
14	Uganda	−19.9		73	Slovak Republic	0.9
15	Ukraine	−19.6		74	Guatemala	1.0
16	Hong Kong SAR	−18.7		75	Switzerland	1.7
17	Israel	−18.6		76	Finland	1.7
18	Philippines	−18.3		77	Slovenia	1.7
19	Dominican Republic	−17.5		78	Malta	1.7
20	Ghana	−17.3		79	Luxembourg	2.6
21	Bolivia	−17.3		80	Croatia	2.7
22	Nigeria	−16.5		81	Austria	2.8
23	Colombia	−15.3		82	Germany	2.9
24	Algeria	−15.3		83	Moldova	3.0
25	Taiwan	−13.5		84	Belgium	3.2
26	Chile	−13.4		85	Korea, Rep.	3.3
27	Nicaragua	−12.9		86	France	3.4
28	Armenia	−12.4		87	United Kingdom	4.1
29	Bahrain	−11.9		88	Denmark	5.6
30	Jamaica	−11.9		89	Cameroon	5.7
31	Mongolia	−11.8		90	Greece	5.8
32	Malaysia	−11.0		91	Portugal	6.0
33	Ethiopia	−10.8		92	Italy	6.4
34	Bangladesh	−10.1		93	Iceland	6.5
35	Tunisia	−9.4		94	Netherlands	6.7
36	Guyana	−9.1		95	Lithuania	7.5
37	Sri Lanka	−9.0		96	Ecuador	7.6
38	Pakistan	−8.9		97	Spain	7.8
39	Peru	−8.8		98	Cyprus	7.8
40	Singapore	−8.6		99	Indonesia	7.8
41	Costa Rica	−8.3		100	South Africa	7.9
42	Panama	−8.2		101	Estonia	8.0
43	Kuwait	−8.0		102	Benin	8.9
44	Cambodia	−7.9		103	Chad	9.0
45	Thailand	−7.6		104	Romania	9.8
46	Kazakhstan	−7.3		105	Canada	10.3
47	Jordan	−7.3		106	Ireland	10.5
48	Japan	−6.9		107	Namibia	10.6
49	United States	−6.5		108	Czech Republic	10.9
50	Mexico	−6.3		109	Turkey	12.5
51	Vietnam	−6.2		110	Albania	13.1
52	United Arab Emirates	−5.6		111	Russian Federation	14.8
53	Mozambique	−5.5		112	New Zealand	15.3
54	China	−5.4		113	Australia	16.2
55	Georgia	−5.1		114	Bulgaria	21.1
56	Mauritius	−4.8		115	Hungary	23.2
57	Macedonia, FYR	−4.0		116	Botswana	28.9
58	Morocco	−3.4			East Timor	n/a
59	Latvia	−2.7				

SOURCE: International Monetary Fund

2.16   Inflation, 2004

Percentage change in consumer price index, 2004

RANK	COUNTRY	HARD DATA
1	Chad	−4.8
2	Mali	−3.1
3	Hong Kong SAR	−0.4
3	Israel	−0.4
5	Macedonia, FYR	−0.3
6	Japan	0.0
7	Finland	0.1
8	Cameroon	0.3
9	Norway	0.4
10	Panama	0.5
11	Bosnia and Herzegovina	0.8
11	Switzerland	0.8
13	Chile	1.1
13	Sweden	1.1
15	Denmark	1.2
15	Lithuania	1.2
17	United Kingdom	1.3
18	Malaysia	1.4
18	Netherlands	1.4
18	South Africa	1.4
21	Taiwan	1.6
22	Singapore	1.7
23	Canada	1.8
23	Germany	1.8
23	Kuwait	1.8
26	Belgium	1.9
27	Austria	2.0
27	Cambodia	2.0
27	Morocco	2.0
30	Croatia	2.1
31	Luxembourg	2.2
32	Australia	2.3
32	Cyprus	2.3
32	France	2.3
32	Ireland	2.3
32	Italy	2.3
32	New Zealand	2.3
38	Portugal	2.5
39	Benin	2.6
40	Ecuador	2.7
40	Malta	2.7
40	Thailand	2.7
40	United States	2.7
44	Czech Republic	2.8
45	Albania	2.9
46	Estonia	3.0
47	Greece	3.1
47	Iceland	3.1
47	Spain	3.1
50	Jordan	3.4
51	Poland	3.5
52	Algeria	3.6
52	Korea	3.6
52	Slovenia	3.6
52	Tunisia	3.6
56	Peru	3.7
57	India	3.8
57	United Arab Emirates	3.8
59	China	3.9

RANK	COUNTRY	HARD DATA
59	Trinidad and Tobago	3.9
61	East Timor	4.1
61	Kyrgyz Republic	4.1
63	Argentina	4.4
63	Bolivia	4.4
63	Mauritius	4.4
66	El Salvador	4.5
67	Tanzania	4.6
68	Guyana	4.7
68	Mexico	4.7
70	Bahrain	4.9
71	Mongolia	5.0
72	Paraguay	5.2
73	Namibia	5.5
73	Philippines	5.5
75	Georgia	5.7
76	Colombia	5.9
76	Uganda	5.9
78	Bangladesh	6.1
78	Bulgaria	6.1
78	Indonesia	6.1
81	Botswana	6.3
81	Latvia	6.3
83	Brazil	6.6
84	Pakistan	6.7
85	Hungary	6.8
86	Kazakhstan	6.9
87	Armenia	7.0
87	Guatemala	7.0
89	Tajikistan	7.1
90	Qatar	7.5
90	Slovak Republic	7.5
92	Sri Lanka	7.6
93	Vietnam	7.7
94	Azerbaijan	8.1
94	Egypt	8.1
94	Honduras	8.1
97	Nicaragua	8.2
98	Ethiopia	9.0
98	Ukraine	9.0
100	Uruguay	9.2
101	Serbia and Montenegro	9.5
102	Turkey	10.6
103	Russian Federation	10.9
104	Jamaica	11.5
104	Kenya	11.5
106	Malawi	11.6
107	Romania	11.9
108	Costa Rica	12.3
108	Moldova	12.3
110	Ghana	12.6
110	Mozambique	12.6
112	Madagascar	13.8
113	Gambia	14.6
114	Nigeria	15.0
115	Venezuela	21.7
116	Dominican Republic	51.5
117	Zimbabwe	282.4

493

SOURCES: IMF World Economic Outlook Database, April 2005

2.17   Interest rate spread, 2004

Average interest rate spread, 2004 (difference between typical lending and deposit rates)

RANK	COUNTRY	HARD DATA		RANK	COUNTRY	HARD DATA
1	United Kingdom	1.4		60	India	5.7
2	Spain	1.5		61	Jordan	5.8
3	Japan	1.7		62	Bulgaria	5.8
4	Luxembourg	1.8		63	Moldova	5.8
5	Taiwan	2.0		64	Venezuela	5.9
6	Korea	2.0		65	Macedonia, FYR	5.9
7	Austria	2.1		66	Ghana	6.3
8	Malta	2.3		67	Pakistan	6.5
9	Netherlands	2.4		68	Trinidad and Tobago	6.5
10	Norway	2.6		69	Azerbaijan	6.5
11	Portugal	2.6		70	Bosnia and Herzegovina[1]	6.6
12	United States	2.8		71	Botswana	6.6
13	Finland	2.8		72	Panama	6.6
14	Switzerland	2.8		73	Bahrain	6.6
15	El Salvador	3.0		74	Bolivia	7.1
16	Kuwait	3.0		75	Iceland	7.2
17	Sweden	3.0		76	Colombia	7.3
17	Tunisia	3.0		77	Russian Federation	7.6
19	Malaysia	3.0		78	Indonesia	7.7
20	Chile	3.2		79	Morocco	7.9
21	Canada	3.2		80	Bangladesh	8.4
22	China	3.3		81	Nicaragua	8.8
23	Germany	3.4		82	Honduras	8.8
24	Estonia	3.5		83	Benin	9.3
25	Denmark	3.6		84	Ukraine	9.6
25	Vietnam	3.6		85	Guatemala	9.6
27	Ethiopia	3.6		86	Tanzania	9.7
28	Cyprus	3.7		87	Croatia	9.9
29	Hungary	3.7		88	Kenya	10.1
30	Poland	3.7		89	Jamaica	10.2
31	Israel	3.8		90	Kazakhstan	10.4
32	Italy	3.8		91	Tajikistan	10.6
33	Philippines	3.9		92	Mongolia	11.2
34	Greece	4.0		93	Mali	11.5
35	Ireland	4.1		94	Peru	11.5
36	Argentina	4.2		95	Dominican Republic	11.5
37	Latvia	4.2		96	Guyana	11.9
38	France	4.4		97	Madagascar	12.0
39	Sri Lanka	4.4		98	Mozambique	12.2
40	United Arab Emirates	4.5		99	Serbia and Montenegro	12.8
41	Thailand	4.5		100	Mauritius	12.9
42	Lithuania	4.5		101	Uganda	12.9
43	Mexico	4.5		102	Cameroon	13.0
44	New Zealand	4.6		102	Chad	13.0
45	South Africa	4.7		104	Armenia	13.7
46	Czech Republic	4.7		105	Costa Rica	13.9
47	Slovenia	4.8		106	Romania	14.5
48	Singapore	4.9		107	Gambia	14.5
49	Slovak Republic	4.9		108	Uruguay	15.0
50	Hong Kong SAR	5.0		109	Cambodia	15.8
51	Qatar	5.0		110	Turkey	16.5
52	Namibia	5.0		111	Kyrgyz Republic	22.6
53	Australia	5.1		112	Malawi	23.1
54	Albania	5.2		113	Georgia	24.0
55	Belgium	5.2		114	Paraguay	28.4
56	Nigeria	5.5		115	Brazil	39.7
57	Algeria	5.5		116	Zimbabwe	175.7
58	Ecuador	5.6			East Timor	n/a
59	Egypt	5.7				

SOURCES: IMF International Financial Statistics, June 2005; Economist Intelligence Unit, and national sources
[1] 2003

2.18   Exports, 2004

Exports of goods and services as a percentage of GDP, 2004

RANK	COUNTRY	HARD DATA
1	Singapore	223.2
2	Hong Kong SAR	189.9
3	Luxembourg	146.2
4	Malaysia	128.6
5	Guyana	117.9
6	United Arab Emirates	93.9
7	Malta	93.2
8	Bahrain	89.8
9	Belgium	83.7
10	Ireland	80.2
11	Estonia	79.7
12	Slovak Republic	76.8
13	Mongolia	74.1
14	Czech Republic	71.3
15	Thailand	70.0
16	Ukraine	67.7
17	Taiwan	65.8
18	Vietnam	65.7
19	Netherlands	65.4
20	Hungary	64.9
21	Panama	64.4
22	Qatar	64.1
23	Slovenia	59.9
24	Kuwait	59.6
25	Cambodia	59.2
26	Bulgaria	58.4
27	Kazakhstan	56.6
28	Trinidad and Tobago	55.6
29	Mauritius	55.2
30	Gambia	54.7
31	Jordan	53.0
32	Lithuania	52.7
33	Austria	50.6
34	Philippines	50.2
35	Moldova	48.9
36	Ghana	48.9
37	Tajikistan	48.0
38	Croatia	47.5
39	Cyprus	46.9
40	Costa Rica	46.4
41	Sweden	46.2
42	Switzerland	45.9
43	Nigeria	45.6
44	Namibia	44.8
45	Tunisia	44.6
46	Algeria	44.1
47	Korea	44.0
48	Norway	43.7
49	Denmark	43.5
50	Israel	42.8
51	Latvia	42.5
52	Azerbaijan	42.1
53	Poland	41.8
54	Jamaica	41.6
55	Chad	41.0
56	Chile	41.0
57	Honduras	40.7
58	Dominican Republic	40.7
59	Botswana	40.3
60	China	40.0
61	Kyrgyz Republic	39.8
62	Paraguay	39.7
63	Macedonia, FYR	39.5
64	Canada	38.2
65	Germany	38.0
66	Sri Lanka	37.6
67	Romania	37.2
68	Finland	37.1
69	Russian Federation	37.0
70	Iceland	36.8
71	Venezuela	36.4
72	Zimbabwe	35.9
73	Indonesia	30.9
74	Portugal	30.9
75	Mexico	30.1
76	Uruguay	29.6
77	Madagascar	29.4
78	New Zealand	29.2
79	Mozambique	28.9
80	Turkey	28.9
81	Kenya	28.8
82	Malawi	28.6
83	Cameroon	28.2
84	Egypt	28.1
85	Mali	27.7
86	El Salvador	27.2
87	Armenia	27.1
87	Georgia	27.1
89	Spain	27.0
90	Italy	26.7
91	Bolivia	26.6
91	Nicaragua	26.6
93	South Africa	26.6
94	Ecuador	26.5
95	France	25.9
96	Morocco	25.5
97	Argentina	25.3
98	United Kingdom	24.7
99	Bosnia and Herzegovina[1]	23.7
100	Greece	21.7
101	Peru	21.0
102	Colombia	20.5
103	Australia	18.2
104	Brazil	18.0
105	Benin	17.2
106	Albania	16.8
107	Guatemala	16.4
108	Ethiopia	16.2
109	Pakistan	16.0
110	India	16.0
111	Tanzania	15.3
112	Bangladesh	14.8
113	Serbia and Montenegro	13.8
114	Uganda	13.5
115	Japan	13.1
116	United States	10.0
117	East Timor[1]	1.8

SOURCES: Economist Intelligence Unit, IMF Country Reports, and national sources
[1] 2003

Macroeconomic Environment

495

2.19 Imports, 2004

Imports of goods and services as a percentage of GDP, 2004

RANK	COUNTRY	HARD DATA
1	Singapore	193.5
2	Hong Kong SAR	181.3
3	Guyana	132.0
4	Luxembourg	124.6
5	Malaysia	106.0
6	Malta	102.1
7	Estonia	87.1
8	Mongolia	86.7
9	Gambia	81.1
10	Belgium	80.7
11	Moldova	80.0
12	Slovak Republic	79.5
13	Bosnia and Herzegovina[1]	79.1
14	Azerbaijan	77.0
15	United Arab Emirates	75.9
16	Czech Republic	71.7
17	Jordan	71.5
17	Vietnam	71.5
19	Bahrain	68.7
20	Bulgaria	68.7
21	Hungary	68.6
22	Cambodia	65.6
23	Thailand	64.9
24	Ireland	64.7
25	Macedonia, FYR	64.2
26	Taiwan	62.0
27	Tajikistan	61.3
28	Slovenia	60.5
29	Ghana	60.5
30	Jamaica	60.3
31	Honduras	60.2
32	Netherlands	60.0
33	Latvia	59.9
34	Panama	59.4
35	Lithuania	59.2
36	Paraguay	58.0
37	Ukraine	57.6
38	Croatia	55.7
39	Mauritius	55.4
40	Nicaragua	53.6
41	Cyprus	50.8
42	Philippines	50.3
43	Costa Rica	49.9
44	Israel	49.1
45	Namibia	48.5
46	Tunisia	47.9
47	Romania	46.0
48	Austria	45.3
49	Sri Lanka	44.6
50	Madagascar	44.4
51	Armenia	44.3
52	El Salvador	44.2
53	Kazakhstan	44.1
54	Kyrgyz Republic	44.0
55	Georgia	43.5
55	Malawi	43.5
57	Poland	43.2
58	Iceland	42.7
59	Mozambique	42.3

RANK	COUNTRY	HARD DATA
60	Trinidad and Tobago	40.9
61	Ethiopia	39.8
62	Korea	39.7
63	Dominican Republic	39.1
64	China	38.5
64	Nigeria	38.5
66	Portugal	38.5
67	Denmark	38.4
68	Switzerland	38.3
69	Sweden	38.2
70	Kuwait	37.5
71	Albania	36.0
72	Kenya	35.1
73	Zimbabwe	34.9
74	Turkey	34.7
75	Botswana	34.6
76	Canada	33.8
77	Germany	33.1
78	Greece	32.7
79	Mali	32.6
80	Chile	31.9
81	Mexico	31.9
82	Morocco	31.9
83	Finland	31.5
84	Spain	30.7
85	Egypt	29.8
86	New Zealand	29.6
87	Norway	29.5
88	Guatemala	28.9
89	Benin	28.7
90	Ecuador	28.2
91	Uganda	28.2
92	United Kingdom	28.0
93	Uruguay	27.9
94	Cameroon	27.4
95	Algeria	27.1
96	South Africa	27.1
97	Serbia and Montenegro	27.0
98	Indonesia	26.9
99	Italy	25.9
100	Bolivia	25.6
101	France	25.4
102	Qatar	23.4
103	Chad	23.0
104	Tanzania	22.4
105	Colombia	22.3
106	Russian Federation	22.1
107	Bangladesh	21.6
108	Australia	21.2
109	Venezuela	20.3
110	Argentina	18.1
111	Peru	18.1
112	East Timor	17.9
113	India	17.9
114	Pakistan	16.2
115	United States	15.2
116	Brazil	13.3
117	Japan	11.2

SOURCES: Economist Intelligence Unit, IMF Country Reports, *World Economic Outlook Database*, April 2005; International Trade Commission, and national sources

[1] 2003

2.20 Government debt, 2004

Government debt as a percentage of GDP, 2004

RANK	COUNTRY	HARD DATA
1	East Timor	0.0
2	Hong Kong SAR	2.0
3	Estonia	5.5
4	Luxembourg	7.5
5	Botswana	7.9
6	Kazakhstan	12.1
7	Chile	12.2
8	Latvia	14.2
9	Azerbaijan	15.5
10	United Arab Emirates	16.9
11	Korea	17.0
12	Australia	17.2
13	Nigeria	19.3
14	Lithuania	19.6
15	Mexico	20.9
16	Romania	21.4
17	Ukraine	22.1
18	New Zealand	22.5
19	Russian Federation	24.7
20	Macedonia, FYR	26.4
21	Guatemala	27.1
21	Zimbabwe	27.1
23	Mauritius	28.8
24	Slovenia	29.1
25	Kuwait	29.2
26	Czech Republic	30.5
27	Ireland	31.5
28	China	31.8
29	Algeria	32.1
30	Armenia	32.8
31	Taiwan	33.2
32	Norway	33.3
33	Venezuela	36.6
34	South Africa	37.9
35	Thailand	38.8
36	Benin	39.7
37	Tajikistan	40.0
38	Finland	40.1
39	Paraguay	40.3
40	Namibia	41.0
41	Bulgaria	41.1
41	Iceland	41.1
41	United Kingdom	41.1
44	El Salvador	42.4
45	Peru	43.5
46	Slovak Republic	43.6
47	Denmark	43.8
48	Bangladesh	44.6
49	Malaysia	46.2
50	Georgia	46.3
51	Poland	48.4
52	Ecuador	49.1
53	Spain	49.2
53	Trinidad and Tobago	49.2
55	Cambodia	49.4
56	Colombia	49.8
57	Qatar	51.2
58	Sweden	51.3
59	Brazil	51.4

RANK	COUNTRY	HARD DATA
60	Dominican Republic	55.2
61	Albania	55.3
62	Switzerland	56.1
63	Netherlands	56.2
64	Croatia	57.3
65	Indonesia	57.9
66	Bosnia and Herzegovina	58.0
67	Tunisia	58.1
68	Pakistan	59.3
69	India	59.8
70	Costa Rica	60.0
71	Hungary	60.4
72	Portugal	60.6
73	Cameroon	62.0
74	Bahrain	63.0
75	Vietnam	63.6
76	Austria	63.7
76	United States	63.7
78	Germany	65.9
79	France	66.0
79	Mali	66.0
81	Kenya	66.6
82	Moldova	67.0
83	Honduras	68.5
84	Canada	70.8
85	Cyprus	72.1
86	Panama	72.8
87	Malta	73.0
88	Chad[1]	73.3
89	Turkey	73.5
90	Uganda	73.8
91	Morocco	74.0
92	Bolivia	74.6
93	Philippines	78.7
94	Serbia and Montenegro	80.0
95	Jordan	81.5
96	Tanzania	85.1
97	Nicaragua	85.4
98	Mongolia[1]	92.9
99	Madagascar	93.4
100	Ghana	93.9
101	Mozambique[1]	94.3
102	Egypt	95.6
103	Belgium	97.3
104	Kyrgyz Republic	97.9
105	Uruguay	100.7
106	Israel	103.0
107	Singapore	103.3
107	Sri Lanka	103.3
109	Italy	106.2
110	Greece	112.7
111	Argentina	115.9
112	Ethiopia	128.2
113	Jamaica	139.4
114	Japan	163.4
115	Guyana	178.5
116	Gambia	194.5
117	Malawi	238.5

SOURCES: IMF *World Economic Outlook*, Winter 2005 published version; IMF Country Reports; IMF *World Economic Outlook Database, April 2005*; Eurostat; IMF International Finance Statistics, June 2005, and national sources.

[1] 2003

2.21 Country credit rating, 2005

Institutional Investor Country Credit Rating, March 2005

RANK	COUNTRY	HARD DATA
1	Switzerland	94.5
2	Norway	93.7
3	Luxembourg	92.8
4	Finland	92.7
4	United Kingdom	92.7
6	United States	92.4
7	France	92.2
8	Denmark	92.1
9	Netherlands	92.0
10	Germany	91.8
11	Sweden	91.6
12	Austria	91.2
13	Canada	90.9
14	Ireland	90.0
15	Singapore	89.5
16	Belgium	89.0
17	Spain	87.6
18	Australia	86.0
19	Japan	84.4
20	Italy	83.6
21	New Zealand	83.0
22	Portugal	81.6
23	Iceland	77.7
24	Taiwan	77.1
25	Greece	76.0
26	Hong Kong SAR	75.7
27	Slovenia	74.2
28	Korea	72.0
29	United Arab Emirates	71.0
30	Malta	70.5
31	Kuwait	70.2
32	Chile	70.0
33	Qatar	68.9
34	Czech Republic	68.6
35	Malaysia	68.2
36	Cyprus	67.2
37	China	66.0
38	Estonia	65.6
39	Poland	65.4
40	Hungary	65.2
41	Slovak Republic	64.0
42	Thailand	62.4
43	Botswana	62.3
44	Israel	62.0
45	Mexico	61.6
46	Lithuania	61.4
47	Bahrain	60.7
48	Latvia	60.5
49	South Africa	59.9
50	Trinidad and Tobago	59.3
51	Mauritius	57.4
52	Tunisia	55.4
53	India	55.3
54	Russian Federation	55.2
55	Croatia	54.0
56	Bulgaria	52.0
57	Kazakhstan	51.8
58	Morocco	50.7
59	Panama	50.6
60	Costa Rica	50.4
61	Romania	48.4
62	Brazil	46.7
62	El Salvador	46.7
64	Egypt	46.5
65	Colombia	46.3
66	Namibia	45.7
67	Peru	44.9
68	Algeria	44.7
69	Turkey	44.3
70	Jordan	44.0
71	Philippines	43.5
72	Guatemala	40.1
73	Vietnam	38.7
74	Venezuela	37.9
75	Indonesia	37.7
76	Ukraine	37.5
77	Uruguay	37.4
78	Azerbaijan	35.0
79	Sri Lanka	34.4
80	Jamaica	32.8
81	Macedonia, FYR	30.2
82	Pakistan	30.1
83	Ghana	29.7
84	Ecuador	29.5
85	Paraguay	29.4
86	Bangladesh	28.8
87	Bolivia	28.6
88	Honduras	27.6
89	Bosnia and Herzegovina	26.9
89	Tanzania	26.9
91	Nigeria	26.6
92	Dominican Republic	26.5
92	Guyana	26.5
94	Kenya	26.0
95	Mozambique	25.7
96	Albania	24.9
97	Mongolia	24.3
98	Armenia	24.1
98	Serbia and Montenegro	24.1
100	Cameroon	23.8
101	Benin	23.4
102	Mali	22.7
102	Uganda	22.7
104	Chad	20.8
105	Nicaragua	20.6
106	Gambia	20.3
107	Argentina	20.1
107	Cambodia	20.1
109	Kyrgyz Republic	20.0
110	Malawi	19.3
111	Georgia	18.7
112	Madagascar	18.5
113	East Timor	17.7
114	Ethiopia	17.6
115	Moldova	16.0
116	Tajikistan	13.3
117	Zimbabwe	10.6

3.01 Technological readiness

Your country's level of technological readiness (1 = generally lags behind most other countries, 7 = is among the world leaders)

RANK	COUNTRY	SCORE	1 MEAN: 3.7 7	SD
1	United States	6.5		0.9
2	Japan	6.3		0.8
3	Finland	6.3		1.2
4	Israel	6.2		0.9
5	Denmark	6.1		0.8
6	Iceland	6.1		1.0
7	Singapore	6.0		0.9
8	Sweden	6.0		0.9
9	Germany	5.9		1.0
10	Switzerland	5.7		1.1
11	United Kingdom	5.4		1.2
12	Norway	5.4		1.1
13	France	5.4		1.1
14	Taiwan	5.4		1.1
15	Malaysia	5.4		1.1
16	Korea, Rep.	5.3		1.0
17	United Arab Emirates	5.3		0.9
18	Canada	5.3		1.2
19	Australia	5.3		1.1
20	Ireland	5.2		1.1
21	Hong Kong SAR	5.2		1.2
22	New Zealand	5.1		1.1
23	Belgium	5.0		1.3
23	Netherlands	5.0		1.2
25	Austria	4.9		1.3
26	Chile	4.9		1.0
27	Estonia	4.8		1.2
28	India	4.7		1.2
29	Czech Republic	4.6		1.3
30	Bahrain	4.6		1.2
31	Spain	4.6		1.3
32	Qatar	4.4		1.2
33	South Africa	4.4		1.3
34	Malta	4.4		1.2
35	Jordan	4.3		1.3
36	Kuwait	4.2		1.1
37	Venezuela	4.2		1.6
38	Mauritius	4.2		1.1
39	Thailand	4.1		1.1
40	Tunisia	4.1		1.3
41	Slovak Republic	4.1		1.3
42	Italy	4.1		1.6
43	Hungary	4.1		1.1
44	Slovenia	4.0		1.1
45	Argentina	4.0		1.3
46	Cyprus	4.0		1.3
47	Luxembourg	3.9		1.5
48	Costa Rica	3.9		1.4
49	Jamaica	3.8		1.5
50	Portugal	3.8		1.1
51	Turkey	3.8		1.3
52	Uruguay	3.8		1.1
53	Dominican Republic	3.8		1.3
54	Namibia	3.8		1.3
55	Ghana	3.8		1.3
56	Brazil	3.7		1.5
57	Panama	3.7		1.5
58	Mexico	3.7		1.4
59	Poland	3.7		1.1
60	Latvia	3.7		1.3
61	Egypt	3.7		1.5
62	Peru	3.6		1.3
63	El Salvador	3.6		1.2
64	Kazakhstan	3.5		1.3
65	Greece	3.5		1.2
66	Lithuania	3.5		1.3
67	Indonesia	3.4		1.1
68	China	3.4		1.3
69	Botswana	3.4		1.2
70	Colombia	3.4		1.2
71	Trinidad and Tobago	3.3		1.3
72	Azerbaijan	3.1		1.4
73	Romania	3.1		1.3
74	Pakistan	3.1		1.4
75	Guatemala	3.0		1.5
76	Philippines	3.0		1.4
77	Russian Federation	3.0		1.4
78	Ukraine	3.0		1.4
79	Sri Lanka	2.9		1.4
80	Kenya	2.8		1.4
81	Morocco	2.8		1.3
82	Vietnam	2.8		1.2
83	Zimbabwe	2.7		1.3
84	Ecuador	2.7		1.1
85	Algeria	2.7		1.3
86	Nicaragua	2.7		1.2
87	Croatia	2.6		1.3
88	Tanzania	2.6		1.2
89	Honduras	2.6		1.3
90	Bulgaria	2.6		1.3
91	Gambia	2.6		1.3
92	Nigeria	2.6		0.9
93	Mali	2.5		1.3
94	Bolivia	2.5		1.3
95	Bangladesh	2.5		1.2
96	Armenia	2.5		1.2
97	Madagascar	2.4		1.2
98	Mongolia	2.4		1.3
99	Paraguay	2.4		1.3
100	Uganda	2.3		1.4
101	Georgia	2.3		1.2
102	Bosnia and Herzegovina	2.3		1.1
102	Cameroon	2.3		1.3
104	Cambodia	2.2		1.2
105	Malawi	2.2		1.0
106	Tajikistan	2.2		1.3
107	Macedonia, FYR	2.2		1.0
108	Moldova	2.1		1.2
109	Albania	2.1		1.2
110	Mozambique	2.1		1.0
111	Guyana	2.0		1.2
112	Kyrgyz Republic	2.0		1.0
113	Serbia and Montenegro	1.9		1.2
114	Benin	1.9		1.1
115	East Timor	1.9		1.5
116	Ethiopia	1.8		0.9
117	Chad	1.7		1.1

500

3.02 Firm-level technology absorption

Companies in your country are (1 = not able to absorb new technology, 7 = aggressive in absorbing new technology)

RANK	COUNTRY	SCORE	1 MEAN: 4.5 7	SD
1	United States	6.3		0.9
2	Japan	6.2		0.9
3	Iceland	6.2		0.8
4	Taiwan	6.1		0.7
5	Finland	6.1		0.7
5	Israel	6.1		0.8
7	Singapore	5.9		0.9
8	Korea, Rep.	5.8		1.0
9	Denmark	5.7		0.9
10	Ireland	5.7		0.9
11	Sweden	5.7		1.2
12	Austria	5.6		0.8
13	Switzerland	5.6		1.0
14	Germany	5.6		0.9
15	United Arab Emirates	5.6		0.8
16	Malaysia	5.5		0.9
17	Norway	5.5		0.8
18	Hong Kong SAR	5.5		1.2
19	India	5.5		1.1
20	New Zealand	5.4		1.0
21	Australia	5.4		1.0
22	Canada	5.4		1.0
23	United Kingdom	5.3		1.1
24	Slovak Republic	5.3		1.0
25	Czech Republic	5.3		1.0
26	Vietnam	5.3		1.2
27	France	5.3		1.0
28	Hungary	5.2		1.0
29	Turkey	5.2		1.1
30	South Africa	5.2		1.1
31	Kuwait	5.1		1.1
32	Bahrain	5.1		1.3
33	Belgium	5.1		1.1
34	Tunisia	5.0		1.2
35	Estonia	5.0		1.1
36	Netherlands	5.0		1.0
37	China	5.0		1.2
38	Thailand	5.0		1.1
39	Spain	5.0		1.0
40	Chile	4.9		1.1
41	Lithuania	4.9		1.1
42	Luxembourg	4.9		1.0
43	Qatar	4.9		1.2
44	Mauritius	4.8		0.6
45	Jordan	4.8		1.3
46	Brazil	4.8		1.2
47	Pakistan	4.7		1.2
48	Portugal	4.7		1.0
49	Armenia	4.6		1.5
50	Egypt	4.6		1.5
51	Azerbaijan	4.6		1.6
52	Latvia	4.6		1.3
53	Malta	4.6		1.0
54	Cyprus	4.6		1.2
55	Algeria	4.6		1.6
56	Costa Rica	4.6		1.2
57	Kenya	4.5		1.6
58	Madagascar	4.5		1.7
59	Kazakhstan	4.5		1.5

RANK	COUNTRY	SCORE	1 MEAN: 4.5 7	SD
60	Slovenia	4.5		1.1
61	Poland	4.5		1.1
62	Namibia	4.4		1.4
63	Russian Federation	4.4		1.5
64	Philippines	4.4		1.2
65	Jamaica	4.4		1.4
66	Venezuela	4.4		1.8
67	Ghana	4.3		1.3
68	El Salvador	4.3		1.2
69	Romania	4.3		1.2
70	Greece	4.3		1.1
71	Dominican Republic	4.3		1.2
72	Morocco	4.2		1.5
73	Panama	4.2		1.5
74	Trinidad and Tobago	4.2		1.3
75	Mexico	4.2		1.3
76	Bangladesh	4.2		1.6
77	Sri Lanka	4.1		1.5
78	Cameroon	4.1		1.8
79	Zimbabwe	4.1		1.2
80	Botswana	4.1		1.2
81	Tanzania	4.1		1.7
82	Indonesia	4.1		1.2
83	Uganda	4.1		1.6
84	Peru	4.1		1.3
85	Mali	4.1		1.8
86	Ukraine	4.0		1.3
87	Mongolia	4.0		1.3
88	Benin	4.0		2.0
89	Argentina	4.0		1.0
90	Gambia	4.0		1.5
91	Italy	4.0		1.3
92	Colombia	3.9		1.2
93	Guatemala	3.8		1.4
94	Croatia	3.8		1.4
95	Uruguay	3.7		1.1
96	Moldova	3.7		1.7
97	Cambodia	3.6		1.6
98	Nigeria	3.6		1.4
99	Mozambique	3.6		1.4
100	Bulgaria	3.6		1.3
101	Serbia and Montenegro	3.6		1.3
102	Honduras	3.5		1.3
103	Albania	3.5		1.5
104	Tajikistan	3.5		1.5
105	Georgia	3.4		1.2
106	Nicaragua	3.4		1.2
107	Ecuador	3.3		1.0
108	Malawi	3.3		1.2
109	Bolivia	3.1		1.1
110	Macedonia, FYR	3.1		1.5
111	Chad	3.1		2.1
112	Ethiopia	3.0		1.5
113	Guyana	3.0		1.1
114	Bosnia and Herzegovina	3.0		1.3
115	Paraguay	3.0		1.1
116	East Timor	3.0		1.9
117	Kyrgyz Republic	2.8		1.4

3.03 Prevalence of foreign technology licensing

In your country, licensing foreign technology is (1 = uncommon, 7 = a common means of acquiring new technology)

RANK	COUNTRY	SCORE	1 MEAN: 4.3 7	SD
1	Taiwan	5.8		1.0
2	Singapore	5.8		1.1
3	South Africa	5.7		1.0
4	Portugal	5.7		1.1
5	Australia	5.6		1.2
6	Ireland	5.5		1.2
7	India	5.5		1.1
7	New Zealand	5.5		1.0
9	Malaysia	5.5		0.9
10	Hong Kong SAR	5.5		1.2
11	United Kingdom	5.5		1.3
12	Japan	5.4		1.4
13	Israel	5.4		1.0
14	Netherlands	5.4		1.0
15	United Arab Emirates	5.4		1.4
16	Thailand	5.3		1.3
17	Denmark	5.3		1.3
18	Czech Republic	5.2		1.2
19	Philippines	5.2		1.2
20	Bahrain	5.2		1.6
21	Canada	5.2		1.4
22	United States	5.2		1.6
23	Germany	5.1		1.4
24	Spain	5.1		1.4
25	Mauritius	5.1		1.3
26	Switzerland	5.1		1.4
27	Belgium	5.0		1.3
28	Kuwait	5.0		1.4
29	Turkey	5.0		1.3
30	Iceland	5.0		1.3
31	Sweden	5.0		1.3
32	Qatar	4.9		1.6
33	Greece	4.9		1.2
34	Korea, Rep.	4.9		1.4
35	Indonesia	4.9		1.3
36	Norway	4.9		1.4
37	Brazil	4.9		1.5
38	Hungary	4.8		1.2
39	Jordan	4.8		1.7
40	Egypt	4.8		1.5
41	Finland	4.8		1.7
42	Poland	4.8		1.2
43	Kenya	4.8		1.7
44	Tunisia	4.7		1.5
45	Jamaica	4.7		1.4
46	Estonia	4.7		1.4
47	Chile	4.7		1.4
48	France	4.7		1.5
49	Austria	4.7		1.4
50	Italy	4.6		1.5
51	Namibia	4.6		1.5
52	Croatia	4.6		1.5
53	Mexico	4.6		1.6
54	Cyprus	4.5		1.6
54	Ghana	4.5		1.8
56	Trinidad and Tobago	4.5		1.5
57	Slovak Republic	4.5		1.5
58	Romania	4.5		1.5
59	Slovenia	4.5		1.4

RANK	COUNTRY	SCORE	1 MEAN: 4.3 7	SD
60	Luxembourg	4.5		1.4
61	Lithuania	4.4		1.4
62	Malta	4.4		1.7
62	Mozambique	4.4		2.0
64	El Salvador	4.4		1.5
65	Morocco	4.4		1.5
66	Botswana	4.3		1.7
67	Argentina	4.3		1.5
68	Latvia	4.3		1.5
69	Uganda	4.2		2.0
70	Costa Rica	4.2		1.6
71	China	4.2		1.4
72	Mongolia	4.1		1.7
73	Zimbabwe	4.0		1.5
74	Panama	4.0		1.7
75	Tanzania	3.9		1.9
76	Nigeria	3.9		1.4
77	Dominican Republic	3.9		1.6
78	Colombia	3.9		1.8
79	Albania	3.9		1.8
80	Sri Lanka	3.9		1.6
81	Venezuela	3.9		1.8
82	Kazakhstan	3.8		1.5
83	Bangladesh	3.8		1.7
84	Peru	3.8		1.3
85	Malawi	3.8		1.8
86	Uruguay	3.7		1.5
87	Gambia	3.7		1.9
88	Pakistan	3.7		1.6
89	Bulgaria	3.6		1.5
90	Georgia	3.6		1.7
91	East Timor	3.6		2.0
92	Ecuador	3.6		1.5
93	Azerbaijan	3.5		1.6
93	Madagascar	3.5		1.9
95	Guatemala	3.4		1.6
96	Ukraine	3.4		1.5
97	Mali	3.4		1.8
98	Cambodia	3.4		1.9
99	Honduras	3.4		1.7
100	Bosnia and Herzegovina	3.3		1.7
101	Russian Federation	3.3		1.6
102	Serbia and Montenegro	3.3		1.9
103	Armenia	3.2		1.7
104	Cameroon	3.2		1.8
105	Macedonia, FYR	3.2		1.8
106	Algeria	3.0		1.8
107	Nicaragua	3.0		1.4
108	Tajikistan	3.0		1.7
109	Vietnam	2.9		1.6
110	Moldova	2.9		1.8
111	Ethiopia	2.7		1.8
112	Paraguay	2.6		1.3
113	Bolivia	2.6		1.3
114	Guyana	2.5		1.6
115	Benin	2.5		1.8
116	Kyrgyz Republic	2.3		1.5
117	Chad	2.3		1.7

3.04 FDI and technology transfer

Foreign direct investment (FDI) in your country (1 = brings little new technology, 7 = is an important source of new technology)

RANK	COUNTRY	SCORE	1 MEAN: 4.7 7	SD
1	Ireland	6.4		0.9
2	Singapore	6.2		0.9
3	Czech Republic	5.9		0.9
4	Slovak Republic	5.9		1.1
5	Costa Rica	5.7		1.1
6	Malaysia	5.7		0.8
7	Hungary	5.6		1.4
8	Qatar	5.6		1.3
9	Kenya	5.5		1.6
10	Serbia and Montenegro	5.5		1.7
11	Hong Kong SAR	5.4		1.2
12	Romania	5.4		1.3
13	Estonia	5.4		1.3
14	Portugal	5.4		1.0
15	Uganda	5.4		1.7
16	United Kingdom	5.4		1.1
17	Jamaica	5.4		1.3
18	Chile	5.4		1.2
19	Malta	5.4		1.4
20	Ghana	5.4		1.5
21	Israel	5.3		1.3
22	Egypt	5.3		1.7
23	Thailand	5.3		1.0
24	Mozambique	5.3		1.6
25	Taiwan	5.3		1.1
26	Luxembourg	5.3		1.5
27	Denmark	5.2		1.2
28	Canada	5.2		1.3
29	Mexico	5.2		1.4
30	Peru	5.2		1.2
31	Brazil	5.2		1.5
32	Trinidad and Tobago	5.1		1.4
33	New Zealand	5.1		1.1
34	India	5.1		1.3
35	Panama	5.1		1.5
36	Poland	5.1		1.3
37	Philippines	5.1		1.6
38	Spain	5.1		1.3
39	South Africa	5.1		1.3
40	Pakistan	5.1		1.7
41	Tanzania	5.0		1.7
42	Australia	5.0		1.3
43	Indonesia	5.0		1.4
44	United Arab Emirates	4.9		1.3
45	Netherlands	4.9		1.3
46	Vietnam	4.9		1.8
47	France	4.9		1.3
48	Dominican Republic	4.9		1.7
49	Bahrain	4.9		1.7
50	Latvia	4.8		1.4
51	Belgium	4.8		1.4
52	Jordan	4.8		1.5
53	Honduras	4.8		1.5
54	Argentina	4.8		1.5
55	Mauritius	4.8		1.5
56	Korea, Rep.	4.8		1.3
57	China	4.7		1.4
58	Guatemala	4.7		1.6
59	Turkey	4.7		1.4

RANK	COUNTRY	SCORE	1 MEAN: 4.7 7	SD
60	Austria	4.7		1.1
61	Morocco	4.7		1.6
62	Sri Lanka	4.7		1.9
63	Switzerland	4.7		1.4
64	Nigeria	4.7		1.5
65	Bulgaria	4.6		1.9
66	Armenia	4.6		1.9
67	Japan	4.6		1.5
68	Cambodia	4.6		2.1
69	Botswana	4.6		1.7
70	Colombia	4.6		1.5
71	Georgia	4.6		2.0
72	Norway	4.6		1.1
73	Lithuania	4.5		1.6
74	El Salvador	4.5		1.5
74	Tunisia	4.5		1.5
76	Uruguay	4.4		1.4
77	United States	4.4		1.6
78	Sweden	4.4		1.4
79	Kuwait	4.4		1.6
80	Gambia	4.4		1.9
81	Nicaragua	4.4		1.9
81	Venezuela	4.4		1.8
83	Bangladesh	4.4		1.9
84	Germany	4.4		1.5
85	Namibia	4.3		1.9
86	Mongolia	4.3		1.9
87	Greece	4.3		1.6
88	Moldova	4.3		1.9
89	Kazakhstan	4.3		1.6
90	Ethiopia	4.2		2.0
91	Albania	4.2		1.9
92	Tajikistan	4.1		1.9
93	Azerbaijan	4.1		1.7
94	Cyprus	4.1		1.5
95	Ecuador	4.1		1.5
96	East Timor	4.0		2.2
97	Malawi	4.0		1.7
98	Russian Federation	4.0		1.7
99	Slovenia	4.0		1.4
100	Bolivia	3.9		1.6
101	Guyana	3.9		1.7
102	Zimbabwe	3.9		2.1
103	Italy	3.9		1.5
104	Finland	3.9		1.6
105	Paraguay	3.9		1.8
106	Macedonia, FYR	3.9		2.0
107	Iceland	3.8		1.4
108	Madagascar	3.8		1.7
109	Croatia	3.8		1.7
110	Mali	3.8		1.9
111	Ukraine	3.7		1.5
112	Kyrgyz Republic	3.5		1.8
113	Cameroon	3.4		1.7
114	Bosnia and Herzegovina	3.3		1.7
115	Algeria	3.0		1.8
116	Benin	2.8		1.8
117	Chad	2.8		1.8

3.05   Quality of scientific research institutions

Scientific research institutions in your country (e.g. university laboratories, government laboratories) are (1 = nonexistent, 7 = the best in their fields internationally)

RANK	COUNTRY	SCORE	1 MEAN: 3.8 7	SD
1	United States	6.4		0.9
2	Switzerland	5.9		0.9
3	United Kingdom	5.8		0.9
4	Israel	5.8		1.0
5	Germany	5.7		0.9
6	Finland	5.7		0.8
7	Japan	5.6		1.1
8	Singapore	5.5		0.9
9	Netherlands	5.5		0.9
10	France	5.5		1.0
11	Canada	5.5		1.0
12	Sweden	5.4		0.9
13	Belgium	5.4		0.9
14	Australia	5.3		1.0
15	Denmark	5.3		1.0
16	Taiwan	5.2		0.9
17	India	5.1		1.1
18	New Zealand	5.1		0.9
19	Korea, Rep.	5.1		1.2
20	Ireland	5.0		1.3
21	Hungary	5.0		0.9
22	Malaysia	5.0		1.0
23	Hong Kong SAR	4.9		1.0
24	Austria	4.8		1.1
25	Norway	4.8		1.1
26	South Africa	4.7		1.2
27	Iceland	4.7		0.8
28	Czech Republic	4.6		1.2
29	Portugal	4.5		0.9
30	Ghana	4.5		1.2
31	Russian Federation	4.4		1.4
32	Kenya	4.4		1.5
33	Estonia	4.4		1.2
34	Costa Rica	4.3		1.0
35	Botswana	4.2		1.2
36	Uganda	4.2		1.5
37	Slovenia	4.2		1.1
38	Jamaica	4.1		1.1
39	Brazil	4.1		1.2
40	Lithuania	4.1		1.3
41	Thailand	4.0		1.2
42	Tunisia	4.0		1.2
43	Spain	4.0		1.2
44	Argentina	4.0		1.3
45	Kuwait	4.0		1.4
46	Azerbaijan	3.9		1.7
47	Ukraine	3.9		1.4
48	Chile	3.9		1.1
49	Indonesia	3.9		1.2
50	Mauritius	3.9		1.2
51	Qatar	3.9		1.5
52	Kazakhstan	3.8		1.4
53	Bulgaria	3.8		1.6
54	Poland	3.8		1.2
55	China	3.8		1.3
56	Turkey	3.8		1.3
57	Mexico	3.7		1.2
58	Jordan	3.7		1.4
59	Armenia	3.7		1.5
60	Croatia	3.7		1.3
61	Serbia and Montenegro	3.7		1.3
62	Sri Lanka	3.7		1.5
63	Pakistan	3.7		1.6
64	Tajikistan	3.6		1.5
65	Tanzania	3.5		1.5
66	Zimbabwe	3.5		1.3
67	Greece	3.5		1.1
68	Uruguay	3.5		1.1
69	Trinidad and Tobago	3.5		1.3
70	Mozambique	3.5		1.7
71	Slovak Republic	3.5		1.1
72	Mali	3.5		1.4
73	Latvia	3.4		1.2
74	Cyprus	3.4		1.4
75	Egypt	3.4		1.5
76	Colombia	3.4		1.2
77	Italy	3.3		1.4
78	Bangladesh	3.3		1.4
79	United Arab Emirates	3.3		1.3
80	Philippines	3.3		1.3
81	Vietnam	3.3		1.1
82	Moldova	3.2		1.4
83	Macedonia, FYR	3.2		1.3
84	Luxembourg	3.2		1.4
85	Georgia	3.2		1.3
86	Nigeria	3.2		1.2
87	Romania	3.2		1.2
88	Ethiopia	3.2		1.2
89	Mongolia	3.2		1.4
90	Morocco	3.1		1.5
91	Malawi	3.1		1.4
92	Cameroon	3.1		1.3
93	Panama	3.1		1.3
94	Madagascar	3.1		1.3
95	Venezuela	3.1		1.3
96	Namibia	3.0		1.2
97	Algeria	3.0		1.3
98	Gambia	3.0		1.4
99	Guatemala	2.9		1.2
100	Benin	2.9		1.4
101	Bosnia and Herzegovina	2.8		1.4
102	Guyana	2.8		1.1
103	Nicaragua	2.8		1.0
104	Peru	2.8		0.9
105	Ecuador	2.7		0.9
106	Malta	2.7		1.2
107	Honduras	2.6		1.0
108	Bolivia	2.5		1.0
109	Kyrgyz Republic	2.5		1.3
110	El Salvador	2.5		1.1
111	Cambodia	2.4		1.3
112	Bahrain	2.3		1.2
113	Chad	2.3		1.3
114	Dominican Republic	2.2		0.9
115	East Timor	2.1		1.3
116	Albania	2.1		1.1
117	Paraguay	2.1		0.8

3.06   Company spending on research and development

Companies in your country (1 = do not spend money on research and development, 7 = spend heavily on research and development relative to international peers)

RANK	COUNTRY	SCORE	1 MEAN: 3.3 7	SD
1	United States	5.9		1.1
2	Japan	5.8		1.0
3	Germany	5.8		0.8
4	Switzerland	5.6		1.3
5	Israel	5.5		0.9
6	Finland	5.4		1.0
7	Sweden	5.3		1.1
8	Korea, Rep.	5.2		1.1
9	Denmark	5.2		0.9
10	Singapore	5.0		1.1
11	United Kingdom	5.0		1.2
12	Taiwan	5.0		1.0
13	France	4.8		1.1
14	Iceland	4.7		1.1
15	Belgium	4.7		1.0
16	Canada	4.7		1.1
17	Netherlands	4.6		1.0
18	Malaysia	4.6		1.3
19	Austria	4.5		1.1
20	Luxembourg	4.3		1.3
21	Ireland	4.2		1.3
22	South Africa	4.1		1.1
23	Norway	4.1		1.2
24	New Zealand	4.0		1.0
25	Czech Republic	3.9		1.4
26	Hong Kong SAR	3.8		1.3
27	India	3.8		1.2
28	Australia	3.8		1.3
29	Brazil	3.8		1.3
30	Slovenia	3.7		1.1
31	China	3.6		1.4
32	Spain	3.6		1.0
33	Kenya	3.6		1.8
34	Costa Rica	3.5		1.2
35	Poland	3.5		1.1
36	Estonia	3.4		1.2
37	Thailand	3.4		1.3
38	Ukraine	3.4		1.5
39	Colombia	3.4		1.2
40	Tunisia	3.4		1.5
41	Azerbaijan	3.3		1.8
42	Portugal	3.3		1.1
43	Russian Federation	3.3		1.5
44	Kazakhstan	3.3		1.4
45	Indonesia	3.3		1.1
46	Lithuania	3.3		1.3
47	Chile	3.2		1.1
48	Latvia	3.2		1.3
49	Hungary	3.2		1.2
50	Jamaica	3.2		0.9
51	Panama	3.2		1.4
52	Greece	3.2		1.2
53	Uganda	3.1		1.6
54	Turkey	3.1		1.1
55	Vietnam	3.1		1.2
56	Slovak Republic	3.1		1.1
57	Ghana	3.1		1.3
58	Argentina	3.0		1.0
59	Botswana	3.0		1.4

RANK	COUNTRY	SCORE	1 MEAN: 3.3 7	SD
59	Mauritius	3.0		1.3
59	Pakistan	3.0		1.5
62	United Arab Emirates	3.0		1.3
63	Mexico	3.0		1.1
64	Namibia	3.0		1.2
65	Zimbabwe	3.0		1.2
66	Malawi	2.9		1.3
66	Philippines	2.9		1.2
68	Nigeria	2.9		1.1
69	Jordan	2.9		1.3
70	Morocco	2.9		1.5
71	Italy	2.9		1.2
72	Romania	2.9		1.3
73	Egypt	2.8		1.5
74	Cyprus	2.8		1.2
75	El Salvador	2.8		1.2
76	Trinidad and Tobago	2.8		1.3
77	Sri Lanka	2.8		1.3
78	Croatia	2.8		1.1
79	Bulgaria	2.8		1.3
80	Mongolia	2.8		1.3
81	Tajikistan	2.8		1.4
82	Tanzania	2.7		1.4
83	Cameroon	2.7		1.5
84	Madagascar	2.7		1.4
85	Macedonia, FYR	2.6		1.4
86	Uruguay	2.6		0.8
87	Venezuela	2.6		0.9
88	Guatemala	2.6		1.1
89	Mali	2.6		1.4
90	Ecuador	2.6		1.0
91	Armenia	2.6		1.1
92	Serbia and Montenegro	2.6		1.2
93	Peru	2.6		0.9
94	Kuwait	2.6		1.2
94	Qatar	2.6		1.5
96	Malta	2.5		0.9
97	Dominican Republic	2.5		1.1
98	Moldova	2.5		1.4
99	Bangladesh	2.5		1.3
100	Mozambique	2.5		1.2
101	Algeria	2.5		1.4
102	Georgia	2.5		1.2
103	Guyana	2.4		0.9
104	Cambodia	2.4		1.4
105	Bosnia and Herzegovina	2.4		1.2
106	Gambia	2.4		1.5
107	Honduras	2.4		1.0
108	Nicaragua	2.3		0.9
109	Albania	2.3		1.3
110	Bolivia	2.3		1.1
111	East Timor	2.2		1.6
112	Ethiopia	2.1		1.1
113	Benin	2.1		1.4
114	Paraguay	2.1		0.8
115	Bahrain	2.1		1.0
116	Chad	2.0		1.3
117	Kyrgyz Republic	1.9		1.1

3.07　University/industry research collaboration

In its R&D activity, business collaboration with local universities is (1 = minimal or nonexistent, 7 = intensive and ongoing)

RANK	COUNTRY	SCORE	SD
1	United States	5.7	1.2
2	Finland	5.4	1.3
3	Switzerland	5.1	1.3
4	Germany	5.1	1.2
5	Singapore	5.0	1.3
6	Sweden	5.0	1.4
7	United Kingdom	5.0	1.1
8	Taiwan	4.9	1.2
9	Denmark	4.9	1.3
10	Korea, Rep.	4.8	1.3
11	Israel	4.7	1.2
12	Malaysia	4.7	1.2
13	Canada	4.7	1.3
14	Belgium	4.6	1.2
15	Japan	4.6	1.3
16	Netherlands	4.6	1.2
17	France	4.5	1.4
18	Iceland	4.4	1.1
19	Austria	4.4	1.4
20	Ireland	4.3	1.1
21	South Africa	4.2	1.3
22	Norway	4.2	1.5
23	Australia	4.1	1.3
24	Hong Kong SAR	4.1	1.3
25	New Zealand	4.1	1.0
26	China	3.9	1.5
27	Czech Republic	3.9	1.5
28	Thailand	3.6	1.4
29	Slovak Republic	3.5	1.4
30	Colombia	3.5	1.2
31	Portugal	3.5	1.2
32	Slovenia	3.5	1.4
33	Costa Rica	3.4	1.4
34	Estonia	3.4	1.2
35	Indonesia	3.4	1.1
36	India	3.3	1.3
37	Spain	3.3	1.4
38	Hungary	3.3	1.9
39	Poland	3.2	1.4
40	Brazil	3.2	1.4
41	Kenya	3.2	1.8
42	Russian Federation	3.2	1.5
43	Jamaica	3.2	1.3
44	Tunisia	3.2	1.4
45	Chile	3.1	1.2
46	Ukraine	3.1	1.6
47	Lithuania	3.1	1.4
48	Uganda	3.1	1.8
49	Turkey	3.1	1.2
50	Mexico	3.0	1.3
51	Serbia and Montenegro	3.0	1.5
52	Argentina	3.0	1.3
53	Azerbaijan	3.0	1.7
54	Kazakhstan	3.0	1.4
54	Panama	3.0	1.2
54	Tanzania	3.0	1.6
57	Ghana	3.0	1.3
58	Greece	3.0	1.3
59	Croatia	2.9	1.4

RANK	COUNTRY	SCORE	SD
60	Kuwait	2.9	1.3
61	Latvia	2.9	1.4
62	Mauritius	2.9	1.5
63	Venezuela	2.9	1.6
64	Zimbabwe	2.8	1.5
65	Jordan	2.8	1.5
66	Italy	2.8	1.4
67	Mongolia	2.8	1.4
68	Philippines	2.7	1.3
69	Botswana	2.7	1.1
70	Vietnam	2.7	1.4
71	Nigeria	2.7	1.1
72	Pakistan	2.7	1.4
73	Luxembourg	2.7	1.4
74	Qatar	2.6	1.7
75	United Arab Emirates	2.6	1.3
76	Bosnia and Herzegovina	2.6	1.5
77	Macedonia, FYR	2.6	1.4
78	Cyprus	2.6	1.1
78	Uruguay	2.6	1.2
80	Trinidad and Tobago	2.6	1.2
81	Egypt	2.6	1.5
82	Armenia	2.5	1.4
83	Sri Lanka	2.5	1.4
84	Tajikistan	2.5	1.4
85	Mozambique	2.5	1.3
86	Bulgaria	2.5	1.3
87	Cameroon	2.5	1.4
88	Namibia	2.5	1.1
89	Peru	2.5	1.0
90	Nicaragua	2.4	1.1
91	Mali	2.4	1.3
92	Guatemala	2.4	1.3
93	Romania	2.4	1.3
94	Moldova	2.4	1.4
95	Madagascar	2.4	1.2
96	Cambodia	2.4	1.4
97	Malawi	2.3	1.1
98	Ecuador	2.3	1.0
99	Honduras	2.3	1.2
100	El Salvador	2.3	1.2
101	Georgia	2.2	0.9
102	Malta	2.2	1.0
103	Morocco	2.1	1.0
104	East Timor	2.1	1.4
105	Bangladesh	2.1	1.4
106	Algeria	2.1	1.1
107	Ethiopia	2.1	1.2
108	Dominican Republic	2.1	1.0
109	Bolivia	2.0	1.2
110	Gambia	1.9	1.1
111	Guyana	1.9	0.9
112	Bahrain	1.9	1.0
113	Kyrgyz Republic	1.8	1.1
114	Chad	1.8	1.2
115	Benin	1.8	1.1
116	Paraguay	1.7	0.8
117	Albania	1.7	1.1

MEAN: 3.1

3.08 Government procurement of advanced technology products

Government purchase decisions for the procurement of advanced technology products are (1 = based solely on price, 7 = based on technical performance and innovativeness)

RANK	COUNTRY	SCORE	1 MEAN: 3.7 7	SD	RANK	COUNTRY	SCORE	1 MEAN: 3.7 7	SD
1	Singapore	5.3		1.1	60	Slovenia	3.6		1.4
2	Taiwan	5.3		1.1	61	Colombia	3.6		1.4
3	Malaysia	5.1		1.2	62	Benin	3.6		1.8
4	France	4.9		1.0	63	Lithuania	3.5		1.4
5	Israel	4.9		1.0	64	Azerbaijan	3.5		1.5
6	Japan	4.9		1.2	65	Italy	3.5		1.4
7	Tunisia	4.8		1.4	66	Zimbabwe	3.5		1.5
8	United States	4.8		1.3	67	Macedonia, FYR	3.5		1.7
9	Finland	4.8		1.4	68	Russian Federation	3.5		1.5
10	Korea, Rep.	4.8		1.3	69	Croatia	3.5		1.5
11	China	4.6		1.1	70	El Salvador	3.5		1.3
12	Denmark	4.6		1.2	71	Romania	3.5		1.4
13	Switzerland	4.6		1.3	72	Turkey	3.5		1.3
14	United Arab Emirates	4.5		1.1	73	Mexico	3.5		1.3
15	Germany	4.4		1.2	74	Greece	3.5		1.3
16	Hong Kong SAR	4.3		1.4	75	Sri Lanka	3.4		1.6
17	Ghana	4.3		1.3	76	Venezuela	3.4		1.5
18	Vietnam	4.2		1.5	77	Armenia	3.4		1.7
19	Qatar	4.2		1.6	78	Malta	3.4		1.3
20	Netherlands	4.2		1.2	79	Morocco	3.4		1.6
21	Luxembourg	4.2		1.5	80	Bahrain	3.4		1.6
22	Canada	4.2		1.3	81	Jamaica	3.4		1.4
23	Thailand	4.2		1.2	82	Cameroon	3.3		1.6
24	Austria	4.2		1.5	83	Poland	3.3		1.3
25	Uganda	4.2		1.9	84	Bulgaria	3.3		1.5
26	Tanzania	4.2		1.8	85	Argentina	3.3		1.3
27	New Zealand	4.2		0.9	86	Costa Rica	3.3		1.4
28	Iceland	4.2		1.1	87	Ukraine	3.3		1.4
29	South Africa	4.1		1.3	88	Namibia	3.3		1.2
30	Botswana	4.1		1.4	88	Philippines	3.3		1.3
31	Mali	4.1		1.6	90	Panama	3.2		1.4
32	Norway	4.1		1.3	91	Guyana	3.2		1.4
33	Portugal	4.1		1.1	92	Gambia	3.2		1.7
34	Ireland	4.1		1.3	93	Egypt	3.2		1.6
35	Sweden	4.0		1.4	94	Latvia	3.2		1.3
36	United Kingdom	4.0		1.2	95	Ethiopia	3.1		1.6
37	Czech Republic	4.0		1.4	96	Malawi	3.1		1.3
38	Nigeria	4.0		1.4	97	Bangladesh	3.1		1.6
39	Indonesia	4.0		0.9	98	Dominican Republic	3.1		1.2
40	Spain	3.9		1.2	99	Uruguay	3.1		1.1
41	India	3.9		1.4	100	Kuwait	3.1		1.8
42	Mauritius	3.9		1.5	101	Cambodia	3.1		1.3
43	Chile	3.9		1.4	102	Tajikistan	3.1		1.7
44	Brazil	3.8		1.4	103	Moldova	3.0		1.6
45	Kazakhstan	3.8		1.5	104	Peru	3.0		1.3
46	Australia	3.8		1.3	105	Mongolia	3.0		1.5
47	Trinidad and Tobago	3.8		1.3	106	Georgia	3.0		1.4
48	Algeria	3.8		1.5	107	Nicaragua	2.9		1.2
49	Estonia	3.8		1.5	108	Chad	2.9		1.8
50	Serbia and Montenegro	3.8		1.6	109	Honduras	2.9		1.3
51	Cyprus	3.8		1.4	110	Bosnia and Herzegovina	2.8		1.3
52	Pakistan	3.8		1.5	111	Guatemala	2.7		1.4
53	Mozambique	3.7		1.6	112	East Timor	2.6		1.7
54	Jordan	3.7		1.6	113	Ecuador	2.5		1.2
55	Kenya	3.7		1.5	114	Bolivia	2.5		1.3
56	Slovak Republic	3.6		1.4	115	Paraguay	2.4		1.2
57	Hungary	3.6		1.0	116	Kyrgyz Republic	2.3		1.4
58	Madagascar	3.6		1.6	117	Albania	2.2		1.3
59	Belgium	3.6		1.5					

3.09 Availability of scientists and engineers

Scientists and engineers in your country are (1 = nonexistent or rare, 7 = widely available)

RANK	COUNTRY	SCORE	1 MEAN: 4.5 7	SD
1	India	6.4		0.7
2	Finland	6.2		0.7
3	Japan	6.2		0.8
4	Israel	6.2		0.7
5	France	6.0		1.0
6	Czech Republic	6.0		1.0
7	Singapore	5.9		0.9
8	Canada	5.9		1.0
9	Switzerland	5.9		1.0
10	Taiwan	5.8		0.8
11	Tunisia	5.7		1.0
12	Denmark	5.7		1.1
13	United States	5.7		1.1
14	Jordan	5.7		1.2
14	Sweden	5.7		1.0
16	Slovak Republic	5.6		1.0
17	Hungary	5.6		1.1
18	Germany	5.6		1.1
19	Iceland	5.6		0.8
20	Austria	5.5		1.1
21	Greece	5.5		1.0
22	Belgium	5.5		1.3
23	Ireland	5.4		1.2
24	Cyprus	5.4		1.4
25	Cameroon	5.3		1.4
26	Armenia	5.3		1.4
27	Australia	5.3		1.2
28	Algeria	5.2		1.4
29	Poland	5.2		1.2
30	Malaysia	5.2		1.0
31	Bulgaria	5.1		1.4
32	Egypt	5.1		1.4
33	Korea, Rep.	5.1		1.2
34	Hong Kong SAR	5.1		1.2
35	Lithuania	5.1		1.2
36	Norway	5.1		1.1
37	Netherlands	5.0		1.4
38	Spain	5.0		1.2
39	Vietnam	5.0		1.4
40	Romania	5.0		1.3
41	United Kingdom	5.0		1.3
42	Turkey	5.0		1.2
43	Ghana	5.0		1.1
44	Russian Federation	4.9		1.5
45	Macedonia, FYR	4.9		1.7
46	Serbia and Montenegro	4.9		1.4
47	Argentina	4.9		1.4
48	Costa Rica	4.9		1.2
49	Portugal	4.9		1.3
50	Estonia	4.8		1.1
51	Georgia	4.8		1.3
52	Chile	4.8		1.2
53	Morocco	4.8		1.6
54	Italy	4.7		1.3
54	Venezuela	4.7		1.7
56	Nigeria	4.7		1.2
57	New Zealand	4.7		1.3
58	Kenya	4.6		1.5
59	Kuwait	4.6		1.5
60	Bangladesh	4.6		1.5
61	Ukraine	4.6		1.8
62	Croatia	4.6		1.4
63	Azerbaijan	4.5		1.6
64	Sri Lanka	4.5		1.3
65	Uruguay	4.5		1.4
66	Indonesia	4.5		1.1
67	Pakistan	4.5		1.5
68	China	4.4		1.3
69	Thailand	4.4		1.2
70	Trinidad and Tobago	4.4		1.5
71	Madagascar	4.3		1.7
72	Brazil	4.3		1.6
73	Qatar	4.3		1.5
74	Mali	4.2		1.8
75	Moldova	4.2		1.7
76	Mongolia	4.2		1.5
77	Malta	4.1		1.4
78	Luxembourg	4.1		1.4
79	Benin	4.1		1.8
80	United Arab Emirates	4.1		1.4
81	Panama	4.0		1.4
82	Slovenia	4.0		1.3
83	Bosnia and Herzegovina	3.9		1.6
84	Albania	3.9		1.5
85	Tanzania	3.9		1.6
86	Philippines	3.9		1.5
87	Colombia	3.8		1.4
88	Kazakhstan	3.8		1.7
89	Jamaica	3.8		1.5
90	South Africa	3.8		1.3
91	Botswana	3.8		1.3
92	Mexico	3.8		1.3
93	Zimbabwe	3.8		1.4
94	Bahrain	3.7		1.6
95	Mauritius	3.7		1.6
96	Peru	3.7		1.4
97	Tajikistan	3.7		1.7
98	Uganda	3.6		1.6
99	Latvia	3.6		1.3
100	Nicaragua	3.6		1.7
101	Ecuador	3.6		1.4
102	Bolivia	3.5		1.3
103	Dominican Republic	3.5		1.5
104	Malawi	3.3		1.4
105	Kyrgyz Republic	3.1		1.8
106	Ethiopia	3.1		1.3
107	Honduras	3.1		1.5
108	Namibia	3.1		1.4
109	Mozambique	3.1		1.3
110	Guatemala	3.1		1.4
111	Guyana	2.9		1.1
112	El Salvador	2.9		1.2
113	Paraguay	2.8		1.3
114	Chad	2.6		1.6
115	Cambodia	2.5		1.0
116	Gambia	2.5		1.1
117	East Timor	2.5		1.5

3.10 Availability of mobile or cellular telephones

Mobile or cellular telephones for your business are (1 = not available, 7 = as accessible and affordable as in the world's most technologically advanced countries)

RANK	COUNTRY	SCORE	MEAN: 6.1	SD		RANK	COUNTRY	SCORE	MEAN: 6.1	SD
1	Germany	6.9		0.3		60	Latvia	6.3		0.9
2	Austria	6.9		0.3		61	South Africa	6.3		0.8
3	Israel	6.9		0.3		62	Sri Lanka	6.2		1.1
4	Finland	6.9		0.3		63	Bolivia	6.2		1.1
5	Hong Kong SAR	6.9		0.4		64	Malta	6.2		0.8
6	Estonia	6.8		0.4		65	Nicaragua	6.2		1.0
7	Denmark	6.8		0.5		66	Botswana	6.1		0.8
8	Chile	6.8		0.4		67	Ireland	6.1		1.0
9	Portugal	6.8		0.4		68	Paraguay	6.1		1.3
10	Japan	6.8		0.6		69	Mexico	6.0		1.0
11	El Salvador	6.8		0.5		70	Morocco	6.0		1.6
12	Iceland	6.8		0.6		71	Algeria	6.0		1.0
13	Sweden	6.8		0.6		72	Panama	6.0		1.4
14	France	6.7		0.5		73	Qatar	6.0		1.1
15	Singapore	6.7		0.5		74	Russian Federation	5.9		1.2
16	Czech Republic	6.7		0.7		75	Bulgaria	5.9		1.3
17	Norway	6.7		0.5		76	Vietnam	5.9		1.0
18	Dominican Republic	6.7		0.5		77	Ghana	5.9		1.0
19	Switzerland	6.7		0.6		78	Namibia	5.9		1.1
20	Netherlands	6.7		0.6		79	Bangladesh	5.9		1.0
21	United Kingdom	6.7		0.6		80	Egypt	5.9		1.1
22	United States	6.7		0.5		81	Azerbaijan	5.9		1.3
23	Philippines	6.7		0.5		82	Honduras	5.8		1.4
24	Luxembourg	6.7		0.7		83	Macedonia, FYR	5.8		1.2
25	Cyprus	6.7		0.6		84	Moldova	5.8		1.4
26	Hungary	6.7		0.6		85	Uganda	5.8		1.1
27	Jamaica	6.7		0.5		86	Kazakhstan	5.7		1.5
28	Slovak Republic	6.7		0.5		87	Kenya	5.7		1.1
29	Canada	6.7		0.6		88	Poland	5.7		1.4
30	Belgium	6.6		0.7		89	Ecuador	5.7		1.5
31	India	6.6		0.6		90	Gambia	5.7		1.1
32	Jordan	6.6		0.6		91	Serbia and Montenegro	5.6		1.2
33	Kuwait	6.6		1.0		92	Malawi	5.6		1.0
34	Spain	6.6		0.7		93	Tanzania	5.6		1.5
35	Slovenia	6.6		0.7		94	Romania	5.5		1.9
36	Greece	6.6		0.7		95	China	5.5		1.4
37	United Arab Emirates	6.6		0.7		96	Guyana	5.4		1.3
38	Lithuania	6.6		0.7		97	Mozambique	5.4		1.3
39	Venezuela	6.5		0.6		98	Mali	5.4		1.6
40	Croatia	6.5		0.7		99	Bosnia and Herzegovina	5.4		1.4
41	Australia	6.5		0.7		100	Albania	5.4		1.5
42	Italy	6.5		0.9		101	Indonesia	5.3		1.0
43	Turkey	6.5		0.9		102	Nigeria	5.3		1.2
44	Georgia	6.5		0.7		103	Ukraine	5.2		1.1
45	Peru	6.5		0.7		104	Tajikistan	5.2		1.6
46	Bahrain	6.4		1.0		105	Trinidad and Tobago	5.2		1.3
47	Mauritius	6.4		0.6		106	Cambodia	5.2		1.6
48	Brazil	6.4		1.0		107	Kyrgyz Republic	5.2		1.5
49	Korea, Rep.	6.4		0.9		108	Cameroon	5.2		1.6
50	Uruguay	6.4		0.8		109	East Timor	5.2		1.6
51	Thailand	6.4		0.7		110	Madagascar	5.1		1.5
52	Taiwan	6.4		0.9		111	Mongolia	5.0		1.6
53	Pakistan	6.3		0.7		112	Zimbabwe	4.7		1.0
54	Malaysia	6.3		0.7		113	Chad	4.5		2.0
55	Argentina	6.3		0.7		114	Benin	4.4		1.8
56	Colombia	6.3		0.9		115	Ethiopia	3.6		1.4
57	Tunisia	6.3		0.9		116	Costa Rica	3.1		1.8
58	New Zealand	6.3		0.8		117	Armenia	2.9		1.7
59	Guatemala	6.3		1.1						

3.11   Internet access in schools

Internet access in schools is (1 = very limited, 7 = extensive—most children have frequent access)

RANK	COUNTRY	SCORE	1 MEAN: 3.8 7	SD
1	Iceland	6.7		0.5
2	Finland	6.6		0.7
3	Denmark	6.4		0.8
4	Singapore	6.4		0.8
5	Estonia	6.3		0.9
6	Korea, Rep.	6.2		1.0
7	Austria	6.2		0.9
8	Netherlands	6.1		0.7
9	Hong Kong SAR	6.1		1.0
10	Sweden	6.1		1.2
11	Taiwan	6.0		0.8
12	Australia	6.0		0.9
13	United States	6.0		1.0
14	Canada	5.9		1.0
15	Switzerland	5.9		1.2
16	United Kingdom	5.8		1.1
17	Luxembourg	5.8		0.9
18	New Zealand	5.7		1.0
19	Israel	5.7		1.0
20	Slovenia	5.6		1.2
21	Japan	5.6		1.1
22	Belgium	5.5		1.2
23	Malta	5.5		1.0
24	Norway	5.5		1.0
25	Malaysia	5.2		1.1
26	Czech Republic	5.2		1.4
27	France	5.2		1.2
28	United Arab Emirates	5.2		1.2
29	Hungary	5.1		1.4
30	Germany	5.1		1.1
31	Slovak Republic	4.9		1.4
32	Cyprus	4.9		1.5
33	Chile	4.8		1.3
34	Kuwait	4.8		1.4
35	Spain	4.8		1.2
36	Lithuania	4.7		1.4
37	Ireland	4.7		1.4
38	Latvia	4.7		1.4
39	Portugal	4.6		1.3
40	Tunisia	4.6		1.5
41	Qatar	4.6		1.5
42	Jordan	4.5		1.4
43	Bahrain	4.4		1.6
44	Greece	4.2		1.3
45	Thailand	4.2		1.5
46	Uruguay	4.1		1.4
47	Poland	4.1		1.3
48	Italy	4.0		1.6
49	India	4.0		1.6
50	Croatia	4.0		1.6
51	Mauritius	3.9		1.8
52	Philippines	3.9		1.8
53	Romania	3.8		1.5
54	China	3.8		1.7
55	Russian Federation	3.6		1.7
56	Kazakhstan	3.6		1.7
57	South Africa	3.6		1.5
58	Turkey	3.6		1.3
59	Bulgaria	3.6		1.7

RANK	COUNTRY	SCORE	1 MEAN: 3.8 7	SD
60	Mexico	3.6		1.5
61	El Salvador	3.6		1.4
62	Indonesia	3.5		1.2
63	Argentina	3.4		1.4
64	Brazil	3.4		1.5
65	Panama	3.4		1.8
66	Pakistan	3.4		1.7
67	Colombia	3.4		1.5
68	Namibia	3.3		1.5
69	Jamaica	3.3		1.4
70	Bosnia and Herzegovina	3.2		1.5
71	Venezuela	3.2		1.5
72	Vietnam	3.2		1.6
73	Morocco	3.2		1.8
74	Egypt	3.2		1.7
75	Peru	3.1		1.5
76	Ghana	3.1		1.4
77	Azerbaijan	3.1		1.6
78	Trinidad and Tobago	3.0		1.5
79	Botswana	3.0		1.5
80	Georgia	3.0		1.5
81	Kyrgyz Republic	2.9		1.6
82	Moldova	2.9		1.7
83	Dominican Republic	2.9		1.5
84	Serbia and Montenegro	2.8		1.4
85	Costa Rica	2.7		1.4
86	Ukraine	2.7		1.4
87	Mongolia	2.6		1.5
88	Tajikistan	2.6		1.6
89	Bolivia	2.6		1.5
90	Macedonia, FYR	2.6		1.6
91	Ecuador	2.6		1.4
92	Honduras	2.5		1.5
93	Sri Lanka	2.5		1.4
94	Nigeria	2.5		1.2
95	Mozambique	2.4		1.5
96	Guatemala	2.3		1.4
97	Zimbabwe	2.3		1.0
98	Gambia	2.2		1.5
99	Nicaragua	2.2		1.4
100	Armenia	2.1		1.3
101	Cambodia	2.1		1.5
102	Algeria	2.1		1.4
103	Madagascar	2.1		1.4
104	Bangladesh	2.0		1.4
105	Tanzania	2.0		1.2
106	Paraguay	2.0		1.3
107	Malawi	2.0		1.3
108	Albania	2.0		1.3
109	Kenya	2.0		1.3
110	Mali	1.9		1.2
111	Guyana	1.9		1.0
112	Uganda	1.8		1.0
113	Ethiopia	1.7		0.8
114	Cameroon	1.7		0.9
115	East Timor	1.6		1.3
116	Benin	1.5		1.0
117	Chad	1.3		0.8

3.12 Quality of competition in the ISP sector

Is there sufficient competition among Internet service providers (ISPs) in your country to ensure high quality, infrequent interruptions, and low prices?
(1 = no, 7 = yes, equal to the best in the world)

RANK	COUNTRY	SCORE	1 MEAN: 4.1 7	SD	RANK	COUNTRY	SCORE	1 MEAN: 4.1 7	SD
1	United States	6.3		1.0	60	Luxembourg	4.0		1.7
2	Japan	6.1		1.0	61	Venezuela	4.0		1.6
3	Korea, Rep.	6.0		1.1	62	Uruguay	3.9		1.6
4	Netherlands	5.9		1.2	63	Tunisia	3.9		1.6
5	Austria	5.8		1.0	64	Bulgaria	3.9		1.8
6	Finland	5.7		1.3	65	Romania	3.9		1.8
7	United Kingdom	5.7		1.4	66	Poland	3.9		1.4
8	Germany	5.7		1.2	67	Mexico	3.9		1.7
9	Canada	5.7		1.5	68	Tanzania	3.9		1.7
10	Hong Kong SAR	5.7		1.3	69	Namibia	3.8		1.7
11	Israel	5.6		1.2	70	Uganda	3.8		1.9
12	Taiwan	5.6		1.0	71	South Africa	3.8		1.9
13	Sweden	5.5		1.3	72	Benin	3.8		2.2
14	Chile	5.5		1.2	73	Kenya	3.8		1.9
15	Singapore	5.5		1.3	74	Honduras	3.8		1.6
16	France	5.5		1.6	75	Bolivia	3.8		1.6
17	Belgium	5.5		1.6	76	Nigeria	3.8		1.6
18	Estonia	5.4		1.6	77	Cameroon	3.7		2.1
19	Australia	5.4		1.4	78	Peru	3.7		1.5
20	Pakistan	5.4		1.1	79	Hungary	3.6		1.8
21	Iceland	5.3		1.6	80	Croatia	3.6		1.5
22	Norway	5.2		1.3	81	Russian Federation	3.6		1.8
23	Denmark	5.2		1.6	82	Mauritius	3.5		2.0
24	India	5.2		1.4	83	Azerbaijan	3.5		1.6
25	Malaysia	5.2		1.4	84	Madagascar	3.5		1.9
26	Philippines	5.2		1.3	85	Ecuador	3.5		1.4
27	Brazil	5.1		1.6	86	Moldova	3.4		1.9
28	Jordan	5.1		1.3	87	Zimbabwe	3.4		1.4
29	El Salvador	5.0		1.3	88	Guatemala	3.4		1.7
30	Switzerland	5.0		1.7	89	Tajikistan	3.4		2.1
31	Malta	5.0		1.3	90	Kazakhstan	3.4		1.8
32	New Zealand	4.9		1.5	91	Mozambique	3.3		1.7
33	Cyprus	4.9		1.4	92	Guyana	3.3		1.6
34	Portugal	4.9		1.6	93	Botswana	3.3		1.6
35	Argentina	4.8		1.5	94	Kyrgyz Republic	3.3		1.8
36	Thailand	4.7		1.3	95	Malawi	3.3		1.8
37	Indonesia	4.6		1.1	96	Nicaragua	3.2		1.6
38	Italy	4.5		1.6	97	Vietnam	3.2		1.6
39	Egypt	4.4		1.5	98	Gambia	3.2		1.8
40	China	4.4		1.4	99	Serbia and Montenegro	3.2		1.7
41	Jamaica	4.4		1.6	100	Algeria	3.1		1.8
42	Georgia	4.3		1.6	101	Paraguay	3.1		1.4
43	Spain	4.3		1.7	102	Ukraine	3.1		1.7
44	Greece	4.3		1.4	103	Mongolia	3.0		1.7
45	Kuwait	4.3		1.7	103	Morocco	3.0		1.9
46	Mali	4.3		2.1	105	Macedonia, FYR	3.0		1.6
47	Turkey	4.3		1.6	106	Cambodia	3.0		1.5
48	Sri Lanka	4.2		1.5	107	Bosnia and Herzegovina	2.8		1.5
49	Latvia	4.2		1.6	108	Albania	2.7		1.7
50	Slovenia	4.2		1.5	109	Armenia	2.4		1.5
51	Lithuania	4.2		1.6	110	East Timor	2.4		1.9
52	Panama	4.2		1.5	111	Trinidad and Tobago	2.2		1.4
53	Ghana	4.2		1.7	112	United Arab Emirates	2.2		1.6
54	Colombia	4.1		1.6	113	Bahrain	2.2		1.6
55	Ireland	4.1		2.1	114	Chad	2.0		1.4
56	Czech Republic	4.1		1.8	114	Costa Rica	2.0		1.4
57	Slovak Republic	4.1		1.5	116	Qatar	1.9		1.5
58	Dominican Republic	4.1		1.9	117	Ethiopia	1.7		1.2
59	Bangladesh	4.1		1.5					

3.13   Government prioritization of ICT

Information and communication technologies (ICT) are an overall priority for the government (1 = strongly disagree, 7 = strongly agree)

RANK	COUNTRY	SCORE	1 MEAN: 4.4 7	SD
1	Singapore	6.1		0.9
2	Malaysia	5.9		0.8
3	Denmark	5.9		1.0
4	Finland	5.9		1.2
5	Taiwan	5.8		1.0
6	Mauritius	5.8		1.1
7	Korea, Rep.	5.7		1.1
8	United Arab Emirates	5.6		1.1
9	India	5.6		1.0
10	Egypt	5.6		1.3
11	Mali	5.6		1.4
12	Jordan	5.5		1.5
13	Japan	5.5		1.0
14	Malta	5.5		1.1
15	Tunisia	5.5		1.5
16	Portugal	5.4		1.0
17	Pakistan	5.4		1.5
18	Ghana	5.3		1.4
19	United States	5.3		1.3
20	Ireland	5.2		1.4
21	Estonia	5.2		1.5
22	Mongolia	5.2		1.7
23	Thailand	5.1		1.2
24	Hong Kong SAR	5.1		1.0
25	France	5.1		1.3
26	Vietnam	5.1		1.5
27	United Kingdom	5.0		1.3
28	Qatar	5.0		1.2
29	Azerbaijan	4.9		1.5
30	Jamaica	4.9		1.6
31	Chile	4.9		1.3
32	South Africa	4.9		1.5
33	Switzerland	4.9		1.3
34	Israel	4.9		1.3
35	Tajikistan	4.8		2.0
36	Sweden	4.8		1.1
37	Iceland	4.8		1.2
38	Benin	4.8		1.9
39	Botswana	4.8		1.6
40	Kazakhstan	4.7		1.5
41	Kyrgyz Republic	4.7		2.0
42	Gambia	4.7		1.6
43	Austria	4.7		1.5
44	Philippines	4.7		1.4
45	Luxembourg	4.7		1.3
46	Bahrain	4.6		1.5
47	Tanzania	4.6		1.5
48	Madagascar	4.6		1.7
49	Netherlands	4.6		1.3
50	Canada	4.5		1.2
51	Norway	4.5		1.3
52	New Zealand	4.5		1.1
53	Germany	4.5		1.3
53	Moldova	4.5		1.9
55	Uganda	4.5		1.8
56	China	4.4		1.4
57	Bangladesh	4.4		1.7
58	Venezuela	4.4		1.7
59	Slovenia	4.3		1.3

RANK	COUNTRY	SCORE	1 MEAN: 4.4 7	SD
60	Romania	4.3		1.5
61	Spain	4.3		1.4
62	Australia	4.3		1.3
63	Slovak Republic	4.3		1.3
64	Armenia	4.3		2.0
65	Dominican Republic	4.3		1.5
66	Belgium	4.3		1.5
67	Croatia	4.2		1.5
68	Lithuania	4.2		1.4
69	Cameroon	4.2		1.7
70	Ukraine	4.1		1.6
71	Greece	4.1		1.3
72	Turkey	4.1		1.5
73	Czech Republic	4.1		1.5
74	Cyprus	4.1		1.4
75	Brazil	4.0		1.5
76	El Salvador	4.0		1.5
77	Mozambique	4.0		1.9
78	Cambodia	4.0		1.9
79	Kuwait	4.0		1.5
80	Albania	4.0		2.2
80	Hungary	4.0		1.4
80	Mexico	4.0		1.4
83	Morocco	4.0		1.7
84	Sri Lanka	4.0		1.7
85	Italy	4.0		1.6
86	Serbia and Montenegro	4.0		1.8
87	Latvia	4.0		1.5
88	Bosnia and Herzegovina	3.9		2.0
89	Algeria	3.9		1.9
90	Bulgaria	3.9		1.8
91	Russian Federation	3.9		1.8
92	Kenya	3.8		1.9
93	East Timor	3.8		2.2
94	Trinidad and Tobago	3.8		1.6
95	Nigeria	3.8		1.6
96	Nicaragua	3.7		1.6
97	Colombia	3.7		1.4
98	Ethiopia	3.7		1.8
99	Poland	3.6		1.3
100	Uruguay	3.6		1.4
101	Indonesia	3.6		1.5
102	Namibia	3.6		1.7
103	Malawi	3.5		1.6
104	Honduras	3.4		1.6
105	Macedonia, FYR	3.4		1.8
106	Panama	3.4		1.5
107	Georgia	3.4		1.6
108	Guyana	3.2		1.6
109	Argentina	3.2		1.4
110	Peru	3.2		1.5
111	Costa Rica	3.1		1.4
112	Zimbabwe	3.1		1.6
113	Chad	3.0		2.0
114	Guatemala	3.0		1.5
115	Bolivia	2.9		1.6
116	Paraguay	2.4		1.4
117	Ecuador	2.3		1.4

3.14 Government success in ICT promotion

Government programs promoting the use of information and communication technologies (ICT) are (1 = not very successful, 7 = highly successful)

RANK	COUNTRY	SCORE	MEAN: 3.9	SD
1	Singapore	5.9		0.9
2	Malaysia	5.5		1.0
3	Taiwan	5.4		0.9
4	Tunisia	5.4		1.2
5	United Arab Emirates	5.3		1.1
6	Korea, Rep.	5.3		1.1
7	Pakistan	5.2		1.5
8	Denmark	5.2		1.2
9	Finland	5.1		1.5
10	Malta	5.1		1.0
11	India	5.0		1.2
12	Estonia	5.0		1.1
13	Portugal	4.8		1.0
14	Qatar	4.8		1.2
15	France	4.8		1.3
16	Thailand	4.8		1.1
17	Israel	4.7		1.2
18	Jordan	4.7		1.3
18	Mauritius	4.7		0.9
20	Egypt	4.7		1.3
21	Hong Kong SAR	4.7		1.3
22	Iceland	4.7		1.2
23	Japan	4.7		1.5
24	United States	4.6		1.2
25	Mali	4.6		1.8
26	Vietnam	4.5		1.4
27	Sweden	4.5		1.1
28	Ghana	4.5		1.2
29	Ireland	4.4		1.2
30	Madagascar	4.4		1.4
31	Tajikistan	4.4		1.8
32	Austria	4.3		1.4
33	Tanzania	4.3		1.4
34	Mozambique	4.2		1.5
35	Jamaica	4.2		1.4
36	Luxembourg	4.2		1.5
37	Chile	4.2		1.4
38	Azerbaijan	4.2		1.8
39	South Africa	4.2		1.2
40	China	4.1		1.2
41	Cameroon	4.1		1.8
42	Canada	4.1		1.3
43	Gambia	4.1		1.4
44	Philippines	4.1		1.3
45	Switzerland	4.1		1.4
46	Norway	4.0		1.4
47	Uganda	4.0		1.7
48	Morocco	4.0		1.7
49	Germany	4.0		1.2
50	Romania	4.0		1.4
51	Netherlands	3.9		1.2
52	United Kingdom	3.9		1.3
53	Australia	3.9		1.2
54	Kazakhstan	3.9		1.4
55	Benin	3.9		2.0
56	Belgium	3.9		1.4
57	Botswana	3.9		1.3
58	Brazil	3.9		1.4
59	Bahrain	3.8		1.3
60	New Zealand	3.7		1.0
61	Hungary	3.7		1.3
62	Cyprus	3.7		1.3
63	Italy	3.7		1.4
64	Mongolia	3.7		1.6
65	Lithuania	3.7		1.4
66	Slovak Republic	3.7		1.2
67	Algeria	3.7		1.7
68	Slovenia	3.7		1.1
69	Czech Republic	3.7		1.4
70	Kuwait	3.6		1.3
71	Turkey	3.6		1.4
72	Spain	3.6		1.3
73	Moldova	3.6		1.6
74	Nigeria	3.6		1.3
75	Sri Lanka	3.5		1.4
76	Croatia	3.5		1.2
77	Trinidad and Tobago	3.5		1.3
78	El Salvador	3.5		1.1
79	Mexico	3.5		1.4
80	Colombia	3.5		1.4
81	Greece	3.4		1.2
82	Indonesia	3.4		1.2
83	Kenya	3.4		1.7
84	Armenia	3.4		1.7
85	Ukraine	3.4		1.3
86	Serbia and Montenegro	3.3		1.4
87	Cambodia	3.3		1.6
88	Uruguay	3.3		1.5
89	Latvia	3.3		1.3
90	Poland	3.2		1.3
91	Bulgaria	3.2		1.5
92	Namibia	3.2		1.2
93	Costa Rica	3.2		1.4
94	Malawi	3.1		1.4
95	Kyrgyz Republic	3.1		1.5
96	Dominican Republic	3.1		1.2
97	Ethiopia	3.1		1.6
98	Honduras	3.1		1.4
99	Russian Federation	3.1		1.5
100	Bangladesh	3.1		1.5
101	Nicaragua	3.0		1.4
102	East Timor	3.0		1.8
103	Panama	3.0		1.5
104	Argentina	3.0		1.5
105	Guyana	2.9		1.2
106	Georgia	2.9		1.4
107	Venezuela	2.9		1.4
108	Macedonia, FYR	2.8		1.3
109	Zimbabwe	2.8		1.3
110	Bosnia and Herzegovina	2.8		1.3
111	Peru	2.7		1.2
112	Guatemala	2.6		1.3
113	Albania	2.6		1.5
114	Chad	2.5		1.6
115	Bolivia	2.4		1.1
116	Ecuador	2.1		1.0
117	Paraguay	2.1		1.1

513

3.15 Laws relating to ICT

Laws relating to the use of information and communication technologies (ICT) (electronic commerce, digital signatures, consumer protection) are (1 = nonexistent, 7 = well developed and enforced)

RANK	COUNTRY	SCORE	1 MEAN: 3.8 7	SD
1	Singapore	5.9		0.8
2	Denmark	5.8		0.9
3	United States	5.8		1.0
4	United Kingdom	5.7		1.0
5	Iceland	5.7		1.1
6	Finland	5.7		0.9
7	Estonia	5.6		1.1
8	Australia	5.6		0.8
9	Germany	5.6		1.0
10	Korea, Rep.	5.5		1.0
11	Norway	5.5		1.0
12	New Zealand	5.4		0.9
13	Ireland	5.4		1.4
14	Malaysia	5.4		1.1
15	Canada	5.4		1.2
16	France	5.3		1.2
17	Switzerland	5.3		1.2
18	Austria	5.2		1.1
19	Taiwan	5.2		0.9
20	Netherlands	5.2		1.1
21	Hong Kong SAR	5.1		1.4
22	Sweden	5.1		0.9
23	Israel	5.0		1.0
23	South Africa	5.0		1.2
25	Malta	5.0		1.2
26	Chile	4.9		1.2
27	Spain	4.8		1.1
28	Portugal	4.7		1.0
29	Luxembourg	4.7		1.2
30	Japan	4.7		1.3
31	Slovenia	4.6		1.2
32	Belgium	4.5		1.2
33	Hungary	4.4		1.3
34	Tunisia	4.3		1.3
35	United Arab Emirates	4.2		1.1
36	Mauritius	4.2		1.8
37	Italy	4.2		1.4
38	Bahrain	4.2		1.6
39	Slovak Republic	4.2		1.3
40	Czech Republic	4.1		1.4
41	Lithuania	4.0		1.3
42	Philippines	4.0		1.2
43	India	4.0		1.3
44	Brazil	3.9		1.4
45	Thailand	3.9		1.3
46	Bulgaria	3.9		1.3
47	Poland	3.9		1.1
48	Turkey	3.8		1.4
49	Mexico	3.8		1.3
50	Kazakhstan	3.8		1.6
51	Cyprus	3.8		1.4
52	Jordan	3.8		1.6
53	Qatar	3.7		1.5
54	El Salvador	3.6		1.6
55	Colombia	3.6		1.5
56	China	3.6		1.5
57	Croatia	3.6		1.4
58	Venezuela	3.6		1.6
59	Latvia	3.5		1.5

RANK	COUNTRY	SCORE	1 MEAN: 3.8 7	SD
60	Peru	3.5		1.3
61	Jamaica	3.5		1.5
62	Greece	3.5		1.3
63	Panama	3.5		1.4
64	Azerbaijan	3.5		1.8
65	Romania	3.4		1.4
66	Ghana	3.4		1.4
67	Indonesia	3.4		1.3
68	Zimbabwe	3.4		1.7
69	Costa Rica	3.3		1.3
70	Botswana	3.3		1.3
71	Argentina	3.3		1.2
72	Namibia	3.3		1.5
73	Serbia and Montenegro	3.3		1.4
74	Nigeria	3.3		1.3
74	Uruguay	3.3		1.3
76	Moldova	3.2		1.7
77	Kenya	3.2		1.6
78	Pakistan	3.2		1.6
79	Russian Federation	3.1		1.4
80	Uganda	3.1		1.6
81	Macedonia, FYR	3.0		1.5
82	Ukraine	3.0		1.4
83	Egypt	3.0		1.5
84	Kuwait	3.0		1.5
85	Mali	3.0		1.4
85	Tanzania	3.0		1.7
87	Sri Lanka	3.0		1.5
88	Morocco	2.9		1.5
89	Ecuador	2.9		1.2
90	Mozambique	2.9		1.3
91	Dominican Republic	2.8		1.4
92	Trinidad and Tobago	2.8		1.2
93	Malawi	2.7		1.6
94	Nicaragua	2.7		1.4
95	Armenia	2.7		1.2
96	Guatemala	2.7		1.3
97	Tajikistan	2.7		1.7
98	Cameroon	2.6		1.6
99	East Timor	2.6		1.9
100	Madagascar	2.6		1.6
101	Gambia	2.6		1.4
102	Benin	2.6		1.6
103	Vietnam	2.6		1.5
104	Honduras	2.6		1.2
105	Bosnia and Herzegovina	2.5		1.3
106	Georgia	2.4		1.2
107	Mongolia	2.4		1.3
108	Algeria	2.4		1.4
109	Kyrgyz Republic	2.4		1.3
110	Albania	2.3		1.5
111	Cambodia	2.3		1.7
112	Paraguay	2.2		1.1
113	Ethiopia	2.2		1.3
114	Bangladesh	2.0		1.3
115	Bolivia	2.0		1.1
116	Chad	2.0		1.3
117	Guyana	1.8		1.2

3.16   Extent of business Internet use

Internet use by businesses in your country to buy and/or sell products and services is (1 = very low, 7 = very widespread)

RANK	COUNTRY	SCORE	MEAN: 3.7	SD
1	United States	6.4		0.8
2	Sweden	5.9		1.1
3	Korea, Rep.	5.8		1.1
4	United Kingdom	5.8		1.1
5	Denmark	5.8		1.0
6	Estonia	5.7		1.3
7	Finland	5.6		1.0
8	Japan	5.6		1.0
9	Canada	5.6		1.3
10	Iceland	5.6		1.2
11	Germany	5.6		1.3
12	Netherlands	5.5		1.2
13	Taiwan	5.4		1.3
14	Australia	5.3		1.2
15	New Zealand	5.3		1.3
16	Austria	5.2		1.3
17	Hong Kong SAR	5.2		1.3
18	Switzerland	5.2		1.5
19	Singapore	5.2		1.2
20	Norway	5.2		1.3
21	Israel	5.1		1.3
22	France	5.1		1.4
23	Chile	4.7		1.1
24	Malaysia	4.7		1.4
25	Belgium	4.7		1.4
26	Ireland	4.6		1.3
27	Czech Republic	4.6		1.6
28	Brazil	4.5		1.5
29	South Africa	4.4		1.4
30	Indonesia	4.4		1.3
31	Slovenia	4.4		1.4
32	Argentina	4.3		1.3
33	Luxembourg	4.3		1.1
34	Portugal	4.2		1.3
35	Panama	4.1		1.6
36	Spain	4.1		1.5
37	Thailand	4.1		1.5
38	Malta	4.1		1.3
39	Hungary	4.0		1.6
40	Latvia	4.0		1.5
41	El Salvador	4.0		1.4
42	Lithuania	4.0		1.5
43	Philippines	3.9		1.6
44	Poland	3.9		1.2
45	United Arab Emirates	3.8		1.7
46	Cyprus	3.8		1.5
47	India	3.8		1.5
48	Slovak Republic	3.8		1.5
49	Mexico	3.8		1.5
50	Venezuela	3.7		1.3
51	Costa Rica	3.7		1.6
52	Dominican Republic	3.6		1.7
53	Peru	3.6		1.4
54	Guatemala	3.6		1.6
55	Italy	3.5		1.5
56	Kazakhstan	3.5		1.9
57	Colombia	3.5		1.5
58	Turkey	3.5		1.5
59	China	3.5		1.6
60	Uruguay	3.4		1.5
61	Bulgaria	3.4		1.6
62	Tunisia	3.4		1.6
63	Egypt	3.4		1.7
64	Azerbaijan	3.4		1.9
65	Kuwait	3.4		1.7
66	Jordan	3.3		1.6
67	Mauritius	3.3		1.7
68	Russian Federation	3.3		1.7
69	Pakistan	3.3		1.7
70	Jamaica	3.2		1.5
71	Ecuador	3.2		1.5
72	Romania	3.2		1.6
73	Croatia	3.2		1.6
74	Honduras	3.2		1.6
75	Ukraine	3.0		1.5
76	Madagascar	3.0		1.8
77	Botswana	3.0		1.7
78	Namibia	3.0		1.4
79	Ghana	3.0		1.7
80	Trinidad and Tobago	3.0		1.4
81	Greece	3.0		1.1
82	Bolivia	2.9		1.5
83	Nigeria	2.9		1.4
84	Sri Lanka	2.8		1.4
85	Kenya	2.8		1.8
86	Zimbabwe	2.8		1.4
87	Nicaragua	2.8		1.4
88	Morocco	2.7		1.8
89	Cameroon	2.7		1.9
90	Qatar	2.7		1.7
91	Armenia	2.7		1.5
92	Mali	2.7		1.8
93	Georgia	2.7		1.6
94	Serbia and Montenegro	2.6		1.6
95	Tanzania	2.6		1.6
96	Macedonia, FYR	2.6		1.5
97	Paraguay	2.5		1.4
98	Mozambique	2.5		1.4
99	Cambodia	2.4		1.6
100	Gambia	2.4		1.8
101	Bangladesh	2.4		1.6
102	Bahrain	2.4		1.5
103	Benin	2.4		1.8
104	Malawi	2.4		1.5
105	Moldova	2.4		1.7
106	East Timor	2.2		1.8
107	Guyana	2.2		1.2
108	Bosnia and Herzegovina	2.2		1.1
109	Mongolia	2.2		1.2
110	Tajikistan	2.2		1.5
111	Uganda	2.2		1.6
112	Vietnam	2.2		1.4
113	Kyrgyz Republic	2.1		1.4
114	Algeria	2.1		1.2
115	Ethiopia	2.1		1.3
116	Albania	1.9		1.5
117	Chad	1.8		1.2

3.17   Utility patents, 2004

US utility patents (i.e., patents for invention) granted per million population, 2004

RANK	COUNTRY	HARD DATA		RANK	COUNTRY	HARD DATA
1	United States	283.7		60	Thailand	0.3
2	Japan	276.6		61	Philippines	0.3
3	Taiwan	263.9		62	Ecuador	0.2
4	Switzerland	177.4		63	Colombia	0.2
5	Finland	176.5		64	Peru	0.2
6	Israel	155.8		65	Kenya	0.2
7	Sweden	144.9		66	Turkey	0.2
8	Germany	130.7		67	Jordan	0.2
9	Canada	106.4		68	El Salvador	0.2
10	Singapore	104.4		69	Kazakhstan	0.1
11	Korea	92.3		70	Azerbaijan	0.1
12	Luxembourg	88.0		71	Tunisia	0.1
13	Netherlands	78.6		72	Zimbabwe	0.1
14	Denmark	76.7		73	Egypt	0.1
15	Austria	66.7		74	Sri Lanka	0.1
15	Iceland	66.7		75	Morocco	0.0
17	Belgium	59.4		76	Algeria	0.0
18	United Kingdom	58.1		77	Indonesia	0.0
19	France	56.0		78	Pakistan	0.0
20	Norway	52.8		79	Vietnam	0.0
21	Australia	47.9		80	Nigeria	0.0
22	Ireland	46.5		81	Albania	0.0
23	Hong Kong SAR	43.8		81	Bahrain	0.0
24	New Zealand	36.4		81	Bangladesh	0.0
25	Italy	27.6		81	Benin	0.0
26	Slovenia	10.5		81	Bolivia	0.0
27	Spain	6.4		81	Bosnia and Herzegovina	0.0
28	Hungary	4.9		81	Botswana	0.0
29	Malaysia	3.2		81	Cambodia	0.0
30	Czech Republic	3.0		81	Cameroon	0.0
31	Malta	2.5		81	Chad	0.0
32	South Africa	2.2		81	Costa Rica	0.0
33	Croatia	2.0		81	Dominican Republic	0.0
34	Portugal	1.7		81	East Timor	0.0
35	Estonia	1.5		81	Ethiopia	0.0
35	Kuwait	1.5		81	Gambia	0.0
37	Cyprus	1.4		81	Ghana	0.0
38	Greece	1.4		81	Guatemala	0.0
39	Russian Federation	1.2		81	Guyana	0.0
40	Argentina	1.2		81	Honduras	0.0
41	Chile	0.9		81	Kyrgyz Republic	0.0
42	Slovak Republic	0.9		81	Macedonia, FYR	0.0
43	Latvia	0.9		81	Madagascar	0.0
44	Mexico	0.8		81	Malawi	0.0
45	Georgia	0.8		81	Mali	0.0
46	Moldova	0.7		81	Mauritius	0.0
47	Venezuela	0.7		81	Mongolia	0.0
48	United Arab Emirates	0.6		81	Mozambique	0.0
49	Panama	0.6		81	Namibia	0.0
50	Brazil	0.6		81	Nicaragua	0.0
51	Ukraine	0.4		81	Paraguay	0.0
52	Poland	0.4		81	Qatar	0.0
53	Romania	0.4		81	Serbia and Montenegro	0.0
54	Bulgaria	0.4		81	Tajikistan	0.0
55	Jamaica	0.4		81	Tanzania	0.0
56	India	0.3		81	Trinidad and Tobago	0.0
57	Armenia	0.3		81	Uganda	0.0
58	China	0.3		81	Uruguay	0.0
59	Lithuania	0.3				

SOURCE: US Patent and Trademark Office, April 2005

3.18   Cellular telephones, 2003

Cellular mobile subscribers per 100 inhabitants, 2003

RANK	COUNTRY	HARD DATA	RANK	COUNTRY	HARD DATA
1	Luxembourg	119.4	60	Venezuela	27.3
2	Taiwan	114.1	61	Dominican Republic	27.2
3	Hong Kong SAR	107.9	62	Philippines	27.0
4	Italy	101.8	63	Mauritius	26.7
5	Sweden	98.1	64	Brazil	26.4
6	Iceland	96.6	65	Russian Federation	24.9
7	Czech Republic	96.5	66	Morocco	24.4
8	Israel	96.1	67	Jordan	24.2
9	United Kingdom	91.2	68	Panama	22.2
10	Finland	91.0	69	China	21.5
11	Spain	90.9	70	Argentina	21.2
12	Norway	90.9	71	Tunisia	19.3
13	Greece	90.2	72	Ecuador	19.0
14	Portugal	89.9	73	Costa Rica	18.1
15	Denmark	88.3	74	El Salvador	17.3
16	Ireland	88.0	75	Guatemala	16.5
17	Austria	87.9	76	Uruguay	15.4
18	Slovenia	87.1	77	Georgia	14.5
19	Switzerland	84.6	78	Colombia	14.1
20	Belgium	83.0	79	Ukraine	13.6
21	Singapore	82.9	80	Moldova	13.2
22	Germany	78.5	81	Bolivia	13.1
23	Estonia	77.7	82	Mongolia	13.0
24	Hungary	76.9	83	Azerbaijan	12.8
25	Netherlands	76.8	84	Namibia	11.6
26	Cyprus	74.4	85	Peru	10.6
27	United Arab Emirates	73.6	86	Guyana[1]	9.9
28	Malta	72.5	87	Indonesia	8.7
29	Australia	72.0	88	Nicaragua	8.5
30	Korea	70.1	89	Egypt	8.5
31	France	69.6	90	Kazakhstan	8.4
32	Slovak Republic	68.4	91	Gambia[1]	7.5
33	Jamaica	68.1	92	Sri Lanka	7.3
34	Japan	67.9	93	Cameroon	6.6
35	New Zealand	64.8	94	Honduras	5.5
36	Bahrain	63.8	95	Kenya	5.0
37	Lithuania	63.0	96	Algeria	4.5
38	Croatia	58.4	97	Ghana	3.6
39	Kuwait	57.2	98	Cambodia	3.5
40	United States	54.6	99	Vietnam	3.4
41	Qatar	53.3	100	Benin	3.4
42	Latvia	52.6	101	Zimbabwe	3.1
43	Chile	51.1	102	Uganda	3.0
44	Bulgaria	46.6	103	Armenia	3.0
45	Poland	45.1	104	Tanzania	3.0
46	Malaysia	44.2	105	East Timor[2]	2.8
47	Canada	41.9	106	Kyrgyz Republic	2.7
48	Trinidad and Tobago	39.9	107	Nigeria	2.6
49	Turkey	39.4	108	India	2.5
50	Thailand	39.4	109	Mozambique	2.3
51	Macedonia, FYR	37.2	110	Mali	2.3
52	South Africa	36.4	111	Pakistan	1.8
53	Albania	35.8	112	Madagascar	1.7
54	Serbia and Montenegro	33.8	113	Malawi	1.3
55	Romania	32.4	114	Bangladesh	1.0
56	Paraguay	29.9	115	Chad	0.8
57	Botswana	29.7	116	Tajikistan	0.7
58	Mexico	29.5	117	Ethiopia	0.1
59	Bosnia and Herzegovina	27.4			

SOURCES: International Telecommunication Union, *World Telecommunications Indicators 2004*, and national sources
[1] 2002
[2] 2004

3.19　Internet users, 2003

Internet users per 10,000 inhabitants, 2003

RANK	COUNTRY	HARD DATA
1	Iceland	6,747
2	Sweden	6,300
3	Korea	6,097
4	United Kingdom	5,919
5	Australia	5,667
6	United States	5,558
7	Canada[1]	5,549
8	Denmark	5,410
9	Finland	5,338
10	New Zealand	5,263
11	Netherlands	5,220
12	Taiwan	5,194
13	Singapore	5,088
14	Japan	4,827
15	Malta	4,750
16	Hong Kong SAR	4,718
17	Austria	4,620
18	Estonia	4,441
19	Italy	4,164
20	Latvia	4,036
21	Slovenia	4,006
22	Germany	3,999
23	Switzerland	3,985
24	Belgium	3,856
25	Luxembourg	3,765
26	France	3,656
27	Norway	3,457
28	Malaysia	3,441
29	United Arab Emirates	3,399
30	Cyprus	3,371
31	Ireland	3,167
32	Czech Republic	3,080
33	Israel[1]	3,014
34	Chile	2,720
35	Portugal	2,569
36	Slovak Republic	2,559
37	Spain	2,391
38	Poland	2,325
39	Hungary	2,322
40	Croatia	2,318
41	Jamaica[1]	2,285
42	Kuwait	2,282
43	Bahrain	2,161
44	Costa Rica	2,157
45	Bulgaria	2,058
46	Lithuania	2,019
47	Qatar	1,993
48	Romania	1,841
49	Uruguay	1,640
50	Greece	1,500
51	Guyana[1]	1,422
52	Mauritius	1,229
53	Mexico	1,197
54	Argentina[1]	1,120
55	Trinidad and Tobago[1]	1,060
56	Peru	1,039
57	Brazil	1,023
58	Thailand	956
59	Turkey	849
60	Panama	834
61	Dominican Republic	832
62	El Salvador	829
63	Jordan	811
64	Moldova	798
65	Serbia and Montenegro	787
66	Russian Federation	683
67	South Africa[1]	682
68	Zimbabwe	680
69	Tunisia	637
70	China	632
71	Macedonia, FYR	605
72	Venezuela	603
73	Mongolia	581
74	Colombia	525
75	Ukraine	525
76	Ecuador	450
77	Philippines[1]	440
78	Egypt	437
79	Vietnam	430
80	Azerbaijan	425
81	Honduras	397
82	Bosnia and Herzegovina	391
83	Kyrgyz Republic	384
84	Indonesia	376
85	Bolivia	369
86	Armenia	368
87	Namibia	338
88	Guatemala[1]	333
89	Morocco	332
90	Georgia	239
91	Botswana	227
92	Paraguay	202
93	Kazakhstan	189
94	Gambia[1]	188
95	India	175
96	Nicaragua[1]	173
97	Algeria[1]	160
98	Sri Lanka	130
99	Kenya[1]	127
100	Benin	100
101	Albania	98
102	Pakistan	80
103	Ghana[1]	78
104	Tanzania	71
105	Nigeria	61
106	Uganda	49
107	Madagascar	43
108	Cameroon[1]	38
109	Malawi	34
110	Mali	32
111	Mozambique	28
112	Cambodia	25
113	Chad[1]	19
114	Bangladesh	18
115	Ethiopia	11
116	Tajikistan	6
117	East Timor[2]	5

SOURCES: International Telecommunication Union, *World Telecommunications Indicators 2004*, and national sources

[1] 2002

[2] 2004

3.20   Internet hosts, 2003

Internet hosts per 10,000 inhabitants, 2003

RANK	COUNTRY	HARD DATA
1	United States	5,577.8
2	Iceland	3,789.7
3	Finland	2,436.5
4	Denmark	2,312.7
5	Netherlands	2,162.7
6	Australia	1,428.1
7	Norway	1,245.9
8	Taiwan	1,228.6
9	New Zealand	1,183.3
10	Singapore	1,155.3
11	Sweden	1,050.7
12	Japan	1,015.7
13	Canada	1,012.0
14	Hong Kong SAR	869.3
15	Korea	797.6
16	Switzerland	748.9
17	Austria	713.4
18	Israel	643.9
19	Luxembourg	624.9
20	United Kingdom	545.3
21	Estonia	474.1
22	France	401.2
23	Ireland	399.2
24	Hungary	357.8
25	Germany	315.4
26	Czech Republic	274.4
27	Uruguay	271.2
28	Spain	222.4
29	Portugal	218.1
30	Slovenia	214.8
31	Slovak Republic	212.2
32	Poland	203.8
33	Belgium	202.6
34	Argentina	200.7
35	Lithuania	192.6
36	Brazil	179.8
37	Malta	177.9
38	Latvia	177.9
39	Greece	170.5
40	United Arab Emirates	139.0
41	Chile	137.6
42	Mexico	130.6
43	Italy	114.0
44	Dominican Republic	82.2
45	Cyprus	77.9
46	Croatia	67.8
47	Bulgaria	66.6
48	South Africa	62.3
49	Trinidad and Tobago	61.4
50	Turkey	50.8
51	Malaysia	42.9
52	Russian Federation	42.2
53	Moldova	33.2
54	Mauritius	32.6
55	Colombia	26.3
56	Costa Rica	25.9
57	Peru	24.0
58	Panama	22.9
59	Romania	21.8

RANK	COUNTRY	HARD DATA
60	Bahrain	19.2
61	Ukraine	19.2
62	Bosnia and Herzegovina	18.9
63	Serbia and Montenegro	18.4
64	Macedonia, FYR	17.3
65	Guatemala	16.5
66	Namibia	16.4
67	Thailand	16.4
68	Paraguay	15.6
69	Venezuela	13.7
70	Kazakhstan	13.5
71	Nicaragua	12.9
72	Kyrgyz Republic	11.0
73	Botswana	10.9
74	Kuwait	10.9
75	Georgia	10.1
76	Bolivia	8.4
77	Guyana	6.9
78	El Salvador	6.2
79	Jordan	5.7
80	Jamaica	5.6
81	Armenia	5.5
82	Gambia	4.2
83	Zimbabwe	3.8
84	Philippines	3.5
85	Qatar	3.1
86	Indonesia	2.9
87	Honduras	2.8
88	Kenya	2.6
89	Ecuador	2.5
90	Mozambique	1.7
91	Tanzania	1.6
92	East Timor	1.3
93	China	1.3
94	Benin	1.2
95	Morocco	1.2
96	Pakistan	1.0
97	Uganda	1.0
98	Sri Lanka	1.0
99	India	0.8
100	Albania	0.8
101	Azerbaijan	0.7
102	Cambodia	0.6
103	Egypt	0.5
104	Madagascar	0.5
105	Cameroon	0.3
106	Tunisia	0.3
107	Algeria	0.3
108	Ghana	0.2
109	Mali	0.2
110	Mongolia	0.2
111	Tajikistan	0.1
112	Nigeria	0.1
113	Vietnam	0.0
114	Malawi	0.0
115	Chad	0.0
116	Ethiopia	0.0
117	Bangladesh	0.0

519

SOURCES: International Telecommunication Union, *World Telecommunications Indicators 2004*, and national sources

3.21 Personal computers, 2003

Personal computers per 100 inhabitants, 2003

RANK	COUNTRY	HARD DATA		RANK	COUNTRY	HARD DATA
1	Switzerland	74.2		60	Bosnia and Herzegovina[3]	6.0
2	United States	68.8		61	Macedonia, FYR	5.7
3	Singapore[2]	62.2		62	Jamaica[2]	5.4
4	Sweden[2]	62.1		63	Zimbabwe	5.3
5	Luxembourg	62.0		64	Bulgaria[2]	5.2
6	Australia	60.2		65	Colombia[2]	4.9
7	Denmark[2]	57.7		66	Jordan	4.5
8	Korea	55.8		67	Turkey[2]	4.3
9	Hong Kong SAR	55.5		68	Peru[2]	4.3
10	Norway[2]	52.8		69	Botswana[2]	4.1
11	Canada[2]	48.7		70	Tunisia	4.0
12	Germany	48.5		71	Thailand[2]	4.0
13	Taiwan	47.1		72	Panama	3.8
14	Netherlands[2]	46.7		73	Georgia	3.5
15	Iceland[2]	45.1		74	Paraguay[2]	3.5
16	Finland[2]	44.2		75	El Salvador	3.3
17	Estonia	44.0		76	Ecuador[2]	3.2
18	Ireland[2]	42.1		77	Egypt	2.9
19	France	41.7		78	Nicaragua[2]	2.9
20	New Zealand[2]	41.4		79	Philippines[2]	2.8
21	United Kingdom[2]	40.6		80	China[2]	2.8
22	Austria	39.6		81	Guyana[2]	2.7
23	Japan[2]	38.2		82	Serbia and Montenegro[2]	2.7
24	Slovenia	32.5		83	Ukraine	2.4
25	Belgium	31.8		84	Bolivia[2]	2.3
26	Cyprus[2]	27.0		85	Moldova[2]	2.1
27	Malta[2]	25.5		86	Morocco	2.0
28	Israel[2]	24.3		87	Sri Lanka	1.7
29	Slovak Republic	23.6		88	Armenia[2]	1.6
30	Italy[2]	23.1		89	Azerbaijan	1.5
31	Costa Rica	21.8		90	Honduras	1.5
32	Spain[2]	19.6		91	Guatemala[2]	1.4
33	Latvia	18.8		92	Kyrgyz Republic	1.4
34	Czech Republic[2]	17.7		93	Gambia[2]	1.4
35	Croatia[2]	17.4		94	Indonesia[2]	1.2
36	Malaysia	16.7		95	Albania[2]	1.2
37	Qatar[2]	16.4		96	Vietnam[2]	1.0
38	Kuwait	16.1		97	Algeria	0.8
39	Bahrain[2]	15.9		98	Bangladesh	0.8
40	Mauritius[2]	14.9		99	India[2]	0.7
41	Poland	14.2		100	Nigeria	0.7
42	Chile	13.6		101	Kenya[2]	0.6
43	Portugal	13.4		102	Cameroon[2]	0.6
44	Uruguay	12.7		103	Tanzania	0.6
45	United Arab Emirates[2]	12.0		104	Madagascar	0.5
46	Dominican Republic[3]	11.0		105	Mozambique[2]	0.5
47	Lithuania[2]	11.0		106	Pakistan[1]	0.4
48	Hungary[2]	10.8		107	Uganda	0.4
49	Namibia	9.9		108	Ghana[2]	0.4
50	Mexico	9.8		109	Benin	0.4
51	Romania	9.7		110	Mali	0.2
52	Russian Federation[2]	8.9		111	Cambodia	0.2
53	Argentina[2]	8.2		112	Ethiopia	0.2
54	Greece[2]	8.2		113	Chad[2]	0.2
55	Trinidad and Tobago[2]	8.0		114	Malawi	0.2
56	Mongolia	7.7			East Timor	n/a
57	Brazil[2]	7.5			Kazakhstan	n/a
58	South Africa[2]	7.3			Tajikistan	n/a
59	Venezuela[2]	6.1				

SOURCES: International Telecommunication Union, *World Telecommunications Indicators 2004*, and national sources

[1] 2001

[2] 2002

[3] 2004

Human Resources: Education, Health, and Labor

4.01   Quality of the educational system

The educational system in your country (1 = does not meet the needs of a competitive economy, 7 = meets the needs of a competitive economy)

RANK	COUNTRY	SCORE	1 MEAN: 3.6 7	SD
1	Singapore	6.1		0.8
2	Finland	6.0		1.0
3	Ireland	5.7		1.1
4	Iceland	5.6		0.9
5	Denmark	5.5		1.1
6	Switzerland	5.4		1.2
7	Taiwan	5.3		0.9
8	Canada	5.2		1.3
9	Belgium	5.2		1.2
10	Malaysia	5.2		1.1
11	France	5.1		1.4
12	Hong Kong SAR	5.0		1.1
13	Austria	5.0		1.3
14	Australia	5.0		1.2
15	Netherlands	5.0		1.2
16	Tunisia	4.9		1.4
17	Israel	4.9		1.2
18	United States	4.9		1.5
19	Czech Republic	4.7		1.4
20	New Zealand	4.7		1.4
21	Cyprus	4.6		1.4
22	Norway	4.6		1.3
23	United Kingdom	4.6		1.3
24	Japan	4.5		1.6
25	India	4.5		1.6
26	Sweden	4.5		1.6
27	Germany	4.4		1.2
28	United Arab Emirates	4.4		1.2
29	Malta	4.3		1.3
30	Ghana	4.3		1.4
31	Korea, Rep.	4.3		1.5
32	Estonia	4.2		1.4
33	Hungary	4.2		1.5
34	Lithuania	4.2		1.5
35	Poland	4.1		1.3
36	Qatar	4.1		1.4
37	Latvia	4.1		1.4
38	Slovenia	4.0		1.4
39	Costa Rica	4.0		1.6
40	Slovak Republic	4.0		1.4
41	Romania	4.0		1.5
42	Bulgaria	4.0		1.7
43	Spain	4.0		1.4
44	Botswana	3.9		1.5
45	Russian Federation	3.9		1.6
46	Macedonia, FYR	3.9		1.7
47	Luxembourg	3.9		1.6
48	Thailand	3.9		1.4
49	Kazakhstan	3.9		1.6
50	Ukraine	3.9		1.6
51	Jordan	3.8		1.8
52	Kenya	3.8		1.7
53	Nigeria	3.7		1.4
54	Zimbabwe	3.7		1.5
55	Armenia	3.6		1.7
56	Indonesia	3.6		1.2
57	Portugal	3.6		1.3
58	Mauritius	3.6		1.4
59	Bosnia and Herzegovina	3.6		1.4
60	Gambia	3.5		1.6
61	Colombia	3.5		1.4
62	China	3.5		1.3
63	Cameroon	3.5		1.8
64	Uruguay	3.5		1.4
65	Kuwait	3.4		1.7
66	Serbia and Montenegro	3.4		1.7
67	Mongolia	3.4		1.5
68	Italy	3.4		1.5
69	Greece	3.4		1.3
70	Turkey	3.3		1.3
71	Croatia	3.3		1.6
72	Trinidad and Tobago	3.3		1.6
73	Chile	3.3		1.5
74	Moldova	3.2		1.7
75	Kyrgyz Republic	3.2		1.6
76	El Salvador	3.1		1.4
77	Argentina	3.1		1.4
78	Philippines	3.0		1.4
79	Mexico	3.0		1.4
80	Tanzania	3.0		1.6
81	South Africa	3.0		1.2
82	Mozambique	3.0		1.4
83	Azerbaijan	3.0		1.6
84	Jamaica	2.9		1.4
85	Bahrain	2.9		1.6
86	Uganda	2.9		1.9
87	Sri Lanka	2.8		1.5
88	Ethiopia	2.8		1.4
89	Pakistan	2.8		1.6
90	Albania	2.8		1.1
91	Cambodia	2.8		1.4
92	Guyana	2.8		1.4
93	Tajikistan	2.7		1.5
94	Brazil	2.7		1.4
95	Egypt	2.7		1.6
96	Algeria	2.7		1.4
97	Morocco	2.7		1.5
98	Benin	2.6		1.7
99	Malawi	2.6		1.4
100	Georgia	2.6		1.3
100	Vietnam	2.6		1.4
102	Namibia	2.5		1.3
103	Bangladesh	2.5		1.3
104	Nicaragua	2.5		1.3
105	Venezuela	2.5		1.5
106	Madagascar	2.4		1.3
107	Panama	2.4		1.2
108	Mali	2.4		1.5
109	East Timor	2.2		1.5
110	Peru	2.2		1.1
111	Bolivia	2.2		1.0
112	Ecuador	2.2		1.0
113	Dominican Republic	2.1		1.2
114	Honduras	2.1		1.0
115	Guatemala	2.1		1.2
116	Paraguay	2.0		1.0
117	Chad	2.0		1.3

4.02 Quality of public schools

The public (free) schools in your country are (1 = of poor quality, 7 = equal to the best in the world)

RANK	COUNTRY	SCORE	1 MEAN: 3.7 7	SD
1	Finland	6.5		0.9
2	Singapore	6.1		0.9
3	Ireland	6.1		0.9
4	Iceland	6.1		0.7
5	Belgium	6.0		1.2
6	France	6.0		1.1
7	Switzerland	5.8		1.1
8	Canada	5.8		0.9
9	Netherlands	5.8		0.9
10	Czech Republic	5.7		1.1
11	Japan	5.6		1.2
12	Australia	5.6		0.9
13	Denmark	5.6		0.9
14	Austria	5.6		1.1
15	Taiwan	5.5		0.9
16	New Zealand	5.4		1.3
17	Estonia	5.4		1.1
18	Malaysia	5.3		1.2
19	Hungary	5.2		1.3
20	Norway	5.2		1.0
21	Germany	5.2		1.0
22	Sweden	5.1		1.3
23	Slovenia	5.1		1.2
24	Luxembourg	5.0		1.0
24	United States	5.0		1.3
26	Hong Kong SAR	5.0		1.2
27	Italy	5.0		1.5
28	Tunisia	4.9		1.2
29	Cyprus	4.9		1.1
30	Israel	4.9		1.3
31	Slovak Republic	4.8		1.3
32	Korea, Rep.	4.7		1.2
33	United Kingdom	4.7		1.4
34	Portugal	4.6		1.1
35	Malta	4.6		1.3
36	Romania	4.6		1.4
37	Latvia	4.5		1.4
38	Spain	4.5		1.4
39	Lithuania	4.4		1.5
40	Kuwait	4.3		1.4
41	Poland	4.3		1.3
42	Croatia	4.2		1.5
43	Bulgaria	4.1		1.7
44	Mauritius	4.1		1.4
45	Qatar	4.1		1.5
46	Russian Federation	4.1		1.7
47	United Arab Emirates	4.1		1.2
48	Botswana	4.0		1.4
49	Greece	3.9		1.3
50	Uruguay	3.9		1.3
51	Macedonia, FYR	3.8		1.6
52	Serbia and Montenegro	3.8		1.5
53	Thailand	3.8		1.4
54	Costa Rica	3.7		1.4
55	Sri Lanka	3.7		1.5
56	Trinidad and Tobago	3.7		1.4
57	Kazakhstan	3.7		1.5
58	Ukraine	3.7		1.6
59	Jordan	3.5		1.3
60	Bahrain	3.5		1.4
61	China	3.5		1.3
62	Vietnam	3.4		1.2
63	Armenia	3.3		1.7
64	Ghana	3.3		1.3
65	Algeria	3.3		1.4
66	Indonesia	3.3		1.3
67	South Africa	3.3		1.3
68	Turkey	3.3		1.2
69	Bosnia and Herzegovina	3.2		1.3
70	Argentina	3.2		1.3
71	Moldova	3.2		1.5
72	Albania	3.1		1.3
73	Colombia	3.0		1.2
74	Kyrgyz Republic	3.0		1.4
75	Jamaica	3.0		1.4
76	Mongolia	2.9		1.4
77	Namibia	2.9		1.5
78	Gambia	2.8		1.2
79	Guyana	2.8		1.1
80	Morocco	2.8		1.2
81	Mexico	2.8		1.2
82	Chile	2.8		1.1
83	India	2.8		1.5
84	Pakistan	2.8		1.4
85	Azerbaijan	2.7		1.5
86	Cameroon	2.7		1.2
87	El Salvador	2.7		1.1
88	Panama	2.7		1.1
89	Kenya	2.7		1.6
90	Benin	2.6		1.3
91	Egypt	2.5		1.4
92	Georgia	2.5		1.3
93	Tanzania	2.4		1.3
94	Mozambique	2.4		1.1
95	Honduras	2.3		1.1
96	Madagascar	2.3		1.2
97	Nigeria	2.3		1.0
98	Cambodia	2.3		1.2
99	Zimbabwe	2.3		1.4
100	Brazil	2.2		1.1
101	Nicaragua	2.2		1.1
102	Bangladesh	2.2		1.1
103	Philippines	2.2		1.2
104	Mali	2.2		1.0
104	Uganda	2.2		1.4
106	Tajikistan	2.1		1.3
107	Bolivia	2.1		0.9
108	Chad	2.1		1.4
109	Ecuador	2.0		0.9
110	Ethiopia	2.0		1.1
111	Paraguay	2.0		1.1
112	Venezuela	2.0		1.1
113	Guatemala	1.9		1.0
114	East Timor	1.8		1.2
115	Peru	1.8		0.8
116	Malawi	1.7		0.9
117	Dominican Republic	1.5		0.7

523

4.03 Quality of math and science education

Math and science education in your country's schools (1 = lag far behind most other countries, 7 = are among the best in the world)

RANK	COUNTRY	SCORE	SD	RANK	COUNTRY	SCORE	SD
1	Singapore	6.5	0.7	60	Vietnam	4.1	1.5
2	Belgium	6.3	1.2	61	Zimbabwe	4.1	1.5
3	Finland	6.0	1.1	62	Mongolia	4.1	1.5
4	France	6.0	1.1	63	Georgia	4.1	1.5
5	India	5.7	1.2	64	Italy	4.0	1.5
6	Czech Republic	5.7	1.1	65	Sri Lanka	4.0	1.5
7	Taiwan	5.6	1.0	66	Costa Rica	4.0	1.4
8	Romania	5.6	1.2	67	Spain	3.9	1.4
9	Switzerland	5.6	1.1	68	Botswana	3.9	1.4
10	Hong Kong SAR	5.6	0.9	69	Luxembourg	3.8	1.5
11	Tunisia	5.5	1.1	70	Kenya	3.8	1.5
12	Japan	5.3	1.3	71	Cameroon	3.8	1.5
13	Hungary	5.3	1.3	72	Colombia	3.8	1.5
14	Canada	5.3	1.2	73	Argentina	3.8	1.4
15	Malaysia	5.2	1.2	74	Morocco	3.7	1.8
16	Ireland	5.2	1.1	75	Kyrgyz Republic	3.7	1.5
17	Slovak Republic	5.2	1.0	76	Norway	3.7	1.3
18	Lithuania	5.2	1.2	77	Benin	3.7	1.7
19	Estonia	5.2	1.2	78	Bahrain	3.6	1.3
20	Bulgaria	5.2	1.5	79	Madagascar	3.5	1.4
21	Russian Federation	5.1	1.5	80	Uruguay	3.5	1.5
22	Netherlands	5.1	1.3	81	Venezuela	3.5	1.6
23	Cyprus	5.1	1.0	82	Azerbaijan	3.5	1.7
24	Poland	5.1	1.1	83	Egypt	3.5	1.4
25	Korea, Rep.	5.1	1.3	84	Portugal	3.5	1.2
26	Australia	5.0	1.3	85	Algeria	3.3	1.4
27	Israel	5.0	1.0	86	Pakistan	3.3	1.5
28	Serbia and Montenegro	5.0	1.3	87	Nigeria	3.2	1.4
29	Jordan	4.9	1.3	88	Chile	3.2	1.3
30	Denmark	4.9	1.3	89	Bangladesh	3.1	1.6
31	Iceland	4.8	1.1	90	Ecuador	3.1	1.1
32	New Zealand	4.8	1.2	91	Tanzania	3.1	1.4
33	Austria	4.8	1.2	92	Mexico	3.0	1.2
34	Greece	4.7	1.3	93	El Salvador	3.0	1.1
35	Ukraine	4.7	1.6	94	Mozambique	3.0	1.5
36	Armenia	4.6	1.6	95	Namibia	3.0	1.5
37	Croatia	4.6	1.5	96	Jamaica	2.9	1.4
38	Malta	4.6	1.2	97	Bolivia	2.9	1.4
39	United States	4.5	1.4	98	Panama	2.9	1.3
40	Qatar	4.5	1.3	99	Nicaragua	2.9	1.3
41	Slovenia	4.5	1.3	100	Brazil	2.9	1.4
42	Sweden	4.5	1.4	101	Guyana	2.9	1.3
43	Latvia	4.4	1.4	102	Mali	2.8	1.4
44	United Arab Emirates	4.4	1.2	103	Ethiopia	2.8	1.3
45	Thailand	4.4	1.2	104	Uganda	2.7	1.6
46	Germany	4.4	1.2	105	South Africa	2.7	1.2
47	United Kingdom	4.4	1.3	106	Malawi	2.7	1.2
48	Moldova	4.4	1.6	107	Gambia	2.7	1.3
49	Kuwait	4.3	1.3	108	Tajikistan	2.6	1.2
50	Macedonia, FYR	4.3	1.7	109	Paraguay	2.5	1.3
51	China	4.2	1.4	110	Peru	2.4	1.1
52	Mauritius	4.2	1.2	111	Cambodia	2.4	1.1
53	Bosnia and Herzegovina	4.2	1.4	112	East Timor	2.4	1.5
54	Turkey	4.2	1.3	113	Philippines	2.4	1.3
55	Indonesia	4.1	1.2	114	Chad	2.4	1.5
56	Albania	4.1	1.2	115	Dominican Republic	2.3	1.1
57	Trinidad and Tobago	4.1	1.5	116	Guatemala	2.3	1.1
58	Ghana	4.1	1.2	117	Honduras	2.3	1.2
59	Kazakhstan	4.1	1.5				

The future impact of malaria on your company is (1 = extremely serious, 7 = not a problem)

RANK	COUNTRY	SCORE	1 MEAN: 5.8 7	SD
1	Sweden	7.0		0.2
2	Austria	6.9		0.2
3	Ireland	6.9		0.3
4	Portugal	6.9		0.3
5	Norway	6.9		0.5
6	Netherlands	6.9		0.4
7	Uruguay	6.9		0.6
8	Chile	6.9		0.5
9	Belgium	6.9		0.8
10	Spain	6.9		0.4
11	Czech Republic	6.9		0.6
12	Argentina	6.9		0.5
13	Estonia	6.9		0.8
14	New Zealand	6.9		0.4
15	Hungary	6.8		0.7
16	Greece	6.8		0.8
17	Germany	6.8		0.7
18	Italy	6.8		0.7
19	Denmark	6.8		0.7
20	Switzerland	6.8		0.6
21	Serbia and Montenegro	6.8		0.7
22	Luxembourg	6.8		0.9
23	Slovenia	6.8		0.6
24	France	6.8		0.9
25	Canada	6.8		0.8
26	United States	6.8		0.9
27	Turkey	6.8		0.7
28	Finland	6.8		1.0
28	Israel	6.8		1.1
30	Iceland	6.7		1.1
31	Croatia	6.7		1.1
32	Slovak Republic	6.7		1.0
33	Latvia	6.7		0.8
34	Malta	6.7		1.0
35	United Kingdom	6.7		1.1
36	United Arab Emirates	6.6		0.6
37	Taiwan	6.6		1.0
38	Australia	6.6		0.9
39	Qatar	6.6		1.1
40	Japan	6.6		0.9
41	Cyprus	6.6		1.3
42	Jordan	6.5		1.3
43	Lithuania	6.5		1.2
44	Egypt	6.5		1.2
45	Mexico	6.5		1.1
46	Bosnia and Herzegovina	6.5		1.3
47	Romania	6.5		1.3
48	Georgia	6.5		1.3
49	Colombia	6.5		1.2
50	Russian Federation	6.4		1.3
51	Albania	6.3		1.5
52	Hong Kong SAR	6.3		1.3
53	Singapore	6.2		1.2
54	Thailand	6.2		1.1
55	Costa Rica	6.2		1.4
56	Bahrain	6.2		1.8
57	El Salvador	6.2		1.3
58	Ukraine	6.2		1.5
59	Tunisia	6.2		1.6

RANK	COUNTRY	SCORE	1 MEAN: 5.8 7	SD
60	Mauritius	6.2		1.2
61	Moldova	6.2		1.6
62	Pakistan	6.1		1.2
63	Kuwait	6.1		1.9
64	Peru	6.1		1.5
65	Bolivia	6.1		1.5
66	Jamaica	6.1		1.6
67	Vietnam	6.0		1.4
68	Bulgaria	6.0		1.8
69	Poland	6.0		1.6
70	Malaysia	6.0		1.2
71	Kazakhstan	6.0		1.6
72	Paraguay	5.9		1.7
73	Korea, Rep.	5.9		1.3
74	Dominican Republic	5.9		1.5
75	Brazil	5.9		1.7
76	Trinidad and Tobago	5.9		1.5
77	Philippines	5.8		1.3
78	China	5.8		1.3
79	Venezuela	5.8		1.9
80	Kyrgyz Republic	5.8		1.7
81	Panama	5.7		1.4
82	Guatemala	5.7		1.6
83	Algeria	5.7		2.1
84	Macedonia, FYR	5.7		2.1
85	Ecuador	5.6		1.8
86	Mongolia	5.6		1.9
87	Sri Lanka	5.6		1.7
88	Azerbaijan	5.5		1.9
89	Bangladesh	5.5		1.6
90	Armenia	5.5		2.1
91	Nicaragua	5.4		1.7
92	Honduras	5.2		1.9
93	India	5.2		1.8
94	Morocco	5.0		2.3
95	South Africa	5.0		1.8
96	Nigeria	5.0		1.4
97	Botswana	5.0		1.6
98	Indonesia	4.6		1.2
99	Cambodia	4.6		1.9
100	Zimbabwe	4.3		1.9
101	Tajikistan	4.2		2.3
102	Ghana	4.1		1.7
103	Cameroon	3.9		2.0
104	Namibia	3.8		1.8
105	Madagascar	3.8		2.0
106	Benin	3.7		2.1
107	Ethiopia	3.6		2.2
108	Kenya	3.5		2.1
109	Guyana	3.4		1.9
110	Mali	3.3		1.9
111	Mozambique	3.3		1.7
112	Uganda	3.3		2.1
113	Gambia	3.2		2.0
114	Malawi	3.0		1.8
114	Tanzania	3.0		1.7
116	Chad	2.1		1.5
117	East Timor	1.9		1.2

4.05 Medium-term business impact of tuberculosis

The future impact of tuberculosis on your company is (1 = extremely serious, 7 = not a problem)

RANK	COUNTRY	SCORE	MEAN: 5.6	SD
1	Luxembourg	6.9		0.3
2	Sweden	6.9		0.3
3	Austria	6.8		0.4
4	Denmark	6.8		0.6
5	Italy	6.8		0.8
6	Israel	6.8		1.0
7	Germany	6.8		0.6
8	Uruguay	6.8		0.7
9	Norway	6.8		0.6
10	Belgium	6.8		0.8
11	Spain	6.7		0.6
12	Switzerland	6.7		0.8
13	Ireland	6.7		0.7
14	Chile	6.7		0.8
15	France	6.7		0.9
16	Greece	6.7		0.9
17	Netherlands	6.7		0.7
18	New Zealand	6.7		0.5
19	Turkey	6.7		0.8
20	Argentina	6.6		0.8
21	Australia	6.6		0.9
22	Finland	6.6		1.1
23	Slovenia	6.6		0.8
24	Iceland	6.6		1.2
25	Hungary	6.6		0.9
26	Croatia	6.6		1.2
27	United States	6.5		1.1
28	Canada	6.5		0.9
29	Malta	6.5		1.1
30	Qatar	6.5		1.3
31	Slovak Republic	6.5		1.1
32	Colombia	6.5		1.2
33	Cyprus	6.4		1.3
34	Jordan	6.4		1.2
35	Serbia and Montenegro	6.4		1.0
36	United Arab Emirates	6.4		1.0
37	Portugal	6.4		1.1
38	Taiwan	6.4		1.1
39	Mexico	6.4		1.2
40	Japan	6.3		1.1
41	United Kingdom	6.3		1.1
42	Egypt	6.3		1.5
43	Estonia	6.3		1.1
44	Tunisia	6.3		1.6
45	Singapore	6.3		1.2
46	Mauritius	6.2		1.2
47	Hong Kong SAR	6.2		1.3
48	Czech Republic	6.2		1.3
49	Costa Rica	6.2		1.5
50	Albania	6.1		1.7
51	Pakistan	6.1		1.2
52	El Salvador	6.1		1.4
53	Bahrain	6.1		1.7
54	Malaysia	6.0		1.2
55	Brazil	6.0		1.5
56	Kuwait	6.0		1.9
57	Bosnia and Herzegovina	6.0		1.5
58	Thailand	6.0		1.3
59	Korea, Rep.	5.9		1.3
60	Lithuania	5.8		1.4
61	Latvia	5.8		1.3
62	Dominican Republic	5.8		1.5
63	Venezuela	5.8		1.8
64	Jamaica	5.8		1.8
65	Nicaragua	5.7		1.6
66	Romania	5.7		1.8
67	Bolivia	5.7		1.6
68	Vietnam	5.7		1.6
69	Sri Lanka	5.6		1.5
70	Bulgaria	5.6		1.9
71	Paraguay	5.6		1.7
72	Russian Federation	5.6		1.7
73	Panama	5.6		1.5
74	China	5.6		1.3
75	Ecuador	5.6		1.7
76	Trinidad and Tobago	5.6		1.6
77	Algeria	5.5		1.9
78	Poland	5.5		1.5
79	Georgia	5.5		1.8
80	Guatemala	5.5		1.7
81	Macedonia, FYR	5.4		2.2
82	Peru	5.4		1.6
83	Bangladesh	5.4		1.7
84	Armenia	5.3		2.1
85	Azerbaijan	5.1		2.1
86	Ukraine	5.1		1.8
87	Kazakhstan	5.0		1.7
88	Honduras	5.0		2.0
89	India	5.0		1.8
90	Ghana	4.9		1.7
91	Philippines	4.9		1.5
92	Morocco	4.7		2.2
93	Moldova	4.6		2.1
94	Nigeria	4.6		1.5
95	Mongolia	4.5		2.0
96	Cambodia	4.3		1.8
97	Indonesia	4.3		1.3
98	Uganda	4.2		1.9
99	Mali	4.1		2.1
100	Kyrgyz Republic	4.1		1.9
101	Gambia	4.1		1.9
102	Madagascar	4.1		2.1
103	Tajikistan	4.1		2.4
104	Cameroon	4.1		2.0
105	Guyana	3.8		1.6
106	Benin	3.8		2.1
107	South Africa	3.8		1.9
108	Botswana	3.7		1.8
109	Kenya	3.7		2.1
110	Tanzania	3.6		1.9
111	Mozambique	3.6		1.8
112	Ethiopia	3.5		1.9
113	Namibia	3.3		1.9
114	Zimbabwe	3.3		1.8
115	Malawi	2.8		1.7
116	East Timor	2.6		1.4
117	Chad	2.5		1.7

4.06 Medium-term business impact of HIV/AIDS

The future impact of HIV/AIDS on your company is (1 = extremely serious, 7 = not a problem)

RANK	COUNTRY	SCORE	MEAN: 5.0	SD	RANK	COUNTRY	SCORE	MEAN: 5.0	SD
1	Hungary	6.6		0.8	60	Kazakhstan	5.3		1.8
2	Austria	6.5		1.0	61	Peru	5.3		1.7
3	Norway	6.5		0.8	62	Sri Lanka	5.2		1.8
4	Sweden	6.5		0.8	63	Azerbaijan	5.2		2.1
5	Germany	6.4		0.9	64	Latvia	5.2		1.7
6	Israel	6.4		0.8	65	Brazil	5.2		1.7
7	Denmark	6.4		1.0	66	Mexico	5.2		1.6
7	Iceland	6.4		1.0	67	Algeria	5.1		2.3
9	Slovak Republic	6.3		1.2	68	Armenia	5.1		2.1
10	Greece	6.3		1.0	69	United States	5.1		1.7
11	Qatar	6.3		1.4	70	Costa Rica	5.1		1.7
12	Belgium	6.3		1.1	71	Macedonia, FYR	5.1		2.4
13	Luxembourg	6.3		1.0	72	Poland	5.1		1.5
14	Turkey	6.2		1.2	73	Moldova	5.0		2.1
15	Egypt	6.2		1.7	74	Bangladesh	5.0		1.8
16	Croatia	6.2		1.3	75	Vietnam	5.0		2.0
17	New Zealand	6.2		1.1	76	Philippines	5.0		1.6
18	Slovenia	6.2		1.1	77	Mauritius	5.0		2.0
19	Ireland	6.2		1.3	78	Panama	4.9		1.6
20	Italy	6.2		1.2	79	Nicaragua	4.9		1.8
21	Jordan	6.2		1.6	80	Dominican Republic	4.9		1.9
22	Malta	6.2		1.0	81	Thailand	4.8		1.8
23	Finland	6.2		1.3	82	Paraguay	4.7		1.8
24	Uruguay	6.1		1.3	83	Kyrgyz Republic	4.7		2.0
25	Serbia and Montenegro	6.1		1.5	84	Pakistan	4.7		2.4
26	Taiwan	6.0		1.2	85	Ecuador	4.7		1.9
27	Switzerland	6.0		1.3	86	Venezuela	4.6		2.0
28	Netherlands	6.0		1.1	87	El Salvador	4.6		1.6
29	France	5.9		1.4	88	Mongolia	4.6		2.4
30	Spain	5.9		1.3	89	Morocco	4.5		2.2
31	Kuwait	5.9		2.0	90	Ghana	4.4		1.7
32	Tunisia	5.9		1.9	91	Guatemala	4.4		1.9
33	Chile	5.9		1.4	92	Indonesia	4.1		1.4
34	United Arab Emirates	5.8		1.4	93	Tajikistan	4.0		2.5
35	Cyprus	5.8		1.6	94	India	4.0		1.9
36	United Kingdom	5.8		1.4	95	Madagascar	4.0		2.0
37	Bosnia and Herzegovina	5.8		1.7	96	Honduras	3.8		2.0
38	Hong Kong SAR	5.8		1.5	97	Gambia	3.7		1.9
39	Japan	5.8		1.5	98	Jamaica	3.5		1.9
40	Bahrain	5.8		1.9	99	Mali	3.5		2.1
41	Albania	5.8		1.8	100	Cambodia	3.2		1.8
42	Portugal	5.7		1.6	101	East Timor	3.2		1.8
43	Lithuania	5.7		1.5	102	Nigeria	3.1		1.5
44	Argentina	5.7		1.3	103	Trinidad and Tobago	3.0		1.9
45	Singapore	5.7		1.4	104	Benin	3.0		2.0
46	Australia	5.7		1.3	105	Cameroon	2.9		1.8
47	Georgia	5.6		1.8	106	Kenya	2.8		1.9
48	Canada	5.6		1.4	107	Ethiopia	2.5		1.8
49	Estonia	5.6		1.6	108	Uganda	2.5		1.6
50	Czech Republic	5.6		1.6	109	Mozambique	2.4		1.4
51	Malaysia	5.6		1.3	110	Namibia	2.3		1.4
52	Bolivia	5.5		1.7	111	Guyana	2.1		1.4
53	Romania	5.5		1.8	112	Tanzania	2.1		1.4
54	Russian Federation	5.5		1.8	113	South Africa	2.1		1.6
55	Korea, Rep.	5.5		1.5	114	Botswana	2.0		1.5
56	Ukraine	5.4		1.7	115	Zimbabwe	1.9		1.4
57	Colombia	5.4		1.6	116	Malawi	1.9		1.3
58	Bulgaria	5.3		2.1	117	Chad	1.8		1.3
59	China	5.3		1.5					

4.07 Ease of hiring foreign labor

Labor regulation in your country (1 = prevents your company from employing foreign labor, 7 = does not prevent your company from employing foreign labor)

RANK	COUNTRY	SCORE	1 MEAN: 4.7 7	SD
1	Armenia	6.1		1.4
2	Georgia	6.0		1.4
3	Dominican Republic	6.0		1.4
4	Uruguay	5.8		1.6
5	Singapore	5.8		1.1
6	Luxembourg	5.8		1.5
7	United Arab Emirates	5.7		1.3
8	Portugal	5.7		1.4
9	Kuwait	5.7		1.5
10	Slovak Republic	5.6		1.2
11	Albania	5.6		1.4
12	Qatar	5.6		1.7
13	Nicaragua	5.5		1.3
14	United Kingdom	5.5		1.3
15	Colombia	5.4		1.6
16	Hong Kong SAR	5.4		1.5
17	Ireland	5.4		1.3
18	Ghana	5.4		1.3
19	Bolivia	5.4		1.5
20	Peru	5.3		1.6
21	Uganda	5.3		1.8
22	Argentina	5.3		1.8
23	Nigeria	5.3		1.1
24	Malaysia	5.3		1.1
25	Chile	5.2		1.7
26	Czech Republic	5.2		1.5
27	Italy	5.2		1.6
28	Gambia	5.2		1.7
29	Guyana	5.2		1.7
30	Paraguay	5.1		1.8
31	Spain	5.1		1.5
32	Benin	5.1		2.0
33	Serbia and Montenegro	5.1		1.7
34	Costa Rica	5.1		1.7
35	Indonesia	5.1		1.4
36	Lithuania	5.1		1.5
37	Azerbaijan	5.0		1.5
38	El Salvador	5.0		1.6
39	Switzerland	5.0		1.6
40	Norway	5.0		1.3
41	Hungary	4.9		1.7
42	Pakistan	4.9		1.9
43	Finland	4.9		1.8
44	Cambodia	4.9		1.9
45	Denmark	4.9		1.8
46	Jamaica	4.8		1.6
47	Latvia	4.8		1.5
48	Iceland	4.8		1.5
49	Ukraine	4.8		1.5
50	Turkey	4.8		1.8
51	Greece	4.8		1.7
52	Estonia	4.8		1.6
53	Honduras	4.7		1.9
54	Taiwan	4.7		1.5
55	Egypt	4.7		1.8
56	Vietnam	4.7		1.6
57	Tajikistan	4.7		1.9
58	Bulgaria	4.7		1.6
59	China	4.7		1.5
60	New Zealand	4.7		1.4
61	Mali	4.7		1.9
62	Venezuela	4.6		1.8
63	Cameroon	4.6		2.1
64	United States	4.6		1.6
65	Mexico	4.6		1.8
66	India	4.6		1.9
67	Canada	4.5		1.7
68	Mongolia	4.5		1.7
69	Ecuador	4.5		1.9
70	Guatemala	4.5		2.0
71	Romania	4.5		1.7
72	France	4.5		1.8
73	Sweden	4.5		1.9
74	Kyrgyz Republic	4.5		1.8
75	Belgium	4.5		2.0
76	Slovenia	4.4		1.5
77	Chad	4.4		2.2
78	Morocco	4.4		1.7
79	Japan	4.4		1.8
80	Tanzania	4.4		1.8
81	Macedonia, FYR	4.4		2.0
82	Croatia	4.4		1.7
83	Trinidad and Tobago	4.3		1.8
84	Kenya	4.3		1.7
85	Germany	4.3		1.6
86	Netherlands	4.3		1.5
87	Malta	4.3		1.5
88	Cyprus	4.3		1.6
89	Korea, Rep.	4.3		1.5
90	Botswana	4.3		1.9
91	Sri Lanka	4.3		1.9
92	Jordan	4.2		2.0
93	Mozambique	4.2		1.8
94	East Timor	4.2		1.9
95	Bosnia and Herzegovina	4.2		1.8
96	Madagascar	4.2		1.8
97	Moldova	4.2		2.2
98	Poland	4.2		1.3
99	Kazakhstan	4.1		1.7
100	Bahrain	4.1		1.9
101	Thailand	4.1		1.8
102	Austria	4.1		1.8
103	Brazil	4.1		1.8
104	Tunisia	4.1		1.8
105	Mauritius	4.0		2.0
106	Algeria	4.0		2.0
107	Malawi	4.0		1.8
108	Australia	3.9		1.7
109	Philippines	3.8		2.1
110	Panama	3.8		1.7
111	Russian Federation	3.7		1.8
112	Ethiopia	3.7		1.8
113	Bangladesh	3.6		1.8
114	South Africa	3.4		1.6
115	Namibia	2.9		1.7
116	Israel	2.8		1.5
117	Zimbabwe	2.7		1.6

4.08   Brain drain

Your country's talented people (1 = normally leave to pursue opportunities in other countries, 7 = almost always remain in the country)

RANK	COUNTRY	SCORE	1 MEAN: 3.5 7	SD
1	United States	6.4		0.8
2	Qatar	5.8		1.4
3	United Arab Emirates	5.8		1.2
4	Norway	5.7		0.8
5	Kuwait	5.6		1.3
6	Japan	5.6		1.1
7	Iceland	5.3		1.0
8	Chile	5.3		1.3
9	Finland	5.2		1.1
10	Singapore	5.2		1.0
11	United Kingdom	5.1		1.1
12	Switzerland	5.1		1.3
13	Taiwan	5.0		0.9
14	Ireland	5.0		1.0
15	Malaysia	5.0		1.3
16	Hong Kong SAR	4.9		1.1
17	Thailand	4.9		1.3
18	Netherlands	4.8		1.1
19	Austria	4.8		1.4
20	Canada	4.7		1.4
21	Germany	4.7		1.2
22	Israel	4.6		1.0
23	Denmark	4.6		1.3
24	Sweden	4.5		1.2
25	Belgium	4.4		1.5
26	Korea, Rep.	4.3		1.5
27	Spain	4.3		1.5
28	Portugal	4.2		1.4
29	Costa Rica	4.2		1.7
30	Luxembourg	4.2		1.2
31	Cyprus	4.2		1.5
32	Indonesia	4.2		0.9
33	Czech Republic	4.1		1.5
34	Bahrain	4.1		1.9
35	France	4.1		1.6
36	Botswana	4.1		1.6
37	Australia	4.0		1.3
38	Malta	4.0		1.3
39	Brazil	3.9		1.6
40	Tunisia	3.9		1.3
41	Cambodia	3.8		1.7
42	China	3.8		1.4
43	Slovenia	3.7		1.4
44	Panama	3.7		1.5
45	Hungary	3.6		1.3
46	Greece	3.6		1.2
47	India	3.6		1.3
48	Estonia	3.6		1.3
49	El Salvador	3.6		1.6
50	Kazakhstan	3.4		1.5
51	Poland	3.4		1.1
52	Italy	3.4		1.4
53	Vietnam	3.3		1.6
54	Turkey	3.3		1.3
55	New Zealand	3.3		1.1
56	Azerbaijan	3.3		1.7
57	East Timor	3.3		1.9
58	Colombia	3.3		1.6
59	Slovak Republic	3.2		1.4
60	Namibia	3.2		1.5
61	Mexico	3.2		1.4
62	Russian Federation	3.2		1.5
63	Ghana	3.2		1.6
64	Mozambique	3.1		1.6
65	Mongolia	3.1		1.6
66	Guatemala	3.1		1.6
67	Latvia	3.1		1.3
68	South Africa	3.1		1.1
69	Dominican Republic	3.0		1.6
70	Ecuador	3.0		1.3
71	Honduras	3.0		1.5
72	Argentina	3.0		1.2
73	Croatia	2.9		1.3
74	Nigeria	2.9		1.3
75	Trinidad and Tobago	2.9		1.3
76	Ukraine	2.8		1.4
77	Lithuania	2.8		1.2
78	Tanzania	2.8		1.5
79	Mauritius	2.8		1.1
80	Mali	2.7		1.6
81	Armenia	2.7		1.3
82	Paraguay	2.7		1.2
83	Venezuela	2.7		1.6
84	Uruguay	2.7		1.1
85	Jamaica	2.6		1.1
86	Peru	2.6		1.0
87	Jordan	2.6		1.3
88	Tajikistan	2.6		1.7
89	Nicaragua	2.6		1.3
90	Uganda	2.6		1.4
91	Pakistan	2.5		1.4
92	Egypt	2.5		1.5
93	Madagascar	2.5		1.5
94	Sri Lanka	2.5		1.3
95	Chad	2.4		1.7
96	Malawi	2.4		1.1
97	Kenya	2.3		1.4
98	Benin	2.3		1.4
99	Bolivia	2.3		1.2
100	Georgia	2.3		1.0
101	Philippines	2.3		1.3
102	Cameroon	2.2		1.2
103	Bosnia and Herzegovina	2.2		1.1
104	Morocco	2.2		1.4
105	Bangladesh	2.2		1.0
106	Gambia	2.2		1.1
107	Algeria	2.1		1.4
108	Romania	2.1		1.1
109	Macedonia, FYR	2.1		1.2
110	Bulgaria	2.1		1.2
111	Kyrgyz Republic	2.1		1.2
112	Ethiopia	2.1		1.3
113	Serbia and Montenegro	2.0		1.2
114	Moldova	1.9		1.1
115	Albania	1.9		1.1
116	Zimbabwe	1.7		0.9
117	Guyana	1.4		0.7

4.09 Private sector employment of women

In your country, private sector employment of women is (1 = limited and usually takes place in less important jobs, 7 = equal to that of men)

RANK	COUNTRY	SCORE	1 MEAN: 4.7 7	SD
1	Singapore	6.1		0.9
2	Denmark	6.0		0.9
3	Malaysia	6.0		1.0
4	Tunisia	6.0		1.1
5	Hong Kong SAR	5.9		1.0
6	Finland	5.7		1.1
7	Philippines	5.7		1.2
8	Georgia	5.7		1.3
9	Thailand	5.6		1.4
10	Estonia	5.6		1.3
11	Canada	5.6		1.0
12	United States	5.6		1.0
13	New Zealand	5.5		1.0
14	Norway	5.5		1.1
15	Iceland	5.4		1.6
16	Jamaica	5.4		1.2
17	Taiwan	5.4		1.3
18	Sweden	5.3		1.3
19	United Kingdom	5.3		1.1
20	Venezuela	5.2		1.4
21	Moldova	5.2		1.7
22	Czech Republic	5.2		1.3
23	Ghana	5.2		1.4
24	Kyrgyz Republic	5.1		1.8
25	Belgium	5.1		1.3
26	Ireland	5.1		1.3
27	Portugal	5.1		1.4
28	Panama	5.1		1.5
29	Luxembourg	5.1		1.2
30	Albania	5.0		1.7
31	Morocco	5.0		1.9
32	Jordan	5.0		1.4
33	Australia	5.0		1.1
34	Azerbaijan	5.0		1.6
35	Botswana	5.0		1.5
36	Colombia	5.0		1.2
37	Sri Lanka	5.0		1.6
38	Latvia	4.9		1.4
39	Mongolia	4.9		1.7
40	Gambia	4.8		1.6
41	Indonesia	4.8		1.2
42	France	4.8		1.3
43	Madagascar	4.8		1.8
44	Bulgaria	4.8		1.8
45	Armenia	4.8		1.7
46	Kuwait	4.8		1.7
47	Lithuania	4.8		1.7
48	Cambodia	4.8		1.8
49	Vietnam	4.7		1.7
50	Cyprus	4.7		1.3
51	Romania	4.7		1.7
52	Netherlands	4.7		1.2
53	Israel	4.7		1.3
54	Kazakhstan	4.7		1.8
55	Nigeria	4.7		1.3
56	Austria	4.7		1.4
57	South Africa	4.7		1.4
58	Slovak Republic	4.7		1.5
59	Cameroon	4.6		1.8

RANK	COUNTRY	SCORE	1 MEAN: 4.7 7	SD
60	Bahrain	4.6		1.3
61	Germany	4.6		1.4
62	Peru	4.6		1.4
63	Algeria	4.6		1.9
64	Uganda	4.5		1.9
65	Costa Rica	4.5		1.3
66	Switzerland	4.5		1.4
67	Greece	4.5		1.3
68	Trinidad and Tobago	4.5		1.5
69	Guyana	4.5		1.7
70	Tajikistan	4.5		2.0
71	Egypt	4.5		1.7
72	China	4.5		1.5
73	Croatia	4.4		1.6
74	Slovenia	4.4		1.5
75	El Salvador	4.4		1.3
76	Zimbabwe	4.4		1.3
77	India	4.4		1.5
78	Turkey	4.4		1.5
79	Macedonia, FYR	4.4		2.1
80	Dominican Republic	4.4		1.4
81	Ecuador	4.4		1.5
82	Italy	4.3		1.5
83	Tanzania	4.3		2.0
84	Poland	4.3		1.4
85	Brazil	4.3		1.6
86	Japan	4.3		1.5
87	Malta	4.3		1.4
88	Argentina	4.3		1.5
89	Hungary	4.2		1.5
90	Russian Federation	4.2		1.8
91	Namibia	4.2		1.7
92	Uruguay	4.2		1.4
93	Kenya	4.1		1.8
94	Mozambique	4.1		1.5
95	Honduras	4.1		1.6
96	Korea, Rep.	4.1		1.6
97	Serbia and Montenegro	4.1		1.8
98	United Arab Emirates	4.1		1.5
99	Bosnia and Herzegovina	4.1		1.8
100	Benin	4.0		2.0
101	Chile	4.0		1.3
102	Qatar	4.0		1.7
103	Spain	3.9		1.4
104	East Timor	3.9		1.8
105	Ukraine	3.9		1.5
106	Mauritius	3.9		1.7
107	Chad	3.9		2.1
108	Mexico	3.8		1.3
109	Mali	3.8		1.8
110	Nicaragua	3.7		1.5
111	Guatemala	3.7		1.6
112	Malawi	3.6		1.6
113	Bolivia	3.6		1.5
114	Bangladesh	3.5		1.7
115	Pakistan	3.3		1.6
116	Paraguay	3.3		1.4
117	Ethiopia	3.2		1.7

4.10 Infant mortality

Infant mortality (aged 0 to 11 months) per 1,000 live births, 2003 or most recent year available

RANK	COUNTRY	HARD DATA		RANK	COUNTRY	HARD DATA
1	Singapore	2		60	Ecuador	16
2	Finland	3		60	Mauritius	16
2	Iceland	3		60	Russian Federation	16
2	Japan	3		63	Argentina	17
2	Norway	3		63	Romania	17
6	Austria	4		65	Georgia	18
6	Czech Republic	4		65	Venezuela	18
6	France	4		65	Vietnam	18
6	Germany	4		68	Brazil	20
6	Hong Kong SAR	4		69	Colombia	21
6	Slovenia	4		69	Kyrgyz Republic	21
6	Spain	4		71	Jordan	22
6	Sweden	4		72	Honduras	23
14	Australia	5		73	Guyana	25
14	Canada	5		73	Sri Lanka	25
14	Greece	5		75	Trinidad and Tobago	28
14	Israel	5		76	Azerbaijan	29
14	Italy	5		77	Dominican Republic	31
14	Korea	5		77	Nicaragua	31
14	Luxembourg	5		79	Peru	33
14	Netherlands	5		80	Mongolia	35
14	Portugal	5		80	Philippines	35
14	Switzerland	5		80	Thailand	35
14	United Kingdom	5		83	Armenia	36
25	Taiwan	5		84	China	37
26	Croatia	6		85	Namibia	38
26	Denmark	6		86	Turkey	43
26	Estonia	6		87	Algeria	44
26	Ireland	6		87	Egypt	44
26	Jamaica	6		89	Guatemala	45
26	Malta	6		89	South Africa	45
32	Bahrain	7		91	Indonesia	46
32	Chile	7		92	Tunisia	48
32	Hungary	7		93	Tajikistan	50
32	Lithuania	7		94	Botswana	57
32	New Zealand	7		94	Ghana	57
32	United States	7		94	Morocco	57
38	Albania	8		97	Kazakhstan	62
38	Belgium	8		98	Zimbabwe	65
38	Poland	8		99	Bangladesh	66
38	Slovak Republic	8		100	Bolivia	67
38	Cyprus	8		101	India	68
43	Latvia	9		102	Kenya	74
44	Kuwait	10		103	Cameroon	77
44	Malaysia	10		104	Gambia	81
44	Paraguay	10		105	Pakistan	86
47	Costa Rica	11		106	Uganda	88
47	El Salvador	11		107	Benin	89
49	Bulgaria	12		108	Cambodia	95
49	Macedonia, FYR	12		109	Madagascar	96
49	Qatar	12		110	Ethiopia	97
52	Mexico	13		111	Tanzania	99
52	Serbia and Montenegro	13		112	Nigeria	100
54	Bosnia and Herzegovina	14		113	Chad	103
54	Moldova	14		114	Malawi	104
54	Panama	14		115	Mali	113
54	Ukraine	14		116	East Timor	124
54	United Arab Emirates	14		117	Mozambique	135
54	Uruguay	14				

531

SOURCES: World Health Organization *The World Health Report 2005*, UNFPA *State of the World Population 2004*, and national sources

4.11　Life expectancy

Life expectancy at birth, 2003

RANK	COUNTRY	HARD DATA		RANK	COUNTRY	HARD DATA
1	Japan	82.0		60	China	71.0
2	Australia	81.0		60	Ecuador	71.0
2	Italy	81.0		60	Estonia	71.0
2	Sweden	81.0		60	Georgia	71.0
2	Switzerland	81.0		60	Jordan	71.0
6	Hong Kong SAR	80.1		60	Latvia	71.0
7	Canada	80.0		60	Morocco	71.0
7	France	80.0		60	Romania	71.0
7	Iceland	80.0		60	Sri Lanka	71.0
7	Israel	80.0		60	Vietnam	71.0
7	Singapore	80.0		70	Algeria	70.0
7	Spain	80.0		70	El Salvador	70.0
13	Austria	79.0		70	Nicaragua	70.0
13	Belgium	79.0		70	Peru	70.0
13	Finland	79.0		70	Thailand	70.0
13	Germany	79.0		70	Trinidad and Tobago	70.0
13	Greece	79.0		70	Turkey	70.0
13	Luxembourg	79.0		77	Brazil	69.0
13	Malta	79.0		78	Armenia	68.0
13	Netherlands	79.0		78	Dominican Republic	68.0
13	New Zealand	79.0		78	Philippines	68.0
13	Norway	79.0		81	Egypt	67.0
13	United Kingdom	79.0		81	Honduras	67.0
24	Cyprus	78.0		81	Indonesia	67.0
24	Ireland	78.0		81	Moldova	67.0
26	Chile	77.0		81	Ukraine	67.0
26	Costa Rica	77.0		86	Guatemala	66.0
26	Denmark	77.0		87	Azerbaijan	65.0
26	Kuwait	77.0		87	Bolivia	65.0
26	Portugal	77.0		87	Mongolia	65.0
26	Slovenia	77.0		87	Russian Federation	65.0
26	United States	77.0		91	Bangladesh	63.0
33	Taiwan	76.2		91	Kyrgyz Republic	63.0
34	Korea	76.0		93	Guyana	62.0
35	Croatia	75.0		93	India	62.0
35	Czech Republic	75.0		93	Pakistan	62.0
35	Panama	75.0		96	Kazakhstan	61.0
35	Poland	75.0		96	Tajikistan	61.0
35	Uruguay	75.0		98	East Timor	58.0
40	Argentina	74.0		98	Ghana	58.0
40	Bahrain	74.0		100	Gambia	57.0
40	Mexico	74.0		100	Madagascar	57.0
40	Qatar	74.0		102	Cambodia	54.0
40	Slovak Republic	74.0		103	Benin	53.0
40	Venezuela	74.0		104	Namibia	51.0
46	Bosnia and Herzegovina	73.0		105	Ethiopia	50.0
46	Hungary	73.0		105	Kenya	50.0
46	Jamaica	73.0		107	South Africa	49.0
46	Serbia and Montenegro	73.0		107	Uganda	49.0
46	United Arab Emirates	73.0		109	Cameroon	48.0
51	Albania	72.0		110	Chad	46.0
51	Bulgaria	72.0		111	Mali	45.0
51	Colombia	72.0		111	Mozambique	45.0
51	Lithuania	72.0		111	Nigeria	45.0
51	Macedonia, FYR	72.0		111	Tanzania	45.0
51	Malaysia	72.0		115	Malawi	42.0
51	Mauritius	72.0		116	Zimbabwe	37.0
51	Paraguay	72.0		117	Botswana	36.0
51	Tunisia	72.0				

SOURCES: World Health Organization *The World Health Report 2005*, UNFPA *State of the World Population 2004*, and national sources

4.12   Tuberculosis prevalence

Estimated tuberculosis cases per 100,000 inhabitants, 2003

RANK	COUNTRY	HARD DATA
1	Iceland	3.0
2	Cyprus	4.0
2	Sweden	4.0
4	Jordan	5.0
4	United States	5.0
6	Australia	6.0
6	Canada	6.0
6	Malta	6.0
6	Norway	6.0
10	Italy	7.0
10	Switzerland	7.0
12	Denmark	8.0
12	Germany	8.0
12	Jamaica	8.0
12	Netherlands	8.0
16	Finland	9.0
16	Israel	9.0
16	Trinidad and Tobago	9.0
19	New Zealand	11.0
20	Czech Republic	12.0
20	France	12.0
20	Ireland	12.0
20	Luxembourg	12.0
20	United Kingdom	12.0
25	Austria	14.0
25	Belgium	14.0
27	Costa Rica	15.0
28	Chile	16.0
29	Slovenia	18.0
29	United Arab Emirates	18.0
31	Greece	20.0
32	Tunisia	22.0
33	Albania	23.0
34	Slovak Republic	24.0
35	Turkey	26.0
36	Kuwait	27.0
36	Spain	27.0
38	Egypt	28.0
38	Uruguay	28.0
40	Hungary	29.0
41	Japan	31.0
41	Macedonia, FYR	31.0
41	Poland	31.0
44	Mexico	33.0
45	Serbia and Montenegro	35.0
46	Singapore	41.0
47	Venezuela	42.0
48	Bulgaria	43.0
48	Croatia	43.0
50	Argentina	44.0
51	Portugal	45.0
52	Bahrain	46.0
53	Panama	48.0
54	Estonia	50.0
55	Colombia	52.0
56	Algeria	53.0
57	Bosnia and Herzegovina	55.0
58	El Salvador	57.0
59	Sri Lanka	60.0

RANK	COUNTRY	HARD DATA
60	Qatar	61.0
61	Brazil	62.0
62	Taiwan	62.4
63	Nicaragua	63.0
64	Mauritius	64.0
65	Armenia	70.0
65	Lithuania	70.0
65	Paraguay	70.0
68	Guatemala	74.0
69	Latvia	75.0
70	Azerbaijan	76.0
71	Hong Kong SAR	77.0
72	Honduras	81.0
73	Georgia	83.0
74	Benin	87.0
74	Korea	87.0
76	Ukraine	92.0
77	Dominican Republic	96.0
78	China	102.0
79	Malaysia	106.0
80	Morocco	112.0
80	Russian Federation	112.0
82	Kyrgyz Republic	124.0
83	Guyana	130.0
84	Ecuador	138.0
85	Moldova	139.0
86	Thailand	142.0
87	Kazakhstan	145.0
88	Romania	149.0
89	India	168.0
89	Tajikistan	168.0
91	Vietnam	178.0
92	Cameroon	180.0
93	Pakistan	181.0
94	Peru	188.0
95	Mongolia	194.0
96	Ghana	210.0
97	Madagascar	216.0
98	Bolivia	225.0
99	Chad	226.0
100	Gambia	234.0
101	Bangladesh	246.0
102	Indonesia	285.0
103	Mali	288.0
104	Nigeria	293.0
105	Philippines	296.0
106	Ethiopia	356.0
107	Tanzania	371.0
108	Uganda	411.0
109	Malawi	442.0
110	Mozambique	457.0
111	Cambodia	508.0
112	South Africa	536.0
113	East Timor	556.0
114	Kenya	610.0
115	Botswana	633.0
116	Zimbabwe	659.0
117	Namibia	722.0

533

SOURCES: World Health Organization *Global Atlas of Infectious Diseases 2003* and national sources

4.13 Malaria prevalence

Estimated malaria cases per 100,000 inhabitants, 2003 or most recent year available

RANK	COUNTRY	HARD DATA		RANK	COUNTRY	HARD DATA
1	Albania	0		60	Moldova	1
1	Australia	0		61	Trinidad and Tobago	1
1	Austria	0		62	Armenia	1
1	Bahrain	0		63	Algeria	1
1	Belgium	0		64	El Salvador	1
1	Bosnia and Herzegovina	0		65	Mauritius	2
1	Bulgaria	0		66	Korea	2
1	Canada	0		67	Uruguay	3
1	Croatia	0		68	China	3
1	Cyprus	0		69	Mexico	4
1	Czech Republic	0		70	Azerbaijan	6
1	Denmark	0		71	Georgia	6
1	Egypt	0		72	Kyrgyz Republic	9
1	Estonia	0		73	Turkey	13
1	Finland	0		74	Dominican Republic	15
1	France	0		75	Costa Rica	17
1	Germany	0		76	Paraguay	24
1	Greece	0		77	Malaysia	26
1	Hong Kong SAR	0		78	South Africa	30
1	Hungary	0		79	Bangladesh	38
1	Iceland	0		80	Vietnam	46
1	Ireland	0		81	Philippines	55
1	Israel	0		82	Sri Lanka	55
1	Italy	0		83	Thailand	59
1	Jamaica	0		84	Pakistan	81
1	Japan	0		85	Tajikistan	86
1	Jordan	0		86	Indonesia	101
1	Kuwait	0		87	Venezuela	123
1	Latvia	0		88	Nicaragua	124
1	Lithuania	0		89	Honduras	147
1	Luxembourg	0		90	India	167
1	Macedonia, FYR	0		91	Brazil	213
1	Malta	0		92	Bolivia	231
1	Mongolia	0		93	Guatemala	253
1	Netherlands	0		94	Panama	290
1	New Zealand	0		95	Peru	292
1	Norway	0		96	Colombia	373
1	Poland	0		97	Kenya	389
1	Portugal	0		98	Ecuador	401
1	Qatar	0		99	Cambodia	505
1	Romania	0		100	Ethiopia	800
1	Russian Federation	0		101	Botswana	1,245
1	Serbia and Montenegro	0		102	Nigeria	2,104
1	Singapore	0		103	East Timor	3,444
1	Slovak Republic	0		104	Guyana	3,453
1	Slovenia	0		105	Cameroon	4,646
1	Spain	0		106	Chad	4,768
1	Sweden	0		107	Mali	6,226
1	Switzerland	0		108	Zimbabwe	9,562
1	Tunisia	0		109	Gambia	10,087
1	Ukraine	0		110	Madagascar	12,152
1	United Arab Emirates	0		111	Benin	12,173
1	United Kingdom	0		112	Ghana	16,999
1	United States	0		113	Namibia	22,204
55	Chile	0		114	Malawi	24,181
56	Kazakhstan	0		115	Mozambique	26,920
57	Taiwan	0		116	Tanzania	28,953
58	Morocco	0		117	Uganda	47,843
59	Argentina	0				

SOURCES: World Health Organization *Global Atlas of Infectious Diseases 2003*, World Health Organization Regional Offices, and national sources

4.14 HIV prevalence

HIV prevalence rate for population aged 15 to 49, in percent, 2003

RANK	COUNTRY	HARD DATA		RANK	COUNTRY	HARD DATA
1	Kuwait	0.00		47	United Kingdom	0.20
2	Mauritius	0.00		61	Austria	0.30
3	Turkey	0.00		61	Bangladesh	0.30
4	Taiwan	0.00		61	Canada	0.30
5	Albania	0.10		61	Chile	0.30
5	Algeria	0.10		61	Ecuador	0.30
5	Armenia	0.10		61	Mexico	0.30
5	Australia	0.10		61	Uruguay	0.30
5	Azerbaijan	0.10		68	France	0.40
5	Bolivia	0.10		68	Malaysia	0.40
5	Bosnia and Herzegovina	0.10		68	Portugal	0.40
5	Bulgaria	0.10		68	Switzerland	0.40
5	China	0.10		68	Vietnam	0.40
5	Croatia	0.10		73	Italy	0.50
5	Cyprus	0.10		73	Paraguay	0.50
5	Czech Republic	0.10		73	Peru	0.50
5	Egypt	0.10		76	Costa Rica	0.60
5	Finland	0.10		76	Latvia	0.60
5	Georgia	0.10		76	United States	0.60
5	Germany	0.10		79	East Timor[1]	0.64
5	Hong Kong SAR	0.10		80	Argentina	0.70
5	Hungary	0.10		80	Brazil	0.70
5	Indonesia	0.10		80	Colombia	0.70
5	Ireland	0.10		80	El Salvador	0.70
5	Israel	0.10		80	Spain	0.70
5	Japan	0.10		80	Venezuela	0.70
5	Jordan	0.10		86	India	0.90
5	Korea	0.10		86	Panama	0.90
5	Kyrgyz Republic	0.10		88	Estonia	1.10
5	Lithuania	0.10		88	Guatemala	1.10
5	Macedonia, FYR	0.10		88	Russian Federation	1.10
5	Mongolia	0.10		91	Gambia	1.20
5	Morocco	0.10		91	Jamaica	1.20
5	New Zealand	0.10		93	Ukraine	1.40
5	Norway	0.10		94	Thailand	1.50
5	Pakistan	0.10		95	Dominican Republic	1.70
5	Philippines	0.10		95	Madagascar	1.70
5	Poland	0.10		97	Honduras	1.80
5	Romania	0.10		98	Benin	1.90
5	Slovak Republic	0.10		98	Mali	1.90
5	Slovenia	0.10		100	Guyana	2.50
5	Sri Lanka	0.10		101	Cambodia	2.60
5	Sweden	0.10		102	Ghana	3.10
5	Tajikistan	0.10		103	Trinidad and Tobago	3.20
5	Tunisia	0.10		104	Uganda	4.10
46	United Arab Emirates	0.18		105	Ethiopia	4.40
47	Bahrain	0.20		106	Chad	4.80
47	Belgium	0.20		107	Nigeria	5.40
47	Denmark	0.20		108	Kenya	6.70
47	Greece	0.20		109	Cameroon	6.90
47	Iceland	0.20		110	Tanzania	8.80
47	Kazakhstan	0.20		111	Mozambique	12.20
47	Luxembourg	0.20		112	Malawi	14.20
47	Malta	0.20		113	Namibia	21.30
47	Moldova	0.20		114	South Africa	21.50
47	Netherlands	0.20		115	Zimbabwe	24.60
47	Nicaragua	0.20		116	Botswana	37.30
47	Serbia and Montenegro	0.20			Qatar	n/a
47	Singapore	0.20				

SOURCES: World Health Organization *2004 Report on the global AIDS epidemic*, US Agency for International Development, and national sources
[1] 2002

4.15   Primary enrollment

Gross primary enrollment rate, 2003 or most recent year available

RANK	COUNTRY	HARD DATA
1	Brazil	147
2	East Timor	143
3	Uganda	141
4	Malawi	140
5	Guyana	125
6	Dominican Republic	124
7	Cambodia	124
8	Madagascar	120
9	Nigeria	119
10	Argentina	119
11	Peru	118
12	Russian Federation	118
13	Ecuador	117
14	Bolivia	115
15	Portugal	115
16	China	115
17	El Salvador	113
18	Philippines	112
19	Sri Lanka	112
20	Israel	112
21	Panama	112
22	Indonesia	112
23	Tunisia	111
24	Tajikistan	111
25	Sweden	111
26	Mexico	110
27	Colombia	110
28	Paraguay	110
29	Morocco	110
30	Uruguay	109
31	Benin	109
32	Algeria	109
33	Nicaragua	108
34	Netherlands	108
35	Slovenia	108
36	Switzerland	108
37	Costa Rica	108
38	Spain	108
39	Cameroon	108
40	India	108
41	Hong Kong SAR	107
42	Guatemala	106
43	Honduras	106
44	Qatar	106
45	South Africa	106
46	Ireland	106
47	Belgium	105
48	Namibia	105
49	Malta	104
50	France	104
51	Denmark	104
52	Venezuela	104
53	Korea	104
54	Mauritius	104
55	Australia	104
56	Albania	104
57	Mozambique	103
58	Botswana	103
59	Austria	103

RANK	COUNTRY	HARD DATA
60	Finland	102
61	Czech Republic	102
62	New Zealand	102
63	Kazakhstan	102
64	Norway	101
65	Italy	101
66	Vietnam	101
67	Canada	101
68	Kyrgyz Republic	101
69	Mongolia	101
70	Greece	101
71	Estonia	101
72	Slovak Republic	101
73	Japan	100
74	Bulgaria	100
75	Hungary	100
76	Trinidad and Tobago	100
77	United Kingdom	100
78	Chile	100
79	Jamaica	100
80	Iceland	100
81	Taiwan	100
82	Poland	99
83	Germany	99
84	Luxembourg	99
85	Jordan	99
86	Romania	99
87	Armenia	99
88	Lithuania	98
89	United States	98
90	Serbia and Montenegro	98
91	Cyprus	98
92	Egypt	97
93	Bahrain	97
94	United Arab Emirates	97
95	Croatia	97
96	Macedonia, FYR	97
97	Thailand	96
98	Bangladesh	96
99	Singapore	95
100	Latvia	94
101	Zimbabwe	94
102	Bosnia and Herzegovina	94
103	Kuwait	94
104	Malaysia	93
105	Ukraine	93
106	Kenya	92
107	Azerbaijan	92
108	Turkey	91
109	Georgia	90
110	Moldova	86
111	Gambia	85
112	Tanzania	84
113	Ghana	79
114	Chad	78
115	Pakistan	68
116	Ethiopia	66
117	Mali	58

SOURCES: UNESCO Institute for Statistics, World Bank *World Development Indicators 2005*, and national sources

4.16　Secondary enrollment

Gross secondary enrollment rate, 2003 or most recent year available

RANK	COUNTRY	HARD DATA	
1	United Kingdom	179	
2	Belgium	161	
3	Australia	154	
4	Sweden	139	
5	Denmark	129	
6	Finland	128	
7	Netherlands	122	
8	New Zealand	118	
9	Spain	117	
10	Norway	115	
11	Iceland	114	
12	Portugal	113	
13	Brazil	110	
14	Slovenia	109	
15	France	109	
16	Ireland	107	
17	Hungary	106	
18	Uruguay	106	
19	Canada	105	
20	Poland	105	
21	Lithuania	102	
22	Japan	102	
23	Germany	100	
24	Austria	100	
25	Argentina	100	
26	Italy	99	
27	Taiwan	99	
28	Singapore	99	
29	Cyprus	98	
30	Bulgaria	98	
31	Switzerland	98	
32	Greece	97	
33	Czech Republic	97	
34	Ukraine	97	
35	Estonia	96	
36	Luxembourg	96	
37	Bahrain	96	
38	Latvia	95	
39	Russian Federation	95	
40	Malta	95	
41	Guyana	95	
42	United States	94	
43	Qatar	94	
44	Israel	93	
45	Kyrgyz Republic	92	
46	Kazakhstan	92	
47	Slovak Republic	92	
48	Korea	90	
49	Croatia	90	
50	Peru	90	
51	Kuwait	89	
52	Chile	89	
53	Serbia and Montenegro	89	
54	South Africa	88	
55	Armenia	87	
56	Bolivia	86	
57	Sri Lanka	86	
58	Jordan	86	
59	Tajikistan	86	

RANK	COUNTRY	HARD DATA	
60	Egypt	85	
61	Macedonia, FYR	85	
62	Romania	85	
63	Jamaica	84	
64	Philippines	84	
65	Mongolia	84	
66	Azerbaijan	83	
67	Trinidad and Tobago	82	
68	Thailand	81	
69	Mauritius	81	
70	Albania	81	
71	Hong Kong SAR	80	
72	Georgia	80	
73	Algeria	80	
74	Turkey	79	
75	Mexico	79	
76	United Arab Emirates	79	
77	Tunisia	78	
78	Moldova	73	
79	Bosnia and Herzegovina	73	
80	Botswana	73	
81	Vietnam	72	
82	Colombia	71	
83	Panama	71	
84	Malaysia	70	
85	China	70	
86	Venezuela	70	
87	Costa Rica	66	
88	Paraguay	65	
89	Namibia	62	
90	Indonesia	61	
91	Nicaragua	61	
92	Ecuador	59	
93	El Salvador	59	
94	Dominican Republic	59	
95	India	53	
96	Bangladesh	47	
97	Morocco	45	
98	Guatemala	43	
99	Zimbabwe	40	
100	Ghana	39	
101	Nigeria	36	
102	East Timor	35	
103	Gambia	34	
104	Malawi	33	
105	Kenya	33	
106	Honduras	32	
107	Cameroon	31	
108	Benin	28	
109	Cambodia	25	
110	Pakistan	23	
111	Uganda	20	
112	Ethiopia	20	
113	Mali	20	
114	Mozambique	16	
115	Chad	15	
116	Madagascar	14	
117	Tanzania	6	

537

SOURCES: UNESCO Institute for Statistics, World Bank *World Development Indicators 2005*, World Bank *World Development Indicators 2004*, and national sources

4.17 Tertiary enrollment

Gross tertiary enrollment rate, 2003 or most recent year available

RANK	COUNTRY	HARD DATA		RANK	COUNTRY	HARD DATA
1	Finland	87.5		60	Philippines	30.0
2	Korea	84.7		61	Moldova	29.8
3	Sweden	83.3		62	Egypt	29.4
4	United States	83.2		63	Malaysia	29.3
5	Norway	80.7		64	Turkey	28.0
6	Australia	74.3		65	Macedonia, FYR	27.5
7	Greece	74.2		66	Armenia	27.3
8	New Zealand	73.9		67	Paraguay	27.0
9	Latvia	72.5		68	Tunisia	26.7
10	Taiwan	72.4		69	Bosnia and Herzegovina	24.7
11	Lithuania	71.6		70	Colombia	24.3
12	Russian Federation	69.4		71	Mexico	22.4
13	Slovenia	68.4		72	Qatar	22.0
14	Denmark	66.9		73	Kuwait	20.9
15	Estonia	66.4		74	Brazil	20.6
16	United Kingdom	64.3		75	Algeria	20.5
17	Iceland	62.7		76	Costa Rica	19.4
18	Spain	61.9		77	Nicaragua	18.3
19	Ukraine	61.8		78	Ecuador	17.6
20	Belgium	61.1		79	Jamaica	17.5
21	Poland	59.9		80	El Salvador	17.4
22	Argentina	59.8		81	Azerbaijan	16.5
23	Netherlands	58.1		82	Tajikistan	16.4
24	Canada	58.0		83	Indonesia	16.4
25	Israel	57.4		84	Albania	16.2
26	Italy	56.9		85	China	15.8
27	Portugal	55.7		86	Mauritius	15.3
28	France	55.5		87	South Africa	15.0
29	Ireland	51.6		88	Honduras	15.0
30	Hungary	51.1		89	Luxembourg	12.1
31	Germany	51.0		90	East Timor	12.0
32	Japan	50.7		91	India	11.9
33	Austria	48.9		92	Morocco	10.8
34	Switzerland	48.7		93	Vietnam	10.0
35	Singapore	46.0		94	Guatemala	9.3
36	Kazakhstan	44.7		95	Trinidad and Tobago	8.9
37	Panama	43.2		96	Nigeria	8.2
38	Chile	42.4		97	Namibia	7.5
39	Kyrgyz Republic	42.2		98	Bangladesh	6.2
40	Venezuela	40.2		99	Guyana	6.1
41	Bolivia	39.4		100	Cameroon	5.5
42	Croatia	39.4		101	Sri Lanka	5.3
43	Bulgaria	39.0		102	Botswana	4.7
44	Georgia	37.9		103	Zimbabwe	4.3
45	Thailand	37.7		104	Benin	3.6
46	Uruguay	37.4		105	Cambodia	3.4
47	Mongolia	37.0		106	Ghana	3.3
48	Serbia and Montenegro	36.0		107	Uganda	3.2
49	Czech Republic	35.5		108	Kenya	3.0
50	Romania	34.9		109	Pakistan	2.8
51	Jordan	34.8		110	Mali	2.5
52	United Arab Emirates	34.7		111	Ethiopia	2.4
53	Dominican Republic	34.5		112	Madagascar	2.1
54	Slovak Republic	33.7		113	Gambia	1.1
55	Bahrain	33.2		114	Tanzania	1.0
56	Cyprus	32.3		115	Chad	0.9
57	Peru	31.9		116	Mozambique	0.6
58	Hong Kong SAR	30.8		117	Malawi	0.4
59	Malta	30.2				

SOURCES: UNESCO Institute for Statistics, World Bank *World Development Indicators 2005*, World Bank *World Development Indicators 2004*, and national sources

Section V: General Infrastructure

5.01 Overall infrastructure quality

General infrastructure in your country is (1 = poorly developed and inefficient, 7 = among the best in the world)

RANK	COUNTRY	SCORE	1 — MEAN: 3.9 — 7	SD
1	Denmark	6.7		0.7
2	Singapore	6.7		0.6
3	Germany	6.7		0.6
4	Switzerland	6.6		0.8
5	France	6.6		0.7
6	United States	6.5		0.8
7	Finland	6.4		0.9
8	Hong Kong SAR	6.3		1.0
9	Austria	6.2		1.0
10	Canada	6.1		0.8
11	Iceland	6.1		0.9
12	Japan	6.0		1.1
13	United Arab Emirates	6.0		0.8
14	Malaysia	6.0		0.7
15	Luxembourg	5.9		0.9
16	Sweden	5.9		1.0
17	Belgium	5.8		1.3
18	Netherlands	5.8		1.3
19	Australia	5.6		0.9
20	Taiwan	5.4		0.9
21	Norway	5.4		1.1
22	United Kingdom	5.3		1.4
23	Korea, Rep.	5.2		1.1
24	Spain	5.2		1.1
25	New Zealand	5.1		1.2
26	South Africa	5.1		1.0
27	Kuwait	5.1		1.3
28	Portugal	5.1		1.0
29	Cyprus	5.0		1.1
30	Israel	5.0		1.1
31	Czech Republic	4.9		1.3
32	Chile	4.9		0.8
33	Thailand	4.8		0.9
34	Jordan	4.8		1.2
35	Slovenia	4.6		1.2
36	El Salvador	4.6		1.0
37	Namibia	4.6		1.4
38	Estonia	4.6		1.3
39	Tunisia	4.6		1.1
40	Bahrain	4.4		1.6
40	Ireland	4.4		1.1
42	Botswana	4.4		1.1
43	Greece	4.3		1.0
44	Lithuania	4.3		1.2
45	Qatar	4.1		1.5
46	Mauritius	4.0		1.0
47	Latvia	3.9		1.2
48	Hungary	3.9		1.3
49	Slovak Republic	3.8		1.2
50	Uruguay	3.8		1.1
51	Ghana	3.8		1.2
52	Italy	3.8		1.6
53	Malta	3.7		1.3
54	Panama	3.6		1.3
55	Jamaica	3.6		1.3
56	Azerbaijan	3.6		1.4
57	Croatia	3.6		1.2
58	Egypt	3.6		1.3
59	Argentina	3.6		1.1

RANK	COUNTRY	SCORE	1 — MEAN: 3.9 — 7	SD
60	Kazakhstan	3.5		1.2
61	Mexico	3.5		1.2
62	Turkey	3.5		1.3
63	Zimbabwe	3.4		1.1
64	Ukraine	3.4		1.3
65	Trinidad and Tobago	3.3		1.2
66	Indonesia	3.3		1.3
67	Algeria	3.3		1.3
68	Poland	3.2		1.1
69	China	3.2		1.3
70	Venezuela	3.2		1.2
71	Tanzania	3.2		1.3
72	Gambia	3.1		1.3
73	Tajikistan	3.1		1.4
74	Dominican Republic	3.1		1.1
75	Morocco	3.0		1.3
76	Honduras	3.0		1.2
77	Pakistan	3.0		1.3
78	India	2.9		1.2
79	Russian Federation	2.9		1.2
80	Armenia	2.9		1.1
81	Macedonia, FYR	2.9		1.2
82	Colombia	2.9		1.0
83	Bulgaria	2.9		1.2
84	Romania	2.8		1.3
85	Brazil	2.8		1.2
86	Ecuador	2.8		1.0
87	Sri Lanka	2.8		1.3
88	Bangladesh	2.7		1.3
89	Nigeria	2.7		1.1
90	Guatemala	2.6		1.0
91	Mali	2.6		1.3
92	Vietnam	2.6		1.1
93	Costa Rica	2.6		1.1
94	Philippines	2.6		1.2
95	Uganda	2.6		1.4
96	Madagascar	2.6		1.1
97	Peru	2.5		1.0
98	Nicaragua	2.4		1.0
99	Mozambique	2.4		1.0
100	Cambodia	2.4		1.1
101	Moldova	2.4		1.2
102	Malawi	2.3		1.0
103	Kenya	2.3		1.1
104	Ethiopia	2.3		1.1
105	Kyrgyz Republic	2.3		1.0
106	Georgia	2.3		1.1
107	Benin	2.3		1.0
108	Guyana	2.2		0.9
109	Cameroon	2.1		1.0
110	Mongolia	2.1		0.9
111	Bosnia and Herzegovina	2.1		1.0
112	Bolivia	2.1		0.8
113	East Timor	2.1		1.4
114	Paraguay	2.0		0.9
115	Serbia and Montenegro	1.9		0.9
116	Albania	1.8		0.8
117	Chad	1.6		0.9

5.02   Railroad infrastructure development

Railroads in your country are (1 = underdeveloped, 7 = as extensive and efficient as the world's best)

RANK	COUNTRY	SCORE	1 MEAN: 3.0 7	SD
1	Japan	6.7		0.5
2	Switzerland	6.7		1.0
3	France	6.7		0.7
4	Germany	6.3		0.8
5	Denmark	6.2		0.9
6	Hong Kong SAR	6.2		1.2
7	Singapore	5.8		1.3
8	Finland	5.7		1.2
9	Netherlands	5.7		1.2
10	Malaysia	5.4		0.9
11	Belgium	5.4		1.5
12	Korea, Rep.	5.4		1.0
13	Canada	5.4		1.4
14	Czech Republic	5.3		1.4
15	Taiwan	5.2		0.9
16	Sweden	5.2		1.1
17	Austria	5.0		1.4
18	United States	4.9		1.5
19	Luxembourg	4.8		1.3
20	Ukraine	4.5		1.4
21	Australia	4.5		1.2
22	Slovak Republic	4.5		1.3
23	Spain	4.4		1.3
24	Russian Federation	4.3		1.5
25	United Kingdom	4.3		1.3
26	Azerbaijan	4.2		1.7
27	India	4.2		1.5
28	Portugal	4.2		1.3
29	Norway	4.2		1.3
30	Tunisia	4.2		1.2
31	Latvia	4.1		1.3
32	Kazakhstan	4.0		1.4
33	Slovenia	3.9		1.3
34	Lithuania	3.9		1.4
35	Namibia	3.9		1.8
36	Hungary	3.7		1.4
37	Poland	3.7		1.5
38	Bulgaria	3.7		1.4
39	Estonia	3.6		1.6
40	New Zealand	3.6		1.3
41	Israel	3.6		1.3
42	China	3.6		1.4
43	South Africa	3.6		1.3
44	Thailand	3.5		1.3
45	Italy	3.5		1.6
46	Romania	3.5		1.4
47	Botswana	3.4		1.4
48	Georgia	3.3		1.4
49	Egypt	3.2		1.5
50	Greece	3.1		1.3
51	Morocco	3.1		1.4
52	Indonesia	3.1		1.3
53	Moldova	3.0		1.5
54	Tajikistan	2.9		1.7
55	Zimbabwe	2.8		1.1
56	Ireland	2.8		1.1
57	Mongolia	2.8		1.3
58	Chile	2.7		1.1
59	Pakistan	2.7		1.2

RANK	COUNTRY	SCORE	1 MEAN: 3.0 7	SD
60	Argentina	2.7		1.3
61	Croatia	2.6		1.3
62	Bangladesh	2.6		1.2
63	Algeria	2.3		1.1
64	Macedonia, FYR	2.3		1.3
65	Vietnam	2.3		1.1
66	Panama	2.3		1.2
67	Sri Lanka	2.2		1.2
68	Mexico	2.2		1.3
69	Tanzania	2.1		1.2
70	Mozambique	2.1		1.2
71	Turkey	2.1		0.9
72	Kenya	2.0		1.3
73	Jordan	1.9		1.3
74	Kyrgyz Republic	1.9		1.1
75	Nigeria	1.9		1.1
76	Armenia	1.8		1.0
77	Brazil	1.8		0.9
78	Bolivia	1.8		0.9
79	Ghana	1.8		1.3
80	Iceland	1.8		1.6
80	Serbia and Montenegro	1.8		0.9
82	Mali	1.8		1.0
83	Cameroon	1.7		0.9
84	Malawi	1.7		0.8
84	Malta	1.7		1.2
86	Kuwait	1.6		1.3
86	United Arab Emirates	1.6		1.5
88	Madagascar	1.6		0.9
89	East Timor	1.6		1.1
89	Mauritius	1.6		1.3
91	Chad	1.6		1.1
92	Peru	1.6		0.8
93	Bahrain	1.6		1.3
94	Uganda	1.6		0.9
95	Bosnia and Herzegovina	1.6		0.7
96	El Salvador	1.5		1.0
97	Cambodia	1.5		0.9
98	Uruguay	1.5		0.7
99	Gambia	1.4		1.1
100	Qatar	1.4		1.0
101	Ethiopia	1.4		0.7
102	Colombia	1.4		0.7
103	Philippines	1.3		0.7
104	Trinidad and Tobago	1.3		0.9
105	Venezuela	1.3		1.1
106	Guatemala	1.3		0.7
107	Benin	1.3		0.6
108	Costa Rica	1.2		0.8
109	Albania	1.2		0.4
110	Ecuador	1.2		0.5
111	Jamaica	1.2		0.4
112	Honduras	1.2		0.4
113	Guyana	1.2		0.6
114	Dominican Republic	1.1		0.3
115	Paraguay	1.0		0.1
116	Cyprus	1.0		0.0
116	Nicaragua	1.0		0.0

5.03　Port infrastructure quality

Port facilities and inland waterways in your country are (1 = underdeveloped, 7 = as developed as the world's best)

RANK	COUNTRY	SCORE	1　　MEAN: 3.8　　7	SD
1	Singapore	6.8		0.6
2	Netherlands	6.7		0.6
3	Denmark	6.6		0.6
4	Hong Kong SAR	6.4		1.1
5	Germany	6.3		0.8
6	Finland	6.2		1.0
7	United Arab Emirates	6.1		0.8
8	Belgium	6.1		1.1
9	France	6.1		1.0
10	United States	6.0		0.9
11	Iceland	6.0		1.3
12	Japan	6.0		1.1
13	Malaysia	5.9		0.8
14	New Zealand	5.7		0.9
15	Canada	5.7		1.2
16	Taiwan	5.6		1.0
17	Sweden	5.6		1.0
18	Norway	5.4		1.1
19	Korea, Rep.	5.3		1.1
20	Estonia	5.3		1.2
21	United Kingdom	5.3		1.1
22	Namibia	5.1		1.4
23	Australia	5.1		1.0
24	Switzerland	5.1		1.6
25	Jamaica	5.0		1.4
26	Mauritius	5.0		0.7
27	Chile	4.9		1.1
28	Slovenia	4.9		1.4
29	Cyprus	4.9		1.2
30	Malta	4.8		1.2
31	Portugal	4.8		1.2
32	Spain	4.7		1.3
33	Bahrain	4.7		1.5
34	Austria	4.7		1.3
35	Israel	4.6		1.2
36	South Africa	4.5		1.2
37	Greece	4.5		1.4
38	Panama	4.5		1.8
39	Thailand	4.4		1.2
40	Uruguay	4.4		1.1
41	Tunisia	4.4		1.1
42	Ghana	4.3		1.5
43	Kuwait	4.3		1.7
44	Luxembourg	4.3		1.1
45	Azerbaijan	4.3		1.6
46	Ireland	4.2		1.3
47	Egypt	4.1		1.5
48	Qatar	4.1		1.4
49	Latvia	4.0		1.4
50	Lithuania	4.0		1.4
51	Honduras	3.9		1.5
52	El Salvador	3.9		1.4
53	Gambia	3.8		1.4
54	Romania	3.7		1.4
55	Jordan	3.7		1.4
56	Russian Federation	3.7		1.4
57	Ukraine	3.7		1.4
58	Poland	3.6		1.2
59	Argentina	3.6		1.3

RANK	COUNTRY	SCORE	1　　MEAN: 3.8　　7	SD
60	Bulgaria	3.6		1.4
61	Georgia	3.6		1.3
62	China	3.6		1.4
63	Czech Republic	3.5		1.7
64	Morocco	3.4		1.4
65	Nigeria	3.4		1.6
66	Dominican Republic	3.4		1.5
66	Sri Lanka	3.4		1.5
68	Pakistan	3.3		1.5
69	Mexico	3.3		1.2
70	Slovak Republic	3.3		1.4
71	Indonesia	3.3		1.3
72	Italy	3.2		1.7
73	Tanzania	3.2		1.4
74	Hungary	3.2		1.4
75	Turkey	3.1		1.2
76	India	3.1		1.4
77	Trinidad and Tobago	3.1		1.5
78	Croatia	3.0		1.5
79	Kenya	3.0		1.5
80	Ecuador	2.9		1.2
81	Kazakhstan	2.9		1.2
82	Botswana	2.9		1.5
83	Algeria	2.9		1.4
84	Philippines	2.8		1.5
85	Colombia	2.8		1.2
86	Venezuela	2.8		1.3
87	Mozambique	2.8		1.3
88	Cameroon	2.8		1.4
89	Vietnam	2.8		1.2
90	Cambodia	2.7		1.3
91	Guatemala	2.7		1.2
92	Brazil	2.7		1.2
93	Bangladesh	2.6		1.2
94	Benin	2.5		1.3
95	Madagascar	2.4		1.1
96	Zimbabwe	2.4		1.2
97	Paraguay	2.3		1.2
98	Nicaragua	2.3		1.2
99	Guyana	2.3		1.0
100	Costa Rica	2.3		1.1
101	Serbia and Montenegro	2.1		1.1
102	Peru	2.1		0.9
103	Macedonia, FYR	2.0		1.2
104	Uganda	1.9		1.1
105	Albania	1.8		1.0
106	East Timor	1.8		1.1
107	Malawi	1.7		0.9
107	Tajikistan	1.7		1.0
109	Chad	1.6		1.2
110	Moldova	1.5		1.1
111	Mongolia	1.5		1.0
112	Ethiopia	1.5		0.9
113	Bolivia	1.4		0.8
114	Mali	1.4		0.8
115	Bosnia and Herzegovina	1.4		0.7
116	Armenia	1.3		0.8
117	Kyrgyz Republic	1.2		0.7

5.04   Air transport infrastructure quality

Passenger air transport in your country is (1 = infrequent and inefficient, 7 = as extensive and efficient as the world's best)

RANK	COUNTRY	SCORE	1 MEAN: 4.5 7	SD
1	Singapore	6.9		0.3
2	United States	6.6		0.7
3	Germany	6.6		0.6
4	United Arab Emirates	6.6		0.7
5	Hong Kong SAR	6.5		1.0
6	Denmark	6.5		0.8
7	France	6.3		0.9
8	Finland	6.3		1.0
9	Netherlands	6.3		1.0
10	United Kingdom	6.2		1.0
11	Australia	6.1		0.8
12	Japan	6.0		1.1
13	South Africa	6.0		1.0
14	New Zealand	6.0		0.7
15	Malaysia	6.0		0.7
16	Canada	5.9		1.0
17	Belgium	5.8		1.2
18	Austria	5.8		1.0
19	Sweden	5.8		1.1
20	Taiwan	5.7		0.8
21	Switzerland	5.7		1.1
22	Chile	5.7		0.9
23	El Salvador	5.6		1.0
24	Norway	5.6		1.1
25	Bahrain	5.6		1.2
26	Spain	5.6		0.9
27	Iceland	5.6		1.4
28	Israel	5.5		1.0
29	Qatar	5.5		1.2
30	Greece	5.5		1.0
31	Korea, Rep.	5.5		1.0
32	Thailand	5.4		1.0
33	Estonia	5.3		1.1
34	Portugal	5.3		1.1
35	Jamaica	5.3		1.2
36	Tunisia	5.3		1.0
37	Jordan	5.2		1.2
38	Cyprus	5.2		1.3
39	Czech Republic	5.2		1.6
40	Malta	5.2		1.1
41	Azerbaijan	5.1		1.5
42	Ireland	5.1		1.2
43	Mauritius	5.0		0.8
44	Luxembourg	5.0		1.2
45	Namibia	4.9		1.3
46	Mexico	4.9		1.1
47	Slovenia	4.9		1.1
48	Latvia	4.8		1.2
49	Dominican Republic	4.8		1.4
50	Kuwait	4.8		1.5
51	Turkey	4.8		1.3
52	Colombia	4.7		1.1
53	Pakistan	4.7		1.3
54	Nigeria	4.6		1.4
55	Brazil	4.5		1.5
56	Costa Rica	4.5		1.3
57	India	4.5		1.5
58	Italy	4.5		1.4
59	Kenya	4.4		1.7
60	Lithuania	4.4		1.3
61	Moldova	4.4		1.5
62	Ecuador	4.4		1.0
63	Ethiopia	4.4		1.6
64	Russian Federation	4.4		1.4
65	Hungary	4.3		1.5
66	Egypt	4.3		1.4
67	Argentina	4.3		1.1
68	Botswana	4.2		1.0
69	Panama	4.2		1.7
70	Indonesia	4.2		0.9
71	Kazakhstan	4.1		1.8
72	Gambia	4.1		1.4
73	Nicaragua	4.0		1.2
74	Poland	4.0		1.0
75	Philippines	4.0		1.1
75	Venezuela	4.0		1.0
77	China	4.0		1.3
78	Trinidad and Tobago	4.0		1.4
79	Romania	4.0		1.6
80	Croatia	4.0		1.4
81	Morocco	3.9		1.5
82	Guatemala	3.9		1.3
83	Ghana	3.8		1.4
83	Madagascar	3.8		1.3
85	Tanzania	3.8		1.4
86	Tajikistan	3.7		1.7
87	Bolivia	3.7		1.4
88	Honduras	3.7		1.4
89	Sri Lanka	3.7		1.6
90	Georgia	3.6		1.4
91	Cambodia	3.6		1.4
92	Vietnam	3.6		1.3
93	Armenia	3.6		1.5
94	Ukraine	3.5		1.4
95	Uruguay	3.5		1.3
96	Malawi	3.5		1.2
97	Kyrgyz Republic	3.5		1.5
98	Bulgaria	3.5		1.3
99	Mozambique	3.4		1.3
100	Macedonia, FYR	3.3		1.4
101	Algeria	3.3		1.5
102	Guyana	3.3		1.1
103	Peru	3.2		1.1
104	Zimbabwe	3.1		1.1
105	Slovak Republic	3.1		1.2
106	Bangladesh	3.1		1.2
107	Uganda	3.1		1.5
108	Benin	3.0		1.5
109	Paraguay	2.9		1.3
110	Serbia and Montenegro	2.9		1.4
111	Mongolia	2.9		1.2
112	East Timor	2.8		1.5
113	Mali	2.7		1.5
114	Albania	2.6		1.6
115	Bosnia and Herzegovina	2.2		1.2
116	Chad	2.1		1.4
117	Cameroon	2.0		1.2

5.05   Quality of electricity supply

The quality of electricity supply in your country (in terms of lack of interruptions and lack of voltage fluctuations) is (1 = worse than in most other countries, 7 = meets the highest standards in the world)

RANK	COUNTRY	SCORE	SD		RANK	COUNTRY	SCORE	SD
1	Iceland	6.9	0.3		60	Brazil	4.7	1.4
2	Germany	6.9	0.4		61	Kazakhstan	4.6	1.3
3	Japan	6.8	0.5		62	Trinidad and Tobago	4.6	1.2
4	Denmark	6.8	0.6		63	Venezuela	4.6	1.5
5	Finland	6.8	0.4		64	Jamaica	4.5	1.3
6	France	6.8	0.5		65	Malta	4.4	1.3
7	Netherlands	6.7	0.6		66	Bolivia	4.4	1.3
8	Switzerland	6.7	1.0		67	Argentina	4.3	1.2
9	Norway	6.6	0.8		68	Macedonia, FYR	4.3	1.7
10	Belgium	6.6	0.8		69	Turkey	4.2	1.3
11	United States	6.6	0.8		70	Bosnia and Herzegovina	4.2	1.7
12	Austria	6.6	1.0		71	Bulgaria	4.2	1.7
13	Singapore	6.5	0.7		72	Algeria	4.1	1.7
14	United Kingdom	6.5	0.9		73	Romania	4.1	1.7
15	Canada	6.5	0.8		74	Russian Federation	4.1	1.6
16	United Arab Emirates	6.4	0.8		75	Ghana	4.1	1.3
17	Hong Kong SAR	6.4	1.4		76	Ukraine	3.9	1.6
18	Ireland	6.3	0.8		77	Sri Lanka	3.8	1.4
19	Kuwait	6.3	0.8		78	Mexico	3.8	1.4
20	Czech Republic	6.3	0.9		79	Moldova	3.8	1.6
21	Luxembourg	6.2	0.9		80	China	3.7	1.4
22	Cyprus	6.2	0.8		81	Armenia	3.7	1.8
23	Australia	6.1	0.9		82	Paraguay	3.7	1.7
24	Israel	6.1	0.8		83	Philippines	3.7	1.3
25	Slovak Republic	6.0	1.1		84	Indonesia	3.6	1.1
26	Sweden	6.0	1.0		85	Honduras	3.6	1.4
27	Korea, Rep.	5.9	1.0		86	Pakistan	3.5	1.5
28	Taiwan	5.9	0.9		87	Guatemala	3.5	1.4
29	Portugal	5.8	1.0		88	Vietnam	3.5	1.5
30	Jordan	5.8	1.0		89	Serbia and Montenegro	3.5	1.7
31	Malaysia	5.8	0.8		90	Kyrgyz Republic	3.4	1.6
32	Slovenia	5.7	1.2		91	Mozambique	3.3	1.4
33	Qatar	5.7	1.1		92	Ethiopia	3.3	1.3
34	New Zealand	5.6	1.3		93	Azerbaijan	3.3	1.6
35	Chile	5.5	1.0		94	India	3.3	1.4
36	Spain	5.5	1.1		95	Ecuador	3.3	1.0
37	Uruguay	5.4	1.2		96	Nicaragua	3.1	1.2
38	Hungary	5.4	1.3		97	Zimbabwe	3.0	1.1
39	Italy	5.4	1.6		98	Kenya	3.0	1.5
40	Tunisia	5.4	1.3		99	Mongolia	3.0	1.2
41	Bahrain	5.3	1.4		100	Mali	2.9	1.4
42	Thailand	5.3	0.9		101	Tanzania	2.7	1.5
43	Costa Rica	5.2	1.2		102	Cambodia	2.6	1.4
44	Latvia	5.2	1.2		103	Madagascar	2.5	1.4
45	Lithuania	5.2	1.3		104	Benin	2.4	1.3
46	Mauritius	5.1	1.0		105	Bangladesh	2.3	1.0
47	Greece	5.1	1.2		106	Nigeria	2.1	1.3
48	Estonia	5.1	1.3		107	Cameroon	2.1	1.1
49	South Africa	5.1	1.3		108	Guyana	2.1	1.0
50	Colombia	5.0	1.3		109	Gambia	2.0	1.0
51	Botswana	5.0	1.2		110	Malawi	2.0	1.1
52	Poland	4.9	1.3		111	Tajikistan	1.9	1.2
53	Croatia	4.9	1.4		112	Uganda	1.8	1.1
54	Namibia	4.9	1.6		113	East Timor	1.8	1.1
55	Peru	4.9	1.1		114	Georgia	1.7	0.7
56	El Salvador	4.8	1.1		115	Albania	1.6	1.0
57	Panama	4.8	1.2		116	Chad	1.4	1.1
58	Morocco	4.7	1.6		117	Dominican Republic	1.3	0.5
59	Egypt	4.7	1.3					

MEAN: 4.6

5.06   Postal efficiency

Do you trust your country's postal system sufficiently to have a friend mail a small package worth US$100 to you? (1 = not at all, 7 = yes, trust the system entirely)

RANK	COUNTRY	SCORE	MEAN: 4.4	SD
1	Iceland	6.8		0.5
2	Japan	6.8		0.7
3	Denmark	6.6		0.8
4	Germany	6.6		0.6
5	Switzerland	6.6		1.1
6	Singapore	6.6		0.7
7	United States	6.5		0.9
8	Hong Kong SAR	6.5		1.0
9	Finland	6.5		0.9
10	Australia	6.4		0.8
11	Taiwan	6.4		0.9
12	Norway	6.4		0.8
13	Luxembourg	6.4		1.0
14	New Zealand	6.3		1.0
15	Slovenia	6.3		1.1
16	France	6.2		1.2
17	Netherlands	6.2		1.0
18	Canada	6.2		1.1
19	Austria	6.2		1.3
20	Sweden	6.1		1.0
21	Portugal	6.0		1.3
22	Cyprus	6.0		1.2
23	Qatar	6.0		1.4
24	Korea, Rep.	5.9		1.0
25	Ireland	5.9		1.1
26	Slovak Republic	5.8		1.5
27	Estonia	5.8		1.6
28	United Kingdom	5.7		1.6
29	United Arab Emirates	5.5		1.7
30	Greece	5.5		1.4
31	Malaysia	5.4		1.3
32	Brazil	5.4		1.8
33	Israel	5.4		1.5
34	Malta	5.3		1.3
35	Vietnam	5.3		1.8
36	Jordan	5.2		1.6
37	Czech Republic	5.2		1.9
38	Tunisia	5.2		1.8
39	Belgium	5.2		1.9
40	Bahrain	5.2		1.8
41	Spain	5.2		1.7
42	Botswana	5.1		1.7
43	Chile	5.1		1.7
44	Mauritius	5.0		1.7
45	Italy	5.0		1.8
46	China	5.0		1.5
47	Croatia	4.9		1.9
48	India	4.9		1.8
49	Thailand	4.9		1.5
50	Morocco	4.8		2.0
51	Romania	4.8		1.7
52	Lithuania	4.7		1.8
53	Serbia and Montenegro	4.7		1.9
54	Hungary	4.7		1.9
55	Latvia	4.5		1.8
56	Egypt	4.5		1.9
57	Azerbaijan	4.5		1.9
58	Kazakhstan	4.5		1.6
59	Bosnia and Herzegovina	4.5		1.9
60	Poland	4.4		1.6
61	Turkey	4.4		1.9
62	Russian Federation	4.3		1.9
63	Macedonia, FYR	4.3		2.1
64	Ghana	4.3		1.8
65	Mongolia	4.2		2.0
66	Ukraine	4.2		1.8
67	Tanzania	4.1		2.2
68	Armenia	4.1		1.9
69	Indonesia	4.1		1.5
70	Mali	4.0		2.0
71	Pakistan	4.0		2.0
72	El Salvador	3.9		2.1
73	Bulgaria	3.8		2.0
74	Namibia	3.7		2.0
75	Trinidad and Tobago	3.7		1.9
76	Benin	3.7		2.1
77	Moldova	3.6		1.9
78	Colombia	3.5		2.2
79	Kyrgyz Republic	3.4		1.6
80	Argentina	3.4		1.9
81	South Africa	3.4		1.9
82	Jamaica	3.3		2.0
83	Kuwait	3.2		2.3
84	Madagascar	3.2		1.8
85	Ethiopia	3.2		1.6
86	Kenya	3.2		1.9
87	Tajikistan	3.2		2.1
88	Algeria	3.1		1.5
89	Uganda	3.1		2.0
90	Nicaragua	3.1		1.8
91	Sri Lanka	3.1		1.9
92	Costa Rica	3.1		2.0
93	Bolivia	3.1		1.7
94	Peru	3.0		1.7
95	Panama	2.9		1.7
96	Uruguay	2.9		1.9
97	Malawi	2.7		1.7
98	Bangladesh	2.7		1.6
99	Guatemala	2.7		1.8
100	Mexico	2.7		1.7
101	Chad	2.7		2.1
102	Georgia	2.7		1.7
103	Philippines	2.7		1.7
104	Cambodia	2.7		1.7
105	Guyana	2.6		1.5
106	Zimbabwe	2.6		1.6
107	Mozambique	2.5		1.7
108	Gambia	2.5		1.7
109	Albania	2.4		1.8
110	East Timor	2.4		1.9
111	Ecuador	2.4		1.7
112	Honduras	2.3		1.6
113	Nigeria	2.1		1.3
114	Paraguay	2.0		1.5
115	Cameroon	2.0		1.5
116	Venezuela	1.6		1.1
117	Dominican Republic	1.5		1.0

5.07　Telephone/fax infrastructure quality

New telephone lines for your business are (1 = scarce and difficult to obtain, 7 = widely available and highly reliable)

RANK	COUNTRY	SCORE	1　MEAN: 5.4　7	SD		RANK	COUNTRY	SCORE	1　MEAN: 5.4　7	SD
1	Germany	6.9		0.4		60	Pakistan	5.7		1.2
2	Japan	6.9		0.4		61	Mexico	5.7		1.1
3	Finland	6.8		0.4		62	Italy	5.6		1.6
4	Singapore	6.8		0.4		63	Panama	5.6		1.5
5	Denmark	6.8		0.7		64	Venezuela	5.6		1.5
6	Switzerland	6.8		0.6		65	Philippines	5.5		1.4
7	Austria	6.8		0.4		66	Sri Lanka	5.5		1.5
8	France	6.8		0.5		67	China	5.5		1.3
9	Iceland	6.8		0.8		68	Macedonia, FYR	5.4		1.6
10	United States	6.7		0.6		69	Georgia	5.4		1.4
11	Norway	6.7		0.5		70	Namibia	5.4		1.3
12	Hong Kong SAR	6.7		0.9		71	Azerbaijan	5.3		1.6
13	Israel	6.7		0.5		72	Tanzania	5.2		1.5
14	Chile	6.7		0.6		73	Jamaica	5.2		1.5
15	Canada	6.6		0.7		74	Guatemala	5.2		1.8
16	Sweden	6.6		0.8		75	Bolivia	5.2		1.7
17	Belgium	6.6		0.8		76	Poland	5.2		1.4
18	New Zealand	6.6		0.6		77	Bosnia and Herzegovina	5.1		1.4
19	Netherlands	6.6		0.8		78	Romania	5.1		1.5
20	El Salvador	6.6		0.7		79	South Africa	5.0		1.6
21	Cyprus	6.5		0.7		80	Bulgaria	5.0		1.5
22	Portugal	6.5		0.7		81	Moldova	5.0		1.5
23	Taiwan	6.5		0.7		82	Kazakhstan	4.9		1.4
24	Jordan	6.5		0.9		83	Uganda	4.9		1.8
25	Slovak Republic	6.5		0.7		84	Mozambique	4.9		1.5
26	United Kingdom	6.5		1.0		85	Nigeria	4.9		1.2
27	Uruguay	6.4		0.8		86	Russian Federation	4.7		1.6
28	Hungary	6.4		0.9		87	Cambodia	4.7		1.7
29	Bahrain	6.4		0.9		88	Tajikistan	4.6		1.8
30	Australia	6.4		0.8		89	Serbia and Montenegro	4.4		1.9
31	Malta	6.3		0.8		90	Indonesia	4.4		1.2
32	Luxembourg	6.3		1.1		91	Ghana	4.4		1.5
33	United Arab Emirates	6.3		1.2		92	Botswana	4.3		1.6
34	Slovenia	6.3		0.9		93	Ukraine	4.3		1.5
35	Peru	6.3		0.7		94	Gambia	4.3		1.9
36	India	6.3		0.9		95	Trinidad and Tobago	4.2		1.7
37	Greece	6.3		0.7		96	Mongolia	4.2		1.7
38	Korea, Rep.	6.3		0.9		97	Mali	4.2		1.9
39	Czech Republic	6.2		1.0		98	Nicaragua	4.1		1.8
40	Brazil	6.2		1.0		99	Paraguay	4.0		1.6
41	Tunisia	6.2		1.1		100	East Timor	3.9		1.9
42	Estonia	6.2		1.3		101	Chad	3.9		2.1
43	Lithuania	6.2		0.9		102	Algeria	3.9		1.9
44	Dominican Republic	6.1		1.1		103	Ecuador	3.9		1.6
45	Malaysia	6.1		1.0		104	Kyrgyz Republic	3.8		1.6
46	Turkey	6.1		1.0		105	Armenia	3.8		1.9
47	Thailand	6.1		0.9		106	Kenya	3.7		1.8
48	Croatia	6.1		1.1		107	Madagascar	3.5		1.8
49	Morocco	6.1		1.4		108	Ethiopia	3.5		1.6
50	Spain	6.0		1.1		109	Malawi	3.5		1.6
51	Ireland	6.0		1.2		110	Albania	3.4		1.8
52	Kuwait	6.0		1.5		111	Honduras	3.3		2.0
52	Qatar	6.0		1.4		112	Guyana	3.3		1.7
54	Egypt	5.9		1.2		113	Costa Rica	3.2		1.6
55	Mauritius	5.9		1.0		114	Cameroon	3.0		1.7
56	Colombia	5.8		1.2		115	Zimbabwe	2.9		1.4
57	Latvia	5.8		1.2		116	Bangladesh	2.5		1.3
58	Vietnam	5.8		1.3		117	Benin	2.4		1.6
59	Argentina	5.8		1.2						

5.08 Telephone lines, 2003

Main telephone lines per 100 inhabitants, 2003

RANK	COUNTRY	HARD DATA		RANK	COUNTRY	HARD DATA
1	Luxembourg	79.7		60	Kuwait	19.6
2	Sweden	76.6		61	Malaysia	18.2
3	Switzerland	72.7		62	Colombia	17.9
4	Norway	71.3		63	Jamaica[1]	16.9
5	Denmark	66.9		64	Mexico	16.0
6	Iceland	66.0		65	Armenia	14.8
7	Germany	65.9		66	Kazakhstan	14.1
8	Canada	65.1		67	Georgia	13.4
9	United States	62.4		68	Egypt	12.7
10	Netherlands	61.4		69	Ecuador	12.2
11	United Kingdom	59.5		70	Panama	12.2
12	Taiwan	59.1		71	Tunisia	11.8
13	Cyprus	57.2		72	Dominican Republic	11.5
14	France	56.4		73	Azerbaijan	11.4
15	Hong Kong SAR	55.9		74	Jordan	11.4
16	Australia	54.2		75	El Salvador	11.3
17	Korea	53.8		76	Venezuela	11.1
18	Malta	52.1		77	Thailand	10.5
19	Finland	49.2		78	South Africa	10.4
20	Ireland	49.1		79	Guyana[1]	9.2
21	Belgium	48.9		80	Albania	8.3
22	Italy	48.4		81	Guatemala	7.7
23	Austria	48.1		82	Kyrgyz Republic	7.6
24	Japan	47.2		83	Botswana	7.5
25	Israel	45.8		84	Bolivia	7.3
26	Greece	45.4		85	Algeria	6.9
27	Singapore	45.2		86	Peru	6.7
28	New Zealand	44.8		87	Namibia	6.6
29	Spain	43.4		88	Mongolia	5.6
30	Portugal	41.1		89	Vietnam	5.4
31	Slovenia	40.7		90	Sri Lanka	4.9
32	Croatia	38.9		91	Honduras	4.9
33	Bulgaria	38.0		92	Paraguay	4.7
34	Czech Republic	36.0		93	Philippines	4.1
35	Hungary	34.9		94	Morocco	4.0
36	Estonia	34.1		95	India	4.0
37	Poland	30.7		96	Indonesia	3.9
38	Uruguay	29.0		97	Tajikistan	3.7
39	Mauritius	28.5		98	Nicaragua	3.7
40	Latvia	28.2		99	Gambia[1]	2.9
41	United Arab Emirates	28.1		100	Pakistan	2.7
42	Costa Rica	27.8		101	Zimbabwe	2.6
43	Bahrain	26.8		102	Ghana	1.3
44	Turkey	26.8		103	Kenya	1.0
45	Qatar	26.1		104	Benin	0.9
46	Russian Federation	25.3		105	Malawi	0.8
47	Macedonia, FYR	25.2		106	Nigeria	0.7
48	Trinidad and Tobago[1]	25.0		107	Cameroon[1]	0.7
49	Bosnia and Herzegovina	24.5		108	Ethiopia	0.6
50	Serbia and Montenegro	24.3		109	Mali	0.6
51	Slovak Republic	24.1		110	Bangladesh	0.5
52	Lithuania	23.9		111	Tanzania	0.4
53	Ukraine	23.3		112	Mozambique	0.4
54	Argentina	22.6		113	Madagascar	0.4
55	Brazil	22.3		114	Cambodia	0.3
56	Chile	22.1		115	Uganda	0.2
57	Moldova	21.9		116	East Timor[2]	0.2
58	China	20.9		117	Chad[1]	0.2
59	Romania	19.9				

SOURCES: International Telecommunications Union, *World Telecommunications Indicators 2004*, and national sources

[1] 2002

[2] 2004

6.01 Judicial independence

Is the judiciary in your country independent from political influences of members of government, citizens, or firms? (1 = no, heavily influenced, 7 = yes, entirely independent)

RANK	COUNTRY	SCORE	1 MEAN: 3.8 7	SD
1	Germany	6.3		1.1
2	Denmark	6.2		1.3
3	Switzerland	6.1		1.2
4	Australia	6.1		1.0
5	Ireland	6.1		1.1
6	Netherlands	6.0		1.4
7	New Zealand	6.0		1.3
8	Norway	6.0		1.2
9	United Kingdom	6.0		1.3
10	Luxembourg	6.0		1.3
11	Iceland	5.9		1.3
12	Finland	5.9		1.6
13	Austria	5.8		1.2
14	Israel	5.7		1.6
15	Portugal	5.6		1.2
16	Canada	5.5		1.5
17	United States	5.5		1.5
18	Cyprus	5.4		1.6
19	Singapore	5.4		1.3
20	Malaysia	5.4		1.4
21	Qatar	5.4		1.7
22	Japan	5.3		1.4
23	India	5.3		1.4
24	Botswana	5.3		1.5
25	Hong Kong SAR	5.2		1.8
26	Uruguay	5.2		1.5
27	Kuwait	5.2		1.8
28	Belgium	5.1		1.8
29	France	5.1		1.5
30	Malta	5.1		1.8
31	Ghana	5.0		1.6
32	Costa Rica	5.0		1.5
33	South Africa	4.9		1.7
34	Tanzania	4.8		1.7
35	Namibia	4.8		1.7
36	Sweden	4.8		1.6
37	Tunisia	4.8		1.6
38	Estonia	4.7		1.8
39	Jordan	4.7		1.6
40	Thailand	4.4		1.5
41	Czech Republic	4.3		1.8
42	Hungary	4.3		1.6
43	Malawi	4.3		1.9
44	Taiwan	4.3		1.4
45	Korea, Rep.	4.2		1.5
46	United Arab Emirates	4.2		1.7
47	Chile	4.1		1.6
48	Greece	4.1		1.6
49	Jamaica	4.1		1.7
50	Slovenia	4.0		1.6
51	Nigeria	3.9		1.6
52	Mali	3.8		2.0
53	Trinidad and Tobago	3.8		1.7
54	Uganda	3.8		1.8
55	Spain	3.8		1.6
56	Bahrain	3.8		2.0
57	Turkey	3.6		1.5
58	Latvia	3.5		1.5
59	Italy	3.5		1.7

RANK	COUNTRY	SCORE	1 MEAN: 3.8 7	SD
60	Mexico	3.5		1.5
61	Gambia	3.4		1.8
62	Poland	3.4		1.5
63	Vietnam	3.4		1.5
64	Mauritius	3.4		1.8
65	China	3.4		1.6
66	Colombia	3.4		1.6
67	Slovak Republic	3.3		1.6
68	Indonesia	3.2		1.3
69	El Salvador	3.1		1.5
70	Morocco	3.1		1.6
71	Tajikistan	3.0		1.5
72	Brazil	3.0		1.5
73	Sri Lanka	3.0		1.7
74	Kazakhstan	2.9		1.6
75	Kenya	2.9		1.6
76	Croatia	2.9		1.5
77	Madagascar	2.9		1.4
78	Lithuania	2.8		1.4
79	Algeria	2.8		1.5
80	Azerbaijan	2.8		1.7
81	East Timor	2.8		1.7
82	Albania	2.8		2.1
83	Bosnia and Herzegovina	2.7		1.2
84	Bangladesh	2.7		1.5
85	Philippines	2.7		1.5
86	Romania	2.6		1.4
87	Pakistan	2.6		1.5
88	Bulgaria	2.5		1.6
89	Panama	2.5		1.3
90	Guatemala	2.5		1.5
91	Serbia and Montenegro	2.5		1.3
92	Ethiopia	2.5		1.5
93	Mozambique	2.5		1.3
94	Moldova	2.4		1.7
95	Benin	2.4		1.7
96	Guyana	2.4		1.3
97	Honduras	2.4		1.5
98	Dominican Republic	2.4		1.2
99	Mongolia	2.4		1.3
100	Georgia	2.4		1.3
101	Cambodia	2.3		1.5
102	Russian Federation	2.3		1.3
103	Ukraine	2.3		1.2
104	Macedonia, FYR	2.3		1.4
105	Argentina	2.2		1.2
106	Bolivia	2.2		1.2
107	Cameroon	2.2		1.4
108	Armenia	2.1		1.4
110	Peru	2.0		1.1
109	Zimbabwe	2.1		1.1
111	Chad	1.9		1.3
112	Kyrgyz Republic	1.7		1.0
113	Paraguay	1.4		0.7
114	Venezuela	1.3		0.8
115	Ecuador	1.2		0.5
116	Nicaragua	1.2		0.5
	Egypt	n/a		n/a

6.02   Efficiency of legal framework

The legal framework in your country for private businesses to settle disputes and challenge the legality of government actions and/or regulations
(1 = is inefficient and subject to manipulation, 7 = is efficient and follows a clear, neutral process)

RANK	COUNTRY	SCORE	1 MEAN: 3.8 7	SD
1	Denmark	6.3		0.7
2	New Zealand	6.0		1.0
3	Iceland	6.0		1.2
4	Germany	5.9		1.1
5	Switzerland	5.9		1.1
6	Netherlands	5.9		1.2
7	Finland	5.9		1.2
8	Singapore	5.8		1.1
9	Luxembourg	5.8		1.1
10	Hong Kong SAR	5.7		1.5
11	United Kingdom	5.7		1.3
12	Austria	5.7		1.2
13	Ireland	5.6		1.2
14	Norway	5.6		1.2
15	Australia	5.6		1.1
16	Malaysia	5.5		1.2
17	United States	5.4		1.3
18	South Africa	5.4		1.3
19	Sweden	5.3		1.5
20	Canada	5.2		1.5
21	France	5.1		1.5
22	Cyprus	5.0		1.4
23	Israel	5.0		1.4
24	Botswana	4.9		1.5
25	Tunisia	4.9		1.3
26	Qatar	4.9		1.6
27	Japan	4.8		1.5
28	Kuwait	4.8		1.8
29	Ghana	4.8		1.5
30	India	4.7		1.5
31	Taiwan	4.7		1.2
32	Belgium	4.6		1.6
33	Estonia	4.5		1.6
34	Jordan	4.5		1.6
35	Chile	4.4		1.5
36	Thailand	4.3		1.3
37	Costa Rica	4.3		1.4
38	Korea, Rep.	4.2		1.4
39	Malta	4.2		1.8
40	Spain	4.2		1.4
41	Uruguay	4.1		1.4
42	United Arab Emirates	4.1		1.5
43	Namibia	4.1		1.7
44	Portugal	4.0		1.3
45	Tanzania	4.0		1.9
46	Jamaica	4.0		1.7
47	Mauritius	4.0		1.6
48	Greece	3.9		1.3
49	Hungary	3.8		1.5
50	Slovenia	3.8		1.3
51	Egypt	3.8		1.6
52	Trinidad and Tobago	3.8		1.5
53	Mali	3.7		1.7
54	Czech Republic	3.6		1.7
55	Gambia	3.6		1.7
56	Morocco	3.6		1.6
57	China	3.6		1.4
58	Colombia	3.5		1.3
59	Malawi	3.5		2.0
60	Bahrain	3.5		1.8
61	Latvia	3.5		1.3
62	Mexico	3.4		1.5
63	Algeria	3.4		1.5
64	Vietnam	3.4		1.4
65	Turkey	3.4		1.3
66	Sri Lanka	3.4		1.6
67	Tajikistan	3.3		1.6
68	Slovak Republic	3.3		1.4
69	Poland	3.3		1.2
70	Uganda	3.3		1.7
71	Azerbaijan	3.2		1.7
72	Kazakhstan	3.2		1.4
73	Indonesia	3.2		1.1
74	Brazil	3.2		1.5
75	Lithuania	3.2		1.4
76	Nigeria	3.2		1.1
77	Italy	3.1		1.5
78	El Salvador	3.1		1.2
79	Croatia	3.0		1.5
80	Cameroon	3.0		1.6
81	Ukraine	2.9		1.3
82	Madagascar	2.9		1.4
83	Panama	2.9		1.3
84	Kenya	2.9		1.5
85	Romania	2.8		1.4
86	Moldova	2.8		1.5
87	Bangladesh	2.7		1.4
88	Serbia and Montenegro	2.7		1.5
89	Benin	2.7		1.7
90	Honduras	2.7		1.3
91	Philippines	2.7		1.3
92	East Timor	2.7		1.5
93	Armenia	2.7		1.3
94	Ethiopia	2.6		1.4
95	Russian Federation	2.6		1.3
96	Mozambique	2.6		1.2
97	Bulgaria	2.6		1.5
98	Argentina	2.6		1.1
99	Zimbabwe	2.5		1.3
100	Bolivia	2.5		1.1
101	Albania	2.5		1.3
102	Dominican Republic	2.4		1.3
103	Georgia	2.4		1.2
104	Cambodia	2.4		1.3
105	Macedonia, FYR	2.4		1.2
106	Pakistan	2.4		1.2
107	Peru	2.4		1.1
108	Kyrgyz Republic	2.3		1.2
109	Bosnia and Herzegovina	2.3		1.0
110	Guatemala	2.3		1.2
111	Mongolia	2.2		1.2
112	Chad	2.2		1.4
113	Guyana	2.1		1.2
114	Paraguay	1.9		0.9
115	Ecuador	1.9		1.0
116	Nicaragua	1.8		1.0
117	Venezuela	1.7		1.2

551

6.03 Property rights

Property rights, including over financial assets, are (1 = poorly defined and not protected by law, 7 = clearly defined and well protected by law)

RANK	COUNTRY	SCORE	MEAN: 4.5	SD	RANK	COUNTRY	SCORE	MEAN: 4.5	SD
1	Germany	6.5		0.6	60	Brazil	4.3		1.7
2	United States	6.5		0.7	61	Vietnam	4.3		1.6
3	Iceland	6.4		0.9	62	Czech Republic	4.3		1.5
4	Switzerland	6.4		0.8	63	Trinidad and Tobago	4.2		1.5
5	Denmark	6.4		0.8	64	Philippines	4.2		1.6
6	Singapore	6.4		0.7	65	Armenia	4.2		1.6
7	United Kingdom	6.4		1.0	66	Mexico	4.2		1.4
8	Austria	6.3		0.8	67	El Salvador	4.2		1.3
9	Australia	6.3		1.0	68	Tanzania	4.2		1.5
10	Ireland	6.2		0.9	69	Kenya	4.2		1.7
11	New Zealand	6.2		1.1	70	Malawi	4.1		1.5
12	Netherlands	6.2		0.9	71	China	4.1		1.3
13	Finland	6.1		1.3	72	Morocco	4.1		1.6
14	Norway	6.1		1.0	73	Kazakhstan	4.1		1.5
15	Hong Kong SAR	6.0		1.4	74	Mali	4.0		1.6
16	France	6.0		1.0	75	Nigeria	4.0		1.4
17	Japan	6.0		1.1	76	Gambia	4.0		1.9
18	Canada	5.9		1.0	77	Azerbaijan	4.0		1.6
19	South Africa	5.8		1.0	78	Romania	3.9		1.4
20	Luxembourg	5.7		1.6	79	Sri Lanka	3.9		1.4
21	Sweden	5.7		1.3	80	Uganda	3.9		1.9
22	Cyprus	5.7		1.3	81	Mozambique	3.8		1.4
23	Malaysia	5.7		1.0	82	Cameroon	3.8		1.6
24	Belgium	5.6		1.4	83	Mongolia	3.8		1.6
25	Portugal	5.6		1.2	84	Madagascar	3.8		1.5
26	Israel	5.6		1.3	85	Bulgaria	3.7		1.6
27	Estonia	5.5		1.3	86	Croatia	3.7		1.5
28	Hungary	5.5		1.3	87	Pakistan	3.7		1.6
29	Taiwan	5.5		1.1	88	Indonesia	3.7		1.2
30	Malta	5.4		1.3	89	Algeria	3.6		1.8
31	Chile	5.3		1.4	90	Tajikistan	3.6		1.8
32	India	5.3		1.2	91	Bangladesh	3.6		1.7
33	Spain	5.2		1.4	92	Georgia	3.6		1.5
34	Botswana	5.2		1.3	93	Nicaragua	3.5		1.5
35	Jordan	5.2		1.4	94	Honduras	3.5		1.4
36	Korea, Rep.	5.2		1.3	95	Dominican Republic	3.5		1.5
37	Tunisia	5.2		1.3	96	Moldova	3.5		1.6
38	Qatar	5.2		1.5	97	Benin	3.5		1.7
39	Greece	5.1		1.2	98	Peru	3.4		1.3
40	Mauritius	5.0		1.7	99	Guyana	3.3		1.5
41	Italy	5.0		1.5	100	Albania	3.3		1.6
42	Slovak Republic	4.9		1.3	101	Ukraine	3.3		1.4
43	Thailand	4.9		1.3	102	Macedonia, FYR	3.2		1.6
44	Bahrain	4.9		1.6	103	Serbia and Montenegro	3.2		1.5
45	Lithuania	4.9		1.3	104	Kyrgyz Republic	3.2		1.5
46	Panama	4.8		1.5	105	Guatemala	3.2		1.4
47	Jamaica	4.7		1.5	106	Zimbabwe	3.1		1.6
48	Kuwait	4.7		1.7	107	Bolivia	3.1		1.4
49	Slovenia	4.7		1.2	108	Russian Federation	3.1		1.3
50	Namibia	4.7		1.9	109	Ecuador	3.1		1.3
51	Colombia	4.7		1.3	110	Argentina	3.1		1.4
52	Uruguay	4.6		1.4	111	Cambodia	3.0		1.5
53	Latvia	4.6		1.4	112	Ethiopia	3.0		1.6
54	Costa Rica	4.5		1.2	113	Bosnia and Herzegovina	2.9		1.2
55	Ghana	4.5		1.4	114	East Timor	2.8		1.9
56	United Arab Emirates	4.5		1.6	115	Chad	2.7		1.8
57	Egypt	4.4		1.6	116	Paraguay	2.6		1.0
58	Turkey	4.4		1.5	117	Venezuela	2.6		1.4
59	Poland	4.3		1.2					

6.04   Intellectual property protection

Intellectual property protection in your country (1 = is weak or nonexistent, 7 = is equal to the world's most stringent)

RANK	COUNTRY	SCORE	1 MEAN: 3.7 7	SD
1	United States	6.4		0.8
2	Germany	6.3		0.9
3	Switzerland	6.1		1.0
4	United Kingdom	6.1		1.1
5	Singapore	6.1		0.8
6	Denmark	5.9		0.9
7	Netherlands	5.9		1.1
8	Finland	5.8		1.3
9	Iceland	5.8		1.1
10	France	5.8		1.0
11	Australia	5.7		1.1
12	New Zealand	5.7		1.1
13	Ireland	5.6		1.0
14	Sweden	5.6		1.1
15	Austria	5.5		1.0
16	Canada	5.5		1.2
17	Norway	5.4		1.2
18	Japan	5.3		1.5
19	Luxembourg	5.2		1.1
20	Malaysia	5.1		1.1
21	Israel	5.1		1.0
22	Portugal	5.0		1.3
23	South Africa	5.0		1.4
24	Belgium	5.0		1.5
25	Hong Kong SAR	5.0		1.5
26	Taiwan	4.9		1.1
27	Korea, Rep.	4.5		1.4
28	Jordan	4.5		1.4
29	Tunisia	4.4		1.3
30	Slovenia	4.4		1.4
31	Spain	4.4		1.5
32	United Arab Emirates	4.3		1.5
33	Qatar	4.3		1.6
34	Italy	4.3		1.5
35	Estonia	4.3		1.4
36	Cyprus	4.2		1.6
37	Thailand	4.1		1.3
38	Bahrain	4.1		1.6
39	Hungary	4.1		1.3
40	Greece	4.1		1.3
41	India	4.0		1.3
42	Malta	3.9		1.5
43	Ghana	3.8		1.5
44	Slovak Republic	3.8		1.4
45	Chile	3.8		1.3
46	Czech Republic	3.7		1.5
47	Mauritius	3.7		1.7
48	Jamaica	3.7		1.3
49	Costa Rica	3.7		1.4
50	Botswana	3.7		1.5
51	Poland	3.6		1.3
52	Uruguay	3.5		1.5
53	Cameroon	3.5		1.6
54	Kuwait	3.4		1.6
55	Egypt	3.4		1.5
56	Zimbabwe	3.4		1.2
57	Colombia	3.4		1.5
58	Panama	3.4		1.3
59	El Salvador	3.4		1.2

RANK	COUNTRY	SCORE	1 MEAN: 3.7 7	SD
60	Mexico	3.3		1.4
61	Latvia	3.3		1.4
62	Kazakhstan	3.2		1.5
63	China	3.2		1.5
64	Mali	3.2		1.6
65	Brazil	3.2		1.5
66	Namibia	3.2		1.6
67	Croatia	3.2		1.4
68	Indonesia	3.2		1.2
69	Lithuania	3.1		1.2
70	Sri Lanka	3.1		1.3
71	Argentina	3.1		1.2
72	Morocco	3.1		1.5
73	Madagascar	3.1		1.4
74	Turkey	3.1		1.2
75	Benin	3.1		1.7
76	Nigeria	3.0		1.4
77	Romania	3.0		1.5
78	Trinidad and Tobago	2.9		1.4
79	Tanzania	2.9		1.5
80	Kenya	2.9		1.4
81	Honduras	2.9		1.1
82	Dominican Republic	2.8		1.2
83	Azerbaijan	2.8		1.4
84	Philippines	2.8		1.2
85	Mozambique	2.7		1.3
86	Tajikistan	2.7		1.4
87	Peru	2.7		1.2
88	Pakistan	2.6		1.2
89	Moldova	2.6		1.4
90	Bulgaria	2.6		1.4
91	Ukraine	2.6		1.2
92	Vietnam	2.6		1.3
93	Nicaragua	2.5		1.2
94	Uganda	2.5		1.4
95	Gambia	2.5		1.5
96	Ethiopia	2.5		1.3
97	Ecuador	2.5		1.2
98	Algeria	2.5		1.4
99	Macedonia, FYR	2.5		1.3
100	Malawi	2.4		1.4
101	Kyrgyz Republic	2.4		1.2
102	Cambodia	2.4		1.3
103	Mongolia	2.4		1.1
104	East Timor	2.4		1.8
105	Russian Federation	2.4		1.2
106	Venezuela	2.4		1.4
107	Guatemala	2.4		1.2
108	Georgia	2.4		1.3
109	Armenia	2.2		1.2
110	Serbia and Montenegro	2.2		1.2
111	Bangladesh	2.2		1.2
112	Albania	2.1		1.3
113	Bosnia and Herzegovina	2.0		0.9
114	Chad	2.0		1.3
115	Paraguay	1.9		0.8
116	Bolivia	1.9		0.9
117	Guyana	1.7		0.9

6.05   Freedom of the press

In your country, can the media publish/broadcast stories of their choosing without fear of censorship or retaliation? (1 = no, 7 = yes, whatever they want)

RANK	COUNTRY	SCORE	1 MEAN: 4.9 7	SD
1	Germany	6.8		0.5
2	Iceland	6.7		0.6
3	Denmark	6.6		1.1
4	Portugal	6.6		0.6
5	Netherlands	6.6		1.0
6	Sweden	6.5		0.8
7	Switzerland	6.5		0.9
8	Norway	6.5		1.1
9	Austria	6.5		0.9
10	Estonia	6.4		1.1
11	Finland	6.4		0.9
12	Canada	6.4		0.9
13	Belgium	6.3		1.1
14	United Kingdom	6.2		1.2
15	France	6.2		1.0
16	United States	6.2		1.3
17	New Zealand	6.2		1.2
18	India	6.2		1.2
19	Australia	6.1		1.1
20	Ghana	6.1		1.1
21	Luxembourg	6.1		1.3
22	South Africa	6.1		1.1
23	Greece	6.1		1.2
24	Slovak Republic	6.0		1.3
25	Bolivia	6.0		1.2
26	Ireland	5.9		1.4
27	Japan	5.9		1.2
28	Philippines	5.9		1.5
29	Uruguay	5.9		1.3
30	Spain	5.9		1.3
31	Israel	5.8		1.2
32	Costa Rica	5.8		1.5
33	Peru	5.8		1.3
34	Czech Republic	5.7		1.5
35	Chile	5.7		1.3
36	Taiwan	5.7		1.2
37	Nicaragua	5.7		1.5
38	Brazil	5.7		1.6
39	Cyprus	5.6		1.6
40	Malta	5.6		1.6
41	Mexico	5.6		1.4
42	Lithuania	5.5		1.6
43	El Salvador	5.4		1.7
44	Hungary	5.4		1.7
45	Poland	5.4		1.4
46	Latvia	5.4		1.5
47	Hong Kong SAR	5.4		1.8
48	Colombia	5.3		1.7
49	Italy	5.3		1.6
50	Slovenia	5.3		1.6
51	Jamaica	5.2		1.8
52	Serbia and Montenegro	5.2		1.8
53	Paraguay	5.1		1.7
54	Korea, Rep.	5.0		1.5
55	Macedonia, FYR	5.0		1.9
56	Mali	5.0		2.0
57	Mauritius	4.9		1.7
58	Albania	4.9		1.9
59	Honduras	4.9		2.0
60	Bulgaria	4.9		1.9
61	Botswana	4.9		1.8
62	Trinidad and Tobago	4.9		1.7
63	Tanzania	4.9		1.7
64	Benin	4.8		2.1
65	Bangladesh	4.8		1.9
66	Romania	4.8		1.8
67	Kuwait	4.7		1.9
68	Namibia	4.7		1.9
69	Thailand	4.7		1.6
70	Croatia	4.6		1.9
71	Georgia	4.6		1.9
72	Uganda	4.6		2.1
73	Qatar	4.6		1.8
74	Indonesia	4.6		1.3
75	Bosnia and Herzegovina	4.5		1.6
76	Nigeria	4.5		1.7
77	Dominican Republic	4.4		2.0
78	Pakistan	4.4		1.9
79	Guatemala	4.4		2.0
80	Argentina	4.3		1.8
81	Kenya	4.2		2.0
82	Moldova	4.2		1.9
83	Malaysia	4.2		1.6
84	Turkey	4.2		1.9
85	Mongolia	4.1		2.0
86	Panama	4.1		2.1
87	Armenia	4.1		1.8
88	Mozambique	4.0		1.8
89	Ukraine	4.0		1.7
90	Ecuador	3.9		1.9
91	Azerbaijan	3.9		1.9
92	Sri Lanka	3.9		1.8
93	Malawi	3.9		2.0
94	Bahrain	3.8		1.9
95	Madagascar	3.8		1.9
96	Russian Federation	3.8		1.9
97	Tunisia	3.7		1.6
98	Jordan	3.7		1.7
99	Kazakhstan	3.7		1.7
100	Morocco	3.7		1.9
101	Guyana	3.7		2.2
102	Cameroon	3.7		2.0
103	East Timor	3.6		2.1
104	Vietnam	3.6		1.7
105	Chad	3.6		2.3
106	Algeria	3.6		2.0
107	Kyrgyz Republic	3.5		1.8
108	Cambodia	3.5		1.8
109	Singapore	3.3		1.6
110	United Arab Emirates	3.2		1.6
111	Tajikistan	3.2		2.0
112	Ethiopia	2.8		1.8
113	Gambia	2.6		1.7
114	China	2.6		1.5
115	Venezuela	2.4		1.6
116	Zimbabwe	1.5		0.9
	Egypt	n/a		n/a

6.06   Wastefulness of government spending

The composition of public spending in your country (1 = is wasteful, 7 = provides necessary goods and services not provided by the market)

RANK	COUNTRY	SCORE	1 MEAN: 3.3 7	SD		RANK	COUNTRY	SCORE	1 MEAN: 3.3 7	SD
1	Singapore	5.9		0.8		60	Greece	3.2		1.2
2	Malaysia	5.1		1.2		61	East Timor	3.2		1.7
3	Qatar	5.1		1.1		62	Slovenia	3.1		1.3
4	Denmark	5.1		1.3		63	Armenia	3.1		1.4
5	United Arab Emirates	5.0		1.0		63	India	3.1		1.3
6	Iceland	5.0		1.1		65	Uganda	3.1		1.6
7	Tunisia	4.9		1.2		66	Colombia	3.0		1.2
8	Norway	4.9		1.2		67	Uruguay	3.0		1.2
9	Netherlands	4.8		1.3		68	Japan	3.0		1.5
10	Finland	4.6		1.4		69	Georgia	3.0		1.3
11	Hong Kong SAR	4.6		1.4		70	Cambodia	2.9		1.6
12	Taiwan	4.5		1.0		71	Tajikistan	2.9		1.6
13	Switzerland	4.4		1.4		72	Mozambique	2.9		1.4
14	South Africa	4.4		1.3		73	Hungary	2.9		1.3
15	Botswana	4.4		1.5		74	Croatia	2.8		1.3
16	Australia	4.3		1.3		75	Trinidad and Tobago	2.8		1.4
17	Thailand	4.3		1.4		76	Turkey	2.8		1.2
18	Luxembourg	4.3		1.5		77	Poland	2.8		1.2
19	Chile	4.2		1.4		78	Czech Republic	2.8		1.4
20	United States	4.2		1.4		79	Malta	2.8		1.1
21	Ghana	4.2		1.3		80	Moldova	2.7		1.5
22	Austria	4.1		1.4		81	Nigeria	2.7		1.2
23	Jordan	4.0		1.3		82	Slovak Republic	2.7		1.2
24	Spain	4.0		1.4		83	Costa Rica	2.7		1.0
25	New Zealand	4.0		1.4		84	Macedonia, FYR	2.7		1.6
26	Tanzania	4.0		1.4		85	Bangladesh	2.7		1.3
27	United Kingdom	3.9		1.5		86	Guyana	2.7		1.3
28	Ireland	3.9		1.5		87	Italy	2.7		1.4
29	France	3.9		1.5		88	Jamaica	2.7		1.3
30	Cyprus	3.8		1.4		89	Bulgaria	2.7		1.2
31	Sweden	3.8		1.5		90	Romania	2.6		1.3
32	Korea, Rep.	3.8		1.4		91	Argentina	2.6		1.2
33	Canada	3.8		1.5		92	Malawi	2.6		1.6
34	Egypt	3.7		1.5		93	Russian Federation	2.6		1.4
35	El Salvador	3.7		1.2		94	Honduras	2.6		1.3
36	Bahrain	3.7		1.5		95	Albania	2.6		1.5
37	Germany	3.7		1.5		96	Ukraine	2.5		1.3
38	Kuwait	3.6		1.5		97	Bolivia	2.5		1.3
39	Kazakhstan	3.6		1.4		98	Sri Lanka	2.5		1.2
40	Indonesia	3.6		1.2		99	Panama	2.5		1.0
41	Israel	3.5		1.4		100	Philippines	2.4		1.2
41	Mauritius	3.5		1.7		101	Nicaragua	2.4		1.4
43	Estonia	3.5		1.3		102	Cameroon	2.4		1.3
44	China	3.4		1.5		103	Peru	2.3		1.0
45	Gambia	3.4		1.4		104	Benin	2.3		1.5
46	Lithuania	3.4		1.0		105	Kenya	2.3		1.4
47	Madagascar	3.4		1.6		106	Guatemala	2.3		1.3
48	Pakistan	3.4		1.7		107	Kyrgyz Republic	2.3		1.3
49	Latvia	3.3		1.2		108	Serbia and Montenegro	2.3		1.1
50	Belgium	3.3		1.6		109	Mongolia	2.2		1.2
51	Algeria	3.3		1.7		110	Bosnia and Herzegovina	2.1		1.2
52	Namibia	3.2		1.7		111	Brazil	2.1		1.0
52	Vietnam	3.2		1.4		112	Zimbabwe	2.0		1.3
54	Morocco	3.2		1.6		113	Ecuador	2.0		0.9
55	Mexico	3.2		1.2		114	Chad	1.8		1.3
56	Mali	3.2		1.6		115	Dominican Republic	1.7		0.8
57	Azerbaijan	3.2		1.7		116	Venezuela	1.7		1.3
58	Portugal	3.2		1.1		117	Paraguay	1.6		0.9
59	Ethiopia	3.2		1.4						

6.07 Burden of government regulation

Complying with administrative requirements (permits, regulations, reporting) issued by the government in your country is (1 = burdensome, 7 = not burdensome)

RANK	COUNTRY	SCORE	MEAN: 3.0	SD
1	Singapore	5.4		1.3
2	Hong Kong SAR	4.8		1.7
3	Malaysia	4.6		1.4
4	Taiwan	4.5		1.3
5	Finland	4.5		1.6
6	Iceland	4.4		1.4
7	United Arab Emirates	4.2		1.5
8	Estonia	4.1		1.4
9	Denmark	4.0		1.6
10	Tunisia	3.9		1.5
11	Thailand	3.8		1.4
12	Jordan	3.8		1.6
13	Switzerland	3.8		1.5
14	Korea, Rep.	3.8		1.4
15	Ireland	3.8		1.7
16	Ghana	3.8		1.5
17	Gambia	3.7		1.7
18	Chile	3.6		1.3
19	Cyprus	3.6		1.3
20	United States	3.6		1.6
21	Qatar	3.6		1.5
22	Norway	3.5		1.4
23	Tanzania	3.5		1.7
24	Sweden	3.5		1.3
25	Spain	3.5		1.3
26	Botswana	3.5		1.8
27	Azerbaijan	3.4		1.7
28	Portugal	3.4		1.2
29	Canada	3.4		1.4
30	China	3.4		1.2
31	Japan	3.4		1.4
32	Austria	3.3		1.4
33	Latvia	3.3		1.4
34	Luxembourg	3.3		1.6
35	Bahrain	3.2		1.6
35	Nigeria	3.2		1.4
37	Uganda	3.2		1.8
38	Israel	3.2		1.3
39	New Zealand	3.2		1.3
40	Mali	3.2		1.8
41	Dominican Republic	3.1		1.6
42	Malawi	3.1		1.5
43	Mozambique	3.1		1.8
44	Namibia	3.1		1.6
45	Indonesia	3.1		1.3
46	El Salvador	3.1		1.3
47	Ethiopia	3.1		1.6
48	Kazakhstan	3.1		1.6
49	Netherlands	3.1		1.5
50	Romania	3.0		1.5
51	United Kingdom	3.0		1.4
52	Australia	3.0		1.3
53	East Timor	2.9		1.7
54	Hungary	2.9		1.2
55	Cambodia	2.9		1.7
56	Panama	2.9		1.4
57	Armenia	2.9		1.5
58	Egypt	2.9		1.6
59	Uruguay	2.9		1.2
60	Kenya	2.9		1.8
61	Lithuania	2.9		1.3
61	Nicaragua	2.9		1.3
63	Morocco	2.8		1.5
64	Czech Republic	2.8		1.2
65	Turkey	2.8		1.3
66	South Africa	2.8		1.3
67	Paraguay	2.8		1.6
68	France	2.8		1.3
69	Greece	2.8		1.3
70	Honduras	2.8		1.4
71	Colombia	2.8		1.4
72	Macedonia, FYR	2.8		1.6
73	Kuwait	2.8		1.6
73	Slovak Republic	2.8		1.2
75	Tajikistan	2.7		1.5
76	India	2.7		1.4
77	Bulgaria	2.7		1.4
78	Trinidad and Tobago	2.7		1.2
79	Slovenia	2.7		1.1
80	Germany	2.7		1.4
81	Poland	2.7		1.2
82	Georgia	2.7		1.4
83	Sri Lanka	2.7		1.4
84	Ukraine	2.6		1.3
85	Chad	2.6		2.0
86	Mongolia	2.6		1.4
87	Costa Rica	2.6		1.3
88	Albania	2.6		1.7
89	Jamaica	2.6		1.4
90	Kyrgyz Republic	2.6		1.4
91	Guatemala	2.6		1.3
92	Madagascar	2.5		1.4
93	Guyana	2.5		1.4
94	Pakistan	2.5		1.3
95	Philippines	2.5		1.6
96	Mexico	2.5		1.1
97	Croatia	2.4		1.1
98	Bangladesh	2.4		1.6
99	Malta	2.4		1.3
100	Zimbabwe	2.4		1.5
101	Argentina	2.4		1.1
102	Vietnam	2.4		1.2
103	Bolivia	2.4		1.3
104	Benin	2.4		1.6
105	Ecuador	2.3		1.2
106	Cameroon	2.3		1.3
107	Algeria	2.3		1.3
108	Moldova	2.3		1.4
109	Belgium	2.2		1.1
110	Russian Federation	2.2		1.3
111	Venezuela	2.2		1.5
112	Mauritius	2.1		1.2
113	Italy	2.1		1.1
114	Peru	2.1		1.0
115	Brazil	2.0		1.2
116	Serbia and Montenegro	2.0		1.1
117	Bosnia and Herzegovina	2.0		1.1

6.08 Favoritism in decisions of government officials

When deciding upon policies and contracts, government officials (1 = usually favor well-connected firms and individuals, 7 = are neutral)

RANK	COUNTRY	SCORE	1 MEAN: 3.2 7	SD
1	Denmark	5.4		1.1
2	New Zealand	5.3		1.2
3	Singapore	5.2		1.5
4	Qatar	4.9		1.7
5	Finland	4.9		1.4
6	Netherlands	4.8		1.2
7	Luxembourg	4.7		1.3
8	Norway	4.7		1.4
9	Sweden	4.6		1.4
10	Ireland	4.6		1.9
11	Malaysia	4.5		1.5
12	Switzerland	4.5		1.6
13	Germany	4.5		1.4
14	Tunisia	4.5		1.4
15	Iceland	4.5		1.6
16	United Kingdom	4.5		1.5
17	Taiwan	4.4		1.3
18	Australia	4.4		1.6
19	Japan	4.3		1.6
20	Chile	4.1		1.6
21	France	4.1		1.5
22	Portugal	4.1		1.5
23	Austria	4.0		1.6
24	United Arab Emirates	4.0		1.6
25	Botswana	3.9		1.8
26	Korea, Rep.	3.8		1.6
27	Uruguay	3.8		1.2
28	Belgium	3.8		1.7
29	Ghana	3.8		1.4
30	Indonesia	3.7		1.0
31	Jordan	3.7		1.5
32	Hong Kong SAR	3.7		1.6
33	United States	3.6		1.5
34	Estonia	3.6		1.3
35	Algeria	3.6		1.7
36	Kuwait	3.5		2.0
37	Tanzania	3.5		1.9
38	El Salvador	3.5		1.4
39	Thailand	3.5		1.3
40	Bahrain	3.5		2.0
41	Panama	3.5		1.6
42	Egypt	3.5		1.6
43	Mali	3.5		1.9
44	Cyprus	3.4		1.4
45	Canada	3.4		1.5
46	Gambia	3.3		1.7
47	Azerbaijan	3.3		1.8
48	Morocco	3.3		1.5
49	Israel	3.3		1.3
50	Slovenia	3.2		1.3
51	Mauritius	3.2		1.4
52	Spain	3.2		1.4
53	India	3.2		1.3
54	Greece	3.1		1.2
55	Kazakhstan	3.1		1.5
56	Czech Republic	3.1		1.3
57	Lithuania	3.1		1.2
58	South Africa	3.0		1.4
59	China	3.0		1.4

RANK	COUNTRY	SCORE	1 MEAN: 3.2 7	SD
60	Costa Rica	3.0		1.3
61	Malta	3.0		1.3
62	Tajikistan	3.0		1.8
63	Latvia	3.0		1.3
64	Turkey	3.0		1.2
65	Mozambique	3.0		1.7
66	Ethiopia	2.9		1.7
67	Nigeria	2.9		1.4
68	Pakistan	2.9		1.5
69	Brazil	2.9		1.3
70	Vietnam	2.9		1.3
71	Mexico	2.9		1.3
72	Italy	2.9		1.4
73	Hungary	2.8		1.3
74	Georgia	2.8		1.5
75	Cameroon	2.8		1.6
76	Macedonia, FYR	2.8		1.6
77	Croatia	2.8		1.2
78	Madagascar	2.7		1.4
79	Jamaica	2.7		1.4
80	Colombia	2.6		1.1
81	Malawi	2.6		1.5
82	Nicaragua	2.6		1.4
83	Moldova	2.6		1.6
84	Bosnia and Herzegovina	2.6		1.3
85	Namibia	2.6		1.5
86	East Timor	2.6		1.6
87	Trinidad and Tobago	2.6		1.2
88	Poland	2.6		1.2
89	Peru	2.5		1.1
90	Chad	2.5		1.8
91	Slovak Republic	2.5		1.0
92	Benin	2.5		1.5
93	Romania	2.5		1.2
94	Cambodia	2.4		1.4
95	Serbia and Montenegro	2.4		1.5
96	Ukraine	2.4		1.3
97	Argentina	2.4		1.2
98	Philippines	2.4		1.2
99	Zimbabwe	2.3		1.2
100	Sri Lanka	2.3		1.4
101	Bulgaria	2.3		1.4
102	Armenia	2.3		1.5
103	Honduras	2.3		1.4
104	Uganda	2.3		1.6
105	Guatemala	2.3		1.4
106	Russian Federation	2.2		1.3
107	Mongolia	2.2		1.5
108	Bolivia	2.2		1.2
109	Kenya	2.2		1.5
110	Bangladesh	2.1		1.2
111	Albania	2.1		1.3
112	Kyrgyz Republic	2.0		1.3
113	Guyana	1.9		1.2
114	Ecuador	1.8		1.0
115	Paraguay	1.7		1.1
116	Venezuela	1.7		1.1
117	Dominican Republic	1.6		0.8

6.09   Extent of bureaucratic red tape

How much time does your firm's senior management spend dealing/negotiating with government officials (as a percentage of work time)?
(1 = 0%, 2 = 1–10%, 3 = 11–20%, 8 = 81–100%)

RANK	COUNTRY	SCORE	1 MEAN: 2.9 8	SD
1	Romania	2.0		1.2
2	Hungary	2.1		1.0
3	Finland	2.1		0.9
4	Croatia	2.1		1.1
5	Sweden	2.2		0.8
6	Bosnia and Herzegovina	2.2		0.7
7	Japan	2.2		0.7
8	Iceland	2.2		1.0
9	Benin	2.2		1.5
10	Czech Republic	2.2		1.1
11	Luxembourg	2.3		0.6
12	Cyprus	2.3		0.8
13	Ireland	2.3		1.1
14	Belgium	2.4		1.1
15	Singapore	2.4		0.7
16	Malta	2.4		1.0
17	Switzerland	2.4		1.0
18	Dominican Republic	2.4		1.2
19	Austria	2.4		0.7
20	United Kingdom	2.4		0.9
21	Italy	2.4		1.4
22	Chile	2.4		1.2
23	Jamaica	2.5		1.0
24	Canada	2.5		1.2
25	Norway	2.5		1.0
26	New Zealand	2.5		1.1
27	Slovak Republic	2.5		1.1
28	France	2.5		1.4
29	Spain	2.5		1.4
30	Estonia	2.5		1.1
31	Taiwan	2.5		1.2
32	Mozambique	2.6		1.2
33	Australia	2.6		0.9
34	Tunisia	2.6		1.2
35	United States	2.6		1.2
36	Denmark	2.6		1.2
37	Poland	2.6		1.5
38	Latvia	2.6		1.1
39	Paraguay	2.6		1.5
40	El Salvador	2.7		1.3
41	Azerbaijan	2.7		1.6
42	Germany	2.7		1.1
43	Korea, Rep.	2.7		1.1
44	Uruguay	2.7		1.4
45	Greece	2.7		1.2
46	Argentina	2.7		1.4
47	Chad	2.7		1.8
48	Indonesia	2.7		1.1
49	Colombia	2.7		1.4
50	Slovenia	2.7		1.3
51	Guatemala	2.7		1.7
52	Lithuania	2.7		1.4
53	Armenia	2.7		1.3
54	Peru	2.8		1.2
55	Macedonia, FYR	2.8		1.7
56	Israel	2.8		1.2
57	Madagascar	2.8		1.5
58	Tanzania	2.8		1.4
59	Trinidad and Tobago	2.8		1.6

RANK	COUNTRY	SCORE	1 MEAN: 2.9 8	SD
60	India	2.8		1.3
61	Algeria	2.8		1.7
62	United Arab Emirates	2.8		1.1
63	Netherlands	2.8		1.4
64	Vietnam	2.9		1.4
65	Kazakhstan	2.9		1.2
66	Serbia and Montenegro	2.9		1.5
67	Hong Kong SAR	2.9		1.3
68	Brazil	2.9		1.5
69	South Africa	2.9		1.2
70	Gambia	2.9		1.6
71	Bolivia	2.9		1.6
72	Panama	3.0		1.7
73	Morocco	3.0		1.6
74	Uganda	3.0		1.6
75	Guyana	3.0		1.4
75	Mauritius	3.0		1.2
77	Mongolia	3.0		1.8
78	Turkey	3.0		1.4
79	Costa Rica	3.1		1.4
80	Pakistan	3.1		1.6
81	Portugal	3.1		1.2
82	Mali	3.1		1.8
83	Cambodia	3.1		1.5
84	Georgia	3.1		1.3
85	Botswana	3.1		1.4
86	Philippines	3.1		1.5
87	Albania	3.1		1.7
88	Ecuador	3.2		1.9
89	Moldova	3.2		1.3
90	Russian Federation	3.2		1.4
91	Kenya	3.2		1.6
92	Thailand	3.2		1.6
93	Bulgaria	3.3		1.6
94	Ghana	3.3		1.4
95	Kyrgyz Republic	3.3		1.6
96	Ukraine	3.3		1.3
97	Namibia	3.3		1.6
98	Ethiopia	3.3		1.6
98	Malawi	3.3		1.4
98	Tajikistan	3.3		1.4
101	Nicaragua	3.3		1.8
102	Bahrain	3.4		1.5
103	Honduras	3.4		1.8
104	Kuwait	3.4		1.6
105	Sri Lanka	3.4		1.7
106	Malaysia	3.4		1.4
107	Mexico	3.4		1.7
108	Cameroon	3.4		1.7
109	Jordan	3.4		1.6
110	Egypt	3.5		1.5
111	Bangladesh	3.5		1.6
112	Qatar	3.6		1.7
113	Zimbabwe	3.6		1.5
114	Venezuela	3.7		1.9
115	Nigeria	3.8		1.6
116	China	3.9		1.4
117	East Timor	4.2		1.9

6.10   Effectiveness of law-making bodies

How effective is your national parliament/congress as a law-making and oversight institution? (1 = very ineffective, 7 = very effective—the best in the world)

RANK	COUNTRY	SCORE	1 MEAN: 3.4 7	SD
1	Singapore	6.2		0.8
2	Denmark	5.5		1.2
3	United Kingdom	5.5		1.1
4	Australia	5.4		1.1
5	Malaysia	5.3		1.1
6	Ghana	5.2		1.1
7	Iceland	5.2		1.1
8	New Zealand	5.2		1.4
9	United States	5.0		1.5
10	Finland	4.9		1.1
11	Ireland	4.8		1.4
12	France	4.7		1.3
13	South Africa	4.7		1.3
14	Canada	4.7		1.3
15	Norway	4.6		1.2
16	Sweden	4.6		1.1
17	Botswana	4.5		1.5
18	Netherlands	4.5		1.5
19	Luxembourg	4.4		1.5
20	Switzerland	4.4		1.5
21	India	4.3		1.4
22	Tanzania	4.3		1.6
23	Malta	4.2		1.2
24	Thailand	4.2		1.3
25	Kuwait	4.2		1.6
26	China	4.1		1.5
27	Turkey	4.1		1.3
28	Israel	4.1		1.2
29	Japan	4.1		1.5
30	Mauritius	4.1		1.4
31	Estonia	4.1		1.2
32	Austria	4.1		1.4
33	Cyprus	4.1		1.3
34	Germany	4.1		1.6
35	Tunisia	4.0		1.4
36	Kazakhstan	4.0		1.5
37	Spain	4.0		1.3
38	Tajikistan	3.9		1.6
39	Greece	3.9		1.2
40	Vietnam	3.9		1.4
41	Portugal	3.9		1.3
42	Taiwan	3.9		1.3
43	Jordan	3.8		1.5
44	Chile	3.8		1.2
45	Mali	3.8		1.5
46	United Arab Emirates	3.7		1.7
47	Hong Kong SAR	3.7		1.4
48	Korea, Rep.	3.6		1.6
49	Uganda	3.6		1.6
50	Jamaica	3.6		1.5
51	Egypt	3.6		1.6
52	Indonesia	3.5		1.1
53	Slovenia	3.5		1.1
54	Namibia	3.5		1.5
55	Hungary	3.5		1.4
56	Qatar	3.4		1.7
57	Belgium	3.4		1.5
58	Azerbaijan	3.3		1.7
59	Albania	3.3		1.5

RANK	COUNTRY	SCORE	1 MEAN: 3.4 7	SD
60	Lithuania	3.3		1.2
61	Latvia	3.3		1.3
62	Georgia	3.2		1.2
63	Ukraine	3.2		1.3
64	Benin	3.2		1.6
65	Slovak Republic	3.2		1.3
66	Gambia	3.1		1.5
67	Italy	3.1		1.3
68	Croatia	3.1		1.3
69	Czech Republic	3.1		1.4
70	Morocco	3.1		1.5
71	Malawi	3.1		1.3
72	Honduras	3.0		1.3
73	Trinidad and Tobago	3.0		1.3
74	Pakistan	2.9		1.5
75	Uruguay	2.9		1.2
76	Moldova	2.9		1.6
77	Poland	2.9		1.3
78	Sri Lanka	2.9		1.4
79	Serbia and Montenegro	2.8		1.5
80	Russian Federation	2.8		1.3
81	Madagascar	2.8		1.1
82	Macedonia, FYR	2.8		1.4
83	Cambodia	2.8		1.4
84	Colombia	2.8		1.3
85	Bahrain	2.8		1.5
86	Kyrgyz Republic	2.8		1.2
87	Algeria	2.8		1.3
88	Bangladesh	2.7		1.4
89	Nigeria	2.7		1.1
90	Romania	2.6		1.1
91	Cameroon	2.6		1.4
92	Brazil	2.6		1.2
93	Philippines	2.6		1.1
94	Mongolia	2.6		1.3
95	Bulgaria	2.6		1.2
96	Mozambique	2.6		1.2
97	Armenia	2.6		1.3
98	Panama	2.5		1.2
99	Zimbabwe	2.5		1.5
100	Kenya	2.5		1.4
101	East Timor	2.5		1.7
102	Ethiopia	2.4		1.4
103	El Salvador	2.2		1.0
104	Guyana	2.2		1.3
105	Argentina	2.1		1.0
106	Bosnia and Herzegovina	2.1		1.0
107	Chad	2.1		1.4
108	Mexico	2.0		1.1
109	Venezuela	1.8		1.2
110	Guatemala	1.8		1.1
111	Dominican Republic	1.8		0.9
112	Bolivia	1.7		0.9
113	Paraguay	1.7		0.9
114	Costa Rica	1.6		0.8
115	Peru	1.6		0.8
116	Nicaragua	1.6		1.0
117	Ecuador	1.4		0.7

6.11   Extent and effect of taxation

The level of taxes in your country (1 = significantly limits the incentives to work or invest, 7 = has little impact on the incentives to work or invest)

RANK	COUNTRY	SCORE	1 MEAN: 3.4 7	SD
1	Hong Kong SAR	6.0		1.3
2	United Arab Emirates	5.9		1.6
3	Bahrain	5.9		1.8
4	Singapore	5.7		1.0
5	Qatar	5.7		1.4
6	Kuwait	5.4		2.1
7	Slovak Republic	5.2		1.3
8	Iceland	5.1		1.3
9	Malaysia	5.0		1.1
10	Ireland	5.0		1.4
11	Cyprus	4.9		1.4
12	Luxembourg	4.9		1.4
13	Estonia	4.9		1.5
14	Botswana	4.9		1.3
15	Switzerland	4.7		1.4
16	Taiwan	4.7		1.3
17	Tunisia	4.7		1.3
18	United States	4.4		1.3
19	Thailand	4.4		1.3
20	El Salvador	4.1		1.2
21	Ghana	4.1		1.5
22	India	4.1		1.5
23	United Kingdom	4.0		1.3
24	Indonesia	4.0		1.4
25	Austria	3.9		1.6
26	Chile	3.8		1.4
27	Korea, Rep.	3.8		1.4
28	Trinidad and Tobago	3.8		1.4
29	Mauritius	3.8		1.2
30	Pakistan	3.8		1.7
31	Philippines	3.7		1.4
32	Namibia	3.7		1.5
33	Cambodia	3.7		1.7
34	South Africa	3.7		1.3
35	Latvia	3.7		1.5
36	Nigeria	3.6		1.5
37	Bangladesh	3.6		1.8
38	Azerbaijan	3.6		1.6
39	China	3.6		1.4
40	Spain	3.6		1.3
41	Japan	3.5		1.3
42	Portugal	3.5		1.3
43	Tanzania	3.5		1.8
44	New Zealand	3.5		1.4
45	Jordan	3.5		1.6
46	Netherlands	3.5		1.4
47	Paraguay	3.5		1.7
48	Norway	3.4		1.5
49	Vietnam	3.4		1.4
50	Gambia	3.4		1.7
51	Armenia	3.3		1.7
52	Costa Rica	3.3		1.4
53	Mozambique	3.3		1.5
54	Serbia and Montenegro	3.3		1.6
55	Venezuela	3.2		1.9
56	Greece	3.2		1.2
57	Sri Lanka	3.2		1.4
58	Poland	3.2		1.4
59	Egypt	3.2		1.8

RANK	COUNTRY	SCORE	1 MEAN: 3.4 7	SD
60	Malta	3.1		1.3
61	Honduras	3.1		1.6
62	Georgia	3.1		1.6
63	Canada	3.1		1.4
64	Madagascar	3.0		1.6
65	Bolivia	3.0		1.4
66	East Timor	3.0		2.0
67	Czech Republic	3.0		1.5
68	Lithuania	2.9		1.4
69	Jamaica	2.9		1.5
70	Algeria	2.9		1.8
71	Albania	2.9		1.6
72	Australia	2.9		1.4
73	Panama	2.9		1.4
74	Uganda	2.9		1.7
75	Israel	2.9		1.4
76	Guatemala	2.8		1.6
77	Kazakhstan	2.8		1.3
78	Croatia	2.8		1.4
79	Ecuador	2.8		1.4
80	Mexico	2.8		1.2
81	Russian Federation	2.7		1.4
82	Hungary	2.7		1.2
83	Germany	2.7		1.3
84	Ethiopia	2.7		1.6
85	Dominican Republic	2.7		1.3
86	Moldova	2.6		1.6
87	Zimbabwe	2.6		1.3
88	Guyana	2.6		1.5
89	Bulgaria	2.6		1.6
90	Peru	2.6		1.2
91	France	2.6		1.4
92	Tajikistan	2.6		1.5
93	Nicaragua	2.5		1.3
94	Romania	2.5		1.4
95	Slovenia	2.5		1.2
96	Uruguay	2.5		1.2
97	Macedonia, FYR	2.5		1.6
98	Bosnia and Herzegovina	2.5		1.4
99	Mali	2.5		1.6
100	Colombia	2.5		1.2
101	Argentina	2.5		1.1
102	Morocco	2.5		1.3
103	Turkey	2.4		1.1
104	Kenya	2.4		1.6
105	Denmark	2.4		1.7
106	Finland	2.3		1.2
107	Mongolia	2.3		1.3
108	Italy	2.3		1.2
109	Sweden	2.3		1.5
110	Cameroon	2.3		1.2
111	Ukraine	2.3		1.1
112	Chad	2.1		1.6
113	Malawi	2.1		1.3
114	Kyrgyz Republic	2.1		1.4
115	Belgium	1.9		1.4
116	Benin	1.9		1.3
117	Brazil	1.6		1.0

6.12 Efficiency of the tax system

Your country's tax system is (1 = highly complex, 7 = simple and transparent)

RANK	COUNTRY	SCORE	MEAN: 3.4	SD
1	United Arab Emirates	6.3		1.3
2	Hong Kong SAR	6.3		1.1
3	Bahrain	6.2		1.4
4	Singapore	5.9		1.0
5	Qatar	5.9		1.3
6	Estonia	5.6		1.3
7	Botswana	5.4		1.3
8	Malaysia	5.3		1.1
9	Slovak Republic	5.3		1.4
10	Kuwait	5.2		2.0
11	Iceland	5.1		1.4
12	Cyprus	5.0		1.2
13	Taiwan	4.9		1.2
14	New Zealand	4.9		1.3
15	Tunisia	4.6		1.3
16	Gambia	4.6		1.8
17	Luxembourg	4.6		1.2
18	Malta	4.6		1.2
18	Trinidad and Tobago	4.6		1.4
20	Thailand	4.5		1.2
21	Ghana	4.4		1.4
22	Ireland	4.4		1.1
23	Mauritius	4.4		1.3
24	Chile	4.3		1.5
25	Namibia	4.1		1.7
26	Azerbaijan	4.1		1.8
27	Guyana	4.0		1.5
28	Spain	3.9		1.4
29	Malawi	3.9		1.7
29	Zimbabwe	3.9		1.3
31	Jordan	3.9		1.6
32	Switzerland	3.8		1.4
33	El Salvador	3.8		1.2
34	Serbia and Montenegro	3.8		1.8
35	Indonesia	3.7		1.1
36	Finland	3.7		1.8
37	Latvia	3.7		1.4
38	South Africa	3.6		1.4
39	Cambodia	3.6		1.8
40	Netherlands	3.6		1.5
41	Bolivia	3.6		1.4
42	Croatia	3.6		1.6
43	Tanzania	3.5		1.6
44	Jamaica	3.5		1.6
45	East Timor	3.5		1.8
46	Korea, Rep.	3.5		1.5
47	Portugal	3.5		1.5
48	Uganda	3.4		1.7
49	Philippines	3.4		1.5
50	Sri Lanka	3.4		1.5
51	China	3.4		1.2
52	Honduras	3.3		1.3
53	Macedonia, FYR	3.2		1.7
54	Pakistan	3.2		1.5
55	India	3.2		1.4
56	Nigeria	3.2		1.3
57	Panama	3.2		1.3
58	Ethiopia	3.1		1.7
59	Japan	3.1		1.3
60	Paraguay	3.1		1.4
61	Norway	3.1		1.4
62	Nicaragua	3.1		1.4
63	Georgia	3.1		1.5
64	Algeria	3.1		1.6
65	Costa Rica	3.1		1.3
66	Venezuela	3.1		1.4
67	United Kingdom	3.0		1.4
68	Benin	3.0		1.7
69	Madagascar	3.0		1.4
70	Kenya	2.9		1.8
71	Israel	2.9		1.5
72	Kazakhstan	2.9		1.5
73	Canada	2.9		1.3
74	Dominican Republic	2.9		1.5
75	Mozambique	2.9		1.3
76	Vietnam	2.9		1.3
77	Ecuador	2.9		1.3
78	Mali	2.9		1.6
79	Bangladesh	2.9		1.5
80	Egypt	2.8		1.4
81	Chad	2.8		1.9
82	Austria	2.8		1.3
83	Czech Republic	2.8		1.3
84	Mongolia	2.8		1.4
85	Peru	2.7		1.3
86	Tajikistan	2.7		1.5
87	Morocco	2.7		1.4
88	Uruguay	2.6		1.4
89	Albania	2.6		1.2
90	Poland	2.6		1.3
91	France	2.6		1.3
92	Cameroon	2.6		1.4
93	Turkey	2.6		1.3
94	Greece	2.6		1.3
95	Russian Federation	2.6		1.3
96	Lithuania	2.6		1.3
97	Bulgaria	2.5		1.3
98	Slovenia	2.5		1.2
99	Armenia	2.5		1.4
100	Guatemala	2.5		1.3
101	Denmark	2.5		1.7
102	Sweden	2.5		1.5
103	Colombia	2.4		1.1
104	Romania	2.4		1.4
105	Bosnia and Herzegovina	2.4		1.5
106	Hungary	2.4		1.2
107	United States	2.3		1.4
108	Moldova	2.3		1.4
109	Australia	2.3		1.3
110	Ukraine	2.3		1.1
111	Kyrgyz Republic	2.3		1.3
112	Mexico	2.1		1.1
113	Argentina	2.1		1.0
114	Italy	2.0		0.9
115	Belgium	1.8		0.9
116	Germany	1.5		0.8
117	Brazil	1.4		0.7

6.13　Centralization of economic policymaking

Economic policymaking in your country is (1 = centralized—national government controls almost all important decisions, 7 = decentralized—states and cities have important decision rights affecting economic development)

RANK	COUNTRY	SCORE	1　MEAN: 3.0　7	SD	RANK	COUNTRY	SCORE	1　MEAN: 3.0　7	SD
1	Switzerland	5.8		1.3	60	Colombia	2.9		1.7
2	Germany	5.1		1.3	61	Bulgaria	2.9		1.6
3	Belgium	5.1		1.4	62	Tanzania	2.9		1.9
4	United States	5.0		1.5	63	Macedonia, FYR	2.9		1.6
5	Canada	4.7		1.5	64	Ethiopia	2.9		1.8
6	Australia	4.7		1.5	65	Namibia	2.8		1.4
7	Iceland	4.7		1.8	66	Honduras	2.8		1.5
8	Spain	4.6		1.6	67	Malawi	2.8		1.9
9	Estonia	4.6		1.6	68	Croatia	2.8		1.5
10	Austria	4.6		1.6	69	Philippines	2.8		1.4
11	Denmark	4.3		1.6	70	Morocco	2.8		1.6
12	Finland	4.1		1.5	71	Thailand	2.7		1.5
13	Slovak Republic	4.1		1.5	72	Egypt	2.7		1.7
14	Hong Kong SAR	4.1		1.9	73	Portugal	2.7		1.5
15	Netherlands	4.1		1.5	74	Botswana	2.7		1.8
16	Bosnia and Herzegovina	4.1		1.8	75	Tajikistan	2.6		1.6
17	Indonesia	4.0		1.2	76	Serbia and Montenegro	2.6		1.4
18	India	4.0		1.5	77	Jordan	2.6		1.6
19	Czech Republic	4.0		1.4	78	Kyrgyz Republic	2.6		1.5
20	United Arab Emirates	3.9		2.0	79	Argentina	2.6		1.3
21	Korea, Rep.	3.8		1.5	80	Cambodia	2.6		1.5
22	Poland	3.7		1.3	81	Greece	2.6		1.3
23	Latvia	3.7		1.6	82	Peru	2.5		1.3
24	Taiwan	3.7		1.7	83	Luxembourg	2.5		1.6
25	Benin	3.6		2.0	84	Malaysia	2.5		1.7
26	China	3.6		1.5	85	Brazil	2.5		1.5
27	Tunisia	3.6		1.6	86	Armenia	2.4		1.4
28	Nigeria	3.6		1.6	87	Guatemala	2.4		1.3
29	Israel	3.6		1.6	88	Ireland	2.4		1.7
30	Uganda	3.5		2.1	89	Bolivia	2.4		1.3
31	Slovenia	3.5		1.5	90	Qatar	2.4		1.7
32	France	3.5		1.7	91	Jamaica	2.3		1.3
33	Italy	3.5		1.4	92	Moldova	2.3		1.3
34	El Salvador	3.5		1.7	93	Sri Lanka	2.3		1.4
35	Sweden	3.5		1.8	94	Malta	2.3		1.3
36	Vietnam	3.4		1.7	95	Georgia	2.2		1.2
37	Norway	3.3		1.5	96	Algeria	2.2		1.4
38	Panama	3.3		2.0	97	Ecuador	2.2		1.1
39	Kazakhstan	3.3		1.3	98	Chad	2.2		1.5
40	South Africa	3.3		1.7	99	Gambia	2.1		1.3
41	Lithuania	3.2		1.4	100	Singapore	2.1		1.6
42	Ukraine	3.2		1.3	101	East Timor	2.1		1.5
43	Mexico	3.2		1.4	102	Turkey	2.1		1.1
44	Chile	3.2		1.8	103	Kenya	2.1		1.6
45	Hungary	3.2		1.6	104	Kuwait	2.1		1.4
46	Ghana	3.2		1.8	105	Pakistan	2.1		1.5
47	Mali	3.2		1.9	106	Costa Rica	2.0		0.9
48	Romania	3.2		1.4	107	Trinidad and Tobago	2.0		1.1
49	United Kingdom	3.1		1.5	108	Dominican Republic	2.0		1.2
50	Azerbaijan	3.1		1.6	109	Mauritius	2.0		1.4
51	Mongolia	3.1		1.6	110	Paraguay	1.9		1.0
52	Russian Federation	3.1		1.6	111	Uruguay	1.9		1.0
53	Mozambique	3.1		1.8	112	Cameroon	1.9		1.2
54	Nicaragua	3.1		1.5	113	Bangladesh	1.8		1.2
55	Japan	3.0		1.7	114	Bahrain	1.7		1.1
55	Madagascar	3.0		1.7	115	Guyana	1.7		0.9
55	New Zealand	3.0		1.5	116	Zimbabwe	1.6		0.9
58	Cyprus	3.0		1.5	117	Venezuela	1.5		0.9
59	Albania	2.9		1.4					

6.14 Reliability of police services

Police services (1 = cannot be relied upon to protect businesses from criminals, 7 = can be relied upon to protect businesses from criminals)

RANK	COUNTRY	SCORE	MEAN: 4.1	SD
1	Singapore	6.5		0.7
2	Denmark	6.4		1.3
3	Finland	6.3		1.3
4	Germany	6.3		0.8
5	Iceland	6.3		0.9
6	Switzerland	6.1		1.1
7	United States	6.1		1.0
8	Hong Kong SAR	5.9		1.2
9	Austria	5.9		1.2
10	Jordan	5.8		1.3
11	United Arab Emirates	5.8		1.3
12	Norway	5.7		1.4
13	Australia	5.7		1.3
14	Qatar	5.6		1.8
15	Luxembourg	5.6		1.5
16	Canada	5.5		1.3
17	France	5.5		1.5
18	Ireland	5.5		1.4
19	Tunisia	5.5		1.4
20	Japan	5.4		1.4
21	United Kingdom	5.4		1.3
22	Netherlands	5.4		1.3
23	Portugal	5.3		1.3
24	Sweden	5.3		1.3
25	Malta	5.3		1.4
26	Taiwan	5.3		1.1
27	Chile	5.2		1.5
28	Kuwait	5.2		1.5
29	Cyprus	5.2		1.4
30	Ghana	5.2		1.3
31	Morocco	5.1		1.7
32	Korea, Rep.	5.0		1.3
33	Belgium	5.0		1.6
33	Greece	5.0		1.3
35	Spain	5.0		1.5
36	New Zealand	4.9		1.8
37	Malaysia	4.9		1.2
38	Egypt	4.8		1.8
39	Israel	4.8		1.2
40	Italy	4.7		1.4
41	Estonia	4.6		1.7
42	Vietnam	4.6		1.5
43	Algeria	4.6		1.8
44	Slovenia	4.5		1.5
45	Hungary	4.5		1.5
46	Thailand	4.4		1.4
47	Nicaragua	4.4		1.6
48	India	4.4		1.4
49	Panama	4.3		1.7
50	Botswana	4.3		1.8
51	China	4.3		1.4
52	Colombia	4.3		1.5
53	Latvia	4.2		1.6
54	Uruguay	4.2		1.5
55	Tanzania	4.2		1.9
56	El Salvador	4.1		1.5
57	Mali	4.0		1.8
58	Poland	4.0		1.3
59	Slovak Republic	4.0		1.4
60	Turkey	3.9		1.6
61	Czech Republic	3.9		1.7
62	Ethiopia	3.9		1.7
63	Georgia	3.9		1.6
64	Costa Rica	3.9		1.5
65	Bahrain	3.8		2.2
66	Armenia	3.8		1.7
67	Macedonia, FYR	3.8		1.7
68	Kazakhstan	3.8		1.5
69	East Timor	3.7		2.0
70	Madagascar	3.7		1.7
71	Croatia	3.7		1.6
72	Gambia	3.7		1.8
73	Malawi	3.6		1.9
74	Honduras	3.6		1.8
75	Romania	3.6		1.6
76	Azerbaijan	3.6		2.0
77	Mauritius	3.5		1.6
78	Indonesia	3.5		1.1
79	Mozambique	3.5		1.7
80	Tajikistan	3.4		2.0
81	Serbia and Montenegro	3.4		1.6
82	Lithuania	3.4		1.6
83	Benin	3.4		1.8
84	Uganda	3.3		1.6
85	South Africa	3.3		1.6
86	Argentina	3.2		1.4
87	Moldova	3.2		1.9
88	Cameroon	3.2		1.5
89	Brazil	3.1		1.6
90	Ukraine	3.1		1.3
91	Zimbabwe	3.1		1.6
92	Albania	3.1		1.7
93	Bulgaria	3.0		1.7
94	Sri Lanka	3.0		1.5
95	Mongolia	3.0		1.6
96	Philippines	3.0		1.5
97	Peru	3.0		1.6
98	Namibia	2.9		1.8
99	Russian Federation	2.9		1.7
100	Jamaica	2.9		1.4
101	Ecuador	2.9		1.3
102	Mexico	2.8		1.4
103	Cambodia	2.8		1.6
104	Kyrgyz Republic	2.7		1.4
105	Kenya	2.7		1.5
106	Bolivia	2.6		1.4
107	Pakistan	2.6		1.6
108	Trinidad and Tobago	2.5		1.4
109	Chad	2.5		1.7
110	Dominican Republic	2.5		1.4
111	Bosnia and Herzegovina	2.4		1.1
112	Nigeria	2.4		1.0
113	Venezuela	2.4		1.2
114	Paraguay	2.3		1.2
115	Bangladesh	2.3		1.2
116	Guyana	2.1		1.0
117	Guatemala	2.0		1.1

6.15   Business costs of crime and violence

The incidence of common crime and violence (e.g. street muggings, firms being looted) (1 = imposes significant costs on businesses, 7 = does not impose significant costs on businesses)

RANK	COUNTRY	SCORE	1 MEAN: 4.3 7	SD
1	United Arab Emirates	6.6		0.6
2	Qatar	6.5		1.0
3	Singapore	6.5		0.8
4	Finland	6.5		0.7
5	Denmark	6.4		0.9
6	Germany	6.3		0.9
7	Iceland	6.3		0.8
8	Jordan	6.3		0.9
9	Hong Kong SAR	6.2		1.2
10	Switzerland	6.2		1.1
11	Norway	6.1		1.0
12	Malta	6.1		1.0
13	Austria	6.0		1.3
14	Portugal	6.0		1.3
15	Luxembourg	5.9		1.2
16	Australia	5.8		1.3
17	New Zealand	5.8		1.4
18	Cyprus	5.7		1.4
19	Kuwait	5.7		1.8
20	Greece	5.6		1.3
21	Sweden	5.6		1.5
22	Taiwan	5.6		1.3
23	Japan	5.6		1.4
24	Ghana	5.6		1.5
25	India	5.6		1.4
26	Malaysia	5.5		1.3
27	Tunisia	5.5		1.4
28	Canada	5.4		1.6
29	Armenia	5.4		1.5
30	United States	5.4		1.5
31	Belgium	5.3		1.3
32	France	5.3		1.4
33	Slovenia	5.3		1.4
34	Ireland	5.2		1.2
35	Estonia	5.2		1.6
36	Israel	5.2		1.5
37	Latvia	5.1		1.4
38	Hungary	5.1		1.7
39	Thailand	5.1		1.3
40	Gambia	5.0		1.9
41	United Kingdom	5.0		1.5
42	Italy	4.9		1.8
43	Slovak Republic	4.9		1.4
44	Ethiopia	4.8		1.7
45	Korea, Rep.	4.8		1.4
46	Netherlands	4.7		1.5
47	Turkey	4.7		1.7
48	Czech Republic	4.6		1.7
48	Serbia and Montenegro	4.6		1.9
50	Chile	4.6		1.7
51	Azerbaijan	4.5		2.0
52	Vietnam	4.5		1.7
53	Spain	4.5		1.8
54	Mali	4.5		2.1
55	China	4.5		1.5
56	Poland	4.4		1.3
57	Bahrain	4.4		2.1
58	Croatia	4.4		1.8
59	Lithuania	4.3		1.5
60	Egypt	4.2		2.0
61	Georgia	4.2		1.5
62	Algeria	4.2		2.1
63	Morocco	4.2		2.0
64	Uruguay	4.2		1.7
65	Botswana	4.2		1.7
66	Indonesia	4.1		1.2
67	Tanzania	3.9		2.1
68	Mauritius	3.9		1.5
68	Nicaragua	3.9		1.6
70	Philippines	3.8		1.8
71	Ukraine	3.8		1.6
72	Kazakhstan	3.8		1.6
73	Moldova	3.8		1.9
74	Romania	3.8		2.0
75	Benin	3.8		2.1
76	Mongolia	3.8		1.9
77	Pakistan	3.7		1.8
78	Zimbabwe	3.7		1.7
79	Sri Lanka	3.7		1.7
80	Madagascar	3.7		1.7
81	Kyrgyz Republic	3.6		1.8
82	Malawi	3.6		1.9
83	Cambodia	3.5		1.6
84	Bolivia	3.5		1.6
85	Albania	3.5		1.9
86	Panama	3.5		1.4
87	Tajikistan	3.4		2.0
88	Russian Federation	3.4		1.6
89	Cameroon	3.4		1.8
90	Nigeria	3.3		1.3
91	Uganda	3.3		2.0
92	Costa Rica	3.2		1.6
93	East Timor	3.2		1.6
94	Bosnia and Herzegovina	3.2		1.6
95	Bulgaria	3.1		1.8
96	Macedonia, FYR	3.1		1.8
97	Colombia	3.0		1.5
98	Dominican Republic	3.0		1.5
99	Chad	3.0		2.0
100	Mozambique	3.0		1.7
101	Namibia	2.9		1.8
102	Argentina	2.9		1.4
103	Bangladesh	2.8		1.6
104	Peru	2.7		1.2
105	El Salvador	2.6		1.3
106	South Africa	2.6		1.4
107	Brazil	2.6		1.5
108	Honduras	2.4		1.3
109	Paraguay	2.4		1.2
110	Kenya	2.4		1.5
111	Venezuela	2.4		1.6
112	Ecuador	2.3		1.2
113	Guyana	2.3		1.3
114	Trinidad and Tobago	2.3		1.3
115	Mexico	2.2		1.2
116	Jamaica	2.1		1.1
117	Guatemala	1.6		0.9

6.16 Organized crime

Organized crime (e.g. mafia-oriented racketeering, extortion) in your country (1 = imposes significant costs on businesses, 7 = does not impose significant costs on businesses)

RANK	COUNTRY	SCORE	1 MEAN: 4.7 7	SD
1	Iceland	6.8		0.5
2	Finland	6.7		0.5
3	Qatar	6.6		1.1
4	Denmark	6.6		0.9
5	Jordan	6.6		0.8
6	Singapore	6.6		0.8
7	Portugal	6.5		0.7
8	United Arab Emirates	6.5		0.8
9	Luxembourg	6.4		1.0
10	Norway	6.4		0.6
11	Malta	6.4		0.9
12	New Zealand	6.3		1.1
13	Germany	6.2		0.8
14	Austria	6.2		1.1
15	Switzerland	6.2		1.1
16	Kuwait	6.2		1.3
17	Sweden	6.1		1.2
18	Bahrain	6.1		1.4
19	France	6.0		1.1
20	Uruguay	6.0		1.2
21	Australia	5.9		1.2
22	Chile	5.9		1.3
23	Ghana	5.9		1.5
24	Belgium	5.9		1.2
25	Cyprus	5.8		1.5
26	Greece	5.8		1.1
27	Estonia	5.7		1.4
28	Hong Kong SAR	5.7		1.2
29	United Kingdom	5.7		1.2
30	Ireland	5.7		1.3
31	Malaysia	5.7		1.2
32	Israel	5.6		1.3
33	United States	5.6		1.3
34	Tunisia	5.5		1.5
35	Gambia	5.5		1.8
36	Ethiopia	5.5		1.7
37	Canada	5.4		1.3
38	Armenia	5.4		1.6
39	Japan	5.3		1.5
40	Botswana	5.3		1.7
41	Taiwan	5.3		1.4
42	Egypt	5.3		2.0
43	India	5.3		1.5
44	Latvia	5.2		1.4
45	Netherlands	5.2		1.4
46	Slovenia	5.1		1.5
47	Tanzania	5.1		2.0
48	Thailand	5.1		1.2
49	Mali	5.1		1.9
50	Hungary	5.1		1.7
51	Spain	5.0		1.6
52	Mongolia	4.9		1.8
53	Azerbaijan	4.9		1.8
54	Zimbabwe	4.9		1.5
55	Korea, Rep.	4.9		1.4
56	Nicaragua	4.8		1.7
57	Malawi	4.8		1.6
58	Czech Republic	4.7		1.6
59	Bolivia	4.7		1.8

RANK	COUNTRY	SCORE	1 MEAN: 4.7 7	SD
60	Algeria	4.6		2.0
61	Mauritius	4.6		1.6
62	Morocco	4.6		1.9
63	Lithuania	4.6		1.5
64	Slovak Republic	4.6		1.3
65	China	4.5		1.5
66	Poland	4.4		1.3
67	Serbia and Montenegro	4.4		2.0
68	Turkey	4.4		1.7
69	Vietnam	4.3		2.0
70	Georgia	4.3		1.6
71	Argentina	4.2		1.8
72	Tajikistan	4.2		2.1
73	Namibia	4.2		1.9
74	Kazakhstan	4.2		1.5
75	Costa Rica	4.1		1.7
76	East Timor	4.1		1.9
77	Benin	4.1		2.1
78	Panama	4.1		1.7
79	Indonesia	4.0		1.2
80	Kyrgyz Republic	4.0		1.9
80	Romania	4.0		1.9
82	Philippines	4.0		1.8
83	Moldova	4.0		1.8
84	Peru	4.0		1.7
85	Croatia	3.9		1.6
86	Dominican Republic	3.9		1.7
87	Uganda	3.9		2.0
88	Cambodia	3.9		1.8
89	Cameroon	3.8		2.0
90	Pakistan	3.8		1.6
91	Bosnia and Herzegovina	3.7		1.8
92	Mozambique	3.7		1.8
93	Madagascar	3.6		1.6
94	Sri Lanka	3.6		1.7
95	Ukraine	3.5		1.4
96	Kenya	3.5		1.9
97	Nigeria	3.5		1.5
98	South Africa	3.5		1.7
99	Brazil	3.5		1.8
100	El Salvador	3.5		1.6
101	Russian Federation	3.5		1.7
102	Guyana	3.4		1.7
103	Italy	3.3		1.7
104	Venezuela	3.3		1.9
105	Bangladesh	3.1		1.6
106	Honduras	3.1		1.7
107	Ecuador	3.1		1.6
108	Albania	3.1		1.8
109	Chad	3.0		2.0
110	Bulgaria	3.0		1.7
111	Trinidad and Tobago	3.0		1.6
112	Paraguay	2.9		1.5
113	Mexico	2.8		1.4
114	Macedonia, FYR	2.6		1.7
115	Colombia	2.6		1.4
116	Jamaica	2.4		1.1
117	Guatemala	2.0		1.3

6.17 Informal sector

How much business activity in your country would you estimate to be unofficial or unregistered? (1 = none, all businesses are registered, 7 = more than 50% of economic activity is unrecorded)

RANK	COUNTRY	SCORE	MEAN: 4.3	SD
1	Singapore	2.3		1.1
2	Iceland	2.3		0.8
3	Qatar	2.4		1.3
4	Switzerland	2.6		1.2
5	Norway	2.6		0.9
6	Netherlands	2.6		0.9
7	Finland	2.6		1.1
8	Luxembourg	2.6		0.9
9	New Zealand	2.7		1.1
10	United Arab Emirates	2.7		1.4
11	United Kingdom	2.7		1.0
12	Kuwait	2.7		1.7
13	United States	2.8		1.2
14	Austria	2.9		1.3
15	Chile	2.9		1.3
16	France	2.9		1.2
17	Estonia	2.9		1.2
18	Bahrain	3.0		1.4
19	Australia	3.1		1.2
20	Lithuania	3.1		1.3
21	Japan	3.1		1.6
22	Ireland	3.1		1.2
23	Jordan	3.1		1.6
24	Denmark	3.2		1.4
25	Slovenia	3.2		1.2
26	Germany	3.2		1.4
27	Hong Kong SAR	3.3		1.5
28	Czech Republic	3.5		1.3
29	Spain	3.5		1.3
30	Cyprus	3.5		1.4
31	Canada	3.5		1.3
32	Israel	3.6		1.4
33	Sweden	3.6		1.5
34	Taiwan	3.6		1.4
35	Slovak Republic	3.7		1.2
36	Mauritius	3.8		1.3
37	Malaysia	3.8		1.4
38	Portugal	3.9		1.2
39	Botswana	4.0		1.4
40	Belgium	4.0		1.2
41	East Timor	4.0		2.1
42	Latvia	4.0		1.3
43	Tunisia	4.0		1.4
44	Thailand	4.0		1.2
45	Korea, Rep.	4.1		1.5
46	Poland	4.1		1.1
47	Vietnam	4.1		1.4
48	Panama	4.2		1.8
49	Colombia	4.2		1.4
50	Hungary	4.3		1.3
51	Malta	4.3		1.2
52	Trinidad and Tobago	4.4		1.4
53	China	4.4		1.3
54	Ecuador	4.4		1.6
55	Romania	4.4		1.5
56	Greece	4.4		1.2
57	Costa Rica	4.5		1.2
58	Albania	4.5		1.6
59	Gambia	4.5		1.7
60	Azerbaijan	4.5		1.4
61	Egypt	4.6		1.7
62	South Africa	4.6		1.1
63	El Salvador	4.7		1.5
64	Croatia	4.7		1.4
65	Uruguay	4.7		1.1
66	Bulgaria	4.7		1.6
67	Tajikistan	4.7		2.1
68	Armenia	4.7		1.4
69	Moldova	4.7		1.5
70	Serbia and Montenegro	4.7		1.3
71	Macedonia, FYR	4.7		1.5
72	Ethiopia	4.8		1.8
73	Italy	4.8		1.3
74	Kazakhstan	4.8		1.4
75	India	4.8		1.3
76	Indonesia	4.9		0.9
77	Tanzania	5.0		1.6
78	Georgia	5.0		1.4
79	Mongolia	5.0		1.6
79	Namibia	5.0		1.5
81	Cambodia	5.0		1.6
82	Philippines	5.0		1.3
83	Bosnia and Herzegovina	5.0		1.2
84	Uganda	5.1		1.7
85	Venezuela	5.1		1.8
86	Malawi	5.1		1.3
87	Nicaragua	5.1		1.4
88	Pakistan	5.1		1.4
89	Dominican Republic	5.1		1.5
90	Algeria	5.1		1.5
91	Nigeria	5.2		1.3
92	Honduras	5.2		1.5
93	Argentina	5.2		1.2
94	Kenya	5.2		1.3
95	Mozambique	5.3		1.5
96	Ghana	5.3		1.3
97	Bangladesh	5.3		1.4
98	Sri Lanka	5.3		1.5
99	Mexico	5.4		1.3
100	Morocco	5.4		1.2
101	Cameroon	5.4		1.5
102	Jamaica	5.4		1.2
103	Guatemala	5.4		1.5
104	Brazil	5.5		1.3
105	Turkey	5.5		1.2
106	Russian Federation	5.5		1.4
107	Mali	5.5		1.6
108	Zimbabwe	5.5		1.2
109	Madagascar	5.6		1.3
110	Guyana	5.7		1.1
111	Chad	5.7		1.7
112	Ukraine	5.7		1.2
113	Paraguay	5.7		1.5
114	Peru	5.9		1.4
115	Benin	6.3		1.1
116	Bolivia	6.3		0.9
117	Kyrgyz Republic	6.3		1.0

6.18 Government effectiveness in reducing poverty and inequality

In your country, the government's efforts to reduce poverty and address income inequality are (1 = ineffective, 7 = effective)

RANK	COUNTRY	SCORE	MEAN: 3.5	SD
1	Denmark	6.1		1.0
2	Singapore	5.7		0.9
3	United Arab Emirates	5.6		1.1
4	Tunisia	5.6		1.4
5	Malaysia	5.6		1.1
6	Netherlands	5.4		1.1
7	Norway	5.4		1.2
8	Luxembourg	5.4		1.2
9	Finland	5.2		1.0
10	Iceland	5.1		1.0
11	Qatar	4.9		1.9
12	Sweden	4.9		1.6
13	Switzerland	4.8		1.2
14	Japan	4.8		1.3
15	Australia	4.7		1.3
16	New Zealand	4.7		1.3
17	Belgium	4.7		1.5
18	Ireland	4.6		1.3
19	Malta	4.6		1.5
20	Vietnam	4.6		1.6
21	South Africa	4.5		1.4
22	Germany	4.5		1.4
23	United Kingdom	4.5		1.2
24	Canada	4.4		1.3
25	Cyprus	4.4		1.3
26	Austria	4.4		1.4
27	Thailand	4.4		1.3
28	Portugal	4.4		1.1
29	China	4.2		1.4
30	France	4.2		1.5
31	Spain	4.2		1.3
32	Taiwan	4.2		1.3
33	Tanzania	4.2		1.7
34	Jordan	4.1		1.4
35	Botswana	4.0		1.5
36	Mozambique	4.0		1.6
37	Hong Kong SAR	4.0		1.3
38	El Salvador	4.0		1.3
39	Korea, Rep.	4.0		1.4
40	Chile	3.9		1.5
41	Ghana	3.9		1.2
42	United States	3.8		1.4
43	Czech Republic	3.8		1.4
44	Indonesia	3.7		1.1
45	Bahrain	3.7		1.8
46	Mauritius	3.7		1.3
47	Gambia	3.7		1.7
48	Kuwait	3.6		1.6
49	Tajikistan	3.6		1.7
50	India	3.6		1.3
51	Uganda	3.5		1.8
52	Greece	3.5		1.2
53	Egypt	3.5		1.7
54	Slovenia	3.5		1.2
55	Kazakhstan	3.5		1.5
56	Morocco	3.4		1.8
57	Mali	3.4		1.9
58	Madagascar	3.3		1.6
59	Bangladesh	3.3		1.5
60	Algeria	3.2		1.6
61	Pakistan	3.2		1.9
62	Italy	3.2		1.5
63	Azerbaijan	3.2		1.7
64	Estonia	3.2		1.3
65	Panama	3.2		1.4
66	Israel	3.1		1.3
67	Slovak Republic	3.1		1.2
68	Mexico	3.1		1.5
69	Uruguay	3.0		1.2
70	Ethiopia	3.0		1.6
71	Brazil	2.9		1.4
72	Poland	2.9		1.2
73	Namibia	2.9		1.7
74	Colombia	2.9		1.1
75	Nigeria	2.9		1.3
76	Malawi	2.8		1.7
77	Turkey	2.8		1.2
78	Latvia	2.8		1.3
79	Cameroon	2.8		1.6
80	Hungary	2.7		1.2
81	Honduras	2.7		1.4
82	Moldova	2.7		1.7
83	Costa Rica	2.7		1.2
84	Trinidad and Tobago	2.7		1.4
85	Romania	2.7		1.3
86	Lithuania	2.6		1.2
87	Croatia	2.6		1.3
88	Cambodia	2.6		1.5
89	Georgia	2.6		1.3
90	Philippines	2.6		1.3
91	Armenia	2.6		1.3
92	Ukraine	2.6		1.4
93	Sri Lanka	2.5		1.3
94	Argentina	2.5		1.3
95	Kyrgyz Republic	2.5		1.3
96	Nicaragua	2.5		1.3
97	Jamaica	2.5		1.2
98	Guyana	2.5		1.4
99	Albania	2.5		1.5
100	Serbia and Montenegro	2.4		1.4
101	Kenya	2.4		1.4
102	East Timor	2.4		1.6
103	Guatemala	2.4		1.3
104	Bolivia	2.3		1.3
105	Macedonia, FYR	2.3		1.3
106	Peru	2.2		0.8
107	Bulgaria	2.2		1.4
108	Mongolia	2.2		1.1
109	Russian Federation	2.1		1.2
110	Chad	2.1		1.5
111	Zimbabwe	2.1		1.4
112	Bosnia and Herzegovina	2.0		1.0
113	Dominican Republic	2.0		1.0
114	Benin	2.0		1.3
115	Ecuador	1.9		1.0
116	Venezuela	1.9		1.2
117	Paraguay	1.5		0.7

6.19 Irregular payments in exports and imports

In your industry, how commonly would you estimate that firms make undocumented extra payments or bribes connected with export and import permits? (1 = common, 7 = never occurs)

RANK	COUNTRY	SCORE	MEAN: 4.7	SD
1	Iceland	6.7		0.5
2	New Zealand	6.6		0.6
3	Singapore	6.5		0.8
4	Finland	6.5		0.9
5	Japan	6.4		0.9
6	Denmark	6.4		1.2
7	Chile	6.3		1.0
8	Norway	6.3		0.8
9	Portugal	6.3		1.0
10	Sweden	6.3		1.0
11	Luxembourg	6.3		0.7
12	Australia	6.2		0.8
13	United Kingdom	6.2		1.1
14	Austria	6.1		1.1
15	United States	6.1		1.0
16	Ireland	6.1		1.3
17	Switzerland	6.1		1.1
18	Germany	6.1		0.9
19	Canada	6.1		1.1
20	Taiwan	6.0		1.2
21	Slovenia	5.9		1.2
22	Netherlands	5.9		1.0
23	United Arab Emirates	5.9		1.2
24	France	5.9		1.3
25	Estonia	5.8		1.2
26	Israel	5.8		1.2
27	Qatar	5.8		1.6
28	Hong Kong SAR	5.7		1.4
29	Colombia	5.7		1.6
30	Spain	5.6		1.3
31	Cyprus	5.6		1.3
32	Jordan	5.6		1.4
33	Hungary	5.6		1.5
34	Bahrain	5.5		1.7
35	Italy	5.5		1.6
36	Malta	5.4		1.4
37	Belgium	5.4		1.5
38	Bulgaria	5.4		1.9
39	Peru	5.3		1.5
40	Slovak Republic	5.3		1.4
41	Lithuania	5.2		1.6
42	Uruguay	5.2		1.6
43	Greece	5.2		1.6
44	El Salvador	5.2		1.6
45	Malaysia	5.0		1.4
46	Moldova	5.0		2.1
47	China	5.0		1.8
48	Tunisia	5.0		1.4
49	Czech Republic	4.9		1.5
50	Thailand	4.8		1.7
51	Korea, Rep.	4.8		1.4
52	Kuwait	4.8		2.0
53	Botswana	4.7		1.5
54	Ghana	4.7		1.7
55	Serbia and Montenegro	4.7		2.1
56	Honduras	4.7		2.0
57	Latvia	4.6		1.7
58	Brazil	4.6		1.8
59	Nicaragua	4.6		1.8
59	South Africa	4.6		1.7
61	Mexico	4.5		1.8
62	Egypt	4.5		1.9
63	Malawi	4.5		1.9
64	Jamaica	4.4		1.7
65	Argentina	4.3		1.9
66	Armenia	4.3		2.1
67	Croatia	4.3		1.8
68	Ethiopia	4.3		1.8
69	Costa Rica	4.2		1.8
70	Mali	4.2		2.0
71	Poland	4.2		1.7
72	India	4.1		1.6
73	Algeria	4.1		2.0
74	Namibia	4.1		2.1
75	Azerbaijan	4.1		2.1
76	Bolivia	4.0		2.0
77	Albania	4.0		1.8
78	Ukraine	4.0		1.9
78	Zimbabwe	4.0		1.8
80	Tanzania	4.0		2.0
81	Turkey	4.0		1.9
82	Mauritius	4.0		1.7
83	Russian Federation	3.9		2.0
84	Kenya	3.9		1.9
85	Mozambique	3.9		2.0
86	Kazakhstan	3.8		1.6
87	Bosnia and Herzegovina	3.8		1.9
88	Macedonia, FYR	3.8		2.1
89	Guatemala	3.8		2.0
90	Paraguay	3.8		2.0
91	Trinidad and Tobago	3.7		1.6
92	Gambia	3.7		1.8
93	Romania	3.7		2.0
94	Dominican Republic	3.7		2.0
95	Madagascar	3.6		1.5
96	Pakistan	3.6		1.8
97	Morocco	3.6		1.7
98	Venezuela	3.5		1.8
99	Uganda	3.5		1.9
100	Georgia	3.5		1.7
101	Panama	3.5		1.9
102	Nigeria	3.5		1.7
103	Tajikistan	3.4		1.8
104	Benin	3.3		1.9
105	Ecuador	3.2		1.8
106	Indonesia	3.2		1.4
107	Mongolia	3.1		1.8
108	Cameroon	3.1		2.0
109	East Timor	3.1		1.8
110	Guyana	3.0		1.8
111	Philippines	2.9		1.8
112	Sri Lanka	2.7		1.8
113	Vietnam	2.7		1.5
114	Chad	2.5		1.7
115	Kyrgyz Republic	2.4		1.6
116	Bangladesh	2.4		1.5
117	Cambodia	2.2		1.6

6.20   Irregular payments in public utilities

In your industry, how commonly would you estimate that firms make undocumented extra payments or bribes when getting connected to public utilities (e.g. telephone or electricity)? (1 = common, 7 = never occurs)

RANK	COUNTRY	SCORE	MEAN: 5.0	SD
1	Iceland	6.8		0.5
2	New Zealand	6.7		0.6
3	Luxembourg	6.7		0.8
4	Austria	6.7		0.7
5	Singapore	6.6		0.9
6	Denmark	6.6		1.2
7	Norway	6.5		0.7
8	Finland	6.5		1.3
9	Australia	6.4		0.8
10	Switzerland	6.4		1.0
11	Sweden	6.4		1.0
12	Chile	6.4		1.1
13	United Kingdom	6.4		0.9
14	Japan	6.4		1.2
15	Estonia	6.4		1.0
16	United States	6.3		1.0
17	France	6.3		1.2
18	Canada	6.3		1.0
19	Portugal	6.3		1.0
20	United Arab Emirates	6.3		1.1
21	Germany	6.2		1.1
22	Netherlands	6.2		1.2
23	Ireland	6.2		1.0
24	Hong Kong SAR	6.2		1.5
25	Spain	6.1		1.1
26	Taiwan	6.1		1.3
27	Slovenia	6.1		1.3
28	Italy	6.1		1.5
29	Cyprus	6.0		1.1
30	Hungary	6.0		1.3
31	Belgium	6.0		1.3
32	Lithuania	6.0		1.3
33	Uruguay	5.9		1.4
34	Slovak Republic	5.9		1.4
35	Colombia	5.9		1.6
36	Jordan	5.9		1.3
37	Qatar	5.8		1.6
38	El Salvador	5.8		1.7
39	Argentina	5.8		1.4
40	Malta	5.7		1.2
41	Peru	5.7		1.7
42	Israel	5.7		1.7
43	Thailand	5.6		1.5
44	Greece	5.6		1.6
45	Moldova	5.6		1.8
46	Bulgaria	5.6		1.8
47	Malaysia	5.5		1.2
48	Latvia	5.5		1.6
49	Korea, Rep.	5.4		1.3
50	Tunisia	5.4		1.8
51	Czech Republic	5.3		1.5
52	China	5.3		1.6
53	Botswana	5.3		1.4
54	Kuwait	5.3		1.8
55	Bahrain	5.3		1.8
56	Armenia	5.2		1.8
57	Jamaica	5.1		1.7
58	Brazil	5.1		2.0
59	Turkey	5.0		1.8
60	Mauritius	5.0		1.7
61	Bosnia and Herzegovina	4.9		1.8
62	Croatia	4.9		1.8
63	Macedonia, FYR	4.9		2.0
64	Namibia	4.9		1.9
65	Poland	4.9		1.6
66	Serbia and Montenegro	4.9		2.1
67	Venezuela	4.9		1.8
68	Bolivia	4.8		1.8
69	Azerbaijan	4.8		2.0
70	Egypt	4.8		2.0
71	South Africa	4.8		1.7
72	Georgia	4.7		1.7
73	Romania	4.7		2.0
74	Mexico	4.6		1.7
75	Ukraine	4.6		1.9
76	Kazakhstan	4.6		1.9
77	Costa Rica	4.5		1.7
78	Russian Federation	4.4		2.0
79	Guatemala	4.4		2.0
80	Ethiopia	4.3		1.8
81	Zimbabwe	4.3		1.7
82	Tanzania	4.3		1.9
83	India	4.3		1.9
84	Mongolia	4.3		1.8
85	Philippines	4.3		2.0
86	Nicaragua	4.2		1.8
87	Trinidad and Tobago	4.2		1.8
88	Morocco	4.2		2.4
89	Panama	4.1		2.0
90	Mozambique	4.1		1.8
91	Dominican Republic	4.0		2.0
92	Honduras	4.0		1.9
92	Mali	4.0		1.9
94	Indonesia	4.0		1.6
95	Vietnam	4.0		1.8
96	Albania	4.0		1.8
97	Sri Lanka	3.9		1.9
98	Malawi	3.8		2.1
99	Madagascar	3.8		1.7
100	Algeria	3.8		1.9
101	Paraguay	3.8		2.0
102	Kyrgyz Republic	3.7		1.7
103	Kenya	3.7		1.8
104	Gambia	3.7		1.8
105	Uganda	3.7		2.0
106	Ghana	3.6		1.6
107	Tajikistan	3.6		1.8
108	Guyana	3.6		1.8
109	Pakistan	3.5		1.8
110	Cambodia	3.5		2.0
111	Ecuador	3.5		1.8
112	East Timor	3.5		2.0
113	Cameroon	2.9		1.7
114	Chad	2.8		2.0
115	Benin	2.7		1.6
116	Nigeria	2.7		1.1
117	Bangladesh	2.1		1.2

6.21   Irregular payments in tax collection

In your industry, how commonly would you estimate that firms make undocumented extra payments or bribes connected with annual tax payments? (1 = common, 7 = never occurs)

RANK	COUNTRY	SCORE	1 MEAN: 4.9 7	SD	RANK	COUNTRY	SCORE	1 MEAN: 4.9 7	SD
1	New Zealand	6.8		0.4	60	Latvia	4.9		1.7
2	Iceland	6.8		0.7	61	Korea, Rep.	4.9		1.4
3	Singapore	6.7		0.9	62	Tunisia	4.8		1.5
4	Denmark	6.6		1.0	63	Poland	4.8		1.4
5	United Arab Emirates	6.6		0.7	64	Croatia	4.7		1.7
6	Norway	6.6		0.6	65	Argentina	4.7		1.6
7	Finland	6.5		1.1	66	Costa Rica	4.7		1.7
7	Japan	6.5		0.9	67	Armenia	4.6		2.0
9	Australia	6.5		0.8	68	Panama	4.6		1.7
10	United Kingdom	6.4		1.0	69	Russian Federation	4.6		2.0
11	Luxembourg	6.4		1.0	70	Ghana	4.5		1.3
12	Ireland	6.4		1.1	71	Honduras	4.5		2.0
13	Austria	6.4		1.0	72	Nicaragua	4.5		1.7
14	Qatar	6.4		1.1	73	Azerbaijan	4.5		2.0
15	United States	6.4		1.0	74	Brazil	4.4		1.9
16	Sweden	6.3		1.0	75	India	4.3		1.7
17	Canada	6.3		1.0	76	Venezuela	4.3		2.1
18	Estonia	6.3		1.2	77	Egypt	4.3		2.1
19	Switzerland	6.3		1.1	78	Bosnia and Herzegovina	4.3		1.9
20	Germany	6.3		1.2	79	Malawi	4.3		2.1
21	France	6.2		1.2	80	Kazakhstan	4.2		1.8
22	Netherlands	6.2		1.2	81	Greece	4.2		1.8
23	Bahrain	6.2		1.4	82	Bolivia	4.2		1.8
24	Chile	6.2		1.2	83	Trinidad and Tobago	4.2		1.8
25	Taiwan	6.1		1.2	84	Ukraine	4.2		1.8
26	Hong Kong SAR	6.1		1.5	85	Tanzania	4.0		1.9
27	Spain	6.1		1.3	86	Ecuador	3.9		2.0
28	Hungary	6.0		1.1	87	Georgia	3.9		1.8
28	Portugal	6.0		1.3	88	Macedonia, FYR	3.9		2.2
30	Slovenia	6.0		1.3	89	Kenya	3.8		1.8
31	Kuwait	5.8		1.7	90	Mongolia	3.8		1.9
32	Colombia	5.8		1.6	91	Sri Lanka	3.8		1.9
33	Bulgaria	5.8		1.6	92	Guatemala	3.8		2.1
34	Cyprus	5.7		1.1	93	Ethiopia	3.8		1.9
35	Lithuania	5.7		1.4	94	Paraguay	3.7		1.9
36	Malaysia	5.7		1.0	95	Guyana	3.7		1.7
37	Italy	5.7		1.6	96	Gambia	3.7		1.9
38	Slovak Republic	5.7		1.4	97	Algeria	3.7		2.0
39	Peru	5.6		1.4	98	Nigeria	3.6		1.3
40	Botswana	5.6		1.3	99	Mozambique	3.6		1.8
41	Belgium	5.6		1.6	100	Albania	3.5		2.0
42	Israel	5.5		1.7	101	Mali	3.5		1.7
43	South Africa	5.5		1.3	102	East Timor	3.5		2.1
44	Malta	5.4		1.3	103	Uganda	3.4		2.0
45	Serbia and Montenegro	5.4		1.8	104	Indonesia	3.3		1.5
46	Thailand	5.4		1.4	105	Madagascar	3.3		1.5
47	Mauritius	5.4		1.2	106	Dominican Republic	3.2		1.8
48	Uruguay	5.3		1.5	107	Morocco	3.1		1.5
49	Czech Republic	5.3		1.4	108	Pakistan	3.1		1.6
50	Moldova	5.2		1.9	109	Kyrgyz Republic	3.0		1.6
51	Turkey	5.1		1.8	110	Benin	3.0		1.8
52	Jordan	5.1		1.7	111	Chad	2.9		2.0
53	Zimbabwe	5.1		1.5	112	Cambodia	2.9		1.8
54	El Salvador	5.1		1.9	113	Cameroon	2.9		1.7
55	Namibia	5.1		1.9	114	Vietnam	2.8		1.5
56	Romania	5.0		1.9	115	Philippines	2.6		1.7
57	Mexico	5.0		1.6	116	Tajikistan	2.6		1.8
58	Jamaica	5.0		1.6	117	Bangladesh	2.2		1.4
59	China	4.9		1.7					

6.22 Irregular payments in public contracts

In your industry, how commonly would you estimate that firms make undocumented extra payments or bribes connected with the awarding of public contracts (investment projects)? (1 = common, 7 = never occurs)

RANK	COUNTRY	SCORE	1 MEAN: 4.1 7	SD
1	New Zealand	6.4		0.7
2	Iceland	6.4		0.8
3	Singapore	6.4		1.0
4	Finland	6.2		1.1
5	Norway	6.2		0.6
6	Denmark	6.1		1.3
7	Australia	5.9		1.0
8	United Kingdom	5.9		1.2
9	Sweden	5.7		1.1
10	Luxembourg	5.7		1.4
11	United States	5.6		1.3
12	Switzerland	5.5		1.3
13	Netherlands	5.5		1.3
14	Japan	5.5		1.5
15	Austria	5.5		1.5
16	Hong Kong SAR	5.5		1.5
17	Ireland	5.5		1.4
18	Taiwan	5.4		1.4
19	Germany	5.3		1.1
20	Canada	5.3		1.3
21	United Arab Emirates	5.3		1.5
22	Portugal	5.3		1.4
23	France	5.2		1.6
24	Qatar	5.0		1.9
25	Malaysia	4.9		1.5
26	Chile	4.9		1.7
27	Israel	4.9		1.7
28	Uruguay	4.8		1.4
29	Jordan	4.8		1.7
30	Moldova	4.7		2.2
31	Cyprus	4.7		1.5
32	Bulgaria	4.7		2.2
33	Slovenia	4.7		1.7
34	Korea, Rep.	4.7		1.5
35	Tunisia	4.6		1.4
36	Italy	4.6		2.1
37	Estonia	4.6		1.7
38	Colombia	4.6		2.2
39	Egypt	4.6		1.9
40	Belgium	4.5		1.6
41	Spain	4.5		1.7
42	Thailand	4.5		1.8
43	Lithuania	4.4		2.0
44	Malta	4.3		1.7
45	Botswana	4.3		1.7
46	Serbia and Montenegro	4.3		2.2
47	Ukraine	4.3		2.0
48	China	4.3		1.9
49	El Salvador	4.1		1.6
50	Jamaica	4.1		1.8
51	Kuwait	4.1		1.9
52	South Africa	4.1		1.7
53	Azerbaijan	4.0		2.0
54	Greece	4.0		1.7
55	Hungary	4.0		1.6
56	Peru	4.0		1.8
57	Bahrain	3.9		1.9
58	Kazakhstan	3.8		1.7
59	Armenia	3.8		2.1
60	Brazil	3.8		2.0
61	Nicaragua	3.8		1.7
62	Costa Rica	3.7		2.0
63	Czech Republic	3.7		1.7
64	Croatia	3.7		1.7
65	Mexico	3.7		1.8
66	Zimbabwe	3.7		1.6
67	Malawi	3.7		2.0
68	India	3.6		1.6
69	Namibia	3.6		1.9
70	Mauritius	3.6		1.7
71	Ethiopia	3.6		1.9
72	Georgia	3.6		1.7
73	Latvia	3.6		1.8
74	Macedonia, FYR	3.5		2.1
75	Turkey	3.5		1.8
76	Poland	3.5		1.7
77	Algeria	3.5		1.9
78	Mozambique	3.5		1.6
79	Honduras	3.5		1.9
80	Tanzania	3.4		2.0
81	Slovak Republic	3.4		1.8
82	Russian Federation	3.4		2.0
83	Gambia	3.4		1.6
84	Indonesia	3.4		1.4
85	Tajikistan	3.3		1.9
86	Mali	3.3		1.8
87	Panama	3.3		1.5
88	Trinidad and Tobago	3.3		1.7
89	Bosnia and Herzegovina	3.3		1.6
90	Nigeria	3.2		1.3
91	Guatemala	3.2		2.0
92	Argentina	3.2		1.7
93	Mongolia	3.2		1.9
94	Kenya	3.1		1.8
95	Romania	3.1		1.9
96	Ghana	3.1		1.6
97	East Timor	3.0		1.9
98	Albania	3.0		2.0
98	Kyrgyz Republic	3.0		1.9
100	Morocco	3.0		1.5
101	Paraguay	2.9		1.9
102	Pakistan	2.9		1.6
103	Bolivia	2.8		1.8
104	Chad	2.8		1.9
105	Uganda	2.8		1.7
106	Madagascar	2.8		1.4
107	Sri Lanka	2.7		1.9
108	Vietnam	2.7		1.4
109	Venezuela	2.7		2.0
110	Cameroon	2.6		1.6
111	Cambodia	2.6		1.6
112	Dominican Republic	2.6		1.7
113	Ecuador	2.5		1.6
114	Guyana	2.5		1.4
115	Benin	2.5		1.7
116	Philippines	2.1		1.5
117	Bangladesh	2.1		1.3

571

6.23   Irregular payments in judicial decisions

In your industry, how commonly would you estimate that firms make undocumented extra payments or bribes connected with getting favorable judicial decisions? (1 = common, 7 = never occurs)

RANK	COUNTRY	SCORE	MEAN: 4.6	SD
1	Iceland	6.8		0.6
2	New Zealand	6.8		0.5
3	Finland	6.7		0.5
4	Germany	6.5		0.9
5	Singapore	6.5		0.9
6	Australia	6.5		0.7
7	Denmark	6.5		1.2
8	United Kingdom	6.5		0.9
9	Austria	6.5		0.9
10	Switzerland	6.4		0.9
11	Luxembourg	6.4		0.7
12	Ireland	6.4		1.1
13	Norway	6.4		0.8
14	Netherlands	6.4		1.0
15	Sweden	6.3		0.9
16	United States	6.2		1.2
17	Japan	6.2		1.2
18	Canada	6.1		1.2
19	Qatar	6.1		1.4
20	Portugal	6.1		0.9
21	France	6.0		1.3
21	Hong Kong SAR	6.0		1.5
23	Israel	5.9		1.6
24	Uruguay	5.8		1.3
25	Cyprus	5.8		1.4
26	United Arab Emirates	5.7		1.2
27	Spain	5.6		1.3
28	Slovenia	5.6		1.5
29	Jordan	5.5		1.4
30	South Africa	5.5		1.4
31	Belgium	5.5		1.5
32	Malta	5.5		1.4
33	Egypt	5.5		1.8
34	Italy	5.5		1.7
35	Taiwan	5.5		1.4
36	Malaysia	5.4		1.1
37	Estonia	5.4		1.6
38	Chile	5.4		1.5
39	Botswana	5.3		1.6
40	Hungary	5.3		1.6
40	Kuwait	5.3		1.7
42	Jamaica	5.2		1.5
43	Colombia	5.2		1.9
44	Costa Rica	5.2		1.5
45	Thailand	5.2		1.6
46	India	5.1		1.6
47	Bulgaria	5.1		2.1
48	Ghana	5.0		1.3
49	Tunisia	5.0		1.3
50	Bahrain	4.8		1.9
51	Namibia	4.8		1.7
52	Malawi	4.8		1.8
53	Mauritius	4.8		1.6
54	Korea, Rep.	4.8		1.5
55	Greece	4.7		1.5
56	China	4.7		1.6
57	Czech Republic	4.7		1.6
58	Zimbabwe	4.6		1.5
59	Serbia and Montenegro	4.5		2.1
60	Lithuania	4.4		1.8
61	Moldova	4.4		2.1
62	Poland	4.3		1.4
63	Gambia	4.2		1.5
64	Brazil	4.2		1.8
65	Turkey	4.2		1.6
66	Nigeria	4.2		1.6
67	Trinidad and Tobago	4.2		1.7
68	Croatia	4.1		1.7
69	Sri Lanka	4.1		1.9
70	Mexico	4.0		1.7
71	Ethiopia	4.0		1.7
72	Latvia	3.9		1.7
73	Ukraine	3.9		1.8
74	Kazakhstan	3.8		1.6
75	Argentina	3.8		1.7
76	Russian Federation	3.7		1.9
77	Tanzania	3.7		1.9
78	Bosnia and Herzegovina	3.7		1.7
79	Slovak Republic	3.7		1.7
80	Armenia	3.7		2.0
81	Azerbaijan	3.7		2.1
82	Uganda	3.7		1.9
83	Romania	3.6		1.8
84	Kenya	3.6		1.8
85	Algeria	3.6		1.8
86	Panama	3.6		1.7
87	Honduras	3.5		1.9
88	Guyana	3.5		1.6
89	Macedonia, FYR	3.5		2.0
90	Dominican Republic	3.5		1.8
91	Mozambique	3.4		1.6
92	El Salvador	3.4		1.6
93	Guatemala	3.4		1.9
94	Bangladesh	3.4		1.7
95	East Timor	3.4		1.6
96	Peru	3.3		1.8
97	Morocco	3.3		1.6
98	Pakistan	3.3		1.7
99	Indonesia	3.3		1.3
100	Vietnam	3.3		1.4
101	Georgia	3.3		1.7
102	Mali	3.2		1.6
103	Tajikistan	3.1		1.7
104	Madagascar	3.0		1.5
105	Venezuela	2.9		2.0
106	Nicaragua	2.9		1.9
107	Albania	2.9		1.6
108	Paraguay	2.8		1.8
109	Mongolia	2.8		1.5
110	Cameroon	2.8		1.6
111	Bolivia	2.7		1.7
112	Kyrgyz Republic	2.7		1.8
113	Benin	2.7		1.7
114	Cambodia	2.6		1.6
115	Philippines	2.6		1.4
116	Ecuador	2.4		1.8
117	Chad	2.4		1.7

6.24   Diversion of public funds

In your country, diversion of public funds to companies, individuals, or groups due to corruption (1 = is common, 7 = never occurs)

RANK	COUNTRY	SCORE	MEAN: 3.7	SD
1	Denmark	6.4		1.1
2	Finland	6.3		0.7
3	Iceland	6.3		1.0
4	Singapore	6.2		0.8
5	Norway	6.1		0.7
6	Switzerland	6.0		1.0
7	New Zealand	5.9		1.2
8	Austria	5.8		1.0
9	Australia	5.8		0.9
10	Luxembourg	5.8		1.0
11	United Kingdom	5.8		1.1
12	Germany	5.7		0.7
13	Hong Kong SAR	5.6		1.2
14	Netherlands	5.6		0.9
15	Sweden	5.5		1.3
16	Ireland	5.5		1.0
17	Qatar	5.4		1.4
18	United States	5.4		1.0
19	United Arab Emirates	5.3		1.1
20	Jordan	5.1		1.5
21	France	5.0		1.3
22	Malaysia	5.0		1.3
23	Cyprus	5.0		1.3
24	Portugal	5.0		1.2
25	Belgium	4.9		1.3
26	Canada	4.9		1.4
27	Taiwan	4.9		1.3
28	Tunisia	4.8		1.3
29	Malta	4.7		1.5
30	Kuwait	4.7		1.7
31	Japan	4.7		1.4
32	Chile	4.7		1.5
33	Spain	4.6		1.3
34	Uruguay	4.6		1.3
35	Bahrain	4.6		1.9
36	Israel	4.4		1.4
37	Botswana	4.4		1.4
38	Estonia	4.3		1.5
39	Slovenia	4.2		1.4
40	Ghana	4.1		1.3
41	Korea, Rep.	4.0		1.5
42	El Salvador	3.9		1.3
43	Greece	3.9		1.4
44	Hungary	3.8		1.4
45	Thailand	3.8		1.4
46	Italy	3.7		1.5
47	Slovak Republic	3.7		1.5
48	South Africa	3.6		1.2
49	Croatia	3.6		1.3
50	Latvia	3.5		1.3
51	Kazakhstan	3.5		1.3
52	Tanzania	3.5		1.6
53	Mauritius	3.5		1.4
54	India	3.4		1.5
55	Tajikistan	3.4		1.8
56	Egypt	3.3		1.8
57	Czech Republic	3.3		1.4
58	Turkey	3.3		1.4
59	Indonesia	3.3		1.3
60	Georgia	3.2		1.4
61	Ethiopia	3.2		1.5
62	Bosnia and Herzegovina	3.2		1.4
63	Jamaica	3.2		1.2
64	Namibia	3.2		1.5
65	China	3.1		1.5
66	Poland	3.1		1.2
67	Algeria	3.1		1.5
68	East Timor	3.1		1.5
69	Costa Rica	3.1		1.4
70	Moldova	3.0		1.5
71	Macedonia, FYR	3.0		1.5
72	Vietnam	3.0		1.3
73	Panama	3.0		1.4
74	Pakistan	3.0		1.4
75	Armenia	3.0		1.6
76	Ukraine	3.0		1.4
77	Gambia	3.0		1.5
78	Malawi	3.0		1.6
79	Lithuania	2.9		1.2
80	Azerbaijan	2.9		1.6
81	Colombia	2.8		1.3
82	Peru	2.8		1.2
83	Nigeria	2.8		1.5
84	Serbia and Montenegro	2.8		1.5
85	Mexico	2.8		1.2
86	Kyrgyz Republic	2.8		1.5
87	Russian Federation	2.8		1.4
88	Mali	2.7		1.4
89	Nicaragua	2.7		1.3
90	Madagascar	2.7		1.3
91	Trinidad and Tobago	2.6		1.2
92	Morocco	2.6		1.4
93	Romania	2.6		1.3
94	Mozambique	2.6		1.2
95	Argentina	2.6		1.1
96	Zimbabwe	2.6		1.2
97	Sri Lanka	2.5		1.5
98	Mongolia	2.5		1.4
99	Brazil	2.5		1.3
100	Bulgaria	2.5		1.4
101	Honduras	2.4		1.2
102	Guyana	2.3		1.2
103	Cambodia	2.2		1.5
104	Bangladesh	2.2		1.1
105	Bolivia	2.2		1.3
106	Kenya	2.2		1.4
107	Philippines	2.1		1.0
108	Guatemala	2.0		1.2
109	Albania	2.0		1.1
109	Dominican Republic	2.0		1.1
111	Uganda	2.0		1.1
112	Cameroon	2.0		1.3
113	Chad	1.8		1.2
114	Ecuador	1.8		1.0
115	Benin	1.6		0.9
116	Paraguay	1.6		0.8
117	Venezuela	1.5		0.7

573

6.25   Business costs of corruption

Do other firms' illegal payments to influence government policies, laws, or regulations impose costs or otherwise negatively affect your firm? (1 = large impact distorting competition, 7 = no impact on competition)

RANK	COUNTRY	SCORE	1 MEAN: 4.4 7	SD		RANK	COUNTRY	SCORE	1 MEAN: 4.4 7	SD
1	Iceland	6.8		0.6		60	Azerbaijan	4.2		1.8
2	Norway	6.6		0.7		61	Zimbabwe	4.1		1.5
3	New Zealand	6.5		1.0		62	Poland	4.1		1.5
4	Finland	6.5		1.1		63	Egypt	4.1		2.1
5	Singapore	6.5		0.9		64	Gambia	4.1		1.9
6	Denmark	6.5		1.0		65	Mexico	4.1		1.7
7	Australia	6.4		0.8		66	Turkey	4.0		1.9
8	Netherlands	6.3		1.0		67	Lithuania	4.0		1.6
9	Ireland	6.2		1.4		68	Mauritius	4.0		1.7
10	Luxembourg	6.2		1.0		69	Indonesia	4.0		1.3
11	Germany	6.2		1.2		70	Tanzania	4.0		1.7
12	Switzerland	6.2		1.2		71	Armenia	3.9		1.9
13	United Kingdom	6.1		1.3		72	Mali	3.8		1.7
14	Austria	6.0		1.5		73	Brazil	3.8		1.9
15	Sweden	6.0		1.4		74	Nigeria	3.8		1.5
16	United States	5.9		1.3		75	Peru	3.8		1.7
17	France	5.8		1.4		76	Algeria	3.8		1.8
18	Canada	5.8		1.4		77	Costa Rica	3.8		1.7
19	Hong Kong SAR	5.7		1.6		78	Sri Lanka	3.8		1.8
20	Israel	5.7		1.5		79	Vietnam	3.7		1.5
21	Portugal	5.6		1.5		80	Nicaragua	3.7		1.5
22	Malaysia	5.5		1.3		81	Ethiopia	3.6		1.8
22	Qatar	5.5		1.7		82	Serbia and Montenegro	3.6		1.9
24	Taiwan	5.5		1.4		83	Argentina	3.6		1.6
25	United Arab Emirates	5.5		1.4		84	Bosnia and Herzegovina	3.6		1.6
26	Estonia	5.3		1.8		85	Kazakhstan	3.5		1.6
26	Malta	5.3		1.5		86	Georgia	3.5		1.6
28	Chile	5.3		1.6		87	Macedonia, FYR	3.4		1.9
29	Belgium	5.3		1.6		88	Mongolia	3.4		1.7
30	Spain	5.3		1.4		89	Panama	3.4		1.4
31	Cyprus	5.2		1.6		90	Bulgaria	3.4		2.0
32	Japan	5.2		1.8		91	Madagascar	3.3		1.5
33	Uruguay	5.1		1.5		92	Kenya	3.3		1.6
34	Jordan	5.0		1.6		93	Pakistan	3.3		1.5
35	Slovenia	5.0		1.7		94	Mozambique	3.3		1.6
36	South Africa	4.8		1.5		95	Ecuador	3.3		1.7
37	Jamaica	4.8		1.8		96	Philippines	3.3		1.6
38	Botswana	4.8		1.8		97	Venezuela	3.3		2.1
39	Czech Republic	4.8		1.5		98	Morocco	3.2		1.3
40	Ghana	4.8		1.5		99	Moldova	3.2		1.8
41	Tunisia	4.7		1.6		100	Cambodia	3.2		1.8
42	Greece	4.6		1.6		101	Guatemala	3.2		1.6
43	Thailand	4.6		1.5		102	Bolivia	3.2		1.4
44	Bahrain	4.6		2.0		103	East Timor	3.1		1.7
45	Korea, Rep.	4.5		1.5		104	Honduras	3.1		1.6
46	Italy	4.5		2.0		105	Romania	3.1		1.7
47	Colombia	4.5		1.8		106	Uganda	3.0		1.7
48	Hungary	4.5		1.8		107	Tajikistan	3.0		1.7
49	Slovak Republic	4.4		1.6		108	Ukraine	2.9		1.2
50	Latvia	4.4		1.6		109	Russian Federation	2.9		1.5
51	Trinidad and Tobago	4.4		1.7		110	Paraguay	2.9		1.6
52	China	4.4		1.7		111	Cameroon	2.8		1.6
53	India	4.3		1.8		112	Dominican Republic	2.8		1.5
54	Malawi	4.3		1.7		113	Bangladesh	2.8		1.5
55	Kuwait	4.3		1.8		114	Benin	2.7		1.6
56	Guyana	4.3		1.8		115	Chad	2.5		1.5
57	El Salvador	4.3		1.6		116	Kyrgyz Republic	2.4		1.3
58	Croatia	4.2		1.6		117	Albania	2.2		1.6
59	Namibia	4.2		2.0						

6.26 Public trust of politicians

Public trust in the financial honesty of politicians is (1 = very low, 7 = very high)

RANK	COUNTRY	SCORE	MEAN: 2.7	SD
1	Singapore	6.4		0.7
2	Denmark	6.1		1.1
3	Finland	5.5		1.3
4	Luxembourg	5.4		1.5
5	Norway	5.3		1.5
6	Iceland	5.3		1.4
7	Switzerland	5.2		1.5
8	Netherlands	4.9		1.4
9	United Arab Emirates	4.8		1.4
10	Malaysia	4.7		1.4
11	Qatar	4.7		1.6
12	New Zealand	4.6		1.5
13	United Kingdom	4.5		1.5
14	Tunisia	4.5		1.5
15	Hong Kong SAR	4.4		1.7
16	Australia	4.3		1.4
17	Austria	4.2		1.7
18	United States	4.1		1.4
19	Botswana	4.0		1.5
19	Sweden	4.0		1.5
21	Taiwan	3.7		1.3
22	Germany	3.7		1.5
23	Chile	3.7		1.5
24	Portugal	3.6		1.4
25	Jordan	3.6		1.5
26	Ireland	3.5		1.5
27	France	3.4		1.5
28	Canada	3.4		1.6
29	China	3.3		1.5
30	Belgium	3.3		1.7
31	Ghana	3.2		1.5
32	Malta	3.2		1.5
33	South Africa	3.1		1.5
34	Spain	3.1		1.3
35	Japan	3.1		1.4
36	Cyprus	3.1		1.3
37	Uruguay	3.1		1.3
38	Korea, Rep.	3.0		1.8
39	Thailand	3.0		1.4
40	Israel	2.9		1.2
41	Estonia	2.9		1.3
42	Indonesia	2.9		1.3
43	Vietnam	2.9		1.6
44	Greece	2.8		1.3
45	Slovenia	2.8		1.2
46	Tanzania	2.8		1.5
47	Tajikistan	2.8		1.7
48	Kuwait	2.8		1.5
49	Namibia	2.7		1.5
50	Bahrain	2.7		1.5
51	Kazakhstan	2.6		1.4
52	Azerbaijan	2.6		1.6
53	Turkey	2.6		1.2
54	Algeria	2.6		1.3
55	Gambia	2.4		1.4
56	East Timor	2.4		1.9
57	Georgia	2.4		1.3
58	Morocco	2.4		1.4
59	Hungary	2.3		1.1
60	El Salvador	2.3		1.1
61	Latvia	2.3		1.2
62	Italy	2.3		1.1
63	Ethiopia	2.3		1.3
64	Mali	2.2		1.2
65	Mozambique	2.2		1.4
66	Czech Republic	2.2		1.5
67	Malawi	2.1		1.4
68	Poland	2.1		1.3
69	India	2.1		1.1
70	Jamaica	2.0		1.1
71	Nigeria	2.0		1.1
72	Lithuania	2.0		1.0
73	Croatia	2.0		1.1
74	Ukraine	2.0		1.1
75	Madagascar	2.0		1.1
76	Romania	1.9		1.1
77	Colombia	1.9		1.0
78	Trinidad and Tobago	1.9		1.1
79	Cameroon	1.9		1.1
80	Uganda	1.9		1.3
81	Cambodia	1.9		1.1
82	Moldova	1.9		1.3
83	Pakistan	1.9		1.0
84	Honduras	1.9		1.0
85	Costa Rica	1.9		1.0
86	Mexico	1.8		0.9
87	Bulgaria	1.8		1.0
88	Slovak Republic	1.8		0.9
89	Macedonia, FYR	1.8		0.9
90	Panama	1.8		1.1
91	Bosnia and Herzegovina	1.8		0.9
92	Serbia and Montenegro	1.7		1.1
93	Brazil	1.7		1.0
94	Russian Federation	1.7		1.0
95	Armenia	1.7		1.1
96	Mauritius	1.7		1.0
97	Kenya	1.7		1.1
98	Mongolia	1.6		0.9
99	Zimbabwe	1.6		0.9
100	Chad	1.6		1.2
101	Albania	1.6		1.0
102	Sri Lanka	1.6		1.1
103	Bangladesh	1.6		0.9
104	Guyana	1.5		0.8
105	Guatemala	1.5		0.9
106	Kyrgyz Republic	1.5		1.2
107	Argentina	1.5		0.7
108	Benin	1.4		0.8
109	Philippines	1.4		0.7
110	Peru	1.4		0.6
111	Bolivia	1.4		0.7
112	Venezuela	1.4		0.8
113	Nicaragua	1.3		0.7
114	Dominican Republic	1.3		0.6
115	Paraguay	1.2		0.5
116	Ecuador	1.2		0.5
	Egypt	n/a		n/a

6.27　Pervasiveness of money laundering through banks

Money laundering through the formal banking system in your country is (1 = pervasive, 7 = extremely rare)

RANK	COUNTRY	SCORE	SD
1	Iceland	6.7	0.7
2	New Zealand	6.6	0.6
3	Denmark	6.6	0.9
4	Finland	6.5	0.8
5	Qatar	6.3	1.0
6	Singapore	6.2	0.9
7	France	6.2	1.1
8	Australia	6.2	1.0
9	Germany	6.2	0.8
10	Norway	6.1	1.0
11	Austria	6.1	1.1
12	United States	6.1	1.0
13	United Kingdom	6.1	1.0
14	Bahrain	6.1	1.2
15	Sweden	6.0	1.1
16	Canada	6.0	1.1
17	Netherlands	5.9	1.1
18	Kuwait	5.9	1.2
19	Jordan	5.9	1.2
20	Chile	5.9	1.1
21	Japan	5.9	1.3
22	Luxembourg	5.8	1.1
23	Malaysia	5.8	1.0
24	Estonia	5.7	1.4
25	Malta	5.7	0.9
26	Tunisia	5.6	1.4
27	Switzerland	5.6	1.3
28	Belgium	5.5	1.5
29	Ghana	5.5	1.4
30	Cyprus	5.5	1.4
31	Ireland	5.5	1.0
32	Taiwan	5.4	1.3
33	South Africa	5.4	1.2
34	Spain	5.4	1.3
35	Botswana	5.4	1.2
36	United Arab Emirates	5.3	1.4
37	Israel	5.3	1.2
38	El Salvador	5.3	1.2
39	Greece	5.3	1.2
40	Portugal	5.3	1.1
41	Hungary	5.3	1.2
42	Hong Kong SAR	5.3	1.3
43	Egypt	5.2	1.6
44	Lithuania	5.1	1.2
45	Slovenia	5.1	1.3
46	China	5.1	1.5
47	Korea, Rep.	5.1	1.2
48	Mali	5.1	1.6
49	Gambia	5.1	1.5
50	Slovak Republic	5.1	1.3
51	Vietnam	5.0	1.4
52	India	4.9	1.3
53	Mauritius	4.9	1.3
54	Czech Republic	4.8	1.5
55	Pakistan	4.8	1.6
56	Croatia	4.7	1.3
57	Namibia	4.7	1.5
58	Italy	4.6	1.5
59	Ethiopia	4.6	1.7
60	Brazil	4.6	1.5
61	Thailand	4.6	1.3
62	Poland	4.6	1.4
63	Malawi	4.6	1.6
64	Nicaragua	4.6	1.4
65	Cameroon	4.5	1.4
66	Zimbabwe	4.5	1.0
67	Macedonia, FYR	4.5	1.9
68	Uruguay	4.5	1.4
69	Argentina	4.5	1.3
70	Panama	4.5	1.3
71	Chad	4.5	1.9
72	Armenia	4.5	1.7
73	Georgia	4.5	1.4
74	Turkey	4.4	1.5
75	Tanzania	4.4	1.3
76	Algeria	4.4	1.8
77	Uganda	4.4	1.5
78	Costa Rica	4.4	1.4
79	Bolivia	4.4	1.3
80	Peru	4.4	1.3
81	Bangladesh	4.4	1.5
82	Benin	4.3	1.6
83	Albania	4.3	1.7
84	East Timor	4.3	1.6
85	Mongolia	4.3	1.6
86	Madagascar	4.3	1.3
87	Sri Lanka	4.3	1.5
88	Serbia and Montenegro	4.2	1.5
89	Kyrgyz Republic	4.2	1.7
90	Kenya	4.2	1.5
91	Morocco	4.2	1.3
92	Tajikistan	4.2	1.9
93	Colombia	4.2	1.5
94	Philippines	4.1	1.4
95	Mexico	4.1	1.4
96	Mozambique	4.1	1.6
97	Trinidad and Tobago	4.1	1.5
98	Bosnia and Herzegovina	4.0	1.7
99	Romania	4.0	1.6
100	Honduras	4.0	1.6
101	Kazakhstan	4.0	1.5
102	Nigeria	3.9	1.3
103	Bulgaria	3.9	1.7
104	Latvia	3.9	1.5
105	Jamaica	3.8	1.3
106	Azerbaijan	3.8	1.7
107	Moldova	3.8	1.5
108	Cambodia	3.8	1.8
109	Venezuela	3.8	1.6
110	Ecuador	3.8	1.2
111	Indonesia	3.6	1.3
112	Paraguay	3.3	1.4
113	Guatemala	3.3	1.4
114	Russian Federation	3.2	1.6
115	Ukraine	3.1	1.4
116	Dominican Republic	3.1	1.3
117	Guyana	3.0	1.5

MEAN: 4.8

Domestic Competition and Cluster Development

7.01 Intensity of local competition

Competition in the local market is (1 = limited in most industries and price-cutting is rare, 7 = intense in most industries as market leadership changes over time)

RANK	COUNTRY	SCORE	1 MEAN: 4.7 7	SD
1	United States	6.3		0.8
2	Germany	6.2		0.8
3	United Kingdom	6.1		1.0
4	Belgium	6.0		0.9
5	Australia	6.0		0.9
6	Netherlands	5.9		0.7
7	Chile	5.9		1.0
8	Japan	5.9		0.9
9	Israel	5.9		1.1
10	Austria	5.8		1.0
11	India	5.8		0.9
12	New Zealand	5.8		0.8
13	Taiwan	5.8		0.8
14	Canada	5.7		1.0
15	Hong Kong SAR	5.7		1.0
16	Finland	5.7		1.3
17	United Arab Emirates	5.7		1.1
18	Estonia	5.6		1.1
19	France	5.6		1.2
20	Malaysia	5.6		0.9
21	Singapore	5.5		1.0
22	Denmark	5.5		1.3
23	Sweden	5.5		1.4
24	Spain	5.5		0.9
25	Cyprus	5.5		1.0
26	Hungary	5.5		1.1
27	Malta	5.4		1.1
28	El Salvador	5.4		1.1
29	Korea, Rep.	5.4		1.0
30	Jordan	5.4		1.1
31	China	5.3		1.1
32	Czech Republic	5.2		1.3
33	Turkey	5.2		1.2
34	Sri Lanka	5.2		1.4
35	Iceland	5.2		1.2
36	Thailand	5.2		0.9
37	Kuwait	5.2		1.2
38	Norway	5.2		1.0
39	Lithuania	5.2		1.2
40	Jamaica	5.1		1.0
40	Portugal	5.1		1.0
42	South Africa	5.1		1.2
43	Ireland	5.1		1.1
44	Bahrain	5.1		1.5
45	Pakistan	5.1		1.5
46	Poland	5.0		1.2
47	Qatar	5.0		1.3
48	Greece	5.0		1.2
49	Slovak Republic	4.9		1.3
50	Slovenia	4.9		1.3
51	Kenya	4.9		1.5
52	Italy	4.9		1.6
53	Philippines	4.9		1.4
54	Colombia	4.8		1.2
55	Indonesia	4.8		1.0
56	Brazil	4.8		1.5
57	Peru	4.8		1.4
58	Luxembourg	4.8		1.6
59	Ghana	4.8		1.2
60	Mauritius	4.8		1.5
61	Tunisia	4.8		1.2
62	Mexico	4.8		1.4
63	Switzerland	4.8		1.5
64	Latvia	4.7		1.3
65	Costa Rica	4.7		1.4
66	Malawi	4.7		1.5
67	Croatia	4.7		1.5
68	Botswana	4.7		1.4
69	Mali	4.7		1.6
70	Trinidad and Tobago	4.6		1.4
71	Vietnam	4.6		1.5
72	Bangladesh	4.6		1.6
73	Russian Federation	4.5		1.7
74	Ukraine	4.5		1.7
75	Uganda	4.4		1.7
76	Tanzania	4.4		1.6
77	Kazakhstan	4.4		1.6
78	Romania	4.3		1.6
79	Egypt	4.3		1.7
80	Morocco	4.3		1.5
81	Argentina	4.3		1.5
82	Serbia and Montenegro	4.3		1.6
83	Gambia	4.3		1.5
84	Namibia	4.2		1.7
85	Georgia	4.2		1.3
86	Bosnia and Herzegovina	4.2		1.6
87	Nigeria	4.2		1.4
88	Cambodia	4.2		1.6
89	Kyrgyz Republic	4.2		1.8
90	Benin	4.1		1.8
91	Cameroon	4.1		1.9
92	Bolivia	4.0		1.5
93	Guyana	4.0		1.5
94	Bulgaria	4.0		1.8
95	Mongolia	4.0		1.6
96	Uruguay	4.0		1.3
97	Venezuela	3.9		1.4
98	Guatemala	3.9		1.6
99	Madagascar	3.9		1.6
100	Dominican Republic	3.8		1.6
101	Azerbaijan	3.8		1.7
102	Albania	3.8		1.6
103	Algeria	3.8		1.6
104	Paraguay	3.7		1.4
105	Tajikistan	3.7		1.7
106	Macedonia, FYR	3.7		1.5
107	Nicaragua	3.6		1.3
108	Ethiopia	3.6		1.7
109	Honduras	3.5		1.6
110	Ecuador	3.5		1.3
111	Panama	3.5		1.6
112	Armenia	3.4		1.7
113	Zimbabwe	3.4		1.2
114	Mozambique	3.4		1.5
115	East Timor	3.3		1.7
116	Moldova	3.2		1.5
117	Chad	3.1		1.8

7.02   Effectiveness of antitrust policy

Anti-monopoly policy in your country is (1 = lax and not effective at promoting competition, 7 = effective and promotes competition)

RANK	COUNTRY	SCORE		SD
1	Germany	6.3		0.8
2	Australia	6.1		0.9
3	United Kingdom	6.0		1.0
4	Finland	6.0		1.2
5	New Zealand	6.0		0.8
6	United States	5.9		1.1
7	France	5.7		1.1
8	Denmark	5.7		1.2
9	Netherlands	5.7		1.1
10	Austria	5.7		1.1
11	Belgium	5.6		1.2
12	Canada	5.6		1.1
13	Norway	5.5		1.0
14	South Africa	5.5		1.0
15	Ireland	5.5		1.4
15	Luxembourg	5.5		0.9
17	Israel	5.5		1.2
18	Sweden	5.3		1.3
19	Iceland	5.3		1.4
20	Taiwan	5.3		1.1
21	Cyprus	5.1		1.1
22	Chile	5.1		1.2
23	Japan	5.1		1.3
24	Singapore	5.0		1.2
25	Portugal	5.0		1.1
26	Czech Republic	4.9		1.1
27	Spain	4.9		1.3
28	Korea, Rep.	4.9		1.2
29	Estonia	4.8		1.4
30	Malaysia	4.7		1.3
31	Switzerland	4.7		1.5
32	Hungary	4.6		1.4
33	India	4.6		1.4
34	Greece	4.6		1.2
35	Malta	4.5		1.3
36	Tunisia	4.5		1.4
37	Turkey	4.4		1.2
38	Brazil	4.4		1.6
39	Poland	4.3		1.1
40	Pakistan	4.3		1.4
41	Slovenia	4.2		1.3
42	Thailand	4.2		1.3
43	Colombia	4.2		1.3
44	Jordan	4.2		1.5
45	Italy	4.2		1.7
46	Hong Kong SAR	4.1		1.6
47	Nigeria	4.1		1.4
48	Lithuania	4.1		1.3
49	Jamaica	4.1		1.4
50	Kuwait	4.0		1.7
51	Latvia	4.0		1.3
52	Kenya	4.0		1.5
53	Slovak Republic	3.9		1.5
54	Ghana	3.9		1.3
55	China	3.8		1.3
56	Mexico	3.8		1.5
57	Bahrain	3.8		1.8
58	Tanzania	3.8		1.7
59	Peru	3.8		1.3
60	Panama	3.7		1.7
61	Indonesia	3.7		1.1
62	Morocco	3.6		1.2
63	Mali	3.6		1.4
64	Benin	3.6		1.5
65	Namibia	3.6		1.6
66	Zimbabwe	3.6		1.3
67	Venezuela	3.6		1.6
68	Mauritius	3.6		1.6
69	United Arab Emirates	3.5		1.6
70	Cameroon	3.5		1.6
71	El Salvador	3.5		1.4
72	Philippines	3.5		1.6
73	Kazakhstan	3.5		1.3
74	Botswana	3.4		1.7
75	Ukraine	3.4		1.2
76	Egypt	3.4		1.7
77	Costa Rica	3.4		1.6
78	Romania	3.4		1.4
79	Argentina	3.4		1.3
80	Qatar	3.3		1.4
81	Malawi	3.3		1.6
82	Uganda	3.3		1.9
83	Sri Lanka	3.3		1.4
84	Algeria	3.3		1.5
85	Mozambique	3.3		1.3
86	Croatia	3.2		1.3
87	Georgia	3.2		1.4
88	Bulgaria	3.2		1.5
89	Tajikistan	3.2		1.6
90	Moldova	3.1		1.4
91	Gambia	3.1		1.6
92	Chad	3.1		1.6
93	Cambodia	3.0		1.6
94	Russian Federation	3.0		1.4
95	Trinidad and Tobago	3.0		1.3
96	Bangladesh	3.0		1.6
97	East Timor	3.0		1.8
98	Madagascar	2.9		1.4
99	Macedonia, FYR	2.9		1.5
100	Guyana	2.9		1.2
101	Mongolia	2.9		1.5
102	Uruguay	2.8		1.0
103	Serbia and Montenegro	2.8		1.5
104	Bolivia	2.8		1.3
105	Azerbaijan	2.8		1.5
106	Guatemala	2.8		1.4
107	Vietnam	2.8		1.4
108	Ethiopia	2.7		1.5
109	Bosnia and Herzegovina	2.7		1.2
110	Armenia	2.6		1.3
111	Paraguay	2.6		1.2
112	Nicaragua	2.5		1.1
113	Kyrgyz Republic	2.5		1.5
114	Honduras	2.4		1.2
115	Ecuador	2.3		1.2
116	Albania	2.3		1.4
117	Dominican Republic	2.3		1.2

7.03 Extent of market dominance

Corporate activity in your country is (1 = dominated by a few business groups, 7 = spread among many firms)

RANK	COUNTRY	SCORE	MEAN: 3.9	SD	RANK	COUNTRY	SCORE	MEAN: 3.9	SD
1	United States	6.3		1.0	60	Jamaica	3.7		1.4
2	Germany	6.3		0.8	61	Mali	3.7		1.9
3	United Kingdom	6.0		1.3	62	Uruguay	3.7		1.3
4	Finland	5.9		1.1	63	Malta	3.7		1.5
5	Austria	5.9		1.3	64	Egypt	3.7		1.7
6	Japan	5.9		1.2	65	Tanzania	3.6		1.8
7	Denmark	5.7		1.2	66	Indonesia	3.6		1.2
8	Belgium	5.6		1.4	67	Lithuania	3.6		1.2
9	Taiwan	5.6		1.1	68	Morocco	3.6		1.7
10	Netherlands	5.6		1.1	69	Kazakhstan	3.6		1.4
11	Canada	5.5		1.3	70	Kenya	3.5		1.9
12	Switzerland	5.5		1.4	71	Italy	3.5		1.6
13	Ireland	5.4		1.6	72	El Salvador	3.4		1.6
14	France	5.3		1.5	72	Philippines	3.4		1.5
15	Australia	5.2		1.4	74	Zimbabwe	3.4		1.1
16	New Zealand	5.2		1.4	75	Cameroon	3.4		1.9
17	India	5.2		1.5	76	Argentina	3.4		1.4
18	Malaysia	5.1		1.2	77	Peru	3.3		1.4
19	Luxembourg	5.0		1.5	78	Tajikistan	3.3		1.7
19	Singapore	5.0		1.5	79	Ukraine	3.3		1.2
21	Tunisia	4.8		1.4	80	Croatia	3.3		1.2
22	Norway	4.8		1.4	81	Mexico	3.2		1.2
23	Hong Kong SAR	4.7		1.9	82	Botswana	3.2		1.5
24	Spain	4.7		1.5	83	Trinidad and Tobago	3.2		1.7
25	Sweden	4.7		1.6	84	Azerbaijan	3.2		1.3
26	Poland	4.5		1.3	85	Sri Lanka	3.2		1.6
27	Slovenia	4.5		1.3	86	Panama	3.2		1.4
28	Cyprus	4.4		1.5	87	Cambodia	3.1		1.7
29	Israel	4.4		1.6	88	Namibia	3.1		1.5
30	Thailand	4.3		1.3	89	Colombia	3.1		1.1
31	Pakistan	4.3		1.6	90	Macedonia, FYR	3.1		1.5
32	Portugal	4.3		1.3	91	Mozambique	3.1		1.3
33	Jordan	4.3		1.7	92	Mauritius	3.1		1.6
34	South Africa	4.3		1.6	93	Russian Federation	3.0		1.4
35	Qatar	4.3		1.5	94	Moldova	3.0		1.5
36	Vietnam	4.3		1.5	95	Georgia	2.9		1.3
37	Romania	4.3		1.6	96	Gambia	2.9		1.6
38	Costa Rica	4.2		1.6	97	Chad	2.9		2.1
39	Hungary	4.2		1.7	98	East Timor	2.9		1.8
40	Greece	4.2		1.4	99	Bolivia	2.9		1.4
41	Brazil	4.2		1.6	100	Venezuela	2.9		1.2
42	Czech Republic	4.2		1.2	101	Dominican Republic	2.9		1.3
43	Ghana	4.2		1.2	102	Guyana	2.8		1.3
44	China	4.1		1.4	103	Serbia and Montenegro	2.8		1.5
45	Korea, Rep.	4.1		1.7	104	Mongolia	2.8		1.3
46	Iceland	4.1		1.9	105	Madagascar	2.8		1.7
47	Benin	4.1		2.1	106	Paraguay	2.7		1.5
48	Algeria	4.0		1.8	107	Guatemala	2.7		1.3
49	Slovak Republic	4.0		1.6	108	Ethiopia	2.6		1.4
50	Turkey	4.0		1.5	109	Bangladesh	2.6		1.5
51	Estonia	4.0		1.4	110	Malawi	2.6		1.3
52	Bahrain	3.9		1.8	111	Honduras	2.6		1.4
53	Latvia	3.9		1.3	112	Albania	2.6		1.3
54	United Arab Emirates	3.9		1.4	113	Uganda	2.5		1.6
55	Kuwait	3.8		1.7	114	Nicaragua	2.5		1.3
56	Bulgaria	3.8		1.8	115	Armenia	2.4		1.2
57	Nigeria	3.8		1.4	116	Kyrgyz Republic	2.3		1.3
58	Chile	3.7		1.6	117	Ecuador	2.3		1.2
59	Bosnia and Herzegovina	3.7		1.6					

7.04 Buyer sophistication

Buyers in your country are (1 = unsophisticated and make choices based on the lowest price, 7 = knowledgeable and demanding and buy based on superior performance attributes)

RANK	COUNTRY	SCORE	1 MEAN: 4.1 7	SD
1	United States	6.2		1.0
2	Luxembourg	6.2		0.7
3	Japan	6.1		1.1
4	Hong Kong SAR	6.1		0.9
5	Germany	5.9		1.1
6	New Zealand	5.9		0.8
7	Australia	5.8		1.2
8	United Kingdom	5.8		1.0
9	France	5.8		1.2
10	Singapore	5.8		0.9
11	Canada	5.8		1.0
12	Denmark	5.8		1.1
13	Taiwan	5.7		0.8
14	Switzerland	5.7		1.1
15	Netherlands	5.6		1.2
16	Korea, Rep.	5.6		1.1
17	Finland	5.6		1.3
18	Belgium	5.6		1.3
19	Sweden	5.5		1.2
20	Norway	5.5		0.8
21	Austria	5.5		1.4
22	Malaysia	5.5		1.1
23	Ireland	5.4		1.3
24	Iceland	5.3		1.3
25	India	5.2		1.3
26	Spain	5.1		1.4
27	Israel	5.1		1.3
28	Slovenia	5.0		1.2
29	Mauritius	4.9		1.7
30	Chile	4.8		1.3
31	Cyprus	4.8		1.4
32	South Africa	4.8		1.3
33	United Arab Emirates	4.8		1.5
34	Italy	4.8		1.6
35	Thailand	4.7		1.3
36	Tunisia	4.7		1.4
37	Sri Lanka	4.6		1.7
38	Indonesia	4.6		1.2
39	Estonia	4.5		1.5
40	Kazakhstan	4.5		1.8
41	Czech Republic	4.5		1.6
42	El Salvador	4.4		1.5
43	Greece	4.4		1.2
44	China	4.4		1.4
45	Costa Rica	4.4		1.5
46	Philippines	4.4		1.6
47	Trinidad and Tobago	4.3		1.4
48	Kuwait	4.3		1.7
49	Ghana	4.3		1.5
50	Nigeria	4.3		1.4
51	Portugal	4.3		1.3
52	Malta	4.2		1.4
53	Jamaica	4.1		1.5
54	Poland	4.1		1.4
55	Bahrain	4.1		1.5
56	Pakistan	4.0		1.5
57	Argentina	4.0		1.3
58	Kenya	4.0		1.9
59	Latvia	4.0		1.4
60	Qatar	4.0		1.6
61	Mexico	3.9		1.5
62	Turkey	3.9		1.3
63	Russian Federation	3.9		1.6
64	Jordan	3.9		1.6
65	Brazil	3.9		1.6
66	Hungary	3.9		1.5
67	Romania	3.9		1.6
68	Vietnam	3.8		1.7
69	Botswana	3.8		1.3
70	Zimbabwe	3.8		1.2
71	Panama	3.8		1.4
72	Slovak Republic	3.6		1.4
73	Lithuania	3.6		1.3
74	Ukraine	3.6		1.5
75	Colombia	3.6		1.5
76	Peru	3.5		1.4
77	Namibia	3.5		1.5
78	Croatia	3.4		1.5
79	Venezuela	3.4		1.5
80	Morocco	3.4		1.7
81	Mongolia	3.4		1.5
82	Bulgaria	3.4		1.6
83	Uruguay	3.3		1.1
84	Bangladesh	3.3		1.4
85	Azerbaijan	3.3		1.6
86	Algeria	3.2		1.7
87	Malawi	3.2		1.7
88	Cambodia	3.2		1.5
89	Macedonia, FYR	3.1		1.7
90	Dominican Republic	3.1		1.5
91	Armenia	3.1		1.4
92	Tanzania	3.0		1.5
93	Kyrgyz Republic	3.0		1.6
94	Georgia	2.9		1.3
95	Ecuador	2.9		1.1
96	Gambia	2.9		1.7
97	Moldova	2.8		1.5
98	Tajikistan	2.8		1.7
99	Serbia and Montenegro	2.8		1.5
100	Guatemala	2.7		1.4
101	Albania	2.7		1.6
102	Guyana	2.7		1.3
103	Cameroon	2.7		1.9
103	Honduras	2.7		1.4
105	Egypt	2.7		1.4
106	Uganda	2.7		1.6
107	Mozambique	2.6		1.4
108	Bosnia and Herzegovina	2.6		1.3
109	Paraguay	2.5		1.2
110	Nicaragua	2.4		1.1
111	Mali	2.4		1.5
112	Ethiopia	2.3		1.4
113	Benin	2.3		1.7
114	Madagascar	2.2		1.4
115	East Timor	2.2		1.4
116	Bolivia	2.1		1.1
117	Chad	1.9		1.5

7.05 Local supplier quantity

Local suppliers in your country are (1 = largely nonexistent, 7 = numerous and include the most important materials, components, equipment, and services)

RANK	COUNTRY	SCORE	1 — MEAN: 4.8 — 7	SD
1	Japan	6.6		0.6
2	Germany	6.4		0.9
3	United States	6.4		0.8
4	Austria	6.1		1.0
5	India	6.0		0.9
6	France	6.0		1.0
7	United Kingdom	5.9		1.0
8	Finland	5.9		1.0
9	Belgium	5.9		1.2
10	Denmark	5.8		1.0
11	Netherlands	5.8		0.9
12	Hong Kong SAR	5.8		1.1
13	Canada	5.8		1.2
14	Taiwan	5.7		0.9
15	Sweden	5.7		1.1
16	Switzerland	5.7		1.2
17	Australia	5.7		1.0
18	Malaysia	5.6		0.9
19	Spain	5.6		1.0
20	Chile	5.5		1.0
21	South Africa	5.5		1.1
22	Korea, Rep.	5.5		1.0
23	Czech Republic	5.5		1.0
24	Italy	5.5		1.2
25	New Zealand	5.5		1.0
26	Ireland	5.4		1.1
27	Brazil	5.4		1.1
28	Luxembourg	5.3		1.4
29	Norway	5.3		1.1
30	Mauritius	5.3		1.3
31	Israel	5.3		1.2
32	Thailand	5.3		1.0
33	Singapore	5.3		1.3
34	Turkey	5.3		1.0
35	Lithuania	5.2		1.0
36	Slovak Republic	5.2		1.0
37	China	5.1		1.1
38	Iceland	5.1		1.2
39	Kenya	5.1		1.3
40	Pakistan	5.1		1.3
41	United Arab Emirates	5.1		1.1
42	Tunisia	5.1		1.2
43	Argentina	5.1		0.9
44	Costa Rica	5.0		1.1
45	Colombia	5.0		1.0
46	Philippines	5.0		1.0
46	Portugal	5.0		1.3
48	Cyprus	4.9		1.4
49	Estonia	4.9		1.3
50	Slovenia	4.9		1.2
51	Morocco	4.8		1.6
52	Poland	4.8		1.2
53	El Salvador	4.8		1.1
54	Sri Lanka	4.8		1.5
55	Kuwait	4.8		1.6
56	Russian Federation	4.8		1.7
57	Dominican Republic	4.8		1.3
58	Hungary	4.8		1.5
59	Ukraine	4.8		1.4

RANK	COUNTRY	SCORE	1 — MEAN: 4.8 — 7	SD
60	Kazakhstan	4.8		1.6
61	Trinidad and Tobago	4.7		1.3
62	Panama	4.7		1.5
63	Mexico	4.7		1.2
64	Bangladesh	4.7		1.4
65	Bulgaria	4.7		1.3
66	Greece	4.7		1.1
67	Nigeria	4.7		1.2
68	Peru	4.6		1.2
69	Cameroon	4.6		1.7
70	Ghana	4.5		1.1
71	Jordan	4.5		1.4
72	Malta	4.5		1.7
73	Armenia	4.5		1.6
74	Bahrain	4.5		1.4
75	Egypt	4.5		1.4
76	Croatia	4.5		1.4
77	Vietnam	4.4		1.4
78	Uruguay	4.4		1.0
79	Algeria	4.4		1.6
80	Latvia	4.4		1.3
81	Indonesia	4.4		1.1
82	Romania	4.4		1.5
83	Tanzania	4.4		1.5
84	Serbia and Montenegro	4.3		1.2
85	Macedonia, FYR	4.3		1.5
86	Guatemala	4.3		1.4
87	Chad	4.3		2.0
88	Mali	4.2		1.8
89	Azerbaijan	4.2		1.4
90	Uganda	4.2		1.5
91	Madagascar	4.2		1.6
92	Qatar	4.1		1.6
93	Zimbabwe	4.1		1.3
94	Ecuador	4.1		1.1
95	Malawi	4.1		1.5
96	Jamaica	4.1		1.3
97	Paraguay	4.0		1.3
98	Gambia	3.9		1.5
99	Bosnia and Herzegovina	3.9		1.6
100	Guyana	3.9		1.4
101	Kyrgyz Republic	3.9		1.6
102	Honduras	3.9		1.4
103	Ethiopia	3.8		1.4
104	Venezuela	3.7		1.3
105	Botswana	3.7		1.4
106	Nicaragua	3.7		1.4
107	Mozambique	3.6		1.4
108	Namibia	3.6		1.7
109	Moldova	3.6		1.7
110	Albania	3.6		1.7
111	Benin	3.6		1.9
112	Tajikistan	3.5		1.8
113	Georgia	3.5		1.4
114	Bolivia	3.4		1.3
115	East Timor	3.3		1.9
116	Cambodia	3.2		1.5
117	Mongolia	3.1		1.3

7.06 Local supplier quality

The quality of local suppliers in your country is (1 = poor, as they are inefficient and have little technological capability, 7 = very good, as they are internationally competitive and assist in new product and process development)

RANK	COUNTRY	SCORE	MEAN: 4.4	SD		RANK	COUNTRY	SCORE	MEAN: 4.4	SD
1	Japan	6.5		0.6		60	Sri Lanka	4.3		1.5
2	Germany	6.5		0.6		61	Jamaica	4.2		1.1
3	United States	6.3		0.9		62	Croatia	4.2		1.2
4	Austria	6.1		1.0		63	Pakistan	4.2		1.4
5	Denmark	6.1		0.8		64	Jordan	4.2		1.2
6	Belgium	6.0		0.9		65	Russian Federation	4.1		1.6
7	France	6.0		0.9		66	Qatar	4.1		1.3
8	Switzerland	5.9		0.9		67	Peru	4.1		1.1
9	Sweden	5.9		0.9		68	China	4.1		1.1
10	Netherlands	5.9		1.0		69	Namibia	4.1		1.3
11	Canada	5.8		0.9		70	Ukraine	4.0		1.2
12	Hong Kong SAR	5.8		0.8		71	Azerbaijan	4.0		1.4
13	Australia	5.8		0.9		72	Uruguay	4.0		1.1
14	New Zealand	5.8		0.9		73	Ghana	4.0		1.1
15	United Kingdom	5.8		0.9		74	Bulgaria	4.0		1.3
16	Taiwan	5.8		0.8		75	Panama	3.9		1.5
17	Finland	5.8		0.9		76	Bangladesh	3.9		1.3
18	Iceland	5.6		1.0		77	Macedonia, FYR	3.9		1.3
19	Ireland	5.6		0.9		78	Dominican Republic	3.8		1.3
20	Singapore	5.5		1.0		79	Morocco	3.8		1.4
21	Norway	5.5		1.0		80	Armenia	3.8		1.3
22	Spain	5.5		1.0		81	Botswana	3.8		1.2
23	Israel	5.4		1.1		82	Guatemala	3.8		1.3
24	Korea, Rep.	5.4		0.9		83	Indonesia	3.8		1.1
25	South Africa	5.3		1.1		84	Romania	3.7		1.3
26	Malaysia	5.3		1.0		85	Egypt	3.7		1.3
27	India	5.3		1.1		86	Zimbabwe	3.7		1.1
28	Czech Republic	5.3		1.1		87	Serbia and Montenegro	3.7		1.3
29	Chile	5.2		1.1		88	Vietnam	3.6		1.3
30	Luxembourg	5.2		1.0		89	Nigeria	3.6		1.3
31	Italy	5.1		1.4		90	Honduras	3.5		1.3
32	Thailand	5.0		1.0		91	Bosnia and Herzegovina	3.5		1.4
33	United Arab Emirates	5.0		1.0		92	Venezuela	3.5		1.1
34	Estonia	5.0		1.0		93	Cameroon	3.5		1.4
35	Slovenia	5.0		1.0		94	Ecuador	3.4		1.0
36	Brazil	4.9		1.4		95	Algeria	3.4		1.3
37	Turkey	4.8		1.1		96	Mali	3.4		1.4
38	Lithuania	4.8		1.2		97	Tanzania	3.4		1.4
39	Poland	4.8		1.1		98	Madagascar	3.3		1.3
40	Slovak Republic	4.8		1.2		99	Moldova	3.3		1.5
41	Cyprus	4.7		1.4		100	Gambia	3.3		1.3
42	Costa Rica	4.7		1.2		101	Malawi	3.3		1.3
43	Mauritius	4.7		1.2		102	Paraguay	3.3		1.3
44	Latvia	4.6		1.3		103	Benin	3.2		1.4
45	Tunisia	4.6		1.1		104	Guyana	3.2		1.1
46	Argentina	4.6		1.0		105	Nicaragua	3.2		1.3
47	Kenya	4.6		1.2		106	Bolivia	3.1		1.1
48	Portugal	4.5		1.1		107	Tajikistan	3.0		1.6
49	Colombia	4.5		1.4		108	Mongolia	3.0		1.2
50	Kuwait	4.5		1.3		109	Georgia	3.0		1.1
51	Hungary	4.5		1.3		110	Uganda	2.9		1.5
52	Greece	4.5		1.1		111	Kyrgyz Republic	2.9		1.2
53	Philippines	4.5		1.1		112	Cambodia	2.9		1.2
54	Trinidad and Tobago	4.4		1.2		113	Ethiopia	2.8		1.2
55	El Salvador	4.4		1.2		114	Mozambique	2.8		1.1
56	Mexico	4.4		1.2		115	Albania	2.7		1.4
57	Kazakhstan	4.3		1.4		116	Chad	2.5		1.6
58	Bahrain	4.3		1.5		117	East Timor	2.0		1.2
59	Malta	4.3		1.1						

7.07 Presence of demanding regulatory standards

Standards on product/service quality, energy, and other regulations (outside environmental regulations) in your country are (1 = lax or nonexistent, 7 = among the world's most stringent)

RANK	COUNTRY	SCORE	1 MEAN: 4.2 7	SD		RANK	COUNTRY	SCORE	1 MEAN: 4.2 7	SD
1	Germany	6.4		0.7		60	Kazakhstan	4.0		1.2
2	Japan	6.2		0.9		61	El Salvador	4.0		1.0
3	Austria	6.2		1.0		62	Nigeria	4.0		1.2
4	United Kingdom	6.1		0.9		63	Russian Federation	4.0		1.4
5	United States	6.1		0.9		64	Mexico	4.0		1.1
6	Switzerland	6.1		0.9		65	Botswana	4.0		1.2
7	France	6.1		0.8		66	Croatia	4.0		1.3
8	Australia	6.0		0.8		67	Namibia	3.9		1.3
9	Belgium	6.0		0.9		68	Argentina	3.9		1.1
10	Finland	6.0		0.7		69	Malta	3.8		1.2
11	Denmark	5.9		0.9		70	Bulgaria	3.8		1.4
12	Singapore	5.9		0.8		71	Peru	3.8		1.1
13	Netherlands	5.9		1.1		72	Trinidad and Tobago	3.8		1.3
14	New Zealand	5.9		0.7		73	Philippines	3.8		1.3
15	Canada	5.8		0.8		74	Sri Lanka	3.7		1.1
16	Iceland	5.8		1.0		75	Indonesia	3.7		1.1
17	Sweden	5.8		1.0		76	China	3.7		1.3
18	Norway	5.7		0.9		77	Romania	3.7		1.3
19	Luxembourg	5.6		0.9		78	Moldova	3.7		1.5
20	Ireland	5.5		1.2		79	Panama	3.6		1.4
21	Hong Kong SAR	5.5		1.1		80	Tanzania	3.6		1.4
22	Israel	5.5		1.0		81	Egypt	3.6		1.4
23	Czech Republic	5.5		1.1		82	Morocco	3.6		1.3
24	Slovak Republic	5.4		1.1		83	Azerbaijan	3.5		1.3
25	Taiwan	5.4		0.9		84	Zimbabwe	3.4		1.4
26	Spain	5.3		0.9		85	Venezuela	3.4		1.2
27	Slovenia	5.3		1.1		86	Serbia and Montenegro	3.4		1.5
28	Hungary	5.2		1.1		87	Algeria	3.4		1.3
29	Malaysia	5.2		0.8		88	Macedonia, FYR	3.3		1.3
30	Korea, Rep.	5.1		1.2		89	Tajikistan	3.3		1.6
31	Estonia	5.1		1.0		90	Malawi	3.3		1.3
32	Italy	5.0		1.3		91	Vietnam	3.2		1.3
33	Thailand	5.0		0.9		92	Kyrgyz Republic	3.2		1.4
34	South Africa	4.9		1.2		93	Bangladesh	3.2		1.3
35	Portugal	4.9		1.1		94	Bolivia	3.2		1.3
36	Chile	4.9		1.1		95	Uganda	3.1		1.3
37	Cyprus	4.8		1.2		96	Mongolia	3.1		1.1
38	Brazil	4.8		1.2		97	Ecuador	3.1		0.9
39	Lithuania	4.7		1.2		98	Armenia	3.1		1.3
40	Latvia	4.7		1.2		99	Nicaragua	3.0		1.1
41	United Arab Emirates	4.7		1.1		100	Guatemala	3.0		1.2
42	Tunisia	4.7		1.2		101	Mali	3.0		1.4
43	Qatar	4.7		1.3		102	Bosnia and Herzegovina	3.0		1.1
44	India	4.6		1.2		102	Mozambique	3.0		1.1
45	Costa Rica	4.4		1.1		104	Honduras	3.0		1.2
46	Kuwait	4.4		1.3		105	Guyana	2.9		0.8
47	Jordan	4.4		1.2		106	Cambodia	2.9		1.2
48	Colombia	4.4		1.3		107	Benin	2.9		1.4
49	Poland	4.4		1.0		108	Madagascar	2.9		1.2
50	Greece	4.3		1.1		109	Dominican Republic	2.8		1.2
51	Kenya	4.3		1.3		110	Ethiopia	2.8		1.1
52	Turkey	4.2		1.0		111	Cameroon	2.8		1.4
53	Bahrain	4.2		1.6		112	Georgia	2.7		1.1
54	Mauritius	4.2		1.2		113	Paraguay	2.7		1.0
55	Jamaica	4.2		1.1		114	Gambia	2.6		1.2
56	Ukraine	4.1		1.2		115	Albania	2.5		1.1
57	Ghana	4.1		1.2		116	East Timor	2.3		1.5
58	Uruguay	4.1		0.9		117	Chad	2.0		1.2
59	Pakistan	4.1		1.3						

7.08 Local availability of process machinery

How is process equipment and machinery specific to your field obtained in your country? (1 = almost always imported, 7 = almost always locally available from capable suppliers)

RANK	COUNTRY	SCORE	MEAN: 2.9	SD
1	Japan	6.0		1.1
2	Germany	5.9		1.1
3	United States	5.3		1.3
4	Finland	4.8		1.4
5	Korea, Rep.	4.7		1.5
6	Italy	4.5		1.7
7	China	4.5		1.3
8	Denmark	4.5		1.5
9	Netherlands	4.5		1.2
10	Switzerland	4.5		1.5
11	Ukraine	4.4		1.6
12	Austria	4.3		1.6
13	United Kingdom	4.3		1.4
14	France	4.1		1.4
15	Sweden	4.1		1.4
16	Spain	4.1		1.5
17	Taiwan	4.1		1.6
18	Brazil	4.1		1.6
19	Canada	4.1		1.5
20	Russian Federation	4.0		1.8
21	Belgium	4.0		1.7
22	India	4.0		1.4
23	Czech Republic	3.9		1.4
24	Malaysia	3.7		1.5
25	Poland	3.6		1.2
26	Kazakhstan	3.5		1.7
27	Azerbaijan	3.4		1.9
28	Israel	3.4		1.7
29	Turkey	3.3		1.5
30	Australia	3.3		1.7
31	Norway	3.3		1.3
32	Ireland	3.3		1.8
33	Slovenia	3.2		1.5
34	Tajikistan	3.2		2.1
35	Bulgaria	3.2		1.7
36	Indonesia	3.2		1.2
37	Singapore	3.1		1.7
38	South Africa	3.1		1.4
39	New Zealand	3.1		1.4
40	Hong Kong SAR	3.0		1.8
41	Hungary	3.0		1.5
42	Lithuania	3.0		1.7
43	Cyprus	3.0		1.8
44	Portugal	3.0		1.6
45	Tunisia	3.0		1.5
46	Iceland	3.0		1.5
47	Nigeria	3.0		1.2
48	Romania	3.0		1.7
49	Panama	2.9		1.5
50	Thailand	2.9		1.2
51	Sri Lanka	2.8		1.8
52	Egypt	2.8		1.7
53	Chile	2.8		1.6
54	Kuwait	2.8		2.1
55	Morocco	2.8		1.4
56	Pakistan	2.8		1.3
57	Argentina	2.8		1.2
58	Jordan	2.8		1.8
59	Slovak Republic	2.7		1.2
60	Vietnam	2.7		1.6
61	Bosnia and Herzegovina	2.7		1.5
62	Macedonia, FYR	2.7		1.7
63	Mexico	2.7		1.2
64	Kenya	2.7		1.7
65	Latvia	2.6		1.4
66	Luxembourg	2.6		1.4
67	Greece	2.6		1.2
68	Croatia	2.5		1.2
68	Estonia	2.5		1.5
70	Serbia and Montenegro	2.5		1.5
71	United Arab Emirates	2.4		1.6
72	Madagascar	2.4		1.6
73	Moldova	2.4		1.5
74	Uganda	2.3		1.7
75	El Salvador	2.3		1.4
76	Philippines	2.3		1.4
77	Chad	2.2		1.8
78	Costa Rica	2.2		1.3
79	Ghana	2.2		1.5
80	Peru	2.2		1.0
81	Guatemala	2.2		1.4
82	Mozambique	2.1		1.3
83	Trinidad and Tobago	2.1		1.4
84	Botswana	2.1		1.4
85	Armenia	2.1		1.3
86	Kyrgyz Republic	2.1		1.4
87	Mali	2.1		1.6
88	Georgia	2.0		1.2
89	Namibia	2.0		1.3
90	Algeria	2.0		1.1
91	Honduras	2.0		1.3
92	Benin	2.0		1.5
93	Tanzania	1.9		1.4
94	Mongolia	1.9		1.3
95	Gambia	1.9		1.3
96	Colombia	1.9		0.9
97	Jamaica	1.9		1.2
98	Qatar	1.9		1.3
99	Cambodia	1.9		1.2
100	Bangladesh	1.9		1.2
101	Uruguay	1.8		0.8
102	Mauritius	1.8		1.2
103	Bolivia	1.8		0.9
104	Guyana	1.8		1.4
105	Bahrain	1.7		1.2
106	Ecuador	1.7		0.8
107	Venezuela	1.7		1.1
108	Nicaragua	1.7		1.0
109	Dominican Republic	1.7		1.0
110	Paraguay	1.6		0.9
111	Cameroon	1.6		1.0
112	Ethiopia	1.6		0.9
113	East Timor	1.6		1.3
114	Malta	1.6		1.1
115	Malawi	1.6		1.0
116	Albania	1.6		0.8
117	Zimbabwe	1.6		1.0

585

7.09 Local availability of specialized research and training services

In your country, specialized research and training services are (1 = not available in the country, 7 = available from world-class local institutions)

RANK	COUNTRY	SCORE	1 MEAN: 4.0 7	SC
1	United States	6.4		0.8
2	United Kingdom	6.1		0.8
3	Germany	6.1		0.8
4	France	6.0		0.9
5	Japan	5.9		0.8
6	Denmark	5.9		0.9
7	Switzerland	5.8		1.2
8	Finland	5.8		1.0
9	Canada	5.7		0.9
10	Israel	5.6		0.9
11	Netherlands	5.5		0.9
12	Australia	5.5		1.0
13	Belgium	5.4		1.4
14	Austria	5.4		1.1
15	Singapore	5.3		1.2
16	Sweden	5.3		0.9
17	Norway	5.2		0.9
18	Taiwan	5.2		1.1
19	New Zealand	5.1		1.0
20	Korea, Rep.	5.0		1.0
21	Czech Republic	4.9		1.2
22	Estonia	4.9		1.4
23	South Africa	4.9		1.2
24	Brazil	4.8		1.3
25	Ireland	4.7		1.4
26	Hong Kong SAR	4.7		1.4
27	Malaysia	4.7		0.9
28	Slovenia	4.7		1.2
29	India	4.7		1.3
30	Italy	4.7		1.4
31	Iceland	4.6		1.2
32	Poland	4.5		1.1
33	Argentina	4.5		1.4
34	Spain	4.5		1.1
35	Lithuania	4.4		1.2
36	China	4.4		1.2
37	Portugal	4.3		1.1
38	Tunisia	4.3		1.4
39	Chile	4.3		1.3
40	Thailand	4.2		1.2
41	Romania	4.2		1.3
42	Latvia	4.2		1.4
43	Costa Rica	4.2		1.3
44	Cyprus	4.2		1.5
45	Uganda	4.1		1.7
46	Panama	4.1		1.5
47	Turkey	4.1		1.2
48	Croatia	4.1		1.2
49	Luxembourg	4.1		1.6
50	Russian Federation	4.1		1.4
51	Indonesia	4.1		1.2
52	Mexico	4.0		1.3
53	Slovak Republic	4.0		1.2
54	Kenya	4.0		1.5
55	Ghana	4.0		1.4
56	Bulgaria	4.0		1.3
57	Jordan	4.0		1.6
58	Kuwait	3.9		1.5
59	Hungary	3.9		1.3
60	Azerbaijan	3.9		1.4
61	Mauritius	3.9		1.6
62	Uruguay	3.9		1.2
63	Serbia and Montenegro	3.8		1.4
64	Egypt	3.8		1.6
65	Colombia	3.8		1.6
66	Morocco	3.8		1.6
67	Greece	3.7		1.2
68	Jamaica	3.7		1.5
69	Kazakhstan	3.7		1.3
70	Sri Lanka	3.7		1.4
71	Ukraine	3.7		1.2
72	Vietnam	3.6		1.5
73	El Salvador	3.5		1.4
74	Guatemala	3.5		1.4
75	Pakistan	3.5		1.6
76	Benin	3.5		1.8
77	Macedonia, FYR	3.5		1.5
78	Cameroon	3.5		1.6
79	Mongolia	3.5		1.7
80	Philippines	3.4		1.5
81	Mali	3.4		1.8
82	Dominican Republic	3.4		1.5
83	Nigeria	3.4		1.4
84	Peru	3.4		1.4
85	Botswana	3.4		1.4
86	United Arab Emirates	3.4		1.6
87	Tanzania	3.3		1.7
88	Trinidad and Tobago	3.3		1.6
89	Nicaragua	3.3		1.6
90	Armenia	3.2		1.5
91	Honduras	3.2		1.5
92	Bosnia and Herzegovina	3.2		1.6
92	Moldova	3.2		1.5
94	Madagascar	3.2		1.6
95	Ecuador	3.2		1.4
96	Georgia	3.1		1.5
97	Malta	3.1		1.5
98	Algeria	3.1		1.5
99	Venezuela	3.0		1.6
100	Bahrain	3.0		1.5
101	Qatar	3.0		1.5
102	Zimbabwe	2.9		1.5
103	Bolivia	2.9		1.3
104	Cambodia	2.9		1.6
105	Malawi	2.9		1.5
106	Mozambique	2.9		1.3
107	Namibia	2.8		1.4
108	Paraguay	2.8		1.4
109	Tajikistan	2.8		1.4
110	Gambia	2.7		1.4
111	Guyana	2.7		1.4
112	Bangladesh	2.6		1.4
113	East Timor	2.5		1.8
114	Chad	2.5		1.8
115	Ethiopia	2.5		1.3
116	Albania	2.4		1.5
117	Kyrgyz Republic	2.3		1.2

7.10 Number of procedures required to start a business, 2005

Number of administrative procedures required to register a business, 2005

RANK	COUNTRY	HARD DATA		RANK	COUNTRY	HARD DATA
1	Australia	2		49	Zimbabwe	10
1	Canada	2		61	Albania	11
1	New Zealand	2		61	Botswana	11
4	Finland	3		61	Cambodia	11
4	Sweden	3		61	Costa Rica	11
6	Belgium	4		61	India	11
6	Denmark	4		61	Japan	11
6	Ireland	4		61	Jordan	11
6	Norway	4		61	Pakistan	11
10	Hong Kong SAR	5		61	Philippines	11
10	Israel	5		61	Portugal	11
10	Morocco	5		61	Serbia and Montenegro	11
10	Romania	5		61	Uruguay	11
10	United States	5		61	Vietnam	11
15	Estonia	6		74	Bosnia and Herzegovina	12
15	Hungary	6		74	Cameroon	12
15	Spain	6		74	China	12
15	Switzerland	6		74	Croatia	12
15	United Kingdom	6		74	El Salvador	12
20	Ethiopia	7		74	Ghana	12
20	France	7		74	Indonesia	12
20	Jamaica	7		74	Kenya	12
20	Latvia	7		74	Korea	12
20	Netherlands	7		74	United Arab Emirates	12
20	Panama	7		84	Egypt	13
20	Singapore	7		84	Honduras	13
27	Bangladesh	8		84	Kuwait	13
27	Benin	8		84	Macedonia, FYR	13
27	Kyrgyz Republic	8		84	Madagascar	13
27	Lithuania	8		84	Mali	13
27	Mexico	8		84	Tanzania	13
27	Mongolia	8		84	Venezuela	13
27	Sri Lanka	8		92	Algeria	14
27	Taiwan	8		92	Azerbaijan	14
27	Thailand	8		92	Colombia	14
27	Turkey	8		92	Ecuador	14
37	Austria	9		92	Mozambique	14
37	Chile	9		97	Argentina	15
37	Georgia	9		97	Bolivia	15
37	Germany	9		97	Greece	15
37	Italy	9		97	Guatemala	15
37	Kazakhstan	9		97	Ukraine	15
37	Malaysia	9		102	Brazil	17
37	Nicaragua	9		102	Paraguay	17
37	Russian Federation	9		102	Uganda	17
37	Slovak Republic	9		105	Chad	19
37	South Africa	9			Bahrain	n/a
37	Tunisia	9			Cyprus	n/a
49	Armenia	10			East Timor	n/a
49	Bulgaria	10			Gambia	n/a
49	Czech Republic	10			Guyana	n/a
49	Dominican Republic	10			Iceland	n/a
49	Malawi	10			Luxembourg	n/a
49	Moldova	10			Malta	n/a
49	Namibia	10			Mauritius	n/a
49	Nigeria	10			Qatar	n/a
49	Peru	10			Tajikistan	n/a
49	Poland	10			Trinidad and Tobago	n/a
49	Slovenia	10				

587

SOURCE: World Bank, *Doing Business in 2005*

Domestic Competition and Cluster Development

7.11 Time required to start a business, 2005

Number of days required to register a business, 2005

RANK	COUNTRY	HARD DATA
1	Australia	2
2	Canada	3
3	Denmark	4
4	United States	5
5	France	8
5	Singapore	8
7	Turkey	9
8	Hong Kong SAR	11
8	Morocco	11
8	Netherlands	11
11	New Zealand	12
12	Italy	13
13	Finland	14
13	Tunisia	14
15	Sweden	16
16	Latvia	18
16	United Kingdom	18
18	Panama	19
19	Mongolia	20
19	Switzerland	20
21	Kyrgyz Republic	21
22	Korea	22
23	Norway	23
24	Ireland	24
24	Pakistan	24
26	Armenia	25
26	Georgia	25
26	Kazakhstan	25
29	Algeria	26
29	Lithuania	26
31	Chile	27
32	Romania	28
33	Austria	29
34	Malaysia	30
34	Moldova	30
36	Jamaica	31
36	Japan	31
36	Poland	31
39	Argentina	32
39	Benin	32
39	Bulgaria	32
39	Ethiopia	32
43	Thailand	33
44	Belgium	34
44	Israel	34
44	Ukraine	34
47	Bangladesh	35
47	Kuwait	35
47	Malawi	35
47	Tanzania	35
51	Jordan	36
51	Russian Federation	36
51	Uganda	36
54	Cameroon	37
55	Greece	38
55	South Africa	38
57	Guatemala	39
58	Czech Republic	40
59	China	41

RANK	COUNTRY	HARD DATA
60	Mali	42
61	Colombia	43
61	Egypt	43
63	Madagascar	44
63	Nigeria	44
65	Germany	45
65	Nicaragua	45
65	Uruguay	45
68	Albania	47
68	Kenya	47
70	Macedonia, FYR	48
70	Taiwan	48
72	Croatia	49
73	Philippines	50
73	Sri Lanka	50
75	Serbia and Montenegro	51
76	Hungary	52
76	Slovak Republic	52
78	Bosnia and Herzegovina	54
78	United Arab Emirates	54
80	Vietnam	56
81	Mexico	58
82	Bolivia	59
83	Slovenia	61
84	Honduras	62
85	Estonia	72
86	Paraguay	74
87	Chad	75
88	Costa Rica	77
89	Dominican Republic	78
89	Portugal	78
91	Ghana	85
91	Namibia	85
93	India	89
94	Ecuador	92
95	Cambodia	94
96	Zimbabwe	96
97	Peru	98
98	Botswana	108
98	Spain	108
100	El Salvador	115
101	Venezuela	116
102	Azerbaijan	123
103	Indonesia	151
104	Brazil	152
105	Mozambique	153
	Bahrain	n/a
	Cyprus	n/a
	East Timor	n/a
	Gambia	n/a
	Guyana	n/a
	Iceland	n/a
	Luxembourg	n/a
	Malta	n/a
	Mauritius	n/a
	Qatar	n/a
	Tajikistan	n/a
	Trinidad and Tobago	n/a

588

SOURCE: World Bank, *Doing Business in 2005*

8.01 Nature of competitive advantage

Competitiveness of your country's companies in international markets is primarily due to (1 = low cost or local natural resources, 7 = unique products and processes)

RANK	COUNTRY	SCORE	1 MEAN: 3.6 7	SD
1	Japan	6.4		0.7
2	Germany	6.3		1.0
3	Switzerland	6.2		1.0
4	Finland	5.9		0.8
5	United States	5.9		1.2
6	Belgium	5.9		1.2
7	Denmark	5.8		1.2
8	Luxembourg	5.7		0.8
9	France	5.7		0.9
10	Sweden	5.7		1.2
11	Austria	5.7		0.9
12	United Kingdom	5.7		0.9
13	Netherlands	5.5		1.0
14	Israel	5.4		1.1
15	Italy	5.3		1.3
16	Korea, Rep.	5.3		0.9
17	Singapore	5.2		1.2
18	Ireland	5.2		1.2
19	Norway	5.0		1.5
20	Taiwan	5.0		1.2
21	Iceland	4.8		1.5
22	Hong Kong SAR	4.7		1.6
23	Cyprus	4.6		1.3
24	Slovenia	4.3		1.1
25	Jamaica	4.3		1.5
26	Spain	4.3		1.3
27	New Zealand	4.1		1.3
28	Botswana	4.1		1.8
29	Canada	4.1		1.6
30	Australia	4.1		1.6
31	Costa Rica	4.0		1.3
32	El Salvador	3.9		1.3
33	Malta	3.9		1.3
34	Czech Republic	3.9		1.3
35	Kenya	3.8		1.8
36	Greece	3.7		1.2
37	United Arab Emirates	3.7		1.5
38	Azerbaijan	3.7		1.5
39	Nigeria	3.6		1.4
40	Croatia	3.6		1.5
41	Panama	3.5		1.8
42	Armenia	3.5		1.5
43	Tunisia	3.5		1.3
44	Namibia	3.5		1.7
45	Mauritius	3.4		1.4
46	South Africa	3.4		1.5
47	Ghana	3.4		1.4
48	Hungary	3.4		1.2
49	Bahrain	3.3		1.9
50	Thailand	3.3		1.3
51	Mexico	3.3		1.4
52	Colombia	3.3		1.2
53	Indonesia	3.3		1.3
54	Portugal	3.3		1.2
55	Malaysia	3.3		1.2
56	Albania	3.2		2.2
57	Lithuania	3.2		1.3
58	Latvia	3.2		1.4
59	Philippines	3.2		1.3

RANK	COUNTRY	SCORE	1 MEAN: 3.6 7	SD
60	China	3.2		1.2
61	Estonia	3.2		1.3
62	Morocco	3.2		1.5
63	Mali	3.2		1.5
64	Jordan	3.2		1.3
65	India	3.2		1.4
66	Benin	3.2		1.5
67	Peru	3.1		1.3
68	Qatar	3.1		1.7
69	Chile	3.1		1.4
70	Guatemala	3.1		1.6
71	Uganda	3.1		1.8
72	Poland	3.1		1.1
73	Georgia	3.1		1.7
74	Pakistan	3.1		1.5
75	East Timor	3.0		1.8
76	Brazil	3.0		1.4
77	Malawi	3.0		1.6
78	Guyana	3.0		1.5
79	Egypt	2.9		1.5
80	Cameroon	2.9		1.4
81	Kazakhstan	2.9		1.5
82	Kuwait	2.9		1.3
83	Ukraine	2.9		1.1
84	Mongolia	2.9		1.9
85	Chad	2.9		1.8
86	Turkey	2.9		1.2
87	Honduras	2.9		1.4
88	Gambia	2.9		1.3
89	Mozambique	2.8		1.3
90	Uruguay	2.8		1.2
91	Trinidad and Tobago	2.8		1.6
92	Bulgaria	2.7		1.4
93	Bosnia and Herzegovina	2.7		1.5
94	Sri Lanka	2.7		1.5
95	Argentina	2.7		1.2
96	Slovak Republic	2.7		1.0
97	Moldova	2.7		1.6
98	Macedonia, FYR	2.7		1.3
99	Russian Federation	2.6		1.3
100	Cambodia	2.6		1.2
101	Tajikistan	2.6		1.4
102	Ecuador	2.6		1.3
102	Nicaragua	2.6		1.5
104	Madagascar	2.6		1.5
105	Venezuela	2.6		1.3
106	Tanzania	2.5		1.5
107	Dominican Republic	2.5		1.5
108	Serbia and Montenegro	2.5		1.3
109	Romania	2.5		1.2
110	Vietnam	2.5		1.3
111	Kyrgyz Republic	2.4		1.4
112	Paraguay	2.4		1.3
113	Algeria	2.4		1.1
113	Zimbabwe	2.4		1.3
115	Ethiopia	2.3		1.4
116	Bolivia	2.2		1.1
117	Bangladesh	2.1		1.1

590

8.02 Value chain presence

Exporting companies in your country are (1 = primarily involved in resource extraction or production, 7 = not only produce but also perform product design, marketing sales, logistics, and after-sales services)

RANK	COUNTRY	SCORE	MEAN: 3.8	SD
1	Japan	6.5		0.9
2	Germany	6.5		0.8
3	Switzerland	6.3		0.9
4	United States	6.3		0.9
5	Austria	6.2		0.7
6	United Kingdom	6.2		0.8
7	France	6.2		1.0
8	Italy	6.2		0.8
9	Belgium	6.1		0.7
9	Luxembourg	6.1		0.7
11	Sweden	6.1		0.9
12	Denmark	6.0		1.3
13	Finland	5.9		1.3
14	Netherlands	5.9		1.0
15	Israel	5.8		1.0
16	Singapore	5.7		0.9
17	Hong Kong SAR	5.7		1.1
18	Korea, Rep.	5.6		0.9
19	Taiwan	5.5		1.0
20	Ireland	5.4		1.1
21	Slovenia	5.1		1.0
22	Czech Republic	5.0		1.1
23	Spain	4.9		1.2
24	Iceland	4.8		1.3
25	Mauritius	4.8		1.1
26	India	4.8		1.3
27	Hungary	4.7		1.3
28	Lithuania	4.6		1.3
29	Malaysia	4.6		1.2
30	Panama	4.6		1.6
31	Tunisia	4.6		1.3
32	New Zealand	4.5		1.2
33	Costa Rica	4.5		1.4
34	Philippines	4.4		1.4
35	Cyprus	4.3		1.3
36	Malta	4.3		1.5
37	Turkey	4.2		1.3
38	Canada	4.2		1.6
39	Portugal	4.2		1.1
40	United Arab Emirates	4.0		1.3
41	Norway	4.0		1.4
42	Estonia	4.0		1.3
43	Colombia	3.9		1.4
44	Poland	3.9		1.3
45	Greece	3.9		1.1
46	Thailand	3.9		1.1
47	Egypt	3.8		1.6
48	Latvia	3.8		1.5
49	Armenia	3.8		1.6
50	Mexico	3.8		1.4
51	Sri Lanka	3.8		1.7
52	China	3.8		1.3
53	Slovak Republic	3.8		1.4
54	El Salvador	3.7		1.5
55	Indonesia	3.7		1.4
56	Brazil	3.7		1.5
57	Pakistan	3.7		1.5
58	Jordan	3.6		1.5
59	Croatia	3.6		1.5
60	Morocco	3.6		1.7
61	Azerbaijan	3.5		1.6
62	Jamaica	3.5		1.4
63	Romania	3.5		1.7
64	Benin	3.5		1.9
65	Chile	3.4		1.6
66	Moldova	3.4		1.8
67	Bulgaria	3.3		1.5
68	Nigeria	3.3		1.3
69	Kenya	3.3		1.8
70	South Africa	3.3		1.5
71	Georgia	3.3		1.5
72	Macedonia, FYR	3.2		1.8
73	Ukraine	3.2		1.4
74	Guatemala	3.2		1.5
75	Ghana	3.1		1.5
76	Uganda	3.1		1.8
77	Australia	3.1		1.5
78	Uruguay	3.1		1.3
79	Peru	3.1		1.3
80	Vietnam	3.1		1.5
81	Honduras	3.1		1.5
82	Cameroon	3.1		1.8
83	Bangladesh	3.0		1.6
84	Argentina	3.0		1.4
85	Bosnia and Herzegovina	3.0		1.5
86	Bahrain	3.0		1.4
87	Dominican Republic	2.9		1.5
88	Trinidad and Tobago	2.9		1.5
89	Cambodia	2.8		1.5
90	Chad	2.8		2.0
91	Tajikistan	2.8		1.6
92	Malawi	2.8		1.5
93	Kazakhstan	2.8		1.6
94	Namibia	2.7		1.4
95	Mali	2.7		1.7
96	Madagascar	2.7		1.3
97	Qatar	2.6		1.7
98	Botswana	2.6		1.5
99	Kuwait	2.6		1.5
100	East Timor	2.6		1.6
101	Ecuador	2.5		1.3
102	Guyana	2.5		1.5
103	Gambia	2.5		1.2
104	Serbia and Montenegro	2.5		1.3
105	Nicaragua	2.4		1.3
106	Venezuela	2.4		1.5
107	Albania	2.3		1.6
108	Kyrgyz Republic	2.3		1.4
109	Tanzania	2.3		1.3
110	Russian Federation	2.3		1.3
111	Mozambique	2.3		1.0
112	Bolivia	2.2		1.0
113	Zimbabwe	2.1		1.1
114	Ethiopia	2.1		1.0
115	Paraguay	2.1		1.2
116	Mongolia	2.0		1.1
117	Algeria	1.9		1.1

8.03   Capacity for innovation

Companies obtain technology (1 = exclusively from licensing or imitating foreign companies, 7 = by conducting formal research and pioneering their own new products and processes)

RANK	COUNTRY	SCORE	SD
1	Germany	6.2	0.8
2	Israel	6.0	0.8
3	Japan	6.0	0.7
4	United States	5.9	1.0
5	France	5.8	0.9
6	Switzerland	5.8	0.9
7	Finland	5.7	1.1
8	Sweden	5.6	1.0
9	Belgium	5.6	0.9
10	Denmark	5.6	1.1
11	United Kingdom	5.5	1.0
12	Netherlands	5.3	1.0
13	Austria	5.2	0.9
14	Korea, Rep.	5.2	1.0
15	Iceland	5.1	1.1
16	Taiwan	5.0	1.1
17	Norway	5.0	1.0
18	Canada	4.8	1.1
19	Italy	4.8	1.2
20	Luxembourg	4.7	1.3
21	Slovenia	4.6	1.0
22	Singapore	4.5	1.3
23	Ireland	4.5	1.3
24	Czech Republic	4.3	1.2
25	Spain	4.3	1.2
26	New Zealand	4.3	1.1
27	Panama	4.3	1.5
28	Malaysia	4.2	1.2
29	Hong Kong SAR	4.1	1.4
30	Australia	4.0	1.2
31	India	3.9	1.2
32	Brazil	3.9	1.3
33	Costa Rica	3.9	1.3
34	China	3.8	1.2
35	Ukraine	3.8	1.4
36	South Africa	3.8	1.3
37	Portugal	3.7	0.9
38	Hungary	3.7	1.1
39	Estonia	3.6	1.1
40	Chile	3.6	1.2
41	Vietnam	3.6	1.2
42	Poland	3.5	1.1
43	Russian Federation	3.5	1.3
44	Turkey	3.5	1.2
45	Azerbaijan	3.5	1.4
46	Lithuania	3.4	1.1
47	Indonesia	3.4	1.3
48	Armenia	3.3	1.4
49	Colombia	3.3	1.3
50	Jamaica	3.3	1.2
51	Latvia	3.3	1.3
52	Tunisia	3.3	1.3
53	Kazakhstan	3.3	1.4
54	Mexico	3.2	1.2
55	Sri Lanka	3.2	1.6
56	Macedonia, FYR	3.2	1.5
57	El Salvador	3.2	1.4
58	Greece	3.2	1.2
59	Benin	3.1	1.6
60	Moldova	3.1	1.6
61	Slovak Republic	3.1	0.9
62	Thailand	3.1	1.2
63	Argentina	3.1	1.1
64	Bosnia and Herzegovina	3.1	1.5
65	Guatemala	3.0	1.4
66	Croatia	3.0	1.4
67	Jordan	3.0	1.3
68	Mongolia	3.0	1.6
69	Cyprus	3.0	1.2
70	Romania	3.0	1.3
71	Kenya	3.0	1.7
72	Egypt	3.0	1.5
73	Malta	3.0	1.2
74	Pakistan	3.0	1.3
75	United Arab Emirates	3.0	1.2
76	Bulgaria	3.0	1.3
77	Philippines	3.0	1.0
78	Uruguay	2.9	1.0
79	Nigeria	2.9	1.2
80	Mauritius	2.9	1.3
81	Peru	2.9	1.1
82	Cameroon	2.8	1.6
83	Uganda	2.8	1.7
84	Tajikistan	2.8	1.5
85	Georgia	2.8	1.4
86	Honduras	2.8	1.3
87	Ghana	2.8	1.5
88	Kyrgyz Republic	2.7	1.5
89	Morocco	2.7	1.4
90	Botswana	2.7	1.3
91	Namibia	2.7	1.3
92	Tanzania	2.6	1.3
93	Mali	2.6	1.5
94	Bangladesh	2.6	1.3
95	Trinidad and Tobago	2.6	1.3
96	Madagascar	2.6	1.2
97	Malawi	2.6	1.4
98	Nicaragua	2.5	1.2
99	Serbia and Montenegro	2.5	1.2
100	East Timor	2.5	1.8
101	Ecuador	2.5	1.0
102	Venezuela	2.5	1.1
103	Dominican Republic	2.5	1.2
104	Mozambique	2.4	1.3
105	Guyana	2.4	1.3
106	Qatar	2.4	1.2
107	Gambia	2.3	1.3
108	Cambodia	2.3	1.2
109	Ethiopia	2.3	1.3
110	Chad	2.2	1.5
111	Zimbabwe	2.2	1.0
112	Algeria	2.2	1.4
113	Bolivia	2.2	1.1
114	Kuwait	2.1	1.1
115	Paraguay	2.1	1.1
116	Bahrain	2.1	1.0
117	Albania	1.9	1.2

8.04 Ethical behavior of firms

The corporate ethics (ethical behavior in interactions with public officials, politicians, and other enterprises) of your country's firms in your industry are (1 = among the world's worst, 7 = the best in the world)

RANK	COUNTRY	SCORE	MEAN: 4.3	SD
1	Denmark	6.3		0.6
2	United Kingdom	6.2		1.0
3	Finland	6.1		1.0
4	New Zealand	6.1		1.0
5	Singapore	6.0		0.8
6	Austria	6.0		0.9
7	Australia	5.9		0.7
8	Iceland	5.9		1.0
9	United States	5.9		1.0
10	Switzerland	5.9		1.0
11	Luxembourg	5.8		0.9
12	Canada	5.8		0.9
13	Ireland	5.8		0.9
14	Norway	5.7		0.8
15	Germany	5.7		0.9
16	Netherlands	5.7		0.9
17	France	5.7		1.0
18	Sweden	5.6		0.8
19	Japan	5.5		1.2
20	Chile	5.3		1.0
21	Belgium	5.3		1.1
22	Malaysia	5.2		1.1
23	Taiwan	5.1		1.0
24	Hong Kong SAR	5.1		1.1
25	Israel	5.0		1.1
26	Spain	5.0		1.0
27	South Africa	5.0		1.0
28	United Arab Emirates	4.8		1.0
29	Portugal	4.7		1.1
30	Qatar	4.7		1.2
31	Estonia	4.7		1.1
32	Tunisia	4.6		0.8
33	Kuwait	4.6		0.9
34	Colombia	4.6		1.2
35	Korea, Rep.	4.6		1.3
36	Jordan	4.5		1.0
37	Bahrain	4.5		1.1
38	India	4.5		1.3
39	Thailand	4.5		0.9
40	Lithuania	4.5		1.0
41	Uruguay	4.5		0.9
42	Slovenia	4.4		1.0
43	Slovak Republic	4.4		1.1
44	Pakistan	4.4		1.4
45	Cyprus	4.4		1.0
46	Ghana	4.4		1.1
47	Botswana	4.3		1.0
48	El Salvador	4.3		1.1
49	Italy	4.3		1.2
50	Jamaica	4.2		1.3
51	Brazil	4.2		1.3
52	Costa Rica	4.2		1.0
53	Turkey	4.2		1.1
54	Czech Republic	4.1		1.4
55	Namibia	4.1		1.4
56	Mexico	4.1		1.3
57	Greece	4.1		1.1
58	Serbia and Montenegro	4.1		1.3
59	Mauritius	4.1		1.1
60	Malta	4.0		0.9
61	Latvia	4.0		1.1
62	Mali	4.0		1.2
63	Hungary	4.0		1.2
64	Azerbaijan	4.0		1.3
65	China	4.0		1.2
66	Egypt	4.0		1.1
67	Kenya	4.0		1.4
68	Tanzania	3.9		1.3
69	Philippines	3.9		1.4
70	Zimbabwe	3.9		1.3
71	Trinidad and Tobago	3.9		1.2
72	Kazakhstan	3.9		1.3
73	Malawi	3.9		1.2
74	Madagascar	3.9		1.1
75	Peru	3.8		1.0
76	Poland	3.8		1.0
77	Vietnam	3.7		1.1
78	Ukraine	3.7		1.0
79	Croatia	3.7		1.1
80	Argentina	3.7		1.1
81	Sri Lanka	3.7		1.0
82	Gambia	3.7		1.2
83	Cameroon	3.7		1.3
84	Panama	3.7		1.2
85	Nicaragua	3.7		1.2
86	Algeria	3.7		1.1
87	Indonesia	3.6		0.9
88	Benin	3.6		1.3
89	Romania	3.6		1.1
90	Russian Federation	3.6		1.4
91	Nigeria	3.6		1.3
92	Bulgaria	3.6		1.3
93	Morocco	3.6		1.2
94	Albania	3.6		1.1
95	Ecuador	3.6		1.2
96	Guatemala	3.5		1.1
97	Armenia	3.5		1.4
98	Venezuela	3.4		1.2
99	Mozambique	3.4		1.0
100	Uganda	3.4		1.4
101	Georgia	3.4		1.2
102	Ethiopia	3.4		1.3
103	Tajikistan	3.4		1.5
104	Bosnia and Herzegovina	3.4		1.2
105	Moldova	3.4		1.5
106	Bangladesh	3.3		1.3
107	Macedonia, FYR	3.3		1.3
108	Honduras	3.3		1.1
109	Mongolia	3.3		1.2
110	Dominican Republic	3.2		1.0
111	Cambodia	3.1		1.3
112	Guyana	3.1		1.0
113	Bolivia	3.0		1.1
114	Kyrgyz Republic	3.0		1.5
115	Chad	2.9		1.5
116	East Timor	2.8		1.3
117	Paraguay	2.8		1.1

8.05 Production process sophistication

Production processes use (1 = labor-intensive methods or previous generations of process technology, 7 = the world's best and most efficient process technology)

RANK	COUNTRY	SCORE	MEAN: 3.8	SD
1	Japan	6.5		0.7
2	Germany	6.3		0.6
3	United States	6.2		0.8
4	Switzerland	6.0		1.1
5	Finland	5.9		0.7
6	Austria	5.9		1.0
7	Denmark	5.9		0.9
8	France	5.9		0.9
9	Singapore	5.8		0.8
10	Belgium	5.8		1.0
11	Sweden	5.7		0.9
12	Taiwan	5.7		0.8
13	Norway	5.6		0.8
14	Netherlands	5.6		0.9
15	Iceland	5.6		1.1
16	Luxembourg	5.5		0.8
17	Israel	5.5		0.9
18	United Kingdom	5.4		0.9
19	Australia	5.4		0.8
20	Ireland	5.3		0.8
21	Korea, Rep.	5.3		0.9
22	Canada	5.3		1.0
23	New Zealand	5.0		0.7
24	Spain	4.9		0.9
25	Italy	4.9		1.2
26	Czech Republic	4.9		1.0
27	Malaysia	4.8		1.1
28	Hong Kong SAR	4.7		1.3
29	Chile	4.7		1.1
30	Qatar	4.7		1.7
31	Slovenia	4.5		1.1
32	Brazil	4.3		1.3
33	India	4.3		1.1
34	Estonia	4.3		1.1
35	United Arab Emirates	4.3		1.4
36	Costa Rica	4.2		1.1
37	Cyprus	4.2		1.2
38	South Africa	4.1		1.2
39	Turkey	4.1		1.1
40	Lithuania	4.1		1.1
41	Greece	4.1		1.0
42	Slovak Republic	4.0		1.1
43	Kuwait	4.0		1.4
44	Hungary	3.9		1.2
45	Tunisia	3.9		1.5
46	Argentina	3.9		1.1
47	Portugal	3.9		1.2
48	Kazakhstan	3.9		1.6
49	Azerbaijan	3.9		1.3
50	Trinidad and Tobago	3.9		1.4
51	Poland	3.8		1.1
52	Malta	3.8		1.0
53	Thailand	3.8		1.3
54	Latvia	3.7		1.3
55	Panama	3.7		1.5
56	Egypt	3.7		1.4
57	Jordan	3.7		1.2
58	Colombia	3.7		1.3
59	Botswana	3.6		1.3
60	Mexico	3.6		1.2
61	Mauritius	3.6		1.2
62	Ukraine	3.6		1.0
63	Bahrain	3.5		1.7
64	El Salvador	3.5		1.2
65	Peru	3.5		1.2
66	Uruguay	3.4		1.0
67	Russian Federation	3.4		1.3
68	Pakistan	3.4		1.6
69	China	3.4		1.3
70	Romania	3.3		1.3
71	Jamaica	3.3		1.1
72	Ghana	3.3		1.4
73	Indonesia	3.3		1.2
74	Croatia	3.3		1.3
75	Namibia	3.2		1.3
76	Venezuela	3.2		1.2
77	Nigeria	3.2		1.2
78	Moldova	3.2		1.5
79	Armenia	3.1		1.2
80	Philippines	3.1		1.1
81	Bulgaria	3.1		1.2
82	Mongolia	3.1		1.4
83	Kyrgyz Republic	2.9		1.2
84	Morocco	2.9		1.2
85	Albania	2.9		1.3
86	Guatemala	2.9		1.2
87	Georgia	2.9		1.2
88	Macedonia, FYR	2.9		1.5
89	Honduras	2.9		1.2
90	Vietnam	2.8		1.1
91	Dominican Republic	2.8		1.2
92	Bosnia and Herzegovina	2.8		1.3
93	Cameroon	2.8		1.4
94	Serbia and Montenegro	2.8		1.3
95	Sri Lanka	2.8		1.2
96	Ecuador	2.7		1.0
97	Tajikistan	2.7		1.4
98	Mozambique	2.7		1.2
99	Algeria	2.6		1.2
100	Bangladesh	2.6		1.3
101	Kenya	2.6		1.4
102	Tanzania	2.4		1.2
103	Nicaragua	2.4		1.0
104	Bolivia	2.4		1.0
105	Paraguay	2.4		1.0
106	Benin	2.4		1.2
107	Uganda	2.4		1.4
108	East Timor	2.4		1.4
109	Madagascar	2.3		1.2
110	Malawi	2.3		1.1
111	Guyana	2.3		1.1
112	Cambodia	2.3		1.2
113	Mali	2.3		1.2
114	Gambia	2.3		1.1
115	Zimbabwe	2.3		1.0
116	Chad	2.1		1.3
117	Ethiopia	2.0		1.0

8.06 Extent of marketing

The extent of marketing in your country is (1 = limited and primitive, 7 = extensive and employs the world's most sophisticated tools and techniques)

RANK	COUNTRY	SCORE	1 MEAN: 4.3 7	SD
1	United States	6.7		0.5
2	United Kingdom	6.4		0.9
3	France	6.1		0.9
4	Germany	6.0		0.8
5	Denmark	6.0		1.1
6	Switzerland	5.9		1.0
7	Japan	5.9		1.0
8	Netherlands	5.8		1.0
9	Canada	5.8		1.0
10	Australia	5.8		1.0
11	Austria	5.7		1.0
12	New Zealand	5.7		0.7
13	Hong Kong SAR	5.7		1.2
14	Belgium	5.7		1.0
15	Sweden	5.5		1.0
16	Israel	5.5		0.9
16	Singapore	5.5		1.0
18	Ireland	5.4		1.3
19	Spain	5.4		1.0
20	Iceland	5.4		1.3
21	South Africa	5.4		1.0
22	Taiwan	5.4		1.0
23	Chile	5.4		1.0
24	Korea, Rep.	5.3		1.0
25	Brazil	5.3		1.2
26	India	5.3		1.0
27	Czech Republic	5.2		1.2
28	Italy	5.2		1.4
29	Norway	5.2		1.0
30	Finland	5.2		1.1
31	Argentina	5.2		1.1
32	Luxembourg	5.1		1.2
33	Cyprus	5.1		1.0
34	Malaysia	5.1		1.1
35	Panama	5.0		1.2
36	Greece	5.0		1.0
37	Poland	5.0		1.1
38	United Arab Emirates	5.0		1.2
39	Estonia	5.0		1.2
40	Philippines	4.9		1.1
41	Jamaica	4.9		1.1
42	Costa Rica	4.8		1.2
43	Portugal	4.8		1.2
44	Slovenia	4.8		1.1
45	Slovak Republic	4.7		1.1
46	Colombia	4.6		1.4
47	Ghana	4.6		1.2
48	Thailand	4.6		1.1
49	Lithuania	4.6		1.1
50	Turkey	4.6		1.2
51	Peru	4.6		1.1
52	Sri Lanka	4.6		1.5
53	Indonesia	4.5		1.1
54	Latvia	4.5		1.2
55	Mexico	4.5		1.3
56	Kuwait	4.5		1.5
57	El Salvador	4.5		1.5
58	Tunisia	4.4		1.2
59	Venezuela	4.4		1.3
60	Hungary	4.4		1.3
61	Dominican Republic	4.3		1.2
62	Trinidad and Tobago	4.3		1.4
63	Mauritius	4.2		1.3
64	Kenya	4.2		1.3
65	Nigeria	4.2		1.4
66	Uruguay	4.2		1.1
67	Pakistan	4.1		1.2
68	Romania	4.0		1.3
69	Croatia	4.0		1.4
70	Ecuador	4.0		1.2
71	Kazakhstan	4.0		1.5
72	Malta	4.0		1.2
73	Jordan	4.0		1.5
74	China	4.0		1.4
75	Qatar	3.9		1.4
76	Guatemala	3.8		1.4
77	Ukraine	3.8		1.3
78	Bahrain	3.8		1.3
79	Botswana	3.8		1.3
80	Morocco	3.8		1.4
81	Cameroon	3.7		1.6
82	Namibia	3.6		1.2
83	Egypt	3.6		1.4
84	Bulgaria	3.6		1.3
85	Zimbabwe	3.6		1.2
86	Madagascar	3.6		1.7
87	Honduras	3.5		1.2
88	Kyrgyz Republic	3.5		1.5
89	Russian Federation	3.5		1.4
90	Mongolia	3.4		1.4
91	Macedonia, FYR	3.4		1.3
92	Vietnam	3.4		1.4
93	Bangladesh	3.3		1.4
94	Azerbaijan	3.3		1.6
95	Albania	3.2		1.4
96	Paraguay	3.2		1.2
97	Nicaragua	3.2		1.2
98	Malawi	3.2		1.3
99	Mozambique	3.2		1.3
100	Georgia	3.2		1.4
101	Tanzania	3.1		1.4
102	Serbia and Montenegro	3.1		1.5
103	Bolivia	3.1		1.2
104	Guyana	3.0		1.1
105	Moldova	3.0		1.5
106	Bosnia and Herzegovina	3.0		1.1
107	Gambia	3.0		1.3
108	Benin	2.9		1.6
109	Cambodia	2.9		1.4
110	Armenia	2.9		1.2
111	Uganda	2.8		1.3
112	Algeria	2.7		1.5
113	Mali	2.7		1.4
114	Tajikistan	2.5		1.3
115	Ethiopia	2.4		1.1
116	East Timor	2.1		1.2
117	Chad	1.8		1.3

8.07　Degree of customer orientation

Firms in your country (1 = generally treat their customers badly, 7 = are highly responsive to customers and customer retention)

RANK	COUNTRY	SCORE	1　MEAN: 4.6　7	SD
1	United States	6.2		0.9
2	Austria	6.1		0.9
3	Japan	6.1		1.0
4	Denmark	6.1		0.9
5	Iceland	6.0		1.0
6	Taiwan	5.9		0.7
7	Egypt	5.8		1.3
8	New Zealand	5.8		0.8
9	Canada	5.8		0.8
10	Hong Kong SAR	5.8		1.0
11	Belgium	5.7		0.8
12	Germany	5.7		1.0
13	Sweden	5.7		1.0
14	Finland	5.7		0.9
15	Switzerland	5.7		1.1
16	Korea, Rep.	5.7		0.9
17	Singapore	5.6		1.0
18	Ireland	5.5		1.2
19	United Kingdom	5.5		1.0
20	Netherlands	5.5		1.1
21	Australia	5.5		0.8
22	Slovenia	5.4		0.9
23	France	5.4		1.2
24	Norway	5.4		0.9
25	Estonia	5.3		1.1
26	Malaysia	5.2		1.1
27	Cyprus	5.2		0.9
28	Lithuania	5.1		1.2
29	Israel	5.1		1.0
30	Colombia	5.1		1.3
31	Thailand	5.1		1.0
32	Spain	5.1		1.2
33	United Arab Emirates	5.0		1.1
34	Mauritius	5.0		1.3
35	Czech Republic	5.0		1.3
36	Italy	5.0		1.5
37	Luxembourg	5.0		1.2
38	Turkey	5.0		1.0
39	Kenya	5.0		1.5
40	Chile	4.9		1.3
41	Kyrgyz Republic	4.9		1.6
42	Pakistan	4.9		1.3
43	India	4.9		1.1
44	Costa Rica	4.8		1.2
45	El Salvador	4.8		1.2
45	Ukraine	4.8		1.1
47	Greece	4.8		1.1
48	Peru	4.8		1.2
49	Kazakhstan	4.7		1.5
50	Panama	4.7		1.3
51	Latvia	4.7		1.1
52	South Africa	4.7		1.3
53	Brazil	4.7		1.4
54	Philippines	4.7		1.3
55	Indonesia	4.6		1.0
56	Sri Lanka	4.6		1.3
57	Slovak Republic	4.6		1.2
58	Ghana	4.6		1.2
59	Poland	4.6		1.2

RANK	COUNTRY	SCORE	1　MEAN: 4.6　7	SD
60	Mexico	4.5		1.2
61	Jordan	4.5		1.3
62	Portugal	4.5		1.0
63	Bahrain	4.5		1.2
63	Kuwait	4.5		1.4
65	Bangladesh	4.5		1.4
66	Russian Federation	4.5		1.5
67	Hungary	4.5		1.3
68	Malta	4.5		0.9
69	China	4.4		1.4
70	Tunisia	4.4		1.3
71	Qatar	4.4		1.4
72	Cambodia	4.4		1.5
73	Bulgaria	4.3		1.5
74	Argentina	4.3		1.3
75	Malawi	4.3		1.3
76	Vietnam	4.3		1.3
77	Jamaica	4.3		1.2
78	Croatia	4.3		1.4
79	Azerbaijan	4.3		1.5
80	Armenia	4.2		1.4
81	Cameroon	4.2		1.8
82	Romania	4.2		1.5
83	Uruguay	4.1		1.1
84	Nigeria	4.1		1.6
85	Gambia	4.1		1.5
86	Morocco	4.1		1.4
87	Guatemala	4.1		1.5
88	Tanzania	4.1		1.6
89	Albania	4.0		1.5
90	Uganda	4.0		1.7
91	Dominican Republic	4.0		1.4
92	Benin	3.9		1.9
93	Tajikistan	3.9		1.8
94	Namibia	3.9		1.4
95	Trinidad and Tobago	3.9		1.2
96	Moldova	3.8		1.7
97	Georgia	3.8		1.4
98	Bosnia and Herzegovina	3.7		1.4
99	Botswana	3.7		1.5
100	Macedonia, FYR	3.7		1.4
101	Ethiopia	3.7		1.4
102	Guyana	3.6		1.4
102	Mali	3.6		1.8
104	Honduras	3.6		1.3
104	Madagascar	3.6		1.5
106	Paraguay	3.6		1.5
107	Mozambique	3.6		1.5
108	Zimbabwe	3.6		1.2
109	Nicaragua	3.6		1.3
110	Venezuela	3.5		1.5
111	Mongolia	3.4		1.4
112	East Timor	3.4		1.7
113	Serbia and Montenegro	3.4		1.6
114	Algeria	3.3		1.7
115	Ecuador	3.2		1.2
116	Bolivia	3.0		1.2
117	Chad	2.7		1.8

8.08   Control of international distribution

International distribution and marketing from your country (1 = takes place through foreign companies, 7 = is owned and controlled by local companies)

RANK	COUNTRY	SCORE	MEAN: 4.1	SD
1	Iceland	5.8		1.0
2	Japan	5.6		1.1
3	Germany	5.6		1.0
4	France	5.5		1.3
5	United States	5.4		1.2
6	Denmark	5.3		1.2
7	Bahrain	5.2		1.2
8	United Kingdom	5.1		1.1
9	Mauritius	5.1		0.9
10	Switzerland	5.1		1.3
11	Luxembourg	5.1		1.4
12	Kuwait	5.1		1.4
13	Taiwan	5.1		1.1
14	Sweden	5.0		1.1
15	Israel	5.0		0.9
16	Korea, Rep.	5.0		1.2
17	Netherlands	5.0		1.2
18	Ireland	4.9		1.0
19	Austria	4.9		1.2
20	Canada	4.8		1.2
21	Jordan	4.8		1.3
22	Panama	4.8		1.5
23	Pakistan	4.8		1.7
24	Slovenia	4.8		1.2
25	Malaysia	4.7		1.2
26	Ukraine	4.7		1.3
27	Turkey	4.7		1.2
28	Hong Kong SAR	4.7		1.2
29	United Arab Emirates	4.7		1.4
30	Finland	4.6		1.5
31	Norway	4.6		1.1
32	New Zealand	4.6		1.3
33	Italy	4.6		1.4
34	India	4.6		1.2
35	South Africa	4.5		1.3
36	Belgium	4.5		1.3
37	Cyprus	4.5		1.5
38	Qatar	4.4		1.6
39	Brazil	4.4		1.4
40	Spain	4.4		1.2
41	Kazakhstan	4.4		1.3
42	Philippines	4.4		1.3
43	Chile	4.4		1.2
44	Tajikistan	4.4		1.8
45	Ghana	4.3		1.3
46	Singapore	4.3		1.2
47	Kyrgyz Republic	4.3		1.7
48	Indonesia	4.2		1.0
49	Australia	4.2		1.3
50	Greece	4.2		1.2
51	Tunisia	4.2		1.4
52	Lithuania	4.2		1.2
53	Egypt	4.2		1.6
54	Albania	4.1		1.7
55	Croatia	4.1		1.3
56	Morocco	4.1		1.7
57	Thailand	4.0		1.1
58	Azerbaijan	4.0		1.3
59	Colombia	4.0		1.5
60	Peru	3.9		1.2
61	Czech Republic	3.9		1.3
62	Estonia	3.9		1.6
63	Romania	3.9		1.4
64	Costa Rica	3.8		1.4
65	Ethiopia	3.8		1.6
66	Macedonia, FYR	3.8		1.4
67	China	3.8		1.2
68	Russian Federation	3.8		1.5
69	Portugal	3.8		1.0
70	Poland	3.7		1.2
71	Mexico	3.7		1.3
72	Latvia	3.7		1.4
73	Bosnia and Herzegovina	3.7		1.6
74	Argentina	3.7		1.3
75	Jamaica	3.7		1.5
76	Mali	3.7		1.8
77	Uruguay	3.7		1.3
78	Trinidad and Tobago	3.7		1.4
79	Guyana	3.7		1.7
80	El Salvador	3.7		1.4
81	Dominican Republic	3.6		1.5
82	Nigeria	3.6		1.3
83	Sri Lanka	3.6		1.5
84	Hungary	3.6		1.4
85	Bulgaria	3.6		1.4
86	Benin	3.6		1.8
87	Guatemala	3.6		1.4
88	Ecuador	3.5		1.3
89	Gambia	3.5		1.7
90	Malta	3.5		1.3
91	Kenya	3.5		1.7
92	Moldova	3.5		1.6
93	Serbia and Montenegro	3.5		1.3
94	Slovak Republic	3.5		1.3
95	Bangladesh	3.5		1.7
96	Algeria	3.5		1.9
97	Malawi	3.5		1.5
98	Uganda	3.4		1.8
99	Georgia	3.4		1.6
100	Namibia	3.4		1.2
101	Zimbabwe	3.4		1.4
102	Mongolia	3.3		1.6
103	Armenia	3.3		1.4
104	Mozambique	3.3		1.5
105	Honduras	3.3		1.3
106	Botswana	3.3		1.3
107	Madagascar	3.3		1.5
108	Vietnam	3.2		1.4
109	Tanzania	3.2		1.3
110	Cameroon	3.2		1.8
111	Venezuela	3.2		1.5
112	Paraguay	3.2		1.3
113	Cambodia	3.1		1.6
114	Bolivia	2.9		1.3
115	Nicaragua	2.9		1.2
116	Chad	2.7		1.9
117	East Timor	2.7		1.5

597

8.09 Extent of regional sales

Exports from your country to neighboring countries are (1 = limited, 7 = substantial and growing)

RANK	COUNTRY	SCORE	1　MEAN: 4.5　7	SD
1	Germany	6.6		0.7
2	Ireland	6.4		0.8
3	Japan	6.3		0.8
4	Austria	6.2		1.0
5	Denmark	6.2		0.9
6	Hong Kong SAR	6.2		1.0
7	Canada	6.2		0.9
8	New Zealand	6.1		0.7
9	Netherlands	6.1		0.8
10	Finland	6.1		0.8
11	France	6.1		0.9
12	Belgium	6.1		0.9
13	Switzerland	6.0		1.0
14	Taiwan	5.9		0.9
15	United Kingdom	5.9		1.0
16	United States	5.9		1.1
17	Luxembourg	5.9		1.4
18	South Africa	5.8		1.0
19	Iceland	5.8		0.8
20	Sweden	5.8		1.1
21	Malaysia	5.7		1.0
22	Singapore	5.6		1.1
23	Thailand	5.6		1.0
24	Australia	5.6		1.0
25	Slovenia	5.5		0.8
26	Slovak Republic	5.5		1.3
27	United Arab Emirates	5.5		1.3
28	Korea, Rep.	5.5		1.1
29	Czech Republic	5.4		1.0
30	Costa Rica	5.4		1.1
31	Trinidad and Tobago	5.4		1.4
32	Mexico	5.3		1.2
33	Brazil	5.3		1.2
34	Norway	5.3		1.1
35	Jordan	5.2		1.4
36	Argentina	5.2		1.0
37	Turkey	5.2		1.3
38	Spain	5.1		1.2
39	China	5.1		1.2
40	Kenya	5.1		1.5
41	Colombia	5.1		1.4
42	Estonia	5.1		1.3
43	Hungary	5.1		1.3
44	Portugal	5.0		1.2
45	Poland	5.0		1.3
46	Italy	5.0		1.2
47	Lithuania	5.0		1.2
48	Greece	5.0		1.2
49	Chile	4.9		1.5
50	Uruguay	4.9		0.9
51	India	4.9		1.5
52	Panama	4.9		1.7
53	Tunisia	4.8		1.3
54	Indonesia	4.8		0.9
55	El Salvador	4.7		1.3
56	Cameroon	4.7		1.8
57	Ghana	4.7		1.5
58	Latvia	4.6		1.3
59	Vietnam	4.6		1.5

RANK	COUNTRY	SCORE	1　MEAN: 4.5　7	SD
60	Pakistan	4.4		1.9
61	Philippines	4.4		1.3
62	Malta	4.3		1.2
63	Sri Lanka	4.3		1.5
64	Mauritius	4.2		1.4
65	Bahrain	4.2		1.7
66	Kazakhstan	4.2		1.5
67	Peru	4.1		1.4
68	Guatemala	4.0		1.6
69	Morocco	4.0		1.4
70	Russian Federation	3.9		1.5
71	Cyprus	3.9		1.3
72	Namibia	3.9		1.5
73	Azerbaijan	3.9		1.8
74	Croatia	3.9		1.5
75	Honduras	3.9		1.6
76	Kuwait	3.8		1.6
77	Tanzania	3.8		1.7
78	Romania	3.8		1.4
79	Ecuador	3.8		1.2
80	Nigeria	3.7		1.3
81	Qatar	3.7		1.9
82	Uganda	3.7		1.9
83	Paraguay	3.7		1.5
84	Venezuela	3.6		1.3
85	Bulgaria	3.6		1.5
86	Zimbabwe	3.6		1.3
87	Egypt	3.6		1.4
88	Jamaica	3.6		1.4
89	Guyana	3.6		1.5
90	Georgia	3.6		1.6
91	Moldova	3.5		1.9
92	Macedonia, FYR	3.5		1.7
93	Dominican Republic	3.5		1.5
94	Armenia	3.4		1.6
95	Mozambique	3.4		1.8
96	Bolivia	3.4		1.4
97	Gambia	3.4		2.0
98	Ukraine	3.4		1.4
99	Serbia and Montenegro	3.3		1.7
100	Cambodia	3.2		1.9
101	Madagascar	3.2		1.4
102	Mongolia	3.1		1.7
103	Malawi	3.0		1.5
104	Botswana	3.0		1.5
105	Mali	3.0		1.8
106	Bosnia and Herzegovina	3.0		1.6
107	Nicaragua	2.9		1.2
108	Kyrgyz Republic	2.8		1.7
109	Benin	2.7		1.9
110	Bangladesh	2.7		1.7
111	Ethiopia	2.7		1.5
112	Israel	2.6		1.8
113	Chad	2.5		1.9
114	Tajikistan	2.5		1.5
115	Algeria	2.2		1.4
116	Albania	2.2		1.5
117	East Timor	1.9		1.2

8.10   Breadth of international markets

Exporting companies from your country sell (1 = primarily in a small number of foreign markets, 7 = in virtually all international country markets)

RANK	COUNTRY	SCORE	1 MEAN: 3.8 7	SD	RANK	COUNTRY	SCORE	1 MEAN: 3.8 7	SD
1	Germany	6.7		0.7	60	Latvia	3.5		1.3
2	Japan	6.5		0.7	61	Malta	3.5		1.4
3	United States	6.4		1.1	62	Nigeria	3.4		1.4
4	Switzerland	6.2		1.2	63	Bahrain	3.4		1.6
5	Netherlands	6.2		0.9	64	Morocco	3.4		1.5
6	United Kingdom	6.1		1.1	65	Azerbaijan	3.4		1.5
7	Hong Kong SAR	6.1		1.1	66	Vietnam	3.4		1.6
8	Sweden	6.1		0.8	67	Romania	3.3		1.4
9	Taiwan	5.8		1.0	68	Mauritius	3.3		1.5
10	Austria	5.8		1.4	69	Kazakhstan	3.3		1.5
11	Denmark	5.8		1.2	70	Trinidad and Tobago	3.3		1.6
12	France	5.7		1.4	71	Kuwait	3.3		1.8
13	Singapore	5.7		1.1	72	Mexico	3.2		1.4
14	Chile	5.7		1.2	73	Jamaica	3.2		1.3
15	Israel	5.6		0.8	74	Ukraine	3.2		1.5
16	Finland	5.6		1.4	75	Cyprus	3.2		1.3
17	Korea, Rep.	5.5		1.2	76	Uruguay	3.1		1.1
18	Ireland	5.4		1.5	77	Cameroon	3.1		1.7
19	Malaysia	5.4		1.2	78	Egypt	3.1		1.5
20	Turkey	5.3		1.2	79	Zimbabwe	3.0		1.4
21	Belgium	5.3		1.6	80	Bangladesh	3.0		1.6
22	Australia	5.3		1.4	81	El Salvador	2.9		1.1
23	New Zealand	5.2		1.4	82	Bulgaria	2.9		1.4
24	Italy	5.2		1.7	83	Ecuador	2.9		1.2
25	Iceland	5.2		1.4	84	Guatemala	2.9		1.4
26	India	5.0		1.4	85	Namibia	2.8		1.2
27	Spain	5.0		1.4	86	Mozambique	2.7		1.3
28	Canada	4.8		1.7	87	Serbia and Montenegro	2.6		1.5
29	Luxembourg	4.8		1.9	88	Croatia	2.6		1.1
30	Thailand	4.7		1.4	89	Armenia	2.6		1.3
31	Brazil	4.7		1.5	90	Madagascar	2.6		1.4
32	Czech Republic	4.7		1.4	91	Mali	2.6		1.7
33	South Africa	4.6		1.4	92	Macedonia, FYR	2.6		1.3
34	Hungary	4.6		1.5	93	Dominican Republic	2.6		1.1
35	Slovenia	4.6		1.4	94	Honduras	2.6		1.1
36	Slovak Republic	4.6		1.5	95	Cambodia	2.6		1.6
37	China	4.5		1.2	96	Botswana	2.6		1.5
38	Panama	4.5		1.8	97	Malawi	2.5		1.3
39	Lithuania	4.4		1.5	98	Nicaragua	2.4		1.1
40	United Arab Emirates	4.4		1.6	99	Tanzania	2.4		1.2
41	Norway	4.4		1.4	100	Bosnia and Herzegovina	2.4		1.2
42	Costa Rica	4.2		1.6	101	Guyana	2.4		1.3
43	Poland	4.2		1.2	102	Bolivia	2.4		1.0
44	Indonesia	3.9		1.0	103	Paraguay	2.4		1.1
45	Argentina	3.9		1.3	104	Uganda	2.4		1.4
46	Qatar	3.9		2.0	105	Moldova	2.3		1.4
47	Estonia	3.8		1.5	106	Algeria	2.3		1.5
48	Tunisia	3.8		1.5	107	Ethiopia	2.3		1.2
49	Pakistan	3.8		1.9	108	Gambia	2.2		1.3
50	Greece	3.7		1.2	109	Venezuela	2.2		1.1
51	Sri Lanka	3.7		1.5	110	Georgia	2.1		0.9
52	Philippines	3.7		1.3	111	Mongolia	2.1		1.0
53	Kenya	3.7		1.8	112	East Timor	2.0		1.4
54	Peru	3.7		1.4	113	Kyrgyz Republic	2.0		1.1
55	Portugal	3.7		1.2	114	Tajikistan	2.0		0.9
56	Jordan	3.7		1.5	115	Benin	2.0		1.1
57	Ghana	3.6		1.5	116	Chad	2.0		1.3
58	Colombia	3.6		1.3	117	Albania	1.8		0.9
59	Russian Federation	3.5		1.5					

8.11   Extent of staff training

The general approach of companies in your country to human resources is (1 = to invest little in training and employee development, 7 = to invest heavily to attract, train, and retain employees)

RANK	COUNTRY	SCORE	1 MEAN: 3.8 7	SD	RANK	COUNTRY	SCORE	1 MEAN: 3.8 7	SD
1	Germany	5.9		0.8	60	Portugal	3.6		1.0
2	Denmark	5.9		0.9	61	Azerbaijan	3.6		1.5
3	Japan	5.9		0.9	62	Panama	3.6		1.5
4	United States	5.8		1.1	63	Qatar	3.6		1.6
5	Sweden	5.8		0.8	64	Argentina	3.5		1.1
6	Austria	5.7		1.0	65	Romania	3.5		1.4
7	Singapore	5.5		1.0	66	Colombia	3.5		1.2
7	Switzerland	5.5		1.2	67	Indonesia	3.5		1.1
9	Belgium	5.5		1.0	68	China	3.5		1.4
10	Norway	5.4		0.8	69	El Salvador	3.4		1.2
11	Luxembourg	5.4		1.1	70	Malawi	3.4		1.3
12	Finland	5.4		1.0	71	Sri Lanka	3.4		1.5
13	Taiwan	5.4		1.0	72	Mexico	3.4		1.1
14	Netherlands	5.4		0.9	73	Kuwait	3.3		1.5
15	United Kingdom	5.4		0.9	74	Macedonia, FYR	3.3		1.6
16	France	5.3		1.3	75	Peru	3.2		1.2
17	Ireland	5.2		1.0	76	Russian Federation	3.2		1.5
18	Korea, Rep.	5.2		1.0	77	Morocco	3.2		1.6
19	Canada	5.2		1.1	78	Cameroon	3.2		1.7
20	Iceland	5.2		1.0	79	Venezuela	3.2		1.4
21	Israel	5.1		1.2	80	Kazakhstan	3.2		1.4
22	Australia	4.9		1.0	81	Bahrain	3.2		1.4
23	New Zealand	4.9		1.1	82	Vietnam	3.1		1.3
24	South Africa	4.8		1.1	83	Croatia	3.1		1.4
25	Hong Kong SAR	4.8		1.1	84	Mozambique	3.1		1.3
26	Malaysia	4.8		1.1	85	Mongolia	3.1		1.5
27	India	4.5		1.3	86	Cambodia	3.0		1.5
28	Czech Republic	4.5		1.4	87	Ukraine	3.0		1.3
29	Thailand	4.4		1.0	88	Uruguay	3.0		1.0
30	Costa Rica	4.4		1.2	89	Bulgaria	3.0		1.5
31	Spain	4.3		1.2	90	Armenia	3.0		1.4
32	Estonia	4.3		1.3	91	Uganda	3.0		1.7
33	Chile	4.3		1.2	92	Kyrgyz Republic	2.9		1.3
34	Brazil	4.3		1.4	93	Bosnia and Herzegovina	2.9		1.4
35	Slovenia	4.3		1.2	93	Gambia	2.9		1.6
36	Tunisia	4.2		1.5	95	Madagascar	2.9		1.3
37	Mauritius	4.1		1.4	96	Guatemala	2.9		1.3
37	Zimbabwe	4.1		1.2	97	Honduras	2.9		1.2
39	Philippines	4.1		1.2	98	Moldova	2.9		1.4
40	Slovak Republic	4.1		1.3	99	Dominican Republic	2.9		1.1
41	Greece	4.0		1.1	100	Guyana	2.8		1.1
42	Turkey	3.9		1.2	101	Ecuador	2.7		1.0
43	Malta	3.9		1.2	102	East Timor	2.7		1.6
44	Hungary	3.8		1.3	103	Algeria	2.7		1.5
45	Poland	3.8		1.0	104	Tanzania	2.7		1.3
46	Namibia	3.8		1.4	105	Georgia	2.7		1.2
47	Nigeria	3.8		1.6	106	Nicaragua	2.7		1.0
48	Botswana	3.8		1.4	107	Pakistan	2.6		1.4
49	Latvia	3.8		1.2	108	Serbia and Montenegro	2.6		1.5
50	Jamaica	3.8		1.2	109	Paraguay	2.5		1.0
51	Cyprus	3.8		1.2	110	Bangladesh	2.5		1.1
52	Kenya	3.7		1.6	111	Albania	2.5		1.6
53	Italy	3.7		1.5	112	Bolivia	2.4		1.0
54	Ghana	3.7		1.2	113	Ethiopia	2.3		1.1
55	Trinidad and Tobago	3.7		1.3	114	Tajikistan	2.2		1.1
56	Egypt	3.7		1.5	115	Mali	2.2		1.2
57	Jordan	3.7		1.4	116	Benin	2.1		1.3
58	Lithuania	3.6		1.3	117	Chad	2.0		1.3
59	United Arab Emirates	3.6		1.3					

8.12   Willingness to delegate authority

Willingness to delegate authority to subordinates is (1 = low; top management controls all important decisions, 7 = high; authority is mostly delegated to business unit heads and other lower-level managers)

RANK	COUNTRY	SCORE	1 MEAN: 3.7 7	SD
1	Denmark	6.0		1.3
2	Sweden	5.9		1.0
3	Norway	5.9		0.8
4	Finland	5.8		0.9
5	United States	5.7		1.1
6	Netherlands	5.6		0.9
7	Belgium	5.3		1.1
8	Germany	5.3		1.3
9	Luxembourg	5.3		1.2
10	United Kingdom	5.3		1.1
11	Canada	5.2		1.1
12	Ireland	5.2		0.9
13	Austria	5.2		1.3
14	New Zealand	5.2		1.0
15	Switzerland	5.2		1.6
16	Australia	5.2		1.2
17	Taiwan	5.1		1.2
18	Japan	5.0		1.4
19	Iceland	4.9		1.4
20	Israel	4.8		1.2
21	Singapore	4.8		1.3
22	France	4.6		1.5
23	Korea, Rep.	4.6		1.3
24	Malaysia	4.5		1.2
25	Hong Kong SAR	4.4		1.4
26	Spain	4.3		1.3
27	South Africa	4.3		1.4
28	India	4.2		1.5
29	Costa Rica	4.1		1.3
30	Estonia	4.1		1.4
31	Zimbabwe	4.1		1.2
32	Philippines	4.1		1.4
33	Slovenia	4.1		1.2
34	Chile	3.9		1.2
35	Nigeria	3.9		1.5
36	Brazil	3.9		1.4
37	Thailand	3.9		1.3
38	Czech Republic	3.8		1.5
39	Lithuania	3.8		1.4
40	Latvia	3.8		1.4
41	Poland	3.8		1.1
42	Slovak Republic	3.8		1.4
43	Tunisia	3.7		1.6
44	Egypt	3.7		1.7
45	Colombia	3.7		1.3
46	Romania	3.7		1.6
47	Indonesia	3.7		1.2
47	Mauritius	3.7		1.7
49	Namibia	3.7		1.3
50	El Salvador	3.7		1.4
51	Argentina	3.6		1.3
52	Kyrgyz Republic	3.6		1.9
53	Italy	3.6		1.4
54	Azerbaijan	3.6		1.6
55	Portugal	3.5		1.1
56	Hungary	3.5		1.4
57	Kenya	3.5		1.9
58	Greece	3.5		1.3
59	Ghana	3.5		1.4

RANK	COUNTRY	SCORE	1 MEAN: 3.7 7	SD
60	China	3.5		1.3
61	Trinidad and Tobago	3.5		1.4
62	Mexico	3.5		1.3
63	Turkey	3.4		1.3
64	Peru	3.4		1.3
65	Moldova	3.4		1.7
66	Botswana	3.3		1.4
67	Macedonia, FYR	3.3		1.7
68	Vietnam	3.3		1.5
69	United Arab Emirates	3.3		1.3
70	Cyprus	3.3		1.2
71	Venezuela	3.3		1.3
72	Croatia	3.3		1.2
73	Sri Lanka	3.3		1.7
74	Jamaica	3.3		1.2
75	Bahrain	3.2		1.4
76	Tanzania	3.2		1.7
77	Kuwait	3.2		1.5
78	Malta	3.2		1.2
79	Jordan	3.2		1.4
80	Malawi	3.2		1.4
81	Kazakhstan	3.1		1.5
82	Ukraine	3.1		1.3
83	Russian Federation	3.1		1.5
84	Qatar	3.0		1.6
85	Guatemala	3.0		1.4
86	Uganda	3.0		1.8
87	Uruguay	3.0		1.0
88	Mozambique	3.0		1.4
89	Cambodia	3.0		1.7
90	Panama	3.0		1.2
91	Cameroon	2.9		1.7
92	Ecuador	2.9		1.3
93	Albania	2.9		1.5
94	Dominican Republic	2.9		1.1
95	Mongolia	2.8		1.4
96	Bulgaria	2.8		1.4
97	Bosnia and Herzegovina	2.8		1.2
98	Armenia	2.8		1.4
99	Gambia	2.8		1.7
100	Guyana	2.7		1.4
101	Honduras	2.7		1.2
102	Pakistan	2.7		1.6
103	Morocco	2.7		1.4
104	Madagascar	2.7		1.4
105	Tajikistan	2.6		1.6
106	Nicaragua	2.6		1.3
107	Bangladesh	2.6		1.5
108	Serbia and Montenegro	2.6		1.4
109	Georgia	2.5		1.2
110	East Timor	2.5		1.5
111	Ethiopia	2.5		1.4
112	Benin	2.4		1.7
113	Algeria	2.4		1.3
114	Mali	2.4		1.3
115	Bolivia	2.3		1.0
116	Chad	2.3		1.6
117	Paraguay	2.3		1.1

8.13 Extent of incentive compensation

Cash compensation of management (1 = is based exclusively on salary, 7 = includes bonuses and stock options, representing a significant portion of overall compensation)

RANK	COUNTRY	SCORE	SD
1	United States	6.4	0.7
2	United Kingdom	5.9	1.0
3	Netherlands	5.6	0.9
4	Germany	5.6	1.0
5	Switzerland	5.6	1.2
6	Canada	5.6	1.0
7	France	5.5	1.2
8	South Africa	5.4	1.3
9	Singapore	5.4	1.0
10	Austria	5.2	1.2
11	Ireland	5.2	1.1
12	Denmark	5.2	1.2
13	Australia	5.2	1.3
14	Korea, Rep.	5.1	1.0
15	Finland	5.1	1.3
16	Iceland	5.1	0.9
17	Spain	5.1	1.1
18	Belgium	5.1	1.3
19	Panama	5.1	1.3
20	Taiwan	5.0	1.5
21	Italy	5.0	1.3
22	Israel	5.0	1.2
23	Hong Kong SAR	4.9	1.4
24	Sweden	4.9	1.2
25	Malaysia	4.9	1.2
26	Chile	4.8	1.2
27	Zimbabwe	4.8	1.0
28	Luxembourg	4.8	1.5
29	Estonia	4.7	1.2
30	Costa Rica	4.6	1.2
31	New Zealand	4.5	1.2
32	India	4.5	1.3
32	Portugal	4.5	1.2
32	Thailand	4.5	1.2
35	Norway	4.4	1.2
36	Argentina	4.4	1.4
37	Hungary	4.4	1.3
38	Philippines	4.4	1.4
39	Mexico	4.4	1.3
40	Greece	4.4	1.2
41	Kuwait	4.4	1.7
42	Poland	4.3	1.3
43	Brazil	4.3	1.5
44	Slovenia	4.3	1.3
45	Trinidad and Tobago	4.2	1.4
46	El Salvador	4.2	1.5
47	Jamaica	4.2	1.3
48	Czech Republic	4.2	1.3
49	Japan	4.2	1.4
50	Romania	4.2	1.5
51	United Arab Emirates	4.1	1.4
52	Latvia	4.1	1.3
53	China	4.1	1.3
54	Croatia	4.0	1.6
55	Venezuela	4.0	1.4
56	Nigeria	4.0	1.5
57	Mauritius	4.0	1.6
58	Russian Federation	4.0	1.6
59	Namibia	3.9	1.3
60	Peru	3.9	1.4
61	Indonesia	3.8	1.3
62	Honduras	3.8	1.5
63	Egypt	3.8	1.7
64	Qatar	3.8	1.4
65	Ukraine	3.8	1.4
66	Dominican Republic	3.8	1.4
67	Slovak Republic	3.8	1.3
68	Kyrgyz Republic	3.8	1.9
69	Vietnam	3.8	1.6
70	Azerbaijan	3.7	1.7
71	Moldova	3.7	1.8
72	Uruguay	3.7	1.2
73	Lithuania	3.7	1.5
74	Cyprus	3.6	1.3
75	Botswana	3.6	1.4
76	Guatemala	3.6	1.5
77	Pakistan	3.6	1.7
78	Bulgaria	3.6	1.8
79	Tunisia	3.6	1.3
80	Malta	3.6	1.3
81	Bahrain	3.6	1.5
82	Turkey	3.5	1.4
83	Ecuador	3.5	1.4
84	Kazakhstan	3.5	1.5
85	Armenia	3.4	1.5
86	Kenya	3.4	1.7
87	Ghana	3.4	1.5
88	Colombia	3.4	1.3
89	Macedonia, FYR	3.4	1.8
90	Mongolia	3.4	1.4
91	Sri Lanka	3.3	1.8
92	Mozambique	3.3	1.6
93	Malawi	3.3	1.4
94	Jordan	3.3	1.6
95	Georgia	3.2	1.5
96	Morocco	3.2	1.5
97	Guyana	3.1	1.3
98	Bolivia	3.1	1.3
99	Nicaragua	3.0	1.2
100	Bangladesh	3.0	1.3
101	Cambodia	3.0	1.7
102	Madagascar	3.0	1.4
103	Cameroon	2.9	1.6
104	Benin	2.8	1.6
105	Uganda	2.8	1.7
106	Serbia and Montenegro	2.8	1.5
107	Tanzania	2.7	1.4
108	Bosnia and Herzegovina	2.7	1.4
109	Tajikistan	2.7	1.6
110	Paraguay	2.6	1.4
111	Gambia	2.6	1.6
112	Albania	2.6	1.4
113	East Timor	2.5	1.4
114	Mali	2.5	1.2
115	Ethiopia	2.4	1.3
116	Algeria	2.4	1.3
117	Chad	2.4	1.7

8.14 Reliance on professional management

Senior management positions in your country are (1 = usually held by relatives, 7 = held by professional managers chosen based on superior qualification)

RANK	COUNTRY	SCORE	1 MEAN: 4.5 7	SD
1	United States	6.4		0.8
2	New Zealand	6.3		0.6
3	United Kingdom	6.3		0.7
4	Germany	6.2		0.7
5	Finland	6.2		0.8
6	Australia	6.1		0.7
7	Norway	6.1		0.7
8	Japan	6.0		0.8
9	Netherlands	6.0		0.9
10	Denmark	6.0		1.0
11	Canada	6.0		0.8
12	Ireland	5.9		0.8
12	South Africa	5.9		0.9
14	Sweden	5.8		1.0
15	France	5.8		1.0
16	Iceland	5.8		0.9
17	Singapore	5.8		1.0
18	Austria	5.7		1.0
19	Luxembourg	5.7		0.8
20	Belgium	5.7		0.9
21	Switzerland	5.6		1.3
22	Zimbabwe	5.5		0.9
23	Malaysia	5.4		1.0
24	Spain	5.4		0.9
25	Taiwan	5.3		1.1
26	Chile	5.3		1.1
27	Estonia	5.3		1.3
28	Botswana	5.2		1.3
29	Hong Kong SAR	5.2		1.2
30	Ghana	5.1		0.9
31	Israel	5.1		1.3
32	Czech Republic	5.1		1.0
33	Hungary	5.1		1.1
34	India	5.1		1.3
35	United Arab Emirates	5.0		1.2
36	Jamaica	4.9		1.3
37	Korea, Rep.	4.9		1.2
38	Malawi	4.9		1.3
39	Argentina	4.9		1.1
40	Tanzania	4.8		1.6
41	Portugal	4.8		1.0
42	Trinidad and Tobago	4.8		1.2
43	Brazil	4.8		1.5
44	Lithuania	4.8		1.2
45	Colombia	4.8		1.3
46	Slovak Republic	4.8		1.3
47	Latvia	4.7		1.2
48	Slovenia	4.6		1.0
49	Venezuela	4.6		1.5
50	Philippines	4.6		1.4
51	Gambia	4.6		1.7
52	Thailand	4.6		1.1
53	Namibia	4.5		1.3
54	Costa Rica	4.5		1.1
55	Nigeria	4.5		1.5
56	Peru	4.5		1.3
56	Poland	4.5		1.1
58	Greece	4.5		1.3
59	Bahrain	4.5		1.6

RANK	COUNTRY	SCORE	1 MEAN: 4.5 7	SD
60	Sri Lanka	4.4		1.6
61	Kenya	4.4		1.8
62	Pakistan	4.4		1.5
63	Qatar	4.4		1.5
64	Romania	4.3		1.5
65	Croatia	4.3		1.2
66	Turkey	4.3		1.2
67	Mauritius	4.2		1.7
68	Cameroon	4.2		1.6
69	Panama	4.2		1.5
70	Uganda	4.2		1.8
71	Benin	4.2		1.8
72	Moldova	4.2		1.7
73	El Salvador	4.1		1.4
73	Georgia	4.1		1.4
75	Egypt	4.1		1.6
76	Russian Federation	4.1		1.6
77	Malta	4.1		1.3
78	Mexico	4.1		1.2
79	China	4.1		1.4
80	Kyrgyz Republic	4.1		2.0
81	Indonesia	4.0		1.3
82	Tunisia	4.0		1.4
83	Ukraine	4.0		1.3
84	Uruguay	4.0		1.1
85	Vietnam	4.0		1.5
86	Algeria	4.0		1.8
87	Jordan	3.9		1.5
88	Guyana	3.9		1.5
89	Kazakhstan	3.8		1.4
90	Kuwait	3.8		1.7
91	Italy	3.8		1.6
92	Madagascar	3.8		1.6
93	Cyprus	3.7		1.3
94	Albania	3.7		1.6
95	Mozambique	3.7		1.5
96	Bangladesh	3.7		1.5
97	Cambodia	3.6		1.8
98	Ethiopia	3.6		1.6
99	Bosnia and Herzegovina	3.5		1.4
100	Mali	3.5		2.0
101	Mongolia	3.5		1.5
102	Bulgaria	3.4		1.5
103	Ecuador	3.4		1.2
104	Guatemala	3.3		1.5
105	Morocco	3.3		1.4
106	Nicaragua	3.3		1.4
107	East Timor	3.3		2.0
108	Tajikistan	3.3		1.9
109	Macedonia, FYR	3.2		1.5
110	Dominican Republic	3.2		1.3
111	Armenia	3.2		1.6
112	Serbia and Montenegro	3.2		1.3
113	Honduras	3.1		1.2
114	Azerbaijan	2.9		1.5
115	Bolivia	2.8		1.2
116	Paraguay	2.8		1.3
117	Chad	2.3		1.5

8.15 Quality of management schools

Management or business schools in your country are (1 = limited or of poor quality, 7 = among the best in the world)

RANK	COUNTRY	SCORE	1 MEAN: 4.1 7	SD
1	United States	6.6		0.7
2	France	6.1		0.9
3	Switzerland	6.0		1.0
4	Canada	6.0		0.7
5	United Kingdom	5.9		0.8
6	India	5.9		0.9
7	Austria	5.7		0.9
8	Spain	5.7		0.8
9	Belgium	5.7		0.9
10	Australia	5.7		0.8
11	Singapore	5.6		1.0
12	Netherlands	5.5		0.9
13	Denmark	5.5		0.8
14	Israel	5.5		1.0
15	Chile	5.5		0.8
16	South Africa	5.5		0.8
17	Ireland	5.4		1.1
18	Finland	5.4		1.2
19	Norway	5.3		0.9
20	Germany	5.3		0.9
21	Costa Rica	5.1		1.0
22	Argentina	5.1		0.9
23	New Zealand	5.1		1.3
24	Tunisia	5.1		1.1
25	Iceland	5.0		0.9
26	Taiwan	5.0		0.9
27	Estonia	5.0		1.1
27	Sweden	5.0		1.2
29	Philippines	5.0		1.1
30	Malaysia	4.9		1.2
31	Hong Kong SAR	4.9		1.0
32	Czech Republic	4.9		1.1
33	Portugal	4.8		0.9
34	Thailand	4.7		0.9
35	Slovenia	4.7		1.1
36	Mexico	4.7		1.2
37	Hungary	4.7		1.1
38	Korea, Rep.	4.6		1.3
39	Colombia	4.6		1.1
40	Italy	4.5		1.4
41	Brazil	4.5		1.3
42	Japan	4.5		1.3
43	Morocco	4.5		1.2
44	Peru	4.4		1.0
45	Turkey	4.4		1.2
46	Latvia	4.4		1.2
47	Ghana	4.4		1.3
48	Poland	4.4		1.1
49	Lithuania	4.4		1.2
50	Jamaica	4.4		1.1
51	Nicaragua	4.3		1.2
52	Trinidad and Tobago	4.3		1.3
53	Uruguay	4.2		1.0
54	Slovak Republic	4.2		1.0
55	Venezuela	4.1		1.5
56	Kenya	4.1		1.5
57	Cyprus	4.0		1.4
58	Pakistan	3.9		1.6
59	El Salvador	3.9		1.3

RANK	COUNTRY	SCORE	1 MEAN: 4.1 7	SD
60	Greece	3.9		1.3
61	Cameroon	3.9		1.6
62	Indonesia	3.9		0.9
63	Sri Lanka	3.8		1.3
64	Benin	3.8		1.6
65	Malta	3.7		1.4
66	Romania	3.7		1.3
67	Kuwait	3.6		1.1
68	Zimbabwe	3.6		1.4
69	Guatemala	3.6		1.2
70	Ukraine	3.6		1.2
71	Macedonia, FYR	3.6		1.6
72	Madagascar	3.6		1.4
73	China	3.5		1.3
74	Russian Federation	3.5		1.2
75	Mauritius	3.5		1.6
76	Jordan	3.5		1.4
77	Kazakhstan	3.5		1.2
78	Mali	3.4		1.4
79	Serbia and Montenegro	3.4		1.3
80	Egypt	3.4		1.3
81	Botswana	3.4		1.4
82	Qatar	3.3		1.4
83	Ecuador	3.3		1.2
84	Bulgaria	3.3		1.3
84	Panama	3.3		1.0
86	Bangladesh	3.3		1.4
87	United Arab Emirates	3.3		1.4
88	Bosnia and Herzegovina	3.2		1.2
89	Algeria	3.2		1.3
90	Uganda	3.2		1.4
91	Dominican Republic	3.2		1.1
92	Croatia	3.2		1.2
93	Nigeria	3.2		1.4
94	Gambia	3.2		1.4
95	Bolivia	3.1		1.0
96	Armenia	3.1		1.2
97	Mozambique	3.1		1.4
98	Honduras	3.1		1.1
99	Tanzania	3.1		1.4
100	Georgia	3.0		1.1
101	Mongolia	3.0		1.2
102	Bahrain	3.0		1.4
102	Malawi	3.0		1.3
104	Paraguay	3.0		1.2
105	Azerbaijan	2.9		1.6
106	Ethiopia	2.9		1.2
107	Moldova	2.8		1.4
108	Kyrgyz Republic	2.8		1.1
109	Luxembourg	2.8		1.4
110	Vietnam	2.7		1.2
111	Cambodia	2.7		1.2
112	Albania	2.5		1.1
113	Tajikistan	2.5		1.1
114	Guyana	2.5		1.2
115	Chad	2.5		1.6
116	Namibia	2.4		1.4
117	East Timor	1.6		0.8

604

8.16 Efficacy of corporate boards

Corporate governance by investors and boards of directors in your country is characterized by (1 = management has little accountability, 7 = investors and boards exert strong supervision of management decisions)

RANK	COUNTRY	SCORE	1 MEAN: 4.6 7	SD
1	United Kingdom	6.1		1.0
2	United States	5.8		1.1
3	Australia	5.8		0.8
4	New Zealand	5.7		0.9
5	Denmark	5.7		1.1
6	Germany	5.7		1.0
7	Finland	5.6		1.1
8	South Africa	5.6		1.0
9	Ireland	5.6		1.0
10	Canada	5.6		1.1
11	Netherlands	5.5		1.0
12	Singapore	5.5		1.1
13	Austria	5.5		1.2
14	Malaysia	5.5		1.1
15	Luxembourg	5.5		1.2
16	France	5.4		1.2
17	Norway	5.3		0.9
18	Belgium	5.3		1.0
19	Sweden	5.3		1.0
20	Iceland	5.2		1.0
21	Estonia	5.2		1.2
22	Switzerland	5.2		1.3
23	Chile	5.2		1.1
24	Israel	5.2		0.9
25	Hungary	5.1		1.0
26	Colombia	5.0		1.0
27	Slovak Republic	5.0		1.2
28	Malawi	5.0		1.0
29	Taiwan	5.0		1.2
30	Zimbabwe	5.0		1.0
31	Spain	5.0		1.1
32	Ghana	5.0		1.2
33	Japan	4.9		1.3
34	Czech Republic	4.8		1.2
35	Malta	4.8		0.9
36	Russian Federation	4.8		1.5
37	Mauritius	4.8		1.4
38	Kazakhstan	4.8		1.3
39	Kenya	4.7		1.5
40	Thailand	4.7		1.1
41	Ukraine	4.7		1.3
42	Hong Kong SAR	4.7		1.3
43	Tanzania	4.7		1.5
44	Kyrgyz Republic	4.7		1.7
45	Latvia	4.7		1.2
46	India	4.6		1.4
47	Botswana	4.6		1.3
48	Portugal	4.6		1.0
49	El Salvador	4.6		1.3
50	Lithuania	4.6		1.1
51	Slovenia	4.6		1.1
52	Korea, Rep.	4.6		1.4
53	United Arab Emirates	4.6		1.1
54	Costa Rica	4.6		1.2
55	Egypt	4.5		1.5
56	Jamaica	4.5		1.0
57	Trinidad and Tobago	4.5		1.3
58	Nigeria	4.5		1.4
59	Brazil	4.5		1.4
60	Argentina	4.5		1.3
61	Moldova	4.5		1.5
62	Gambia	4.4		1.6
63	Namibia	4.4		1.2
64	Italy	4.4		1.3
65	Turkey	4.4		1.2
66	Peru	4.4		1.2
67	Ethiopia	4.4		1.7
68	Benin	4.3		1.9
69	Poland	4.3		1.1
70	Mali	4.3		1.7
71	Mozambique	4.3		1.3
72	Cameroon	4.3		1.7
73	Mexico	4.3		1.3
74	Uganda	4.3		1.8
75	Cambodia	4.3		1.7
76	Indonesia	4.3		1.0
77	Philippines	4.3		1.3
78	Sri Lanka	4.2		1.5
79	Qatar	4.2		1.4
80	Romania	4.2		1.3
81	Bulgaria	4.2		1.5
82	Tajikistan	4.2		1.9
83	Croatia	4.2		1.1
84	Albania	4.2		1.5
85	Vietnam	4.2		1.5
86	Georgia	4.2		1.5
87	Guyana	4.1		1.4
88	Jordan	4.1		1.5
89	Uruguay	4.1		1.3
90	Armenia	4.1		1.5
91	Greece	4.1		1.2
92	Honduras	4.1		1.3
93	Macedonia, FYR	4.1		1.6
94	Kuwait	4.1		1.5
95	Tunisia	4.0		1.3
96	Cyprus	4.0		1.3
97	Guatemala	4.0		1.5
98	Madagascar	4.0		1.5
99	Morocco	4.0		1.4
100	Azerbaijan	4.0		1.5
101	China	3.9		1.4
102	Nicaragua	3.9		1.3
103	Panama	3.9		1.3
104	Bosnia and Herzegovina	3.9		1.5
105	Bahrain	3.8		1.3
106	Ecuador	3.8		1.3
107	Venezuela	3.8		1.6
108	Serbia and Montenegro	3.8		1.3
109	Mongolia	3.8		1.7
110	Bangladesh	3.7		1.6
111	Dominican Republic	3.7		1.6
112	East Timor	3.6		1.9
113	Paraguay	3.6		1.6
114	Algeria	3.5		1.5
115	Bolivia	3.5		1.4
116	Pakistan	3.4		1.5
117	Chad	2.8		1.6

8.17 Hiring and firing practices

Hiring and firing of workers is (1 = impeded by regulations, 7 = flexibly determined by employers)

RANK	COUNTRY	SCORE	1 MEAN: 3.8 7	SD
1	Singapore	5.9		1.2
2	Hong Kong SAR	5.8		1.4
3	Iceland	5.4		1.5
4	Kazakhstan	5.4		1.5
5	Switzerland	5.4		1.4
6	Denmark	5.4		1.6
7	United States	5.3		1.4
8	Russian Federation	5.0		1.6
9	United Arab Emirates	5.0		1.6
10	Uganda	5.0		2.0
11	Kyrgyz Republic	4.9		1.7
12	Armenia	4.9		1.8
13	El Salvador	4.9		1.6
14	Georgia	4.9		1.5
15	Kenya	4.9		1.8
16	Albania	4.8		1.8
17	Ukraine	4.8		1.7
18	Slovak Republic	4.8		1.6
19	Tajikistan	4.7		1.9
20	Azerbaijan	4.7		1.5
21	Qatar	4.7		1.8
22	Mongolia	4.6		1.8
23	Taiwan	4.6		1.7
24	Kuwait	4.5		1.7
25	Nigeria	4.5		1.5
26	China	4.5		1.6
27	Guyana	4.5		1.5
28	Bulgaria	4.5		1.8
29	Pakistan	4.5		1.5
30	Estonia	4.4		1.5
31	Ghana	4.4		1.6
32	United Kingdom	4.4		1.5
33	Israel	4.4		1.2
34	Moldova	4.4		1.9
35	Gambia	4.3		1.9
36	Canada	4.3		1.5
37	Vietnam	4.2		1.7
38	Thailand	4.2		1.5
39	Tunisia	4.2		1.6
40	Costa Rica	4.1		1.8
41	Korea, Rep.	4.1		1.5
42	Benin	4.1		2.0
43	Malaysia	4.0		1.8
44	Bangladesh	4.0		1.8
45	Trinidad and Tobago	4.0		1.5
46	Jamaica	4.0		1.5
47	Hungary	4.0		2.0
48	Egypt	3.9		1.8
49	Latvia	3.9		1.5
50	Dominican Republic	3.9		1.9
51	Cambodia	3.9		1.9
52	Colombia	3.8		1.7
53	Serbia and Montenegro	3.8		1.9
54	New Zealand	3.8		1.5
55	Austria	3.8		1.8
56	Croatia	3.8		1.8
57	Morocco	3.7		1.6
58	Botswana	3.7		1.4
59	Uruguay	3.7		1.5

RANK	COUNTRY	SCORE	1 MEAN: 3.8 7	SD
60	Tanzania	3.7		1.8
61	Nicaragua	3.7		1.8
62	Chad	3.6		2.0
63	Madagascar	3.6		1.8
64	Japan	3.6		1.7
65	Bosnia and Herzegovina	3.6		1.8
66	Finland	3.6		1.9
67	Indonesia	3.6		1.5
68	Mozambique	3.6		1.6
69	Mauritius	3.6		1.7
70	Cameroon	3.6		1.9
71	Ethiopia	3.6		1.7
72	Guatemala	3.6		1.9
73	Turkey	3.5		1.7
74	Poland	3.5		1.4
75	Australia	3.5		1.5
76	Malawi	3.5		1.6
77	Czech Republic	3.5		1.5
78	Algeria	3.4		1.6
79	Ireland	3.4		1.4
80	Mali	3.4		1.9
81	Jordan	3.4		1.6
82	Chile	3.4		1.7
83	Cyprus	3.3		1.6
84	Macedonia, FYR	3.3		1.8
85	Peru	3.3		1.6
86	Luxembourg	3.2		1.5
87	Lithuania	3.1		1.6
88	Romania	3.1		1.7
89	Brazil	3.1		1.8
90	Bahrain	3.1		1.7
91	Honduras	3.1		1.7
92	Bolivia	3.1		1.9
93	East Timor	3.0		1.8
94	Panama	3.0		1.2
95	Ecuador	3.0		1.5
96	Malta	3.0		1.6
97	Mexico	3.0		1.5
98	Namibia	3.0		1.5
99	Norway	3.0		1.4
100	Greece	2.9		1.5
101	Spain	2.9		1.5
102	Slovenia	2.9		1.3
103	Netherlands	2.8		1.5
104	Portugal	2.8		1.2
105	Paraguay	2.7		1.6
106	Sri Lanka	2.7		1.5
107	Argentina	2.7		1.4
108	Italy	2.6		1.5
109	Philippines	2.6		1.4
110	Belgium	2.6		1.7
111	India	2.6		1.6
112	France	2.4		1.2
113	Sweden	2.4		1.4
114	Germany	2.3		1.1
115	South Africa	2.3		1.1
116	Zimbabwe	2.2		1.0
117	Venezuela	1.9		1.2

8.18   Flexibility of wage determination

Wages in your country are (1 = set by a centralized bargaining process, 7 = up to each individual company)

RANK	COUNTRY	SCORE	1 MEAN: 4.9 7	SD
1	Hong Kong SAR	6.4		0.9
2	Uganda	6.3		1.4
3	United Arab Emirates	6.3		0.7
4	Estonia	6.2		1.0
5	Taiwan	6.2		0.7
6	Bahrain	6.2		0.8
7	Chile	6.1		0.8
8	Kuwait	6.1		1.0
9	United States	6.1		1.0
10	Georgia	6.0		1.1
11	Singapore	6.0		1.0
12	Qatar	6.0		1.0
13	Egypt	5.9		1.3
14	Mongolia	5.9		1.3
15	Japan	5.9		1.1
16	Jordan	5.9		1.3
17	United Kingdom	5.9		1.0
18	Kyrgyz Republic	5.8		1.3
19	Bosnia and Herzegovina	5.8		1.5
20	Switzerland	5.8		1.2
21	Lithuania	5.8		1.2
22	New Zealand	5.8		0.9
23	Pakistan	5.7		1.3
24	Latvia	5.7		1.4
25	Gambia	5.7		1.4
26	Albania	5.7		1.5
27	Hungary	5.7		1.1
28	Peru	5.7		1.0
29	Ethiopia	5.7		1.2
30	Malaysia	5.6		0.8
31	Armenia	5.6		1.4
32	Slovak Republic	5.6		1.3
33	Bulgaria	5.6		1.4
34	Romania	5.6		1.5
35	Kazakhstan	5.6		1.6
36	Russian Federation	5.6		1.5
37	Canada	5.6		1.3
38	Colombia	5.5		1.4
39	El Salvador	5.5		1.3
40	Macedonia, FYR	5.5		1.7
41	Nicaragua	5.5		1.3
42	Korea, Rep.	5.5		1.1
43	Jamaica	5.5		1.4
44	Czech Republic	5.4		1.4
45	Bolivia	5.4		1.5
46	Chad	5.4		1.9
47	India	5.4		1.5
48	Vietnam	5.4		1.5
49	Madagascar	5.3		1.7
50	Moldova	5.3		1.7
51	Benin	5.3		2.0
52	Bangladesh	5.3		1.5
53	Azerbaijan	5.2		1.7
54	China	5.2		1.2
55	Croatia	5.1		1.5
56	Malta	5.1		1.1
57	Israel	5.1		1.2
58	Dominican Republic	5.1		1.6
59	Turkey	5.1		1.5
60	Guyana	5.1		1.6
61	Morocco	5.1		1.7
62	Botswana	5.1		1.6
63	Ukraine	5.0		1.6
64	Poland	5.0		1.3
65	Kenya	5.0		1.9
66	Malawi	5.0		1.8
67	Uruguay	5.0		1.5
68	Mexico	5.0		1.2
69	Serbia and Montenegro	5.0		1.7
70	Cambodia	4.9		2.0
71	Trinidad and Tobago	4.9		1.5
72	Spain	4.8		1.4
73	Cameroon	4.8		2.2
74	Thailand	4.7		1.5
75	Tajikistan	4.7		2.1
76	France	4.6		1.6
77	Australia	4.6		1.3
78	Slovenia	4.6		1.4
79	Nigeria	4.6		1.4
80	Tanzania	4.5		2.0
81	Mali	4.5		2.1
82	Ecuador	4.5		1.7
83	Sri Lanka	4.5		1.8
84	Iceland	4.5		1.6
85	Guatemala	4.4		2.0
86	Portugal	4.4		1.3
87	Mozambique	4.4		1.8
88	Costa Rica	4.4		1.8
89	East Timor	4.4		1.8
90	Philippines	4.4		1.8
91	Luxembourg	4.3		2.0
92	Honduras	4.3		1.9
93	Namibia	4.3		1.8
94	Indonesia	4.2		1.4
95	Denmark	4.2		1.4
96	Cyprus	4.2		1.6
97	Venezuela	4.2		1.9
98	Brazil	4.1		1.8
99	Argentina	4.0		1.5
100	Panama	4.0		1.7
101	Norway	3.9		1.5
102	Algeria	3.9		2.0
103	Paraguay	3.8		2.1
104	Ghana	3.7		1.9
105	Tunisia	3.7		1.7
106	South Africa	3.4		1.5
107	Greece	3.4		1.6
108	Sweden	3.3		1.4
109	Italy	3.3		1.4
110	Ireland	3.2		1.7
111	Netherlands	3.1		1.3
112	Mauritius	3.1		1.4
113	Belgium	3.0		1.5
114	Zimbabwe	2.8		1.7
115	Germany	2.8		1.3
116	Austria	2.7		1.6
117	Finland	2.5		1.5

8.19 Cooperation in labor-employer relations

Labor-employer relations in your country are (1 = generally confrontational, 7 = generally cooperative)

RANK	COUNTRY	SCORE	1 MEAN: 4.5 7	SD	RANK	COUNTRY	SCORE	1 MEAN: 4.5 7	SD
1	Singapore	6.3		0.7	60	China	4.5		1.3
2	Denmark	6.1		0.8	61	Tajikistan	4.5		1.6
3	Japan	6.1		0.9	62	Slovenia	4.4		1.1
4	Switzerland	6.0		0.9	63	Indonesia	4.4		1.2
5	Austria	5.9		1.0	64	Mongolia	4.4		1.6
6	Hong Kong SAR	5.8		0.9	65	Russian Federation	4.4		1.5
7	Finland	5.7		1.2	66	Cameroon	4.4		1.9
8	Malaysia	5.6		0.9	66	Lithuania	4.4		1.2
9	Norway	5.6		0.9	68	Egypt	4.3		1.5
10	Luxembourg	5.6		1.1	69	Nicaragua	4.3		1.2
11	Taiwan	5.5		1.0	70	Mali	4.3		1.8
12	Iceland	5.5		1.0	71	Malawi	4.3		1.6
13	Netherlands	5.4		1.1	72	Benin	4.3		1.9
14	Costa Rica	5.4		1.1	73	Mozambique	4.2		1.4
15	United Kingdom	5.3		1.0	74	Greece	4.2		1.5
16	Sweden	5.3		1.2	75	Bangladesh	4.2		1.6
17	Qatar	5.3		1.3	76	Belgium	4.1		1.5
18	United Arab Emirates	5.3		1.3	77	Jamaica	4.1		1.6
19	Thailand	5.2		1.1	78	Brazil	4.1		1.5
20	United States	5.2		1.3	79	Uruguay	4.1		1.1
21	Ireland	5.2		1.3	80	Turkey	4.1		1.3
22	New Zealand	5.2		0.9	81	Korea, Rep.	4.1		1.5
23	Slovak Republic	5.1		1.0	82	Honduras	4.0		1.4
24	El Salvador	5.1		1.1	83	Paraguay	4.0		1.3
25	Kuwait	5.0		1.3	84	Bulgaria	4.0		1.4
26	Ghana	5.0		1.1	85	Bosnia and Herzegovina	4.0		1.5
27	Hungary	5.0		1.3	86	Cambodia	4.0		1.5
28	Colombia	5.0		1.2	87	Argentina	4.0		1.2
29	Armenia	5.0		1.4	88	Guatemala	4.0		1.4
30	Dominican Republic	5.0		1.2	89	Peru	3.9		1.3
31	Chile	5.0		1.1	90	Algeria	3.9		1.6
32	Moldova	4.9		1.3	91	Madagascar	3.9		1.6
33	Cyprus	4.8		1.3	92	Uganda	3.9		1.7
34	Botswana	4.8		1.2	93	Ecuador	3.9		1.3
35	Gambia	4.8		1.3	94	East Timor	3.9		1.9
35	Germany	4.8		1.3	95	Chad	3.8		2.2
37	Jordan	4.8		1.3	96	Namibia	3.8		1.6
38	Czech Republic	4.8		1.2	97	Croatia	3.8		1.4
39	Pakistan	4.8		1.4	98	Italy	3.8		1.4
40	Albania	4.7		1.6	99	Poland	3.8		1.1
41	Kazakhstan	4.7		1.3	100	Philippines	3.8		1.2
42	Tunisia	4.7		1.3	101	Morocco	3.8		1.4
43	Vietnam	4.7		1.5	102	Macedonia, FYR	3.7		1.6
44	Kyrgyz Republic	4.7		1.3	103	Malta	3.7		1.4
45	Georgia	4.7		1.2	104	South Africa	3.7		1.4
46	Australia	4.6		1.3	105	Kenya	3.7		1.6
47	Canada	4.6		1.3	106	Nigeria	3.7		1.4
48	Tanzania	4.6		1.5	107	Bolivia	3.6		1.4
49	Spain	4.6		1.3	108	Ethiopia	3.6		1.4
50	Israel	4.6		1.1	109	Trinidad and Tobago	3.6		1.3
51	Estonia	4.6		1.3	110	Venezuela	3.6		1.3
52	Azerbaijan	4.6		1.4	111	Serbia and Montenegro	3.6		1.3
53	Mexico	4.6		1.3	112	Zimbabwe	3.5		1.5
54	India	4.6		1.2	113	Guyana	3.5		1.4
55	Portugal	4.5		1.3	114	Panama	3.4		1.4
56	Mauritius	4.5		1.4	115	France	3.3		1.4
57	Latvia	4.5		1.2	116	Sri Lanka	3.3		1.4
58	Ukraine	4.5		1.3	117	Romania	3.1		1.7
59	Bahrain	4.5		1.6					

8.20   Pay and productivity

Pay in your country is (1 = not related to worker productivity, 7 = strongly related to worker productivity)

RANK	COUNTRY	SCORE	MEAN: 4.0	SD
1	Hong Kong SAR	5.9		1.0
2	Singapore	5.9		0.9
3	Taiwan	5.7		0.8
4	United States	5.5		1.0
5	Malaysia	5.4		1.0
6	Switzerland	5.3		1.2
7	Estonia	5.1		1.1
8	Kyrgyz Republic	5.1		1.4
9	United Kingdom	5.1		0.9
10	Slovak Republic	4.9		1.4
11	New Zealand	4.9		0.9
12	Moldova	4.9		1.6
13	China	4.9		1.2
14	Denmark	4.8		1.1
14	Japan	4.8		1.3
16	Czech Republic	4.8		1.3
17	Kazakhstan	4.8		1.4
18	Chile	4.8		1.1
19	Iceland	4.8		1.2
20	Canada	4.8		1.3
21	Vietnam	4.7		1.5
22	Latvia	4.7		1.3
23	Romania	4.7		1.6
24	Korea, Rep.	4.7		1.4
25	Hungary	4.7		1.2
26	Lithuania	4.7		1.4
27	Mongolia	4.6		1.7
28	Thailand	4.6		1.3
29	Albania	4.6		1.7
30	El Salvador	4.6		1.4
31	Azerbaijan	4.5		1.8
32	Armenia	4.5		1.7
33	United Arab Emirates	4.5		1.5
34	Australia	4.5		1.2
35	Israel	4.4		1.3
36	Tajikistan	4.4		1.8
37	Russian Federation	4.4		1.5
38	Austria	4.4		1.3
39	Slovenia	4.3		1.2
40	Ukraine	4.3		1.8
41	Bulgaria	4.3		1.8
42	Poland	4.3		1.2
43	France	4.2		1.3
44	Ireland	4.2		1.5
45	Egypt	4.2		1.8
46	Indonesia	4.1		1.2
47	Costa Rica	4.1		1.5
48	Jordan	4.1		1.6
49	Qatar	4.1		1.6
50	Cambodia	4.1		1.9
51	India	4.0		1.3
52	Turkey	4.0		1.4
53	Georgia	4.0		1.6
54	Luxembourg	4.0		1.3
55	Norway	4.0		1.2
56	Germany	3.9		1.3
57	Tunisia	3.9		1.4
58	Spain	3.9		1.3
59	Madagascar	3.9		1.8
60	Nigeria	3.9		1.4
61	Peru	3.8		1.4
62	Panama	3.8		1.9
63	Kuwait	3.8		1.7
64	Macedonia, FYR	3.8		1.9
65	Finland	3.8		1.5
66	Bosnia and Herzegovina	3.8		1.4
67	Bahrain	3.8		2.0
68	Mexico	3.8		1.3
69	Morocco	3.8		1.8
70	Portugal	3.8		1.3
71	Botswana	3.7		1.6
72	Jamaica	3.7		1.5
73	Sweden	3.7		1.5
74	Nicaragua	3.7		1.5
75	Dominican Republic	3.7		1.5
76	Cyprus	3.6		1.4
77	Brazil	3.6		1.6
78	Croatia	3.6		1.6
79	Philippines	3.6		1.5
80	Greece	3.6		1.3
81	South Africa	3.6		1.4
82	Malawi	3.6		1.9
83	Netherlands	3.5		1.4
84	Belgium	3.5		1.5
85	Italy	3.5		1.6
86	Kenya	3.5		1.7
87	Gambia	3.5		1.6
88	Serbia and Montenegro	3.5		1.6
89	Ghana	3.5		1.4
90	Colombia	3.5		1.4
91	Argentina	3.4		1.4
92	Mauritius	3.4		1.4
93	Honduras	3.4		1.7
94	Cameroon	3.3		1.9
95	Benin	3.3		2.0
96	Chad	3.3		2.3
97	Tanzania	3.3		1.7
98	Malta	3.3		1.4
99	Bangladesh	3.3		1.6
100	Bolivia	3.3		1.4
101	Guatemala	3.3		1.6
102	Namibia	3.2		1.5
103	Trinidad and Tobago	3.2		1.4
104	East Timor	3.1		1.9
105	Venezuela	3.1		1.5
106	Uruguay	3.1		1.2
107	Algeria	3.0		1.7
108	Mozambique	3.0		1.7
109	Pakistan	3.0		1.5
110	Ecuador	2.9		1.3
111	Zimbabwe	2.9		1.3
112	Guyana	2.8		1.4
113	Ethiopia	2.8		1.4
114	Sri Lanka	2.8		1.7
115	Mali	2.7		1.8
116	Uganda	2.7		1.7
117	Paraguay	2.7		1.2

8.21 Protection of minority shareholders' interests

Interests of minority shareholders in your country are (1 = not protected by law and seldom recognized by majority shareholders, 7 = protected by law and actively enforced)

RANK	COUNTRY	SCORE	MEAN: 4.4	SD
1	United Kingdom	6.2		1.1
2	New Zealand	6.0		1.1
3	Germany	6.0		0.9
4	Denmark	6.0		1.2
5	Finland	6.0		1.1
6	Australia	6.0		1.0
7	United States	5.9		1.2
8	Norway	5.8		0.9
9	Austria	5.8		1.2
10	Ireland	5.7		1.4
11	Canada	5.6		1.3
12	Sweden	5.6		1.3
13	Singapore	5.6		1.1
14	Belgium	5.5		1.4
15	South Africa	5.5		1.2
16	Malaysia	5.5		1.2
17	Israel	5.4		1.0
18	Iceland	5.3		1.4
19	Netherlands	5.3		1.3
20	Zimbabwe	5.3		1.0
21	Portugal	5.3		1.3
22	France	5.3		1.4
23	Chile	5.2		1.4
24	Greece	5.2		1.2
25	Hungary	5.2		1.2
26	India	5.2		1.5
27	Pakistan	5.1		1.5
28	Ghana	5.1		1.4
29	Jordan	5.0		1.8
30	Qatar	5.0		1.7
31	Namibia	4.9		1.5
32	Malta	4.9		1.5
33	Tunisia	4.9		1.3
34	Switzerland	4.8		1.5
35	Hong Kong SAR	4.8		1.7
36	Botswana	4.8		1.3
37	Cyprus	4.8		1.5
38	Thailand	4.7		1.3
39	Taiwan	4.7		1.3
40	Estonia	4.6		1.6
41	United Arab Emirates	4.6		1.4
42	Japan	4.6		1.5
43	Korea, Rep.	4.6		1.4
44	Spain	4.6		1.5
45	Panama	4.6		1.5
46	Malawi	4.6		1.7
47	Mali	4.6		1.6
48	Mauritius	4.5		1.8
49	Kenya	4.5		1.7
50	Jamaica	4.5		1.5
51	Brazil	4.5		1.6
52	Poland	4.5		1.3
53	Slovenia	4.4		1.5
54	Turkey	4.4		1.6
55	Kuwait	4.4		1.6
56	Philippines	4.4		1.7
57	Vietnam	4.4		1.4
58	Cameroon	4.4		1.6
59	Colombia	4.4		1.6
60	Bahrain	4.4		1.9
61	Egypt	4.4		1.6
62	Indonesia	4.3		1.2
62	Trinidad and Tobago	4.3		1.4
64	Algeria	4.3		1.9
65	Sri Lanka	4.3		1.7
66	Uruguay	4.3		1.4
67	Peru	4.2		1.6
68	Costa Rica	4.2		1.4
69	Tanzania	4.2		1.7
70	Benin	4.2		1.8
71	Czech Republic	4.2		1.5
72	Gambia	4.1		1.6
73	Nigeria	4.1		1.4
74	Mexico	4.1		1.5
75	Slovak Republic	4.1		1.7
76	El Salvador	4.1		1.5
77	Ethiopia	4.1		1.7
78	Chad	4.0		2.0
79	Bangladesh	4.0		1.7
80	Argentina	4.0		1.4
81	Macedonia, FYR	4.0		2.0
82	Madagascar	3.9		1.7
83	Italy	3.9		1.7
84	Lithuania	3.9		1.5
85	Morocco	3.9		1.4
86	Azerbaijan	3.8		1.6
87	Latvia	3.8		1.5
88	Mozambique	3.8		1.4
89	Luxembourg	3.8		2.0
90	Kazakhstan	3.7		1.4
91	Uganda	3.7		1.8
92	Tajikistan	3.7		1.7
93	Venezuela	3.6		1.7
94	Romania	3.6		1.6
95	Croatia	3.5		1.7
96	Honduras	3.5		1.7
97	East Timor	3.4		1.8
98	Bosnia and Herzegovina	3.4		1.7
99	Kyrgyz Republic	3.4		1.6
100	Guyana	3.4		1.4
101	Cambodia	3.4		1.7
102	Albania	3.3		1.4
103	Dominican Republic	3.3		1.5
104	Georgia	3.3		1.4
105	Ecuador	3.2		1.5
106	Armenia	3.2		1.7
107	Paraguay	3.1		1.5
108	China	3.1		1.4
109	Bolivia	3.1		1.4
110	Bulgaria	3.1		1.5
111	Mongolia	3.0		1.5
112	Guatemala	3.0		1.5
113	Moldova	3.0		1.5
114	Serbia and Montenegro	3.0		1.6
115	Nicaragua	2.9		1.4
116	Russian Federation	2.8		1.5
117	Ukraine	2.8		1.5

8.22 Foreign ownership restrictions

Foreign ownership of companies in your country is (1 = rare, limited to minority stakes, and often prohibited in key sectors, 7 = prevalent and encouraged)

RANK	COUNTRY	SCORE	1 MEAN: 5.0 7	SD		RANK	COUNTRY	SCORE	1 MEAN: 5.0 7	SD
1	Luxembourg	6.5		0.6		60	Benin	5.0		1.5
2	Hong Kong SAR	6.4		1.1		61	Korea, Rep.	5.0		1.1
3	Ireland	6.4		0.9		62	Azerbaijan	5.0		1.6
4	Singapore	6.4		0.8		63	Mali	4.9		1.6
5	Slovak Republic	6.3		0.8		64	Honduras	4.9		1.5
6	United Kingdom	6.3		0.9		65	Georgia	4.9		1.4
7	Finland	6.2		0.7		66	Thailand	4.9		1.4
8	Chile	6.1		0.8		67	Guyana	4.9		1.3
9	Hungary	6.1		0.8		68	Tanzania	4.9		1.7
10	Ghana	6.1		1.1		69	Indonesia	4.8		1.4
11	New Zealand	6.0		1.1		70	Brazil	4.8		1.3
12	Sweden	5.9		1.1		71	Uruguay	4.8		1.3
13	Australia	5.9		1.0		72	Mozambique	4.8		1.3
14	United States	5.9		1.1		73	Colombia	4.8		1.3
15	Austria	5.9		1.0		74	Armenia	4.8		1.7
16	Jordan	5.9		1.0		74	Cambodia	4.8		1.7
17	Gambia	5.8		1.2		76	Nicaragua	4.8		1.2
18	Germany	5.8		1.0		77	Madagascar	4.8		1.6
19	Estonia	5.8		0.9		78	Japan	4.7		1.3
20	Costa Rica	5.7		1.0		79	Egypt	4.7		1.6
21	Netherlands	5.7		1.0		80	China	4.7		1.3
22	Czech Republic	5.7		1.1		81	Mauritius	4.7		1.5
23	Belgium	5.7		1.0		82	Turkey	4.6		1.5
24	Denmark	5.6		1.4		83	Croatia	4.6		1.3
25	Canada	5.6		1.1		84	Namibia	4.6		1.6
26	Jamaica	5.6		1.1		85	Cyprus	4.5		1.5
27	Malta	5.6		1.2		86	Romania	4.5		1.4
28	Switzerland	5.6		1.0		87	Bosnia and Herzegovina	4.4		1.6
29	South Africa	5.6		1.1		88	Venezuela	4.4		1.3
30	Spain	5.6		1.0		89	Albania	4.4		1.6
31	Pakistan	5.5		1.1		90	Chad	4.3		1.9
32	Israel	5.5		1.0		91	Slovenia	4.3		1.2
33	Taiwan	5.5		1.1		92	Italy	4.3		1.3
34	Uganda	5.5		1.7		93	Guatemala	4.3		1.5
35	Norway	5.5		0.8		94	Tajikistan	4.3		1.7
36	India	5.5		1.1		95	Iceland	4.3		1.8
37	Malaysia	5.4		1.1		96	Serbia and Montenegro	4.3		1.5
38	France	5.4		1.2		97	Bolivia	4.3		1.5
39	Botswana	5.4		1.2		98	Panama	4.3		1.7
40	Cameroon	5.4		1.4		99	Kyrgyz Republic	4.3		1.8
41	Portugal	5.4		1.0		100	Mongolia	4.2		1.8
42	Mexico	5.3		1.3		101	United Arab Emirates	4.2		2.0
43	Sri Lanka	5.3		1.6		102	Kazakhstan	4.2		1.2
44	Dominican Republic	5.3		1.4		103	Bulgaria	4.1		1.5
45	Bangladesh	5.3		1.5		104	Paraguay	4.0		1.4
46	Latvia	5.3		1.1		105	Macedonia, FYR	4.0		1.8
47	Malawi	5.3		1.4		106	East Timor	4.0		1.9
48	Greece	5.3		1.0		107	Philippines	4.0		1.9
49	Trinidad and Tobago	5.3		1.1		108	Algeria	4.0		1.8
50	Argentina	5.2		1.0		109	Qatar	3.9		1.8
51	Bahrain	5.2		1.6		110	Ecuador	3.9		1.3
52	El Salvador	5.2		1.1		111	Vietnam	3.9		1.7
53	Kenya	5.2		1.5		112	Zimbabwe	3.9		1.5
54	Tunisia	5.2		1.4		113	Russian Federation	3.6		1.3
55	Lithuania	5.2		0.9		114	Moldova	3.6		1.6
56	Morocco	5.1		1.6		115	Ukraine	3.5		1.2
57	Nigeria	5.1		1.2		116	Ethiopia	3.5		1.8
58	Peru	5.1		1.2		117	Kuwait	3.3		1.6
59	Poland	5.1		1.1						

8.23 Strength of auditing and accounting standards

Financial auditing and reporting standards regarding company financial performance in your country are (1 = extremely weak, 7 = extremely strong—among the best in the world)

RANK	COUNTRY	SCORE	1 MEAN: 4.7 7	SD	RANK	COUNTRY	SCORE	1 MEAN: 4.7 7	SD
1	United Kingdom	6.6		0.7	60	Tunisia	4.7		1.1
2	United States	6.5		0.8	61	El Salvador	4.7		1.0
3	Ireland	6.4		0.6	62	Brazil	4.7		1.5
4	Australia	6.4		0.6	63	Turkey	4.7		1.4
5	South Africa	6.3		0.7	64	Egypt	4.6		1.3
6	Finland	6.3		0.6	65	Kenya	4.6		1.4
7	Denmark	6.2		0.6	66	Mexico	4.6		1.3
8	New Zealand	6.2		0.6	67	Bulgaria	4.5		1.4
9	Iceland	6.2		0.7	68	Peru	4.5		1.3
10	Germany	6.2		0.7	69	Tanzania	4.4		1.3
11	France	6.1		0.8	70	Croatia	4.4		1.3
12	Norway	6.1		0.6	71	Macedonia, FYR	4.3		1.5
13	Austria	6.1		0.9	72	Costa Rica	4.3		1.1
14	Singapore	6.0		0.8	73	Italy	4.2		1.5
15	Netherlands	6.0		0.8	74	Argentina	4.2		1.3
16	Canada	6.0		0.9	75	Romania	4.2		1.2
17	Hong Kong SAR	6.0		1.1	76	Nigeria	4.1		1.5
18	Luxembourg	5.9		1.0	77	Panama	4.0		1.4
19	Malaysia	5.9		0.8	78	Indonesia	4.0		1.1
20	Switzerland	5.9		1.0	79	Mongolia	3.9		1.4
21	Malta	5.8		0.9	80	Kazakhstan	3.9		1.2
22	Sweden	5.8		0.8	81	China	3.9		1.4
23	India	5.8		0.9	82	Serbia and Montenegro	3.9		1.4
24	Japan	5.7		1.0	83	Armenia	3.9		1.5
25	Belgium	5.7		1.1	84	Morocco	3.8		1.5
26	Israel	5.7		0.6	85	Ukraine	3.8		1.1
27	Bahrain	5.6		1.1	86	Guyana	3.8		1.4
28	Portugal	5.6		1.0	87	Azerbaijan	3.8		1.5
29	Estonia	5.6		0.9	88	Vietnam	3.8		1.5
30	Cyprus	5.6		1.0	89	Russian Federation	3.8		1.2
31	Jamaica	5.5		1.2	90	Kyrgyz Republic	3.8		1.3
32	Kuwait	5.4		1.2	91	Bosnia and Herzegovina	3.7		1.3
33	Zimbabwe	5.4		1.1	92	Gambia	3.7		1.5
34	Mauritius	5.3		1.0	93	Bangladesh	3.7		1.4
35	Hungary	5.3		1.0	94	Georgia	3.7		1.4
36	Taiwan	5.3		0.9	95	Moldova	3.7		1.5
37	Thailand	5.3		0.9	96	Ecuador	3.7		1.4
38	Chile	5.3		1.0	97	Uganda	3.7		1.5
39	Botswana	5.3		1.1	98	Nicaragua	3.6		1.2
40	Jordan	5.2		1.1	99	Honduras	3.6		1.6
41	Spain	5.2		1.0	100	Albania	3.5		1.5
42	Namibia	5.2		1.4	101	Mali	3.5		1.4
43	Slovenia	5.1		0.9	102	Mozambique	3.5		1.4
44	Ghana	5.1		1.2	103	Venezuela	3.4		1.4
45	Korea, Rep.	5.1		1.2	104	Dominican Republic	3.4		1.5
46	Greece	5.0		0.9	105	Uruguay	3.4		1.3
47	Trinidad and Tobago	5.0		1.2	106	Benin	3.4		1.5
48	Poland	5.0		1.1	107	Cameroon	3.4		1.7
48	United Arab Emirates	5.0		1.2	108	Ethiopia	3.3		1.5
50	Pakistan	5.0		1.3	109	Bolivia	3.2		1.2
51	Malawi	4.9		1.2	110	Algeria	3.2		1.5
52	Lithuania	4.9		1.0	111	Guatemala	3.2		1.4
53	Sri Lanka	4.9		1.2	112	Tajikistan	3.1		1.5
54	Czech Republic	4.9		1.0	113	Madagascar	3.1		1.4
55	Qatar	4.9		1.4	114	Cambodia	3.0		1.5
56	Philippines	4.9		1.3	115	Paraguay	3.0		1.2
57	Colombia	4.8		1.3	116	East Timor	2.5		1.3
58	Latvia	4.8		1.2	117	Chad	2.3		1.4
59	Slovak Republic	4.8		1.2					

8.24   Importance of corporate social responsibility

In your country, corporate codes of conduct and other aspects of corporate social responsibility are (1 = rare or nonexistent, 7 = frequent)

RANK	COUNTRY	SCORE	1 MEAN: 4.2 7	SD
1	United Kingdom	6.2		0.8
2	United States	6.2		1.0
3	Denmark	6.1		0.9
4	Germany	6.0		0.9
5	Australia	6.0		0.9
6	Canada	6.0		1.0
7	Netherlands	5.9		0.9
8	South Africa	5.9		0.8
9	Finland	5.9		1.4
10	Ireland	5.9		1.0
11	Sweden	5.8		1.0
12	Switzerland	5.8		1.0
13	Norway	5.8		0.9
14	New Zealand	5.7		1.0
15	Singapore	5.7		1.0
16	Japan	5.7		1.2
17	France	5.5		1.3
18	Austria	5.4		1.4
19	Malaysia	5.4		1.1
20	Belgium	5.3		1.3
21	Taiwan	5.2		1.1
22	Iceland	5.1		1.0
23	Hong Kong SAR	5.0		1.2
24	Korea, Rep.	5.0		1.2
25	Luxembourg	5.0		1.5
26	Chile	4.9		1.2
27	Israel	4.9		1.2
28	Spain	4.8		1.2
28	Zimbabwe	4.8		1.1
30	India	4.6		1.3
31	Mauritius	4.6		1.5
32	Colombia	4.6		1.4
33	Thailand	4.5		1.2
34	Slovenia	4.5		1.3
35	Tunisia	4.5		1.3
36	Ghana	4.5		1.1
37	Botswana	4.4		1.5
38	Philippines	4.4		1.4
39	Cyprus	4.4		1.2
40	Lithuania	4.3		1.3
41	Nigeria	4.3		1.3
42	Brazil	4.2		1.5
43	Portugal	4.2		1.3
44	Qatar	4.2		1.8
45	Egypt	4.2		1.6
46	Italy	4.2		1.6
47	Namibia	4.2		1.5
48	Costa Rica	4.2		1.3
49	Jamaica	4.1		1.4
50	Slovak Republic	4.1		1.4
51	Uganda	4.1		1.5
52	Malawi	4.1		1.3
53	Greece	4.1		1.2
54	China	4.1		1.3
55	United Arab Emirates	4.0		1.2
56	Malta	4.0		1.3
57	Poland	4.0		1.3
58	Czech Republic	4.0		1.2
59	Kenya	4.0		1.5
60	Vietnam	4.0		1.6
61	Mexico	4.0		1.4
62	Estonia	3.9		1.3
63	Morocco	3.9		1.4
64	Jordan	3.9		1.5
65	Tanzania	3.8		1.5
66	Argentina	3.8		1.3
67	Mali	3.8		1.6
68	Turkey	3.8		1.3
69	Sri Lanka	3.8		1.5
70	El Salvador	3.8		1.4
71	Trinidad and Tobago	3.8		1.4
72	Venezuela	3.8		1.8
73	Bahrain	3.8		1.5
74	Latvia	3.8		1.4
75	Uruguay	3.8		1.3
76	Cameroon	3.7		1.6
77	Benin	3.7		1.8
78	Indonesia	3.7		1.1
79	Romania	3.7		1.5
80	Kuwait	3.7		1.3
81	Kazakhstan	3.7		1.5
82	Peru	3.6		1.2
83	Pakistan	3.6		1.4
84	Hungary	3.6		1.5
85	Panama	3.6		1.4
86	Croatia	3.6		1.4
87	Macedonia, FYR	3.5		1.7
88	Madagascar	3.4		1.5
89	Gambia	3.4		1.6
90	Algeria	3.4		1.6
91	Albania	3.3		1.5
92	Kyrgyz Republic	3.3		1.7
93	Azerbaijan	3.2		1.4
94	Mozambique	3.2		1.1
95	Ecuador	3.2		1.2
96	Russian Federation	3.2		1.4
97	Bulgaria	3.2		1.4
98	Serbia and Montenegro	3.2		1.5
99	Guatemala	3.2		1.5
100	Nicaragua	3.2		1.4
101	Guyana	3.1		1.3
102	Bangladesh	3.1		1.4
103	Honduras	3.1		1.5
104	Mongolia	3.1		1.4
105	Cambodia	3.0		1.6
106	East Timor	3.0		1.7
106	Georgia	3.0		1.3
108	Moldova	3.0		1.6
109	Ethiopia	3.0		1.6
110	Tajikistan	3.0		1.4
111	Ukraine	2.9		1.2
112	Armenia	2.9		1.2
113	Paraguay	2.8		1.3
114	Bolivia	2.7		1.0
115	Dominican Republic	2.7		1.2
116	Bosnia and Herzegovina	2.7		1.3
117	Chad	2.6		1.5

613

9.01 Stringency of environmental regulations

How stringent is your country's environmental regulation? (1 = lax compared to most countries, 7 = among the world's most stringent)

RANK	COUNTRY	SCORE	1 MEAN: 4.0 7	SD
1	Germany	6.7		0.6
2	Denmark	6.6		0.9
3	Austria	6.5		0.8
4	Switzerland	6.3		0.8
5	Norway	6.3		0.9
6	Sweden	6.2		0.9
7	Finland	6.2		0.8
8	Luxembourg	6.2		1.0
9	Netherlands	6.2		0.9
10	New Zealand	6.1		0.8
11	Belgium	6.0		1.1
12	Japan	5.9		0.9
13	Iceland	5.9		1.0
14	United Kingdom	5.8		0.9
15	Australia	5.8		0.9
16	Canada	5.8		0.9
17	France	5.8		1.0
18	Singapore	5.7		0.9
19	United States	5.5		1.2
20	Ireland	5.3		1.3
21	Taiwan	5.3		1.0
22	Slovenia	5.2		1.2
23	Czech Republic	5.2		1.4
24	Hungary	5.2		1.2
25	Brazil	5.0		1.6
26	Malaysia	4.9		1.1
27	Spain	4.9		1.2
28	Italy	4.9		1.6
29	Estonia	4.9		1.3
30	Qatar	4.9		1.5
31	Israel	4.8		1.2
31	Portugal	4.8		1.3
33	South Africa	4.8		1.3
34	Slovak Republic	4.8		1.3
35	Chile	4.7		1.1
36	Korea, Rep.	4.7		1.3
37	Tunisia	4.6		1.1
38	Costa Rica	4.6		1.2
39	Lithuania	4.5		1.4
40	United Arab Emirates	4.5		1.2
41	Colombia	4.3		1.4
42	Hong Kong SAR	4.3		1.2
43	Thailand	4.2		1.1
44	Greece	4.2		1.4
45	Ghana	4.2		1.3
46	Poland	4.2		1.1
47	India	4.0		1.6
48	Jordan	4.0		1.3
48	Latvia	4.0		1.3
50	Cyprus	4.0		1.4
51	Croatia	4.0		1.6
52	Philippines	3.7		1.7
53	Mexico	3.7		1.3
54	Namibia	3.7		1.4
54	Nigeria	3.7		1.5
56	Argentina	3.6		1.2
57	Uruguay	3.6		1.2
58	Panama	3.5		1.2
58	Uganda	3.5		1.6
60	Zimbabwe	3.5		1.7
61	Honduras	3.5		1.6
62	Turkey	3.5		1.2
63	Mauritius	3.4		1.4
64	Indonesia	3.4		1.1
65	Madagascar	3.4		1.4
66	Kenya	3.4		1.7
67	Tanzania	3.4		1.7
68	Gambia	3.4		1.5
69	El Salvador	3.3		1.6
70	Peru	3.3		1.4
71	Venezuela	3.3		1.7
72	Ukraine	3.3		1.4
73	Botswana	3.3		1.3
74	Romania	3.3		1.5
75	Jamaica	3.3		1.3
76	Kuwait	3.2		1.3
77	Malta	3.2		1.3
78	Egypt	3.2		1.6
79	Kazakhstan	3.2		1.5
80	Bulgaria	3.2		1.7
81	Russian Federation	3.2		1.5
82	Moldova	3.2		1.7
83	Sri Lanka	3.1		1.3
84	Mozambique	3.1		1.3
85	Trinidad and Tobago	3.1		1.3
86	Cameroon	3.1		1.5
87	Bahrain	3.1		1.6
88	China	3.1		1.3
89	Algeria	3.1		1.3
90	Bangladesh	3.0		1.5
91	Benin	3.0		1.4
92	Azerbaijan	3.0		1.4
93	Pakistan	3.0		1.3
94	Morocco	2.9		1.3
95	Vietnam	2.9		1.3
96	Mali	2.9		1.3
97	Nicaragua	2.9		1.3
98	Armenia	2.9		1.4
99	Georgia	2.8		1.2
100	Bolivia	2.8		1.5
101	Serbia and Montenegro	2.8		1.4
102	Tajikistan	2.7		1.4
103	Guyana	2.7		1.3
104	Malawi	2.6		1.2
105	East Timor	2.6		1.4
106	Ecuador	2.6		1.0
107	Guatemala	2.6		1.2
108	Macedonia, FYR	2.5		1.4
109	Cambodia	2.4		1.3
110	Mongolia	2.4		1.3
111	Dominican Republic	2.4		1.2
112	Paraguay	2.4		1.2
113	Ethiopia	2.3		1.0
114	Bosnia and Herzegovina	2.3		1.2
115	Chad	2.3		1.4
116	Kyrgyz Republic	2.2		1.1
117	Albania	2.1		1.2

9.02   Clarity and stability of regulations

Environmental regulations in your country are (1 = confusing and enforced erratically, 7 = stable and enforced consistently and fairly)

RANK	COUNTRY	SCORE	MEAN: 3.8	SD
1	Denmark	6.2		0.8
2	Singapore	5.9		0.9
3	Switzerland	5.9		1.1
4	Germany	5.8		1.4
5	Norway	5.8		0.9
6	Japan	5.6		1.0
7	Austria	5.6		1.2
8	Sweden	5.5		1.2
9	Finland	5.5		1.3
10	Australia	5.3		1.1
11	Netherlands	5.3		1.3
12	United Kingdom	5.3		1.0
13	France	5.3		1.1
14	Canada	5.3		1.2
15	New Zealand	5.3		1.2
16	Iceland	5.1		1.3
17	United States	5.0		1.3
18	Taiwan	5.0		1.1
19	Ireland	4.9		1.2
20	Malaysia	4.8		1.2
21	Luxembourg	4.8		1.7
22	Slovenia	4.8		1.2
23	Korea, Rep.	4.7		1.2
24	Estonia	4.7		1.3
25	Czech Republic	4.6		1.4
26	Qatar	4.5		1.6
27	Slovak Republic	4.5		1.3
28	Tunisia	4.5		1.1
29	Israel	4.5		1.2
30	Spain	4.4		1.2
31	United Arab Emirates	4.4		1.2
32	South Africa	4.4		1.3
33	Portugal	4.2		1.2
34	Hungary	4.2		1.2
35	Hong Kong SAR	4.2		1.3
36	Belgium	4.2		1.5
37	Thailand	4.2		1.3
38	Chile	4.1		1.2
38	Ghana	4.1		1.4
40	Latvia	4.0		1.3
41	Cyprus	4.0		1.2
42	Lithuania	4.0		1.3
43	Namibia	4.0		1.3
44	Italy	3.9		1.5
45	Costa Rica	3.9		1.4
46	Jordan	3.9		1.4
47	Gambia	3.9		1.5
48	Brazil	3.9		1.5
49	Poland	3.8		1.2
50	Colombia	3.8		1.4
51	Greece	3.7		1.3
52	Uruguay	3.7		1.2
53	Nigeria	3.7		1.5
54	Botswana	3.7		1.3
55	India	3.6		1.5
56	Tanzania	3.6		1.6
57	Kazakhstan	3.6		1.4
58	Croatia	3.6		1.4
59	Uganda	3.5		1.8
60	China	3.5		1.3
61	Zimbabwe	3.5		1.5
62	Kenya	3.4		1.6
63	Argentina	3.4		1.2
64	Mexico	3.4		1.3
65	Indonesia	3.4		1.1
66	Azerbaijan	3.3		1.4
67	Mauritius	3.3		1.6
68	Mozambique	3.3		1.2
69	Panama	3.3		1.5
70	Ukraine	3.3		1.3
71	Turkey	3.3		1.2
72	Russian Federation	3.2		1.4
73	Tajikistan	3.2		1.5
74	Bahrain	3.2		1.5
75	Jamaica	3.2		1.3
76	Moldova	3.2		1.5
77	Romania	3.2		1.4
78	Peru	3.2		1.1
79	Armenia	3.2		1.3
80	Kuwait	3.1		1.3
81	Egypt	3.1		1.4
82	El Salvador	3.1		1.1
83	Madagascar	3.1		1.4
84	Sri Lanka	3.0		1.2
85	Trinidad and Tobago	3.0		1.2
86	Cameroon	3.0		1.5
87	Bulgaria	3.0		1.5
88	Malta	2.9		1.0
89	Vietnam	2.9		1.2
90	Honduras	2.9		1.1
91	Bangladesh	2.9		1.4
92	Nicaragua	2.9		1.2
93	Georgia	2.9		1.4
94	Pakistan	2.9		1.4
95	Kyrgyz Republic	2.9		1.2
96	Morocco	2.8		1.3
97	Ethiopia	2.8		1.3
98	Philippines	2.8		1.1
99	Bolivia	2.8		1.2
100	Cambodia	2.8		1.3
101	Bosnia and Herzegovina	2.8		1.5
102	Venezuela	2.8		1.3
103	Malawi	2.8		1.3
104	Benin	2.8		1.4
105	Mali	2.8		1.6
106	Guyana	2.7		1.1
107	Mongolia	2.7		1.2
108	Macedonia, FYR	2.7		1.5
109	Algeria	2.7		1.2
110	Ecuador	2.6		1.1
111	Guatemala	2.5		1.2
112	East Timor	2.5		1.3
113	Serbia and Montenegro	2.4		1.3
114	Dominican Republic	2.4		1.1
115	Paraguay	2.3		1.1
116	Chad	2.0		1.3
117	Albania	2.0		1.1

617

9.03   Extent of government-mandated environmental reporting

Government-mandated disclosures of environmental performance and pollutant releases in your country are (1 = nonexistent, 7 = widely used and effective)

RANK	COUNTRY	SCORE	SD
1	Denmark	6.2	1.0
2	Germany	6.1	0.9
3	Norway	5.9	0.9
4	Finland	5.8	0.9
5	Sweden	5.8	0.8
6	Japan	5.6	1.0
7	Singapore	5.5	1.1
8	Austria	5.5	1.2
9	United States	5.4	1.1
10	Netherlands	5.4	1.1
11	United Kingdom	5.4	1.0
12	Switzerland	5.3	1.2
13	Australia	5.3	1.2
14	Canada	5.3	1.3
15	France	5.3	1.3
16	Iceland	5.2	0.9
17	New Zealand	5.0	1.3
18	Taiwan	5.0	1.0
19	Slovenia	5.0	1.2
20	Estonia	4.9	1.3
21	Ireland	4.9	1.3
22	Belgium	4.9	1.1
23	Slovak Republic	4.9	1.2
24	Czech Republic	4.9	1.3
25	Malaysia	4.8	1.2
26	Korea, Rep.	4.7	1.2
27	Hungary	4.6	1.2
28	Israel	4.5	1.4
29	Spain	4.4	1.2
30	Lithuania	4.4	1.1
31	Portugal	4.3	1.2
32	Qatar	4.3	1.7
33	South Africa	4.2	1.3
34	Italy	4.2	1.5
35	Tunisia	4.2	1.3
36	Thailand	4.1	1.1
37	United Arab Emirates	4.1	1.5
38	Hong Kong SAR	4.1	1.4
39	Luxembourg	4.1	1.8
40	India	4.1	1.4
41	Turkey	4.0	1.2
42	Cyprus	4.0	1.3
43	Ghana	4.0	1.3
44	Panama	4.0	1.6
45	Chile	4.0	1.4
46	Brazil	3.9	1.6
47	Poland	3.9	1.1
48	Latvia	3.9	1.3
49	Jordan	3.8	1.6
50	Costa Rica	3.8	1.4
51	Greece	3.7	1.3
52	Nigeria	3.7	1.5
53	Kenya	3.7	1.7
54	Kazakhstan	3.6	1.5
55	China	3.6	1.3
56	Indonesia	3.6	1.2
57	Croatia	3.4	1.3
58	Colombia	3.4	1.4
59	Namibia	3.4	1.5
60	Mexico	3.4	1.2
61	Gambia	3.4	1.7
62	Botswana	3.3	1.4
63	Tanzania	3.3	1.5
64	Uganda	3.3	1.6
65	Egypt	3.3	1.6
66	Azerbaijan	3.3	1.6
67	Romania	3.2	1.3
68	Bulgaria	3.2	1.4
69	Mauritius	3.2	1.5
70	Mozambique	3.2	1.4
71	Uruguay	3.2	1.2
72	Sri Lanka	3.1	1.3
73	Vietnam	3.1	1.5
74	Ukraine	3.1	1.2
75	Kuwait	3.1	1.3
76	Philippines	3.1	1.3
77	Madagascar	3.0	1.6
78	Tajikistan	3.0	1.6
79	Bangladesh	3.0	1.4
80	Macedonia, FYR	3.0	1.4
81	Moldova	3.0	1.7
82	Bahrain	2.9	1.5
83	Armenia	2.9	1.3
84	Russian Federation	2.9	1.3
85	Benin	2.9	1.8
86	Argentina	2.8	1.1
87	Peru	2.8	1.2
88	Morocco	2.8	1.4
89	Malta	2.8	1.1
90	Zimbabwe	2.8	1.6
91	Serbia and Montenegro	2.7	1.2
92	Cambodia	2.7	1.4
93	Mali	2.7	1.6
94	El Salvador	2.7	1.1
95	Pakistan	2.7	1.2
96	Jamaica	2.7	1.3
97	Georgia	2.7	1.2
98	Trinidad and Tobago	2.7	1.2
99	Nicaragua	2.7	1.0
100	Algeria	2.6	1.4
101	Cameroon	2.6	1.5
102	Honduras	2.4	1.2
103	Malawi	2.4	1.2
104	East Timor	2.4	1.6
105	Bolivia	2.3	1.1
106	Guyana	2.3	1.2
107	Ethiopia	2.3	1.2
108	Albania	2.3	1.0
109	Ecuador	2.3	1.1
110	Venezuela	2.3	1.2
111	Bosnia and Herzegovina	2.3	1.1
112	Chad	2.2	1.6
113	Guatemala	2.2	1.1
114	Kyrgyz Republic	2.2	1.3
115	Mongolia	2.2	1.1
116	Paraguay	2.1	1.1
117	Dominican Republic	2.1	1.0

MEAN: 3.7

9.04 Effects of compliance on business

Complying with environmental standards in your country (1 = significantly reduces competitiveness, 7 = helps long-term competitiveness by encouraging improvements in products and processes)

RANK	COUNTRY	SCORE	MEAN: 4.3	SD
1	Denmark	5.7		1.1
2	Japan	5.6		1.0
3	Singapore	5.6		0.9
4	Norway	5.5		1.0
5	Switzerland	5.4		1.0
6	Taiwan	5.4		0.9
7	Finland	5.3		1.6
8	France	5.3		1.2
9	Sweden	5.3		0.9
10	United Kingdom	5.2		1.1
11	United States	5.2		1.3
12	Germany	5.1		1.4
13	Malaysia	5.1		1.0
14	Iceland	5.1		1.3
15	Australia	5.1		1.2
16	Israel	5.0		1.0
17	Austria	5.0		1.3
18	Netherlands	5.0		1.2
19	Canada	5.0		1.4
20	Korea, Rep.	4.9		1.2
21	Tunisia	4.9		1.1
22	Estonia	4.9		1.1
23	Qatar	4.8		1.4
24	Ireland	4.8		1.2
25	New Zealand	4.8		1.3
26	Slovenia	4.7		1.3
27	Mali	4.7		1.4
28	Uganda	4.7		1.6
29	South Africa	4.7		1.2
30	Kenya	4.7		1.5
31	Cyprus	4.7		0.9
32	Hong Kong SAR	4.6		1.3
33	Egypt	4.6		1.6
34	Thailand	4.6		1.0
35	United Arab Emirates	4.6		1.0
36	Ghana	4.6		1.2
37	Chile	4.5		1.2
38	Czech Republic	4.5		1.2
39	Botswana	4.5		1.0
40	Benin	4.5		1.5
41	Tanzania	4.5		1.4
42	Jordan	4.5		1.3
43	India	4.5		1.3
44	Luxembourg	4.5		1.6
45	Croatia	4.4		1.4
46	Costa Rica	4.4		1.2
47	Panama	4.4		1.4
48	Namibia	4.4		1.1
49	Gambia	4.4		1.3
50	Portugal	4.4		1.0
51	Nigeria	4.4		1.4
52	Hungary	4.4		1.3
53	Spain	4.4		1.2
54	Romania	4.4		1.4
55	Slovak Republic	4.3		1.2
56	Italy	4.3		1.3
57	Madagascar	4.3		1.3
58	Brazil	4.3		1.4
59	Lithuania	4.3		1.0
60	Jamaica	4.3		1.2
61	Bahrain	4.3		1.5
62	Turkey	4.3		1.4
63	Trinidad and Tobago	4.2		1.2
64	Mauritius	4.2		1.0
65	Poland	4.2		0.9
66	Morocco	4.2		1.4
67	Indonesia	4.2		0.9
68	Latvia	4.2		1.1
69	China	4.2		1.4
70	Greece	4.1		1.1
71	Cameroon	4.1		1.4
72	Chad	4.1		1.8
73	Mexico	4.1		1.2
74	Uruguay	4.1		1.0
75	Pakistan	4.1		1.8
76	Vietnam	4.1		1.5
77	Sri Lanka	4.1		1.2
78	Colombia	4.1		1.5
79	Ukraine	4.0		1.3
80	Malta	4.0		1.1
81	Moldova	4.0		1.4
82	Philippines	4.0		1.3
83	Malawi	4.0		1.3
84	Belgium	4.0		1.6
85	Zimbabwe	4.0		1.1
86	Kuwait	3.9		1.4
87	Ethiopia	3.9		1.6
88	Peru	3.9		1.3
89	Kazakhstan	3.9		1.3
90	Algeria	3.9		1.5
91	Mozambique	3.9		0.9
92	Argentina	3.8		1.1
93	Bangladesh	3.7		1.4
94	Bulgaria	3.7		1.5
95	Cambodia	3.7		1.4
96	Russian Federation	3.7		1.3
97	Guyana	3.7		1.3
98	El Salvador	3.7		1.2
99	Serbia and Montenegro	3.6		1.6
100	Bosnia and Herzegovina	3.6		1.6
101	Macedonia, FYR	3.6		1.5
102	Azerbaijan	3.6		1.4
103	Nicaragua	3.5		1.2
104	Armenia	3.5		1.3
105	East Timor	3.5		1.6
106	Honduras	3.4		1.3
107	Georgia	3.4		1.1
108	Albania	3.4		1.8
109	Bolivia	3.3		1.3
110	Tajikistan	3.3		1.6
111	Venezuela	3.2		1.1
112	Guatemala	3.2		1.4
113	Kyrgyz Republic	3.2		1.6
114	Ecuador	3.1		1.3
115	Dominican Republic	3.0		1.1
116	Paraguay	3.0		1.4
117	Mongolia	2.9		1.2

9.05   Effects of privitization on competition and the environment

Privatization of major sectors in your country (1 = distorts competition and encourages inefficient use of energy and materials, 7 = improves long-term competitiveness and efficient use of energy and materials)

RANK	COUNTRY	SCORE	MEAN: 4.8	SD
1	Germany	6.1		0.8
2	Iceland	6.1		0.8
3	Denmark	5.9		0.8
4	Finland	5.9		0.8
5	Chile	5.9		0.9
6	United Kingdom	5.9		1.0
7	Japan	5.8		0.9
8	Austria	5.8		1.1
9	India	5.8		0.9
10	Switzerland	5.7		1.1
11	United States	5.7		1.4
12	Singapore	5.7		0.9
13	Israel	5.7		0.8
14	Canada	5.6		1.2
15	Australia	5.6		1.0
16	New Zealand	5.6		1.1
17	Jordan	5.5		1.1
18	Taiwan	5.5		0.9
19	France	5.5		1.2
20	Bahrain	5.4		1.3
21	Uganda	5.4		1.3
22	Portugal	5.4		1.0
23	Belgium	5.4		1.1
24	Norway	5.4		1.0
25	Qatar	5.4		1.2
26	Turkey	5.3		1.2
27	Ireland	5.3		1.4
28	Spain	5.3		1.1
29	Brazil	5.3		1.2
30	Hong Kong SAR	5.3		1.1
31	Vietnam	5.3		1.4
32	Nigeria	5.2		1.3
33	Tunisia	5.2		1.1
34	South Africa	5.2		1.1
35	Sweden	5.2		1.3
36	Colombia	5.2		1.1
36	United Arab Emirates	5.2		1.2
38	Mauritius	5.2		1.0
39	Malaysia	5.2		0.9
40	Netherlands	5.2		1.0
41	Egypt	5.1		1.5
42	Bangladesh	5.1		1.4
43	El Salvador	5.1		1.4
44	Korea, Rep.	5.1		1.0
45	Greece	5.1		1.1
45	Tanzania	5.1		1.4
47	Ghana	5.1		1.1
48	Pakistan	5.1		1.5
49	Luxembourg	5.1		1.1
50	Malta	5.1		1.2
51	Kenya	5.1		1.6
52	Philippines	5.0		1.3
53	Estonia	5.0		1.4
54	Italy	5.0		1.4
55	Morocco	5.0		1.4
56	Thailand	5.0		1.1
57	Poland	5.0		1.3
58	Kuwait	4.9		1.2
59	Czech Republic	4.9		1.2

RANK	COUNTRY	SCORE	MEAN: 4.8	SD
60	Cyprus	4.9		1.1
61	Hungary	4.9		1.4
62	Peru	4.9		1.5
63	Mozambique	4.9		1.3
64	Romania	4.9		1.5
65	Slovenia	4.9		1.1
66	Panama	4.9		1.7
67	Zimbabwe	4.9		1.4
68	Botswana	4.8		1.1
69	Slovak Republic	4.8		1.4
70	Trinidad and Tobago	4.8		1.3
71	Jamaica	4.8		1.4
72	Sri Lanka	4.8		1.4
73	Indonesia	4.8		0.6
74	Lithuania	4.7		1.3
75	Algeria	4.7		1.5
76	Ethiopia	4.7		1.9
77	Mali	4.7		1.6
78	Albania	4.7		2.1
79	Georgia	4.6		1.5
80	Costa Rica	4.6		1.7
81	Uruguay	4.6		1.2
82	Namibia	4.5		1.1
83	Gambia	4.4		1.5
84	Guatemala	4.4		1.6
85	Cameroon	4.4		1.8
86	Malawi	4.3		1.3
87	Mexico	4.3		1.4
88	Benin	4.3		1.9
88	Guyana	4.3		1.5
90	Argentina	4.3		1.5
91	Latvia	4.3		1.2
92	Madagascar	4.2		1.5
93	Serbia and Montenegro	4.1		1.7
94	Venezuela	4.1		1.8
95	Moldova	4.1		1.7
96	Dominican Republic	4.0		1.5
97	China	4.0		1.4
98	Macedonia, FYR	4.0		1.7
99	Croatia	3.9		1.5
100	Cambodia	3.9		1.6
101	Bosnia and Herzegovina	3.9		1.6
102	Bolivia	3.8		1.5
103	East Timor	3.8		1.6
104	Azerbaijan	3.8		1.6
105	Chad	3.7		1.9
106	Paraguay	3.7		1.5
107	Kazakhstan	3.7		1.5
108	Ecuador	3.7		1.3
109	Armenia	3.7		1.6
110	Nicaragua	3.6		1.4
111	Tajikistan	3.6		1.7
112	Mongolia	3.5		1.6
113	Bulgaria	3.5		1.7
114	Honduras	3.4		1.5
115	Russian Federation	3.3		1.5
116	Ukraine	3.3		1.3
117	Kyrgyz Republic	2.6		1.6

9.06 Prioritization of energy efficiency

In your country, energy efficiency and transition to new and renewable sources of energy are (1 = a low priority, 7 = a high priority)

RANK	COUNTRY	SCORE	SD	RANK	COUNTRY	SCORE	SD
1	Denmark	6.3	0.9	60	Peru	3.6	1.7
2	Germany	6.2	1.0	61	Mozambique	3.6	1.5
3	Iceland	6.0	1.1	62	Turkey	3.6	1.5
4	Japan	5.9	1.1	63	Uganda	3.6	1.8
5	Finland	5.8	1.3	64	Latvia	3.6	1.4
6	Austria	5.8	1.2	65	Uruguay	3.6	1.6
7	Sweden	5.6	1.3	66	Poland	3.6	1.2
8	New Zealand	5.4	1.2	67	Hungary	3.6	1.4
9	Singapore	5.4	1.3	68	Italy	3.6	1.7
10	Netherlands	5.3	1.2	69	Jordan	3.6	1.7
11	Switzerland	5.3	1.1	70	Vietnam	3.6	1.6
12	Canada	5.2	1.1	71	United Arab Emirates	3.5	1.6
13	Korea, Rep.	5.2	1.1	72	Bangladesh	3.5	1.8
14	Norway	5.2	1.3	73	Qatar	3.5	2.3
15	United Kingdom	5.1	1.3	74	Azerbaijan	3.5	1.7
16	Taiwan	5.1	1.2	75	Indonesia	3.5	1.1
17	Tunisia	5.0	1.2	76	Botswana	3.5	1.5
18	Luxembourg	4.9	1.4	77	Mongolia	3.5	1.6
19	France	4.8	1.4	78	Slovak Republic	3.5	1.3
20	Malaysia	4.8	1.2	79	Kazakhstan	3.5	1.6
21	Spain	4.7	1.3	80	Gambia	3.4	1.9
22	Israel	4.7	1.4	81	Bulgaria	3.4	1.6
22	Portugal	4.7	1.3	82	Chad	3.4	2.2
24	Belgium	4.6	1.5	83	Madagascar	3.3	1.6
25	Brazil	4.6	1.6	84	Panama	3.3	1.4
26	Thailand	4.5	1.3	85	Argentina	3.3	1.4
27	China	4.5	1.6	86	Georgia	3.3	1.8
28	Lithuania	4.5	1.5	87	Ethiopia	3.3	1.7
29	South Africa	4.5	1.6	88	Romania	3.2	1.5
30	Chile	4.4	1.5	89	Ukraine	3.1	1.3
31	Armenia	4.4	1.9	90	Serbia and Montenegro	3.1	1.7
32	Ireland	4.4	1.5	91	Honduras	3.1	1.7
33	Australia	4.3	1.4	92	Cambodia	3.1	1.7
34	Egypt	4.3	1.6	93	Zimbabwe	3.1	1.6
35	Ghana	4.3	1.5	94	Bahrain	3.0	1.7
36	India	4.3	1.5	95	Croatia	3.0	1.4
37	United States	4.2	1.6	96	Mexico	3.0	1.4
38	Slovenia	4.2	1.3	97	East Timor	3.0	2.0
39	Mali	4.1	2.0	98	Russian Federation	3.0	1.5
40	Costa Rica	4.1	1.6	99	Guatemala	3.0	1.5
41	Czech Republic	4.1	1.6	100	Algeria	3.0	1.7
42	Estonia	4.1	1.4	101	Moldova	3.0	1.9
43	Pakistan	4.1	2.0	102	Cameroon	2.9	1.8
44	Colombia	4.0	1.5	102	Malawi	2.9	1.4
45	Philippines	4.0	1.4	104	Nicaragua	2.9	1.6
46	Greece	4.0	1.2	105	Macedonia, FYR	2.9	1.6
46	Morocco	4.0	1.6	106	Trinidad and Tobago	2.9	1.6
48	Tajikistan	3.9	2.2	107	Malta	2.7	1.3
49	Cyprus	3.9	1.3	108	Guyana	2.6	1.6
50	Mauritius	3.9	2.0	109	Dominican Republic	2.6	1.7
51	Hong Kong SAR	3.8	1.4	110	Paraguay	2.5	1.3
52	Tanzania	3.8	1.7	111	Kyrgyz Republic	2.5	1.7
53	Kenya	3.8	1.8	112	Albania	2.5	1.9
54	El Salvador	3.8	1.7	113	Bolivia	2.4	1.3
55	Benin	3.7	1.9	114	Kuwait	2.4	1.4
56	Namibia	3.7	1.6	115	Bosnia and Herzegovina	2.4	1.3
57	Sri Lanka	3.7	1.9	116	Ecuador	2.3	1.2
58	Nigeria	3.7	1.7	117	Venezuela	2.1	1.5
59	Jamaica	3.6	1.7				

MEAN: 3.9

9.07 Importance of environment in business planning

Business and project planning in your country now considers long-term factors such as global climate change to be (1 = unimportant, 7 = important)

RANK	COUNTRY	SCORE		SD
1	Japan	5.8		1.2
2	Finland	5.7		1.1
3	Germany	5.5		1.3
4	Sweden	5.4		1.2
5	Norway	5.3		1.3
6	Netherlands	5.2		1.3
7	Denmark	5.2		1.5
8	New Zealand	5.2		1.3
9	Iceland	5.1		1.2
10	Canada	5.1		1.3
11	Singapore	5.1		1.3
12	United Kingdom	4.9		1.3
13	Luxembourg	4.9		1.3
14	Taiwan	4.8		1.3
15	Korea, Rep.	4.8		1.3
16	Ireland	4.8		1.1
17	Malaysia	4.7		1.3
18	Switzerland	4.7		1.7
19	Uganda	4.7		2.0
20	France	4.6		1.5
21	Belgium	4.5		1.5
22	Australia	4.5		1.4
23	Slovenia	4.5		1.5
24	Kenya	4.4		1.9
25	Spain	4.4		1.3
26	South Africa	4.3		1.4
27	Austria	4.3		1.7
28	Panama	4.3		1.7
29	Thailand	4.3		1.5
30	Brazil	4.2		1.6
31	Portugal	4.2		1.4
32	Ghana	4.2		1.4
33	Morocco	4.1		1.7
34	Israel	4.1		1.5
35	Czech Republic	4.0		1.7
36	United Arab Emirates	4.0		1.5
37	Mali	4.0		1.9
37	Tunisia	4.0		1.5
39	Tanzania	4.0		2.0
40	Mauritius	4.0		1.8
41	Botswana	3.9		1.8
42	Nigeria	3.9		1.5
43	Egypt	3.9		1.9
44	China	3.9		1.6
45	Gambia	3.8		2.0
46	Tajikistan	3.8		1.9
47	United States	3.8		1.6
48	India	3.8		1.7
49	Costa Rica	3.7		1.6
50	Moldova	3.7		2.4
51	Pakistan	3.7		1.7
52	Indonesia	3.7		1.1
53	Chad	3.7		2.0
54	Qatar	3.7		1.9
55	Cyprus	3.7		1.5
56	Kazakhstan	3.6		1.8
57	Azerbaijan	3.6		1.8
58	Madagascar	3.6		1.8
59	East Timor	3.6		2.2
60	Cambodia	3.6		1.9
61	Bangladesh	3.6		1.8
62	Benin	3.6		1.8
62	Jamaica	3.6		1.8
64	Hong Kong SAR	3.6		1.5
65	Greece	3.5		1.5
66	Colombia	3.5		1.6
67	Chile	3.5		1.6
68	Mongolia	3.5		1.7
69	Cameroon	3.4		1.8
69	Macedonia, FYR	3.4		2.0
71	Ethiopia	3.4		1.7
72	Sri Lanka	3.4		1.7
73	Namibia	3.4		1.6
74	Mozambique	3.4		1.7
75	Jordan	3.4		1.9
76	Turkey	3.3		1.5
77	Philippines	3.3		1.6
78	Nicaragua	3.3		1.6
79	Guyana	3.3		1.6
80	Poland	3.3		1.5
81	Vietnam	3.2		1.7
82	Slovak Republic	3.2		1.5
83	Estonia	3.2		1.5
84	Italy	3.2		1.7
85	Honduras	3.1		1.7
86	Trinidad and Tobago	3.1		1.6
87	Lithuania	3.1		1.6
88	Kuwait	3.1		1.8
89	Guatemala	3.1		1.6
90	Malawi	3.1		1.7
90	Ukraine	3.1		1.6
92	Mexico	3.0		1.5
93	Croatia	3.0		1.5
94	El Salvador	3.0		1.6
94	Hungary	3.0		1.5
96	Peru	3.0		1.5
97	Armenia	3.0		1.7
98	Algeria	2.9		1.7
99	Latvia	2.8		1.4
100	Bulgaria	2.8		1.6
101	Zimbabwe	2.8		1.9
102	Malta	2.8		1.5
103	Argentina	2.7		1.4
104	Kyrgyz Republic	2.7		2.0
105	Serbia and Montenegro	2.6		1.6
106	Bahrain	2.6		1.7
107	Uruguay	2.6		1.4
108	Albania	2.6		1.8
109	Romania	2.6		1.5
110	Russian Federation	2.6		1.6
111	Bosnia and Herzegovina	2.6		1.4
112	Paraguay	2.6		1.6
113	Dominican Republic	2.4		1.6
114	Georgia	2.3		1.6
115	Venezuela	2.3		1.8
116	Ecuador	2.3		1.3
117	Bolivia	2.1		1.2

MEAN: 3.7

9.08   Protection of ecosystems by business

In your country, companies that harvest or process natural resources such as food, forest or fishery products (1 = rarely concern themselves with the degradation of ecosystems, 7 = frequently take steps to preserve the ecosystems they depend on)

RANK	COUNTRY	SCORE	MEAN: 3.8	SD	RANK	COUNTRY	SCORE	MEAN: 3.8	SD
1	Iceland	5.8		1.0	60	Argentina	3.5		1.4
2	Finland	5.8		1.3	61	Kuwait	3.5		1.7
3	Germany	5.8		1.0	62	Croatia	3.5		1.4
4	New Zealand	5.8		1.0	63	Indonesia	3.4		1.0
5	Switzerland	5.8		0.9	64	Kazakhstan	3.4		1.6
6	Denmark	5.5		1.3	65	Panama	3.4		1.3
7	Sweden	5.5		1.1	66	Turkey	3.4		1.3
8	Austria	5.5		1.2	67	China	3.4		1.5
9	Canada	5.4		1.1	68	Mali	3.4		1.8
10	Norway	5.4		1.0	69	Uganda	3.4		1.7
11	Netherlands	5.4		1.0	70	Madagascar	3.3		1.9
12	United Kingdom	5.3		1.0	71	Hong Kong SAR	3.3		1.4
13	Japan	5.2		1.1	72	Tanzania	3.3		1.6
14	Australia	5.2		1.3	73	Macedonia, FYR	3.3		1.7
15	United States	5.2		1.3	74	Gambia	3.3		1.7
16	Luxembourg	5.2		1.2	75	Romania	3.3		1.5
17	France	5.2		1.2	76	Bahrain	3.3		1.5
18	Ireland	5.1		1.3	77	Tajikistan	3.3		1.5
19	Belgium	5.0		1.3	78	El Salvador	3.2		1.4
20	Malaysia	5.0		1.3	79	Philippines	3.2		1.3
21	Singapore	4.9		1.2	80	Benin	3.2		1.8
22	South Africa	4.8		1.3	81	Malawi	3.2		1.7
23	Chile	4.7		1.3	82	Mexico	3.2		1.3
24	Tunisia	4.7		1.5	83	Peru	3.2		1.3
25	Slovenia	4.6		1.3	84	Vietnam	3.1		1.5
26	Korea, Rep.	4.5		1.2	85	Sri Lanka	3.1		1.5
27	Czech Republic	4.5		1.4	86	Morocco	3.1		1.5
28	Israel	4.5		1.3	87	Cameroon	3.1		1.6
29	Slovak Republic	4.4		1.2	88	Venezuela	3.1		1.6
30	Portugal	4.4		1.2	89	Honduras	3.1		1.5
31	Namibia	4.4		1.6	90	Ukraine	3.0		1.3
32	Estonia	4.3		1.3	91	Moldova	3.0		1.5
33	Taiwan	4.3		1.3	92	Malta	2.9		1.2
34	Lithuania	4.3		1.4	93	Trinidad and Tobago	2.9		1.3
35	Cyprus	4.3		1.2	94	Mozambique	2.8		1.4
36	Spain	4.2		1.3	95	East Timor	2.8		1.7
37	Ghana	4.2		1.5	96	Algeria	2.8		1.4
38	Brazil	4.1		1.5	97	Bangladesh	2.8		1.5
39	Hungary	4.1		1.5	98	Cambodia	2.8		1.5
40	Mauritius	4.1		1.3	99	Guyana	2.8		1.3
41	Costa Rica	4.0		1.3	100	Kyrgyz Republic	2.8		1.5
42	Qatar	4.0		1.9	101	Guatemala	2.8		1.4
43	Thailand	4.0		1.3	102	Chad	2.8		1.9
44	Zimbabwe	3.9		1.3	103	Dominican Republic	2.7		1.2
45	Colombia	3.9		1.6	104	Pakistan	2.7		1.2
46	Greece	3.9		1.4	105	Ecuador	2.7		1.2
47	Latvia	3.8		1.5	106	Russian Federation	2.7		1.4
48	Jordan	3.8		1.5	107	Serbia and Montenegro	2.7		1.6
49	United Arab Emirates	3.8		1.3	108	Bosnia and Herzegovina	2.7		1.4
50	Nigeria	3.8		1.4	109	Armenia	2.7		1.4
51	Italy	3.8		1.4	110	Nicaragua	2.7		1.1
52	Kenya	3.8		1.8	111	Ethiopia	2.6		1.3
53	Botswana	3.7		1.3	112	Georgia	2.6		1.4
54	Egypt	3.7		1.7	113	Bolivia	2.4		1.1
55	Jamaica	3.7		1.4	114	Bulgaria	2.4		1.4
55	Uruguay	3.7		1.3	115	Paraguay	2.3		1.2
57	Azerbaijan	3.6		1.5	116	Mongolia	2.1		1.0
58	India	3.6		1.5	117	Albania	1.9		1.3
59	Poland	3.6		1.3					

9.09 Prevalence of corporate environmental reporting

Corporate environmental reporting in your country is (1 = nonexistent, 7 = widespread)

RANK	COUNTRY	SCORE	MEAN: 3.6	SD
1	Denmark	5.9		1.0
2	Norway	5.9		1.0
3	Germany	5.9		0.9
4	Sweden	5.8		0.9
5	Finland	5.7		1.0
6	Japan	5.7		1.3
7	United Kingdom	5.6		0.9
8	Netherlands	5.5		1.0
9	United States	5.4		1.4
10	Canada	5.3		1.2
11	Switzerland	5.2		1.2
12	France	5.2		1.2
13	Australia	5.2		1.3
14	New Zealand	5.1		1.1
15	Slovenia	5.0		1.3
16	Belgium	4.9		1.4
17	Taiwan	4.9		1.2
18	Singapore	4.8		1.5
19	Austria	4.8		1.6
20	South Africa	4.7		1.3
21	Hungary	4.7		1.5
22	Luxembourg	4.6		1.7
23	Korea, Rep.	4.6		1.3
24	Israel	4.6		1.4
25	Iceland	4.6		1.2
26	Malaysia	4.6		1.3
27	Ireland	4.5		1.3
28	Lithuania	4.3		1.4
29	Kazakhstan	4.3		1.7
30	Estonia	4.1		1.3
31	Spain	4.1		1.3
32	Brazil	4.1		1.3
33	Ukraine	4.0		1.7
34	Tunisia	4.0		1.4
35	Czech Republic	4.0		1.3
36	Chile	4.0		1.4
37	Slovak Republic	3.9		1.8
38	India	3.8		1.6
39	Portugal	3.8		1.3
40	Poland	3.8		1.4
41	Uganda	3.8		1.7
42	Qatar	3.8		1.5
43	Ghana	3.7		1.4
44	Nigeria	3.7		1.4
45	Moldova	3.7		1.8
46	Thailand	3.7		1.4
47	Indonesia	3.6		1.1
48	Italy	3.6		1.5
49	Botswana	3.6		1.5
50	Hong Kong SAR	3.5		1.5
51	Costa Rica	3.5		1.4
52	Zimbabwe	3.5		1.4
53	Cyprus	3.4		1.4
54	Romania	3.4		1.5
55	Kenya	3.4		1.6
56	United Arab Emirates	3.4		1.5
57	Greece	3.4		1.5
58	China	3.4		1.4
59	Colombia	3.4		1.6

RANK	COUNTRY	SCORE	MEAN: 3.6	SD
60	Tajikistan	3.4		1.7
61	Namibia	3.4		1.4
62	Croatia	3.4		1.5
63	Russian Federation	3.3		1.7
64	Tanzania	3.3		1.6
65	Madagascar	3.3		1.5
66	Egypt	3.3		1.6
67	Latvia	3.3		1.3
68	Turkey	3.2		1.4
69	Mali	3.2		1.6
70	Jordan	3.2		1.6
71	Sri Lanka	3.2		1.5
72	Mexico	3.1		1.4
73	Philippines	3.1		1.6
74	Pakistan	3.1		1.3
75	Gambia	3.1		1.5
76	Mauritius	3.0		1.5
77	Morocco	3.0		1.3
78	Argentina	3.0		1.1
79	Malawi	3.0		1.5
80	Mozambique	3.0		1.2
81	Cameroon	3.0		1.5
82	Panama	3.0		1.6
83	Vietnam	2.9		1.5
84	Azerbaijan	2.9		1.4
85	El Salvador	2.9		1.3
86	Trinidad and Tobago	2.8		1.4
87	Bahrain	2.8		1.3
88	Peru	2.8		1.2
89	Jamaica	2.7		1.4
90	Uruguay	2.7		1.2
91	Armenia	2.7		1.5
92	Kuwait	2.7		1.2
93	Bulgaria	2.7		1.4
94	Cambodia	2.6		1.4
95	Albania	2.6		1.6
96	Malta	2.5		1.4
97	Honduras	2.5		1.3
98	Macedonia, FYR	2.5		1.4
99	Venezuela	2.5		1.5
100	Bolivia	2.4		1.0
101	Ecuador	2.4		1.2
102	Bangladesh	2.4		1.1
103	Algeria	2.4		1.4
104	Guyana	2.4		1.1
105	East Timor	2.4		1.4
106	Benin	2.4		1.4
107	Ethiopia	2.4		1.5
108	Nicaragua	2.4		1.1
109	Serbia and Montenegro	2.3		1.4
110	Guatemala	2.3		1.2
111	Georgia	2.3		1.1
112	Bosnia and Herzegovina	2.2		1.2
113	Chad	2.2		1.4
114	Mongolia	2.1		1.2
115	Paraguay	2.1		1.1
116	Kyrgyz Republic	2.0		1.2
117	Dominican Republic	2.0		0.9

9.10 Grassroots involvement in development projects

In your country, development projects that have the potential to impact specific communities (1 = rarely consult or gain support from these communities, 7 = do not proceed without consultation and community support)

RANK	COUNTRY	SCORE	1 MEAN: 4.3 7	SD
1	New Zealand	6.0		0.9
2	Australia	5.9		0.9
3	Denmark	5.8		1.2
4	United Kingdom	5.8		1.0
5	Canada	5.8		1.2
6	United States	5.7		1.2
7	Switzerland	5.6		1.3
8	Japan	5.6		1.1
9	Finland	5.6		1.0
10	Taiwan	5.5		1.0
11	Germany	5.5		1.3
12	South Africa	5.5		1.2
13	Norway	5.4		1.0
14	Iceland	5.4		1.0
15	Netherlands	5.4		1.3
16	Ireland	5.3		1.4
17	Austria	5.3		1.1
18	Malaysia	5.2		1.3
19	Sweden	5.2		1.2
20	France	5.1		1.3
21	Singapore	5.1		1.2
22	Belgium	5.1		1.3
23	Luxembourg	5.0		1.5
24	Hungary	4.9		1.3
25	Portugal	4.9		1.2
26	Spain	4.9		1.1
27	Ghana	4.9		1.1
28	Hong Kong SAR	4.8		1.4
29	Chile	4.7		1.5
30	Korea, Rep.	4.7		1.2
31	Slovenia	4.7		1.1
32	Israel	4.6		1.3
33	Philippines	4.6		1.5
34	Thailand	4.6		1.5
35	Greece	4.6		1.4
36	Cyprus	4.6		1.3
37	Botswana	4.6		1.4
38	Estonia	4.6		1.2
39	Nigeria	4.6		1.7
40	Gambia	4.5		1.6
41	Tunisia	4.5		1.1
42	Tanzania	4.5		1.4
43	Mauritius	4.5		1.3
44	Brazil	4.5		1.5
45	Mali	4.5		1.8
46	Colombia	4.5		1.4
47	Italy	4.4		1.7
48	Zimbabwe	4.4		1.0
49	Czech Republic	4.4		1.2
50	Kenya	4.4		1.6
51	Namibia	4.4		1.3
52	Malawi	4.3		1.6
53	Cameroon	4.3		1.7
54	Peru	4.3		1.5
55	Costa Rica	4.3		1.5
56	Jamaica	4.3		1.4
57	Slovak Republic	4.2		1.3
58	India	4.2		1.3
59	Poland	4.2		1.2

RANK	COUNTRY	SCORE	1 MEAN: 4.3 7	SD
60	Latvia	4.2		1.3
61	Lithuania	4.1		1.1
62	Bolivia	4.1		1.6
63	Malta	4.1		1.4
64	Uruguay	4.0		1.4
65	China	4.0		1.5
66	Vietnam	4.0		1.6
67	Pakistan	3.9		1.6
68	Jordan	3.9		1.5
69	Indonesia	3.9		0.9
70	Morocco	3.9		1.3
71	Mexico	3.9		1.5
72	El Salvador	3.9		1.5
73	Romania	3.9		1.5
74	Croatia	3.9		1.5
75	Tajikistan	3.8		1.8
75	Uganda	3.8		1.9
77	Armenia	3.8		1.5
78	Madagascar	3.8		1.5
79	Venezuela	3.7		1.8
80	Kazakhstan	3.7		1.4
81	Macedonia, FYR	3.7		1.4
82	Honduras	3.7		1.3
83	Serbia and Montenegro	3.7		1.7
84	Trinidad and Tobago	3.7		1.4
85	Ukraine	3.7		1.2
86	Azerbaijan	3.7		1.4
87	United Arab Emirates	3.7		1.3
88	Turkey	3.7		1.3
89	Benin	3.7		1.9
90	Panama	3.6		1.4
91	Georgia	3.6		1.2
92	Sri Lanka	3.6		1.6
93	Argentina	3.6		1.4
94	Nicaragua	3.6		1.5
95	Ecuador	3.6		1.5
96	Qatar	3.6		1.6
97	East Timor	3.6		1.9
98	Cambodia	3.5		1.5
99	Bulgaria	3.5		1.4
100	Bangladesh	3.5		1.5
101	Kyrgyz Republic	3.5		1.5
102	Mozambique	3.5		1.4
103	Guyana	3.5		1.5
104	Dominican Republic	3.4		1.2
105	Egypt	3.4		1.6
106	Moldova	3.4		1.6
107	Bahrain	3.3		1.7
108	Ethiopia	3.2		1.6
109	Guatemala	3.2		1.5
110	Algeria	3.1		1.4
111	Russian Federation	3.1		1.4
112	Chad	3.1		2.0
113	Mongolia	3.0		1.5
114	Bosnia and Herzegovina	2.9		1.2
115	Kuwait	2.8		1.3
116	Paraguay	2.8		1.2
117	Albania	2.8		1.5

625

Technical Notes and Sources

The data used in this *Report* represent the best available estimates from various national authorities, international agencies, and private sources at the time the *Report* was prepared (July/August 2005). It is possible that some data will have been revised or updated by national sources after publication. Throughout the statistical tables in this publication, "n/a" denotes that the value is not available.

The following outlines some notes on sources for specific variables listed in the Data Tables of this *Report*. All of these variables are related to the Growth Competitiveness Index, the Business Competitiveness Index, or the Global Competitiveness Index.

Section I: Aggregate Country Performance Indicators

1.01 Total GDP, 2004. Gross domestic product (GDP) in current US dollars. Source: The International Monetary Fund's *World Economic Outlook Database, April 2005*. Available online at http://www.imf.org/external/pubs/ft/weo/2005/01/data/index.htm

1.02 Total population, 2004. Source: The United Nations Population Fund's (UNFPA) *State of World Population 2004*. Available online at http://www.unfpa.org/swp/2003/english/ch1/index.htm; Economist Intelligence Unit, and national sources.

1.03 GDP per capita (PPP), 2004. Per capita GPD adjusted for puchasing power across countries. Source: The International Monetary Fund's *World Economic Outlook Database, April 2005*. Available online at http://www.imf.org/external/pubs/ft/weo/2005/01/data/index.htm

Section II: Macroeconomic Environment

2.13 Government surplus/deficit, 2004. Source: The International Monetary Fund's *World Economic Outlook, Winter 2005* (Published Version).

2.14 National savings rate, 2004. Sources: The International Monetary Fund Country Reports; Economist Intelligence Unit, and national sources.

2.15 Real effective exchange rate, 2004. Real effective exchange rate 2004 relative to the 1997 - 2003 average. Source: The International Monetary Fund.

2.16 Inflation, 2004. Source: The International Monetary Fund's *World Economic Outlook Database, April 2005*. Available online at http://www.imf.org/external/pubs/ft/weo/2005/01/data/index.htm

2.17 Interest rate spread, 2004. The difference between the typical short-term lending and deposit rates over the 2004 period. Source: The International Monetary Fund's *International Financial Statistics, June 2005*; Economist Intelligence Unit, and national sources.

2.18 Exports, 2004. Exports of goods and services as a percentage of GDP, 2004. Sources: The International Monetary Fund Country Reports; Economist Intelligence Unit, and national sources.

2.19 Imports, 2004. Imports of goods and services as a percentage of GDP, 2004. Sources: The International Monetary Fund Country Reports; International Monetary Fund's *World Economic Outlook Database, April 2005*; International Trade Commission; Economist Intelligence Unit, and national sources.

2.20 Government debt, 2004. Sources: The International Monetary Fund's *World Economic Outlook, Winter 2005* (Published Version); International Monetary Fund Country Reports; International Monetary Fund's World Economic Outlook Database, April 2005; Eurostat; International Monetary Fund's International Finance Statistics, June 2005, and national sources.

2.21 Country Credit Rating, 2005. Source: Institutional Investor, available online at http://www.institutionalinvestor.com © Institutional Investor, 2005. No further copying or transmission of this material is allowed without the express permission of Institutional Investor. mailto:publisher@institutionalinvestor.com

Section III: Technology: Innovation and Diffusion

3.17 Utility patents, 2004. Source: The United States Patent and Trademark Office, *Patent Counts by Country/State and Year, Utility Patents*, April 2005. Available online at: http://www.uspto.gov. Utility patents (i.e., patents for invention) are recorded such that the origin of the patent is determined by the first-named inventor at the time of the grant. Patents per million population are calculated by dividing the number of patents granted to a country in 2004 by that country's population in the same year.

3.18 Cellular telephones, 2003. Sources: The International Telecommunication Union, *World Telecommunications Indicators 2004*. Some data is available online at http://www.itu.int/ITU-D/ict/statistics, and national sources.

3.19 Internet users, 2003. Sources: The International Telecommunication Union, *World Telecommunications Indicators 2004*. Some data is available online at http://www.itu.int/ITU-D/ict/statistics, and national sources.

3.20 Internet hosts, 2003. Sources: The International Telecommunication Union, *World Telecommunications Indicators 2004*. Some data is available online at http://www.itu.int/ITU-D/ict/statistics, and national sources.

3.21 Personal computers, 2003. Sources: The International Telecommunication Union, *World Telecommunications Indicators 2004*. Some data is available online at http://www.itu.int/ITU-D/ict/statistics, and national sources.

Section IV: Human resources: Education, Health, and Labor

4.10   Infant mortality. Sources: The World Health Organization's *World Health Report 2005*; The United Nations Population Fund's (UNFPA) *State of the World Population 2004*, and national sources.

4.11   Life expectancy. Sources: The World Health Organization's *World Health Report 2005*; The United Nations Population Fund's (UNFPA) *State of the World Population 2004*, and national sources.

4.12   Tuberculosis prevalence. Sources: The World Health Organization's *Global Atlas of Infectious Diseases 2003*, and national sources.

4.12   Malaria prevalence. Sources: The World Health Organization's *Global Atlas of Infectious Diseases 2003*; World Health Organization Regional Offices, and national sources.

4.14   HIV prevalence. Sources: The World Health Organization's *Global Atlas of Infectious Diseases 2003*; World Health Organization Regional Offices, and national sources.

4.15   Primary enrollment. Sources: UNESCO Institute for Statistics; World Bank *World Development Indicators 2005*, and national sources. According to the *World Development Indicators*, the gross primary enrollment rate is the ratio of total enrollment, regardless of age, to the population of the age group that officially corresponds to the primary education level. Primary education provides children with basic reading, writing, and mathematics skills along with an elementary understanding of such subjects as history, geography, natural science, social science, art and music.

4.16   Secondary enrollment. Sources: UNESCO Institute for Statistics; World Bank *World Development Indicators 2005*; World Bank *World Development Indicators 2004*, and national sources. According to the *World Development Indicators*, the gross secondary enrollment rate is the ratio of total enrollment, regardless of age, to the population of the age group that officially corresponds to the secondary education level. Secondary education completes the provision of basic education that began at the primary level, and aims at laying the foundations for lifelong learning and human development, by offering more subject- or skill-oriented instruction using more specialized teachers.

4.17   Tertiary enrollment. Sources: UNESCO Institute for Statistics; World Bank *World Development Indicators 2005*; World Bank *World Development Indicators 2004*, and national sources. According to the *World Development Indicators*, the gross tertiary enrollment rate is the ratio of total enrollment, regardless of age, to the population of the age group that officially corresponds to the tertiary education level. Tertiary education, whether or not leading to an advanced research qualification, normally requires, as a minimum condition of admission, the successful completion of education at the secondary level.

Section V: General Infrastructure

5.08   Telephone lines, 2003. Sources: The International Telecommunication Union, *World Telecommunications Indicators 2004*. Some data is available online at http://www.itu.int/ITU-D/ict/statistics, and national sources.

Section VII: Domestic Competition and Cluster Development

7.10   Number of procedures required to start a business, 2005. Source: The World Bank *Doing Business in 2005*.

7.11   Time required to start a business, 2005. Source: The World Bank *Doing Business in 2005*.

627

About the Authors

Jagdish Bhagwati

Jagdish Bhagwati is University Professor at Columbia University and Senior Fellow in International Economics at the Council on Foreign Relations. He was Economic Policy Adviser to the Director General, GATT (1991–93) and also served as Special Adviser to the United Nations on Globalization and External Adviser to the Director General of the World Trade Organization. Currently, he is a member of UN Secretary General Kofi Annan's High-level Advisory Group on the NEPAD process in Africa. Five volumes of his scientific writings and two of his public policy essays have been published by MIT press. He is the recipient of three Festschrifts, and has received numerous awards and honorary degrees. Professor Bhagwati's latest book *In Defense of Globalization* was published by Oxford University Press in 2004, to worldwide acclaim.

Jennifer Blanke

Jennifer Blanke is Senior Economist and Associate Director of the Global Competitiveness Programme at the World Economic Forum. She has written and lectured extensively on issues related to national competitiveness. From 1998 to 2001, she was Senior Program Manager responsible for developing the business, management, and technology section of the World Economic Forum's Annual Meeting. Before joining the Forum, Blanke worked for a number of years as a management consultant for Eurogroup (Mazars Group) in Paris, France, where she specialized in banking and financial market organization. Blanke obtained an MA in International Affairs from Columbia University and an MA and a PhD in International Economics from the Graduate Institute of International Studies, Geneva.

Margareta Drzeniek

Margareta Drzeniek is Senior Program Manager, Economics with the Global Competitiveness Programme at the World Economic Forum. She is responsible for developing the economics section of the program for the Annual Meeting of the World Economic Forum in Davos, and also contributes to other projects within the Forum's Centre for Strategic Insight, such as scenario building and analysis of global risks. Before joining the Global Competitiveness Team, she worked for several years with the International Trade Centre in Geneva, where she designed and managed trade promotion projects for Central and Eastern European countries. Drzeniek received a diploma in Economics from the University of Münster, and holds a PhD in International Economics from the University of Bochum, both in Germany.

Nicholas Eberstadt

Nicholas Eberstadt holds the Henry Wendt Chair in Political Economy at the American Enterprise Institute in Washington, DC, and is Senior Adviser to the National Bureau of Asian Research in Seattle, Washington. Dr. Eberstadt is a member of the Visiting Committee for the Harvard University School of Public Health (HSPH), of the Board of Scientific Counselors for the United States National Center for Health Statistics, and of the Advisory Committee for Voluntary Foreign Aid for the U.S. Agency for International Development. Dr. Eberstadt regularly consults for governmental and international organizations, and is often invited to offer expert testimony before the US Congress. Dr. Eberstadt has published over three hundred studies and articles in scholarly and popular journals, mainly on topics in demography, international development, and East Asian security. He has authored or edited more than a dozen books and monographs, including *Poverty in China, Fertility Decline in the Less Developed Countries, The Tyranny of Numbers, The End of North Korea, Prosperous Paupers and Other Population Problems, Fault Lines In China's Economic Terrain* (co-author), and most recently, *A New International Engagement Framework For North Korea? Contending Perspectives*. Dr. Eberstadt earned his AB, MPA, and PhD degrees from Harvard, and his MSc from the London School of Economics.

Allen Hammond

Allen Hammond is Vice President for Innovation and Special Projects at the World Resources Institute, a nonprofit, non partisan policy research institute located in Washington, DC. His responsibilities include institute wide leadership in Internet strategy and digital technologies, and development of new initiatives. He also directs WRI's Digital Dividends project and works on private sector development strategies with foundations, development agencies, and major corporations. His book, *Which World? Scenarios for the 21st Century,* focused on long-term sustainability issues. Dr. Hammond holds degrees from Stanford and Harvard Universities in engineering and applied mathematics. Prior to joining WRI, he helped to edit the international journal *Science,* and went on to found and edit several national publications, including *Science 80–86* (American Association for the Advancement of Science), *Issues in Science and Technology* (National Academy of Science), and the *Information Please Environmental Almanac* (Houghton Mifflin). Dr. Hammond has published extensively in the scientific, policy, research, and business literature.

Richard Layard

Richard Layard is Emeritus Professor of Economics at the London School of Economics, where he was until recently Director of the Centre for Economic Performance. He now heads the Centre's Programme on Well-Being. Since 2000 he has been a member of the House of Lords (Lord Layard of Highgate). He has written widely on unemployment, inflation, education, inequality, and post-communist reform. He was an early advocate of the welfare-to-work approach to unemployment, and co-authored the influential book *Unemployment: Macroeconomic Performance and the Labour Market* (OUP 1991). He is currently working on happiness, and his book *Happiness—Lessons from a New Science* was published by Penguin in spring 2005. In Britain, he founded the Employment Institute to press for action to prevent long-term unemployment, and served as Chairman from 1987–92. From 1997–2001 he was consultant to the UK Department of Education and Skills on policies toward unemployment (including the New Deal). Outside Britain, he was Chairman of the European Commission's Macroeconomic Policy Group in the 1980s, and subsequently Co-Chairman of the World Economy Group set up by the World Institute for Development Economics Research. From 1991–97 he was an economic adviser to the Russian government's economic staff.

Emma Loades

Emma Loades is Senior Manager of the Global Competitiveness Programme at the World Economic Forum, where her responsibilities include articulating the findings of *The Global Competitiveness Report* for the media and the website, and integrating the work of over 100 Partner Institutes. She has also presented the results of the *Report* at several national and international conferences. Since joining the Forum, she has held several positions in the Communications Department, most prominently as editor. Ms. Loades has also participated in a coordinating capacity in many of the key regional summits and country meetings held by the World Economic Forum, including the Annual Meeting in Davos. She has a BA (Honours) degree from University College, London.

Augusto Lopez-Claros

Augusto Lopez-Claros is Chief Economist and Director of the Global Competitiveness Programme at the World Economic Forum in Geneva. Before joining the Forum he was Senior International Economist and Executive Director with Lehman Brothers International (London). He was the International Monetary Fund's resident representative in the Russian Federation (Moscow) from 1992 to 1995. Dr. Lopez-Claros was educated in England and the United States, receiving a diploma in Mathematical Statistics from Cambridge University and a PhD in economics from Duke University. Before joining the IMF, he was Professor of Economics at the University of Chile in Santiago. He has written and lectured extensively in South America, the United States, Asia, and Europe on a broad range of subjects, including aspects of economic reform in transition economies, economic integration, interdependence and cooperation, governance, peace, and issues in the reform of international organizations. He is the editor of the World Economic Forum's *Global Competitiveness Report*.

Daniel Kaufmann

Daniel Kaufmann is Director of Global Programs and Governance at the World Bank Institute in Washington, DC. Regarded as a leading expert, researcher, and adviser on governance and development, he has helped pioneer new empirical approaches and survey methodologies in good governance, anti-corruption programs, and capacity building. Previously, Dr. Kaufmann held positions at the World Bank in Capacity Building for Latin America, Finance, Regulation and Governance, and served as Lead Economist in Economies in Transition in the research department. He co-authored the World Development Report on the *Challenges of Development*. In the early 1990s, he was the first Chief of Mission of the World Bank to Ukraine, and subsequently Visiting Scholar at Harvard University. He is currently a member of the World Economic Forum (Davos) Faculty. His research articles on economic development, governance, the unofficial economy, trade and exchange rate, investment, corruption, privatization, and urban and labor economics have been published in leading journals. A Chilean national, Daniel Kaufmann received his MA and PhD in economics from Harvard University, and a BA in Economics and Statistics from the Hebrew University of Jerusalem.

Irene Mia

Irene Mia is Senior Economist with the Global Competitiveness Programme at the World Economic Forum. Her responsibilities include researching competitiveness issues and developing the economic content for World Economic Forum activities. She is in charge of the technical coordination of *The Global Information Technology Report*. Before joining the Forum, she worked at the Headquarters of Sudameris Bank in Paris, holding various positions in the international affairs and international trade divisions. Dr. Mia has an MA in Latin American studies from the Institute of Latin American Studies, London University, and a PhD in International Economic and Trade Law from Bocconi University, Milan.

Michael E. Porter

Michael E. Porter is Bishop William Lawrence University Professor at the Institute for Strategy and Competitiveness at the Harvard Business School. He is a leading authority on competitive strategy and international competitiveness. The author of 16 books and over 100 articles, Professor Porter's ideas have guided economic policy throughout the world, led competitiveness initiatives in nations and states such as Canada, India, New Zealand, and Connecticut, and currently guides regional projects in Central America and the Middle East. Dr. Porter is co-chairman of *The Global Competitiveness Report*. In 1994, Professor Porter founded the Initiative for a Competitive Inner City, a nonprofit private sector initiative formed to catalyze business development in distressed inner cities across the United States. The holder of eight honorary doctorates, Professor Porter has won numerous awards for his books, articles, public service, and influence on several fields.

629

Kenneth Rogoff

Kenneth Rogoff is Thomas D. Cabot Professor of Public Policy and Professor of Economics at Harvard University. From 2001–2003, he served as Chief Economist and Director of Research at the International Monetary Fund. He is the former Director of the Center for International Development at Harvard, and an elected member of the American Academy of Arts and Sciences, as well as the Econometric Society, Research Associate of the National Bureau of Economic Research, and Fellow of the World Economic Forum. Dr. Rogoff received his BA and PhD degrees from Yale and Harvard Universities. After serving as Research Economist in International Finance Division of the Federal Reserve System, Dr. Rogoff taught at the University of Wisconsin-Madison, the University of California at Berkeley, and Princeton University, where he was Charles and Marie Robertson Professor of International Affairs, from 1995 to 1999. He has published widely on a broad range of topics in international finance, including exchange rates, international debt, and financial globalization. Dr. Rogoff holds the life title of international grandmaster of chess.

Nouriel Roubini

Professor Nouriel Roubini is Professor of Economics at the Stern School of Business, New York University and is co-founder and Chairman of Roubini Global Economics LLC, a Web-based economic and geo-strategic information service and economic consultancy. As a senior academic researcher in the field of international macroeconomics, with broad policy experience, his views are regularly cited in the press and media, and his global economics website (http://www.rgemonitor.com) has been ranked by *The Economist* as the premiere economics website in the world. Professor Roubini received his BA from Bocconi University, Milan, and his PhD in economics from Harvard University, and from 1988 to 1995, taught economics at Yale University. He was Senior Economist for International Affairs on the White House Council of Economic Advisers, later Senior Adviser to the Under Secretary for International Affairs, and Director of the Office of Policy Development and Review at the United States Treasury Department, working on the resolution of the Asian and global financial crises of 1997–1998, and the reform of the international financial architecture. He has published over 70 theoretical and empirical and policy papers on international macroeconomic issues, Europe and the US economy, the Asian and global financial crisis, emerging markets, the reform of the international financial system, and global economic imbalances. He co-authored several books, including *Political Cycles: Theory and Evidence,* and *Bailouts or Bail-ins? Responding to Financial Crises in Emerging Markets.*

Brad Setser

Brad Setser is Senior Economist at Roubini Global Economics, and Research Associate at the Global Economic Governance Programme at University College, Oxford. He is the author, with Nouriel Roubini, of *Bailouts or Bail-ins? Responding to Financial Crises in Emerging Economies*. He was an International Affairs Fellow at the Council on Foreign Relations, and Visiting Scholar at the International Monetary Fund (IMF). He served in the United States Treasury from 1997 to 2001, where he worked extensively on the reform of the international financial architecture, sovereign debt restructurings, and US policy toward the IMF. He ended his tenure at the Treasury as the acting director of the US Treasury's Office of International Monetary and Financial Policy. He received his undergraduate and graduate degrees from Oxford University, Sciences-Po (Paris), and Harvard University.

Camilla Toulmin

Camilla Toulmin is Director of the International Institute for Environment and Development (IIED), formerly founder and Director of its Drylands Programme from 1987–2002. An economist by training, Dr. Toulmin's work, mainly in francophone West Africa, has focused on social, economic, and environmental development in drylands. This has combined field research, policy analysis, capacity building, and advocacy with people at many different levels, from farmers and researchers to national governments, NGOs, donor agencies, and international bodies. Dr. Toulmin received an MSc in Economics from the London School of Economics, and a DPhil in Economics from Oxford University. She was a member of the International Expert Panel supporting the preparation of the Convention to Combat Desertification. Her current work includes research on land tenure in West Africa, livelihoods and poverty in Mali, challenges and opportunities relating to decentralization, and collective management of common resources. She is a member of several boards, including ISNAR, the Scientific Committee of the agricultural Policy Network in West and Central Africa, and the UK Centre for Ecology and Hydrology, of which she became a Senior Fellow in 2002.

Beatrice Weder di Mauro

Beatrice Weder di Mauro is Professor of Economics at the University of Mainz, Member of the German Council of Economic Experts, and Research Affiliate at the Centre for Economic Policy Research, London. Previously she worked as an economist with the International Monetary Fund and the World Bank, in Washington, served on the Council of Economic Advisors of Switzerland, and as a consultant for various international organizations including the International Finance Corporation, the World Bank, the IMF, the United Nations University, and the OECD Development Centre. She was Visiting Professor at Harvard University and at the United Nations University, and holds a PhD in Economics from the University of Basel. Her research interests are in the fields of international macroeconomics, international finance, capital markets, and monetary policy.

John Williamson

John Williamson is Senior Fellow of the Institute for International Economics, with which he has been associated since 1981 as a specialist in international monetary issues. He was Project Director for the United Nations High-Level Panel on Financing for Development (the Zedillo Report) in 2001, and on leave as Chief Economist for South Asia at the World Bank from 1996–99. He received his education at the Universities of York, and Warwick, England, and at the Pontifícia Universidade Católica of Rio de Janeiro, Brazil, where he taught economics from 1978–81. After several years teaching at the University of Warwick, Massachusetts Institute of Technology, the University of York, and Princeton University, he served as adviser to the International Monetary Fund on questions of international monetary reform related to the work of the Committee of Twenty, and as economic consultant to the UK Treasury. He is author, co-author, editor, or co-editor of numerous studies on international monetary and development issues, some of the most recent including *Dollar Adjustment: How Far? Against What?* (2004), *After the Washington Consensus: Restarting Growth and Reform in Latin America* (2003), *Delivering on Debt Relief: From IMF Gold to a New Aid Architecture* (2002), and *Exchange Rate Regimes for Emerging Markets: Reviving the Intermediate Option* (2000).

Saadia Zahidi

Saadia Zahidi is an economist with the Global Competitiveness Programme at the World Economic Forum, where her responsibilities include analysis for *The Global Competitiveness Report*, and for other brief studies and reports of the Competitiveness Programme, including the recent *Women's Empowerment: Measuring the Global Gender Gap*. She has also presented the results of the *Reports* at national and international conferences. Ms. Zahidi holds a BA in economics from Smith College, Massachusetts, and an MA in international economics from the Graduate Institute of International Studies, Geneva. Her research interests include transparency, financial crises, and gender issues.

The World Economic Forum would like to thank FedEx, Gallup International, and USAID for their invaluable support of this *Report*.

FedEx is proud to support the World Economic Forum by continuing to provide reliable global transportation services for the distribution of its annual *Global Competitiveness Report*. FedEx supports the Forum's commitment to improve the state of the world by engaging leaders in regulatory, industry and economic cooperation.

Recently FedEx Express announced plans for a new Asia Pacific hub at the Guangzhou Baiyun International Airport in Southern China. A joint study by China's Development Research Commission and Campbell-Hill Aviation Group of the United States estimates that the direct impact of FedEx hub on China's economy will be $11 billion in 2010, increasing to $63 billion by 2020.

FedEx Corporation provides customers and businesses worldwide with a broad portfolio of transportation, e-commerce and business services. With annual revenues of $29 billion, the company offers integrated business applications through operating companies competing collectively and managed collaboratively, under the respected FedEx brand. Consistently ranked among the world's most admired and trusted employers, FedEx inspires its more than 250,000 employees and contractors to remain "absolutely, positively" focused on safety, the highest ethical and professional standards and the needs of their customers and communities. For more information, visit fedex.com.

Gallup International was founded in 1947 and is a not-for-profit Association, registered in Switzerland. We continue to believe surveys are an integral part of democracy and that policymakers should take account of the views of ordinary citizens. In the reality of today's globalized world, public opinion has a powerful influence on political, social and economic events—increasingly at a global, as well as country level.

Our unique international survey, Voice of the People, is dedicated to interviewing the general population in more than 65 countries. In this way, the views and attitudes of almost 2 billion global citizens can be taken into account in important decision-making. Politicians, business leaders and key NGOs from across the world now regularly discuss results from the Voice of the People at the Forum's Annual Meeting in Davos.

As international research experts, Gallup International is proud to work with the World Economic Forum on the Executive Opinion Survey and *The Global Competitiveness Report 2005—2006*.

USAID is an independent federal government agency that receives overall foreign policy guidance from the Secretary of State.

The USAID mission is to create a more secure, democratic, and prosperous world for the benefit of the American people and the international community.

Our work supports long-term and equitable economic growth and advances US foreign policy objectives by supporting: economic growth, agriculture and trade; global health; and democracy, conflict prevention and humanitarian assistance.

We provide assistance in four regions of the world: Sub-Saharan Africa; Asia and the Near East; Latin America and the Caribbean, and Europe and Eurasia.

With headquarters in Washington, D.C., USAID's strength is its field offices around the world. We work in close partnership with private voluntary organizations, indigenous organizations, universities, American businesses, international agencies, other governments, and other U.S. government agencies. USAID has working relationships with more than 3,500 American companies and over 300 US-based private voluntary organizations.

For further information about USAID and its programs, visit www.usaid.gov.